ECONOMICS

the science of choice

Irwin Publications in Economics

Advisory Editor Martin S. Feldstein *Harvard University*

Lloyd C. Atkinson

Deputy Assistant Director
Fiscal Analysis Division
Congressional Budget Office
and
The University of Maryland

ECONOMICS

the science of choice

1982

RICHARD D. IRWIN, INC.
Homewood, Illinois 60430

ISBN 0-256-02486-3

Library of Congress Catalog Card No. 81–82447

Printed in the United States of America

1 2 3 4 5 6 7 8 9 0 H 9 8 7 6 5 4 3 2

To Sherry, Scott, and Stefan

Preface

The quotation succinctly captures the character of the present text. We have witnessed dramatic changes in the field of economics in the last decade or so. In macroeconomics, a veritable explosion of knowledge has altered substantively the profession's views regarding the appropriate conduct of monetary and fiscal policies. Monetarism, supply-side economics, and rational expectations, ideas that were largely ignored or unheard of in the late 1960s and early 1970s, have all assumed center stage in today's macroeconomic policy debates. Microeconomics has undergone major transformations as well, as has the economist's view of the role of government in promoting efficiency in the allocation of resources. Relatively obscure specialties, such as the economics of exhaustible resources, externalities, poverty and discrimination, and health and safety regulation, have all emerged as major branches of the science. Even the staples of microeconomic analysis—the economics of market structure, antitrust policy, and international trade, for example—have not been left untouched.

The traditional tools of analysis have proved equal to the task of accommodating these rapid advances in economic knowledge. To put it differently, those tools of long standing in the economics profession, such as the demand and supply model, the production possibilities apparatus, and the aggregate demand–aggregate supply framework, have all proved to be sufficiently expansive and versatile to admit both a growing knowledge base and diverse points of view. "The more things change, the more they remain the same."

The focus in *Economics: The Science of Choice* is on the tools of economic analysis, with special emphasis on their varied and versatile uses. In my view, a thorough grounding in those tools is essential to an understanding of the major economic problems of our times—inflation, unemployment, the energy crisis, inequities in the distribution of income and wealth, poverty, discrimination, pollution, an eroding natural resource base worldwide. Many introductory economics textbooks are written with a similar point of view. However, the study of the tools of analysis is pushed further in *Economics: The*

Science of Choice. In my estimation, this does not make the study of economics more difficult for the student. On the contrary, in fourteen years of teaching the introductory course I have found that familiarizing the student with the rich and varied features of the traditional tools of analysis makes the nature of our economic problems and of the policy options more understandable than otherwise. Going the extra distance enables the student to acquire a more thorough understanding of the implications of the diverse points of view found within the economics profession. This enhanced understanding is not accomplished by introducing the student to new and more sophisticated tools, but by extending and then exploiting the student's understanding of a few traditional tools.

Some highlights of *Economics: The Science of Choice*

The Table of Contents provides an overview of the coverage of topics in *Economics: The Science of Choice.* Upon reading it, you will be struck by three things. First, this text is not an encyclopedia of issues in economics. To keep the length of the text moderate and to provide depth of coverage, I had to pick and choose from among the many and varied interests of economics. I limited my selection to what I believe are the major issues in macroeconomics and microeconomics.

Second, you will note the general absence of chapters specifically devoted to "policy applications." The policy issues are fully integrated with the theoretical discussions; in many instances, the policy issue itself provides the frame of reference for the study of the tools of the economic analysis.

Third, certain features of this text can be identified that set it apart from the competition.

General equilibrium analysis is introduced early in the text, at the end of Chapter 3. In my view, students have enough tools to readily handle the discussion there. They have been introduced to the production possibilities curve and to the demand and supply model. The point of the exercise is to show the interdependencies between product markets and resource markets.

The broad outlines of President Reagan's *Economic Recovery Tax Act of 1981,* perhaps the most dramatic fiscal policy initiative undertaken in U.S. history, are set forth in Chapter 4. The theoretical underpinnings of that tax proposal are explored in Chapter 14.

The concept of the natural rate of unemployment is introduced in Chapter 5. The familiar demand and supply model is all that is required to illustrate this important idea. The discussion makes clear that the natural rate of unemployment is not some immutable constant, but depends on the distribution of excess demand and excess supply markets and the speeds of adjustment of wages in both.

The Keynesian and classical models of income determination are compared in Chapter 7. This discussion is an important prelude to the study of rational expectations in Chapters 13 and 14.

An unusually lengthy discussion is accorded to hotly debated issues surrounding budget deficits and the national debt in Chapters 8 and 11.

The Depository Institutions and Monetary Control Act of 1980, the most significant piece of legislation affecting U.S. financial institutions since the mid-1930s, is examined in Chapters 9 and 10.

Chapters 12, 13, and 14 constitute the heart of the macroeconomics portion of the text. The student is taken step by step from the comparative statics aggregate demand–aggregate supply framework (where the focus is on the theoretical determinants of the price level and real output) to a fully dynamic aggregate demand–aggregate supply model (where the focus is on inflation, unemployment, and growth). The model in Chapter 13 is then applied in Chapter 14 to the study of the major macroeconomics policy issues of our time.

In view of the importance of international monetary relations to the conduct of macroeconomic policy, the macroeconomics portion of the text closes with a discussion of the U.S. balance of payments and the international monetary system.

The focus of the discussion in Chapters 19 through 21 is efficiency in the allocation of resources under alternative market structures.

Chapter 25 focuses on the economics of exhaustible resources. There it is demonstrated that the usual marginal cost pricing criterion for efficiency would often result in resource misallocation.

Chapters 27 and 28 bring together a wide variety of issues dealing with the role of government in our economic system. The point of the entire discussion is simple: In the face of monopoly power and externalities, government intervention is often required in the interests of efficiency. How well government performs its role is touched on peripherally.

Chapters 29 and 30 present an in-depth examination of the costs and benefits of free trade and trade restrictions.

Teaching and learning aids

Great care has been exercised to make *Economics: The Science of Choice* and accompanying supplementary materials, including a Student Guide, Instructor's Manual, Newsletter, and Test Bank, a highly effective package of teaching and learning aids. Considerable attention was given to clarity of presentation at a level of difficulty corresponding to the reading abilities of today's introductory economics students. Particularly important arguments and notable points of view are screened in blue for emphasis.

Student guide. One of the exciting learning aids accompanying *Economics: The Science of Choice,* is *Concepts and Language of Economics: A Student Guide,* written by my good friend and highly respected colleague, Dennis Sullivan of Miami University in Oxford, Ohio. *Concepts and Language of Economics* is extremely closely coordinated with the text and pedagogically is an important complement to the text and to the study and teaching of economics. I strongly urge its use along with the text.

Instructor's Manual. The Instructor's Manual is designed to serve three purposes. First, it provides a detailed list of the learning objectives for each chapter of the text. Second, outline answers to the questions at the end of each chapter reduce the instructor's burdensome chore of preparing answers for distribution to students. Third, for each chapter in the text the Instructor's Manual provides Tips and Suggestions in the form of case studies, supplementary readings, and teaching ideas that I have found useful over the years. Transparency masters are available upon request.

Test Bank. A Test Bank, available on request to users of the text, has been prepared by myself and Dennis Sullivan. The Test Bank contains both multiple choice and true-false questions, each coded to one of three levels of difficulty. Recognizing the problems instructors encounter when they use text banks containing ambiguous items or incorrectly answered questions, we have drawn extensively from our own personal test banks to ensure, as far as possible, that each question has been classroom tested. The Test Bank is available in computerized format.

Newsletter. Twice yearly, a Newsletter will be prepared by the author and made available to all instructors adopting the text. The Newsletter will not have any preset format. Generally, it will be used as a vehicle for updating statistical charts and tables contained in the text, for discussing current policy issues, and for drawing attention to new theoretical and empirical discoveries.

Acknowledgments

In an undertaking as large as *Economics: The Science of Choice,* one incurs a large stack of debts. I seem to owe an unusually large number. Indeed, I am hard-pressed to find very much to offset the huge gifts of time and energy that have been given to me over the course of the past four years while this text was being written, rewritten, and rewritten again.

First, I want to express my deepest appreciation and thanks to my colleague and close friend, Edward F. McKelvey, chief of the Capital Markets Section of the Board of Governors of the Federal Reserve, who not only collaborated with me in writing Chapters 4, 5, and 9 of the book, but who also volunteered to serve as proofreader of the text when it was in pages. I doubt that I will ever be able to repay these debts. Of course, Ed's contributions to this text are his own and do not necessarily represent the views of the Board of Governors of the Federal Reserve System or any of its other staff members.

An equally large debt is owed to Dennis Sullivan, author of *Concepts and Language of Economics: A Student Guide* that accompanies *Economics: The Science of Choice*. Not only did he leave his mark on this undertaking with the publication of his invaluable Student Guide, but he also served as my finest critic through each of the several drafts of the text. His detailed comments so heavily influenced the final product that I am tempted to shift some of the responsibility for any remaining errors onto his shoulders. But, alas, any remaining errors are mine and mine alone. However, if any credits are to be given, Dennis should share in them.

Next, I want to thank the many reviewers who offered valuable comments on the several drafts of the manuscript: Robert M. Aduddell, Loyola University; Richard K. Anderson, Texas A&M University; Orley Ashenfelter, Princeton University; Frank J. Bonello, University of Notre Dame; Martin S. Feldstein, Harvard University; Harold D. Flint, Montclair State College; J. Fred Giertz, University of Illinois; Robert J. Korbach, University of North Dakota; Peter H. Lindert, University of California-Davis; Roger Magyar, Sacramento City College; Virginia Owen, Illinois State University; Robert L. Pennington, George Mason University; Andrew J. Policano, University of Iowa; Richard Roehl, University of Michigan-Dearborn; John C. Soper, Northern Illinois University; Robert Strom, University of Missouri-Columbia; Craig West, Federal Reserve Bank of Kansas City; Donald Yankovic, University of Toledo.

A very special thanks goes to Linda Maisel, typist extraordinaire, who cheerfully accepted my completely unreasonable deadlines without complaint. My apologies at the time seemed inadequate, so let me emphasize again, "I'm sorry."

The tally of these debts, sizable though it is, is small by comparison with the debt I owe to my family—to my wife, Sherry, and to my two sons, Scott and Stefan. Sherry performed an unusual number of roles in the production of this text. As an economist in the Banking Section of the Board of Governors of the Federal Reserve System, she was extremely valuable as a critic and as a sounding board for my ideas. Her patience, understanding, and encouragement, and her willingness to take on much more than her fair share of household chores and family obligations, were critical ingredients to the successful completion of this work. I owe her a great deal, and I trust that she will now accept my profuse thanks as but a small down payment for a debt piled high. To my sons: I know I cannot turn the clock back to retrieve the hundreds of weekends when I was locked away in my study. But I *can* promise to share with you future weekends.

Lloyd C. Atkinson

Contents

The Alfred Nobel Memorial Prize in Economic Science was officially established in 1968 under a donation by the Central National Bank of Sweden to mark its 300th anniversary. Alfred Nobel, who died in 1896, was a millionaire best known for his invention of dynamite. His will established a fund for monetary awards to persons who have worked for peace as well as to persons who have benefited mankind through their contributions in the fields of literature, physics, chemistry, medicine, and psychology. The awards have been given annually since 1901. However they have occasionally been withheld in one or more categories, especially the peace prize.

The award for Economic Science is the only addition to the five categories as set up by the Nobel Foundation. It is administered in the same way as the others and the cash value is identical—in 1981 the equivalent of $180,000. The Swedish Academy of Sciences is responsible for determining the recipients for all of the prizes. The criteria for selecting the winners in economics is based on "the achievements on their scientific merits," and the rules generally require a "discovery," though that may be broadly defined to include a different approach or use of previous works. Although the public is most eager to know what the "work" implies for public policy, invariably the technical or scientific contributions of its economic laureates are stressed in the citation.

Between 1969, when the first Economic Science award was made, and 1981, 19 persons have received or shared one of the 13 coveted awards—6 were joint awards. Several of the recipients have been politically active; however the citations have carefully avoided any commentary on their political or social orientations.

Ragnar Frisch and Jan Tinbergen were joint winners of the first Alfred Nobel Memorial Prize in Economic Science in 1969. Both were recognized by the Nobel committee for their pioneering work in the areas of econometrics and mathematical economics. Their work brought greater precision to economic policymaking.

Ragnar Frisch (1895–1972)

A pioneer in the development of mathematical methods for analyzing economic phenomena, Ragnar Frisch—a Norwegian—was noted for his contributions in mathematical economics and applied econometrics.

Wide World Photos

Frisch was one of the founders of the Econometrics Society in 1931 and was chief editor of its journal, *Econometrica*, until 1955. He is perhaps best known for his writings on the use of models as tools for the design of economic policies. Today, his ideas are widely accepted in all parts of the world. The Oslo model, a statistical-economic planning system is the product of his many years of research at the Oslo University.

Frisch was one of a group of university professors whom the Nazis imprisoned in a concentration camp during World War II. A huge, intense, strong-willed man, Frisch was also a beekeeper and an expert in the genetics of bees.

Jan Tinbergen (1903–)

Working principally in applied econometrics and occasionally in the field of mathematical economics, Jan Tinbergen is associated with the Netherlands School of Economics in Rotterdam. His work in the development of the first large-scale model of the U.S. economy during the Great Depression of the 1930s served as the main stimulus to the development of the modern techniques of economic forecasting.

Subsequent to World War II Tinbergen served as advisor to the governments of several developing and emerging nations in Africa, Asia, and Latin America, devoting most of his efforts to improving economic planning for long-term growth. More recently his chief activity has been to focus on problems of income distribution and a program for world economic development.

Wide World Photos

PART ONE

Basic concepts

Tinbergen's work has been called a marriage between theoretical economics and a very deep concern for social justice. A colleague described his style as "a hard-boiled approach as a theoretician with a practical application of work for human betterment."

An unassuming man, Tinbergen is known for his gentleness and modesty as well as for his dedication to the cause of human welfare. He lives a quiet, secluded life. Indeed, when asked how he planned to spend his share of the prize money, Tinbergen said he intended to spend it entirely for research: "As a nonsmoker, nondrinker, and nonmotorist, I don't think that the prize will bring much change in my life."

From the moment you picked up this book and began leafing through its pages you made a choice that cost you something. There were many other things you could have done with your time. But the fact that you chose as you did kept you from experiencing those alternatives at that instant. Even now you must decide whether to go on reading this chapter or to do something else. If you are still with me, then it is natural to ask why. If you are rational, the answer must be that, *for one reason or another,* you value this use of your time more than any alternative available to you at this very minute. That is, at this moment, you must value reading this material more highly than you value alternatives such as playing, sleeping, or studying other subjects. Otherwise, why would you continue reading as you are? And what about the cost that you are now incurring as a result of your decision to stick it out? It is the value you place on the most attractive of the many alternatives you now face; it is a cost because it is something that you must forego in order to do what you are doing.

THE ELEMENTS OF AN ECONOMIC PROBLEM

The above example contains all of the essential elements of any economic problem. *There is a scarce resource—the time you have available—and alternative uses of that resource. This creates a problem of choice—an economic problem. By choosing to use that resource in one way you forego the opportunity of using it in some other way. The highest valued alternative foregone is the cost—the* **opportunity cost**—*of making the choice that you do.*

The key ingredient here is **scarcity.** In the absence of scarcity all possible uses of the resource could be completely satisfied and no problem of choice––no economic problem—would arise.

Scarcity: A fact of life

Unfortunately, we live in a world of scarce resources. As a consequence, the world abounds

Chapter 1

The study of economics

with economic problems; they are part and parcel of our daily existence.

The time we have available is limited, so we must make choices about its use. Likewise, our incomes are limited. Thus, we must decide how much to budget for food and clothing, how much to spend on transportation, how much to set aside for entertainment, how much to give to charity, and how much to save. We simply cannot have everything we would like. If we choose to spend our money on one thing, we must give up something else.

Our federal, state, and local governments face similar difficulties—namely, how to allocate public revenues among all possible competing uses. *Choices must be made.* Higher salaries for public officials means less funds for needed public services; increased expenditures for national defense means less funds for other things—for health or education or welfare.

The nation faces precisely the same economic problem. The resources used in the production of our nation's output are limited. The economic problem we face is that of determining the appropriate allocation of our scarce national resources among all possible alternative uses. If the government takes over more resources, fewer resources will be available to produce all the private goods and services we want; or, if more resources are used to produce autos, less will be left over for the production of other things.

Scarcity is also a fact of life for the entire world economy. The larger the quantity of the world's resources at the disposal of any one country, the smaller will be the quantity available for use by the rest of the world.

The nature of our scarce resources

Let us focus for the moment on the kinds of resources that are used to produce goods and services. Traditionally, we divide them into three categories: **land, labor,** and **capital.** Since these resources are used in production, we refer to them as **factors of production.** The factor of production we call **land** includes everything provided by our *natural environment.* It includes land itself in its many forms: farmland, parkland, open space. It also includes our water, air, mineral, and fossil fuel resources. Moreover, our environment is a *receptacle* for the deposit of waste materials, a use of land that has important economic implications.

By **labor** we mean not only the time and muscle power but the brainpower of those people who constitute the *labor force.* The U.S. labor force consists of that part of the population aged 16 and over that is either working or seeking work.

Capital is a *produced* resource. It refers to those produced factors of production such as factory buildings, office buildings, machinery, equipment, roads, and bridges used in the production and/or distribution of goods and services. The **capital stock** consists of the sum total of those produced resources. **Investment** is the process of adding to the stock of capital.

Our land, labor, and capital resources can also be classified on the basis of whether they are *reproducible* or *exhaustible.* Capital and labor can be reproduced; fossil fuels, such as coal and oil, by contrast, are exhaustible.

The common thread: Scarcity

What all these resources share in common is the fact that they are scarce. However, scarcity is *not* determined by whether a resource is exhaustible or reproducible. Nor is it determined by the fact that there may be only a limited amount of the resource available. *A resource is scarce only if there is less of it than people want during any time period.* Although hardworking individuals outnumber lazy bums, the former are a scarce resource but the latter are not!

The point that needs emphasis is this: The sum of our individual and collective wants far outstrips the resources that are available to satisfy those wants. No matter how well off we are—individually or as a nation—we can always produce a long list of unsatisfied wants and needs. These desires are unmet simply because we do not have the means—the resources—to satisfy them. The U.S. economic system is often described as affluent, perhaps the most affluent in the world. But it is important to note that the quantities of goods and services we produce and consume would have to increase significantly if the *average* American were to be as well off as our nation's moderately wealthy people. Imagine how large our total output would have to be if the average American were to be as well off as those whose wealth and incomes run into the millions.

However, by comparison with living standards elsewhere in the world, ours is truly an affluent society. When we consider that almost 800 million people—nearly one-fifth of the world's population—goes to bed hungry each night, could we ever seriously question that resources are scarce?

Moreover, many people think that conditions are getting worse, especially in view of the rate at which we are now depleting our supply of exhaustible resources, such as oil and natural gas. Indeed, some think that if we continue to use up resources at the current rate, the most we can hope for by the turn of the next century is an average standard of living at the level of bare physiological necessity.

Scarcity and the choices we make

Because land, labor, and capital are scarce, it is critically important that we use those resources wisely. In order to discover the meaning of wise use, however, we must come to an understanding of how those resources are actually used. Basically, *how our resources are used is determined by people;* in particular, it is determined by those who own or have control of the resources. In our economic system, ownership and control are divided between the private sector and government. In other more centrally controlled economic systems, government plays a decidedly more important role.

It is important to understand who decides how our resources are used and how they decide, for they determine the very dimensions of our economy. **What** goods and services are produced by our economic system, **How** those goods and services are produced (i.e., what resources are used in their production), and **For whom** the resultant output is produced are all resolved by those decisionmakers. In addition, these people determine **How extensively** our resources will be used—whether some of them will remain idle or whether they will be fully employed.

What, how, for whom, and **how extensively** constitute the four basic questions that need to be resolved by decisionmakers in any economic system. There are a great many ways to resolve these questions; no single way is necessarily *the* correct one. However, we do know that all of the troubling economic issues confronting our society—for example, inflation, unemployment, inequities in the distribution of income and wealth, pollution, and monopoly power—result from decisions made by people about the use of our scarce resources. Any modification of those problems will demand modifications of the decisions made.

Scarcity, choice, and mutual dependence

This last observation—namely, that many characteristics of our economy are determined by the decisions people make in regard to the use of scarce resources—is important because it highlights the fact that we live in an economic system characterized by **mutual dependence.** Each of us produces a mere fraction of the goods and services we consume. We depend on others to produce everything else we want and need. And since everyone else also depends on the decisions of other people, our economy involves a very high degree of mutal dependence.

In Chapter 2 we discuss how *capital accumulation, specialization,* and *exchange* have contributed to the high degree of mutual dependence that exists in our economy. These forces, as we will see, have been important in generating the high standards of living we now enjoy. However, not all aspects of mutual dependence benefit everyone. Women, blacks, and other minorities who are the targets of discrimination often suffer as a consequence of the decisions of others. And what about the effect of inflation on elderly people forced to live on fixed pension incomes? Isn't inflation largely the outcome of decisions made by other people elsewhere in the economy? And what about the impact on those who are forced into unemployment as a result of government policies?

In sum, a high degree of mutual dependence implies that our individual well-being depends to a significant degree on the decisions of others. For the majority of Americans, the decisions of others have been favorable in the sense of providing them with ample opportunity to achieve higher standards of living. For a large number of people, however, the decisions of others have clearly inhibited chances for advancement.

ECONOMICS: THE SCIENCE OF CHOICE

No definition of *economics* would completely satisfy all economists. Part of the difficulty lies in the fact that economists are concerned with the behavior of people, and the complexities of people's behavior cannot be easily captured in a single definition. As a result, some economists have suggested, only half in jest, that "economics is what economists do."

Nonetheless, there is broad agreement about some of the essential ingredients of a definition, even if these ingredients are not all-inclusive. *Economics is the study of how scarce resources are allocated among alternative uses. It is the study of the choices people make with respect to the use of scarce resources, and how they make their choices.*

There are two fundamental elements in this definition—*scarce resources* and *alternative uses* of those resources. When both elements are present, a problem of choice arises; that problem we designate an economic problem.

The imbalance between people's available resources and people's wants is *the* economic problem. Our land, labor, and capital resources can be employed to produce a wide variety of goods and services desired by people. But if we were to sum up all people's wants, we would soon discover that those wants far outstrip the resources available to satisfy them. Therein lies the problem: What use should we make of our resources when we can't get everything we want?

If the problem involves choice, it is an economic problem. Thus, even marriage and children are economic problems! They are not exclusively economic problems because sociological, psychological, anthropological, and other considerations enter into people's decisions about these matters. Nor are any of the other problems noted in this chapter exclusively economic problems. But in each of the examples cited, the fact that a scarce resource exists for which there are alternative uses is enough to make each an economic problem.

Evaluating choices: Opportunity costs

Whenever we make choices, we give up something. In other words, in making the choices we incur a cost; the cost is measured by what we forego. To illustrate, you incurred a cost when you decided to go to college for four years. Part of the cost can be measured by the other goods and services you could have purchased with the money spent on books, tuition, and room and board. The remaining cost can be measured by the opportunities foregone because you decided to remain in college for four years. You forego, for example, the income you could have earned had you taken a full-time job immediately after high school.

In recognition of the notion that alternatives must be foregone when choices are made, economists have developed what is perhaps the central concept in economics—the concept of **opportunity cost.** Each time we make a choice, we incur an opportunity cost. That cost is measured by the opportunities we forego in making the choice that we do. Formally, opportunity cost is measured as *the sacrifice of the next most highly valued alternative.* Why the highest-valued sacrificed alternative? Because that is the best measure of what we must give up in choosing as we do. That's the price we pay.

A word of caution

Although the idea of opportunity cost is simple enough, it is often extremely difficult to conceptualize and measure. The reason? *Just as the benefits we expect to receive from the choices we make are determined subjectively, so are the opportunity costs.* That is, the value that people attach to each of the alternatives they face are determined subjectively, not objectively. Since people value things differently, it is therefore reasonable to expect not only differences in the choices people make, but also differences of opinion about the value of those choices. Your decision to go to college was subjective. Other alternative uses of your time and money were available but, for some reason, you attached greater value to the choice you made than to the alternatives. On the other hand, some of your high school classmates turned down the opportunity to go to college and chose to go to work instead. Were they wrong? Who is to say? In their minds, they made the decision they believed was right for them.

"I really don't think college would be right for me, Dad. Could I just have $6,000 a year in CASH instead?"

Reprinted by permission *The Wall Street Journal.*

The same kinds of differences of opinion exist about the use of our nation's scarce resources. To some people, what we forego by spending as much as we do on national defense is a decent standard of living for the poor. By the same token, others argue that we should spend less on poverty programs and more on national defense to better protect ourselves against a hostile world. Who's right? Who knows? It is strictly a matter of judgment. Thus what constitutes the best use of our resources cannot be determined objectively; what is best can only be determined in the mind of the decisionmaker. The "best" choice

of one person could very easily be the "worst" choice of another.

Despite the highly subjective nature of opportunity cost, the concept is important because it forces us to think in terms of what we must give up in making the choices we make. If we fail to conceptualize these costs properly, the possibility exists that we will make incorrect decisions about the use of our resources. As we shall see in later chapters, many government actions might never have been undertaken had the costs of those actions been properly conceptualized— that is, if the costs considered by our representatives had been opportunity costs.

THE METHODOLOGY OF ECONOMICS

Economics is a science. As such, its fundamental objective is the establishment of *valid generalizations* about certain aspects of human behavior. These generalizations are sometimes called *laws* (as in *laws* of supply and demand). However, because it is commonplace to think of laws as immutable truths, which economic laws are not, it is more accurate to describe these generalizations as *theories.*

Why is the establishment of valid generalizations about economic phenomena so important? Because it better enables us to *predict.* Prediction is important because it allows the possibility that we can control or influence outcomes.

In the context of our earlier discussion, the crux of our scientific inquiry is this: Economics is the science of choice. In our study of economics we seek valid generalizations about the principles underlying the choices people make. That knowledge will better enable us to predict the outcomes of people's behavior, which in turn will better enable us to formulate policies to alter those outcomes if alterations are deemed appropriate.

While the statement of our objective seems simple enough, the attainment of that objective is by no means simple. The difficulty of economics stems from its concern with people's behavior and the outcomes of their behavior—a subject that is quite complex. We live in an economic system in which literally millions of economic decisions are made daily by households, producers, and government. The results of all of this decisionmaking are reflected in the dimensions of our economy—in the goods and services that are daily produced and consumed, in the distribution of income and wealth, in the quality of our environment, in the unemployment rate, in the inflation rate, and in the growth rate, to mention just a few. The task we have set for ourselves in this book is to try to understand and explain all of this interrelated activity.

The need to simplify, to abstract

We might begin by attempting to inquire into all of the reasons *why* people make the economic decisions they do. However, such an investigation would ultimately be doomed to failure. Human motivation is simply too complex to be comprehended fully. Why people do what they do is itself an inquiry into all the factors that make people tick—an impossible task, to say the least!

But even if we were able to compile such a list, what would we do with it? We would still have to discover some way to *give meaning* to all of those facts. We would need to discover, that is, some *organizing principle* or set of organizing principles on which to arrange and interpret these facts. It is the objective of *economic theory* to provide the appropriate organizing principles.

For economic theory to give meaning to reality, it must simplify reality and abstract from it. This statement may at first appear to be contradictory. How can economic theory enhance our understanding of reality if it simplifies and abstracts from the reality we wish to understand? The answer has two parts. The first part has already been alluded to: The economy is so complicated, such a maze of actions and reactions, that there is no hope whatsoever of understanding it all fully. The best we can hope for is a partial understanding. To accomplish even that objective, therefore, we need to simplify reality— to divest reality of its complexity. The second part of the answer has to do with abstraction: Abstraction is the groundwork of classification, the means by which things can be separated and organized.

To illustrate these ideas, let us focus for a moment on a single economic event—the quantity of steak purchased over the course of a week. There is no way we can understand all of the reasons why people bought steak during that week. We could ask everyone who bought steak that week, Why? "What about you, Fred?" "Well, my in-laws came to visit and I figured if I served steak it would impress them." "And what about you, Joan?" "I hadn't had steak in months; the craving became so intense that I rushed out to buy one." "Susie?" "The store had a steak sale." "J. B.?" "I eat steak every week."

We could, of course, go on and on. But what purpose would that serve? Even if we interviewed everyone who bought steak that week—a huge task, to say the least—what would we have at the end? A roomful of interview sheets and several thousand different reasons for people buying steak that week. Assuming we could digest all those facts, is there any reason to think that those same people would be similarly motivated the next week? It is not likely. Some of those people will not buy steak the next week; others will, but for different reasons; and some new people will buy steak the next week who did not buy any the week before.

As you can see, acquiring more and more facts, week after week, will not necessarily help you to understand reality in this single instance. And what about all of the other economic decisions people make besides whether or not to buy steak? There must be a better way.

There *is* a better way. Let's step back—abstract—from reality and attempt to simplify the problem. We acknowledge that people's motivations are complex; many of the reasons for buying steak are unique. However, instead of focusing on the factors that are unique to each individual—the factors that are different for each—suppose we attempt to discover those factors that are the same. Thus, abstracting from the problem, we might discover that three important factors are present in almost everyone's decision to purchase steak. The first might be the price of steak itself. Almost everyone will be influenced by its price per pound. A second factor might be people's incomes. Incomes certainly differ, but each person is influenced by their income level as far as the purchase of steak is concerned. A third common factor might be the prices of other meats.

Think carefully about what we have just done. We have taken a problem that is extremely complex, too complex to understand completely. We have abstracted from reality and simplified the problem. We have hypothesized that most people make their decisions about steak *partly* on the basis of three common factors—the price of steak, their incomes, and the prices of other meats. Perhaps if we search hard enough, we will be able to discover yet another common factor. But enough has been said to illustrate the process.

To recap, by abstracting from the details of reality—by discarding those factors that are different for each person and focusing our attention on the common aspects—we are able to reduce the problem to more manageable proportions. Being confronted with fewer facts, we are in a much better position to formulate theories to enhance our understanding of reality. What is needed is a theory that explains how people's steak purchases are influenced by the three common factors identified.

Of course, the usefulness of any theory will depend on how well it is supported by the facts— i.e., on how well it conforms to reality. The ultimate test of a theory is its ability to predict— to explain the facts again and again as economic circumstances change. Once we develop a theory to explain people's steak purchases based on the three common factors, we will need to test the theory to make sure it is consistent with the facts. Then, if the theory appears to be consistent with reality, we will want to see how well it predicts. If the price of steak changes, will we be able to predict how people's steak purchases will change using the theory we have developed? And will the theory accurately predict how people's pur-

chases will be influenced if their incomes or the prices of other meats change? If the theory is able to predict fairly accurately, then there is reason to hold on to it; if it fails to predict accurately, then we will have to go back to the drawing board to discover what went wrong.

A LABORATORY METHODOLOGY APPLIED TO REAL-WORLD EXPERIENCE: *CETERIS PARIBUS* AND ALL THAT

Economic laws (or theories), like all scientific laws, should never be interpreted as exact, precise relationships for which there are no exceptions. On the contrary, there are *always* exceptions to *all* scientific laws. In the development of a theory, we simplify and abstract from reality; there are bound to be exceptions as a consequence of the workings of factors that were excluded.

Our ability to *identify* the factors responsible for exceptions to theories, and *our understanding of the consequences of those factors,* are as important as the formulation of the theories themselves. One method of determining the circumstances under which a theory is true—which means also determining the circumstances under which there could be exceptions—is *controlled experimentation.* For example, in order to discover the effects of streptomycin on a living organism, biologists will undertake experiments to control—to hold constant or unchanged—the *other* factors that affect the organism (heat, light, oxygen, etc.). In this manner, they can isolate the effects of streptomycin on the organism and study its effects separately from the effects of other factors.

Unfortunately, controlled experimentation is seldom possible for the economist. We can rarely identify the impact of changes in one factor in isolation from all the rest. Specifically, the impact of a change in the price of steak on the amount purchased can rarely be isolated, as in a laboratory, from the effects caused by changes in income because both factors are often changing at the same time. The real world is the economist's laboratory. Accordingly, controlled experiments of the sort undertaken by biologists are not possible. Nevertheless, the methodology of controlled experiments plays an important role in economics. It must, however, be adapted to fit the circumstances facing economists. Before examining how the laboratory methodology is adapted, let us examine in more detail the nature of the laboratory methodology itself.

Scientists who undertake controlled experiments isolate the particular phenomena of interest by explicitly holding unchanged all factors other than those under consideration. Isolating phenomena in this way is an essential first step toward understanding them. Nevertheless, the ability of the scientific law to predict real-world phenomena depends on those other factors remaining unchanged. If the other factors do not remain unchanged, the law may fail to predict accurately.

The law or theory may fail to predict accurately because it is too simple. By conducting more complex experiments—i.e., by sequentially allowing for the influence of previously excluded factors—more complex laws that potentially possess greater predictive power can be constructed.

When scientific inquiry advances from the simple to the more complex, two important results emerge. First, since greater complexity implies fewer excluded forces, the predictive ability of the law or theory is enhanced. Second, and equally important, as each new force is introduced one at a time, the researcher is able to identify how the results change; it is thus possible to identify the separate influence of each force on the phenomenon in question. In this manner, an assessment can be made of the importance of each factor under consideration.

Using our earlier example, biologists could determine the influence of streptomycin on the organism under different intensities of light and then under different temperatures. Finally, different combinations of light and temperature could be examined. These experiments complicate the results but allow for greater accuracy in prediction. They improve the biologist's ability to predict the impact of streptomycin on living organisms in real-life situations.

Although economists cannot engage in controlled experiments, they isolate the phenomena to be studied by *assuming* all other factors remain unchanged. As was the case with the biologist, isolating the phenomena is a necessary first step toward understanding them. Of course, the accuracy or validity of an economic theory will depend on the validity of the assumptions. If the factors assumed to remain constant are in fact changing, the results of real-world experience may differ from the economic theory.

More complex laws can be devised by assuming fewer and fewer factors remain unchanged. As before, the results of this greater complexity are twofold. First, the increased complexity enhances the predictive ability of the law or theory. And second, as each additional factor is allowed to vary sequentially, the economist can identify and assess the importance of each factor under consideration.

Thus the counterpart of the controlled experiment for the economist is the assumption that all factors other than those being examined in isolation remain unchanged. Such assumptions are referred to as *ceteris paribus* assumptions. *Ceteris paribus* is a Latin phrase that, literally interpreted, means "other things being equal" or "other things being unchanged."

Economic theory: An illustration

These ideas can be illustrated with the so-called **law of demand.** This law states that the quantity demanded of good X will be inversely related to the price of X: If the price of X increases, the quantity demanded will fall; if the price of X falls, the quantity demanded will rise. Here, the factors isolated are the price of X and the quantity of X demanded. In devising the law, we assume that certain things are unchanged—namely, all of the factors other than the price of X that could possibly affect the purchase of X. The validity of the law depends on these factors remaining constant.

However, we know that the amount purchased depends not only on the price of the good in question, but on other factors as well. Income and the prices of *other* goods and services are just two of the additional considerations that enter into people's decisions about how much to buy. Thus the law of demand will be true only if, among other things, people's income and the prices of other goods and services remain unchanged. In Chapter 3 we examine the law of demand in detail. In that chapter we will also examine how a more complex theory of demand can be devised by varying income and the prices of other goods and services in addition to the price of X.

ECONOMIC LAWS: PROBLEMS

Considerable care must be exercised both in the formation and interpretation of economic laws. We highlight here only some of the major problem areas.

Different interpretations of real-world experiences. Economists are unable to conduct controlled experiments. Therefore they are forced to develop their scientific laws or theories on the basis of their interpretations of real-world experience. Since real-world phenomena are so complex and interrelated, it is often possible to interpret any given event in several different ways. As a consequence, we could formulate several competing theories to explain the *same* phenomenon. As we shall see later, the existence of several competing theories can prove very troublesome for government decisionmaking. Which theory is judged "correct" will often dictate which government policy ought to be pursued.

Post hoc, ergo propter hoc **fallacy.** Literally interpreted, the Latin phrase *post hoc, ergo propter hoc* means "after this, therefore on account of this." Specifically, this Latin phrase means that if event A occurred before event B, event A caused B. This is not necessarily true; it may be a fallacy.

Sometimes it is true that event A preceded event B *and* that A caused B. But it would be incorrect to conclude that A caused B *because* A preceded B. The point can be illustrated by the following example. Some people argue that large corporations and not labor unions are the source of the inflationary pressures in the U.S. economy *because* price increases occur in ad-

vance of wage increases; if the situation were reversed, labor unions could be blamed. But did the large corporations raise their prices in *anticipation* of higher union wage demands? If so, wouldn't it be correct to conclude that wage increases caused price increases even though prices went up first?

The dynamics of economic change. Even if we are lucky enough to formulate an economic theory that corresponds closely to real-world events, that successfully predicts people's behavior, it may not always be an accurate predictor. Economics is concerned with human behavior, and human behavior changes, sometimes rapidly and unpredictably; many economic laws will not retain their validity in the face of such changes. We must constantly examine our economic theories in the light of changing reality to see if they remain valid. And we must discard or modify them if experience so dictates.

The fallacy of composition. This fallacy can arise when we automatically assume that what is true for an individual or other small entity must be true for the whole. It is reasonable to assume, for example, that I personally can have no influence on the price of gasoline. Whether I drive my car a little or a lot will not affect the price at the pump. However, if *we all* decide to, say, double our driving, the result is likely to be a substantial increase in the price of motor gasoline. What is true for the individual is often not true for the group or the whole. To assume otherwise is to commit a fallacy of composition.

This distinction between the small and the large is also reflected in the way this book (and the study of economics) is divided between **macroeconomics** and **microeconomics.**

Microeconomics is the study of individual market participants—the individual consumer, the individual firm—and individual markets—the market for oil, the market for cars. In microeconomics we focus our attention on individual *parts* of the economy, not on the whole. Macroeconomics, on the other hand, is concerned with the behavior of people in the aggregate—with the aggregate of consumers, the aggregate of businesspeople, and with government overall.

Until very recently, microeconomics and macroeconomics were viewed by most economists as quite distinct fields of study because of their (generally) quite distinct methods of analysis. Although this view is still the dominant one in the profession, a large body of literature has recently developed that aims at linking the methods of analysis. Formally, that literature is entitled the *microeconomic foundations of macroeconomics.* This book will reflect at least some of these advances.

Values: Normative versus positive economics

Earlier we stated that the objective of our scientific inquiry was the establishment of valid generalizations about the choices people make. These generalizations are important because they enable the economist to predict. Prediction, in turn, serves as the basis for the formation of policies designed to alter the outcomes of people's behavior.

Up to this point, we have been concerned exclusively with the formation of valid generalizations—with scientific laws or theories—and their predictive abilities. We have been concerned, that is, with the question of how we go about constructing theories of people's behavior. We have been concerned with the economy *as it is.* Analyzing the economy *as it is* is known as **positive economics.**

Since positive economics is the study of the choices people make, without judging those choices, it is a value-free science; it is an objective science. However, to keep the laws of economics value-free, it is essential that researchers avoid letting value judgments influence their theories.

On the other hand, the design of policy for the purpose of altering people's behavior is **normative economics;** it is concerned with what *ought to be.* It is *not* an objective science; it is *not* value-free.

Policy measures are designed to change people's behavior. But whether their behavior ought to be changed is itself a value judgment. Whether the outcomes resulting from people's choices are "good" or "bad," or whether they could be improved can only be determined by subjective evaluation. What an "appropriate" distribution of income is cannot be determined objectively;

it is completely subjective. The same is true of the other goals we set for ourselves: high employment, price stability, a clean environment, rapid growth, and so forth. We may all want to achieve these goals in general. But when it comes to specifics, sharp disagreements—subjective disagreements—can and do arise. This is especially so in view of the conflicts that exist in attaining these goals. Rapid growth and a clean environment seem to clash head-on; high employment and price stability appear to be unattainable simultaneously.

It is essential that we understand the relationship between positive and normative economics. Positive scientific knowledge is clearly a prerequisite to effective policymaking, even though the goals to be attained by the recommended policy actions are determined completely subjectively. In order to recommend a given policy, it is important to know whether the policy will actually promote the goal. Put differently, the knowledge of how behavior will be altered as a result of a recommended economic policy, and an understanding of the likely outcome of these behavioral changes, are essential to the normative judgment of what constitutes the desired course of action. As Milton Friedman, the 1976 Nobel laureate in economics, puts it:

> The Road to Hell is paved with good intentions precisely because of the neglect of this rather obvious point. . . . Many countries around the world are today experiencing socially destructive inflation, abnormally high unemployment, misuse of economic resources, and, in some cases, the suppression of human freedom not because evil men deliberately sought to achieve these results, nor because of differences in values among their citizens, *but because of erroneous judgments about the consequences of government measures:* errors that at least in principle are capable of being corrected by the progress of positive economic science.[1]

The estimation of economic relationships

The testing of theory against fact is an essential part of economics, as it is for any science.

[1] Milton Friedman, "Nobel Lecture: Inflation and Unemployment," *Journal of Political Economy,* June 1977, p. 453.

Increasingly, economists are using highly sophisticated statistical techniques both to verify (or refute) economic theories and to predict economic events. The branch of economics that deals with the quantitative analysis of people's economic behavior is called **econometrics.**

The most difficult problem in econometrics is how to provide reliable quantitative estimates of the relationships suggested by economic theory. You will recall our earlier discussion of the law of demand in which we posited an inverse relationship between the quantity demanded and price. We further stated that the amount demanded also depended on income. Therefore, if price and income both change, we will need some technique that allows us to identify the magnitude of the influence of *each* on the quantity demanded. It is the task of econometrics to provide us with such techniques.

It is necessary to develop such techniques because the economist cannot engage in controlled experimentation. Real-world experience rarely provides us with isolated economic phenomena. The *ceteris paribus* condition that all other things remain unchanged—a condition that is required to test our theories—is rarely true in the real world. The challenge faced by econometricians is the development of techniques that can, in effect, artificially hold other influences constant. In this way, the econometrician can test theory against fact and measure the magnitude of the influence of one factor on another.

Of course, we are a long way from the development of any foolproof techniques. But we have witnessed some remarkable improvements in our estimation capabilities in the past two decades. The world is an extremely complicated place. Is it any wonder then that we face formidable problems in *statistically* sorting out all of the relevant economic relationships in view of the challenge we face in sorting them out *conceptually?*

SUMMARY

1. When confronted with scarce resources and alternative uses of those resources, a problem of choice arises—an economic problem.

2. By choosing to use our scarce resources as we do we incur an *opportunity cost*—the foregone opportunity of using those resources in other ways.

3. Scarcity is *not* determined by whether a resource is exhaustible or reproducible, nor is it determined by the fact that there may be only a limited amount of the resource available. A resource is scarce only if there is less of it than people want during any time period.

4. The sum of our individual and collective wants far outstrip the resources available to satisfy those wants. It is important, therefore, that we use those resources wisely. It is also important to understand how resources are actually used.

5. How our resources are used is determined by those who own or control the resources. They determine **What, How, For whom,** and **How extensively**—the four basic questions that must be resolved by decisionmakers in any economic system.

6. Economics is a science. It has as its fundamental objective the establishment of valid generalizations about the principles underlying the choices people make. This is important because it better enables us to predict.

7. The valid generalizations we seek take the form of economic theories. The objective of a theory is to give meaning to reality. To give meaning to reality, an economic theory must simplify reality and abstract from it.

8. In the development of their scientific theories, economists cannot undertake controlled experiments as biologists or physicists can do. Nevertheless, the methodology of controlled experiments plays an important role in economics. It must, however, be adapted to fit the different circumstances facing economists.

9. Scientists who undertake controlled experiments isolate the phenomena of interest by explicitly holding unchanged all factors other than those under consideration. Economists, however, isolate the phenomena of interest by *assuming* all other factors remain unchanged. Such assumptions are referred to as *ceteris paribus* assumptions.

10. Considerable care must be exercised in formulating and interpreting economic laws. Be-

cause it is possible that any given economic event can be interpreted in several different ways, several competing theories may well exist to explain the *same* phenomenon. We must avoid the *post hoc, ergo propter hoc* **fallacy.** We must recognize that changes in people's behavior may render earlier validated theories invalid. We must avoid committing *fallacies of composition.*

11.   *Positive economics* is the study of the economy *as it is.* As such, positive economics is an objective (i.e., value-free) science. *Normative economics* is the study of what *ought to be.* As such, normative economics is *not* an objective science.

CONCEPTS FOR REVIEW

Resource

Opportunity cost

Scarcity

Factors of production

Land

Labor

Capital

Capital stock

Investment

Mutual dependence

**Laboratory methodology of controlled
    experimentation**

Ceteris paribus

Post hoc, ergo propter hoc **fallacy**

Fallacy of composition

Macroeconomics

Microeconomics

Positive economics

Normative economics

Econometrics

QUESTIONS FOR DISCUSSION

(Those marked with an asterisk (*) are more difficult.)

1.   Explain why it is appropriate to view each of the following as an economic problem.

   a.   George and Helene decide to get married.

   b.   Fred decides that he will study harder to raise his grade point average.

   c.   The government passes legislation that calls for the installation of "scrubbers" in smokestacks to reduce the amount of particulate matter being emitted into the air.

   d.   John decides to join the army.

   e.   Mary decides to go to business school.

2.   You have often heard the expression "the price of success." Explain what this means in terms of the concept of opportunity cost.

3.   "Economics is useless. It deals too much with theory and not enough with facts." Evaluate critically.

4.   "Economists are always disagreeing with each other. Put a dozen economists in a room and you are likely to get a dozen different opinions—perhaps more. Economics can't be much of a science if that much disagreement exists." Evaluate critically.

5.   Kenneth Boulding once stated, "Theories without facts may be barren, but facts without theories are meaningless."[2] Explain.

6.   "What is good for GM is good for the country." Critically evaluate.

*7.   The labor force in the United States is defined as that portion of the population aged 16 or older that is either working or seeking work. The unemployment rate is defined as the percentage of the labor force that is unemployed—that is, the ratio of the number of people unemployed to the labor force.

Most economists believe that the unemployment rate is very sensitive to changes in *total* spending. Specifically, there is a theory that increased total spending will bring about a reduction in the unemployment rate.

   a.   Does this economic theory state that the unemployment rate will *necessarily* decline if total spending increases? Under what circumstances would an increase in total spending be accompanied by an *unchanged* unemployment rate? Could an increase in total spending ever be accompanied by a rise(!) in the unemployment rate? (*Hint:* Remember that the unemployment rate is defined as the ratio of two numbers; you have to look at both.)

   b.   If government spending alone is increased, does the law state that the unemployment rate will decline? Explain. (*Hint:* Is government spending synonymous with *total* spending?)

---

[2] Kenneth E. Boulding, *Economic Analysis: Microeconomics,* 4th ed. (New York: Harper & Row, 1966), p. 5.

Our economic system is a maze of complicated relationships involving millions of people who daily make billions of economic decisions regarding the use of our scarce resources. The results of all this decisionmaking are reflected in the basic dimensions of our economy and in the economic problems—such as inflation, unemployment, poverty, and pollution—to which we devote so much of our attention.

Underlying all of this complexity are a few fundamental principles that hold the key to our understanding of the way our economic system operates. Each of these principles has been identified in the title to this chapter: **Scarcity, choice, and mutual dependence.** An understanding of each is essential if we are to answer the four basic questions that confront the people of this economy, as well as the peoples of all other economies: **what** to produce, **how** to produce each good and service, **for whom** goods and services shall be produced, and **how extensively** resources shall be used. It is our purpose in this chapter to undertake a thorough examination of these important principles.

THE ECONOMIC PROBLEM

We live in a world of limited resources. However, because resources are limited does not mean they are necessarily scarce. **Scarcity** arises because our resources are not sufficient to satisfy all our wants. Put simply, the sum of our individual and collective wants far outstrips the land, labor, and capital resources available to satisfy those wants.

Thus, choices must be made as to which wants will be satisfied and which will not. *Who* will be allowed to make those choices and for what ends are issues that each economic system—capitalist, socialist, communist, etc.—must settle. But whatever the ends or whoever decides, the necessity of having to choose is a fact of life for decisionmakers in every economic system.

The central problem all economies face is this: *How do we **best** allocate scarce resources among alternative uses?* What constitutes the *best* uses of scarce resources cannot be determined inde-

Chapter 2

Scarcity, choice, and mutual dependence

pendently of the goals each society establishes for itself. Since our goals and those of the Soviet Union are so different, for example, the best uses of our own resources will certainly be different from the best uses of resources in the Soviet Union.

Are we to conclude, then, that the best uses of scarce resources are determined completely subjectively? After all, are not the goals of any society determined subjectively and therefore a matter of **normative** economics? Yes and no. Yes, because resources ought to be used in a manner that will promote the goals society sets for itself; no, because different uses promote those goals differently. Although decisions about resource use aim at attaining society's goals, not all uses will promote those goals equally *efficiently*. Efficient resource use means *getting the most (in terms of the chosen goals) from available resources*. In principle, efficiency can be determined objectively. Efficiency is a matter of **positive** economics.

Why is efficiency such an important consideration? Because our resources are scarce. We cannot possibly hope to satisfy all our wants—to attain fully all our goals. Thus it is critical that we do the best with what we have. It is critical, that is, that we use our scarce resources in efficient ways.

Production possibilities

These points can be illustrated with the aid of a **production possibilities table** and its graphic counterpart, a **production possibilities curve**. Three principles underlie this illustration:

1. Given some interval of time (such as a year), there is a limit to the quantity of goods and services that can be produced. That limit is determined by the quantity and quality of the land, labor, and capital resources, which, we assume, are fixed in supply over the given time interval.

2. If resources are being used fully, the increased production of any one good will necessitate the reduced production of some other good(s); to increase the production of any one

good, resources must be withdrawn from employment elsewhere. There is a cost—an **opportunity cost**—to increasing the production of any one good. This opportunity cost we measure as the value of the good(s) whose production is reduced.

3. Finally, to shift more and more resources toward the production of any one good, *increasing* amounts of some other good(s) must be given up to achieve the same quantity increase in the good desired. The reason? The increased production of the desired good will lead, *increasingly,* to the employment of resources that are less and less adaptable to the production of that good. Thus, to achieve the same quantity increase of the good in question, more resources than before must be withdrawn from employment elsewhere; and therefore increasing amounts of other goods must be given up. This phenomenon is called the **law of increasing (opportunity) costs.**

These principles are highlighted in Figure 2.1. For illustrative purposes, we imagine an economy in which there is a fixed quantity of resources available for the production of two goods only—pickles and pumps. This example is an obvious simplification of reality; our economic system produces not two but literally millions of goods and services. Nevertheless, the example is completely general in the sense that it captures the essence of the economic problem. We could let "pumps" represent "all other goods," in which case the production possibilities example would involve the two goods "pickles" and "all other goods"; or pickles could be used as the symbol for private goods and pumps the symbol for government-produced goods; or pickles could represent consumer goods and pumps capital goods; and so forth.

In any event, as Figure 2.1 makes clear, the limited resources in our hypothetical economy could be employed in a number of alternative ways. All resources could be devoted to the production of pickles alone (production alternative A), pumps alone (production alternative F), or some combination of the two goods (production alternatives B, C, D, or E). However, regardless of which production alternative is selected, two basic facts cannot be avoided:

Figure 2.1
Production possibilities of pickles and pumps

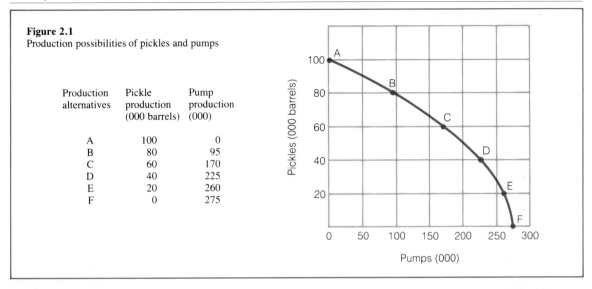

Production alternatives	Pickle production (000 barrels)	Pump production (000)
A	100	0
B	80	95
C	60	170
D	40	225
E	20	260
F	0	275

1. *Since resources are limited, there is a limit to the amount that can be produced. This defines the outer edge or limit of the production possibilities curve.*

2. *If resources are being used fully, the increased production of one good necessitates the reduced production of the other good. This requires a downward-sloping* **production possibilities curve.**

Opportunity costs

As a consequence of these facts, 100,000 barrels of pickles and 275,000 pumps cannot *both* be produced at the same time. Instead, one or the other alternative, or some combination in between, must be chosen. Decisionmakers must choose the production alternative that best satisfies their wants or goals.

Suppose production alternative C is chosen. (*Why* C was selected is not important at the moment.) Suppose, that is, that the limited resources are used to produce 60,000 barrels of pickles and 170,000 pumps. By choosing this combination of goods, decisionmakers have incurred an opportunity cost. By choosing to use their limited resources in one way they forego the opportunity of using them in some other way. In our example, the opportunity cost of producing 60,000 barrels

of pickles is the 105,000 additional pumps that could have been produced with the resources that were instead employed in the production of pickles. If all of the resources had been devoted to the production of pumps, 275,000 pumps would have been produced; in order to produce 60,000 barrels of pickles, pump production had to be reduced by 105,000. The opportunity cost of producing 60,000 barrels of pickles is, therefore, 105,000 pumps.

What is the opportunity cost of producing 170,000 pumps? Forty thousand barrels of pickles; that is, 40,000 barrels of pickles were effectively given up when production alternative C was selected over alternative A.

To carry the analysis one step further, suppose decisionmakers decided that production alternative C is not the desired combination of pickles and pumps, but, rather, alternative D now represents the preferred combination. To bring about that change, resources will have to be transferred from the production of pickles to the production of pumps; pump production will rise and pickle production will fall. And what is the opportunity cost of increasing pump production from 170,000 units to 225,000? The 20,000 barrels of pickles whose production must be given up to provide the resources needed for the increased production of pumps.

Law of increasing (opportunity) costs. Suppose the most preferred position for our hypothetical economy changes from production alternative D to E. Again pickle production must fall so that pump production can increase. But the 20,000-barrel reduction in pickle production in moving from D to E results in a much smaller increase in pump production than did the movement from C to D. Pump production increases by 35,000 in the movement from D to E at a cost of 20,000 barrels of pickles; in the movement from C to D, however, pump production increased by 55,000 at the *same cost* of 20,000 barrels of pickles. The shift from D to E was thus more costly than from C to D. Our hypothetical economy *got less* for the 20,000 barrels of pickles it gave up in moving from D to E than it did in its move from C to D.

This is an example of the phenomenon known as the **law of increasing (opportunity) costs.** A given quantity reduction in the production of any one good will yield less and less of an increase in the production of other goods. The law of increasing costs is responsible for the bowed (concave-to-the-origin) shape of the production possibilities curve.

What accounts for the law of increasing costs? Earlier we hinted at the answer to this question. The increased production of the desired good would lead increasingly to the employment of resources that are less adaptable to the production of that good. What precisely is meant by resources being "less adaptable"?

The answer is rather complex and will be the subject of a lengthy discussion in Part Four of this book. For the moment, let us be satisfied with an incomplete but intuitive explanation:

The law of increasing costs depends, fundamentally, on two things:

1. The fact that land, labor, and capital are used in differing proportions to produce different products. The land-labor-capital combination used to produce automobiles certainly differs from the way those resources are combined to produce wheat; and the same is true of most other goods, including pumps and pickles.

2. The law of diminishing returns; or, more generally, the law of variable proportions. To illustrate, consider the production of any good—wheat, for example. Suppose 1,000 bushels of wheat can be produced using X amount of land, Y amount of labor, and Z amount of capital. Now let the amount of land devoted to wheat production increase by 10 acres (to X + 10 acres) *holding fixed the amount of labor and capital used.* What will happen to the output of wheat? Presumably it will increase; we assume that wheat production rises by 100 bushels to 1,100. Now let 10 acres more be added (raising the total to X + 20 acres), again holding fixed the amount of labor and capital. Output will increase further, but in all likelihood, output will rise by less than 100 bushels. *That is, the output added by the second 10-acre increase will be smaller than the output added by the first 10-acre increase.* This outcome is not the result of the fact that the last 10 acres are of inferior quality (though reduced quality will bring about the same outcome). It is a consequence of the *fixed* amounts of labor and capital being spread ever more thinly across more and more acres of land. This is what the law of diminishing returns is all about.

The law of diminishing returns can be stated formally as follows: As equal amounts of one input are added to fixed amounts of the other inputs, total output will rise but at a diminishing rate. Why is it at a diminishing rate? Because that one input will have less and less of the fixed inputs to work with.

The law of diminishing returns can be stated somewhat more generally as the **law of variable proportions.** In the above example we varied the proportions in which the inputs were used by varying the land input holding *constant* all other inputs. Consider now a situation in which all inputs are allowed to vary but not in the same proportion. Specifically, allow all inputs to increase, some to a greater extent than others. Under these circumstances, the **law of variable proportions** states that as the factor proportions are changed in any one direction the successive additions to total output will get smaller and smaller. And the reason? The inputs that are growing most rapidly will increasingly have less of the other inputs with which to work.

Combining these two ideas, the law of increasing costs can be explained as follows:

a. Pumps and pickles use land, labor, and capital in different proportions.

b. Increasing pump production requires that resources be shifted from pickle production.

c. Absorbing the resources released from pickle production will bring about a *change* in factor proportions in the production of pumps.

d. As a result of changing factor proportions, successive additions to the output of pumps will get smaller and smaller.

SCARCITY AND THE OPTIMUM PRODUCT MIX

With the aid of our production possibilities curve, *scarcity* can be given a simple graphic interpretation. Since the sum of all our wants far outstrips the resources available to satisfy those wants, we *prefer* a position well beyond our production possibilities curve. We always want more than we can get, but we are limited by our production possibilities. If the position we desired was less than our production possibilities, scarcity would cease to exist and our economic problem would disappear. All wants would be completely satisfied without exception.

Since our preferred position lies beyond our production possibilities, the *best* we can do is attain a position on the curve itself. To allow our resources to be used otherwise—i.e., to allow our economy to operate at a position *inside* the curve—would be a waste. It would mean an inefficient use of our resources since superior attainable alternatives exist.

These ideas are illustrated in Figure 2.2. Point H is unattainable since it lies beyond our production possibilities. On the other hand, points A, B, C, and F (and any other point on that contour) are all attainable. What is notable about each of these points is that each represents a full utilization of our resources; **full employment** of available resources exists at each and every point on the production possibilities curve.

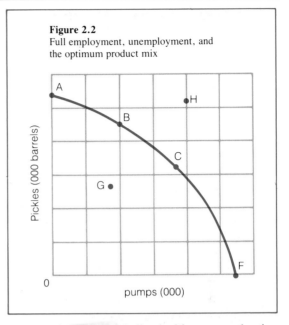

Figure 2.2
Full employment, unemployment, and the optimum product mix

At point G, which lies inside our production possibilities curve, **unemployment** exists. Resources are being used inefficiently at point G. Our preferred position lies well beyond our production possibilities curve. Thus, by operating at point G we are not even doing as well as we could. What a waste! Indeed, there can be more goods and services without having to reduce the output of other things. This means it does not cost us anything—the opportunity cost is zero—to move from, say, G to C.

The fact that resources are not being used as extensively as they could be raises the question, Why would decisionmakers permit such a state of affairs? Some answer this by arguing that it is appropriate to allow the economy to operate at a point like G for a time if other goals are thereby promoted. One goal that many people believe is promoted by having unemployed resources is that of greater price stability. Specifically, a lower rate of inflation is believed to accompany higher rates of unemployment. This highly controversial issue will be dealt with at length in Part Two of this book. For now, we will assume that departures from full employment cannot be justified on policy grounds.

Although the production possibilities curve provides us with several alternative full-employ-

Figure 2.3
The production possibilities for public
and private goods and services

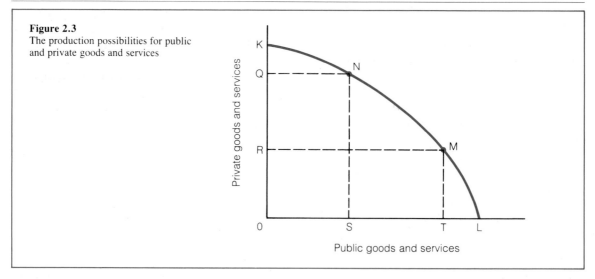

ment positions, there is no objective way of determining what single point on the curve is most
desirable. Simply put, the optimum product mix
cannot be determined objectively. It is subjective;
it is a matter of normative economics. Objectively, we cannot say whether we ought to be
producing more or less pickles relative to pumps.

The point can perhaps be best illustrated by
a brief examination of the debate over the appropriate size of government. The essence of that
problem is captured in the production possibilities curve of Figure 2.3, where *private* goods and
services are measured on the vertical axis and
public goods and services—those produced by
government—are measured on the horizontal.
(The units used to measure these different goods
and services are immaterial at the moment.)
Thus, either OK units of private goods (involving
the complete absence of government), OL units
of public goods (meaning no private sector), or
some combination in between can be produced.

Those who subscribe to a capitalistic philosophy of less government would undoubtedly prefer
a position closer to point K, such as point N.
On the other hand, those who take the position
that more should be spent on public goods and
services and less on private would prefer a position to the right of point N, perhaps point M.

Who is right? Does point N represent the optimum mix of public and private goods? Or is point
M better? Who knows? There is no way to settle

the issue objectively. But note: The opportunity
cost of producing at point N as opposed to point
M is the amount of public goods and services—
the amount ST—that must be sacrificed to produce more private goods and services. Those who
prefer a point like M can get very heated if decisionmakers fail to choose to produce what they
think is the appropriate mix. By the same token,
the opportunity cost of producing at point M
as opposed to point N is the amount of private
goods and services we must forego—QR units—
to have more public needs met. People who prefer
point N can get just as heated as those who prefer
point M. Unfortunately, all this heat casts little
light on what the optimum product mix ought
to be, nor can it!

**Behind optimum product mix: Optimum resource
mix**

The quantity and quality of our land, labor,
and capital resources effectively establish a limit
to the amount that we can produce. But whether
we get a little or a lot out of our resources will
depend on how efficiently they are used. Efficiency, however, is an elusive concept. It is important, therefore, that we examine it closely.
Once we have nailed down its meaning, we can
proceed to an analysis of how efficiency has been
enhanced through *(a)* **specialization,** *(b)* **exchange,** and *(c)* the use of **money.**

Efficiency

Generally, efficiency means using scarce resources in the *best ways possible* to produce the goods and services society *wants*. Consider this definition in parts.

1. Our first concern is with the production of goods and services that society *wants*. It matters little that we can produce large quantities of things that nobody wants. It would be inefficient to employ resources in their production when we do not have enough resources to produce all of the things that society does want.

2. Economic efficiency is *not* synonymous with engineering or technical efficiency. An engineer would argue, for example, that a plant producing pickles would be operating at peak efficiency only if it were producing *that level of output for which output per unit of input was at its maximum.* But if, *with given resources,* society wants more pickles than could be produced efficiently (from an engineering point of view) and it is willing to give up other goods to satisfy its wants, of what consequence is the engineer's definition? Would we produce less just because we are not producing that level of output for which output per unit of input is at its maximum? No. If society's wants are better satisfied with the production of more pickles, then it is *economically* efficient to produce more pickles. (This is not to suggest that efficiency from an engineering point of view is unimportant. Quite the contrary. As we shall see in Chapter 19, some forces operate in the long run to ensure that all producers produce at the point where output per unit of input is maximized. *With given resources,* however, there is no guarantee that producers will be operating at that point *at each instant in time.* Nor should they necessarily be doing so if society desires a different rate of output.)

3. As was emphasized earlier, the existence of unemployment implies an inefficient use of resources. When unemployment exists, wants that could be satisfied go unsatisfied. Therefore, only at full employment can efficiency be attained.

4. Finally, *given society's wants,* it is important, in the interests of efficiency, that our land,

labor, and capital resources be employed in activities that produce the greatest *relative* contribution. In the jargon of the economist, efficiency demands that resources be used in those activities in which they have a **comparative advantage.**

This means, for example, that we should not use experienced picklers to produce pumps at the same time that pump engineers produce pickles. By simply rearranging inputs, the total output of both pickles and pumps would rise. This is illustrated in Table 2.1.

Table 2.1

Comparative advantage and efficiency: Output per day of picklers and pump engineers

	Pickles (barrels per day)	Pumps (units per day)
Pickler	8	10
Pump engineer	6	14

Note in Table 2.1 that a pickler can produce 8 barrels of pickles per day or 10 pumps per day. The pump engineer, on the other hand, can produce 6 barrels of pickles or 14 pumps per day. Thus, if the pickler is producing pumps and the pump engineer is producing pickles, resources are not being used efficiently. Each ought to be employed where he or she has a comparative advantage. If they would simply switch jobs, the total output of *both* goods would rise; the total output of pickles would rise by two barrels per day; pump output would go up by four units per day.

Comparative advantage can be defined in fairly simple terms. Consider again Table 2.1. What is the opportunity cost of the pickler producing eight barrels of pickles? It is the 10 pumps that could otherwise have been produced. What is the opportunity cost of the pump engineer producing eight barrels of pickles (the same number as the pickler). First, it would take the pump engineer $1\frac{1}{3}$ days to produce eight barrels; in that time almost 19 pumps could have been produced. Thus, the opportunity cost of the pump engineer producing eight barrels of pickles is the almost 19 pumps that could otherwise have been produced. The fact that the opportunity cost of producing pickles for the pickler is less than that for the pump engineer—10 pumps as opposed to almost 19—means that the pickler has a comparative advantage in producing pickles. (It is left to the reader to show that the opportunity cost of producing 14 pumps for the pump engineer is smaller than the opportunity cost producing the same number of pumps for the pickler. Thus, the pump engineer has a comparative advantage in producing pumps.)

The same kind of rearrangement of resources would be called for even if the pickler was absolutely more efficient in the production of both goods. This is illustrated in Table 2.2, where it is evident that the output of *either good* per day for the pickler is much greater than that for the pump engineer. The pickler is said to possess an *absolute advantage* in the production of pickles and pumps.

Table 2.2
Absolute advantage, comparative advantage, and efficiency: Output per day of picklers and pump engineers

	Pickles (barrels per day)	Pumps (units per day)
Pickler	12	18
Pump engineer	4	10

Nevertheless, the pickler has a comparative advantage in the production of pickles; he or she is *relatively* more efficient in the production of pickles. An examination of the opportunity cost of producing pickles makes this clear. The opportunity cost of producing 12 barrels of pickles for the pickler is 18 pumps; the opportunity cost of 12 barrels of pickles for the pump engineer is 30 pumps. Likewise, the pump engineer has a comparative advantage in the production of pumps. The opportunity cost of the pump engineer producing 18 pumps is a bit more than 7 barrels of pickles, whereas for the pickler the opportunity cost of 18 pumps is 12 barrels of pickles.

Specialization. There can be no disputing that ours is a highly specialized economic system.

Virtually everyone and everything is specialized. Labor is specialized. Capital is specialized. And so is land.

Production processes are continuously being divided and subdivided in ever-increasing degrees of specialization. The extent to which specialization has been carried in this country is astounding. Whole industries specialize in the production of goods that are used as inputs in the production of other goods that are, in turn, used as inputs in the production of still other goods. Within each of these plants, the production process is broken down into hundreds of distinct operations, each involving the assignment of separate workers. Even managerial and administrative functions are divided minutely, with each narrow task performed by a specialist. And a high degree of specialization is evident in capital goods where machinery and structures are specifically designed to perform specialized tasks.

Moreover, as industries grow, specialization increases. Plants become more and more mechanized and automated. Accompanying these developments is an ever-greater division of labor, creating and maintaining new and sophisticated techniques of production.

An important source of increased efficiency that often accompanies growth and greater mechanization is **economies of scale.** Technically, economies of scale refer to the savings in resources made possible by increases in the size—the scale—of productive facilities. When the scale of the operation is small, complex assembly-line techniques may not be profitable; when the scale is large, such mass-production techniques often become feasible. When these economies are possible the result will be greater output per unit of input. However, such economies are not achievable to the same extent in *all* production processes. Economies of scale may be very limited in the textile industry, for example; in the production of autos, though, they are apparently tremendous.

It is not difficult to discover why specialization contributes to increased efficiency. Consider the **division of labor.** As people become more and more specialized, they acquire ever-increasing skill and dexterity in the performance of their jobs. By concentrating on a limited number of tasks, the time that would be spent in moving from task to task is saved. And, as tasks become more routine and standardized, greater mechanization of production techniques become possible, permitting substantial savings in the use of labor.

Machines contribute to efficiency largely because they are faster, more powerful, and/or more accurate than the labor they replace. In addition, they release labor for the production of other goods and services and contribute to the further division of labor.

Although the specialization of labor and capital enables each resource to become *absolutely* more efficient in the task to which it is assigned, efficiency demands that these resources be assigned to tasks for which they are best suited—i.e., for which they have a **comparative advantage.** Both picklers and pump engineers can become more efficient as a result of specialization in *either* occupation, but maximum overall efficiency will be attained only if they specialize in the occupations for which they are best suited. In general then, *efficiency is best served when* **specialization** *is undertaken in accordance with the principle of* **comparative advantage.**

And finally, efficiency can be further enhanced by the **regional specialization** of resources—both nationally and internationally. This is because different regions are differently endowed with land, labor, and capital resources. Regions vary in climate, qualities of soil, mineral resources, and the quantity and quality of capital and labor resources. As a result, wheat is produced in Kansas, tobacco in Virginia; Colombia specializes in coffee, the Mideast in oil.

However, such regional specialization will result in an increase in efficiency only if it is also in accord with the principle of comparative advantage. If instead, Virginia specialized in the production of wheat and Kansas in the production of tobacco, we would probably get less of both products, even if the same amount of land were devoted to the production of each. And consider what would happen if the Mideast specialized in the production of coffee while Colombia specialized in the production of oil!

Exchange and mutual dependence. Specialization is possible only in an economy characterized by the exchange of goods and services—an **exchange economy.** In such an economy, individuals produce a mere fraction of what they consume. Indeed, most people do not even produce an entire single product alone. Thus, a system must be developed whereby goods and services can be exchanged. Individuals in developed economies are not jacks-of-all-trades, islands unto themselves. Rather, they are mutually dependent on each other for the satisfaction of their wants.

We could, of course, devise a system in which each kind of good and service is exchanged directly for others—a **barter exchange system.** Such a system would not only be extremely complicated; it would be highly inefficient as well. Think of the difficulties it would entail. If you specialized in the production of pumps and you wanted pickles, you would have to find a pickler who also wanted pumps. In the absence of such a **coincidence of wants,** satisfactory exchange would be impossible. You might be able to devise a more complicated set of exchanges to ensure that you ultimately got what you wanted. For example, suppose the pickler wants to exchange pickles for shoes; the shoemaker, on the other hand wants bread; the baker wants pumps; you want pickles. For mutually satisfactory exchanges to take place, all participants would have to agree on a set of satisfactory **exchange ratios.** These exchange ratios are known formally as **terms of trade**—the amount of one good given up in exchange for another. It is unlikely, though, that such trades would be completely satisfactory. There is no guarantee that you will get as many pickles as you want. It will depend on how many pumps the baker wants, on how much bread the shoemaker wants, *and* on how many pairs of shoes the pickler wants. If you got more or less pickles than you wanted, off you would have to go in search of yet other exchange arrangements. What a waste of time.

There are yet further difficulties with barter exchange. Think about the problems confronting an aircraft producer who wants to nibble on a pickle now and then. At an exchange ratio of 500,000 barrels to one airplane, that's an awful lot of nibbling—assuming, of course, that a pickler can be found who has 500,000 barrels of pickles and also wants an airplane. Formally, this is referred to as the **indivisibilities problem.** A plane is a huge, indivisible good; it cannot easily be divided into smaller, less costly units.

Money. It would be so much simpler and more efficient if all exchanges were consummated with the aid of yet another good—**a medium of exchange**—which *everyone was willing to accept* in exchange for their goods and services. As a producer of pumps, you would no longer have to concoct elaborate exchanges in order to get what you wanted. People who want pumps would buy them from you with the medium of exchange; and you could then use that same common good—the medium of exchange—to buy the things that you wanted. The recipients of this common good could use it in turn to buy the things that they wanted. How simple and efficient!

This generally acceptable medium of exchange is called **money.** Its use converts a barter exchange system into a **monetary exchange system.** Moreover, it permits more specialization, enabling resources to be used much more efficiently than in a barter system. The coincidence-of-wants problem is resolved handily and the indivisibilities problem disappears when money is introduced into the system.

Money is not desired for its own sake. It is, instead, a means to an end; it is the medium— the medium through which goods and services are ultimately exchanged for other goods and services. Because people worry so much about the amount of money they have, this point is easily obscured. Thus, fundamentally, people exchange their labor services, not for money, but for other goods and services. Yes, they are paid for their labor services with money. But money is just the means to acquire those other goods and services. Money, as the so-called classical economists argued, is just a veil that masks the true underlying exchange relations. Strip away the veil and you will observe exchanges exactly

analogous to those that characterized a barter economy. However, money enables people to effect those exchanges more efficiently.

THE GROWTH PROCESS

It was demonstrated earlier that the quantity and quality of our land, labor, and capital resources establish an effective limit to our production possibilities. If existing resources are being used efficiently, an expansion of our production possibilities is feasible only if the quantity and/ or quality of those resources increase. Such increases are what the growth process is all about.

The growth process is depicted graphically by the outward shifting of the production possibilities curve. This is illustrated in Figure 2.4. In the analysis presented there, the assumed source of the increased production possibilities is **capital accumulation.**

Measuring quantities of capital goods on the vertical axis and quantities of consumer goods on the horizontal axis, the curve labeled ABC depicts our economy's 1980 production possibilities. Given the quantity and quality of the resources available in 1980, our hypothetical econ-

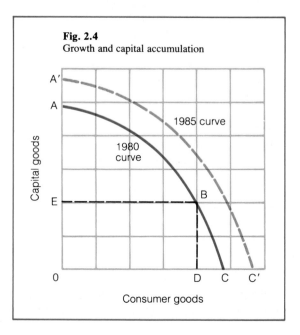

Fig. 2.4
Growth and capital accumulation

omy could produce OA units of capital goods, OC units of consumer goods, or some combination in between (such as OE units of capital goods and OD units of consumer goods at production point B).

If production point B is selected, the economy, as will be seen below, *might* add capital goods to its existing stock of capital, thereby enabling an expansion of its production possibilities. The 1985 production possibilities curve, labeled A′C′, reflects the cumulative effect of such capital accumulation over the period 1980–1985.

It is important to note, however, that capital accumulation—a process we formally refer to as **investment**—is costly. There is an opportunity cost to investment; investment takes resources away from the production of other goods and services. In our example, the opportunity cost of investment (or capital accumulation) is the consumer goods that could otherwise have been produced with the resources used in the production of capital goods. The opportunity cost of OE units of capital goods is the DC units of consumer goods that could otherwise have been obtained.

Although present capital accumulation requires the loss of consumer goods today, the likelihood of a payoff in the future does exist. By investing now, the economy will have the capacity to produce even more in the future, including more consumer goods. Indeed, *the fundamental objective of investment is the expansion of our potential to produce other goods and services in the future.* Capital goods are not desired for their own sake. They are a means to an end. They are a means to the attainment of increased production possibilities. It is for this reason that investment is often called **roundabout production.** Resources are diverted from the production of other goods *now* to produce capital goods; these capital goods will be used, in turn, to produce even greater quantities of other goods and services in the future.

Gross investment and net investment

Although investment is the process of adding to the stock of capital goods, not *all* investment adds to our productive capacity. Indeed, in the course of production, some capital goods are used up—that is, they are consumed, or *depreciated.* As a result, some investment must take place simply to maintain a given stock of capital goods. Only investment over and above what is necessary to maintain the stock of capital and to replace worn machinery constitutes an increase in our productive capacity. Thus economists distinguish between **gross investment** and **net investment.** Gross investment refers to the total of all capital goods produced during a given period of time. Net investment, on the other hand, refers to that part of gross investment that represents a net change in the **stock of capital** goods. It excludes that portion of gross investment that is used to replace depreciated capital goods. Formally,

Net investment = Gross investment − Depreciation.

Figure 2.5 illustrates the importance of this distinction. Assume, for example, that 2 million units of capital wear out, or depreciate, annually. In this case, gross investment must be at least 2 million just to maintain the existing stock of capital. Thus, if the economy is operating at production point D, its productive capacity would be maintained in the future.

At any point above point D—say, point B—there would be a positive net accumulation of capital goods; net investment would be positive. Gross investment at point B equals 4 million units, 2 million of which offset depreciation, leaving 2 million units to add to our productive capacity. Our production possibilities would thus expand, shifting the production possibilities out and to the right to, say, A′C′.

If, in contrast, the economy were operating at production point E, depreciation would exceed gross investment and net investment would therefore be negative. Accordingly, our future productive capacity would decline; our production possibilities would shrink, shifting the production possibilities curve down and to the left to, for example, A″C″.

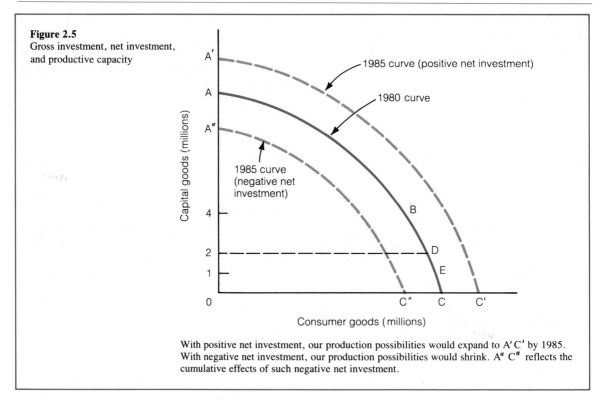

Figure 2.5
Gross investment, net investment, and productive capacity

With positive net investment, our production possibilities would expand to A′ C′ by 1985. With negative net investment, our production possibilities would shrink. A″ C″ reflects the cumulative effects of such negative net investment.

Growth and some aspects of the problem of underdevelopment

The production possibilities framework and our analysis of the investment process can illustrate some of the problems faced by less developed nations in their efforts to achieve rising standards of living. For living standards to improve, total output must grow more rapidly than population. A rise in the average standard of living necessitates an increase in *output per capita*. In the analysis presented below, we consider the production of two goods only: consumer goods and capital goods. We will define a rise in the standard of living as an increase in the output of consumer goods per capita.

One fundamental problem confronting most less developed countries (LDCs) is portrayed in Figure 2.6. Note that both capital goods and consumer goods are measured on a per capita basis. Thus the curve measures the per capita production possibilities of the country in question. The LDC's per capita production possibilities curve is drawn close in to the origin. The developed

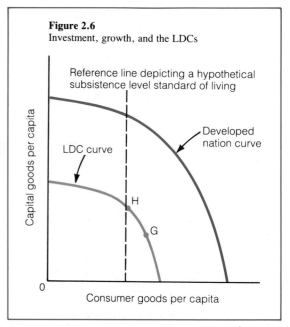

Figure 2.6
Investment, growth, and the LDCs

nation curve, by contrast, is drawn a considerable distance from the origin, reflecting the higher average living standard in the developed nation.

Suppose that the LDC is currently producing at point G. Assume further that at point G, *total* output is growing at the same rate as population. In this case, the per capita production possibilities are, for the moment, constant. If the LDC is to have any hope of achieving a standard of living comparable to the standard experienced in the developed nation, its per capita production possibilities must expand. In order to accomplish this, though, the per capita output of consumer goods must be *reduced* to divert more resources toward the production of additional capital goods. Increased capital goods production today will increase the LDC's potential to produce all goods in the future, shifting the LDC production possibilities curve closer to that of the developed country. However, many LDCs face a dilemma. *For countries whose standards of living are already absymally low, the opportunity cost of yet more investment is a reduction in current living standards; however, without more investment, there is little prospect of improving those standards in the future.*

The movement from G to H in Figure 2.6 dramatizes these costs; here the effect of greater investment is to reduce current living standards

from above subsistence to barely subsistence levels.

The additional investment necessary for growth need not always require reduced standards of living. If output per capita is already growing, the *additional* investment could come out of the *additional* output. This is illustrated in Figure 2.7. If the economy were to follow the path depicted by the series of points G, H, J, K, and L, the output of consumer goods per capita would rise continuously. Investment would also be growing in a manner consistent with an expanding per capita production possibilities. The points A, B, C, D, and E represent, respectively, the capital goods/consumer goods combinations that will cause no net increase in the stock of capital goods for each production possibilities curve; gross investment equals depreciation at each of these points.

Growth and other investments

An economy's productive capacity is also advanced by other forms of investment: investment in **human capital**—the use of resources to educate and train the labor force; investment in **social overhead capital**—the use of resources by government to provide transportation, communication and health systems, and other public goods and services; and investment in **research and development (R&D)**—the use of resources to advance the technical capabilities of capital goods and to improve the efficiency with which resources are utilized.

Like investment in physical capital, all of these other forms of investment are roundabout production. They are, therefore, not ends in themselves, but means to an end—means to the attainment of an enlarged production possibilities. Thus, from an analytical point of view, the impact of these activities on our production possibilities is the same as investment in physical capital.

Growth and technology

Technological change has historically been one of the most important factors responsible for the rapid growth of our production possibili-

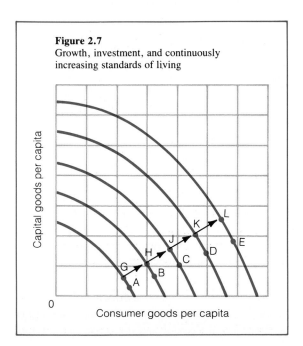

Figure 2.7
Growth, investment, and continuously increasing standards of living

ties. *By improving the efficiency with which resources are used, technological change enables a larger quantity of goods and services to be produced with a given quantity of resources.* Such improvements, however, are almost always connected in one way or another with the investment process. Indeed to the extent that all technical advance is a product of brainpower, technical progress can in large measure be attributed to investments in human capital.

Moreover, since many technical advances are embodied in new capital goods, investment in physical capital is often required before the effects of technical change can be seen. But this is not always the case. Technological advance is sometimes possible through a rearrangement of existing resources. Time-and-motion studies, aimed at the more efficient use of time, and crop rotation practices in agriculture are perhaps the best-known examples of this kind of technological change.

THE ECONOMIC PROBLEM: THE FOUR FUNDAMENTAL QUESTIONS

The stage is now set for a more detailed analysis of the economic problem: how best to allocate scarce resources among alternative uses. What constitutes the best allocation of resources for any society can only be determined on the basis of the answers to four fundamental questions.

What to produce

Every society must determine what goods and services to produce with its scarce resources. A great many different products could be produced, but because resources are scarce, choices must be made. We cannot have everything that we want, so it is important that we do the best with what we have. The optimum product mix must somehow be discovered. What kinds of private, public, consumer, and capital goods should be produced? This question must somehow be answered.

In addition to determining what to produce, decisions must be made about how much to produce of each good and service: How many auto-

mobiles? How many parks? How many capital goods? How many pickles? How many pumps? And all these decisions must somehow be made consistent with one another. If society decides in favor of more public goods, it will be at the expense of private goods; if it decides in favor of more consumer goods, it will be at the expense of capital goods, which has implications for future growth.

The answers to both questions—what to produce and how much of each—can be shown graphically as the production alternative selected on the production possibilities curve.

How to produce

Society must next determine *how* resources will be employed both to produce the things people want and to attain the optimum product mix. Basically, this is a question of determining how the resources will be combined: Who will produce what? Where will production take place? And what specific resources will be used in what combinations? Of course, if we are to make the best use of our resources, production must be organized efficiently.

How to distribute output

Having determined the optimum collection of goods and services to produce and the most efficient ways of producing them, society must then determine *who* will receive the fruits of this productive effort. How should the total output be distributed among the population? Should it be divided evenly irrespective of ability or productive effort? Or should it be divided on the basis of ability and productive effort alone? If neither of these alternatives, then somewhere in between? And if in between, does some generally agreed-upon desirable position exist? As we shall see, answers to these questions, like those to the fundamental question of what to produce, are largely matters of normative economics, for which there are no "correct" value-free answers.

How extensively to use resources

We come at last to the question of the optimum utilization rate of our resources. This might seem at first to be a question with an obvious answer. After all, since we can never hope to satisfy *all* our wants, shouldn't we use our resources to the fullest extent possible? But what does it mean to use our resources "to the fullest extent possible"? Should we all work 80 hours a week? Why not 120? Should we enter the labor force at the age of 2 or 3 and work until the very hour of death? Should we operate productive facilities continuously around the clock?

Most people would agree that such high levels of resource use would not be optimal. First, leisure time is a good that most people value. If people are willing to give up the goods and services that could have been produced during leisure time, then working only 40 hours a week might be optimal.

In regard to the employment of children, child labor laws were motivated by concerns for their health and welfare. Moreover, if children do not remain in school—if a smaller investment is made in human capital—the impact on our future production possibilities could be decidedly negative.

As you can see, determining the optimum utilization rate of our resources is not simple. Most of Part Four of this book will deal with these issues in depth. For now it is important to recognize that our production possibilities are defined subject to these resource-use limitations. That is, *our production possibilities are determined on the basis of the "normal" number of working hours, the optimum amounts of investment in human capital, the optimal rates of natural resource extraction,* etc. Thus, to say that it is *impossible,* to attain a production point beyond our production possibilities is incorrect. Indeed, during World War II we surpassed our normal production possibilities by a considerable margin as a result of overtime work and the employment of people who would not have normally participated in the labor force.

On the other hand, to select a production point to the interior of our production possibilities curve would constitute a nonoptimal and inefficient use of our resources. The failure of the economy to operate at full employment implies a failure to use resources optimally. It is in this sense that unemployment is inefficient.

Solving the economic problem

In an effort to solve the economic problem, each society must determine for itself the answers to these four fundamental questions. In highly individualistic societies of the **free enterprise, capitalist** type—known, formally, as **laissez-faire**—the societal answers to these questions are determined by the **free choices** of all those people who own privately the means of production. The emphasis in these societies is on the private ownership of resources. The allocation of those resources is thus determined by the decisions of those private individuals who own them.

In collectivist societies, on the other hand, of the **socialist** or **communist** type, the societal answers to these questions are largely determined centrally by the government. The emphasis in these economic systems is on public ownership of the means of production. Resource allocation is determined in large measure by the dictates of those in authority.

Finally, there are **mixed economies** that combine elements of both private decisionmaking in the allocation of some resources and collectivist or government control over the rest.

Regardless of the kind of economic system, each must also decide the means or *the mechanism whereby the many decisions can be coordinated and made consistent.* Free enterprise systems rely on market prices—which reflect the choices made by individual consumers and producers—to perform the requisite coordinating function. Many collectivist states use planning agencies and government directives to allocate resources. And increasingly, these centrally controlled economies are discovering the advantages of using market prices for the purpose of achieving plan objectives. *Just as market prices in capitalist systems determine resource use, so prices can be established in socialist systems to promote state objectives.* The differences in resource allocation between a capitalist state and a socialist state will be reflected in the different sets of prices in each. The set of prices in a capitalist system reflects the aggregate of individual choices; the set of prices in a socialist system reflects the choices made by the central planning agency.

Similarly, the prices that emerge from a **mixed system** reflect individual and collectivist objectives. We undertake a detailed treatment of these issues in the next chapter.

SUMMARY

1. The nature of **the economic problem** is clear. The sum total of our wants far outstrip the resources available to satisfy those wants. Choices must be made as to which wants will be satisfied and which will not. By choosing to use our scarce resources in one way, we forego the opportunity of using them in some other way at the same time.

2. **The economic problem** can be illustrated with the aid of a *production possibilities* table or curve. Three principles underlie this production possibilities concept:

   a. Given the quantity and quality of our resources, there is a limit to the amounts of various goods and services that can be produced in a given interval of time.

   b. If resources are being fully employed, the increased production of any one good requires the reduced production of some other good(s). The cost—the *opportunity cost*—of increasing the production of that one good is measured by the value of the good(s) whose production is reduced.

   c. Resource shifts are subject to the *law of increasing (opportunity) cost*. This law accounts for the bowed (concave-to-the-origin) shape of the production possibilities curve.

3. The *law of increasing cost* can be defined in two ways: (a) equal reductions in the quantity produced of any one good will yield less and less of an increase in the production of other goods; or (b) equal increases in the quantity produced of any one good will necessitate larger and larger reductions in the production of other goods.

4. The *law of increasing cost* depends fundamentally on two things: (a) the fact that land, labor, and capital are used in differing proportions to produce different commodities; and (b)

the *law of diminishing returns,* or, more generally, the *law of variable proportions.*

5. To ensure that we get the most out of our resources, it is important that they be used efficiently—i.e., that they be used in the *best ways possible* to produce what society wants. The assignment of resources to tasks for which they are best suited—i.e., for which they have a *comparative advantage*—is extremely important to promote efficiency. Efficiency is further enhanced through *specialization, exchange,* and the use of *money.*

6. Growth can be described as the process of adding to the quantity and/or quality of our nation's resources. The growth process is depicted graphically by the outward shifting of the production possibilities curve.

7. One of the most important sources of growth is *capital accumulation.* Not all *investment* adds to our productive capacity; only investment over and above what is necessary to maintain the stock of capital constitutes an increase in our productive capacity—i.e., only when *net investment* (the difference between *gross investment* and *depreciation*) is positive will the stock of capital goods, and our productive capacity, increase.

8. To solve **the economic problem,** each society must answer four fundamental questions:

   a. What to produce.

   b. How to produce.

   c. How to distribute output.

   d. How extensively to use resources.

9. Different kinds of societies answer these four questions in different ways. In *free enterprise, capitalist*—i.e., *laissez-faire*—societies, resource allocation is largely determined by the decisions of those private individuals who own resources through market prices; in *socialist* or *communist* systems, the answers are largely determined by government.

CONCEPTS FOR REVIEW

Scarcity
Production possibilities
Opportunity cost

Law of increasing (opportunity) costs

Law of diminishing returns

Law of variable proportions

Efficiency

Comparative advantage

Specialization

Economies of scale

Division of labor

Mutual dependence

Exchange

Barter exchange system

Coincidence-of-wants problem

Indivisibilities problem

Terms-of-trade

Money

Monetary exchange system

Growth

Capital accumulation

Roundabout production

Investment

Gross investment

Net investment

Depreciation

Stock of capital

Output per capita

Human capital

Social overhead capital

Research and development (R&D)

Technological change

The four fundamental questions
1. What to produce
2. How to produce
3. How to distribute output
4. How extensively to use resources

Laissez-faire

QUESTIONS FOR DISCUSSION

(Those marked with an asterisk (*) are more difficult.)

1. The military draft was abolished a number of years ago and replaced by an all-volunteer army. Under which of the following conditions could we conclude that the opportunity costs of maintaining an army has dropped?

a. The defense budget is reduced.
b. Less skilled men and women enter the army.
c. Military pay is reduced.
Explain.

2. Suppose that, instead of increasing opportunity costs, our economy was characterized by *constant* opportunity costs. What would our production possibilities curve look like under such circumstances? Explain.

3. Using Figure 2.1, illustrate the principle of increasing opportunity costs. Use as your starting point production alternative E and proceed from there to points D and C.

4. Consider Figure 2.1 again. Suppose we are initially producing at production alternative C. If society decides to move to production alternative D, this requires the movement of land, labor, and capital resources out of pickle production into pump production. Because some experienced picklers are producing pumps, does it mean that we are using our resources inefficiently? Explain carefully.

5. "As the accompanying chart makes clear, the average length of the workweek in the United States has declined significantly since the turn of the century. Doesn't the fact that we have more and more leisure mean that an economic problem no longer exists? After all, by working longer hours we could produce more goods and services." Critically evaluate.

Manufacturing workweek

6. The following table shows the output per hour of work in countries A and B in the production of two goods—wheat and wine. Using the idea of opportunity cost, indicate whether A or B has a comparative advantage in wine. Which, therefore, has a comparative advantage in wheat? Explain carefully.

	Output per hour of work	
	Wheat (bushels harvested per hour)	Wine (bottles filled and corked per hour)
Country A	6	6
Country B	8	4

7. In 1933, in the depths of the Great Depression, gross private domestic investment amounted to $1.4 billion; depreciation for that year amounted to $7.0 billion. Ignoring all other considerations, what conclusions can you draw about U.S. production possibilities in 1933?

*8. "One of the economic arguments in favor of foreign aid is that it provides LDCs with additional resources with which they can expand their capital investment. However, since a lot of our foreign aid is in the form of food, not capital goods, it cannot help the development processes in these countries." Evaluate critically.

*9. Suppose technological advances occur at a more rapid rate in the production of pickles than in the production of pumps. What, as a result, will happen to the production possibilities curve over time? Will it move out uniformly over time or not? Be very explicit.

*10. The law of diminishing returns is assumed to hold. Pumps and pickles are produced using labor and capital in differing proportions. Suppose now that capital and labor grow at different rates over time. Ignoring all else, what impact will these differing rates of growth have on the production possibilities curve over time? Will it move out uniformly over time or not? Explain.

*11. As resources are shifted from pickle production to pump production, the opportunity cost of producing pumps rises. But suppose that, as pump production increases, pump producers experience economies of scale in the production of pumps. What would the attainment of such economies imply about the shape of the production possibilities curve? Would it matter if the economies of scale were small or large? Explain.

We now undertake an analysis of one of the most remarkable systems for allocating scarce resources among alternative uses—**the system of markets and prices.** This system is remarkable because of the ease with which it *coordinates* the many decisions required to ensure that the *right* kinds of goods and services in the *right* quantities get to the *right* places and into the *right* hands at the *right* time. It performs this coordinating function for millions upon millions of goods and services involving billions of decisions day in and day out. And all of this is accomplished without the aid of any central planning agency!

We approach an understanding of this system in steps. In the first section we examine the system of markets and prices in a laissez-faire capitalist economy. All scarce resources are privately owned in this type of economy. All decisions regarding the use of those resources are made by the individuals who own them. In the context of such an economy, we look first at how price is determined in a single market, ignoring all else; i.e., we look at a part of the economy in isolation from all the rest. This approach is called a **partial equilibrium** approach. We will then proceed to analyze the interrelationships between markets, demonstrating how this system of markets and prices answers the four fundamental questions—*what, how, for whom,* and *how extensively.* The method of analysis used there is called the **general equilibrium** approach.

A laissez-faire capitalist system provides us with *one* possible solution to **the economic problem**—one set of answers to the four fundamental questions. Some other more centrally controlled economic system will provide us with some *other* solution, some *other* set of answers. Interestingly, it is possible to translate the different answers to the four fundamental questions into a different set of prices. Specifically, if the *desired* answers to the four fundamental questions differ from the answers emerging from a laissez-faire capitalist system, the possibility arises that policies could be devised and implemented that generate a different set of prices, a different allocation of resources, and a different set of answers. We explore this important issue in the second section of this chapter, where we attempt to show how

Chapter 3

Prices, markets, and resource allocation

the price system can be used to promote the goals of different kinds of economic systems.

Finally, in the third section, we will examine carefully the concept known as the **circular flow of economic activity,** which illustrates succinctly the flows of both goods and money among consumers, producers, and government in all markets.

PRICES AND MARKETS: LAISSEZ-FAIRE CAPITALISM

The answers to the four fundamental questions vary from nation to nation. Not only are the economic goals often different among the various nations of the world, but the institutions and methods of organizing resources are frequently different as well. The question is: What determines the means chosen by the various societies to answer the four fundamental questions?

Basically, the means chosen reflect the philosophical principles on which each society is organized. And generally speaking, most industrialized societies at least are organized on the basis of one or both of two different philosophies. At one extreme are socialism and communism, which stress public ownership of resources and central planning as the mechanism of coordination. At the other extreme is laissez-faire capitalism, which stresses private ownership of resources and freedom of choice for each decision-maker; the coordinating mechanism is to be found in the system of markets and prices characterized by the absence of any central planning authority. In this chapter we focus on the latter ideology—laissez-faire capitalism.

Before proceeding, though, it should be noted that laissez-faire capitalism has never existed in its pure form. Neither have socialism and communism. Most industrialized nations are organized around principles that mix elements of both philosophies. Why, then, do we study laissez-faire capitalism? We hinted at the answer to this question in Chapter 1. Isolating certain aspects of the economy—in this instance, those that correspond most closely to the capitalist ideology—is a necessary first step toward understanding the maze of actions and reactions in real-world economies. To understand reality, we must simplify reality and abstract from it.

The circular flow of economic activity: A first view

It is useful to begin our discussion of laissez-faire capitalism by briefly examining the interrelationships between resource markets and product markets. The essential features of those interrelationships are captured in the so-called circular flow of economic activity, which is graphically illustrated in Figure 3.1.

Study first the inner loop in Figure 3.1. In order to produce goods and services, producers require the use of resources—land, labor, and capital. Those resources are supplied by consumers; and consumers are the ones for whom the goods and services are produced. In this circular flow, consumers and producers both take on roles as buyers and sellers. Consumers act as sellers in **resource markets**—selling the services of their resources to producers. In **product markets,** consumers act as buyers—purchasing the goods and services produced by businesses. Producers, on the other hand, act as buyers in resource markets and as sellers in product markets.

The outer loop in Figure 3.1 highlights the money flows that correspond to the flows of goods and services through resource and product markets. The expenditures consumers make for goods and services become the receipts for businesses. And the business costs—the costs incurred to pay for resources—become the income received by the resources. Finally, the wherewithal to pay for the use of resources comes from business receipts; and the wherewithal for consumer expenditures comes from resource income. The flow of economic activity is circular. Moreover, under laissez-faire capitalism, resource and product markets perform the important function of linking up—coordinating—the decisions of producers and consumers.

Price determination in a single market

To understand the details of the circular flow under laissez-faire capitalism, let us simplify the

Figure 3.1
The circular flow of economic activity

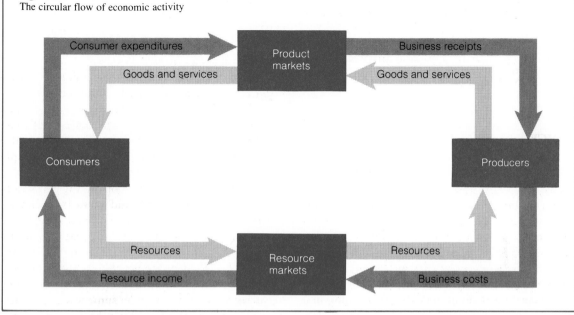

problem further to focus on the role of *price* and the determination of price in a *single* market. As will soon be discovered, it is fairly easy to state how prices are determined. *Individual prices are determined by the demand for and supply of each good and service.* Unfortunately, a lot of unnecessary confusion exists about *how* demand and supply determine price. There is also a lot of unnecessary confusion about the concepts of demand and supply themselves. It is our purpose here to develop these ideas in ways that avoid confusion.

Demand

The term **demand** has a very definite meaning to an economist. *The demand for a particular good or service expresses a "willingness and ability to buy."* The emphasis given to the "willingness and ability to buy" is important. While the demand for some good or service may reflect a *want* or a *desire* for that item, demand expresses much more than that. There are many things I want and desire. But some I cannot afford, and

others would necessitate my having to give up many things I now buy in order to have those other goods and services. The importance attached to "willingness and ability to buy" is therefore clear. *Demand for a good or service expresses a willingness and an ability to pay, a willingness to forego other goods and services in order to acquire it.* The notion of opportunity cost is central to the concept of demand.

Demand for a good, therefore, cannot be viewed as independent of the demand for other goods; it reflects people's relative preference for some given good or service. In product markets, the demand for a product expresses a preference for that product vis-à-vis others that could be purchased. In resource markets, the demand for a resource expresses a relative preference for that resource.

Moreover, how much people are willing and able to buy of a product or a resource must be given an explicit time dimension. How much steak you are willing and able to purchase in a week is doubtless different from the amount you are willing and able to purchase in a year or

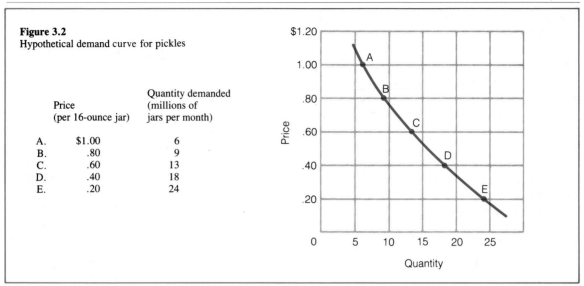

Figure 3.2
Hypothetical demand curve for pickles

	Price (per 16-ounce jar)	Quantity demanded (millions of jars per month)
A.	$1.00	6
B.	.80	9
C.	.60	13
D.	.40	18
E.	.20	24

over your lifetime; the quantity of labor services producers are willing and able to pay for in a week is different from the quantity they are willing and able to pay for over an entire year. Thus, demand expresses a willingness and an ability to buy *during some given period of time*—an amount per unit of time.

Since the factors that determine the demand for *resources* are different from the determinants of the demand for *products,* we will analyze each separately. We will first consider the demand for products.

Product demand. What determines the quantity of a product—any product—people are willing and able to purchase during some well-defined time period—say, a month? Many factors influence this decision. Suppose the product in question is pickles. The demand for pickles—the number of jars of pickles people are willing and able to buy per month—will be determined by the price of pickles, the prices of other goods and services, people's income and wealth, and family sizes, among other things. Let us focus for the moment on only one of these determinants—the price of pickles—and ignore all else. That is, let us *assume as unchanged* all of the *other* factors that could influence the quantity of pickles people would be willing and able to

buy. We can then record how the quantity bought varies as the price of pickles varies.

The results of our experiment are displayed in the hypothetical **demand schedule** and its graphical counterpart—the **demand curve**—in Figure 3.2. Note that at a price of $1 a jar, 6 million jars of pickles are purchased each month. At a price of 60 cents a jar, the quantity demanded per month jumps to 13 million. And at the very low price of 20 cents per jar, the quantity demanded rises to 24 million.

This inverse relationship between the price and quantity demanded of a good—shown as a downward-sloping demand curve—is known as the **law of demand.** *Ceteris paribus*—that is, holding everything else constant—a reduction in price leads to an increase in the quantity demanded. Alternatively, an increase in price leads to a reduction in the quantity demanded.

Rationale for the law of demand

The law of demand can be understood intuitively. Each of us has a limited income. We cannot buy all the things we would like, so we have to make choices—satisfying some wants and foregoing the satisfaction of others. Our objective is to get the most satisfaction possible from our limited incomes—i.e., to get the most value for each dollar we spend.

In making the choices we do, we look at the price tag of good X and compare the satisfaction we expect to get from good X with the satisfaction expected from a similar outlay of money for other things. Sometimes we reject the good in question with statements like, "I can't afford it," "It isn't worth it," "What a rip-off," and "I've got better things to do with my money." Had the price been lower, the product might have been given more serious consideration.

If prices change, people will reassess their purchases. What the law of demand states is that, if the price of any good increases, the quantity demanded will decline, *ceteris paribus;* or, if the price falls, the quantity demanded will rise, *ceteris paribus.* Basically, this inverse relationship between price and the quantity demanded (shown by the downward-sloping demand curve) can be explained as the consequence of *two* factors. Consider again, for illustrative purposes, people's decisions regarding the purchase of pickles.

1. If pickle prices rise, consumers are poorer in the sense that they can't buy as much of *all* goods as they did before the price rise without spending more. Their *real* income—what their money income will purchase—has been reduced. As a result of a reduced real income, they will spend less on most goods, *including pickles.* This phenomenon is referred to as the **income effect** of a price change.

2. If pickle prices rise, people may substitute other things for pickles in their diet. *People substitute away from higher-priced products toward products carrying relatively lower price tags.* People do not necessarily reduce to zero their consumption of the product; they may only reduce it somewhat—for example, from three to two jars of pickles a month. This phenomenon is technically referred to as the **substitution effect** of a price change.

Accordingly, when the price of pickles goes up, the operation of both the income effect and the substitution effect serve to reduce the quantity of pickles demanded. (To be sure you understand these ideas, explain how both of these would work in reverse if the price of pickles declined.)

Individual demand and market demand

Not everyone responds in precisely the same way to a change in the price of pickles. Some people hate pickles and wouldn't eat them even if their price fell to zero. Pickle lovers, on the other hand, might also be very unresponsive to a change in price. Whether the price is 20 cents or $1, they would continue to buy the same number of jars each month. Other people might not buy a single jar until the price falls to 40 cents (meaning that their behavior is unaffected by price changes in the 40 cents to $1 range). Still others might not enter the market until the price falls to 20 cents.

Does this mean that the law of demand has only limited applicability—valid only for some people in some cases some of the time? No. The law of demand was never intended to apply to everyone in all circumstances. Its usefulness is to be determined by whether it is valid *on average.* Thus, the law of demand states that, *on average,* a reduction in price will induce an increase in the quantity demanded, *ceteris paribus* (i.e., holding constant all things other than the price of the good in question).

This point is illustrated in the hypothetical numerical example set forth in Figure 3.3, which illustrates the *individual* and *market* demands for beets. As the figure shows, David won't buy beets at any price; his demand curve lies on or is coincident with the vertical axis in Figure 3.3. Jimmy, on the other hand, will not buy any beets until the price reaches 10 cents each, at which price he buys 5; he will increase his purchases to 12 only if the price falls to 5 cents each. Andrea loves beets; she eats 40 beets a week whether the price is 20 cents or 5 cents each. Mimi's demand schedule suggests a smooth downward-sloping curve up until 20 units, at which point it becomes vertical. A lower price will not induce Mimi to purchase any more pickles. *The market*

Figure 3.3
Individual demand and market demand for beets

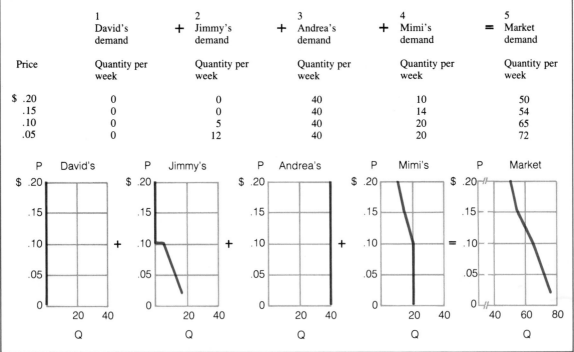

Price	1 David's demand Quantity per week	+	2 Jimmy's demand Quantity per week	+	3 Andrea's demand Quantity per week	+	4 Mimi's demand Quantity per week	=	5 Market demand Quantity per week
$ .20	0		0		40		10		50
.15	0		0		40		14		54
.10	0		5		40		20		65
.05	0		12		40		20		72

demand schedule is obtained by summing up the individual demand schedules.

As the above example makes clear, the law of demand does hold on average—that is, the *market* demand curve slopes downward to the right. And it holds in spite of individual idiosyncrasies. Indeed, though all our hypothetical people behave differently, and none (except Jimmy, perhaps) in strict accordance with the predictions of the law of demand, we can still conclude that, *for the market,* lower beet prices lead to increases in the quantity of beets demanded.

Changes in the quantity demanded and changes in demand

The amount that people are willing and able to buy is determined by more than the price of the product alone. Income, wealth, tastes, the prices of other products, and a great many other factors influence people's spending.

Suppose that people's incomes rise by 10 percent and that, as a result, they express a willingness to buy 2 million additional jars of pickles a month. If, for example, they were previously willing to buy 6 million jars of pickles, they will now be willing to step up their consumption to 8 million; if they had been willing to consume 18 million before, they will now be willing to purchase 20 million. The new demand schedule is presented in Figure 3.4 along with the original demand schedule of Figure 3.2. Note how we have incorporated the influence of a change in income on the demand schedule for pickles. The quantity that people are willing to purchase has been increased by 2 million *at each and every price.* And, as Figure 3.4 makes clear, such a change is represented graphically by a rightward shift of the entire demand curve from D_0 to D_1.

A single graph can be used to illustrate the impact of more than one factor on the amount that people are willing and able to purchase.

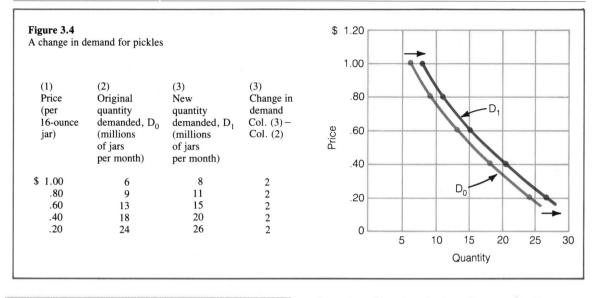

Figure 3.4
A change in demand for pickles

(1) Price (per 16-ounce jar)	(2) Original quantity demanded, D_0 (millions of jars per month)	(3) New quantity demanded, D_1 (millions of jars per month)	(3) Change in demand Col. (3) − Col. (2)
$ 1.00	6	8	2
.80	9	11	2
.60	13	15	2
.40	18	20	2
.20	24	26	2

Economists have therefore adopted the following convention whereby the influence of price on demand is kept analytically distinct from the effect of other forces on demand:

1. If the price of good X changes, people will alter the amount they are willing to buy. This change in quantity caused by a change in price is referred to as a **change in the quantity demanded.** Graphically, it is depicted as a movement from one point on the demand curve to another point on the *same* curve—that is, as a movement *along* the demand curve.

2. If some force *other than a change in the price of good X* induces people to alter the amount of good X they are willing to buy, this change in quantity is referred to as a **change in demand.** Graphically, it is portrayed as a *shift* in the entire demand curve—a change in quantity at *each and every price.*

Using this terminology, *a reduction in the price of pickles* from $1 to 80 cents leads to *an increase in the quantity of pickles demanded*—a movement along the demand curve. An increase in income, on the other hand, induces *an increase in demand* for pickles—an outward shift of the demand curve at each and every price.

As an additional example, consider the impact on the demand for one product of a change in the price of some *other* good or service. Suppose, for example, that the price of pork increases. What impact will this have on the demand for beef? To the extent that pork and beef are substitute products, people will have a tendency to buy more beef and less pork. There will be a *reduction in the quantity demanded* of pork but an *increase in demand* for beef. The higher price for pork causes a movement along the demand curve for pork; the demand curve for beef shifts outward at each and every price. This is illustrated in Figure 3.5.

Supply

The concept of supply is analogous to that of demand, but refers to the seller's side of the market rather than the buyer's side. Like demand, supply has a very definite meaning to an economist. *The supply of a particular good or service expresses a "willingness to sell" on the part of sellers.* Like demand, supply of a good cannot be determined independently of the supply of other goods. A willingness to use scarce resources to supply one product precludes the use of those same resources to produce something else (at the same time). A willingness to sell a resource for use in some particular productive activity implies a willingness to forego alternative uses of that

Figure 3.5
A change in demand and a change in the quantity demanded: A change in the price of substitute goods

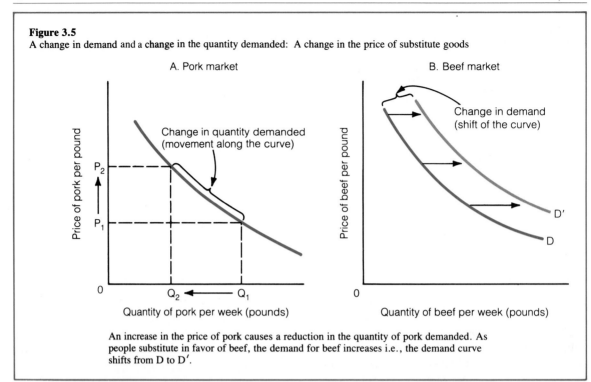

An increase in the price of pork causes a reduction in the quantity of pork demanded. As people substitute in favor of beef, the demand for beef increases i.e., the demand curve shifts from D to D′.

resource. The notion of opportunity cost is central to the concept of supply. And finally, supply, like demand, must be given an explicit time dimension. The amount that can be produced in a week using given techniques is certainly different from the amount that can be produced in a year. Thus, supply is expressed as so much per unit of time.

We defer for the moment any discussion of resource supply in order to concentrate on product supply.

Product supply

How much producers are willing to sell during some period—say, a month—will depend on many things—the price of the product, the prices of other goods and services, resource prices, the technology used in production, etc. Let us concentrate for the moment on the price of the product itself, holding all else constant. Using pickles as our example, let us record how the quantity

of pickles supplied varies as the price of pickles is varied.

The results of this experiment are recorded in the **supply schedule** and the **supply curve** of Figure 3.6. At a price of 20 cents, producers are willing to sell only 4 million jars per month; but at a price of 80 cents, the quantity supplied jumps to 16 million per month.

The positive relationship between the quantity supplied and price—shown graphically as an upward sloping supply curve—is known as the **law of supply.** *Ceteris paribus, an increase in price leads to an increase in the quantity supplied; or, alternatively, ceteris paribus, a reduction in price leads to reduction in the quantity supplied.*

Rationale for the law of supply

The law of supply—the upward-sloping supply curve—can be understood intuitively as the consequence of two fundamental forces: the law of increasing costs and the desire of producers

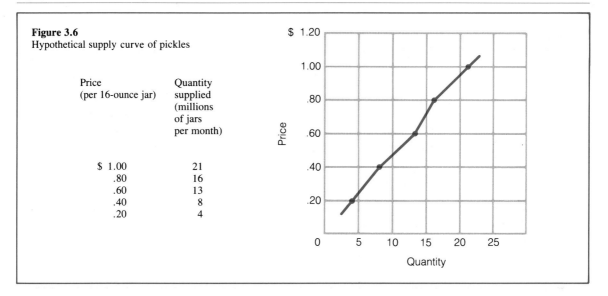

Figure 3.6
Hypothetical supply curve of pickles

Price (per 16-ounce jar)	Quantity supplied (millions of jars per month)
$ 1.00	21
.80	16
.60	13
.40	8
.20	4

to maximize profits. Let us examine each of these in turn.

The law of increasing costs. As you will recall from Chapter 2, the **law of increasing costs** states that it becomes increasingly costly to produce equal increases in the output of any good or service, *ceteris paritus.* In other words, *costs per unit of output increase as the level of production is increased, holding everything else constant.* The operation of the law of increasing costs was portrayed in Chapter 2 by the bowed (concave-to-the-origin) shape of the production possibilities curve; the law is portrayed here by the upward slope of the supply curve.

To ensure that this important idea is understood thoroughly, let us illustrate the law of increasing costs by examining a law that underlies it—the **law of diminishing returns.** Consider the production of any good—wheat, for example. Its production involves the use of land, labor, and capital. Hold fixed for the moment the amount of capital and land that are used and observe what happens to the total output of wheat as we add more and more labor to its production. The law of diminishing returns states that total output will rise but at a diminishing rate. Put formally, *the law of diminishing returns states that the additions to total output will diminish as equal amounts of one input are added to fixed*

amounts of other inputs. The reason? Because that one input will have less and less of the fixed inputs to work with.

This point is best illustrated by a simple numerical example. Table 3.1 shows how the total output of wheat varies as more and more labor is added to its production, *holding land and capital fixed.* Thus, whereas the addition of the sixth worker results in a 4,000-bushel expansion of output, the addition of the seventh worker causes an expansion of output of only 3,000; adding an eighth worker adds only 1,000 to total output.

Let us go one step further. Holding fixed the amounts of capital and land means that the capital and land costs do not vary as output is in-

Table 3.1
Diminishing returns illustrated

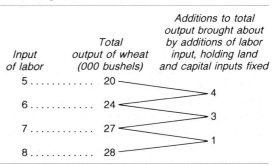

Input of labor	Total output of wheat (000 bushels)	Additions to total output brought about by additions of labor input, holding land and capital inputs fixed
5	20	4
6	24	3
7	27	1
8	28	

creased. On the other hand, the amount of labor employed is increased, which adds to total costs. Suppose each worker costs $10,000 per year. Adding the sixth worker adds $10,000 to total costs; the fact that output increases by 4,000 bushels means that the added cost per additional bushel is $2.50 (i.e., $10,000 divided by 4,000). The seventh worker adds another $10,000 to total cost; *had* output increased by 4,000 bushels, we would not have had a situation we could characterize as increasing costs. Yes, total costs increase because we have added another worker; but if output had increased by 4,000 bushels, the added cost per additional bushel would have been the *same* as for the sixth worker—a situation of constant, not increasing, costs. However, the fact that total output increased by only 3,000 bushels with the addition of the seventh worker means that the added cost per additional bushel was $3.33 (i.e., $10,000 divided by 3,000)—an amount much higher than for the sixth worker. *The fact that the additional cost per added bushel rises as output is increased means that the production of wheat is subject to increasing costs.*

Maximizing profits. The second force that accounts for the positive relationship between price and the quantity supplied is the notion that producers seek to maximize their profits. *Profits* are defined as the difference between the receipts from the sale of the product and the costs of the product.

Under laissez-faire capitalism, businesspeople will seek to employ resources in those activities that seem to promise the highest profit. If using a given quantity of resources to produce good X appears to be more profitable than using those resources in good Y, more resources will be devoted to the production of X and fewer to Y.

Combining these two ideas, the intuitive basis for the law of supply can be explained in the following terms. *Faced with increasing costs, and to ensure at least as much profit as could be had using additional resources elsewhere, producers would, in general, have to receive higher prices to willingly increase the production of wheat* (or any other good, for that matter). The supply curve slopes upward.

Two further notes on supply

As was the case with the law of demand, the law of supply was never intended to apply without exception to all producers. It is presumed to be valid *on average*—i.e., on average, an increase in price will induce an increase in the quantity supplied, *ceteris paribus*. Thus, like our earlier discussion of demand, it is important to distinguish between individual supply and market supply. The market supply curve is the combined willingness of all actual and/or potential producers to supply a good or service. Therefore, the market supply curve tells us how much of a product will be offered for sale at different prices by all producers as a group.

It is also important to distinguish between a change in the quantity supplied and a change in supply. The change in quantity caused by a change in price we refer to as a change in the quantity supplied. Graphically it is depicted as a movement along the supply curve. On the other hand, the change in quantity caused by a change in some factor other than price (e.g., a change in production technique or a change in resource prices) we refer to as a change in supply. Graphically such a change is shown as a shift in the entire supply curve—a change in quantity at each and every price.

A shift in the supply curve is illustrated in Figure 3.7 A change in technology is assumed to have taken place causing pickle producers to willingly increase their production by 12 million jars per month *at each and every price*. The increase in supply is depicted as a rightward shift of the supply curve, from S to S'.

As a final example, consider the effect of an increase in resource prices on the amount that producers would be willing to sell. Since the costs of producing *each* level of output are now higher as a consequence of the hike in resource prices, producers will insist on higher prices to produce and sell the *same* quantities as before. The increase in resource prices will be reflected in a shift of the supply curve upward and to the left. This *reduced supply* shift is shown in Figure 3.8.

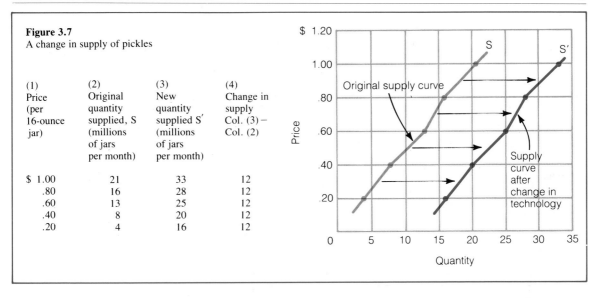

Figure 3.7
A change in supply of pickles

(1) Price (per 16-ounce jar)	(2) Original quantity supplied, S (millions of jars per month)	(3) New quantity supplied S′ (millions of jars per month)	(4) Change in supply Col. (3) − Col. (2)
$ 1.00	21	33	12
.80	16	28	12
.60	13	25	12
.40	8	20	12
.20	4	16	12

Product market equilibrium

Demand expresses a willingness to buy; supply, a willingness to sell. But what people are *willing* to do and what they might be permitted to do may be very different matters. This is illustrated in Figure 3.9, which is simply a reproduction of data from Figures 3.2 and 3.6. From the figure we see that people are willing to buy 24 million jars of pickles a month at a price of 20 cents each, but producers are not willing to offer 24 million jars at that price; producers are willing

to sell only 4 million a month at a price of 20 cents each. Similarly, at the high price of $1 per jar, producers are willing to sell 21 million jars per month, but consumers are willing to buy only 6 million per month. At a price of $1 each, 15 million jars would just pile up on grocers' shelves each month.

The reason for these mismatches is obvious. A price of 20 cents is too low. The quantity demanded exceeds the quantity supplied. On the other hand, a price of $1 is too high. The quantity

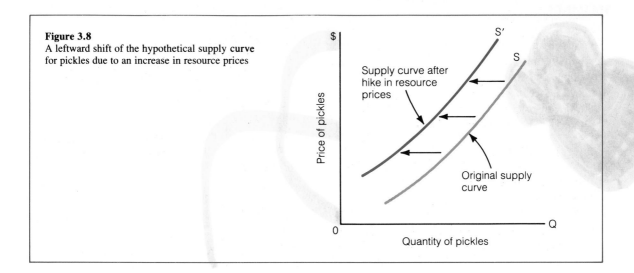

Figure 3.8
A leftward shift of the hypothetical supply curve for pickles due to an increase in resource prices

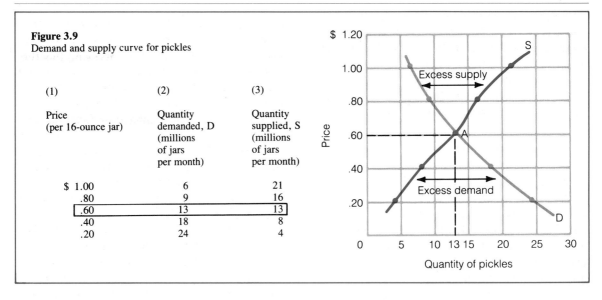

Figure 3.9
Demand and supply curve for pickles

(1)	(2)	(3)
Price (per 16-ounce jar)	Quantity demanded, D (millions of jars per month)	Quantity supplied, S (millions of jars per month)
$ 1.00	6	21
.80	9	16
.60	13	13
.40	18	8
.20	24	4

supplied exceeds the quantity demanded. Can we, then, find a price at which the quantity demanded is equal to the quantity supplied—i.e., a price at which the amount consumers are willing to buy is matched by the amount producers are willing to sell? Yes. At a price of 60 cents producers and consumers are willing to sell and buy 13 million jars of pickles per month; quantity supplied equals quantity demanded. This is portrayed graphically by the intersection of the demand and supply curves at a price of 60 cents and a quantity of 13 million.

The intersection point is referred to as a **market equilibrium.** But in what sense is this an equilibrium? An equilibrium exists if there is no *tendency* for further change. And since the quantity producers are prepared to sell is equal to the quantity consumers are willing to purchase at 60 cents per jar, there is no tendency for the quantity or price to change. At the point of intersection, the market has "cleared."

In order to better understand this concept of equilibrium, let us select some price other than 60 cents, and then examine the forces that are set in motion to push the price toward 60 cents. Suppose a price of 80 cents per jar is selected. As Figure 3.9 makes clear, the quantity supplied at 80 cents is 16 million; the quantity demanded,

on the other hand, is only 9 million. Thus, at a price of 80 cents there is an *excess supply* of pickles. This means that *some producers are not able to find customers willing to buy all that they are willing to sell at that price.* As a consequence, they will cut the price. The reduced price will in turn have two effects:

1. At a lower price, producers will reduce the quantity they are willing to place on the market for sale.
2. As price falls, the quantity consumers are willing to purchase rises.

As a result of these effects, the *excess supply is reduced.* And the process of price reduction will continue until a price of 60 cents per jar has been reached.

Suppose, on the other hand, that a price of 20 cents is selected. At that price, there is an *excess demand* for pickles. The quantity demanded (24 million) exceeds the quantity supplied (4 million). This means that some consumers are not able to get all the pickles they want at a price of 20 cents. They will therefore bid the price up. And the increased price will have two effects:

1. At a higher price, the quantity demanded will decline.
2. As price rises, the quantity supplied rises.

As a consequence of these effects, the *excess demand is reduced.* Of course, the price will continue to be bid up until the excess demand has been eliminated entirely—until a price of 60 cents has been reached.

Such is the manner by which demand and supply determine both price and quantity.

Surpluses and Shortages

We are now in a position to give meaning to the concepts of **surplus** and **shortage,** terms that are, at best, poorly understood and often misused. An excess supply of a commodity is referred to as a surplus. Note that a surplus exists *only because the price is too high to clear the market;* that is, the quantity suppliers are willing to sell *at that price* exceeds the quantity demanded *at that price.* An excess demand, on the other hand, is referred to as a shortage. Again, a shortage exists *only because the price is too low to clear the market.* These points are illustrated in Figure 3.10.

How can surpluses and shortages be eliminated? Through a change in prices. A surplus is eliminated when price is reduced to its market clearing level; a shortage is eliminated when price is raised to its market clearing level. In this way, prices perform an important **rationing function.** That is, once an equilibrium price is discovered, the available supply is distributed—rationed—to those who are willing and able to buy. Likewise, prices perform an **allocation function.** That is, since the equilibrium *quantity* is determined at the point of intersection of demand and supply, we are able to gauge the amount of resources markets will allocate to this good.

Examples of shortages and surpluses, and the confusion surrounding these concepts, abound. To cite just one example, during the 1973–74 Arab oil embargo and the ensuing fourfold increase in world energy prices there was ample evidence of a gasoline shortage—long lines at gasoline stations. At the official, government-controlled price, an excess demand existed for motor gasoline. An increase in price to the market clearing level would have eliminated these lines; the shortage would have been eliminated.

At the time, many people were skeptical regarding the possible effects of price hikes on the gasoline lines. "After all," they argued, "people have to have gasoline to drive and they will pay

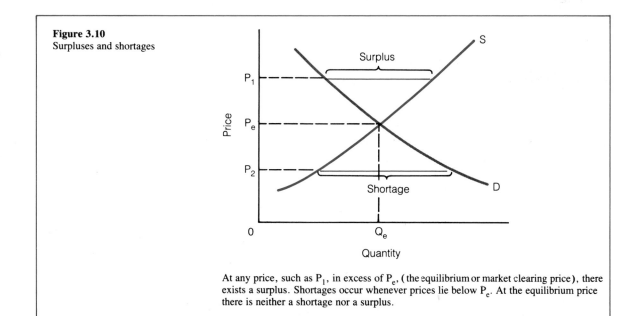

Figure 3.10
Surpluses and shortages

At any price, such as P_1, in excess of P_e, (the equilibrium or market clearing price), there exists a surplus. Shortages occur whenever prices lie below P_e. At the equilibrium price there is neither a shortage nor a surplus.

anything to get it. The lines will not go away just because the price is increased." However, if one thinks about the problem carefully, it should be clear that it is always possible to find a price that is high enough to "force" people to curtail their gasoline consumption. Two dollars per gallon might not have done it in 1974, but what about $8 or $10 per gallon or more? Now, raising the price to these levels might have had a number of undesirable effects, which might have recommended against electing that means to "solve" the gasoline line problem. But there is no question that enough of a price hike could have wiped out the shortage.

Changes in demand and supply

It is now clear how the forces of demand and supply determine the equilibrium price and quantity. It follows that the equilibrium will change if demand and supply change—that is, if the demand or supply curves *shift*. A number of possible changes in the equilibrium price and quantity are illustrated in Figure 3.11.

Suppose buyers experience an increase in income and, as a result, they increase their demand for the product in question. What happens? The demand curve shifts to the right from D to D', as is illustrated in panel A of Figure 3.11. And then what? At the initial price there is an excess demand, a shortage. Buyers will bid the price up; at the higher price, producers will be willing to place a larger quantity on the market for sale. Thus, an increase in demand results in an increase in both the equilibrium price and quantity.

In panel B we show how a reduction in demand leads to a reduction in the equilibrium price and quantity. This could come about, for example, because of a change in tastes away from the good in question, or because of a reduction in consumer income.

In panel C we investigate the impact of an increase in supply on the market equilibrium. Assume that producers, for one reason or another, are now paying less for their material inputs and that, as a consequence, they are willing to sell a larger quantity of their product at each

and every price. What will happen? The supply curve will shift to the right from S to S'. Then what? At the initial price there is an excess supply, a surplus. The price will be reduced and consumers will respond by increasing the quantity demanded. The equilibrium price will fall and the quantity will rise.

In panel D it is clear that a reduction in supply will lead to a reduction in the equilibrium quantity and an increase in price.

Panel E shows the impact on market equilibrium of an increase in supply *and* an increase in demand. The equilibrium quantity will definitely rise, but price might rise or fall depending on the relative shifts of the demand and supply curves. An increase in demand is a force that, by itself, exerts upward pressure on price; an increase in supply exerts downward pressure on price. What happens to the equilibrium price will thus depend on which change dominates.

Finally, in panel F the quantity change is ambiguous, but the price change is clear. The reduction in supply and the increase in demand both operate to push the price up. The increase in demand, which on its own signals an increase in quantity, is offset more or less by a reduction in supply.

Ceteris paribus revisited

The law of demand posits an inverse relationship between price and quantity; the law of supply, a positive relationship. But each of these laws is presumed to hold *ceteris paribus*—everything else unchanged. Specifically, the law of supply is presumed to hold only if all of the other factors affecting supply, such as resource prices and technology, remain unchanged. The law of demand holds, it is hypothesized, only if all of the other factors affecting demand, such as income and tastes, are unchanged.

Our previous discussion highlights the importance of these *ceteris paribus* assumptions. Suppose, for example, that the equilibrium price goes up and the equilibrium quantity purchased rises. Does this mean that the law of demand is therefore invalid? Not necessarily. Consider again the situation presented in panel A of Figure 3.11.

Figure 3.11
Changes in demand and supply: Changing market equilibrium

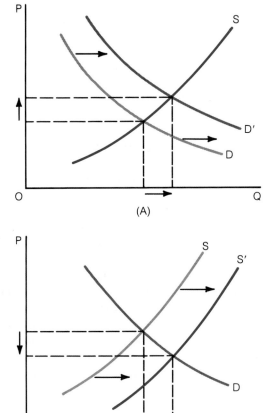

(A)

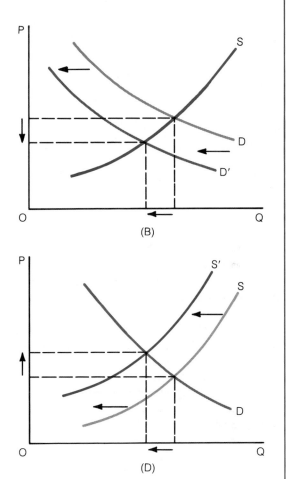

(B)

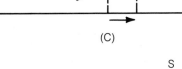

(C)

(D)

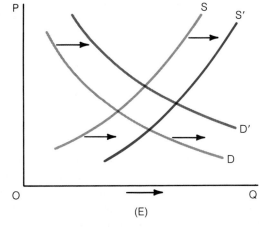

(E)

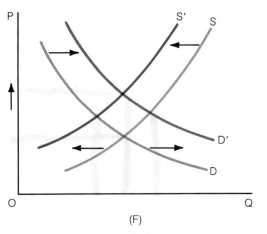

(F)

There the increase in demand caused the price increase. But the law of demand is still valid. *Ceteris paribus,* an increase in price will lead to a reduction in the quantity demanded—that is, the demand curve has a negative slope. The reason price rose and the quantity bought also rose was that the *ceteris paribus* assumption was violated; one of the things assumed constant in formulating the law did, in fact, change.

In the above example, the law of demand failed to predict because demand changed—i.e., the demand curve shifted. But the law of supply predicted accurately. Why? Because the supply curve did not change its position in face of the change in demand. Conversely the law of demand predicts accurately the outcomes in panels C and D of Figure 3.11, but the law of supply does not. Be sure you can explain why.

This distinction—between a movement *along* a demand or a supply curve, for which *ceteris paribus* applies, and a *shift* in the demand or supply curve, for which *ceteris paribus* does not apply—is critical to our understanding of markets. A failure to keep them analytically distinct can lead to absurd results. For example, suppose you observed Americans consuming record quantities of motor gasoline at record high prices. Would you conclude that the demand curve for motor gasoline had a positive slope and that, therefore, another oil embargo that reduced the supply would cause gasoline prices to fall?

Or suppose you observed higher prices for agricultural commodities but sharply reduced levels of production. Would you conclude that the supply curve was downward sloping? And would you be willing to assume that agricultural prices would fall if people stepped up their purchases? You would probably do better to predict higher prices and to search out the factors responsible for the leftward shift of the supply curve (such as, for example, poor weather conditions).

Demand and supply in resource markets

The equilibrium prices and quantities of our scarce resources are also determined by the forces of demand and supply—specifically, by the demand for and supply of each of the resources in question. Because resource markets function in much the same way as product markets, they will be discussed only briefly.

Since resources are used to produce goods and services, the demand for resources is a **derived demand**—derived from the demand for products. Moreover, like the law of product demand, the law of resource demand states: *Ceteris paribus, an increase in the price of a resource leads to a reduction in the quantity demanded. Conversely, a reduction in the price of a resource will induce an increase in the quantity demanded.* There are fundamentally two reasons for this inverse relationship:

1. If resource prices rise, producers may reduce production and their use of those resources. This effect is analogous to the income effect.

2. An increase in the price of one resource may cause producers to substitute in favor of other resources. For example, firms faced with an increase in the price of labor may substitute in favor of labor-saving techniques of production. This is the substitution effect.

The demand for a resource is affected by more than the price of the resource. One of the most important other factors is the demand for the product that uses the resource in its production. An increase in demand for a *product* generally leads to an increase in demand for the *resources* used in its production—that is, the demand curve for the resource shifts to the right at each and every price. Conversely, a reduction in product demand will induce a reduction in the demand for the resource. The distinction between a change in demand and a change in the quantity demanded is as important in resource markets as it is in product markets.

Looking to the supply side of resource markets, the law of resource supply states: *Ceteris paribus, an increase in price leads to an increase in the quantity supplied. Conversely, a reduction in price leads to a reduction in the quantity supplied.* And the reasons? In the case of some resources, the reasons are identical to those used to explain the law of product supply. The production of capital goods requires the use of scarce resources, as does the production of any other product. Capital goods producers are subject to diminishing returns. In the face of increasing costs, profit maximization requires that prices increase in order that capital goods production increase.

Moreover, since the extraction of resources from the earth's crust also requires the use of other scarce resources, the production of these natural resources being subject to diminishing returns, higher prices are often necessary in order to increase the quantities supplied. In addition, more arable land might be made available for the production of agricultural commodities the higher the price of arable land. More labor services might be made available the higher the price of labor, either because some people are willing to give up some leisure in order to work longer hours or because others can now be induced by the high price of labor to enter the labor force for the first time. Thus it seems reasonable to assume upward-sloping resource supply curves.

Finally, as we have emphasized repeatedly, it is critical that we maintain a distinction between a change in the quantity supplied and a change in supply.

The factor price equalization theory

Although the reasons for the distinction between a change in supply and a change in the quantity supplied should by now be obvious, there is one aspect of the problem in resource markets that warrants further analysis. The problem is that, *according to one celebrated theory, unless a resource is paid the same price in all of its alternative employments, resource supply changes will take place until equality is established.* This theory is sometimes referred to as the **factor-price equalization theory.** There are many reasons why, in the real world, the theory does not hold precisely (which we will investigate more fully in later chapters). However, it does have enough merit to warrant discussion here. It is illustrated in Figure 3.12.

Assume for simplicity that only one kind of labor exists and that all laborers are identical. Labor can work in the production of A goods or B goods. Suppose initially that 125 people work in the production of A goods at a wage

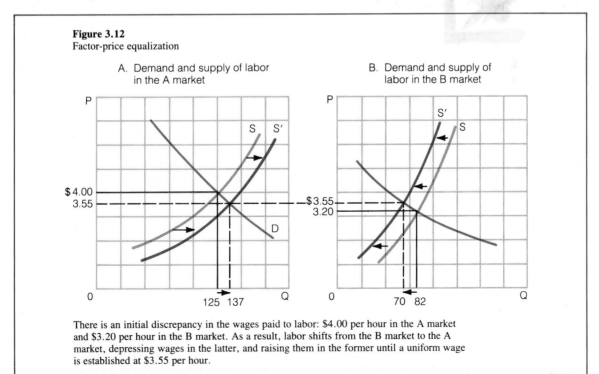

Figure 3.12
Factor-price equalization

A. Demand and supply of labor in the A market

B. Demand and supply of labor in the B market

There is an initial discrepancy in the wages paid to labor: $4.00 per hour in the A market and $3.20 per hour in the B market. As a result, labor shifts from the B market to the A market, depressing wages in the latter, and raising them in the former until a uniform wage is established at $3.55 per hour.

of $4 per hour; 82 work in the production of B goods at a wage of $3.20 per hour. As a result of the discrepancy in wages, workers will shift from the B market to the A market in search of higher wages. What happens as a result of this movement? The increased supply of workers in the A market drives down the wage rate there; the reduced supply of workers in the B market causes wages to be bid up there. This movement of workers from the B market to the A market will continue until a uniform wage is established. We have assumed in Figure 3.12 that $3.55 per hour is the final equilibrium wage. The factor price has been equalized.

PARTIAL EQUILIBRIUM AND GENERAL EQUILIBRIUM: RESOURCE AND PRODUCT MARKETS

When we analyze the forces of demand and supply in any *single* market or small group of markets, we refer to this as **partial equilibrium analysis.** That is, we analyze a single market or group in isolation from all the rest. We look only at part of the economic system. Although this approach is a useful first step toward understanding any economic system, it is important that we deal explicitly with the interrelationships of all markets. Thus we must deal with the **general equilibrium** aspects of demand and supply phenomena.

Since it is clear that market participants can choose from literally millions of different combinations of goods and services, we must seek to determine how the forces of demand and supply operate in a laissez-faire capitalist economy to yield the combinations selected. Moreover, since the goods and services selected can be produced in many different ways, we must also discover how the forces of demand and supply operate to determine how and where our resources will be employed.

If we are to make any headway, we must make a number of simplifying assumptions. Let us assume, for the moment, that our economy produces two goods only—pickles and pumps. Suppose further that the economy is initially produc-

ing at point C on the production possibilities curve in panel A of Figure 3.13. (The production possibilities curve used here is a reproduction of Figure 2.1.) At this point, 60,000 barrels of pickles and 170,000 pumps are produced each month.

There will be no tendency for producers to alter their production plans, nor for resources to shift from the production of one good to the other as long as 60,000 barrels of pickles and 170,000 pumps represent the equilibrium quantities of these two goods. The results presented in panel B of Figure 3.13 suggest that this is the case initially. The original demand and supply curves (labeled D and S, respectively) for pickles and pumps imply, respectively, the equilibrium quantities of 60,000 barrels of pickles and 170,000 pumps.

Finally, assume that both products are produced with the aid of a single input—labor. Note in panel C the existence of a uniform wage initially.

Suppose, as a result of a change in tastes, consumers desire more pickles and fewer pumps. Specifically, assume that people desire the product mix represented by point B. Under the circumstances, how does a system of markets and prices in a laissez-faire capitalist economy bring about the requisite shift of resources?

First, the increased demand for pickles and the reduced demand for pumps leads to an increase in the price of pickles and a reduction in the price of pumps. These results are reflected in panel B of Figure 3.13. The demand for pickles increases from D to D', causing both the equilibrium quantity and price of pickles to rise. The demand for pumps declines, reducing its equilibrium price and quantity.

Second, the increased demand for pickles leads to an increased demand for labor, forcing up the price of labor in the pickling sector. The reduced demand for labor on the part of pump producers lowers the price of labor in the pump sector.

Third, the discrepancy in wages that now exists provides an incentive for labor resources to shift toward the sector paying the highest wage. Specifically, the higher wage paid by pickle pro-

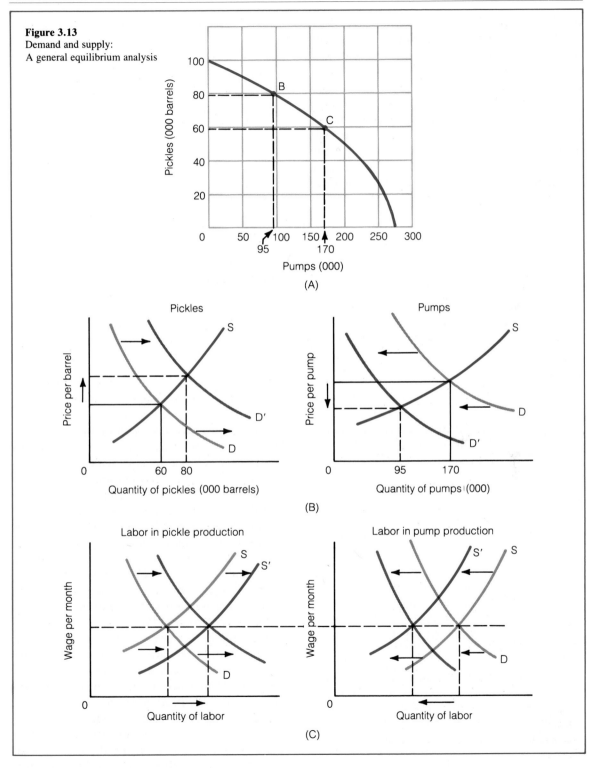

Figure 3.13
Demand and supply:
A general equilibrium analysis

ducers acts as a lure attracting workers away from pump production. The result? An increase in the supply of labor in the pickling sector and a reduced supply of labor in the pump sector. Such shifts will continue until a uniform wage is reestablished. These results are depicted in panel C Figure 3.13. In order to avoid cluttering the diagram any more than it is now, we have assumed in panel C that the uniform wage existing after the shift of labor resources is the same as that which existed initially; this need not occur.

Relative prices

Just as labor will shift from the production of one good to the production of another as a result of discrepancies in wages, so will other resources shift in response to differences in the payments received for their services. Indeed, one of the fundamental premises of a laissez-faire capitalist system is that all resources—land, labor, and capital alike—have an incentive to move into those activities that "pay" the most. And such movement of resources from one activity to another will cease only when differences in resource payments have been eliminated.[1] Not only will all labor be paid the same wage, but similarly, each activity will yield the same *rate of profit*— that is, *the same profit per dollar invested.* The profit rate in pickle production will be the same as in pump production. If such were not the case, producers would shift resources from low-profit activities to those offering higher returns. This would, as we have seen before, tend to bring about the equalization of returns in all activities.

It is on the basis of such considerations that a state of equilibrium is defined. As noted earlier, an equilibrium is said to exist if there is no *ten-*

---

[1] We are assuming for simplicity that labor, capital, and land are each homogeneous. Thus each laborer is paid the same wage; the return on capital investment is likewise uniform. And to the extent that labor is *not* homogeneous— some workers are healthier, stronger, more intelligent—wage differentials can and will exist to reflect those differences. In a sense, different kinds of labor can be viewed as different resources. The same is true of capital and land. This will be discussed in greater depth in Part Four.

dency for further change. Therefore, an equilibrium will exist only if resource payments discrepancies have been eliminated. Otherwise, resources will shift until the payments are equalized. Once resource payments are equalized there will be no tendency for further change; the system will be in equilibrium.

Corresponding to equilibrium in resource markets, there is also equilibrium in product markets. Indeed, *equilibrium in product markets reflects equilibrium in resource markets.* To see this, return to the analysis presented in Figure 3.13. Point C on the production possibilities curve is an initial equilibrium point because consumers are willing to purchase and producers are willing to supply 60,000 barrels of pickles and 170,000 pumps *at the prices then prevailing for pickles and pumps.* This is evident in panel B. And producers are willing to supply those respective quantities at those prices only if the profit rates for the two goods are the same. This implies, in turn, that labor and other resources are paid at uniform rates. Otherwise, resources will shift and resource prices will change, affecting producer profits and the quantities they are willing to supply at any given price.

We can express this equilibrium set of prices in relative terms. Indeed, from the point of view of resource allocation, it is *relative prices* that are important, not the absolute price of each good. This derives from the fact that both demand and supply are relative concepts. As noted earlier, the demand for any given product reflects people's relative preferences. It reflects a preference for this good vis-à-vis other goods. Similarly, the supply of any good suggests a willingness to use scarce resources to produce and sell one particular good rather than another. If people, *for whatever reason,* want more of one good relative to others, the price of that good will rise *relative* to the price of other goods. This relative price change provides a signal to producers that resources should be redirected toward the good whose price has risen relatively. Relative price changes bring about resource shifts.

This can be seen from an examination of Figure 3.13. The economy is initially producing at point C. As long as consumers are willing to purchase 60,000 barrels of pickles and 170,000 pumps at the prevailing prices for pickles and pumps, there will be no tendency for producers to alter their production plans or for resources to shift. Suppose, on the other hand, that, at the prices quoted for pickles and pumps, consumers desire more pickles than are produced and less pumps. This disequilibrium situation will result in a change in relative prices. At the initial prices, there is a shortage of pickles and a surplus of pumps. This shortage and surplus can be rectified by allowing the relative price of pickles to rise. Since it is now more profitable to produce pickles than pumps, resources will shift away from pump production to pickle production. And such resource shifts will continue until the profit differential has been eliminated. *The increase in the relative price of pickles caused the resource shift.*

Suppose the shift takes place and we arrive at point B (where we are producing 80,000 barrels of pickles and 95,000 pumps). Can point B be considered an equilibrium point in the sense that when we reach it there is no further tendency to change? It all depends. If consumers are willing to purchase 80,000 barrels of pickles and 95,000 pumps *at the prices prevailing at point B,* the situation can be described as one of equilibrium. Panel B of Figure 3.13 suggests that this is the case.

Consumer sovereignty

In the laissez-faire capitalist system we have been describing, the consumer in a fundamental sense dictates how scarce resources will be allocated. We have already seen that it was profitable for producers to move resources out of pump production and into pickle production because of the increase in the relative price of pickles that resulted from changed consumer preferences.

Why all this emphasis on the consumer? Isn't the producer important? Yes, the producer is important, but as will become clear, it is the response of the producer *to the consumer* that is important. To illustrate, suppose producers were to shift resources away from the production of

one good toward the production of another. Would the resource shift be more profitable or less? It all depends. *In the absence of any changes in (1) demand or (2) the quantity and/or quality of resources, it would be less profitable.* The fact that the resource shift brings about a *reduction* in the relative price of the good whose production is expanded is sufficient to reflect this decline in relative profitability. Put differently, the movement from C to B in Figure 3.13 is profitable only if the relative price of pickles *rises.* But such a change in relative price will take place only if the demand for pickles rises relative to the demand for pumps (assuming no change in the quantity and/or quality of resources). In the absence of any change in consumer demand, the increased production of pickles and the reduced production of pumps would create a surplus of pickles and a shortage of pumps, reducing the relative price of pickles. Since pickle production is less profitable than pump production, resources will shift back to where they were before. *It is the consumer therefore who dictates how much of each good will be produced; the consumer is sovereign.*

General equilibrium and "the invisible hand"

The points we have made in our discussion of just two goods and a few resources are also true of many goods and many resources. Equilibrium in all markets obtains only when the prevailing prices for the millions of goods and services that are daily being produced and consumed are at their equilibrium levels. This equilibrium set of product prices also reflects equilibrium in resource markets. In equilibrium, not only is the demand for and supply of each resource equilibrated, but each resource earns the same return in all activities. Not only is each part of the economy in equilibrium, but the whole economy is in equilibrium; *general equilibrium* exists.

Moreover, if for some reason consumer preferences change, this will be translated into a relative price change. This in turn dictates a shift of resources in the direction of those goods whose prices have risen relatively. And note: This shift of resources comes about *not as a result of actions undertaken by some central authority (e.g., by government),* but solely because producers discovered that it was more profitable in the face of the relative price change to alter production plans. It is as if resources were guided by an **invisible hand.** (The suggestion that resources are allocated in a laissez-faire capitalist system as if by an invisible hand was first made in 1776 by Adam Smith, the true grandfather of economics, in one of the most famous books ever, *The Wealth of Nations.*)

Laissez-faire capitalism and the four fundamental questions

We are now in a position to show how a laissez-faire capitalist system answers the four fundamental questions—*what, how, for whom,* and *how extensively.*

What is determined on the basis of consumer preferences as reflected in the demand for goods and services. Recall the meaning of demand. It expresses a *willingness and ability to pay.* What goods will be produced in what quantities will depend on what consumers are willing and able to pay (given the quantity and quality of the available resources).

How resources will be used to produce *what* is partly a technical question and partly a matter of profits. For each of the various techniques of production—that is, for each way any given good can be produced—a technical relationship exists between the quantity that can be produced with varying amounts of each of the inputs. Given the prices of the various inputs, however, businesspeople will select those techniques that are the most profitable.

For whom is more complicated. We have already emphasized the fact that *what* is determined by people's willingness and ability to pay. But my willingness to pay depends on how much I have available to spend, which in turn depends on how much I can get for the resources that I own (including my labor resources). The worth of those resources depends on how much they contribute to the production of the goods and services people demand. If they make little or

no contribution, they will command a small or a zero return.

The above-described process is often put differently. Depending on the contribution that any given resource makes to the production of goods and services, the owner receives a certain number of "dollar votes"; these dollar votes can be cast by the owner of the resources to obtain the goods and services wanted. Thus, *for whom* will be determined on the basis of how the dollar votes are distributed.

From this interaction between product and resource markets, *how extensively* resources will be used in a laissez-faire capitalist system is determined.

Laissez-faire capitalism: A preliminary evaluation

The laissez-faire capitalist system is often portrayed as ideal. After all, look at the ease with which that system *coordinates* the many millions of decisions required to insure that the *right* things are produced in the *right* quantities and are distributed to the *right* people. Could we ask for anything more? Perhaps.

Let us examine the system more carefully. First, the laissez-faire capitalist system will allocate resources in accordance with the wants of consumers (in the way we have described) *only if each participant*—buyer and seller alike—exerts a negligible influence on price. If either a buyer or seller (or a group of buyers or sellers) can influence price, it then becomes possible for the market to be rigged to the advantage of some and disadvantage of others. This is easily illustrated.

We have already seen how a reduction in supply (i.e., a leftward shift of the supply curve) will cause the price to rise. Thus, if any single seller (or group sellers) dominates the market, in the sense of producing a sizable proportion of the total output, then it might be possible for that seller (or group) to withhold output (i.e., restrict supply). This could force up the price to his or her advantage. Consumer sovereignty would be undermined by the actions of such producers, and the system would fail to operate in accordance with that dictum. Consumer sovereignty will prevail only when sellers produce such a trivial proportion of the total output that they are unable to change price to their advantage through changes in the rate of production. In an economy where several hundred pump producers each produce a small fraction of the total output of pumps, it will matter little whether any *single* producer decreases output or even shuts down completely. The *total* supply, and therefore price, will not be altered noticeably.

The same is true of the buyers' side of the market. If any single person, or a group acting in concert, is able to affect the price of any good or service, it is natural to expect that he or she will try to turn things to their own advantage, thereby distorting the allocation of resources. The point is that the goals of laissez-faire capitalism can be furthered only if power is so widely diffused that no one is able to rig the market in such a way as to advance his or her own interest at the expense of others.

There are other senses in which laissez-faire capitalism may be far from ideal. Who is to judge that the *right* things get produced in the *right* quantities for the *right* people? How is "rightness" determined? In a laissez-faire capitalist system the answers are obvious. The right goods are produced in the right quantities if they accord with how dollar votes are cast. And the number of dollar votes each of us has at our disposal will be determined by the worth of the resources we own. But is it just and equitable for people who have little in the way of resources (because of physical or mental handicaps, or because they are not lucky enough to have property resources bequeathed to them) to be denied access to even the basic necessities of life? This is not something that economists as economists can answer. But it is a question every society must answer: What is the "just" distribution of income and wealth? To the extent that society's answer to this question differs from that which emerges from a laissez-faire capitalist system, such a system is less than ideal.

Even if the distribution of income and wealth were not in question, there are many who would argue that laissez-faire capitalism does not necessarily produce the right goods in the right quantities because of the presence of *externalities*—**external costs** or **external benefits** associated with the production or consumption of goods. These externalities are best illustrated by example. Consider first external costs. In the process of producing many goods and services, we foul the air and dirty the water. Often these costs are not reflected in the prices of those goods and services. Left to their own devices, the only costs business people would be willing to incur would be those associated with the acquisition of resources, not the costs imposed on others—costs that are external to the production processes. Thus, there is every reason to expect that more of these goods and services will be produced than is desirable, because the market prices does not reflect all of the costs of production. The internal (or direct) costs are reflected but not the *external* costs.

Or consider goods that yield external benefits like life-saving vaccines. Those who pay for the vaccines receive benefits, but so do those who are not vaccinated because the likelihood of the disease spreading is reduced. Those benefits received by those not vaccinated—the external benefits—are not reflected in product prices because the benefits were received without any dollar votes being cast. Since the price system only reflects the dollar votes that are cast, there is likelihood that too few resources will be devoted to the production of goods yielding external benefits.

More will be said on these matters in Chapter 4 and again in Chapter 27.

Prices and markets: Mixed and planned economies

On the basis of the above considerations it is clear that laissez-faire capitalism will not necessarily produce the best mix of goods or the most desirable distribution of income and wealth. Indeed, many people argue that the outcomes of the laissez-faire capitalist system are far from ideal. In terms of our earlier discussion, what this means is that many people would not accept as ideal a capitalist system's answers to the four fundamental questions—*what, how, for whom,* and *how extensively*. Their answers would be different.

It is possible to use the system of markets and prices to achieve outcomes that differ from those resulting from a purely laissez-faire system—that is, to achieve outcomes that have different answers to the four fundamental questions. It is our purpose here to explore in a limited way how mixed and planned economies use the price system to accomplish a different allocation of resources.

Consider the situation portrayed in Figure 3.14. The economy in question produces two goods—automobiles and corn. Assume for the moment that the product mix represented by point A—200 units of automobiles and 60 units of corn—represents the *initial* equilibrium product mix arising from a laissez-faire capitalist system.

Suppose further that society, through government, decides for one reason or another (e.g., automobile production creates an excessive amount of pollution) that the most desirable product mix is represented instead by point B, not point A. How can the price system be used to bring about the requisite shift of resources away from the production of automobiles to the

production of corn? *By taxing the production of automobiles and subsidizing the production of corn.* This is shown in Figure 3.15.

Initially, the equilibrium quantity of 200 automobiles sells for a price of P_0 each. Consumers can be induced to cut back their consumption of automobiles to 150 only if the price of automobiles rises to P_1. This can be seen by an examination of the demand curve for automobiles in Figure 3.15. Producers, on the other hand, will be willing to cut back their production of automobiles to 150 units only if the price of autos falls to P_2. Thus, if the government were to levy a tax on each unit sold—an *excise* tax equal to the distance P_1P_2—it could accomplish the goal it desires. The *gross price*—the price paid by consumers—would be P_1. The *net price*—the price received by the sellers—would be P_2. The quantity supplied (150) would equal the quantity demanded (150). In effect, the supply curve has been shifted upward by the amount of the tax to S'. The new market equilibrium occurs where the new supply curve, S', crosses the demand curve, D.

Similarly, the production and consumption of corn can be stimulated through a government *subsidy*. Consumers will increase their consumption of corn to 90 only if the price falls to P_3; corn producers, on the other hand, are willing to supply 90 only if the price rises to P_4. By providing producers with a subsidy (which is passed on to the consumer) equal to the distance P_3P_4 for each unit produced, the government is able to accomplish its objective.

There are, of course, other ways government can obtain a different allocation of scarce resources and a different set of answers to the four fundamental questions, but we leave a consideration of these issues for Part Three of this book. The point that needs to be made here, however, is as follows.

> The laissez-faire capitalist system provides one set of answers to the four fundamental questions through the prices established in product and resource markets. If a different set of prices were to prevail, there would emerge a different allocation of resources and a different set of answers

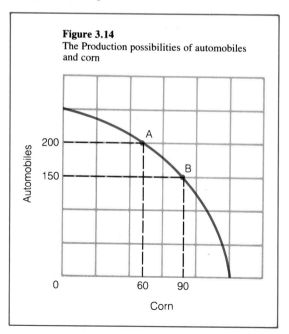

Figure 3.14
The Production possibilities of automobiles and corn

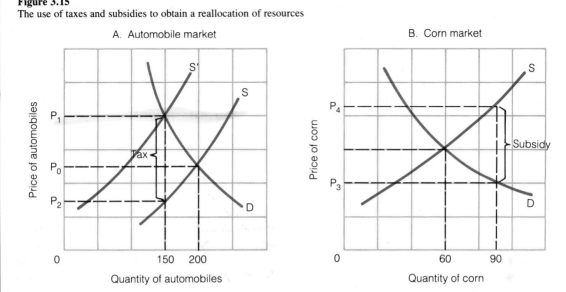

Figure 3.15
The use of taxes and subsidies to obtain a reallocation of resources

A. Automobile market

B. Corn market

to the four fundamental questions. It is possible, therefore, to devise policies that can change prices and the allocation of resources in ways that better enable the achievement of society's objectives. As a consequence, the price system can be used by mixed and planned economies to obtain answers to the four fundamental questions different from the answers provided by laissez-faire capitalism.

THE CIRCULAR FLOW OF ECONOMIC ACTIVITY

Figure 3.16 deserves your very close attention. It captures in a succinct way many of the diverse ideas presented in this chapter. It summarizes the complex interrelationships between product and resource markets, pictorially capturing how a system of markets and prices determines *what, how, for whom,* and *how extensively.*

Consumers cast dollar votes for various goods and services. They obtain these dollars from the sale of the services of the resources that they own. The producers of products pay for those resource services. And the wherewithal to make

such payments is obtained from the sale of their products to consumers. Thus the expenditures that are made by consumers for goods and services are matched by a return flow of funds to consumers as owners of resources. The flow of economic activity is circular.

SUMMARY

1.   *Demand* for a commodity expresses a willingness to buy, a willingness to forego other goods and services in order to acquire it. The notion of opportunity cost is central to the concept of demand.

2.   The demand for any commodity will be influenced by many things—the price of the commodity itself, the prices of other goods and services, people's income and wealth, etc. The *law of demand* hypothesizes that an inverse relationship exists between the price and quantity demanded of a good, *ceteris paribus.* Holding everything else constant, a reduction in price leads to an increase in the quantity demanded. The *income* and *substitution effects* of a price change explain this inverse relationship.

3.   The change in the quantity willingly pur-

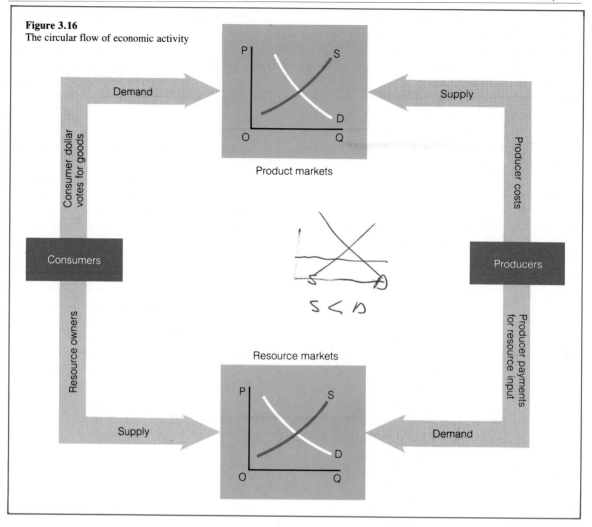

Figure 3.16
The circular flow of economic activity

Product markets

Consumers

Producers

Resource markets

chased caused by a change in price is referred to as a *change in the quantity demanded;* the change in quantity caused by something other than a change in the price of the good in question is referred to as *a change in demand.* A change in the quantity demanded is represented by a movement along the demand curve; a change in demand is represented by a shift of the demand curve at each and every price.

4. *Supply* of a commodity expresses a willingness to sell, a willingness to use scarce resources in this activity as opposed to the production of something else. The notion of opportunity cost is central to the concept of supply.

5. The supply of any commodity will be influenced by many things—the price of the commodity itself, the prices of land, labor and capital, etc. The *law of supply* hypothesizes that a direct, positive relationship exists between the price and quantity supplied of a good, *ceteris paribus.* Holding everything else constant, a reduction in price leads to a reduction in the quantity supplied. The law of increasing costs and the desire of producers to maximize profits explain this direct positive relationship.

6. The change in the quantity willingly sold caused by a change in the price of the good in question is referred to as a *change in the quantity*

supplied; it is represented by a movement along the supply curve. The change in quantity caused by a change in some factor other than its price is referred to as a *change in supply;* it is represented by a shift of the supply curve at each and every price.

7. *Market equilibrium* occurs at the point of intersection of the market demand and supply curves. At that point, quantity supplied equals quantity demanded.

8. A *surplus* refers to a condition of excess supply; a surplus exists only because the price is *too high* to clear the market. A *shortage* refers to a condition of excess demand; a shortage exists only because the price is *too low* to clear the market.

9. *Ceteris paribus,* a change in demand will cause price *and* quantity to change in the same direction as the demand shift. A change in supply will cause quantity to change in the same direction but price to move in the opposite direction. Accordingly, in the face of shifts of *both* demand and supply, it is possible that the equilibrium price or quantity change will be ambiguous.

10. The forces of demand and supply are as relevant in resource markets as they are in product markets. The functioning of resource markets is much the same as product markets.

11. Analysis of a single market or group in isolation from other markets is referred to as *partial equilibrium analysis.* Analysis of the interrelationships of the many markets is referred to as *general equilibrium analysis.*

12. In a laissez-faire capitalist system, market prices perform the function of coordination and guiding, as if by an *invisible hand,* the millions upon millions of economic decisions that cause the emergence of a general equilibrium. In this system, the consumer is sovereign. It is the establishment of the set of *relative prices* by the sovereign consumer that guides the allocation of resources in a laissez-faire capitalist system.

13. The system of markets and prices provides answers to the four fundamental questions. *What* is determined by the preferences of sovereign consumers. *How* is determined partly by the technical relationships between the goods produced and the inputs used in their production and partly by the profit-maximizing behavior of producers. *For whom* is determined on the basis of the distribution of "dollar votes" (i.e., the distribution of income and wealth). And *how extensively* is determined by the interaction between resource and product markets.

14. The laissez-faire capitalist system is ideal only in a limited sense. First, this economic system will allocate resources in accordance with the wants of consumers *only if* each buyer and seller exerts a negligible influence on price. Second, the distribution of dollar votes may not square with society's view of what is a just and equitable distribution. Third, resources may be misallocated as a result of the existence of external costs (e.g. pollution) or external benefits (e.g., vaccinations).

15. Although laissez-faire capitalism may not produce the "best" mix of goods and services or the most desirable distribution of income and wealth, one can make use of the system of markets and prices to produce outcomes that are different. For example, by taxing goods we desire less of and subsidizing goods we desire more of—the taxes and subsidies causing changes in relative prices—we are able to accomplish a different set of outcomes than those under laissez-faire capitalism.

CONCEPTS FOR REVIEW

Circular flow of economic activity

Demand

Product demand

Resource demand

Law of demand

Change in demand versus change in quantity demanded

Income effect of a price change

Substitution effect of a price change

Supply

Product supply

Resource supply

Law of supply

Change in supply versus change in quantity supplied

Law of diminishing returns

Market equilibrium

Excess demand

Excess supply

Shortage

Surplus

The rationing function of prices

Derived demand

Factor price equalization

Partial equilibrium analysis

General equilibrium analysis

Relative prices

Consumer sovereignty

The "invisible hand"

Externalities

External costs

External benefits

Excise tax

Subsidies

QUESTIONS FOR DISCUSSION

(Those marked with an asterisk (*) are more difficult.)

1. Automobile prices are reduced. According to the law of demand, the quantity of automobiles demanded will increase. Explain this increase in terms of the income and substitution effects of the automobile price change. Be explicit.

2. Explain what is wrong with the following statement. "If supply is reduced, the price will increase. The increase in price will reduce demand, which in turn will bring the price back down."

3. State whether you agree or disagree with each of the following statements. Explain your reasoning carefully in each instance.
   a. If demand and supply are both reduced, both the equilibrium price and quantity will fall.
   b. If the demand for good X is reduced and the equilibrium quantity is unchanged, this could imply that the supply curve of X is vertical (i.e., perpendicular to the horizontal axis).
   c. If demand is increased and supply is reduced, the equilibrium price will increase but the equilibrium quantity will increase or decrease de-

pending on the relative magnitude of the demand and supply shifts.
   d. If supply is increased and the equilibrium price is unchanged, the demand curve *necessarily* is horizontal (i.e., parallel to the horizontal axis). (*Hint:* Always be suspicious of any statement that says "necessarily." Ask yourself, "Is it true that the price would remain unchanged if the demand curve were horizontal?" Then, once that is answered, ask yourself, "Are there any other circumstances under which this could be true?" If you are having trouble with the latter question, consult Figure 3.11, panel E.)

4. Assume that the supply of motor gasoline is fixed. Assume further that there is a gasoline shortage. Explain *why* long lines at gasoline pumps can be taken as evidence of the existence of a gasoline shortage. Explain some of the ways higher gasoline prices will induce people to alter their driving habits so as to reduce or eliminate those gasoline lines. Finally, how would you respond to those who argue that higher gasoline prices can never be successful in eliminating lines at the gasoline pumps?

5. "Both the law of demand and the law of supply are *ceteris paribus* relationships." Explain precisely what this statement means. In particular, explain how, for example, an increase in price *accompanied* by a larger amount purchased does not necessarily mean that the law of demand has been violated.

*6. The factor price equalization theory suggests that labor, for example, will be paid the same wage in all of its alternative employments. We know that this conclusion is not true. Can you identify some of the reasons there are wage differences among workers? Explain circumstances under which the theory would hold true. On the basis of your answer, would you suggest throwing the theory out, or can it still offer us some insight into one of the reasons resources shift from one activity to another, or from one area of the country to another?

7. In Figure 3.13, panel A, suppose we begin initially at production point B, which we assume is an equilibrium position. Now assume that people's tastes change in the direction of pumps and that, as a consequence, people desire the output combination represented by point C. Trace through the effects of this change in tastes in the markets for pickles and pumps, and in the labor market. What happens to the absolute and relative prices of pickles and pumps? What happens to the amount of labor employed in each, and what accounts for the shift of labor resources?

In a laissez-faire capitalist economic system, the forces of demand and supply play the critical role of determining how scarce resources will be allocated among alternative uses. In such an economic system, the outcomes are the consequence of the interaction of households and business firms.

The U.S. economic system is not a pure laissez-faire capitalist system. Heavy reliance is placed on private incentives to allocate the bulk of our national resources, but over 20 percent of total national production is determined by our federal, state, and local governments. However, the role of government in our economic system is not limited to the production of goods and services for government use. Indeed, the fundamental purpose of government is to bring about socially desirable results that a laissez-faire capitalist system would probably not generate on its own. Whether government is successful in its endeavors is a matter of considerable dispute. What is not in dispute is the fact that government influences in one way or another virtually every facet of private market activity.

Given the nature of the interrelationships between government and the private sector, it is inappropriate to study the private sector or government in isolation from one another. Ours is not a purely capitalist system with a government sector added; it is a system of **mixed capitalism,** a system in which economic outcomes are the by-product of the interaction of government and the private sector.

It is the purpose of this chapter to provide an overview of our system of mixed capitalism. We begin with a brief description of the private business sector and an examination of the basic production unit—the business firm. We then turn our attention to the government sector, examining its role in allocating scarce resources among alternative uses and its activities designed to effect changes in the overall level of economic activity.

THE PRIVATE BUSINESS SECTOR

In the private sector of the economy, the basic unit of production is the business firm. Business

Chapter 4

Mixed capitalism: Business firms and the government

firms come in many shapes and sizes—from the local candy store to the international conglomerate with offices around the world. In this section we examine the various types of business enterprises in the United States, the advantages and drawbacks of each, and the basic accounting relationships that are central to the operation and analysis of private business.

The sole proprietorship. Of the nearly 15 million business enterprises in the United States, the overwhelming majority—nearly 11.5 million—are **sole proprietorships;** the remainder consists of **partnerships** (1.2 million) and **corporations** (2.2 million). These numbers, however, give a distorted view of the relative importance of the various kinds of business enterprises. Despite their huge numbers, sole proprietorships account for only about 10 percent of total business receipts; the bulk of business receipts—around 85 percent—are accounted for by corporations.

Sole proprietorships are individually owned businesses and farms. For the most part, they are easy to set up and operate. Usually they are operated by the owner. And typically, though not invariably, they are small in size. About three fourths of all sole proprietorships have sales of less than $25,000 a year; 85 percent have sales of less than $50,000; and only one half of one percent have sales in excess of $500,000 per year. (By contrast, about 24 percent of corporations have sales in excess of $500,000 per year.) Over 70 percent of all proprietorships are concentrated in three industries—agriculture (farms), retail trade (hardware stores, automobile dealerships, bicycle shops, etc.) and services (barber shops, dry cleaners, etc.).

One unique aspect of a proprietorship is the fact that all the risks—the prospects for failure as well as success—are borne by one person—the owner. This provides a strong incentive for the sole proprietor to work hard and a potential for immense satisfaction if the effort pays off. Moreover, such a form of enterprise may be particularly appealing to those who like to make their own decisions without having to consult with others.

There are, of course, potential disadvantages to sole proprietorships. First, there are generally fairly severe limits on the amount of capital that can be raised to finance this kind of business enterprise. A sole proprietor is limited to his or her own resources and to the amount that can be borrowed from financial institutions and friends. Generally speaking, sole proprietors do not have access to the amounts of credit or financing available to other forms of business enterprise, especially corporations.

Second, a related problem is that sole proprietors bear **unlimited liability** in the eyes of the law. Indeed, in a legal sense, the sole proprietorship and the owner are one and the same. Thus, if the assets of the sole proprietorship are not sufficient to satisfy a claim, the personal assets of the owner can be taken.

The partnership. A partnership is formed when two or more individuals enter into a legal agreement to share in some specified manner the rights of ownership in a business enterprise. This form of organization is most common in industries that provide financial services (e.g., brokerage houses) and legal services.

Like a proprietorship, a partnership is fairly easy to set up and operate. The legal requirements are not difficult to meet, and generally they are small enough in size that they can be easily managed. But the main reason partnerships are formed is to take advantage of the expanded set of resources and talents that a group of owners may offer. Indeed, very often a partnership comes into being when a sole proprietor decides to take on an additional owner in order to attract additional capital, expand operations, or obtain managerial expertise of one sort or another. If the objective is to raise capital, the advantage may go beyond the additional resources that the new owner brings to the firm. Usually lenders will also be more willing to extend credit because there is one more person to share the responsibility of discharging the obligation.

However, although the partnership form of organization may offer some advantages over a sole proprietorship, it shares with the proprietorship one major drawback and has a couple more of its own. The common disadvantage is unlimited liability. Thus, if the firm owes money in excess of its assets, the personal property of *each and every* partner may be taken in order to satisfy the obligation. This is true even if only one of the partners was responsible for incurring the debt in the first place.

This problem is closely related to another difficulty encountered in operating a partnership—namely, that the decisions of any one of the partners is binding on *all* of them. For this reason, partnerships tend to work best in areas where decisions can be compartmentalized to some extent—that is, where each partner assumes responsibility for his or her specialty without the need to consult extensively with the other partners. This is perhaps the main reason law and finance are more conducive to the formation of partnerships. Difficulties in reaching mutually acceptable decisions are a major reason many partnerships do not last.

Although it might appear that the existence of more than one partner would provide continuity and extend the life of the firm, in practice this may not happen. From a legal point of view, the withdrawal or death of any partner automatically terminates the partnership agreement; a new agreement must be drawn up if the organization is to survive. Similarly, the entry of a new partner can only be accomplished by the execution of a new agreement. Therefore, partnerships—especially those with many partners—are very fluid organizations. Those that survive must be able to adapt to changing membership with a minimum of disruption.

The corporation. While the sole proprietorship and partnership forms of business enterprise offer many attractions, they do entail certain drawbacks and impose some limitations. Many of these are overcome in the corporation form of business enterprise. Unlike the other two organizational forms, the corporation is a separate entity in the eyes of the law—legally distinct from those people or groups who may own shares of the business. This distinction between the corporation and its owners is particularly advantageous when it comes to raising capital. However, managerial problems may also arise.

Ownership of a corporation takes the form of ownership of common stocks. Each share of common stock represents the contribution of a certain amount of capital and entitles the person holding it to a proportionate vote in the affairs of the firm. The **stockholders,** as owners of the corporation, elect managers to run the firm's everyday operations. If a single individual or small group of people owns a significant percentage of the outstanding stock, that person or group can often "control" the elections and either elect themselves or others sympathetic to their views.

The financial stake of the owners is limited to the amount of their investment as represented by the total value of the stock outstanding. Thus, if the firm cannot satisfy all of its debts, the owners may lose whatever they invested, but their personal assets are shielded from claims in excess of that amount. This feature of **limited liability** stands in marked contrast to the unlimited liability to which sole proprietorships and partnerships are exposed.

Shareholders typically receive returns on their investment in one or both of two forms: **dividends** and **price appreciation.** As the firm earns profits from its operations, the management can either distribute or retain the earnings. That portion of earnings that is distributed to stockholders is called **dividends;** that portion not distributed to stockholders is called **retained earnings.** Retained earnings are generally "ploughed back" to expand the business enterprise.

Price appreciation refers to the increase in the price of the stock over time. Of course, there are no guarantees of price appreciation (or, for that matter, of dividends). However, expected future earnings are an important determinant of a stock's price. If future earnings are expected to increase, this will often be reflected in an increase in the price of the stock and in an increase in the stock's **price/earnings ratio**—the ratio of the price of the stock to current earnings. Conversely, if future earnings are expected to fall, this will often show up in the form of **price depreciation** and a reduced price/earnings ratio.

It is important to note that, in our interdependent economic system, the expected future earnings of any corporation are affected by more than just its own actions. Stock prices can be affected by all sorts of events—by good or bad news on the state of the economy generally, by announced changes in economic policy, by major international and domestic political developments, and so forth.

One principal advantage of the corporate form of business enterprise is that corporations can usually amass much greater quantities of financial resources than proprietorships and partnerships. The limited liability feature makes it easier for corporations to tap the financial resources of large numbers of people. And the larger size frequently, though not always, enables corporations to gain greater access to the markets for borrowed funds.

Despite these advantages, the corporate form of organization involves some clear drawbacks. One is the difficulty of organizing and operating a corporation. The laws governing the establishment and operation of corporations are not only complex, but they vary from state to state; the legal costs are frequently substantial.

Another drawback is taxation. Corporations are subject to their own federal and state income taxes, and the dividends they distribute after these taxes are paid are then taxed *again* as part of the incomes of those who receive them. (This is referred to as the *double taxation* business income.)

Finally, the corporate form of organization raises important questions regarding the relationship between the owners and managers of the firm. Recall that one principal advantage of the sole proprietorship is that owner and manager are generally one and the same; if they are not the same, there is at least frequent communication and the owner can easily replace the manager if he or she is dissatisfied with the manager's performance. With the corporation, ownership is constantly changing—minute by minute as shares are traded on the stock exchanges. In addition, most stockholders own such a small fraction of the outstanding stock that they are hardly in a position to exercise control over the firm's activities.

In this environment, management can frequently operate with considerable autonomy—that is, without interference from the owners. Under the circumstances, managers could become less sensitive to stockholders' interests than stockholders would like. Managers could spend much time trying to feather their own nests at the expense of the owners. In an effort not to rock the boat, they could try to avoid the larger risks that could ultimately produce larger payoffs.

In spite of these potential problems, the corporation remains the most important kind of business organization from the point of view of the amount of output produced. This is largely because, among the three basic forms of business enterprise, the corporate form of organization is the most conducive to large-scale operations. Thus, as the economy has grown, the corporation has grown with it and expanded in relative importance. As we have seen, this has much to do with the facility with which corporations can attract financing. We now turn to this subject in more detail.

Corporate finance: Equity, debt, safety, and leverage

All firms need money to run their businesses. Typically when they begin operations they need to finance their start-up needs even before they open their doors. Once in business, they continue to need funds to buy inventories of raw materials, pay their costs during periods when sales may be slow, and, it is hoped, expand their operations once they get going. While it is possible in some instances that the financial resources of the owner or owners of the firm will be sufficient to cover these financial needs, in most cases they will not be. Accordingly, the firm, whether a sole proprietorship, a partnership, or a corporation, will at times have to borrow money. As we have seen, the ability to raise funds through borrowing—that is, through **debt financing**—is one principal advantage of the corporate form of ownership.

Debt financing. Because of its status as a separate and distinct legal entity, the corporation can borrow funds in its own name rather than in those of its owners. The assets that the corporation acquires through such borrowing (or through the use of its own funds) are also held in the name of the corporation. These assets provide the ultimate means by which debts can be settled if the cash required to discharge them is not available when needed.

There are a number of ways corporations can borrow money. For example, they can borrow from banks or other financial institutions, they can sell bonds, or they can issue commercial paper. In addition, they can borrow for short-term or long-term periods. Also, although any activity can be financed using either short-term or long-term borrowed funds, the method of financing that a corporation chooses is often related in a general way to the purposes for which the funds are being obtained. Short-term borrowing generally is used by business firms to even out fluctuations in their cash flow and to finance the carrying of inventories. This borrowing usually takes the form of **bank loans** or **commercial paper.** Bank loans are self-explanatory. Most corporations have some kind of ongoing relationship with a bank or several banks whereby they can borrow funds quickly on an as-needed basis. Nowadays the interest rate on these loans fluctuates with the **prime rate**—the rate of interest charged by banks to those firms regarded as the best credit risks. Firms with lesser standing will generally be charged an interest rate somewhat above prime. (In recent years the meaning of the prime rate has been called into question, as many loans have been extended at rates below prime.)

Commercial paper is a form of credit whereby firms issue short-term notes, or IOUs, to whoever will buy them. By law, commercial paper has a maturity of 270 days (nine months) or less. Through this mechanism, firms can greatly expand their sources of short-term financing, as a variety of nonbank financial institutions and some wealthier individuals will often purchase commercial paper. One advantage of this form of financing, in contrast to bank loans, is that the commercial paper can be resold to other investors prior to the maturity date.

In contrast to bank loans and commercial paper, **corporate bonds** are generally used to raise cash for new plant and capital equipment investment projects to replace, modernize, or expand productive capacity. The maturities on corporate bonds range from a few years to as long as 40 years. Investors in these borrowing instruments typically receive their interest at intervals of six months or one year, clipping coupons from the bond and sending them to the corporation for payment.

Equity financing. As an alternative to borrowing, the corporation does have the option of raising new funds by issuing new shares of ownership. This is called **equity financing** because a shareholder's financial interest in a corporation is also known as his or her equity.

Under what circumstances would a firm choose to issue new equity instead of debt? One obvious consideration would be the price of its stock. If the stock is currently trading at a high price, then issuing new shares may be a relatively cheap source of new financial capital—cheap in the sense that raising the same amount of funds by issuing bonds may commit the firm to interest payments that are higher per dollar of funds raised than the payment of dividends on the new shares of stock.

Another important reason firms may issue new stock is that their debt positions may be considered to be too high—either by the firms themselves or by potential buyers of new debt issues. In this regard, one commonly and closely watched index of a firm's financial condition is its **debt/equity ratio**—that is, the value of its total indebtedness relative to the value of the owners' equity. The higher this ratio is, the greater the risk to investors when they purchase the bonds of the firm in question. One way for a firm to reduce its debt/equity ratio is to sell new stock. However, the price of its stock may not be all that high if the debt/equity ratio is a matter of general concern. While no precise standards can be spelled out as to how high this ratio should be, bondholders and other creditors clearly get concerned if this number rises substantially relative to the past experience of the firm in question or relative to that of other firms in the same or closely related industries.

If equity financing can be used to keep the debt position of the firm in control, what are the limits to using this method of financing? One has already been suggested. If the price of a firm's stock is relatively low, this can be an expensive source of funds. But, even if this is not a problem, firms tend to rely on equity financing only occasionally. Issues of new stock must be authorized by the existing owners of the firm, and they typically will be reluctant to dilute their ownership rights by making more shares available to others. Their voice in the affairs of the firm will be reduced. From a financial point of view, the amount of profits to be distributed by the corporation will have to be shared with more people. For these reasons, when a firm decides to issue more stock, existing stockholders often get the first opportunity to buy more.

The concept of leverage. This discussion focuses our attention on an important financial concept—the concept of **leverage.** Leverage refers to the level of the debt/equity ratio. If a firm has a high ratio, then it—and implicitly its stockholders—is said to be highly leveraged. From the point of view of potential earnings per share, the amount of leverage is quite important. Consider the following example. Suppose the values of debt and equity in a firm are each $5 million, which implies a debt/equity ratio of one. Assume the firm earns $2 million after deducting all expenses *except* interest and taxes. Assume further a 10 percent rate of interest on the firm's debt. Thus, $5 million in debt will require payment of $500,000 in interest (0.10 × $5 million = $500,000). After deducting interest expenses, the firm's earnings before taxes will amount to $1.5 million. Assuming a 50 percent tax rate, the firm will earn $750,000 *after taxes.* Earnings of $750,000 on $5 million of *equity* implies a 15 percent aftertax return to the owners ($750,000 ÷ 5 million = 0.15).

Now suppose the firm borrows an additional $10 million in an effort to double the size of its operations. Total debt outstanding rises to $15 million, increasing the debt/equity ratio to 3, raising the leverage of its stockholders. Suppose the firm is successful in sharply increasing its sales; its income after all expenses *other than interest and taxes* comes to $4 million. Payment of $1.5 million in interest (10 percent of $15 million) leaves $2.5 million; assuming a 50 percent tax rate, this amount is divided evenly between taxes and net profits. The *stockholders* thus earn

$1.25 million, or a handsome 25 percent return on their $500,000 equity investment. The higher rate of return results from the greater degree of leverage. The firm has successfully used the borrowed money of its creditors to make more money for its stockholders.

Of course, leverage has its risks. If the firm only earns $3 million, then the return to its stockholders remains at 15 percent ($750,000). And if earnings fail to rise at all, the stockholders get only $250,000, or 5 percent. Can you verify these calculations?

From the point of view of the investor, this exercise illustrates the difference between equity and debt with regard to their *safety.* Because the corporation must first satisfy the obligations associated with its debt, including interest payments, the risks of success or failure fall on the stockholders, who are the owners of the firm. To compensate for this risk, the return to stockholders often tends to be somewhat higher than the interest return to bondholders. Of course, bondholders and other creditors also bear some risk that the firm will not earn enough to satisfy its interest obligations, or the repayment of borrowed funds. These risks, however, are not as large as those of the stockholders.

Business accounting relationships

The financial condition and operations of a business firm can be summarized in two related statements: the **balance sheet** and the **income statement.**

The balance sheet. The *balance sheet*—or statement of condition—shows the financial condition of the firm at a given point in time. Business firms, whether corporations, partnerships, or sole proprietorships, usually prepare their balance sheet once each year to show their owners how they stand at year end. A typical balance sheet is presented in Figure 4.1.

The left-hand side of the balance sheet lists all those items owned by the firm—its *assets*—and shows next to each item its value as of December 31, 1981. In the example given, we see that the Nitty-Gritty Sand and Gravel Company

Figure 4.1

Nitty-Gritty Sand and Gravel Company
Statement of Condition
as of December 31,1981

Assets		Liabilities and net worth	
Cash on hand	$ 20,000	Accounts payable	$ 4,000
Accounts receivable	6,000	Bank loans	17,000
Inventory	9,000	Mortgage	49,000
Equipment	70,000	Bonds outstanding	80,000
Land and structures	95,000	Total liabilities	150,000
Total assets	$200,000	Net worth	50,000
		Total liabilities and net worth	$200,000

had cash on hand of $20,000 on December 31, 1981; its accounts receivable—the amounts owed to the firm by other business enterprises or by individuals—amounted to $6,000; and so forth.

On the right-hand side of the balance sheet are shown all the *liabilities* of the firm—the amounts it owes. Again, these items range the gamut from short-term obligations, such as accounts payable and bank loans, to longer-term debt, such as the firm's bonded debt and the mortgage on its building.

The difference between the firm's assets and its liabilities represents the value of the firm to its owners. That difference is known as the *net worth* of the firm. Net worth is always calculated so as to satisfy the basic accounting identity:

Assets = Liabilities + Net worth.

The concept of net worth has a very intuitive interpretation. If the owners of the firm decided to liquidate the operation (or convert it to cash)— that is, to go out of business—they could presumably sell off the assets and use the proceeds to pay off all the liabilities. Assuming that the balance sheet had been figured properly, in the sense that all relevant items had been included, and that estimates of value for buildings, inventories, and the like were accurate, the owners would walk away from the business with an amount of cash in their pockets equal to the net worth of the firm.

As time passes, the firm's balance sheet changes. New assets are acquired, others are disposed of, and money is borrowed and repaid. The effects of all of these activities on the balance

sheet of the firm can be kept track of through the method of **double-entry bookkeeping.**

Double-entry bookkeeping. The principle behind double-entry bookkeeping is that any transaction affecting the balance sheet must show up in two places. Thus, if Nitty-Gritty uses cash to pay off the accounts payable, the accounting of this transaction would look like:

Changes in assets		Changes in liabilities and net worth	
Cash on hand	−4,000	Accounts payable	−4,000

Or the purchase of a new truck for $10,000 in cash would show up as follows:

Changes in assets		Changes in liabilities and net worth
Cash on hand	−10,000	
Equipment	+10,000	

Can you set up an account to show the sale of $100,000 in bonds to finance the construction of a new building? Or the payment of accounts payable by borrowing from the bank? Presumably, if all these transactions are recorded properly, figuring out the balance sheet at the end of the next accounting period, whenever that might be, is straightforward.

The income statement. In contrast to the balance sheet, which displays the condition of a firm at an *instant* of time, the **income statement** summarizes the activities of the firm over a *period* of time—usually a quarter of a year or a full year. The income statement is also called a *profit and loss statement* because it indicates whether the firm made or lost money over the period covered by the statement. An example is given in Figure 4.2 for the Nitty-Gritty Sand and Gravel Company.

Figure 4.2

Nitty-Gritty Sand and Gravel Company
Profit and loss statement
For the period from January 1, 1981, through December 31, 1981

Total revenues
Sales of sand and gravel	$143,000
Interest income on investments	4,000
Leasing of dump trucks	12,000
Other income	7,000
	166,000

Total expenses
Wages and salaries	61,000
Purchases of goods and services, including inventories (of rocks)	27,000
Interest paid	13,000
Other expenses (depreciation, office, and administrative costs, etc.)	14,000
	115,000

Net income before taxes
(Total revenues minus total expenses) ...	51,000
Taxes	12,000
Net income	39,000
Distributed to stockholders	(20,000)
Retained earnings	(19,000)

The top portion of the income statement records all the receipts of the firm over the period covered by the statement, in this case, one year. These include not only the sale of its basic products, but also income that may be derived from its assets. For example, the firm may receive interest on bank deposits or it may lease some of its equipment to other firms. Similarly the expense portion of the statement shows all of the costs incurred by the firm for the year in question.

Once the firm has listed all its receipts and expenditures, its *net income before taxes* can be calculated. If net income before taxes is positive, the firm will generally have to pay taxes. Once taxes have been subtracted, the true bottom line is reached. This is the amount of earnings availa-

ble for distribution to the owners, or for reinvestment in the business.

The income statement and the balance sheet: Stocks versus flows

On the face of it, the income statement and the balance sheet of the firm provide different types of information about the firm, and indeed they do. The income statement summarizes the *flows* that characterize the firm's activities over a given period. The time dimension is a crucial consideration for all items on the **income statement.** It would make no sense to ask what the firm's sales were unless you also specified the period over which they occurred. The same holds true for each entry on the income statement.

The **balance sheet,** on the other hand, summarizes the *stocks* of assets and liabilities and the net worth of the firm on a given date. The balance sheet thus applies to a particular moment, not to a time interval. To ask what the firm's cash on hand or total assets are, for example, you must specify the date for which you want the information. The same is true for any item shown on the balance sheet.

Although the income statement and balance sheet convey different types of information, they are closely related. In particular, some of the flows shown on the income statement tell us how corresponding stocks on the balance sheet are changing. If the receipt of payments on accounts receivable shows up in the revenue portion of the income statement, then the next balance sheet should show a lower level of accounts receivable, *ceteris paribus.* Similarly, the payment of debts should show up as lower levels of indebtedness on the next balance sheet and the acquisition or disposal of inventories should also be appropriately affected. Finally, of course, the net income earned after taxes should bear a close relation to the reported *change* in net worth. Indeed, an examination of Figures 4.1 and 4.2 should indicate the following. Since the firm's retained earnings for the calendar year 1981 amounted to $19,000, the December 31, 1981, balance sheet for Nitty-Gritty will show a *net worth* $19,000 higher than it otherwise would have been.

THE ECONOMIC ROLE OF GOVERNMENT

What are the proper functions of government in an economy that relies heavily on private decisionmaking to determine the allocation of our scarce resources? In Chapter 3 we saw how the forces of demand and supply could be relied upon to provide us with one set of answers to the four fundamental questions—*what, how, for whom,* and *how extensively.* We also discovered in Chapter 3 that the price mechanism could be relied upon to channel resources to their "best" uses, but only if certain conditions were met, and only if everyone played by the rules of the game. Unfortunately, not everyone plays according to the rules that would make laissez-faire capitalism operate efficiently and effectively. Therefore, there is a need for government to help set and then enforce the rules. Moreover, in the face of *externalities*—costs or benefits that are external to particular production or consumption activities— laissez-faire capitalism will fail to produce the right quantities of various goods and services, overallocating resources to some goods and underallocating resources to others. Accordingly, there is need for government to step in to help correct the misallocation. And in some instances it may be appropriate for government to assume responsibility for the production of some goods (e.g., national defense) outright.

In addition, there are no guarantees that laissez-faire capitalism will produce the distribution of income that society would agree was correct; government intervention may therefore be required. And what guarantees do we have that millions of people making billions of decisions day after day would produce the appropriate level of resource use? We don't. Again, government may play a useful role in promoting optimum levels of resource use.

It is the purpose of this section to examine some of these issues in greater depth in order to gain deeper insight into the role of government in promoting the best use of our scarce resources. The fact that government does have an important role to play does not mean that government necessarily does a good job. That controversial issue is quite separate and will *not* be evaluated here.

Government regulation

Through a variety of mechanisms, the government establishes or clarifies certain economic rules of the game. Some of these are so thoroughly accepted that it is easy to overlook the fact that they really are forms of economic regulation. For example, the laws designed to enforce contracts, prevent fraud, or protect private property are all essential if the private economy is to function properly. Few people would quarrel with the claim that government interference in these matters is appropriate.

Matters can easily become more controversial, however. There are many ways the economy, if left to its own devices, would not produce the conditions of perfect competition outlined in Chapter 3. In some industries, for example, *collusion* among producers could result in sharply increased prices to the detriment of the public welfare. The federal antitrust laws are intended to prevent such collusion and to place limits on those activities that would significantly reduce competition. In other markets, on the other hand, considerations of efficiency may actually dictate that one firm be given an exclusive franchise to produce some good or service. Public utilities are a case in point. It is often cheaper to have one telephone company or one electric company providing services in a given locale than to have several competing producers. In such instances where government grants individual producers *monopoly* rights in a given market, that same government usually steps in to establish the maximum prices that can be charged so as to prevent those producers from operating contrary to the public interest.

What makes these types of regulation controversial? There are two things. First, not all people will agree in specific situations that regulation is called for. Therefore, there may be reasonable arguments on either side about whether the merging of two or more large firms is anticompetitive. Also, the granting of exclusive franchises to individual producers is becoming increasingly controversial. (Witness the intense price competition among the different telephone companies for long-distance telephone calls.) Decisions on matters such as these usually pit strong economic interests against each other, which, naturally enough, gives rise to much debate.

Second, even where regulation is widely regarded as appropriate and the regulatory mechanism is in place, it is not precisely clear how to strike the appropriate balance between government interference and private enterprise. Those who support the existence of regulation in a particular industry or circumstances may still take issue with how it is exercised. For example, those state commissions charged with regulating the prices of the public utilities frequently use the profits earned by the utilities to guide them in setting prices. The public utility companies accept, if somewhat reluctantly, government's role in setting prices. But often, they argue, the public utility commissions go too far. For example, the U.S. Congress passes tax legislation designed to encourage businesses to modernize their equipment. The tax breaks raise profits, which, in the case of public utilities, the commissions take away by lowering prices (or by not granting price increases that would otherwise have been justified). This leaves the utilities with little funds and little incentive to modernize!

The source of greatest controversy, however, are those government regulations designed to accomplish social welfare objectives such as a safe and clean environment and occupational health and safety. After the mid-1960s, new government regulations in these areas proliferated at a very rapid pace largely in response to an intense public insistence. In recent years, however, the weight of public opinion has shifted in the opposite direction. A widespread view now exists that government has gone too far, or that the methods used by government to realize these social objectives are all wrong. Slowing the proliferation of government regulations, as is well known, is one of the major objectives of the Reagan Administration.

Changing views regarding government regulation are not limited to such areas as the environment, health, and safety. Other areas where government regulation has been longstanding are also being questioned and altered. For example, in 1977 the airline industry was successfully deregulated. And in 1980 landmark legislation was passed that set in motion forces designed to largely deregulate U.S. financial institutions.

Government regulation and "externalities." Without attempting to assess the merits or demerits of the waves of regulation and deregulation actions over the past several years, let us try to examine in greater detail one of the important reasons for government regulation in the first place—to correct for the existence of **external benefits** and **external costs.**

An external benefit is said to exist when benefits provided by goods or services are received without having to pay for them. One simple example where external benefits are present is trash collection. We all benefit not only from the removal of our own garbage but from that of our neighbors as well. The neighborhood will look neater and disease will be easier to control. The benefits we each receive are of two sorts—the benefits received by having our own trash removed (called the private benefit) and the (external) benefits received when the neighbors have theirs removed. If we relied on market prices to accomplish the "right amount" of trash removal, we might not be all that satisfied. What if several people in the neighborhood did not have their trash removed because they were unable or unwilling to pay the price? In such instances, there may be a need for government to step in and subsidize the local garbage company, or take over the whole operation, financing the costs through additional taxation. Here, even though the cost per household may not change, the *total* benefit received by each household is higher. In general, goods and services such as trash removal that confer external benefits are underproduced by the private economy. The government may intervene to stimulate more.

External costs are the opposite of external benefits. They arise when uncompensated costs are imposed as the result of the production or consumption of some goods services. Perhaps the classic example of an external cost is pollution: air pollution from automobiles, airplanes and steel production; water pollution from industrial chemicals; and noise pollution from construction activity and your neighbor's stereo. The costs of these activities can be divided into two types—the costs to the producer or consumer of the good or service (called **private cost**), and the (external) costs imposed on others. If we relied on market prices to accomplish the right amount of those goods that cause pollution, we might not be particularly satisfied with the results. As long as steel producers do not have to pay for the costs imposed on others, and as long as drivers of automobiles do not have to pay for the costs that their driving imposes on others, an overproduction of these kinds of goods and services is likely to result. Through taxes and regulation, government can raise the cost. The higher prices that would result would, according to the law of demand, reduce the quantity demanded.

Public goods

In general, goods that confer external benefits are, to that extent, **public goods.** Specifically, public goods refer to those goods and services whose benefits people cannot be excluded from consuming regardless of who pays. By contrast, goods such as bananas, apples, and steak are called **private goods** since your consumption of those items effectively excludes others from consuming *precisely* the same items.[1]

National defense is the most commonly cited example of a public good. Every citizen "consumes" national defense once it is produced, no matter who pays for it; no one can be *excluded* from the benefits it provides. Police and fire protection, the administration of justice, broadcast air waves, road maintenance, public beautification programs, and trash removal are all services that, to some extent, have the nonexclusion characteristic of a public good.

It is a feature of laissez-faire capitalism that goods possessing public good features would be underproduced; some public goods would proba-

bly not be produced at all. The reason this would be so will be explored at length in Chapter 27. To anticipate our discussion there somewhat, the reason can be put as follows. In the case of private goods, I get no satisfaction from them unless I purchase them; other people's purchases of those private goods yield no external benefits. The amount of satisfaction we *all* receive from these private goods is reflected in the amount we are willing and able to purchase. In the case of public goods, on the other hand, I get some satisfaction from other people's purchases even if I do not pay; if I do purchase some, other people will benefit. Now here is the point that needs emphasis: The amount I am willing and able to purchase will be determined by how much satisfaction I receive personally, *not* by the amount of satisfaction others receive. Since everyone else feels as I do, the amount that will be purchased in the market will be determined only by the *private* benefits of people. Yet, because external benefits are present, the total (or social) benefits received will exceed the sum of the individual private benefits. The amount of resources allocated to each good will be determined by the private benefits alone. Thus, since the social benefits exceed the private benefits, too few resources will be allocated to the production of public goods.

It is clear, then, why many public goods, such as national defense, might never be produced in a laissez-faire capitalist system. If I were to purchase a defense system that effectively protected me from nuclear attack, everyone around me would have the *same* protection. But those people around me have no incentive to pay. Therefore the amount of national defense that will be purchased will be determined by the person who is willing and able *to pay the most.* However, no single individual would be willing and able to pay the tens of *billions* of dollars required to purchase such a defense system. In a laissez-faire capitalist economy, therefore, no national defense would be purchased.

Of course, people have an incentive to get together to have such a defense system purchased. But because each of us has an incentive to pay as little as possible in the hope that others will

---

[1] Of course, others consume apples and bananas, but *not* the *same* apples and bananas you consume.

pay—after all, if they do pay, I get the same benefits as they do—there is need for government to distribute the burden of paying fairly.

Income redistribution

One social goal that the government attempts to achieve is an adequate standard of living for all people. By itself, laissez-faire capitalism may not provide this. Mental and physical handicaps may prevent some people from earning a living. Sometimes people experience long periods of unemployment when labor markets fail to clear properly, seriously disrupting their incomes.

The government has a variety of mechanisms with which it can try to ensure that people receive adequate incomes. The most obvious are programs such as welfare and unemployment compensation. The tax system, as we will see below, provides another means by which the government can more systematically alter the distribution of income.

Economic stabilization

Another major function of government is its **stabilization function.** Generally speaking, this function is best described as one of trying to provide an economic environment that is conducive to high employment, price stability, and the absence of booms and busts in the economy. The laissez-faire capitalist economic system may not provide the kind of stable economic environment people want. Without in any way suggesting that instability would arise inevitably under laissez-faire capitalism, it is possible to imagine that millions upon millions of different economic decisions being made daily *could* bring about less stability than would be desirable. One may easily see why there might be need for the steadying influence of government.[2]

In this regard, history would seem to suggest that government has an important role to play.

Up through the first part of this century, economic history was characterized by repeated cycles of booms and panics. And, in the 1930s, the United States and the general world economy experienced probably the worst depression of all times. In response, after World War II, Congress passed the Employment Act of 1946, which, among other things, declared the federal government's intent to pursue policies designed to foster conditions conducive to full employment and stable prices. More recently these goals have been clarified in the Humphrey-Hawkins Full Employment and Balanced Growth Act of 1978. In Chapter 5 we analyze in more detail the government's success in defining and achieving these objectives.

Noneconomic functions of government

Many government activities are not aimed primarily to influence the economy. The making of foreign policy and the administration of justice are obvious examples. However, the decisions that get made in the execution of these functions almost inevitably have economic consequences, some of which can be quite significant. For instance, the imposition of the Soviet grain embargo in 1980 was an action undertaken primarily for international political purposes, but it certainly had important implications for U.S. commodity markets. Similarly, judicial decisions about civil rights may have dramatic economic effects on both those discriminated against and those in the favored groups of citizens.

Federal, state, and local governments

Some perspective on the importance of the government's role in the economy can be gained by examining its size and influence in our lives. There are a number of different ways to do this—including by calculating the government's share of total expenditures in the economy, or by looking at the total amount of resources it commands through taxation, borrowing, and regulation. These approaches give different answers to the question of how big government is. However,

---

[2] By the same token, one could imagine that government might be the *source* of economic instability. We will explore this dimension further in Chapter 14.

as we will see, they convey one basic message: Government plays a large role in our lives, and, until recently, its importance has been growing over time.

Throughout much of the discussion to this point we have discussed the government as if it were one single entity. But, of course, in the United States we have a **federal system** of government. This means we must deal with government at state and local, as well as national, levels. Indeed, given that the focus of so much attention these days is on the federal government, you may be surprised to learn that, by some measures, state and local governments together are larger than the federal government.

How big is government?

Government purchases of goods and services. One way to get a feel for the size of government is to compare government purchases of newly produced goods and services with the total amount of newly produced goods and services in the United States. This is done in Figure 4.3. There we plot government purchases of goods and services as a percent of gross national product (GNP) for the years 1929 to 1980. (GNP, the most comprehensive measure of our nation's total production, will be studied in detail in Chapter 6.)

Two facts emerge distinctly from an examination of Figure 4.3. First, the effect of wartime is clear. As big and pervasive as government seems today, it is not nearly as important as it was during our protracted involvement in World War II. (Effects of the Korean and Vietnam wars are harder to see.) Underlying these war-related bulges, however, is a trend that has been distinctly upward over time, although for considerable lengths of time the proportion of output being purchased by government has remained essentially flat. Whereas the government share was less than 10 percent in 1929, it is now above 20 percent. The major increases occurred in the early 1930s as a result of the Great Depression and in the 1950s. Since the late 1950s, there has been no marked increase in total government spending relative to GNP. Moreover, throughout

the entire period—except for the wartime years—state and local government spending has accounted for the bulk of total government purchases.

Whether total government spending as a share of GNP will decline in future years is still an open question despite the best efforts of the Reagan Administration. There are two reasons for this. First, defense spending relative to GNP is slated to increase for the next several years. Second, although *federal* nondefense spending as a percent of GNP may decline, state and local officials may feel obligated to pick up projects abandoned by the federal government.

Taxes and government. Government purchases of goods and services may understate the degree to which government affects our lives. Why is this so? As we shall see later, a significant part of the government's budget, particularly at the federal level, reflects transfers of income to individuals and organizations. These **income transfers**—including outlays for social security, federal employee retirement, welfare, etc.—are *not* part of government purchases of newly produced goods and services. To that extent, government purchases understate the size of government. A somewhat more comprehensive measure of government influence is provided by the amount of revenue government derives in the form of taxes; taxes provide us with a better measure of the command of government over our scarce national resources, a better measure of the resources used by government for newly produced goods and services and for income transfers.

Figure 4.4 displays the relevant data on taxation for selected years from 1929 to 1980; we present there federal government tax receipts as a percent of GNP, state and local tax receipts as a percent of GNP, and *total* tax receipts as a percent of GNP. It is plainly clear that this measure does indeed show a more pervasive influence of government. In 1980, taxes at all levels of government absorbed nearly one third of our nation's GNP as opposed to a figure of 20 percent for government purchases of goods and services. Moreover, in contrast to the purchases-of-goods-and-services measure, where state and local gov-

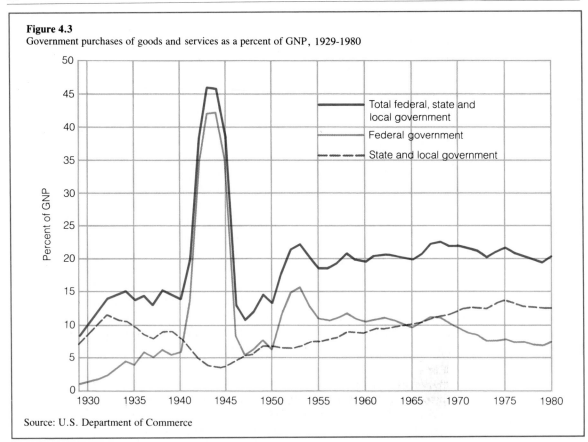

Figure 4.3
Government purchases of goods and services as a percent of GNP, 1929-1980

Source: U.S. Department of Commerce

ernments dominated the picture, from the point of view of taxes, the federal government is clearly more important.

How can this be reconciled? In two ways. First, since income transfers are significantly more important at the federal level, the goods-and-services measure of relative government size tends to understate the importance of the federal government. Second, since income is transferred from the federal government to state and local units (accounting for nearly one quarter of total state and local government receipts in 1980), the amount of taxation required by state and local governments to carry out their functions is that much less.

Whether tax receipts as a percent of GNP will decline in future years is also an open question despite the fact that the Reagan Administration accomplished the most massive tax cut in

U.S. legislative history in 1981, slashing taxes by a whopping $750 billion below what they might otherwise have been for the first half of the 1980s. There are two reasons for this view. First, because of the huge budget cuts for social welfare programs accompanying the tax cuts, state and local governments may feel compelled to augment their social welfare services, raising *their* taxes to pay for those extra services. Second, unless the federal government cuts social security benefits or federal employee retirement benefits, outlays under those programs are likely to continue to grow rapidly for the next several years, necessitating tax increases either in the form of social security tax hikes or higher income taxes. The political difficulties the government faces in cutting these programs are formidable.

Taxes and government borrowing. Actually, the measure, government tax receipts as a percent

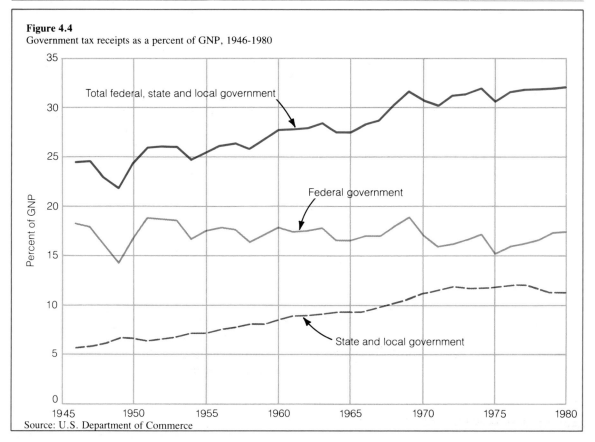

Figure 4.4
Government tax receipts as a percent of GNP, 1946-1980

Source: U.S. Department of Commerce

of GNP, may understate government's influence in terms of its command over our nation's resources. Many would argue that account needs to be taken of the government borrowing that is required to finance the excess government **budget outlays** (expenditures for goods and services plus income transfers) over tax receipts. The reason is that, when government borrows to finance its programs, those funds are withdrawn from alternative uses, and what remains to finance private sector activity will be that much more expensive. In 1980, total government deficit borrowing amounted to about 5 percent of total government tax receipts; for the federal government alone, deficit borrowing amounted to over 12 percent of federal tax receipts. As one might expect, borrowing during wartime is extremely high. In 1944, deficit borrowing *exceeded* total government tax receipts!

Taxes, borrowing, and government regulation. Many people go farther and argue that even taxes and borrowing combined understate the size and influence of government. When government issues regulations that require business firms to incur expenditures in order to be in compliance, those expenditures ought to be included in the government column; they are, indirectly, a form of taxation. No one knows how much larger government is as a consequence of the regulatory costs that it imposes on the private sector. But some estimates put this amount at more than $100 billion for 1980.

Distribution of government expenditures and taxes

It is instructive to examine briefly the *distribution* of government expenditures by type of government and type of expenditure in order to gain some appreciation of the diverse activities of government. Figure 4.5 summarizes the distribution of government expenditures at the federal level; Figure 4.6 summarizes the distribution at the state and local levels. In both Figures 4.5 and 4.6, the data are for fiscal years. (Fiscal year 1980 started on October 1, 1979, and ended September 30, 1980.)

As is apparent from Figure 4.5, at the federal level, **income security programs**—including outlays for social security, federal employee retirement, unemployment compensation, and income assistance to the poor—absorbed the largest share of government spending in 1980 (33 percent), with national defense second (24 percent). This relative ranking, which may surprise you, has not always been the case. For example, in 1970, national defense made up 40 percent of federal government budget outlays, whereas income security accounted for only 22 percent. The change between 1970 and 1980 reflects the influence of two forces—sharp increases in outlays for social security and other income maintenance

programs, and much smaller increases for national defense. As is well known, one of the objectives of the Reagan Administration is to slow the growth of income security programs and to increase outlays for defense. In combination, this shift, concurred with by the Congress in 1981, will reduce the income security share of federal outlays to about 29 percent, and raise the national defense share to 38 percent, by 1986.

The third largest expenditure category at the federal level is interest on the national debt. It comprised a little more than 11 percent of federal budget outlays in 1980. (In recent years, interest on the national debt has absorbed an increasing share of federal outlays, rising from about 9 percent in 1970. This increase reflects the combined influence of both larger deficits and dramatically higher interest rates over the course of the 1970s.)

These three programs alone—income security, national defense, and interest—account for almost 70 percent of federal government budget outlays. All other federal government programs—for education, health, housing, the environment, the administration of justice, interna-

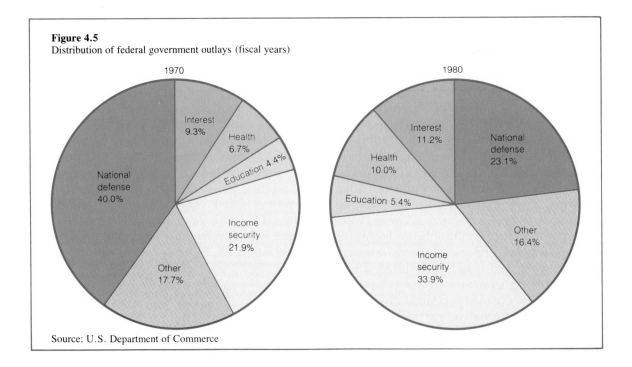

Figure 4.5
Distribution of federal government outlays (fiscal years)

Source: U.S. Department of Commerce

tional affairs, energy, and the running of the federal government—are financed out of the remaining 30 percent.

As Figure 4.6 makes clear, the distribution of expenditures by state and local jurisdictions is much different from the federal government. Clearly, these government units do not have to worry about national defense, and income maintenance programs figure much less prominently in their outlays. Instead, state and local governments spend most of their money providing or subsidizing services of more immediate interest to their local citizens. Education and highways together absorb more than 45 percent of the state and local spending dollar. Other items of significance include public welfare, hospitals and health programs, and public utilities.

The social balance question

Not surprisingly, the sheer size and pervasive influence of government is a source of intense debate. Put bluntly, just how big and pervasive should government be? In spite of fairly general

agreement that government should be involved in each of the areas noted earlier, considerable dispute remains about the appropriate form and extent of these involvements.

Those who argue that government should be small are typically on the conservative end of the political spectrum. They stress the ability of the price system, if left to its own devices, to achieve an efficient allocation of resources. Government intervention, they argue, produces many inefficiencies because the process of acquiring resources, producing public goods, and distributing benefits operates to a considerable extent outside the price system. Thus the power of the government to levy taxes and to commandeer other resources, such as the services of military draftees, releases it from the discipline of the price system to which others are subjected in obtaining scarce resources. Also, when government provides goods, services, and other benefits free of separate charge, or at below-market cost, excessive demand for government-provided benefits is stimulated. On either account, there is a built-in bias for government to overproduce—i.e., to

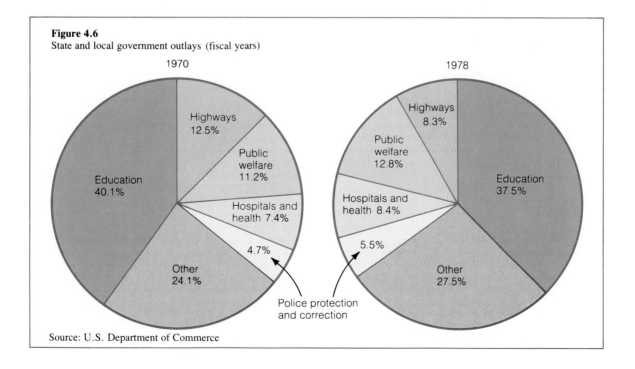

Figure 4.6
State and local government outlays (fiscal years)

1970

Highways 12.5%
Public welfare 11.2%
Hospitals and health 7.4%
Education 40.1%
4.7%
Other 24.1%

1978

Highways 8.3%
Public welfare 12.8%
Hospitals and health 8.4%
Education 37.5%
5.5%
Other 27.5%

Police protection and correction

Source: U.S. Department of Commerce

become more important than it really should be.

On the other side of the debate, others (who usually find themselves labeled as liberals) argue that there are many situations in which the market by itself will not produce the "right" solutions. In a great number of instances, they claim, the conditions required to achieve an efficient and socially desirable allocation of resources simply do not exist. In such cases, the government as the ultimate determiner of social priorities must intervene.

There is no easy way to resolve the question of the "proper" size and influence of government. It is largely a matter of normative economics, and the answer each of us gives will reflect to a considerable extent our own philosophical orientation. True, the size and influence of government has increased substantially over the course of the 20th century, and the relative shift of resources toward government was, for the most part, accepted, if somewhat reluctantly, by the American people. Recently, though, there has been a strong resistence to this trend. Politicians rail against big government; they promise to return more income (and power) to the people to

dispose of as they see fit. This was apparently a very important reason President Reagan and the Republicans generally scored as impressive a victory at the polls as they did in 1980. It also helps to explain the unprecedented legislative victories scored by the Reagan Administration to sharply curtail both federal government spending and federal taxes in 1981. Moreover, as part of this conservative trend, the past several years have witnessed a wave of initiatives, referendums, propositions, constitutional amendments, and the like—primarily at the state and local levels—designed to circumscribe the taxing authority of government units. These efforts have met with considerable success at the polls, but it is too early yet to know whether the trend is decisively toward a sharply reduced role for government.

The U.S. tax system

We turn our attention now to a brief examination of the U.S. tax system. Figures 4.7 and 4.8 provide a summary of the kinds of taxes collected by the federal government on the one hand and

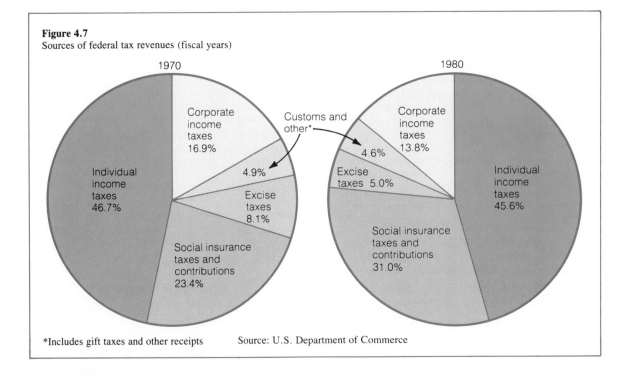

Figure 4.7
Sources of federal tax revenues (fiscal years)

1970

Corporate income taxes 16.9%

Customs and other*

4.9%

Individual income taxes 46.7%

Excise taxes 8.1%

Social insurance taxes and contributions 23.4%

1980

Corporate income taxes 13.8%

4.6%

Excise taxes 5.0%

Individual income taxes 45.6%

Social insurance taxes and contributions 31.0%

*Includes gift taxes and other receipts   Source: U.S. Department of Commerce

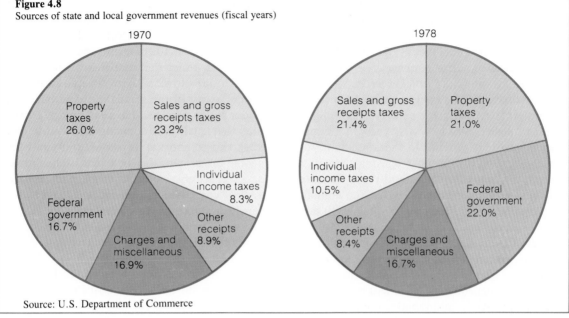

Figure 4.8
Sources of state and local government revenues (fiscal years)

Source: U.S. Department of Commerce

state and local governments on the other. As is apparent, there are marked differences in the kinds of taxes levied by the various taxing jurisdictions.

At the federal level, the personal income tax is the most important source of revenue, accounting for nearly 46 percent of federal government revenues in 1980. Second in importance is the payroll tax—the primary source of funding of our social security system. Next in importance is the corporate income tax. Customs taxes (taxes on goods imported from abroad) and excise taxes (sales taxes on items such as gasoline, automobile tires, tobacco, and liquor) provide a relatively small amount of revenue at the federal level.

Sources of revenue for state and local governments are considerably more varied. Federal government **grants-in-aid** transfers were the most important source of revenue at the state level in 1978; the sales tax was next in importance, followed by the property tax, the most important source of revenue at the local level. The income tax is much less important at the state level; its importance varies considerably across states (ranging from 58 percent of total revenues in

Massachusetts to zero in Texas and Wyoming).

In the remainder of this section we will highlight various features of our different systems of taxation.

The U.S. federal tax system

1981 witnessed a dramatic restructuring of the U.S. federal tax system. The tax law changes signed into law by President Reagan as part of his Economic Recovery Program were viewed as very controversial at the time they were proposed and they continue to be the source of much debate. In view of the unusual and unprecedented nature of the 1981 tax law changes, and in further view of the importance that President Reagan and others attach to those changes—matters that we will examine in more detail in Chapters 13 and 14—we will undertake here a detailed study of several features of our restructured tax system.

The U.S. individual income tax. The law governing the individual income tax in the United States is extremely complicated. It is our purpose here to review only a few of its key features. First, the individual income tax is levied on *taxa-*

ble income, not *gross* income. Second, the tax schedule is *progressive* in structure. Third, different kinds of income are treated differently for tax purposes. Fourth, individual income taxes are levied on people's money incomes, which, in an inflationary environment, gives rise to a phenomenon known as **bracket creep.** And finally, many married taxpayers who both work are subject to a "marriage penalty" tax.

Gross income versus taxable income. **Gross income** refers, in general, to the amount of income received in the form of wages, salaries, tips, interest, dividends, royalties, and rents. **Taxable income** is gross income reduced by the amount of **exemptions** and **deductions** to which each taxpayer is legally entitled. Under current law, the number of exemptions that each taxpayer is permitted to take is determined by the number of dependents. (Each taxpayer counts himself or herself as one dependent. Dependent relatives are then added. And, additional exemptions are granted in cases of old age and blindness.) Currently, each exemption reduces gross income by $1,000. Beginning in 1985, the value of each exemption will be increased at a rate equal to the rate of inflation of the previous year. Thus, if inflation in 1984 amounted to 10 percent, each exemption in 1985 would be worth $1,100—10 percent more than its value in 1984. This adjustment in the value of the exemption was passed by Congress as part of the *Economic Recovery Tax Act of 1981.* It is designed to prevent inflation-induced tax increases. Other inflation adjustments were made as well, as will be noted later.

Most taxpayers elect the standard deduction—called the **zero bracket amount**—in calculating their taxable income. This amount varies depending on the taxpayer's filing status. The amount is $2,300 for unmarried individuals, $3,400 for married individuals filing jointly and for surviving spouses, and $1,700 for married individuals filing separately. (This standard deduction is called the zero bracket amount because income from zero up to that amount is taxed at a zero tax rate. All tax tables published by the federal government, such as those in Figure 4.9, have these amounts incorporated, as can be

seen by the first rows in each table. Beginning in 1985 the value of the zero bracket amount will be increased at a rate equal to the rate of inflation of the previous year. Thus, if inflation in 1984 equals 10 percent, the zero bracket amount for unmarried individuals will rise from $2,300 in 1984 to $2,530 in 1985.) To elect deductions in excess of the standardized amounts, taxpayers must itemize. Those itemized expenditures that qualify as deductions include, among other things, interest expenses, state and local income taxes, state and local real estate and sales taxes, charitable contributions, and excessive medical costs. Since each taxpayer receives the benefit of a zero bracket amount in the tax rate schedules, itemizers are entitled to deduct only **excess itemized deductions** in arriving at taxable income.

Once taxable income is determined (there are many other miscellaneous adjustments that we ignore here), the actual tax—or tax liability—is calculated by reference to the appropriate tax schedules. Two commonly used tax schedules are shown in Figure 4.9. (Your filing status—married versus single, joint versus separate returns, etc.—determines which schedule you should use.)

There are several points to note about these tax rate schedules:

First, we show in Figure 4.9 the tax rate schedules for 1982, 1983, and 1984 as mandated in the *Economic Recovery Tax Act of 1981.* We ignore for the time being the 1983 and 1984 schedules, concentrating our attention on the 1982 schedule.

Second, in each schedule, the lowest taxable income amount is the zero bracket amount. Thus, for unmarried individuals, the zero bracket amount is $2,300; for married individuals filing joint returns, the zero bracket amount is $3,400.

Third, we see from Schedule X that single individuals earning more than $2,300 but less than $3,400 pay 12 percent in taxes on the excess over $2,300. The 12 percent is called the **marginal tax rate** for the first taxable income bracket. It is the *extra* tax paid on the *extra* dollars earned above $2,300 up to the bracket limit of $3,400. If they earn exactly $3,400, they pay $132 (i.e., $(0.12) \times (\$3,400 - \$2,300)$).

Figure 4.9

Tax rate schedules for 1982, 1983, and 1984

A. Schedule X—Unmarried individuals (other than surviving spouses and heads of households)

If taxable income is:		1982 tax is:		1983 tax is:		1984 tax is:	
Not over $2,300		–0–		–0–		–0–	
Over—	But not over—		Of the amount over—		Of the amount over—		Of the amount over
$ 2,300	$ 3,400	12%	$ 2,300	11%	$ 2,300	11%	$ 2,300
$ 3,400	$ 4,400	$ 132 + 14%	$ 3,400	$ 121 + 13%	$ 3,400	$ 121 + 12%	$ 3,400
$ 4,400	$ 6,500	$ 272 + 16%	$ 4,400	$ 251 + 15%[1]	$ 4,400	$ 241 + 14%	$ 4,400
$ 6,500	$ 8,500	$ 608 + 17%	$ 6,500	$ 566 + 15%[1]	$ 6,500	$ 535 + 15%	$ 6,500
$ 8,500	$ 10,800	$ 948 + 19%	$ 8,500	$ 866 + 17%	$ 8,500	$ 835 + 16%	$ 8,500
$ 10,800	$ 12,900	$ 1,385 + 22%	$ 10,800	$ 1,257 + 19%	$ 10,800	$ 1,203 + 18%	$ 10,800
$ 12,900	$ 15,000	$ 1,847 + 23%	$ 12,900	$ 1,656 + 21%	$ 12,900	$ 1,581 + 20%	$ 12,900
$ 15,000	$ 18,200	$ 2,330 + 27%	$ 15,000	$ 2,097 + 24%	$ 15,000	$ 2,001 + 23%	$ 15,000
$ 18,200	$ 23,500	$ 3,194 + 31%	$ 18,200	$ 2,865 + 28%	$ 18,200	$ 2,737 + 26%	$ 18,200
$ 23,500	$ 28,800	$ 4,837 + 35%	$ 23,500	$ 4,349 + 32%	$ 23,500	$ 4,115 + 30%	$ 23,500
$ 28,800	$ 34,100	$ 6,692 + 40%	$ 28,800	$ 6,045 + 36%	$ 28,800	$ 5,705 + 34%	$ 28,800
$ 34,100	$ 41,500	$ 8,812 + 44%	$ 34,100	$ 7,953 + 40%	$ 34,100	$ 7,507 + 38%	$ 34,100
$ 41,500	$ 55,300	$12,068 + 50%[2]	$ 41,500	$10,913 + 45%	$ 41,500	$10,319 + 42%	$ 41,500
$ 55,300	$ 81,800	$18,968 + 50%[2]	$ 55,300	$17,123 + 50%[2]	$ 55,300	$16,115 + 48%	$ 55,300
$ 81,800	. . .	$32,218 + 50%[2]	$ 81,800	$30,373 + 50%[2]	$ 81,800	$28,835 + 50%[2]	$ 81,800

[1] Due to rounding the marginal tax rate for the $4,400–$6,500 bracket is the same as the $6,500–$8,500 bracket.

[2] In 1982, the top marginal tax rate of 50 percent applies to all taxable income in excess of $41,500; in 1983, the top marginal tax rate of 50 percent applies to all taxable income in excess of $55,300; in 1984, the top marginal tax rate of 50 percent applies to all taxable income in excess of $81,800.

B. Schedule Y—Married individuals filing joint returns and surviving spouses

If taxable income is:		1982 tax is:		1983 tax is:		1984 tax is:	
Not over $3,400		–0–		–0–		–0–	
Over—	But not over—		Of the amount over—		Of the amount over—		Of the amount over—
$ 3,400	$ 5,500	12%	$ 3,400	11%	$ 3,400	11%	$ 3,400
$ 5,500	$ 7,600	$ 252 + 14%	$ 5,500	$ 231 + 13%	$ 5,500	$ 231 + 12%	$ 5,500
$ 7,600	$ 11,900	$ 546 + 16%	$ 7,600	$ 504 + 15%	$ 7,600	$ 483 + 14%	$ 7,600
$ 11,900	$ 16,000	$ 1,234 + 19%	$ 11,900	$ 1,149 + 17%	$ 11,900	$ 1,085 + 16%	$ 11,900
$ 16,000	$ 20,200	$ 2,013 + 22%	$ 16,000	$ 1,846 + 19%	$ 16,000	$ 1,741 + 18%	$ 16,000
$ 20,200	$ 24,600	$ 2,937 + 25%	$ 20,200	$ 2,644 + 23%	$ 20,200	$ 2,497 + 22%	$ 20,200
$ 24,600	$ 29,900	$ 4,037 + 29%	$ 24,600	$ 3,656 + 26%	$ 24,600	$ 3,465 + 25%	$ 24,600
$ 29,900	$ 35,200	$ 5,574 + 33%	$ 29,900	$ 5,034 + 30%	$ 29,900	$ 4,790 + 28%	$ 29,900
$ 35,200	$ 45,800	$ 7,323 + 39%	$ 35,200	$ 6,624 + 35%	$ 35,200	$ 6,274 + 33%	$ 35,200
$ 45,800	$ 60,000	$11,457 + 44%	$ 45,800	$10,334 + 40%	$ 45,800	$ 9,772 + 38%	$ 45,800
$ 60,000	$ 85,600	$17,705 + 49%	$ 60,000	$16,014 + 44%	$ 60,000	$15,168 + 42%	$ 60,000
$ 85,600	$109,400	$30,249 + 50%[1]	$ 85,600	$27,278 + 48%	$ 85,600	$25,920 + 45%	$ 85,600
$109,400	$162,400	$42,149 + 50%[1]	$109,400	$38,702 + 50%[1]	$109,400	$36,630 + 49%	$109,400
$162,400	. . .	$56,149 + 50%[1]	$162,400	$65,202 + 50%[1]	$162,400	$62,600 + 50%[1]	$162,400

[1] In 1982, the top marginal tax rate of 50 percent applies to all taxable income in excess of $85,600; in 1983, the top marginal tax rate of 50 percent applies to all taxable income in excess of $109,400; in 1984, the top marginal tax rate of 50 percent applies to all taxable income in excess of $162,400.

Now, for income above $3,400 but less than $4,400, single taxpayers pay $132 (the amount of tax on their first $3,400 of income) *plus* 14 percent of the amount over $3,400. In this instance, we say the single taxpayer is subject to a marginal tax rate of 14 percent in the second bracket.

Consider the following example. Mr. Flood, a single man, has gross income of $26,000 in 1982. He files a return as a single individual and claims itemized deductions of $4,000. His taxable income is $23,300 ($26,000, less $1,000 exemption, less $1,700 excess itemized deductions). Referring to Schedule X, the tax is $4,775 ($3,194 on the first $18,200 plus 31 percent of the amount over 18,200 = 0.31 × $5,100 = $1,581).

Schedule Y, the schedule used by married individuals and surviving spouses, is interpreted in the same way as Schedule X. (Another schedule, *married taxpayers filing separately,* is not shown in Figure 4.9.)

Fourth, a careful examination of each of the tables in Schedules X and Y reveals that successively higher taxable income brackets are subject to successively higher marginal tax rates up to a maximum marginal rate of 50 percent. For every dollar received in excess of $85,600, the married taxpayer filing a joint return pays 50 percent to the federal government in the form of taxes.

The tax schedule is progressive in structure. Because increases in taxable income subject taxpayers to increases in marginal tax rates, the tax schedules imply that the income tax is progressive in structure. Let us make sure we thoroughly understand this important idea.

A tax structure is said to be progressive if increases in income result in more than proportionate increases in taxes. If income rises by 10 percent, taxes will increase by more than 10 percent; taxes as a percentage of taxable income increase with taxable income.

To illustrate this, look at Schedule X again. Suppose the taxpayer initially has a taxable income of $15,000; the taxpayer pays $2,330 in taxes in 1982. Now let the taxpayer's 1982 taxable income double to $30,000; the tax liability is now $7,172—an amount that is more than *three* times the former tax liability of $2,330.

Under a proportional tax structure, a doubling of taxable income would have resulted in a doubling of the tax liability. A proportional tax structure implies a constant ratio of tax liability to taxable income. The marginal tax rate does *not* increase as taxable income increases. For completeness, a regressive tax structure would be one in which tax liability declines as taxable income increases. Alternatively, marginal tax rates decline as taxable income increases.

An aside: The fact that taxpayers are subject to higher and higher marginal tax rates as taxable income increases is a matter of considerable controversy. The progressive structure was introduced into our tax system on grounds that those with higher incomes ought to pay more in taxes since they have the ability to pay more. However, increasing marginal tax rates can have adverse effects on incentives to work and to save. For example, if you are a single taxpayer in the 49 percent marginal tax bracket, you apparently have less incentive to work harder and save more than the person in the 21 percent bracket because Uncle Sam takes almost half of the extra money you earn. More will be said on this subject in our discussion below of "bracket creep."

Different types of income are treated differently for tax purposes; and tax credits. Although the tax tables imply a fairly progressive income tax structure at the federal level, it is much less progressive in practice. We touch on only a few of the reasons here.

Capital gains income. When you purchase an asset—a house or common stock—and sell it one or more years later at a higher price, the difference (adjusted for various expenses incurred in the interim) is called **capital gains income.** Capital gains income is given preferential treatment under the U.S. tax code. Persons aged 55 or over who sell their personal residences are not taxed on the first $125,000 of capital gains income; on the amount over $125,000, the tax they pay is determined in the same way as the tax for most other sources of capital gains income. That is, most capital gains income is computed by first *excluding* 60 percent of capital gains income from any tax whatever and multiplying the remaining 40 percent times the appropriate marginal tax rate. To illustrate using Schedule X, suppose Mr. Smith's taxable income before the sale of his common stock was $15,000. Suppose further that the sale of his stock nets him a capital gains income of $5,000. Sixty percent of that $5,000 is excluded, leaving him with $2,000 of extra taxable income. Given Mr. Smith's 1982 tax bracket, the extra tax he pays is $540 (0.27 × $2,000). What was the effective marginal tax rate on Mr. Smith's capital gains income? It was only 11 percent ($540 ÷ $5,000 = 0.11). In general, the effective tax rate can be calculated by taking the percentage that is *not* excluded—40 percent—and multiplying it times the appropriate marginal tax rate. (For Mr. Jones the appropriate marginal tax rate was 0.27; and 0.27 × 0.40 = 0.11.) Can you see that the *maximum* effective marginal tax rate on capital gains income is only 20 percent? (Hint: what is the maximum marginal tax rate on taxable income? That value times the percentage of the capital gain *not* excluded gives you the answer. *The Economic Recovery Tax Act of 1981* reduced the top marginal tax rate from 70 percent to 50 percent. Thus, prior to this most recent tax bill the maximum effective tax rate on capital gains income was 28 percent. Can you explain why?)

Exclusions and tax deferrals. Many types of income are not subject to any tax whatever. As a result of the 1981 tax bill, taxpayers can exclude from gross income up to $2,000 in interest income if that interest income comes from special tax-exempt savings certificates (popularly known as "all saver" certificates). For most taxpayers, estate and gift taxes were all but eliminated by this law. Citizens of the United States living abroad can exclude from their gross income up to $75,000 of the income they earn abroad (rising to $95,000 in 1986) plus their housing costs abroad. Moreover, there are a great many ways people can *defer* their taxes: If people sell their principal residence and realize a capital gain, the tax on that gain is deferred if they purchase another higher valued principal residence within 2 years; and, within limits, most taxpayers can elect to join pension plans, which defer the tax

on the amount contributed until it is withdrawn. (When taxes are deferred it is like getting an interest-free loan. You have a tax liability and Uncle Sam says, in effect, "keep it for now, and pay me later—without interest charges." Moreover, tax deferral schemes often permit taxpayers to pay less in taxes. Often your income will be lower when, for example, you retire; drawing down your tax deferred retirement account puts you in a *lower* tax bracket than you were in when you were working.)

Tax credits. When taxpayers are eligible to receive **tax credits,** their tax liability is reduced dollar for dollar by the amount of the credit. There are all sorts of tax credits in U.S. tax law: an investment tax credit (a credit given for the purchase of machinery); a credit for individuals aged 65 or over; a credit for political contributions; an earned-income credit (a credit to help reduce the tax liability of certain low income workers); a child and dependent care credit; and credits for energy saving expenditures and for foreign taxes paid.

The net effect of all of these provisions in our tax code—and we have only touched the surface here—is to complicate considerably the matter of determining just how progressive the U.S. tax structure is. Many studies of our tax system have concluded that, after taking account of all the exemptions, deductions, the different treatment of different types of income and the plethora of tax credits, actual tax payments tend to be much less progressive than is normally believed, especially at the upper end of the income scale. What is the reason for the absence of much progressivity higher up on the income scale? Higher-income people have more of these tax-reducing devices available to them and a stronger incentive to use them given the high marginal tax rates they would otherwise be subjected to.

The phenomenon of "bracket creep." Although most of the provisions of the tax law discussed above serve to make taxes much less progressive than the tax rate schedules imply, one major factor has been operating over the decade of the 1970s to make taxes *more* progressive. That factor has been inflation, and the phenomenon in question that has caused the increase in progressivity is called **bracket creep.** Bracket creep is not another name for your local IRS agent; it refers rather to the way in which inflation and the progressive tax structure interact to increase your tax in real terms. That is, to increase your tax in purchasing power terms.

The Economic Recovery Tax Act of 1981 went a long way toward correcting the problem of bracket creep—particularly the provisions of that Act that apply beginning in 1985. Nevertheless, the tax rate schedules in Figure 4.9 can be used to illustrate the concept of bracket creep.

Suppose that your taxable income for 1982, as a single taxpayer, is $23,000. According to schedule X, your federal income tax would be $4,682 ($3,194 + 31% of the amount over $18,200), leaving $18,318 available for other purposes. Now suppose that prices rise by 10 percent over the course of 1982 and that your taxable income just keeps pace with inflation. In 1983 your taxable income would be $25,300 (i.e., 10 percent more than in 1982). Now, *assuming that the tax rate schedule in 1983 was the same as the tax rate schedule in 1982,* your taxes in 1983 would be $5,467 ($4,837 + 35% of the amount over $23,500). Your aftertax income would thus be $19,833—higher than before, to be sure, but not 10 percent higher. Indeed, after taxes, your income would be only 8 percent higher; your tax liability, on the other hand, would rise by over 17 percent. After adjusting for the 10 percent increase in prices, you would find yourself with enough to buy only $18,030 worth of goods in *1982* prices—a loss of more than $288. In this example, the government has, in effect, taxed your inflation induced gains in income.

It is important to understand what happened in this numerical example. As a result of the increase in income from $23,000 to $25,300, you moved—you crept—from a tax bracket with a 31 percent marginal tax rate to a bracket having a 35 percent marginal tax rate. Your real tax burden increased even though your real income—your real purchasing power—*before taxes* remained unchanged. Accordingly, your real income *after taxes* declined.

The phenomenon of bracket creep has been the source of a great deal of controversy. Many economists—most notably those associated with *supply-side economics*—have argued that bracket creep provides strong disincentives to work and to save, outcomes that, in their view, have been responsible for many of the economic ills plaguing us today.

The Reagan Administration addressed the bracket creep problem in two ways in its *Economic Recovery Tax Act of 1981.* First, this tax bill called for cuts in marginal tax rates for three successive years beginning in October 1981. Those cuts in marginal tax rates are reflected in the tax rate schedules in Figure 4.9. Look again at schedule X. Consider the tax bracket $23,500 to $28,800. The marginal tax rate for that bracket is 35 percent in 1982. In 1983 it drops to 32 percent, and then to 30 percent in 1984. All other tax brackets are subject to marginal tax rate reductions over time; the magnitude of the rate reductions is given in Figure 4.9.

How do marginal tax rate reductions address the problem of bracket creep? To answer this, let us retrace our earlier example. In 1982 your taxable income as a single taxpayer was $23,000 which put you in the 31 percent marginal tax rate bracket. Your income rises by 10 percent which raises your taxable income to $25,300 causing you to creep into the next higher tax bracket. However, whereas in our earlier example (where we assumed that the 1982 tax rate schedule applied in 1983 as well), the bracket creep raised your marginal tax rate from 31 to 35 percent, the fact of the reduction in marginal tax rates between 1982 and 1983 means that your marginal tax rate will be 32 percent in 1983. This particular result is clear by examining the tax bracket row $23,500–$28,800 in Figure 4.9 and discovering the 1983 marginal tax rate for that bracket.

(In this particular numerical example, your marginal tax rate actually increased: in 1982 your marginal tax rate was 31 percent in the $18,200–$23,500 tax bracket; in 1983, your marginal tax rate was 32 percent. True, the marginal tax rate was lower in 1983 than it would otherwise have been had there been no marginal tax rate reduction but it is, for you, nonetheless higher.

Other numerical examples can be constructed in which, for some taxpayers, the marginal tax rate would be unchanged. In still other instances, taxpayers would discover that they had lower marginal tax rates in 1983. If you experiment with the numbers in Figure 4.9 you will see that the magnitude and direction of change of the marginal tax rate, if any, will depend on the initial income, the rate of inflation, and the size of the marginal tax rate change.)

Changing marginal tax rates is not a perfect way to offset bracket creep. Of course, as we will see in Chapter 14, this was not the purpose of the mandated changes in tax rates in the 1981 tax law; the offset to bracket creep—more for some taxpayers than for others—was merely a by-product of an effort to reduce all tax rates.

The second way bracket creep was addressed in the *Economic Recovery Tax Act of 1981*—the way specifically aimed at the bracket creep problem—was through **indexation** of the individual income tax. Thus, under the 1981 tax law, various adjustments are made starting in 1985, to prevent inflation induced tax increases. Basically, three kinds of adjustments are called for:

1. As noted before, beginning in 1985, the value of each personal exemption will be increased at a rate equal to the rate of inflation of the previous year.

2. As noted before, beginning in 1985, the value of the zero bracket amount will be increased at a rate equal to the rate of inflation of the previous year.

3. Beginning in 1985, the tax brackets will be adjusted by the rate of inflation of the previous year. This is done by adjusting up the minimum and maximum dollar amounts for each bracket by the rate of inflation of the previous year. To illustrate, consider the bracket amount in Schedule X (Figure 4.9), $6,500–$8,500. Suppose inflation rises by 10 percent in 1984. In 1985, that tax bracket would be increased to $7,150–$9,350. $7,150 is 10 percent more than $6,500 and $9,350 is 10 percent more than $8,500. It should be

clear, therefore, that for taxpayers in the $6,-500–$8,500 tax bracket in 1984 who experience taxable income increases in 1984 equal to the assumed 10 percent rate of inflation that they will stay in the *same* tax bracket in 1985 except that in 1985, that tax bracket will be defined by the values $7,150 and $9,350. Because they are not kicked into a higher tax bracket because of inflation, there is no bracket creep. Thus, they will be subjected to the *same* marginal tax rate in 1985 as in 1984.

More will be said on the issue of indexation in Chapter 14.

The marriage penalty tax. There is one final aspect of the individual income tax that needs to be understood. This is the marriage penalty tax. The penalty is this: if married taxpayers both earn income, their combined tax will exceed the sum of the amounts they each would have paid as single taxpayers. To illustrate, suppose John and Sue each have taxable incomes of $18,200 in 1982. If they were single, they each would have a tax liability of $3,194; the sum of their tax liabilities would be $6,388. Suppose now that John and Sue marry; their combined taxable income is $36,400. If they file jointly, their joint tax liability in 1982 would be $7,791—$1,403 *more* because they got married. Even in these inflationary times, a marriage license shouldn't cost that much!

The Economic Recovery Tax Act of 1981 provides a deduction to couples filing a joint return to correct for the marriage penalty. Specifically the Act allows couples to deduct from their gross income (not taxable income) 10 percent of the lower earning spouse's earned income (up to a $3,000 maximum deduction). (For 1982, the percentage reduction is 5 percent.)

How this works for our hypothetical couple, John and Sue, for 1982 can be explained as follows: This couple can deduct from their gross income 5 percent of one of the spouse's income (which one is immaterial since it is assumed that they both earn the same amount). Suppose this amounts to $1,200 in 1982. This reduces their taxable income by $1,200, bringing that amount to $35,200. They stay in the same tax bracket in 1982. And, since their taxable income is $1,200 less, their tax liability is reduced by $468—the marginal tax rate times the amount taxable income was reduced. This offsets only part of the marriage penalty for John and Sue. They will probably do better in 1983. Why?

The social security tax. Most taxpayers are also subject to another federal tax besides the individual income tax—the **social security tax** (or, as it is sometimes called, the **payroll tax**). This tax is levied on the earnings of employees. Half the tax is paid for by the employers; half is paid for by the employees. The proceeds of the tax are used to finance the federal government's social security system.

The structure of this tax is quite simple, especially in comparison with the personal income tax. Basically the payroll tax is calculated as a percentage of earnings up to a certain amount. In 1981, for example, the combined rate for employers and employees was 13.3 percent—6.65 percent apiece—levied on the first $29,700 of income. There are no exemptions, deductions, or the like; all those who are subject to the tax, which basically includes the vast majority of workers in the private (nongovernment) sector, pay at the same rate. (Self-employed individuals pay a rate of 9.3 percent on self-employment income through $29,700.)

Two points should be noted about the payroll tax. First, it is a proportional income tax up through $29,700, but a *regressive* income tax thereafter; the greatest relative burden of the social security tax is borne by people earning less than $29,700. Anyone with earnings of more than $29,700 currently pays exactly the same social security tax as someone with $29,700 in earnings. (In future years, the *base* $29,700 is scheduled to increase.)

The second point is that the payroll tax is truly a tax rather than a retirement savings plan. Many people regard it as a form of saving, in which you contribute now for income to be paid back later. The notion of a social security account number reinforces this impression. But the key difference is that there is no necessary direct link between the amount you pay in and your claim to the benefits. (There is a requirement that you

contribute for 20 quarters, but this just establishes eligibility to receive payments. The actual amounts you can receive depend on your highest income years and a great many other factors.) Indeed, the funds being paid in today are *not* being held back to finance—even in a general way—the future benefits of those paying the taxes. Rather, they are going directly to today's recipients.

Reform of the social security system is highly probable in future years. However, any and all changes are likely to prove controversial as well.

The corporation income tax. The business incomes earned by sole proprietorships and partnerships are taxed at the individual income tax rates. Income earned by corporations, however, is taxed at the corporation income tax rates.

The *taxable income* of corporations is based on the *net income* concept introduced earlier in this chapter. Basically, corporate taxable income subtracts out of the gross proceeds of the corporation all those costs associated with doing business—wages and salaries, office expenses, interest payment on debt, depreciation, etc. The remainder is taxed according to the schedule laid out in Figure 4.10. Like the personal income tax schedules, this schedule is progressive, with the marginal tax rate beginning at 16 percent in 1982 on the first $25,000 of taxable income and work-

Figure 4.10
Corporation income tax rates
For 1982

Corporations

On taxable income through $25,000	16%
On taxable income over $25,000 through $50,000	19%
On taxable income over $50,000 through $75,000	30%
On taxable income over $75,000 through $100,000	40%
On taxable income over $100,000	46%

For 1983 and later years:

On taxable income through $25,000	15%
On taxable income over $25,000 through $50,000	18%
On taxable incomes above $50,000	Same as for 1982

ing its way up to 46 percent on that portion of taxable income over $100,000. Beginning in 1983, the tax rates on the two lowest brackets are scheduled to be lowered.

As was the case with our discussion of the individual income tax, we will merely highlight here a few features of the corporation income tax. Two features that have captured headlines over the course of the past few years are the **investment tax credit** and **accelerated depreciation.** Both features are frequently referred to as **capital cost recovery** items.

The investment tax credit is easily explained. For most equipment purchases, businesspeople are permitted to deduct from their tax liability an amount up to 10 percent of the purchase price. This credit against taxes was first introduced by President Kennedy in 1962 to enhance capital spending incentives by business firms.

Accelerated depreciation is a bit more involved. Depreciation expenses represent the deductions businesspeople are permitted to make for those portions of their capital goods that are used up, consumed, or depreciated during the production process. The depreciation laws were originally written so that the amounts deducted corresponded to the income flows generated by the various types of capital goods. Accelerated depreciation methods permit businesspeople to write off, or expense, their capital goods at *faster* rates. There are two ways to speed up the write-offs: (1) reducing the number of years over which capital goods can be written off; and (2) increasing the percentage deduction in the early years. *The Economic Recovery Tax Act of 1981* substantially shortened the number of years capital goods can be written off. And, although the percentage deduction in the early years was *increased* for the first few years of the law (in order to lessen the impact on Treasury revenues), the original percentage amounts will be restored in steps in 1985 and 1986.

One other feature associated with the corporate income tax is the **double taxation of corporate dividends.** Those who own stock in effect pay taxes *twice* on that portion of their earnings that they receive as dividends. Why? Because

the corporation first pays taxes on its net income, then—once the earnings have been distributed—they count as income on the individual income tax return and are thus taxed again. The personal income tax code allows taxpayers to exclude from income the first $100 of dividends ($200 for a joint return), but this may be a relatively small benefit for some taxpayers. This double-taxation characteristic is the subject of intense debate. Those who want it changed claim that it is unfair and provides reduced incentives to undertake investment. Those who are opposed to changing the law argue that dividends accrue primarily to those in the upper income brackets, individuals who are not overly burdened by taxes anyway.

State and local taxes. As noted earlier, state and local governments derive their tax income from three principal sources—individual and corporate income, the value of property, and sales taxes. Not all state and local jurisdictions rely to the same degree on these various types of taxes. The taxes faced by any given individual or business firm will depend on the particular blend of taxes used by the states and municipalities in which she or he resides.

As a rule, states depend less on personal and corporate income taxes than the federal government does, and only a few municipalities have income taxes. Those jurisdictions that do tax income directly generally do so at much lower rates than the federal government, and they use schedules that are simpler and less progressive. Indeed, many of the state systems simply *piggyback* on the federal tax system in the sense that they use the same definitions of income and the same principle deductions and exemptions.

For the most part, state and local jurisdictions rely on two forms of *indirect* taxes—taxes not based on the incomes of those taxed: sales taxes and property taxes. **Sales taxes** are familiar to all of us in everyday life. Virtually everything we purchase is subject to a sales tax of one kind or another. For the most part, sales taxes tend to be regressive because consumer expenditures (on which the tax is based) absorb a larger fraction of lower-income budgets. (The regressive feature is reduced somewhat when necessities like food and drugs are exempted from such taxation.)

Property taxes are those that are assessed on certain items of personal property—real estate, automobiles, and luxury items such as boats.

It is difficult to tell whether property taxes are progressive, proportional, or regressive. To the extent that the value of property held, and the property taxes paid, rise more or less in line with income, the property tax would tend to be proportional. However, because different jurisdictions tax at different rates, it is almost impossible to assess the degree of progressivity in a general way.

SUMMARY

1. The overwhelming majority of business enterprises in the United States are *sole proprietorships*. However, despite their huge numbers, sole proprietorships account for only about 10 percent of total business receipts; the bulk of business receipts—around 85 percent—are accounted for by *corporations*. For the most part, sole proprietorships are easy to set up and operate; usually they are operated by the owner; typically they are small in size. One unique aspect of a proprietorship is that all the risks—the prospects for failure as well as success—are borne by one person—the owner. Moreover, such a form of enterprise may be particularly appealing to those who like to make their own decisions without having to consult with others. The disadvantages of a sole proprietorships are the generally severe limits of capital that can be raised to finance this business enterprise and *unlimited liability* in the eyes of the law.

2. Like a proprietorship, a *partnership* is fairly easy to set up and operate. Partnerships have one distinct advantage over sole proprietorships—namely, the expanded set of resources and talents that a group of owners may offer. On the other hand, one major disadvantage of a partnership is that the decisions of any one of the partners are binding on *all* partners. In addition, the partnership form of organization shares one

major drawback with the sole proprietorship—namely, unlimited liability.

3. Many of the drawbacks and limitations of sole proprietorships and partnerships are overcome in the *corporation* form of business enterprise. First, the *limited liability* feature makes it easier for corporations to tap the financial resources of large numbers of people. Second, the larger size frequently enables corporations to gain greater access to the markets for borrowed funds. However, with these advantages come certain disadvantages. First, from a legal standpoint, it is not as easy to organize and operate a corporation. Another drawback is taxation: corporations are subject to their own income taxes, and the dividends they distribute after these taxes are paid are then taxed again as part of the incomes of those who receive them. Finally, the corporate form of organization raises important questions regarding the relationship between the owners and managers of the firm. In spite of these potential problems, the corporation remains the most important kind of business organization because it is the most conducive to large-scale operations. This has a lot to do with the ease with which corporations can attract financing.

4. The financing of business activity can take one or both of two forms: *debt financing* or *equity financing*. Bank loans and commercial paper constitute the dominant forms of short-term debt financing; corporate bonds constitute the dominant form of long-term debt financing. Equity financing could be an attractive alternative to borrowing if the price of the firm's stock is high or its debt/equity ratio is large. For the most part, however, firms rely on equity financing only occasionally because issues of new stock must be authorized by the existing owners of the firm, and they typically will be reluctant to dilute their ownership rights by making more shares available to others.

5. *Leverage* refers to the level of the debt/equity ratio. From the point of view of potential earnings per share, the amount of leverage possessed by owners is quite important.

6. The financial condition and operations of a business firm can be summarized in two related

statements: the *balance sheet* and the *income statement*. The balance sheet shows the financial condition of the firm as of a given moment. The income statement, on the other hand, summarizes the activities of the firm over a period of time.

7. The proper functions of government in an economy that relies heavily on private decisionmaking to determine the allocation of scarce resources are as follows. Since many economic agents do not play according to the rules of the game that would make laissez-faire capitalism operate efficiently and effectively, there is a need for government to help set and then enforce the rules. Moreover, in the face of externalities, laissez-faire capitalism will fail to produce the right quantities of various goods and services, overallocating resources to some goods and underallocating resources to others. In addition, there are no guarantees that laissez-faire capitalism will produce a distribution of income that society would agree was correct. Also, there are no guarantees that the millions of people making billions of economic decisions day after day would produce the optimum—that is, full employment—level of resource use.

8. There are several ways to answer the question, How big is government? One measure is government purchases of goods and services as a percent of gross national product. A more comprehensive measure is provided by the amount of revenue government derives in the form of taxes; taxes provide us with a better measure of the command of government over our scarce national resources. Even this measure, however, may understate the influence of government. Account needs to be taken of the government borrowing that is required to finance the excess of government budget outlays over cash receipts. One also needs to add to this those government regulations that require business firms to incur expenditures in order to be in compliance.

9. At the federal level, income security programs, national defense, and interest on the national debt account for fully 70 percent of outlays. At the state and local level, education and highways together absorb more than 45 percent

of the spending dollar. Other items of significance include public welfare, hospitals and health programs, and public utilities.

10. At the federal level, the personal income tax is the most important source of revenue, accounting for nearly 46 percent of federal government revenues in 1980. Second in importance is the payroll tax. Next in importance is the corporate income tax. At the state and local level, federal government *grants-in-aid* transfers are the most important source of revenue. Sales tax is next in importance followed by the property tax.

11. Several aspects of the U.S. federal income tax are worth noting:

a. The individual income tax is levied on taxable income, not on gross income.

b. The tax schedule is progressive in structure.

c. Different kinds of income are treated differently for tax purposes.

d. Many types of income are excluded from taxation altogether and the taxes on some other kinds of income can be deferred.

e. Individual income taxes are levied on people's money incomes, which, in an inflationary environment, gives rise to a phenomenon known as *bracket creep*.

f. Many married taxpayers who both work are subject to a "marriage penalty" tax.

12. The social security tax is the second important revenue source at the federal level. This tax is levied on the earnings of employees. Half the tax is paid for by the employer; half is paid by the employees. The proceeds of the tax are used to finance the federal government's social security system.

13. The business incomes earned by sole proprietorships and partnerships are taxed at the individual income tax rates. Income earned by corporations, however, is taxed at the corporation income tax rates. In examining the corporation income tax, one needs to take account of its progressive rate structure, the investment tax credit, accelerated depreciation, and the double taxation of dividends.

14. State and local governments derive their tax income from three principal sources: sales

taxes, property taxes, and individual and corporate income taxes.

CONCEPTS FOR REVIEW

Sole proprietorship

Partnership

Corporation

Unlimited liability

Limited liability

Common stocks

Stockholders

Dividends

Price appreciation

Price depreciation

Debt financing

Equity financing

Prime rate

Commercial paper

Debt/equity ratio

Leverage

Balance sheet

Income statement

External benefits

External costs

Public goods

The social balance question

Taxable income versus gross income

Progressive versus proportional versus regressive taxes

Economic Recovery Tax Act of 1981

Exemptions and deductions

Zero bracket amount

Excess itemized deductions

Marginal tax rate

Capital gains income

Tax credits

Bracket creep

Accelerated depreciation

Capital cost recovery

Double taxation of dividend income

QUESTIONS FOR DISCUSSION
(Those marked withan asterisk (*) are more difficult.)

1. Suppose the laws were changed to eliminate the limited liability feature for corporations. How do you think this would affect the ability of new firms to amass large amounts of funds? What about the ability of well-established firms to acquire funds? If limited liability had never existed, how would this have affected American economic development? Explain carefully.

2. Explain and illustrate the relationship between a firm's income statement and balance sheet.

3. Explain the concept of leverage and illustrate its relationship to a firm's debt/equity ratio. From the point of view of the stockholders, is increased leverage always a good thing? Why or why not. Explain.

4. From an external benefits perspective, can you make a case for government support of "the arts" and education? Be explicit.

5. Many coal miners suffer from so-called black lung disease. Can a case be made, on the basis of external costs, for government regulations requiring coal producers to compensate those coal miners afflicted with the disease for their medical costs and reduced life expectancies?

*6. *a.* Suppose Freddie, a single man, has a gross income of $35,000, itemized deductions of $9,000, and two dependent children. What amount of federal income tax would Freddie pay in 1982? What about 1983? Suppose Freddie meets and marries Freda, who also has a gross income of $35,000, itemized deductions of $9,000, and two dependent children. What amount of federal income tax would the new family pay if Freddie and Freda filed jointly? (Make the calculation inclusive of the adjustment for the marriage penalty discussed in the text. Assume the taxable year in 1983.) Is there indeed a marriage penalty tax?

b. Suppose the general price level increases by 10 percent and Freddie and Freda both experience 10 percent increases in their incomes. If they file jointly in 1982, are they subject to bracket creep? Explain.

7. Explain the difference between the investment tax credit and accelerated depreciation.

Paul Samuelson (1915–   )

The second Nobel Prize in Economics (1970) was awarded to a man who, in the words of the Swedish Academy of Sciences, did "more than any other contemporary economist to raise the level of scientific analysis in economic theory." Paul Samuelson was the first American to receive the award.

Wide World Photos

A witty and prolific writer, educator, and commentator, Samuelson has played a major role in the shaping of economic thinking among both academics and policymakers. Under his leadership the economics department at the Massachusetts Institute of Technology has become preeminent.

Although not cited for his specific contribution to what was then termed the 'new economics,' Samuelson declared that "I'd like to think that it's a pat on the back for the new economics which I represent generally, as well as for my own efforts."

New economics is described by Samuelson as "simply the economics of the mixed economy." It is the view that government has an obligation to *manage* monetary and fiscal policies to realize the broad macroeconomics objectives of full employment, rapid growth, and price stability. Samuelson's writings on the subject have been the source of much controversy. The reason is clear—he is widely regarded as the leading exponent of the Keynesian school of thought.

The Swedish Academy gave heavy weight to Samuelson's *Foundations of Economic Analysis,* a classic that is used in most graduate programs in economics. The work was largely completed when he was a 22 year old graduate student at Harvard. He followed with a popular undergraduate textbook which has been translated into 25 languages and used around the world.

A father of six children (including one set of triplet boys), Samuelson is a dedicated tennis player (which he calls his passion), a columnist for *Newsweek* magazine, and an avid reader of detective novels.

Simon Kuznets (1901–   )

A man who devoted almost all of his professional life to the systematic statistical measurement of economic behavior was awarded the third Nobel Prize in Economics (1971). Simon Kuznets—often referred to as the "father of GNP" because of his work in the development of the national income and product accounts—was cited for his 25 years of labor ferreting out the quantative characteristics of long-term economic growth in the world's economies. The citation stated that Kuznets "more than any other scientist has illuminated with facts—and explained through analysis—the economic growth from the middle of the last century."

Wide World Photos

PART TWO

Macroeconomics: Employment, inflation, fiscal policy, monetary policy, economic stability, and economic growth

Although precise quantative work of the sort that occupied Kuznets' attention lacks the glamour of other endeavors in the field of economics, his work is of the upmost importance. Careful documentation of statistical facts is essential to the testing of economic theories. The national income and product accounts form the basic factual foundation for the economists' study of inflation, unemployment, and growth.

A quiet, slender, and warmhearted man who is Professor of Economics, emeritus, at Harvard University, is described as a person "without enemies in a most competitive profession. And that's a very rare thing." His favorite recreation is listening to classical music.

Wassily Leontief (1906–   )

An engaging Russian émigré, the intellectual father of input-output analysis, was awarded the fifth Nobel Prize in Economics (1973) by the Swedish Academy. The work of Wassily Leontief on input-output theory represented a breakthrough in the analysis of the components of an economic system and their interrelationships.

United Press International

Input-output analysis, a clear example of Leontief's genius for blending theory with practical detail, is used extensively in almost every country of the world—most notably in those with centrally planned economies.

An an undergraduate at the University of Leningrad Leontief first studied philosophy and mathematics. Later he shifted to sociology and then to economics. As he said of this transition, "I began in philosophy and logic but found them too speculative, too abstract. Then I changed to sociology, but the only interesting part of it was its title. Then I sank lower, into economics, the field nearest to philosophy."

Known widely for his outspoken liberal political views—views for which he was jailed several times while an undergraduate in Russia—Leontief has been sharply critical of university faculty who are not dedicated to the teaching of their students. He frequently prefers to eat lunch in the student cafeteria rather than the faculty club. "Because," he says in his high-pitched, heavily accented voice, "I like undergraduates best. They're excited about ideas. They're not afraid to say what they think."

The New York University Professor has a passion for classical music, opera, and ballet and a zeal for trout fishing and photography.

Milton Friedman (1912–   )

The Swedish Academy of Sciences acknowledged the "independence and brilliance" of Milton Friedman in awarding the eighth Nobel Prize in Economics in 1976. "It is very rare for an economist to wield such influence directly and indirectly, not only on the direction of scientific research but on actual policy," the citation read.

This statement by the academy is telling in two respects. On the one hand it was precisely because of his *conservative* influence on actual policies that kept him 'waiting in line' for the prize; on the other hand, in spite of his political views, his "achievements in the fields of consumption analysis, monetary history and theory, [and] his demonstration of the complexity of stabilization policy" were so major that it was inevitable that the prize would be awarded to him. Perhaps this explains, in part, his response to the announcement: "It is not the pinnacle of my career." He emphasized that he cared more for the verdict of his peers than that of the seven members of the Swedish Academy.

Wide World Photos

Wide World Photos

As a leader of the Chicago school of economic philosophy, Friedman has been more than a mere expositor of the conservative point of view; he has been an important architect of the conservative philosophy. His work attests to his profound respect for the marketplace as the best and most efficient means to economic improvement for everyone, and to his resentment of government encroachment on individual freedoms.

As an eloquent proponent of monetarism Friedman "alone turned the world's economic attention back to money"—back to the view that money is basic to the determination of the rate of change of the price level.

Friedman is known to the public for his regular column in *Newsweek* magazine and, more recently, as the narrator and star of the public television series "Freedom to Choose."

Lawrence Klein (1920–   )

A professor of Economics at the University of Pennsylvania's Wharton School of Economics was awarded the twelfth Nobel Price in Economics (1980). Lawrence Klein was cited by the Swedish Academy for his three decades of research "in the field of economic science which deals with the construction of empirical models of business fluctuations."

Described as the father of 'forecasting models' that are used throughout the world to forecast trends and analyze business conditions, Klein was cited for his work on how oil price increases had influenced inflation, employment, and trade balances in different countries of the world.

Klein's work is not only the forerunner of the famous Wharton Model, which he continues to administer, but of the numerous other commercial econometric models on which the business community and the government have come to rely for market analyses and for assessment of changed economic policies.

A soft-spoken, modest man, Klein is described as "a prince of a guy . . . who actually does worry about his students."

In the eyes of many of his friends and colleagues Klein's Nobel award represented "the ultimate triumph of good sense over prejudice." In the early 1950s, Klein was one of the victims of the late Senator Joseph McCarthy's anti-communist drives. Klein ultimately lost tenure at the University of Michigan, despite the fact that early on McCarthy dropped the charges against him.

It is not difficult to set forth our major national economic goals. They include:

Full employment.
Price stability.
Rapid economic growth.
A fair and equitable distribution of income.
A safe and clean environment.
A proper mix of goods and services.

At this level of generality, it is hard to imagine many people disagreeing with these ideals. Of course we would like to achieve all of these objectives. However, as soon as we begin to inquire into the specifics of each of these goals, very sharp disagreements among people can and do surface.

To illustrate, what do we mean by the goal of "full employment?" Do we mean zero unemployment? As we will see in this chapter, there is good reason to define *full employment* as some positive amount of unemployment. However, there is very little agreement over precisely what positive amount of unemployment is "acceptable." Some argue that full employment will be reached only when the overall unemployment rate falls to 3 percent; others argue that the "full-employment–unemployment rate" is 4 percent; and still others argue that it is 6 percent or more. Some people sidestep the issue completely by restating the goal as one of **high employment,** which is, admittedly, a vaguer idea than full employment.

What about the goal of price stability? Do we mean that each and every price should remain fixed? If you recall our discussion of demand and supply in Chapter 3 where we emphasized the important role that changing prices play in the allocation of resources, it is doubtful that we would want to choose as our goal of price stability the complete absence of any price changes whatsoever. If that's the case, then how should we define price stability? Often people mean by price stability the absence of *inflation*— that is, the absence of increases in the general level of prices, or the absence of price increases *on the average* (the price increases for some goods and services being offset by price reductions elsewhere). However, given the problems of defining

Chapter 5

National economic goals and goal conflicts: An analysis of the record

the price level, or the average rate of price change (as we will see), and given the difficulties our policymakers have had in solving inflation, should we stick with zero inflation as our goal or something a bit more "realistic" or "reasonable?" As soon as we admit qualifying words like "realistic" or "reasonable," defining the goal precisely becomes very difficult; those words mean different things to different people.

Similar problems arise as we attempt to set forth the specifics of the other economic goals. What is meant by a "fair and equitable" distribution of income? Should everyone's income be exactly the same, or is some degree of inequality to be permitted? And if so, how much? What about a "safe and clean environment?" Does this mean that we should eliminate all nuclear reactors because they are potentially dangerous? Does this mean that we should stop all productive activity where there are potential problems of toxic waste disposal? Does this mean the complete absence of any air or water pollution, or is some "minimal" amount consistent with our definition of "clean?"

Does a "proper mix" of goods and services mean that we should devote one third of our nation's output to our federal, state, and local governments, or should we devote even more? Or less? Within the public sector, should we devote more or less to national defense? And within the private sector, should we devote more or less to the accumulation of capital goods? Unfortunately, there are no generally accepted answers to these questions.

The matter of defining our national economic goals is even more complicated than the discussion above implies. There are at least three reasons for this. First, as our economic system evolves over time, a change in goal specifics, though not necessarily the general goals themselves, might be called for. A 4 percent unemployment goal might have been reasonable 20 years ago. But a comparable, reasonable rate today might be 5 percent in view of the structural changes that have taken place in our nation's labor force. This will be examined in detail later.

Second, goal specifics may change over time as the political climate changes. What constitutes a clean and safe environment or a fair and equitable distribution of income under one administration may not be the same under another.

Third, the specific goals set forth by our nation's leaders may not all be attainable simultaneously because the realization of one goal may conflict with the realization of another. For example, it is often argued that the realization of a 4 percent unemployment rate in today's economy will almost inevitably result in ever-accelerating price level increases. Moreover, it is argued by certain environmentalists that any positive rate of economic growth would only serve to further degrade our environment. And still others argue that it is not possible to step up the rate of economic growth sharply without worsening the distribution of income.

It is the purpose of this chapter to examine in detail these several aspects of our national economic goals. It is not our purpose, however, to set forth the specifics of the goals themselves. Put simply but bluntly, there is no easy way to be precise about our economic goals. In part, this is a reflection of the complexities inherent in our economic system. It is hoped that you will come to an appreciation of these complexities by chapter's end.

THE GOAL OF FULL EMPLOYMENT

The goal of full employment has long been a stated objective of our society. This objective was first enunciated in a formal but vague way in the **Employment Act of 1946** and reaffirmed more explicitly in the **Humphrey-Hawkins Full Employment and Balanced Growth Act of 1978.**

The reason full employment is given so much prominence is straightforward. From a national point of view, the failure to achieve and maintain full employment is a waste of resources. We cannot possibly satisfy all our wants with the limited resources at our disposal. When unemployment is present, we are not even doing as well as we could. Moreover, the output we fail to produce because of unemployment is output that is lost

forever. Yes, we might have full employment tomorrow, but we cannot relive yesterday.

Second, at the personal level, the vast majority
of people depend for their livelihood on the sale
of their labor services. If they were forced to
join the ranks of the unemployed, they could
not long provide for their families or themselves;
they could not continue to meet their house payments; nor could they do the other things with
their money that they often did before. Moreover,
although short spells of umemployment may not
be too painful, spells of unemployment of very
long duration are very damaging, both economically and psychologically.

These considerations would seem to suggest
that the only viable full employment goal is zero
unemployment. However, as will be explained
below, there are many reasons zero umemployment is not only not viable but even not necessarily desirable. To understand this point, we need
to first familiarize ourselves with how employment and unemployment are defined and measured by the U.S. government.

Measuring employment, unemployment, and the labor force

We begin by defining the **civilian labor force.**
It is the civilian (nonmilitary) population aged
16 and over that is either working (employed)
or actively seeking work (unemployed). From
this definition, the overall **national unemployment rate** can be defined. It is the percentage
of the civilian labor force that is unemployed:

National unemployment rate
$$= \frac{\text{Number of labor force members unemployed}}{\text{Number in labor force}}$$

The national unemployment rate is reported
monthly by the Bureau of Labor Statistics (BLS).
It is one of the most closely watched statistics
published by the U.S. government. And it is in
terms of this number that our national goal for
full employment is often defined. The official labor force and unemployment data for 1980 are
presented in Figure 5.1. As can be seen, the na-

"Stop worrying. Politicians always promise full employment — but
I've yet to see one of them deliver."

Reprinted by permission *The Wall Street Journal.*

tional unemployment rate averaged 7.1 percent
during 1980.

The unemployment rate as a measure of the problem of unemployment

It is important at the outset to emphasize what
the unemployment rate does and does not tell
us.

The discouraged-worker problem. Note the
people excluded from the definition of the civilian
labor force: those members of the working-age
population that are not working and not actively
seeking work. Included in this group are most
full-time college students, people who are retired,
people who for one reason or another choose
to remain in the home, people who drop out,
and so on. However, also included in this group
are those workers who have given up their search
for jobs because, as far as they are concerned,
there aren't any. In other words, **discouraged
workers** are not counted as part of the labor force.
Since they are not in the labor force, they are
not officially counted among the unemployed.
Because of the discouraged worker phenomenon,
the overall unemployment rate does not provide
us with an accurate representation of the unemployment problem. According to official BLS statistics, had discouraged workers been included

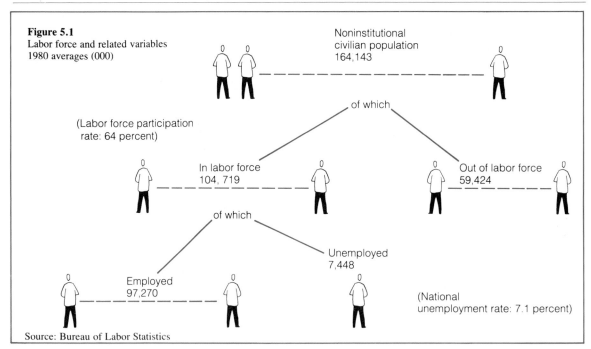

Figure 5.1
Labor force and related variables
1980 averages (000)

Noninstitutional
civilian population
164,143

of which

(Labor force participation
rate: 64 percent)

In labor force
104, 719

Out of labor force
59,424

of which

Unemployed
7,448

Employed
97,270

(National
unemployment rate: 7.1 percent)

Source: Bureau of Labor Statistics

(in both the labor force and unemployed numbers), the 1980 unemployment rate would have averaged about 8.1 percent, 1.0 percentage point higher than the official national unemployment rate. As you might expect, the number of reported discouraged workers increases when business conditions deteriorate.

The part-time unemployment problem. According to the official measure, no distinction is made between *part-time* and *full-time* employment. This would be of no consequence if all part-time employment represented the voluntary choices of those working part time. But not all part-time employment is voluntary. Indeed, when business activity slows down, many employees are put on reduced hours; in effect, those employees are laid off part-time. The official unemployment rate measure does not recognize part-time unemployment. To that extent, the unemployment rate may be a misleading indicator of the unemployment problem. Indeed, if instead of laying off workers, employers were to simply shorten the hours of work, the overall unemployment rate would be unaffected!

Of course, the BLS does publish separate data on the average number of hours worked per month. However, it is difficult to know how much of any change in hours is voluntary or involuntary.

The duration-of-unemployment problem. The **duration of unemployment** for those who experience unemployment is important to any assessment of our nation's unemployment problem. The official unemployment rate does not adequately capture this phenomenon. Indeed, to take an extreme example, if over the course of a year 6 million people experienced unemployment for the entire year while all others remained fully employed, that would be quite a different unemployment problem from one where 52 million people each experienced six weeks of unemployment. Either situation would yield the same average unemployment rate for the year,[1] but they are hardly the same.

Figure 5.2 presents data on the duration of unemployment for the period 1962–1980. What is striking is the relatively *short* time most unem-

[1] Why is there the same unemployment rate? Remember that we are measuring the *average* unemployment rate over the course of a year, a period of 52 weeks. Six million unemployed for all 52 weeks yields the same unemployment rate, on the average, as 52 million unemployed for six weeks each.

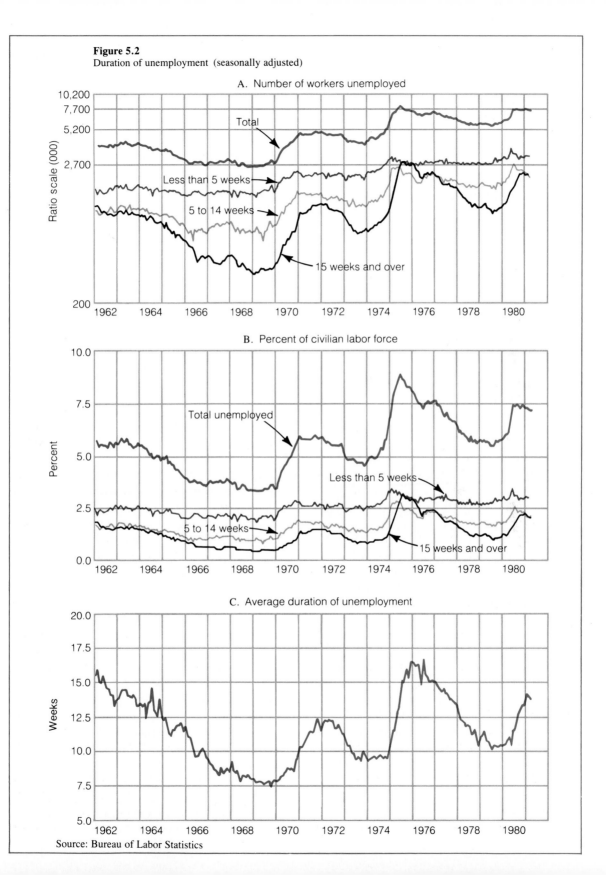

Figure 5.2
Duration of unemployment (seasonally adjusted)

A. Number of workers unemployed

B. Percent of civilian labor force

C. Average duration of unemployment

Source: Bureau of Labor Statistics

ployed people are actually without jobs. Even in periods of *relatively* high unemployment, such as 1975 and 1980, two out of every five unemployed people either found a job or left the labor force within five weeks.

Two important implications can be drawn from the data in Figure 5.2. First, *the total number of people who actually experience unemployment over the course of any year is considerably larger than the "average" number of unemployed people for that year.* To illustrate, the average number of people unemployed over the course of 1980 was 7.4 million. However, the pool of unemployed people in 1980 was not made up of the same people. It was constantly changing, with people entering and reentering the labor force, with some people moving into a state of unemployment while others were moving out, and so on. Although the number of people unemployed "averaged" 7.4 million, over 22 million people actually experienced some unemployment during 1980.

Second, *because the spells of unemployment are of such different lengths, the costs of unemployment are far from uniform.* While any disruption of income poses hardships, most families can make adjustments for short periods by postponing certain purchases and by drawing down savings. Moreover, most workers who lose their jobs are eligible to receive some form of **unemployment compensation,** which helps to cushion the blow. However, a protracted period of unemployment could prove very burdensome, especially after savings and unemployment compensation run out.

Who are the groups of people that experience the longest durations of unemployment? The data in Table 5.1 provide us with an answer in broad terms; although the data there are for one year only, 1980, the same general pattern is evident in earlier years. Note first that, for broad occupational groupings, blue-collar workers experienced, on the average, the longest duration of unemployment in 1980. Moreover, whereas 48 percent of unemployed service workers experienced less than five weeks of unemployment, only 38 percent of blue-collar workers had similarly short periods of unemployment.

Table 5.1
Duration of unemployment by type of worker—1980

Type of unemployed worker	Average (mean) duration	Percent unemployed	
		Less than 5 weeks	15 weeks or more
All unemployed workers	11.9	43.1	24.6
Occupational Status			
Blue-collar	13.2	38.0	29.1
White-collar	11.4	44.3	23.2
Service	10.8	48.3	20.8
Race			
White	11.5	43.7	23.8
Nonwhite	13.4	40.8	27.1
Sex and age			
Males, all ages	13.2	38.9	28.1
Females, all ages ......:...	10.3	48.3	20.1
Teenagers, both sexes, 16–19	8.0	53.7	13.8

Source: Bureau of Labor Statistics, *Employment and Earnings,* January 1981, pp. 176–177.

We note further than the average duration of unemployment was longer for nonwhites than for whites, and that a larger proportion of whites than nonwhites experienced less than five weeks of unemployment. Interestingly, adult women and teenagers experienced *shorter* durations of unemployment than adult males. Part of the explanation for this is attributable to what some call a generally "weaker labor force attachment" on the part of teenagers and adult women. That is, adult women and teenagers tend to enter and leave the labor force more frequently than adult males, and often their reasons for doing so are voluntary—that is, they return to school, take time off, have children, raise families, and so forth. Many of those who leave their jobs leave the labor force altogether and—by definition—are not counted as "unemployed" until they try to reenter. This is a factor that tends to bring down the average duration of unemployment for these groups as a whole.

The reason-for-unemployment problem. It is important to inquire into the reasons people are unemployed. Are people unemployed because they lost their jobs? In the technical jargon of the BLS, are they *job losers?* Or are they unemployed because they voluntarily quit? That is, are they *job leavers?* Or are they unemployed because they are *new entrants* to the labor force and are spending some time searching out their best prospects? Or are they *reentrants*—returning to the labor force after having completed more training and education or after having raised their children? It should be clear that the unemployment problem will differ dramatically depending on the reasons people are unemployed. Indeed, if the source of the increase in the unemployment rate is an increase in the number of people losing their jobs, the situation is very different from the increase being the consequence of new entrants to the labor force. According to BLS statistics, job losers constitute the largest proportion of those unemployed, followed by reentrants. The numbers of people unemployed

according to reason for unemployment for the period 1967–1980 are presented in Figure 5.3.

The problem of distribution of unemployment by occupation, race, sex, and age. The overall national unemployment rate hides from view the rather considerable differences in unemployment rates experienced by different groups of people. Figures 5.4 through 5.6 provide some summary information on the distribution of unemployment by occupational status, race, age, and sex for the period 1962–1980.

Figure 5.4 shows quite clearly that, on the average, blue-collar workers have borne a disproportionate share of unemployment compared with white-collar workers. Moreover, when the overall unemployment rate *increases,* such as occurred in 1975 and 1980, the blue-collar unemployment rate tends to rise even further. Swings in blue-collar unemployment rates tend to be wider than swings in the overall national unemployment rate.

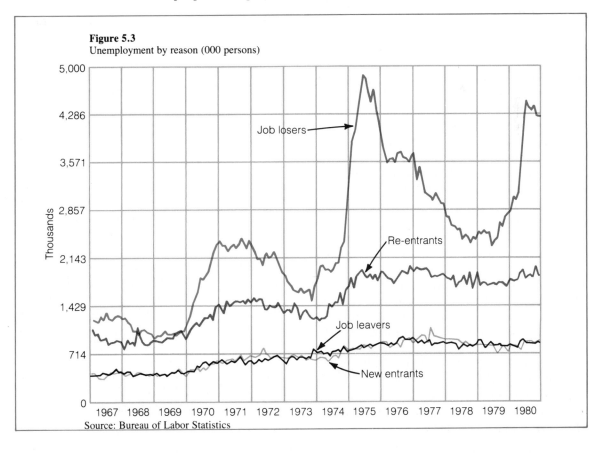

Figure 5.3
Unemployment by reason (000 persons)

Source: Bureau of Labor Statistics

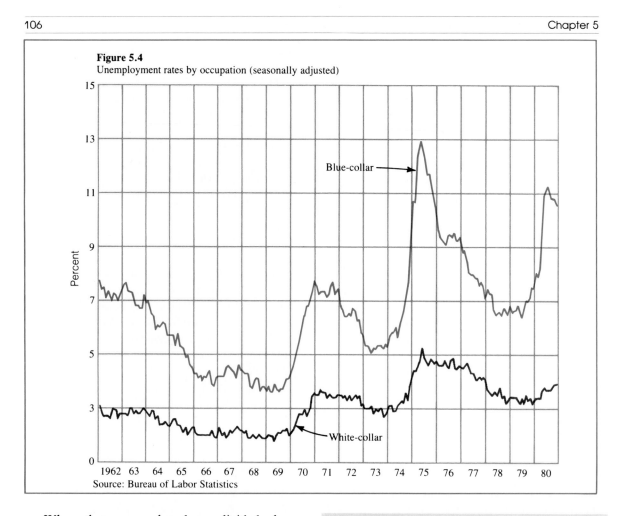

Figure 5.4
Unemployment rates by occupation (seasonally adjusted)

Source: Bureau of Labor Statistics

When those unemployed are divided along race lines, as is done in Figure 5.5, it is clear that nonwhites have suffered much higher rates of unemployment than whites. Not only has the nonwhite unemployment rate averaged about twice the white unemployment rate, but, during recessions when the overall unemployment rate is rising, the nonwhite unemployment rate tends to increase disproportionately.

Figure 5.6 highlights the large difference between teenage and adult unemployment experiences and the systematic differences between male and female unemployment rates.

Summing up. The point of this entire discussion can be put as follows: The national official unemployment rate is but one of many statistical measures we should use in the evaluation of our unemployment problem. It is a summary measure. Like most summary measures, it provides us with only limited information; it does not tell us the whole story. Despite the attention that this single statistic is accorded, it is important to be aware of its limitations. It is not an unambiguous indicator of how fully we employ our nation's labor resources. And it masks the marked differences in the burden of unemployment borne by various groups in our society.

Kinds of unemployment

While the above discussion is useful to our study of the unemployment problem in the

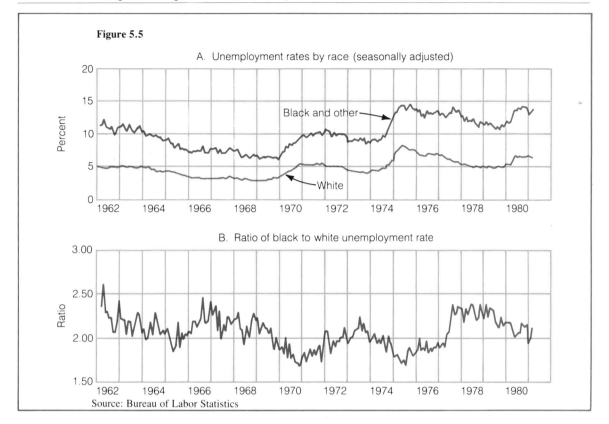

Figure 5.5

A. Unemployment rates by race (seasonally adjusted)

B. Ratio of black to white unemployment rate

Source: Bureau of Labor Statistics

United States, it is not of much help in answering the question, What level of unemployment constitutes full employment? To better enable us to answer this question, economists traditionally have found it worthwhile to focus attention not so much on who the unemployed are, but on the social significance of various *kinds* of unemployment.

Unemployment clearly affects different people in different ways. For some it is a transitional state through which they pass as they move from one job to another or as they enter or reenter the labor force. Others find unemployment to be a chronic problem. For one reason or another, they experience continuous difficulty in nailing down jobs and then have difficulty holding on to them.

Frictional unemployment. Unemployment viewed as a temporary, transitional state of affairs is called **frictional unemployment.** It arises because of certain "frictions" in the economy, the most important friction being the absence of complete information on the part of buyers or sellers of labor services.

There are many examples of frictional unemployment. People who first enter or reenter the labor force will not necessarily take the first job offer that comes along. They will often spend time looking around, acquiring information about various job prospects, before ultimately deciding. Moreover, employers will not necessarily hire the first job candidates they interview. They too will often search for a while before deciding on the job candidates they would like to make offers to. Presumably, if both buyers and sellers had perfect information—that is, if employees had all the information they needed about all jobs and employers, and if employers knew all they needed to know about job candidates—these frictions would disappear. Job vacancies and job candidates would be matched very quickly; the transitional state of unemploy-

Figure 5.6
Unemployment rates by sex and age
(seasonally adjusted)

Source: Bureau of Labor Statistics

ment would be very short or nonexistent. However, information is not perfect and the transitional period of unemployment is not zero. Therefore, for some period, many entrants and reentrants will experience temporary spells of unemployment.

Consider another important source of frictional unemployment. In an economy as complex as ours, with many labor markets, in which production is constantly changing in response to shifting demands, technological advances, and new products, there will always be workers moving from one job to another. Some people are able to make these job transitions without experiencing unemployment in the interim. Some people, for example, line up new jobs before quitting their existing jobs or before being laid off. Many other people, however, experience some joblessness in transit. They may be suddenly and unexpectedly displaced, for example, as conditions

change. Or they may simply find that it is more efficient to quit existing jobs to devote full time to locate jobs more suitable to their training, skills, and liking.

How long will this transitional period of unemployment be? There are no "normal" periods. The duration of unemployment will depend on several factors: Are there other appropriate job vacancies in the same geographical area, or is it necessary to relocate? Will some additional training be required to raise skill levels to meet the new job requirements? How much time are people willing and able to take off to search? We could go on and on, but the point that needs emphasis is this: For the frictionally unemployed, unemployment is a transitional state of relatively short duration.

Structural unemployment While many frictions in our economic system are the source of short, transitional spells of unemployment, some frictions are the source of chronic unemployment problems. These frictions might best be described as *structural* in nature; the unemployment they give rise to is, accordingly, termed **structural unemployment.**

More specifically, structural unemployment arises because of the presence of fundamental mismatches of jobs and job candidates. The qualifications of those unemployed do not match the requirements of the jobs that are vacant. To a certain extent, frictional unemployment was the result of mismatches as well. The difference in the case of structural unemployment is that the mismatches are very fundamental (rather than, for example, informational). This gives rise to extended (and perhaps permanent) spells of unemployment.

Perhaps the most important source of structural unemployment is the absence of education and training on the part of large numbers of people. A lot of youth unemployment can be so characterized. However, education and training are not the only causes. Many allege that discrimination on the basis of sex, race, age, weight, and so forth are also contributing factors. Some even argue that the minimum wage is a source of structural unemployment: the excess supply of workers at the minimum wage creates unemployment attributable to a structural characteristic of the economy (namely, the minimum wage). Finally, just as too little education and training can cause structural unemployment, the "wrong kind" of training and education can also be a cause as well. Too many engineers or too many physicists have, at times, been evident in certain labor markets.

In any event, the point that needs emphasis regarding structural unemployment is that the mismatches between jobs and job candidates will, under the best of circumstances, take a long time to remedy. In some cases they will never be remedied. Unlike the frictionally unemployed, there are no self-correcting or "quick-fix" solutions.

Cyclical unemployment. Frictional and structural unemployment can exist even if there is no overall shortage of jobs. Indeed, the way we defined those concepts, it is clear that jobs are available. It will, however, take time to fill

them from the ranks of the unemployed—a short time in the case of the frictionally unemployed, and a much longer time in the case of the structurally unemployed.

In contrast, **cyclical unemployment** occurs when there is a general shortage of jobs. This shortage arises because the economy produces at less than its potential. Typically such shortages are associated with the *recession* phase of the business cycle, hence the term *cyclical* unemployment. The causes of cyclical unemployment will be discussed at length later in this book. Suffice it to say for now that extraordinary events such as very sharp increases in OPEC prices or policy actions undertaken by the government can be contributing causes.

Defining "full employment." What relevance does this discussion of the various kinds of unemployment have to do with the definition of full employment? Actually, it is very relevant. It makes clear why zero unemployment is neither viable nor necessarily desirable.

First, regarding frictional unemployment, zero unemployment is not viable because frictions of the sort that give rise to this kind of unemployment are part and parcel of the dynamic, evolving economic system we live in. Zero unemployment is not necessarily desirable because the dynamic changes that give rise to these labor market frictions are the stuff of which rapid growth and rising living standards are made. If we want rapid growth and rising living standards, we want entrants and reentrants to the labor force to look for jobs where they will be the most productive. We want resources to move out of declining and into expanding industries. We want the lure of profits to spur rapid technological advance and greater efficiency. Of course, acceptance of some positive amount of frictional unemployment should not be construed as a rejection of policies designed to reduce it (such as improving the flow of information in job markets about both job applicants and job vacancies). It simply should be a recognition of the fact that we would probably never eliminate it totally. To try to do so would be tantamount to trying to throw away the advantages that accrue as a result of dynamic change. Moreover, because frictional unemployment is temporary and transitional, it does not represent a major social or economic problem. Indeed, zero frictional unemployment could represent a bigger problem because of what it would imply—a rigid and unchanging society.

Second, regarding structural unemployment, a different set of difficult issues is raised. The long spells of joblessness experienced by the structurally unemployed impose severe hardships on certain people and therefore constitute a social evil. The elimination of structural unemployment, however, requires that policies be specifically tailored to meet the needs of the structurally unemployed—policies that frequently take a long time to have the desired effects. Worker education, training, and retraining programs do not perform miracles overnight.

It is on the basis of considerations such as these that policymakers have attempted to define *full employment:*

1. A first requirement is that cyclical unemployment be zero. A fully employed economy cannot be characterized by a *general* shortage of jobs.
2. Frictional unemployment is tolerable, though efforts to reduce the duration of unemployment of the frictionally unemployed should be beefed up.
3. In view of the long time required to solve the structural unemployment problem, little can be done to reduce the number of structurally unemployed *in the short run*. Any unemployment targets set for the short run, therefore, should be interim targets only.

Defining full employment indirectly. One of the real problems we encounter in trying to define *full employment* using this approach is that we have no precise knowledge of the magnitudes of frictional and structural unemployment. These kinds of unemployment are analytical concepts; people who are unemployed do not designate themselves as either frictionally or structurally unemployed. (They have probably never heard of the concepts!) Accordingly, it is not possible to determine via direct methods what overall

level of (frictional plus structural) unemployment is consistent with zero cyclical unemployment.

Accordingly, policymakers have attempted to figure out using *indirect methods* what the overall unemployment rate would have to be with zero cyclical unemployment. Crudely, the approach can be described as follows. If cyclical unemployment were zero, the economy would be operating at (or very close to) its potential. Some unemployment would exist at the economy's potential—namely, the amount of frictional and structural unemployment. An unemployment rate *below* the frictional plus structural amount would imply that the economy was operating beyond its potential, beyond its "normal" capacity to produce. Such an outcome would be reflected ultimately in upward pressure on the general level of prices. At higher unemployment rates, on the other hand, the opposite would be true. By producing below our potential, we could expect some downward pressure on the general level of prices. Thus one indirect method used to discover the "full-employment-unemployment rate" was to find that particular overall unemployment rate that was consistent with a stable general price level.

The Kennedy Administration in 1962 was the first to use this indirect approach to establish its interim full employment target of 4.0 percent unemployment. In setting this goal, Kennedy's Council of Economic Advisers stressed the interim nature of the target, noting that policies designed to reduce frictional and structural unemployment would eventually justify an adjustment of the interim target to lower and lower rates.

Because of the difficulties encountered in reaching 4.0 percent unemployment, the word *interim* was frequently ignored in many subsequent policy discussions. More important, as the unemployment rate approached 4.0 percent, there was a noticeable increase in the general level of prices, an outcome that caused policymakers to question whether 4.0 percent was "high enough." Indeed, in the early days of the Ford Administration, it was hinted that 4.9 percent unemployment might be a more appropriate interim target. Since that time, other administrations have hinted that even 4.9 percent might be too low; it is not uncommon to hear numbers like 6.0 or 6.5 percent being discussed today, though, given the political sensitivity of the issue, no administration would dare declare rates of this magnitude even as interim targets. Interestingly, in an effort to avoid the issue of numerically specifying an unemployment goal, our nation's leaders often speak in terms of the goal of **high employment,** rather than full employment. Although the two concepts presumably mean the same thing, high employment is a less specific notion.

This background helps us to understand some of the controversy that continues to surround the Humphrey-Hawkins Full Employment and Balanced Growth Act of 1978. In that act, the Congress reaffirmed a 4.0 percent unemployment rate as an interim target. But it was not an immediate interim target; the target was to be achieved in 1983—a full five years after the enactment of the legislation. The hope was that the country by then would have made considerable process in reducing structural unemployment. Progress was not rapid enough and so, just before leaving office, President Carter in 1980 pushed back the target date to 1985. What the Reagan Administration intends in this regard is unknown at the time of this writing.

The natural rate of unemployment

In an effort to come to a clearer understanding of these many issues, we will now develop a concept known as the **natural rate of unemployment.** The natural rate is the unemployment rate toward which the economy is alleged to gravitate automatically. In the minds of many economists, the natural rate is the only viable "full-employment–unemployment rate" candidate.

Two considerations are of utmost importance to an understanding of the natural rate concept. First, although it is often convenient to talk about the U.S. labor market as though it were just one huge market, in fact there are literally thousands of different labor markets in the United States. The sources of the differences in these markets are not difficult to discover. Some markets are

different because they are geographically separated from one another (the market for bricklayers in New York City being geographically separate and therefore different from the market for bricklayers in Seattle); other markets are different because of skill differences among workers and because of differences in the attractiveness of various kinds of jobs.

The second important consideration is the idea that wages do not adjust quickly in response to the emergence of excess demands or excess supplies. If in the labor market for electricians in Los Angeles an excess demand emerges, wages for electricians will go up in Los Angeles, but not quickly. As a consequence of this slow adjustment of wages, the excess demand will persist for some time. Similarly, if an excess supply of bricklayers develops in Washington, D.C., bricklayer wages in Washington, D.C. will fall, but not quickly. Because of this slow adjustment of wages, the excess supply will persist for some time.

What is the reason for the sluggish adjustment of wages? In part it is attributable to the existence of labor contracts that spell out in detail the wage scales for employees. Many of these contracts run for up to three years, and the terms of the contracts are not generally adjustable in the face of excess demands or supplies. In addition, many workers who do not operate under formal labor contracts often operate under "implicit" wage contracts. For example, it is frequently *understood* that changes in workers' wages will occur only once a year. Finally, it takes time for both employees and employers to come to realize what is going on in their markets and how this affects both what employees will try to get and what employers will be willing to offer.

The natural rate of unemployment illustrated. Figure 5.7 illustrates the implications of these two ideas. For simplicity, we are assuming that there are only two different labor markets; we call them labor market A and labor market B. Suppose that what makes them different is their geographical separation from one another.

We show in Figure 5.7 the demand and supply curves for labor in each of the two markets.

Figure 5.7
Multiple labor markets and the natural rate of unemployment

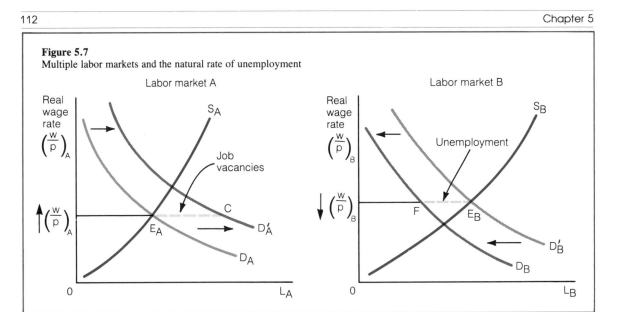

Drawing on our study of markets in Chapter 3, equilibrium will occur in each market at the point of intersection of the respective demand and supply curves.

Before proceeding with the analysis here, two points need to be emphasized. First, you will note that on the vertical axis of each graph we are measuring the **real wage**—the money wage (w) the employee receives (or the employer pays) divided by the general price level (p). This is as it should be. From the point of view of the suppliers of labor services, what is important is *not* the money wage they receive, but what that money wage will buy. If money wages rise by less than inflation, each week's wages will buy fewer goods and services than the week before. To be sure that this is understood, ask yourself the following question: If workers were willing to work 35 hours a week at a wage of $10 per hour before, how many hours per week would they be willing to work at $10 per hour if the price the goods and services they buy rose by 20 percent? Presumably, they would work less; that's what the upward-sloping supply curve implies.

From the point of view of employers, what matters is not the money wage they pay, but the money wage compared to the prices at which they can sell their goods and services in the mar-

ketplace. What matters to employers is their **real wage costs**—the wages they pay divided by the prices for their products.

The fact that the vertical axis measures the *real wage rate* means we must be careful when we talk about changing wages. For example, if money wages were to increase by 10 percent, and if the general price level also increased by 10 percent, the real wage would remain unaltered. Falling real wages do not necessarily imply falling *money* wages; money wages rising at a less rapid pace than the general price level implies a falling real wage.

The second point that needs emphasis is this: Any point on the supply curve of labor in each labor market represents a position of full employment in that labor market. To see this, ask yourself what the supply curve means: it tells us how much labor is willingly offered at each real wage rate. If employers are willing to hire the number of workers offering their services at any given real wage, there can be no unemployment in that market.

Now let us turn to the task at hand. Assume, to begin with, that we have equilibrium in both labor markets, given by points E_A *and* E_B respectively in Figure 5.7. Suppose, for one reason or another, these equilibrium positions are disturbed by shifts in the demand for labor in each of these markets. Specifically, assume that the demand for labor in market A increases from D_A to D'_A and that the demand for labor in market B decreases from D_B to D'_B. The results? There will now emerge at the initial real wage in market A, $(w/p)_A$, an excess demand for labor. As a consequence, the real wage for labor in A will tend to go up as the arrow indicates. However, because the adjustment of the real wage does not occur quickly, the excess demand for labor in market A will persist for some time. Also note that the excess demand for labor in market A will take the form of *job vacancies*. Employers are willing at the real wage, $(w/p)_A$, to hire the quantity of labor services represented by point C; the amount offered, however, is given by point E_A; the difference, E_AC, represents the number of unfilled positions—the number of vacant job openings—in market A.

The reverse of these events occurs in market B. The reduced demand for labor in market B creates an excess supply of labor at the real wage, $(w/p)_B$; there will be a tendency for the real wage in market B to fall, but because the real wage change will be slow, the excess supply will persist for some time. Also note that the excess supply of labor in market B takes the form of *unemployed labor resources*. The quantity of labor services willingly offered at $(w/p)_B$ exceeds the demand for labor at that real wage; that excess supply results in FE_B of *unemployment* in market B.

Vacancies and unemployment simultaneously. Figure 5.7 is very useful in pointing out why the existence of unemployment and vacancies simultaneously is not so strange. That is, it is sometimes argued that those people who are unemployed must not want to work because if they looked around they would see that there are lots of job vacancies. It is undoubtedly true that there are people who do not want to work. But that alone can hardly explain the existence of unemployed labor resources or the simultaneous existence of unemployment and job vacancies. Recall the reasons emphasis was given to there being many different labor markets—geographical separation, skill differences, and so on. Yes, there

may be job vacancies, but the skills of those unemployed may not match the job requirements of vacant positions. Geographically, job vacancies may be present in markets that are very distant from where the unemployed workers are; and time is required for these adjustments to take place.

Persistence of vacancies and unemployment in a dynamic world. If nothing else happened in labor markets A and B, equilibrium would ultimately be restored through real wage adjustments or through resource shifts. Ultimately, therefore, job vacancies in market A and unemployment in market B would cease to exist. However, in a dynamically changing economy such as the United States, an economy characterized by not two but many thousands of labor markets, the movement toward equilibrium in any group of labor markets could be nullified by yet further shifts of demand and supply. Or the movement toward equilibrium in one group of markets could be occurring simultaneous with demand and supply shifts in *other* labor markets. Indeed, these changes take place continuously, with the result that unemployed labor resources always exist along with job vacancies. The important point to note, however, is that the location of unemployment and vacancies often changes continuously as well.

The natural rate of unemployment defined. We are now in a position to define the *natural rate of unemployment. Despite the dynamic, ever-changing character of the economy, the overall unemployment rate has a tendency to gravitate toward that value—the natural rate—where the real wage for the economy as a whole remains fixed.* Real wages in individual labor markets could be rising (because of excess demand pressures) or falling (because of excess supply pressures). But, for the economy as a whole, these real wage changes would offset one another at the natural rate.

What is the significance of a constant overall real wage? It is significant for the following reason: If there were just one large labor market in the United States, a *changing* real wage would be taken as evidence of disequilibrium; a constant real wage would be taken as evidence of equilibrium. This notion is carried over and applied to a situation in which there are *many* labor markets. Overall equilibrium will prevail only when the real wage overall remains constant.

This might seem like a strange notion of equilibrium, and indeed it is. Because the economy is ever changing, no single labor market need be in equilibrium but, overall, the excess demands and the excess supplies together produce an equilibrium characterized by the absence of a changing real wage.

Why does the economy have a tendency to gravitate toward the natural rate? We are not ready now to answer this question. It is, however, a subject that will occupy much of our attention in Chapter 13.

Note one very important implication of the condition that the real wage is constant: The overall real wage can be constant if the general price level rises at 5 percent, 10 percent, 15 percent or any other rate *as long as* the money wages workers receive overall advance at the *same* rate. A constant real wage is also consistent with a constant (stable) price level as long as the money wage is also constant. And finally, a constant real wage is consistent with a *declining* price level *as long as* money wages decline at the *same* rate.

Put differently, the natural rate of unemployment does not depend on how rapidly the price level changes. A rapidly changing price level or a stable price level are all consistent with the *same* natural rate of unemployment. The only requirement is that money wages overall change at the same rate as the price level.

Let us carry the analogy with a single market a bit further. If there were just one large labor market in the United States, a *rising* real wage would suggest the presence of excess demand. In the same manner, under the natural rate concept, a rising real wage overall would be taken as evidence of excess demand in the aggregate. The upward real wage pressures in excess-demand labor markets outweigh the downward real wage pressures in excess-supply labor markets. Conversely, a declining real wage overall would

suggest the presence of excess supply in the aggregate.

The natural rate: An amendment. Actually, we need to amend the above discussion in one technical respect. The natural rate should be defined as that level of unemployment where the real wage *adjusted for productivity change* remains constant. Let us illustrate this point.

Suppose workers are paid $10 per hour. Suppose further that, on average, output per hour per worker—**average labor productivity**—is 10 units. What is the labor cost per unit of output—the **unit labor cost?** As you can see, unit labor cost comes to $1 (i.e., $10 per hour divided by 10 units per hour). Now let workers' wages rise to $11. If average labor productivity also rises from 10 to 11 units, then what happens to unit labor costs? They remain at $1. Because unit labor costs have not increased—that is, because the labor costs for each unit produced have not increased—there are no cost increases producers feel compelled to try to pass on. Hence, prices will remain unchanged. However, although prices did not increase, real wages did. But real wages adjusted for the productivity increase—that is, unit labor costs—did not rise. And it is unit labor costs that are important as far as the natural rate is concerned.

Let us now restate the natural rate concept. If real wages overall grow at the same rate as average labor productivity (so that real wages adjusted for productivity remain constant), the associated level of employment will be the natural rate. If real wages grow more rapidly than average labor productivity, this is evidence of excess demand in the aggregate. And if real wages grow less rapidly than average labor productivity, this is evidence of excess supply in the aggregate.

Is the natural rate some fixed rate of unemployment? The answer to this question is, Not necessarily. The "natural rate" of unemployment depends on the distribution of excess demand and excess supply labor markets. One could imagine finding a certain distribution that would produce a constant real wage (adjusted for productivity) and an associated natural rate of unemployment. However, the distribution of excess demand and excess supply markets is subject to change. And the speed with which real wages adjust in different labor markets is not likely to be the same as in the original distribution. Accordingly, there is no necessary reason the natural rate should be some fixed constant number. This, of course, complicates matters for policymakers since there is no single rate toward which policy should necessarily be aimed if they are trying to hasten the move of the economy toward the natural rate. At one time, the "appropriate" rate could be 5 percent; at another time it could be closer to 7 percent. However, while there is no single number for the natural rate, the results of most research efforts suggest that it is in the neighborhood of 6.0 to 7.0 percent in today's economy (1981).

What general characteristics are present in labor markets at rates of unemployment in the neighborhood of 6.0 to 7.0 percent? At overall rates of unemployment in that neighborhood, there is generally a lot of unemployment in *unskilled* labor markets (where real wages are falling), but little unemployment in *skilled* markets (where real wages are rising somewhat). If policy actions were undertaken that had the effect of lowering the unemployment rates in *both* types of markets, real wages (adjusted for productivity change) would tend to increase overall.

If the 6.0 to 7.0 percent range is correct, does this not pose serious problems for the realization of the 4.0 percent unemployment target mandated by the Humphrey-Hawkins Act? Yes. Indeed, many argue that the 4.0 percent target is unrealistically low and can never be reached. Others argue that it might be possible to reach the 4.0 percent rate, but not by undertaking policies that have the effect of lowering unemployment rates in *all* markets. It would have to be achieved by policies that are specifically tailored to meet the needs of those in unskilled labor markets who are for the most part structurally unemployed. More will be said on this in Chapters 13 and 14.

Three final notes on the natural rate. First, in view of the ever changing distribution of excess demands and excess supplies in labor markets, and the variable speeds of real wage changes in those markets, it is perhaps best to think of the natural rate not as a single, easily calculable number but as encompassing a *range* of values. The 6.0 to 7.0 percent range embraces the values currently found in most economic research. However, there is no universal agreement on this matter. Some economists think the natural rate is lower; others think it is higher.

Second, it is important to distinguish between the natural rate of unemployment and the goal of full employment. At times they may be the same. For example, the reasoning used by the Kennedy Administration in 1962 in establishing the 4.0 percent interim target suggests that there was then no conflict between the natural rate (although, at that time they did not call it the natural rate) and the goal of full employment. The Kennedy Administration at that time set its full employment target at a rate believed to be consistent with a stable price level. Kennedy's Council of Economic Advisers were very clear that a stable price level would prevail only if money wages advanced at the same rate as average labor productivity. In other words, in setting its full employment goal, the Kennedy Administration implicitly chose that rate where real wages adjusted for productivity change were constant—that is, the natural rate.

The 4.0 percent interim goal in the Humphrey-Hawkins Act, however, would appear to be far below the natural rate. The framers of the Humphrey-Hawkins Act were aware of this, which is one reason they initially put off the date for the realization of the goal until five years *after* the act became law. In view of our discussion earlier of the relationship between skilled and unskilled labor markets at the natural rate, the idea behind the Humphrey-Hawkins Act was that, if the supply of *skilled* workers could be increased enough (through the education and training of the unskilled), it might be possible to eliminate the upward pressure on *skilled* real wages that is evident when the unemployment rate overall is in the 6.0 to 7.0 percent range. If that could be accomplished, then it might be possible to lower the natural rate to the Humphrey-Hawkins target. Of course, achieving the requisite increase in the supply of skilled workers takes time, which is why the target was initially set at 1983 and why President Carter in 1980 set it back to 1985. Unless significant progress is made in the near future, the date for the realization of the Humphrey-Hawkins target is likely to be pushed back again.

There is an important conclusion from all of this. The natural rate is a very useful concept because it forces us to focus on the structure of labor markets as the means of accomplishing some rate of unemployment different from the current natural rate. Indeed, if we want to avoid excess demand in the aggregate (and the resultant increases in the price level that such a situation would entail), and an unemployment rate *below* the current natural rate, we must change the structure of labor markets in appropriate ways (such as increasing the supply of skilled workers). *Put differently, if we want to accomplish an unemployment rate below the current natural rate, we are going to have to bring about the structural changes required to lower the natural rate to the targeted rate.*

Third, if President Kennedy's advisers were correct that the natural rate of unemployment in 1962 was around 4.0 percent, and if the consensus view is that the natural rate is in the 6.0 to 7.0 percent range today, there has been a very sharp increase in the natural rate of unemployment over the course of the past two decades. The question is, What accounts for this 2 to 3 percentage point increase?

Actually, we do not have a complete understanding of this phenomenon. One explanation is that the natural rate has increased as a consequence of changes in the demographic composition of the labor force. Specifically, teenagers and adult women now constitute a much larger percentage of the labor force than they did in the early 1960s. The evidence for this is found in the increasing labor force participation rates of teenagers and women and in the decline in the labor force participation rate of adult males.

The **labor force participation rate** is defined as the proportion of the working age population that is either working or actively seeking work; it is given by the ratio of the labor force to the working age population. The labor force participation rate for any *subgroup* of the population is given by the number of labor force members in that subgroup divided by the number in that group of working age.

As is clear from Figure 5.8, the labor force participation rate of adult females has increased from around 38 percent in 1962 to around 52 percent in 1981. Teenagers have increased their participation rate by about 10 percentage points over the same period. The labor force participation rate of adult males, on the other hand, has declined somewhat.

Now, so the argument goes, since teenagers and adult women, on the average, have weaker labor force attachments than adult males—reflected in their relatively high rates of entry and exit from the labor force, which in part accounts for their higher rates of unemployment—the natural rate occurs at a higher level of unemployment today than in the early 1960s. The reason? Because of the increased labor force participation rates of adult women and teenagers, we now have a *relatively* larger number of less skilled, less experienced and, in the case of teenagers, less educated people in the labor force. Therefore, the upward real wage pressures emanating from skilled labor markets occurs at a higher overall unemployment rate today than in the early 1960s when the teenage and adult women participation rates were lower.

According to the Council of Economic Advisers in 1979, these changes in the demographic composition of the labor force explain only a small part of the increase in the natural rate. These demographic changes have added only about one half of 1 percentage point to the natural rate.

What accounts for the additional 1½ to 2½ percentage point increase in the natural rate? We do not yet have a good understanding of this. However, one apparently very important contributing factor has been the slowdown in the

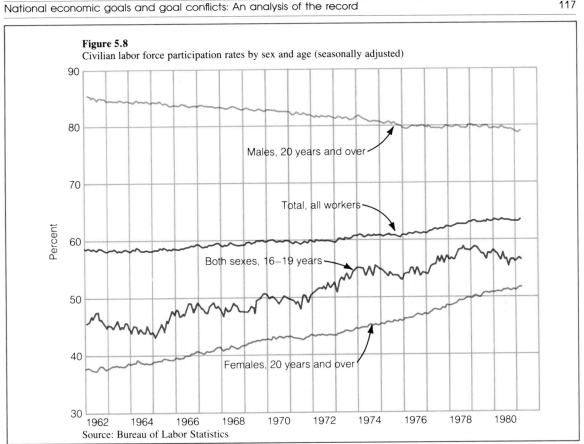

Figure 5.8
Civilian labor force participation rates by sex and age (seasonally adjusted)

Males, 20 years and over

Total, all workers

Both sexes, 16–19 years

Females, 20 years and over

Percent

Source: Bureau of Labor Statistics

growth of the stock of capital goods during the late 1960s and the 1970s. This factor will be examined closely in Chapter 14.

THE GOAL OF PRICE STABILITY

Another widely acknowledged national economic goal is **price stability**—or, as it is sometimes stated, "reasonable" price stability. What is meant by this goal? And why is it deemed so important? These and other questions form the basis of our discussion here.

In an economy as diverse and complex as the U.S. economic system, there are literally millions of different prices. One possible definition of *price stability* would be the absence of any change in any price. However, in an economy that relies heavily on private markets to allocate scarce re-sources among alternative uses, that kind of price stability would not be desirable. Put simply, in a dynamic, ever-changing economic system such as ours, changing prices—in particular, changing *relative* prices—are essential to "properly" direct the flow of resources to uses that best satisfy people's wants.

Generally speaking, most people mean *the absence of increases in prices on average* when they refer to price stability. Yes, there can be considerable movement up and down in the prices of individual goods and services. But, on the average, price stability demands that price increases be canceled out by price reductions.

Measuring price stability and inflation

The first problem we encounter is that of trying to define what is meant by the "average of prices" or the "average price level." First, not all prices are of equal importance. Some goods and services take big chunks of our income; others take very little. Therefore, we need to weight the various price changes by the importance of each item in our budgets. If housing takes 20 percent of our incomes, housing prices should be given a 20 percent weight; if food takes 15 percent, the price of food should be given a weight of 15 percent; and so forth. However, as prices change—especially as *relative* prices change—the weights are likely to change as well. Suppose, for example, that you are currently spending 3 percent of your income on beef; beef prices would get a weight of 3 percent. Now let beef prices increase sharply. In response, you might curtail your expenditures on beef, substituting in favor of pork or chicken. After the adjustment, you could end up spending only 1 percent of your income on beef. Now, in evaluating the change in prices, should you use the initial 3 percent weight or the 1 percent weight? There is no definitive answer to this question. Some argue that the initial 3 percent weight should be used since 3 percent of the budget is really what the consumer would have liked to have spent on beef before being forced to cut back. Others argue that the use of the fixed 3 percent weight makes no sense. If beef prices had initially been much lower, people probably would have spent *more* than 3 percent on beef. Different (relative) prices will affect how much people are willing and able to spend; at the new set of prices, they are willing and able to spend only 1 percent of their income on beef. Accordingly, the 1 percent weight should be used.

Because of these different points of view, the government publishes price level statistics using both fixed weights and variable weights. One of the most widely watched fixed weight statistics is the **consumer price index (CPI).** This statistic measures the changes in prices of a "basket" of consumer goods. (The basket includes most of the important goods and services consumers buy.) A less well-known statistic that also purports to measure the change in consumer prices is the **personal consumption expenditure deflator.** This statistic is a variable weight measure.

The difference between the consumer price index and the personal consumption expenditure deflator is given in Figure 5.9. As is clear, they tend to be fairly close to one another over long stretches of time. But during shorter intervals there are marked differences between the two. The major factor responsible for these differences is the fact that one is a fixed-weight index (the CPI), while the other is a variable-weight measure (the personal consumption expenditure deflator). Thus, if large relative price changes occur, the fixed-weight index will attach more importance to those items whose prices have increased the most. The variable-weight index, because it reflects people's adjustments to changes in prices, will attach a smaller weight. There is also another important reason: The basket of goods used in the CPI is not the same as in the personal consumption expenditure deflator, the most important difference being the much greater influence of housing- and mortgage-related expenditures in the CPI.

There are a great many other measures of inflation. Each is designed for a particular purpose and the coverage of goods differs among them. One carefully watched measure is the **producer price index for finished goods.** This is a fixed-weight index designed to measure the change in prices of finished goods at the wholesale level. It is watched carefully because many people believe that increases in wholesale prices will ultimately show up in the form of increases in retail prices; in other words, an increase in this index is often used by some to try to forecast future increases in the CPI.

The most general measure of inflation, the one that covers *all* goods and services, is the **gross national product implicit price deflator.** This is a variable-weight measure. In addition, there are price indexes for housing, for business investment, for government purchases of goods and services, for exports and imports, and so on; some are fixed weight indexes, others are not.

The point that needs emphasis is this: There is no single universally accepted measure of inflation. Economists generally prefer the gross national product implicit price deflator as the best overall measure of inflation, but it is not a univer-

Figure 5.9

Comparison of the consumer price index (CPI) and the personal consumption expenditure (PCE) deflator 1960-1981 (quarterly data; percent change from previous period, seasonally adjusted at an annual rate)

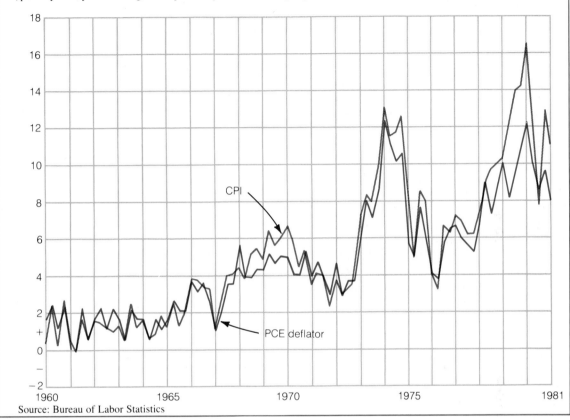

Source: Bureau of Labor Statistics

sally accepted measure. There are sharp disagreements among economists about whether the CPI or the personal consumption expenditure deflator is the best measure of inflation in consumer goods. Some people take the existing measures of inflation and adjust them to calculate new indexes that they believe give a more accurate picture. Thus, some people take the CPI index and remove energy prices (among other things) on grounds that sharp increases in energy prices will not be sustained in the future; inclusion of energy prices misrepresents the trend of inflation. Others disagree. And, as will be explained in Chapter 13, some economists believe that the best measure of inflation is given by the "core" rate—the rate determined primarily by the pace of increases in unit labor costs.

Defining inflation

We now come to the more difficult question, that of defining what we mean by **inflation.** Actually, there are many possible definitions. One could define it broadly—including the prices of a great many goods and services—or narrowly—including only a few goods. We could talk in terms of inflation in consumer goods prices, inflation in auto prices, and so on. One could say that inflation occurs any time the relevant price index registers an increase. Or one could reserve use of the term for *sustained* increases only.

However, when policymakers talk about the U.S. inflation problem, they usually have in mind broadly based, sustained price increases. For our purposes, we will define *inflation* as *a sustained and broadly based increase in the general price level.* There are two key terms in this definition: *sustained* and *broadly based.*

By a *sustained* increase we mean that prices rise fairly consistently over some significant stretch of time. That is, the price indexes generally go up month by month, not necessarily every month, or by the same amount each month, but consistently enough so that increases are the rule rather than the exception. Thus, the term *inflation* as it is normally used does not characterize a situation in which a price index registers a one-shot increase, even if the increase is sizable.

The second requirement is that price increases be *broadly based.* Normally the price indexes commonly used in economic analysis will not show significant, sustained increases unless most prices are rising; prices of a few specific goods and services, for the most part, do not have sufficient weight to move the overall index by themselves. This is not to say that some items, such as food, energy, and costs of home ownership, may not dominate price movements at times, but simply to underscore the meaning of inflation as a phenomenon of widespread price increases.

In this context, it is important to note that prices of various goods and services can change *relative to each other* in an environment that would not necessarily be defined as inflationary. This is an important distinction. As noted earlier, changes in relative prices are necessary if resources are to be directed to their most profitable uses; relative price changes per se, therefore, are desirable. Generalized inflation, on the other hand (which may arise from or be aggravated by sharp or prolonged relative price changes, among other things), is not critical to the functioning of our economic system. Indeed, inflation usually is regarded as undesirable because of the adverse effects it can have on income distribution and on output and employment as well.

Acceptance of this definition of inflation, however, does not imply acceptance of any particular measure of inflation. The gross national product implicit price deflator is a more broadly based index than the consumer price index. But both

can legitimately be used as measures of inflation because they are both broadly based. They will each yield different measures of inflation, partly because the coverage of prices is different and partly because the former uses variable weights while the latter uses fixed weights. On the other hand, one would not want to take a very narrowly based index, such as the index of used automobile prices, as a measure of inflation.

The costs of inflation

There are many costs to inflation, but often they are misunderstood. It is frequently alleged, for example, that we are all worse off as a result of inflation. The reason? A dollar will not buy as much today as it did in some earlier time.

This is what is meant by statements like, "A dollar today is worth only a few cents." However, what is often ignored is the fact that, on average, the number of dollars we have to spend today is much greater than the number we had to spend in that earlier time. So, is it true that we are really worse off, on average, as a result of inflation?

This is not an easy question to answer, so let us examine it in parts. At one level, the argument that we are all worse off is nonsense. If I have to pay more to purchase a car today than years ago, the extra amount I pay must end up as somebody's income. Perhaps the auto dealer is just making more profit income; perhaps the dealer has to pay more to the producer, in which case the producer's income is higher; perhaps the producer has to charge more to cover added wage costs, in which case the incomes of auto workers are higher. The point is that the extra expenditure must show up somewhere as extra income for someone; the extra expenditure does not get "lost."

Let us put the issue somewhat differently. Suppose the total quantity of goods and services produced remains fixed. Suppose further that, as a result of inflation, these goods and services sell for 10 percent more, on the average. Total spending being 10 percent higher means that the total income generated is 10 percent higher. Here, total income rises by the same amount as total spend-

"We're making more now than he ever did!"
Reprinted by permission The Wall Street Journal.

ing. The increase in total income is sufficient to cover the price increases.

With regard to this statement, two important points require emphasis. First, although total income increased by the same amount as total spending—by 10 percent—there is no necessary reason *everyone's* income should increase by 10 percent. Indeed, it is unlikely that everyone will experience the same percentage increase. Some might experience no increase whatever; others will experience an increase in excess of 10 percent. Mathematically speaking, if the average increase is 10 percent and some people register an increase of less than that, others *must* register an increase of more than 10 percent. Those who get more than 10 percent will find that their incomes now enable them to purchase more goods and services than before; those who get less than 10 percent find their incomes—their *real* incomes—are "worth less." Thus inflation may be accompanied by a redistribution of *real* purchasing power among people.

The second point has to do with the effects of inflation on total production and employment. We assumed earlier that the total quantity of goods and services produced remained fixed. Is that a legitimate assumption? Many would say no. The total production of goods and services could suffer a decline as a result of inflation.

Let us examine each of these points in greater detail.

Redistribution effects of inflation

Identifying the gainers and losers in an inflationary environment is often difficult. For one thing, not all prices rise by the same percentage amount during a period of inflation; some rise more, others rise less. Also, not everyone purchases the same bundle of goods to begin with. Thus, with prices rising by different percentage amounts, even two people who experience the same increase in their money incomes will not necessarily experience equivalent changes in the *real* purchasing power of their incomes. Also, people earn their incomes from widely different sources. During an inflationary period, these different types of income frequently behave quite differently. For example, if interest rates rise in line with inflation, people's *interest income* will keep up with general price level increases even though their *wage and salary incomes* might not.

Some of the redistributive effects of inflation depend on whether inflation is correctly *anticipated*. That is, people form expectations as to how much, if any, inflation there will be. If they expect prices to rise, they will act to try to offset the effects of those rising prices on their incomes. For example, creditors will often insist on higher interest rates on loans if they anticipate large price increases. The reason? To ensure that the dollars that are paid back in the future will enable them to buy as much as today. Labor unions will often demand larger wage increases as the expected rate of inflation goes higher. If business managers share these price expectations, they will tend to pay higher interest rates and wages on the assumption that they will be able to recoup those higher costs by charging higher prices.

The success of these efforts in insulating the incomes of creditors and workers from the effects of inflation obviously depends on whether the expectations about inflation are right. If prices rise more quickly than anticipated, then these creditors and workers will find that the real purchasing power of their incomes are lower than they thought they would be; debtors and business firms will gain, relatively speaking. The opposite redistribution of purchasing power will occur if actual inflation turns out to be less than anticipated.

There is, of course, one important way to avoid having to gamble about whether or not the inflation you expect now will be realized: try to incorporate clauses into contracts that adjust current incomes and current interest rates for past price increases. For example, many labor contracts include so-called **cost-of-living adjustment (COLA) clauses** that automatically adjust workers' incomes by the amount of inflation in the recent *past.* And so-called **variable-rate mortgages** adjust up or down the mortgage interest rates home owners must pay in response to changes in the lending institution's costs of funds, costs which are heavily influenced by current and expected rates of inflation.

However, even if inflation is correctly anticipated, there is likely to be considerable redistribution of purchasing power anyway. How can this be? Put simply, although everyone might anticipate inflation correctly, not everyone has the ability to adjust his or her income to reflect the change in the price level. For example, many people continue to receive income from private pensions that provide the *same* dollar amount month in and month out; the real value of that pension income deteriorates with inflation. Moreover, many people for years have had their savings in savings accounts whose interest return was limited by government regulation to levels that happened to be much less than the rate of inflation; the real value of their savings declined as a consequence. Moreover, a great many financial contracts remain outstanding that were written at a time when very few people expected inflation ever to reach high levels; the best known examples are **fixed-rate home mortgages,** especially those fixed-rate mortgages issued years ago at rates of interest of 5 or 6 percent, rates well below the rates of inflation since then.

Finally, one highly publicized form of income redistribution occurs as a consequence of *bracket creep,* a phenomenon discussed at length in Chapter 4. Thus, because inflation pushes people into higher and higher tax brackets characterized by higher and higher marginal tax rates, *real* incomes *after taxes* rise more slowly than real income *before taxes.* Real federal government tax receipts, on the other hand, rise more

rapidly. Some people refer to this inflation-induced increase in real tax receipts as an *inflation tax,* for good reason. Cynics have suggested that our elected officials have an interest in *not* stopping inflation because inflation makes it easier to balance the budget and provides government with more funds to increase spending. Whatever the merits of this argument, the inflation tax will soon be "repealed." That is, beginning in 1985, the individual income tax system will be *indexed* to arrest the phenomenon of bracket creep.

What general conclusions can we draw regarding the redistribution of real incomes as a result of inflation? First, the amount of real income that is redistributed is unknown. Proportionately, it is much less today than years ago because the use of **indexing** is so widespread. COLA clauses in labor contracts are a form of indexation; variable-rate mortgages represent another form of indexing; and many government transfer payments—social security and government pensions—are indexed as well. As a consequence of the widespread use of indexing schemes, many economists believe that the one big remaining redistribution problem is from the taxpaying public to the federal government. And this, as we have seen, is scheduled to be corrected beginning in 1985.

Output and employment effects of inflation

The capricious redistribution of real incomes that occurs in an inflationary environment is reason enough to want to stop inflation. But there is another important reason—the apparent slowdown in the growth of output and employment as a consequence of inflation. Two reasons are often given for these adverse outcomes.

First, an inflationary environment often fosters *uncertainty,* which interferes with good business planning. If businesspeople had some assurance that inflation would be steady, this would not be as important a consideration. However, inflation is frequently not steady. Accordingly, business profits bounce around more than otherwise, which serves to depress business investment generally. Moreover, in an inflationary environment, there is uncertainty regarding the actions policymakers will undertake. If the policy authorities seem willing to risk a recession to slow the pace of inflation, this might not be the time to undertake any new projects. Business investment spending could suffer as a consequence.

Second, it is frequently alleged that inflation, in combination with our tax system, serves to depress business investment spending directly by reducing the real aftertax income return to investment. We will take up this issue in depth in Chapter 14, but the central idea can be illustrated fairly simply.

In arriving at their taxable incomes, firms are permitted to deduct from earnings their production costs. Generally, labor costs are deducted in the taxable year those costs are incurred; the same is true of most other costs like those for energy and raw materials. However, the costs of capital goods are not generally deductible immediately; these costs are spread out over time in recognition of the fact that most capital goods generate revenues over time. The allowable deductions are called *depreciation expenses.*

Now here is the problem. Suppose all prices rise by 10 percent per year. The firm's revenues will rise by 10 percent, as will the replacement cost of capital goods. However, our tax laws do not permit firms to depreciate capital on the basis of the replacement cost of capital; capital can be depreciated only in amounts equal to the original cost—that is, the historic cost. In an inflationary environment, historic cost depreciation means that the firm's taxable income rises by more than 10 percent. (Remember, revenues are rising by 10 percent but depreciation expenses are not rising at all; therefore, taxable income rises by more than 10 percent.) The fact that taxable income is higher means that profit taxes will be higher—higher than if taxable income had just increased in pace with inflation. The extra tax reduces the return to investment and thereby reduces the incentive to invest.

There is considerable controversy surrounding this argument, which we will attempt to evaluate in Chapter 14. However, if the argument is valid,

it means that inflation, by reducing the growth of investment spending, slows the growth of our nation's production possibilities; our potential output growth is smaller than it might be otherwise. This is very important from the point of view of policy. Indeed, some economists would argue that we must change policy to slow inflation, or alter the tax system (to permit, for example, firms to deduct amounts equal to replacement costs), or both. If we don't, we are not likely to see significant improvements in American living standards; we will witness an erosion of our competitive position internationally; and we will not be able to reach the 4.0 percent Humphrey-Hawkins unemployment target because we will fail to put into place the increases in capital equipment needed to employ the additional labor resources. Significant progress was made in this direction with passage of the Economic Recovery Tax Act of 1981. In that act, firms were permitted to substantially shorten the number of years over which they write off their capital equipment and structures.

Creeping versus double- or triple-digit inflation: How much inflation is too much?

The costs of inflation, whether in the form of redistributed incomes or reduced growth, depend in part on how much inflation there is. This focuses our attention on some questions raised earlier: What is meant by "reasonable price stability"? Does it require that prices on average remain unchanged? And if inflation entails costs, should we strive for *deflation*—a sustained broadbased decline in prices?

One way to provide insight to these questions is to look at the history. Figure 5.10 shows the record from the 1920s to the present. One striking aspect of the chart is that there have been no substantial periods since the 1920s, aside from those associated with wartime controls, when the average price level remained unchanged. In recent decades price stability, like full employment, has eluded us.

The chart also shows only one period when prices declined in a sustained fashion—the early 1930s. This deflation was associated with the

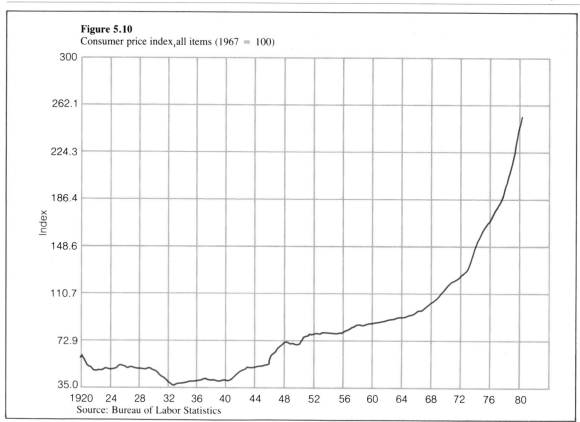

Figure 5.10
Consumer price index, all items (1967 = 100)

Source: Bureau of Labor Statistics

worst depression in modern times. During the early 1930s, unemployment soared to around 25 percent of the labor force. While this episode by itself may not establish the undesirability of some more moderate amount of deflation, it certainly gives an inkling of the costs that *could* be incurred.

More recently, prices have shown a clear upward trend. Within the last 40 years, however, there is one period—lasting from the early 1950s to the mid-1960s—that does stand out as a time when prices were increasing at a relatively slow pace. Between 1950 and 1965 the consumer price index rose at an average annual rate of only 1.4 percent—a rate that seems unimaginably slow by today's standards! This period is now known as one of **creeping inflation.**

It can be argued that the creeping inflation of the 1950s and early 1960s was as close to "reasonable" price stability as we can hope to get. After all, price indexes are constructed to

measure an elusive and ill-defined concept called the "average price level," and they may be subject to considerable error in measurement. For example, the CPI does not make timely adjustments in weights for the shifts in expenditures that are brought about by price changes. While some corrections are made for improvements in the quality of some goods in the index, such corrections are not made for all goods, nor is there any way of measuring accurately how good these adjustments are.[2]

Since the mid-1960s, prices have exhibited a more pronounced upward trend. More signifi-

_____

[2] The question of quality change is a tricky one. For example, if the 1980 version of goods is superior to the 1975 version, and if the higher price for the 1980 version reflects only the cost of introducing the improvements, has there really been a price increase? For some goods, the Bureau of Labor Statistics says no, and so the index does not increase. For other goods, no corrections are made for quality change, and so the index will rise even though the increase might be inappropriate.

cantly, the rates of increase in the last 15 years generally have gotten larger, and in several recent years, we have experienced **double-digit inflation**—rates of increase of 10 percent or more per year.

Obviously, the notion of double-digit inflation is largely a symbolic one. There is little real difference (approximately 0.1 percent) between price increases of 10 percent and 9.9 percent per year. At rates of inflation such as these, however, the costs of inflation can become quite substantial. Under creeping inflation, those on fixed pension incomes, for example, lose relatively little purchasing power year by year. But at double-digit rates these losses—and the adjustments required to absorb them in terms of lower consumption and living standards—are large. (This is sometimes portrayed vividly by news stories documenting the suffering endured by many elderly people on fixed incomes; some live in roach-infested apartments eating canned dog and cat food.) Also, efforts to avoid the risks of inflation may be more pronounced as the expected course of future price changes becomes more uncertain.

Fortunately, the United States has never experienced inflation of the *triple-digit* variety. Price increases of this magnitude are described as **runaway inflation** or **hyperinflation.** The classic historical example of hyperinflation is the German experience of 1922–1923, which culminated in price increases of 250 percent *per day* in 1923 and ultimately in the breakdown of the entire German monetary system.

What makes hyperinflation so serious is that people develop a tremendous incentive to get rid of money. Of course, inflation of any degree provides some such inducement (just as deflation may encourage people to hoard money). But at rapid rates of inflation it begins to have strong reinforcing effects. When prices are rising quickly, money becomes the hot potato of the system. Everyone is trying to spend it before it loses more value. The efforts to get rid of money ultimately push prices up faster, and the situation quickly becomes unstable. Production may fall substantially as people divert their attention away from their jobs towards ways of disposing of their money. Eventually, the economy, if it doesn't

break down completely, reverts to a system of barter exchange; people trade goods and services directly for other goods and services instead of for money. As we saw in Chapter 2, this is a much less efficient form of exchange than one that involves money.

Hyperinflation can thus impose quite significant costs on the economy as a whole. The redistributive effects, and even the employment and output effects, of an inflation of more moderate dimensions pale by comparison. In an ultimate sense, one might say that a significant cost of inflation is the possibility that it will develop into a hyperinflation. This risk clearly increases with the rate of inflation itself.

Are the goals of full employment and price stability in conflict?

It is often alleged that it is not possible to achieve simultaneously the goals of full employment and price stability. As you might suspect, this is a highly controversial issue. It is hard to imagine politicians admitting to its truth. But interestingly, there is also little agreement among economists on this matter.

The allegation of conflict between the two goals rests on a fundamental proposition—namely, that a "systematic relationship" exists between the amount of unemployment and the rate of inflation. Specifically, it is often argued that efforts to achieve full employment will result in more rapid inflation; or policy efforts aimed at slowing inflation will force the unemployment rate up. This view was a very popular one during the 1960s and early 1970s; it was formally enshrined in the so-called **Phillips curve,** which we will describe momentarily. In the late 1960s, a literal revolution in thinking began to occur and it persists to this day. It suggests that there is no necessary or simple systematic relationship between inflation and unemployment. As a consequence, there need be no policy conflict. Let us look at each of these views briefly.

A view from the 1960s: The Phillips curve. The relationship between inflation and unemployment has long been intensely debated among economists. One important milestone in that debate occurred in 1958 with the publication of an article by Australian economist A. W. Phillips. The article explored statistically (as opposed to theoretically) the relationship between inflation and unemployment for the United Kingdom. Phillips found that these two variables—inflation and unemployment—displayed a clear—and apparently stable—negative relationship over a very long span of time beginning in 1867 and ending in 1957. Appropriately enough, this inverse relationship became known as the *Phillips curve*.

A hypothetical, *stable* Phillips curve is illustrated in Figure 5.11. If this curve really does represent accurately the nature of the relationship between unemployment and inflation, then it suggests that policymakers confront a menu of policy choices. Using the hypothetical data of Figure 5.11, policymakers could presumably conduct policy in a manner so as to accomplish the inflation-unemployment combination given by point A—a 5.0 percent unemployment rate and a 4.2 percent rate of inflation. Alternatively, policymakers might try to attain point C; the lower rate of unemployment (3.0 percent) is bought at the expense of much greater inflation (9.1 percent). If we could just identify the precise nature of this inverse relationship—this "trade-

off"—we could finally answer the question of how much additional inflation would have to be tolerated to reduce the unemployment rate by a given amount.

What do the data tell us about the nature of the relationship between inflation and unemployment in the U.S. economy? Figure 5.12 depicts the combinations of unemployment and inflation for each of the 20 years 1961 to 1980 inclusive; all points are connected up chronologically. Do you see a Phillips curve relationship here? It's certainly not obvious. Actually, it looks like a mess—like unemployment and inflation are not related as Phillips suggested. However, look carefully at the data for the decade of the 1960s. What pattern do you see formed there? Although

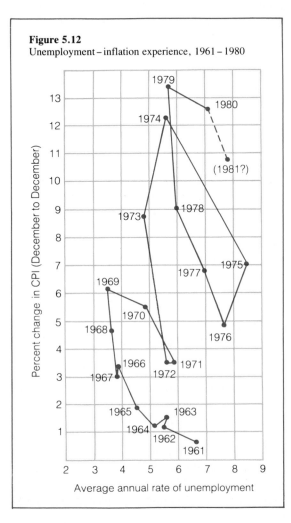

Figure 5.12
Unemployment–inflation experience, 1961–1980

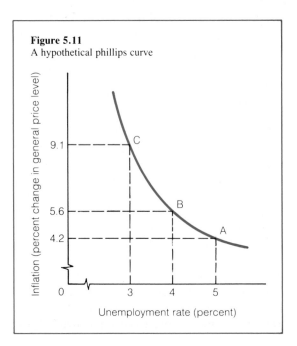

Figure 5.11
A hypothetical phillips curve

the relationship is not precise, it certainly does look like a Phillips curve. At the beginning of that decade, the economy was operating at a level of unemployment—6.7 percent—that was then considered to be extremely high. Prices were rising at a rate of less than 1 percent per year. As the decade unfolded, the economy progressed along a path that generally produced lower and lower unemployment rates and ever-higher rates of inflation. By the end of the decade, the economy had reached a level of unemployment of only 3.5 percent, and prices were rising at a 6 percent clip. The Phillips curve certainly looked valid enough for the U.S. economy.

The 1970s—A more sober experience. Beginning in 1970, a strange thing happened. Unemployment increased substantially, but inflation did not decline as much as the Phillips curve would have predicted it would. Indeed, the Phillips curve for the 1960s would have led policy-makers to expect an inflation rate in 1970 closer to the rates registered in 1964 or 1965 (1.0–2.0 percent). Instead, inflation continued to advance at a nearly 6.0 percent pace.

Inflation fell fairly sharply in 1971 and 1972 (largely the result of the wage and price controls instituted by President Nixon on August 15, 1971). But in 1973 and again in 1974, inflation literally exploded. The Phillips curve of the 1960s would not have predicted this kind of explosion, especially at such high rates of unemployment as were prevalent in those years. Yes, some of this extraordinary inflation experience could be attributed to "special factors," such as the Arab oil embargo in late 1973 and early 1974 and the subsequent 400 percent increase in the price of imported oil. However, increasing numbers of economists began to question seriously whether the Phillips curve relationship was in fact valid any longer, or indeed whether it ever had been valid. (Some well-known economists questioned its validity as early as 1967, but widespread disaffection with the Phillips Curve did not occur until the early 1970s.)

Nevertheless, if you study Figure 5.12 carefully, you should be able to see a Phillips curve type of relationship for the period 1976–1979. However, this relationship is substantially above

and to the right of the curve formed for the 1960s. That is, for any given unemployment rate, the rate of inflation implied by the Phillips curve relationship for the latter half of the 1970s was substantially above the inflation rate implied by the 1960s Phillips curve relationship. Moreover, just as the year 1970 seemed to "fall off track" (i.e., not follow the Phillips curve formed by the 1960s), 1980 seemed also to fall off track.

What conclusions, if any, can we draw from the data plotted in Figure 5.12?

1. There have been periods in the past when an inverse relationship between unemployment and inflation appeared to reveal itself. However, it is clear that no single curve describes that relationship. Put differently, the data do *not* suggest the existence of a stable Phillips curve.

2. Note also that, *on the average,* unemployment and inflation have both increased over time. What this would seem to suggest is that, although for some subperiods—1961–1969 and 1976–1979—a trade-off (or inverse relationship) existed between unemployment and inflation, the two variables are positively related over the 20-year span. The latter apparent relationship has caused some people to throw their hands in the air and declare that neither goal is attainable; it is not simply a question of there being a conflict between the two.

Where does all this leave us? Chapters 13 and 14 will examine these issues in detail. However, enough has been said in this chapter to indicate, in broad terms, one possible answer to the question of whether the goals of full employment and inflation are in conflict.

First, recalling the concept of natural rate of unemployment, it would appear that full employment and inflation are not in conflict—*as long as full employment is defined as the natural rate of unemployment.* Thus, since the natural rate is presumably consistent with any (steady) rate of inflation, including complete price stability, there is no necessary conflict between the natural rate of unemployment and the goal we set for inflation. A conflict can and will arise if the full employment goal is set at a rate *below* the natural rate. Of course, if the full employment goal is below the *current* natural rate, it is possible, in principle, to devise policies aimed at lowering the natural rate itself in order to bring it into alignment with the full employment target.

Second, as was suggested earlier, the natural rate of unemployment has apparently increased dramatically since the early 1960s. If this is so, there may be an *increasing* conflict between the inflation goal and an *unchanged* full employment goal. Put differently, it is often suggested that the long-run positive relationship between unemployment and inflation noted earlier can be explained as having been the result of policy actions that, on the average, kept the unemployment rate below the natural rate. The result? Higher and higher rates of inflation; and, in order to ease the upward pressure on inflation, higher rates of unemployment were permitted, although publicly the goal of "full employment" was never abandoned.

In short, the concept of natural rate of unemployment suggests that there is a conflict between unemployment and inflation *only if* the full employment goal is defined differently from the natural rate.

THE GOAL OF RAPID ECONOMIC GROWTH

Rapid economic growth has always figured prominently in the list of U.S. economic goals. The reason is not difficult to discover. Although we can never hope to satisfy all our wants, rapidly expanding production possibilities permit the satisfaction of more wants over time than otherwise; economic growth is the means of reducing scarcity.

It is important at the outset that we have a clear understanding of what is meant by economic growth. At first glance, defining growth would appear to present no unusual problems. The simplest definition of a growing economy would be one in which the output of goods and services expands from one year to the next. With this definition, the most natural measure of growth would seem to be the percentage increase in output between successive years.

What this definition lacks is precision. Does the definition refer to the *actual* growth of goods and services production or the *potential* growth? It refers to the actual growth. However, further and further increases in production, year after year, are not possible without an expanding output potential—that is, without expanding production possibilities. Accordingly, a rapidly expanding economy requires a rapidly expanding output potential. For this reason, when we talk about economic growth we are referring to the rate of expansion of our economy's productive potential.

The distinction between growth as measured by actual and potential output can be conveniently illustrated by the production possibilities apparatus introduced in Chapter 2. Recall that the production possibilities curve identifies all those combinations of goods and services that the economy could produce if all factors of production were fully employed. Points interior to the curve represent situations in which the productive resources of the economy are less than fully employed.

Consider an economy that is currently at interior point A in Figure 5.13. If in the next period it moves to point B on the production possibilities

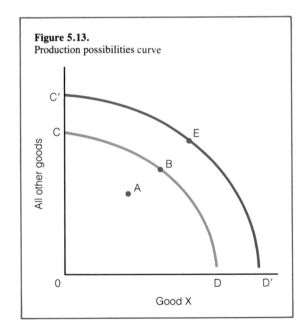

Figure 5.13.
Production possibilities curve

curve, CD, some growth in actual output will be recorded, even if the productive capacity of the economy remains unchanged. This growth from A to B simply represents the employment of previously unused resources; further growth is not possible unless the production possibilities curve is pushed out. In other words, further increases in the total amount of goods and services produced cannot be realized unless there occurs an outward shift in the production possibilities curve, say from CD to C'D'. In short, if the production possibilities curve does not shift out over time, or shifts out slowly, the scope for growth will be very limited. Yes, there can be rapid growth for certain periods under these circumstances, but only if resources are unused or underutilized initially. Rapid growth over time requires a rapidly expanding production possibilities.

An aside. Is it ever possible for the economy to produce more than its potential—that is, to operate outside its production possibilities frontier? As noted in Chapter 2, the answer to this question depends on what interpretation is given to the production possibilities curve. If the curve were defined as the absolute maximum amount obtainable from a given set of resources, then the answer would clearly be no.

More often, however, the production possibilities curve, and its empirical counterpart, **potential output,** are defined on the basis of levels of resource utilization considered to be the largest possible from a practical point of view—the largest "normally." We saw earlier, for example, that a zero level of unemployment simply is unrealistic as a definition of full employment, so a higher than zero rate is typically used to calculate potential output. Similar assumptions are used for other factors of production as well. If the economy uses resources more intensively for a while, then actual output will exceed "normal" potential. But this situation cannot persist indefinitely if the definitions of full resource utilization are at all realistic.

The growth process

Because growth is an important goal of economic policy, it is important to identify the factors that determine the rate at which the productive capacity of the economy expands. Fundamentally, increases in our nation's productive capacity will be determined by increases in the quantity and quality of our land, labor, and natural resources, as was emphasized in Chapter 2. For some purposes, it is useful to examine these phenomena within the following framework: Total output produced (Q) can be defined as equal to "output per unit of labor" (Q/L) times the amount of labor employed (L). Symbolically,

$$Q = (Q/L) \times L.$$

If L is set at its full employment level and other productive resources are also fully employed, then Q can be interpreted as potential output—a point on the production possibilities curve.

Let us examine this relationship more closely. What it tells us is that the quantity produced is equal to the amount of labor employed times *average labor productivity*—the amount produced per unit of labor. Does this mean that labor is the only important factor of production? What about all the other factors of production besides labor? The influence of the other factors is summarized in the term *average labor productivity*. Let us illustrate this point. Suppose that the labor input remains fixed. Suppose now that the stock of capital goods is increased. What will happen as a consequence to our nation's productive potential? It will increase. That increase will show up on the left-hand side of the above expression as an increase in Q, and on the right-hand side as an increase in Q/L—that is, an increase in average labor productivity.

An aside. Examining labor productivity in this manner avoids a common confusion. All too often it is argued that, if labor productivity falls, it is because employees are not working as hard as they used to. Reduced work effort could cause labor productivity to fall. But any recorded decline in labor productivity could also be the result of a wide variety of other factors that affect both the quantity and quality of our other resources.

Focusing on labor input and labor productivity. Focusing on labor input and labor productivity is understandable from a policy point of view. After all, the stated objective of most policies aimed at increasing economic growth is the improvement of average living standards. One frequently used definition of the average living standard is **output per capita**—total output divided by population. And one very important determinant of output per capita is average labor productivity.

To illustrate, over the long haul it is reasonable to expect that the pace of labor force growth will keep close pace with population growth. If labor force and population both grow at exactly the same rate, a constant labor force participation rate is implied.[3] There may be periods when the labor force participation rate may vary—the result, for example, of changing mores as reflected in the increased labor force participation rate of women. But there cannot be persistent movement in one direction.[4] Ultimately, therefore, improvements in average living standards (output per person) will require improvements in labor productivity (output per worker). It is appropriate in our discussion of the growth process, therefore, to focus our attention on the growth in labor productivity.

The growth of labor productivity: A look at the record. In recent years, the growth of American labor productivity has assumed center stage, along with inflation, in virtually all national economic policy discussions. The reason is clear. Since 1965, and particularly since 1973, labor productivity growth in the United States has slowed sharply. Whereas labor productivity (in the nonfarm business sector) grew at an average annual rate of 2.7 percent between 1948 and 1965, it declined to 2.0 percent on average from 1965 to 1973, and to 0.7 percent on average from 1973 to 1980.

This very sharp fall-off in the growth of U.S. labor productivity has been the source of widespread alarm. The alarmed reaction is perfectly

understandable. In the absence of productivity gains, there can be no *general* improvement in living standards.

This point is sometimes confused. Some people, for example, look at hourly earnings (or hourly compensation) for these three periods and conclude that living standards have increased. After all, for the three periods noted above, hourly earnings have increased sharply from an average annual rate of increase of 4.6 percent to 5.5 percent to 9.1 percent. However, what happened to *real* hourly earnings—hourly earnings corrected for increases in the general level of prices—over these three periods? Using the consumer price index as our measure of inflation, the growth of *real hourly earnings actually declined in step with the slowdown in productivity growth*—from an average annual rate of growth of 2.9 percent from 1948 to 1965, to 2.1 from 1965 to 1973, to 0.7 percent from 1973 to 1980.

The lesson to be learned from this is simple: productivity growth, not wage growth, determines the growth of real income per worker. If productivity fails to increase, wage increases will simply inflate unit labor costs. If other input costs increase by the same percentage as labor costs, and if profit margins are maintained, output prices will rise in proportion to the increase in unit labor costs. Under these circumstances, the output price increases cancel the wage increases, leaving *real* income per worker unaltered; increased real incomes for some must come at the expense of reduced real incomes for others.

Causes of the slump in productivity growth. Identifying the factors responsible for the slowdown in the growth of labor productivity requires focusing attention on those factors that have caused the growth of our production possibilities to slow relative to the growth of labor. This means we need to focus attention on changes in the quantity and quality of *all* factors of production relative to changes in the labor force since this is what determines the expansion of our production possibilities.

Almost all economists would agree with this general statement. However, the quantitative sig-

---

[3] Since the labor force participation rate is defined as the ratio of labor force to population, a constant rate means that both the numerator and denominator grow at exactly the same rate.

[4] For example, there is a physical upper limit to the labor force participation rate, namely, one. If the labor force participation rate were equal to one, every person of working age would be a member of the labor force.

nificance of each of the many factors that might be pointed to is hotly disputed. Rather than try to settle this issue, let us just identify what appear to be the major contributing factors.

Growth of the capital-labor ratio. Many studies of productivity emphasize the important role played by changes in the **capital-labor ratio**— that is, changes in the amount of capital that labor works with. Specifically, it is alleged that increases in the capital-labor ratio cause productivity—output per unit of labor—to increase; the converse situation is also held to be true.

And what has happened to the growth of the capital-labor ratio since the end of World War II? Between 1948 and 1969, the capital-labor ratio for the private business sector advanced at an average annual rate of nearly 2.5 percent; between 1969 and 1980, the capital-labor ratio grew by only about 0.4 percent annually. It is hardly surprising, therefore, that many economists point to this decline as having been responsible for the precipitous fall off in productivity growth through the 1970s.

What matters is the *ratio* of capital to labor. This means we need to examine changes in both the numerator (capital) and the denominator (labor). In this regard, part of the slowdown in productivity growth may be attributed to the sharp increase in labor force growth, the result of the influx of new workers who were part of the baby boom after World War II, and the result of the increases in labor force participation rates of adult females and teenagers. After advancing at an annual rate of increase of about 1.3 percent between 1948 and 1969, the civilian labor force increased by about 2.3 percent between 1969 and 1980. This inordinately rapid increase in the labor force during the 1970s is expected to slow dramatically in the 1980s, a factor that many believe will help to reverse the slump in productivity growth.

However, although labor force growth increased substantially, the growth in the capital-labor ratio during the 1970s was slowed further by a slowdown in the growth of the stock of capital. For the private business sector of the economy, the stock of capital slowed from an

annual rate of increase of about 4.6 percent between 1948 and 1969 to an annual rate of increase of about 2.7 percent between 1969 and 1980.

What accounted for the reduced growth rate of the stock of capital goods during the 1970s? The reasons are many and varied, and the quantitative significance of each is in considerable dispute. Some argue that high rates of inflation, in combination with the current tax treatment of income, have served to depress real aftertax returns to investment. The result? A slower rate of capital formation and, therewith, a slower rate of productivity growth. Thus, as we noted before, since firms are allowed to depreciate their plant and equipment on an historic cost basis only, even though inflation raises their replacement costs, inflation automatically causes taxable profits to overstate "true" profits. This reduces the return to investment after taxes and, in turn, reduces the incentive to invest.

However, even though historic cost depreciation tends to reduce the aftertax return on investment, there is another feature of our tax laws that offsets this disincentive (at least in part)— the fact that the interest costs incurred by businesses when they borrow are fully deductible from income before taxes to arrive at taxable income. To illustrate, suppose inflation is zero, the cost of borrowing is 4 percent, and the marginal tax rate on business income equals 50 percent. Then, for each dollar borrowed, businesspeople will deduct 4 cents; and because the tax rate is 50 percent, their cost after taxes is only 2 cents. Moreover, because there is no inflation, their *real* costs after tax are also 2 cents.

Now let there be a 10 percent inflation rate. Suppose further that lenders insist on a 14 percent rate of interest to ensure the same *real* 4 percent return as before. That is, the 14 percent rate consists of a 10 percent rate (to offset 10 percent inflation) plus a 4 percent rate (to give them what they were receiving before). What is the cost to businesspeople for each dollar after taxes? Seven cents. (That is, because they are in the 50 percent bracket, the aftertax cost is one half the before-tax cost.) And what is the cost *after* inflation? That is, what is the *real after-*

tax cost? It is *minus* 3 cents—the 7 cent aftertax cost minus the 10 percent inflation rate. One very important conclusion follows from this illustration: Even though the *real before-tax* cost of funds has not changed, the fact that interest expenses can be deducted means that the *real* aftertax cost varies *inversely* with the rate of inflation. In an inflationary environment, therefore, the real cost of borrowing is reduced which means that real reported profits are understated.

Combining the inflation-induced overstatement of profits arising from historic cost depreciation with the inflation-induced understatement arising from the reduction in the real aftertax cost of borrowing, it is *not* obvious that real aftertax returns on investment necessarily suffer in an inflationary environment. We will examine this issue in more detail in Chapter 14.

The role of energy price increases. It is widely acknowledged that higher energy prices have been a major contributing factor to our inflationary spiral. In line with our earlier discussion, this energy-induced increase in our overall inflation rate, in combination with heightened risks and uncertainties concerning the availability of energy supplies, has probably contributed to a slower rate of investment spending than would be the case otherwise. But independent of their influence on our general rate of inflation, higher energy prices affect capital expenditure decisions directly. The available empirical evidence suggests that energy and capital are, in the short run at least, *complementary* as opposed to *substitutable* inputs. The implication of this is clear: An increase in the price of one decreases the quantity demanded for *both*. Not only has the energy-induced price increase for the complementary energy-capital input induced the search for technologies that are more labor using—a factor contributing directly to the slowdown in the growth of labor productivity—it has also, so it has been conjectured, made a significant part of the capital stock economically obsolete; that is, many capital goods that would have continued to be profitable before the energy price hikes ceased to be profitable afterwards.

The role of cyclical swings in the economy. Cyclical swings in the economy can adversely affect the rate of productivity growth in several ways. First and foremost is the effect of an economic slowdown on the rate of capital formation. When the economy falls below its productive potential and remains below it for a considerable period, business investment spending suffers. Why? A decline in the level of economic activity means a diminished capacity to sell goods and services at high rates of return. Accordingly, many capital expansion plans are either shelved or abandoned. And if the slump persists, even the incentive to replace capital that wears out is diminished. In addition, an economic slowdown may also adversely affect business spending for capital goods by adversely affecting business expectations. In this regard, the magnitude and duration of the 1974–75 U.S. recession—the worst in our post-World War II history—coming as it did on the heels of the OPEC oil embargo and subsequent oil price hikes, is widely viewed as having seriously inhibited business investment in the latter half of the 1970s, a contributing factor to the productivity growth slump.

The role of government regulation. The 1970s witnessed a significant increase in both the pace and scope of federal regulation in the U.S. economy. The increase affected such diverse areas as consumer product safety, occupational health and safety, water and air pollution control, toxic waste disposal, and strip-mining control, to name only the most important. Despite the rapid growth in government regulation, it is difficult to determine by how much productivity growth declined as a consequence. Nevertheless, it is fairly clear how regulation might adversely affect our productivity performance. To the extent that regulatory costs divert funds that would otherwise have gone into investment, research and development, or other business activities that serve to increase labor productivity, government regulation has contributed to the productivity slowdown.

The rapid growth in federal regulation could also have contributed to a decline in productivity growth by diverting the time and attention of top-level management from the task of running their businesses to the task of complying with federal controls and demands. To the extent that this has occurred, and there is widespread belief that it has, business efficiency would be reduced. In addition, regulatory programs may have diverted business research and development talents from the more traditional tasks of developing new products and cutting the costs of old products toward meeting regulatory goals.

The proliferation of new regulatory programs and new regulations has likely discouraged business investment by increasing the complexity as well as the cost of business investment decisions. In the estimation of some people, many of the new federal regulatory programs have acted to increase inordinately the capital costs of new business investments. Some regulations—particularly those dealing with health and safety regulations and the environment—require the use of the best available technology, even if less expensive nontechnical alternatives exist that could do just as well. Others require the use of equipment or processes that would not have been used in the absence of regulation. Still others require studies or the gathering of permits and approvals from a variety of agencies; this significantly prolongs the gestation period of investment. The effect is to raise the capital cost of many business investments.

Regulations reduce the incentive to invest in a number of other ways. First, the rapid proliferation of new regulations during the past decade, along with changes, amendments, recisions, and conflicts among agencies, has created a great deal of uncertainty in the business environment. It has become very difficult at the time of planning a new undertaking to determine what the regulatory environment will look like at the end of the road; the longer the period, the more uncertainty involved. Unfortunately, it is now impossible to estimate the extent to which this has discouraged investment.

It was considerations such as these that led the Reagan Administration to attempt to reduce both the number and scope of government regulations, and also to reduce the compliance costs associated with remaining regulations, in order to enhance productivity growth.

The role of research and development (R&D) and technological innovation. It is a generally accepted proposition that technological progress is one of the most important factors influencing productivity growth. Put simply, technological progress enables us to get more out of our existing resources. For any given quantity of labor input, technological progress permits the production of a larger quantity of goods and services, which raises labor productivity.

It is often alleged that the pace of technological progress slowed beginning around 1965. Two factors are largely responsible for this reduced trend. First, since many technological improvements are "embodied" in new plant facilities and equipment, the lower rate of growth of capital spending in the 1970s lowered the *actual* rate of technological advance. Second, since many technological innovations are believed to result from research and development (R&D) expenditures, the reduced share of our total national output being devoted to R&D has, so it is alleged, contributed to the slower pace of technological progress.

Unfortunately, this is an area where our understanding is far from complete. First, in most instances we are unable to measure technological progress directly; indirect methods, while understandable, are often suspect. For example, it is frequently claimed that increases in production *not* explained by other things (such as increases in the quantities of capital and resources) *must* have been the result of technological progress.

Second, the link between R&D spending and technological innovation is not precise. Sometimes huge amounts will be spent on R&D to no avail (i.e., no technical improvements will emerge as a result). Sometimes technological advances are discovered "by luck," with little or no R&D outlays. And R&D expenditures in one industry may be much more successful than in other industries. Nevertheless, the Economic Recovery Tax Act of 1981 provided substantial tax incentives to those undertaking R&D spending.

The goal of rapid economic growth and the goals of full employment and price stability

Rapid economic growth—which, to repeat and to avoid confusion, means rapid growth of our productive potential—is widely viewed as important to the realization of both full employment and price stability. Put differently, many economists argue that the sharp increases in the natural rate of unemployment and the rate of inflation noted earlier were due in part to the sluggish growth performance of the American economy.

What are the reasons for these apparent adverse effects? First, recall the meaning of the natural rate of unemployment. It is that rate of unemployment consistent with a stable inflation rate. According to many economists, the natural rate increased because capital formation was so sluggish. Efforts today to achieve rates of unemployment that *earlier* were believed to be "natural" would necessitate the use of older, less efficient capital that would have increased unit production costs and inflation even further. A stable inflation rate was possible only at a higher rate of unemployment because capital was the restraining factor.

Second, it is popularly maintained that the reduced rate of productivity growth has been a major factor responsible for the accelerated pace of inflation. Many people attempt to explain this phenomenon by appeal to the following definition:

$$\text{Growth in unit labor costs} = \text{Growth in employee earnings} - \text{Growth in labor productivity}$$

By exploiting the additional factual evidence that shows a close statistical relationship between the growth in unit labor costs and the growth in output prices, one conclusion seems all but inevitable: Slower productivity growth will result in a higher rate of inflation, and faster productivity growth will slow the inflation rate.

Actually, this "explanation" is not an explanation at all. The connection between productivity growth and the growth in unit labor costs cannot be deduced directly from the above definitional relationship. That relationship tells us nothing more than that the growth in unit labor costs *must* equal the difference between the growth of employee earnings and the growth of labor productivity. If the decline in productivity growth is accompanied by a corresponding decline in employee earnings, unit labor costs will *not* increase; conversely, if productivity growth increases and employee earnings increase by a corresponding amount, unit labor costs will *not* decline. The question is, How are employee earnings affected by changes in productivity growth? We do not have a good answer to this question. Some argue that changes in productivity growth do not affect growth in employee earnings. If that's the case, reductions in productivity growth will raise the growth in unit labor costs and therewith inflation. And it also means that higher rates of productivity growth will help to bring inflation down. Other economists argue, however, that reductions in productivity growth will not be met with a reduced growth of employee earnings, but that increases in productivity growth will cause faster growth in employee earnings. If that's the case, decreases in productivity growth will cause inflation to worsen, but increases in productivity growth (because they are partly matched by higher employee earnings) will not provide much, if any, inflation relief. This argument will be examined in more detail in Chapter 14.

Moreover, with respect to the relationship between inflation and productivity growth, we may have a Did-the-chicken-come-before-the-egg? problem. That is, as we saw earlier, some economists have argued that inflation, in combination with our tax laws, have reduced incentives to invest with the result that productivity growth has suffered. Therefore, if one finds lower productivity growth associated with higher inflation, should one conclude that high inflation caused lower productivity growth, or is the reverse true?

Growth and other economic goals

Although rapid economic growth may facilitate the realization of our full employment and inflation goals, it may come in conflict with other policy objectives. For example, high-growth policies are viewed by many, with some justification, as encouraging productive activities that damage the environment through pollution, that upset the ecological balance, and that deplete our natural (and exhaustible) resources too quickly. Implicitly, these concerns emanate from a point of view that believes that increases in material wealth, per se, should not be the sole or overriding objective of economic policy.

The question policymakers all face is, How should the goal of rapid growth be modified to meet legitimate concerns over the environment and natural resource use? The answer to this question has varied over time and from one administration to the next. Between about 1964 and 1980, the federal government paid less attention to rapid growth per se. This is reflected in part in the myriad environmental and safety regulations promulgated during that period. However, beginning with the Reagan Administration, the relative emphasis has shifted in the direction of more rapid growth.

The pace of economic growth can also have important implications for the achievement of a "fair and equitable distribution of income." To illustrate, suppose we set as our goal the achievement of a redistribution of income toward those at the lowest end of the income scale. A high rate of growth, if suitably accompanied by other policies, may facilitate the attainment of this goal in the following sense: If growth is high and policies can be devised to make lower-level incomes grow faster than higher-level incomes, then the redistribution may be accomplished with a minimum of difficulty, since all incomes can be rising. On the other hand, a situation of low or nonexistent growth forces the government to engineer the redistribution of income by reducing absolutely the incomes of those in the higher-level brackets, a course of action that obviously is unlikely to be well received.

OTHER GOALS

At the beginning of this chapter, two other goals were cited as objectives of economic policy: fair and equitably distributed incomes, and a proper mix of goods and services. These goals generally receive less attention because they are more difficult to define, and because they are very controversial. More so than the other goals, they pit the interests of different groups within

the society against each other. This conflict makes it extremely difficult to establish policies that will be effective in achieving the stated ends.

A fair and equitable distribution of income

It is difficult to identify with precision the nature and extent of the government's commitment to an equitable distribution of income. High incomes can be achieved through policies that promote employment and growth, and, as noted previously, rapidly increasing incomes can make efforts to redistribute incomes easier. But equity in the distribution of income is an elusive concept. Clearly, whatever else it may mean, it does not mean that government is committed to a policy of achieving absolute equality. Such a policy probably would be impossible; even if it were possible, the successful attainment of absolute equality might have serious effects on economic incentives. People would not have incentives to work harder, study longer, invest in risky ventures, etc. The effect of complete equality, therefore, could be economic stagnation.

This reduces the question to one of determining how much inequality is appropriate. The government has never addressed this question in any comprehensive way. Rather, its objective has generally been a more limited one: to improve the lot of those at the lower end of the income distribution. More specifically, the government has defined a level of income thought to be consistent with a minimally acceptable standard of living and then attempted, through a variety of policies, including welfare programs, training and education programs, and employment subsidies, to move people *above* this poverty line.

A desirable mix of goods and services

The goal of achieving a desirable mix of output may be even more problematical than that of ensuring an equitable distribution of income. In this area, even crude definitions are very hard to come by. As with income distribution, choices to be made usually involve pitting the interests of one person or group against another.

Like a fair and equitable distribution of income, the attainment of a desirable mix of output may or may not necessitate government intervention. It depends on what the desirable mix is. However, national governments frequently do adopt principles regarding the appropriate mix, even if their role in producing the right mix is largely passive. For one thing, national priorities such as a strong defense capability, rapid economic growth, and expanded educational opportunities may be deemed sufficiently important to justify specific efforts to encourage production of certain goods or services.

An important determinant of the government's role in these matters is the type of economic system with which the nation operates. In a command or centrally planned economy, the government gets heavily involved in setting production schedules. In a market economy, on the other hand, determination of the output mix is left largely to the marketplace, with the end result depending on the number of dollar votes cast for each possible mix.

To close this chapter, one very important mix-of-output question currently being debated in the U.S. Congress merits attention. It concerns the issue of how to achieve the goal of a reduced share of federal government expenditures relative to total, economy-wide expenditures. In 1980, federal government expenditures accounted for over 23 percent of total expenditures. The Reagan Administration wants that percentage reduced to below 20 percent by 1984. Can the Administration succeed, and should it?

Without answering these questions, here are some of the issues that will undoubtedly affect the outcome:

There is likely to be a sharp increase in expenditures for national defense, which would serve to increase the federal government's share of total expenditures.

Social security outlays and outlays for retired federal government employees are likely to rise steadily because the aged will continue to comprise ever larger percentages of the population. This also would serve to increase the federal share.

To reduce the federal share, policymakers could attempt to trim other federal government expenditures. But this is difficult to do because almost all government programs have strong vested interests, and many enjoy the support of groups with considerable political clout. One constituency that appears to be the weakest politically is the poor, which helps explain why, in the fiscal year 1982 budget, programs targeted at the poor were cut so sharply. Obviously, cuts such as those accomplished by the Reagan Administration have important implications for the goal of a "fair and equitable distribution of income."

One way to reduce the share is to realize a much faster rate of economic growth. To the extent that the economy grows very rapidly, it is that much easier to accomplish a reduced federal share of total expenditures. In a stagnant, slow-growing economy, a reduced federal share might be nearly impossible. For this reason, among others, it is apparent why the Reagan Administration is trying to focus national attention on economic growth and growth of labor productivity.

SUMMARY

1. There are a number of reasons the overall unemployment rate is an inadequate measure of the "problem of unemployment." First, because *discouraged workers* are not counted as part of the labor force, they are not officially counted among the unemployed. Second, the official unemployment rate measure does not recognize the distinction between *part-time* and *full-time employment.* Third, the official unemployment rate does not adequately capture differences in the *duration of unemployment* of different groups. And fourth, it hides from view both why people are unemployed and the *distribution* of unemployment by occupation, race, sex, and age.

2. Unemployment viewed as a temporary, transitional state of affairs is called *frictional unemployment.* Frictions that are structural in nature, that give rise to chronic unemployment

problems, are the source of *structural unemployment*. *Cyclical unemployment* occurs when there is a general shortage of jobs.

3.   The existence of frictional and structural unemployment clarifies why zero unemployment is neither viable nor necessarily desirable. A requirement for *full employment* is that cyclical unemployment be zero.

4.   In a dynamic, ever-changing economic system, the overall unemployment rate has a tendency to gravitate toward a *"natural rate" of unemployment,* where the real wage (adjusted for productivity change) for the economy as a whole remains fixed. Real wages in individual markets may be rising or falling but, for the economy as a whole, these real wage changes offset one another at the natural rate. There is no necessary reason to assume that the natural rate is some *fixed* rate since what determines the natural rate is the distribution of excess supply and excess demand labor markets and the speeds of real wage changes in those markets.

5.   We do not mean by "price stability" the absence of any change in any price. We mean, rather, the absence of changes in prices *on average.* We define *inflation* as a *sustained* and *broadly based* increase in the general price level.

6.   Generally speaking, there are two types of costs associated with inflation: *(a)* the capricious redistributions of real purchasing power, and *(b)* the output and employment effects.

7.   It is often alleged that the goals of full employment and price stability are in conflict; specifically, efforts to achieve one or the other goal require abandoning the other. This view, which was very popular during the 1960s and early 1970s, was formally enshrined in the *Phillips curve.* Today, many economists argue that the Phillips curve, depicted as a *stable* and *permanent* relationship, misrepresents the relationship between unemployment and inflation. Some argue, by way of contrast, that there is no *necessary* systematic relationship between inflation and unemployment.

8.   A rapidly expanding economy requires a rapidly expanding output potential.

9.   The very sharp fall-off in the growth of U.S. labor productivity has been the source of widespread alarm. The alarmed reaction is understandable. In the absence of productivity gains, there can be no *general* improvement in living standards. It is productivity growth, not wage growth, that determines the growth of real income per worker.

10.   Many factors are pointed to as having been responsible for the slowdown in productivity growth. They include: reduced growth of the capital-labor ratio; sharply increased energy prices; sharper cyclical swings in the economy; increased government regulation; and an apparent reduction in the pace of technological advance.

11.   Sluggish economic growth apparently diminshes the prospects of realizing our full employment and price stability goals.

12.   The goal of rapid economic growth may conflict with the goal of a safe and clean environment. On the other hand, rapid growth may facilitate policies aimed at redistributing incomes.

CONCEPTS FOR REVIEW

Employment Act of 1946

Humphrey-Hawkins Full Employment and
    Balanced Growth Act of 1978

Civilian labor force

National unemployment rate

Discouraged workers

Part-time-unemployment problem

Duration-of-unemployment problem

Reasons-for-unemployment problem

Distribution-of-unemployment-by-occupation,
    race, sex, and age problem

Frictional unemployment

Structural unemployment

Cyclical unemployment

The problem of defining full employment

High employment

Natural rate of unemployment

Real wage

The problem of defining price stability

Consumer price index (CPI)

Personal consumption expenditure deflator

Producer price index for finished goods

Gross national product implicit price deflator

Redistribution of real purchasing power effects of inflation

Effects of inflation on real output and employment

Cost-of-living adjustment (COLA) clauses

Variable-rate mortgages

Inflation tax

Indexing for inflation

Deflation

Creeping inflation

Double-digit inflation

Hyperinflation

Phillips curve

Potential output

Output per capita

QUESTIONS FOR DISCUSSION

(Those marked with an asterisk (*) are more difficult.)

1. Carefully evaluate: "The government must be lying. They tell us that the unemployment rate for 1979 averaged 6.7 percent. However, I just read in the newspaper that 17 million people experienced unemployment in 1979. Since the labor force numbered 100 million people in 1979, that implies an unemployment rate of 17 percent, not 6.7 percent!"

2. *a.* Suppose average labor productivity is advancing at a rate of 3 percent per year. Suppose further that the general level of prices is increasing at a rate of 7 percent per year. If the economy is at its natural rate of unemployment, what will be the average rate of increase be in money wages? Explain.

b. If money wages happened to be growing at a rate faster than the rate given in your answer to *(a)*, would the actual rate of unemployment be above or below the natural rate of unemployment? What if money wages grew at a slower pace? Explain your reasoning carefully. (Use the analogy to a single, large, economy-wide labor market if you wish.)

3. *a.* Explain why there need not be any conflict between the goals of full employment and price stability as long as the full employment target is the same as the natural rate.

b. Explain why the Phillips curve implies the possibility of an inherent conflict between the goals of full employment and price stability.

*4. Suppose everyone's income was indexed to the general price level so that if the general price level rose by 10 percent, so too would people's wage and salary incomes, interest incomes, pension incomes, etc. Would such indexing eliminate the redistributive effects of inflation? (*Hint:* What about the fact that different commodity prices rise at different rates? What about people who hold their savings in the form of currency and coin hidden under their beds? What if the tax system were *not* indexed?)

5. Explain how inflation can result in a slower growth of output and employment over time. Can inflation, therefore, be said to be partly responsible for the increase in the natural rate noted early in this chapter?

6. From the point of view of the framework developed in the text—that is $Q = (Q/L) \times L$—explain how changes in the rate of capital formation and technological advance can serve to change average labor productivity.

*7. Carefully evaluate: "Although rapid economic growth may make it easier to redistribute income from those higher up to those lower down on the income scale, any redistribution in that direction will slow economic growth because of the adverse effects that redistributive policies have on those at the upper end. Accordingly, the goal of rapid economic growth conflicts with the goal of a fair and equitable distribution of income."

The well-being of each of us depends very heavily on how our economic system functions. Therefore, it is important, from a policy point of view, to be able to measure accurately our economic performance. We need reliable data on the quantity and quality of our land, labor, and capital resources to determine how the actual performance of our economy compares with its potential capabilities—that is, to determine how close we are to our production possibilities. We also need accurate statistics on the nature of the goods produced by our economic system: What is the mix of public and private goods? How much of our total output is devoted to capital accumulation? How much to national defense? To social welfare? In addition, we require accurate measures of the distribution of income and wealth, of leisure time, and of the condition of our environment. In short, we require a system of accounts that provides us with a record of how our economic system answers the four fundamental questions—*What, how, for whom,* and *how extensively.* These are the matters that concern us in the present chapter; the focus of our attention will be the **national income and product accounts** of the U.S. economy.

GROSS NATIONAL PRODUCT (GNP)[1]

One of the most important statistical measures of our economic performance is the widely used **gross national product (GNP).** The reason for its widespread use is that it summarizes, in a single number, the total value of all the goods and services our nation produces in a given interval of time; it is a summary measure of *our overall economic performance.* Of course, since GNP measures only the aggregate value of the *goods and services* produced, it is far from being a perfect measure of well-being. It does not provide us with any indication of how much leisure we enjoy, how the goods and services are distributed, what kinds of goods and services are produced, or what the condition of our environment is like.

Chapter 6

The national income and product accounts

---

[1] Some of the material in this chapter is adapted from Lloyd C. Atkinson and Bradley R. Schiller, *A Guide to the Economy* (Prentice-Hall, 1975), ch. 30.

And, like all summary measures, it suffers from the defect of hiding from view the details of the operation of our economic system. Nevertheless, insofar as the measurement of our overall material well-being is important, GNP is a useful concept.

GNP defined

GNP is defined as the *market value of all final goods and services produced during some period of time*. There are five aspects to this definition and each must be clearly understood. They are:

1.   GNP is a **market value** concept. The value of each good and service is defined by its market price as opposed to some other method of valuation.

2.   GNP measures the value of **final goods and services**—goods and services acquired for final use, not for resale or further processing. (Goods and services acquired for resale or further processing are called **intermediate goods and services.**)

3.   GNP refers only to the value of the goods and services that are *produced* during some interval of time, as opposed to the value of the goods and services that are *sold*.

4.   GNP refers to the production that takes place over some interval of *time*. The fact that more can be produced in a year than in a month means that GNP must be given an explicit time dimension.

5.   With few exceptions, GNP refers only to the value of goods and services produced for the marketplace. Nonmarket activities, such as "do-it-yourself" projects and volunteer work, are excluded.

Each of these five concepts will now be examined in turn.

Market value

Our economic system produces literally millions of different goods and services. So that all of these diverse goods and services can be added together in a meaningful way—that is, so that the production of apples can be added to that of oranges, automobiles, battleships, postal services, etc.—we need some common unit of measurement and some basis for identifying the relative worth of each good and service. *Money* is the common unit of measurement, and *market prices* are the measures of relative worth. Thus, an orange that sells for 20 cents and an automobile that sells for $8,000 can be added together using the money prices of each as the relevant measures of value. The **market value** of each final good and service is then obtained by multiplying the price of each times the quantity produced. And GNP is obtained by adding together all those market values. *GNP is a market value aggregate.*

These relationships are readily illustrated with the aid of Table 6.1. There we consider a hypothetical economy that produces three goods only—meat, bread, and candlesticks. Because a pound of meat sells for $3 while a loaf of bread sells for 50 cents, each pound of meat carries a *weight* in the calculation of GNP that is six times the *weight of each* loaf of bread. On the basis of market prices, a pound of meat is worth six times as much as a loaf of bread.

The market values of the three final goods are arrayed in column (3); the GNP for this hypothetical economy is simply the sum of those market values. Thus, for the hypothetical economy consisting of butchers, bakers, and candlestick makers, the GNP is $3,250.

Real versus nominal GNP.   Because GNP is a price-times-quantity relation, GNP can change either because the prices of goods and services change, the quantities produced change, or both. Since, from a welfare point of view, we have an interest in *how much* our economic system produces and how that quantity changes over time, it is important to be able to abstract from the GNP changes brought about by price movements in order to focus on quantity changes. It is for this reason that economists make a sharp distinction between *nominal GNP* and *real GNP*.

Nominal GNP—or, as it is often called, **current dollar GNP**—is a value arrived at by using the prices prevailing in the year the goods and services were produced. The nominal GNP for

Table 6.1
GNP: A market value aggregate (hypothetical data)

	(1) Final output produced in a year	(2) Market price (per unit)	(3) Market value
Meat	1,000 pounds	$3.00	$3,000
Bread	400 loaves	.50	200
Candlesticks	50 sticks	1.00	50
Total			$3,250

The GNP for the hypothetical economy described above is $3,250. It is obtained by adding together the *market value* of all final goods—meat, bread, and candlesticks—produced during the year. The market value of each good is obtained by multiplying its price times the quantity produced.

1981 refers to the market value of all final goods and services produced during 1981 using 1981 prices as the measures of value. **Real GNP,** on the other hand, is calculated using prices prevalent during some previous, or *base,* year. If 1970 happens to be the relevant base year, the year selected for purposes of comparision, the *real GNP for 1981* refers to the market value of all final goods and services produced during 1981 using *1970* prices as the measures of value. Thus, real GNP is sometimes referred to as "GNP at constant prices"; or, if the base year happens to be 1970, "GNP at 1970 prices" or "GNP in 1970 dollars," or further still, "constant dollar GNP."

The differences between nominal and real GNP can be illustrated with the aid of Tables 6.1 and 6.2. Suppose the prices in Table 6.1 are those that prevailed in 1981. Therefore, the nominal (or current dollar) GNP for 1981 is $3,250.

What is the real GNP for 1981? It all depends. *It depends on the base year selected and the prices prevailing in the base year.* Assume the appropriate base year is 1970 and that base year prices for the three goods were as follows:

Meat	$2.00 per pound
Bread	.50 per loaf
Candlesticks	.80 each

By valuing the quantities produced in 1981 at *1970* prices, it is clear, as shown in Table 6.2, that the real GNP for 1981 is $2,240.

The calculation of real GNP is an important one for it enables us to determine whether, and to what extent, the *quantities* of goods and services produced change from one year to the next. If the quantities produced in two different years are *both* valued at 1970 prices, any difference in GNP between those two years will reflect a difference in the amounts produced. By comparing the nominal GNP between two years, one

Table 6.2
Real GNP versus nominal GNP
(hypothetical data)

	(1) Final output produced in 1981	(2) 1981 prices	(3) Market value at 1981 prices (col. (1) × col. (2))	(5) 1970 prices	(4) Market value at 1970 prices (col. (1) × col. (4))
Meat	1,000 lbs.	$3.00	$3,000	$2.00	$2,000
Bread	400 loaves	0.50	200	0.50	200
Candlesticks	50 sticks	1.00	50	0.80	40
Total			$3,250		$2,240

Nominal GNP is given in column (3). It tells us the market value of the output produced in 1981 using 1981 prices.
Real GNP is given in column (5). It tells us the market value of the output produced in 1981 using 1970 prices.

cannot tell whether, and to what extent, the difference is caused by a difference in the amounts produced or by a difference in prices.

The real GNP concept is important for a second reason. It enables us to abstract from the price changes that occurred between the year in question and the base year. Whereas the nominal GNP for 1981 was $3,250, the real GNP was only $2,240; the difference between these two figures reflects the price level change that took place between the base year (1970) and the year in which the goods were produced (1981). One can calculate the percentage change in the level of prices over that period by first calculating the ratio of nominal GNP to real GNP. Specifically, calculate the ratio,

$$\frac{\text{Nominal GNP for year X}}{\text{Real GNP for year X}}.$$

Using the numerical example above, dividing $3,250 (nominal GNP) by $2,240 (real GNP) gives us an answer of 1.45, suggesting a price increase of 45 percent between 1970 and 1981 for our hypothetical economy. The number 1.45 is a **price index**—a GNP price index—using 1970 prices as the basis. Normally, this price index is multiplied by 100 and expressed as 145 instead of 1.45.

It is obvious from the above relationship that if the value of the GNP price index *and* the nominal GNP were known, we could readily calculate real GNP as follows:

$$\text{Real GNP} = \frac{\text{Nominal GNP}}{\text{GNP price index}} \times 100.$$

(In this calculation, since the price index is multiplied by 100, the numerator, nominal GNP, must be multplied by 100 as well.) Thus, given a GNP price index equal to 145 and a nominal GNP of $3,250, it is clear that real GNP is $2,240, (i.e., $\frac{\$3,250}{145} \times 100 = \$2,240$).

This last relationship among real GNP, nominal GNP, and the GNP price index is useful because it accords more precisely with the way real GNP is actually calculated by government statisticians. That is, *real GNP is arrived at by taking nominal GNP and "deflating" that figure by the appropriate GNP price index.* For obvious reasons, then, the appropriate GNP price index is called the **GNP implicit price deflator.** Let us examine this process a little more closely.

A base year is selected and the price index for that base year is set equal to 100—*prices in the base year are 100 percent of themselves.* If prices rise on average by, say, 25 percent between the base year and the year in question, then the price index for the year in question will be 125. The figure of 125 can be used to deflate the nominal GNP of that year to arrive at the real GNP. Consider the following example. Suppose 1960 is selected as the base year. The GNP price index (the GNP implicit price deflator) for 1960 is therefore equal to 100. Suppose that prices rose an average of 50 percent between 1960 and 1970. What will be the GNP implicit price deflator for 1970? It will equal 150. And if nominal GNP for 1970 was $450, what would real GNP for 1970 equal? It would equal $300 (i.e., $\frac{\$450}{\$150} \times 100$).

Final goods

To arrive at an accurate measure of GNP, it is necessary to count only *final* goods and services—goods and services produced for final use, not for resale or further processing. The reason? We want to be sure to count each good and service that is produced during the specified period, but we want to count each only *once.* By adding up only the value of the final goods produced, we have some assurance of arriving at the measure we want. This can be illustrated quite easily.

For simplicity, consider the production of two goods only—automobiles and automobile radios. Assume that automobile companies produce 20 automobiles with a market price of $5,000 each; the market value of all of the automobiles is therefore $100,000. *All automobiles have factory-installed radios.*

Radio manufacturers, on the other hand, are assumed to produce 30 automobile radios. Twenty of these were sold to the automobile companies for installation in their new cars; 10 were sold to other retail radio outlets. The market price of each radio is $100; the market value of all of these radios is therefore $3,000.

Now, following the rule that we must count everything that has been produced *once,* should we simply add together the market value of each good in order to arrive at a measure of GNP, or should we subtract out from that total the sale of automobile radios to automobile manufacturers? *We should subtract out the sale of automobile radios to the automobile manufacturers.* The reason is this: *The value of each radio has already been included in the $5,000 automobile price.*

If we were to add the $3,000 market value of automobile radios to the $100,000 market value of automobiles to arrive at our measure of GNP, we would be **double-counting** the production of 20 automobile radios—once as part of the $3,000 figure, and once again as part of the $100,000 figure. Properly calculated, GNP is $101,000, *not* $103,000.

The $2,000 worth of radios sold to the automobile manufacturers are referred to as **intermediate products.** To arrive at the appropriate GNP value, it is necessary to net out all intermediate products. Otherwise, we would end up counting some items twice. Indeed, in many instances, if we did not net out intermediate goods and services, we would count some items several times. (For instance, steel sheets are sold to stamping plants and stamping plants sell their output to automobile manufacturers.) In arriving at a measure of GNP, we could perform the following calculation:

$$\text{GNP} = \frac{\text{Market value of \textit{all} goods and services produced}}{\textit{minus} \text{ market value of \textit{all intermediate products.}}}$$

All goods and services can be classified as either *intermediate or final.* Therefore it is clear that the difference between the value of *all* goods and services and intermediate products is, simply, the value of all final goods and services. Accordingly, GNP is nothing other than the market value of all *final* goods and services produced. We shall have more to say about the nature of *final* goods and services later.

GNP is equal to the sum of values added. There is another essentially equivalent procedure for calculating GNP. That is to sum up the **values added** of each production unit within the economy. Value added is calculated by *subtracting the value of the intermediate products used in the production of a good or service from the value of the output produced. The result is the value added by the production unit in question.* This can be illustrated with the aid of Table 6.3.

In this example of auto production from the ground up, start with the production of mined ore. Using scarce land, labor, and capital resources, $100,000 worth of ore is produced and sold to the steel mill. The mill uses scarce resources to convert the mined ore into steel sheets. *The steel sheets are sold to the stamping manufacturer for $400,000. The difference between the value of the ore and the value of the steel sheets represents the value added by the steel mill.* The stamping manufacturer adds an additional $500,000 in value to produce $900,000 worth of auto parts. Finally, the auto manufacturers add $1.1 million of value to the $900,000 worth of parts to produce $2 million worth of autos. Note particularly that the market value of the *final* output of autos is identically equal to the sum of the values added at each stage of production—from the ground up.

An input-output approach. The above example is oversimplified. Indeed, automobile manufacturers purchase goods and services not from just a few concerns but from literally hundreds of different producers. Each of these producers in turn purchases goods and services from other industries as well. The complex nature of these interdependencies is captured in an **input-output transactions table;** a simplified hypothetical table is presented in Table 6.4.

The input-output table allows us to identify at a glance the distribution of both inputs and outputs throughout the economy. Reading *across* any given row in the table, we are able to identify how an industry's *output* is distributed among the economy's participants. Consider the "Manufactures" row. We see there that manufacturing firms sell $5 billion worth of goods and services to agriculture, $5 billion to mining, $8 billion

Table 6.3
Automobile production from the ground up

Good produced	Value of output produced (and sold)	Value added
Mined ore (using scarce land, labor, and capital resources)	$100,000	$100,000
↓		
Sold to steel mill		
↓		
Steel sheets (using scarce land, labor, and capital resources)	$400,000	$300,000
↓		
Sold to stamping manufacturers		
↓		
Stamped automobile parts (using scarce land, labor, and capital resources)	$900,000	$500,000
↓		
Sold to automobile manufacturers		
↓		
Automobiles (using scarce land, labor, and capital resources)	$2 million	$1.1 million

Final output of automobiles = $2 million = Total value added

Table 6.4
Input–output transactions table
($ billions, hypothetical data)

Outputs → / ↓ Inputs	Output sold as intermediate products to						Output sold as final product	Total output
	Agriculture	Mining	Construction	Manufactures	Services	Total		
Agriculture	10	1	4	6	1	22	38	60
Mining	2	3	3	7	0	15	5	20
Construction	4	2	1	5	0	12	18	30
Manufactures	5	5	8	6	3	27	25	52
Services	2	1	3	6	3	15	12	27
Imports	1	2	0	3	0	6	4	
Total input	24	14	19	33	7	97	Total final product	102
Total output	60	20	30	52	27	189	Minus imports	−10
Value added	36	6	11	19	20	92	Equals GNP	92

to construction, and so forth; total *intermediate sales*—sales to other industries for resale or further processing—amount to $27 billion. *Final sales*—sales to final users—amount to $25 billion. Total output—the sum of intermediate and final sales—is $52 billion. All other rows in the table are interpreted similarly, with one exception—imports. The import row shows how the goods and services imported (i.e., purchased) from foreign countries are distributed. As Table 6.4 makes clear, $6 billion worth of imported goods and services are used as inputs by the five designated industries; $4 billion of imported goods are sold as final product. The important point to note here is that *imports are not part of our nation's output.*

Reading *down* a column, we are able to identify the sources of an industry's *inputs.* Thus, the construction industry purchases $4 billion worth of inputs from agriculture, $3 billion from mining, $1 from itself, and so forth. The total is $19 billion worth of inputs. *Value added* for the construction industry amounts to $11 billion—that is, the difference between the value of its total output ($30 billion) and the value of the inputs purchased ($19 billion).

The GNP for our hypothetical economy can be obtained by summing up the values added of all five industries—here it amounts to $92 billion. Similarly, GNP can be calculated by adding up the value of all final products *minus* the value of imports. Imports are subtracted because they represent the output produced by *other* countries; imports amount to $10 billion. Thus, the value of the final product ($102 billion) minus the value of imports ($10 billion) yields a value of $92 billion for GNP—which is identical to the sum of the values added.

Production versus sales

As the definition of GNP makes clear, we are concerned with the value of the final goods *produced,* not strictly with the value of the final goods sold. The distinction is important because goods sold in one period may have been produced in an earlier period.

Since the emphasis is on production in a given

time interval, it is clear that goods produced in *previous* periods but sold in the current period are *not* part of the current period's GNP. Because GNP is frequently calculated using final *sales* numbers, those goods produced in an earlier period will have to be subtracted from final sales. Similarly, there will be goods produced in the current period that will not be sold until another accounting period. We must be sure, however, that we count these goods as part of our current period GNP.

In principle, these calculations can be done quite simply if we know the value of beginning-of-period and end-of-period *inventories*—that is, the value of the *stock* of goods on hand at the beginning of our accounting period and the value at the end. Figure 6.1 illustrates the procedure schematically. We see in Figure 6.1 that, at the beginning of our accounting period, there is an inventory of $50 billion worth of goods. These goods are *not* part of current period GNP because they were produced in a previous time period.

During the year, $900 billion worth of goods and services are *sold.* This is not, however, the GNP for the current period. Some of those sales may have been out of beginning-of-period inventories. Moreover, some of the goods produced in the current period will not be sold until some future period. Indeed, we notice in Figure 6.1 that at the end of the accounting period, there is $62 billion worth of inventories. *Since inventories at the beginning of the period amounted to $50 billion and inventories at the end were valued at $62 billion, this implies that the value of the goods produced during the current period was $12 billion more than sales ($62 billion minus $50 billion).* GNP was therefore equal to $912 billion in the current period. Hence, we can arrive at the value of production by simply looking at the value of final sales plus or minus (+ or −) the *net change* in the value of inventories:

Value of final output produced = Value of final sales
(+ or −) Net change in the value of inventories.

If inventories had fallen during the period, the value of the final output produced would have

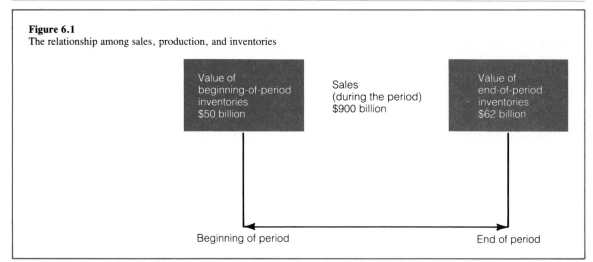

Figure 6.1
The relationship among sales, production, and inventories

Value of beginning-of-period inventories $50 billion

Sales (during the period) $900 billion

Value of end-of-period inventories $62 billion

Beginning of period   End of period

fallen short of sales by the amount of the *change* in inventories.

Now it is often useful to *define* terms so that the value of final production is identical to the value of final expenditures—that is, by defining the net change in inventories as a positive (if inventories rise) or negative (if inventories fall) final expenditure. In effect, if businesspeople run up their inventories, they "sell" that much of their output to themselves; the converse is true for a decline in inventories.

This is precisely the procedure followed by U.S. government statisticians. If business firms increase their inventories, this increase is recorded as **inventory investment;** a *decline* in inventories is recorded as **inventory disinvestment.** Thus GNP can be defined as the market value of all final expenditures. What expenditures do we classify as final? Broadly speaking, there are four categories—personal consumption expenditures, gross private domestic investment, government purchases of goods and services, and net exports of goods and services.

Personal consumption expenditures are largely self-explanatory. They include expenditures by consumers for *durable goods* (such as automobiles, furniture and household equipment), *nondurable goods* (such as food, clothing, and motor gasoline), and *services* (such as hair cuts and transportation).

Gross private domestic investment refers to the sum total of all expenditures made by the private (i.e., nongovernment) sector for investment goods produced in the current period. There are two major categories of investment. First, there is **fixed investment,** which includes both structures (i.e., buildings) and producers' durable equipment; fixed investment is frequently subdivided into the two categories—nonresidential fixed investment and residential fixed investment. The **change in business inventories** represents the second major kind of investment. Gross private domestic investment equals the sum of fixed investment and the *change* in business inventories.

Not all investment constitutes an increase in the stock of capital. As emphasized in Chapter 2, capital goods are used up—that is, *depreciated* or *consumed*—during the production process. The purchase of a building or a piece of equipment represents the purchase of a certain quantity of usefulness; that quantity of usefulness is "consumed" over the course of the asset's useful life. *Depreciation measures the reduction in the asset's quantity of usefulness over some interval of time.*

The reduction in the quantity of usefulness—the depreciation—of our nation's stock of capital goods as a consequence of production activity serves to effectively reduce that stock of capital goods over time unless offset by new investment. Some investment must take place simply to keep the stock of capital goods intact. Only investment over and above what is necessary to keep the stock of capital intact constitutes an increase in our capital stock. A sharp distinction is made between **gross investment** and **net investment,** the difference being the depreciation of capital goods. In the national income and product accounts, such "consumption" of capital is called **capital consumption allowance (CCA).** Using this concept, net investment can be defined as:

Net investment = Gross investment − CCA.

Net investment measures the change, plus or minus, in our nation's stock of capital goods over some interval of time.

Government purchases of goods and services include all expenditures for currently produced goods and services by federal, state, and local governments. It includes expenditures for such things as national defense, police protection, education, and welfare.

Net exports are defined as **exports** minus **imports.** *Exports* refer to the market value of goods and services produced in this country and sold abroad; *imports* are goods and services produced abroad and purchased here at home.

On the basis of the above considerations it is clear that:

GNP = Personal consumption expenditures + Gross private domestic investment + Government purchases of goods and services + Net exports.

Symbolically, if we let **GNP** = Y, personal consumption expenditures = C, gross private domestic investment = I_g, government expenditures = G, exports = X, and imports = M, the above relationship can be written as:

$$Y = C + I_g + G + (X - M).$$

Table 6.5 summarizes these concepts using data for 1980; these data reflect the **product side** of the national income and product accounts. We see that GNP for 1980 amounted to $2.6

Table 6.5:
GNP: The expenditures approach, 1980
($ billions)
Product side

Personal consumption expenditures		$1,672.8
Gross private domestic investment		395.3
(CCA)	($287.3)	
(net investment)	(108.0)	
Government purchases of goods and services		534.7
Net exports (exports − imports)		23.3
Nominal GNP		$2,626.1
GNP in 1972 dollars		$1,480.7
(GNP implicit price deflator, 1972 = 100)		(177.36)

Source: *U.S. Department of Commerce.*

trillion. Personal consumption expenditures, by far the largest component, were $1.7 trillion. Government purchases amounted to about $0.5 trillion. And gross private domestic investment was $0.4 trillion. Also note that real GNP—GNP in 1972 dollars—amounted to about $1.5 trillion; this, combined with the nominal GNP of $2.6 trillion, yields the GNP implicit price deflator value of about 177 for 1980.

The time period

Time is the fourth important aspect of the definition of GNP. Indeed, as we narrow the time frame, the amount that can be produced will be smaller. *Production takes time.*

The most common time period is a year. That is, we talk in terms of the GNP for 1979 or for 1980. This, as the definition of GNP implies, tells us how much was produced in those years.

Sometimes we use **calendar years** (January 1 through December 31) or we use **fiscal years** (usually October 1 of a particular year through September 30 of the following year). We could also calculate quarterly values or monthly values of GNP. For example, we could calculate GNP for the first quarter of 1980, which would tell us the value of the output produced in the first three months of 1980.

Often, the value of GNP for a period less than

a year will be reported as that value at an **annual rate.** Thus, the value of GNP for the first quarter of the year will be reported as GNP "for the first quarter at an annual rate." To convert a quarterly value into an annual rate value, the government multiplies the quarterly value by four. This is justified on the grounds that if the quarterly value were to persist for four quarters then GNP for the year would be precisely four times that quarterly value.

Market versus nonmarket activities

The fifth aspect of the definition of GNP is that it generally includes only market activities. Thus, GNP excludes a large number of economic activities that are *not* transacted in the marketplace but that do have implications for our material economic welfare. These activities include, for example, do-it-yourself projects, volunteer charity work, and the cleaning and cooking activities we do for ourselves in the home. If a payment were made to people in the marketplace for any of these services, such payments would show up (in principle, at least) in our GNP; since these activities are not transacted in the marketplace, they are excluded. The results of this procedure can at times be strange. If you marry your housekeeper, for instance, the GNP will decline.[2]

It would, of course, be possible to make estimates of the value of such nonmarket activities and to include those estimates in our GNP calculations. In practice such estimates are rarely made because of the difficulties associated with determining the value of such activities.

There are exceptions, however. First, the government regularly makes a calculation that is called the **implicit rental value of owner-occupied houses.** Housing is considered to be an **investment good** that, if rented, would yield the owner rental income. Corresponding to that value of rental income there is an equivalent value—the value of housing services consumed. The value

is *implicit* because it represents the implied rent that could have been obtained if owners had, in fact, rented. Second, an estimate is regularly made of the food that is consumed by farmers out of their own crops. In societies where the agricultural population is large, such a calculation is important. Finally, since many government services are not transacted in markets, their value cannot be determined by market forces— that is, there is no market price for such services. As a result, GNP statisticians value such services at the cost to the government of providing them. For example, if a police department has a payroll and other expenses of $2 million, we say the value of police services is $2 million. The value of output is based only on the value or cost of the inputs. Many people might value the law and order that is provided at more than $2 million, but since such evaluations are very subjective (after all, how much is a human life worth?), government statisticians stick with costs (which are easier to measure anyway).

GROSS NATIONAL INCOME

We turn now to an examination of the *income side* of the national income and product accounts. Before proceeding to an in-depth study of the income side, however, it is worthwhile examining the significance of there being an income side that corresponds to the product side.

The equivalence of income and the value of output

A lot of needless confusion can be avoided if one understands the following proposition: *The production of a dollar's worth of final product generates a dollar of income.* This equivalence is easily demonstrated. Consider the example presented in Table 6.6.

The automobile manufacturer of Table 6.6 produces $500,000 worth of output. For simplicity, assume that all of this output is sold to consumers. Given intermediate goods purchases of $200,000, the value added by the manufacturer comes to $300,000; the $300,000 value added rep-

---

[2] Illegal market activities are also generally excluded in the calculation of GNP. Statistically, then, the legalization of prostitution, gambling, and drugs would raise our GNP significantly.

Table 6.6
Value added and the income generated by
an automobile manufacturer

Value added		Income generated	
Value of output	$500,000	Indirect business taxes	$ 50,000
Less: Intermediate goods			
purchased from other firms....	200,000	Employee compensation	150,000
		Interest	10,000
		Rent	10,000
		Residual	80,000
		Depreciation $20,000	
		Corporate profits 60,000	
Value added	$300,000	Total income	$300,000

resents this firm's contribution to the nation's GNP. Importantly, the income generated by this auto manufacturer is exactly $300,000—the same as its value added.

The value added and the amount of income generated *must be* identical. The producer receives $500,000 for the output it produces. $200,000 is distributed to the suppliers of the intermediate goods. The remaining $300,000 is distributed as follows: $50,000 is government income in the form of excise and sales taxes (so-called indirect business taxes) paid by car purchasers and collected by the producer; $150,000 represents *employee compensation*, the income earned by the firm's workers; $10,000 in *interest income* is paid on debt outstanding to the firm's creditors; $10,000 in *rental income* is paid to the landlords of the property leased by the firm; the *residual*—what is left over after all other income claims have been satisfied—amounts to $80,000. The residual is not all profit, however. Depreciation must be subtracted as an allowance for the capital "consumed" during the production process; the residual claim *after* allowance for depreciation is *profit*.

The reason the income generated is precisely equal to the value added is clear. After the payment of all other income claims, there is a residual income claim representing what is left over (which could, by the way, be negative). Moreover, since income generated is precisely equal to value added, and since the GNP for the whole nation is defined as the sum of all values added,

GNP has as its counterpart, an identical value, **gross national income (GNI).** (Because they are identical, it is commonplace to simply let GNP represent both the market value of the final goods produced *and* the aggregate income generated.)

This identity of GNP and GNI has a number of important implications. First and foremost, the nation's real income will increase only if more goods and services are produced. Second, any increase in nominal GNP brought about by an increase in the general level of prices (i.e., inflation), will be reflected in an *equal* change in the value of nominal income. If inflation results in a 10 percent increase in nominal GNP, nominal GNI will rise by a like amount. This does *not* mean that *everyone's* income within the economy will rise by 10 percent. But it does mean that corresponding to those whose incomes rise by less than 10 percent, there are others whose incomes rise by more than 10 percent.

GNP and NNP

Although GNP is one useful summary measure of our economic well-being, there are a number of other income and product concepts that economists have found to be useful in analyzing economic activity. One of these concepts is **net national product (NNP),** defined as GNP minus capital consumption allowances (CCA). That is,

$$NNP = GNP - CCA.$$

The NNP measure is important because it tells us how much of total output is available for distribution while still keeping the stock of capital intact. That is, if the economy is to maintain its existing stock of capital, it is necessary that the capital that is used up or "consumed" in production be replaced. NNP, therefore, gives us some idea of how much we can consume as a nation without impairing our productive capacity. Of course, if gross private domestic investment exceeds CCA (i.e., net investment is positive), our productive capacity will expand; negative net investment, on the other hand, implies a reduction in our productive capacity. For 1980, NNP equaled $2.3 trillion, $287 billion less than GNP.

National Income (NI)

Neither GNP nor NNP, however, gives us an accurate measure of how much income is actually earned by the various factors of production— by land, labor, and capital. The most important reason? Product prices are augmented by various **indirect business taxes (IBT),** the value of which is not part of the earnings of the factors of production. Thus, the measure that most accurately reflects the income earned is called **national income** (NI), which is defined as:[3]

$$NI = NNP - IBT.$$

---

[3] Actually, going from NNP to NI is a bit more involved than this. First, there are a number of government enterprises (the Post Office and Amtrak, for example) that produce goods and services for sale to the public. If these enterprises are subsidized, then this tells us that the payments to the various factors of production exceeded the market value of the output produced. Accordingly, to arrive at our measure of national income we need to *add* to NNP the subsidies of government enterprises. If government enterprises have surpluses, which are returned to the government, the value of those surpluses should be subtracted from NNP.

Second, in conducting business, many firms give gifts to clients and customers—technically called **business transfer payments.** Since these are not payments to factors of production, they are deducted from NNP in arriving at NI. However, in arriving at *personal income*—income received by individuals—these business transfer payments are added back in.

Third, for a number of complicated reasons, government statisticians adjust NNP up or down by the amount of the *statistical discrepancy* in arriving at NI.

In our discussion in the text, we ignore the complications introduced by these further adjustments to NNP. Specifically we include in indirect business taxes adjustments for business transfer payments, for subsidies to government enterprises, and for the statistical discrepancy.

National income consists of the sum of wages and salaries (employee compensation), proprietor's income, rental income of individuals, corporate profits, and interest income. For 1980, national income amounted to $2.1 trillion.

Personal income (PI)

National income is not a good measure of the amount of income that *individuals* receive. Another concept, **personal income (PI),** has therefore been developed. To arrive at personal income, a number of adjustments must be made to national income. The important items are these:

1. Part of employee compensation is subject to social security taxes that go to the government to pay for our social insurance programs. These payments, technically referred to as **contributions for social insurance,** are part of the income earned, but they are not part of personal income. Contributions for social insurance must be subtracted from national income.

2. Not all corporate profits become part of personal income. Corporations do pay dividends out of profits to people who own shares of corporate stock. (This part is distributed and does become part of personal income.) But the taxes that are paid to the government on profits (corporate profits taxes) and the profits that are not distributed to individuals (undistributed corporate profits) are not part of personal income. Therefore, corporate profits taxes and undistributed corporate profits must be subtracted from national income. (Technically, this is done by subtracting from NI all corporate profits except those distributed as dividend income.)

3. The government makes various forms of **transfer payments** to individuals. The transfer itself does not have associated with it the production of goods and services. It is, therefore, not included in value added, nor is it part of earned income. But it does add to personal income. These transfer payments—which include payments to welfare recipients, veterans, farmers, and the unemployed—are *added* to national income.

Table 6.7
National income and product accounts, 1980 ($billions)

Product side		Income side	
Personal consumption expenditures	$1,672.8	Indirect business taxes*	$ 217.5
Gross private domestic investment	395.3	Employee compensation (wage and salaries)	1,596.5
CCA $287.3			
Net investment 108.0		Rent and interest	211.6
Government purchases of goods and services	534.7	Business income	600.6
		Proprietors' income† ... $130.6	
Net exports of goods and		Corporate profits 182.7	
services (exports − imports)	23.3	CCA 287.3	
GNP	$2,626.1	GNI	$2,626.1

Note: Columns may not total because of rounding.
* Includes adjustments for business transfer payments, for subsidies to government enterprises and for the statistical discrepancy.
† Proprietors' income refers to income of businesses that are not incorporated.
Source: U.S. Department of Commerce, *Survey of Current Business.*

Combining all of these items, personal income is defined as follows:

PI = NI
  − Contributions for social insurance
  − Corporate profits taxes
  − Undistributed corporate profits
  + Government transfer payments.

In 1980, PI amounted to about $2.2 trillion.

Disposable personal income (DPI)

Personal income does not tell us how much income people have available to spend for the goods and services they want. To arrive at **disposable personal income (DPI)** we need to subtract out personal income taxes.

Thus:

DPI = PI − Personal income taxes.

In 1980, DPI equaled $1.8 trillion. All of these concepts are summarized in Tables 6.7 and 6.8 using data for 1980.

The various income concepts and their interrelationships: A summary

Figure 6.2 illustrates the relationships among these concepts diagrammatically. You would do well to study Figure 6.2 carefully since a thorough understanding of the financial flows depicted there is essential to everything that follows in this part of the book. Let's break into the flowchart at the top.

1. Land, labor, and capital resources are used to produce both intermediate and final

Table 6.8
Relation of gross national product to national income personal income, and disposable personal income, 1980 ($billions)

Gross national product	$2,626.1
Less capital consumption allowance	− 287.3
Equals net national product	2,338.9
Less indirect business taxes*	− 217.3
Equals national income	2,121.6
Less contributions for social insurance	− 203.7
Less corporate profits taxes	− 82.3
Less undistributed corporate profits	− 44.4
Plus government transfer payments†	+ 370.2
Equals personal income	2,160.2
Less personal taxes	− 338.5
Equals disposable personal income	$1,821.7

Note: Columns may not total because of rounding.
* Includes adjustments for business transfer payments, for subsidies to government enterprises and for the statistical discrepancy.
† This includes adjustments for net interest, personal interest income and business transfer payments.
Source: U.S. Department of Commerce, *Survey of Current Business.*

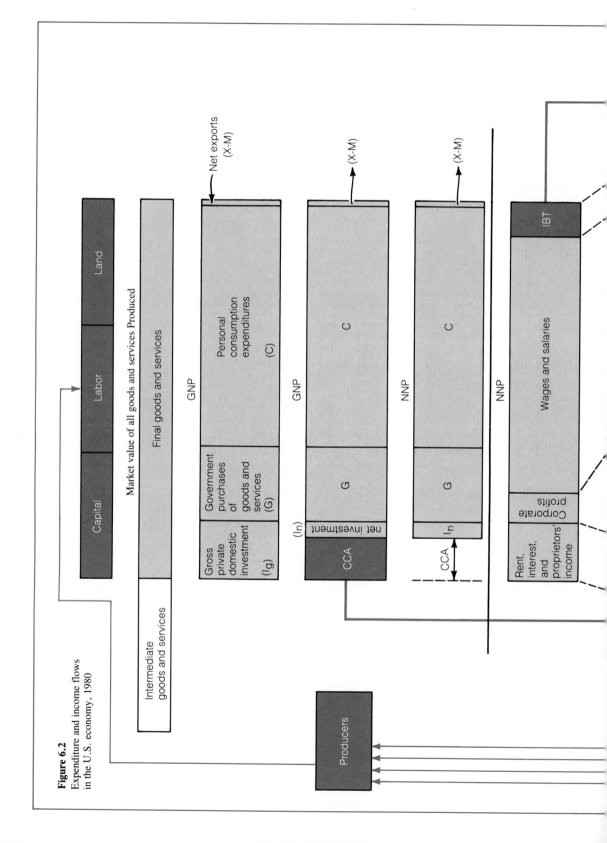

Figure 6.2
Expenditure and income flows in the U.S. economy, 1980

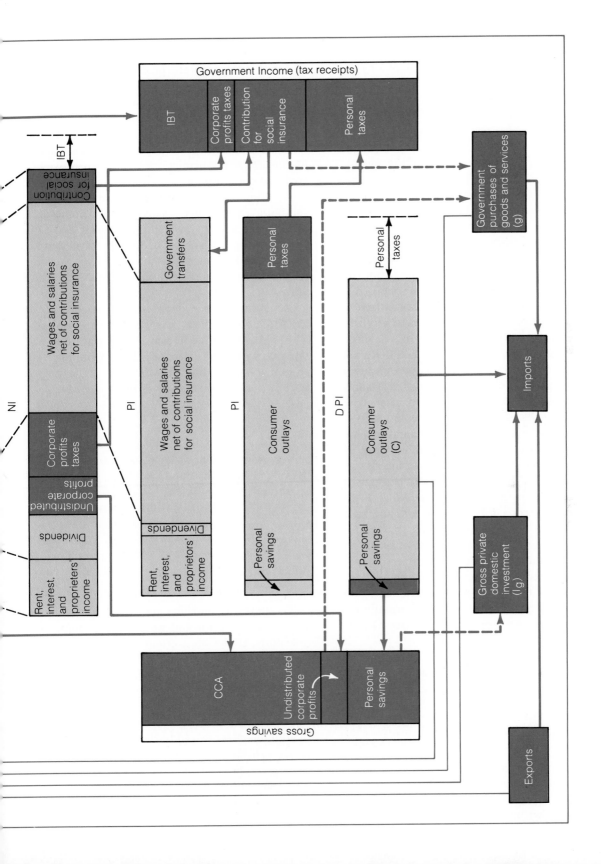

goods and services. The market value of all *final* goods and services produced yields our GNP, a value that is identically equal to GNI. Part of our GNI is siphoned off in the form of capital consumption allowances (CCA), which become part of **gross savings.** Subtracting out indirect business taxes (which become part of the government's income), we are left with national income. Contributions for social insurance and corporate income taxes are paid to government out of national income. After subtracting out undistributed corporate profits (which also become part of gross savings), and adding in government transfers we arrive at personal income. After the payment of personal income taxes, we obtain disposable personal income, which can either be saved or spent on consumer goods and services; personal savings become part of gross savings.

2. As is apparent from Figure 6.2, there are four sources of government income—indirect business taxes, contributions for social insurance, corporate income taxes, and personal income taxes. A portion of government income is used to make transfer payments; government income is also used to purchase goods and services. If government purchases exceed government income (net of transfers), the government runs a **budget deficit;** in general, such a deficit is financed by government borrowing. The purchase of government bonds by individuals or corporations constitutes one use of gross savings. If, on the other hand, the government runs a **budget surplus** (defined as an excess of government income—net of transfers—over government purchases), some government bonds are usually retired (i.e., some of the previously borrowed funds are paid back).

3. Gross savings consists of CCA, undistributed corporate profits, and personal savings. For some purposes it is useful to define a **net savings** concept; it is:

Net savings = Gross savings − CCA.

Gross savings is an important source of funds for the financing of gross private domestic investment. That financing can be direct—corporations using their own internal funds (i.e., CCA plus

undistributed corporate profits) and/or issuing bonds or stocks, which are purchased directly by individuals and corporations—or indirect—savings placed with various financial institutions (e.g., commercial banks, savings and loan institutions, mutual savings banks, credit unions, and life insurance companies), who in turn provide credit to corporations.

4. Finally, some portion of personal consumption expenditures, gross private domestic investment, and government purchases consist of imported goods and services. Exports measure the expenditures made by the rest of the world for the goods and services produced in the United States.

An aside: The savings-investment identity. On the basis of these accounting relationships, we are able to derive in a formal way a proposition that will prove very useful later in our analysis of macroeconomic behavior. This proposition is known as the **savings-investment identity.**

The idea behind the savings-investment identity is straightforward. This identity states that, on the one hand, all income not spent on consumer goods is defined as *savings,* and that, on the other hand, all output produced other than consumer goods is defined as *investment.* Thus, since GNP is identical to GNI, it is clear that savings must be identical to investment since the value of consumer goods subtracted from GNP leaves you with investment and the value of consumer goods subtracted from GNI leaves you with savings.

To illustrate, consider an economy without a government sector and without either imports or exports. Under these circumstances, GNP (Y) would be defined as the sum of consumer expenditures (C) and gross private domestic investment (I_g):

$$Y = C + I_g.$$

In addition, GNI would be divided between consumer expenditures (C), on the one hand and gross savings (S) on the other. That is, GNI not spent on consumer goods would consist of the sum of CCA, undistributed corporate profits, and personal savings (i.e., gross savings):

$$Y = C + S.$$

Combining the last two expressions, it is clear that

$$C + I_g = C + S$$

and that, therefore

$$I_g = S.$$

Or consider a more realistic economic system in which a government sector is admitted. GNP would then be defined as the sum of consumer expenditures (C), gross private domestic investment (I_g), and government purchases of goods and services (G):

$$Y = C + I_g + G.$$

On the income side, that portion not spent on consumer goods will take the form of taxes (T) and gross savings (S):

$$Y = C + T + S.$$

Combining the last two expressions, it is clear that

$$\underbrace{I_g + G}_{} = \underbrace{T + S}_{}$$
"Investment" = "Savings."

For some purposes it is useful to rearrange this expression as,

$$I_g - S = T - G.$$

What this tells us is that the government surplus (if T exceeds G), must be identical to the excess of I_g over S; or the government deficit (if T is less than G) must be identical to the excess of S over I.

Finally, taking into account all sectors of the economy, foreign and domestic, GNP can be defined as

$$Y = C + I_g + G + (X - M),$$

where X = exports, and M = imports. The income generated by both foreign and domestic activity can be either consumed or "saved"

$$Y = C + S + T,$$

where S + T is defined as *savings*.

Thus, defining *investment* as $I_g + G + (X -$

M),[4] it is clear from the last two expressions that "savings is identical to investment."

$$\underbrace{I_g + G + (X - M)}_{} = \underbrace{S + T}_{}$$
"Investment" = "Savings."

Again, for some purposes it is useful to rearrange this expression as

$$(I_g - S) + (X - M) = T - G.$$

This tells us that the sum of the difference between the two pairs of values on the left-hand side *must* equal the value of the budget surplus or deficit.

This savings-investment identity is, as noted earlier, a source of considerable confusion. It is important, therefore, that we identify explicitly the source of this confusion in order that we can avoid it. The savings-investment identity described above is true by *definition*. It holds whether the economy is at full employment or far below; it holds whether there is a little inflation or a lot; and it holds whether the economy *is or is not* in equilibrium.

Later, we will encounter the notion of **macroeconomic equilibrium,** in which the condition for equilibrium is that savings equal investment. But this latter relationship should never be confused with the above accounting identity. That is, equilibrium will occur only when *planned* investment is equal to *planned* savings; the accounting identity defined above deals with *actual* investment and savings.

The source of the difference between these two concepts lies in the national income accounts treatment of changes in inventories. If business firms experience an increase in their inventories, we record this in the national income accounts as an investment; a decline in inventories is recorded as a disinvestment. But if the *actual* change in inventories differs from the change business people *intended* or *planned* to make, this will probably call forth changes in the level

---

[4] Net exports are viewed as foreign investment in the sense that if the value of exports exceeds the value of imports, U.S. residents build up claims against foreigners. If imports exceed exports, foreign investment will be negative.

of production and income. The economy will not be in equilibrium because *actual* investment differs from *planned* investment. Since the plans of business people were frustrated, future adjustments will be called forth to right the situation.

A simple example will illustrate these ideas. Suppose business firms produce $100 billion worth of final goods based on sales forecasts of $100 billion; included in those sales forecasts is a *desired* net increase in inventories of $10 billion. If the *actual* change in inventories happens to be not $10 billion but $20 billion, business firms would have actually sold $10 billion less than they had forecast. This *unintended* increase in inventories will in all likelihood lead to a cutback in future production levels as businesspeople seek to work off those excess inventories, the more so if they revise downward their sales forecasts. If, on the other hand, the actual change had been $10 billion, no revision in production plans would be called for. The economy would be in equilibrium. Thus, the equality of savings and investment will reflect macroeconomic equilibrium only if the *actual* change in inventories is equal to the *planned* change. More will be said on this matter in Chapter 7.

POTENTIAL GNP

Up until this point we have been concerned exclusively with the amount of output we actually produce during some period of time; that is, we have been concerned with our *actual GNP*. It is now time to consider our **potential GNP**— the potential quantity of goods and services we could produce with our available land, labor, and capital resources. Potential GNP is the empirical counterpart of our production possibilities.

Given the quantity and quality of our resources, there is a "normal" maximum amount that we could produce during any period. That potential GNP (GNP*) can be described by the following simple formula: Let L* denote the number of people that would be employed if we were at full employment; let h* represent the normal number of hours that would be worked *per person during the year* if full employment prevailed; (L*h*) therefore represents the poten-

tial number of hours available for the year in question. Multiplying this number by the value of the *average output per hour of work* (π^*) (i.e., average productivity) that would exist if full employment were a reality, we obtain

$$GNP^* = \pi^* \times (L^* \times h^*).$$

Thus, if $\pi^* = \$5.00$, $h^* = 2,000$, and $L^* = 100$ million, then GNP* = $1 trillion. Let us examine this relationship carefully.

GNP is the "normal" maximum output of final goods and services.* During any given period, actual GNP may be more or less than this potential. During recessions, actual production falls short of its potential as workers are laid off or work fewer hours. The actual number employed, L, or the actual average number of hours worked, h, fall below L* and h* respectively. Similarly, during emergencies such as war, larger numbers of people can be recruited into the labor force and almost everyone can work longer hours; actual L and h rise above L* and h*.

Although our potential GNP is determined by the quantity and quality of all our resources, the formula given above seems to place emphasis on the quantity of labor services only. This is an illusion. *The contribution of land, capital, and labor quality to our potential GNP is summarized in π^*.* Increases in the quantity and quality of land and capital, as well as improvements in labor quality, raise labor productivity—that is, raise the output produced per hour of work. This can best be illustrated with a simple example. Suppose, as above, that $\pi^* = \$5$ and that L* × h* = 200 billion, yielding a potential GNP of $1 trillion. Suppose further that, as a result of capital accumulation, improvements in the quality of labor, technological advances, etc., our potential GNP rises by $200 billion with the result that GNP* rises from $1 trillion to $1.2 trillion. With a given 200 billion available hours (i.e., L* × h*), this $200 billion increase would be reflected in an increase of π^* from $5.00 to $6 (i.e., the new GNP* = $6 × 200 billion = $1.2 trillion).

L*, the number of people employed if the economy were at full employment, is determined by numerous complex factors. In the first place, the size of L* will be determined by the size of the labor force. You will recall our discussion in Chapter 5 in which we defined the labor force as those adults who are either working or seeking work. And you will recall further that full employment was defined as a situation in which there existed, *not* zero unemployment, but some "small" positive amount of frictional and structural unemployment. L* is defined subject to these limitations. Therefore, if full employment is defined as 5 percent unemployment, L* will be equal to 95 percent of the labor force. (In the 1950s and 1960s, 4 percent unemployment was considered full employment; today the benchmark unemployment rate is 5.1 percent.)

But the size of the labor force is not some given, immutable constant. Rather, it is determined by a variety of socioeconomic forces. This can be seen most clearly by an examination of the following definition of the labor force: Letting N represent the total population and LF represent the labor force, it is true that

$$LF = N \times \frac{LF}{N}$$

where LF/N, the percentage of the population in the labor force, is the aggregate **labor force participation rate.** Therefore, increases in population and/or increases in the labor force participation rate lead to an increased labor force.

But care must be exercised in the use of the above definition. Changes in population and changes in the labor force participation rate are often *not* independent of one another. In the first place, if population increases through an increase in the birth rate, the labor force participation rate will, for some time at least, decline. Since the labor force consists of adults, an increase in the number of children will not lead to an expansion of the labor force until those children attain working age; LF/N will decline. In addition, if there is an increase in the birth rate, this will often be accompanied by more adults staying at home to rear the children; the labor force participation rate declines. And the converse of these propositions is also often true: A declining birth rate is generally accompanied by an increasing labor force participation rate.

If, on the other hand, population increases as a result of immigration, the labor force participation rate may rise or fall depending on the composition of the families immigrating.

Other factors also affect the labor force participation rate. An increase (decrease) in the proportion of adults who remain in school will lower (raise) the participation rate. If, as a result of social, cultural, or religious factors, increasing numbers of women join the labor force, the participation rate will rise. These issues were discussed in Chapter 5.

The average number of normal working hours, h*, is also not some given constant. Indeed, the average length of the workweek in the United States has declined significantly since the turn of the century—from nearly 54 hours per week in 1900 to about 40 hours in 1946; 40 hours has been pretty much the norm ever since World War II.

Productivity advance, as summarized in π*, has historically been one of the most important sources of increase in our potential (and actual) GNP. Specialization, economies of large-scale operation, technological advance, capital accumulation, improved health care, education, and political stability have all contributed to the high levels of productivity we enjoy in this country.

π*, h*, and L* are not, in general, independent factors. In the first place, changes in productivity (π*) have historically exerted an important influence on both h* and L*. The slowdown in our population growth (which in turn led to a somewhat slower growth in our labor force) and the reduced length of the workweek are traceable in large measure to the rapid advancement in our standards of living; and the rapid advance of our living standards is largely attributable to the rapid pace of productivity change. Historically at least, increases in productivity have contributed to a decline in both h* and L*.

Second, education is an important determinant of productivity advance. To the extent that high levels of education imply a somewhat lower aggregate labor force participation rate (since people remain in school longer), implying in turn a somewhat lower L* for any given population,

π^* and L^* will not be independent of one another.

Potential GNP versus actual GNP

Figure 6.3 portrays graphically the gap between our potential GNP and our actual GNP for the period 1952–1980. The **"GNP gap"** is defined as the difference between potential GNP and actual GNP. It is a measure of the economic slack or the waste of resources due to high levels of unemployment.

The disturbing fact reported in Figure 6.3 is readily apparent. In a great many years since 1952, our actual GNP has fallen below our potential; at times it was far below. Of course, the GNP gap measures the foregone production of goods and services—goods and services that we had the capability of producing but didn't! The explanation of this GNP gap and the reasons for its persistence are among the central questions facing us in this section of the book.

Growth and unemployment: Okun's Law. As actual GNP approaches potential GNP, the unemployment rate approaches its full employment value. This relationship is fairly straightforward. What is not so straightforward is the relationship between *growth* in GNP and the unemployment rate. The problem is this: as a result of increases in the quantity and quality of productive resources, potential GNP tends to rise overtime. In order for the unemployment rate to stay at its full employment level, actual GNP must grow as rapidly as potential GNP. Thus, if potential GNP grows at 3 percent per year, actual GNP must grow that fast *just to keep the rate of unemployment constant.*

Empirically, what is the relationship between growth in real GNP and the unemployment rate? The answer is given by a useful rule of thumb known as **Okun's Law,** named afters its founder, the late Arthur Okun. The law can be summarized as follows:

1. Suppose potential GNP grows at x percent per year.
2. If the growth in actual GNP exceeds the growth of potential GNP by 2½ percent for

a year, the unemployment rate will decline by one percentage point.

To illustrate, if potential GNP grows at 3 percent per year, and actual GNP grows at 5½ percent per year, each year we will reduce the unemployment rate by one percentage point. This is a useful guide to policy because it enables us to answer the following question. How rapidly can we reduce the unemployment rate to its full employment value? The answer depends on the difference between the actual and full employment unemployment rates and on how fast the economy grows. Suppose the actual unemployment rate is 8 percent whereas full employment is defined as 6 percent unemployment. If potential GNP advances at a rate of 3 percent per year, full employment will be realized in *two* years if actual GNP grows at 5½ percent per year. At 4¼ percent actual GNP growth year after year, the full employment unemployment rate would be realized in 4 years. Can you explain why?

Okun's Law is not an exact relationship. It need not hold year in and year out; it holds *on average* only.[5] It is, nonetheless, a useful rule of thumb.

GNP—A measure of welfare?

Obviously, the quantity of goods and services we produce as a nation is important to our welfare. But our welfare is determined by much more than material goods and services. Peace, justice, freedom, love, and equality of opportunity are all things that would make us better off as a nation. However, these things are not included in our GNP, though the extent to which they are realized would be included in some more comprehensive measure of welfare.[6] Even if we

---

[5] The original Okun's Law used to be 3 to 1, not 2½ to 1. Some economists now believe it to be as low as 2 to 1.

[6] We need to be careful here. To the extent that resources are used by government to produce services designed to bring about peace, justice, equality, etc., at least some aspects of these social phenomena are included in our measured GNP. But the fact that we choose to use our scarce resources in

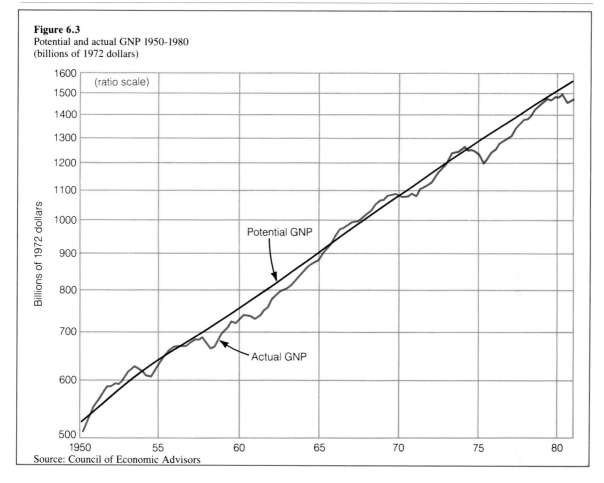

Figure 6.3
Potential and actual GNP 1950-1980
(billions of 1972 dollars)

Source: Council of Economic Advisors

abstract from all of these considerations and focus our attention on the construction of some index of material well-being, GNP would not prove to be a suitable index. In the first place, it fails to account for a large number of nonmarket transactions—such as the services of those who cook and clean—or illegal activities, even though such activities have an important bearing on our economic well-being.

Second, we count as a plus the production of goods and services; but we also count as a plus the production of goods and services designed to reduce the amount of pollution associated with our production and consumption activity. Can we really argue that we are better off

as a result? And what about all the pollution that we fail to do anything about? How do our GNP accounts handle this? They don't! If it does not represent an expenditure for a final good and service as defined by the government, it is not included in our GNP.

Third, as a result of significant improvements in our living standards we as a nation have opted in favor of a shortened workweek in order to increase our leisure. Is not leisure a good that we "consume" like other goods and services? And does not the amount of leisure time we have have implications for our well-being? It surely does. But leisure is not counted as part of our GNP.

Fourth, what about the product mix and our economic well-being? If we spend $10 billion more on military equipment *or* $10 billion more

these ways means we must give up other goods and services. Clearly, we would be better off if peace and justice were a reality, releasing resources for the production of other things.

on a life-saving vaccine, in either case our GNP accounts would show an increase of $10 billion. But can we really argue that our welfare is independent of the use we make of our resources? Some would argue that our welfare would rise by more as a result of the production of an additional $10 billion worth of military equipment; others would argue in favor of $10 billion more for the life-saving vaccine. But virtually no one would argue that it didn't matter!

Finally, even in the limited sense in which GNP is a measure of well-being, it is much more meaningful to represent our output on a *per capita* basis—that is, to divide GNP by population. The reason is simple. Although GNP may grow at a rather rapid rate, if it grows less rapidly than population, the average "standard of living" will actually decline.

The conclusion from all of this is rather straightforward. GNP was never intended to be used as an exclusive measure of well-being, not even of material well-being. It measures one thing only—the market value of all final goods produced during some period. Although this is an important indicator of social welfare, it is only one such indicator, and a very crude and imperfect one at that.

SUMMARY

1. *GNP* is defined as the market value of all final goods and services produced during some period. There are five aspects to this definition and each must be clearly understood.

a. GNP is a *market value* concept; the value of each good and service is defined by its market price. *Nominal GNP* is arrived at using prices prevailing in the year the goods and services were produced; *real* GNP is calculated using prices prevalent during some selected base year. Nominal GNP divided by the *GNP implicit price deflator* yields *real GNP*.

b. GNP measures the value of *final* goods and services—goods and services produced for final use, not for resale or further processing.

In arriving at this measure, one could calculate the market value of *all* goods and services produced *less* the market value of *all* intermediate goods. An essentially equivalent procedure for calculating GNP is to sum up the *values added* by all producing units in the economy. The nature of relationships among final goods, intermediate goods, and values added are summarized in the *input-output transactions table.*

c. GNP refers to the value of the goods and services *produced,* as opposed to sold, during some time interval. Value of output produced can readily be calculated as the value of final sales plus or minus the *net change* in the value of inventories. If we define an increase in inventories as a positive final sale (producers, in effect, "selling" the goods to themselves) and a decrease in inventories as a negative final sale, the value of final goods and services produced must be identical to the value of final goods and services "sold."

Accordingly, we can define GNP as the sum of four broad categories of final expenditures—*personal consumption expenditures, gross private domestic investment, government purchases of goods and services,* and *net exports of goods and services.* Symbolically, this relationship can be written as

$$Y = C + I_g + G + (X - M).$$

d. GNP refers to the production that takes place over some interval of *time;* GNP must be given an explicit time dimension.

e. With few exceptions, GNP refers only to the value of goods and services produced for the marketplace; most nonmarket activities, and illegal activities (i.e., markets that are not recognized for accounting purposes) are excluded.

2. The production of a dollar's worth of final product generates a dollar of income. This identity has two important implications. First, a nation's real income can increase only if more goods and services are produced. Second, any increase in the general level of prices will be reflected in an *equal* change in the value of nominal income.

3. *Net national product* (NNP), defined as

GNP − CCA, measures how much of our nation's output we can consume without impairing our productive capacity.

4. *National income* (NI) measures the amount of income earned by the various factors of production—by land, labor, and capital. To arrive at NI, one subtracts from NNP the value of *indirect business taxes* (plus some other items).

5. *Personal income* (PI) measures the amount of income individuals receive. To arrive at PI, one subtracts from NI *contributions for social insurance, corporate profits taxes,* and *undistributed corporate profits,* and adds in *government transfer payments.*

6. *Disposable personal income* (DPI) measures the amount of income individuals have to dispose of. To arrive at DPI we subtract from personal income the value of personal income taxes.

7. The *savings-investment identity* merely states that if *savings* is defined as all income not spent on consumer goods and if *investment* is defined as all output produced other than consumer goods, then, by definition, savings will equal investment. This identity is not to be confused with the idea of macroeconomic equilibrium, which we will encounter in subsequent chapters; macroeconomic equilibrium calls for the equality of savings and investment, not of *actual* values, but of *planned* values.

8. *Potential GNP* is the empirical counterpart of our *production possibilities.* It is defined as the product of L* (the number of people that would be employed if we were at full employment), h* (the normal number of working hours per person per year if full employment prevailed), and π^* (the average output per hour of at full employment):

$$GNP^* = \pi^* \times L^* \times h^*.$$

9. GNP is a very imperfect measure of economic welfare. It fails to account for a large number of nonmarket transactions and illegal activities that have a bearing on our well-being. The production of goods and services to eliminate pollution, crime, and so on are treated in the same way as the production of food, clothing, and shelter. It fails to account for the increased leisure enjoyed by U.S. citizens. It also ignores the effects of changes in the product mix on our economic well-being. But GNP was never intended to be used as an exclusive measure of well-being. It measures only one thing—the market value of all final goods produced—an important welfare indicator, but a crude and imperfect one.

CONCEPTS FOR REVIEW

Gross National Product (GNP)

Nominal GNP

Real GNP

GNP implicit price deflator

Final goods and services

Intermediate goods and services

Value added

Input-output transactions table

Final sales versus value of final output produced

Inventories

Inventory investment

Inventory disinvestment

Personal consumption expenditures

Gross private domestic investment
    Fixed investment
    Structures
    Producers' durable equipment
    Nonresidential fixed investment
    Residential fixed investment
    Change in business inventories

Net investment

Capital consumption allowance (CCA)

Government purchases of goods and services

Net exports
    Exports
    Imports

Product side of national income and product accounts

Calendar year vs. fiscal year

Equivalence of income and value of output

Net national product (NNP)

Gross national income (GNI)

Indirect business taxes (IBT)

Personal income (PI)

Employee compensation

Contributions for social insurance

Corporate profits

Dividends

Undistributed corporate profits

Transfer payments

Disposable personal income

Gross savings

Savings-investment identity

Actual versus planned savings and investment

Potential GNP versus actual GNP

Okun's Law

Average output per hour of work (average labor
    productivity)

Labor force participation rate

"GNP gap"

QUESTIONS FOR DISCUSSION

1. Suppose the economy of Alpha reported the following list of statistical data:

Net investment	125
Net exports	15
Gross savings	160
Capital consumption allowance	50
Government transfer payments	100
Indirect business taxes	25
Government purchases of goods and services	200
Employee compensation	500
Contributions for social insurance	150
Indirect business taxes	50
Personal consumption expenditures	500
Dividends	60
Undistributed corporate profits	100
Corporate profits taxes	50
Personal income taxes	80
Purchases of common stock	50

a. Calculate for the economy of Alpha GNP, NNP, NI, PI, and DPI.

b. What is the value for personal savings? (There are two ways to figure this out; show both.) What is the value of the personal savings rate, savings divided by DPI?

c. What is the value of "rent, interest, and proprietors' income"?

d. What is the value of gross private domestic investment?

e. What is the size of the government surplus or deficit?

2. Explain the circumstances under which net investment can be negative. What are the implications of negative net investment? Can gross private domestic investment ever be negative?

3. It often said, "You can't compare apples and oranges." Show how they can be compared using the money-measuring rod.

4. Many items are not included in our measure of GNP. Explain why the following are *not* included: *(a)* government transfer payments; *(b)* the purchase of a used car; and *(c)* the purchase of common stock.

5. The value of illegal activities is not included in our measure of GNP. However, according to the Internal Revenue Service (IRS), it is illegal not to report income derived from illegal sources. Suppose that all sources of illegal income were reported to the IRS. (After all, these people would not want to do anything illegal.) What would happen to our *measured* overall tax burden—i.e., taxes as a proportion of GNP?

6. Statistically, what would be the effect of an increase in social security taxes on GNP, NNP, NI, PI, and DPI? Explain.

7. According to Figure 6.3, actual GNP has at times been larger than potential GNP. How can potential GNP have any meaning if this can happen?

Now that we have a clear understanding of the *concept* of national income, we turn our attention to the more difficult problem of how the level of national income is determined.

We know the meaning of *potential* income and we know what determines it—the quantity and quality of land, labor, and capital resources. However, potential income is not the same as actual income and they are seldom equal to one another. Indeed, on the basis of our discussion of the GNP gap in Chapter 6, it is clear that our actual income has been below our potential income more often than not; sometimes it has been tens of billions of dollars below for several years in a row. What accounts for this failure of our economic system to produce at its potential? Why is our actual GNP what it is? And what causes it to go up and down? It is the purpose of this chapter to *begin* an investigation of questions such as these.

The need to simplify

To arrive at answers to the questions posed above, we need to acquire a thorough understanding of how our economic system functions. However, because our economy is so complicated, it is necessary to approach such an understanding in steps. Accordingly, we will first study the operation of a highly simplified economic system. Having mastered that, we will proceed, in increasing degrees of complexity, to the consideration of an economy that more accurately portrays the American economic system. In this chapter we will analyze a simplified economic system only, leaving the analysis of more complicated phenomena to later chapters.

However, although the framework developed here is highly simplified, it is a necessary building block toward a fuller understanding of the U.S. economy.

Some simplifying assumptions. In an effort to advance our understanding, we make the following simplifying assumptions:

1. We ignore any and all complications introduced by the existence of depreciation. That is, the focal point of our attention is on the forces

Chapter 7

Static models of income determination: The classical and Keynesian approachs

determining net national product (NNP), not GNP. When we speak of "investment" we are referring to "net investment."

2. We assume that our economy is *closed* in the sense that it has no contact whatever with the rest of the world economy. Exports and imports are therefore assumed to be zero.

3. We assume the complete absence of government activity of any sort; our hypothetical economy is exclusively private. Government expenditures, transfer payments, and tax receipts are all zero.

4. Finally, we assume that all corporate profits are distributed to individuals in the form of dividend payments; undistributed corporate profits are zero.

With these assumptions we can simplify considerably the national income accounting relationships developed in Chapter 6. Specifically:

1. Net national product, national income, personal income, and disposable personal income (DPI) are all equal to one another; in the absence of any taxes or business saving (i.e., capital consumption allowances (CCA) plus undistributed corporate profits), this must be so.

2. All saving is personal saving.

3. The savings-investment accounting identity now simplifies to:

Personal savings = Net investment.

Letting personal savings = S and net investment = I_n, this can be written symbolically as

$$S = I_n$$

4. NNP, defined as the sum of expenditures for final goods and services, is now simply the sum of personal consumption expenditures (C) and net investment (I_n):

$$NNP = C + I_n$$

The fundamental questions are these: What determines how much output and income will be produced by our hypothetical private closed economy? Do any automatic forces exist to ensure that our economy will produce at its poten-

tial—that is, at full employment? Before we can answer these questions, however, we must acquire a clear understanding of the meaning of equilibrium in our simplified macroeconomy.

THE CONCEPT OF MACROEQUILIBRIUM

In general, an equilibrium is said to exist when there is no further tendency to change. This notion was illustrated in Chapter 3 by the point of intersection of the demand and supply curves. At the intersection point, the amount buyers are willing and able to buy equals the amount sellers are willing to sell. Applying this idea to a macroeconomy, a **macroequilibrium** is said to exist when the amount that buyers in the aggregate are *willing and able to buy* of goods and services is equal to the amount that producers in the aggregate are *willing to sell.*

In our simplified macroeconomy, there are two groups of buyers—households and businesses. Personal consumption expenditures are made by the household sector; investment expenditures (for plant and equipment and for inventory) are undertaken by the business sector. Restating the idea of macroequilibrium in terms of our simplified economy, macroequilibrium will exist when the amount of goods and services that consumers and investors (i.e., businesses) are *willing and able to buy* equals the amount that producers are *willing to sell.* There are several ways to express this concept.

Suppose consumers in the aggregate are willing to spend, for whatever reasons, $700 billion on consumer goods and services. Suppose further that businesspeople, for whatever reasons, are willing to make investment expenditures totaling $200 billion—to expand their plant and equipment or to add to their stocks of inventories. If producers are willing to sell $900 billion worth of goods and services, the economy is said to be in equilibrium; consumers buy $700 billion worth of that output and investors buy the remaining $200 billion. Both consumers and investors are satisfied in the sense that each group purchases the quantities of goods and services they desire; producers are satisfied because they sell as much as they are willing to sell. The $900 billion NNP is, therefore, the equilibrium NNP.

We can express the notion of macroequilibrium more generally. Letting C represent personal consumption expenditures and I_n^d represent *desired* or *planned* net investment expenditures, we define **aggregate demand** as the sum of $C + I_n^d$. That is,

$$\text{Aggregate demand} = C + I_n^d.$$

Defining NNP (represented symbolically by the letter Y) as **aggregate supply,** it is clear that equilibrium will occur when aggregate demand is equal to aggregate supply. That is, equilibrium occurs when

$$Y = C + I_n^d.$$

Note one very important characteristic of this equilibrium NNP: since the value of the output produced is identical to the value of the income generated, and since, by our assumptions, NNP = DPI, *planned savings is equal to planned investment in equilibrium.* Since DPI is $900 billion (because NNP is $900 billion), and since consumers spend $700 billion on goods and services, their savings amount to $200 billion—which is exactly equal to planned investment.

We saw above that equilibrium occurs when $Y = C + I_n^d$. This can, of course, be rewritten as $Y - C = I_n^d$. But $Y - C$ is nothing other than savings, S. Therefore, macroequilibrium can be expressed as

$$S = I_n^d.$$

It is clear, then, that macroequilibrium can be expressed either as aggregate demand equal to aggregate supply or as planned savings equal to planned investment.

There is yet one other way to express macroequilibrium. This way, in many respects, is more meaningful intuitively: *macroequilibrium will exist when actual investment equals desired investment.* This follows naturally from the equilibrium condition $Y = C + I_n^d$. Therefore, since aggregate supply, Y, is equal to $C + I_n$ (actual investment)—i.e., since NNP is defined in our simplified economy as the sum of personal consumption

expenditures and actual net investment—and since aggregate demand is equal to $C + I_n^d$ (desired or planned investment), the aggregate supply equals aggregate demand condition implies that, in equilibrium,

$$C + I_n = C + I_n^d.$$

Since C is the same on both sides of this expression, macroequilibrium will occur when

$$I_n = I_n^d.$$

To illustrate the significance of the equilibrium condition expressed in this equation, consider another example. Suppose $C = \$600$ billion and $I_n^d = \$250$ billion. Aggregate demand, therefore, will equal $850 billion. Suppose, on the other hand, that NNP = $900 billion. Can $900 billion be viewed as an equilibrium level of output and income? No. The amount that producers are willing to sell ($900 billion) exceeds by $50 billion the amount that consumers and investors are willing to buy. As a consequence, businesspeople will be running up their inventories by $50 billion more than they had intended; this we refer to as **unintended inventory investment.** The magnitude of unintended inventory investment is given by the difference between desired or planned investment, I_n^d, and actual investment, I_n. Since NNP = $900 billion and C = $600 billion, actual investment *must* equal $300 billion. However, planned investment amounts to only $250 billion. The excess of actual investment, I_n, over planned investment, I_n^d—$50 billion in this example—represents unintended inventory investment.

Because the expectations of businesspeople were unfulfilled, there is considerable likelihood that they will cut back their levels of production, both to work off their excess holdings of inventories and to meet a lower-than-expected aggregate demand. *Since aggregate supply exceeds aggregate demand there will be a tendency for further change.* Another way of stating that aggregate supply exceeds aggregate demand is that I_n exceeds I_n^d.

Let us examine this disequilibrium situation further. Although an NNP of $900 billion is not an equilibrium, actual saving *does* equal actual investment at this NNP level. Because of the

Table 7.1
Macroequilibrium and disequilibrium: A summary

Aggregate demand $(C + I_n^d)$ and aggregate supply (expressed as Y or as $C + I_n$)	Planned savings (S) and investment (I_n^d)	Planned investment (I_n^d) and actual investment (I_n)	Actual savings (S) and actual investment (I_n)
$Y = C + I_n^d$ (Equilibrium)	$S = I_n^d$	$I_n^d = I_n$	$S = I_n$
$Y > C + I_n^d$ (Above equilibrium production)	$S > I_n^d$	$I_n^d < I_n$ (Unintended inventory investment)	$S = I_n$
$Y < C + I_n^d$ (Below equilibrium production)	$S < I_n^d$	$I_n^d > I_n$ (Unintended inventory disinvestment)	$S = I_n$

Note: Actual saving is *always* equal to actual investment whether the economy is in equilibrium or not. Planned saving equals planned investment, and planned investment equals actual investment, only when the economy is in equilibrium.

equality of output and income, DPI = $900 billion; given that C = $600 billion, S must equal $300 billion. And since actual investment is defined as output not sold to consumers—including both intended and unintended inventory investment—actual investment must equal actual saving.

But planned investment does not equal planned saving at an NNP of $900 billion. Indeed, planned saving is $300 billion but planned investment is only $250 billion; actual investment amounted to $300 billion, but $50 billion of that represented an unintended increase in inventories. *There is yet another way of stating that aggregate supply exceeds aggregate demand—planned saving exceeds planned investment.*

What if aggregate demand exceeds aggregate supply? Suppose C = $650 billion, I_n^d = $250 billion, and NNP = $800 billion. Under these circumstances, aggregate demand of $900 billion exceeds aggregate supply of $800 billion. Businesspeople sell $100 billion more than they had intended and this **unintended inventory disinvestment** will probably call forth higher levels of production in the future to restore depleted inventories and to meet the higher-than-expected level

of aggregate spending. An NNP of $800 billion does *not* represent an equilibrium level of output and income.

I leave it to the reader to show that, when aggregate demand exceeds aggregate supply, planned investment exceeds planned saving and planned investment exceeds actual investment.

A summary of these relationships is provided in Table 7.1.

TWO APPROACHES TO INCOME DETERMINATION

On the basis of the discussion of equilibrium in a macroeconomy given above, it is clear that the equilibrium level of income will be determined at the point where aggregate demand is equal to aggregate supply (or, in other terms, where planned investment is equal to planned saving, or where planned investment equals actual investment). The question, then, is: Do any forces exist to ensure that aggregate demand will equal aggregate supply at full employment?

There are two different answers to this question. According to so-called classical economists—with whom we associate the names John Stuart Mill, F. Y. Edgeworth, Alfred Marshall, and A. C. Pigou—*automatic* forces do exist that, given enough time, will bring about an equilibrium level of income that fully employs our nation's resources. A second view—the one put forward by John Maynard Keynes in 1936 in his famous book, *The General Theory of Employment, Interest and Money*—is that automatic forces pushing our economic system toward full employment do not exist, *at least not in the short run* (which, to Keynes, could mean a period of several years); if they do exist, they operate with such weak force that they are largely irrelevant. Consider each of these views in turn.

The classical theory of employment and income

The classical view that automatic forces exist ending to push the economy toward full employment rests on two fundamental propositions:

1. *It is not possible for there to be overproduction or underproduction; aggregate demand is always equal to aggregate supply.* This idea, developed by 19th-century French economist J. B. Say, is known as **Say's Law.**

2. *Wages and all other prices are completely flexible in the sense that whenever a discrepancy exists between the demand for and supply of any good or service, the price of that good or service will adjust, either up or down* (depending on whether an excess demand or an excess supply exists) *by an amount sufficient to clear that market.* Frequently, classical economists would argue, implicitly at least, that discrepancies between the amounts demanded and supplied would be eliminated rather *quickly*. Let us examine each of these propositions in turn.

Say's Law. Say's Law is deceptively simple. It is based on the proposition, which we know to be true, that the value of the output produced is identical to the value of the income generated. What this means is that the act of producing goods and services provides the wherewithal to purchase all of the goods and services produced. However, although this proposition merely indi-cates that the wherewithal exists, Say's Law states something quite different—that all of the income generated *will be* used to acquire the goods and services produced; aggregate demand must equal aggregate supply at all times. Moreover, since production is the source of the income generated, it is proper to state, according to Say's Law, that *supply creates its own demand*. There can never be overproduction or underproduction in the aggregate. There can be overproduction of *some* goods and services (i.e., the amount of income spent on some goods and services can be less than the amount of income produced by those goods and services). But this must be matched by an underproduction of other things (i.e., the income spent on other things must exceed the value of the income produced by those other things). Given the value of the output produced, equivalent amounts of income and spending are generated. Put differently, all production results in payments to factors of production, and all those income payments will be used to purchase the goods and services produced.

Flexibility of wages and prices. By itself, Say's Law is insufficient to guarantee that aggregate demand will equal aggregate supply at full employment. Say's Law, if true, merely tells us that aggregate demand must equal aggregate supply at any given level of income, whether it be the full employment level or not. According to classical theory, another condition is required to bring about full employment. That condition is the complete flexibility of wages and prices.

If wages and prices are completely flexible, then any time the quantity demanded differs from the quantity supplied in any market, the price will change by an amount sufficient to clear the market. Moreover, if wages and prices adjust *quickly* in response to shifts of demand and supply, a state of near-continuous equilibrium will exist.

When all product markets are in equilibrium a state of macroeconomic equilibrium, as we defined it earlier, must exist. The fact that in each and every product market the quantity demanded equals the quantity supplied means that, when everything is added up, aggregate demand will

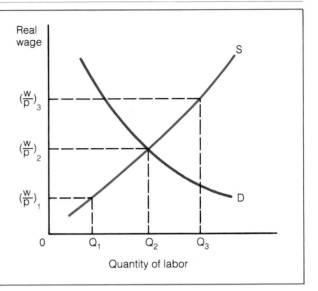

Figure 7.1
Wage and price flexibility and full employment

equal aggregate supply. The complete flexibility of wages and other resource prices means that this state of macroeconomic equilibrium will occur at full employment, as Figure 7.1 suggests.

Recalling our discussion of the labor market in Chapter 5, each point on the supply curve of labor represents a possible position of full employment. Therefore, if the real wage $\left(\frac{w}{p}\right)$ happens to be $\left(\frac{w}{p}\right)_1$, and Q_1 of labor is hired, full employment will obtain; the quantity of labor that is willing to work at a real wage of $\left(\frac{w}{p}\right)_1$, is Q_1. Similarly, at a real wage of $\left(\frac{w}{p}\right)_3$, if the amount labor hired is Q_3, the economy will have reached full employment.

Given the demand for labor, full employment will occur only at a real wage equal to $\left(\frac{w}{p}\right)_2$. At that real wage, the amount of labor producers are willing to hire is equal to the amount of labor willingly supplied. At a real wage equal to $\left(\frac{w}{p}\right)_3$, on the other hand, there is an excess supply of labor—that is, unemployment. At a real wage of $\left(\frac{w}{p}\right)_3$, producers are willing to hire less labor than is supplied; if wages and prices were flexible,

the real wage would be bid down to $\left(\frac{w}{p}\right)_2$ and full employment would be restored.[1]

In sum, then, Say's Law, in combination with wage and price flexibility and speedy adjustments of wages and prices to market-clearing levels in the face of differences in demand and supply, would, according to many classical economists, bring about a state of near-continuous macroeconomic equilibrium at full employment.

---

[1] In Figure 7.1, the positively sloping supply curve means that full employment will be reached partly because some labor services are withdrawn from the market. Indeed, as the real wage declines from $\left(\frac{w}{p}\right)_3$ to $\left(\frac{w}{p}\right)_2$, the quantity of labor supplied declines from Q_3 to Q_2. This need not always be the case. Suppose that the labor curve is vertical, which means that the same quantity of labor will be supplied no matter what the real wage. Then full employment will be restored solely as a result of the fact that producers will hire more labor at a lower real wage. This is demonstrated in the accompanying diagram.

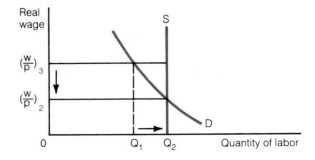

Say's Law and wage and price flexibility. Although virtually all classical economists believed that wages and prices were sufficiently flexible that the forces of demand and supply could be relied upon to bring about full employment, not all of them believed in Say's Law. Indeed, some of them rejected Say's Law outright, maintaining that wage and price flexibility alone were sufficient to produce full employment and macroeconomic equilibrium. Those who did reject the law were perfectly right in doing so.

The basic difficulty with Say's Law is that it confuses the meaning of the equivalence of income and output. Say's Law is valid in a barter economy where the act of supplying a good or service is itself a demand for something else; in that sense, supply does create its own demand. But it is not necessarily valid in a money-exchange economy. In the latter type of economy, each good or service is exchanged for money; there is no necessary reason people must spend *all* of the money so acquired on goods and services. They could well decide, for a whole host of reasons, to spend less than they receive; they could **hoard** money. Under these circumstances, aggregate demand would be less than aggregate supply. Similarly, people could spend more than their incomes by **dishoarding**—by drawing down their previously hoarded money balances; aggregate demand would then exceed aggregate supply. Given the existence of money, then, overproduction and underproduction are clearly possible.

A number of classical economists disputed this possibility even in a money-exchange economy. To their way of thinking, money was used *exclusively* by people for the purpose of facilitating the exchange of goods and services. Hoarding (and, therefore, dishoarding) were impossible; no one would hoard money when they could have goods and services. What this argument ignores is the fact that money held back today can be used to acquire goods and services at some time in the future. Money is, therefore, also a **store of value;** a dollar hoarded today can be used to buy a dollar's worth of goods and services tomorrow. People can plan to spend their money at times different from when they earn it; and they often do. Say's Law must be rejected.

Once Say's Law is discarded, the possibility of overproduction and underproduction must be admitted—that is, aggregate demand need not equal aggregate supply at all times. Those classical economists who did recognize the incorrectness of Say's Law were quite prepared to admit that aggregate demand need not equal aggregate supply at every instant. Nevertheless, they continued to maintain that automatic forces—wage and price adjustments—would be set in motion to bring about the equality of demand and supply in each and every market. In their view, these automatic forces could be relied upon for the most part to restore equilibrium rather quickly. Automatic forces would quickly restore the equality of aggregate demand and aggregate supply whenever they moved apart from one another; such a macroeconomic equilibrium would obtain at full employment.

The Keynesian critique

Keynes began his critique of the classical theory of employment and income with a simple observation. If indeed automatic mechanisms existed to ensure full employment, how could the classical economists explain the existence of huge amounts of unemployment year after year such as existed during the Great Depression of the 1930s? Writing during the Great Depression, Keynes maintained that they couldn't. He concluded, therefore, that either wages and prices are not flexible or they are *so slow* to adjust that they do little to eliminate unemployment in the short run. They might operate with sufficient strength to eliminate unemployment in the long run, but as Keynes was fond of saying, "In the long run we're all dead!"

Keynes supported his attack on the classical economists by pointing out that wages and prices, and especially wages, are notoriously "sticky," at least on the down side. Even in the face of a great deal of unemployment, workers steadfastly resist cuts in their wages. This resistance can persist for relatively long periods despite continued high unemployment rates.

Keynes went on to argue that even if wages were cut, such reductions might not do much to reduce the unemployment rate anyway; wage reductions could actually make things worse. In particular, *if* wage reductions lowered the *real* incomes of workers, they might be forced to cut back on their *real* spending. This would drive the unemployment rate up further as producers laid off more workers.[2]

In light of both of these considerations, Keynes concluded that no automatic mechanism exists that would operate *within a reasonable amount of time* to bring about full employment. In his view, the existence of unemployed resources was the result of inadequate spending in the aggregate. And, since wage and price reductions could not be counted on to increase spending—at least in the short run—*it was necessary for government to intervene to raise total aggregate spending to reduce the unemployment rate directly.*

To understand completely the full import of Keynes' message, let us examine carefully the determination of income in a world characterized by the absence of government. Following Keynes, we will assume the existence of unemployed resources initially and wage and price rigidities throughout the economy.

The Keynesian theory of employment and income

Since the level of employment was thought to be determined by the amount of aggregate spending, Keynes naturally focused his attention on the determinants of aggregate demand—on the determinants of consumer spending (C) and planned investment (I_n^d). Consider first consumer demand for goods and services.

The consumption function. The amount we spend on any *particular* good or service is deter-

mined by all sorts of factors—the price of the good or service, the prices of other goods and services, our income, our tastes, and so on. But what is the single most important factor that determines how much we spend on *all* goods and services? What determines our overall level of spending for consumer goods? To Keynes, and to the huge majority of economists since, the answer was clear—disposable income. *An increase in disposable income acts as a powerful inducement to consumers to increase their total spending; alternatively, a decrease in disposable income induces a reduction in the overall level of spending for consumer goods.*

This relationship between consumer spending and disposable income—known formally as the **consumption function**—is illustrated in Table 7.2. As is apparent from the data presented in columns (1) and (2), increases in disposable income lead to increases in consumer spending. As disposable income rises from $300 billion to $1 trillion, consumption expenditures rise from $340 billion to $900 billion; *consumption expenditures are positively related to disposable income.*

Since people can either spend their disposable income or save it, it is also clear that *saving is*

Table 7.2

The consumption function: The relationship between consumer spending and disposable income ($ billions)

(1) Disposable income (Y)	(2) Consumption expenditures (C)	(3) MPC	(4) APC
300	340		1.13
400	420	0.80	1.05
500	500	0.80	1.00
600	580	0.80	0.97
700	660	0.80	0.94
800	740	0.80	0.93
900	820	0.80	0.91
1,000	900	0.80	0.90

$$MPC = \frac{\text{Change in consumption}}{\text{Change in disposable income}} = \frac{\Delta C}{\Delta Y}$$

$$MPS = \frac{\text{Change in savings}}{\text{Change in disposable income}} = \frac{\Delta S}{\Delta Y}$$

$$APC = \frac{\text{Level of consumption}}{\text{Level of disposable income}} = \frac{C}{Y}$$

$$APS = \frac{\text{Level of savings}}{\text{Level of disposable income}} = \frac{S}{Y}$$

---

[2] This latter argument is highly controversial. Note that the emphasis in the text is placed on the word *if: If wage reductions lowered the real incomes of workers,* Keynes' conclusion might follow. But is there any reason this must necessarily be so? If the general level of prices fell by more than wages, the real incomes of workers would rise and stimulate real spending. We shall take up this issue in greater detail in Chapter 13.

positively related to disposable income. Saving is defined as the difference between disposable income and consumption expenditures. At a disposable income of $600 billion, saving amounts to $20 billion (i.e., $600 billion minus consumer expenditures of $580 billion); with an increase in disposable income to $700 billion, saving rises to $40 billion. But note that when disposable income is equal to $500 billion, saving is zero; and for levels of disposable income *below* $500 billion, saving is negative! How can saving be negative? How can people spend more than their disposable income? By drawing down their accumulated past savings—by dissaving—and/or by borrowing.

We make use of these simple relations to develop two concepts that are of utmost importance to the study of the Keynesian theory of income determination. The first is known as the **marginal propensity to consume (MPC),** which measures the extent to which consumption expenditures *change* in response to a *change* in disposable income; it is defined as *the change in consumption divided by the change in disposable income.* Letting the Greek symbol Δ ("delta") represent "change in," we can show this relationship symbolically as,

$$MPC = \frac{\Delta C}{\Delta Y}.$$

To illustrate, consider the impact on consumption of an increase in disposable income from $600 billion to $700 billion. As Table 7.2 suggests, consumption rises by $80 billion—from $580 billion to $660 billion. Therefore, the MPC in that range of disposable income is 0.80. (i.e., $\frac{80}{100} = 0.8$). And what is the MPC as disposable income rises from $700 billion to $800 billion? Since consumption again rises by $80 billion, MPC = 0.8. Indeed, we see from column (3) that MPC = 0.8 over the entire range of income. It should be noted, however, that the existence of a constant MPC is solely the result of the nature of the relationship *assumed* in Table 7.2; that is, we assumed there that consumption and disposable income were related to one an-

other linearly.[3] Of course, the relationship need not be linear. Indeed, Keynes suggested that the MPC might decline somewhat at high levels of income. However, in the interest of simplicity we will retain the linearity assumption; we will, that is, assume that the MPC is constant over the entire range of variation of disposable income.

A related concept is the **marginal propensity to save (MPS),** defined as the *change* in savings brought about by the *change* in disposable income. This relationship can be represented as

$$MPS = \frac{\Delta S}{\Delta Y}.$$

Using the data in Table 7.2, it is clear that MPS = 0.20. Since consumer expenditures increase by $80 billion for each $100 billion increase in disposable income, savings must increase by $20 billion for each $100 billion increase in disposable income. This follows from the fact that people can either spend or save their changed incomes. Put differently, since any change in income that is not spent must be saved, it is clear that MPS and MPC must add up to one:

$$MPC + MPS = 1.$$

The MPS, therefore, must equal the value (1 − MPC). Accordingly, since MPC = 0.80, MPS must equal 0.20 (i.e., 1 − 0.80 = 0.20).

The second important concept is the **average propensity to consume (APC);** its related concept is the **average propensity to save (APS).** The APC tells us the proportion or percentage of disposable income that is consumed; it is defined as consumption divided by disposable income. Thus,

$$APC = \frac{C}{Y}.$$

The APS is defined in a similar way—as the proportion of disposable income that is saved.

---

[3] Those who are somewhat more mathematically inclined will recognize that we have assumed a specific linear relationship of the form C = 100 + 0.8Y.

The APS, commonly referred to as the **savings rate,** is defined as

$$APS = \frac{S}{Y}.$$

Because consumption and saving exhaust disposable income, the APC and the APS must sum to one. Thus,

$$APC + APS = 1.$$

Accordingly, it is clear that APS must equal the value $(1 - APC)$.

The APC (and, therefore, the APS) implied by our assumed linear relation of consumption and disposable income is presented in column 4 of Table 7.2. Unlike the MPC, which has a constant value throughout, *the APC declines as income rises*—that is, *consumption expenditures rise less than in proportion to income*. At a disposable income of $500 billion, the APC = 1.00; at a disposable income of $800 billion, APC = 0.93. Given the relationship of APC and APS, the decline in APC as income rises implies a corresponding increase in APS as income rises. In other words, the consumption function assumed here implies that the savings rate increases with increases in disposable income.

To sum up, then, the consumption function presented in Table 7.2 implies that (1) consumption expenditures and disposable income are positively related, an increase in disposable income inducing an increase in consumption expenditures; and (2) consumption rises less than in proportion to disposable income (which, in turn implies, that saving rises more than in proportion).[4]

These relationships are shown graphically in Figure 7.2 using the data from Table 7.2. Plotting consumption expenditures on the vertical axis

and disposable income on the horizontal axis, we obtain in the top diagram the positively sloping linear consumption function, C, implied by our data. *Since MPC is defined as the change in consumption divided by the change in income, it is clear that MPC is the slope of the consumption function.* Before proceeding to an analysis of the other relationships discussed above, however, a word of explanation is in order concerning the *45° line* that is plotted in the upper diagram.

The 45° line bisects the angle formed by the consumption and disposable income axes. It is, therefore, extremely useful as a reference line because the vertical distance from any point on the horizontal axis to the 45° line is exactly equal to the horizontal distance from that point to the origin. A disposable income of $400 billion measured horizontally can also be measured as the vertical distance above $400 billion to the 45° line; and likewise, a disposable income of $700 billion can be measured as the vertical distance above $700 billion to the 45° line.

On the basis of these considerations, it is clear that if consumption were equal to disposable income at all levels of income, the consumption function would be coincident with the 45° line. However, using the data of Table 7.2, it is evident that consumption and disposable income are equal to one another only at a disposable income of $500 billion. At income levels above $500 billion, disposable income exceeds consumption; at income levels below $500 billion, disposable income is less than consumption. These are all captured graphically in the upper diagram of Figure 7.2. The consumption function, labeled C, intersects the 45° line at a disposable income level of $500 billion (meaning that consumption is equal to disposable income at that point). At income levels *below* $500 billion, the consumption function lies above the 45° line (meaning that consumption exceeds disposable income); at income levels *above* $500 billion, the consumption function lies below the 45° line (meaning consumption is less than disposable income). Therefore, it is apparent from the upper diagram of Figure 7.2 that consumption rises with disposable income, but it rises less than in proportion (meaning APC falls as income rises).

---

[4] Although these conclusions were arrived at on the basis of a linear consumption function, the linearity assumption is not a critical one. Thus, many economists who posit a nonlinear relationship between C and Y discover a positive MPC and an APC that declines with income. At least this is true of the *short-run* consumption function. The generally accepted *long-run* consumption function, on the other hand, implies a constant MPC *and* a constant APC. This is discussed in the appendix to this chapter.

Figure 7.2.
The consumption function and the savings function

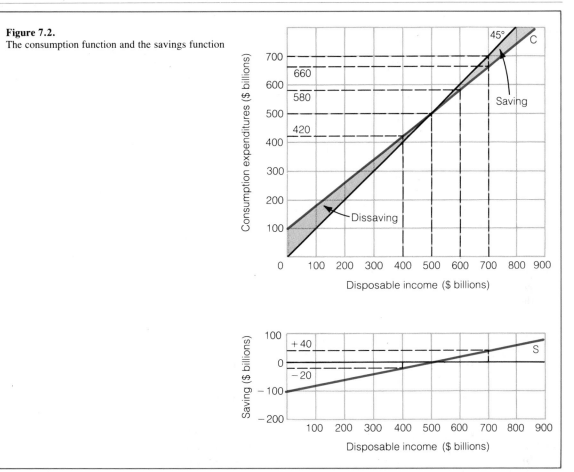

Moreover, since disposable income can be either spent or saved, and since disposable income can be measured as the vertical distance to the 45° line, the vertical difference between the consumption function and the 45° line measures the amount saved or dissaved at each level of income. Accordingly, at a disposable income level of $700 billion, the amount saved ($40 billion) is measured as the distance between the amount consumed at that level of income and the 45° line. Similarly, the amount dissaved at a disposable income of $400 billion ($20 billion) is measured as the distance between the amount consumed at that income level and the 45° line.

For some purposes it is useful to graph separately the relationship of saving to disposable income. This is done in the lower portion of Fig-

ure 7.2. Note the correspondence between the upper and lower diagrams. At a disposable income of $500 billion, consumption equals disposable income and saving is zero. At that income level the consumption function in the upper diagram crosses the 45° line; the saving function, labeled S in the lower diagram, crosses the horizontal axis (implying a zero level of saving). At income levels in excess of $500 billion, saving is positive; below, it is negative. The vertical distance between the 45° line and the consumption function in the upper diagram is matched by the vertical distance between the S function and the horizontal axis in the lower diagram at each income level.

The second component of aggregate demand: Net investment. Let us turn our attention now to the second component of aggregate demand in our simplified economy—desired net investment. Recall the meaning of *investment*—expenditures for newly produced plant and equipment (i.e., residential and nonresidential structures and equipment) plus the change in business inventories. Recall further that, to avoid the complications introduced by depreciation, we are focusing on net national product and therefore on net investment—gross investment minus capital consumption allowances (i.e., depreciation).

What determines the volume of net investment that will be undertaken in our private closed economy? Unfortunately, this question is not easy to answer. Fundamentally, the amount of net investment businesspeople will undertake will depend on the profits they *expect* from these kinds of expenditures. However, the expected profitability of investment is itself determined by a whole host of complex forces almost too numerous to mention. Since these matters are discussed in depth in Chapters 11 and 14, we will assume, for our purposes here, a very simple relationship for net investment, leaving to later chapters a fuller treatment of its determinants. Specifically, we will assume here that *desired* or *planned* net investment is some constant value equal to, say,

$60 billion per year *regardless of the level of NNP*. Whether income is $400 billion or $900 billion, the net investment businesspeople desire to undertake is exactly $60 billion.

The equilibrium level of national income. Now that the components of aggregate demand in our private closed economy have been specified, we are in a position to show how the equilibrium level of NNP is determined. Recall our earlier discussion of the concept of equilibrium in a macroeconomy: *Equilibrium will occur at the income level where aggregate supply is equal to aggregate demand.* Therefore, in order to discover equilibrium, it is necessary to find the level of NNP that is equal to the sum of consumption expenditures plus *planned* or *desired* net investment. Given the consumption function and the assumed level of *desired* net investment, the equilibrium level of NNP can thus be determined readily. This result is shown in Table 7.3.

First, a word about Table 7.3. The first two columns of Table 7.3 duplicate the information provided in the first two columns of Table 7.2. Since the assumptions made at the outset of this chapter imply that NNP equals disposable income, the consumption function in our private

Table 7.3
Aggregate supply and the components of aggregate demand ($ billions)

(1) NNP (Disposable income) (Y)	(2) Consumption expenditures (C)	(3) Desired net investment (I_n^d)	(4) New desired net investment ($I_n^{d'}$)
300	340	60	80
400	420	60	80
500	500	60	80
600	580	60	80
700	660	60	80
800	740	60	80
900	820	60	80
1,000	900	60	80

1. Given the consumption function and $I_n^d = $60 billion, the equilibrium NNP = $800 billion.
2. Given the consumption function and $I_n^{d'} = $80 billion, the equilibrium NNP = $900 billion.
3. Thus, a change in desired net investment of $20 billion induces a $100 billion change in the equilibrium NNP.

closed economy can be expressed as a relation between C and NNP or C and disposable income. The data in column (3) reflect our assumptions concerning *desired* net investment. Ignore for now the data presented in column (4).

Do we have enough information to determine the equilibrium level of NNP? Yes. Since *desired* net investment is fixed at $60 billion, the equilibrium level of NNP can be found by identifying that level of consumption in column (2) that, when added to *desired* net investment, is equal to the level of NNP in column (1). And, as is apparent, such an equality takes place at an NNP of $800 billion: *The equilibrium level of NNP is equal to $800 billion.*

How can we be sure that $800 billion is the equilibrium NNP? By selecting some other value for NNP and establishing that it does not meet the requirements for equilibrium. Consider an NNP of $600 billion. Could this also be an equilibrium? No. Since consumers will spend $580 billion and businesspeople *desire* to spend $60 billion, aggregate demand (equal to $640 billion) exceeds aggregate supply (equal to $600 billion). Since aggregate demand exceeds aggregate supply, this will induce businesspeople to step up production. Why? Because, although *desired* net investment equals $60 billion, the *actual* net investment business people undertake will be only $20 billion. Since NNP is defined as the sum of *actual* expenditures for consumption and investment, and since at an NNP of $600 billion consumers spend $580 billion, *actual* net investment must be only $20 billion. There is, therefore, an unintended inventory disinvestment of $40 billion. Assuming that investors do not change their *desired* investment plans, producers will increase production in an effort to restore depleted inventories and to meet the higher-than-expected level of aggregate spending. *NNP will rise above $600 billion.* And NNP will continue to rise until it reaches $800 billion.

Could an NNP of $1,000 billion be considered an equilibrium? No. Aggregate supply (equal to $1,000 billion) exceeds aggregate demand ($960 billion), leading to an unintended inventory investment of $40 billion; this overstocking of inventories will induce businesspeople to cut back

production levels until an equilibrium NNP of $800 billion is attained.

Therefore, given our consumption function and a desired net investment of $60 billion, the only candidate for equilibrium is an NNP of $800 billion. And note that at an NNP of $800 billion, planned saving of $60 billion is equal to planned investment. This is exactly what we should have expected since the equality of planned saving and planned investment is nothing other than an alternative way of expressing the fact that aggregate demand is equal to aggregate supply. Moreover, actual investment of $60 billion equals desired investment at an NNP of $800 billion, yet another indication that the economy has attained equilibrium.

These results are shown graphically in Figure 7.3. Looking at the upper diagram first, we measure consumption expenditures (C) and net investment (I_n) on the vertical axis, and NNP (Y) on the horizontal axis. The curve labeled C is nothing other than the consumption function of Figure 7.2. The curve labeled $C + I_n^d$ is the aggregate demand curve obtained by adding consumption and *desired* net investment. And note that the $C + I_n^d$ curve is parallel to the C curve. This must be so. Since aggregate demand is arrived at by adding $60 billion of desired net investment to consumption at *each level of income,* the $C + I_n^d$ curve must lie above the C curve by an amount equal to $60 billion. Finally, recalling the meaning of the 45° line and noting that NNP is identical to the sum of expenditures for consumption and *actual* investment, then *actual* aggregate spending equals NNP all along the 45° line. Equilibrium will be discovered on the 45° line at that point where *actual* spending (NNP) equals desired spending (aggregate demand).

Graphically, then, the equilibrium level of NNP can be determined at the point of intersection of the aggregate demand schedule and the 45° line. At that point, aggregate demand is equal to NNP, aggregate supply; at that point there will be no further tendency to change. Consumption expenditures at an NNP of $800 billion amount to $740 billion and *desired* net invest-

Figure 7.3
The equilibrium NNP:
A graphical representation

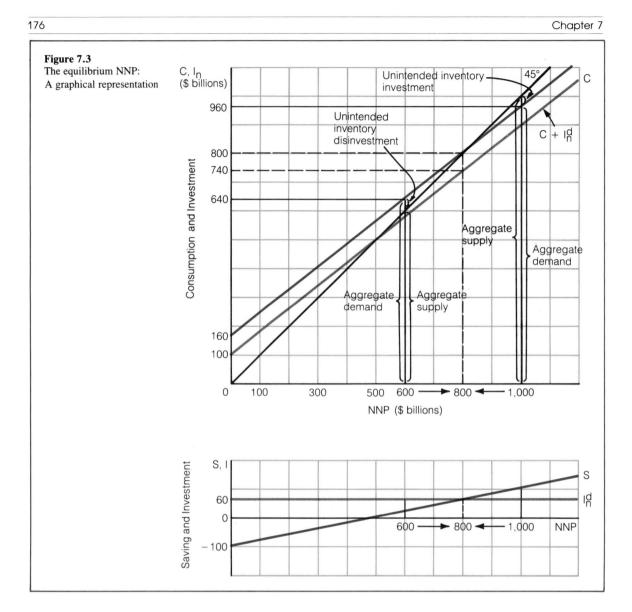

ment of $60 billion is equal to *actual* net investment: $Y = C + I_n^d$.

At an NNP of $600 billion, on the other hand, aggregate demand equals $640 billion causing an unintended inventory disinvestment of $40 billion; in response, producers will increase their production levels, thereby increasing NNP and income. By how much will NNP increase? Since aggregate demand exceeds aggregate supply at all levels of income below $800 billion, producers will continue to raise production until an NNP of $800 billion is attained.

Similarly, at an NNP of $1,000 billion, aggregate supply, as measured by the 45° line, exceeds aggregate demand. The unintended inventory investment of $40 billion induces producers to curtail production, forcing down NNP and income. Given the consumption function and a level of desired net investment of $60 billion, NNP will continue to fall until it reaches $800 billion.

Note one final graphical result. Since the difference between the 45° line and the consumption function measures the amount saved, only at an NNP of $800 billion does planned saving equal planned investment. To the right of the equilibrium NNP, planned saving exceeds planned investment; to the left of equilibrium, planned investment exceeds planned saving. These same results are also displayed in the lower diagram of Figure 7.3. Note there that desired net investment is represented by the horizontal straight line I_n^d; this is because I_n^d is independent of the level of NNP—that is, it is equal to $60 billion whether NNP is $600 billion, $800 billion, or $1,000 billion. As that diagram makes clear, planned saving is equal to planned investment only at an NNP of $800 billion.

The simple multiplier.

Suppose that businesspeople, for one reason or another, decide to increase their *desired* net investment from $60 billion per year to $80 billion. What will happen to the equilibrium level of income? It will rise. By how much? By $100 billion. This can be seen by examining once again the data presented in Table 7.3. The new level of desired net investment ($I_n^{d\prime}$) is presented in column (4). With desired investment fixed at its new level of $80 billion, the new equilibrium level of NNP can be found by identifying that level of consumption in column (2) that, when added to the new level of desired net investment in column (4), is equal to the level of NNP in column (1). As Table 7.3 makes clear, such an equality takes place at an NNP of $900 billion: *the new equilibrium level of NNP is equal to $900 billion.* Thus, according to the results presented in Table 7.3, a $20 billion increase in desired net investment will lead to a $100 billion increase in the level of income. Income rises by a multiple of the increase in desired investment spending. *The multiple by which income increases is called the multiplier.* And the value of the multiplier here is 5—that is, income rises by an amount five times the change in desired net investment.

Let us examine this multiplier process in detail. The initial increase of $20 billion in desired investment will induce producers to initially expand their production and income by $20 billion to meet the new higher level of aggregate demand. However, this increase in income will generate yet further increases in aggregate demand. Indeed, the consumption function tells us that a $20 billion increase in income will induce consumers to step up their spending by an additional $16 billion—that is, with MPC = 0.8, consumers will increase their spending by 0.8 × $20 billion = $16 billion. This in turn will induce producers to increase production and income by an *additional* $16 billion to meet the new higher level of aggregate demand. But *that* $16 billion increase in income will induce consumers to increase their spending by another $12.8 billion (0.8 × $16 billion), which in turn causes producers to increase production and income by yet *another* $12.8 billion. Does the process stop here? No. That $12.8 billion increase in income induces a further increase in consumption, and a further increase in income, and so on.

What we see here is that the initial increase in desired net investment sets in motion a number of "rounds of spending," causing income and production to rise by some multiple of the initial increase in desired spending. *By adding up all of the changes in income brought about by all of the increases in spending, we obtain the ultimate increase in aggregate demand and NNP.*

The flow chart of Figure 7.4 illustrates the multiplier process. The change in desired investment initially leads to an equal dollar change in NNP. This change in NNP induces a change in consumption; by assumption, each dollar change in NNP induces a 0.80 dollar change in consumption; that 0.80 dollar change in consumption changes NNP by a like amount; that in turn induces yet another change in consumption equal to 0.80 of the increase in NNP; and so on.

Returning to our numerical example, the initial $20 billion increase in desired investment leads to an initial $20 billion increase in the level of income. Thus, at the end of *round one,* income has increased by $20 billion. Out of that increased income, 80 percent will be spent on additional consumption, inducing a further increase in production and income of $16 billion (0.80 × $20 billion). By the end of *round two,* income has

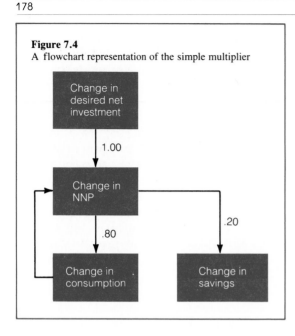

Figure 7.4
A flowchart representation of the simple multiplier

$20 billion + 0.80 × $20 billion + 0.80²
× 20 billion + 0.80³ × 20 billion + · · ·
+ 0.80ⁿ⁻¹ × 20 billion + · · ·.

Factoring out the common $20 billion value, we get:

Ultimate change in NNP
= $20 billion (1 + 0.80 + 0.80²
+ 0.80³ + · · · + 0.80ⁿ⁻¹ + · · ·).

The expression inside the parentheses is the sum of an infinite series, the general solution to which is given as follow[5]:

$$(1 + 0.80 + 0.80^2 + · · ·) = \frac{1}{(1 - 0.80)}.$$

Accordingly,

$$\text{Ultimate change in NNP} = \$20 \text{ billion} × \frac{1}{(1 - 0.80)}.$$

Since 0.80 is the numerical value of the marginal propensity to consume (MPC), the expression inside the parentheses can be written as $1/(1 - \text{MPC})$. And since the MPS + MPC = 1, this expression can be rewritten as 1/MPS. This is known as **the simple multiplier.**

It is readily apparent that the multiplier in the numerical example above has a value equal to 5 (i.e., $1/(1 - 0.80)) = 1/0.20 = 5$). And $100 billion (5 × $20 billion) is the increase in income we noted earlier. That is, a $20 billion increase in desired investment will ultimately lead to a $100 billion increase in the equilibrium NNP.

Generalizing,

Change in equilibrium NNP	=	Change in desired net investment	×	Simple multiplier.

Let us show these results graphically. In Figure 7.5, the aggregate demand curve is shifted upward by $20 billion to $C + I_n^{d'}$. The equilibrium

gone up by $36 billion (round one of $20 billion + round two of $16 billion). What about *round three?* Out of the $16 billion increase in income in round two, 80 percent of that increase will be spent on additional consumption, inducing yet a further increase in production and income of $12.8 billion. After three rounds of spending, then, income has increased by $48.8 billion (rounds one and two of $36 billion + round three of $12.8 billion).

A pattern should be evident at this point. *The increase in income that occurs in every round but the first is exactly 80 percent of the increase in income in the previous round.* Thus, the income increase in round two is 0.80 of the income increase in round one; the increased income in round three is 0.80 of the income increase in round two (that is, 0.80 × $16 billion = 0.80 × (0.80 × $20 billion) = 0.80² × $20 billion); the increased income in round four is .80³ × $20 billion; and so on. In general, the increased income in *round n* is (0.80ⁿ⁻¹ × $20 billion). If we add up *all* of the changes in income that take place in all rounds, we arrive at the ultimate increase in income. The ultimate increase in income will therefore be:

---

[5] In general, the sum of any infinite series $(1 + r + r^2 + r^3 + · · ·)$ where $|r| < 1$ is given by $\frac{1}{1 - r}$.

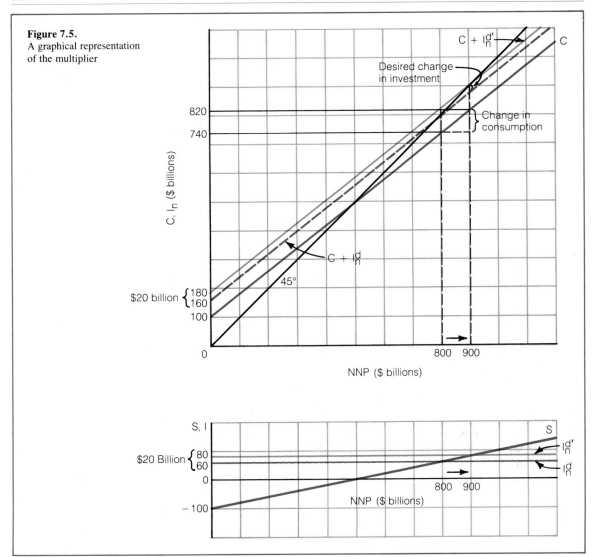

Figure 7.5.
A graphical representation
of the multiplier

NNP occurs at the point where the new aggregate demand curve crosses the 45° line. The new equilibrium NNP is $900 billion. Similar results are displayed in the lower diagram of Figure 7.5. There, the desired investment line shifts from I_n^d to $I_n^{d'}$; planned saving now equals planned investment at an NNP of $900 billion.

Can we be sure that an NNP of $900 billion is in fact the new equilibrium NNP? Yes. Why? Because the change in aggregate supply of $100 billion is equal to the change in consumption ($80 billion) plus the desired change in invest-

ment ($20 billion); or alternatively, because the change in planned saving ($20 billion) equals the change in planned investment. These results are all shown graphically in Figure 7.5; a careful study of the data in Table 7.3 reveals the same conclusion.

Two final notes on the simple multiplier. First the multiplier process we have been describing here is *symmetrical* in the sense that decreases in desired net investment will lead to reductions in the equilibrium net national product in a manner that is exactly analogous to, but the reverse of, an increase in desired investment. This can be readily demonstrated using the above numerical examples. Suppose desired net investment equals $80 billion initially. Given our consumption function, it is clear that equilibrium NNP will equal $900 billion. Consider now a reduction in desired net investment from $80 billion per year to $60 billion. As a result of the $20 billion decline in desired investment, the equilibrium NNP will, via the multiplier process, decline from $900 billion to $800 billion. The implied value of the multiplier is therefore 5.

Second, it should be noted that the value of the multiplier varies directly with the value of the MPC. Indeed, suppose the value of the MPC had been 0.75 instead of 0.80. What would happen to the value of the multiplier? It would decline from a value of 5 to a value of 4 (i.e., $1/(1 - 0.75) = 1/0.25 = 4$). The reason for this result is clear: *the smaller the MPC, the smaller the additional income generated on each round of spending, and the smaller, therefore, the cumulative total.* Analogously, the value of the multiplier varies inversely with the value of the MPS: the higher the value of the MPS, the smaller the multiplier.

By focusing our attention on the saving-income relation we can provide an intuitive explanation for the numerical value of the multiplier. Assume that the MPS equals 0.20. This tells us that saving rises by 20 cents for every dollar increase in income. Since equilibrium requires that planned saving equal planned investment, then for every dollar increase in planned investment, income must rise by $5 in order to generate the necessary increase in saving to restore the above equality; the multiplier must, therefore, be equal to 5 when the MPS equals 0.20.

Shifts in the consumption function. Up to this point we have focused our attention on only one of the determinants of consumer spending—income. However, consumer spending is determined by more than income. Two of the most important additional factors are consumer *wealth* and consumer *expectations.* If consumers experience an increase in their wealth, higher levels

of consumer spending normally will result; decreases in consumer wealth frequently cause reduced levels of consumer spending. Generally, consumer wealth does not change significantly in the short run. We should, therefore, not expect sizable wealth-induced changes in consumer spending in the short run as a result. However, wealth is a very important factor in the long run. This is discussed in greater detail in the appendix to this chapter.

Consumer expectations, on the other hand, exert an extremely powerful influence on the level of consumer spending, especially in the short run. Indeed, on the basis of studies conducted at the Survey Research Center at the University of Michigan and elsewhere, the changing attitudes of consumers about unemployment, inflation, the oil crisis, and like matters are so important that they can cause dramatic changes in the level of consumer spending in the short run. If consumer attitudes sour, such pessimism is often reflected in a decline in consumer spending; optimistic attitudes regarding the state of the economy, on the other hand, often lead to increases in consumer spending.

What is important for our purposes here is that changes in consumer spending brought about by changes in wealth or changes in consumer expectations cause *shifts* in the consumption function. *Since changes in wealth and expectations cause changes in the level of consumer spending independent of changes in income, the consumption function will shift.* Accordingly, an increase in wealth and/or greater optimism on the part of consumers will cause the consumption function to shift upwards at each and every level of income; a reduction in wealth and/or greater consumer pessimism will cause a downward shift in the consumption function.

A change in consumption brought about by changes in these other determinants has an impact on the equilibrium level of income that is exactly analogous to the impact of a change in the desired level of investment. This is easily demonstrated. Assume, as before, that desired net investment equals $60 billion. Given the original consumption function, the equilibrium level of NNP will be $800 billion, as we have already shown.

Suppose now that, as a result of greater consumer optimism, consumers decide to increase their expenditures by $20 billion independent of any change in income. Then, on the assumption that the marginal propensity to consume remains unaltered—that is, that consumers will continue to increase their consumer spending by 80 percent of any subsequent change in income—that $20 billion increase in consumption will lead ultimately to a $100 billion increase in the equilibrium net national product. That is, the equilibrium level of income will rise from $800 billion to $900 billion as a result of the $20 billion increase in consumer spending. This is precisely the amount by which income changed in response to the $20 billion increase in desired net investment.

The explanation for these identical results is straightforward. Just as the $20 billion increase in desired net investment led initially to a $20 billion increase in production and income and to a subsequent additional $80 billion increase in income via the multiplier, the $20 billion increase in consumer spending attributable to consumer optimism will do precisely the same thing.

This particular result is probably easier to understand graphically. Since an upward shift of the consumption function by $20 billion causes the aggregate demand ($C + I_n^d$) schedule to shift upward by $20 billion, just as a $20 billion increase in desired net investment would do, it is hardly surprising that the equilibrium level of income rises by the same amount. This is shown pictorially in Figure 7.6.

The $20 billion increase in consumer spending causes the consumption function to shift upwards by $20 billion from C to C′, which in turn raises the aggregate demand schedule from $C + I_n^d$ to $C′ + I_n^d$; the equilibrium level of income rises from $800 billion to $900 billion. Here, consumption rises ultimately by precisely the same amount as income. The initial $20 billion increase in consumer spending, by raising income by $100 billion, induces an additional $80 billion increase in consumer spending.

Similar results are displayed in the lower portion of Figure 7.6. The upward shift of the consumption function has, as its counterpart, a downward shift of the saving function from S to S′. Planned saving will once again be brought into line with planned investment only if income rises by $100 billion. Since saving declines initially by $20 billion, planned investment (fixed at $60 billion), will exceed planned saving by $20 billion. Income must, therefore, rise by an amount sufficient to restore the equality of planned saving and planned investment; with MPS equal to 0.20, income must rise by $100 billion. And note that *the amount saved at an income level of $900 billion is exactly equal to the amount saved at $800 billion.* This result is hardly surprising once it is recognized that planned investment remains fixed at $60 billion throughout and that equilibrium requires that planned saving equal planned investment. To cement this idea completely, note the implications of an increase in planned savings: *If people decide, for whatever reason, that they want to increase their savings—that is, become more thrifty—those plans will ultimately be frustrated, and they will end up saving no more than they did before.* At least this is true as long as desired net investment remains fixed at some constant level. The reason for this is clear. A higher desired rate of savings implies a reduced level of consumer spending. This, via the multiplier, reduces the level of income *and* the level of saving. Put differently, since net investment remains fixed throughout, and since equilibrium involves the equilibration of planned investment and planned savings, savings must ultimately return to their original level (via a reduction in income).

The paradox of thrift. It is even possible that attempts to increase the level of saving will ultimately cause the level of savings to *decline!* This is known as the **paradox of thrift.** It is easily demonstrated.

Suppose we drop the assumption that desired net investment is fixed at some constant level. Instead assume that businesspeople desire to undertake varying amounts of investment depending on the level of income. In particular, let us assume that desired net investment is positively related to the level of income. Increases (decreases) in the level of income will induce

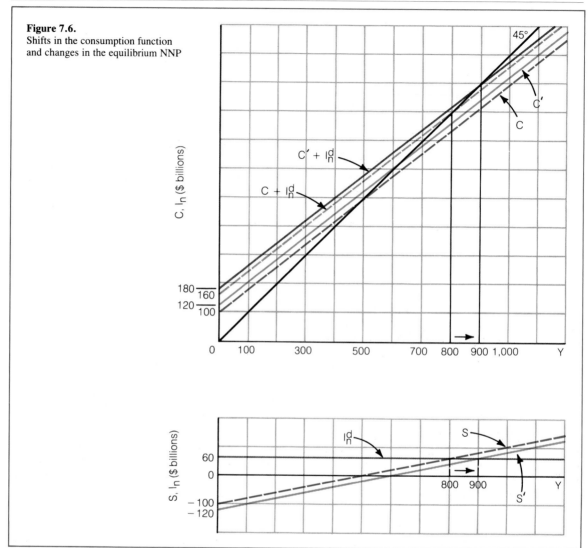

Figure 7.6.
Shifts in the consumption function and changes in the equilibrium NNP

an increase (decrease) in the level of desired net investment. Such an upward-sloping investment function is portrayed in Figure 7.7.

Given the initial savings function, S, the initial equilibrium will occur at E. This gives us the level of income Y_1 and a level of savings (equal to desired net investment) of OA (or Y_1E). Suppose consumers desire to increase their savings from Y_1E to Y_1F. As a result, the equilibrium level of income will fall from Y_1 to Y_2 and, at the new level of income, people will actually be

saving *less* than they were at Y_1 (OB as compared to OA). Isn't this paradoxical?!

Actually, the paradox is easily explained. Equilibrium will occur only when planned net investment is equal to planned saving. We have already noted that an increase in savings will cause, via the multiplier, a reduction in income and savings. However, by our earlier assumption, *the reduction in income will cause a reduction in desired net investment*, meaning that the new

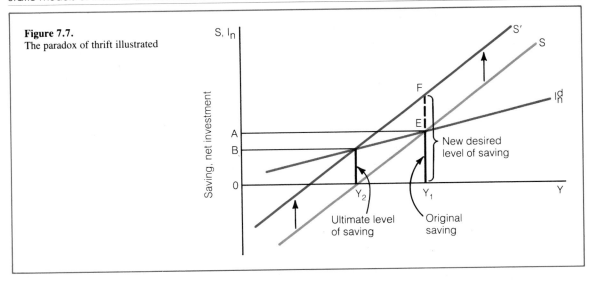

Figure 7.7.
The paradox of thrift illustrated

equilibrium level of income will be one in which both planned saving and planned net investment are both lower than they were originally.

To cement this idea, consider the following simple numerical example. Suppose that, for each $100 billion *increase* in income, desired investment rises by $10 billion, (which implies that, for each $100 billion *decrease* in income, desired investment is reduced by $10 billion). In our example, savings and desired investment are both initially equal to $200 billion. Now let savings increase to $210 billion. Consumption will fall; therefore, so will income. But the decline in income will cause desired investment to fall, further reducing income. The reduction in income will cause savings to fall below $210 billion (a movement along the savings function). And, most important, the income reduction that forces a reduction in investment *below* $200 billion means that, ultimately, savings must be reduced *below* the original value of $200 billion. The increase in savings is not only frustrated; the increase actually turns into a *decrease*.

Ben Franklin and the fallacy of composition. Isn't saving *always* a good thing? Indeed, didn't Benjamin Franklin teach us that "a penny saved is a penny earned"? How is it then that we can arrive at a result that suggests that we are worse

off in terms of output and income as a result of increased saving?

The paradox can be resolved by recognizing that what may be virtuous for each person separately may not be good for the nation as a whole. That is, we must take care not to commit a **fallacy of composition.** Since the increased savings on the part of any one person or small group of people will have no noticeable effect on the total amount saved by society, such "prudent" behavior will not affect noticeably the aggregate level of income and output produced. However, if everyone were to *attempt* to increase their savings, the level of income and output would decline, making the nation as a whole worse off. Such an attempt to increase savings would not, *under these circumstances,* be very prudent socially.

We should not, however, jump to the conclusion that efforts to increase the volume of savings is socially undesirable *under all circumstances.* Indeed, the above results emerged only because of the assumptions we made concerning saving and investment. Since planned saving initially equaled planned investment at an income of Y_1, any attempts to increase saving at Y_1 would actually reduce income and therewith the level of saving and investment.

But consider a situation in which the economy is actually producing at its potential. If desired investment *exceeded* savings at that potential level of income, an increase in saving might well be an appropriate action socially. Since we are at full employment, more resources can be devoted to the production of capital goods only if fewer resources are devoted to consumer goods. An increase in the overall level of saving would, by reducing consumption expenditures, release resources for the production of capital goods. Under these circumstances, the reduction in consumption would be offset by the increase in investment, thereby enabling the maintenance of full employment. In addition, since more resources are being devoted to capital formation, the economy could achieve higher levels of output in the future. Increased saving need not, therefore, be a social evil; it could well be very prudent.

The point that needs to be made is this: If equilibrium occurs at levels of income below full employment, any attempts to increase the overall level of saving may be frustrated and lead to reductions in income and employment. If the economy has already attained full employment and if desired investment exceeds saving, an increase in the overall level of saving could well be consistent both with the maintenance of full employment and greater growth of our capital resources. In the first instance, attempts to increase aggregate savings would be social folly; in the latter, a higher level of savings would be socially desirable.

Equilibrium at full employment?

Now that we have completed our analysis of income determination in a private closed economy characterized by the absence of wage and price flexibility, we are in a position to provide Keynes' answer to the question posed at the outset of this chapter—Do any automatic forces exist to ensure that our economy will produce at its potential? The Keynesian answer is a simple no. The equilibrium level of income is determined by aggregate demand and aggregate supply, and there is no necessary reason such an equilibrium should occur at full employment. Indeed, it it very likely that our economy will attain an **under-**

employment equilibrium—that is, a less-than-full employment equilibrium—or it will attain an **overemployment equilibrium.** Unless something happens to change either desired net investment or the level of consumer spending, there will be no tendency for that equilibrium level of income to change. It is possible that aggregate demand could equal aggregate supply at the full employment level of income. But no mechanism exists in the Keynesian system described above to guarantee such a result.

Deflationary and inflationary gaps. Figure 7.8 illustrates the case of an underemployment equilibrium. The full employment (or potential) level of income is given by Y_{FE}. However, given the aggregate demand schedule, $C + I_n^d$, it is clear that the equilibrium level of income is not Y_{FE}, but Y_e, a level of income that is below full employment. Equilibrium would occur at full employment only if aggregate demand were sufficiently far above $C + I_n^d$ that it intersected the 45° line at point A, the point corresponding to Y_{FE}. *This gap between the actual aggregate demand and the higher level of aggregate demand required to bring about full employment is called the deflationary or recessionary gap.* It measures the magnitude of the increase in aggregate demand required to reach full employment. It is called a deflationary or recessionary gap in order

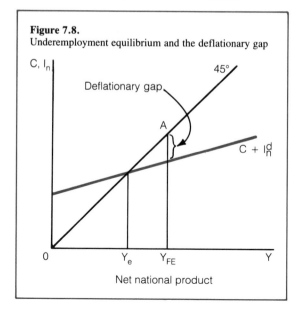

Figure 7.8.
Underemployment equilibrium and the deflationary gap

to highlight the fact that it is the deficiency of aggregate demand that keeps our level of income depressed below its full employment potential.

With the assistance of our multiplier concept it is possible, in principle, to figure out by how much the aggregate demand schedule must shift up to eliminate the deflationary gap. Suppose, as our earlier example implied, the multiplier is equal to 5. If the gap between our actual and potential income is equal to $100 billion—that is, if the difference between Y_{FE} and Y_e equals $100 billion—then an increase in the aggregate demand schedule of $20 billion (due either to an increase in desired net investment, an upward shift of the consumption function, or both) will do the trick. The $20 billion increase in aggregate demand times the multiplier of 5 gives us the required $100 billion increase in net national product. In general, the magnitude of the upward shift in the aggregate demand schedule can be calculated as the difference between Y_e and Y_{FE} divided by the value of the multiplier. In our example, the $100 billion difference between Y_e and Y_{FE} divided by a multiplier value of 5 gives us the $20 billion shift.

The countercase, that of an overemployment equilibrium, is presented in Figure 7.9. There, the only possible equilibrium level of income consistent with the aggregate demand schedule,

$C + I_n^d$, is a level of income in excess of full employment. A lower level of aggregate demand would be required in order to establish Y_{FE} as an equilibrium. *This gap between the actual aggregate demand and the lower level of aggregate demand required to bring about full employment is called the **inflationary gap.*** It measures the magnitude of the reduction in aggregate demand required to achieve full employment. It is called an inflationary gap for one simple reason. Since the equilibrium level of income, Y_e, exceeds the full employment level of income, it is not sustainable; it is beyond our production possibilities. The excess demand can lead to one result only— rising prices, or *inflation.* Analogous to our discussion of the deflationary gap, the magnitude of the downward shift of the aggregate demand schedule to reach Y_{FE} can be calculated as difference between Y_e and Y_{FE} divided by the value of the multiplier.

A final note. As far as the classical economists were concerned, underemployment and overemployment equilibriums were not possible except for very short time periods. Both types of situations—underemployment and overemployment—would *ultimately* give rise to wage and price adjustments sufficient to bring about full employment. Equilibriums at levels of income other than full employment could not long be sustained.

The real difficulty that Keynes had with this kind of thinking was with the word *ultimately.* Ultimately, wage and price adjustments might do the trick, but the necessary wage and price adjustments might take several years before accomplishing their task. Indeed, to Keynes, prices and wages were so sticky in the short run that it would be more appropriate to assume that no automatic mechanism existed whatsoever in the short run to bring about full employment. And, as was apparent to Keynes at least, the short run could last for quite some time.

This absence of an automatic mechanism has two important consequences. First, not only does an economy lose the production of valuable goods and services when unemployed resources exist, but unemployment itself is a social evil that imposes a heavy burden on society, most

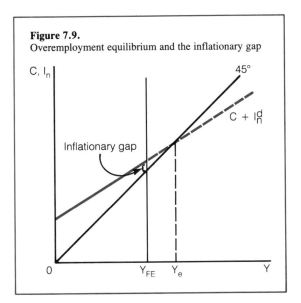

Figure 7.9.
Overemployment equilibrium and the inflationary gap

notably on those who are unemployed. Second, depressed levels of spending can lead to the formation of pessimistic expectations on the part of both consumers and businesspeople, further depressing consumption and investment expenditures and lowering further still the levels of income and employment. In order to rectify the situation, it is necessary for government to intervene by either increasing its spending for goods and services directly or by pursuing policies that have the effect of stimulating private expenditures. These issues will be the main topics of discussion in the next three chapters.

SUMMARY

1. In the simplified economy studied in this chapter there are two groups of buyers—households and businesses. Personal consumption expenditures are made by the household sector; investment is undertaken by the business sector.

2. Macroequilibrium will exist when the amount consumers and investors (i.e., businesses) in the aggregate are *willing to buy* equals the amount producers are willing to sell. The notion of macroequilibrium can be expressed in several different ways:

   a. Defining *aggregate demand* as the sum of personal consumption expenditures (C) and *desired* or *planned* net investment (I_n^d) and *aggregate supply* (Y) as the actual level of the net national product, macroequilibrium will occur when

$$Y = C + I_n^d.$$

   b. Defining planned saving as the difference between NNP (Y) and consumption (C), macroequilibrium will occur when

$$S = I_n^d.$$

   c. Macroequilibrium will occur when

$$I_n = I_n^d.$$

3. When aggregate demand exceeds aggregate supply, this disequilibrium can be expressed alternatively as *(a)* I_n^d exceeds I_n or *(b)* planned investment exceeds planned saving. Likewise,

when aggregate supply exceeds aggregate demand, this disequilibrium can be expressed alternatively as *(a)* I_n exceeds I_n^d or *(b)* planned saving exceeds planned investment.

4. According to the classical theory of income determination, *automatic* forces exist that will bring about an equilibrium level of income that fully employs our nation's resources. *Say's Law,* which hypothesizes that overproduction and underproduction are impossible, is *not* an essential element of the classical position. Complete wage and price flexibility is the essential feature. Assuming that wages and prices adjust quickly enough to eliminate market disequilibrium, a near-continuous state of equilibrium will obtain, according to the classical economists.

5. John Maynard Keynes maintained that automatic forces do not exist to bring about full employment—at least not in the short run. Either wages and prices are not flexible or they are *so slow* to adjust that they do not eliminate unemployment within a reasonable length of time.

Keynes maintained that wages and prices, and especially wages, were notoriously sticky, at least on the down side. Wage and price flexibility could not, therefore, be counted on to eliminate unemployment. In order to reduce unemployment, it was necessary for government to intervene to raise total aggregate spending.

6. Since Keynes believed that the level of employment was determined by the level of aggregate spending, he naturally focused his attention on the determinants of aggregate demand—that is, the determinants of consumer expenditures and desired net investment.

7. *The consumption function* implies that consumption expenditures increase as disposable income increases, but that consumption expenditures rise less than in proportion to disposable income.

8. If aggregate demand increases (the result of either an increase in desired net investment or an upward shift of the consumption function), the equilibrium level of NNP will rise by a multiple of that initial increase in aggregate demand. The multiple by which NNP increases is given by the multiplier. The *simple multiplier* is given by the formula $1/(1 - \text{MPC})$, or what is the

same thing, 1/MPS. As is apparent, the value multiplier varies directly with the value of the MPC and inversely with the value of the MPS.

9. In the simplified economy assumed in this chapter, if desired net investment is fixed at some level, say $60 billion per year, it will not be possible for people in the aggregate to change the total volume of savings. Efforts to increase savings from $60 billion to $80 billion per year will be frustrated. Since equilibrium requires that planned savings equals planned investment, income will change by the amount necessary to ensure that savings is brought into alignment with the assumed unchanged desired net investment. If desired net investment is positively related to income, the *paradox of thrift* will result—attempts to increase savings will actually cause the level of savings to *decline!*

10. A *deflationary gap* arises whenever aggregate demand equals aggregate supply at a less than full employment level of income. The gap measures the change in aggregate demand required to bring about full employment. The required increase in aggregate demand can be calculated as the difference between the actual and full employment levels of income divided by the value of the multiplier.

An *inflationary gap* arises whenever aggregate demand equals aggregate supply at a greater than full employment level of income. The reduction in aggregate demand required to achieve full employment can be calculated as the difference between the actual and full employment levels of income divided by the value of the multiplier.

CONCEPTS FOR REVIEW

Macroequilibrium

Aggregate demand

Aggregate supply

Desired or planned net investment (I_n^d)

Unintended inventory investment

Unintended inventory disinvestment

Disequilibrium

Classical theory of income determination

Say's Law

Wage and price flexibility

Keynesian theory of employment and income

"Sticky" wages and prices

Consumption function

Marginal propensity to consume

Marginal propensity to save

Average propensity to consume

Average propensity to save (the savings rate)

Simple multiplier

Paradox of thrift

Underemployment equilibrium

Overemployment equilibrium

Deflationary (or recessionary) gap

Inflationary gap

QUESTIONS FOR DISCUSSION

(Those marked with an asterisk (*) are more difficult.)

1. Carefully evaluate the following statement: "If savings always equals investment, and if equilibrium requires the equality of savings and investment, the economy must be in a continuous state of equilibrium."

2. According to the simplified Keynesian model developed in this chapter, if planned investment exceeds planned savings, will net national product increase or decrease? Explain.

3. "If planned savings exceeds planned investment by $50 billion, actual investment must exceed planned investment by $50 billion." Do you agree or disagree? Illustrate your answer with a numerical example.

*4. It is sometimes alleged that redistributing income from the rich to the poor will raise aggregate demand. The reason? Those with high incomes save a larger percentage of their income than those with low incomes. If the well-to-do save a larger fraction of their incomes, does it follow that redistributing income from them to lower-income people will raise aggregate spending? (*Hint:* As far as the *change* in consumer expenditures is concerned, is it the average propensity to save of the different income groups that is important, or is it the marginal propensity to save?)

5. What changes in the economy cause a movement along the aggregate demand schedule, $C + I_n^d$?

What changes would cause the aggregate demand schedule to shift?

6. If the MPC were to increase, what would happen to the value of the simple multiplier? Why? What effect would an increase in the MPC have on the aggregate demand schedule, $C + I_n^d$?

7. Frequently we hear it said that economic policy should be changed to foster an increase in the savings rate. In terms of the Keynesian model presented in this chapter, what effect would an increase in the savings rate have on the equilibrium level of income? Why?

8. Explain carefully why the *deflationary gap* is defined as the difference between the actual and full employment levels of income divided by the value of the multiplier.

Appendix

THE SHORT-RUN AND LONG-RUN CONSUMPTION FUNCTION

Several economists have attempted to estimate empirically the consumption function discussed in Chapter 7. Their purposes were twofold: (1) to determine whether such a relationship as described in the text is actually supported by the facts; and (2) to obtain numerical estimates of both the marginal and average propensity to consume. In general, the conclusions derived from these studies can be classified on the basis of whether they used short-run data (i.e., data that reflect the short-run responsiveness of consumers to changes in income) or long-run data. The general conclusions from these research efforts can be stated as follows:

1. In studies employing *short-run* data, the MPC has been shown to be positive and ranging in value from 0.65 to 0.84 (depending on the time period used in studying the consumption-income relation and the statistical methods employed). These same studies showed that the APC declined with income. Both results lend

support to the consumption function discussed in the text.

2. In studies focusing on the *long-run* relationship of consumption to disposable income, the MPC was also shown to be positive, but its numerical value was significantly larger than the MPC estimated using short-run data; the estimates ranged from 0.88 to 0.94. In addition, these studies came to the conclusion that, contrary to the short-run results, the APC did *not* decline with income. *The percentage of income saved and consumed did not change significantly with changes in income.*

Although these two types of studies appear to yield contradictory results, they can be reconciled by focusing on yet another determinant of consumer spending—wealth. While it is widely recognized that increases in wealth will induce consumers to increase their expenditures at any given level of income, it is also acknowledged that wealth changes by very little in the short run, though it can grow considerably in the long run. Therefore, the short-run consumption function shows the consumption-income relation under circumstances in which wealth is relatively constant. Over time, however, as wealth accumulates, the short-run consumption function shifts upward, "tracing out" a long-run consumption function. This is shown in Figure 7.A1.

Consider the short-run consumption function labeled C_{SR}. If, in the short run, income rises by an amount Y_1Y_2, then consumption will rise by CD. However, with the passage of time and the accumulation of greater wealth, consumers will increase their spending, which shifts the consumption function upwards to, say, C_{SR}'. Thus, whereas the short-run consumption function implies that consumption will rise from A and D in response to an increase in income from Y_1 to Y_2, in the long run, as wealth accumulates, we will observe that consumption rises to point B—that is, the consumption function will shift up at each and every level of income. In the long run, then, consumption rises from A to B. Therefore, the long-run consumption function has a larger MPC than the short-run function (since the long-run function is steeper than the short-run function).

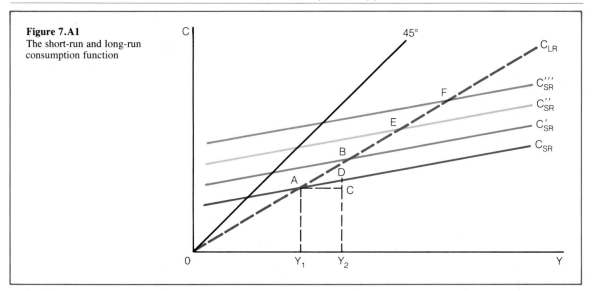

Figure 7.A1
The short-run and long-run consumption function

Points E and F can be found similarly. The consumption expenditures represented at those points reflect both growing income and growing wealth over time. The points ABEF form the long-run consumption function, labeled C_{LR}. We have extended this line to the origin (since this is what the statistical results from the long-run studies seem to indicate), which implies that consumption, in the long run, rises in proportion to income. The APC does not decline in the long run, though in the short run it does. The reconciliation is complete.

Chapter 8

Fiscal policy and national income determination: A static approach

It is widely accepted that government has an obligation to pursue policies designed to bring about full employment without inflation. This obligation is set forth formally in the Employment Act of 1946 and in the Full Employment and Balanced Growth Act of 1978 (popularly referred to as the Humphrey-Hawkins Act). Technically, this area of government responsibility is referred to as the **stabilization function** of government. In general, the policies used in the pursuance of these goals fall into two broad categories—**fiscal policy** and **monetary policy.**

Monetary and fiscal policy encompass all of those policy actions used by government for the purpose of influencing or controlling the general level of economic activity. Although the aims of both policies are similar—to influence the levels of income and employment and the rate of change of prices—the policy tools, or instruments of control, are not. Specifically, the tools of fiscal policy are government expenditures and taxes; the tools of monetary policy consist of those measures designed to control the money supply and interest rates. The focal point of our attention in this chapter will be fiscal policy; the issue of monetary policy will be taken up in Chapters 9 and 10.

Background material:
Our assumptions modified

To come to a better understanding of the role and significance of fiscal policy, let us expand the analytical framework developed in Chapter 7 to incorporate a government sector. Toward that end we make the following assumptions:

1. We will continue to ignore the complications introduced by the existence of depreciation. The focal point of our attention will again be on the determinants of net national product (NNP); accordingly, all investment will be "net investment."

2. We will continue to assume that our economy is *closed;* exports and imports, therefore, are zero.

3. With respect to government, we assume that all tax receipts are derived from personal income taxes. Thus, indirect business taxes, social security taxes, and corporate profits taxes are all zero. In addition, we ignore government transfer payments by assuming that they are zero.

4. Finally, we assume, as before, that all corporate profits are distributed; undistributed corporate profits are therefore zero.

With these assumptions we can modify a number of the national income accounting relationships developed in Chapter 6. Specifically:

Net national product (NNP), national income (NI), and personal income (PI) are all equal to one another. In the absence of any business taxes, social security taxes, transfer payments, or business saving, this must be so. However, disposable personal income (DPI) is smaller than PI (or NNP) by the amount of personal income taxes (T). That is,

$$DPI = NNP - T.$$

All saving is personal saving.

The "savings-investment" accounting identity is now personal savings + personal taxes = net investment + government expenditures. This can be written symbolically as:

$$S + T = I + G.$$

Defining a government budget deficit as the excess of government spending over tax receipts, and a budget surplus as the excess of tax receipts over government spending, the above identity can be rewritten as:

$$(T - G) = (I - S.)$$

That is, *it is always true that a budget surplus (deficit) is matched by the excess of actual investment (saving) over actual saving (investment).*

NNP, defined as the sum of expenditures for final goods and services, is now the sum of personal consumption expenditures (C), net investment (I_n), and government purchases of goods and services (G). Thus,

$$NNP = C + I_n + G.$$

The concept of macroequilibrium reconsidered

Recalling our discussion of equilibrium in Chapter 7, the equilibrium level of income will occur at the point where aggregate demand is equal to aggregate supply. Defining aggregate demand as the sum of personal consumption expenditures (C), *desired* (or planned) net investment (I_n^d), and government purchases of goods and services (G), and NNP as aggregate supply (Y), we can represent this condition as

$$Y = C + I_n^d + G.$$

Moreover, since the value of the output produced is identical to the value of the income generated, and since, by our assumptions, NNP = DPI + T, *planned savings (the difference between NNP and C) plus taxes is equal to planned investment plus government spending in equilibrium.* That is, equilibrium occurs when[1]

$$S + T = I_n^d + G.$$

Recalling the meaning of a budget surplus or deficit, this last condition can further be rewritten as

$$T - G = I_n^d - S.$$

Thus, in equilibrium, a budget surplus is matched by the excess of *desired* investment over saving; the converse is true for a budget deficit.

Macroequilibrium illustrated. These ideas can all be illustrated with the aid of a simple numerical example. Suppose personal consump-

---

[1] Actually, this last condition is nothing more than a different way of expressing the fact that, in equilibrium, aggregate demand is equal to aggregate supply. This can be seen as follows: We know in equilibrium that

$$Y = C + I_n^d + G,$$

and that

$$Y = DPI + T.$$

Thus,

$$DPI + T = C + I_n^d + G.$$

But (DPI − C) is nothing other than personal savings. Therefore

$$(DPI - C) + T = I_n^d + G,$$

or

$$S + T = I_n^d + G.$$

tion expenditures (C) are $600 billion, desired net investment (I_n^d) is $200 billion, and government expenditures (G) are $200 billion. Aggregate demand, therefore, will equal $1,000 billion. Suppose, on the other hand, that net national product is $1,100 billion. Can $1,100 billion be viewed as an equilibrium level of output and income? No. The amount that producers are willing to sell ($1,100 billion) exceeds by $100 billion the amount that consumers, investors, and the government are willing to buy. As a consequence, businesspeople will be running up their inventories by $100 billion more than they had intended. This unintended inventory investment will in all likelihood lead to production cutbacks. An NNP of $1,100 billion cannot, therefore, be an equilibrium level of income and output.

In the above example, aggregate supply exceeds aggregate demand. Another way of stating this is that savings plus taxes exceeds *desired* investment plus government spending. This is easily illustrated. Suppose personal income taxes (T) amount to $150 billion. Given an NNP of $1,100 billion, personal disposable income is therefore $950 billion. Since consumption expenditures are $600 billion, personal saving (S) is equal to $350 billion. Thus, personal savings plus personal taxes (S + T) ($500 billion) exceeds ($I_n^d$ + G) ($400 billion) by $100 billion, the amount of the unintended inventory investment.

But note that S + T is exactly equal to *actual* investment plus government spending. That is, since actual investment is equal to desired investment plus the unintended inventory investment, S + T = $500 billion = I_n + G, which is nothing more than our familiar accounting identity.

Similarly, it is easy to show that, if aggregate demand exceeds aggregate supply, desired investment plus government spending will exceed savings plus taxes, and production will increase. I leave it to the reader to demonstrate these conclusions.

A summary of the above-described relationships is provided in Table 8.1. As is apparent, if we define taxes as a form of "saving" and government expenditures as a form of "investment," the conditions for equilibrium are exactly analogous to those presented in Chapter 7.

Table 8.1
Macroequilibrium and disequilibrium with government included: A summary

Aggregate demand ($C + I_n^d + G$) and aggregate supply (Y)	Planned "savings" (S + T) and planned "investment" ($I_n^d + G$)	Actual "savings" (S + T) and actual "investment" ($I_n + G$)
$Y = C + I_n^d + G$ (Equilibrium)	$S + T = I_n^d + G$	$S + T = I_n + G$
$Y > C + I_n^d + G$ (Above equilibrium production)	$S + T > I_n^d + G$	$S + T = I_n + G$
$Y < C + I_n^d + G$ (Below equilibrium production)	$S + T < I_n^d + G$	$S + T = I_n + G$

Actual "savings" (S + T) is always equal to actual "investment" (I_n + G) whether we are in equilibrium or not. But only in equilibrium will planned "savings" (S + T) be equal to planned "investment" (I_n^d + G). Moreover, only in equilibrium will actual investment equal planned investment.

THE THEORY OF EMPLOYMENT AND INCOME WITH GOVERNMENT INCLUDED

We are now in a position to examine the determination of income and employment in a more realistic framework than that presented in Chapter 7. As before, we will assume the existence of unemployed resources initially, and wage and price rigidities throughout the economy.

With respect to the determinants of aggregate demand, we assume, in line with our discussion in the previous chapter, that *consumption expenditures are positively related to disposable income* and that the marginal propensity to consume out of disposable income (MPC) is equal to 0.75—that is, consumption expenditures rise by 75 percent of any increase in disposable income. *Desired net investment,* on the other hand, *is assumed fixed* at a value of $100 billion per year, independent of the level of income. Finally, to keep the analysis as simple as possible, we assume that *government expenditures are also fixed by Congress at some constant value* equal to $200 billion per year, *no matter what the level of income.*

As far as *tax receipts* are concerned, we assume that they *are positively related to NNP in a very simple way.* Specifically, it is assumed that for every dollar *increase* in NNP, tax receipts *rise* by 20 cents. Defining the **marginal tax rate (MTR)** as the change in tax receipts brought about by a change in NNP, it is clear by our assumption that the MTR equals 0.20. That is,

$$MTR = \frac{\Delta T}{\Delta Y} = 0.20.$$

Therefore, if net national product rises by $100 billion, tax receipts will rise by $20 billion; similarly, disposable income will rise by $80 billion for each $100 billion increase in NNP. The data in Table 8.2 reflect all of these assumptions.

The equilibrium level of national income

Having specified all of the relationships in our mixed (government and private) closed economy, we are now in a position to show how the equilibrium level of NNP, or national income, is determined. Recalling the condition for equilibrium, it is clear that equilibrium occurs when aggregate demand is equal to aggregate supply. Therefore, what we need to do is find that level of NNP

that is equal to the sum of consumption expenditures, *desired* net investment, and government expenditures. Thus, using the data in Table 8.2, we can find the equilibrium NNP by identifying that level of consumption in column (4), which, when added to desired net investment and government expenditures in columns (5) and (6), is equal to the level of NNP in column (1); the aggregate demand total is given in column (7). As is apparent, such an equality takes place at an NNP of $1,000 billion. *The equilibrium level of national income is $1,000 billion.*

Can we be sure that $1,000 billion is *the* equilibrium NNP? Yes. Any other level of income fails to meet the requirements for equilibrium. That is, given our consumption function, a desired net investment of $100 billion and government expenditures of $200 billion, the only candidate for equilibrium is an NNP of $1,000 billion. And note that at that level of national income, savings of $60 billion plus tax receipts of $240 billion are exactly equal to planned investment plus government expenditures. This is precisely

Table 8.2
Aggregate supply and the components of aggregate demand ($ billions)

NNP (= NI = PI) (Y) (1)	Tax receipts (T) (2)	Disposable income (3)	Consumption expenditures (C) (4)	Desired net investment (I_n^d) (5)	Government expenditures (G) (6)	Aggregate demand $(C + I_n^d + G)$ (7)
300	100	200	280	100	200	580
400	120	280	340	100	200	640
500	140	360	400	100	200	700
600	160	440	460	100	200	760
700	180	520	520	100	200	820
800	200	600	580	100	200	880
900	220	680	640	100	200	940
1,000	240	760	700	100	200	1,000
1,100	260	840	760	100	200	1,060
1,200	280	920	820	100	200	1,120
1,300	300	1,000	880	100	200	1,180
1,400	320	1,080	940	100	200	1,240
1,500	340	1,160	1,000	100	200	1,300

1. NNP − T = disposable income.

2. $MPC = \dfrac{\Delta C}{\Delta \text{ Disposable income}} = 0.75.$

3. $MTR = \dfrac{\Delta T}{\Delta Y} = 0.20.$

4. I_n^d is fixed at $100 billion per year.

5. G is fixed at $200 billion per year.

what we should have expected, since that equality is nothing other than an alternative way of expressing the fact that aggregate demand is equal to aggregate supply.

These results are shown graphically in Figure 8.1. In that diagram, we measure consumption expenditures (C), net investment (I_n), and government expenditures (G) on the vertical axis, and NNP (Y) on the horizontal axis. The curve labeled $C + I_n^d + G$ is the aggregate demand curve obtained by adding together consumption, desired net investment, and government expenditures. Note that the $C + I_n^d + G$ curve is parallel to the C curve. This is because I_n^d and G are independent of the level of income. Finally, recalling the meaning of the 45° line and noting that NNP is identical to the sum of *actual* expenditures, *actual* aggregate spending is equal to NNP all along the 45° line.

Graphically, then, the equilibrium level of NNP can be determined at the point of intersection of the aggregate demand schedule and the 45° line. At that point, aggregate demand is equal to aggregate supply and there will be no further tendency to change.

On the basis of our analysis in Chapter 7, most of this is pretty familiar territory. All we have done is add another component to aggregate demand. By equating aggregate demand to aggregate supply we are able to discover the equilibrium level of national income. There is, however, one rather critical difference between our graphical representation of equilibrium in this chapter and that of our previous chapter. Specifically, the curve labeled C in Figure 8.1 is *not* our familiar consumption function; it is *related to* the consumption function, but it is not the consumption function. The reason for this is clear. The consumption function expresses a relationship between consumption expenditures and *disposable income*. However, it is national income, *not* disposable income, that is measured along the horizontal axis. Therefore, the curve labeled C in Figure 8.1 expresses a relation between consumption expenditures and national income.

However, because disposable income is defined here as national income minus personal income taxes, the consumption function and the C curve in Figure 8.1 are related to one another. Specifically, since 20 cents of each additional dollar of national income goes to the government in the form of taxes, 80 percent (or 1 minus 20 percent) of each additional dollar of national income ends up in the hands of consumers as disposable income. And, assuming that MPC equals 0.75, consumers will increase their spending by 75 percent of that increase in their disposable

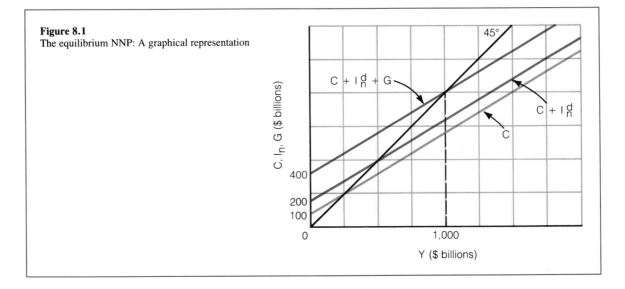

Figure 8.1
The equilibrium NNP: A graphical representation

income. Thus, for each additional dollar of national income earned, consumers will increase their spending by 60 cents (i.e., 0.75 × 0.80 = 0.60). The C curve reflects this pass-through from national income to disposable income to consumption expenditures. Accordingly, the C curve has a slope equal to 0.60, summarizing the responsiveness of consumer spending to changes in national income after taking account of the change in personal income taxes.

We can express these important relationships more generally. Letting the marginal tax rate be represented by t, it is clear that for any change in national income, ΔY, tax receipts rise by $t \times \Delta Y$ and disposable income rises by $(\Delta Y - t \times \Delta Y)$. And consumption rises by the MPC times the change in disposable income; that is, $\Delta C = MPC \times (\Delta Y - t \times \Delta Y)$, or

$$\Delta C = MPC \times (1 - t) \times \Delta Y.$$

Therefore, the change in consumption brought about by a change in national income is given by

$$\frac{\Delta C}{\Delta Y} = MPC \times (1 - t).$$

Thus, consumer spending will rise by a larger amount per dollar change in national income the *greater* the MPC and the *lower* the marginal tax rate. The reasoning behind this result is straightforward. The lower the marginal tax rate, the greater will be the change in disposable income per dollar change in national income; and the higher the MPC, the higher will be the change in consumption for any given change in disposable income.

Note one final result. Given the meaning of the C curve in Figure 8.1, it can be shown that the distance between the C curve and the 45° line measures not savings alone but savings (or dissavings) plus taxes. That is, since Y = disposable income + taxes, and since disposable income = C + S, then Y = C + S + T; the difference between Y and C is S + T. Therefore, since NNP is measured along the 45° line, the distance be-

tween that line and the C curve equals saving (or dissavings) plus taxes.

Government spending and the multiplier

Suppose government expenditures suddenly rise from $200 billion per year to $280 billion. As a result, the equilibrium level of income will rise by $200 billion, from $1,000 billion to $1,200 billion. This can be seen by once again examining the data presented in Table 8.2 and by replacing the value in column (6) by the constant value $280 billion, and by adding $80 billion to each value in column (7). With government spending fixed at its new level of $280 billion, the new equilibrium level of NNP can be found by identifying the level of consumption in column (4) that, when added to desired net investment of $100 billion and government expenditures of $280 billion, is equal to the NNP of column (1). This equality takes place at an NNP of $1,200 billion.

Thus, an $80 billion increase in government spending leads ultimately to a $200 billion increase in the level of national income; income rises by a multiple of two-and-one-half times the change in government spending. On the basis of the above numerical example, therefore, the multiplier has a value of 2.5.

Let us examine carefully the process that led to this particular result. The $80 billion increase in government spending leads initially to an $80 billion increase in output and income as businesspeople step up production in response to the higher level of government spending. Of that increase in national income, 20 percent goes back to the government in the form of taxes (0.20 × $80 billion = $16 billion), implying that disposable income rises by $64 billion. Of that, consumers will increase their expenditures $48 billion (0.75 × $64 billion). The $48 billion increase in C will lead to a further $48 billion increase in production and income. Of that increase, 20 percent will go to the government in taxes (0.20 × $48 billion = $9.6 billion) and the remainder adds to disposable income ($48 billion − $9.6 = $38.4 billion). Of that increase in disposable income, 75 percent gets spent on additional consumption, leading to a further increase in production and income, and yet another increase in disposable income and consumption. And on and on and on.

A pattern very similar to the one noted in Chapter 7 is emerging. *What is important is that each dollar change in national income will lead to a 60 cent change in consumption on each round of spending.* That is, a dollar increase in Y leads to an 80 cent increase in disposable income; of that, 75 percent gets spent on additional consumption, meaning that consumption rises by 60 percent of the change in Y (i.e., $0.75 \times 0.80 = 0.60$). Accordingly, an $80 billion increase in G leads, in round one, to an $80 billion increase in national income. That $80 billion increase in Y leads to a $48 billion increase in consumption and income in round two ($0.60 \times \$80$ billion = $48 billion). In round three, consumption and income rise by another $28.8 billion ($0.60 \times \$48$ billion = $0.60^2 \times \$80$ billion = $28.8 billion); in round four, consumption and income go up yet another $17.28 billion ($0.60^3 \times \$80$ billion = $17.28 billion); and so forth. The ultimate change in income is, therefore

$$\overset{(1)}{\Delta Y = \$80 \text{ billion}} + \overset{(2)}{0.60 \times \$80 \text{ billion}}$$
$$\overset{(3)}{+ 0.60^2 \times \$80 \text{ billion}} + \overset{(4)}{0.60^3 \times 80 \text{ billion}} + \cdots$$

or,

$$\Delta Y = \$80 \text{ billion} (1 + 0.60 + 0.60^2 + 0.60^3 + \cdots).$$

The expression inside the parentheses is a sum of an infinite series that has the solution value, $1/(1 - 0.60)$. Accordingly,

$$\Delta Y = \$80 \text{ billion} \times \frac{1}{1 - 0.60}$$
$$= \$80 \text{ billion} \times 2.5 = \$200 \text{ billion},$$

which is exactly what we expected. Here, the multiplier, $1/(1 - 0.60)$, has a numerical value of 2.5. And this tells us the multiple by which national income changes per dollar change in government spending.

Figure 8.2 displays these results graphically. There, the aggregate demand schedule is shifted upwards by $80 billion from $C + I_n^d + G$ to $C + I_n^d + G'$, raising the equilibrium level of national income from $1,000 billion to $1,200 billion. Moreover, at the new equilibrium level of national income, savings plus taxes is equal to planned investment plus government spending. By now you should be able to demonstrate this result. You should also be able to show that the equilibrium level of national income would rise by $200 billion if the consumption function had shifted upward by $80 billion. Can you explain why this is the case?

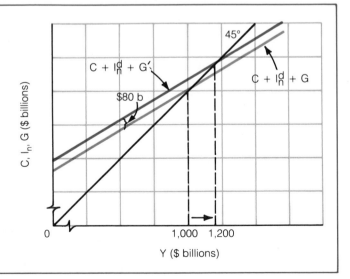

Figure 8.2
The government expenditure multiplier illustrated

The multiplier (more generally)

All of the above results can be restated more generally. It is clear on the basis of our numerical example that the value of the multiplier can be readily determined once we know the percentage change in spending per dollar change in national income.

Here, the percentage change in spending per dollar change in national income had a numerical value equal to 0.6; that is, out of every dollar increase in national income, 60 percent gets respent. However, this is nothing more than the change in consumption brought about by a change in national income after taking account of the taxes paid to government. Moreover, we have already demonstrated that this can be represented as

$$\frac{\Delta C}{\Delta Y} = MPC \times (1 - t).$$

Therefore, the multiplier, which is called the **expenditure multiplier** for reasons that will soon become obvious, can be written generally as

$$\text{Expenditure multiplier} = \frac{1}{1 - [MPC \times (1 - t)]}.$$

Using the values assumed above for MPC and t, we get a multiplier value of 2.5 (i.e.,

$$\frac{1}{1 - (0.75 \times 0.80)} = \frac{1}{1 - 0.6} = 2.5).$$

Consider an entirely different example. Suppose that aggregate demand equals aggregate supply at an income level of $800 billion. Suppose further that the MPC equals 0.50 and that the marginal tax rate, t, is also equal to 0.50. The expenditure multiplier, therefore, has a value of approximately 1.33; thus, a $100 billion increase in aggregate demand brought about by an increase in G or I_n^d (or a shift of the C curve for that matter) will cause the equilibrium level of national income to rise by about $133 billion.

It is clear from these examples that the value of the expenditure multiplier depends on both the marginal tax rate, t, and the marginal propensity to consume out of disposable income, MPC.

If the marginal tax rate is increased, the expenditure multiplier will fall in value. Why? Because out of every increase in national income, less will be added to disposable income and less, therefore, will be spent on each round. Similarly, if the marginal propensity to consume declines, the expenditure multiplier will fall since less gets respent on each round of spending.

Taxes and the multiplier

It is now clear that changes in the level of government spending can effect changes in the level of income and employment. Moreover, the magnitude of the change in income occasioned by a change in government spending can be inferred on the basis of the multiplier. However, the fiscal authorities also have at their disposal another stabilization tool—taxes. That is, government, by changing taxes, can bring about changes in the level of economic activity. Let us examine this process closely.

If government decides to *reduce* taxes, an increase in people's disposable income will immediately result. Out of that increase in disposable income, people will increase their spending, via the consumption function, setting off a series of spending rounds, which we have come to know as the multiplier process.

But, although the multiplier process associated with a change in taxes is similar to that associated with a change in government spending (or desired investment, or consumption), a dollar change in taxes does *not* in general have the same impact on the level of income and employment as does a dollar change in government spending. And the reason?

A dollar increase in government spending constitutes at the outset a dollar increase in aggregate demand. A dollar reduction in taxes, on the other hand, leads *first* to an increase in disposable income, part of which will be saved; the first-round increase in aggregate demand will be the induced increase in consumption brought about by the change in disposable income, which is equal to the MPC times the change in disposable income.

Therefore, if the MPC equals 0.75, a dollar reduction in taxes will lead to a first-round increase in aggregate demand of only 75 cents, unlike the dollar increase in aggregate demand associated with a dollar increase in government spending.

Income taxes versus income tax rates. Before proceeding with a detailed analysis of the multiplier effects of changes in tax policy, it is worthwhile to distinguish between *income taxes* and *income tax rates.* Income taxes refer to the tax revenues collected by government through the taxation of people's incomes. Income tax rates refer to the taxes levied *per dollar* of income.

Average tax rates must be distinguished from *marginal* tax rates. The average income tax rate refers to the proportion of income paid in taxes; it is defined by the ratio of taxes (T) to income (Y). The marginal income tax rate, on the other hand, measures the *change* in taxes brought about by a *change* in income; it is defined by the ratio of the change in taxes (ΔT) to the change in income (ΔY).

There is no reason why the average and marginal income tax rates should equal one another. On the contrary, they will in general not be equal. For example, if your income is $40,000 a year and you pay $10,000 in taxes, your average tax rate is 25 percent ($10,000 \div $40,000 = 0.25). But, with an income of $40,000, you could be in a 44 percent marginal tax bracket, meaning that for each extra dollar of income your tax liability goes up by 44 cents.

In our illustrations below we will assume that changes in tax policy take the form of changes in average tax rates, *not* marginal tax rates. If an income tax reduction is being illustrated, we will assume that people pay a smaller portion of their income to government in the form of taxes but that, for each extra dollar of income, they have the same marginal tax rate as before. A simple numerical example will clarify this point. Suppose the tax system can be described by the following simple equation:

$$T = \$120 \text{ billion} + 0.20\,Y.$$

This tells us that taxes (T) equal $120 billion plus 20 percent of income (Y); 0.20 is the marginal tax rate. If Y equals $1,000 billion, total taxes amount to $320 billion ($120 billion + (0.20 × $1,000 billion) = $320 billion); the average tax rate is equal to 32 percent (i.e., 320/1,000). Let government now reduce taxes by $60 billion. The new tax equation could be written as follows:

$$T = \$60 \text{ billion} + 0.20Y.$$

Here the marginal tax rate is the same as before, 0.20. The average tax rate, however, has been reduced. If total income equaled $1,000 billion, taxes would amount to $260 billion ($60 billion + (0.20 × $1,000 billion) = $260 billion), implying an average tax rate of only 26 percent (i.e., 260/1,000).

(As far as the analysis of fiscal policy in this chapter is concerned, it does not matter whether we discuss tax policy changes in terms of changing average tax rates or changing marginal tax rates. We choose to illustrate changes in taxes with changes in average tax rates because it is easier. We leave until Chapter 14 a detailed analysis of changing marginal tax rates; changing marginal tax rates are discussed there in terms of *supply side economics.*)

Returning to the problem at hand: Taxes and the multiplier process. To illustrate the macroeconomic effects of a change in tax policy, consider a tax reduction of $80 billion; assume throughout that MPC = 0.75 and t = 0.20. As a consequence of the $80 billion tax cut, disposable income will rise by $80 billion, inducing an increase in consumption expenditures of $60 billion (i.e., 0.75 × $80 billion). This in turn will lead to an initial $60 billion increase in income and output. *At the end of the first round of spending, the $80 billion reduction in taxes has induced a $60 billion increase in income.* Twenty percent of that increase ($12 billion) will go to the government in the form of taxes; the remainder ($48 billion) will add to disposable income, inducing a further $36 billion (0.75 × $48 billion) increase in consumption, income, and output. As before, income will rise in each round of spending by 60 percent of the increase in the previous round.

Therefore, the ultimate change in income is given by

$\Delta Y = \$60$ billion
$$\times (1 + 0.60 + 0.60^2 + 0.60^3 + \cdots),$$

which reduces to

$$\Delta Y = \$60 \text{ billion} \times \frac{1}{1 - 0.60}$$
$$= \$60 \text{ billion} \times 2.5 = \$150 \text{ billion.}$$

That is, an $80 billion reduction in taxes leads ultimately to a $150 billion increase in national income.

This particular result is displayed graphically in Figure 8.3. *Note there that the $80 billion reduction in taxes causes the C curve to shift upwards by $60 billion (0.75 × $80 billion), which in turn raises the aggregate demand schedule by $60 billion; the equilibrium level of income rises from $1,000 billion to $1,150 billion.*

Since the $60 billion increase in consumption is equal to the MPC times the $80 billion reduction in taxes, we can express the above results more generally as

$$\Delta Y = -\Delta T \times MPC \times \frac{1}{1 - [MPC \times (1 - t)]}$$

or

$$\Delta Y = -\Delta T \times \left[\frac{MPC}{1 - [MPC \times (1 - t)]} \right].$$

The expression given inside the large brackets is called the **tax multiplier.** As is apparent, *the tax multiplier is equal to the MPC times the expenditure multiplier.* Given an MPC equal to 0.75, the tax multiplier is 75 percent of the expenditure multiplier; *as long as the MPC is less than one, the tax multiplier will be smaller than the expenditure multiplier.* With MPC = 0.75 and t = 0.20, the expenditure multiplier will equal 2.5 and the tax multiplier will equal 1.875 (0.75 × 2.5).

The balanced budget multiplier

Since a change in government spending will exert a larger impact on the level of national income than an equivalent change in taxes, economists have been led to inquire into the impact on national income of a *balanced change* in government expenditures and taxes. To illustrate, suppose that government spending is increased by $80 billion, financed by an $80 billion *increase* in taxes. What will happen to the level of national income? Will it remain unaltered or will it go up? *It will go up.* The reason for this is clear. With an expenditure multiplier of 2.5, the $80 billion increase in government spending will tend to cause a $200 billion increase in national income (i.e., 2.5 × $80 billion). This increase in national income will not be completely offset by

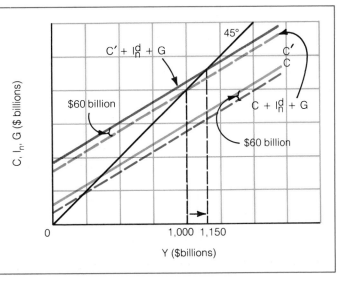

Figure 8.3
The tax multiplier illustrated

A tax reduction of $80 billion increases disposable income by $80 billion and increases consumption by $60 billion (.75 x $80 billion).

the increase in taxes. Indeed, with a tax multiplier of 1.875, the offsetting reduction in national income brought about by the $80 billion *increase* in taxes will be only $150 billion (−$80 billion × 1.875 = −$150 billion). Therefore, national income will rise on balance by $50 billion ($200 billion − $150 billion).

Let us examine this result more closely. Since the ultimate change in income is equal to the change in government spending times the expenditure multiplier *minus* the change in taxes times the tax multiplier, it is clear that

$$\Delta Y = (\$80 \text{ billion} \times 2.5) - (\$80 \text{ billion} \times 1.875)$$

or

$$\Delta Y = \$80 \text{ billion} \times (2.5 - 1.875)$$
$$= \$80 \text{ billion} \times 0.625 = \$50 \text{ billion}.$$

In other words, *the ultimate change in national income associated with a balanced change in government spending and taxes can be found by multiplying that balanced change times the difference between the expenditure multiplier and the tax multiplier.* The difference between these two multipliers is referred to as the **balanced budget multiplier;** the balanced budget multiplier in the above example has a numerical value of 0.625.

Consider another example. Suppose the expenditure multiplier for some hypothetical economy is 3.0, while the tax multiplier is 2.4. The balanced budget multiplier is therefore 0.6. Under these circumstances, a balanced *decrease* in government spending and taxes of $100 billion will lead ultimately to a $60 billion *decrease* in the level of national income (0.6 × $100 billion = $60 billion).

FISCAL POLICY AND THE INFLATIONARY AND DEFLATIONARY GAPS

We are now in a position to demonstrate how *fiscal policy* may be used for the purpose of eliminating the *inflationary* or *deflationary gap*—that is, how fiscal policy may be used for the purpose

of achieving our potential or full employment level of income.

Consider again the numerical example presented in Table 8.2. Given the consumption function, a desired net investment of $100 billion, and government spending of $200 billion, the equilibrium level of national income will be $1,000 billion. Suppose that the potential or full employment level of national income is $1,200 billion. Since the equilibrium level of national income lies below the full employment level a *deflationary gap* exists. But how big is the deflationary gap? We can figure this out as follows. The deflationary gap measures the change in aggregate demand required to bring about the full employment level of national income. Since the gap between our actual and potential national income amounts to $200 billion, and since the expenditure multiplier implied by our data is 2.5, an $80 billion increase in aggregate demand is required in order to attain full employment. If aggregate demand rises by $80 billion, national income will rise via the multiplier by $200 billion. The deflationary gap, therefore, is $80 billion. This is illustrated in Figure 8.4.

The question we now need to answer is this: How much of a change in government spending or taxes is required to achieve the full employment level of national income? Armed with information about the value of the expenditure and tax multipliers, the answer to this question is relatively straightforward. Given an expenditure multiplier of 2.5, an increase in government spending of $80 billion will generate the requisite $200 billion increase in national income (i.e., 2.5 × $80 billion = $200 billion). In general, the required change in government spending can be discovered as follows:

Required change in G

$$= \frac{\text{Gap between full employment NNP and actual NNP}}{\text{Expenditure multiplier}}.$$

Similarly, with a tax multiplier of 1.875, a $106.67 billion *reduction* in taxes is required in order to achieve the desired $200 billion increase

Figure 8.4
Using fiscal policy to eliminate the deflationary gap

The initial equilibrium level of national income is $1,000 billion; the full employment level of output is $1,200 billion. Either an increase in G of $80 billion or a reduction in the level of taxes of approximately $106.67 billion is required to eliminate the $80 billion deflationary gap, assuming MPC = .75 and t = .20.

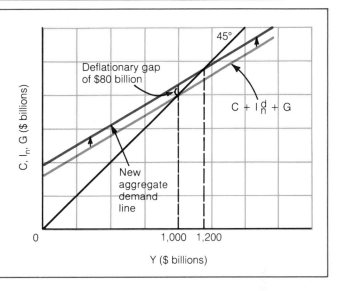

in national income (i.e., $1.875 \times \$106.67$ billion = \$200 billion). In general, the required change in taxes can be found by:

Required change in taxes

$$= \frac{\text{Gap between full employment NNP and actual NNP}}{\text{Tax multiplier}}.$$

Why is it necessary to reduce taxes by more than the required increase in government spending? Because a dollar reduction in taxes will, assuming MPC = 0.75, induce a first-round increase in aggregate demand of only 75 cents, whereas a dollar increase in G induces a first-round increase in aggregate demand of $1; in order to generate a first-round increase in aggregate demand of $80 billion, taxes must be reduced by $106.67 billion (i.e., the change in consumption on the first round will be $0.75 \times \$106.67$ billion = \$80 billion).

Finally, how much of a *balanced* increase in government spending and taxes would be required to bring about full employment? Given a balanced budget multiplier of 0.625, government spending and taxes would have to rise by $320 billion ($200 billion $\div$ 0.625)!

Fiscal policy can also be used to eliminate the *inflationary gap*. Suppose the equilibrium

level of income happened to be $1,500 billion—not that $1,500 billion is attainable but, given aggregate demand, $1,500 billion is the only candidate for equilibrium. Since the equilibrium level of national income exceeds our potential by $300 billion, an inflationary gap of $120 billion exists ($300 billion divided by 2.5, the expenditure multiplier). Thus, a $120 billion reduction in government spending or a $160 billion *increase* in taxes would be required to achieve a $1,200 billion level of national income. Can you figure out what a balanced reduction in government spending and taxes would have to be?[2]

It should be obvious from the above discussion that the fiscal authorities require reliable information on the numerical values of various multipliers for the implementation of fiscal policy. In an effort to obtain such information, government makes use of large-scale econometric models that specify literally hundreds of relations—for example, different consumption functions are specified for different types of consumer goods—in order to come as close as possible to the real values of the multipliers characterizing the actual economy. However, although these models are much more complex than the model developed here, the principle of the multiplier is the same. For

---

[2] $480 billion! ($300 billion $\div$ 0.625).

the U.S. economy, estimates for the expenditure multiplier range from 2.0 to 2.5.

AUTOMATIC STABILIZERS

If we compare the model developed in this chapter with the one presented in Chapter 7, the one developed here is more *stable.* We mean by this that changes in the level of national income brought about by changes in aggregate demand are much less pronounced in an economy characterized by a tax system of the sort we have assumed here. This difference in the degree of stability of the two models is reflected in the different values of the respective expenditure multipliers. This is easily illustrated.

Imagine two different economies, one *private* and the other *mixed* (private-government). Assume that desired investment in both is fixed at some constant value and that government spending in the mixed economy is likewise fixed. Assume further that the MPC in both is equal to 0.75 and that the marginal tax rate in the mixed economy is equal to 0.20. On the basis of these assumptions, it is clear that the expenditure multiplier is much larger in the private economy than in the mixed. Whereas the expenditure multiplier in the mixed economy has a value of 2.5 (i.e., $\frac{1}{1 - [0.75 \times (1 - 0.20)]} = 2.5$), the expenditure multiplier in the private economy is 4 (i.e., $\frac{1}{1 - 0.75} = 4.0$). Thus, if desired investment were to change by $100 billion, national income in the private economy would change by $400 billion in contrast to the much smaller change of $250 billion in the mixed economy. And if desired investment is a fairly unstable component of aggregate demand in both economies, the private economy would experience much sharper swings in its level of economic activity—that is, it would be less stable.

It is not difficult to discover the source of the greater stability in the mixed economy. It can be found by examining the way the tax system operates. Thus, when aggregate demand declines as a result of, say, a decline in desired investment, this will lead to a reduction in na-

tional income and disposable income. But the reduction in disposable income will be *smaller* than the reduction in national income for the simple reason that tax receipts also decline (by an amount equal to the marginal tax rate times the change in national income). As a result, consumption expenditures will not decline by as much as otherwise; the *cumulative* decrease in national income will therefore be smaller. Similarly, when aggregate demand increases, disposable income will rise by less than national income (because tax payments rise), moderating the induced increase in consumption expenditures and reducing, therefore, the *cumulative* increase in national income.

Accordingly, *the rise and fall of tax revenues as the level of economic activity increases and decreases act as an **automatic stabilizer**, moderating the swings in national income automatically.*

The value of the multiplier measures the extent of this automatic or built-in stability: *The smaller the value of the multiplier, the greater the amount of built-in stability.* Since the value of the multiplier will be lower the higher is the marginal tax rate, greater built-in stability is achieved with higher marginal tax rates.

While the functioning of our tax system acts as an automatic stabilizer, the U.S. economic system is characterized by still other automatic stabilizers. One of the most important of these is **unemployment compensation.** As the level of economic activity declines and unemployment rises, many workers become eligible to receive unemployment compensation, which is another factor limiting the decline in disposable income. Similarly, virtually all welfare payments tend to rise as national income declines, further limiting the decline in disposable income. Finally, if a slump in economic activity extends to agriculture, price or income support programs are often triggered to maintain farm incomes at a higher level than otherwise.

Fiscal drag

Although the automatic stabilizers operate to limit the decline in economic activity—generally viewed as a plus—they also operate to limit the increase, making it more difficult for an economy to extricate itself from a recession. Since this difficulty is often viewed with dismay by many congressional leaders and others as well, they tend to consider built-in stability which inhibits recovery as undesirable. As a reflection of that thinking, they term such built-in stability during an upswing as **fiscal drag.**

Automatic stabilizers and passive changes in the budget

One rather important and often misunderstood feature of our tax system is that the automatic stabilizers operate to produce automatic and passive changes in the value of our government's budget. That is, *even if government does not actively pursue policies to change either the level of government spending or the level of taxes, the value of the budget will tend to change automatically and passively with changes in the level of national income.* As the level of national income rises, the automatic stabilizers tend to increase surpluses (or reduce deficits); declines in the level of economic activity tend to increase deficits (or reduce surpluses). This is illustrated in Table 8.3, using the data presented earlier in Table 8.2.

If we assume that government expenditures

Table 8.3
Automatic stabilizers and passive changes in the budget ($ billions)

(1) National income	(2) Tax receipts	(3) Government expenditures	(4) Budget (T − G)
$ 300	100	200	−100
400	120	200	− 80
500	140	200	− 60
600	160	200	− 40
700	180	200	− 20
800	200	200	0
900	220	200	20
1,000	240	200	40
1,100	260	200	60
1,200	280	200	80
1,300	300	200	100
1,400	320	200	120
1,500	340	200	140

are fixed at $200 billion per year and that tax *laws* are unaltered, then as income changes from $300 billion per year to $1,500 billion, the budget changes passively from a $100 billion deficit to a $140 billion surplus. The reason for this change in the value of the budget is clear. With government expenditures fixed, tax receipts rise relative to government expenditures as national income rises. This relationship between passive changes in the budget and changes in national income is also portrayed graphically in Figure 8.5, using the data from Table 8.3.

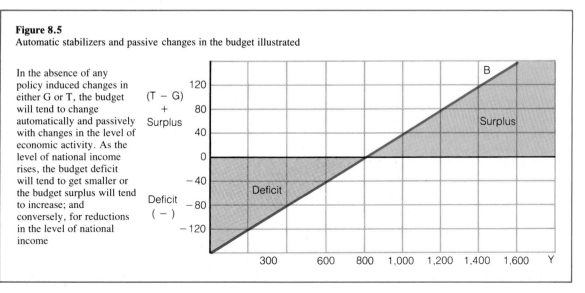

Figure 8.5
Automatic stabilizers and passive changes in the budget illustrated

In the absence of any policy induced changes in either G or T, the budget will tend to change automatically and passively with changes in the level of economic activity. As the level of national income rises, the budget deficit will tend to get smaller or the budget surplus will tend to increase; and conversely, for reductions in the level of national income

Table 8.4
Policy-induced changes in the budget
($ billions)

(1) National income	(2) Tax receipts	(3) Initial level of government spending	(4) Initial budget	(5) New level of government spending	(6) New budget
$ 300	100	200	−100	280	−180
400	120	200	− 80	280	−160
500	140	200	− 60	280	−140
600	160	200	− 40	280	−120
700	180	200	− 20	280	−100
800	200	200	0	280	− 80
900	220	200	20	280	− 60
1,000	240	200	40	280	− 40
1,100	260	200	60	280	− 20
1,200	280	200	80	280	0
1,300	300	200	100	280	20
1,400	320	200	120	280	40
1,500	340	200	140	280	60

Policy-induced changes in the budget

Not all changes in the budget are passive. Indeed, if government actively seeks to change the level of economic activity by changing its expenditures or the level of its taxes, such changes will have rather obvious impacts on the value of the budget. These we refer to as **policy-induced budget changes.**

To illustrate, consider the example presented in Table 8.4. Suppose the equilibrium level of income is initially $1,000 billion. Given an initial level of government spending of $200 billion and tax receipts of $240 billion, there is an initial budget surplus of $40 billion. Suppose that government, in an effort to achieve full employment, increases its expenditures by $80 billion, from $200 billion to $280 billion. The immediate impact of this increase in government spending is to cause the budget to shift from a surplus to a deficit. At the *initial* level of national income—at the $1,000 billion level—the budget changes by $80 billion from a $40 billion surplus to a $40 billion deficit. And note that the new budget at each and every level of income is $80 billion below its initial value. The policy-induced change in the budget brought about by the $80 billion increase in government spending can be represented graphically as a downward displacement of the budget line (labeled B) in Figure 8.5 by

$80 billion. This is shown in Figure 8.6. Exactly the same result would have occurred if government had, instead, *reduced* the level of taxes by $80 billion at the initial level of income. This follows directly from the definition of the budget—the difference between government spending and tax receipts. Moreover, if government were to pursue a policy of either reducing its expenditures or raising the level of its taxes, on the other hand, such changes would tend to cause the budget line to shift upwards.

We refer to an increase in the level of government spending and/or a reduction in the level of taxes as an **expansionary fiscal policy.** By contrast, an increase in taxes and/or a reduction in government expenditures is referred to as a **contractionary fiscal policy.** It is clear, then, that an expansionary fiscal policy can be represented by a downward displacement of the budget line, whereas a contractionary fiscal policy will cause the budget line to be displaced upwards. This is summarized in Figure 8.7.

Policy-induced and passive changes in the budget combined

Although a change in fiscal policy will bring about a policy-induced change in the budget that is *initially* equal to the change in government spending or taxes, such a policy-induced budget

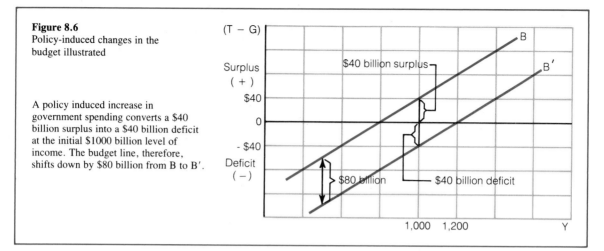

Figure 8.6
Policy-induced changes in the
budget illustrated

A policy induced increase in
government spending converts a $40
billion surplus into a $40 billion deficit
at the initial $1000 billion level of
income. The budget line, therefore,
shifts down by $80 billion from B to B'.

change does not reflect the *ultimate* change in the budget. Indeed, since a change in fiscal policy causes the level of national income to change, this will cause further changes in tax receipts and further changes, therefore, in the budget. *Any change in fiscal policy will bring about policy-induced changes in the budget and subsequent passive changes in the budget as the level of national income changes.* This is best illustrated by example.

Suppose equilibrium occurs at a level of national income of $1,000 billion. Assume, as before, an initial budget surplus of $40 billion. Now, suppose that government spending increases by $80 billion. This will cause a policy-induced reduction in the budget from a surplus of $40 billion to a deficit of $40 billion. But the $80 billion

increase in government spending will, via the multiplier, cause an increase in the equilibrium level of national income. If MPC = 0.75 and t = 0.20 (implying a multiplier of 2.5), the equilibrium level of national income will rise by $200 billion, from $1,000 billion to $1,200 billion. And this $200 billion increase in national income will cause tax receipts to rise passively by $40 billion (0.20 × $200 billion).

At the new equilibrium level of income, the budget is balanced. The ultimate change in the budget from a $40 billion surplus to a balanced budget is the result of both a policy-induced change and a passive change in the budget. Figure 8.8 illustrates this graphically.

In Figure 8.8, the $80 billion increase in government spending causes the aggregate demand

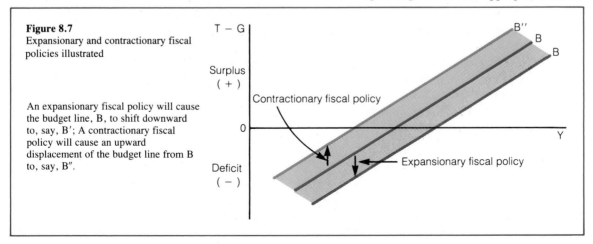

Figure 8.7
Expansionary and contractionary fiscal
policies illustrated

An expansionary fiscal policy will cause
the budget line, B, to shift downward
to, say, B'; A contractionary fiscal
policy will cause an upward
displacement of the budget line from B
to, say, B".

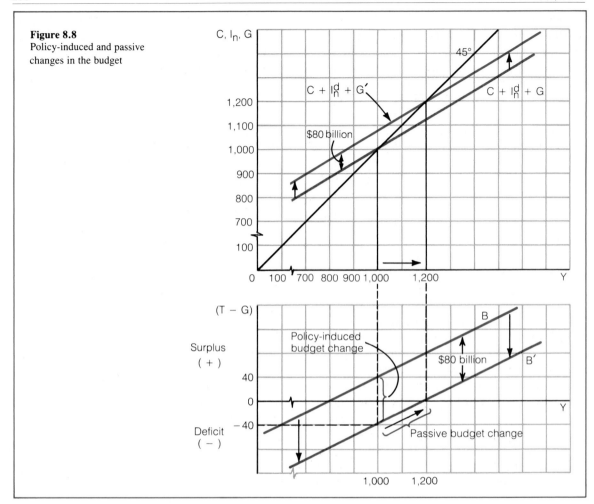

Figure 8.8
Policy-induced and passive changes in the budget

schedule in the upper diagram to shift upwards by $80 billion from $(C + I_n^d + G)$ to $(C + I_n^d + G')$. In like manner, the budget line in the lower diagram is shifted downward by $80 billion from B to B'. The policy-induced change in the budget is $80 billion. The $200 billion increase in the level of national income, however, causes the budget to change passively from a deficit of $40 billion to a balanced budget.

The full employment (or high employment) budget

On the basis of the above considerations, it is obvious that we cannot infer from actual changes in the budget whether fiscal policy has become more or less expansionary. This is because the budget changes in response to both changes in economic conditions (passively) *and* changes in policy (policy-induced). Thus, a sizable deficit might arise if the economy were to become severely depressed, or it might arise because the government actively increased its expenditures and/or reduced its taxes. It is only the latter change in the budget that reflects a change in fiscal policy; the former change is passive.

In order to keep separate and identify those changes in the budget that are policy-induced from those that are brought about by changes in the level of economic activity, the Council of Economic Advisers under President Kennedy developed a widely used concept called the **full employment** (or **high employment**) **budget.** The idea behind this concept is really quite simple. *The full employment budget is defined as the value of the budget if the economy were at full employment, assuming the existing level of government expenditures and the existing tax structure.* It could be either a surplus or a deficit, depending on the level of government spending and the existing tax structure. Assume, for purposes of illustration, that the full employment budget happens to be a full employment deficit. The budget line labeled B_1 in Figure 8.9 depicts this case.

If the actual level of income just happened to be the full employment level of income, Y_{FE}, the actual budget deficit would equal the full employment budget deficit. If the actual level of income was Y_1, on the other hand, the actual deficit would exceed the full employment deficit. The meaning that one would attach to the full employment deficit is this: *If the level of income were to rise from Y_1 to Y_{FE} without any policy-induced change in government spending or taxes (say, because desired investment increased), the actual budget deficit would decline passively until at full employment it equaled the full employment deficit.* The actual budget change was exclusively passive. And in the absence of any policy change, the full employment budget remained unaltered.

Consider now the impact of a change in fiscal

policy on the full employment budget. Suppose government pursues an expansionary policy designed to raise the level of income from Y_1 to Y_{FE}. This, as we have already shown, will cause the budget line to shift down by the amount of the policy-induced change in G or T. However, not only will the initial deficit at Y_1 rise by the amount of the change in G or T; so too will the full employment deficit. In other words, *the magnitude of the fiscal stimulus provided by the expansionary fiscal policy will be reflected in, and can be measured by, the rise in the full employment deficit.* The shift in the budget line from B_1 to B_2 and the resultant change in the full employment deficit are illustrated in Figure 8.9. Symmetrically, a contractionary fiscal policy would cause a reduction in the full employment deficit; the budget line would shift up rather than down.

Similarly, if the initial situation was one characterized by a full employment surplus, an expansionary fiscal policy would be reflected in a reduction in the full employment surplus. A contractionary fiscal policy, on the other hand, would result in an increase in the full employment surplus.

Summing up. We can sum up this analysis with the following conclusions:
1.   The existence of a deficit or a surplus by

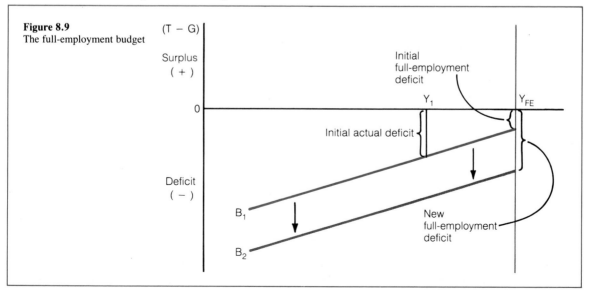

Figure 8.9
The full-employment budget

$(T - G)$

Surplus
$(+)$

Initial full-employment deficit

Y_1 Y_{FE}

0

Initial actual deficit

Deficit
$(-)$

B_1

B_2

New full-employment deficit

itself tells us nothing about the direction of fiscal policy—whether it is expansionary, contractionary, or neutral.

2. On the basis of a change in the *actual* deficit or surplus, it is not in general possible to infer the direction of change of fiscal policy. Just knowing that the budget has changed does not in itself, tell us whether it was a passive change or a policy-induced change.

3. The existence of a full employment surplus or a full employment deficit tells us nothing about the direction of fiscal policy. It merely tells us what the budget would be at full employment given the existing level of government expenditures and the existing tax structure.

4. A *changing* full employment budget, on the other hand, does provide us with information about the direction of change of fiscal policy; it also provides us with some measure of the degree of fiscal expansion and contraction.

   a. An expansionary fiscal policy will be reflected in a decline of the full employment budget—either a smaller full employment surplus or a larger full employment deficit. The magnitude of the decline in the full employment budget is itself a measure of the magnitude of the fiscal stimulus, a measure of the change in aggregate demand occasioned by the policy change.

   b. A contractionary fiscal policy will be reflected in a rise of the full employment budget—either a larger full employment surplus or a smaller full employment deficit. The magnitude of the rise in the full employment budget is itself a measure of the magnitude of the fiscal contraction.

Measuring fiscal stimulus and contraction: Problems with the full employment budget

Although in general it is possible to measure the degree of fiscal stimulus or contraction on the basis of changes in the full employment budget, it is not always an unambiguous measure and it needs to be used with caution. In this respect, there are at least two fundamental problems with the measure.

The first problem relates to our earlier discussion of the balanced budget multiplier. As is well known, a balanced increase in government spending and taxes will cause an increase in the equilibrium level of national income. Such a balanced increase is, therefore, an expansionary policy. However, the balanced increase will leave unaltered the full employment budget; the downward shift of the budget line due to the increase in G would be offset by the upwards shift of the budget line due to the increase in T. We would err, however, if we were to conclude that fiscal policy had not changed on the basis of this zero change in the full employment budget. Put differently, although a dollar change in government spending exerts a larger impact on national income than a dollar change in taxes, a dollar change in either will be reflected in the *same* change in the full employment budget. But obviously, a change in the full employment budget brought about by a change in G has a larger impact on national income than that for a change in T. Two conclusions follow from this. First, an *unchanged* full employment budget does not necessarily imply the absence of fiscal policy change. Second, a change in the full employment budget of a certain amount will mean a different degree of fiscal restraint or ease depending on whether taxes have changed or government expenditures have changed.

A second problem arises when the fiscal stimulus or contraction takes the form of policy-induced changes in taxes. It is frequently the case that tax changes alter more than just the level of taxes. They also change the marginal tax rate. And changes in the marginal tax rate change the slope of the budget line. In particular, a lowering of the marginal tax rate will reduce the slope of the budget line; and conversely, an increase in the marginal tax rate increases the slope of the budget line. Why is this so? Because a reduction in the marginal tax rate means that for every dollar increase in national income, tax receipts rise by less than otherwise. The result is that the budget rises by a smaller amount per dollar increase in Y; the converse holds true for an increase in the marginal tax rate.

Figure 8.10 illustrates the problems of inter-

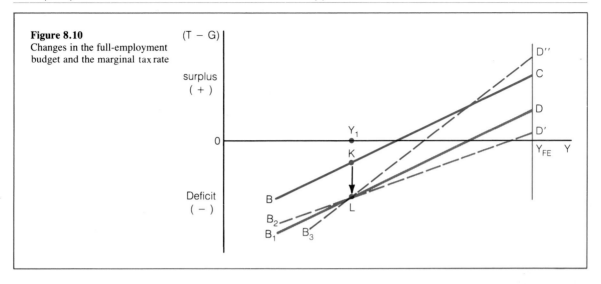

Figure 8.10
Changes in the full-employment budget and the marginal tax rate

pretation that can arise as a consequence of changes in the marginal tax rate. Assume, to begin with, that the equilibrium income level is Y_1. Assume further an initial budget deficit given by point K. Suppose government reduces the level of taxes by an amount KL *without* changing the marginal tax rate. The budget line will shift from B to B_1; the new budget line will be parallel to the original one (because the marginal tax rate did not change). The reduction in the full employment budget by CD is a fairly unambiguous measure of the fiscal stimulus provided by the reduction in taxes.

Now suppose that government reduces the level of taxes by an amount KL via, in part, a lowering of the marginal tax rate. The budget line will be lowered (as a result of the reduced level of taxes); and the new budget line will be less steep than the original one (as a result of the reduced marginal tax rate). The dashed line B_2 represents such a change in policy. (The dashed line passes through point L because the reduction in taxes at the income level Y_1 is the same as the original tax reduction, KL.) Note what this difference implies: as Figure 8.10 makes clear, this policy change causes the full employment budget to decline by CD[1]—by more than CD. This is as it should be. A reduction in the marginal tax rate raises the value of the multiplier, meaning that a given reduction in the level

of taxes now exerts a more expansionary influence on national income.

Symmetrically, it would be reasonable to expect that a tax reduction accompanied by an *increase* in the marginal tax rate would cause the full employment budget to decline by less than CD. But if, for example, B_4 in Figure 8.10 happens to be the new budget line, the full employment budget will actually rise, implying a contractionary fiscal policy. That is, this illustration suggests that a tax cut will actually serve to reduce the equilibrium level of national income.

The moral. Changes in the full employment budget can frequently be used to indicate both the direction and magnitude of change in fiscal policy. But in some instances, the change in the full employment budget will provide us with incorrect answers with respect to the magnitude of the fiscal policy change. And in still other instances, it will provide us with incorrect answers, even with respect to the direction of change of fiscal policy. It is clear, then, that such changes need to be interpreted with caution.

DEFICITS, SURPLUSES, AND THE NATIONAL DEBT

Few economic issues create as much public outcry as deficit spending and a growing national debt. Indeed, to a great many people, the mere existence of a deficit provides convincing evidence that the government is fiscally irresponsible. How many times have you heard that charge leveled at our government?

There are others, on the other hand, including the vast majority of economists, who argue that the existence of deficits per se tells us nothing about how fiscally responsible or irresponsible the government is. To their way of thinking, government behaves in a fiscally responsible manner only if it actively pursues policies designed to achieve a full employment, noninflationary level of income and output. At times, the achievement of this objective will call for deficit spending; at other times, it will call for a surplus. The philosophy underlying this kind of thinking has been termed **functional finance,** and it is best illustrated by the following two cases.

Case I. If equilibrium occurs at a level of national income below the full employment level (i.e., a deflationary gap exists), government has an obligation to pursue an expansionary policy—increasing government expenditures and/or reducing taxes—for the purpose of bringing about full employment. If the budget is initially in surplus, government has a responsibility to cut that surplus by the amount necessary to accomplish its full employment goal. This may call for only a smaller surplus, or it may call for a deficit,[3] depending on the size of the initial surplus, the value of the multiplier and the magnitude of the deflationary gap. Or, if the budget were initially in deficit, the "correct" policy would call for an even larger deficit.

Case II. If an inflationary gap exists initially, government has an obligation to reduce its spending and/or raise its taxes. If the budget is initially in surplus, this will call for a larger surplus; if the budget is initially in deficit, the required contractionary policy will necessitate government pursuance of a smaller deficit, or perhaps even a surplus.

According to the functional finance philosophy, then, government should not be concerned with the issue of a balanced budget to the exclusion of its concern with the economy. Government has an overriding obligation to undertake policies to ensure a full employment noninflationary level of income and output. If the fulfillment of that obligation demands budget deficits, so be it. Balancing the budget is clearly of secondary importance.

One of the obvious implications of deficit spending, however, is that it raises the level of the national debt. When the government runs a deficit, it must borrow funds sufficient to cover the deficit; it does so by issuing government bonds, which raises the outstanding debt. Because so many people consider the national debt to be intolerably burdensome, Congress and the executive branch of government are under continuous pressure to balance the budget. In view of the functional finance philosophy, however, is it appropriate to insist that government balance the budget at each instance? What about requiring that government deficits now be offset by government surpluses later so that, *on average,* the budget is balanced? Even if this latter question were answered in the affirmative, there is little agreement on how this should be accomplished. A number of different balanced budget strategies have therefore emerged. We shall evaluate these strategies first, and then we shall examine the question of the burden of the national debt.

Alternative budget strategies[4]

Fundamentally, there are three philosophies or strategies for balancing the budget. They are (1) **the annually balanced budget, (2) the cyclically balanced budget,** and (3) **the balanced full**

---

[3] Of course, if government decides to increase aggregate demand by increasing both its spending and its taxes, it is possible that it could achieve its full employment objective with a somewhat *higher* surplus. This is a logical conclusion derived from the balanced budget multiplier concept. But while such an approach is perfectly consistent with the philosophy underlying functional finance, it is unlikely, in practice, that government would pursue such a policy. Why? Because of the small value of the balanced budget multiplier, the necessary changes in G and T might be inordinately large.

---

[4] In shorter courses this section can be ignored without loss of continuity.

employment budget. Let us analyze each in turn.

The annually balanced budget. According to this philosophy, government should pursue policies designed to balance the budget each year; any deficits occurring *during* the year must be offset by surpluses in the same year. This philosophy was very popular during the 1920s and 1930s. Now it has very few supporters within the economics profession. The reason for this change in attitude is simple. *If government were to attempt to balance the budget annually, fiscal policy could well exert a destabilizing influence on the general level of economic activity. Instead of fiscal policy being countercyclical, it could be procyclical.* This is easily demonstrated.

Suppose the budget is initially balanced. And suppose, for one reason or another, consumer spending or desired investment is reduced. As a result, the budget will move *passively* towards a deficit because of reduced tax receipts caused by the decline in national income. If the government were to attempt to balance the budget, it would have to *reduce* its expenditures and/or raise its taxes, which means it would have to pursue a *contractionary* policy. A contractionary policy would tend to magnify the reduction in national income; it would, that is, be procyclical, magnifying the decline in the level of economic activity.

Similarly, if national income rises, generating a surplus, fiscal policy would have to be expansionary. Can you explain why this is so? Balancing the budget annually would necessitate that fiscal policy be procyclical, exacerbating swings in the level of economic activity.

Cyclically balanced budget. In view of the obvious defect associated with the annually balanced budget philosophy, proponents of a balanced budget have suggested an alternative approach—balancing the budget over the business cycle. According to this view, government deficits that occur during downswings in the economy would be offset by surpluses on upswings.

There are at least three problems with this approach. First, upswings and downswings in the level of economic activity are not uniform in length. There is, therefore, no reason to believe that deficits on downswings will be exactly offset

by surpluses on upswings. Worse yet, if the downswing lasts longer than the upswing, the government might have to pursue a *contractionary* policy at some point *on the downswing* (reducing government spending or increasing taxes) *or a less expansionary policy on the upswing,* in order to ensure an overall balance over the cycle; the converse would be true for upswings longer than downswings. Thus, policy could at times be procyclical, at other times countercyclical, and at still other times neutral. The point is, under this philosophy, the obligation of government to pursue countercyclical policy in order to bring about a noninflationary full employment level of income and output is a matter of secondary importance; the prime objective is budgetary balance.

A second problem arises when we seek an answer to the question, At what level of income should the budget be in balance? At the full employment level of income or at some point below full employment? If it is at full employment, then the cyclically balanced budget philosophy has the same defect as the annually balanced budget. It implies that fiscal policy will have to be procyclical in nature in order to ensure a cyclically balanced budget. This is illustrated in Figure 8.11.

We have assumed in Figure 8.11 that budget balance occurs at full employment. Thus, if the business cycle swings from Y_{FE} to Y_1 and back to Y_{FE}, the budget, *in the absence of any change in fiscal policy,* will be in deficit over the entire cycle. As the level of income declines from Y_{FE} to Y_1, the budget will change passively from balance to deficit; and as income swings back to Y_{FE}, the budget deficit will decline until, at Y_{FE}, it is once again in balance. The budget will not, therefore, be in balance over the cycle; it will be in deficit. A procyclical policy would be called for to ensure surpluses on the upswing; but a procyclical policy would magnify the decline in national income and delay or completely forestall the recovery. Even if government were to pursue an expansionary policy on the downswing, thereby raising the deficit, it would have to pursue an *even stronger* contractionary policy on the upswing to ensure budget balance at Y_{FE}, assuming that there were, in fact, natural forces operat-

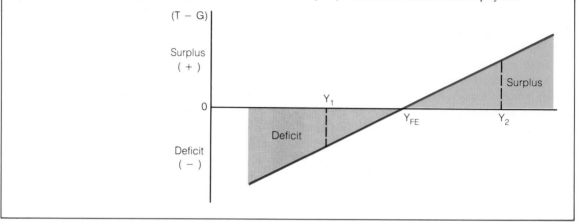

Figure 8.11
The cyclically balanced budget and the procyclical behavior of fiscal policy when balance obtains at full employment

ing with sufficient strength to overcome the contractionary fiscal policy, enabling us to reach full employment.

If, on the other hand, the swings in national income were between Y_1 and Y_2, where Y_2 exceeds the full employment level of income, cyclical budget balance might be feasible, with surpluses at levels of income above full employment offsetting deficits at income levels below full employment. However, our history has been one in which, for the most part, national income has fluctuated between Y_{FE} and points below full employment. All of this implies, therefore, that cyclical balance will be achieved only if balance obtains at some level of income *below* full employment, and perhaps considerably below to the extent that downswings are longer than upswings.

This brings us to the third problem. Assuming that we are able to identify the income level below full employment at which balance should occur (which implies a surplus at full employment), what assurances do we have that the surplus generated at full employment will be consistent with equilibrium at full employment? That is, how do we know that the requirement for equilibrium—aggregate demand equaling aggregate supply—will be consistent with a budgetary surplus? We don't. This is easily seen.

Recall our earlier discussion wherein it was

demonstrated that equilibrium occurs when $S + T$ equals $I_n^d + G$. Stated differently, this condition implies that, in equilibrium, a surplus must be matched by the excess of desired investment over saving:

$$T - G = I_n^d - S.$$

What is to guarantee that I_n^d will exceed S by exactly the amount that taxes must exceed G in order for there to be a cyclically balanced budget? In general, there is no such guarantee. However, as we shall see in later chapters, investment spending is in part determined by interest rates, which are in turn influenced by monetary policy. Therefore, if a particular monetary policy generates an interest rate structure that ensures the requisite amount of I_n^d, then it is possible to have an equilibrium at full employment that is consistent with a budget surplus of the magnitude required to balance the budget cyclically. Otherwise, full employment equilibrium and budget balance will be incompatible. The point is, however, that the feasibility of a cyclically balanced budget consistent with the attainment and maintenance of full employment depends heavily on the posture of monetary policy. This, as we shall see, is a pretty tall order and, in general, an unlikely outcome.

The balanced full employment budget. These difficulties with the cyclically balanced budget have led some to propose that the budget be balanced at full employment. In this regard, there are two possibilities—balancing the full employment budget annually, or seeking that balance at some time in the future and maintaining balance thereafter.

Consider the annually balanced full employment budget. If the full employment budget is initially in deficit, this would call for a contractionary fiscal policy (to shift up the budget line) no matter what the initial level of income—whether there was a deflationary gap, an inflationary gap, or no gap at all. If the full employment budget were initially in surplus, an expansionary policy would be called for no matter what the state of the economy. And finally, if the full employment budget were balanced, it would not be possible for the fiscal authorities to pursue either an expansionary or contractionary policy since that would violate the goal of a balanced full employment budget. Thus, while the philosophy underlying this approach pays no heed to actual deficits or surpluses (except those that exist at full employment), it does put budgetary balance ahead of all other considerations. If the economy were severely depressed but the full employment budget was balanced, this philosophy would demand that fiscal policy remain unchanged. Worse still, if the economy were depressed and the full employment budget was in

deficit, this philosophy would demand that fiscal policy become *contractionary*. The only time fiscal policy could become expansionary would be if an initial full employment surplus existed. *Policy is completely dictated by the value of the full employment budget.*

What if we seek balance in the full employment budget by the gradual adjustment of government expenditures and taxes over time? Would this not leave room for the adoption of expansionary or contractionary fiscal policies as dictated by the needs of the economy, yet still enable the attainment of balance at full employment sometime in the future? Possibly.

Let us look at the thinking underlying this approach. Suppose government is currently running a deficit of $80 billion at income level Y_1, below the full employment level of income, Y_{FE}^1. Suppose further that the full employment budget has a deficit value of $40 billion. Assuming that the full employment level of income rises over time as a result of the accumulation of capital, growth in the labor force, technological advance, and the like, there is a tendency for the full employment budget to rise as well. The growth in the full employment level of income over time raises full employment tax receipts; with government expenditures fixed, the budget at full employment will move steadily in the direction of a surplus. This is illustrated in Figure 8.12; con-

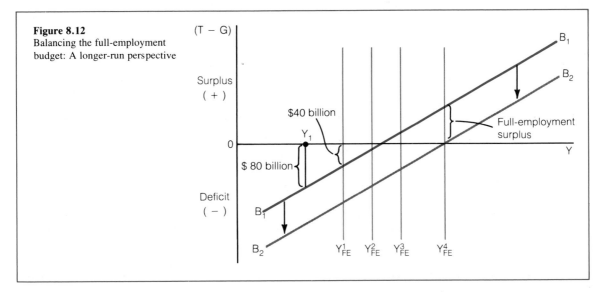

Figure 8.12
Balancing the full-employment budget: A longer-run perspective

centrate for the moment on the budget line labeled B_1.

Given existing tax laws and the current level of government spending (summarized in the budget line labeled B_1), there is at the income level Y_1 an actual deficit of $80 billion and a full employment deficit amounting to $40 billion (at the initial full employment level Y_{FE}^1). As the full employment level of income rises from Y_{FE}^1 to Y_{FE}^4, the full employment deficit is whittled away until at Y_{FE}^4 a full employment surplus exists; and at higher full employment levels, the full employment surplus becomes larger still.

Recognizing this fact, suppose that government adopts a strategy of balancing the full employment budget—not at income level Y_{FE}^1 but at income level Y_{FE}^4—and balancing it at full employment each year thereafter. What this strategy does is enable the government to pursue an expansionary policy *now*—represented by the shift of the budget line from B_1 to, say, B_2—in order to extricate itself from the current recession evidenced by the fact that Y_1 is below Y_{FE}^1, allowing the growth in full employment tax receipts to reduce with time the full employment deficit.

However, while such a strategy gives the government some degree of flexibility initially in dealing with inflationary and deflationary gaps, that flexibility is diminished both with the passage of time and the implementation of the changed fiscal policy. If at some future date government decides that the economy needs additional stimulus—greater than that represented by the shift of the budget line from B_1 to B_2—that expansionary policy will have to be offset by some future contractionary policy in order that balance can be attained at Y_{FE}^4. Moreover, the closer we get to having the full employment level of income, Y_{FE}^4, the less the government's flexibility will be. Since balance must be attained at a certain time in the future, the policy choices are reduced.

Once balance is attained at Y_{FE}^4, the strategy from there on out has associated with it the same problems as the annually balanced full employment budget, with one difference: in a growth context, this means balancing the growth in government expenditures with the growth in full employment tax receipts.

Let us note one final problem with these strategies. Can we be sure that a balanced full employment budget is consistent with the requirements for equilibrium at full employment? If G must equal T at full employment, can we be sure that I_n^d will equal S at full employment? As before, this particular result will depend heavily on the posture of monetary policy.

Summing up the balanced budget strategies. The basic problem with all of these balanced budget strategies is that they often conflict with the goal of producing a full employment noninflationary level of output. Budget balance becomes the primary objective of government fiscal policy; the full employment goal becomes secondary. Indeed, the implications of a balanced budget strategy are clear: Fiscal policy can be used to assist the economy to achieve a full employment noninflationary level of output *as long as such policies are consistent with an ultimate balancing of the budget.* Contrast this with the implications of the functional finance philosophy: Budget balance can be pursued *as long as such policies are consistent with the attainment of a full employment noninflationary level of output.* Budget balance is of secondary importance.

Although considerable support exists for a strategy that ultimately results in a balanced budget, very few people would argue that we ought to pursue a balanced budget *no matter what.* Indeed, most proponents of a balanced budget would argue that we need to be somewhat flexible; at least we ought not to pursue policies that aggravate swings in the level of economic activity. Nevertheless, the objective of a balanced budget can severely constrain fiscal policy actions, delaying or forestalling the use of policy for the purpose of achieving full employment. It is this characteristic of balanced budget strategies that most economists find distasteful.

The national debt

In general, it is not the presence of budget surpluses that creates concern; it is budget deficits. Why? Because *budget deficits, financed as they must be by borrowing, lead to increases in the national debt.* And the existence of a national debt, especially one as large as ours (around $1 trillion in 1981), is disturbing to many people. It provides convincing evidence that the nation is in deep financial straits. We refuse to live within our means and that spells trouble, if not for the present generation then for future generations.

The fears that many people associate with a growing national debt are derived in large measure from personal experience. If you or I were to live continuously beyond our means, piling up debt year after year, we'd discover soon enough the meaning of trouble. If our personal debt rises to such an extent that we are unable to make the required interest and principal payments, we will be forced to declare bankruptcy. Even if the final outcome is not bankruptcy, all of the debt we have run up will have to be paid off at some time. Is this not true as well for the nation as a whole as a consequence of our growing national debt? How shall we ever be able to pay it all off?

Unfortunately (or fortunately), proponents of this view have overlooked the fallacy of composition: What is true for each of us may not be true for the nation as a whole. While each of us will ultimately have to settle all of our debts in one way or another, the same is not necessarily true for the whole nation. Our own personal financial affairs have a definite terminating point— *death.* The same is not true of our nation.

Consider a more relevant comparison. Do people get particularly upset at the growing debt of Exxon, AT&T, or any of our other successful corporations? Do we view such debt growth as unsound? Not generally. *As long as these corporations are able to acquire assets that generate revenues sufficient to cover the interest payments and periodic refundings, such debt growth is often viewed as sound and proper finance.* Of course, one could imagine catastrophic events that could bankrupt these companies. But it is apparent that the public attaches a very low probability to such occurrences. This is evidenced by the fact that the public is willing to lend so much to these companies. Indeed, this is exactly what a growing corporate debt implies—a willingness on the part of the public to acquire ever-increasing quantities of corporate bonds. If people were generally alarmed and fearful of such debt growth, they would refuse to lend as much as they do; they would limit that growth either by their refusal to buy corporate bonds or by their insistence on very high rates of return to cover the added risk. *It is largely a matter of confidence.* In large measure, the public is reasonably confident that the successful corporations will at least be able to meet their interest obligations and repay the principal when the debt matures. As a result of this confidence and the fact that corporations can continue in existence indefinitely, such corporate debt can continue to rise year after year without any apparent limit.

The problem of the national debt can be viewed in much the same light. As long as the public is confident that the government will be able to meet its interest obligations and repay the principal when the debt matures, it will be willing to lend to government; it will be willing to acquire ever-increasing quantities of government bonds. And, given the fact that government bonds are viewed as almost risk-free by the public, considerable confidence must exist in the government's ability to pay off its debts.

There is, however, one very important difference between the corporation and the government as far as debt growth is concerned. The corporation relies on increasing revenues from the sale of its output to meet its increasing debt obligation. The government, on the other hand, relies on the taxable capacity of our nation's income and output in order to meet its debt obligations. What is important, therefore, is the magnitude of the interest payments on the national debt relative to our GNP. As Table 8.5 makes clear, interest payments on the national debt amount to less than 3 percent of our GNP— hardly what you would call an overwhelming burden. It has grown slightly in recent years as a result of sizable government deficits and record high interest rates, but it is still relatively small.

The burden of the national debt. From the point of view of the nation as a whole, then, the overall tax burden of the interest payments on our national debt is slight. There are, however,

Table 8.5

Interest payments on the national debt relative to gross
national product, selected years ($ billions)

Year	National debt	Interest payments on the national debt	GNP	Interest payments as a percent of GNP
1930	16.2	0.7	90.7	0.8
1935	28.7	0.8	72.5	1.1
1940	43.0	1.0	100.0	1.0
1945	258.7	3.6	212.4	1.7
1950	256.1	5.7	286.5	2.0
1955	272.8	6.4	400.0	1.6
1960	284.1	9.2	506.5	1.8
1965	313.8	11.3	691.1	1.6
1970	370.1	19.3	992.7	1.9
1975	533.2	32.7	1,549.2	2.1
1980	907.7	64.5	2,626.1	2.5

Source: U.S. Department of the Treasury, and U.S. Department of Commerce

a number of other burdens associated with a growing national debt that are potentially quite troublesome. Let us consider some of them.

If a growing national debt results in a lower rate of capital formation than otherwise, we impose a burden on future generations by leaving them a smaller stock of capital goods. A lower rate of capital formation—that is, a lower level of investment—implies slower growth and a reduced production potential in the future. There are a number of complicated issues here, and we would do best to consider each of them in turn.

If the economy is currently at full employment and *if* the growth in the national debt (i.e., deficit spending) causes the Congress to hold down the growth of government capital formation and *if* private investment must be held down by various policy measures so that aggregate demand does not exceed aggregate supply at full employment, a growing national debt will impose a burden on society in the form of a reduced rate of capital formation. However, this proposition involves a lot of "ifs." In the first place, deficit spending could well involve some government capital formation that need not displace private capital formation; in this instance, there could be an increase in the overall stock of capital goods. Second, equilibrium, defined as $S + T = I_n^d + G$, need not imply that private investment must be held down. If the investment busi-

nesspeople desire to undertake relative to saving just happens to equal the value of the deficit, no policy measures to hold down private investment would be required.

If the economy is producing a less-than-full employment level of output, this implies that producers are operating their plants at less than full capacity, which, in general, is not conducive to a high rate of capital formation. If deficit spending and a growing national debt raise the level of national income and capacity utilization, such actions could well raise the rate of capital formation; that would be a plus, a *negative* burden on future generations as opposed to a positive burden because the future stock of capital goods would be larger.

Investment spending on the part of the business community is sensitive to interest rates. To the extent that increased government borrowing to finance deficits results in higher interest rates, there will be a reduced rate of capital formation—a burden on future generations. Here, people's holdings of government bonds come partially at the expense of their holdings of corporate bonds.

Interest payments on the national debt can result in a redistribution of income from the general taxpaying public toward those who own government bonds. This redistribution effect may not be sizable, however, in view of the fact that the bondholders themselves are part of the taxpaying public. Nevertheless, since bondholders tend to be wealthier and have higher incomes, there will be some redistribution of income toward those individuals.

Part of our national debt is owned by residents in foreign countries. This external debt imposes a burden on our residents to the extent that we must give up goods and services to residents of foreign countries to pay our interest obligations. Again, relative to GNP, this burden is not large.

A question of opportunity cost. There are, admittedly, a number of burdens associated with an existing and growing national debt. The question is, however, do the benefits exceed the costs? Put differently, what would be the opportunity costs of balancing the budget or reducing the national debt? They could be sizable.

As we have emphasized repeatedly, attempts to balance the budget could mean a refusal on the part of the government to pursue policies designed to achieve a noninflationary, full employment level of income and output. Worse yet, it could mean the pursuit of procyclical policies, which have the effect of aggravating swings in the level of economic activity. As a result of these facts, the bulk of the economics profession takes the view that, although there are burdens associated with the national debt, these are minor in comparison with the burdens of unemployment and inflation. Fiscal policy ought to be used, therefore, for the pursuit of balancing the economy at full employment, not balancing the budget. If such policies are consistent with a balancing of the budget, so much the better. But balancing the budget ought not to be the primary motivational consideration.

PROBLEMS WITH THE IMPLEMENTATION OF FISCAL POLICY

Although the theoretical case for the use of fiscal policy to balance the economy at full employment is clear, it is essential that we be aware of a number of problems associated with its implementation.

First, fiscal policy, at least in the United States, is not a flexible stabilization tool in the sense

that it can be changed quickly to meet the demands of a changing economy. On the contrary, changes in government spending and taxes for the purpose of effecting changes in the level of economic activity are often subject to *long congressional lags*. Legislative bills get bogged down in committee; they are often the subject of extensive hearings; they are frequently debated at length on the floors of both houses of Congress; differences between the two houses must be thrashed out in conference. Although there may be general agreement in favor of an increase in government spending, there is often little agreement over how the increase is to be spent. Bills introduced to change taxes are frequently used as vehicles for the purpose of discussing tax reform. When President Kennedy attempted to introduce a tax cut in 1962, it was not implemented until 1964. Likewise, it took a year before the tax surcharge suggested by President Johnson was finally enacted. And President Ford's tax cut of 1975 took almost a year before it was finally passed. President Reagan was able to get his proposed expenditure cuts and tax cuts in only about 5 months, but this was truly the exception historically.

As a result of all of these delays, fiscal policy might not be implemented at times when it is needed. Worse still, if the economic outlook changes in the interim, the fiscal policy change could, in fact, make matters worse. For these reasons, a number of economists have suggested that the President be given some discretionary authority to change taxes or spending without prior congressional approval to better enable the economy to achieve balance at full employment. Whatever the merits of this argument, there does not appear to be any prospect in the near future that Congress will grant the President this kind of authority. We will therefore probably continue to be plagued by delays.

A second problem concerns the impact of a change in fiscal policy on other components of private demand. It is alleged, for example, that an expansionary fiscal policy will exert upward pressures on interest rates, leading to offsetting reductions in desired investment. The result will be that there might not be any net increase in aggregate demand at all. Fiscal policy would, under these circumstances, be impotent. We will evaluate this argument in depth in Chapter 11 and again in Chapter 14.

Third, although Congress often appears to be amenable to tax cuts, most legislators steadfastly resist tax hikes. The same asymmetry is frequently encountered with respect to government spending. It often seems easier for government to approve a spending increase than to approve a spending cut.

Finally, there is the whole question of whether a change in fiscal policy ought to take the form of a change in taxes or a change in government spending. It is true that a change in government spending brings about a larger change in the level of economic activity than an equivalent change in taxes does. But this should not be the prime consideration. It is a question of the optimum mix of public and private goods. If government spending is already too large and a deflationary gap exists, the required expansionary policy should take the form of tax cuts; and of course, the converse holds true.

SUMMARY

1. With government added to our simplified economy, the planned savings equals planned investment condition for macroequilibrium needs to be redefined. It is now seen as planned savings plus taxes equals planned investment plus government spending.

2. In the more complex economy with government included, the simple multiplier of Chapter 7 is no longer sufficient. Thus, assuming that, for every dollar *increase* in NNP, tax receipts rise by t (where t represents the marginal tax rate), a more realistic *expenditure multiplier* is given by $1/[1 - (\text{MPC} \times (1 - t))]$. From this formula it is clear that the expenditure multiplier will vary inversely with the *marginal tax rate* but directly with the *marginal propensity to consume* out of disposable income.

3. In general, the *tax multiplier* will have a numerical value that is less than the *expenditure multiplier*. More precisely, the tax multiplier is

equal to MPC times the expenditure multiplier. Whereas a dollar increase in government spending, for example, causes an initial $1 increase in aggregate demand, a dollar reduction in taxes causes an initial increase in aggregate demand of only MPC times the change in taxes. A dollar reduction in taxes leads first to an increase in disposable income, part of which will be saved (MPS times the change in disposable income), part of which will be spent (MPC times the change in disposable income).

4. The fact that the tax multiplier is smaller than the expenditure multiplier means that balanced changes in government spending and taxes will *not* be neutral as regards aggregate demand. Specifically, a balanced increase in government spending and taxes will *raise* national income by an amount equal to the difference between the expenditure and tax multipliers times the balanced change.

5. Fiscal policy, in the form of changes in government spending or taxes, can be used to eliminate either the *inflationary gap* or the *deflationary gap*.

6. The rise and fall of tax revenues as the level of economic activity increases and decreases act as *automatic stabilizers,* moderating the swings in national income automatically. The degree of automatic built-in stability is inversely related to the numerical value of the multiplier. A relatively high multiplier value implies a relatively low degree of automatic built-in stability; the converse is also true.

7. Automatic stabilizers operate to produce automatic and passive changes in the value of the government budget. Thus, as the level of national income increases, the automatic stabilizers tend to increase surpluses (or reduce deficits). Declines in the level of economic activity tend to increase deficits (or reduce surpluses).

8. The *full employment* (or *high employment*) *budget* concept was developed to separate and to identify those changes in the budget that are policy-induced and those that arise passively. Any change in the actual budget unaccompanied by a change in the full employment budget represents a passive budget change. A policy-induced budget change is reflected in a change in the

full employment budget. An expansionary fiscal policy will be reflected in a decline of the full employment budget (either a smaller full employment surplus or a larger full employment deficit); a contractionary fiscal policy will be reflected in a rise of the full employment budget.

9. Although deficit spending is often viewed as a fiscally irresponsible course for government policy, the *functional finance* philosophy emphasizes that the objective of a full employment noninflationary level of income and output takes precedence over budget balance. At times the needs of the economy will call for deficit spending; at other times they will call for surpluses. Nevertheless, the pressures to balance the government's budget have led to the development of a number of alternative budget balancing strategies.

a. One strategy is the *annually balanced budget* that calls for government to pursue those expenditure and tax policies required to balance the budget year in and year out. The problem with this strategy is that fiscal policy could become procyclical in nature rather than countercyclical.

b. A second strategy is the *cyclically balanced budget*—balancing the budget over the business cycle. There are a great many problems with this strategy. Depending on the length of downswings versus upswings in the economy, fiscal policy could be countercyclical, procyclical, or neutral. If the economy swings between full and less-than-full employment positions, budget surpluses at full employment would be required, according to this strategy, to ensure budget balance over the business cycle; and there is no guarantee that budget surplus would be consistent with equilibrium at full employment.

c. A third strategy is the *balanced full employment budget.* An approach that calls for the balancing of the full employment budget annually has some of the same defects as the annually balanced budget strategy. An alternative balanced full employment budget strategy—that of gradually adjusting government expenditures and taxes over time until a balanced full

employment budget is attained—provides some degree of fiscal policy flexibility initially. But that flexibility is diminished both with the passage of time and with the implementation of the changed fiscal policy.

10. Budget deficits, financed as they must be by borrowing, lead to increases in the *national debt.* The existence and growth of the national debt are troubling to many people because they imply that we as a nation live beyond our means. They come to this conclusion by analogy with the consequences for individuals of ever-increasing debt burdens. A more relevant comparision is that between the debt positions of corporations and the government. Considering the relatively small value of interest payments relative to GNP and the general belief that government bonds are the least risky of all bonds, serious doubts exist as to how burdensome our national debt is. Nevertheless, if the national debt *(a)* does result in a lower rate of capital formation generally, *(b)* redistributes income from those lower down on the income ladder to those higher up, and *(c)* forces us to give up goods and services to residents of foreign countries to pay our interest obligations owed them, future (and present) generations of American residents will be burdened. Given these burdens, the question is: Would the benefits of balancing the budget and reducing the growth of the national debt exceed the costs of doing so, the costs being measured in terms of our failure to use policy to achieve a noninflationary full employment level of income and output?

11. Because of lengthy congressional lags, fiscal policy is not a flexible stabilization tool.

CONCEPTS FOR REVIEW

Fiscal policy
Monetary policy

Marginal tax rate

Average tax rate

Expenditure multiplier

Tax multiplier

Balanced budget multiplier

Automatic stabilizers

Fiscal drag

Passive budget changes

Policy-induced budget changes

Full employment (or high employment) budget

Full employment deficit

Full employment surplus

Functional finance

The annually balanced budget

The cyclically balanced budget

The balanced full employment budget

National debt

QUESTIONS FOR DISCUSSION

(Those marked with an asterisk (*) are more difficult.)

1. Which is the "better" tool of fiscal policy—a change in government spending or a change in taxes? Justify your answer in terms of both the effects of each tool on the equilibrium level of net national product (NNP) and on the mix of private versus public goods and services.

2. Is fiscal policy more or less effective as the marginal tax rate moves higher? Be explicit.

3. Explain why the economy is said to have greater "built-in" stability the higher the marginal tax rate goes?

4. State whether you agree or disagree with each of the following statements. Explain your reasoning carefully in each instance.

    a. "The greater the value of the multiplier, the greater will be the amount of *fiscal drag* in the economic system."

    b. "As actual NNP rises toward the given full employment level of income, the full employment budget will increase (i.e., move in the direction of a surplus or an enlarged surplus), assuming an unchanged fiscal policy."

    c. "As the full employment level of income increases over time because of economic growth, the full employment budget will increase, even if fiscal policy is unchanged."

    d. "If the full employment budget registers a surplus, this can be taken as evidence that fiscal policy has turned contractionary."

    e. "If government spends more than it receives in tax revenue—that is, if government runs a budget deficit—this can be taken as evidence that fiscal policy has become expansionary."

5. Explain precisely what is meant by the following statement: "Fiscal policy is procyclical in nature rather than countercyclical."

*6. Sometimes it is argued that the level of government spending should be set on the basis of the "correct" mix of public versus private goods without regard to their macroeconomic effects; in addition, taxes should be adjusted in accordance with the degree of fiscal stimulus or contraction the economy requires. What do you think of such a policy? Would this approach be consistent with the *functional finance* philosophy?

*7. Sometimes it is argued that economic prosperity is possible only if government undertakes "mega-buck" spending on defense. After all, look at the prosperity that occurred around World War II and the Korean and Vietnam wars. How would you evaluate this argument, especially in view of our statement of *the economic problem* in Chapter 2?

In Chapter 2 we identified money as a key element promoting efficiency in the production and exchange of goods and services. Without money, exchange would be cumbersome and specialization would be inhibited. Money helps solve these problems because it is a good that is generally acceptable as a medium of exchange. This means that each of us is willing to sell goods and services for money, confident that the money we receive will be acceptable to those from whom we wish to purchase other goods and services. We do not have to waste time concocting elaborate arrangements to effect the exchanges desired. Therefore the advantages of specialization can be realized.

Given the importance of money to the functioning of our economic system, it is critical that we thoroughly understand its nature and the role it plays in our economic system. It is the purpose of the next three chapters to explore these important matters.

The first question we ask in this chapter is: What is **money?** This might strike you as a rather odd question since the answer seems so obvious. But, as you will soon discover, the answers to this question are many, varied, and hotly debated.

We then want to turn our attention to the question of how much money should be in circulation and who should provide it. As you will see, some of the answers given here are far from clear-cut.

Finally, we will examine in detail the institutional makeup of the U.S. financial system, including a discussion of the Federal Reserve System, commercial banks, "thrift" institutions, and their interrelationships. We leave to Chapter 10 the analysis of the credit creation process, and to Chapter 11 the study of the relationship between money and the pace of economic activity.

Chapter 9

Money and the U.S. financial system

FUNCTIONS OF MONEY

The meaning and importance of money can best be understood by first examining its several functions. One of these functions is its role as the **unit of account.** Just as distances are measured in miles or meters, and weights in pounds or grams, so the values of goods and services are measured in dollars and cents; as miles and meters are units of account for distance measurement, dollars and cents are units of account for measuring the value of goods and services.

The second important function of money is its role as a **medium of exchange**—a medium through which each good and service can be exchanged for other goods and services. To illustrate, consider the main reason most people work. The object of their work effort is not the money they are paid, but the goods and services that are ultimately purchased with the money received. Put simply, the main reason most people work is to "make a living"—to acquire other goods and services. Money is simply an intermediate good—a medium—that facilitates the exchange of our labor services for these other goods and services. Two transactions are involved in this process. We receive money as payment for our work effort; and subsequently we use the money to buy goods and services.

If our ultimate aim is to consume those other goods and services, why not simply exchange our labor services for them directly? Because it is too difficult! Imagine the problems you would encounter in getting what you wanted in a **barter economy**—an economy without money. You would have to find those people who not only had what you wanted, but also happened to want your labor services. Barring this fortuitous **coincidence of wants,** you would have only two other options in a barter economy: (1) produce for yourself all the goods and services you wanted (imagine how difficult it would be to produce from scratch the items you normally purchase— a home, food, clothes, automobiles, televisions, pens, paper clips, etc.); or (2) exchange your labor services for whatever products you could get, then search out those people who would be willing to take those products in exchange for the ones you really wanted. Even if such people could be found, the trade might not be easy: 500,000 barrels of pickles might trade for one airplane, but what would the airplane producer do with half a million barrels of pickles? By comparison, the trading of some goods and services for others

through the medium of money looks marvelously simple.

Finally, money serves a **store of value** function. This means we can take the money we receive in exchange for our labor services and *store it* for later use to buy goods and services as we want or need them. Unlike a barter economy, the sale of our labor services need not be synchronized with the purchase of the goods and services we demand.

Defining money

What characterics should money possess to best fulfill the various functions of money? What about the unit of account function? That's easy. Any good or service can serve equally well as the unit of account. This is so because each good and service can be expressed in terms of so many units of *any other* good or service. No good is unique as far as the unit of account function is concerned.

What about the store of value function of money? This is a more difficult problem. All goods do not serve equally well as stores of value; some goods are much better stores of value than others. To satisfy the store of value function, the good in question should maintain a relatively stable value over time. This means that its purchasing power—the real quantity of goods and services that a given amount of *this good* will "buy"—should not vary much from one time period to another. If its future value is likely to deteriorate—meaning that a greater amount of this good will be required to "purchase" some given quantity of other goods and services—people will try to get rid of it; they will either purchase now the goods and services they want or exchange this "money" for other assets that will maintain their relative value. Conversely, if its relative value is expected to rise, people will try to acquire more of it and hoard it.

What about the medium of exchange function of money? Here again, not all goods would be equally desirable. To serve as the medium of exchange, money should be convenient to carry around and transfer to others. It should be durable enough to be passed from one person to an-

Table 9.1
Definitions: Checkable deposits

Demand deposit accounts. Checking accounts at depository institutions. The overwhelming amount of these deposits is located in commercial banks. Withdrawals from these accounts are made simply by writing checks. By law, demand deposits pay no interest.

Negotiable order of withdrawal (NOW) accounts. Savings accounts at depository institutions that pay interest. In all other respects, however, they are like demand deposits since withdrawals can be made simply by writing a checklike draft, technically called a negotiable order of withdrawal. NOW accounts are generally acceptable as a medium of exchange. The interest they pay are subject of federally mandated ceilings. Prior to January 1, 1981, NOW accounts were restricted to certain northeastern states; beginning January 1, 1981, NOW accounts were authorized on a nation-wide basis. NOW accounts quickly have become very popular.

Automated transfer service (ATS) accounts. Savings accounts that pay interest. However, unlike some other savings accounts, these accounts are different in that, for banks offering the service, the owner of the account and the bank have entered into an arrangement whereby the bank automatically transfers funds from this account to the customer's demand deposit account whenever needed to pay a check. ATS accounts were permitted to enable commercial banks in particular to circumvent the law prohibiting the payment of interest on demand deposits and thereby to more effectively enable these institutions to compete with NOW accounts and share draft accounts. Like NOW accounts, ATS accounts (and other savings accounts) pay interest subject to federally mandated ceilings.

Share draft accounts. Except for some technical differences, these accounts—offered by credit unions—are identical to NOW accounts.

other or held for a while between transactions. And it should be available in units of a standard size sufficiently divisible to accommodate easily the purchase and sale of goods and services over a very wide range of prices. Most important of all, to serve as a medium of exchange it must be generally acceptable.

What is important to recognize is that those items that might serve as the best stores of value are not necessarily those that possess the most desirable characteristics from the point of view of the medium of exchange function of money; the best stores of value, for example, might be too bulky or not easily divisible. Oil paintings or real estate might be very good stores of value, but they are not easily divisible (indeed, what is the value of half a painting?), nor are they convenient to carry or transfer.

Conflicts between the store of value and medium of exchange functions of money create problems in defining the term *money.* It is possible, therefore, to define *money* differently depending on the relative emphasis one gives to the medium of exchange and store of value functions. One could define money *narrowly* as *anything that is generally acceptable as a medium of exchange.* In the United States, this narrow definition would mean that money consists of two things: (1) **currency** (dollar bills in various de-

nominations) and **coins;** and (2) **checkable deposits**—*accounts in depository institutions against which checks can be written.* There are principally four basic kinds of checkable deposits that satisfy the general acceptability criterion. They are **demand deposit accounts, negotiable order of withdrawal (NOW)** accounts, **automated transfer service (ATS)** accounts, and **share draft** accounts. These different accounts are described in detail in Table 9.1. The money supply measure that corresponds to this narrow definition of money is known as **M1.**[1]

Although M1 includes generally acceptable mediums of exchange, thereby satisfying the medium of exchange function of money, it is widely agreed that this measure of money excludes many assets that are better stores of value than those assets that are included. Moreover, because of the ease with which these other assets can be exchanged for any of the items comprising M1, and because many people do acquire such other assets as "temporary abodes of purchasing power" until such time as they are needed to

---

[1] As of this writing, the Federal Reserve publishes two narrowly defined money supply measures, M1-A and M1-B. In 1982 the Federal Reserve intends to focus its attention on only one narrow money measure, M1, whose coverage is the same as M1-B. As employed here, M1 and M1-B are interchangeable.

finance transactions, at which point they are exchanged for the medium of exchange, many economists believe that the narrow M1 measure of money should be expanded (or broadened) to include many of these "near monies."

The monetary and credit aggregates in the United States

Broadening the definition of money poses some difficult problems. Once you begin to admit assets other than those that are generally acceptable as mediums of exchange, where do you stop? There are many assets that could qualify as good stores of value. But to include them for just that reason might not be appropriate for a variety of reasons that will become clear later on. Moreover, some economists question the wisdom of broadening the definition of money on grounds that these other assets are not mediums of exchange and must be exchanged for items already included in M1 in order to finance transactions.

In recognition of the legitimacy of the different sides of this debate, the Federal Reserve, the nation's central bank, publishes many different measures of money. And just in case researchers do not like the particular measures selected, the Federal Reserve publishes separately all of the individual components used in their various definitions. This permits people to "roll their own"—that is, to construct their own favorite monetary aggregate.

The monetary and credit aggregates officially published by the Federal Reserve are M1, M2, M3, and L. Figure 9.1 presents these various definitions along with their dollar volumes as of May, 1981. Let us examine briefly each of these aggregate measures.

M1 has already been discussed. It is the measure that best satisfies the definition of money

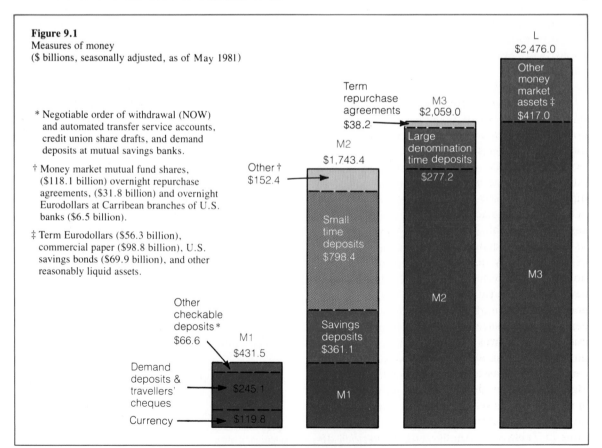

Figure 9.1
Measures of money
($ billions, seasonally adjusted, as of May 1981)

* Negotiable order of withdrawal (NOW) and automated transfer service accounts, credit union share drafts, and demand deposits at mutual savings banks.

† Money market mutual fund shares, ($118.1 billion) overnight repurchase agreements, ($31.8 billion) and overnight Eurodollars at Carribean branches of U.S. banks ($6.5 billion).

‡ Term Eurodollars ($56.3 billion), commercial paper ($98.8 billion), U.S. savings bonds ($69.9 billion), and other reasonably liquid assets.

as a generally acceptable medium of exchange. *In contrast to M1, the broader definitions of money (i.e., M2 and M3, for example) contain items that must be converted into the medium of exchange before they can be used to pay for goods and services.* To understand the distinctions among these other definitions of money, we must introduce the concept of **liquidity.**

Basically, liquidity refers to the ease with which deposits, financial assets, or other items can be transformed into the medium of exchange, or means of payment, without loss. The transfer of funds from a savings to a checking account, if not already done automatically by your bank in an ATS account, involves no loss of funds and only a small expenditure of time and effort. Savings accounts are thus highly liquid. On the other hand, houses are highly illiquid. If you were to try to sell a house to obtain spendable funds, the transaction would be much more difficult than the savings account transfer just described. Normally, the sale would require much time and effort. If you had to sell quickly, you could be forced to sell at a price far below its value.

Liquidity thus refers to the ease with which various assets can be converted into the medium of exchange quickly and without loss. In an economy as complex as ours, with many different kinds of financial assets, there are many gradations of liquidity. M2, M3, and L are distinguished from one another on the basis of these different gradations of liquidity. The **M2** measure adds to M1 those items considered to be the most easily substitutable for cash and checkable deposits—assets that can be converted into the means of payment very quickly and, in most cases, at no loss whatsoever. These include such items as **savings deposits** (non-ATS type), **small time deposits, money market certificates, small saver certificates, all-saver certificates, money market mutual fund shares** (most of which are held by individuals or small business enterprises), and certain types of assets—**overnight RPs** and **overnight Eurodollar deposits**—that have emerged in recent years as vehicles in which large corporations tend to park funds temporarily. (See definitions in Table 9.2.) All of these financial assets

can be transformed into the means of payment within a day or so without any uncertainty as to the amount of funds that can be obtained. Only the conversion of small time deposits might entail a significant cost to the depositor (in the form of a penalty for early withdrawal), but at least this cost is known in advance.

The **M3** aggregate incorporates assets that are somewhat less liquid—**large-denomination time deposits** of $100,000 or more, and **repurchase agreements** that are arranged for more than one day (called **term RPs**). These assets, held almost exclusively by larger corporations, are a bit harder to convert quickly into the means of payment than their counterparts in M2. Term RPs obviously take longer to mature than overnight RPs, and large-denomination time deposits, unlike small time deposits, are traded in markets where price variability creates the risk of some loss.

Finally, the most comprehensive aggregate of all is **L**, the aggregate referred to as **liquid assets.** This aggregate is not formally regarded as a measure of money, but simply represents the sum total of all those items that, in the entire spectrum of financial assets, are considered to be either a medium of exchange or reasonably close substitutes for it. The additional assets included in L—**term Eurodollars, U.S. Savings Bonds, and commercial paper**—offer business firms and individuals a wide array of alternatives in which funds can be placed for short periods at little risk of loss in case the funds be needed quickly to finance transactions.

A final note on the monetary and credit aggregates. For purposes of analysis, the quantity of money is defined as the quantity in the hands of the public. Currency and coin in the vaults of banks are *not* part of the money supply. (That would mean double counting, as will become clear in Chapter 10.) Also, government checking account balances are *not* part of the money supply. This latter point might seem strange at first. But given that the nature of government decision-making is different from that of the public, there is justifiable cause to keep the two aspects separate.

Table 9.2
Definitions: Other deposit and nondeposit savings instruments

---

Savings (passbook-type) accounts. Traditionally the most common form of liquid saving, these accounts provide the depositor with an interest-bearing asset from which funds can readily be withdrawn. The interest returns these accounts pay are subject to federally mandated ceilings.

Small time (certificates of) deposit. In contrast to savings accounts, these instruments require the depositor to maintain funds on deposit for a specified time period (maturity), with penalties for premature withdrawal specified by federal regulations. They are available in maturities ranging from three months to eight years and offer higher (though also regulated) rates of interest than savings accounts. The term *small* means that they are less than $100,000 in size.

All-saver certificates. These are a special type of one-year certificate whose interest yield is equal to 70 percent of the 52-week Treasury bill yield. The interest income on these certificates is tax-exempt (up to $2,000 on a joint return). As of this writing, the tax-exempt status of these certificates was to expire on December 31, 1982.

Money market certificates. These are a special type of small certificate whose maximum rate of interest changes weekly according to a formula that keeps it about equal to yields (rates of return) available on six-month U.S. Treasury securities. These six-month money market certificates require a minimum deposit of $10,000 and pay a fixed rate of interest for the six-month period.

Small saver certificates. These certificates are another special type of small certificate whose interest rate ceiling varies periodically (biweekly) to reflect changes in yields on marketable U.S. government securities of similar maturity. These certificates can be offered in any denomination, carry a minimum maturity of 2½ years, and pay rates of interest only slightly less than 2½-year Treasury securities. They pay a fixed rate of interest for 2½ years.

Large-denomination time deposits. These are deposit certificates of $100,000 or more, which can pay any rate of interest without restriction. They typically are held by larger corporations. They generally are issued for short maturities (14 days to 1 year). Most of them can be traded to other corporations (or individuals) before the date of maturity (i.e., they are tradable but cannot be redeemed before maturity except at a stiff penalty).

Money market mutual fund shares. There are a number of money market instruments—large denomination time deposits, commercial paper, and Eurodollar deposits, for example—that offer the highest rates of return possible but are out of reach of most people because they generally require minimum investments of $100,000 or more. Money market mutual funds get around this problem by pooling the financial investments of many people and purchasing these assets with the pooled funds. Each account holder purchases a "share" of the fund for as little as $1,000 and earns a portion of the interest that the fund receives on its investments (called its *portfolio*) in the high-yield money market instruments. Funds can be deposited or withdrawn quickly, and many funds even offer check-writing privileges; however, for most funds, the minimum size of the check they will honor is $500. Because of these check-writing privileges, money market mutual fund shares are very much like other checkable deposits; if there were no minimum size restrictions, there would be no reason to exclude these funds from the definition of M1.

Repurchase agreements (RPs). Here a commercial bank or savings and loan institution sells a security to a customer—typically a large corporation or a state or local government—with an agreement that it will purchase it back at a higher price at a later time; the interest the customer earns is reflected in the price differential. There are two basic types of RPs—*overnight RPs* (the depository institution agrees to buy back the security the *next* business day) and *term RPs* (any RPs that are for a longer period than overnight).

Eurodollar deposits. These are deposits in foreign financial institutions, (including branches of U.S. banks abroad). The deposits are denominated not in the currencies of the countries in which the financial institutions are located but in dollars. The name *Eurodollar* was derived from the fact that, initially, most dollar-denominated deposits outside the United States were located in European financial institutions. Nowadays, one finds dollar-denominated deposits in almost all major financial centers of the world; though increasingly inappropriate, all of them are called Eurodollars. There are two basic types of Eurodollar deposits—*overnight Eurodollar deposits* and *term Eurodollar deposits.*

Commerical paper. This is a promissory note that varies in maturity from just a few days to several months. Commercial paper does not yield interest explicitly; rather, it is sold at a *discount*—i.e., a 60-day piece of commercial paper with a face value of $100,000 might sell for $97,000. The difference in price reflects the interest return. Rather than go to financial institutions to acquire short-term loans, many large corporations and finance companies will issue commercial paper instead.

Federal funds. These are reserves of depository institutions that are traded among those institutions, often for one day and seldom for periods exceeding several days. Organized originally to facilitate the exchange of reserves by banks to meet their reserve requirements, this market has expanded in recent years to provide a general source and outlet for short-term funds.

The changing definition of money

As the foregoing discussion illustrates, defining *money* is not an easy matter. Controversy exists over how wide the net should be cast. Moreover, changes in the regulatory environment and financial innovations have made the job of defining the term even harder. Indeed, in light of changes in government regulations in the late 1970s that permitted depository institutions to offer the six-month money market certificates and the 2½-year small saver certificates, and other regulatory changes that permitted the development of the popular NOW accounts, ATS accounts, and other innovations, the Federal Reserve Board found it necessary in 1980 to redefine its monetary measures—to adopt new measures of money to replace the old outmoded measures. In all probability, developments such as those that occasioned the 1980 redefinitions will continue to occur, requiring yet other changes in our concepts of money in the future.

The importance of defining money

Despite the difficulties of defining *money,* it is important that we continue to search for meaningful measures of money. The reason is clear. Money plays a very important role in our economic system. It affects not only the efficiency of the economy, but changes in its quantity affect the levels of output, employment, growth, and prices. In short, the quantity of money in circulation and the rate at which this quantity changes over time critically affect our success in achieving our nation's economic goals.

Unfortunately, there is no single measure of money that adequately captures the many complex links between the U.S. financial system and the overall performance of the economy. The narrow definition of money—M1—is important for some purposes; the other more broadly defined aggregates are useful for other purposes. Accordingly, the Federal Reserve attempts to exert its control not over any single measure of money to the exclusion of others but over all the measures described in Figure 9.1. As we will see, this makes the task of interpreting monetary policy difficult. However, this complexity is justified by the complexities inherent in the U.S. financial system.

In what follows, we will focus our attention on M1. We will focus our attention, therefore, on the medium of exchange aspect of money. This is justified on grounds that all transactions must be financed using either currency and coin or checkable deposits. No other assets are generally acceptable as means of payments. All other assets must be converted to the means of payment before they can be used to finance business transactions.

THE OPTIMUM QUANTITY OF MONEY

In a money-exchange economy such as ours, nearly every market transaction is financed using money. Sellers of goods and services accept money because they are confident that they will be able to turn around and use the money to buy other items that they themselves want. Money thus passes continuously from hand to hand. The question of interest is, How much money should be circulating in our economy? Or, putting the question differently, *What is the optimum quantity of money?*

Because money plays such a central role in executing transactions, *it is important that there be enough in circulation to finance that volume of transactions that permits the full realization of our nation's productive potential, the full employment level of output.* Exactly how this objective should be translated into policy is a matter of considerable debate. An appropriate framework for discussing this debate is the famous **equation of exchange.**

The equation of exchange

Focusing our attention on final goods and services, a fairly simply relationship exists between the quantity of money in circulation and the volume of final goods and services it finances. This relationship is given by the identity known as the *equation of exchange:*

$$MV \equiv PQ.$$

This identity states that the amount of money in circulation (M) multiplied by the **velocity of circulation** (V) must equal the nominal value of GNP (PQ), where P is the price level index known as the GNP implicit price deflator, and Q is real GNP.

Once we understand the meaning of the *velocity of circulation* (V) it will become clear why the equation of exchange *must* be true. The idea behind the velocity of circulation is straightforward. Over any interval of time, such as a year, a given amount of money can be used again and again to finance people's purchases of goods and services. The money one person spends for goods and services at any given moment can be used later by the recipient of that money to purchase yet other goods and services. *The number of times a dollar "turns over" in this fashion, on average, during the relevant period is the velocity of circulation.* If the stock of money has a value of $300 billion and its velocity—the number of times it "turns over"—is equal to five, the nominal value of GNP *must* be equal to $1,500 billion. If each dollar, on average, financed $5.00 worth of final goods and services, $300 billion must have financed $1,500 billion of final goods and services.

Considerable care must be exercised when the equation of exchange is used to interpret economic events. By itself, the relationship is only an identity; it says nothing whatsoever about causation. For example, we could not assume necessarily that a change in M would result in a change in nominal GNP (PQ). An increase in M could be offset by a reduction in V such that the product, MV, would be unaltered. Or, if nominal GNP increased, it would be incorrect on the basis of this identity to conclude that the increase in MV *caused* the increase in PQ. All we can say is that the increase in PQ *must be accompanied by* an increase in MV; we cannot say the increase in MV caused the increase in PQ any more than we can say the increase in PQ caused the increase

in MV. In short, no causal connections can be inferred from this identity.

Alternative theories of money and the equation of exchange. It is possible, however, to use the factors identified in the equation of exchange to *hypothesize* certain causal relationships. Such hypotheses usually involve making some assumption about one or more of the four relevant variables. One hypothesis known as the **naive version of the quantity theory of money** states that there is a direct causal link running from the quantity of money to prices. According to this theory, changes in the money supply affect prices only, not real GNP or the velocity of circulation. In a static world with both V and Q constant (the velocity of circulation and real GNP being determined by forces other than the quantity of money), changes in M can have only one result—to change the price level. Specifically, according to the naive version, a 10 percent increase in M will *cause* a 10 percent increase in the level of prices.

In a dynamic world where both V and Q grow over time—the growth of V the consequence of ever-improving cash management practices, and the growth of Q the consequence of labor force growth and capital accumulation—a similar kind of relationship can be derived between the money supply and the price level. From the equation of exchange. MV = PQ, it can be shown that

$$\frac{\text{Percent}}{\text{change in M}} + \frac{\text{Percent}}{\text{change in V}}$$
$$= \frac{\text{Percent}}{\text{change in P}} + \frac{\text{Percent}}{\text{change in Q}}$$

If V rises at 3 percent per annum and Q grows at 4 percent—the growth of both V and Q being independent of the growth in M, according to the naive version—price stability will obtain (i.e., the percent change in the price level will equal zero) only with a money supply growth of 1 percent per annum. If M grows at 2 percent, so that MV grows at 5 percent, prices will rise by 1 percent; or, if the money supply remains fixed, the price level will *fall* by 1 percent per annum.

The optimum quantity of money, according to the naive version of the quantity theory, is easy to discover. It depends on what goal society establishes for the price level or the rate of change in prices. Indeed, according to this view, almost any quantity of money is enough to finance the volume of transactions associated with the full employment level of output. This is because real GNP is *not* determined in any way by the quantity of money; only the price level is affected. If the money supply is "small," the same real quantity of goods and services can be transacted as with a "large" money supply. The only difference will be the price level at which that *same* quantity is transacted.

More sophisticated modern versions of the quantity theory are less assertive than the naive version. It is no longer assumed that the velocity of circulation is determined independent of M. However, it is assumed that changes in V are highly predictable. Moreover, it is no longer assumed that the link between M and P is direct and exclusive. Rather, the hypothesized link is between M and nominal GNP, with the direction of causality running from M to PQ. This latter difference between the naive and modern versions is important because it suggests that changes in M affect real GNP. However, how any given change in PQ brought about by a change in M is *divided* between P and Q is frequently not specified. Nevertheless, proponents of the modern version maintain that changes in M can effect changes in Q only in the short run (though it should be emphasized that the short run can be two or three years or more). In the long run, the level of real GNP and its rate of growth are independent of M. This means that in the long run the direct link between M and P reasserts itself.

Most proponents of the **modern version of the quantity theory** believe in the efficacy of wage and price adjustments in the long run to bring about full employment. This is in line with the thinking of the classical economists. Accordingly, in the long run, almost any quantity of money will be optimum, as the naive version implied. Not so in the short run.

To illustrate the short-run problem, consider the dilemma that has faced policymakers for the past several years. Inflation has been running at about 10 percent per annum. To adherents of the quantity theory of money, inflation can be licked only by slowing the growth of the money supply. However, any abrupt slowing in the growth of money would risk throwing the economy into a severe recession, the consequence of the adverse effects of slower money growth on real output. Accordingly, many quantity theory proponents argue for a *gradual* slowing in the growth of money to permit the economy to make the necessary *real* adjustments that can and do come about only gradually. As is apparent, the quantity of money that is optimum from a "short-run" perspective is much different from the optimum longer-run quantity.

There are, of course, competing theories of money. Critics of the quantity theory argue that changes in M influence real output in both the short run and long run. They argue that changes in V are much less stable and less predictable than the quantity theorists would have us believe. And they also argue that causality runs from nominal GNP to M, as well as from M to nominal GNP. Under these circumstances, determining the optimum quantity of money is much more complicated.

It is not our intent to try to sort out all of these differences between the quantity theorists and their critics in this chapter. This we will attempt to do in Chapters 11 and 14. What is important to recognize here is that the determination of the optimum quantity of money—the amount of money sufficient to finance the level of transactions associated with full employment—depends in large measure on what theory of money is correct. No hard and fast rules can be established until the differences between the different schools of thought have been resolved. This, as we will see, is not easy to do.

A final note on the optimum quantity of money. Throughout this discussion we have implicitly assumed that the appropriate definition of money was M1. This need not be the case, a point that should by now be clear given the different views regarding which assets ought to be included in the aggregate called "money." However, more is at issue here than mere definitional matters. If one of the monetary aggregates is closely and predictably related to nominal GNP, there is no reason to conclude that any of the other aggregates will be as closely related. This point reinforces an idea alluded to earlier—namely, that each aggregate may be more important for some purposes that others. Moreover, it cautions against trying to generalize on the basis of a single measure of money.

The value of money

The values of most goods and services are usually expressed in terms of the number of dollars they can fetch. A six-pack of beer may be worth $3, whereas a pair of fancy shoes is worth $150. Reverse these relationships and one can discover the value of money. Its value is given by the quantity of goods and services each dollar will buy. If the prices of all goods and services doubled, then each dollar could buy one half of what it bought before. *The value of money is inversely related to the general price level:* the higher the level of prices, the less a given amount of money is worth. Put differently, *the value of a dollar is given by 1/P.*

It is therefore clear that, in order for money to have a stable value, the general level of prices must be stable. And since a stable value for money is an important characteristic of a generally acceptable medium of exchange, price stability figures prominently in the determination of the optimum quantity of money.

Proponents of the naive version of the quantity theory would argue that the attainment of price stability is easy—stabilize the money supply. Proponents of the more modern version of the quantity theory, on the other hand, would argue that the road to price stability is nowhere near so clear-cut as simply stabilizing the quantity of money—at least that would not necessarily give us price stability in the short run. On this point, their critics would agree. These issues will be examined at length in Chapter 14.

Should the money supply be backed? A related matter concerns the question of whether the money supply should be "backed" by gold, silver, or other precious items—that is, whether the quantity of money in circulation should be fixed by the amount of the precious items that the government guarantees money to be convertible into. Two important issues are raised here. First, many advocates of backing argue that the quantity of money should be based on items that have *inherent* or *intrinsic* value. Most economists reject this proposition, emphasizing that there is nothing intrinsic about the value of, say, gold; its value, like the value of other goods and services, is determined by the forces of demand and supply. Rather than let the quantity of money be fixed by the amount of the precious metal in the hands of the government, we should instead seek that quantity that is optimal from the point of view of the realization of our nation's productive potential. There is no guarantee that the quantity of gold would yield the "correct" money supply; it could be too small or too large. To adherents of the naive version of the quantity theory, "too large" or "too small" make no sense since, no matter what its quantity, only the price level and *not* the quantity of real output will be different. However, to adherents of the modern version of the quantity theory and other theories of money—hypotheses that enjoy much stronger empirical support than the naive version—"too large" and "too small" are alarming possibilities. If the money supply were too small, we would be forced to operate at a position of less than full employment; if it were too large, it could ignite inflation. Moreover, given that the bulk of the world's gold production is mined in the USSR and South Africa, converting to a system where those two countries could so materially affect our economic well-being is not generally viewed as highly desirable.

The reason many people advocate a return to the **gold standard**—a standard that formally enshrines the convertibility of money into gold—is to stop government from recklessly increasing the money supply and adding to inflation. Few would disagree with this objective. However, not everyone would agree that all increases in the money supply are reckless or inflationary. Nor would everyone agree that linking the money supply tightly to gold would necessarily ensure a stable quantity of money. A major new gold discovery, for example, would cause the money supply to swell sharply with possibly very harmful effects on the economy. Or, if we were forced to settle payments deficits with foreign nations in gold, a sharp, abrupt reduction in the quantity of money could result, to the detriment of production and employment domestically.

In the United States and most countries of the world, the money supply is not backed. The quantity of money in circulation is determined in large measure by the central bank—in the United States, by the **Federal Reserve System.** Frequently, this nonbacked money is described as **government fiat money.** It is money because the government tells us that it is money. Actually, this view is not entirely accurate. True, government has the exclusive authority to mint coins and to print paper currency; and true, government can declare currency and coin to be **legal tender,** which means that, to government, they are a legally acceptable and enforceable means of discharging debts. However, whether the currency and coin issued by government function as forms of money will be determined *not* by government fiat but by their general acceptability by the public. Indeed, as the experience of Germany after World War I illustrates, if government prints so much "money" that it becomes "worthless" (due to the hyperinflation ignited by inordinately large, ever-increasing supplies), it will lose its quality of general acceptability and cease to function as money.

Moreover, although it is possible to imagine the government issuing orders to the effect that various kinds of deposits at depository institutions are legal tender, it has not done so. Yet the bulk of the money supply known as M1 consists of checkable deposits at depository institutions. True, these deposits are convertible into government-issued currency and coin that do enjoy legal tender status. However, there are many deposits that are not generally acceptable as mediums of exchange that also are convertible into currency and coin. It is not obvious, therefore,

what convertibility to currency and coin means in this context.

In any event, at the heart of the debate over the question of whether the money supply should be backed is the issue of confidence in government officials to conduct monetary policy in a responsible manner. Many people do not trust government officials to perform in a responsible manner—which, in the context of our earlier discussion, means that they do not trust government officials to produce the optimum quantity of money. They want, therefore, to remove from those officials the discretionary flexibility to change the money supply. Backing the money supply is viewed as an effective means of accomplishing that goal. However, as we saw earlier, there are no guarantees that backing the money supply would produce the optimum quantity of money or that the quantity produced would be stable. Under the circumstances, government has decided in favor of an approach that entrusts to government officials the responsibility of ensuring that monetary policy is conducted responsibly. Admittedly, there are flaws in this system. But a policy of rigidly backing money with gold is also flawed. Nevertheless, a return to some form of gold standard is apparently strongly supported by some high level officials in the Reagan administration. Whether much will come of this support is, at this writing, an open question.

THE U.S. FINANCIAL SYSTEM

The major portion of the U.S. money supply is supplied by private financial institutions. Taking M1 as the basic measure of money, we note that about one half of this aggregate is composed of demand deposits at commercial banks. A smaller but rapidly growing portion of M1 consists of other checkable deposits at banks and **thrift institutions** (savings and loan associations, mutual savings banks and credit unions). Thus, a basic understanding of how money is provided to the economy requires a discussion of these institutions and of the agency responsible for regulating them and the money supply—the Federal Reserve System.

The Federal Reserve System

The Federal Reserve System—commonly referred to as *the Fed*—is the nation's central bank. The Fed was established by the Federal Reserve Act of 1913 in the wake of the financial panic of 1907; it was restructured by the *Banking Acts of 1933 and 1935* and the *Depository Institutions Deregulation and Monetary Control Act of 1980*. The Fed is charged with the responsibility of controlling the money supply for the good of the nation and of overseeing the U.S. financial system.

Structure of the Fed. The Fed is structured something like a pyramid. At the top sits the Board of Governors. Next is the **Federal Open Market Committee (FOMC).** Below these are the 12 district Reserve Banks. At the base are the member banks and other depository institutions.

Board of Governors of the Federal Reserve System. This is without question the most powerful group in the Federal Reserve System. For all intents and purposes, it is the Board that has final say in all regulatory matters involving the banking system and in the conduct of monetary policy.

The Board consists of seven members, each of whom is appointed by the president, subject to Senate approval, for a term of 14 years. Governors can serve only one full 14-year term, though they may serve a partial term (completing the term of a former governor) in addition. The governors' terms are relatively long and each is appointed rather than elected. This assures some degree of independence from partisan politics. The terms are staggered—with one appointment every two years—so as to provide continuity of membership. The chairman of the board—frequently described as "first among equals"—is appointed by the president to serve in that capacity for four years; the chairman may be reappointed.

The Board meets regularly in Washington, D.C., and exercises a wide range of decisionmaking authority on questions involving monetary policy and bank regulation. The Board sets **reserve requirements**—that is, specifies the reserves that financial institutions must hold against various types of deposits. It has the authority to approve or disapprove changes in the rates of interest (**"discount rates"**) charged by the regional Federal Reserve Banks on loans made to financial institutions. It has the responsibility to regulate certain types of credit (such as the credit extended for purchasing stocks and bonds). It has the authority to approve or disapprove bank mergers. It specifies and enforces a wide range of regulations dealing with appropriate banking and credit practices. Finally, since the Board has 7 of the 12 seats on the Federal Open Market Committee, the monetary policymaking organ of the Federal Reserve System, it has de facto control over the conduct of monetary policy as well.

Federal Open Market Committee (FOMC). **Open market operations**—the purchase and sale of securities in the open market by the Fed—are the principal means by which the Federal Reserve System attempts to implement national monetary policy. It is the job of the Federal Open Market Committee (FOMC) to set the basic objectives of monetary policy—such as the growth rates of the money aggregates—and to decide on how open market operations should be conducted to achieve these objectives.

There are 12 members of the Federal Open Market Committee. The seven members of the Board of Governors constitute a majority; the other five members are drawn from the presidents of the 12 regional banks. One of these—the president of the Federal Reserve Bank of New York—is a permanent member of the committee. The presidents of the other 11 banks fill the remaining four slots on a rotating basis, each term lasting one year. By tradition, the committee "elects" the chairman of the Board of Governors as its chairman and the president of the Federal Reserve Bank of New York as its vice chairman.

The Federal Reserve Banks. When the Federal Reserve Act was passed in 1913, its framers were anxious to prevent the concentration of too much authority in the hands of a single centralized agency. The dispersion of power regionally was considered important. The failure to strike the correct regional balance had been a major stumbling block in previous efforts to establish a national central bank. Accordingly, as a compromise solution, Congress established not one but 12 regional Federal Reserve Banks. Initially, considerable power was vested in the regional banks. However, as a consequence of the restructuring that took place through the Banking Act of 1935, the regional banks lost much of their power to the Board of Governors in Washington, D.C. What remained with the regional banks was the authority to carry out the day-to-day operations of the Federal Reserve system—an important function, but one that is nonetheless subject to the overall directive of the Board of Governors.

The regional banks are located in various cities around the country; several of the regional banks have branches. The boundaries of the Federal Reserve districts are shown on the map in Figure 9.2, along with the locations of the regional banks and their branches.

The regional banks are essentially privately owned institutions set up to implement the policies and directives of the Board of Governors and the Federal Open Market Committee. Those commercial banks that are members of the Federal Reserve system must hold shares of stock of the Federal Reserve Bank in their district.

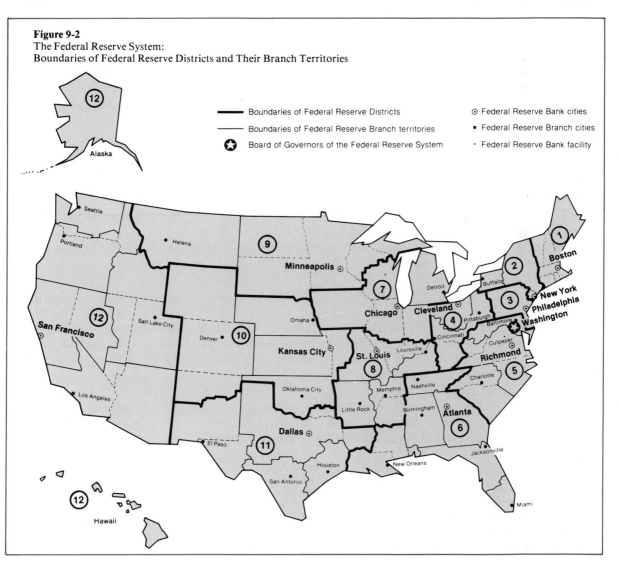

Figure 9-2
The Federal Reserve System:
Boundaries of Federal Reserve Districts and Their Branch Territories

The directorship of each regional bank is divided among representatives of its member banks, representatives of the nonbanking community that are elected by member banks, and others (also nonbankers) that are appointed by the Board of Governors. Under the overall supervision of the Board of Governors, the board of directors of each regional bank oversees its operations. Each board of directors decides on the interest rates its regional bank will charge on loans to financial institutions; these decisions, however, are subject to approval by the Board of Governors.

Functions of the Federal Reserve System. Together, the Board of Governors, the FOMC, and the regional banks provide several critical services to the financial community and to the federal government. Clearly the most important of these is the *regulation of the money supply.* This is achieved through a variety of mechanisms that have already been mentioned—reserve requirements, loans from regional banks to financial institutions, and, most significantly, open market operations. The Federal Reserve Bank of New York occupies a preeminent position in the regulation of money because it is at this regional bank that open market operations are executed. That is, the FOMC at its regular meetings issues what is called the **open market directive.** That directive provides instructions to the New York Federal Reserve Bank regarding how the FOMC's policies are to be carried out. More will be said about all of these policy tools in Chapter 10.

Another responsibility of the Federal Reserve System is to ensure *an adequate supply of paper currency.* Thus, since all the paper currency in the United States today consists of **Federal Reserve Notes**—paper currency issued by all 12 Federal Reserve Banks—depository institutions in each district look to their regional bank to supply them with the currency they need to meet customer withdrawals. Is the paper currency simply given to the depository institutions in whatever quantities they need or want? No. Depository institutions maintain accounts at their regional Federal Reserve Bank much like the accounts you and I maintain at depository institutions. When depository institutions want more currency to meet their customer demands, they draw down their accounts at the Fed and receive in exchange the currency they asked for. If the currency in the vaults of the depository institutions increases as a consequence of customer deposits, the depository institutions can rid themselves of what they do not need by sending the currency to their regional bank in exchange for an increase in their accounts there.

The regional Federal Reserve Banks also act essentially as *bankers for depository institutions;* the Fed is the "bankers' bank." Not only do depository institutions hold funds on deposit at the Fed, but the Fed also loans funds to those same depository institutions. However, although this banking function is analagous to the function that depository institutions play for individual households and businesses, there is one important difference. These depository institutions are required by law to maintain deposits at the Fed to satisfy the Fed's reserve requirements; more on this in Chapter 10.

Another important function the Fed performs is **check clearing.** The reason check-clearing operations are required is easy to see. There are literally tens of thousands of different depository institutions in the United States. When checks are drawn on one institution and deposited with another, some easy means must be found to settle the resultant claims among those institutions. When one considers that there are hundreds of millions of such claims that have to be settled daily, the magnitude of the chore the Fed must perform is truly mind-boggling. Actually, the methods used are really very straightforward, as we will see in Chapter 10.

One other very important purpose served by the Federal Reserve System is to *supervise the activities of financial institutions,* principally those commercial banks that are members of the system—the so-called **member banks.** By law, all commerical banks operating under *national* charters are required to join—become members of—the Federal Reserve System. Banks under state charter can elect to join; about 10 percent have chosen to do so. The lending and deposit-taking activities of member institutions are subject to review by the Federal Reserve to ensure that they conform to the Fed's guidelines for sound banking practices.

Until recently, membership conferred certain advantages, including access to check-clearing facilities and the right to borrow from the Fed. However, these benefits were purchased at the cost of having to hold higher proportions of deposits on reserve in cash or in non-interest-bearing accounts at the Fed. The opportunity cost represented by the interest on these reserves remained relatively low until the mid-1960s, when interest rates began to rise; as rates drifted upward, more and more banks left the Federal Reserve System. Partly in response to this trend, Congress passed the Depository Institutions Deregulation and Monetary Control Act of 1980. This law, among other things, requires uniform reserve requirements for all depository institutions, regardless of whether or not they are members of the Federal Reserve system. In addition, this act eliminated the most significant differential benefits of membership by permitting all depository institutions the right to borrow from the Fed and to have access to the Fed's check-clearing facilities.

Finally, the Federal Reserve System acts as a bank for the U.S. Treasury. It often deals as an agent of the Treasury with foreign governments and foreign central banks on international monetary matters. In short, the Federal Reserve is a central bank in every sense of the term.

Interestingly, in performing its functions as a central bank, the Federal Reserve earns a profit on its operations. That is, the income it receives on its assets more than covers the Fed's costs of operations. However, unlike other financial institutions, the Federal Reserve does not seek to maximize its profits. Indeed, the portion of the Fed's earnings that is not used to defray costs is returned each year to the Treasury Department.

Other financial institutions

We now turn our attention to the private financial institutions, which collectively supply the economy with not only two thirds of its money supply but many other financial services as well. Indeed, it is the provision of *financial* services rather than the production of *physical* goods or services of a nonfinancial nature that sets financial institutions as a whole apart from other business enterprises. Examples of financial institutions include such diverse organizations as commercial banks, savings and loan associations (S&Ls), mutual savings banks (MSBs), credit unions, money market mutual funds, insurance companies, mortgage companies, finance companies, and others—the list goes on. All of these institutions have in common the fact that they accept deposits (i.e., borrow funds) from individuals or business firms and then turn around and lend these funds to other people or organizations. In this way they act as go-betweens; they act as **financial intermediaries.**

Of all the types of intermediaries, we shall concentrate primarily on those issuing checkable deposit accounts or close substitutes for such accounts. These are the institutions that are intimately involved in the money supply process to be discussed at length in Chapter 10. They include commercial banks, savings and loan associations, mutual savings banks, credit unions, and money market mutual funds.

Historically, these financial institutions were classified into two groups—commercial banks on the one hand, and other depository institutions (or "thrifts") on the other. This distinction was based in large measure on the fact that commercial banks were the only institutions authorized by law to issue checkable deposits. However, as a consequence of financial innovations and regulatory changes that led to the development of NOW accounts, ATS accounts, share draft accounts, and money market mutual funds, this distinction between financial institutions became blurred and progressively outmoded. The death blow to this distinction came in 1980 in the form of the Depository Institutions Deregulation and Monetary Control Act of 1980.

The Depository Institutions Deregulation and Monetary Control Act of 1980. No discussion about modern-day financial institutions can go very far without a review of the basic provisions of the Depository Institutions Deregulation and

Monetary Control Act of 1980 (also known as the Monetary Control Act, or MCA). Many regard this act as the most significant and far-reaching piece of banking legislation since the 1930s. Generally, the act removes or diminishes the differences among institutions with regard to the deposits they can offer, the interest they can pay, the reserves they must hold, and the access they have to Federal Reserve services. Other parts of this law relate to such diverse areas as the loan and investment powers of nonbank depository institutions, state usury laws, truth in lending, simplification of financial regulation, foreign control of U.S. financial institutions, and various amendments to previous banking laws. Let us examine some of these features.

Deposit issuing authority. In this area the new law formally sanctioned and extended the development of new checkable deposits that had been occurring since 1972. NOW accounts, which had first appeared in Massachusetts and New Hampshire in 1972, and which had been authorized on a piecemeal basis to other northeastern states, were extended to banks and all other depository institutions nationwide effective January 1, 1981. The law also permitted credit unions to offer share draft accounts—instruments similar to NOW accounts—and banks to offer automated transfer service (ATS) accounts, whereby funds are automatically transferred from interest-bearing savings accounts to ordinary, noninterest-bearing checking accounts when checks are presented to banks for payment. The net effect of these and other related provisions was to make it easier for individuals and nonprofit organizations (the account holders to whom these actions principally applied) to earn interest on funds held for transactions purposes. It also permitted more competition between commercial banks and other institutions in attracting those funds.

Interest rate ceilings on deposits. The 1980 act also provided for a six-year phaseout of interest rate ceilings on time and savings accounts at banks and other depository institutions. These ceilings were first imposed in 1933, in the midst of the Great Depression, in the wake of large numbers of bank failures. Under the authority

of **Regulation Q**—popularly called "Reg Q"—the Federal Reserve instituted ceiling rates on *commercial banks* to induce them to follow more sensible and sound lending policies. The notion was that interest rate competition among banks for deposits had caused interest rates to increase; to cover these costs, so it was argued, banks were led to make increasing numbers of higher-yield, higher-risk loans. When many of those risky ventures failed, borrowers defaulted. This caused banks holding large amounts of these risky loans to fail.

At best, the rationale for imposing ceiling rates was a dubious one; no one has ever successfully demonstrated that bank competition was responsible for higher interest rates, or that banks, as a consequence of higher interest costs, would load up their loan portfolios with high-risk ventures. Nevertheless, the ceilings persisted.

The existence of ceiling rates was not all that important until the early and mid-1960s. Prior to that time, actual rates paid to depositors were almost always less than the ceilings. And, if rates did move up to press against the ceilings, the Federal Reserve Board would raise them a notch, removing the constraint. The problems with ceiling rates really started in the early 1960s. During those years, open market interest rates often moved above the ceiling rates imposed on commerical banks, forcing deposit rates up to the ceiling. Savings and loan associations and mutual savings banks, however, were not constrained by ceilings. During the periods when ceiling rates were effective in limiting rates paid by commercial banks, thrift institutions would offer their depositors just a little bit more. This put commercial banks at a competitive disadvantage. Accordingly, they would press for further upward adjustments in the ceiling rates, which usually were accommodated. But once open market rates moved above the new ceilings, the problem with the thrift institutions would recur.

However, there was a limit to how much the thrifts could increase their interest rates in the short run. The reason? The loan portfolios of savings and loan associations and mutual savings banks consisted largely of home mortgages. Home mortgages are long-term loans and, at that time, virtually all such loans were granted at fixed rates of interest. Therefore, when interest rates rose, these thrift institutions were able to raise their lending rates on *new* mortgage loans only. But new mortgages made up only a small fraction of their total loan portfolio. Therefore, their overall rate of return—the rate of return on both old and new mortgages—moved up much more slowly than did open market rates. This outcome constrained these institutions from raising the interest rates they could pay to their depositors. By about 1965, so the thrift industry argued, they had reached the upper limit of what they could pay.

Under pressure from the thrift industry, Congress in 1966 extended the ceiling rates to savings and loan associations and mutual savings banks. Congress also made the important move of establishing an interest rate differential that favored the thrift institutions—that is, ceiling rates on thrift deposits were set above the ceiling rates on commercial bank deposits. It was hoped that the interest rate differential would ensure a flow of funds through the thrift institutions to the housing market.

As expected, the commercial banks complained bitterly about the ceiling rate differential, arguing that it put them at a distinct competitive disadvantage. They did get some relief in the early 1970s when the ceiling rates on large-denomination time deposits were first relaxed, then eliminated altogether. The banks wanted more; the regulatory officials, at first, were reluctant to give more.

In any event, it soon became apparent that the ceiling rates were not serving their intended purpose—namely, to ensure a supply of funds to housing. The problem was this. Suppose open market rates rose above even the thrift ceiling rates? What would depositors do? They would have a tendency to withdraw their funds from *both* commercial banks and the thrifts and to place those funds into higher-yielding open market assets. This is exactly what happened in 1966, 1969, and 1974 when, as a consequence of explosive increases in open market interest rates, the funds for housing literally dried up. This phe-

nomenon—of depositors withdrawing funds from both the thrifts and commercial banks, and placing those funds directly in higher-yielding instruments—was called **disintermediation** to reflect the fact that, at very high interest rates, the ceiling rates on deposits encouraged people to lend directly to ultimate borrowers rather than indirectly through the financial intermediaries. Because the housing market suffered badly during periods of disintermediation, the case for retaining ceiling rates was weakened considerably.

The question Congress and the regulators faced was how to get rid of ceiling rates. To eliminate them all at once would impose severe burdens on the thrift institutions, whose loan portfolios were largely frozen by mortgage loans granted in periods when interest rates were low. The same kind of problem did not plague the commercial banks because the bulk of their loan portfolios have always been decidedly shorter in nature. Because their loans turned over much more rapidly, they were in a better position to raise their interest rates as open market rates rose.

At first, regulators chipped away at the ceiling rate problem by permitting depository institutions to offer instruments not subject to ceilings or that had ceiling rates well above those that applied to instruments that were subject to Reg Q-type ceilings. Therefore the ceiling rates on large-denomination time certificates were eliminated altogether in 1973. This was followed years later by other changes, the most important of which was the introduction of the six-month money market certificate in June 1978, followed one year later by the 2½-year small saver certificates. These instruments—particularly the money market certificates—proved so popular that they diminished sharply the effectiveness of ceiling rates. By transferring funds to these instruments, people were able to get around the restrictive ceilings. Of course, people who did not have $10,000 (the minimum for the six-month money market certificate) or who could not tie up their funds for 2½ years were largely left out; ceiling rates continued in effect for them. By 1986, the ceilings will be gone.

Reserve requirements. The monetary control portion of the 1980 act establishes, for the first time, Federal Reserve requirements on the deposits of *all* depository institutions rather than, as formerly, just banks that are members of the Federal Reserve System. Such requirements provide an important lever for the Fed to control the money supply. However, as noted before, member banks had been leaving the Federal Reserve System in increasing numbers throughout the 1970s as ever-higher interest rates raised the opportunity cost of holding reserves. The imposition of uniform reserve requirements, to be phased in over an eight-year period, thus removes an important but arbitrary difference between member banks and other financial institutions offering similar and in some cases identical services.

Access to Federal Reserve services. Finally, the new act equalizes financial institutions in another important dimension—their access to Federal Reserve services. Specifically, upon passage of the legislation in March 1980, all depository institutions were granted the privilege of borrowing from the Federal Reserve "discount window" and given access to check-clearing and other services facilitating the transfers of funds between banks.

In time, these and other parts of this extensive piece of legislation are expected to diminish the differences among various types of financial institutions. Nevertheless, it is useful in our description of the financial system to organize our discussion along the traditional lines of classification.

Commercial banks. In spite of recent financial innovations and regulatory changes, commercial banks are still the most versatile and, as a group, the largest of the depository institutions. Thrift institutions, however, have been steadily narrowing the gap. As of early 1981 (March), there were 14,447 domestically chartered commercial banks in operation with over $1.5 trillion in assets. Of these banks, 4,443 were nationally chartered; the remainder were state-chartered. A total of 5,444 banks, including (by law) all those with national charters, were Federal Reserve System members; these institutions held about 70 percent of total bank assets. As indicated earlier in this chapter, however, legal changes in 1980 had rendered Federal Reserve System membership largely meaningless. By size, 216 banks held assets of more than $1 billion, while 13,882 had less than $250 million.

Banks extend loans for a wide variety of purposes, including short-term business investment and inventory holding, consumer financing of automobiles and other durables, mortgages, agricultural finance, and many other activities. In this respect, they differ significantly from most other depository institutions, whose loans tend to be more restricted in purposes and recipients. However, the Monetary Control Act and other recent legislation have liberalized such restrictions somewhat. Banks also invest a significant proportion of their assets in securities, both of the U.S. Treasury and of private business firms, and hold the remainder as reserves against their deposits or as working balances.

The funds obtained for these purposes come from a wide variety of sources. Commercial banks accept deposits, from individuals and corporations alike, in several forms—ordinary checking accounts, other checkable deposits such as ATS and NOW accounts, savings deposits, and a host of small certificates of deposit (in amounts less than $100,000) ranging from terms of three months to eight years or more. All but the standard checking accounts pay interest. Aside from the funds in these accounts, which generally are deposited and withdrawn at the initiative of the customer, commercial banks actively seek funds through a number of devices collectively known as **managed liabilities.** These include large certificates of deposit (those issued in denominations of $100,000 or more), federal funds purchases, repurchase agreements, and Eurodollar liabilities.

Thrift institutions. The term *thrift institutions* is commonly applied to three types of financial institutions—savings and loan associations, mutual savings banks, and credit unions. All three originated as organizations designed primarily as outlets for the liquid savings of individuals and as sources of credit either for home purchase (in the case of savings and loans and mutual savings banks) or the financing needs of their own depositors (credit unions). As time passed, however, these institutions generally have become more diversified in both their sources and uses of funds; this diversification has been most apparent in the 1970s. The liberalization of certain restrictions on these institutions in recent legislation can be expected to foster continued diversification.

Of the three, **savings and loan associations** are by far the largest in terms of total assets, with 4,535 associations holding nearly $650 billion in June 1981. Savings and loans receive most of their funds from individuals and businesses in the form of small time and savings deposits, although in recent years they also have become more aggressive in searching out funds, as banks do through money market instruments. About four fifths ($515 billion) of their assets are invested in mortgages; the remainder are held primarily in U.S. government securities and other liquid assets. One of the principal provisions of the 1980 financial institutions legislation was to loosen existing restrictions on savings and loans to give them broader investment powers.

Mutual savings banks are quite similar to savings and loan associations in terms of their deposit-taking and lending activities. About 460 savings banks, located mostly in the Northeast, held $175 billion in total assets in the middle of 1981. In comparison to savings and loan associations, mutual savings banks, all of which are state-chartered, have more flexibility in their investment powers, with authority to purchase corporate bonds as well as mortgages. Nevertheless, by tradition, they have placed well over half of their assets in home mortgages. On the deposit side, these institutions tend to rely less on managed liabilities. But they pioneered the way in many states for the development of NOW accounts.

Like the other thrifts, **credit unions** obtain their funds largely (indeed, almost exclusively) from small time and savings deposits. These institutions are unique in that credit union depositors and loan customers must be drawn from a group of individuals sharing some specifically defined "common bond" (generally their place of work).

This restriction has kept credit unions relatively small and localized; there are about 22,000 of them holding $74 billion in total assets as of June 1981. The common bond requirement also has prevented credit unions from tapping the sources of funds available to other depository institutions. Nevertheless, they have participated in recent financial innovations by offering share draft accounts. Traditionally, they used their funds primarily to make installment loans to their members. But more recently they have gained authority to extend mortgage credit as well.

Money market mutual funds. No description of financial institutions important to the money supply process would be complete without a discussion of money market mutual funds. These organizations first appeared in 1971. In the span of one decade they garnered over $150 billion in assets—more than twice as much as the credit unions during their entire existence. Growth was especially rapid in the late 1970s and early 1980s. Their importance in the context of this chapter derives from the characteristics of the shares they offer their customers. For minimum amounts, generally ranging from $1,000 to $2,500, individuals and business firms can buy shares in these funds that are highly liquid and that earn rates of interest generally quite a bit higher than most standard deposit accounts. These interest rates vary from day to day and week to week, depending on the investments that the funds make with the money so deposited. These investments are in a wide variety of so-called money market instruments, about which we have more to say below. What makes the shares in these funds so attractive, apart from their interest, is that the money placed in them can be retrieved quickly, frequently by a check in the amount of $500 or more.

MONEY AND CAPITAL MARKETS

To function efficiently in channeling savings into productive investments, the economy needs both institutions to act as financial intermediaries and markets in which financial assets can be bought and sold. Such markets—known collec-

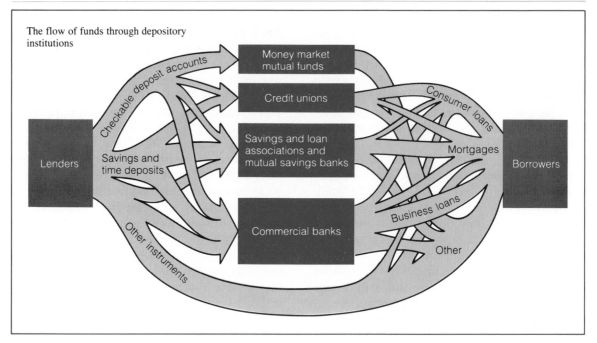

The flow of funds through depository institutions

tively as **money and capital markets**—facilitate the exchange of these assets for money and therefore enhance their liquidity. Many of these markets have been referred to explicitly or implicitly in our discussion of financial institutions. In this section we describe them briefly, concentrating primarily on the money markets that financial institutions use frequently in their daily operations.

Money markets. The term *money markets* is used to describe a set of markets for assets of fairly short maturities. The term arises from the fact that many financial intermediaries and other business enterprises (and occasionally individuals) use these markets as a way to obtain a quick return on funds they do not need immediately. They are thus an important factor in the **reserve management** decisions of financial institutions, as well as in the **cash management** strategies of corporations that want to maximize the return on their temporarily idle funds.

Money markets have evolved rapidly in the past 20 years or so. Historically, the first money market of any significance was the **federal funds market.** This market originated in the 1920s as a means by which commerical banks with excess

reserves could lend to other banks with reserve deficiencies to satisfy their reserve requirements. Reflecting this purpose, trades were arranged for overnight or a few days at the most. The rate seldom, if ever, exceeded the Federal Reserve's discount rate (the rate of interest charged by the Federal Reserve on its loans to depository institutions); and the volume of funds traded in any given day fluctuated depending on the overall supply of reserves to commercial banks as a whole. For the first 40 years of its life, the federal funds market retained its essential character. The volume of trading expanded only gradually, reaching an estimated $2 to $3 billion per day during the early 1960s. However, beginning in the mid-1960s, the federal funds market broadened as other money markets developed and as banks began to use this market for more than strictly reserve adjustment. Eventually other institutions began to participate. The market grew many times over (to well over $100 billion per day in 1980), with transactions occurring at rates more reflective of conditions in other related markets. Nevertheless, the federal funds market is still predominantly a market among banks and other financial institutions. It is primarily a source of overnight money, and one whose course is highly affected by the supply of reserves relative to requirements.

One of the most important innovations in the development of money markets was the issuance of large-denomination time **certificates of deposit (CDs)** by Citibank (then First National City Bank of New York) in 1962. These instruments, issued in denominations of $100,000 or more, proved to be a convenient way in which corporations could hold funds temporarily in an interest-bearing form. They quickly became quite popular. Maturities were arranged at the mutual convenience of the bank and the corporation. A key feature was that most of them were negotiable; that is, they could be sold to a third party prior to maturity. Needless to say, a market soon developed, making these instruments highly attractive liquid assets. However, throughout the 1960s, CDs were subject to federal interest rate ceilings, a feature that limited their usefulness in attracting funds during periods when other rates were higher. In the early 1970s, the ceilings were suspended and the growth of this market was assured.

A third market that has developed in recent years involves **security repurchase agreements,** known for short as either RPs or "repos." A repurchase agreement is an arrangement whereby one institution (say, a bank) obtains funds by selling a security, such as a U.S. government security, to another institution or corporation, agreeing to buy it back at a prespecified price and time in the future. This market has grown rapidly since its beginning in the late 1960s, when the interest rate limits on CDs induced many banks to offer their corporate customers RPs instead.

The market for short-term U.S. government securities, known as **Treasury bills,** also qualifies as a money market, because banks, financial institutions, and corporations can purchase and resell these items easily and at relatively little risk of loss. Indeed, individual investors can also participate in this market if they have $10,000 or more; other markets generally require considerably more. One such market is for **commercial paper,** or corporate short-term debt, which usually is issued in denominations of $25,000 or more.

Finally, there are **Eurodollars,** which are deposits held in financial institutions located overseas but denominated in U.S. dollars. At times, these obligations have been an important source of funds for banks, particularly as an alternative to deposits on which reserves were required. In fact, from time to time, the Federal Reserve has found it necessary to impose reserve requirements on Eurodollars as well, in order to improve its control over credit flows in the U.S. economy.

Capital markets. In addition to the money markets, there are markets in a number of long-term securities. These include mortgages, U.S. Treasury notes and bonds, obligations of state and local governments, corporate bonds, and corporate stocks. Banks and depository institutions are important participants in many of these markets; indeed, thrift institutions, as already noted, are the major suppliers of mortgage credit. Investments in these and other long-term instruments are generally undertaken to generate income over some period of time, rather than as a means of managing reserves. This is because of the risks associated with selling these securities on short notice for cash.

SUMMARY

1. *Money* performs several functions. It is the *unit of account,* the *medium of exchange,* and a *store of value.* Conflicts between the store of value and medium of exchange functions of money create problems as far as the definition of the term *money* is concerned. Changes in the regulatory environment and financial innovations can and do change the definition of money.

2. It is important that there be enough money in circulation to finance the volume of transactions that permits the full realization of our nation's productive potential, the full employment level of output. Exactly how this should be translated into policy is a matter of considerable debate. The *equation of exchange* provides us with a framework for discussing this debate.

3. According to the *naive version of the quantity theory,* almost *any* quantity of money will

be the optimum quantity, depending on the goal society establishes for the price level or the rate of change of prices. The *modern version of the quantity theory* asserts that "almost any quantity" is valid in the long run only. Critics of the quantity theory, on the other hand, argue that changes in the amount of money in circulation (M) influence real output in both the short run and long run. They argue that changes in the velocity of circulation (V) are less stable and less predictable than the quantity theorists believe. And they argue that causality can also run from GNP to M. Given these differing views, it is clear that determining the optimum quantity of money is very complicated.

4. The *value of money* is determined by how much it will buy. In general, the value of a dollar is given by 1/P, where P is a measure of the general price level.

5. Most economists reject the notion that the money supply should be "backed" by gold, silver, or other precious items. Backing does not guarantee that there will be just the *right* amount—the optimum amount—at all times. Indeed, it is possible to envision haphazard changes in the money supply under a *gold standard.*

6. The *Federal Reserve System* is the nation's central bank. The Fed is structured like a pyramid. At the top sits the *Board of Governors,* the most powerful group in the Federal Reserve System; next is the *Federal Open Market Committee* (FOMC), the monetary policy making organ of the Fed; third comes the 12 regional Federal Reserve Banks; and finally, there are the member and nonmember depository institutions.

7. The most important function of the Federal Reserve System is the regulation of the money supply. In addition, the Fed has the responsibility to ensure an adequate supply of paper currency. It acts as a banker for depository institutions. It performs check-clearing operations for depository institutions. It supervises the activities of financial institutions. And it acts as a bank for the U.S. Treasury.

8. Many regard the Depository Institutions Deregulation and Monetary Control Act of 1980 as the most significant and far-reaching piece of banking legislation since the 1930s. The new law

formally sanctioned and extended the development of checkable deposits: NOW accounts were authorized nationwide; credit unions were permitted to offer share draft accounts; and commercial banks were authorized to offer automated transfer service (ATS) accounts. This act provided for a six-year phaseout (by 1986) of interest rate ceilings on time and savings accounts at banks and other depository institutions. It established uniform reserve requirements on the deposits of all depository institutions. And it equalized financial institution access to Federal Reserve services.

CONCEPTS FOR REVIEW

Money

Unit of account

Medium of exchange

Store of value

Barter economy

Coincidence of wants

Currency and coin

Checkable deposits
    Demand deposit accounts
    Negotiable order of withdrawal (NOW) accounts
    Automated transfer service (ATS) accounts
    Share draft accounts

Monetary aggregates
    M1, M2, M3, L

Liquidity

Savings deposits

Money market mutual fund shares

Overnight RPs

Term RPs

Overnight Eurodollar deposits

Term Eurodollars

Large-denomination time deposits

U.S. Savings Bonds

Commercial paper

Federal funds

Optimum quantity of money

Equation of exchange

Naive version of the quantity theory of money

Modern version of the quantity theory of money

Value of money

"Backing" money

Gold standard

Government fiat money

Legal tender

Thrift institutions

The Federal Reserve System

Board of Governors of the Federal Reserve System

Federal Open Market Committee (FOMC)

Reserve requirements

Discount rates

Open market operations

Open market directive

Federal Reserve Notes

Member banks

Depository Institutions Deregulation and Monetary Control Act of 1980

Commercial banks

Savings and loan associations (S&Ls)

Mutual savings banks (MSBs)

Credit unions

Money market mutual funds

Insurance companies

Mortgage companies

Finance companies

Financial intermediaries

Regulation Q ("Reg Q")

Ceiling rate differential

Disintermediation

Discount window

"Managed liabilities"

Money and capital markets

U.S. Treasury bills

QUESTIONS FOR DISCUSSION

(Those marked with an asterisk (*) are more difficult.)

1. Explain how conflicts between the store of value and medium of exchange functions of money make it difficult to arrive at a single definition of money, and therefore at a single monetary aggregate.

2. "Demand deposits do not pay interest; NOW accounts offer less than 6.0 percent interest. In the face of 10 percent inflation, neither asset is a good store of value. True, the NOW account is a better store of value than the demand deposit. But the 'real' return on both is negative. Neither asset, therefore, can be considered 'money.' " Carefully evaluate. (*Hint:* Review again the definition of *money*. In addition, what effects, if any, will the elimination of interest rate ceilings have in this regard? Be explicit.)

3. If money is not "backed," and if the cost of producing money is almost zero (after all, how much does it cost to print a $1,000 bill?), then what determines the value of money?

4. Using numerical examples, show why the naive version of the quantity theory of money implies that almost any quantity of money will be sufficient to finance the volume of transactions associated with the full employment level of output.

*5. Explain carefully what is meant by "disintermediation" and the circumstances under which it can occur. Will disintermediation cease altogether once interest rate ceilings are eliminated? (*Hint:* Suppose interest rates rise very sharply. What will happen to those institutions whose loan portfolios are largely frozen because of mortgages issued in prior years?)

*6. More and more financial institutions are offering "variable rate mortgages." The interest rate charged to the homeowner on these mortgages can vary substantially over the life of the loan—rising or falling with movements in interest rates on the open market. How would your answer to Question 5 be affected by the existence of these mortgages? Be explicit.

Chapter 10

Credit expansion and contraction

In this chapter we undertake an analysis of how the instruments of monetary policy are used to effect changes in the volume of credit in our economic system. The question of how monetary policy affects the level of economic activity will be addressed in Chapter 11.

We begin our analysis with an examination of the processes of credit expansion and credit contraction in the U.S. financial system. In order to keep the discussion manageable, we start by making the following simplifying assumptions:

1. The public's holdings of currency are fixed at some constant level independent of the size of the other components of the money supply.
2. All noncheckable deposits—for example, non-ATS passbook savings accounts, small time (certificates of) deposits, and large-denomination time deposits—are likewise assumed to be fixed in size at some constant level.
3. Other components of the broader M2 and M3 definitions of money, such as money market mutual fund shares, Eurodollars, and RPs, are also assumed to be constant.

What these assumptions enable us to do is to focus our attention on changes in the money supply brought about by changes in the volume of checkable deposits alone. Moreover, it is clear by these assumptions that a *change* in M1, which we will use as our basic measure of money, is identical to the *changes* in M2 and M3. All components of these money supply aggregates have been assumed constant except checkable deposits. For the moment at least, we can talk unambiguously in terms of a change in "the money supply" without having to make distinctions among M1, M2, and M3. We will, of course, modify these assumptions as the analysis proceeds.

CREDIT EXPANSION AND CONTRACTION: A FIRST APPROXIMATION

Let us look at the processes whereby the public increases and decreases its holdings of checkable deposits. In order to facilitate the analysis, we will make use of a concept developed in Chapter 4—the **T-account.** The T-account simply shows the *change* in the balance sheet position of the economic unit under consideration. A balance sheet, as you will recall, displays the assets, liabilities, and net worth of the economic unit. By convention, assets are arrayed on the *left-hand side* of the balance sheet, liabilities and net worth on the *right-hand side.* Since the difference between assets and liabilities is the net worth, the balance sheet must add to the same total on both sides.

Money creation via loans

The simple act of acquiring a loan from a depository institution creates money. This is easily illustrated. Suppose you want to borrow $5,000 from a commercial bank to purchase a new car. You go to the bank and fill out an application form. If your loan is approved, you may return to the bank, sign the required forms, and leave with $5,000 more in your checkable deposit account. This process illustrates the most common method by which money is created. The loan for $5,000 is tantamount to the *creation* of $5,000. Why? Because prior to the granting of the loan, you had less purchasing power; after the loan is granted, you have $5,000 in additional purchasing power, and nobody else has any less. (We will qualify this statement later.) The T-account below illustrates the process in greater detail:

YOUR BANK

Assets		Liabilities	
Loans	+5,000	Checkable deposits	+5,000

The loan granted by your bank is an asset from the point of view of the bank. The bank has a claim on you to the extent of the loan plus interest. On the other hand, the $5,000 in your checkable deposit account is a liability of the bank. It promises to pay that amount to you or to the legitimate bearer of a check written by you, on demand. This balancing of assets and liabilities is reflected in the bank T-account.

As a result of this $5,000 loan, the money supply has been increased by $5,000. Checkable deposits are up by $5,000 with no offsetting reduction in any other component of the money supply. And, of course, as the loan is being paid off, money is being destroyed. You pay off the loan by writing checks against your checkable deposit; corresponding to the reduction in your liability to the bank there is a reduction in the volume of checkable deposits. Money is destroyed. In this manner, money is continuously being created and destroyed. As each new loan is granted, money is being created; and as loans are paid off, money is being destroyed.

Money creation via bank financial investments

Loans are not the only means by which money is created. *Money is created each time a depository institution purchases a bond from a member of the public.* To illustrate, suppose Zenith National, a commercial bank, purchases a $50,000 U.S. government bond from Ms. Aberdeen through its broker. The bank will issue a check for $50,000 payable to its brokerage house, and the brokerage house, in turn, will write a check for $50,000 payable to Ms. Aberdeen. Ms. Aberdeen will then deposit this check in her checkable deposit account. (To keep the example simple we will suppose that Ms. Aberdeen maintains her checkable deposit account with Zenith National.) As a result of these transactions, Zenith National will end up holding $50,000 more in its portfolio of bonds, and its checkable deposits will have increased as well. This increase in checkable deposits constitutes an increase in the money supply. The following T-account summarizes this fact.

ZENITH NATIONAL

Assets		Liabilities	
U.S. government bonds	+50,000	Checkable deposits	+50,000

Symmetrically, commercial bank sales of securities to members of the public reduce the money supply. Can you explain why this is so?

The deposit expansion potential: The volume of reserves and the reserve requirement

Depository institutions earn interest income on their loans and financial investments. They therefore have a strong incentive to expand their loans and financial investments until it ceases to be profitable to do so. However, if profitability were the only factor limiting the volume of deposit expansion, an almost unlimited increase in the money supply could result. Since it is virtually costless to create money in this way—"by the stroke of a pen"—banks would continue to expand their loans and financial investments as long as the interest rate payable to checkable deposit customers was less than the interest return on loans and financial investments. But long before this point was reached, money *as we have defined it,* would probably cease to be generally acceptable as a medium of exchange. Inflation would be so rampant that money would become worthless. There are historical examples that lend support to this view. During the hyperinflation in Germany after World War I, it was a common sight to see people scurrying from their place of work to stores carrying their money in large baskets hoping to buy goods that day—any goods!—before another 200 to 300 percent markup the following morning. If they left their basket of money unattended for a moment, it was likely that someone would steal the basket and leave the money!

In most economies today, it is not the potential profitability of loans and financial investments that limit the expansion of the money supply. On the contrary, *the deposit expansion potential is limited by the volume of reserves in the financial system and the reserve requirement.* This is easily illustrated.

All depository must maintain a certain level of **reserves** for a given level of checkable deposits. The required amount of reserves is determined by the **reserve requirement.** If the reserve requirement is 20 percent (0.20), then 20 cents of reserves must be maintained for every dollar on deposit in a checkable deposit account. If the bank has $100,000 in checkable deposits, it must maintain $20,000 in reserve assets.

What constitutes a reserve asset? *In the Federal Reserve System, reserve assets take two forms—the currency and coin that depository institutions keep in their vaults (so-called **vault cash**) and the deposits of depository institutions at the Federal Reserve Banks.* If the vault cash of all depository institutions amounted to $10 billion, and if their deposits at the Fed totaled $40 billion, total reserves in the U.S. banking system would add up to $50 billion.

What volume of checkable deposits can be supported by these $50 billion of reserve assets? That is, what is the maximum amount of deposits that can exist when there is $50 billion in reserves? It depends on the reserve requirement. If the reserve requirement is 20 percent, each dollar of reserves can support $5 of deposits. Therefore, $50 billion of reserves can support $250 billion of deposits. What would the deposit potential have been if the reserve requirement had been 0.25 instead of 0.20? $200 billion. Since each dollar of reserves can then support only $4 of deposits, $50 billion of reserves can support only $200 billion of deposits.

In general, the checkable deposit potential can be figured quite simply by dividing the volume of reserves by the reserve requirement. Letting R denote total reserves and r_r the reserve requirement on checkable deposits, this conclusion can be represented symbolically as

$$\text{Checkable deposit potential} = \frac{R}{r_r}.$$

Total reserves, required reserves, and excess reserves

There is, of course, no necessary reason why the volume of checkable deposits should exactly equal its potential at all times. Sometimes deposits will be less than their potential, sometimes (though infrequently) more. If the volume of deposits is less than its potential, **excess reserves** will exist in the financial system; if more, a **reserve deficiency** will exist.

To illustrate, suppose checkable deposits amount to $150 billion. With a reserve requirement of 20 percent, *required reserves* will be $30 billion (0.20 × $150 billion). If total reserves amount to $40 billion, there will be *excess reserves* of $10 billion—$10 billion in excess of what is required. Those excess reserves can, therefore, be used to support a volume of checkable deposits in excess of the current $150 billion. How much more? Since each dollar of reserves can support $5 in deposits, $10 billion of excess reserves can support an *additional* $50 billion of deposits. Letting R^e represent the volume of excess reserves, this can be written generally as

$$\text{Potential change in deposits} = \frac{R^e}{r_r}.$$

On the basis of the above discussion, it is clear that a given volume of reserves can support a multiple of checkable deposits, and that the existence of excess reserves can lead to a multiple expansion of deposits, the multiple in either instance being determined by the value of the reserve requirement. For this reason, the system has been dubbed a **fractional reserve system;** reserves are but a fraction of the potential volume of checkable deposits. But note that, *although the system of depository institutions has the capability of expanding checkable deposits by a multiple of the system's excess reserves, an individual depository institution can prudently expand its deposits* (via loans and financial investments) *only by the amount of its excess reserves, not by a multiple of those excess reserves.* This is a further illustration of a concept we have encountered repeatedly before—the fallacy of composition: What may be true for an individual entity may not be true for the whole. Before illustrating this idea, however, it is necessary that we familiarize ourselves with the **check-clearing process,** as it is essential to our understanding.

The check-clearing process

There are more than 40,000 financial institutions in the United States eligible to offer checkable deposits, and every day **payers** with accounts in these institutions write checks to **payees** located all over the country. The check-clearing process is concerned with how the ownership of deposits is transferred from the payer to the payee.

If the payer and the payee maintain deposits at the same depository institution, the process of transferring ownership is very simple. The institution merely increases the deposit of the payee and reduces by like amount the deposit of the payer. But if the payer and the payee maintain deposits at different depository institutions, the process becomes more complicated. The payee's bank acquires a claim against the payer's bank, and some means must be developed to transfer ownership of deposits from the payer's bank to the payee's bank. This function is performed by a **clearinghouse.**

The clearinghouse function is undertaken at three different levels—local, intradistrict (i.e., within the same Federal Reserve district), and interdistrict (i.e., between Federal Reserve districts). Let us examine each of these in turn.

Local clearinghouse. Depository institutions in the same locality have found it in their interest to form a local clearinghouse, which is nothing other than an association of local depository institutions whose purpose it is to clear deposit balances between local members. Daily, representatives from each of these depository institutions bring checks drawn on all of the other local depository institutions to the clearinghouse; the claims of each are netted out and only the residual claims are actually transferred. Generally, settlement is made through the district Federal Reserve Bank. The example presented in Table 10.1 illustrates the process.

Suppose the local clearinghouse consists of four depository institutions—A, B, C, and D. On the day in question, representatives from these institutions bring a total of $133,000 in claims against each other. Clearinghouse personnel then net these claims. Thus A brings claims of $10,000, $16,000, and $14,000 against B, C, and D, for a total of $40,000; B's, C's, and D's claims against A amount to $23,000; A has, therefore, a net claim of $17,000. Similarly, depository institution C has a net claim of $8,000. B and D, on the other hand, register *negative* net claims of $5,000 and $20,000, respectively. The clearinghouse then sends a wire to the dis-

Table 10.1

A local clearinghouse: A summary of a day's transactions

Claims of	Claims against				
	Depository institution A	Depository institution B	Depository institution C	Depository institution D	Total
Depository institution A	—	$10,000	$16,000	$14,000	$ 40,000
Depository institution B	$ 6,000	—	13,000	9,000	28,000
Depository institution C	14,000	12,000	—	18,000	44,000
Depository institution D	3,000	11,000	7,000	—	21,000
Total.................	$23,000	$33,000	$36,000	$41,000	$133,000

A presents claims totaling $40,000 against B, C, and D; claims against A total $23,000. Thus A has a net claim of $17,000 at the clearinghouse. C has a net claim of $8,000 ($44,000 − $36,000).

In the cases of B and D, claims against them exceed the value of their claims by $25,000—by $20,000 in the case of D, by $5,000 in the case of B.

trict Fed instructing it to increase A's account by $17,000 and C's account by $8,000, and to reduce B's and D's accounts by $5,000 and $20,000, respectively. Note that the combined increase in A's and C's accounts matches exactly the reductions in B's and D's. The T-account summarizing this transaction at the district Fed is as follows:

DISTRICT FED

Assets	Liabilities
	Depository institution A deposits +17,000
	Depository institution B deposits −5,000
	Depository institution C deposits +8,000
	Depository institution D deposits −20,000

Note one very important conclusion that emerges from this example. Deposits of depository institutions at the Fed constitute part of the reserves of the Federal Reserve System. Thus, A and C experience an increase in their reserves while B and D experience an offsetting decrease. Moreover, since the reserve gains by A and C are exactly offset by the reserve losses of B and D (as they must), total reserves within the system are unaltered; only the ownership of those reserves has changed.

Intradistrict check clearing. If the payer and the payee maintain deposit balances in different depository institutions in different localities within the same Federal Reserve district, the district Fed will be responsible for clearing the check. Suppose the payer maintains an account at Zenith National while the payee has an account at Acme Federal, both in the same Federal Reserve district.

The payer writes a check payable to the payee for $10,000. The payee deposits the check in Acme Federal. Acme Federal sends the check to the Fed for payment (i.e., clearing). The Fed increases Acme Federal's balance and reduces that of Zenith National. When Zenith National receives the check back from the Fed, it reduces the payee's balance by $10,000. These transactions are summarized below.

Zenith National

Reserves	−10,000	Payer's checkable deposit	−10,000

District Fed

		Zenith National deposits	−10,000
		Acme Federal deposits	+10,000

Acme Federal

Reserves	+10,000	Payee's checkable deposit	+10,000

Note again that the reserve losses of Zenith National are completely offset by the reserve gains of Acme Federal leaving total reserves unchanged.

Interdistrict check clearing. When the payer and the payee hold accounts in depository institutions in different Federal Reserve districts, the Federal Reserve System uses its own clearinghouse facility known as the **Interdistrict Settlement Fund,** where all 12 Federal Reserve Banks maintain accounts. The payee's depository institution submits the payer's check to its district Federal Reserve Bank; that bank in turn submits it for payment (i.e., clearing) to the Interdistrict Settlement Fund; its account at the fund is increased and that of the other district bank is reduced. The net result of these transactions is the same as before. The payer's deposit balance is reduced and the payee's is increased; the reserves of the payer's depository institution are reduced while the reserves of the payee's depository institution are increased.

So much for the mechanics of check clearing. Let us now resume our discussion of the process of deposit expansion in a system composed of thousands of depository institutions.

Loan expansion: A single depository institution versus the system of depository institutions

To see how the system of depository institutions creates money, consider a system consisting of three depository institutions only: University National, American Liberty, and Patriotic Appeal. We assume first that all depository institutions except Patriotic Appeal are initially "loaned up"; second, the reserve requirement on checkable deposits is equal to 0.20.

Suppose Patriotic Appeal has $1,000 in excess reserves. With a reserve requirement of 0.20, can Patriotic Appeal grant loans of $5,000? No! Prudently, it can grant loans only in the amount of its excess reserves—namely, $1,000. Let us show why.

Suppose Patriotic Appeal lends $1,000 to Honest Ed, a used-car dealer who intends to use the money to buy paint and (used) tires for some

of the automobiles on his lot. The loan assets of Patriotic Appeal will increase by $1,000 and checkable deposits will increase by a like amount, reflecting the newly approved credit to Honest Ed's account. Thus,

Patriotic Appeal

Loans	+1,000	Checkable deposits	+1,000

Note two matters at this point:

1. The money supply has been increased by $1,000.
2. Patriotic Appeal's excess reserves are now only $800; as a result of the $1,000 increase in checkable deposits, $200 of the excess were converted to required reserves (i.e., 0.20 × $1,000 = $200).

What happens when Honest Ed spends his money? The dealers who sell paint and tires will deposit Ed's check in *their* accounts. Suppose these dealers have their accounts at American Liberty. After American Liberty receives the checks, they are ultimately forwarded, via the Fed, to Patriotic Appeal. This results in the following T-account transaction.

Patriotic Appeal

Reserves	−1,000	Checkable deposits	−1,000

American Liberty

Reserves	+1,000	Checkable deposits	+1,000

Note several matters at this point:

1. The decline in checkable deposits at Patriotic Appeal is offset by the deposit gains at American Liberty. This second-stage set of transactions, therefore, does not lead to any changes in the money supply.
2. Patriotic Appeal loses $1,000 in reserves to American Liberty; total reserves are therefore unchanged.
3. Patriotic Appeal is now "loaned up"; its required reserves fall by $200 as a result of

the $1,000 reduction in checkable deposits. This as well as the $800 that it had as excess reserves is lost to American Liberty.

4. American Liberty now has $800 in excess reserves. Its total reserves went up by $1,000, but $200 of those are required to support the $1,000 increase in its checkable deposits.

Let us go on. Suppose American Liberty lends $800—its excess reserves—to Charlie Duzit. This would cause the following changes in American Liberty's T-accounts:

American Liberty

Loans	+800	Checkable deposits	+800

This transaction causes the money supply to be increased by *another* $800. Additionally, American Liberty's excess reserves are reduced to $640. The reason? The $800 increase in checkable deposits increases American Liberty's required reserves by $160 (i.e., 0.20 × $800 = $160).

Suppose Charlie uses the money to purchase carpeting for his home. The carpet dealer deposits $800 in University National; University National, via the Fed, sends the check to American Liberty for payment. The following T-accounts summarize these transactions:

American Liberty

Reserves	−800	Checkable deposits	−800

University National

Reserves	+800	Checkable deposits	+800

Again, note the results of these transactions:

1. The decline in checkable deposits at American Liberty is offset by the deposit gains at University National. The money supply is unaltered by this transaction.

2. American Liberty loses $800 in reserves to University National. Total reserves are unaltered.

3. American Liberty is now "loaned up." Do you know why? (*Hint:* Calculate the reduction in required reserves caused by the deposit transfer plus the loss of excess reserves.)

4. University National now has excess reserves totaling $640. Why is this so?

University National is therefore in a position to make new loans—that is, to create more money. A $640 loan by University National will cause checkable deposits and the money supply to expand by *yet another* $640. That will eventually make possible further increases in the money supply. As the $640 lent out by University National is spent, other institutions will receive new reserves, thereby increasing their lending capacity. What will be the ultimate increase in the money supply made possible by the initial $1,000 of excess reserves? Given a reserve requirement equal to 0.20, the potential increase is $5,000. This is summarized in Table 10.2.

The reason it is prudent for any individual depository institution to extend loans only by the amount of its excess reserves is now clear. *Given the existence of more than 40,000 different depository institutions, there is little likelihood that a check written by any one depositor will be redeposited with the same institution.* When bank A uses its excess reserves to extend a loan to Mr. Jones, it is not likely that the recipient of the check written by Mr. Jones will redeposit the check in bank A. As a result, bank A will

Table 10.2
Money creation potential in a system of many depository institutions

	Initial excess reserves = $1,000 Reserve requirement = 0.20		
Bank	Loans	Change in money supply
Patriotic Appeal	$1,000	$1,000
American Liberty	800	800
University National	640	640
Depository Institution E	512	512
Depository Institution F	409.60	409.60
.	.	.
.	.	.
.	.	.
Total	$5,000	$5,000

lose reserves in an amount equal to Mr. Jones' check to some other depository institution; the excess reserves of bank A will be eliminated via the clearing process. This does not limit the lending potential of the *system* of depository institutions, since the reserves lost by bank A are acquired by some other depository institution. But the lending potential of bank A has been reduced dramatically.

In our earlier example, Patriotic Appeal initially had $1,000 in excess reserves. It extended a $1,000 loan to Honest Ed, leaving it with $800 of excess reserves. However, after the clearing process, Patriotic Appeal was left with no excess reserves. If Patriotic Appeal had lent more than $1,000, it would have had fewer reserves when the clearing process was completed than it was required to have in order to support its existing checkable deposits.

The deposit expansion potential:
An alternative presentation

There is an alternative, more appealing way of examining the deposit expansion potential of the system of depository institutions that is analogous to our discussion of the multiplier in Chapters 7 and 8. Given a reserve requirement of 20 percent, the loans granted on each "round of lending" are 80 percent of the loans extended on the previous round. Patriotic Appeal's initial loan amounted to $1,000. On the second round of lending, American Liberty granted a loan equal to $800—80 percent of the initial $1,000 loan. On the third round, University National loaned $640—80 percent of $800. By the end of the third round, then, the money supply had been increased by $2,440 (i.e., $1,000 + $800 + 640). In general, the ultimate potential change in the money supply can be expressed as:

$$
\begin{aligned}
&\text{Ultimate potential change in the money supply} \\
&\quad (1) \qquad (2) \qquad\qquad (3) \\
&= (\$1,000) + (0.8 \times \$1,000) + (0.8^2 \times \$1,000) \\
&\qquad\qquad\qquad\qquad (n) \\
&\quad + \cdots + (0.8^{n-1} \times \$1,000) + \cdots.
\end{aligned}
$$

Factoring out the $1,000 figure, we get

$$
\begin{aligned}
&\text{Ultimate potential change in the money supply} \\
&= \$1,000\,(1 + 0.8 + 0.8^2 + 0.8^3 \ldots) = \frac{1}{1 - 0.8}.
\end{aligned}
$$

This latter result is referred to as the **checkable deposit expansion multiplier.** And since $(1 - 0.8) = 0.2$ is nothing other than the reserve requirement on checkable deposits, the checkable deposit expansion multiplier can be generally expressed as:

$$
\text{Checkable deposit expansion multiplier} = \frac{1}{r_r}.
$$

Given a checkable deposit expansion multiplier of 5 (i.e., $\frac{1}{1 - 0.8} = \frac{1}{0.2} = 5$), $1,000 of excess reserves can support a $5,000 increase in the volume of checkable deposits and the money supply. It is clear, moreover, that the checkable deposit expansion multiplier varies inversely with the reserve requirement. A reserve requirement of 0.25 would imply a checkable deposit expansion multiplier value of 4.

The federal funds market

The example above showing how a given volume of excess reserves can lead to a multiple increase in the volume of deposits and money is a little unrealistic. It implies that no loan expansion will take place unless and until Patriotic Appeal grants its initial loan, and that no subsequent loan expansion will take place until the various depository institutions down the line receive deposits and make loans. What if Patriotic Appeal discovers no creditworthy customers clamoring for loans? Does this mean that the loan expansion process cannot get started? Suppose some other depository institution did have creditworthy customers seeking loans, but had no excess reserves. If they could have access to Patriotic Appeal's excess reserves, the loan demand could be met. Or consider another possible problem. Because of an excess of claims generated via the clearing process—referred to as an **adverse clearing drain**—a depository institution finds itself with a deficiency in its reserves. The *total volume* of deposits within the entire system may not be too large relative to the total volume of reserves, but this institution is deficient. If access could be had to Patriotic Appeal's excess reserves, the deficiency could be eliminated.

These possibilities create a strong incentive on the part of depository institutions to develop a mechanism whereby the excess reserves of some depository institutions can be lent to those who have deficient reserves or who have loan demands that cannot be met with their own existing reserves. There is, in fact, such a mechanism. It is called the **federal funds market.** In that market, institutions that want to lend their excess reserves do so by granting *overnight* loans to institutions seeking additional reserves. The rate of interest paid by the borrowing institution to the lending institution for the use of those reserves is called the **federal funds rate.** Obviously, the higher the rate, the higher the cost of borrowing. We shall see later that Federal Reserve policies, by affecting the supply of reserves, can have a substantial effect on the federal funds rate.

The federal funds market is not the only means whereby depository institutions can acquire the additional reserves that they want or need. They can sell off some of their holdings of U.S. government securities, acquiring the desired reserves through the clearing process. Because of the ease with which this can be accomplished, bank holdings of U.S. government securities are often referred to as **secondary reserves.** However, at times, depository institutions may be reluctant to sell off these securities, especially if the sale results in a capital loss—that is, selling securities at prices below their original cost. The federal funds market is often a preferred alternative.

In addition, depository institutions that want to acquire more reserves can often do so by borrowing them from the Fed through the so-called **discount window.** But some banks are reluctant to use the discount window, especially if they are already heavily indebted to the Fed, and the Fed at times openly discourages its use. Because of these problems, the federal funds market offers an avenue that is often preferred. We shall have more to say about this market in Chapter 11. What is important for our purposes here is that, with the existence of a federal funds market, the

expansion process associated with a given volume of excess reserves can occur even if the excess reserves may not initially be located in the "right" place.

THE TOOLS OF MONETARY POLICY AND THE DEPOSIT EXPANSION POTENTIAL

It is obvious, on the basis of the above considerations, that the deposit expansion potential is determined by two factors—the volume of reserves and the reserve requirement. An increase in the volume of reserves and/or a reduction in the reserve requirement will increase the deposit expansion potential; the converse is of course also true. Herein lies the key to our understanding of the principles underlying the tools of monetary policy.

There are three main tools of monetary policy—**open market operations, the discount rate,** and **the reserve requirement.** Each tool is used by the Fed to alter the deposit expansion potential of the system of depository institutions. Open market operations and the discount rate affect that potential by changing the volume of reserves; the impact of a change in the reserve requirement is obvious from our preceding examples. Let us consider each tool in turn.

Open market operations

Open market operations are by far the most dominant and flexible tool of monetary control. These operations involve nothing more than *the purchase or sale of U.S. government securities by the Fed in the (open) securities market.* In large measure, it is the Federal Open Market Committee (FOMC) that takes responsibility for determining the types of operations to be undertaken; the actual buying and selling is done by the so-called **trading desk** of the Federal Reserve Bank of New York through a network of private securities dealers.

Through its open market operations, the Fed is able to alter the volume of reserves in the financial system. If the Fed wants to expand reserves, it will engage in an **open market purchase**—buying U.S. government securities in the open market. An **open market sale,** on the other hand, reduces reserves. Let us examine these activities closely.

Suppose the Fed deems it appropriate to expand system reserves by $1 million. The trading desk will then place bids for $1 million worth of U.S. government securities with its securities dealers. The open market purchase is completed when the Fed issues $1 million worth of checks to the securities dealers. These dealers, in turn, issue $1 million in checks to their customers who actually sold bonds. Once these checks are deposited, they will be sent to the Fed for "payment." The Fed pays by merely increasing the deposit balances of the depository institutions presenting the checks. Since such deposits at the Fed are part of the system's reserves, the volume of reserves is increased. The following T-accounts summarize these transactions.

Depository institutions

Reserves	+1 million	Checkable deposits	+1 million

The Fed

U.S. government bonds	+1 million	Depository institutions' deposits	+1 million

We have assumed here that all bond purchases by the Fed were made from individual households. Therefore, when these people deposit their checks for $1 million, the money supply is immediately increased by $1 million. Moreover, when the depository institutions present the checks to the Fed for clearing, reserves also go up by $1 million. Corresponding to the $1 million increase in the deposit liabilities of the Fed is a $1 million increase in its assets representing its increased holdings of U.S. government securities.

Note two points here:

1. Since checkable deposits rose by $1 million, not all of the increase in reserves are excess reserves. Indeed, if the reserve requirement on checkable deposits happens to be 0.10, required reserves will rise by $100,000, leaving $900,000 as excess reserves. That $900,000 of excess reserves can be used to support an additional $9 million in loans and deposits. Can you explain why?

2. All told, then, the $1 million increase in reserves associated with the $1 million open market purchase can support a $10 million increase in checkable deposits, assuming a 10 percent reserve requirement. With a reserve requirement of 20 percent, on the other hand, only $5 million worth of additional deposits could be supported.

Of course, not all bond sellers need be households. If instead, **depository institutions** are the ones from whom the Fed (indirectly) purchases its bonds, the following T-account transactions would be recorded:

Depository institutions

U.S. government bonds	−1 million	
Reserves	+1 million	

The Fed

U.S. government bonds	+1 million	Depository institutions' deposits	1 million

The only difference here is that all of the increased reserves are excess reserves since, as yet, there has been no increase in checkable deposits. Nevertheless, assuming a 10 percent reserve requirement, the $1 million hike in reserves can support a $10 million increase in checkable deposits and the money supply, as before.

An open market sale would have exactly the opposite result. A $1 million open market sale would reduce system reserves by $1 million. This means that the banking system could support $10 million less in checkable deposits than before—assuming, of course, a 10 percent reserve requirement. Can you illustrate these results?

The discount rate

All depository institutions issuing checkable deposits have "borrowing privileges" at the Fed.

If they exercise that privilege by borrowing, say, $500,000 from the Fed, system reserves will rise by $500,000, enabling a multiple expansion of deposits and the money supply. The converse happens when bank loans from the Fed are repaid. The **discount rate** is the rate of interest charged by the Fed on these loans; it is the cost of borrowing at the Fed. Loans from the Fed are secured by three types of collateral—U.S. government securities (or other debt guaranteed by the U.S. government); "eligible commerical, industrial, and agricultural paper" (i.e., promissory notes); and other securities deemed acceptable by the Fed. Most borrowing is secured by U.S. government securities. This is facilitated by the fact that many depository institutions keep their holdings of securities at the Federal Reserve Banks for safekeeping.

During the 1920s, the discount rate was considered *the* major tool of monetary control. The idea behind the use of this tool was really quite simple. During periods of economic expansion, when loan demand was strong, banks would send their promissory notes to the Fed to be "discounted"; in return, the banks would receive reserves on the basis of which new loans could be extended and the money supply would expand. During periods of economic slack, on the other hand, banks would send very few promissory notes to the Fed for discounting because loan demand was weak. Thus the money supply would be "elastic," rising or falling as dictated by the needs of the business community. The essential difficulty with this kind of monetary policy was that these kinds of elastic changes in the money supply—up during periods of expansion, down during recessions—could and did have disastrous implications for the economy as a whole. Such an elastic money supply policy is procyclical in nature, reinforcing swings in the level of economic activity rather than offsetting them. We shall analyze this issue in greater depth in the next chapter.

But even if discount rate policy were used by the Fed to effect countercyclical changes in the money supply, just how effective changes in the discount rate would be is a debatable proposition. Suppose the Fed lowers the discount rate

in an effort to increase system reserves. If commercial banks have a lot of excess reserves and are unable to find creditworthy customers who want to borrow, a lowering of the discount rate will not send them scurrying to the discount window to borrow more. If the banking system is nearly loaned up, on the other hand, a lowering of the discount rate might have a substantial impact. The impact depends, of course, on the relationship of the discount rate to other interest rates—that is, the relationship between the discount rate, as a cost of borrowing, and the rate of return depository institutions can get by using those funds to acquire financial investments or to make loans. The point is that the impact of a change in the discount rate on system reserves is not highly predictable.

In today's economic system, the Fed's discount policy is a relatively minor tool of monetary control—at least compared with the importance of open market operations. Many economists view the discount window as a "safety valve"; it enables depository institutions to borrow to meet either seasonal reserve deficiencies or those unexpected shortages that can arise as a result of adverse clearing drains. Borrowing at those times minimizes the disruptive influences of reserve shortages on their other asset holdings. Under this interpretation, the discount rate can be characterized as a "penalty rate," penalizing those banks that fail to manage their portfolios so as to avoid reserve deficiencies.

Like all privileges, the use of the discount window can be abused. Sometimes depository institutions borrow reserves simply because it is very profitable to do so. When reserves are not really in short supply, they may borrow reserves at a relatively low interest rate and use the proceeds to make loans or other financial investments at significantly higher rates of interest. Or, when there are reserve deficiencies that could be corrected by borrowing federal funds or liquidating secondary reserves, the use of the discount window may often provide a cheaper alternative. To prevent such abuses, the Federal Reserve often adjusts the discount rate to align it more closely with other interest rates. When increases in other interest rates give depository institutions a strong incentive to make greater use of the discount window, the Fed will frequently raise the discount rate in an effort to reduce this incentive. Such "technical adjustments" of the discount rate should not be interpreted as a sign that monetary policy has changed direction. Indeed, if the Fed did not adjust the discount rate upwards in the face of an upward movement in other interest rates, depository institutions would enlarge their borrowings and expand reserves, thereby enabling a multiple expansion of deposits. In a sense, the failure to raise the discount rate would be tantamount to the pursuance of a more expansionary policy.

For example, if the FOMC engages in open market sales as part of a contractionary policy, higher interest rates will often occur. Failure to raise the discount rate would encourage borrowing at the discount window, which would diminish, at least in part, the desired contraction in reserves. In an effort to forestall this increased borrowing, the Fed will frequently make an upward technical adjustment of the discount rate.

Although many adjustments in the discount rate are made simply to align that rate more closely with the other interest rates, announcements of such changes are often viewed in the pages of the financial press as signaling a change in the direction of monetary policy. Upward movements are interpreted as implying that the Fed intends to pursue a contractionary policy; downward movements imply an expansionary policy. In other words, discount rate changes have associated with them certain **announcement effects;** that is, such changes are frequently interpreted as tantamount to announcements by the Fed of a fundamental policy change. Obviously, if the Fed were really interested in announcing a policy change, there are certainly more efficient methods of accomplishing that goal than through a discount rate change. They could simply announce their intentions via press releases or news conferences. However, given the general secrecy that surrounds monetary policy formulation, financial observers seem willing to latch onto any change as reflecting a policy change and boldly interpret its implications.

It is precisely because of these alleged implica-tions that changes in the discount rate frequently send tremors throughout the financial community—sometimes good and sometimes bad. Because of the possible adverse consequences associated with announced changes in the discount rate, many economists have proposed that the discount rate be *pegged* to some other interest rate, such as the interest rate on Treasury bills. This would eliminate the need for periodic technical adjustments in that rate. It would also eliminate undesirable announcement effects. Some critics would go further. They would make the discount rate a "true" penalty rate by pegging it *above* the interest rate on Treasury bills. This would discourage many of the abuses of the discount window that exist currently.

The reserve requirement

It should be obvious by now how a change in the reserve requirement can affect the deposit lending potential. A *lowering* of the reserve requirement means that a given volume of reserves can support a larger volume of deposits. A reduction in the reserve requirement does *not* increase the total volume of reserves but alters only the proportion of the reserves that are required—in this instance, the proportion is reduced. Accordingly, a reduction in the reserve requirement causes, as its initial effect, an increase in excess reserves. The converse is true of an increase in the reserve requirement.

The reserve requirement is a powerful tool of monetary control. But, in a sense, it is *too* powerful a tool. Through a very small change in the reserve requirement, the Fed can achieve a rather significant change in the lending potential of the financial system. Such changes are not as flexible as open market operations for making the continuous day-to-day adjustments in the lending potential deemed necessary by the monetary authorities.

Some minor tools of monetary growth

The Fed is also able to affect the lending potential of the financial system through the use of a number of other tools. These other tools are minor by comparison with open market operations, the discount rate, and the reserve requirement. But at times their use can affect outcomes materially. These other tools consist of moral suasion and selective credit controls.

Moral suasion. Moral suasion is nothing more than "jawboning"—an attempt to persuade financial institutions that it is in their interests, or in the interests of the country, to pursue certain types of lending policies. Most often, moral suasion takes the form of policy statements or press releases by the Fed; on some occasions the Fed makes an outright appeal to certain institutions or to the financial community generally. If the Fed feels it is desirable to restrict lending somewhat but is reticent, for one reason or another, to use open market operations to bring about the desired result, it may appeal to the financial institutions to pull in their reins.

Historically, the importance of moral suasion as a tool of monetary control has varied considerably. It was used extensively by the Fed immediately after World War II and during the Korean conflict. This was largely because the Fed was unable to use open market operations in a way consistent with its goal of restricting credit to slow down the inflation rate. During that period, the Fed entered into an *accord* with the U.S. Treasury to keep interest rates down in order to minimize the interest costs of federal government borrowing to finance the U.S. war effort. But because the demand for credit was so high, this agreement required the Fed to pursue policies designed to expand reserves; otherwise, interest rates would have risen. The Fed had to resort to moral suasion to induce financial institutions to restrict credit voluntarily. Ever since the termination of the accord in March 1951, the Fed has used moral suasion much less frequently. It has relied for the most part on open market operations to bring about its objectives.

Selective credit controls. On occasion the Fed has placed selective restrictions on certain types of credit. At these times, the President, under enabling legislation by the Congress, has given wide-ranging authority to the Federal Reserve Board to restrict credit by such devices as minimum down payments and maximum re-

payment periods for loans for real estate and consumer durables. If the Fed wanted to curb spending on real estate, it could establish larger down payments and a shortened repayment period as a requirement for obtaining credit. Such requirements were used extensively during World War II and the Korean War, but very infrequently since. One notable exception was in 1980, when selective credit controls were applied to reduce growth in money and credit as part of an overall effort to slow inflation. Those controls were lifted a few months after they were instituted.

In addition, the Fed has the authority to specify the **margin requirement** for loans used to finance stock market purchases. The margin requirement establishes the percentage of the stock purchase that must be made in cash—that is, *not* loaned. A 75 percent margin requirement means that only 25 percent of the stock purchase can be financed via loans; 75 percent must be made in cash. By varying the size of this requirement, the Fed can either discourage or encourage loans for stock market purchases.

Finally, until very recently, the Fed had the authority, under **Regulation Q**—popularly called Reg Q—to establish the maximum or ceiling rates that member banks could pay on their savings and time deposits. Other financial regulatory agencies—the Federal Home Loan Bank Board, for example—exercised similar authority for nonmember banks and other depository institutions. The Depository Institutions Deregulation and Monetary Control Act of 1980 consolidated this authority in a Depository Institutions Deregulation Committee (composed of all the major financial regulatory agencies). The act also mandated the phaseout of rate ceilings over a six-year period, to be completed by 1986.

CREDIT EXPANSION AND CONTRACTION: SOME COMPLICATIONS

Given our previous discussion, it would appear that determining the deposit expansion potential of the system is a relatively simple matter.

Once the volume of excess reserves and the reserve requirement are known, the deposit expansion potential can be calculated readily as the ratio of excess reserves to the reserve requirement. The simplicity of this calculation, however, is the direct result of the assumptions we made at the outset of this chapter. If the assumptions are removed, the analysis becomes more complicated. Let us now analyze the implications of eliminating these assumptions.

Currency holdings

We began this chapter by assuming that the public's holdings of currency were fixed at some constant level independent of the size of other components of the money supply. What happens to the deposit expansion potential if people do alter their holdings of currency? Let us examine this one step at a time. Suppose people decide to reduce their currency holdings by $2 million, increasing their checkable deposits by a like amount. What effect will this have? After people have deposited their currency, the following T-account transaction will be recorded.

Depository institutions

Vault cash	+2 million	Checkable deposits	+2 million

Has the money supply been changed? No! Checkable deposits have increased by $2 million *but* people's holdings of currency and coin have been reduced by $2 million. The money supply has not changed; only its composition has changed. But note that *the deposit of currency has increased the volume of system reserves.* Why? Because the deposit of currency increases vault cash, and vault cash constitutes part of the system's reserves. The increase in vault cash obtained in this way therefore enables a further multiple expansion of loans and deposits.

Symmetrically, the withdrawal of currency by the public reduces reserves. The volume of deposits that can be supported is thereby reduced. Can you explain why?

This relationship between the public's holdings of currency and the volume of reserves is highly significant because it illustrates one way the behavior of the public affects the deposit expansion potential of the financial system. Although deposits and withdrawals of currency do not affect the money supply *directly,* they do alter the volume of system reserves and thereby the volume of deposits and money that can be supported. *A currency withdrawal reduces the lending potential precisely as a Fed open market sale does; a currency deposit has an effect analogous to an open market purchase.*

As a result of these facts, the Fed must keep a close eye on currency deposits and withdrawals in formulating its policy. The Fed and the depository institutions have virtually no control over the public's holdings of currency. But changes in those holdings that affect the deposit expansion potential in ways deemed undesirable by the Fed can be offset by an appropriate policy change. To illustrate, suppose the Fed wants to expand the deposit expansion potential of the financial system; this will usually be accomplished via an open market purchase. However, if at the same time the public is in the process of reducing its holdings of currency, system reserves will rise even further. If the desired increase in the deposit expansion potential is to be reached, the magnitude of the open market purchase deemed appropriate by the Fed will have to be smaller than otherwise. Indeed, if currency deposits are large enough, the Fed may have to engage in an open market *sale* in order to avoid too rapid an increase in system reserves. Here, an open market sale would be perfectly consistent with the Fed's objective of expanding the deposit expansion potential of the financial system

Of course, the Fed would like to be able to predict in advance changes in the public's holdings of currency. This would enable the Fed to formulate its policies more precisely. In this respect, Fed researchers have had only limited success. They have been able to identify some systematic variations in the public's holdings of currency. But considerable unsystematic and as yet unexplained variations still remain. In general, *the public's holdings of currency tend to vary seasonally and with the general level of economic activity.* During the last few months of the year (around Christmas), there tends to be a sharp upswing in the public's holdings of currency, sometimes by as much as $4 billion or more. Then, in the first few months of the following year, an equally sharp decline occurs. The Fed is quite cognizant of this fact and can easily offset these movements if it so desires through open market operations.

Additionally, it is well documented that *the public's holdings of currency are strongly influenced by the level of income, rising and falling as the level of income rises and falls.* These changes are regularly accounted for in the formulation of Fed policy.

Since changes in the public's holdings of currency alter the volume of system reserves, and since the Fed adjusts its policies in accordance with these changes, monetary economists have devised a very useful concept called the **monetary base** (or, as it is sometimes called, **high-powered money**). This concept is defined as *system reserves plus currency and coin in the hands of the public.* Letting B represent the monetary base, R represent reserves, and C represent currency in the hands of the public, this relationship can be written symbolically as

$$B = R + C.$$

The importance of this concept derives from the fact that the money supply is more closely related to the monetary base than to the volume of reserves. In order to maintain a money supply target, the Fed will engage in policies designed to increase the volume of reserves by more or less, depending upon whether the public is withdrawing or depositing currency. Reserves tend to fluctuate by more than the monetary base; there is, therefore, a more stable relationship between the money supply and the monetary base than between the money supply and reserves.

The deposit expansion multiplier and the public's holdings of currency.[1] There is a relatively simple way of capturing the impact of changes in the public's holdings of currency on the deposit

expansion potential of the financial system—namely, through the deposit expansion multiplier. Suppose, for simplicity, that people desire to hold 5 cents in currency for every dollar they have in checkable deposits. Then, if deposits expand by $100, currency holdings will rise by $5. What is important to recognize here is that the $5 increase in currency holdings implies a $5 reduction in the reserves of the financial system. *Just as an expansion of checkable deposits reduces excess reserves because required reserves rise, a currency withdrawal also reduces excess reserves.* If the reserve requirement on checkable deposits is equal to 0.10, and if the currency-to-checkable-deposit ratio equals 0.05, then a $100 increase in deposits will reduce excess reserves by $15; $10 of that $15 is converted from excess to required reserves, and the remaining $5 in excess reserves is lost because of the currency withdrawal. Therefore, compared with our earlier presentation, a currency-to-deposit ratio of 0.05 affects the deposit expansion potential in exactly the same way as an increase in the reserve requirement from 0.10 to 0.15; out of every dollar increase in checkable deposits, excess reserves decline by 15 cents. We can formalize this as follows. Letting r_r represent the reserve requirement on checkable deposits, and c, the currency-to-checkable-deposit ratio, the deposit expansion multiplier can be represented as

$$\text{Checkable deposit expansion multiplier} = \frac{1}{r_r + c}.$$

Thus, if $r_r = 0.10$ and $c = 0.05$, the multiplier will equal 6.67 (i.e., $\frac{1}{0.10 + 0.05} = \frac{1}{0.15} = 6.67$).

Let us illustrate this with a simple numerical example. Suppose the financial system has $1,000 in excess reserves. What is the deposit expansion potential? With a deposit expansion multiplier of 6.67, total checkable deposits could increase by $6,670 (6.67 × $1,000 excess reserves). Would the system then be "loaned up"? Yes. The $6,670 increase in deposits increases required reserves by $667 (0.10 × $6,670). It is also accompanied by a $333 increase in currency withdrawals (0.05 × $6,670 is approximately equal to $333). Excess

---

[1] In shorter courses, this section can be skipped over without loss of continuity.

reserves are now zero. The following T-account summarizes all of these transactions.

Depository institutions

Vault cash	−333	Checkable	
Loans and finan-		deposits	+6,670
cial investments	+7,003		

Let us examine this numerical example carefully. All told, the financial system was able to expand its loans and financial investments by $7,003. Each time a depository institution granted a loan or made a financial investment, it increased its checkable deposits by a like amount. But people, in an effort to maintain a currency-to-checkable-deposit ratio of 0.05, drew down their checkable deposits somewhat by withdrawing cash, with the result that vault cash declined. We see in the above numerical example that loans and financial investments totaling $7,003 leads ultimately to an expansion of checkable deposits of $6,670 and a reduction in vault cash of $333 as people try to maintain a currency-to-checkable-deposit ratio of 0.05 (i.e., $333/$6,670 is approximately equal to 0.05).

Checkable deposits increased by $6,670. But by how much did the money supply increase? Since currency in the hands of the public rose by $333, the money supply increased by $7,003 ($6,670 + $333 = $7,003). *Here again, the change in the money supply is equal to the change in the volume of loans and financial investments.*

Note one final result. If, because of a change in the level of economic activity, the public decides to alter its holdings of currency relative to checkable deposits, the deposit expansion potential of the financial system will be affected in precisely the same way as if the reserve requirement were changed. *If the currency-to-checkable-deposit ratio is increased, the deposit expansion potential is reduced in a way that is exactly analogous to an equivalent increase in the reserve requirement; the converse is true for a reduction in the currency-to-checkable-deposit ratio.* Therefore, if, as some observers suggest, it is true that the currency-to-checkable-deposit ratio rises during an economic expansion, the deposit expansion

multiplier will be reduced; and the converse holds during a contraction.

Desired excess reserves

We have defined the financial system as being "loaned up" if zero excess reserves exist. This may be true in a technical sense, but it may have no operational significance if, for one reason or another, depository institutions desire to hold some volume of excess reserves. Technically, excess reserves may be present. But if depository institutions refuse to make additional loans on the basis of those excess reserves, the deposit expansion potential will be smaller than we have described it.

Why would financial institutions desire to hold excess reserves? For the most part, they desire to hold some excess reserves to provide a cushion against unexpected reserve losses associated with either the clearing process or customer currency withdrawals. However, since depository institutions are in business to make profits, how much they desire to hold in excess will be determined by comparing the costs and benefits of doing so. If they do incur a reserve deficiency, there are generally alternative sources for obtaining reserves—through the discount window, the federal funds market, or the liquidation of secondary reserves. There are interest costs associated with the use of these other sources, but there are also costs associated with keeping reserves in excess of what is required—namely, the foregone interest income that could otherwise have been obtained from loans and financial investments. This is the opportunity cost of holding excess reserves.

In deciding the amount of reserves to hold in excess, depository institutions will be influenced by the magnitude of the spread between the costs of borrowing reserves and the expected yield from loans and financial investments. The smaller this spread, the greater is the likelihood that depository institutions will hold larger volumes of excess reserves; the larger the spread, the less the likelihood.

How do these changes affect the deposit expansion potential of the financial system? Quite obviously, the deposit expansion potential is increased as desired excess reserves fall and reduced as desired excess reserves rise. Let us examine this phenomenon more closely.

The deposit expansion multiplier and holdings of excess reserves.[2] As in the case of currency holdings by the public, let us assume, for simplicity, that depository institutions desire to hold 5 cents in excess reserves for each dollar of checkable deposits. Then, if deposits rise by $100, *excess reserves available for making loans and financial investments will decline by $5* since depository institutions desire to hold these in excess. This $5 decline in excess reserves is *in addition to* the reduction in excess reserves that comes about as a result of the expansion of checkable deposits, shifting those reserves from excess to required. If the reserve requirement is equal to 0.10, the currency-to-checkable-deposit ratio to 0.05, and the desired ratio of excess reserves to checkable deposits to 0.05, a $100 increase in deposits will reduce excess reserves by $20; $10 of that $20 are converted from excess to required, $5 are lost because of the currency withdrawal, and the remaining $5 represents the increase in *desired* excess reserves that are now unavailable for further deposit expansion. Therefore, as in the analysis of currency withdrawals, the desired increase in excess reserves affects the deposit expansion potential exactly as an increase in the reserve requirement from 0.10 to 0.15. Letting e represent the ratio of desired holdings of excess reserves to checkable deposits, we can represent this result formally in terms of the deposit expansion multiplier. The new multiplier is given as

$$\frac{\text{Checkable deposit}}{\text{expansion multiplier}} = \frac{1}{r_r + c + e}.$$

Thus, if $r_r = 0.10$, $c = 0.05$, and $e = 0.05$, the multiplier will equal 5 (i.e., $\frac{1}{0.10 + 0.05 + 0.05}$ $= \frac{1}{0.2} = 5$).

---

[2] In shorter courses this section can be skipped over without loss of continuity.

Let us illustrate this again with a simple numerical example. Suppose the financial system has, as before, $1,000 in excess reserves. Given a deposit expansion multiplier of 5.0, it implies that checkable deposits could potentially expand by $5,000 (5.0 × $1,000 excess reserves). Would the system be "loaned up"? Technically no, but operationally yes. The $5,000 increase in checkable deposits increases required reserves by $500 (0.10 × $5,000); the currency drain sopped up an additional $250 (0.05 × $5,000); and the remaining $250 in excess reserves are now part of the financial system's holdings of *desired* excess reserves. Since there is no further room for expansion, from an operational point of view, the financial system is loaned up. The following T-account example summarizes these results:

Depository institutions

Vault cash	− 250	Checkable	
Loans and finan-		deposits	+5,000
cial investments	+5,250		

Can you explain why loans and financial investments amounted to $5,250 whereas checkable deposits increased by only $5,000? Also, why is the change in the money supply equal to the change in the volume of loans and financial investments? (*Hint:* Loans and financial investments are the means used by depository institutions to convert their excess reserves into profitable ventures; it is the public that decides how any increase in checkable deposits, initially equal to loans and investments, will be divided ultimately between currency and coin and checkable deposits.)

One final note: *If the desired ratio of excess reserves to checkable deposit rises, the deposit expansion multiplier will be reduced; if the ratio falls, the multiplier will be increased.*

Noncheckable deposits and other financial assets

The deposit expansion potential of the financial system is also affected by the behavior of the public with respect to its holdings of passbook savings accounts, time deposits, and other liquid assets. Up until now we have assumed these to be fixed. However, people's holdings of these assets are not fixed. They vary with the amount of income people save. And, as you will recall from our discussion of the consumption function in Chapter 7, the amount people save is heavily influenced by the level of disposable income. In addition, if interest rates on these noncheckable deposits and assets rise relative to the interest return on checkable deposits, it is reasonable to expect that people will increase their portfolio holdings of these other financial instruments at the expense of checkable deposits. The checkable deposit expansion potential of the financial system will be affected as a consequence.

In this regard, it is important to understand the following two observations.

First, as we have noted before, all depository institutions that issue checkable deposits are subject to the same uniform reserve requirements on checkable deposits. Under the Depository Institutions Deregulation and Monetary Control Act of 1980, the Board of Governors of the Federal Reserve has the authority to set the reserve requirement between 8 and 14 percent on that portion of checkable deposits above some predetermined minimal level; for the predetermined minimal level of checkable deposits, each depository institution is subject to a 3 percent reserve requirement. What complicates matters is that the predetermined minimal level is *not* fixed but changes over time. As of December 31, 1981, the minimal amount was set at $25 million of checkable deposits; in subsequent years, after December 31 of each year, this minimal amount changes by 80 percent of the percentage change in *aggregate* checkable account balances. To illustrate, suppose aggregate checkable account balances—the total of all checkable deposits in all depository institutions—increased by 12.5 percent in any given calendar year. The minimal amount subject to the 3 percent reserve requirement would rise by 10 percent (80 percent of 12.5 percent equals 10 percent). If at the end of 1981 it was determined that checkable deposits in total had increased 12.5 percent, the minimal

amount subject to the 3 percent reserve requirement would have increased by $2.5 million, from $25 to $27.5 million; deposits in excess of $27.5 million in each institution would be subject to the higher reserve requirement.

In addition to the reserve requirements on checkable deposits, depository institutions are required to meet reserve requirements on certain types of noncheckable deposits. Specifically, the Board of Governors has the authority under the Monetary Control Act to vary the reserve requirement from 0 to 9 percent on nonpersonal time deposits (e.g., corporation-owned time deposits, large or small); personal time deposits and passbook savings accounts were exempted from reserve requirements.

The differences between these reserve requirements are important. If people shift from checkable deposits to noncheckable deposits or other kinds of liquid assets, in general this will change the volume of reserves required—not total reserves, but the division of the total between required and excess—and affect the lending potential of the financial system. To illustrate, suppose personal depositors at Virginia Federal shift $10 million from their checkable deposits to small time deposits. Assume further that the reserve requirement on checkable deposits is 0.10; on small time deposits it is zero. The decline in checkable deposits reduces required reserves by $1 million (i.e., 0.10 × $10 million); the increase in time deposits has no effect on required reserves. Excess reserves thus increase by $1 million. Those excess reserves are then available to expand the volume of loans and financial investments. Of course, the converse of these propositions holds if individuals switch from small time deposits to checkable deposits.

As a general rule, the following significant conclusion can be drawn regarding the consequences of shifts of funds among classes of assets. If depositors shift funds from accounts having higher reserve requirements to accounts with lower ones (or none at all), system *excess* reserves will increase. This permits depository institutions to expand their loans and financial investments.

If, on the other hand, the shift is to accounts having higher reserve requirements, excess reserves will decline. This reduces the loan and financial investment potential of depository institutions.

Second, in the face of changes in the public's holdings of noncheckable deposits and other liquid assets, we can now no longer assume that changes in M1 will equal changes in M2, M3, and L. For example, suppose depositors reduce their holdings of checkable deposits in favor of an increase in small time deposits. The reduction in checkable deposits causes M1 to fall, but M2 is unaltered. The reason? M2 includes both checkable deposits *and* small time deposits. By extension, if people switch funds from checkable deposits or small time deposits to commercial paper (a component of L, but not of M1, M2, or M3), M1, M2, and M3 will all decline but L will not change. Do you know why?

Combining these two points—the first having to do with effect on the loan and financial investment potential of shifts between accounts having different reserve requirements, and the second having to do with the nonequivalence of *changes* in M1, M2, and M3 and changes in L—it becomes clear why an exclusive focus on M1, or any other aggregate, could be misleading. To show this, assume the financial system is "loaned up." Now suppose that checkable deposits are reduced as people substitute in favor of small time deposits. M1 will fall, but M2 will remain unchanged; excess reserves will increase, an outcome that permits depository institutions to expand their loans and financial investments. Looking at M1 might be interpreted as evidence that the Fed was pursuing a contractionary policy. What about M2? You would be correct in interpreting an unchanged M2 as evidence of an unchanged monetary policy. How would you interpret the increase in loans and financial investments? True, there was no change in policy that caused the increase in loans and financial investments. However, insofar as the Fed views its job as one of controlling the money aggregates to

effect the desired changes in aggregate spending, it may feel compelled to offset these increases. In any event, as should be apparent, no single money aggregate provides the Fed with all the information it needs.

The deposit expansion potential: A summary. On the basis of the foregoing points, it is clear that the credit expansion process is by no means as simple as we presented it initially. There is generally not a simple one-to-one relationship between changes in the volume of checkable deposits and the volume of credit extended by depository institutions. Nor is it necessarily true that depository institutions will extend credit to the maximum extent technically possible. It is not difficult to discover the sources of these complications. They derive from the behavior of the public with respect to its holdings of currency, noncheckable deposits, and other liquid assets, and from the behavior of depository institutions with respect to their desired holdings of excess reserves. Thus, *for any given volume of excess reserves,* the deposit and credit expansion potential of the system will be determined by the Fed, depository institutions, *and* the public.

Of course, *if* the public were to maintain a *predictable* ratio of currency to checkable deposits, and *if* depository institutions were to maintain a *predictable* ratio of excess reserves to checkable deposits, and *if* people did shift their accounts around in *predictable* ways from one type of asset to another with different reserve requirements, the effects of all of these complicating factors on the volume of credit extended could readily be calculated by the Fed in the formulation of its policies. It would then be relatively simple for the Fed to calculate how much of a change in reserves would be required to effect a given change in the volume of credit.

However, there are a lot of ifs that would have to be met—ifs that are *not* met in the real world. The public's holdings of currency do not move in predictable ways with checkable deposits. And people do shift their accounts around in unforeseen ways. As a result, Fed policy is much less precise than otherwise—sometimes overshooting, sometimes undershooting, its targets. A great deal of research has been undertaken by the Fed to enhance its predictive powers with respect to these relationships. But because of the inherent complexities of human behavior, the Fed is frequently confronted with the unpredictable. The Fed is in a position to anticipate changes in these relationships only imperfectly. It can therefore have only imperfect knowledge of the credit and deposit expansion potential of the system.

THE DIFFICULT TASK OF INTERPRETING MONETARY POLICY

Because of changes in the value of the deposit expansion multiplier, the Fed must continually adjust the magnitude of its open market purchases or sales in order to effect any given desired change in the volume of credit extended by the financial system. We must never make the mistake, therefore, of concluding that Fed policy in some given period is necessarily more expansive than that of some other period solely on the basis of differences in the magnitude of open market purchases between the two. A $2 million open market purchase combined with a large deposit expansion multiplier could be more expansionary than a $3 million open market purchase if the latter occurred when the deposit multiplier was relatively small.

This is not, however, the only problem we encounter in attempting to interpret monetary policy. *A second problem arises because system reserves are affected by more than just the actions of the Fed itself. System reserves are influenced not only by Fed policies, but by the behavior of the public, financial institutions, the U.S. Treasury, and residents of foreign countries as well.* In other words, the actions of any one of these economic agents can serve to increase or decrease reserves independent of actions undertaken by the Fed. Let us examine some of these factors carefully.

The public's holdings of currency

The amount of currency in circulation is determined in large measure by the public. Depository institutions maintain cash in their vaults primarily for the purpose of meeting the currency needs of their depositors. If the public desires more currency, these institutions will experience a decline in their vault cash—that is, a decline in system reserves. Moreover, if depository institutions find it necessary to obtain more vault cash to meet the currency drain, they can obtain it from one of the Federal Reserve Banks by drawing down their deposits at the Fed. In this latter case, there will be an increase in the amount of Federal Reserve Notes outstanding. But such an increase comes at the expense of deposits at the Fed. In any event, increased currency holdings on the part of the public reduce system reserves; and the converse is true for cash deposits.

Depository institition borrowings from the Fed

Whenever depository institutions make use of the discount window to acquire loans from the Fed, system reserves rise. The Fed grants these loans by increasing these institutions' deposits, which are part of the system's reserves.

Treasury deposits at the Fed

The U.S. Treasury maintains deposit balances at both the Federal Reserve Banks and selected depository institutions. Whenever the Treasury draws down its account at the Fed in order to pay its bills, system reserves rise. This is easily illustrated.

Suppose the Treasury writes a check for $100,000 payable to one of its defense contractors, Acme International. When Acme receives the check, it is deposited in a depository institution. The check is then sent to the Fed for payment. The Fed reduces the Treasury account by $100,000 and increases by a like amount the depository institution's deposit. *System reserves have gone up.* The following T-account illustrates these transactions.

Depository institution			
Reserves	+100,000	Checkable deposits	+100,000

The Fed			
		Depository institution deposits	+100,000
		U.S. Treasury deposits	−100,000

Similarly, if the Treasury receives checks from the public representing payments for taxes or U.S. government securities, the Treasury account at the Fed will rise and system reserves will decline. Can you explain why?

Gold sales and purchases

When the Treasury purchases gold from a domestic producer, it usually issues a **gold certificate** to the Fed as a claim against that gold. In return the Treasury receives an increase in its deposit balance at the Fed. The Treasury then writes a check payable to the domestic gold producer. The latter, in turn, deposits the check in a depository institution. The check is then sent to the Fed for payment. The Fed then reduces the Treasury account and increases the deposit balance of the depository institution. *The gold purchase, therefore, increases system reserves.* Can you explain how a gold sale by the Treasury would reduce system reserves?

Foreign deposits at the Federal Reserve

A number of foreign central banks maintain deposit balances at the Federal Reserve Banks. If these foreign central banks issue checks to U.S. residents, these checks will ultimately be deposited in U.S. depository institutions. Once these checks are sent to the Fed for payment, foreign deposit balances will be reduced and deposits of U.S. financial institutions will be increased; system reserves rise. If foreign central banks receive checks from the U.S. public and deposit them

in U.S. Federal Reserve Banks, system reserves will decline. Can you explain why?

Foreign exchange purchases and sales

Part of Federal Reserve assets consists of foreign exchange holdings. When the Fed purchases foreign exchange from U.S. residents or U.S. depository institutions, it pays for the foreign exchange by writing a check on itself. When the check is deposited and has cleared, system reserves will rise.

Changes in bank reserves: A summary

Although the volume of system reserves is readily changed as a result of open market purchases and sales, it is clear that these operations are not the only sources of change. Indeed, system reserves change as a result of changes in the behavior of the public, depository institutions, the U.S. Treasury, and nonresidents. Under these circumstances, it is often difficult for the Fed to achieve precisely the change in reserves it deems necessary for carrying out its policies. These complicating factors would not prove so troublesome if the changes could be predicted in advance. For instance, if the Fed were able to predict that the behavior of all of these agents would cause reserves to rise by $50 million and it wanted to expand reserves by $100 million, it would find it necessary to engage in an open market purchase to the tune of $50 million only. Fed actions, plus the actions of all the other agents, would then cause reserves to rise by the desired amount. Unfortunately, it has proved difficult to predict such behavioral changes in advance, despite considerable research efforts. As a result, the manager at the trading desk must keep a close eye on all sources of changes in reserves and make adjustments in its sales or purchases of U.S. government securities accordingly.

Dynamic versus defensive operations

All of these considerations complicate considerably the task of interpreting monetary policy.

To illustrate, suppose, as before, that the Fed wants to expand system reserves by $100 million. If there were no offsetting changes in the other factors that affect system reserves, the Fed would merely engage in an open market purchase equal to $100 million. If the other factors caused system reserves to rise by $100 million, the Fed would not undertake any purchase at all. If the other factors caused system reserves to rise by more than $100 million, the Fed would have to undertake an open market *sale* in order to offset an excessive expansion of reserves.

In light of these considerations, economists have found it useful to distinguish the **dynamic operations** of the Fed from its **defensive operations.** The dynamic operations of the Fed refer to those open market purchases and sales undertaken to effect a desired change in reserves. Defensive operations are undertaken to offset undesired changes in reserves brought about by the other factors that affect reserves. In light of our earlier example, the dynamic operations would involve those purchases of sales necessary to effect a $100 million change in system reserves. In order to "defend" that target, the Fed might have to engage in offsetting purchases and sales in order to prevent the other factors from bringing about an undesired change in reserves. A recognition of these distinctions is essential to your understanding of the conduct of monetary policy.

SUMMARY

1. When depository institutions extend loans to their customers or purchase securities from members of the public, money is created.

2. The checkable deposit potential of the financial system is limited by the volume of *reserves* in the financial system and the *reserve requirement*. Specifically, the checkable deposit potential, under certain assumptions, can be calculated by dividing the volume of reserves (R) by the reserve requirement (r_r):

$$\text{Checkable deposit potential} = \frac{R}{r_r}.$$

3. When excess reserves are present, the system of depository institutions has the capability of expanding checkable deposits by a multiple of those excess reserves. However, each depository institution can prudently expand its own deposits only by the amount of its excess reserves, not by a multiple of its excess reserves. Given the existence of over 40,000 different depository institutions, there is little likelihood that a check written by any one depositor will be redeposited with the same institution. As a result, the loan extended by depository institution A will quickly result in a loss of reserves for A equal to the amount of the loan. But, although A loses reserves, the system of depository institutions does not, because the reserves lost by A will be picked up by some other depository institution.

4. The *federal funds market* facilitates the realization of the deposit expansion potential and eases the adjustments resulting from adverse clearing drains. In that market, institutions that want to lend their excess reserves do so by granting overnight loans to institutions seeking additional reserves.

5. There are three main tools of monetary policy—open market operations, the discount rate, and the reserve requirement. Minor tools of control include *moral suasion* and *selective credit controls.*

6. *Open market operations*—the purchase or sale of U.S. government securities in the (open) securities market—are by far the most dominant and flexible tool of control. System reserves expand as a consequence of *open market purchases; open market sales* reduce system reserves.

7. The *discount rate*—the rate of interest charged by the Fed on loans it grants to those depository institutions having "borrowing privileges"—is, compared with open market sales, a relatively minor tool of control. The basic problem is that the impact of changes in the discount rate on system reserves is very unpredictable. The *discount window* is retained largely because it serves as a "safety valve" to depository institutions caught with reserve deficiencies. But the borrowing privilege can be abused, especially when open market rates rise above the discount rate. In view of the abuses and the adverse "an-

nouncement effects" accompanying changes in the discount rate, many economists are seeking to reform this policy tool.

8. Changing the reserve requirement does not change the volume of system reserves, but it does change the deposit potential of the system. This is not a flexible tool of control and the Fed uses it sparingly.

9. The deposit expansion multiplier, defined simply as $1/r_r$, is misleading; it is based on a number of assumptions that enjoy no empirical support. Relaxing those assumptions complicates the calculation of the deposit expansion potential for the financial system. Thus, as people adjust their holdings of currency or as they shift their portfolio holdings between checkable and noncheckable deposits, on the one hand, and various kinds of noncheckable deposits, on the other, and as depository institutions alter their holdings of desired excess reserves, the deposit expansion potential and loan potential of the financial system will be affected. At times the changes brought on by these shifts can be dramatic.

10. The unpredictability of changes in the value of the deposit expansion multiplier represents only one of the difficulties we encounter in attempting to interpret monetary policy. A second problem arises because system reserves are affected not only by the actions of the Fed, but by the behavior of the public, financial institutions, the U.S. Treasury, and residents of foreign countries as well. Accordingly, it is useful to distinguish the *dynamic operations* of the Fed from its *defensive operations.*

CONCEPTS FOR REVIEW

Reserves

Reserve requirement

Vault cash

Required reserves

Excess reserves

Fractional reserve system

Clearinghouse

Interdistrict Settlement Fund

Checkable deposit expansion multiplier

Adverse clearing drain

Federal funds market

Federal funds rate

Secondary reserves

Discount window

Discount rate

Penalty discount rate

Open market operations

Moral suasion

Selective credit controls

Regulation Q (Reg Q)

Monetary base (high-powered money)

Dynamic operations

Defensive operations

QUESTIONS FOR DISCUSSION

(Those marked with an asterisk (*) are more difficult.)

1. Using T-accounts where appropriate, illustrate the effects of each of the following transactions on the quantity of M1, the volume of system reserves, the volume of required reserves, and the volume of excess reserves. Briefly explain your reasoning in each instance.

   a. Gloria finally persuades her Uncle Freddy to take his money ($10,000) out of his mattress and to put it into the bank for safekeeping.

   b. Honest Ed, seeking a greater return for his funds, removes $20,000 from his checkable deposit account at Security Mutual to purchase a six-month money market certificate.

   c. The Federal Reserve lowers the discount rate from 9.75 percent to 9.0 percent.

   d. The Federal Reserve lowers the reserve requirement on checkable deposits by one percentage point.

   e. University National sends a wire to the Federal Reserve Bank in its district requesting $200,000 in currency.

   f. The U.S. Treasury writes checks totaling $2 million on its account at the Fed to pay private contractors for work done on one of the Senate office buildings.

2. Suppose Security Federal, a depository institution, has $100,000 in excess reserves. Suppose further that the checkable deposit expansion multiplier is given

by $1/r_r$, and that r_r, the reserve requirement, is equal to 0.10. Explain carefully why Security Federal would probably get into difficulty if it granted loans totaling $1 million, but why the financial system would not.

*3.   As a follow-up to Question 2, suppose Security Federal were the *only* depository institution in the nation. That is, suppose Security Federal held monopoly rights on all checkable deposits. Under these circumstances, could Security Federal prudently grant loans totaling $1 million? Explain your answer carefully.

*4.   Vault cash—the currency and coin in the vaults of depository institutions—is not counted as part of the money supply. Some people think this is strange. However, suppose people were to deposit $10,000 in cash in exchange for checkable deposits. Can you show that, if vault cash were counted as part of the money supply, this transaction would result in "double counting" part of the money supply?

5.   "Controlling the money supply (M1) is very difficult. Not only does the Fed have to contend with changes in the checkable deposit expansion multiplier brought about by factors over which it has only limited control, but the volume of system reserves is affected by more than just Federal Reserve actions." Do you agree or disagree? Explain your answer carefully, illustrating how the actions of the Fed, the public, the depository institutions, and the U.S. Treasury can affect both the deposit expansion potential and the volume of system reserves.

6.   As a follow-up to Question 5, explain how the Fed's control over the money supply would be improved if it could predict fairly accurately the behavioral changes of the public and the banks that cause changes in the deposit potential and volume of system reserves.

Chapter 11

Money and the level of economic activity: A static analysis

We now turn our attention to the very important question of the role of money in determining income, output, and employment. This is a highly controversial subject for which a consensus within the economics profession does not as yet exist. It is also a subject about which there is much needless confusion.

One difficulty we encounter is in discovering the appropriate definition of money itself. If we are attempting to determine the relationship between the money supply and the level of economic activity, it is important that we settle the question, Which money supply? Is the appropriate definition of money M1? Or is some broader-based measure, such as M2 or M3, more appropriate? Unfortunately, there is as yet no generally accepted "appropriate" definition of *money*. In order to keep the analysis manageable, we *assume* here that the appropriate definition of money is M1, which, as you will recall, includes virtually all kinds of checkable deposits.

A second difficulty we encounter has to do with the question of the nature of the relationship between GNP and the amount of money required to finance that level of income. One group of economists—often referred to as **monetarists**—argue that there exists a very close relationship between changes in the money supply and changes in nominal income; and that in the absence of a change in the money supply, fiscal policy will be ineffective. If true, it would imply that the conclusions of Chapter 8 are all wrong. Another group of economists—which for lack of a better term we call **nonmonetarists**—disagree. They argue that a given money supply can be used to finance a wide range of GNP levels with the result that the level of economic activity can be altered, perhaps significantly, through fiscal policy without any accompanying change in the money supply. This important debate and its policy implications will be taken up in the final section of this chapter.

This chapter provides us with an introduction to the economics of money. We begin our study with an examination of the important relationship between bond prices and interest rates. We then analyze how interest rates are determined. Then we turn our attention to the impact of monetary policy on interest rates and the level of economic activity.

Before analyzing these issues, however, it is essential that we be very clear on one matter. We should never make the mistake of confusing money with income or output. They are not the same. GNP refers to the market value of all final goods and services produced during some time period. Aggregate income is identical to that value. The stock of money, however, is not part of our income or output. Money is virtually costless to produce. Very few resources are required to expand the money supply by $10 billion, $20 billion, $50 billion, or any other amount—just a little paper and ink. Unlike an increase in spending, which is by definition an expansion of income and output, an increase in the money supply does not *by itself* constitute an increase in output. Therefore, an expansion of the money supply will generate an increase in the level of output and income only to the extent that it induces people to step up their spending. In other words, an increase in the money supply leads to an increase in income and output *indirectly*. It is the central purpose of this chapter to spell out the mechanisms whereby changes in the money supply generate changes in the level of aggregate spending.

THE INVERSE RELATIONSHIP BETWEEN BOND PRICES AND INTEREST RATES

If there is one relationship that is essential to our understanding of monetary economics it is the inverse relationship between the prices of bonds and open market interest rates. In other words, as interest rates rise, bond prices fall; as interest rates fall, bond prices increase.

To illustrate this important relationship, recall our earlier discussion of bonds. **Bonds** are instruments of **debt** that possess one critically unique characteristic—they yield to the holder a fixed income per time period. The fixed interest income is usually paid annually or semiannually until the bond matures, at which point the holder is paid its **face value;** the face value is sometimes called the **par value** or **redemption value** of the bond. Attached to most bonds are a number of **coupons** representing the number of fixed income payments to maturity; the fixed income payment is often referred to as the **coupon payment.** The **coupon rate** is defined as the ratio of the coupon payment to the face value of the bond. Thus,

$$\text{Coupon rate} = \frac{\text{Coupon payment}}{\text{Face value of bond}}.$$

A bond with a face value of $1,000 paying a fixed income of $60 a year therefore has a coupon rate of 6 percent (i.e., $60/$1,000 = 0.06).

It is important to note that the face value of any bond does not necessarily represent its market price. Sometimes a bond will have a market price in excess of its face value; sometimes market price will be below. How can this be? Shouldn't a bond that has stamped on it a face value of $1,000 always sell for $1,000 since that represents the amount the holder will receive when the bond matures? Not necessarily.

As will be made clear in the discussion below, there are two considerations that are essential to the determination of the price of a bond.

1. Although it is true that a bond with a face value of $1,000 will yield $1,000 to the holder when the bond matures (because the holder must wait until maturity before collecting that amount), $1,000 *today* is worth less than $1,000 in the future. How much less will depend on the years to maturity and the **market interest rate** (*not* the coupon rate).

2. At any particular time other bonds will be on the market that are *similar in quality* to the $1,000 bond in question. These bonds will, in general, have different face values and different coupon rates. The prices of all these bonds must be such that they yield to would-be purchasers approximately the same **rate of return.** Different quality bonds need not yield the same rate of return. But bonds that are equal in quality will yield approximately the same return.

Present discounted value (PDV)

These two propositions are easily demonstrated once we familiarize ourselves with the

present discounted value (PDV) concept. Consider the following simple illustration.

Suppose you were to place $1,000 in a savings account paying an annual rate of interest equal to 6 percent. How much would that $1,000 be worth one year from now? That's easy: $1,000 plus $60 interest, for a total of $1,060. Algebraically, this can be represented as follows:

$$\$1,000 \times (1 + 6\%) = \$1,000 \times (1 + 0.06)$$
$$= \$1,000 \times 1.06 = \$1,060.$$

What if you left that sum in the savings account for yet another year? What would your $1,000 be worth two years from now? $1,123.60. How did we arrive at that figure? You earn 6 percent interest on $1,060 ($63.60) and that plus $1,060 gives you $1,123.60. In other words,

$$\$1,060 \times 1.06 = \$1,123.60.$$

But $1,060 is nothing more than the value of $1,000 one year hence—that is, $1,060 = $1,000 $\times$ 1.06. Replacing $1,060 with ($1,000 $\times$ 1.06) in the last expression we get

$$(\$1,000 \times 1.06) \times 1.06 = \$1,000 \times 1.06^2$$
$$= \$1,123.60.$$

That is, the value of $1,000 two years hence earning 6 percent interest is equal to $1,000 $\times$ 1.06^2. What would be its value three years hence? $1,000 $\times$ 1.06^3. Can you explain why? In general, the future value of $1,000 n years hence (where n is any positive number), earning an interest rate of i percent, works out as follows:

Future value of $1,000 = $1,000 $\times$ $(1 + i)^n$
n years from today.

Let us now examine these numerical examples somewhat differently. Suppose you know that one year hence you will have $1,060. What is the worth of that $1,060 *today*—that is, *what is the present value of $1,060?* With a rate of interest of 6 percent, it will be worth only $1,000. The reason? Since $1,060 represents the value one year in the future of $1,000 earning 6 percent, $1,000 represents the present value of $1,060 one year from now. *The $1,060 to be received one year from now is therefore equivalent to $1,000*

today. Formally, since $1,000 $\times$ 1.06 = $1,060, then

$$\$1,000 = \frac{\$1,060}{1.06}.$$

This last expression is referred to as the **present discounted value (PDV)** of $1,060 due one year from today. It is arrived at by "discounting" the future value by one plus the rate of interest.

Similarly, what is the PDV of $1,123.60 due two years from today? Using the same reasoning as before, it is easily shown to be equal to $1,000. Since $1,123.60 represents the value two years in the future of $1,000 earning 6 percent per year, $1,000 must be the PDV of $1,123.60. That is, since $1,000 $\times$ 1.06^2 = $1,123.60, then

$$\$1,000 = \frac{\$1,123.60}{1.06^2}.$$

Letting i represent the (assumed constant) interest rate, we can readily calculate the PDV of any future value n years hence as follows:

$$PDV = \frac{\text{Future value n years from today}}{(1 + i)^n}.$$

This expression is called the **discount** or **capitalization formula**. As is apparent, it is nothing more than the reverse of the formula used to calculate the future value of a present sum.

The present discounted value of a bond. Let us now apply these concepts to calculate the PDV of a bond. This calculation will enable us to discover the present worth of the bond—the price that the bond can fetch in the marketplace.

Suppose you possess a bond with a face value of $1,000. Suppose further that the bond matures in five years. The coupon payment on the bond is fixed at $60 a year. This means that once a year you can "clip the coupon" and cash it for $60. At the end of five years, you cash in the last coupon *and,* at the same time, you can receive the face value of the bond. Thus, you will receive over the next five years five annual payments of $60 and at the end of the fifth year you will also be able to redeem the bond for $1,000. *But these are future values.* What is the PDV of the bond? The PDV of the first coupon payment will equal $60/(1 + i)$; the PDV of the second coupon payment will be $60/(1 + i)^2$; and so on through the fifth. Moreover, the PDV of the face or redemption value of the bond will be $1,000/(1 + i)^5$. By summing up all of these PDVs, we arrive at the PDV of the bond. Thus,

$$PDV = \frac{\$60}{(1 + i)} + \frac{\$60}{(1 + i)^2} + \frac{\$60}{(1 + i)^3}$$
$$+ \frac{\$60}{(1 + i)^4} + \frac{\$60}{(1 + i)^5} + \frac{\$1,000}{(1 + i)^5}.$$

Assume, for the purposes of illustration, that the rate of interest happens to be 6 percent—which, by the way, is identical to the coupon rate. What would the PDV of the bond be then? Using a standard present value table,[1] this is easily calculated:

$$PDV = \frac{\$60}{(1.06)} + \frac{\$60}{(1.06)^2} + \frac{\$60}{(1.06)^3} + \frac{\$60}{(1.06)^4}$$
$$+ \frac{\$60}{(1.06)^5} + \frac{\$1,000}{(1.06)^5}$$
$$= \$56.60 + \$53.39 + \$50.38 + \$47.52$$
$$+ \$44.83 + \$747.20$$
$$= \$1,000 \text{ (approximately).}$$

The inverse relation between bond prices and interest rates. This bond, therefore, is worth $1,000 which is approximately the price it can be sold for in the marketplace. In this instance, the bond has a value equal to its face value. This need not always be the case, however. Indeed, *this particular result emerged solely because we assumed an interest rate equal to the coupon rate.* Suppose that the interest rate happened to be 8 percent instead of 6 percent. What would the PDV of the bond be under these circumstances? The bond would be worth approximately $920 as the following calculations make abundantly clear:

[1] See, for example, Samuel M. Selby, ed., *Standard Mathematical Tables*, 22d ed. (Cleveland, Ohio: CRC Press, 1973), pp. 643–50.

$$PDV = \frac{\$60}{(1.08)} + \frac{\$60}{(1.08)^2} + \frac{\$60}{(1.08)^3} + \frac{\$60}{(1.08)^4}$$
$$+ \frac{\$60}{(1.08)^5} + \frac{\$1,000}{(1.08)^5}$$
$$= \$55.55 + \$51.44 + \$47.63 + \$44.10$$
$$+ \$40.83 + \$681$$
$$= \$920 \text{ (approximately).}$$

At a rate of interest of 8 percent, therefore, the bond will sell at a price that is *below* its face value. And note that, *when the rate of interest rises from 6 percent to 8 percent, the price of the bond falls from $1,000 to $920.* **The bond price and the interest rate are inversely related.**

Consider another example. Suppose the interest rate happened to be 3 percent. Performing the same calculations as before, it is easy to show that the bond will have a PDV equal to $1,137.40. At that low rate of interest the bond will sell for $137.40 *above* its face value. Note again how the price of the bond and the interest rate are inversely related: As the interest rate declined, the price of the bond rose.

It is not difficult to discover the explanation for the inverse relationship between bond prices and interest rates. *Bonds are fixed-income securities.* The coupon payment is fixed at the date the bond is issued and remains fixed throughout the life of the bond. If interest rates rise, future fixed coupon payments will be more heavily discounted, meaning that their present worth is reduced. The PDV of the bond, and hence its price, is reduced.

One final note on PDV. On the basis of the previous discussion, it is clear that the farther into the future a payment is received, the smaller its PDV will be. Why? Because distant future values are more heavily discounted than less distant ones. Moreover, if interest rates change, bonds with a long maturity will fluctuate more in price than bonds that mature earlier. This is readily apparent from Table 11.1. All calculations in that table were made on the assumption that the bond in question had a face value of $1,000 with a fixed coupon payment of $60 payable annually. Note two points:

1. How the bond price varies for any given rate of interest as the maturity date varies. At a 3 percent rate of interest, a bond with a one-year maturity will sell for $1,029.20, a little above face value; a 20-year bond on the other hand will sell for $1,449.50. This should occasion no surprise since the closer the bond is to maturity, the closer its value will be to the face value. If a bond were to mature tomorrow, it would sell today for almost exactly $1,000—its face value. There is one exception to this rule. At a 6 percent rate of interest, bonds of any maturity sell at face value. Can you explain why?

2. How much the price of the bond varies as the interest rate varies. As the interest rate changes from 3 percent to 15 percent, a one-year bond changes in price from $1,029.20 to $922.20. But a 20-year bond will change in price from $1,449.50 to $436.60, a whopping change of $1,012.90! The price variability for any given change in the interest rate is much larger in the case of long-term bonds.

Bond prices, interest rates, and consols.[2] For some purposes it is useful to extend and simplify this discussion of the inverse relationship between bond prices and interest rates. Consider a bond that has no maturity date whatsoever. Since there is no maturity date, the bond does not possess a face or redemption value; it simply yields a perpetual stream of income payments. Such a bond is called a **consol.** These bonds are not familiar to most Americans, but some European governments issue consols.

In the case of consols, there is a very simple relationship between bond prices and interest rates. Suppose a consol yields to its holder a fixed income payment of A dollars per year. What is the PDV of this consol? That's easy. Since the consol yields a perpetual stream of revenues, its PDV can be expressed as

$$\text{PDV of a consol} = \frac{A}{(1+i)} + \frac{A}{(1+i)^2}$$
$$+ \cdots + \frac{A}{(1+i)^n} + \cdots.$$

---
[2] In shorter courses, this section can be skipped over without loss of continuity.

Table 11.1
Present discounted value of a bond—1-year, 5-year, 10-year, and 20-year maturities

Face value = $1,000
Coupon payment = $60 payable annually

maturity↓	Interest rate			
	3%	*6%*	*8%*	*15%*
1-year . . .	$1,029.20	$1,000	$981.60	$922.20
5-year . . .	1,137.40	1,000	920.00	698.20
10-year . . .	1,255.90	1,000	865.50	548.20
20-year . . .	1,449.50	1,000	804.10	436.60

Factoring out the common term, $A/(1+i)$, we get

$$\text{PDV of a consol} = \frac{A}{(1+i)} \times [1 + \frac{1}{(1+i)}$$
$$+ \cdots + \frac{1}{(1+i)^{n-1}} \cdots].$$

The sum inside the parentheses will be recognized as the sum of an infinite series whose general solution is given by $\frac{1+i}{i}$.[3] Thus,

$$\text{PDV of a consol} = \frac{A}{(1+i)} \times \frac{(1+i)}{i} = \frac{A}{i}.$$

And since the PDV of the consol is its price, this result implies that

$$\text{Price of a consol} = \frac{A}{i}.$$

The inverse relationship between bond prices and interest rates is now obvious. For a consol that yields a perpetual stream of income at the rate of $100 per year, its price will be $2,000 at a rate of interest of 5 percent (i.e., $100/0.05 = $2,000), and $1,000 at a rate of interest of 10 percent (i.e., $100/0.10 = $1,000). Can you

---
[3] This is easily demonstrated. Let $b^j = 1/(1+i)^j < 1$. Then, the series can be written as

$$1 + b + b^2 + \cdots + b^{n-1} + \cdots.$$

We have seen this kind of expression before. Its solution value is $\frac{1}{1-b}$. Substituting for b, this is equal to

$$\frac{1}{1-b} = \frac{1}{1 - \frac{1}{1+i}} = \frac{1}{\frac{1+i-1}{1+i}} = \frac{1}{\frac{i}{1+i}} = \frac{1+i}{i}.$$

figure out the prices of a consol yielding $60 per year at each of the rates of interest given in Table 11.1?

INTEREST RATE DETERMINATION: A FIRST APPROXIMATION

Having established the inverse relationship of bond prices to interest rates, it is now time to undertake an examination of the forces that determine interest rates (or, in other words, the forces that determine bond prices). Two widely used and essentially equivalent approaches to this problem—the **loanable funds theory** and the **liquidity preference theory**—have been suggested by economists. The loanable funds theory hypothesizes that interest rates are determined by the demand for and supply of loanable funds. The liquidity preference theory hypothesizes that the interest rate is determined by the demand for and supply of money. The liquidity preference theory has one distinct advantage over the loanable funds theory: It better enables us to clarify the issues that are hotly debated by different groups of economists. The liquidity preference theory, therefore, will be used in the subsequent analysis.

The demand for money

Assuming that the appropriate definition of money is M1, we define the money supply as the amount of currency and coin plus checkable deposits *in the hands of the public.* The money supply, therefore, is defined as the amount of money that people are *actually* holding—the amount of money that is actually in the hands of the public.

The demand for money, on the other hand, refers to the amount of money that the public is *willing* to hold. How much money people are willing to hold need not be the same as the amount they are actually holding. As a result, the demand for money can differ from the money supply. Our purpose here is to inquire into the forces that bring about the equality of the demand for and the supply of money.

What determines how much money people are willing to hold—that is, what determines the demand for money? Theoretically, the demand for money is determined by three factors—the level of economic activity, interest rates, and people's wealth. Let us examine each factor in turn.

The transactions demand for money. Money is the medium of exchange. As such, it is used to finance the billions of financial transactions that daily take place within the economy. The mere fact that money is used in this way, however, is not sufficient to establish the existence of a demand for money. *A transactions demand for money arises because the times when we receive income and the times when we make purchases are not perfectly synchronized.* Take an extreme example. Suppose you receive a paycheck once a month. If you made all of the purchases you intended to make for the month *at the same instant* you received the check, your transactions demand for money would be zero. You would not hold any money for the purpose of financing transactions later on in the month prior to the receipt of your next paycheck.

This example is clearly an extreme case. Normally, some time elapses between the receipt of income and its disbursement. That is, people normally deposit the bulk of their paycheck into their checkable deposit accounts. Over the month they write checks to pay for various items, gradually depleting that balance. Some people will run down their checkable deposit account balance very quickly as they write checks against their accumulated bills, leaving very little in the account for subsequent purchases later in the month. Others will spread their spending more or less evenly over the month. In any event, the *average* amount that people are willing to hold in their checkable deposit accounts or in the form of currency for the purpose of financing transactions over the month constitutes their monthly demand for money for transactions purposes.

In general, as the dollar volume of transactions within the economy rises, so will the quantity of money demanded for transactions purposes. Since the dollar volume of transactions is closely related to the nominal GNP—it is not precisely the same since the total amount of business transacted includes both intermediate and final sales, whereas GNP refers to the final sales only—we should expect to find a close association between the quantity of money demanded for transactions purposes and the level of economic activity. Figure 11.1 illustrates this relationship. Note in Figure 11.1 how the amount of money demanded for transactions purposes rises from $60 billion to $200 billion as the nominal GNP rises from $300 billion to $1,000 billion.

Note one important implication of Figure 11.1 and its accompanying table: Each dollar finances $5 worth of final purchases. How can this be so? Well, when you spend $50 for groceries, that $50 can be used by the grocer to buy other goods and services; and when the grocer spends that $50, it becomes available for use by someone else; and so on. In other words, *depending on the time period under consideration,* any given dollar can be used over and over again to make purchases. For simplicity, we assume that Figure 11.1 summarizes the transactions that take place over a year. Thus, on average, each dollar finances $5 worth of final purchases during the year; the *velocity of transactions balances*—the rate of turn-

over of transactions balances per year—is therefore equal to 5.

The transactions demand for money is also affected by the rate of interest. That is, the amount of money that many individuals and businesses are willing to hold in their checkable deposit accounts for the purpose of making their planned expenditures between income periods is sensitive to the rate of interest. There is an opportunity cost to holding money—the foregone higher interest earnings that could have been obtained from higher interest-yielding assets. The higher the interest rate on nonM1 assets, the higher that opportunity cost is; and the greater the opportunity cost, the greater the incentive will be for people to hold as little as possible in their low-interest-bearing checkable deposit accounts. The demand for money for transactions purposes, therefore, is inversely related to the rate of interest: the higher the rate of interest, the smaller the demand for money for transactions purposes. *As interest rates rise, people economize on their holdings of transactions balances.*

This inverse relation between the amount of money demanded for transactions purposes and

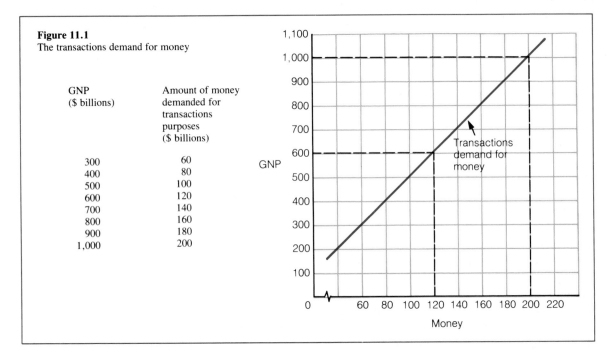

Figure 11.1
The transactions demand for money

GNP ($ billions)	Amount of money demanded for transactions purposes ($ billions)
300	60
400	80
500	100
600	120
700	140
800	160
900	180
1,000	200

the interest rate is important—it indicates that a given level of economic activity can be financed with a smaller volume of transactions balances. The velocity of transactions balances therefore increases. Whereas our earlier discussion implied a transactions velocity of 5, at an increased rate of interest, the transactions velocity could rise above 5 to perhaps 6 or more.

A simple numerical example will illustrate this point. Suppose you now get a paycheck once a month for $1,000 that you spend evenly over the course of each month. Suppose further that you put your entire paycheck in your checkable deposit account and draw on it as you make your expenditures. Under these circumstances, you will maintain an *average* balance of $500 in your account each month—you start out with $1,000 at the beginning and end up with zero at the end meaning that, on average, you maintain $500 in your account. If interest rates rise, you might be induced to place one half of your paycheck in some higher interest earning asset (not part of M1) for a two week period. The other half is put in your checkable account to cover your expenses for a two week period. At the end of two weeks, you *cash in* your higher interest earning asset and put the proceeds in your checkable deposit account to meet expenses for the last two weeks of the month. In this instance, your average balance in your checkable deposit account is $250. Yet you continue to finance as many purchases per month as before: fewer dollars in transactions balances enable the same value of transactions as before. If other people react as you do, there will be fewer transactions balances generally to finance a given volume of transactions. As a result, the velocity of transactions balances increases.

The asset (or speculative) demand for money. People are also willing to hold money—in their wallets, checkable deposit accounts, safes, and cookie jars—as one of the assets constituting their net worth or wealth. Such money holdings are desired for a number of very good reasons. Money is a very convenient form in which to hold your assets. It is the essence of liquidity

and is less risky than bonds or stocks; whereas the *nominal* value of stocks and bonds can change rather dramatically as a result of fluctuations in the stock market and changing interest rates, the *nominal* value of money is immune from such fluctuations. Moreover, if some people feel that interest rates are likely to rise in the near future, they may be willing to hold money in lieu of bonds. Why? Because if interest rates do rise, bond prices will fall. Not only will these people hold money hoping to buy bonds later at a lower price, they will probably also sell off some of their existing bond holdings now in order to avoid a future capital loss if and when interest rates rise. In effect, they hold money speculating on a rise in interest rates. The amount of money that people are willing to hold for these reasons is called the **asset** or **speculative demand for money.** *It represents the amount of money that people are willing to hold, over and above the amount they are willing to hold for transactions purposes.*

What determines the asset or speculative demand for money? In large measure it is determined by the interest rate and people's wealth. Let us focus our attention first on the interest rate. Since currency and coin do not earn interest, and since most checkable deposit accounts offer lower interest returns than noncheckable deposit account assets, there is an obvious opportunity cost to holding money. Therefore, it is reasonable to expect an inverse relationship between the interest rate and people's holdings of money for asset purposes. The higher the interest rate, the greater the desire of people will be to hold less money and more noncheckable deposit account assets in their asset portfolios. This hypothesized inverse relationship is illustrated in Figure 11.2.

First a word of explanation about Figure 11.2. We assume for simplicity that the financial wealth of people consists of two assets only—bonds and money. We also assume that the stock of financial wealth is initially fixed at some constant level equal to $500 billion. How much of that $500 billion people will be willing to hold in the form of money will depend on the rate of interest. At an interest rate of 3 percent, we

Figure 11.2
The asset or speculative demand for money

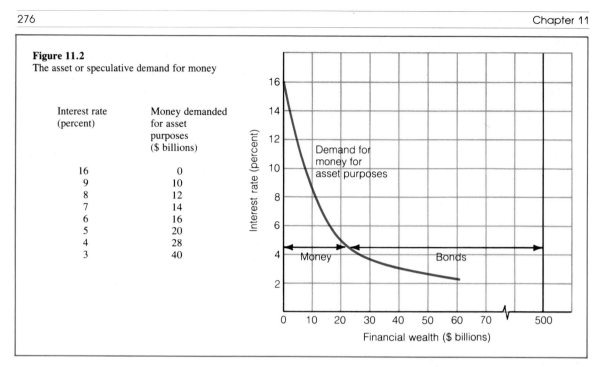

Interest rate (percent)	Money demanded for asset purposes ($ billions)
16	0
9	10
8	12
7	14
6	16
5	20
4	28
3	40

assume people will be willing to hold $40 billion in the form of money balances. As the rate of interest rises, people will reduce their money holdings in order to acquire more bonds. As the interest rate rises from 3 percent to 9 percent to 16 percent, the amount of money demanded for asset purposes is reduced, respectively, from $40 billion to $10 billion to zero.

Besides interest rates, the asset (or speculative) demand for money will also depend on the amount of wealth people possess. As wealth increases, people will attempt to increase their holdings of both bonds *and* money. The asset demand for money is therefore positively related to wealth. In terms of Figure 11.2, changes in the asset demand for money because of changes in wealth will be reflected in a *shift* of the demand curve—an increase (in the case of an increase in wealth) or a decrease (in the case of a reduction in wealth) in the asset demand curve at each and every interest rate.

The total demand for money

The total demand for money (M_d) is made up of the sum of its two component parts—the

transactions demand (M_{dt}) and the asset demand (M_{da}). Formally,

$$M_d = M_{dt} + M_{da}.$$

We are now in a position to integrate the various factors influencing people's demands for money.

The transactions demand is determined by the level of income and the interest rate. The higher the level of income, the higher the quantity of money demanded for transactions purposes; the higher the interest rate, the smaller the quantity demanded for transactions purposes.

The asset demand for money is determined by the level of wealth and the interest rate. The greater the stock of wealth, the greater the quantity of money demanded for asset purposes; the higher the interest rate, the smaller the amount of money demanded for asset purposes.

These relationships are illustrated graphically in Figure 11.3. To begin the analysis, assume that the level of income and wealth are fixed initially at Y_0 and W_0 respectively. Examine first the upper left-hand portion of Figure 11.3. We show there the transactions demand for money for a given level of income, Y_0. The curve labeled

$M_{dt}(Y_0)$ reflects the relationship between the transactions demand for money and the interest rate on the assumption of a fixed level of income, Y_0. Note that, as the interest rate rises from i_1 to i_4, the quantity of money demanded for transactions purposes declines from M_{dt}^1 to M_{dt}^4.

The upper right-hand portion of Figure 11.3 represents the asset demand for money for some given level of wealth, W_0. The curve labeled $M_{da}(W_0)$ reflects the relationship between the asset demand for money and the interest rate on the assumption of a given fixed level of wealth, W_0. Note that, at an interest rate of i_4, the asset demand for money is zero; at the low interest rate i_1, it equals M_{da}^1.

By adding together the transactions and asset demands for money we arrive at the total demand for money. This is done in the lower portion of Figure 11.3. The dashed curve labeled $M_{dt}(Y_0)$ is simply a reproduction of the transactions de-

mand for money relationship discussed above; the curve labeled $L(Y_0, W_0)$ is the total demand for money curve obtained by adding together the transactions and asset demands for money at each and every rate of interest. This is called the **liquidity preference** schedule. Liquidity preference is the convention used by economists to express the public's demand for money. Note once again that this curve is drawn on the assumption that income and wealth are both fixed initially.

As is apparent from the liquidity preference schedule, at an interest rate of i_4 or above, the total demand for money consists of the transactions demand only. The reason? At i_4 the asset demand for money is zero. At the interest rate i_1, on the other hand, the total demand for money, M_d^1, consists of a transactions demand of M_{dt}^1 plus an asset demand of M_{da}^1.

A final note. It is useful to break up the de-

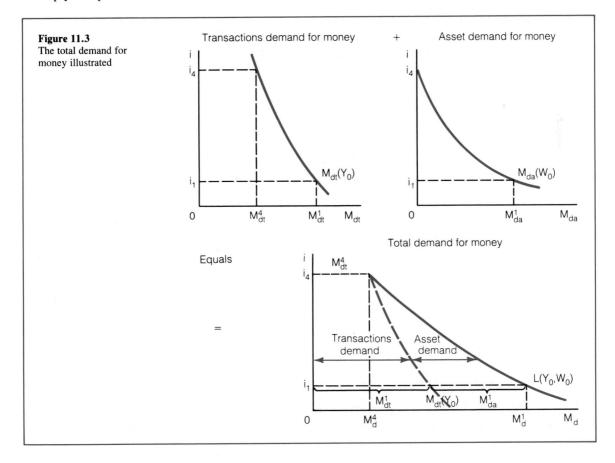

Figure 11.3
The total demand for money illustrated

mand for money into a transactions demand and an asset demand to emphasize the *motives* for holding money. However, it would be incorrect to conclude that one could identify a "bundle A" as people's transactions balances and a "bundle B" as people's asset balances. It is best, therefore, to think in terms of the total demand for money, and to recognize that the amount of money people are willing to hold will depend on their income, their wealth, and interest rates.

Liquidity preference and changes in income and wealth

What happens to the total demand for money as nominal income rises from Y_0 to Y_1? Since the increase in nominal income increases the demand for money for transactions purposes, the liquidity preference schedule *shifts* to the right at each and every rate of interest. This is shown in Figure 11.4A as a rightward displacement of the liquidity preference schedule from $L(Y_0, W_0)$ to $L(Y_1, W_0)$.

Likewise, since the asset demand for money is also positively related to wealth, an increase in wealth will cause a rightward displacement

of the liquidity preference schedule—that is, an increase in the demand for money will result at each and every rate of interest. This is shown graphically in Figure 11.4B as a shift of the schedule from $L(Y_0, W_0)$ to $L(Y_0, W_1)$.

Equilibrium in the money market

Money market equilibrium will occur when the total demand for money is equal to the money supply. To illustrate this idea, we will assume a fixed supply of money initially. This is tantamount to assuming that the monetary authorities engage in whatever actions are necessary to keep the stock of money fixed. If the actions of the public, the commercial banks, or the Treasury lead to increases in the money supply, the Fed will undertake offsetting policies designed to return the money supply to its assumed fixed level.

Recall our earlier definition of the money supply—currency and coin plus checkable deposits *in the hands of the public.* By definition, then, the money supply is held by the public. However, as is apparent from the forces that affect the demand for money, whether people are *willing* to hold the amount of money that they are in fact

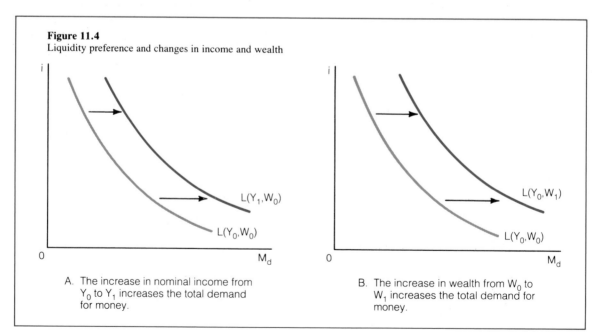

Figure 11.4
Liquidity preference and changes in income and wealth

A. The increase in nominal income from Y_0 to Y_1 increases the total demand for money.

B. The increase in wealth from W_0 to W_1 increases the total demand for money.

holding will depend on the levels of income (Y) and wealth (W) and the rate of interest (i). *If people actually hold more money than they are willing to hold, an excess supply of money will exist. An excess demand for money is said to exist if the amount of money that people are willing to hold exceeds what they actually hold.* Since these ways of expressing excess supply and excess demand are somewhat novel, let us examine their meaning in greater detail.

To illustrate, suppose the money supply is fixed at $200 billion. Suppose further that income and wealth are both fixed initially at Y_0 and W_0 respectively. Finally, assume an initial interest rate of 9 percent.

Given an income level equal to Y_0, a quantity of wealth equal to W_0, and an interest rate of 9 percent, let the total demand for money equal $170 billion. Since the money supply equals $200 billion, people are actually holding $30 billion more than they want to hold given the 9 percent rate of interest. As a result, they will attempt to reduce their money holdings by buying non-money interest-yielding bonds (or other non-money interest-bearing assets). However, *while it is possible for individuals to reduce their money balances, it is impossible for money balances in the aggregate to be reduced. Money balances are merely transferred from those who buy bonds to those who sell them.* Does this mean that an excess supply of money will always exist? No. The reason is this. As people attempt to reduce their money balances by buying bonds, the price of bonds will be driven up. Because of the inverse relationship between bond prices and interest rates, interest rates will fall. But as interest rates decline, more and more people will be willing to hold larger and larger amounts of money; in other words, *the excess supply of money will force interest rates down until the demand for money is brought into line with the money supply.* This is illustrated in Figure 11.5.

The money supply being fixed at $200 billion is represented as a vertical straight line above $200 billion. At a 9 percent rate of interest, a $30 billion excess supply of money exists. As people attempt to reduce their money balances, the interest rate will decline, *raising* the quantity of money demanded for transactions and asset purposes. Equilibrium will occur only at a 5 percent rate of interest.

At a rate of interest of 3 percent, on the other hand, an excess demand for money will exist. Can you explain what this means? If people attempt to increase their money balances, what will happen to bond prices? Interest rates? The

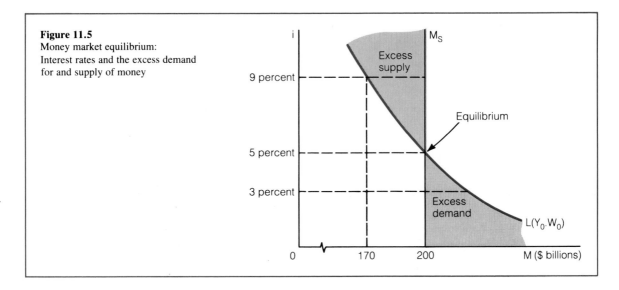

Figure 11.5
Money market equilibrium:
Interest rates and the excess demand
for and supply of money

quantity of money demanded for transactions and asset purposes? Can you explain why the interest rate will rise to 5 percent?

The money supply and the interest rate

What will happen to the interest rate if the monetary authorities increase the money supply? On the basis of the foregoing discussion, it is clear that interest rates will fall. This can be explained in a number of ways. If the Fed expands system reserves and the money supply via an open market purchase, interest rates will be lowered directly because an open market purchase raises bond prices and lowers interest rates. Moreover, the open market purchase will increase excess reserves in the banking system. If banks use these excess reserves to increase their holdings of bonds, bond prices will rise further and interest rates will lower. If banks use the excess reserves to expand their loan portfolios, loan rates on business and consumer loans will frequently be reduced in order to induce people to step up their borrowing. These changes in interest rates are summarized in Figure 11.6. As the money supply is increased from M_s to M_s^1, the interest rate declines from i_1 to i_2. Conversely,

a reduction in the money supply causes the interest rate to rise.

THE IMPACT OF INTEREST RATES ON AGGREGATE DEMAND

It is a widely held view that reductions in the interest rate are an important means of stimulating expenditures for consumer durables, housing, and business fixed investment. The reason for this is straightforward: Lower interest rates reduce the costs of financing these expenditures. To illustrate, let us examine the effect of interest rates on business fixed investment.

Consider the problem confronting a business executive who is attempting to ascertain whether the purchase of some piece of capital equipment is profitable or not. The cost of the machine is $1,000. It is expected to have a useful life of 10 years, at the end of which time it will be junked. For each of the 10 years the machine is in use, the business executive *expects* to receive $150 in additional revenues. Is it profitable to purchase the machine? Not necessarily. It is true that the machine costs only $1,000 and is expected to yield $1,500 in additional revenues. But this $1,500 represents the stream of expected *future* revenues. Whether or not it is profitable depends largely on the rate of interest.

The influence of the rate of interest on the investment decision can be looked at in three ways. In the first place, if the business must borrow funds to purchase the machine, repaying the loan in installments over the 10-year period, the $1,500 in revenues may not be sufficient to cover the principal of the loan (the $1,000) plus interest costs. Indeed, if the interest rate happens to be 8 percent per annum, the assumed $1,500 in revenues will be just sufficient to cover costs; a higher rate of interest would make the purchase a distinctly unprofitable venture. This will become apparent shortly.

Second, if the business executive does not need to borrow but uses instead the firm's internal funds (business savings) to purchase the machine, the interest costs are avoided but an opportunity cost is incurred. By using internal funds to pur-

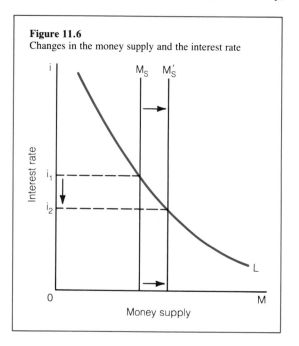

Figure 11.6
Changes in the money supply and the interest rate

Interest rate (vertical axis, i); Money supply (horizontal axis, M). Curve labeled L. Vertical lines M_S and M_S'. Horizontal dashed lines at i_1 and i_2.

Table 11.2
The PDV of an investment project illustrated

Cost of machine = $1,000
Useful life = 10 years

(1) Revenues	(2) PDV (i = 0.05)	(3) PDV (i = 0.07)	(4) PDV (i = 0.08)	(5) PDV (i = 0.10)	(6) PDV (i = 0.12)
$ 150	$ 142.86	$ 140.19	$ 138.89	$136.36	$133.93
150	136.05	131.01	128.60	123.97	119.58
150	129.58	122.45	119.07	112.70	106.77
150	123.41	114.43	110.25	102.45	95.33
150	117.53	106.95	102.09	93.14	85.11
150	111.93	99.95	94.53	84.67	75.99
150	106.60	93.41	87.52	76.96	67.85
150	101.53	87.30	81.04	69.98	60.58
150	96.69	81.59	75.04	63.62	54.09
150	92.09	76.25	69.48	57.83	48.30
$1,500	$1,158.27	$1,053.53	$1,006.51	$921.68	$848.53

chase the machine, the business executive foregoes the opportunity of using those funds in other ways that could yield interest income. If the interest rate at which the firm can borrow is the same as the interest rate at which the firm can lend its funds, the use of internal funds means that the firm foregoes in profit an amount exactly equal to what the interest costs would have been had the funds been borrowed. To ascertain the profitability of the purchase, this opportunity cost must be reckoned with on the same terms as the interest costs of borrowing.

A third approach—and the one most commonly employed—is to calculate the present discounted value (PDV) of the revenues associated with the machine and compare that value with its costs. If the present discounted value of the stream of revenues associated with the investment exceeds its cost, it is profitable to make the investment; otherwise, it is not.

What is the PDV of the stream of revenues associated with the machine described above? Letting i represent the interest rate and assuming a useful life of 10 years, the PDV of the assumed $150 per year in revenues can readily be calculated as follows:

$$PDV = \frac{\$150}{(1+i)} + \frac{\$150}{(1+i)^2} + \frac{\$150}{(1+i)^3}$$
$$+ \cdots + \frac{\$150}{(1+i)^{10}}.$$

Obviously, the PDV will depend on the interest rate. The higher the interest rate, the smaller the PDV; the lower the rate, the larger the PDV. Table 11.2 illustrates this principle using interest rates of 5, 7, 8, 10, and 12 percent. As is apparent, it is profitable to undertake this investment project only if the interest rate is 8 percent or less; at an interest rate exceeding 8 percent, it is unprofitable.

The marginal efficiency of investment (MEI)

These ideas can be looked at somewhat differently. Depending on the value of the interest rate, the PDV of the stream of revenues for any given investment project represents the *maximum* amount the firm will be willing to pay to undertake it. If the interest rate is 5 percent, the firm would be willing to pay a maximum of $1,158 for a machine that yields a 10-year stream of revenues of $150 per year; at a rate of interest of 12 percent, on the other hand, the firm would be willing to pay a maximum of only $848. Since the machine costs $1,000, the maximum rate of interest the firm is willing to pay (either to borrow or to use its internal funds) is 8 percent. This maximum rate is called the **marginal efficiency of investment (MEI),** or alternatively, the **rate of return** on the investment project.[4] If the rate

---

[4] Specifically, the *rate of return* on an investment is defined as *that rate of interest, r, which discounts the stream of reve-*

of interest exceeds the rate of return (or the MEI), it will not be profitable to proceed with the project; if the rate of interest is less than the rate of return, it is profitable. Letting r represent the rate of return or MEI, this can be represented as follows:

If: $i > r$, the project is unprofitable
        $i < r$, the project is profitable.

Returning to our original problem—namely, determining the relationship between the interest rate and the volume of investment—it is clear that at any particular time, millions of business firms will be looking at millions of investment projects seeking to ascertain their profitability. For each one of these projects, it is possible to calculate the expected rate of return or MEI. By comparing the various rates of return with the interest rate, we can determine which projects are profitable and which are not.

Suppose we were to rank order all of these projects on the basis of their various rates of return. If we were to look at all projects earning a return of 20 percent or more, that list would be much smaller than one that contained all projects earning 5 percent or more. Using this rank ordering procedure, then, we could construct an MEI schedule like the one presented in Figure 11.7. Such an MEI schedule could be called an **investment demand schedule,** because it depicts how the volume of investment will vary as the rate of interest is varied. At very high rates of interest, the volume of investment will be relatively small because few projects in the economy yield a sufficiently high rate of return. At lower rates of interest, a larger volume of projects will be undertaken since more projects yield the necessary rate of return, with the result that investment demand will be higher. This is illustrated in Figure 11.7.

On the vertical axis we represent both the rate

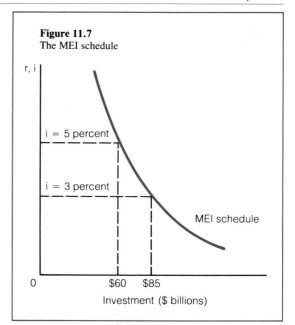

Figure 11.7
The MEI schedule

of return and the rate of interest. Given the rate of interest, all those investment projects having a rate of return *equal to or above* that interest rate will be undertaken. Therefore, when i equals 5 percent, $60 billion worth of investment projects will be undertaken because that many projects have a rate of return of at least 5 percent. And if the rate of interest falls to 3 percent, the volume of investment will expand from $60 billion to $85 billion. Can you explain why?

One final note. We should emphasize that the position of the MEI schedule depends very much on business expectations. Recall that the stream of revenues associated with any investment project consists of revenues that are *expected.* If expectations are altered, the MEI schedule will shift so that there will be different levels of investment at each and every rate of interest. For example, during recessions, businesspeople often have a rather pessimistic outlook, at least for the near future. This implies that they expect a smaller stream of revenues associated with any given investment project. Such pessimism causes the MEI schedule to shift to the left; at each and every interest rate there will be a smaller volume of investment. The converse is true if businesspeople become optimistic

---

nues associated with the investment to an amount equal to its cost. Letting C equal the cost of the investment, and R_1, R_2, . . ., R_n represent the expected stream of revenues for n periods, the rate of return is found by identifying an r such that:

$$C = \frac{R_1}{(1+r)} + \frac{R_2}{(1+r)^2} + \frac{R_3}{(1+r)^3} + \cdots + \frac{R_n}{(1+r)^n}.$$

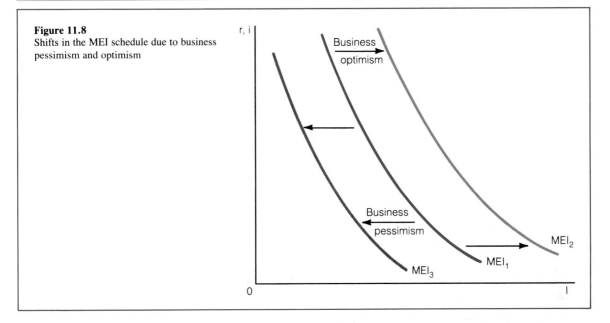

Figure 11.8
Shifts in the MEI schedule due to business pessimism and optimism

about their future sales prospects. This is illustrated in Figure 11.8.

Money, investment, the multiplier, and the level of economic activity

It is now a relatively simple task to indicate how monetary policy can be used to effect changes in the level of economic activity. If the monetary authorities desire to pursue an expansionary policy to expand production, income, and employment, they will usually undertake an open market purchase to expand system reserves and therewith the money supply. The level of economic activity will be altered as a result of the following chain of events:

1. The increased money supply will lead to a reduction in interest rates.
2. The reduced interest rates will stimulate business investment spending (and consumer spending on durable goods and housing as well).
3. The increased spending constitutes an increase in aggregate demand, which, via the expenditure multiplier, generates a multiple increase in income and production.

Whether or not monetary policy is effective in expanding the level of economic activity depends on the degree to which interest rates are lowered and, in turn, the degree to which expenditures are responsive to reduced interest rates. There are other channels of monetary influence besides interest rates, which we will discuss later. But the interest rate channel of transmission is the one that has been the most thoroughly studied.

There is general agreement among economists that monetary policy *normally does* affect interest rates in the manner described above. In addition, interest rates *are* an important determinant of business spending for investment. However, there is much less agreement concerning the efficacy of monetary policy when economic conditions become severely depressed. Under conditions characterized by very high rates of unemployment, high levels of excess capacity, and bearish (i.e., pessimistic) expectations, monetary policy may lose much of its effectiveness. Several arguments have been advanced in favor of this view.

First, commercial banks may not expand their loans much, even if they experience an increase in their excess reserves as a result of the expansionary monetary policy. With business conditions so poor, there may be considerable risk of default on the part of would-be borrowers; loan expansion could be very risky.

Second, there may not be much of a demand for loans on the part of the business community and consumers even if interest rates do fall. If consumers become fearful that they might lose their jobs, or if they are already unemployed, they are likely to put off some of their spending plans for consumer durables and other credit purchases until business conditions improve; they are likely to tighten their belts rather than step up their spending. Moreover, if businesspeople are pessimistic about their future sales prospects, or find themselves with a lot of idle (excess) capacity, they are not likely to expand their plant and equipment expenditures by very much, if at all, in response to a reduction in interest rates.

Third, it is also unlikely that banks will expand the money supply by much by using their excess reserves to acquire bonds from the public. If interest rates are low—as is usually the case during severely depressed economic conditions—bankers may come to feel that such rates have no place to go but up in the future, meaning that they could experience a future capital loss that could wipe out any gain they might receive in the form of interest income on their bond holdings. Therefore, they will simply run up their holdings of excess reserves.

Under these circumstances, monetary policy could well prove to be very ineffective in extricating us from the depths of a depression.

MONETARY POLICY AND THE INFLATIONARY AND DEFLATIONARY GAPS

Despite some doubts regarding the efficacy of monetary policy during periods when the level of economic activity is severely depressed, most economists are in agreement regarding its potency at other times. Monetary policy can generally be used for the purpose of eliminating inflationary and deflationary gaps. Thus, if the economy is confronted with an inflationary gap—that is, a level of aggregate demand in excess of the full employment level of output—the monetary authorities could pursue a restrictive or contractionary policy in order to bring aggregate demand down to the full employment level. The restrictive monetary policy, by raising interest rates, would reduce interest-sensitive spending and, therewith, the level of aggregate demand. This is illustrated in Figure 11.9. By inducing a reduction in aggregate demand from AD_0 to AD_1, monetary policy is capable of eliminating the inflationary gap. Can you explain how mone-

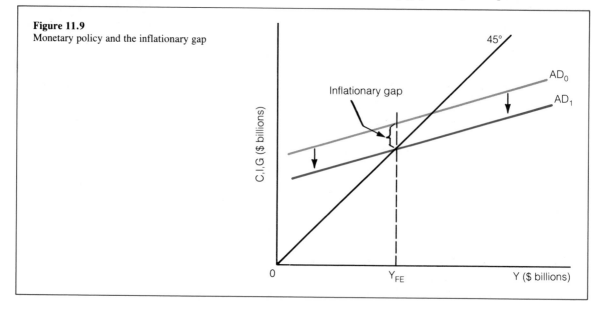

Figure 11.9
Monetary policy and the inflationary gap

tary policy would be used to eliminate a deflationary gap?

OTHER CHANNELS OF MONETARY INFLUENCE

Up to this point we have focused our attention exclusively on the "money supply–interest rate, interest rate–investment" channel of transmission of monetary policy. But while this channel of monetary influence is widely viewed as one of the most important channels through which monetary policy affects the economy, some economists have stressed the importance of yet other channels of monetary influence. Of these other channels, two have been emphasized in the economics literature. They are the **interest-induced wealth effect** and **credit rationing.**

The interest-induced wealth effect can best be understood by recalling our earlier discussion of the inverse relationship between bond prices and interest rates. As interest rates decline due to an expansion of the money supply, the fact that bond prices rise means that the value of the bonds that people hold in their portfolios rises. As a result, people are wealthier. And in response to this increase in wealth, people will increase their consumer expenditures; the consumption function shifts up, further increasing aggregate demand.

The credit-rationing mechanism is frequently invoked as an explanation of the effectiveness of monetary policy, especially during periods of credit restriction. That is, during periods when the Fed is pursuing a restrictive monetary policy, lending institutions may not raise their interest rates sufficiently, preferring instead to ration their loanable funds selectively among their borrowing customers. Rather than use higher interest rates as the exclusive means to discourage borrowing, lending institutions will often turn down some loan applications and/or provide fewer funds than many borrowers want, using the argument that loanable funds are simply unavailable.

But why would lending institutions ration credit selectively rather than raise interest rates by enough to restrict borrowing to a level consistent with available funds? It is often argued that higher interest rates would irritate many long-standing bank customers; if they decided to go elsewhere with their banking business, the longer-term profits of the bank would suffer. Banks would therefore prefer to ration their credit selectively in the interest of maintaining better long-term customer relations. Thus, although lending rates might not rise significantly as a result of restrictive Fed policies, monetary policy can still be very effective in restricting overall credit. The interest rate channel of transmission is not the only important mechanism during periods of "tight money."

THE MONETARIST-FISCALIST DEBATE[5]

There is fairly general agreement among economists that changes in the money supply can bring about changes in the level of economic activity. The question is, Can the level of economic activity be changed without changing the money supply? One group of economists—the **monetarists**—argue that, in the long run, a stable and relatively fixed relationship exists between the money supply and nominal GNP. According to many monetarists, nominal income can increase in the long run *only if* the money supply is increased. If this proposition is true, it leads us to the following highly significant conclusion: If government undertakes an expansionary fiscal policy—either increasing government spending or reducing taxes—for the purpose of expanding income and output, it will fail to bring about that result unless the fiscal policy change is accompanied by an increase in the money supply; fiscal policy unaccompanied by an accommodating change in the money supply is incapable of altering, except temporarily, the level of economic activity. The reasoning underlying this argument can be stated, in its essentials, as follows:

Virtually all spending in our economy is financed using money. At any moment in time,

---

[5] In shorter courses this section may be skipped over without loss of continuity.

there is a fixed quantity of money available for use by the participants of an economy. If it is true that a given quantity of money has associated with it one, and only one, long-run level of nominal GNP, then in the absence of a change in the money supply, increased spending by any one group must come at the expense of the spending of others. If government spending is increased, there will be an offsetting reduction in spending in the private sector. An increase in government spending "crowds out" an equivalent amount of private spending. Therefore, fiscal policy unaccompanied by an accommodating change in the money supply is incapable of altering our economy's nominal GNP.

Nonmonetarist economists sharply disagree with this line of reasoning. They take exception with the monetarist view that a stable and fixed relationship exists between the money supply and nominal GNP. To their way of thinking, it is *not* true that a given quantity of money has associated with it one, and only one, level of nominal GNP. Indeed, they argue that *significantly different levels of economic activity can be financed with the same given fixed stock of money*. To the extent that this is true, there is then no reason to accept, as a matter of logical necessity, the monetarist proposition that an increase in government spending unaccompanied by an accommodating increase in the money supply will "crowd out" an equivalent amount of private spending. There may be *some* offsetting reduction in private spending, *some* crowding out, but much less than dollar for dollar. What is the conclusion according to the nonmonetarists? Fiscal policy, by itself, can and does lead to changes in the level of economic activity; fiscal policy is *not* impotent.

This debate between monetarists and nonmonetarists is extremely important from the point of view of policy. If the monetarists are correct, the policy choices are fairly clear and simple. By controlling the growth of the money supply we control growth of nominal GNP; fiscal policy, being impotent, cannot alter this outcome. Moreover, if policymakers are anxious to pursue policies designed to achieve a relatively stable rate of economic growth, the monetarist argument implies a simple solution: *Engage in policies designed to ensure a stable growth in the money supply.* Indeed, some monetarists, most notably Nobel laureate Milton Friedman, have suggested that the Federal Reserve pursue a **fixed monetary growth rule.** This rule states that the growth of the money supply be fixed at a rate approximately equal to the growth of our potential GNP and left there. Discretionary changes in the money supply are not undertaken, no matter what. Erratic changes in the money supply, according to the rule, can lead ultimately to only one result—erratic changes in the level of economic activity.

If the nonmonetarists are correct, on the other hand, the policy choices are considerably more complicated. If a wide range of output levels can be financed with a given stock of money, there is no reason to think that a fixed monetary growth rule will bring about less pronounced swings in the level of economic activity; the swings in the level of economic activity could, in fact, be very pronounced. There is, therefore, considerable scope for discretionary action on the part of policymakers to pursue policies designed to moderate swings in nominal GNP. Moreover, in view of the potency of fiscal policy, *both* monetary and fiscal policy can be used to produce greater economic stability.

What accounts for these sharply differing views regarding the conduct of macroeconomic policy? Fundamentally, these differences arise because of differing views regarding the **velocity of circulation.**

Velocity of circulation revisited

The importance of the velocity of circulation is easy to understand. Money is used in virtually all economic transactions. Therefore, each transaction involves an exchange of a good or service for money. Armed with this information, it is easy to determine the numerical value of the velocity of circulation for the economy as a whole. If nominal income equals $1,000 billion and if the money supply equals $250 billion, the velocity of circulation *must* equal 4 (i.e., 1,000 ÷

250 = 4). Since $1,000 billion of final sales were effected with a money supply of $250 billion, *on average* each dollar of money financed $4 worth of final sales; the velocity of circulation equals 4.

This relationship is captured in the famous **equation of exchange.** It states that the quantity of money (M) multiplied by the velocity of circulation (V) is *identical* to the nominal value of GNP (P × Q). Thus,

$$M \times V = P \times Q,$$

where P is an index of the prices of the goods and services produced (i.e., the GNP implicit price deflator) and Q is a measure of real output.

Considerable care must be exercised in using this identity (or any identity) to interpret economic events. One cannot infer, for example, that a change in M will lead unequivocally to a change in nominal income; an increase in M could be offset by a reduction in V such that M × V would be unaltered. Or suppose that we observe an increase in both nominal income and M × V (as we must, since they are equal). Can we say that it was the change in M × V that *caused* the change in P × Q? Or should we say that the change in P × Q *caused* the change in M × V? From the identity alone, we cannot determine which statement is true.

However, it is possible to make use of this identity to say something meaningful about the velocity of circulation. If the stock of money is fixed, there can be no increase in nominal GNP *unless* velocity increases. Or, putting it differently, if nominal income increases without an accompanying increase in the money supply, the velocity of circulation must have increased. Here it is the increase in V that "finances" the increase in nominal GNP.

Interest rates and the velocity of circulation. Our earlier study of the demand for and supply of money would seem to indicate that the velocity of circulation will increase as interest rates increase, and that the converse is also true. Let us see why.

If aggregate income increases, an increase in the demand for money will result. As a result of that, interest rates will rise. Why? In order

to finance an increased volume of transactions, more money will be required for transactions purposes. If the money supply is fixed, where will these additional transactions balances come from? Obviously, the additional transactions balances can be attained only through a reduction in people's asset holdings of money or through greater economies in the use of transactions balances. How is this accomplished? Through an increase in interest rates. And what causes interest rates to rise? Increased borrowing by those who have increased their spending, which puts upward pressure on interest rates. In effect, higher interest rates are the means whereby at least some portion of people's asset balances are converted to transactions balances. Higher interest rates also provide people with an incentive to economize on their transactions balances. Figure 11.10 summarizes this outcome. Note there that the increased demand for money associated with the increase in nominal income from Y_0 to Y_1 causes the interest rate to rise from i_1 to i_3.

Note carefully one critically important implication of this discussion: The money supply was assumed fixed, yet that given money supply was capable of supporting an increase in the level of economic activity. This outcome was possible because the velocity of money increased. And the velocity of money increased because interest rates rose. This positive relationship between the velocity of circulation and interest rates, as we will see below, is critically important to the monetarist-fiscalist debate.

Fiscal policy, money, and the level of economic activity

To illustrate, consider an expansionary fiscal policy unaccompanied by any change in the money supply. Suppose government steps up its expenditures. The increase in aggregate demand will, via the multiplier, tend to increase the equilibrium level of income. However, the increased level of income raises the transactions demand for money. As a result, interest rates rise. Because of higher interest rates, private investment spend-

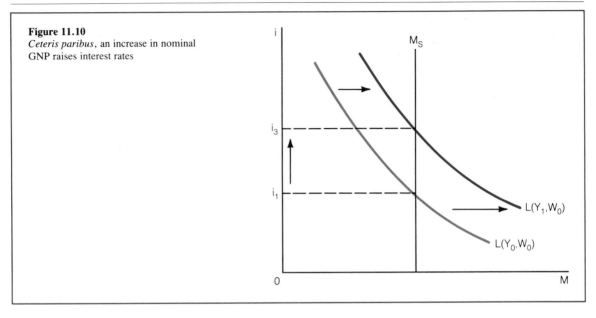

Figure 11.10
Ceteris paribus, an increase in nominal GNP raises interest rates

ing (and other interest-sensitive spending) is reduced. These interest-induced reductions in private spending reduce aggregate demand. As a result, *the increase in aggregate demand brought about by an increased level of government spending is at least in part offset by reduced levels of private spending.* In the jargon of economists, the increase in government spending **crowds out** at least some private spending. This is because higher levels of government spending unaccompanied by an increase in the money supply force up interest rates. *The ultimate impact on the level of GNP of an increase in government expenditures, therefore, will depend on the extent of the reduction in private expenditures caused by higher interest rates.* If the reduction in private spending is less than the increase in government spending, the equilibrium level of income will rise. However, if the increase in government expenditures crowds out an equivalent amount of private expenditures, the equilibrium level of income will remain unaltered. Fiscal policy will then be incapable of altering the level of economic activity.

The crowding-out hypothesis. The monetarist school of thought hypothesizes that increases in government expenditures *do* crowd out an equivalent amount of private expenditures. This

is called, appropriately enough, the **crowding-out hypothesis.** Nonmonetarists, on the other hand, argue that there is only a partial crowding out; the crowding out is incomplete and, as a result, fiscal policy is capable of altering the level of income independent of any changes in the money supply.

Is it possible to resolve this debate one way or another? Maybe. Everything will depend on what happens to the velocity of circulation. This should be obvious from our earlier discussion of the equation of exchange. If the money supply is fixed, the nominal GNP can increase only if velocity increases. So what happens to velocity? The monetarists argue that it will remain unaltered; the nonmonetarists argue that it will increase. Let us examine this issue more closely.

We noted earlier that the public will reduce its holdings of money for asset and transactions purposes as a result of an increase in interest rates. On this the monetarists and nonmonetarists both agree. *If this were the only relevant factor under consideration,* the velocity of circulation would most definitely increase. In other words, monetarists and nonmonetarists agree that the velocity of circulation is positively related to interest rates.

If nothing else happened, then, there would be a *partial* crowding out of private expenditures only. Part of the increase in government spending would come at the expense of private spending; but the rest would be financed through an increase in the velocity of circulation.

Since people do reduce their holdings of money at higher rates of interest, and since velocity increases as a consequence, does this mean that fiscal policy is therefore potent? The monetarists say no.

There is one other factor that needs to be taken account of before the issue can be settled. It is as follows. Since government finances its increased expenditures by borrowing—by issuing bonds—an increase in private wealth will result. Why has wealth increased? Because the stock of money does not change when the government borrows, but the stock of bonds in the hands of the public is increased: when government borrows, those buying bonds reduce their money holdings; the government uses these funds to pay for its goods and services. Therefore, the money supply is not changed; it merely changes hands, from those who lend funds to the government to those who receive checks from the government. However, because the stock of bonds in the hands of the public has increased, total wealth has increased. And what happens to the demand for money as wealth increases? The demand for money rises. And what will happen, therefore, to interest rates as a result? They will rise, crowding out even more private expenditures. This wealth effect reduces the velocity of circulation since a given stock of money now supports a smaller level of aggregate spending; a smaller level of aggregate spending is supported because the wealth-induced increase in interest rates causes even greater reductions in investment spending.

If the crowding-out hypothesis is correct, it implies that the increase in velocity brought about by increased government spending is offset by the reduced velocity associated with the wealth-induced increase in the demand for money, leaving V unaltered. Fiscal policy is, as a result, impotent.

The nonmonetarists argue that the offset is only partial; fiscal policy is still a potent weapon.

The differences between the monetarists and the nonmonetarists are empirical

It becomes apparent that the monetarist-fiscalist debate cannot be settled at the theoretical level. It can be settled only by an appeal to the facts. On the basis of our discussion up to this point, this would *seem* to be a relatively simple task. After all, would not a stable velocity of circulation lend considerable support to the monetarist stance that fiscal policy by itself is a relatively ineffective stabilization tool? Indeed, if we observed changes in the level of government spending and/or changes in taxes and, *in addition,* observed little or no change in the velocity of circulation, would this not be proof positive that fiscal policy was ineffective? And would not a highly variable velocity of circulation lend support to the fiscalist stance? Not necessarily!

Observed changes in velocity: A problem of interpretation. The problem is that the observed velocity of circulation is an ambiguous indicator of the effectiveness or ineffectiveness of fiscal policy. This can easily be explained. Recalling the equation of exchange—$M \times V = P \times Q$—it is obvious that the velocity of circulation will change any time the *aggregate* rate of spending changes relative to the money supply. That is, since $V = \dfrac{P \times Q}{M}$, and since $P \times Q$, the nominal value of GNP, equals the sum of expenditures for consumption, investment, government, and net exports, any change in the *sum total* of those expenditures relative to the money supply during any given period will change the velocity of circulation.

Suppose, for the sake of argument, that fiscal policy *is* an effective stabilization tool in the sense that, *other things unchanged,* an expansionary fiscal policy will raise velocity. Suppose further that consumers or businesspeople, because they are pessimistic about the near-term outlook, reduce their rate of spending during the same period (for reasons unrelated to changes in interest rates) as government spending is increased. If this decline in private spending were offset exactly by the increase in government spending, the overall, or aggregate, rate of spending would be unchanged and the velocity of circulation would remain constant. However, it would be wrong to conclude that fiscal policy was ineffective simply because the velocity of circulation did not change. Indeed, in this example, it is precisely because fiscal policy was effective that the velocity remained unchanged. Had fiscal policy been ineffective, the velocity of circulation would have declined because of the reduction in the private spending rate. That the velocity of circulation did not decline can be taken, in this example, as evidence that fiscal policy is an effective tool. *The decline in velocity attributable to the slower rate of private spending was offset by the rise in velocity associated with the more rapid rate of government spending.*

There is another important sense in which the velocity of circulation is a doubtful indicator of the effectiveness of fiscal policy. It is frequently argued—by monetarists and nonmonetarists alike—that the money supply will often adjust in a rather *passive* way to meet the "needs of trade." An increase in aggregate demand will frequently be accompanied by an increase in the money supply as commercial banks either *(a)* reduce their holdings of excess reserves or *(b)* increase their borrowings at the Federal Reserve in an effort to meet the new, higher level of loan demand. This phenomenon is referred to as **reverse causation;** it is the increase in the level of economic activity that *causes* the change in the money supply, rather than the other way around. The usually assumed direction of causation—a change in M leading to a change in GNP—is reversed. Of course, whether or not the money supply actually increases will depend on whether or not the monetary authorities are *accommodative* in the sense of pursuing policies designed to allow an increase in the money supply. It is conceivable that they could undertake a contractionary policy to offset the increase in M that would otherwise take place. In any event, to the extent that the Federal Reserve is accommodative, and to the extent that GNP and M

change more or less in proportion, the velocity of circulation will hardly vary at all. It should be obvious, however, that it would be inappropriate to use such evidence as demonstrating the ineffectiveness of fiscal policy. Indeed, if fiscal policy were an effective tool (in the sense of increasing V), and if an increase in government spending "caused" an increase in the money supply, such an increase in M would offset the increase in V that would otherwise have taken place.

As the above examples make clear, even if the velocity of circulation were to remain constant, it would be wrong to conclude, on the basis of a constant V, that fiscal policy is proved to be ineffective. All we can conclude is that the constancy of V is, at best, an inconclusive indicator. Just as it is possible to conclude on the basis of an unchanged V in the face of a change in fiscal policy that the latter is ineffective, it is also possible to construct a reasonable case in support of its effectiveness.

By the same token it would be wrong to conclude that increases in V accompanying an expansionary fiscal policy (or decreases in V accompanying a contractionary fiscal policy) necessarily prove that fiscal policy is an effective stabilization tool. To illustrate, the *immediate* impact of an increase in government spending and/or a reduction in taxes is an increase in the velocity of circulation. An increase in government spending, for example, implies—*initially, at least*—an increase in the rate of aggregate spending relative to the money supply, raising the velocity of circulation. However, this increase in velocity may not be permanent. Interest rates will rise in the face of the expansionary fiscal policy; it takes time for the private economy to adjust its rate of spending to these new higher interest rates. When private spenders do adjust, they will cut their spending. In the months following the change in fiscal policy, the velocity of circulation will decline as a consequence of the crowding-out phenomenon.

Cannot this decline in V following its initial increase be taken as evidence in support of the monetarist position? Perhaps. Some decline in V is to be expected; the partial crowding out of private expenditures, a hypothesis that enjoys widespread acceptance, implies that V would decline from its initial high value. However, the question is, How far will V decline?

Even if we could answer this question in some instances, it is unlikely that we would ever be able to answer it unambiguously. The reason? What determines the velocity of circulation over any period is very complicated and often unpredictable. This state of affairs should occasion no surprise. For any given period, the velocity of circulation will be determined by the *rate* of aggregate spending relative to the stock of money. If the rate of total spending is high, velocity will be high; if the rate of total spending is low, velocity will be low. Since the rate of aggregate spending is determined by the decisions of literally millions of families, individuals, businesses, and government, and since the spending behavior of these decisionmakers can vary dramatically from one period to the next, it is hardly surprising that the velocity of circulation moves up and down sharply over time.

What all this means in the context of the monetarist-fiscalist debate is clear. If the private sector, for whatever reason, steps up its spending at the same time as government does, the velocity of circulation may not fall—at least not for quite some time. Or velocity may not change at all when government spending increases because, for one reason or another, private spending slows. Or velocity may actually decline because private spending slows more than government spending increases.

One final example makes clear why there are problems interpreting movements of V. Consider the case of an expansionary monetary policy. Generally, there is a rather long lag between the time when the policy change is undertaken and the time when such a change affects the level of economic activity. It takes time, for example, for the business community and consumers to adjust their spending in response to the reduction in interest rates. Initially, therefore, an expansion of the money supply will be accompanied by little or no change in spending; the velocity of circulation declines. It is reasonable to expect that velocity will increase in subsequent months as people

step up their spending in response to the lower interest rates. But when and by how much is not clearly understood. And it is possible that this increase in spending will be offset by reduced spending elsewhere for any number of reasons. If that happened, V might not recover. Would it then be appropriate to conclude that monetary policy was an ineffective tool of policy because V remained at its low level? Hardly.

For all of these reasons, it is very difficult to settle the question of how effective fiscal (or monetary) policy is on the basis of the velocity of circulation. We will return to this debate, and other aspects of this debate, in Chapter 14. For now, suffice it to say that the crowding-out hypothesis has not been proved valid. That there is likely to be *some* crowding out is not in dispute; that crowding out is complete is hotly contested.

SUMMARY

1. Bond prices and interest rates are inversely related. The reason for the inverse relationship is clear: Bonds are fixed-income securities. If interest rates rise, future fixed coupon payments will be more heavily discounted; the *present discounted value* (PDV) of the bond will be reduced, and hence, so will its price.

2. The demand for money is distinguishable from the money supply. The *money supply* refers to the amount of money actually held by the public; the *demand for money* refers to the amount of money the public is *willing* to hold.

3. The amount of money people are willing to hold—for both transactions and asset purposes—will be determined by their wealth, their income, and interest rates. Specifically, the total demand for money varies directly with income and wealth, and inversely with the interest rates.

4. Money market equilibrium will occur when the total demand for money is equal to the money supply. If an excess demand for money exists, the interest rate will decline until the demand for money is brought into equilibrium with the (assumed fixed) money supply. In the face of an excess supply of money, the interest rate will rise until the amount of money people are

willing to hold is brought into alignment with the amount they are actually holding.

5. Changes in the money supply brought about by, say, Federal Reserve actions will cause the interest rate to change. Specifically, an increase in the money supply will lower the equilibrium interest rate; a decrease will raise the interest rate.

6. The *marginal efficiency of investment* (MEI)—sometimes referred to as the *rate of return on investment*—refers to the maximum rate of interest investors are willing to pay (either to borrow or to use internal funds) to acquire investment projects. If the market rate of interest exceeds the MEI on an investment project, it is not profitable to undertake it; if the interest rate is less than the MEI, it is profitable.

7. Ranking investment projects on the basis of their prospective MEIs, or rates of return, one can construct a downward sloping schedule—called an *MEI schedule*—that measures cumulatively, at each interest rate, the value of all investment projects having a rate of return at least as high as the interest rate. This MEI schedule we call the *investment demand schedule,* showing the inverse relationship between the interest rate and the amount of investment activity.

8. Changes in the money supply lead to changes in interest rates, which, in turn, change business investment spending (and other interest-sensitive expenditures). This change in spending, via the multiplier, generates a multiple increase in income and production.

9. While few economists seriously question the idea that changes in the money supply can effect changes in the level of economic activity, some economists—most notably the *monetarists*—question whether a change in fiscal policy unaccompanied by a change in the money supply can do anything other than change the *mix* of goods and services produced. Specifically, monetarists argue, for example, that increases in government spending unaccompanied by an increase in the money supply will "crowd out" an equivalent amount of private spending, leaving total spending unchanged; private spending will have been reduced and replaced with public spending.

10. Nonmonetarists argue that there will be only a partial crowding out, *not* a complete crowding out. In their view, as interest rates rise in the face of an expansionary fiscal policy, private spending will be reduced. But since the velocity of circulation will increase in the wake of the aggregate demand-induced increase in interest rates, crowding out will be incomplete. Monetarists agree that the aggregate demand-induced increase in interest rates will increase velocity, but argue that the wealth-induced increase in the demand for money caused by the financing of the expansionary fiscal policy will lower V. This will cause, after everything is added up, a complete crowding out. Nonmonetarists disagree.

11. The differences between the monetarists and nonmonetarists can only be settled by an appeal to the facts. However, for a variety of reasons, an appeal to data on the velocity of circulation will not settle the issue entirely one way or the other; observed movements in the velocity of circulation are, at best, ambiguous indicators of the effectiveness or ineffectiveness of fiscal policy alone.

CONCEPTS FOR REVIEW

Face value (or par value, or redemption value) of a bond

Coupon payment

Coupon rate

Present discounted value (PDV)

Capital gain

Consol

Loanable funds theory

Liquidity preference theory

Demand for money

Money supply

Transactions demand for money

Asset (or speculative) demand for money

Marginal efficiency of investment (MEI)

Investment demand schedule

Monetarists versus nonmonetarists

Velocity of circulation

Crowding-out hypothesis

QUESTIONS FOR DISCUSSION

(Those marked with an asterisk (*) are more difficult.)

1. A friend of yours complains, "Years ago my father left me a $10,000 bond that matures in the year 2000. My brother told me to sell it because it did not yield a very high return; the coupon payment only amounts to $500 per year. So I went to a broker to sell it and she offered me only $8,000 for it. I told her I was being ripped off; the bond was worth $10,000, not $8,000. She said that it was worth a lot less than $10,000 because interest rates are much higher today than when my father purchased it. I told her she was crazy. Can you tell me what's wrong here?" Using nontechnical language, explain to your friend exactly what the problem is.

2. Explain verbally why a 1 percent reduction in all rates of interest will cause the price of bonds that mature in the distant future to rise by more than the price of bonds that mature more quickly.

3. If money is defined as the quantity of currency and coin plus checkable deposits *in the hands of the public,* how can the money supply differ from the demand for money?

*4. In Chapter 8 the value of the expenditure multiplier was given as:

$$\text{Expenditure multiplier} = \frac{1}{1 - [\text{MPC} \times (1 - t)]}.$$

Thus, if MPC = 0.75 and t = 0.20, the expenditure multiplier would have a numerical value of 2.5.

One message in this chapter is that the expenditure multiplier is *not* 2.5, but substantially less, unless any expenditure change is accompanied by an accommodating change in the money supply. Specifically, if the crowding-out hypothesis is correct, the numerical value of the government expenditure multiplier will be zero; in other words, a *pure* fiscal policy change (i.e., a fiscal policy change unaccompanied by a change in the money supply) will have no effect on the overall level of aggregate spending.

Explain why the crowding-out hypothesis implies a numerical value of zero for the expenditure multiplier. Explain why nonmonetarists would disagree, yet would agree that its numerical value is less than 2.5. (Hint: take into account partial crowding out.)

*5. If the Federal Reserve were to pursue a policy of "pegging" the interest rate at its current level, r_0, how would the effectiveness of fiscal policy be affected? Given the numerical values for MPC and t of 0.75 and 0.20, respectively, what would be the numerical value of the expenditure multiplier? Would it be equal to 2.5, or would it be less in view of the crowding-out effect? Explain carefully.

*6. There is a deflationary gap. Government desires to both close that gap and promote rapid growth by stimulating investment spending. Assume that either monetary or fiscal policy can be used to close the deflationary gap. On the basis of the discussion in this chapter, which policy tool should be used—expansionary monetary or expansionary fiscal policy? Explain your reasoning carefully.

7. Explain *why* monetarists and nonmonetarists have differing views regarding movements in the velocity of circulation. Also explain why appeal to the data on the velocity of circulation cannot resolve the debate unambiguously.

Aggregate demand, aggregate supply, and the price level

Up to this point, we have virtually ignored the problem of inflation. In Chapter 5 we *defined* the problem—that of a sustained upward movement in the general level of prices. In that chapter we emphasized the reasons economists and policymakers alike view inflation as a destructive phenomenon, so destructive in fact that inflation control has become, during the past several years, the top priority in the U.S. federal government.

There is, of course, no shortage of people who think they understand the problem and no shortage of policy prescriptions for bringing inflation under control. To some, inflation is the result of "too much money chasing too few goods," conjuring up the image of goods with feet frantically trying to escape the onslaught of dollar bills that are similarly outfitted with feet. Of course, the goods get caught and sell henceforth at higher prices. Here, the inflation problem arises because the Federal Reserve Board adopts policies that result in excessive money creation. The solution is simple: Slow the growth of the money supply and you will slow inflation.

Others argue that inflation is caused by government deficit spending. Reduce the deficit and you will observe a corresponding reduction in inflation.

Powerful unions and large corporations are frequently tagged as being the source of inflation. Apparently, it is their greed that causes unions to raise their wages and corporations to raise their prices at very rapid rates. The solutions to these sources of inflationary pressure are varied, ranging from government policy actions designed to reduce the market power of these groups (e.g., through the stricter enforcement of antitrust laws, or through the implementation of "right-to-work" laws), to control their wage and price decisions in one way or another.

People's expectations regarding the future course of inflation are often identified as being yet another source of inflation. If people believe that prices will rise by 7 percent next year, they will undertake actions that ultimately result in the realization of a 7 percent inflation rate. Workers demand higher wages due to higher prices to ensure that their work effort yields at least the same amount of *real* purchasing power as before; in line with increased labor and other costs, firms raise prices as expected.

Finally, there are a whole host of other factors that are seen as inflationary: increased energy prices occasioned by the pricing policies of the world's oil producers (OPEC); increased food prices attributable to adverse domestic or foreign weather conditions; government regulations applied to domestic industries for environmental and social purposes; minimum wage laws; social security and other payroll taxes; tariffs, quotas, and other restrictive trade practices; a decline in the value of the dollar in world currency markets; an aging capital stock that is less productive; a changing labor force that is younger, less skilled, and less educated.

It is the purpose of this chapter and the next to unravel much of the mystery surrounding our inflation problem. We do not as yet have a complete answer as to what has caused, sustained, and accelerated the pace of inflation in the United States. And, as a result, the discovery of foolproof solutions for bringing inflation under control have eluded us. But we have a much more complete understanding of the causes of inflation today than we had 5 to 10 years ago. As a conquence, we are much closer to the desired solutions.

This chapter opened with a brief discussion of some of the factors frequently identified by many people as being the cause or causes of inflation. The message the reader should be left with at the end of these two chapters is that all of the factors cited have played their part in determining our rate of inflation. According to most economists, each factor alone is not sufficient to explain the past U.S. inflation rate; exclusive reliance on any single factor yields a grossly distorted picture of our inflation problem. The trick, however, is to put each factor in proper perspective. The development of that proper perspective is not easy, but it is essential. This is the task we have set for ourselves in this and the following chapter.

In this chapter, the focus of our attention will not be so much on inflation per se as on the price level. In particular, we will examine how aggregate demand and aggregate supply interact to determine the overall level of prices in the American economy. However, understanding how the price level is determined is not the same as understanding inflation; it is only a necessary first step. An understanding of inflation requires an understanding of the complex forces that propel the price level upwards on a sustained basis over time. That issue is taken up in Chapter 13.

AGGREGATE SUPPLY AND THE PRICE LEVEL

The relationships described in this section are absolutely essential to an understanding of the unemployment and inflation problems in the United States. We begin with a brief discussion of the importance of a theory of aggregate supply. We then present a number of alternative views of the relationship between aggregate supply and the price level that are frequently cited—either explicitly or implicitly—in many discussions. Finally, we develop the theory underlying the relationship between aggregate supply and the price level, focusing on a few key determinants.

The importance of a theory of aggregate supply

The question that concerns us for the moment is this: What is the nature of the relationship between the aggregate quantity of goods and services produced and the general level of prices? Put differently, if government pursues policies aimed at expanding production and employment, what will happen to the general price level? Will prices rise? If so, by how much will they rise?

GNP, the market value of the final goods and services produced during some period, is a price-times-quantity relationship. An increase in the general price level, or an increase in the quantity of goods and services produced, or both, will raise GNP. *The theory of aggregate supply is concerned with the question of how a change in nominal GNP is divided between a change in output and a change in the general price level.*

It is a relatively mechanical procedure to calculate the division of any *past* change in GNP into that part that was the result of price level change and that part that was the result of quantity change. We make the calculation using the following three pieces of data: (1) nominal (or current dollar) GNP, (2) real (or constant dollar) GNP, and (3) the GNP implicit price deflator.[1] Thus, if nominal GNP rises by 12 percent from one year to the next and the GNP implicit price deflator rises by 9 percent, real GNP will have increased by 3 percent. The following general relationship always holds:

Percent change in nominal GNP	=	Percent change in GNP implicit price deflator	+	Percent change in real GNP

What we are anxious to discover, however, is the nature of the relationship between real GNP and the GNP implicit price deflator. Will efforts to increase real GNP result simply in an increase in the price level with little or no increase in the quantity of goods and services produced? Or will the quantity increase be large and the price level increase insignificant? From the point of view of economic policy, it is important that we be able to answer this question.

Alternative views of the aggregate supply relationship

Many different answers have been offered to the question stated above, depending on how close actual GNP is to its potential. If actual GNP is at or very close to potential—if the "GNP gap" is negligible—efforts to increase real GNP via expansionary monetary and fiscal policies will be largely unsuccessful, and the increase in aggregate demand will simply force up the price level. Thus, if the economy is already operating at its productive potential, the aggregate supply curve—the curve depicting the relationship between real output and the price level—will be a vertical straight line. This is illustrated in Figure 12.1. On the vertical axis we measure the price level; on the horizontal axis real GNP

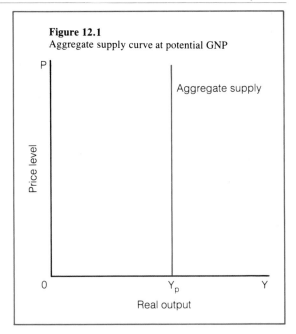

Figure 12.1
Aggregate supply curve at potential GNP

is measured. Y_p represents our nation's potential GNP. Expanding output beyond our potential is extremely difficult, demanding a "larger than normal" number of people in the work force, "longer than normal" working hours, and "longer than normal" hours of plant operation. For simplicity, we assume for now that it is not possible to produce a rate of real output larger than our potential. Any increase in aggregate demand will result simply in a higher price level with no increase in real output. The aggregate supply curve is vertical at the point of our potential GNP.

There is almost no disagreement among economists on this point. Attempts to increase aggregate demand beyond our productive potential will only cause the price level to rise. Thus the first tenet of the theory of aggregate supply can be stated as follows: *When real GNP is equal to potential GNP, changes in aggregate demand will influence only the price level, not real output.*

Potential GNP: An aside

Although all economists agree with the principle just stated, there is much less agreement over whether we are able to determine with much

---

[1] These concepts were discussed in detail in Chapter 6.

precision what our potential GNP is at any given moment. It is true that our potential GNP can be defined relatively easily in abstract terms, as was done in Chapter 6. But attaching a number to our potential GNP is more difficult.

In abstract terms, our nation's potential real GNP for a given time period can be defined by the following relationship:

$$\text{Potential GNP} = \begin{array}{c}\text{Number of}\\\text{people in}\\\text{the labor}\\\text{force}\end{array} \times \begin{array}{c}\text{Average}\\\text{output}\\\text{per hour}\\\text{of work}\end{array} \times \begin{array}{c}\text{Average}\\\text{number}\\\text{of hours}\\\text{worked per}\\\text{time period}\end{array}$$

The immediate problem we encounter is that we do not know precisely what numbers to attach to the three component parts. Take the labor force. It is a well-known fact that the labor force is not an immutable constant. Among other things, its size depends on the state of the economy generally. When the economy is in a slump, job opportunities are limited and many people "choose" to remain outside the labor force. Because they perceive jobs as being generally unavailable, they do not actively look for work. They are therefore not counted as part of the work force. When economic conditions improve, the labor force swells in response to the (correctly) perceived view that job opportunities abound. Because the size of the labor force is so sensitive to changing economic conditions, it is difficult to pin down a number for the size of the potential labor force.

The problem of defining the potential labor force is more difficult than this, however. We have to allow for some margin of unused labor resources represented by the so-called *natural rate of unemployment.* As we saw in Chapter 5, a 4 percent unemployment rate was generally viewed as the (interim) natural rate of unemployment in the mid-1960s. However, in the late 1960s and 1970s, most economists revised upwards their estimate of the natural rate. Although the discussion of this issue is carefully hedged by our national leaders, there is an emerging consensus among economists that the natural rate of unemployment today (1981) is 6.0 to 7.0 percent or more.

But, not all economists agree that a 6.0 to 7.0 percent unemployment rate represents our natural rate. Some believe it is much lower. Accordingly, it is not altogether clear what to include for the labor force in the calculation of potential GNP.

Similarly, it is not clear what number to include for *productivity*—output per hour of work. Among other things, productivity depends on the amount of capital with which labor works (i.e., the capital-labor ratio) and on the state of technology. These, in turn, depend on both the size of the labor force and the state of the economy generally.

To illustrate, many new techniques of production are "embodied" in capital goods; business investment is often required in order to bring new techniques into use. But how much capital investment businesses are willing to undertake depends on the returns they expect. Generally, the expected returns are higher, the higher the level of economic activity. When the economy is in a slump, many industries use less of their productive capacity than they have available, which serves to brake the amount of investment they are willing to undertake. This slows the growth of our productive resources and therewith the future growth of our potential GNP. Productivity will be lower as a result.

Moreover, the larger the labor force is, the smaller the value of labor productivity will be for any given stock of capital resources. Labor productivity will be lower because, on average, each worker has less capital to work with. Thus the value of productivity used in the calculation of our potential GNP is not independent of the size of the labor force.

Because we are unable to pin down precisely either the size of the labor force that would exist under ideal, full employment economic circumstances or the level of labor productivity, it is not entirely clear what our potential GNP is equal to for any given period. The average number of hours worked per time period—the third element required in the calculation of our GNP potential—is easier to get a fix on. But that is not of much assistance in the absence of fairly accurate numbers on the other two elements. In any event, because of these difficulties, we do not know precisely at what level of real GNP to fix our vertical aggregate supply curve.

Aggregate supply below potential GNP

Trying to get a fix on our potential GNP is the first major hurdle we must overcome. However, assuming we are successful in determining our GNP potential—a big assumption, but a necessary one if we are to "get off square one"— we encounter a second problem. What is the nature of our aggregate supply relationship at real GNP levels below our potential? That is, *for levels of real GNP less than potential GNP, how will a given change in nominal GNP be divided between a change in real GNP and a change in the price level?*

This, again, is not an easy question to answer, nor is it one for which there is a universally accepted answer. Indeed, some economists would argue that the question itself is not relevant from the point of view of policy. This group of economists believes, much as the classical economists did, that the economy is in an almost continuous state of full employment and that policy actions aimed at changing the unemployment rate will be ineffective. To be sure, there are some periods in history—the Great Depression of the 1930s, for example—when the economic system failed to function properly, yielding a state of less than full employment for an extended period of time. But such historical incidents are the exception, not the rule. Certainly since World War II, so they argue, there is no evidence to suggest that the economy was in anything but a virtually continuous state of full employment.

The short-run aggregate supply curve: A classical view

How can this be? Over the entire period since World War II, the unemployment rate has varied considerably, ranging from lows of below 4 percent to almost 9 percent. It has bounced up and down frequently over this period as well. How can anyone argue that the economy was in a near-continuous state of full employment in the face of such evidence?

The classical economists reply that, with few exceptions, virtually all of the observed unemployment in the post-World War II era was "voluntary." By this they mean not *all* unemployment in an absolute sense, but only that unemployment over and above the number of people categorized as structurally unemployed. (This is an unemployment problem that virtually all economists would agree cannot be solved by conventional monetary and fiscal policies alone. Instead, it requires either the creation of jobs matching the skills and education levels of those who are structurally unemployed or the alteration of those skills and levels of education to meet existing job requirements.) The rate of unemployment constituting full employment is not some constant, never-changing number. It varies continuously in response to the voluntary choices people make in the face of dynamic changes in the economy. New products, new industries, sluggish growth in some sectors of the economy, and rapid growth elsewhere are characteristic, ever-changing features of our economic system. These changes influence employment conditions and opportunities constantly. On the one hand, they result in the displacement of labor and low wage increases in some areas of the economy. On the other hand, they result in expanded job opportunities and sizable wage increases in other areas. Labor must adapt to changed circumstances; by and large, it does so in a reasonably orderly manner. People who are laid off require time to discover new opportunities. They will not necessarily take the first job they are offered, preferring instead to look around for a while to acquire more information on their market prospects generally. Technically, these people are unemployed. But most of this unemployment, according to classical economists, is frictional, as is the state of unemployment of most of those who quit existing jobs to search for others and of those who enter the labor force for the first time (or who reenter after a period of time outside the labor force).

The point of the classical thesis is this: Except for those who are structurally unemployed, virtually all unemployment is frictional. There is no necessary reason in an economy that is subject to *irregular, ever-changing conditions* for the full employment rate of unemployment to be 4 percent, 5 percent, or any other constant percentage. It may be 8 percent at one point and 4 percent at another. What is important is the fact that the unemployment rate itself cannot be altered, except perhaps temporarily, by the government's monetary and fiscal policies. (These classical economists usually go one step further. They say that fiscal policy is certainly not a potent weapon to alter either employment or the level of economic activity. It can only alter the *composition* of employment between the private and public sectors, and the *composition* of our nation's output. And monetary policy too is not effective in altering the level of employment and output; it can only affect the level of prices.)

What all of this means in terms of our aggregate supply relationship is clear: *The aggregate supply curve is vertical at almost any level of real output* (except, perhaps, at severely depressed levels of output such as those that prevailed during the 1930s). The government cannot alter either output or employment; the changes that occur in output and employment take place independent of government policy. Moreover, a change in fiscal policy will affect neither the price level nor real output; a change in monetary policy will change *nominal* GNP, but all of it will take the form of price change only.

The majority of economists do not subscribe to the beliefs of these classical economists. Most economists agree there is some truth in the classical view. It has merit from a very long-run perspective. But from a short-run policy perspective (a period lasting perhaps several years), the government has the ability to effect significant changes in output and employment.

The Keynesian perspective

At the opposite extreme from the classical economists are a few extreme Keynesian economists. Their view is that the attainment of an equilibrium level of real output at less than full employment is not only possible, but highly likely. Additionally, until the economy reaches its full employment position—its potential GNP—there will be little or no upward pressure on prices.

The Keynesian position—though not necessarily the position maintained by Keynes himself—has been detailed in earlier chapters and need not be repeated here. What is important to recognize is the implications of this Keynesian view for our analysis of the aggregate supply relationship. *It implies that the aggregate supply curve is horizontal up to the point of our GNP potential; thereafter it is vertical.* Thus, until we reach full employment, all changes in nominal GNP will take the form of changes in output—that is, changes in real GNP. The resultant aggregate supply curve looks like a backwards L. This is illustrated in Figure 12.2. Therefore, if real GNP rises from Y_1 to Y_2 or from Y_2 to Y_p, the price level will not change. This means that changes in nominal GNP will equal changes in real GNP. Once our economy reaches its GNP potential, any further increases in nominal GNP will take the form of price increases only.

Note two additional important features of this Keynesian aggregate supply relationship. First, suppose we are at our potential and the price

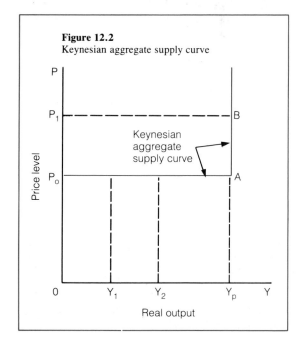

Figure 12.2
Keynesian aggregate supply curve

level is equal to P_0. If nominal GNP falls, all of the reduction will take the form of a reduced level of real output; the price level will not fall below P_0. The reason prices will not fall is that they are "rigid downward." Second, suppose we are at our potential and the price level is again initially equal to P_0. If nominal GNP rises, only the price level will rise. Suppose the new price level is P_1. What will happen if nominal GNP now falls? Will the price level fall to P_0? No. Because prices are rigid downward, the price level will remain fixed at P_1 and all of the reduction in nominal GNP will take the form of a reduced level of real output. What this means is that the horizontal portion of the aggregate supply curve will now occur at point B—the point corresponding to the price level P_1. This is shown in Figure 12.2 by the dashed line starting at point B.

The upward-sloping aggregate supply curve

The majority of economists reject both the extreme classical and Keynesian views. They take, rather, an intermediate position that can be summarized as follows.

1.   The aggregate supply curve is vertical at the point of our potential GNP. At this point, increases in nominal GNP will take the form of price increases only; real GNP will not rise.

2.   At very depressed levels of economic activity—at levels of real GNP *far* below our potential—the aggregate supply curve is horizontal, *at least in the short run*. The price level is unaffected by changes in nominal GNP in this depressed range of output; all changes in nominal GNP take the form of changes in real GNP. In this range, the aggregate supply curve is horizontal.

3.   In the intermediate range, between some depressed level of real output and our potential real GNP, the aggregate supply curve is upward sloping, becoming increasingly steep the closer we get to our potential.

The resultant aggregate supply curve is illustrated in Figure 12.3. For levels of real output *lower than* Y_1, the aggregate supply curve is horizontal. This we will refer to as the **Keynesian range**. The intermediate range portion is upward sloping and increasingly steep the closer we get to our potential. This implies that, over this range of output, any change in nominal GNP will be divided between changes in real output and prices, the division increasingly taking the form of price change the closer we get to our potential. The final portion of the aggregate supply curve

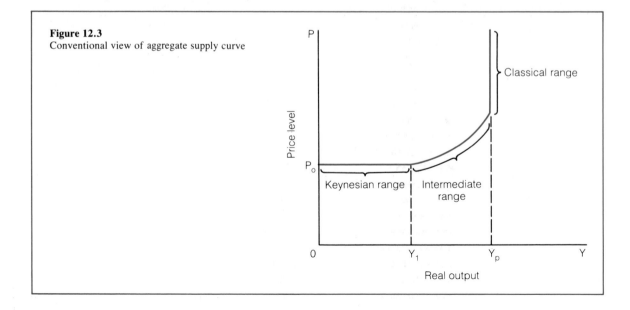

Figure 12.3
Conventional view of aggregate supply curve

is vertical. This occurs at the point corresponding to our GNP potential. The vertical portion we will refer to as the **classical range.**

What accounts for the upward-sloping, intermediate range of the aggregate supply curve? Several factors are responsible for this relationship.

1. Even if *excess capacity* exists in the aggregate, not all firms and industries will have the same degree of excess capacity. Some firms may be utilizing their plants to the fullest extent possible while others are operating far below capacity. Under these circumstances, increases in aggregate demand will put pressures at least on those industries operating at full capacity to raise their prices. This causes the price level to rise. Moreover, the closer we get to full capacity in the *aggregate,* the greater will be the number of firms and industries that are operating at full capacity and the greater, therefore, will be the upward pressure on prices in response to any increase in aggregate demand.

2. Although the level of unemployment in the aggregate may be sizable, sharp regional discrepancies will generally exist in unemployment rates. Some regions of the country may be experiencing unemployment rates as low as 2 or 3 percent, while others may have 12 percent or more of their labor force unemployed. Increases in aggregate demand will intensify the tight labor market conditions existing in low unemployment regions, generating higher wage settlements and higher prices in those regions—and a higher price level in the aggregate. Additionally, not all labor markets for different occupations will be uniformly tight or loose. Indeed, labor markets for skilled workers generally tighten up before those for the less skilled. Even though we are at less than full employment in the aggregate, increases in aggregate demand will result in increasingly large wage hikes in skilled labor markets, which in turn forces up the general level of prices.

3. As the overall unemployment rate drops, labor costs per unit of output—**unit labor costs**—tend to rise for yet other reasons, rising more rapidly the lower the unemployment rate. There are at least two explanations for this. First, in order to generate higher levels of production,

employers may find it necessary to hire people who are less qualified than existing personnel. If the same hourly wage is paid to the new employees, unit labor costs will rise because the output produced per hour of work—**productivity**—of the new workers is lower than that of better qualified and more experienced employees. Second, unions often become increasingly militant in their wage demands the lower are the numbers of union personnel *unemployed.*

The reasons for this are fairly clear. First, unions in general do not insist upon wage levels that would be detrimental to the rank and file. Although the union may have considerable power in determining what wage should be paid to workers, it is usually the employer who determines *how many* workers will be employed. Excessive wage demands, therefore, could wreak havoc within the union if too many of the rank and file cannot obtain employment at the new high wage. As a result of these considerations, it is probably fair to say that wage demands will be higher the lower the rate of unemployment within the union. When the aggregate level of unemployment is high, we are unlikely to witness any significant number of inordinately large wage settlements. When the overall level of unemployment is low, on the other hand, conditions are ripe for sizable wage settlements. Second, employers find it easier to pass along labor (and other) cost increases in the form of higher prices during boom conditions in the economy. The loss in sales volume attributable to the higher prices will often be more than offset by the increased sales volume implied by the higher levels of aggregate demand. In the aggregate, high and growing levels of demand provide an environment within which prices can be raised with less fear of reduced sales or profits.

4. Finally, the upward-sloping aggregate supply curve in the *short run* can be explained by the law of diminishing returns. Because capital expansion generally requires long lead times, short-run increases in output are often realized by increasing the amount of labor that is employed—and, most important, the amount of labor employed relative to capital. Since each worker, on the average, has less capital with

which to work, output per unit of labor increases less rapidly. As a result, for given money wages, unit labor costs increase. This, in turn, raises the general level of prices.

Three additional notes on aggregate supply

For the purposes of our discussion here, we will adopt the conventional view of the aggregate supply relationship as depicted in Figure 12.3. However, for the tool to be useful, it is necessary to add a few refinements and caveats.

Aggregate supply ratcheting up. Consider Figure 12.4. Suppose initially that real output is at Y_1 and that the price level is P_1. In response to an increase in aggregate spending, both real output and the price level will rise, moving along the aggregate supply curve labeled ABCD in the direction of the arrows. The economy reaches its potential GNP at point B; thereafter all increases in nominal GNP take the form of price level increases.

Suppose prices continue to rise to point C (corresponding to the price level of P_3 and the real output level Y_p), at which point aggregate demand is reduced (the result, say, of a contractionary monetary policy designed to stop the price level rise). Will the price level and real output

follow the path given by the aggregate supply curve labeled ABCD? The answer most economists give is *no!* Price and output are more likely to follow the path given by the curve labeled ECD. In other words, the fall in real output from Y_p to Y_2 will be accompanied by a fall in the price level from P_3 to P_2, *not* to P_4 as would be implied by the original aggregate supply curve. The price level associated with any given level of real output has ratcheted up; the price level P_4 that was associated with the real output level Y_2 has now ratcheted up to P_2.

Why did the aggregate supply curve ratchet up? This can be explained by the fact that it is more difficult to accomplish a price level reduction than a price level increase. Prices may not be completely rigid downward (as evidenced by the fact that the price level fell from P_3 at point C to P_2 at point E). But they are sufficiently sticky in the downward direction that, *in the short run at least,* the price level will not return to the level implied by the original aggregate supply relationship ABCD (e.g., P_4 at point F).

Aggregate supply in the face of complete downward price rigidity. Some economists would go farther than the description in the previous section. They would argue that the ratcheting up is more extreme. Although they would

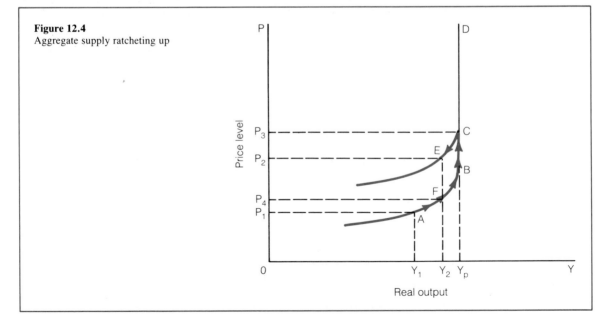

Figure 12.4
Aggregate supply ratcheting up

agree that, for *upward* movements in the economy, the price level and real output would follow a path like ABC, they would not agree with the proposition that, for *downward* movements, the economy would follow a path like C to E in the *short run*. In their view, the price level would not fall below P_3, and all reductions in nominal GNP would take the form of reductions in real output only. Because prices are extremely rigid in a downward direction, the aggregate supply curve is horizontal for declines in the level of economic activity. Of course, if the level of economic activity starts to move upwards again, the price level will once again climb upwards. This is illustrated in Figure 12.5.

Suppose the economy is initially at point A. In response to an increase in the level of economic activity, price and output will both increase until we reach point B; thereafter, only the price level will rise. Suppose the economy reaches point C, at which point the level of economic activity is reduced (in response to, say, a tighter monetary policy). According to those who maintain that prices are extremely rigid downward, the economy will move to D (meaning that there will be no price level decline), instead of to point E, as suggested before. If the economy turns around and starts its upward climb again, the

price level and real output will follow the new higher path given by the curve labeled DG. The extreme form of downward price rigidity illustrated in Figure 12.5 is most closely identified with the work of the Keynesians.

The short-run and long-run aggregate supply curves. Virtually all economists agree that, in the short run at least, there is considerable downward rigidity in the general level of prices. There is some dispute over whether prices are as rigid downward as some Keynesians allege. But the fact that there is some downward rigidity *in the short run* is not hotly disputed. At a minimum, it needs to be recognized that it takes time for wages and prices to be adjusted downward in response to declines in the pace of economic activity. Wages and salaries are frequently negotiated agreements, even in the nonunion sectors of the economy. In response to a decline in the level of economic activity, firms will lay off workers with no immediate adjustment being made in the wages and salaries of those who remain on the job. Those who are dismissed are frequently let go with an understanding—sometimes explicit, sometimes implicit—that they will probably be called back in the near future to resume work at their old wages and salaries. Meanwhile, they can often soften the blow by

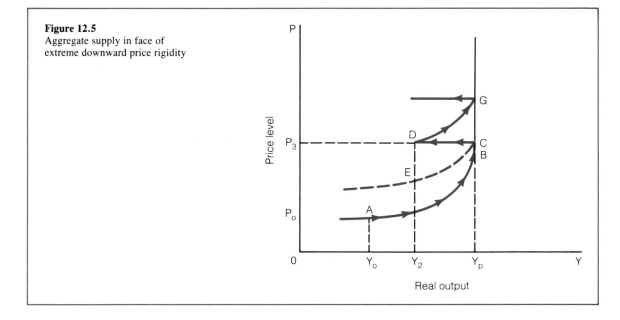

Figure 12.5
Aggregate supply in face of
extreme downward price rigidity

applying for and receiving unemployment compensation (which, on average, pays up to about two thirds of workers' take-home pay for at least 26 weeks and often 39 weeks or more), and supplementary union benefits, and/or by drawing down their accumulated savings. Under the circumstances, there is little incentive to search for new jobs immediately. And certainly there is little incentive to accept permanent employment elsewhere at reduced levels of wages and salaries.

Many unemployed workers may seriously search for new jobs. But they will, for a time at least, be very reluctant to accept employment at wages and salaries less than they were receiving before. They honestly believe they are "worth" at least that much. Even if that is not the case, they are not anxious to cut their wages and salaries below those of their co-workers who are still on the job. To be sure, some workers who are in more desperate straits will seek out and accept jobs at reduced wages and salaries. But during the early stages of an economic slowdown, they are the exception, not the rule.

Eventually, however, resistance to wage and salary cuts will wither. After an extended period of unemployment, workers will begin to doubt that they will be called back, unemployment compensation and union benefits will begin to run out, and savings account balances will be depleted. When faced with the prospect of a job at a reduced wage or salary versus continued unemployment, the former state becomes increasingly more attractive.

Likewise, many other prices in our economic system are set by contract—for the construction and delivery of plant and equipment, for material inputs, etc. When existing contracts expire, it is possible that they will be renegotiated at lower prices. But it takes time for contracts to run out.

The implications of these considerations are clear. In the short run at least, there is considerable downward rigidity in prices. If the level of economic activity slows, the decline at first will take the form of a reduction in real output and an increase in unemployment. Wages and prices will fall little, if at all, in the short run. The aggregate supply curve will be relatively flat, if not horizontal, in the very short run.

Gradually over time, however, wages and prices will adjust downward. What this means is that, over time, the aggregate supply curve will become increasingly steep.

Some economists go farther. Eventually, in the long run, the aggregate supply curve will become vertical and be positioned over the point of our potential GNP. The achievement of this result may take a very long time—a matter not of months but of years—but it *must* occur eventually. People who are currently unemployed can resist lower wage offers for only so long. Ultimately they will make a reassessment of their positions and accept available lower-wage jobs. Additionally, suppliers of material inputs can only hold out so long hoping to find a contract at the old price. If such contracts are not forthcoming, they will be forced to cut their prices.

These outcomes are a reflection of the operation of the laws of demand and supply. On the down side at least, it takes time for prices to adjust. The brunt of any falloff in the pace of economic activity falls initially on the "quantities"—on real output and employment. In time, in the face of continued excess supplies—as evidenced by inordinately high rates of unemployment and bulging inventories—prices will come down, ultimately resulting in a clearing of markets. Once markets are cleared, the economic system will settle down to an equilibrium position. At this long-run equilibrium position our economy will be at the point of its potential GNP. The short-run–long-run distinction is illustrated in Figure 12.6.

The vertical straight line over our potential GNP point, Y_p, represents the long-run aggregate supply curve. (It is labeled AS_{LR}.) The fact that it is vertical *and* positioned directly over Y_p tells us two things. First, the economic system has a *tendency* to gravitate on its own toward full employment, toward the realization of our potential. There is no magic number representing full employment; it could occur at 3 percent un-

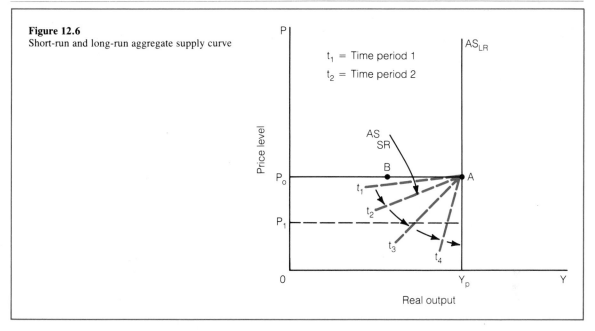

Figure 12.6
Short-run and long-run aggregate supply curve

t_1 = Time period 1
t_2 = Time period 2

employment, 5 percent, or some other number. What needs emphasis is that whatever unemployment rate emerges in the long run, it will reflect the voluntary choices people make. If all unemployment is voluntary, there can be no disputing the fact that we *must* be at full employment; full employment here is the natural rate of unemployment. Second, our potential GNP is *independent* of the price level. This is what is meant by the *vertical* slope of the AS_{LR} line. Whether the price level is high or low will in no way affect our nation's output potential. Y_p *is determined by the quantity and quality of our nation's resources, not by the general level of prices.*

The second point is not particularly controversial, but the first point is. Is there a natural tendency for the economy to gravitate toward full employment? Does this not fly in the face of Keynes' view that there was no such tendency, that the economy could attain an equilibrium position *below* full employment?

In the first place, Keynes was concerned with the short run. In the short run—a period that could last for several years—Keynes saw no automatic tendency for the economy to move toward full employment. In the long run, such a ten-

dency might exist, but, as Keynes was fond of saying, "In the long run, we're all dead." In the short run, the monetary and fiscal authorities have an obligation to pursue policies designed to direct the economy toward its full employment position.

There is nothing contradictory between the Keynesian view and the view of those who maintain that the economy has a natural *long-run* tendency toward full employment. In the short run, the economy can fall far below its ultimate full employment position. The fact that it may take the economy a long time to reach full employment on its own leaves considerable room for the use of monetary and fiscal policies to effect changes in the level of economic activity. Moreover, adherence to the view that the economy has a natural long-run tendency to move toward full employment does not mean that full employment will necessarily emerge in five or six years as long as we are just patient enough to wait. On the contrary, full employment might never be realized by just waiting. The economy could easily be shocked off its path toward full employment by external forces (e.g., production and pricing decisions of the OPEC nations) or by policy actions. There is still considerable scope for the use of discretionary policies.

The distinction between the short-run and long-run aggregate supply curves is important because of what it implies about the ability of policymakers to achieve a reduction in the general level of prices. Examine Figure 12.6 carefully for a moment. Suppose the economy is initially at point A. Policymakers are anxious to reduce the price level below P_0. What will happen if they adopt contractionary policies aimed at slowing the level of economic activity? Will the price level drop quickly, permitting the economy to continue to operate at or close to its potential? According to the "conventional view," no. The brunt of the adjustment at first will fall on output and employment, with little or no change in the price level. With the passage of time—as we move from time period t_1 to time period t_2 to t_3, etc.—output and employment will tend to move back in the direction of Y_p and the price level will fall. This is shown in Figure 12.6 by the movement of the short-run aggregate supply schedule (labeled AS_{SR}) from a horizontal or near-horizontal position to successively steeper positions. The policy conclusion that emerges from all of this is worth emphasizing.

It is extremely difficult to achieve a reduction in the price level without suffering a loss of output and employment for a while—and perhaps a long while. Contractionary policies can result in a lower price level, but not quickly. In an effort to reduce the price level from P_0 to P_1, output at first will fall to, say, point B, with no change in prices. Gradually, output will rise above B toward our potential and prices will fall. Only in the long run will P_1 be achieved at Y_p.

As we shall see shortly, the precise path followed by P and output will depend on how aggregate demand varies as the price level varies. To conclude this part of the discussion, one further point needs to be emphasized. Suppose the economy is at point A in Figure 12.6 and the level of economic activity is raised, say, in response to expansionary monetary and fiscal policies. In this case the price level will rise rapidly and real output will increase only marginally.

Why will real output rise at all? Does not the fact that we are at our potential mean that no further increases in real output are possible? Not necessarily. Remember that our potential output is not defined as the absolute limit, but rather the "normal" real output limit. It is possible for employees to work, for a while, for an "abnormally" long number of hours and for plants to operate a longer than normal number of hours as well. In any event, *what is important to recognize is that the upward movement of the price level in response to an increase in the pace of economic activity is more marked than the downward movement due to a decline in the level of economic activity.* This asymmetrical response is illustrated in Figure 12.7. The aggregate supply curve for increases in the level of economic activity is much steeper than for declines. The arrows point the direction of movement of the aggregate supply curve over time.

AGGREGATE DEMAND AND THE PRICE LEVEL

It is time now to turn our attention to the relationship between aggregate demand and the price level—that is, to the relationship between the amount of real output demanded and the general level of prices. The generally accepted relationship is portrayed in Figure 12.8. As is apparent, the relationship is an inverse one: the higher the price level, the smaller the quantity of real output demanded; the lower the price level, the greater the quantity of real output demanded.

This inverse relationship looks like the ordinary demand curve we studied way back in Chapter 3. However, the explanation of why an increase in the price level will cause a reduction in the quantity of goods and services demanded *in the aggregate* is much different from the explanation of why an increase in the price of some good or service will result in a reduction in the quantity of it demanded. We approach an under-

Figure 12.7
Short-run aggregate supply curve, above and below Yp

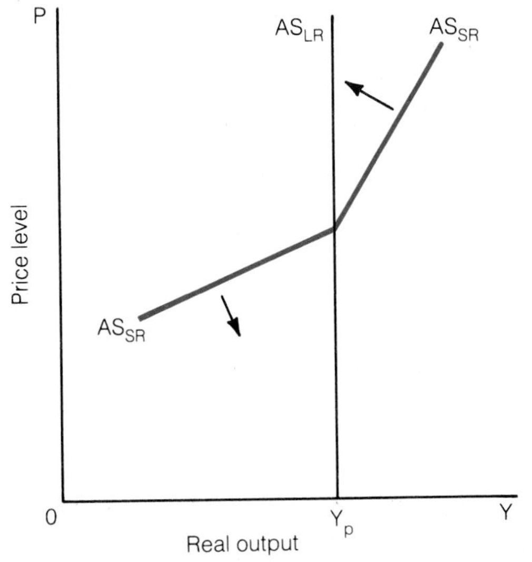

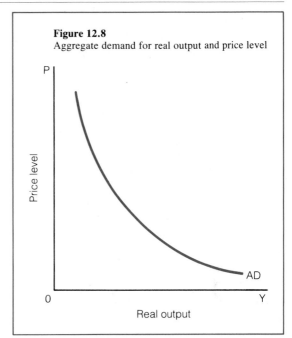

Figure 12.8
Aggregate demand for real output and price level

standing of this inverse aggregate relationship in steps.

First, recall again the definition of GNP. It is the market value of all final goods and services produced during some time period. Recall also the fact that GNP and gross national income are one and the same. The implication of this identity is clear. If the price level goes up by 10 percent *and if the same quantity of goods and services is produced as before,* then *both* nominal GNP and nominal aggregate income will rise by 10 percent. Since nominal GNP and nominal aggregate income are equivalent, the higher prices we all pay for goods and services will show up in the form of higher levels of money income in the aggregate. That 10 percent increase in money income is sufficient to purchase the same quantity of goods and services as before even if they now carry price tags that are 10 percent higher. The fact that the quantity of goods and services produced is unchanged means that real income—nominal income adjusted for (i.e., deflated by) the price level increase—is also unchanged. This implies that, in the face of a price level change, real income *could* be *unchanged*

and real aggregate demand *could be unchanged. This is an important point because it is often stated that price level increases in and of themselves necessarily reduce the purchasing power of people's incomes. However, since the higher prices received for any given level of output imply a corresponding increase in nominal aggregate income, the purchasing power of people's incomes need not be reduced necessarily. The source of the inverse relationship must lie elsewhere.*

Next, let us look at each of the components of aggregate demand to discover why the aggregate demand for real output may decline as a result of an increase in the general level of prices.

Government expenditures. There is no necessary reason government expenditures in *real* terms should remain constant in the face of an increase in the general level of prices. The level of government spending is determined by the Congress, state legislatures, and local governments. If the government wishes to maintain the same real incomes of its employees, some increase in nominal government spending will be required unless, of course, the number of people on government payrolls is cut back. If government desires to maintain the same level of *real* benefits for those on welfare or social security, or the same *real* level of government services, some increase in nominal spending will be required to maintain these programs as well. But there is no guarantee whatsoever that government will act in these ways. Our elected officials may try to hold the line on the magnitude of government spending in nominal terms, implying a *reduced* level of real spending when prices rise. They may opt for an increase in spending at a rate exceeding the rate of prices increase, causing an increase in *real* government expenditures. The point is, we do not know what actions government will take; that will depend on the give and take of government officials. *For our purposes we will assume that government expenditures in real terms will not be changed because of a change in the level of prices. If the aggregate demand for real output falls because of an increase in prices, the source of the fall will be elsewhere.*

Net exports. If the prices of U.S. exports rise by 10 percent while U.S. import prices remain unchanged, both U.S. consumers and foreign consumers will tend to substitute to some extent in favor of non-U.S. goods. U.S. exports will fall and U.S. imports will rise—that is, net exports will fall in the face of an increase in the U.S. price level. *Since net exports are one component of aggregate demand, real aggregate demand will decline as a consequence of an increase in the price level.* (We need to be careful here. If U.S. export prices *and* U.S. import prices *both* rise by 10 percent, no change should result in our real net exports; after all, there has been no change in relative prices. Thus, the inverse relationship noted here depends on import prices rising less than export prices.)

Consumer expenditures. In response to an increase in the price level there is good reason to expect a reduction in real consumption expenditures. It is a generally accepted proposition that *real* consumer expenditures on *real* disposable income and the *real* value of people's wealth. In addition, if interest rates increase, there is likely to be some reduction in demand for those consumer durables financed by borrowing. For the moment we will ignore the effect of an in-

crease in the price level on the real value of people's wealth. And we leave until the next section any discussion of the effects of increases in interest rates brought about by a price level increase. We will concentrate, then, on the effect that a hike in the price level will have on real disposable income.

We must approach this question cautiously. At the outset, it is important to recognize that it is not the increase in the price level itself that reduces people's real disposable income and therefore real consumer expenditures. *The reduction in people's real disposable income is a consequence of the fact that people's real tax liabilities increase.* Let us examine this relationship.

Recall that the increase in the price level that raises nominal GNP increases aggregate nominal income by a like amount. This does not mean that everybody's nominal income goes up in the same proportion. It may or may not. However, if one group experiences an increase in nominal income that is less than in proportion to the price level increase (meaning that their *real* income declines), someone or some other group *must* experience a more-than-proportionate increase in their nominal income (meaning that their *real* income increases). If the reduced real spending by those who experience real income declines is offset by the increased spending of those registering real income gains, *no* decline need result in real aggregate demand as a consequence of the price level increase.

There is, however, one important reason to expect that real aggregate demand will decline as a result of the increase in the level of prices— the phenomenon of "bracket creep" discussed in Chapter 4. Even if all people experience the same percentage increase in their nominal *before-tax* incomes, the taxes they must pay to the federal government at least will rise by a larger percentage. This means that their *aftertax* incomes will rise by a smaller percentage than the price level increase, resulting in a *decline* in their *real* disposable income. This in turn will induce a decline in real consumer spending. Tax receipts by the government, on the other hand, rise more than in proportion to the increase in the price level, with the result that *real* tax revenues rise.

This outcome emerges because federal income taxes, and some state income taxes, are progressive, taking larger and larger percentages of people's nominal incomes as those incomes increase. The fact that the federal income tax code taxes people's nominal incomes at progressively higher rates means that people's *real* tax liabilities increase more than in proportion to their real taxable incomes.

The conclusion that emerges from all of this is straightforward. *If people's before-tax incomes rise by the same proportion as prices, their real disposable incomes will fall, inducing them to cut back on their real consumption expenditures. This is one factor responsible for the decline in real aggregate demand as a consequence of a price level rise.* If, in addition, the real value of people's wealth declines because of the price level increase, a further reduction in real consumer spending will occur.

Gross private domestic investment. Investment spending by businesses is sensitive to the interest rate. Recalling our discussion of the MEI schedule in Chapter 11, a higher interest rate will induce businesspeople to cut back on their real expenditures for plant and equipment. If interest rates increase in the wake of a price level increase, real aggregate demand will fall as a result. We turn to an analysis of this issue now.

If the price level increases, there is good reason to expect that interest rates will rise, causing reductions in both real expenditures for investment and real expenditures for consumer durables. The reason the interest rate will rise is that the price level hike increases the demand for money. If the stock of money remains fixed (or rises by less than the increase in the demand for money), interest rates will rise.

The explanation for the increase in interest rates is straightforward. The amount of money people demand for transactions purposes depends on the value of the expenditures they undertake. If the goods and services they purchase increase in price by 10 percent, more money will be demanded in order to effect the purchases desired. The demand for money increases. Put another way, the amount of money demanded for transactions purposes depends on the *nominal* value of

aggregate income. Since a price level increase raises nominal income, the demand for money will increase. The amount of nominal money balances people's desire to hold for transactions purposes depends on their nominal incomes.

If we assume that the monetary authorities maintain the stock of money at its original level, the increase in the demand for money will force up interest rates. The monetary authorities need not behave in this way. Indeed, sometimes it is alleged that the monetary authorities will desire to keep interest rates at their original levels. If that were so, the Fed would undertake to expand the money supply (through open market purchases) in response to the price level hike. The reason? The increased demand for money would tend to cause interest rates to rise. To offset the interest rate increase the monetary authorities would have to embark on a policy to raise the money supply.

It is not at all obvious what policy initiatives the Fed will take. We will assume, as we have in earlier chapters, that the monetary authorities desire to fix the stock of money at its original level. Any changes in the stock of money will be interpreted as a change in policy. If the Fed desires to keep the interest rate fixed at its original level, the increase in the stock of money to meet the new higher demand will be viewed as a change in monetary policy.

Summing up the aggregate demand relationship

The reason for the inverse relationship between the aggregate demand for real output and the price level is now clear. In response to an increase in the price level:

1. The real demand for consumer goods and services will fall. This is the result of two factors: (a) real disposable income will fall, the consequence of the increased real tax liabilities as people are pushed into higher tax brackets; and (b) the increase in interest rates causes people to curtail their interest sensitive expenditures.
2. The level of real investment will fall. This is the result of higher interest rates.
3. Real net exports *could* fall.

AGGREGATE SUPPLY, AGGREGATE DEMAND, AND THE PRICE LEVEL

We are now finally in a position to show how aggregate demand and aggregate supply interact to determine the general level of prices. We will examine this relationship from two points of view—the long run and the short run.

The long-run equilibrium price level

The price level that will prevail in the long run is illustrated in Figure 12.9. The long-run aggregate supply curve (AS_{LR}) is vertical and positioned over the point representing our potential GNP. The aggregate demand schedule (AD) is downward sloping in accordance with the factors discussed earlier. Their point of intersection yields the long-run equilibrium price level, P_e.

Consider the long-run adjustments that would come about if the price level happened to be different than P_e. Suppose the price level were P_1. At that price level, the aggregate demand for real output is less than our potential. This implies that unemployed resources exist. The unemployment rate is above its natural or full employment rate; some firms and industries are confronted

with excess capacity. *Ultimately,* in the absence of changes in monetary and fiscal policy, wages will be reduced and firms will cut their prices, lowering the price level. The lower price level will cause an increase in the quantity of real output demanded. And, as long as the price level exceeds P_e, further long-run price reductions can be expected until P_e is reached. *The problem at P_1 is that, given the stock of money, interest rates are too high to induce consumers and businesses to purchase a level of output corresponding to our potential.*

At a price level P_2, which is below the long-run equilibrium price level, P_e, real aggregate demand exceeds our output potential. The problem here is that, given the stock of money, interest rates are so low that consumers and businesses desire to purchase more than our potential. The price level will be forced up in the wake of wage increases and price increases.

Changes in the price level in the long run

Assuming for the moment that our potential GNP remains fixed at Y_p, changes in the long-run equilibrium price can occur only if the aggregate demand schedule shifts up or down. What

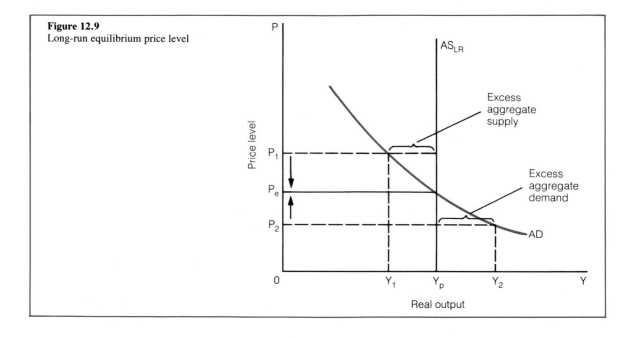

Figure 12.9
Long-run equilibrium price level

can cause the AD schedule to shift? Many factors. Let us consider some of the more important factors.

If consumers *expect* the general level of prices to increase in the future, they may try to step up their spending now in an effort to beat the price rise. They are willing, therefore, to increase their spending *at each and every price level.* This will cause the AD schedule to shift to the right. This is illustrated in Figure 12.10. In the long run, the increase in AD from AD_1 to AD_2 causes the price level to increase from P_1 to P_2. In the absence of an increase in the money supply, the price level increase comes about because the velocity of circulation increases. Can you interpret the equation of exchange—$MV = PY$—to explain why this must be so?

The same result as shown in Figure 12.10 could come about if consumers, for whatever other reason, cut their rate of savings and boosted their spending for consumer goods and services. Similarily, if businesspeople increase their expenditures for capital goods—because, for example, they expect capital goods prices to rise in the future or because they expect their sales performance to be greater in future years—the MEI schedule will shift out, which in turn raises the AD schedule. An increase in our net exports, brought about, say, because of a higher demand for American goods on the part of foreign consumers, will also cause our AD schedule to shift up and to the right.

Of considerable importance is the fact that changes in monetary and fiscal policy can bring about shifts in the AD schedule. An expansionary monetary policy, by lowering interest rates and stimulating the demand for investment goods and for consumer durables, will cause the AD schedule to shift to the right, raising in turn the long-run equilibrium level of prices.

The effect that a change in fiscal policy will have on the price level is a more controversial issue. According to those economists wedded to the monetarist line, any change in government spending or taxes *unaccompanied* by a change in the stock of money will leave aggregate demand unaltered. An expansionary fiscal policy will simply "crowd out" an equivalent amount of private spending, with the result that the AD schedule will not change. As you will recall from our discussion of this issue in Chapter 11, this monetarist conclusion will hold *only* if the velocity of circulation does not change. Nonmonetarists argue that the velocity of circulation will rise as a result of an expansionary fiscal policy.

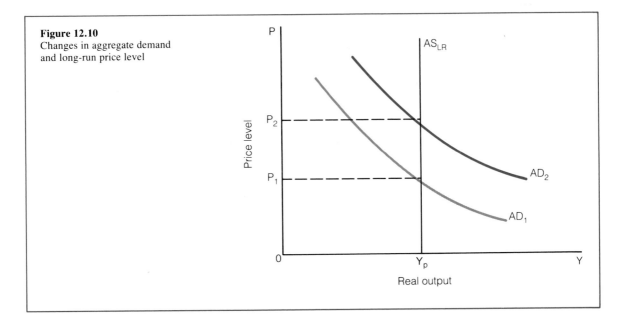

Figure 12.10
Changes in aggregate demand
and long-run price level

If that happens, the AD schedule will shift to the right, in turn raising the long-run equilibrium level of prices. In view of our discussion in Chapter 11, we will assume in our discussion here and in Chapter 13 that aggregate demand will rise (or fall) in response to an expansionary (or contractionary) fiscal policy.

Output and price level determination in the short run

The intersection of the AD schedule with the upward-sloping short-run aggregate supply schedule (AS_{SR}) gives us the short-run equilibrium price level and the short-run equilibrium level of real output. One possible short-run equilibrium position is illustrated in Figure 12.11. There, at point A, we show a short-run equilibrium price level equal to P_1 and a short-run equilibrium level of output, Y_1. Real output, in this example, is below our potential output, Y_p; the equilibrium price in the short run is above P_e, the long-run equilibrium price level.

In an important sense, short-run equilibrium—unless it happens to correspond to the long-run equilibrium position of the economy—is a temporary state of affairs. Therefore, it is

not reasonable to assume that the economy will remain at point A in Figure 12.11 in the long run. Point A is only a short-run equilibrium position. In the long run, in the absence of shifts in the AD schedule or shocks that could cause shifts in the AS_{SR} schedule, the economy will tend to move in the direction of point B—the long-run equilibrium position. Since point A represents a level of output below our potential— a level of output characterized by an unemployment rate above the "natural" rate and an inordinately low rate of capacity utilization—it is reasonable to expect that wages and prices will fall in the long run and that the level of output will increase, moving the economy toward point B. After a period, the AS_{SR} schedule will become steeper, enabling us to reach point C by t_2; in the long run, we will reach point B.

The conclusion reached on the basis of these considerations is that, if we wait long enough, we will gravitate toward our long-run equilibrium position. However, the fact that it may take *years* to move from point A to point B means that the monetary and fiscal authorities can exert considerable influence over the level of economic activity in the short run. Indeed, given the time required to achieve long-run equilibrium, most people would argue that the monetary and fiscal

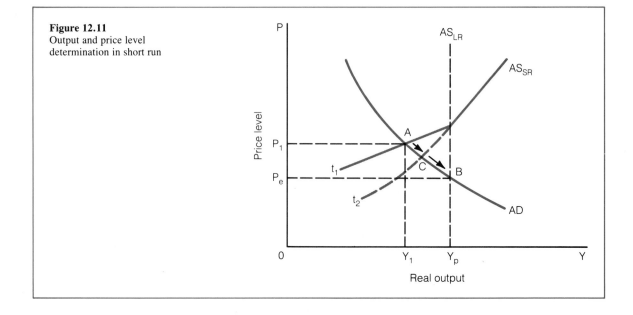

Figure 12.11
Output and price level determination in short run

authorities have the *obligation* to pursue policies designed to ensure that the economy operates most of the time at or near its potential, pursuing expansionary policies when the economy falls below its potential and contractionary policies when it tends to rise above its potential. We will leave to the next chapter a detailed analysis of these policy questions. For now let us examine the short-run relationship between the price level and the level of output, as well as the corresponding short-run relationship between the price level and the rate of unemployment. We will study two different sets of relationships—one where the source of variation is attributable to shifts in AD, and the other where the source of variation is attributable to shifts in AS$_{SR}$.

Short-run price, output, and employment changes: Shifts in AD

Consider the aggregate demand and aggregate supply relationships depicted in Figure 12.12. We start out at point E, the long-run equilibrium position for the economy. Suppose, for one reason or another, that the AD curve shifts to the left. The short-run effect of this decline in AD will

be a reduced level of output, a higher rate of unemployment, and a somewhat lower price level; in the very short run—a period of perhaps three to six months—the reduction in the price level is likely to be miniscule. Thus, in the short run, the economy will move from point E to, say, point F as a result of a decline in AD from AD$_1$ to AD$_2$.

Aggregate demand could shift down in response to several factors: consumers, for one reason or another, decide to curtail their spending and boost their savings rate; businesspeople decide to cut their investment spending because of an anticipated reduction in future sales; net exports fall off because of a reduced demand for our goods from abroad; the government, in an effort to balance its budget, cuts its spending; the monetary authorities, in an effort to achieve a reduced price level, cut the money supply. Any and all of these factors could lead to a reduced level of aggregate demand.

The reduction in aggregate demand will cause, in the short run, a reduced level of output and a somewhat lower level of prices. The reduced level of output will also cause the unemployment

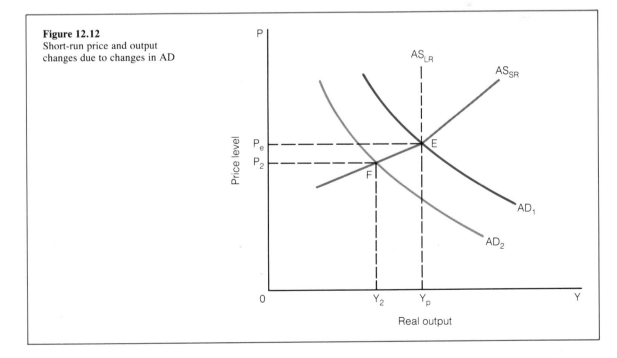

Figure 12.12
Short-run price and output changes due to changes in AD

rate to rise above its natural or full employment rate. When the source of the disturbance is a falloff in aggregate demand, the price level and the level of output will move in the same direction in the short run; the unemployment rate and the price level will move in opposite directions.

Short-run price, output, and employment changes: Shifts in AS$_{SR}$

Output, employment, and price changes can also be brought about by shifts in the short-run aggregate supply schedule. The factors responsible for possible shifts in AS$_{SR}$ are reasonably clear. The position of the short-run aggregate supply schedule is determined in large measure by production costs—by labor costs, capital costs, energy costs, and other input costs. If, for one reason or another, these production costs increase, the short-run aggregate supply schedule will shift up. If unions are able to win for their members inordinately large wage increases—wage increases in excess of productivity increases so that unit labor costs rise—the short-run aggre-

gate supply schedule will shift up. If the OPEC nations force up the level of energy prices, AS$_{SR}$ will shift up. If government regulations raise business capital costs, AS$_{SR}$ will shift up.

The effect of an upward shift in AS$_{SR}$ is shown in Figure 12.13. The important point to note here is that the movement of the short-run aggregate supply schedule from AS$_{SR}^1$ to AS$_{SR}^2$ will cause the price level to rise and cause output and employment *to fall*. In other words, when the source of the variation in price, output, and employment is a shift of AS$_{SR}$, the price and output movements and the price and unemployment movements are opposite to those brought about by changes in AD. *In particular, if AS$_{SR}$ shifts up in response to, say, production cost increases, the price level increase will be accompanied by a falling rate of output and a higher rate of unemployment.* This kind of price, output, and unemployment variation is frequently called **stagflation**—the phenomenon where rising prices are accompanied by both a reduced level of output and a higher rate of unemployment.

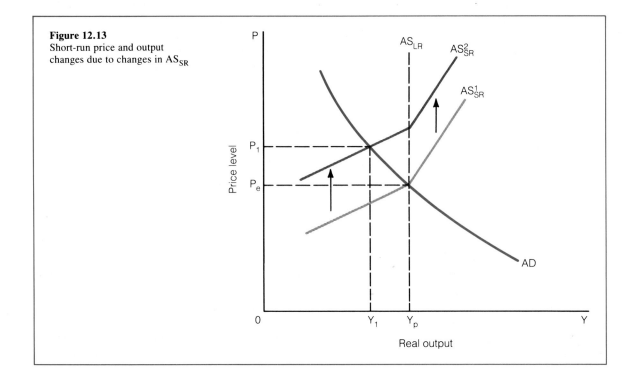

Figure 12.13
Short-run price and output changes due to changes in AS$_{SR}$

Frequently it is alleged that a rise in the price level in conjunction with an increase in the unemployment rate and a reduced level of output provides us with the proof we need that the economy is not operating in the manner economists tell us it should. This conclusion is incorrect. If the source of the variation in price, output, and the unemployment rate is a shift in AD, then a reduced level of output and a higher unemployment rate will be associated with a lower price level. But if the source of variation is a shift in AS_{SR}, then a higher price level will be associated with a reduced level of output and a higher rate of unemployment. The stagflation problem is here the product of shifts in AS_{SR}.

SUMMARY

1. The theory of aggregate supply is concerned with the question of how a change in GNP is divided between a change in output and a change in the general price level. The first tenet of the theory of aggregate supply states: When real GNP is equal to potential GNP, changes in aggregate demand will influence only the price level, not real output. For levels of real GNP less than potential GNP, how a given change in nominal GNP will be divided between a change in real GNP and a change in the price level is a matter of considerable dispute. According to the so-called classical economists, the aggregate supply curve is vertical at almost any level of real output. The extreme Keynesian view is that the aggregate supply curve is horizontal up to the point of our potential GNP; thereafter it is vertical. The majority of economists reject both the extreme classical and Keynesian positions. Rather, they take an intermediate position that can be summarized as follows: (1) the aggregate supply curve is vertical at the point of our potential GNP; (2) at very depressed levels of economic activity, the aggregate supply curve is horizontal, *at least in the short run;* and (3) in the intermediate range, the aggregate supply curve is upward sloping, becoming increasingly steep the closer we get to our potential.

2. Adopting the conventional view, the aggregate supply curve has a tendency to *ratchet up* over time in the face of increases in real output. This is because prices are more rigid downward than they are upward. This has very important implications for policy. In the short run, the economy can fall far below its ultimate full employment position. The fact that it may take the economy a long time to reach full employment on its own leaves considerable room for monetary and fiscal policies to effect changes in the level of economic activity. Moreover, it is extremely difficult to achieve a reduction in the price level without suffering losses of output and employment for a while—perhaps a very long while.

3. Generally speaking, there is an inverse relationship between the amount of real output demanded and the general level of prices. This relationship holds because, in response to an increase in the price level, three things happen. First, the real demand for *consumer goods and services* will fall. This is the result of two factors: *(a)* real disposable income will fall, the consequence of increased real tax liabilities as people are pushed into higher tax brackets, and *(b)* the increase in interest rates causes people to curtail their interest-sensitive expenditures. Second, the level of *real investment* will fall as a result of higher interest rates. And third, real net exports could fall if the prices of U.S. exports rise relative to the prices of U.S. imports.

4. The point of intersection of the aggregate demand schedule and the long-run aggregate supply schedule yields the long-run equilibrium price level. Changes in the long-run equilibrium price level can be brought about by changes in aggregate demand and/or changes in potential GNP. Of considerable importance is the fact that changes in monetary and fiscal policy can bring about shifts in the aggregate demand schedule to effect changes in the level of prices. In view of the monetarist-fiscalist debate, considerable controversy surrounds the proposition that changes in fiscal policy can have permanent effects on the price level.

5. The intersection of the aggregate demand schedule with the upward-sloping short-run ag-

gregate supply schedule gives us the short-run equilibrium price level and the short-run equilibrium level of real output. Unless the short-run equilibrium just happens to correspond to the long-run equilibrium position of the economy, the short-run equilibrium is a temporary state of affairs.

6. When the source of the disturbance of the short-run equilibrium is a change in aggregate demand, the price level and output will move in the same direction; the unemployment rate and the price level will move in opposite directions. On the other hand, if the source of the disturbance is a shift in the aggregate supply schedule, the price and output movements and the price and unemployment movements will be opposite to those brought about by changes in aggregate demand. The *stagflation* problem is the product of shifts in the short-run aggregate supply schedule.

CONCEPTS FOR REVIEW

Theory of aggregate supply

Long-run aggregate supply

Short-run aggregate supply

Problem of defining potential GNP

Classical view of the short-run aggregate supply curve

Keynesian view of the short-run aggregate supply curve

Conventional view of the aggregate supply curve

Ratcheting up of the aggregate supply curve

Short-run versus long-run aggregate supply curves

Relation of aggregate demand to price level

Bracket creep

Long-run equilibrium price level

Stagflation

QUESTIONS FOR DISCUSSION

(Those marked with an asterisk (*) are more difficult.)

*1. *a.* Although we hypothesized an inverse relationship between the price level and real aggregate demand, we emphasized that the reason for this was *not* the same as the inverse relationship between the quantity demanded of some particular good and its price. State the law of demand and explain why it is not applicable at the aggregate level. (*Hint:* Does the *ceteris paribus* condition for the law of demand hold at the aggregate level?)

b. Explain why the hypothesized upward-sloping aggregate supply curve is *not* based on the same reasoning used to justify the upward-sloping supply curve in the case of a single commodity.

2. Assume monetary policy is tightened, causing the AD curve to shift to the left. Explain how the outcomes would differ between the classical economists and the extreme Keynesians in the short run. Would they differ from one another in the long run? What general conclusions can you draw?

3. Assume fiscal policy is tightened. How would a monetarist evaluate the output and price effects of this policy change? Why? What about nonmonetarists?

4. What factors would cause changes in the position of the long-run aggregate supply curve over time? (*Hint:* What factors determine our potential GNP?)

5. *a.* Explain carefully why a change in the AD schedule, whatever its cause, is not capable of explaining a stagflation kind of relationship—that is, a rising price level and a rising rate of unemployment.

b. Explain how a change in OPEC oil prices or a dramatic change in food prices (perhaps caused by a sharp increase in world demand for food or by adverse weather conditions domestically) can lead to a stagflation kind of relationship.

*6. Suppose government reduces the marginal tax rates on individuals and businesses. And suppose the reduced marginal tax rates spur additional work effort and higher levels of real business investment. What effect will this have on the long-run price level? (*Hint:* How is AS_{LR} affected?)

7. Investment is both a component of aggregate demand and a source of increased growth. Using the aggregate demand and aggregate supply apparatus developed in this chapter, show the effects of changes in the levels of real business investment on real output and the price level.

In the previous chapter we examined how aggregate demand and aggregate supply interacted to determine the overall *level of prices* in the American economy. In this chapter we will extend the analysis to show how aggregate demand and aggregate supply interact to determine *inflation*. To extend the analysis in this way does not require the development of a new theory. After all, if the theory developed in Chapter 12 is capable of explaining how the price level is determined, the *same* theory must also be capable of explaining how inflation is determined since *inflation is defined in terms of the rate of change of the price level.*

We open the chapter with a brief definition of *inflation*. This is followed by a brief overview of the inflation process. It is here that we introduce the one critically important difference between the analysis presented in Chapter 12 and our analysis here—the role of inflationary expectations.

Having been presented with a view of the forest, we then turn to an examination of the trees. Specifically, we develop again the tools of aggregate demand and aggregate supply, focusing on the rate of inflation—that is, the rate of change in the level of prices—rather than on the price level.

THE MEANING OF INFLATION

It must be recognized at the outset that no single unambiguous definition of *inflation* exists. In a loose sense, *inflation* can be defined as the upward movement in the general level of prices. However, a one-shot increase in the general level of prices has markedly different implications for the economy than does an increase that is sustained over a prolonged period. Consider the following situations:

1. The price level has remained relatively stable for a number of years. Then, for one reason or another, the price level shoots up. After a short time, the price level stops rising. Thereafter, it remains stable at its new higher level.

2. The price level has remained relatively stable for a number of years. Again, the price

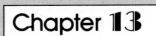

Chapter 13

The macrodynamics of aggregate demand and aggregate supply

level shoots up, only this time it does not settle down, but continues to rise year after year, perhaps at an accelerating rate, perhaps at varying rates, but ever increasing.

In the first situation, inflation was temporary. Whatever caused the price level to increase was not repeated; if repeated, it was offset in future periods by other forces. Moreover, the one-shot increase in the price level did not set off forces to propel the price level upwards over time. The fact that the price level ceased its upward movement meant that the inflation problem was gone. Whatever caused the upward movement in the price level may still be considered a problem but it is no longer an *inflation problem*. The price level increase may have been because of a sharp increase in the price of energy, the result of, say, OPEC raising its oil prices. We may worry about our heavy dependence on imported oil, and we may try to devise ways to reduce that dependence. But, though this energy problem remains, the fact that the price level stabilized meant that the inflation problem was gone.

The second situation is quite different. The price level did not stabilize, but continued to move upwards over time. Perhaps the initial causal factor continued to be repeated; or perhaps it set in motion forces to sustain the upward movement of the price level year after year. In any event, the failure of the price level to settle down to a stable level meant that whatever other problems were caused, the inflation problem persisted. It is the persistence of inflation, characterized by the sustained upward movement in the price level over time that constitutes the inflation problem. Thus, we will not view a once-and-for-all change in the price level as an inflation problem, at least not a permanent one.

We mean by inflation the *sustained* upward movement in the general level of prices over time.

An aside. An interesting but little known fact is the definition of inflation in *Webster's Dictionary:* "an increase in the volume of money and credit relative to available goods resulting in a substantial and continuing rise in the general price level."

Many economists find this definition objectionable. First, it attempts to define inflation in terms of what causes it. Second, the only cause of inflation is assumed to be "an increase in the volume of money and credit relative to available goods." Third, to qualify as inflation, the rise in the general price level must be "substantial." When you complete your study of this chapter you might want to evaluate this definition for yourself.

THE INFLATION PROCESS: AN OVERVIEW

As will be explained at length in the remainder of this chapter, the actual rate of inflation during any given time period can be viewed as consisting of the sum of three separate forces: **the demand-pull rate of inflation, the price-shock rate of inflation,** and **the core rate of inflation.**

The demand-pull rate of inflation

The **demand-pull rate of inflation** is determined by the state of aggregate demand in relation to our potential or full employment level of output. When aggregate demand exceeds the full employment level of output, the price level will be "pulled up." On the other hand, when aggregate demand falls below our GNP potential, the demand-pull pressure on prices will cease. Whether the price level will actually fall when aggregate demand drops below the full employment level of output is a matter on which there is not universal agreement. However, the conventional view among economists is that very little if any reduction in the price level can be expected in the short run in view of the notorious downward stickiness of wages and prices. In the long run, some downward adjustment is likely. This matter was discussed in detail in Chapter 12.

An alternative way of presenting the demand-pull argument is in terms of the relationship between the actual rate of unemployment and the natural rate. As noted in earlier chapters the *natural rate* of unemployment is defined loosely as that equilibrium rate of unemployment characterized by the absence of overall excess demand or excess supply in labor markets. Upward wage pressures emanating from markets with excess demands (markets with job vacancies) are offset by downward wage pressures in markets that are in excess supply (markets with unemployed workers). When aggregate demand exceeds the full employment level of output, the actual rate of unemployment is below the natural rate, pulling up wage and price levels. Demand-pull pressures are eliminated at rates of unemployment above the natural rate.

According to the demand-pull argument, inflation arises because the unemployment rate is pushed below the natural rate. To eliminate demand-pull pressures is easy—use restrictive monetary and fiscal policies to reduce aggregate spending. And note one important consequence of these restrictive aggregate demand measures. The reduction in inflation will be accompanied by an increase in the unemployment rate.

The fact that inflation slows in response to an increase in the unemployment rate *in this instance* does not mean that inflation will be reduced as the unemployment rate rises under all circumstances. This point is not well understood. Many people have been led to believe by some theories that higher rates of unemployment necessarily result in lower rates of inflation. But this need not be true. *Higher rates of unemployment will reduce the demand-pull rate of inflation. But demand-pull is only one source of inflationary pressure.* One must also take into account the fact that other sources of inflation may be causing inflation to rise at the same time as unemployment is rising, more than offsetting the reduction caused by a slowing of aggregate spending. And what are these other sources? The **price-shock rate of inflation** and the **core rate of inflation.**

The price-shock rate of inflation

Sudden increases in the prices of particular goods and services can push the inflation rate up. When OPEC raised its oil prices by a whopping 400 percent in 1973–74 and again by about 125 percent over the course of 1979 and 1980, the inflation rate was pushed up in each instance. Large increases in the price of food, brought about by adverse crop and weather conditions, can cause an increase in inflation. Increases in social security taxes, by boosting labor costs, raise inflation. Increased tariffs that raise the prices of imported goods and services add to inflation. A sharp increase in the costs businesses must incur to comply with new governmental regulations will cause inflation to rise. And increased minimum wages, which raise labor costs, also add to inflation.

A number of other price-shock forces could be identified, but we must be careful not to overdo it. Since we are concerned with the overall level of prices, it is important that we do not get bogged down in the examination of price and cost changes, which, though perhaps huge when viewed in isolation, have only a tiny influence on the general level of prices. An increase in the price of haircuts—from, say, $5 to $8—would have almost no effect on the general price level (although the magnitude of the change in haircut prices is huge) because the "weight" of haircut prices in the overall measure of prices is small. Oil and food price increases, on the other hand, are quite another matter.

Moreover, although oil and food are important in the determination of the overall level of prices, it would be inappropriate to view *all* oil and food price increases as *adding* to inflation. If oil and food prices rise at roughly the same rate as the general level of prices, they will not raise the inflation rate. In this instance, the price-shock rate of inflation attributable to these factors is zero. The price-shock rate turns positive—that is, adds to inflation—when the prices of these goods rise at rates in excess of the general level of prices. The price-shock rate becomes negative—that is, causes lower inflation—when the prices of these items rise less rapidly than other prices.

One other point needs emphasis. It concerns the question of whether a *one-shot* sudden increase in oil or food prices, for example, will cause a temporary or more permanent increase in the rate of inflation. This question can be answered in two parts.

1. From the point of view simply of the price-shock rate of inflation, a one-shot sudden increase in oil or food prices will raise the inflation rate only temporarily. To illustrate, suppose oil prices have been increasing at the same rate as other prices—say, 6 percent annually. Then, as a result of OPEC actions, oil prices suddenly rise by 50 percent, rising thereafter at the same rate as other prices. As a consequence, the price level will jump up faster than otherwise, raising the rate of inflation above 6 percent. However, since oil prices advance in subsequent years at the same rate as other goods and services, the shock rate of inflation is reduced to zero. Whether or not the *actual* inflation rate, after the shock increase, settles down to its old 6 percent rate depends on how future costs and prices are influenced by the inordinately large shock increase in the inflation rate.

2. As we shall see below, there is good reason to expect that the higher inflation rate will cause an increase in the **core rate of inflation.** That is, since the increased rate of inflation raises the cost of living, and since cost-of-living wage increases are granted almost automatically to many workers, the one-shot increase in energy prices could result in an increased rate of inflation over a long period. Thus, although the shock rate of inflation ceases, the one-shot increase in the price level will cause more than a one-shot increase in the rate of inflation if that increase spills over and raises the core rate of inflation. *The inflation effect of a one-shot increase in oil prices could be more than temporary.*

The core rate of inflation

There is yet another factor responsible for inflation—inflationary expectations. Inflationary expectations determine the **core** or **underlying rate of inflation.** The core rate is the rate of inflation that would occur over the long term, provided the economy was not subjected to price shocks and aggregate demand was neutral—neutral in the sense of neither contributing to nor subtracting from inflation.

What determines people's inflationary expectations, and therefore the core rate, is a matter of considerable controversy among economists, as we shall see later. One popular view, and the one we will address for now, holds that inflationary expectations are formed largely on the basis of previous experience—that people *gradually* adjust, or adapt, their expectations regarding future rates of inflation on the basis of *past* actual inflation rates. Appropriately enough, this view is called the **theory of adaptive inflationary expectations.**

And why are people's inflationary expectations so important? Because anticipated price level increases lead to wage demands and wage offers that raise costs and prices. In an environment in which people expect future price increases, we can expect them to devise mechanisms to protect their real incomes from the effects of inflation. One means of accomplishing this objective is to **index** the compensation they receive to the price increases that actually occur. Thus, workers will seek compensation for past increases in their cost of living and protection from future price increases. And producers will seek compensation from those to whom they sell their products for past increases in their costs and protection against future cost increases.

Cost-of-living adjustments (COLAs) are today a standard feature in many labor union contracts with employers; with COLAs, wages are periodically increased *automatically* as a result of past (cost-of-living) price increases. And COLAs are frequently built into employer contracts with individual employees. But even where there are no explicit contracts, employers frequently grant cost-of-living wage increases as part of an *implicit* contract with their workers. Failure to grant such wage increases would ultimately cause many workers in these establishments to quit to take jobs elsewhere that offer higher wages. Employers cannot expect workers to stay on if the wages they offer fall ever-farther below wages received elsewhere.

Producers as well attempt to protect themselves from the effects of inflation in their labor and other costs. It is common practice for producers to mark up the prices they charge their customers as a result of increased costs. This is true of both their explicit and implicit contracts with customers.

As a result of these explicit and implicit contracts, past rates of inflation become embedded in future costs and future prices. The fact that these contracts often remain in force for fairly long periods—union contracts are generally negotiated only every two or three years, and even implicit wage contracts with individual employees are often reviewed only once a year—means that past rates of inflation are likely to persist well into the future.

On the basis of these considerations, we can define the core rate of inflation as follows. The core rate of inflation measures those price increases that result from increases in the trend of production costs, that cost trend being determined by past price increases. Fundamentally, the core rate is a reflection of people's underlying expectations. It is because of their inflationary expectations that workers and producers seek—in both their explicit and implicit contracts—guarantees of increased compensation to make up for past price and cost increases.

Since the core rate of inflation, reflecting people's inflationary expectations, is assumed here to be the result of *past* price increases, inflationary expectations cannot be viewed as the force that initiates an inflationary movement. If prices have been stable for some time, there is no historical reason for believing that prices will rise in the future. The source of any inflationary movement must be found elsewhere—in particular, in the past history of demand-pull and price-shock inflation.

Viewed from this perspective, it is fair to say that inflation is ultimately "caused" by demand-pull and price-shock forces. However, inflationary expectations serve to maintain inflation's momentum. Even if the demand-pull and price-shock factors cease to propel inflation upward, inflation can persist as a consequence of people's inflationary expectations. What is particularly troubling is that it appears to be very difficult

to break the inflation momentum quickly. This, however, is a matter of considerable dispute, as our discussion of *rational expectations* below will reveal.

The remainder of this chapter is designed to bring together the three components of inflation—the demand-pull rate, price-shock rate, and core rate—into a coherent and understandable theory of the inflation process. We begin by redefining the aggregate supply and aggregate demand relationships, where, as noted earlier, the focus is on inflation as opposed to the price level.

AGGREGATE DEMAND, AGGREGATE SUPPLY, AND INFLATION

The aggregate demand and aggregate supply relationships developed in Chapter 12 can be generalized to aid us in our understanding of the inflation process. These generalizations are summarized in Figure 13.1. There are three pairs of graphs in Figure 13.1. The diagram on the left of each pair represents the relationship developed in Chapter 12; the diagram on the right represents its generalization. Let us make sure we understand the generalizations.

In Figure 13.1A, the left diagram tells us that aggregate supply in the long run corresponds to our potential GNP and is independent of the *price level*. This diagram we are familiar with from Chapter 12. The right diagram of Figure 13.1A illustrates the generalization of the aggregate supply relationship on the left. The difference here is that the vertical axis on the right diagram measures *not* the price level but the *rate of change of the price level*—that is, *inflation*. What the diagram on the right of Figure 13.1A tells us is this: Aggregate supply in the long run corresponds to our potential GNP and is independent of the rate of inflation. Whether inflation is high, low, or nonexistent, our nation's productive potential will be unaffected; Y_p is determined by the quantity and quality of our nation's resources, *not* by the rate of inflation. Moreover, the vertical line is called the **long-run aggregate**

Figure 13.1
Aggregate supply and aggregate demand relationships generalized

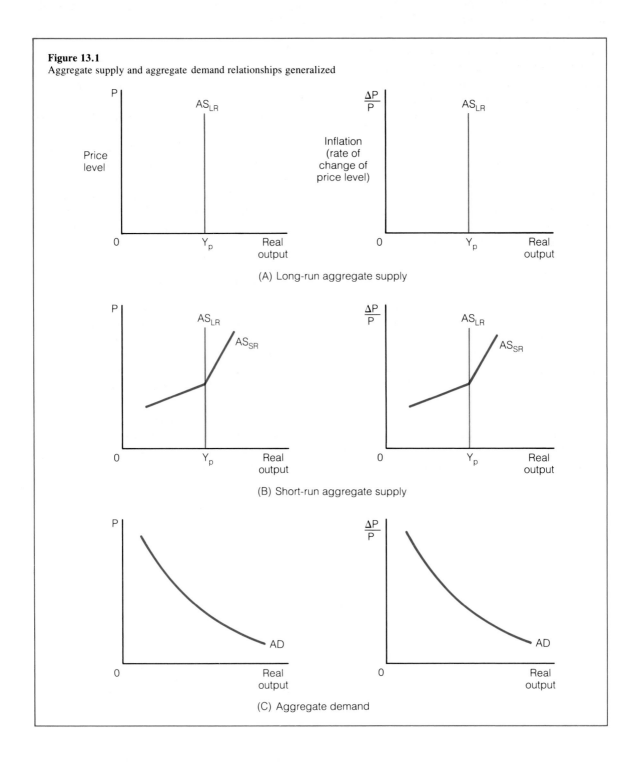

(A) Long-run aggregate supply

(B) Short-run aggregate supply

(C) Aggregate demand

supply curve to emphasize, as in Chapter 12, that the economic system has a tendency to gravitate toward full employment (or the natural rate of unemployment), toward the realization of our productive potential, in the long run. Since the right side of Figure 13.1A is a generalization of the left side, there is no reason to label the long-run aggregate supply curves differently; they are both labeled AS_{LR}.

In Figure 13.1B, the left side shows the short-run aggregate supply curve developed in Chapter 12; on the right side is its generalization. The generalized short-run aggregate supply curve tells us that the quantity produced in the short run and the rate of *inflation* are positively related. Because the right side of Figure 13.1B is a generalization of the left side, the curves in both diagrams are labeled AS_{SR}.

Finally, Figure 13.1C shows the generalization of the aggregate demand relationship. Whereas in Chapter 12 we hypothesized an inverse relationship between the real quantity demanded and the price level, its generalization (on the right side of Figure 13.1C) hypothesizes an inverse relationship between the real quantity of output demanded and *inflation.*

An examination of Figure 13.1 seems to suggest that all we did for each of the hypothesized relationships was replace the price level on the vertical axis with the *rate of change* of the price level. However, it is not that simple, as we will see below.

Long-run aggregate supply and inflation

To see why long-run aggregate supply is independent of inflation, consider Figure 13.2. For simplicity we have assumed that the multiplicity of demand and supply relationships in our nation's many labor markets can be summarized in a single set of demand and supply curves, such as those in Figure 13.2. On the horizontal axis we measure the quantity of labor resources; on the vertical axis is measured the *real* wage—the money wage, w, divided by the general price level, p. The intersection of the demand and supply curves yields both the equilibrium real wage, $\left(\dfrac{w}{p}\right)_0$, and the equilibrium level of employment, E_0. (Because the demand and supply apparatus used in Figure 13.2 summarizes the demand and supply relationships in all labor markets, the level of employment, E_0, should *not* be interpreted to mean a zero unemployment rate. Rather, it should be interpreted to mean that the economy has reached its natural rate of unemployment— the rate characterized by the absence of any *overall* excess demand for or excess supply of labor. If this is all fuzzy to you, go back and see the discussion in Chapter 5.)

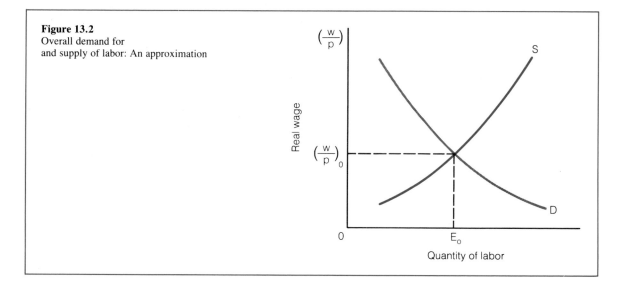

Figure 13.2
Overall demand for
and supply of labor: An approximation

What is important to note about Figure 13.2 is this: As long as the real wage remains fixed at $\left(\dfrac{w}{p}\right)_0$, the level of employment of our nation's labor resources will remain fixed at E_0. However, there are many combinations of wage and price level changes that are consistent with a fixed *real* wage. If wages and the price level *both* increase at the *same* 4 percent rate, the real wage will stay fixed, as will the level of employment. If wages and the price level both remain constant, the real wage will stay where it is and employment will remain at E_0.

As long as the rate of change of money wages equals the rate of change of the price level—whatever that rate happens to be—the amount of labor resources employed will remain fixed. The level of production corresponding to this fixed amount of labor input will remain fixed as well. Moreover, assuming that the presence of overall excess demand or excess supply will correct itself in time through real wage adjustments, aggregate supply in the long run—that is, in equlibrium—will be independent of inflation.

(*An amendment:* Actually, we need to amend the discussion above in one technical respect. The level of employment will remain fixed at E_0 if the real wage *adjusted for productivity change* remains constant. Put differently, in long-run equilibrium, real wages on average will increase at the same rate as the growth of *average labor productivity*. For simplicity, we are here assuming zero growth in average labor productivity. For more details see the discussion of this issue in Chapter 5.)

Long-run aggregate supply and inflationary expectations. The mechanism that ensures that real wages will adjust appropriately to yield the long-run equilibrium level of employment is **inflationary expectations.** It is important, therefore, that we thoroughly understand this mechanism.

Inflationary expectations influence both the wage-setting behavior of workers and the price-setting behavior of producers. In long-run equilibrium, the inflationary expectations of different groups are consistent with one another, on the average, producing wage changes (adjusted for productivity change) equal to price level changes. Several points are worth making in this regard.

1. It is not just people's expectations of inflation that bring about the long-run result described above. It is, rather, the *changes in behavior* induced by people's expectations of inflation that are, in part, responsible for the wage and price patterns in evidence during periods of inflation.

2. Although the expression "inflationary expectations" is concerned with inflation in the future, it need not be the case that workers and producers will set wages and prices today at rates that correspond with the expectations of future inflation that they hold today. It is more common for workers and producers to set forth rules—either in the form of explicit or implicit contracts—that provide them with some guarantees that their real incomes will not be eroded as a result of wage and price inflation. It is often understood—either explicitly or implicitly—that workers will receive cost-of-living adjustments for *past* price level increases, and that producers will pass along such wage increases in the form of higher prices. What is important to note is that workers and producers both try to establish such rules because they expect inflation in the future.

3. In long-run equilibrium, the inflationary expectations of producers and workers are consistent with one another. That is, workers and producers are each adjusted fully to the wage and price inflation that is taking place. Put differently, adjustment is complete in the sense that the equilibrium condition—a constant real wage—is as if there were no inflation.

4. In long-run equilibrium, the *actual* rate of inflation will equal the *expected* rate. Actually, this is really nothing more than a restatement of number 3 above—that is, that workers and producers are each fully adjusted to the wage and price inflation. And again, the notion that the actual and expected rates of inflation are equal does not mean necessarily that people hold the belief that the rate of inflation in the future will be the same as today. Rather, it means that

the wage and price increases that are occurring are consistent with a constant real wage.

Short-run aggregate supply and inflation

Figure 13.2 is also helpful in explaining how the short-run aggregate supply curve on the right side of Figure 13.1B can be a generalization of the short-run aggregate supply curve presented on the left side. Associated with any real wage, say $\left(\dfrac{w}{p}\right)_1$, there is some level of employment (E_1, for example). But there are many combinations of wage and price level changes consistent with $\left(\dfrac{w}{p}\right)_1$. Thus, one can associate the level of employment E_1, and the corresponding less than potential level of output, with a given price level (assuming a wage level appropriate to yield $\left(\dfrac{w}{p}\right)_1$), or with a given rate of inflation, assuming a given appropriate rate of change of wages. All other points on the short-run aggregate supply curve are defined similarly. What the short-run aggregate supply curve means can best be seen by comparing it with the long-run aggregate supply curve.

Since the long-run aggregate supply curve is vertically positioned over the point representing our potential real GNP, Y_p, we know the answer to the question of how, in the long run, changes in the growth of nominal GNP will be divided between changes in real output growth and changes in inflation. Since real output is fixed in the long run—in equilibrium—all long-run changes in nominal GNP will take the form of changes in the level of prices. What about the short run? According to our representation of the short-run aggregate supply curve in Figures 13.1B, changes in nominal GNP will be divided between changes in real output and changes in prices, the division between the two being determined by the slope of the AS_{SR} curve. Before explaining this relationship, it needs to be understood that a small but influential group of economists do not agree that the short-run aggregate supply curve is upward sloping. Like the classical economists discussed in the previous chapter,

they argue that the short-run aggregate supply curve, like the long-run relationship, is vertical and positioned over the point representing our real potential GNP. These economists are known as the **rational expectationists.** Let us examine their thinking first.

The rational expectations hypothesis. The notion of *rational expectations* is perhaps best understood by comparing it with the theory of adaptive expectations, discussed earlier. According to the theory of adaptive expectations, people revise their inflationary expectations—that is, revise their wage and price decisions—only when the actual rate of inflation differs from previously held expectations regarding inflation. One of the problems with this theory is that it leads us to the prediction that people's inflationary expectations will almost always turn out to be wrong. The reason? The theory is based on the proposition that people adjust their inflationary expectations only on the experience of *past* inflation. Consider the following example. Suppose inflation is accelerating—rising from 6 percent to 7 percent to 8 percent over time. With each upward movement in inflation, people revise upward their inflationary expectations—that is, revise upward their wage and price demands. But as long as inflation continues to accelerate, people will, according to the theory, always be expecting a rate of inflation that is less than the actual rate because their inflationary expectations are determined by past (lower-than-current) inflation. Or suppose the rate of inflation fluctuates—rising at 6 percent one year, 4 percent the next, and 8 percent the year after that. Again, if people adjust their inflationary expectations solely on the basis of past inflation, they will consistently expect a rate of inflation different from the rate that actually occurs.

The only time people will be right in their expectations—the only time they will make the "right" wage and price decisions—according to this theory, is when prices advance at a steady rate and people are fully adjusted to it. Otherwise, they will be fooled. This idea—that people can be fooled almost all of the time—has been sharply criticized by many economists. According to these critics, it is wrongheaded thinking to presume that people—at least most people—can be *persistently* fooled. It is also unreasonable, so they argue, to presume that people form their inflationary expectations solely on the basis of the past history of price movements. Will people's inflationary expectations be unaffected by the outcomes of presidential and congressional elections? Will their expectations be unaffected by dramatic changes in the direction of monetary and fiscal policies, by sizable changes in OPEC's prices, or by the imposition of wage and price controls? Probably not.

This kind of criticism has led to the development of an alternative theory of inflationary expectations—the so-called **rational expectations hypothesis.** This theory presumes two things on the part of people: (1) they make good use of all relevant information at their disposal in forming their inflationary expectations, and (2) the information they use is complete in the sense that they have a complete understanding of the factors that determine inflation. If both of these criteria are met, then, on the average, people's expectations regarding inflation, and the wage and price decisions based on those expectations, will be correct.

The implications of the rational expectations hypothesis are profound. What this theory tells us is that those actions *that are correctly foreseen* that could otherwise cause the real wage to be different from overall labor market equilibrium ($\left(\frac{w}{p}\right)_0$ and E_0 in Figure 13.2) would bring about corrective wage and price adjustments to ensure that overall equilibrium would be maintained. There might be temporary departures from equilibrium, caused, for example, by unforeseen events. But *systematic* departures can, according to this theory, be ruled out. What this means, if true, is that the aggregate supply curve in the short run is vertical and positioned over Y_p. Since the real wage is constant at the equilibrium level of employment, we are assured of being at our potential almost all the time, except in instances of temporary, accidental departures. What is important, then, is that real output and employment cannot be altered, except perhaps temporarily,

and only because people are fooled by the government's monetary and fiscal policies. Changes in aggregate demand do not systematically influence real output because people make the "correct" wage and price changes necessary to maintain the employment equilibrium; only prices can be systematically changed by aggregate demand policies. (The rational expectationists usually go one step further. Fiscal policy cannot change aggregate demand; it can only alter the *composition* of employment between the private and public sectors and the *composition* of our nation's output. Monetary policy, too, cannot affect the level of employment and output; it can affect inflation only.)

The conventional-view, short-run aggregate supply curve. Critics of the rational expectationists argue that it is difficult to accept all the requirements of the rational expectations hypothesis—particularly the argument that the information people use is *complete*. Not only does this requirement presume that people have sufficient information about the forces that affect inflation. It also presumes that people know *how* the inflation rate will be affected by these forces. In other words, *the rational expectations hypothesis assumes that people operate on the basis of the correct theory of the inflation process.* However, it is not at all clear what *the* correct theory is; indeed, what *the* correct theory is, is a matter of considerable dispute.

The point that needs emphasis is this. In the face of both confusion and conflict over the importance that should be attached to the many forces that determine inflation, it is hardly reasonable to expect that people's information will be complete enough to ensure that, on the average, their inflationary expectations will be correct nearly all the time. If they turn out to be correct, on the average, it will probably be accidental. Of course, there is no reason to think that people's inflationary expectations will be incorrect in precisely the way implied by the theory of adaptive expectations. This is because people's expectations are formed by more than just past price changes. However, in view of the widespread use of indexing in the form of cost-of-living adjustment (COLA) clauses in labor contracts and other explicit and implicit contracts that adjust for past inflation, people's expectations will, on average, be correct or rational in the *long run*. Ultimately, both workers and producers, on average, catch up to inflation by making wage and price changes today based on *past* inflation. But the adjustment process takes time. The possibility therefore arises that real wages can depart from their long-run equilibrium values and remain apart for quite some time.

To illustrate these ideas, consider Figure 13.3. Assume, to start with, that we are in long-run equilibrium at point A in Figure 13.3A. At that point, the economy is producing at its potential and the actual and expected rates of inflation are equal to one another. Both the actual and expected rates of inflation are equal to 4.0 percent at an annual rate at point A. The long-run equilibrium in Figure 13.3A corresponds to the long-run equilibrium portrayed in Figure 13.3B; Figure 13.3B is just a reproduction of Figure 13.2.

Now suppose that the monetary authorities pursue a contractionary monetary policy, slowing the growth of the money supply below its former rate. As we saw in Chapter 12, the reduc-

tion in aggregate demand occasioned by the "tighter" money policy will reduce the price level below what it would otherwise have been. The pace of inflation will slow to a rate below 4.0 percent. What will happen to wages? According to proponents of the rational expectations hypothesis, wages will adjust quickly, maintaining the real wage at $\left(\frac{w}{p}\right)_0$, and the economy will move from point A to, say, point B (a 3.0 percent rate of inflation) in Figure 13.3A—the long-run equilibrium.

However, according to the conventional view, because the *past* rate of inflation was running at 4.0 percent, workers will attempt to have 4.0 percent wage increases incorporated in their future paychecks. This poses a problem. On the one hand, given the new conditions of aggregate demand, the quantity Y_p can be sold only if prices rise by 3.0 percent; wages rising at more than 3.0 percent are inconsistent with the 3.0 percent increase in prices. The result? We are likely to see prices rising less rapidly than 4.0 percent (because of the reduction in aggregate demand) but more rapidly than 3.0 percent (because wages are rising more rapidly than prices due to cost-of-living adjustments). As a result, the real wage

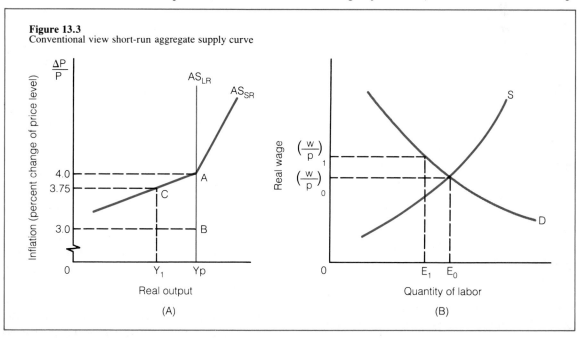

Figure 13.3
Conventional view short-run aggregate supply curve

(A) Real output

(B) Quantity of labor

will rise above $\left(\dfrac{w}{p}\right)_0$, to $\left(\dfrac{w}{p}\right)_1$. In view of the fact that employers will not hire more than the quantity represented by the demand curve for labor, employment will be cut back from E_0 to E_1 in Figure 13.3B. Correspondingly, total production will be cut from Y_p to Y_1. In this instance, we see that the reduction in the growth of nominal GNP from 4.0 percent to 3.0 percent was divided between inflation and real output in the short run as follows: Real output was reduced from Y_p to Y_1, and inflation was reduced from 4.0 to 3.75 percent.

These particular results are just hypothetical, of course. Different combinations of real output and inflation rate adjustments are possible. However, what is important to note is that the upward-sloping aggregate supply curve is the consequence of the sluggish adjustment of wages and prices to the changed economic conditions.

In time, wages and prices will adjust toward long-run equilibrium. The slower rate of advance of prices will cause reduced inflationary expectations and slower wage increases; the increase in unemployment above the natural rate will slow the pace of wage increases further still. Ultimately, wages will slow relative to prices, causing the real wage to return to its equilibrium value.

Increases in aggregate demand, brought about by, say, an expansionary monetary policy, would result in an increase in real output above Y_p and an increase in the inflation rate. In the short run, however, the magnitude of the increase in the inflation rate would be less than its ultimate increase. The sequence of possible events might be described as follows. Ultimately, the increase in inflation occasioned by "easier money" will be, say, 5.0 percent; and ultimately, wages will rise at 5.0 percent, the same as prices. But wages will rise at first by less than 5.0 percent (because past inflation was only 4.0 percent) and initially, prices will rise faster than wages (because aggregate demand is up). Real wages will *fall;* more workers will be hired[1]; employment will rise

above E_0; and real output will rise above Y_p. This is what accounts for the upward-sloping short-run aggregate supply curve beyond Y_p in Figure 13.3A.

Four important additional notes on aggregate supply

1. Aggregate supply ratcheting up. Consider Figure 13.4. Suppose the economy is initially at point G. In response to an increase in aggregate demand, both real output and inflation will rise, moving along the aggregate supply curve AS_{SR}^1 in the direction of the arrows. Potential GNP is reached at point H. Thereafter, we assume, all increases in nominal GNP take the form of higher rates of inflation.

Suppose inflation rises to the rate given by point J, at which point aggregate demand is reduced (the result, say, of a contractionary monetary policy designed to stem the rising inflation rate). Will the inflation rate and real output move down the "same" path they came up—that is, will inflation and output move back along AS_{SR}^1? In general, the answer is *no*. It is more likely that inflation and output would move along the path given by AS_{SR}^2. Thus the inflation rate associated with any given level of real output has ratcheted up.

Why did the short-run aggregate supply curve ratchet up? Basically, it did so because the increase in the rate of inflation from point G through point J increased people's inflationary expectations. For example, workers will attempt to incorporate into their paychecks the higher wages "justified" by the now higher rates of inflation.

To sum up, associated with the curve AS_{SR}^2 there is a higher level of inflationary expectations than is true of AS_{SR}^1. The movement from point G to point H produces a higher rate of inflation but, initially, no change in inflationary expectations. The shift up of the short-run aggregate supply curve reflects the new higher level of infla-

---

[1] How is it possible for more workers to be hired? Is that not inconsistent with the supply curve in Figure 13.3B? Not necessarily. If workers adhere to the belief that prices will rise by only 4.0 percent and interpret increases in their

wages above 4.0 percent (because the increase in aggregate demand increased the overall demand for labor) as an increase in their real wage, the quantity of labor supplied will increase.

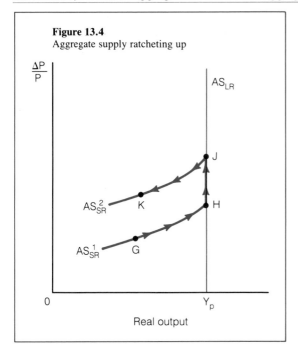

Figure 13.4
Aggregate supply ratcheting up

tionary expectations. Thus, the movement along any given short-run aggregate supply curve captures the real output and actual inflation changes in the face of unchanged inflationary expectations. The shift of the short-run aggregate supply curve is caused by changes in inflationary expectations.

This discussion can be generalized. As we emphasized earlier, in long-run equilibrium, the actual and expected rates of inflation equal one another. Moreover, any point on the long-run aggregate supply curve is a possible long-run equilibrium position; and along the long-run aggregate supply curve, each point represents a different expected inflation rate. Each short-run aggregate supply curve has associated with it a different expected rate of inflation. It is that expected rate given at the point of intersection of the short-run aggregate supply curve (AS_{SR}) with the long-run aggregate supply curve (AS_{LR}). This is shown in Figure 13.5.

Suppose we are initially at point K; the actual and expected rates of inflation equal 3 percent. Suppose aggregate demand increases or decreases; in either case the expected rate of infla-

tion will remain at 3 percent for a while since the actual pace of inflation in the past has been running at 3 percent. Indeed, it is because inflationary expectations do not adjust quickly to the new realities that real output departs from Y_p. However, because changes in aggregate demand do change the rate of inflation, inflationary expectations will eventually change. Those changed inflationary expectations will cause the short-run aggregate supply curve to shift (up in the case of increased inflationary expectations and down in the case of reduced inflationary expectations). Moreover, because movements away from long-run equilibrium imply departures from the natural rate of unemployment, there will be further wage and price adjustments, which will affect inflationary expectations and cause additional shifts of the short-run aggregate supply curve.

In Figure 13.5, we see that the expected rate of inflation associated with AS_{SR}^0 is 3 percent; the expected rate of inflation associated with AS_{SR}^1 is 7 percent.

2. Short-run versus long-run adjustment.
In Chapter 12, the reason given for the absence of quick adjustment of real output to potential

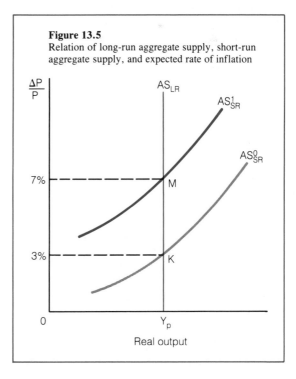

Figure 13.5
Relation of long-run aggregate supply, short-run aggregate supply, and expected rate of inflation

real output in the face of changes in aggregate demand was the stickiness of wages and prices, particularly on the downside. The absence of quick adjustment in the analysis here is the stickiness of inflationary expectations. Time is required for wage inflation and price inflation to be adjusted downward in response to declines in aggregate demand. The rates of increase in many wages and salaries are frequently determined by negotiated agreements, even in nonunion sectors. In response to a decline in economic activity, firms will at first lay off some workers, making no immediate adjustment in the wages and salaries of those who remain. Those who are laid off are frequently let go with the understanding that they will be recalled; they are often eligible for unemployment compensation; and even if they search for new jobs, they will be reluctant at first to accept jobs offering less than their co-workers who are still on the job.

Eventually, however, resistance to more moderate wage and salary increases will wither. In part, this will result from the presence of overall excess supplies in labor markets (which will eventually cause the real wage to fall) and from reduced inflationary expectations (the result of less rapid price increases).

The implications of these considerations are clear: As we move from the short run to the long run, the short-run aggregate supply curve will gradually shift down over time in the face of a maintained lower level of aggregate demand (the down shifts of the short-run aggregate supply curves being the result of reduced inflationary expectations). Moreover, the reduction in the real wage over time will induce higher levels of employment and cause real output to rise toward its potential.

One possible path of adjustment is given by the direction of the arrows in Figure 13.6. Initially, we are in long-run equilibrium at point R. Aggregate demand is reduced; real output is reduced below Y_p; inflation slows somewhat, to S in the short run. In time, the reduced pace of inflation will lower people's inflationary expectations causing the short-run aggregate supply curve to shift down. Eventually, in the face of reduced inflationary expectations and excess sup-

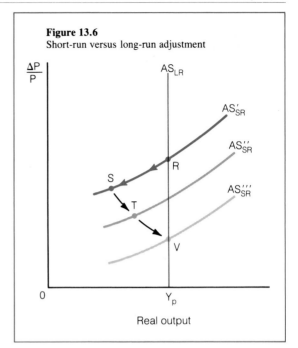

Figure 13.6
Short-run versus long-run adjustment

ply pressures in labor markets, the economy will move toward T and, ultimately, toward point V. (The precise path can only be determined by the interaction of aggregate demand and aggregate supply, as will become clear later.) The achievement of the new long-run equilibrium may take a very long time—a matter of years—but will occur eventually, as long as the economy is not bumped off its path of adjustment by external forces or by policy actions on the part of the government.

3. Asymmetrical inflation responses. It is often argued that the upward movement in inflation in response to an increase in aggregate demand is more marked than the downward movement caused by a decline in the pace of economic activity. This may in part reflect the popular notion that people will fight as strongly to get increases in their nominal incomes when excess demands are present as they will resist reductions in their nominal incomes in the face of excess supplies. This asymmetrical short-run response is illustrated in Figure 13.7, where the curve labeled AS_{SR} is steeper for increases in aggregate demand from point A than for decreases.

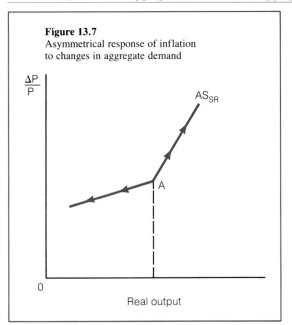

Figure 13.7
Asymmetrical response of inflation
to changes in aggregate demand

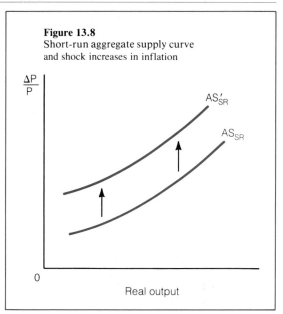

Figure 13.8
Short-run aggregate supply curve
and shock increases in inflation

4. The short-run aggregate supply and the price-shock rate of inflation. Up to this point we have focused most of our attention on the real wage—the relationship of labor costs to output prices. The question might therefore be asked: Does this focus imply that *nonlabor costs* and *profit markups over costs* are unimportant to determining inflation? The answer is no. First, it is true that wage and salary income make up about 75 percent of national income, meaning that labor costs are by far the most important determinant of business costs. Second, because the *share* of national income that accrues to labor and the other factors of production tends to remain relatively constant over time, growth of labor costs for each unit of output will be approximately the same as the growth of nonlabor costs per unit of output and profits per unit of output. If that were not true, the shares of national income accruing to the various factors would change over time. Therefore, growth of labor costs per unit of output can serve as a proxy for *total* costs and profits per unit of output.

There are times, however, when this relationship will not hold. For example, in the face of OPEC price actions, the rate of inflation may be shocked up above the rate implied by the growth of unit labor costs. Increases in inflation rates caused by such actions will also have the effect of raising people's inflationary expectations; these will cause the short-run aggregate supply curve to shift up, as Figure 13.8 illustrates. More will be said on this later.

Aggregate demand and inflation

In Chapter 12 we explained the inverse relationship between aggregate demand and the *price level* as follows:

1. An increase in the U.S. price level relative to foreign prices would reduce net exports and, therewith, aggregate demand.
2. Because of the equivalence of GNP and GNI, an increase in the price level for any given level of production would increase people's nominal incomes. Since the tax rate structure is progressive, people's real tax burdens would increase, lowering real disposable income and, therewith, aggregate consumer spending and aggregate demand.
3. For a given quantity of money in circulation, an increase in the price level, by raising total spending in nominal terms, would increase interest rates and thereby reduce interest-

sensitive spending for investment and consumer durables, and reduce aggregate demand.

For our purposes here we want to focus attention on the latter relationship. Toward that end, we will assume that U.S. and foreign inflation rates are the same. This means that there will be no *relative* price changes to cause net exports to be different from what they would otherwise have been. We leave a more detailed analysis of this issue until Chapter 15.

With respect to the increase in real tax burdens that occurs in an inflationary environment as a consequence of progressive tax rates, we will assume that whatever reduction in aggregate demand is caused by this phenomenon is offset by increases in government spending, reductions in taxes, or both. The rationale for this assumption can be put as follows. Had there been no inflation, any increase in real tax burdens (at some given level of real GNP) would have been the result of a change in government policy to raise people's taxes. An unchanged real tax burden is taken as evidence, in this instance, of an unchanged tax policy. In order for there to be an unchanged fiscal policy in an inflationary environment, there needs to be an offset (through spending changes, tax changes, or both) to the increases in real tax burdens that occur automatically as a result of inflation. In other words, failure to offset the automatic increases in real tax burdens is taken here as evidence of a policy change in the direction of reducing aggregate demand. More will be said on this later.

Having put aside the first two factors for the time being, we will now concentrate on the third—namely, the links among aggregate demand, inflation, and the growth of money. Before examining this triangular relationship, it is critical that we understand the relationship between money and the rate of inflation.

Money and the rate of inflation. Consider the familiar equation of exchange: $MV = PY$. Assume, to begin with, that the economy is in long-run equilibrium with real GNP, Y, fixed at its potential level, and with inflation advancing at some constant rate to which everyone is fully

adjusted. In addition, assume for simplicity that the velocity of circulation, V, is fixed in long-run equilibrium. Under the circumstances, it is clear the rate of increase of prices *must* equal the growth rate of the money supply:

Growth rate of **M** = Rate of increase in **P**.

It is important that we be clear on the meaning of this important relationship. Because the equation of exchange is a definitional relationship, it does not tell us anything about the direction of causality. There are different hypotheses concerning the causes, of course. To the monetarists, the direction of causation is clear and simple: Inflation is caused by money growth in excess of real output growth. Nonmonetarists, on the other hand, agree that money growth in excess of real output growth will cause inflation, but they also argue that price-shock forces, for example—such as sharply increased prices for energy brought about by OPEC—may also cause inflation. However, what the above relationship tells us is that forces such as energy-induced increases in inflation cannot be sustained in the long run unless the higher inflation rate is ratified (i.e., financed) by more rapid money growth; in the absence of more rapid money growth, inflation will ultimately return to its former rate—the rate equal to the rate of growth of the money supply.

What this means from the point of view of policy is that slower money growth is, in the long run, essential to slowing inflation. In addition, this relationship provides the basis for the view that inflation is a monetary phenomenon. This does not necessarily mean that excessive money growth is the only cause of inflation. But it does mean that, whatever the cause of inflation, it cannot be sustained without money expansion.

In thinking about this relationship, it is important to remind ourselves of the conditions that have been set forth that make the rate of growth of money equal to the rate of inflation—a fixed V and a fixed rate of output. Changes in fiscal policy may change the velocity of circulation, although, as we saw in Chapter 11, whether the effect is temporary or permanent is a matter of considerable dispute. Also, the velocity of circulation may change for yet other reasons. For example, changing financial regulations, discussed in Chapter 9, may induce people to economize on their holdings of money which could raise V. Moreover, over time, the level of real output tends to move upward. These matters will be dealt with in greater depth in Chapter 14. What is important to note is that changes in V and Q make the relationship between the growth of money and inflation less exact than otherwise. This is confirmed in Figure 13.9, which shows the relationship between the growth of M1 and the rate of change of the GNP deflator for the years 1963 through 1980. In order to "smooth" the data series to focus on the long term, the rates shown for each year are average rates over the previous four years; technically, this procedure is called a four-year moving average. The rate of growth of M1 shown for 1965 is an average of the years 1962, 1963, 1964, and 1965; the rate of growth of M1 for 1966 is an average

of the years 1963, 1964, 1965, and 1966; and so on. The same four-year moving average procedure was applied to the series on the GNP deflator.

Why a four-year moving average? Implicitly, this procedure assumes that the adjustment of people's behavior to a change in money growth, as reflected in the inflation rate, should be reasonably complete within four years.

In any event, as Figure 13.9 makes clear, the rate of inflation and the rate of money expansion move fairly closely together over long periods. However, the relationship is far from exact, a fact that we will explore at greater length in Chapter 14.

The inverse relationship between inflation and aggregate demand. Let us hold fixed, for the moment, both the growth of the money supply and fiscal policy. Now suppose that the rate of inflation is increased. What will happen to aggregate demand—the quantity of aggregate real out-

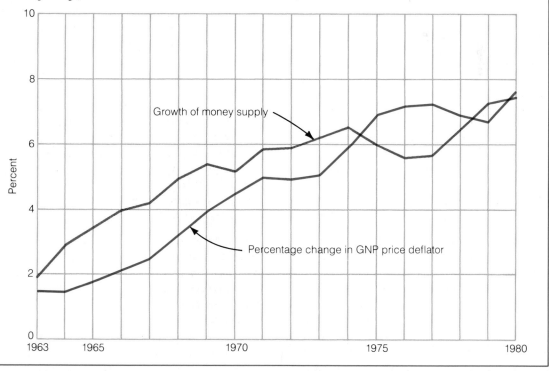

Figure 13.9
Money growth and inflation 1963-1980
(4-year moving average)

put demanded? It will decline. The reason? For any given level of real output purchased, the higher rate of inflation will increase the value of spending in nominal terms, which, in the face of an unchanged rate of growth of money, raises interest rates. The increase in interest rates reduces interest-sensitive spending for investment and some consumer expenditures. Aggregate demand and the rate of inflation are inversely related, as we hypothesized in Figure 13.1.

Real interest rates, nominal interest rates, and inflation. At this juncture it is important to note that what matters to consumers and investors is the *real* rate of interest, not the *nominal* rate. The relationship between real and nominal interest rates is as follows:

$$\text{Nominal interest rate} = \text{Real interest rate} + \text{Expected rate of inflation.}$$

The nominal interest rate is the one observed in the marketplace. It is the rate of interest at

which funds are loaned. How the nominal rate is split between the real rate and the expected rate of inflation is generally unknown since the expected rate of inflation is not known with precision.

What is the rationale for this relationship between the nominal and real rates of interest? Consider first a situation in which inflation is expected to be zero. And suppose the interest rate happens to be 4 percent per year. Under the circumstances, a lender granting, say, a one-year loan, could reason that, when the loan is paid back, the proceeds will permit him or her to purchase *in quantity terms* 4 percent more than now. In other words, the real rate of interest is 4 percent.

Now imagine that the lender expects the rate of inflation to be 10 percent at an annual rate. In order for the lender to receive the *same* real return, the interest rate must be high enough to offset the expected 10 percent inflation rate

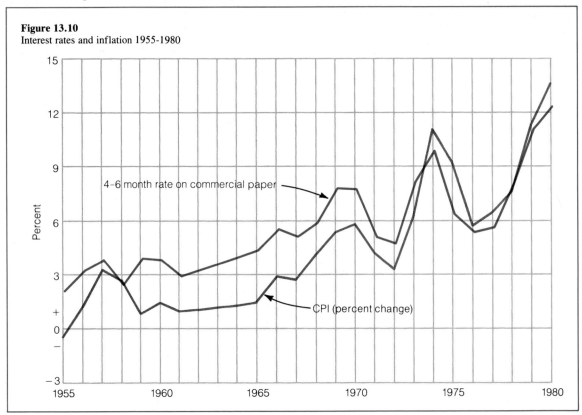

Figure 13.10
Interest rates and inflation 1955-1980

plus 4 percent. In other words, if the interest rate happens to be 14 percent, 10 percentage points of that 14 percent rate will just offset the inflation that is expected between now and one year from now; the 4 percentage points over and above the **inflation premium** represents the *real* return. To receive the same real return, lenders must receive a *nominal* rate that exceeds the real rate by the amount of inflation that is expected. And will borrowers who were willing to pay 4 percent when inflation was zero now be willing to pay 14 percent? Consider producers who are borrowing to finance new equipment purchases. If the prices they expect to receive for their products are 10 percent higher than otherwise, presumably they will be willing to pay the nominal 14 percent rate; a nominal 14 percent rate in the face of an expected rate of inflation of 10 percent implies a real interest cost of only 4 percent. Or consider those who are borrowing to purchase, say, a new car. If the alternative to borrowing is waiting a year and paying 10 percent more for the car, a 14 percent nominal rate is essentially the same as a 4 percent rate when inflation was zero.

Because the expected rate of inflation tends to converge toward the actual rate of inflation, there should be a fairly close relationship between the inflation rate and interest rates. Figure 13.10 confirms this observation. We show there the movement of the nominal interest rate—in this instance, the four-to-six-month interest rate on commercial paper being taken as representative of short-term rates—along with the inflation rate between 1960 and 1980. Again, the relationship is not exact, but it is close enough to be suggestive. In general, the rising trend of the nominal interest rate is widely acknowledged to be the result of rising inflationary expectations.

Aggregate demand, inflation, and inflationary expectations. It is now time to bring together the various elements discussed to this point in order to fashion the aggregate demand curve as a useful tool of analysis.

1. In long-run equilibrium, with fixed output and a given velocity of circulation, the inflation rate will be identical to the growth of money.
2. In long-run equilibrium, the actual and expected rates of inflation will equal one another.
3. In long-run equilibrium, the real rate of interest will be the difference between the nominal rate of interest and the expected rate of inflation.

Let us begin in long-run equilibrium in Figure 13.11 at point B. The money supply is growing at an annual rate of 4.0 percent and the actual and expected rates of inflation are equal to 4.0 percent. Now disturb the equilibrium by increasing the rate of money growth from an annual rate of 4.0 percent to 5.3 percent. In the long run, a *permanent* increase in the growth of money by this amount would cause the equilibrium to change from B to C. In addition, the nominal rate of interest will be 1.3 percentage points higher at point C than at point B.

What about the short run? According to the conventional view, the increase in the growth of the money supply *given the rate of inflation* will lower the nominal rate of interest. Since inflationary expectations are unchanged for the moment, the reduction in the nominal rate of interest will bring about a corresponding reduction in the *real* interest rate. Interest-sensitive expenditures that depend on the real rate of interest will therefore increase, in turn raising real aggregate demand. In time, the excess real aggregate demand will raise the inflation rate above the former 4.0 percent level. The higher rate of inflation in combination with the new steady rate of money growth will tend to raise nominal interest rates from their former lows (because the nominal value of expenditures will be increasing and because inflationary expectations will be rising). This increase in nominal interest rates pulls up the real interest rate, the magnitude of the increase in the real rate being modified by the extent of the increase in inflation expectations. In the new long-run equilibrium, the nominal rate will have increased from the old long-run equilibrium by the magnitude of the increase in

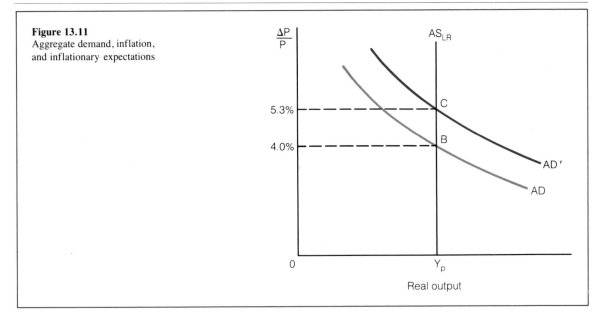

Figure 13.11
Aggregate demand, inflation, and inflationary expectations

inflation (1.3 percentage points), which also happens to be the amount by which inflationary expectations have increased. The real rate of interest will therefore equal its former value. Those interest-sensitive expenditures that depend on the real interest rate will also be at their former levels. Real aggregate demand will be where it was originally.

The rational expectationists, while not disagreeing with the change in long-run equilibrium that will take place as a consequence of more rapid money growth, disagree with the conventional view concerning the path followed in getting from B to C in Figure 13.11. According to the rational expectationists, the increase in the growth rate of the money supply will cause people to quickly revise upward their inflationary expectations by the "correct" amount. This, in turn, will quickly raise the actual rate of inflation and the nominal interest rate by the correct amounts. Accordingly, the real rate of interest will not change, except perhaps very temporarily, which means that the real quantity demanded will not change, except perhaps very temporarily. The movement from B to C is accomplished very quickly.

AGGREGATE DEMAND, AGGREGATE SUPPLY, INFLATION, AND INFLATIONARY EXPECTATIONS: PUTTING THE PIECES TOGETHER

It is time to bring all the pieces together to present a coherent theory of the inflation process. We start out by assuming that the economy is in long-run equilibrium in Figure 13.12; this occurs at the point of intersection—point E_1—of AS_{SR}, AS_{LR}, and AD. The characteristics of long-run equilibrium are easily summarized.

1. The actual and expected rates of inflation are equal to $\left(\frac{\Delta P}{P}\right)_1$. This rate of inflation we will call the "core" rate.

2. The real wage is constant, which means that the nominal wage rate is increasing at the rate $\left(\frac{\Delta P}{P}\right)_1$.

3. The rate of growth of the money supply is equal to the rate of inflation, $\left(\frac{\Delta P}{P}\right)_1$.

4. The real rate of interest is constant and equal to the difference between the nominal interest rate and $\left(\frac{\Delta P}{P}\right)_1$.

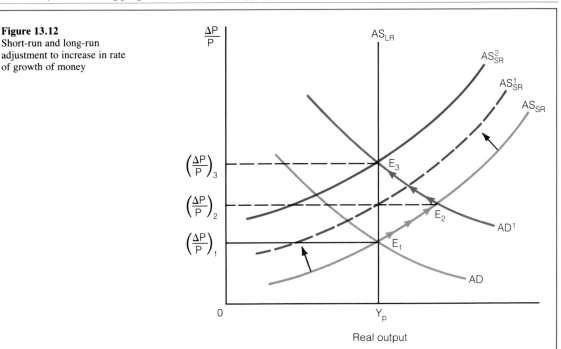

Figure 13.12
Short-run and long-run adjustment to increase in rate of growth of money

We now wish to examine the economic consequences of departures from long-run equilibrium. We will illustrate the effects of four kinds of disturbances: *(a)* a permanent increase in the rate of growth of money; *(b)* a permanent decrease in the rate of growth of money; *(c)* a change in fiscal policy; and *(d)* a price-shock change in the price level.

A permanent increase in the rate of money growth

Figure 13.12 can be used to illustrate the effects of a permanent increase in the growth of the money supply. The increase in the rate of growth of money will cause the aggregate demand curve to shift up from AD to AD^1. Ultimately, the long-run equilibrium will change from E_1 to E_3. Real output will not be changed in the long run, but the rate of inflation will be increased by the magnitude of the increase in the growth of money. In the short run, the economy might follow a path like the one outlined by the arrows. In the short run, both inflation

and real output will increase; the increase in real output will eventually *reverse* itself; and despite subsequent reductions in real output toward Y_p, inflation will continue to rise.

The movement of the economy, first from E_1 to E_2, then ultimately from E_2 to E_3, can be explained by the pattern of change of people's inflationary expectations. The assumption that inflationary expectations are sticky and adjust largely in response to changes in the actual rate of inflation, brings about the following two economic adjustments.

First, the increase in the money supply at first lowers both the nominal and real rates of interest. The reduction in the real rate of interest raises the level of spending in real terms. This is what drives the rate of inflation up.

Second, real output increases because the level of employment increases. At first, this employment increase comes about because both the demand for and supply of labor increases. Consider the demand for labor. The increase in aggregate demand raises prices, which makes it profitable for producers to go out and hire more workers.

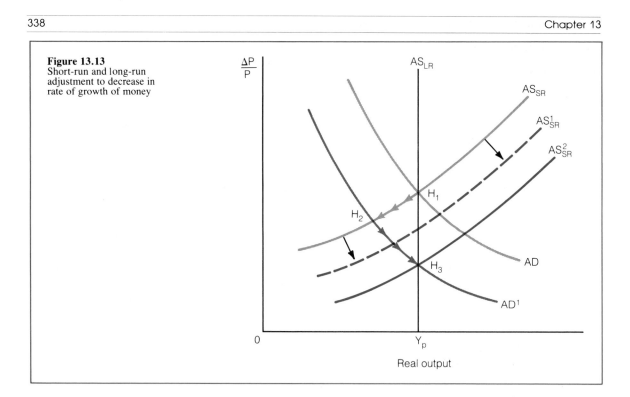

Figure 13.13
Short-run and long-run
adjustment to decrease in
rate of growth of money

Higher nominal wages will probably have to be paid to attract more workers. Now consider the supply of labor. Because inflationary expectations are at first unchanged, the higher nominal wages are viewed by workers as higher real wages, which coaxes out additional labor hours.

These two considerations explain the movement of the economy from E_1 to E_2—a pattern of change that involves both increasing inflation and higher real output. What about the movement from E_2 to E_3? This can be explained by the following two factors.

First, as inflationary expectations adapt to the increased rate of inflation, real interest rates will move closer to their former levels. Real aggregate spending will, at some point, begin to decline.

Second, the reduction in real aggregate spending will cause the demand for labor to decline, which will tend to slow the rate of wage increases. Moreover, the quantity of labor supplied will also decline as workers adjust their inflationary expectations to higher, more realistic rates—that is, the expected real wage begins to fall. Accordingly, the short-run aggregate supply curve will

tend to shift up and to the left. (Gradually, the short-run aggregate supply curve will shift from AS_{SR} to AS_{SR}^1, and finally to AS_{SR}^2.) Despite the reduction in employment, inflation continues to increase because the upward adjustment of wages to catch up with past increases in inflation more than offsets the reduced aggregate demand pressures that are operating to slow the rate of inflation. Ultimately, the rate of inflation will stabilize at E_3.

A word of caution The way the arrows are drawn in Figure 13.12, it appears as though real output and inflation move up along AS_{SR} to E_2, and thereafter along AD^1 to E_3. Actually, it is unlikely that the path would be exactly the same as the arrows suggest. The economy is much too complicated to be described in such simple terms. At a minimum, as inflation changes, inflationary expectations will be changing continously which causes shifts in both aggregate demand and short-run aggregate supply. However, despite these complexities, real output and inflation are likely to generally follow the following path. At first inflation and real output will increase; after a time, real output will tend toward Y_P while inflation will tend toward $\left(\dfrac{\Delta P}{P}\right)_3$. The movement toward equilibrium need not be steady.

A number of conclusions follow from this analysis of a permanent increase in the rate of growth of the money supply. First, as the adjustment from E_1 to E_2 and from E_2 to E_3 indicate, there is no necessary relationship between the *change* in real output and the *change* in the rate of inflation. Inflation rises continuously, but real output rises over one time period and falls over another. Second, the fact that real output rises above Y_p is the consequence of inflationary expectations lagging behind the actual rate of inflation. The pattern of real output and inflation adjustments, as well as the speed with which the economy moves from one long-run equilibrium to the other, depend on how *rapidly* inflationary expectations adjust. According to the rational expectationists, the speed of adjustment is very rapid. The result? The economy moves quickly from E_1 to E_3, with perhaps only very temporary real output adjustments.

Finally, in line with our discussion at the beginning of this chapter, this illustration is an example of a demand-pull force raising the inflation rate.

A permanent reduction in the rate of money growth

A permanent reduction in the rate of money growth will set in motion patterns of real output and inflation rate changes that are the opposite of those described above. This case is illustrated in Figure 13.13. Because the pattern of adjustment can be explained in terms opposite to those discussed in first case, we can be brief.

A permanent reduction in the growth of the money supply will, in the long run, cause the equilibrium to change from H_1 to H_3. Real output will not be changed in the long run, but the rate of inflation will be decreased by the magnitude of the reduction in the growth of money. In the short run, however, the economy might follow

a path like the one from H_1 to H_2 to H_3. Thus, in the short run, both inflation and output decrease. Eventually the reduction in real output will reverse itself and begin to rise toward Y_p, the inflation rate all the while declining. Again, the cautionary note given above is relevant here. The general pattern of change of real output and inflation is likely to correspond to the path described by the arrows, though it is unlikely to follow exactly that path.

The short-run pattern of real output and inflation rate changes can be explained by the pattern of change of people's inflationary expectations. In the face of sticky inflationary expectations, the decline in the growth of money will at first raise both nominal and real interest rates, which reduces real aggregate spending and in turn slows inflation. Employment will fall as the real wage rises; the real wage rises because, although inflation is slowing, inflationary expectations keep wages rising more rapidly than prices. These factors account for the movement of the economy from H_1 to H_2 in Figure 13.13.

Eventually, inflationary expectations begin to adjust to the slower pace of inflation and the economy begins its trek from H_2 to H_3. The real interest rate and the real wage tend to move back toward their former levels.

Given the short-run pattern of adjustment depicted in Figure 13.13, it is clear that there is no necessary single relationship between the *change* in real output and the change in the rate of inflation. Moreover, had inflationary expectations adjusted immediately in the face of the changed growth of money, as the rational expectationists tell us will happen, the economy will quickly move from H_1 to H_3. Finally, this illustration is an example of how a reduction in demand-pull forces can lower the inflation rate.

Summing up the first two cases. What is important to note about each of the cases discussed above is that departures from our real output potential are temporary phenomena only. The reason real output ever departs from its potential level is because inflationary expectations do not adjust immediately to forces that are causing the actual rate of inflation to change. The importance of inflationary expectations, therefore, is critical.

Having said that departures of real output from potential output are only temporary, we need to add that "temporary" may be a long time indeed; some have suggested several years. For example, some economists have suggested that reliance on monetary policy to slow inflation from the near 10 percent rate prevalent in 1980 to 5 percent would require severely depressed levels of real output characterized by an overall unemployment rate of 9 percent or more maintained for a period of five to six years. If these economists are correct, slowing inflation could prove to be a very painful process indeed.

Of course, one needs to recognize that the upward adjustment of the inflation rate in the face of more rapid money growth may occur much more rapidly than the reduction of inflation as a consequence of slower money growth. As noted before, the adjustment process may be asymmetrical. Indeed, some have suggested that for a period as long as 12 or 18 months there may be an almost extreme Keynesian response to a reduced rate of money growth—that is, an aggregate supply curve that is nearly horizontal for this period. If the process of achieving a lower inflation rate is so difficult, lengthy, and painful, it is easy to understand why our political leaders find it so difficult to pursue anti-inflation policies with vigor, determination, and perseverence.

A change in fiscal policy

In Chapter 12 we argued that an expansionary fiscal policy would have the effect of raising permanently the price level. Given an initial long-run equilibrium position, an increase in aggregate demand via an increase in government spending and/or a reduction in taxes would shift the aggregate demand curve up; the increase in the price level, by raising spending in nominal terms, would raise the rate of interest (assuming no increase in the money supply), "crowding out" private spending. The new long-run equilibrium would involve the *same* real output as originally; the price level would be higher; total nominal

spending would therefore be higher (since real output is the same and the price level is higher); and, with a given money supply, interest rates would be higher. In the new long-run equilibrium, the higher price level, and therefore the higher interest rate, is the mechanism that permits the fiscal policy authorities to alter the mix of output.

In terms of the equation of exchange, $MV = PY$, the expansionary fiscal policy raises the velocity of circulation, V, permanently. This accounts for the new higher price level in the long run. (Of course, as we saw in Chapter 11, monetarists would not agree that V was increased permanently. However, for the moment, we will accept the view that V has increased.)

The issue of fiscal policy and its effect on *inflation* is more complicated. We suggested earlier that the inflation rate would be identical to the rate of money growth. This relationship will hold true as long as the velocity of circulation and real output both remain fixed. Let us continue to assume for now that real output remains fixed, but now permit V to vary. Then, definitionally, the rate of inflation will be identical to the *sum* of the rates of growth of M and V:

$$\text{Growth rate of } \mathbf{M} + \text{Growth rate of } \mathbf{V} = \text{Growth rate of } \mathbf{P}.$$

The issue before us is this: *Will a change in fiscal policy cause a permanent change in the growth rate of V?* That is, even if we accept that V will increase in the face of an expansionary fiscal policy, is there any reason to think that the *growth rate* of V will increase? If the answer is yes, then fiscal policy, like monetary policy, could influence the long-run rate of inflation. If the answer is no, then we must reject the notion that fiscal policy can influence the inflation rate in the long run.

There is almost no disagreement among economists on this issue. Fiscal policy may be able to change the level of velocity, but it is *not* able to affect its long-run rate of growth. As a consequence, the inflation rate in the long run is independent of fiscal policy. This notion can best be understood intuitively. Potential output is fixed;

an increase in government spending in real terms, for example, must in the long run come at the expense of other kinds of real spending; the increase in V is the mechanism whereby the government share of total output is increased. However, there is a limit to the increase in government's share of total output. Once government's share stabilizes, there will be no further increase in velocity.

We need to be cautious here. Changes in fiscal policy cannot affect the rate of inflation in the long run, but its short-run impact can be sizable. And, as has been emphasized repeatedly, the short run can persist for a very long time. An expansionary fiscal policy will raise aggregate demand and increase the rate of inflation in the short run; the higher rate of inflation tends to increase inflationary expectations, which further adds to inflation. True, in the absence of an increase in the growth rate of money, the higher inflation rate cannot persist forever. But it could persist for several years.

This brings us to a second consideration. What will the response of the monetary authorities be to an expansionary fiscal policy? Will the Federal

Reserve step up the rate of money expansion to permit government to realize its objectives? In other words, will Federal Reserve policy be accommodative of an expansionary fiscal policy? If Fed policy is accommodative, then fiscal policy can affect the inflation rate in the long run. (Many would object to this statement, emphasizing that the higher inflation rate was caused by an expansionary monetary policy, *not* an expansionary fiscal policy. This is certainly true. However, the question that nonmonetarists ask is this: Would the Fed have undertaken an expansionary monetary policy had it not been for the change in fiscal policy?) More will be said on these issues in Chapter 14.

Price-shock changes in the price level

What will be the economic effect of, for example, sharp price level increases caused by inordinately large oil price hikes (such as those oil price increases engineered by OPEC in 1974 and again in 1979) or by inordinately large food price increases (such as occurred in 1973–74)? Figure 13.14 illustrates the consequences.

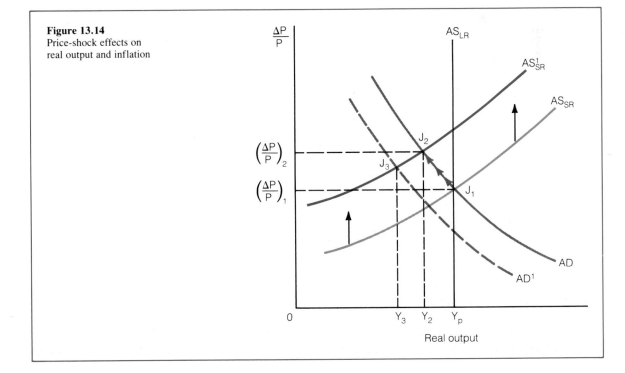

Figure 13.14
Price-shock effects on
real output and inflation

We begin by assuming that we are in long-run equilibrium at J_1. Now assume a shock increase in the price level occurs, the result of sharp food price increases caused by adverse weather conditions. Initially, this will cause the short-run aggregate supply curve to shift up and to the left, causing a higher rate of inflation and a reduced level of real output and employment—that is, **stagflation.** If nothing else happens—in particular, if money supply growth is maintained at its former rate—the economy will ultimately gravitate back toward J_1. However, given the sluggishness of inflationary expectations and the fact that those expectations were aggravated by the price shock itself (which would cause the short-run aggregate supply curve to shift further up and to the left beyond AS_{SR}^1), the adjustment to the former rate of inflation and to Y_p could be a long time in coming.

Several comments are in order regarding the price-shock increase in the price level. First, price shocks like the one illustrated in Figure 13.14 are the classic source of stagflation—a higher rate inflation combined with increasing unemployment. Second, by themselves, price-shock increases can have only a temporary effect on the rate of inflation; that "temporary" effect, however, may persist for years as the price-shock increases in inflation become imbedded in wage and price decisions as a consequence of the increase in inflationary expectations. The only way the price-shock increase in inflation can persist is through an accommodative increase in the growth of money. Third, attempts to offset the higher inflation rate caused by price-shock phenomena will cause, in the short run, further departures of real output from potential. Thus we see in Figure 13.14 that a contractionary monetary policy, say, will cause the aggregate demand curve to shift to the left, reducing real production to Y_3; depending on the changes in people's inflationary expectations, the reduction in inflation in the short run could be negligible. This kind of contractionary monetary policy was pursued in the wake of the sharply increased rate of inflation resulting from OPEC price actions in 1974.

Following the 1979 OPEC price hikes, a similar tight money policy was put into place.

A SUMMARY NOTE ON THE INFLATION PROCESS

The model of the inflation process described in this chapter is reasonably complete. It is important, therefore, that we take stock of what we have accomplished and the problem areas that remain.

Insofar as inflationary expectations are determined by *past* rates of inflation, they can hardly be said to be the *cause* of inflation. The causes can be found in the demand-pull and price-shock forces. However, there is no reason to think that inflationary expectations are determined exclusively by past inflation rates. They therefore could be a cause of inflation. Also, the effects of an increase in inflationary expectations could be examined in exactly the same way as price-shock forces. Increased inflationary expectations would cause the short-run aggregate supply curve to shift up and to the left.

What makes the analysis of the inflationary process so complicated is that we have only a very imperfect understanding of inflationary expectations. In each of the diagrams we shifted the aggregate demand and short-run aggregate supply curves in ways that implied we could track real output and inflation rather closely. Actually, we are able to track real output and inflation changes only *roughly* in the face of demand-pull, price-shock, and inflationary expectations changes.

In each of the diagrams used to study the inflation process, we began from a position of long-run equilibrium. This made the analysis of any disturbance fairly easy. However, in the real world, we observe continuous demand-pull and price-shock disturbances that interfere with forces that are operating to push us toward long-run equilibrium. New disturbances, when added to old ones, complicate considerably the study of the inflation process. In addition, the fact that the economy is subject to frequent demand-pull and price-shock forces means that we may never arrive at our long-run equilibrium "resting place."

One very important conclusion derived from our study to this point is the notion that inflation is a monetary phenomenon. Ultimately, the rate of inflation will be determined by the rate of growth of the money supply. What this means is that slowing inflation will require slowing the growth of money. Having acknowledged the relationship between money growth and inflation, one should not draw the conclusion that inflation is caused by rapid money growth only. Rapid money growth is but one of the many causes of inflation. However, as the above relationship implies, inflation caused by forces other than rapid money growth *cannot* be sustained without an accommodative change in the rate of money expansion. That being the case, it is fair to ask, Why don't the monetary authorities merely keep money growth fixed at its noninflationary growth rate? The answer, which will be explored in greater depth in the next chapter, is that the adjustment of real output to a disturbance is very slow. Thus the *costs* of an unchanged monetary policy (in terms of lost output and unemployment) could be viewed as larger (in both economic and political terms) than the costs of added inflation.

Up to this point we have assumed that the velocity of circulation, V, was fixed in the long run. In fact, it is not fixed, but grows over time largely as a consequence of improved efficiencies in the payments system. What does the fact of an ever-growing V do to our earlier conclusions? Very little. First, if V grows over time at 3 percent per year, this has the *same* effect on the inflation rate as a 3 percent higher rate of money growth. With V growing, there is no longer a one-to-one correspondence between money growth and inflation. The rate of change of the price level will equal the sum of velocity growth and money growth, given a fixed level of output. For a zero rate of inflation in the long run, the monetary authorities would have to set money growth at

a rate that offset the growth rate of V. Second, although V is growing, there is no evidence to suggest that fiscal policy can change the *rate of growth* of V in the long run. Fiscal policy, therefore, cannot affect the long-run inflation rate.

Throughout we have assumed real output was fixed. This was a convenient assumption, but an unrealistic one that we will rectify in the next chapter. What is important to note here is that with real output growing overtime, the relationship between money growth and inflation is less precise than has been implied to now. As we will see, increases in the growth of our real productive potential may serve to slow the inflation rate over the long haul. As will also become clear, fiscal policy can be used to alter the mix of our nation's output in ways to change our real growth potential. Accordingly, fiscal policy may have important effects on inflation.

SUMMARY

1. We mean by inflation the *sustained* upward movement in the general level of prices over time.

2. The actual rate of inflation during any given period can be viewed as consisting of the sum of three separate forces: the *demand-pull rate of inflation,* the *price-shock rate of inflation,* and the *core rate of inflation.*

3. Long-run aggregate supply is independent of inflation. The reason? The level of employment is independent of the rate of inflation. What is important as far as employment is concerned is the *real wage.* As long as the rate of change of money wages equals the rate of change of the price level—whatever that rate happens to be—the amount of labor resources employed will remain fixed. The level of production corresponding to this fixed amount of labor input will remain fixed as well.

4. The mechanism that insures that real wages will adjust appropriately to yield the long-run equilibrium level of employment is *inflationary expectations.*

5. According to proponents of the *rational*

expectations hypothesis, the short-run aggregate supply curve is indistinguishable from the long-run aggregate supply curve. The conventional view of the short-run aggregate supply curve, however, is very different: The short-run aggregate supply curve is upward sloping, reflecting the apparent fact that expectations of inflation adjust sluggishly.

6.   Each short-run aggregate supply curve has associated with it a different expected rate of inflation. The expected rate is given at the point of intersection of the short-run and long-run aggregate supply curves. As inflationary expectations increase, the aggregate supply curve will ratchet up. The upward movement of inflation in a response to an increase in aggregate demand is generally more marked than the downward movement of inflation caused by a decline in the level of economic activity.

7.   Assuming that both the velocity of circulation and the level of real output are fixed in the long run, the growth rate of prices must equal the growth of the money supply. From the point of view of policy, slower money growth is essential for slowing inflation in the long run. This relationship between money growth and the rate of inflation provides the basis for the view that inflation is a monetary phenomenon. This does not necessarily mean that excessive money growth is the only cause of inflation. But it does mean that whatever the cause of inflation, it cannot be sustained without money expansion.

8.   There is an inverse relationship between inflation and the quantity of aggregate real output demanded. For any given level of real output purchased, the higher rate of inflation will increase the value of spending in nominal terms, which, in the face of an unchanged rate of money growth, raises interest rates.

9.   In an inflationary environment it is important to distinguish between the *nominal interest rate* and the *real interest rate.* They are related as follows: The nominal interest rate is equal to the real interest rate plus the expected rate of inflation.

10.   In response to a permanent increase in the rate of money growth, the following long-run and short-run adjustments can be expected.

In the long run, real output will be unaffected, but the rate of inflation will be increased by the magnitude of the increase in the growth of money. In the short run, both inflation and real output will increase, the increase in real output eventually reversing itself and, in the long run, returning to its former level. Sticky inflationary expectations account for the differences in the short-run and long-run adjustments. A permanent reduction in the rate of money growth will set in motion patterns of real output and inflation rate changes that are the opposite of those associated with a permanent increase in the rate of money growth.

11.   Fiscal policy may be able to change the level of velocity, but it cannot affect its long-run rate of growth. As a consequence, the inflation rate in the long run is independent of fiscal policy. However, changes in fiscal policy may exert a sizable impact on inflation in the short run.

12.   Price level increases caused by inordinately large increases in the prices of "important" products will cause a higher rate of inflation in the short run and a condition known as *stagflation.* However, the effect on the inflation rate is only temporary.

CONCEPTS FOR REVIEW

Demand-pull rate of inflation

Price-shock rate of inflation

Core rate of inflation

Adaptive inflationary expectations

Rational expectations hypothesis

Aggregate supply ratcheting up

Asymmetrical aggregate supply responses to inflation

Relationship of aggregate demand and inflation

Real versus nominal interest rates

Stagflation

QUESTIONS FOR DISCUSSION

(Those marked with an asterisk (*) are more difficult.)

1.   Carefully evaluate: "Since in long-run equilibrium the rate of inflation equals the rate of money

expansion, the only cause of inflation worth considering is excessive money creation; and the only way to slow inflation is to slow money growth."

2. Explain the economic implications of the differences between the rational expectations hypothesis and the theory of adaptive expectations.

3. *a.* Explain the difference between the real and nominal interest rate.

b. In the face of sticky inflationary expectations, an expansionary monetary policy will at first cause a reduction in the nominal interest rate, but ultimately a higher nominal interest rate than before. Explain.

*c. If the rational expectations hypothesis holds, then an increase in the money supply will cause only an increase in nominal, not real, interest rates. Explain.

4. "It is not possible to have rising unemployment and rising inflation simultaneously." Demonstrate that this statement may be wrong as a result of price-shock effects. Next, demonstrate that rising inflation may accompany rising unemployment in the latter stages of the adjustment of the economy to, say, a more rapid increase in the rate of money growth.

5. Suppose that national policymakers strive to maintain a rate of growth of real output higher than our productive potential. If they are successful, is it possible for inflation to advance at a steady pace, or will inflation be ever accelerating? Explain.

*6. Suppose the monetary and fiscal authorities pursue what might be called "stop-go" policies—expanding aggregate demand when unemployment rises too much, slamming on the policy brakes when inflation accelerates too rapidly, and then expanding aggregate demand again because the "stop" policy pushed the unemployment too high. If you were to plot the inflation rate on the vertical axis and the unemployment rate on the horizontal axis, what would the pattern of movement of unemployment and inflation be? That is, would the unemployment-inflation points move in a clockwise or counterclockwise direction over time?

7. Explain carefully the distinctions among the demand-pull rate of inflation, the price-shock rate of inflation, and the core rate of inflation.

Chapter 14

Unemployment, inflation, and growth: Demand management and supply-side policy issues

During the Kennedy and Johnson Administrations in the early and mid-1960s, it was widely believed that we had the ability to fine tune the economy. We could rely on monetary and fiscal policies to keep the economy close to our productive potential at all times. We could be assured of steady advances in our productive potential over time and steady improvements in average living standards as well. We could achieve a permanent reduction in the unemployment rate to 4 percent or less. And we could contain inflation.

The performance of the economy during the 1970s and the early 1980s has shattered those earlier beliefs. In 1974 and 1975 we witnessed the worst recession in our post-World War II history. We were forced to suffer through yet another recession in 1980. Double-digit rates of inflation have been commonplace. The growth of our productive potential has slowed sharply, relative to historical performance, as have improvements in average living standards. And we find ourselves reluctantly taking comfort if we succeed in holding the unemployment rate below 6.5 percent.

The employment, inflation, and growth problems plaguing the U.S. economy today are so severe that many people have almost given up hope that we will ever be able to achieve the goals of the Humphrey-Hawkins Full Employment and Balanced Growth Act of 1978, which called for a permanent reduction in the unemployment rate to 4 percent or less and an overall inflation rate of 3 percent. These goals were originally to have been achieved by 1983. However, early in 1981 the timetable for their realization was set back to 1985. The fact that we are still far removed from attaining those goals has caused many to doubt that they will ever be achieved.

It is the purpose of this chapter to clarify the major macroeconomic policy issues facing the United States in the 1980s. Toward this end, we will adopt the aggregate demand–aggregate supply model of the inflation process developed in the previous chapter to focus attention directly on the critical areas of policy concern—unemployment, inflation, and growth. We will proceed in steps. First, we will examine the macrodynamics of unemployment and inflation on the assumption that our potential output remains fixed. With this model we will explore the potential of **demand management policies** to "solve" our unemployment and inflation problems. We mean by *demand management policies* those monetary and fiscal policy initiatives aimed at effecting changes in the overall level of aggregate demand.

Next we will turn our attention to the **supply side**—to the forces that determine the growth of our nation's productive potential. We will explore there the potential of **supply-side economic policies** to help "solve" our unemployment and inflation problems. We mean by *supply-side economic policies* primarily those fiscal policy initiatives aimed at improving people's incentives to save, to invest, and to work, behavioral changes that will serve to enhance the growth of our real potential GNP over time.

UNEMPLOYMENT AND INFLATION DYNAMICS

The achievement of full employment and price stability have long been the stated objectives of policymakers. However, it is clear from the record that we have been notoriously unsuccessful in our efforts to realize these twin objectives. This raises two related questions: Are full employment and price stability compatible goals? If they are compatible, what accounts for our poor track record?

Among economists and policymakers the belief is widespread that these goals are compatible; that is, we should be able to design policies that will enable us to achieve and sustain the full employment of our nation's resources, maintaining all the while a stable level of prices. It is one of the objectives of this chapter to show the circumstances under which these two goals are compatible.

This leads us to the second question: What accounts for our poor track record? Actually, the answer to this question follows from the answer to the first. If it is possible to show the circumstances under which full employment and price stability are compatible, then we should be able to show the circumstances under which they are incompatible using that information to interpret the historical record. The ultimate empirical test will be the extent to which the interpretation of the historical record derived from the "model" accords with events as they occurred in the past.

The relationship between unemployment and inflation: The facts

For decades economists have sought to discover whether some simple and predictable relationship between unemployment and inflation existed. If such a relationship could be found, then it might be possible to offer rather definitive answers to the questions posed above. When we appeal to the facts, however, it is apparent that, if such a relationship exists, it is far from simple and predictable. It is not all obvious that unemployment and inflation are even related!

Consider the data displayed in Figure 14.1. On the vertical axis is measured the annual rate of inflation; we select as our inflation measure the percentage increase in the consumer price index (CPI) from the month of December of one year to the month of December of the next. On the horizontal axis we measure the average unemployment rate for each calendar year. Each point in the figure represents the particular inflation rate–unemployment rate combination that actually occurred in each year since 1953.

A quick glance at Figure 14.1 reveals the obvious. Either there is no systematic relationship between unemployment and inflation, or, if such a relationship exists, it is a complicated one.

In an effort to identify a pattern, let us connect the points chronologically—in the sequence of their occurrence. This we do in Figure 14.2. Although the connecting lines appear at first to form no discernible pattern, a careful examination of Figure 14.2 reveals a number of rough patterns.

1. The unemployment rate and the inflation rate appear to have moved in "swirls." The direction of movement of the swirls is *clockwise;* the

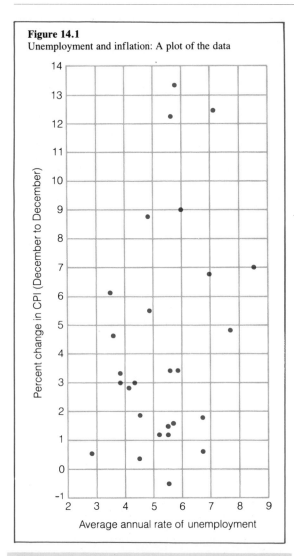

Figure 14.1
Unemployment and inflation: A plot of the data

formed by connecting the points chronologically become steeper and steeper— that is, each little reduction in the unemployment rate is accompanied by increasingly higher rates of inflation. Finally, the curve traced out in the subperiod 1976–1979 is much steeper than the curve traced out in the sub period 1961–1969; and the curve formed in the subperiod 1976–1979 is above and to the right of the earlier curve.

Smooth curves of the sort just identified—showing an inverse relationship between inflation and unemployment—are often referred to as

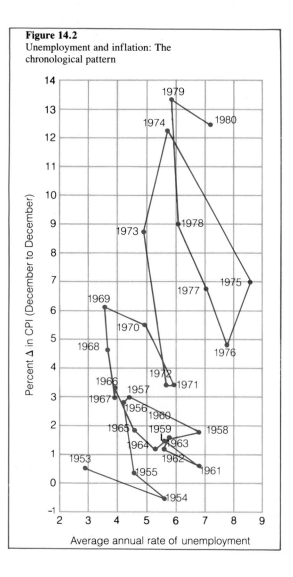

Figure 14.2
Unemployment and inflation: The chronological pattern

swirl movements have been in an upward direction; and there is a decided northeast tilt to the swirl movements. This northeast tilt tells us that, over time, with some acknowledged exceptions, both the *average* rate of inflation and the *average* rate of unemployment have increased. Some have referred to this tilt as evidence of **secular stagflation**—a long-run trend of increasing unemployment *and* inflation.

2. Note carefully the two subperiods 1961–1969 and 1976–1979. In each of those subperiods, declining rates of unemployment were accompanied by rising rates of inflation. Also, the curves

Phillips curves, so named because Australian economist A. W. Phillips discovered that a curve of this general shape fit the data for Britain for the period 1861–1957.

When examining these two sub periods—1961–1969 and 1976–1979—we will seek answers to two fundamental questions: What is the economic explanation for these Phillips curves? Why is the Phillips curve for 1976–1979 above and to the right of the Phillips curve for 1961–1969?

3. Let us look at some individual year-to-year movements. One pattern stands out clearly. When the unemployment rate increases from one year to the next the rate of inflation may fall (as it did from 1960 to 1961, from 1970 to 1971, and from 1974 to 1975); or it may rise (as it did from 1956 to 1957, from 1969 to 1970, and from 1973 to 1974); or it may remain virtually unchanged (as it did from 1953 to 1954 and from 1957 to 1958). However, by the end of *two* years, there is, in each instance, a decisive downward trend in inflation. In some instances inflation is higher than two years earlier, but it is nevertheless coursing downward.

Making sense of the unemployment-inflation facts

In this section we want to show how the aggregate demand-aggregate supply model developed in Chapter 13 can be used to explain the above-described movements of inflation and unemployment. Specifically, what we want to show is how the **demand-pull rate, price-shock rate,** and **core rate** forces can interact to produce almost any conceivable directional movement of unemployment and inflation. We start first with a discussion of the Phillips curve and show how it can be derived from the aggregate supply curve. We then examine a number of demand management policy issues.

The Phillips curve. The Phillips curve defined earlier implies that an unemployment-inflation trade-off exists. In particular, it implies that reduced rates of inflation can be achieved by undertaking policies that result in higher rates of unemployment. Conversely, lower rates of unem-

ployment can be realized, but only at the cost of higher inflation.

A hypothetical Phillips curve is illustrated in Figure 14.3. On the vertical axis we measure inflation—the percentage change in the general level of prices from one time period to another; on the horizontal axis we measure the unemployment rate—the number of people unemployed as a percent of the labor force.

It was widely believed by economists in the 1960s that the Phillips curve constituted a realistic representation of the relationship between unemployment and inflation in the U.S. economy. Given the actual experience of unemployment and inflation during the 1960s (shown in Figure 14.2), it should be no surprise that these economists felt justified in thinking that it was possible to conduct policy in ways that would permit the realization of a wide variety of unemployment and inflation combinations. According to this view, the monetary and fiscal authorities could set policies to achieve a 5 percent rate of unemployment and a 2 percent rate of inflation—point A on the Phillips curve in Figure 14.3. By pursuing more expansionary policies, it would be possible to achieve a 4 percent unemployment rate, though the cost of doing so meant a 4 percent rate of inflation—point B in Figure 14.3. Complete price stability—point C—would be possible only by maintaining the unemployment rate at around 6 percent.

Although these numbers are hypothetical, they illustrate accurately enough the nature of the choices policymakers believed they could make. Specifically, policymakers were led to believe, on the basis of the Phillips curve, that, if they chose stable prices, they would have to reconcile themselves to a fairly high rate of unemployment. And conversely, they believed that, if they chose as their target a low rate of unemployment, they would have to reconcile themselves to a fairly high—but *stable*—rate of inflation.

The Phillips curve: A stable relationship? Many thought so in the 1960s. For years, policymakers and their economic advisers operated on the assumption that the relationship between unemployment and inflation portrayed by the

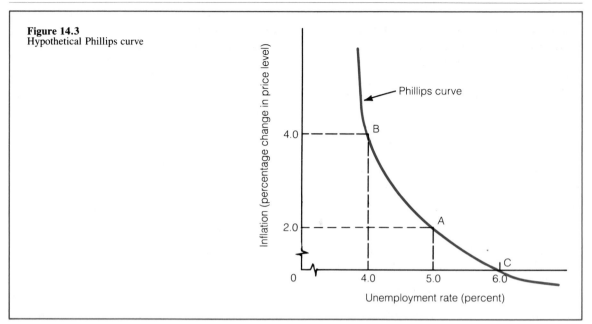

Figure 14.3
Hypothetical Phillips curve

Phillips curve was *stable*. That is, the Phillips curve appeared to offer policymakers a menu of particular unemployment-inflation choices that were presumed to be reasonably fixed. Expansionary monetary and fiscal policies could presumably be used to move the economy up the Phillips curve from choice A to choice B in Figure 14.3. If we persisted in maintaining the unemployment rate at 4 percent, we could reasonably (so it was believed) expect a rate of inflation in the neighborhood of 4 percent indefinitely. There was no presumption that maintenance of a 4 percent unemployment rate might result in an accelerating rate of inflation. Conversely, it was also assumed that it was possible to move back down the Phillips curve—back to choice A—through the use of restrictive monetary and fiscal policies. Restrict the growth of aggregate demand and you would end up with less inflation.

It was widely acknowledged that "price shocks" of one sort or another could jar the Phillips curve from its relatively fixed position. But if the price shock was a one-shot occurrence, the upward displacement of the Phillips curve could only be temporary. Why? Because a one-shot increase in the *price level* can have only a temporary effect on the rate of inflation. True,

dislodging the Phillips curve from its relatively fixed position could generate bizarre patterns of movements of unemployment and inflation for a while. But according to the vast majority of economists in the 1960s, bizarre patterns were the exception, not the rule; they were the result of particular temporary dislocations. In their estimation, the Phillips curve reflected *the* true and permanent relationship between unemployment and inflation.

A stable Phillips curve: A statistical relation in search of a theory. It must be emphasized that few economists, at least in the early 1960s, felt that it was necessary to set forth a theoretical justification for the Phillips curve trade-off between unemployment and inflation. It seemed reasonable to expect an unemployment and inflation trade-off. The "reasonable" argument usually went as follows. Although the unemployment rate is not a perfect measure of the pressure of demand in labor markets, it is a fair barometer of such pressures. Reductions in the unemployment rate, reflecting a shift in the direction toward excess demand for labor, should drive up wages and therewith prices. And conversely, when the unemployment rate is increased, wages should rise less rapidly, slowing inflation.

As we will make clear later, this kind of reasoning was sloppy and highly misleading. However, at the time, this was not well understood. In any event, the most important justification for the existence of a stable Phillips curve was believed to reside in the statistical evidence purporting to demonstrate the existence of a trade-off. The original 1958 essay by A. W. Phillips covering a period of almost 100 years—from 1861 to 1957—demonstrated rather conclusively that periods of low unemployment were characterized by much higher rates of inflation than were periods of high unemployment. Early investigations by American economists in the late 1950s showed a somewhat similar kind of relationship for the U.S. economy. The actual experience of the U.S. economy during the 1960s seemed to settle the issue.

The late 1960s: The trade-off worsens. The data, then, tended to confirm the existence of a Phillips curve for the U.S. economy. Almost immediately upon discovery of the relationship, economists applied their statistical tools in an effort to obtain more precise quantitative estimates on the nature of the trade-off—estimates of the rate of inflation that could reasonably be expected to be associated with each rate of unemployment.

Toward the end of the 1960s, economists began to discover a problem. They noticed that prices were rising at a faster rate for given unemployment rates than their earlier estimates of the Phillips curve would have predicted. Although earlier estimates using the Phillips curve relationship led economists to predict an inflation rate of 4 percent at an unemployment rate of 4 percent, for example, they discovered that, once we reached that 4 percent unemployment rate, inflation was actually much greater than 4 percent. The conclusion most economists reached was that the Phillips curve had shifted up; the trade-off between unemployment and inflation had worsened.

Is there a trade-off? The fact that inflation was actually worse than would have been predicted on the basis of the historical relationship between unemployment and inflation caused many economists in the late 1960s to question

the whole idea of a Phillips curve. Although *historical data* seemed to suggest the existence of a trade-off, many questioned whether such historical evidence could be used as a guide for predicting the future.

The first real challenge to the idea of a trade-off between unemployment and inflation was provided in a series of papers by Milton Friedman of the University of Chicago and Edmund S. Phelps of Columbia University. They argued that, from a theoretical point of view, there was no justification for the existence of a Phillips curve—at least in the long run. Two central propositions emerged from the Friedman-Phelps contributions:

1. In the short run it is possible to discover a Phillips curve type of relationship. In the long run, on the other hand, there is no trade-off. In the long run, the unemployment rate will settle down to its natural rate independent of the inflation rate.

2. A trade-off relationship will be revealed because the actual rate of inflation differs from the rate expected. When the actual and expected rates of inflation coincide, there will be no trade-off. The actual and expected rates of inflation may diverge in the short run; in the long run they will tend to equal one another.

Rationale for Friedman-Phelps arguments. Equipped with the model of the inflation process developed in Chapter 13, it is easy to see the validity of the Friedman-Phelps arguments. Specifically, we wish to show that:

1. A Phillips curve relationship, exhibiting a trade-off between unemployment and inflation, is a short-run relationship only (recognizing, of course, that the short run may be a lengthy period).

2. Corresponding to the vertical long-run aggregate supply curve there is a "vertical" Phillips curve—a curve that tells us that unemployment is independent of inflation in the long run.

3. Just as changes in inflationary expectations cause the short-run aggregate supply curve to shift, such inflationary expectations

changes also cause the trade-off relationship—the short-run Phillips curve—to shift.

Consider Figure 14.4. Figure 14.4A reproduces the short-run aggregate supply curve developed in Chapter 13. Figure 14.4B illustrates the same idea, the difference being that whereas in Figure 14.4A real output is measured along the horizontal axis, in Figure 14.4B the unemployment rate is measured along the horizontal axis.

The correspondence between Figures 14.4A and 14.4B is straightforward. Associated with the level of real output Y_0 is an unemployment rate U_0. Increasing real output to Y_1 lowers the unemployment rate to U_1. Moreover, the increase in the rate of inflation from $(\Delta P/P)_0$ to $(\Delta P/P)_1$ as real output rises to Y_1 corresponds to the *same* increase in the inflation rate as the unemployment rate falls to U_1. To emphasize the close correspondence between the short-run aggregate supply curve and the curve in Figure 14.4B, it would perhaps be most accurate to call the latter curve *the short-run unemployment-inflation aggregate supply curve*. However, it is more consistent with its usage by economists to refer to the curve in Figure 14.4B as the **short-run Phillips curve** (PC_{SR}).

It should also be clear that, just as the long-run aggregate supply curve is positioned vertically over the output level corresponding to our productive potential, the **long-run Phillips curve** will be vertically positioned over the unemployment rate corresponding to the natural rate of unemployment. This result is shown in Figure 14.5.

In a crude sense, the natural rate of unemployment represents the "equilibrium" unemployment rate. In equilibrium the real wage (adjusted for productivity advance) will remain constant. But as long as wages (adjusted for productivity change) and prices both change at the *same* rate, the (adjusted) real wage will remain constant, as will the equilibrium level of unemployment. In other words, the rate of unemployment will not change, whatever the rate of inflation or deflation, as long as (adjusted) wages change at the same rate as the price level; *there is no trade-off between unemployment and inflation in the long run.*

In Figure 14.5B, point U_N represents the natural rate of unemployment. The vertical line constructed above U_N, the long-run Phillips curve (PC_{LR}), implies that there is no trade-off between unemployment and inflation. Unemployment

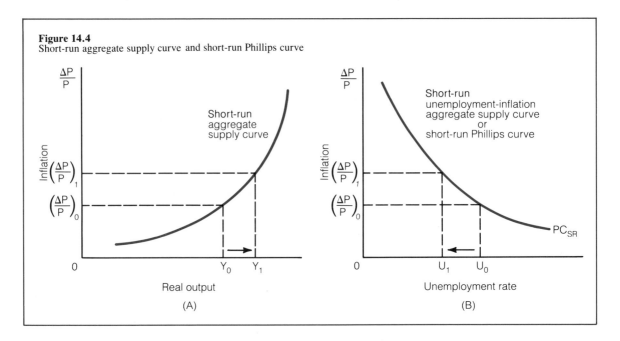

Figure 14.4
Short-run aggregate supply curve and short-run Phillips curve

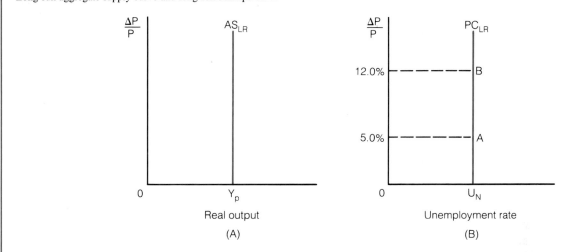

Figure 14.5
Long-run aggregate supply curve and long-run Phillips curve

does not depend on the rate of inflation. Whether inflation advances at a 5 percent rate (point **A**) or a 12 percent rate (point **B**), the rate of unemployment in the long run will stay at U_N. This outcome is not surprising in view of the independence of Y_P and the inflation rate illustrated in Figure 14.5A.

Finally, in Figure 14.6 we show how inflationary expectations affect the vertical positioning of the short-run Phillips curve. Recall from

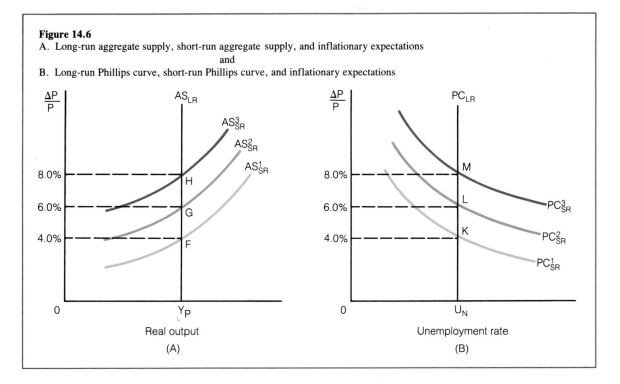

Figure 14.6
A. Long-run aggregate supply, short-run aggregate supply, and inflationary expectations
and
B. Long-run Phillips curve, short-run Phillips curve, and inflationary expectations

Chapter 13 that any point along the long-run aggregate supply curve is a potential candidate for equilibrium; in equilibrium, the actual and expected rates of inflation are equal. Recall as well that associated with each short-run aggregate supply curve is a particular expected rate of inflation, that rate being given by the point of intersection of the short-run and long-run aggregate supply curves. In Figure 14.6A, associated with the short-run aggregate supply curve AS^1_{SR} is a 4.0 percent expected rate of inflation; at a 6.0 percent expected rate of inflation the relevant short-run aggregate supply curve is AS^2_{SR}; and so forth.

Since there is a one-to-one relationship between each short-run aggregate supply curve and each short-run Phillips curve, it follows that *(a)* any point along the long-run Phillips curve is a potential candidate for equilibrium, each point on PC_{LR} representing the required equality of actual and expected rates of inflation, and *(b)* associated with each short-run Phillips curve is a particular expected rate of inflation, that rate being given by the point of intersection of the short-run and long-run Phillips curves. For example, just as AS^1_{SR} has associated with it a 4.0 percent expected rate of inflation, the *same* expected rate of inflation is associated with PC^1_{SR},

since PC^1_{SR} is derived from AS^1_{SR}; the other short-run Phillips curves are similarly interpreted.

The short-run Phillips curve: An unstable relationship. One very profound conclusion emerges from this discussion: *If the aggregate demand–aggregate supply theory of the inflation process is correct, there is no permanent, stable trade-off relationship between unemployment and inflation of the sort that many economists in the 1960s believed existed.* We hinted earlier that most economists were misled by sloppy reasoning into believing that a trade-off relationship existed. And what was sloppy about their reasoning? They failed to take into proper account the role played by inflationary expectations. Specifically, they failed to recognize that what accounts for the trade-off relationship is the departure of the actual rate of inflation from the expected rate. Once people are fully adjusted to the actual rate of inflation—that is, once the actual and expected rates of inflation are brought into equality with one another—the trade-off pattern will cease to exist.

These important ideas are illustrated in Figure 14.7. To begin with, suppose the economy is in equilibrium at the natural rate of unemployment, U_N. Suppose further that the actual and expected

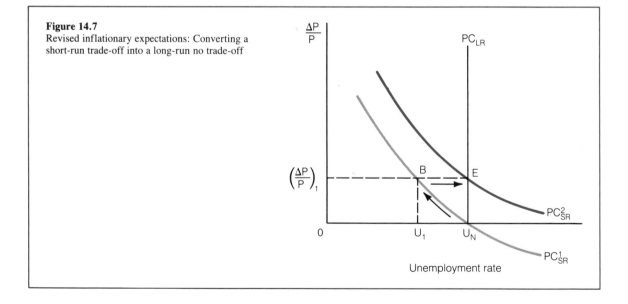

Figure 14.7
Revised inflationary expectations: Converting a short-run trade-off into a long-run no trade-off

rates of inflation are both zero—that is, the price level is stable and people expect it to remain so.

Consider now the effects of an expansionary monetary policy. Assuming that people continue to behave as if the price level will remain stable, the higher level of aggregate spending will both raise the price level and reduce the unemployment rate below the natural rate. In the short run, the economy might move to a position like point B, characterized by an unemployment rate of U_1 and a rate of inflation of $\left(\dfrac{\Delta P}{P}\right)_1$.

However, what is important to recognize is that point B is *not* a stable position. At point B the price level is increasing at a nonzero rate whereas the expected rate of inflation is zero. As workers adjust their money wages to reflect the increase in the inflation rate, the economy will move from B in the direction of E—that is, back toward the natural rate of unemployment. Thus, as people adjust upwards their inflationary expectations, the short-run Phillips curve will shift up from PC_{SR}^1 to, say, PC_{SR}^2. Put differently, point B is not a sustainable equilibrium position. *The only sustainable equilibrium is a point somewhere along the long-run Phillips curve, PC_{LR}.*

At this juncture we need to be very cautious. We know that in the face of an expansionary monetary policy and unchanged inflationary expectations, the economy will move up the short-run Phillips curve toward B. And we know that B is an unstable position in the sense that once people adjust their inflationary expectations to match the new realities, the economic system will tend to move back toward the natural rate of unemployment. However, there is no good reason to expect that the economy will necessarily move to point E; it might or might not, depending on what happens to monetary policy. Let us briefly consider three possible policy responses.

1. The monetary authorities increase permanently the rate of growth of the money supply from the rate consistent with a zero inflation rate to a rate consistent with $(\Delta P/P)_1$ in Figure 14.7.

We started out at a position where the unem-

ployment rate was equal to the natural rate. The increased rate of money expansion raises nominal GNP by raising both real output (reflected in a decline in the unemployment rate to U_1) and the general level of prices (reflected in a measured rate of inflation of $(\Delta P/P)_1$). Once inflationary expectations are revised upwards, wages and prices will probably rise at an even faster rate than $(\Delta P/P)_1$ *for a while*. If that happens, and if the rate of money expansion is unchanged, real output will fall, which means that the unemployment rate will tend to rise above U_1.

Once people become fully adjusted to the new economic realities, inflation will advance at the steady rate $(\Delta P/P)_1$ and the economy will settle down at point E. Point E is a stable equilibrium position. The unemployment rate is equal to the natural rate *and* the actual rate of inflation is equal to the rate people expect. With wages (adjusted for productivity growth) and prices both advancing at a rate equal to $(\Delta P/P)_1$, the (adjusted) real wage will remain constant; and a constant (adjusted) real wage at the natural rate of unemployment means that, on the average, labor markets are in equilibrium.

2. The monetary authorities reverse their previous policy of higher money growth and reestablish a rate of money growth consistent with a zero inflation rate.

According to our aggregate demand–aggregate supply model of the inflation process, a policy of reduced money expansion will set in motion forces opposite to those described earlier. This is shown in Figure 14.8; for completeness we have reproduced the adjustment of the economy from U_N and zero inflation to point B, and ultimately to point E, described in Figure 14.7.

Suppose the policy of slower money growth occurs after the economy has finally settled down to point E. At first, in the face of unchanged inflationary expectations, the economy will move from point E toward point F. The reduction in aggregate demand will slow the pace of inflation and raise the unemployment rate above the natural rate. Again, the rise in the unemployment rate is the consequence of the departure of the actual from the expected rate of inflation. Even-

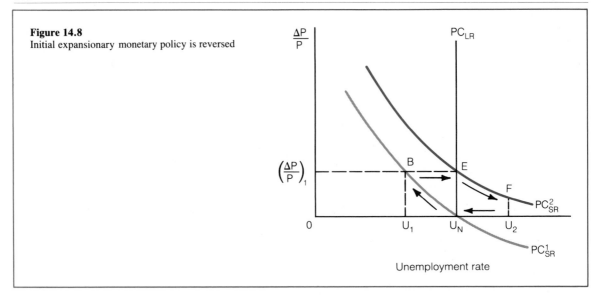

Figure 14.8
Initial expansionary monetary policy is reversed

tually, however, the economy will move from point F back toward the natural rate of unemployment and a stable rate of inflation. And what is the mechanism that brings about this new long-run result? It comes about because inflationary expectations adjust to the actual rate of inflation.

Two final comments are in order regarding this case. First, although the adjustment path of unemployment and inflation in response to a reduced rate of money growth is the opposite of the path that results from more rapid money growth, the downward stickiness of wages and prices and of inflationary expectations may make the ultimate adjustment from E to U_N very prolonged. Put differently, although the movement from U_N to E may be fairly quick, the movement back to U_N may take a very long time.

Second, note the clockwise "swirl" formed by the movement from point U_N to B to E to F and back to U_N. This pattern could arise, for example, by the following sequence of policy initiatives. The monetary authorities, starting at point U_N, pursue expansionary policies in an effort to lower the unemployment rate. In the wake of the increased rate of inflation, they at first slow up the rate of demand expansion, then put restrictive policy initiatives into place in an effort to bring inflation back down. Switching from a

policy of demand expansion to one of demand contraction generates a swirl-like clockwise movement of unemployment and inflation.

3. The monetary authorities seek to hold the unemployment rate below the natural rate of unemployment.

This policy objective will give rise to the so-called **accelerationist thesis.** That is, monetary policy actions aimed at maintaining the unemployment rate below the natural rate will result in an ever-accelerating rate of inflation. This possibility is illustrated in Figure 14.9.

Suppose, initially, that the economy is at point U_N where the actual and expected rates of inflation are both zero. Let the monetary authorities undertake a more rapid rate of money expansion aimed at lowering the unemployment rate to U_1. The unemployment rate will fall below U_N because the expected rate of inflation lags behind the actual inflation rate. As people revise upward their inflationary expectations, there is a tendency for the unemployment rate to move back toward the natural rate. To offset this tendency, the monetary authorities must undertake to expand aggregate demand even further. The increase in wages and prices resulting from the upward revisions of inflationary expectations, in combination with the further increase in aggre-

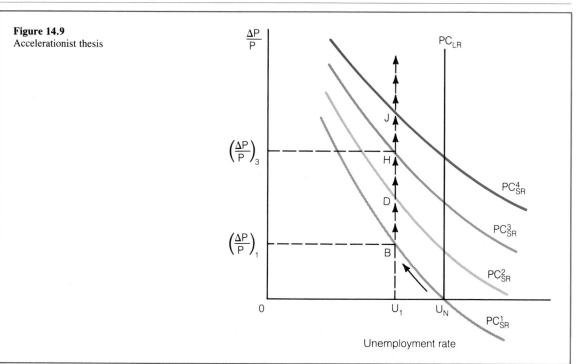

Figure 14.9
Accelerationist thesis

gate demand, will cause the inflation rate to accelerate from point B to D. Again, the economy will tend to move toward the natural rate unless offset by yet another increase in the rate of money growth which pushes the inflation rate higher to $\left(\dfrac{\Delta P}{P}\right)_3$ at point H; and on and on.

In this illustration, the tendency for the unemployment rate to move back toward the natural rate is offset by the increase in aggregate demand. The reason why the unemployment rate remains unchanged is because the monetary authorities keep the inflation rate running ahead of the rate people expect. Thus, because people revise upwards their inflationary expectations, the monetary authorities must continuously keep expanding aggregate demand, ever raising the rate of inflation to keep ahead of ever increasing inflationary expectations. In this way, efforts to keep the unemployment rate at U_1 will cause the inflation rate to continue to accelerate from point H to point J and beyond.

A final note on these three cases. All three cases were examined using a changed rate of

money growth as our policy tool. Why all the emphasis on monetary policy? Is fiscal policy unimportant? The reason for this policy emphasis was made clear in Chapter 13. In the *short run,* a change in fiscal policy will change aggregate demand and the rate of inflation just as a change in money growth will. However, because fiscal policy cannot change the rate of inflation permanently—it can change the velocity of circulation (V), but *not* the rate of growth of the velocity of circulation—fiscal policy changes are of less interest from a longer-run perspective.

The demand-pull, price-shock, and core rates of inflation

In Chapter 13 we distinguished the core rate of inflation from the demand-pull rate and the price-shock rate. The **core rate of inflation** measures those price level increases that occur because of increases in the trend of production costs, that cost trend being determined by past price increases. The trend in unit costs is basically a reflection of people's inflationary expectations.

It is because of their inflationary expectations that people seek—in both their explicit and implicit contracts—guarantees of increased compensation to make up for past price and cost increases and protection from future increases. The core rate is the rate of inflation that would occur over the long term, provided the economy was not subjected to price shocks and aggregate demand was neutral—neutral in the sense of neither contributing to nor subtracting from inflation.

The **demand-pull rate of inflation** is determined by the state of aggregate demand in relation to our productive potential. When aggregate demand exceeds our potential GNP—that is, when the actual rate of unemployment is pushed below the natural rate of unemployment—the price level will be pulled up. When aggregate demand falls below our potential GNP—that is, when the unemployment rate rises above the natural rate—the demand-pull pressure on prices will cease and, in time, inflation will be slowed.

The **price-shock rate of inflation** captures the effects of sudden increases in the prices of particular "important" goods and services on the overall rate of inflation.

The distinctions between these various "kinds" of inflation can be illustrated easily in terms of our unemployment and inflation dynamics. Consider first the relationship between the core and demand-pull rates of inflation.

The core and demand-pull rates of inflation. In Figure 14.10 examine points U_N, C, E, K, and L along the long-run Phillips curve PC_{LR}. What do each of these points have in common? They each represent possible long-run equilibrium inflation-unemployment positions. The (adjusted) real wage is constant at each point and the actual rate of inflation is equal to the rate people expect.

The existence of a short-run Phillips curve—a curve showing a trade-off between unemployment and inflation—arises because the inflation rate differs from the rate people expect. For each expected rate of inflation a different short-run Phillips curve exists.

Finally, given the growth rate of the velocity of circulation and assuming a fixed potential GNP, the long-run equilibrium rate of inflation can be determined once we know the rate of money expansion. If this calculation yields a long-run inflation rate of 4.0 percent, long-run equilibrium would occur at point E in Figure 14.10—the point of intersection of PC_{SR}^3 with

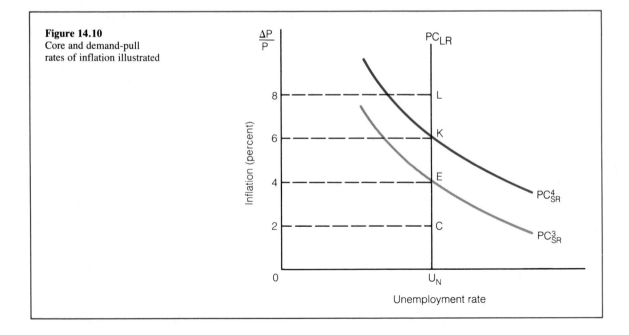

Figure 14.10
Core and demand-pull rates of inflation illustrated

PC_{LR}. (Corresponding to PC_{SR}^3 is an expected rate of inflation of 4.0 percent.) The core rate of inflation in this instance equals 4.0 percent.

Now let the rate of money growth increase. For a while, the actual rate of inflation will rise above the expected rate and unemployment will fall below the natural rate. This is represented by a movement along the Phillips curve labeled PC_{SR}^3. Inflationary expectations will be revised upwards, causing the short-run Phillips curve, PC_{SR}^3, to be displaced upwards. Suppose the economy ultimately settles down to point K. There, the actual and expected rates of inflation equal 6 percent. And through point K one can draw another Phillips curve, PC_{SR}^4, corresponding to the new higher core rate of inflation.

In this case it was the increase in aggregate demand brought about by the more rapid pace of money growth that caused the actual rate of inflation to rise above the core rate and therefore to raise the core rate itself. Conversely, decreases in aggregate demand that lower the actual rate below the core rate cause a lowering of the core rate.

This analysis is important because it indicates fairly clearly what kinds of demand management policies must be pursued to ultimately bring inflation under control. In order to get people to revise their inflationary expectations downward—in order, that is, to lower the core rate—it is necessary to slow the rate of money growth by enough to raise the unemployment rate above the natural rate so as to reduce the actual inflation rate below the rate expected. Of course, if people revise their inflationary expectations downward very slowly, the unemployment rate would hold above the natural rate for an extended period (measured in years, not months)—a policy option that many policymakers find difficult to accept politically, especially since the empirical evidence seems to indicate that the natural rate of unemployment may be as high as 6.5 percent, or even higher. Moreover, it is precisely because inflationary expectations adjust sluggishly that fiscal policy can also be used to drive the unemployment rate up above the natural rate. However, absent a slowing in the rate of money growth, fiscal policy

will not bring about a permanent slowing in inflation.

Adding the shock rate. We complete our analysis of unemployment-inflation dynamics by examining the implications of the third component of inflation—the price-shock rate. Consider Figure 14.11. To start out with, assume we are at point E with the actual and expected rates of inflation equal to 4 percent. Now let there be a sudden one-time "shock" increase in the price level caused by a sharp increase in oil prices. The immediate effect will be an increase in the short-run Phillips curve from PC_{SR}^1 to PC_{SR}^2. In the face of unchanged demand management policies, the oil price hike will push the inflation and unemployment rates in a northeast direction from E to, say, K; *both inflation and unemployment will increase.*

Since the price shock is a one-time affair—not repeated—the inflation rate should, in subsequent periods, come down from the high level recorded at K. With given demand management policies this decline in inflation should be accompanied by a lowering of the unemployment rate. However, it may take a very long time to get back to E. Since the increase in the actual inflation rate above the expected rate will induce people to revise their inflationary expectations upward, and since inflationary expectations tend to be relatively sticky on the down side, the unemployment rate could remain above U_N for years until people adjust their inflationary expectations back down to E.

It is quite possible that demand management policies will be used to offset the higher inflation rate caused by the oil price increase. To attain that objective would require restrictive demand management policies. The effect of these policies would be to increase further the unemployment rate with some modest relief on the inflation front; how much inflation relief will depend on the speed of wage and price adjustments and the speed of adjustment of inflationary expectations. In response to restrictive demand management policies, the economy might move to a point like L in Figure 14.11.

If instead the monetary and fiscal authorities

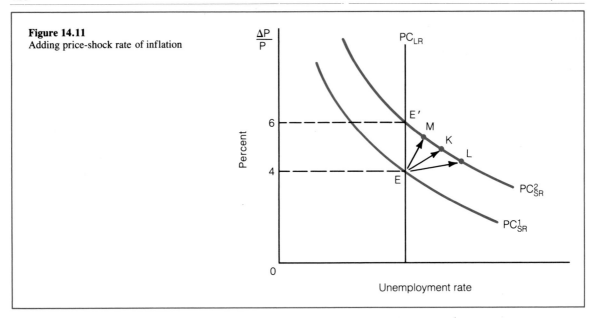

Figure 14.11
Adding price-shock rate of inflation

try to offset the negative employment effects of the oil price hike, they will pursue expansionary policies. The immediate effect of these policy actions will be to cause the inflation rate to rise and the unemployment rate to fall relative to point K in Figure 14.11; the combination of oil price hike and expansionary demand management policies could move the economy to point M. It is important to recognize the consequence of expansionary demand management policies aimed at negating the employment effects of price shocks. Although the price-shock increase in the rate of inflation may be only temporary, a policy of *accommodation* in the form of a higher rate of money expansion could well result in a *permanently* higher rate of inflation than at point E. That is, a permanent increase in the rate of money expansion could cause the long-run equilibrium position to shift from E to E'. This, in the minds of many economists, is the danger inherent in a policy of accommodating the price increases occasioned by price shocks. In an effort to negate the employment effects, such a policy results in a permanently higher inflation rate. To get the long-run inflation rate back down to 4 percent (point E in Figure 14.11) it might be necessary to suffer for a while with an unemployment rate above U_N. This might be necessary to negate the

rise in inflationary expectations occasioned by the shock increase in the price level.

Demand management versus an incomes policy to slow inflation

From a policy point of view, the foregoing discussion can be summarized fairly readily.

According to the conventional view of the inflation process, our inflation woes are the consequence of demand-pull and price-shock factors. Inflationary expectations, as reflected in the core rate of inflation, play the critical role of maintaining the inflation momentum. Put differently, inflationary expectations may not be the source of inflationary pressures, but they maintain the momentum of inflation once underway.

From a long-run perspective, no anti-inflation program can succeed unless slower money growth plays an integral part. This does not mean that excessive money growth is the only source of inflation. However, to repeat what we said before, other causes of inflation cannot be sustained in the long run without an accommodating change in the growth of money. (Changes in velocity growth and real output growth cause the relationship between money growth and inflation over the long haul to be less precise than one to one.)

Slowing the growth of money will, in the long run, slow inflation. However, in order to be successful according to the conventional view, the unemployment rate must be maintained above U_N while inflationary expectations adjust to lower rates. This may take a very long time to accomplish, which, if true, means the unemployment rate must be held above U_N for a long time. Some economists argue that it may take years of high unemployment—an unemployment rate 2 or 3 percentage points above the natural rate—to cut the inflation rate by a few percentage points.

To understand why inflationary expectations adjust so slowly, briefly recall our discussion of this issue in the previous chapter. Although the notion of inflationary expectations is forward-looking, it is often *past* price increases that determine the behavioral response. It is because of their inflationary expectations that people attempt to enter into new contracts—implicit or explicit—to "guarantee" that their real incomes will not be eroded by inflation. Generally, it is *past* wage and price increases that determine how much wages and prices will be marked up *currently.* Even if people believe that inflation in the future might be lower than at present, the fact that their current wages will be marked up by an amount determined by the high inflation rates of the recent past means that, at first, little inflation relief will come from this belief. According to this view, the only way to bring down inflation is to hold the unemployment rate sufficiently far above U_N so that excess supply pressures in labor markets will work to moderate the wage increases resulting from *past* price increases. If successful, the slower rate of wage increase will slow inflation. This, in subsequent time periods, will slow the cost-of-living markup of wages, and so on.

The conventional view is that using restrictive demand management policies to push the unemployment rate above U_N will work, *ultimately.* However, the excess supply conditions may not exert much downward pressure for quite a while.

Several reasons can be given for this state of affairs. First, many of those who are laid off are given to understand that they will be recalled. These workers have little incentive to search out and accept job offers that pay less than what they were receiving. Second, the vast majority of workers are eligible to receive unemployment compensation. It provides benefits, on the average, equal to about two thirds of their former take-home pay. The financial pressures to accept jobs at lower wages are thereby reduced. However, unemployment compensation does not last forever (26 to 39 weeks currently). After a lengthy bout of unemployment, most workers will doubt that they will be called back. Under these circumstances, when the choice is between a job that offers a lower (real) wage and no job or other sources of funds, the lower-wage job will win hands down. It has been estimated that 12 to 18 months is required before significant downward pressures are exerted on wage increases as a result of increased unemployment rates. This helps to explain the empirical observation made at the beginning of the chapter that approximately two years are required for reduced rates of unemployment to show up in the form of a reduced rate of inflation.

The apparent fact that high rates of unemployment must be suffered for long periods to slow inflation has caused many economists to examine alternatives to demand management policies. One alternative that some find appealing is an **incomes policy.** In general, an incomes policy refers to any of a number of actions government might undertake to intervene in the wage and price decisions of workers and producers. At one extreme, the incomes policy may consist of nothing more than a rather loose set of guidelines that may be enforced more or less vigorously; at the other extreme, the government might introduce explicit wage and price controls.

The most frequent argument in favor of an incomes policy is that it can aid in the effort to slow the wage and price momentum—that is, dampen inflationary expectations. To illustrate, consider a fairly extreme kind of incomes policy: The government orders that all wages and prices be frozen for a certain period; the government then orders that all contracts calling for cost-of-living wage increases be thrown out; and finally, the government insists that all future cost-of-living clauses be based on price level increases dating from the time of the freeze.

There is no question but that a wage and price freeze of this sort could slow the wage and price momentum—at least for a while. But many questions would be raised by the policy just described. Wouldn't a freeze of this sort be unfair? After all, some workers will have just received large wage increases while others will lose theirs simply because the effective date of the increase occurs *after* the date of the freeze. And some producers will have just increased their prices, whereas others who were planning to do so will lose out. Yes, a freeze of the kind described here would be unfair in the sense that some people would be forced to shoulder a disproportionate share of the burden. In response, government will have to decide whether it wants to permit some adjustments after the fact or to hold firm against any and all adjustments.

But there are other problems with this kind of incomes policy. A freeze on all wages and prices means a freeze on relative prices. This can distort the allocation of resources. Since changing relative prices are the means whereby resource shifts are signaled in a market economy, a wage and price freeze essentially does away with that important signaling mechanism.

The distortions caused by a wage and price freeze are probably relatively small in the very short run (six months or so). But in the long run, they could become sizable. Since resource shifts will generally take place only in response to relative price changes deemed to be permanent, and since time is often required for people to form some assured judgment on the matter, the cost of a wage-price freeze in the form of misallocated resources is unlikely to be large in the short run. In the long run, the distortions could be so extensive as to raise doubts about whether slowing inflation via this approach was worthwhile. Moreover, the greater the distortions, the greater the pressures are to trade goods and services outside the law—that is, to trade goods and services in **black markets.** For these

reasons, most proponents of wage-price controls emphasize the need for their removal after a short period.

It is also important to note that an incomes policy is *not* a substitute for sound monetary and fiscal policies. Just because a wage-price freeze is instituted does not mean that the monetary and fiscal authorities can forget about inflation. On the contrary, unless demand management policies are conducted in ways consistent with price level stability, pressures will mount during the freeze to cause very sharp price level increases after the freeze is removed.

An analogy at this point might be helpful. Inflation can be likened to the steam coming from the spout of a kettle. Apply greater heat (more rapid money growth) and more steam (more inflation) will result. Cut down the heat source, and the steam will diminish. But even if the stove element is turned off, steam will continue to be emitted for some time (that is, inflation will continue for some time after demand pressures are removed). Now suppose the kettle is emptied, refilled with cool water, and the spout plugged—that is, a wage-price freeze of the sort described above is instituted. If the kettle is put back on the stove with no temperature adjustment, or worse yet, a higher setting, a head of steam will form. Once the stopper is removed (once the freeze is lifted), steam will be emitted with great force (wages and prices will explode upwards). The lesson is clear: If the wage-price freeze is to accomplish its objective, demand management policies must be supportive. Otherwise, the inflation gains made during the period of controls will be quickly nullified after their removal. It is frequently argued that *expansionary* monetary and fiscal policies during the time of the wage and price controls instituted under the Nixon Administration were responsible, in part, for the explosive burst of inflation almost immediately after the controls were lifted.

The "swirl" movements of unemployment and inflation. Stop-go demand management policies are capable of generating patterns of movement of unemployment and inflation that have the appearance of swirls. What accounts for the northeast movement of those swirls is not completely understood. Two hypotheses that have a lot of appeal in terms of our discussion of the inflation process are worth noting.

First, if the speedup of inflation in response to expansionary demand management policies is more rapid than the slowdown in inflation in the face of contractionary policies, then it may be necessary to wait a much longer time on the down side to wipe out the increase in inflation that took place on the up side; this is difficult to do politically. Thus, if demand management policies are reversed before the earlier rate of inflation has been attained, there will be a higher inflation base from which the next round of higher inflation begins. If true, this would help to explain the general northerly movement of inflation over time.

The second hypothesis relates to the general easterly movement of the swirls. This general movement is consistent with an increase in the natural rate of unemployment over time. The question is, What accounts for the apparent increase in the natural rate? We addressed this issue briefly in Chapter 5. As was emphasized there, part of the explanation has to do with slow rates of capital formation during the course of the 1970s in combination with rapid increases in the labor force. Increasingly, capital became the restraining factor inhibiting further expansions of output and employment without adding to inflation. That is, efforts to achieve the lower rates of unemployment that were previously consistent with a stable rate of inflation increasingly required the use of older, less efficient capital, resulting in more rapid increases in unit production costs and higher inflation. The next section of this chapter will discuss this supply-side issue more explicitly.

The above discussion was intended to reflect the "conventional view" of unemployment and inflation dynamics. There is, however, a markedly different view—that of the rational expectationists. This group of economists believes that systematic deviations of the actual rates from the expected rates of inflation do not occur. The implications of this hypothesis are profound. In the absence of any systematic departures of actual

and expected rates of inflation, there can be no systematic departures of the actual from the natural rate of unemployment. There may be temporary, accidental departures, but never anything systematic. The short-run Phillips curve is coincident with the long-run Phillips curve, which means there is no trade-off between inflation and unemployment either in the short run or long run.

SUPPLY-SIDE POLICIES AND THE ANTI-INFLATION POTENTIAL OF FISCAL POLICIES

Up to this point we have been assuming that our real productive potential was fixed. This was a useful assumption for a while, an important building block toward a more complete understanding of the policy problems plaguing the United States today. It is now time to drop the fixed productive potential assumption in order to deal with the economics of the supply side—the economics of growth.

The buzzword in policy circles since the end of the 1970s has been **supply-side economics.** Widely touted by some as the new, revolutionary school of thought destined to replace the thinking of John Maynard Keynes and his followers, supply-side economics has been the source of much heated debate within the economics profession.

There is no clear-cut, generally accepted definition of supply-side economics. However, the dominant issue of concern among the so-called supply siders is economic growth.

To the extent that economic growth is the central issue, supply-side economics is not a new field of inquiry. Indeed, a strong case can be made that the study of supply-side economics is as old as the study of economics itself, since economic growth and the improvement of the material human condition have always figured prominently in the list of important areas of study in economics.

There is, however, a difference in emphasis in the debate that has been raging in the economics profession since at least the late 1970s. The difference is this: *Whereas economists have always been concerned with the general principles governing changes in the quantity and quality of our land, labor, and capital resources, the new supply-side economics is concerned more specifically with the effects of changes in marginal tax rates on incentives to work, save, and invest.*[1]

The basic argument of the new supply-side economics can be stated in a very straightforward manner. Taxes drive a wedge between the incomes earned by individuals and businesses, and the incomes they get to keep; appropriately enough, this wedge is often called the "tax wedge." Incentives to work, invest, and save are all affected by the nature of the tax wedge. Specifically, if the tax wedge gets larger and larger (meaning that the government gets an increasing share of the incomes earned by individuals and businesses), incentives for saving, investing, and working will diminish. After all, if government takes an ever larger share of what each of us earns, leaving us with a smaller percentage with which to do as *we* want, why should we work so hard or risk our savings on ventures having highly uncertain payoffs? According to the supply siders, we are likely to pull our resources back. The consequence will be a slowing in the growth of the quantity and quality of our productive resources and a corresponding slowing in the growth of our nation's productive potential.

The importance of marginal tax rates

The key to understanding the new supply-side economics is to recognize the importance that is accorded to *marginal* tax rates. The marginal tax rate measures the *extra* or *added* tax that is paid per extra dollar of taxable income. If the marginal tax rate is high, the taxpayer gets to keep only a relatively small amount of the extra income that is earned. If you don't get to keep much of the additional amount earned, why go to all the extra trouble and effort to earn it?

[1] At the time of this writing, some proponents of supply-side economics were arguing that an essential other element is the return to some kind of gold standard. This point is not evaluated here. For an analysis of the issues on gold backing, see Chapter 9.

To illustrate, suppose a taxpayer is subject to a 50 percent marginal tax rate. What this means is that for each additional dollar of taxable income, government takes 50 cents, which leaves only 50 cents for the taxpayer. The taxpayer could well argue, "If I work a little harder or save a bit more, half the extra income will go to government, not me. Why should I put in the extra hours or increase my saving when the extra benefit to me is so small? Put bluntly, it's simply not worth it to work harder or to save more."

Marginal tax rates and inflation. The problem of the tax wedge becomes especially acute in an inflationaty environment. The reason? The tax liabilities of individuals and corporations are determined on the basis of their money incomes, *not* their real incomes. Since tax schedules are progressive, *real* tax liabilities will rise over time even if *real* before-tax incomes remain unchanged. This is the phenomenon that is popularly known as **bracket creep.**

Marginal tax rates and work effort. The matter of bracket creep was dealt with at length in Chapter 4. We can, therefore, be very brief. The basic idea is straightforward. Suppose your money income rises at precisely the same rate as inflation. Since your income is taxed at progressively higher rates, the percentage of your income that you pay in taxes will rise; correspondingly, the percentage of your income you get to keep for yourself falls. Although your real income *before* taxes remains constant (since your money income keeps pace with inflation), your real income *after* taxes actually declines. What all of this means is that for the same amount of work effort (reflected in the same income before taxes), you actually fall farther behind in terms of the purchasing power of your income *after* taxes.

How people respond to this situation is a matter of some controversy. On the one hand, there are those who argue that the reduction in real income after taxes will induce people to work harder—to take a second job, to be willing to work additional hours overtime, and to encourage spouses to enter the labor force on a part-time or full-time basis—in order to offset the increased real tax burden. Supply-side theorists, on the other hand, argue that a reduced economic reward for the same work effort will cause people to reduce that work effort or to search for legal (or illegal) means to shelter their incomes from heavy taxes (by moving some of their activities *underground* or by purchasing assets whose economic returns are taxed at lower rates than other sources of income). Moreover, because inflation moves people into higher and higher tax brackets (meaning that they are subjected to higher and higher marginal tax rates over time), any *additional* work effort they might contemplate would yield them progressively less in terms of the real purchasing power of their take home pay—hardly much of an incentive to work more, according to the supply-side view.

The supply-side view of the effect of marginal tax rates on work effort can easily be summarized: Increasing marginal tax rates reduce the rewards for extra work effort and cause work effort to be less than otherwise; this serves to slow the growth of our real productive potential by slowing the growth of labor resources below what they would otherwise have been. In an inflationary environment this effect is compounded. Because people are subjected to increasing marginal tax rates for the *same* amount of work effort, they have an incentive to reduce their work effort continuously. This also serves to reduce the growth of our real productive potential. It is not surprising, therefore, that supply-side theorists call for reductions in marginal tax rates to spur additional work effort and therewith the growth of our potential GNP. This was one of the central arguments used by President Reagan and his economic advisers to persuade Congress to pass the Economic Recovery Tax Act of 1981 that, among other things, reduced marginal tax rates by about 25 percent over the three year period 1981–1983.

Marginal tax rates and saving incentives. Higher marginal tax rates reduce savings incentives as well. Since most income from savings is taxed at the same rate as the income earned from the sale of labor services, the fact that you get to keep less of the extra income from savings

at higher marginal tax rates means that you have a reduced incentive to save more, just as you had a reduced incentive to work more.

The problem of saving incentives is made much worse in an inflationary environment. Not only do taxpayers have to contend with higher marginal tax rates because of bracket creep, but the fact that they have to pay taxes on the full amount of the interest income they earn, including that portion that represents nothing more than an *inflation premium,* means that the income from savings is taxed at very heavy rates.

To illustrate, consider a very simple numerical example. Assume, first, that there is no inflation, that people earn 4 percent interest on their savings, and that, on average, they are subject to a 25 percent marginal tax rate. After taxes, people earn 3 percent on their savings; because inflation is zero, this represents a 3 percent *real* aftertax return. Now let inflation run at 8 percent, and assume that the interest rate on savings rises to 12 percent. Implicitly, this assumes an 8 percent inflation premium and, therefore, a *before-tax* real rate of 4 percent, the same as before. Assume further a marginal tax rate of 25 percent. Now, since government will take one quarter of the interest income on savings, people earn, after taxes, 9 percent. But, after inflation, they earn only 1 percent. *Although the before-tax real return is the same as it was with no inflation, after taxes and after inflation, the real return is only 1 percent in contrast to 3 percent before.* As inflation rose from zero to 8 percent, the real aftertax return on savings *fell* from 3 percent to 1 percent. The incentive to save is, accordingly, reduced. Had the 8 percent inflation premium not been subject to the tax, the real rate of return would have remained at 3 percent. Exempting the 8 percent premium would have meant a reduction of 1 percent from the before-tax return of 12 percent (since 0.25 times the 4 percent rate that is taxed goes to the government); an 11 percent money return minus 8 percent inflation yields an aftertax real return of 3 percent.

To enhance the incentive to save, supply-side theorists suggest one or both of two routes: cut marginal tax rates, and/or exempt from taxation the inflation premium component of interest rates. (In practice, the second method is extremely difficult to do since it is not known what amount represents the inflation premium; in the above example we *assumed* an inflation premium of 8 percent.)

The reason increased saving is viewed as desirable is to permit the release of resources from current consumption to enable more capital formation. It is important to emphasize, however, that increased saving in and of itself does not automatically raise capital formation. In order to undertake more investment, business people must have the incentive to do so. Their future sales prospects and their capital costs are important determinants of the amount of capital formation they will willingly undertake. And tax policy can be used to change those capital costs and also to change the income returns to investing.

Because increased saving will not, in general, necessarily boost capital formation on its own, supply-side theorists often argue in favor of tax incentives for investment *in combination with* increased tax incentives for saving. This makes sense. Tax incentives for investment without any added incentives for saving could fuel greater inflation (in the short run) and raise interest rates as added investment spending is piled on top of consumer spending. This second outcome is all the more likely the closer the economy is to its productive potential to start with.

Taxes, inflation, and incentives to invest. In Chapter 5 we discussed briefly the problem of the tax treatment of depreciation in an inflationary environment. The problem is this: Business firms must spread the cost of their capital goods purchases over time. Each year, they are permitted to deduct from current income some percentage of the original (or historic) cost. Ultimately, they will recover all of their capital costs. However, because they are permitted to recover only an amount equal to the original cost, even though replacement costs are rising in an inflationary environment, their deductions are inadequate. Why are they inadequate? Let us compare two situations—one where inflation is zero, and the other where inflation is positive. In the absence of any inflation, business firms will recover

amounts sufficient to replace capital that is wearing out. In an inflationary environment, on the other hand, since firms can only recover an amount equal to original cost, they do not recover enough to replace capital that is wearing out. True, the presence of inflation means that the firms (on average) have been selling their goods at higher (and rising) prices than in the no-inflation situation. However, because their depreciation deductions did not rise with inflation, their profits were overstated and their tax liabilities were correspondingly higher. The result? In an inflationary environment they effectively have to pay higher taxes, which reduces the aftertax return to investment. The so-called depreciation reform proposals enacted by the Congress in 1981 were at least in part aimed at rectifying the disincentive to invest caused by historic cost depreciation.

In line with our earlier discussion on savings, most supply-side theorists couple depreciation reform (to make the tax treatment of depreciation allowances more inflationproof) with enhanced savings incentives.

Supply-side economics, economic growth, and inflation

This brief discussion of supply-side economics reveals one extremely important conclusion—namely, the role of the tax system in affecting incentives to work, save, and invest. Precisely how adversely those incentives have been affected as a consequence of our tax laws, especially our tax laws in combination with inflation, are matters of much dispute. The Council of Economic Advisers under President Carter sifted through the available empirical evidence and concluded that the increase in potential real GNP, occasioned by reductions in marginal tax rates, would be quite modest. Specifically, the Council of Economic Advisers concluded in its January 1981 report that a 10 percent reduction in personal income tax rates would induce an increase in labor supply between 0.3 and 1.0 percent, and increase the saving rate—the share of personal saving in disposable income—by only 0.2 percentage points. Combined, these labor supply and savings effects would lead to an increase in potential real GNP of between 0.5 and 0.9 percent, a rather modest change. Many staunch supply-side advocates believe the increase in real potential GNP would be much larger. In any event, the empirical evidence would seem to suggest that, at a minimum, the supply-side theorists are correct in pointing out the *direction of change* in incentives caused by our tax laws.

If the supply-side theorists are correct, the distinct possibility arises that fiscal policy can be used to help in the fight against inflation, even from a long-run point of view. Whereas we suggested earlier that fiscal policy from a demand management perspective could affect inflation in the short run only (with the added important qualifier that the short run could last for several years), supply-side economics tells us that fiscal policy can affect inflation in the long run by influencing incentives to work, save, and invest.

To illustrate the role of tax policy in the fight against inflation, recall that, by definition,

$$\begin{array}{c} \text{Growth of} \\ \text{money} \\ \text{supply} \end{array} + \begin{array}{c} \text{Growth} \\ \text{of} \\ \text{velocity} \end{array} = \begin{array}{c} \text{Growth of} \\ \text{price} \\ \text{level} \end{array} + \begin{array}{c} \text{Growth} \\ \text{of real} \\ \text{output.} \end{array}$$

Assuming for simplicity that velocity growth is zero, the equation of exchange tells us that growth of the money supply is identical to growth of the price level plus growth of real output. To the extent that fiscal policy actions can alter incentives to work, save, and invest, fiscal policy can affect the growth of real output. For a given money supply growth, so the argument goes, appropriate tax incentive policies, by raising the growth of our real productive potential, can result in a permanently lower rate of inflation in the long run.

A few comments on this result are in order. First, as the above discussion makes clear, it is not true that the only way to slow inflation is to slow the rate of money growth; nor is it true that fiscal policy cannot affect the long-run rate of inflation. However, it is through the effect of fiscal policy actions on incentives to work, save, and invest that fiscal policy acquires its potency with respect to the long-run rate of inflation. A pure demand-oriented change in fiscal policy—

if such a thing exists—cannot influence the long-run inflation rate.

Second, although the long-run effect of a supply-side tax cut on the rate of inflation is clear, the short-run effects could be just the opposite. That is, the *immediate* effect of a tax cut could be an increase in aggregate demand with little or no change in the growth of our productive potential. The result? A worsened inflation picture in the short run because the increase in aggregate demand exceeds the aggregate supply increase (though, how much of a worsened inflation picture will depend on how close actual GNP is to potential GNP). In time, however, inflation will diminish below its initial rate as the supply-side effects take hold and as the policy-induced change in velocity settles down. This was an important point in the debate over the 1981 tax bill proposed by President Reagan. The Reagan Administration argued that its tax proposals would unleash an increase in savings, investment, and work effort and thereby reduce inflation. Opponents argued, however, that the proposed tax changes would generate higher rates of inflation. According to the theoretical structure developed here, both sides of the debate could have been correct. If Reagan's proposals do have the supply-side effects that were promised, the *long-run* rate of inflation will slow. However, in the short run, inflation could worsen because the demand-side effects exceed the short-run supply-side effects. Thus, as President Carter's Council of Economic Advisers estimated a 10 percent cut in personal income tax rates would induce a 2 percent increase in aggregate demand in contrast to a less than 1.0 percent increase in potential real GNP in the short run. President Reagan's economic advisers disagreed, suggesting that the supply-side response would be larger than the demand-side effects. As of this writing, the debate is far from settled.

SUMMARY

1.   For decades economists have sought to discover whether some simple and predictable relationship existed between unemployment and

inflation. When an appeal is made to the facts, however, it is apparent that, if such a relationship exists, it is far from simple and predictable. Yet we do observe some patterns. The unemployment rate and the inflation rate appear to move in clockwise swirls; for some subperiods, one observes a *Phillips curve* type of relationship. And two years after an unemployment rate increase, we notice decisive downward trends in inflation.

2. The Phillips curve implies that an unemployment-inflation trade-off exists. The data for the U.S. economy for the 1960s seemed to confirm the existence of the Phillips curve. Toward the end of the 1960s, however, economists began to discover a problem. They noticed that prices were rising at a faster rate for given unemployment rates than their estimates of the Phillips curve would have predicted. The conclusion most economists reached was that the Phillips curve had shifted up; the trade-off between unemployment and inflation had worsened.

3. The fact that inflation was worse than predicted on the basis of the historical relationship between unemployment and inflation caused many economists in the late 1960s to question the whole idea of a Phillips curve. Two central propositions emerged as a consequence of that questioning. First, in the short run, it is possible to discover a Phillips curve type of relationship; in the long run, there is no trade-off. Second, a trade-off relationship will be revealed because the actual rate of inflation differs from the rate expected; when the actual and expected rates of inflation coincide, there will be no trade-off.

4. According to the *accelerationist thesis,* monetary policy actions aimed at maintaining the unemployment rate below the natural rate will result in an ever accelerating rate of inflation.

5. It is reasonably clear what kinds of demand-management policies must be pursued to ultimately bring inflation under control. In order to get people to revise their inflationary expectations downward—in order, that is, to lower the core rate—it is necessary to slow the rate of money growth to raise the unemployment rate above the natural rate to bring about the outcome of an actual inflation rate below the rate expected.

6. Supply-side theorists emphasize the role

of taxes in affecting incentives to work, save, and invest. Since changing incentives to work, save, and invest affect the growth of our productive potential, fiscal policy can affect inflation in the long run.

CONCEPTS FOR REVIEW

Secular stagflation

Phillips curve

Demand-pull rate of inflation

Price-shock rate of inflation

Core rate of inflation

Accelerationist thesis

Incomes policy

Bracket creep

Supply-side economics

QUESTIONS FOR DISCUSSION

(Those marked with an asterisk (*) are more difficult.)

1. Explain (in words, not graphs or equations) why there is no inflation-unemployment trade-off in the long run. Explain why, according to the conventional view, there is a Phillips curve type of relationship in the short run and why, according to the rational expectations view, there is no trade-off even in the short run.

2. At the beginning of this chapter we said we wanted to explain the patterns of movement of unemployment and inflation shown in Figure 14.1. How can the analysis of this chapter be used to explain:
   a. The clockwise swirls of unemployment and inflation.
   b. A Phillips curve type of relationship between unemployment and inflation.
   c. Periods of increasing unemployment and inflation (i.e., stagflation).
   d. Secular stagflation.

3. Starting from a position of long-run equilibrium, explain how an increase in the growth of money by itself will affect the unemployment and inflation rates over time. Repeat the exercise for a reduced rate of money growth.

4. Some people argue that supply-side tax cuts will reduce inflation; others argue that inflation will

be made worse because of the effects of the tax cuts on aggregate demand. Can you reconcile these two views?

*5.   "The natural rate of unemployment has increased over time because of slower rates of capital formation. Supply-side tax cuts targeted to increase capital formation can therefore reduce the natural rate and bring us closer to the realization of the goals of the Humphrey-Hawkins Act." Evaluate.

6.   Explain, in words, the meaning and implications of the accelerationist thesis.

*7.   Explain, in words, the importance of inflationary expectations to the analysis of patterns of movements of unemployment and inflation over time. (*Hint:* How would the results of this chapter and Chapter 13 differ if the expected rate of inflation *always* equaled zero?)

Chapter 115

The balance of payments and the international monetary system

We live in an interdependent world economy in which the well-being of each nation depends greatly on its economic relations with other countries. For the United States, imports and exports each amount to about 13 percent of our GNP; for most other developed nations, the proportion is much higher. In the Netherlands, for example, fully 50 percent of its GNP is imported.

International economic interdependence carries with it decided advantages. As a consequence of international trade, standards of living both in the United States and elsewhere in the world economy are higher, in many instances very much higher, than they would otherwise be. On the other hand, economic interdependence carries with it unavoidable problems. The energy crisis and the shock to the world economy caused by OPEC pricing and production policies are perhaps the most evident problem areas. However, other problem areas exist as well. Because inflation is a worldwide phenomenon, and because the world's nations are so closely linked, it is extremely difficult for any one country acting on its own to bring inflation under control; trade and capital movements internationally, and changes in exchange rates, all provide channels through which inflation is transmitted from one country to another. These transmission channels can, at times, serve to frustrate the best-intentioned efforts of the monetary and fiscal authorities to slow inflation.

It is the purpose of this chapter to examine some of the economic consequences for the U.S. economy and U.S. policymaking of our interdependent ties with the rest of the world community. In large measure, the focus here will be on the macroeconomic consequences of this interdependency; the microeconomic aspects will be dealt with at length in Chapters 29 and 30.

More specifically, it is the purpose of this chapter to undertake a careful study of our international monetary system—to study the structure and meaning of our country's **balance of payments,** to analyze the **foreign exchange market** and the determination of **exchange rates,** and to explore the significance of the differences between fixed and floating exchange rates.

In order to deal adequately with the macroeconomic aspects of our ties to the world economy, we have to lay the appropriate groundwork. We open the chapter with an examination of the meaning of our nation's balance of payments. This we follow with a detailed analysis of the foreign exchange market, which will take us through some familiar, and some not-so-familiar, territory on demand and supply. Once that is completed, we will be in a position to take up the critical macroeconomic questions of how the performance of our economy is influenced by our monetary relations with the rest of the world and of how U.S. policymaking is hampered or assisted by economic events abroad.

Over the course of the past several years, there has been growing awareness of our monetary relations with foreign nations. Daily the press carries stories reporting the latest changes in the value of the dollar on the world's currency markets. Movements in the international value of the dollar are given as much play as are movements in stock market averages. And there is no shortage of commentary on the meaning of the reported changes in the value of the dollar. Almost all newspaper accounts view declines in the international value of the dollar as undesirable: The dollar is "weak"; the dollar is "battered"; the once mighty dollar has "fallen." Increases in the value of the dollar, on the other hand, are widely heralded. Unfortunately, these stories frequently confuse what they are intended to clarify. This is due in no small part to the fact that the nature and implications of our financial relations with foreign countries are shrouded in mystique and widely misunderstood. It is hoped that this chapter will eliminate much of this mystique and misunderstanding.

THE BALANCE OF PAYMENTS

This country's **balance of payments** *is a summary statement of the financial transactions between residents of this country—the home country—and residents of all other countries during some specified period of time.* Our nation's imports and exports of goods and services constitute one important aspect of our financial dealings

with foreign countries. In addition, the purchase of foreign financial assets—foreign stocks, bonds, and commercial paper—by residents of this country and the purchase of U.S. financial assets by residents abroad constitute yet another important part of our financial dealings with foreign nations.

It is useful to divide the balance of payments into two distinct kinds of transactions—those transactions that involve **inpayments** and those that involve **outpayments.** *Inpayments are those financial payments made, for whatever reason, by residents of other countries to residents of the home country.* **Outpayments,** *on the other hand, are those financial payments made by residents of the home country to residents in other countries.*

Our exports of goods and services are classified as an inpayment. In exchange for the goods and services we ship abroad, foreign residents make financial payments to U.S. residents. Similarly, **capital inflows**—the acquisition of U.S. financial assets by residents of foreign countries—are classified as an inpayment because they result in financial payments being made to home residents from residents of foreign countries. Examples of outpayments include U.S. imports of goods and services and U.S. capital outflows, because they result in financial payments being made by U.S. residents to foreigners.

The U.S. balance of payments

The inpayments and outpayments for the United States in 1980 are summarized in Table 15.1. A brief explanation of each of the items in Table 15.1 will reveal the nature and magnitude of our financial relationships with foreign countries.

The balance of merchandise trade (or, the balance of trade) and the balance on goods and services. The **balance of trade**—the difference between the dollar value of the *goods* we export abroad and the dollar value of the *goods* we import—is one of the most widely publicized statistics of our financial dealings with foreign countries. Economists have long been critical of the importance the press and many government officials attach to this figure. In the first place, the balance of trade refers to our trade in *goods* alone; it excludes the trade in services (sometimes called the trade in **invisibles**). The trade balance excludes, for example, the travel expenditures made by foreign travelers in the United States, and those made by U.S. travellers abroad for lodging, food, transportation, entertainment, gifts, etc. It excludes freight payments made to U.S.-operated ocean, air, rail, truck, and pipeline carriers by foreign residents, and similar payments made by U.S. residents to foreign-operated carriers. It excludes the payments to and from foreigners for insurance and for fees and royalties. It also excludes the receipt of income on U.S. assets abroad (an export of a service), and the payment of income on foreign assets in the United States (an import of a service).[1]

Focusing so much attention on our trade in goods, in contrast to our trade in goods *and* services, can be highly misleading. If we are concerned with the impact of our trade on domestic employment and income, it would be wrong to focus our attention exclusively on our trade in goods; our service industries are sources of income and employment as well. In this context, the trade balance may be very misleading to a public that views imports as a source of foreign employment (and perhaps as representing the loss in domestic employment opportunities), and exports as a source of domestic employment. Whereas the trade balance was in *deficit* by $27.3 billion in 1980, the balance on *goods and services* was in *surplus* by $7.1 billion; this was because we had in 1980 a *services* export surplus of almost $35 billion.

There is a second reason economists do not favor the emphasis given to the trade balance.

---

[1] It may seem a bit strange to refer to receipts of income on U.S. assets abroad as an export of a service and payments of income on foreign assets in the United States as an import of a service. However, when we lend money abroad or make a financial investment in a foreign corporation, we are providing a service to foreign residents; the interest and dividend income we receive represents the payment for the service provided. Similarly, the interest and dividend payments we make to foreigners who have made loans and financial investments in the United States represent the payments we make for the use of the services of their assets.

The balance of trade gives us *only* a partial balance. It reflects only part of our financial dealings with residents of foreign countries. For the same reason, economists do not favor an exclusive emphasis on our trade in goods *and* services. It too gives us only a partial balance. We need to focus at least as much attention on capital inflows and outflows—both private and official—if we are to understand the whole picture. More on this later.

Given the shortcomings of the trade balance as a measure of our financial dealings with the rest of the world, why is it given so much play? Simply put, because statistics on trade in goods are made available to the public before other international financial statistics for the same time period. Trade in goods is easier to measure accurately and promptly than trade in services or international capital flows.

The current account. Referring to Table 15.1 again, if we add to our balance on goods and services, the balance on *unilateral transfers,* we arrive at a figure known as the **balance on current account.** Unilateral transfers, the bulk of which are best classified as gifts, include *(a)* U.S. government payments used to finance the transfer of goods and services to foreign countries under foreign assistance programs for which no repayment is expected; *(b)* payments of government pensions to eligible persons residing abroad; *(c)* payments abroad under U.S. educational and cultural exchange programs, and U.S. grants supporting individual or institutional research abroad; *(d)* cash and goods distributed abroad by U.S. religious, charitable, educational, scientific, other nonprofit organizations, and private individuals; and *(e)* remittances received from foreign residents for similar kinds of transactions (e.g., German and Canadian government pension payments to U.S. residents). In 1980, net *unilateral transfers*—transfers to U.S. residents less transfers abroad—amounted to some $7 billion.

The current account balance is important because it tells us, for the designated accounting period (here, the year 1980), the extent to which we are a net lending or a net borrowing nation with respect to the rest of the world. When we purchase goods and services from abroad or send

Table 15.1

The U.S. balance of payments, 1980 ($ billions)

1.	U.S. exports of goods, excluding military	+221.8
2.	U.S. imports of goods, excluding military	−249.1
3.	*Balance on merchandise trade* (lines 1 and 2)	−27.3
4.	U.S. exports of goods and services	+340.9
5.	U.S. imports of goods and services	−333.8
6.	*Balance on goods and services* (lines 4 and 5)	+ 7.1
7.	Unilateral transfers (excluding military grants of goods and services), net	− 7.0
8.	*Balance on current account* (lines 6 and 7)	+ 0.1
9.	U.S. assets abroad, net (capital outflow)	− 84.5
10.	Foreign assets in the U.S., net (capital inflow)*	+ 84.4
11.	*Balance on capital movements** (lines 9 and 10)	− 0.1

Transactions in U.S. official reserve assets and in foreign official assets in the United States

12.	Increase in U.S. official reserve assets, net (capital outflow)	− 8.2
13.	Increase in foreign official reserve assets in the United States, net (capital inflow)	+16.2

Note: Inpayment (+); outpayment (−).
* The balance on capital movements has been adjusted to incorporate the statistical discrepancy.
Source: *Survey of Current Business,* June 1981.

gifts to foreign nations, the payments made by U.S. residents to foreigners raise the financial claims of foreign countries on the United States. Similarly, the payments received by U.S. residents for goods, services, and gifts from foreign nations raise the financial claims of the United States on the rest of the world. The difference—the current account balance—measures the net change in financial claims between the United States and other countries. A current account deficit means that we have *increased our indebtedness* to foreign countries. We are more of a net international debtor (or less of a net international creditor). A current account surplus, on the other hand, means that foreign countries have increased their indebtedness to us. We are more of a net international creditor (or less of a net international debtor).

On the basis of these considerations, economists refer to the balance on U.S. current account as a measure of our net foreign investment or disinvestment position with the rest of the world. A U.S. current account surplus for any given period tells us that U.S. residents have increased their claims on the rest of the world during that period; the magnitude of the surplus is a measure of magnitude of U.S. net foreign investment. A U.S. current account deficit, on the other hand, is a measure of U.S. net foreign investment—a measure of the reduction in our claims on the rest of the world (or, alternatively—since a U.S. current account deficit implies that the rest of the world has a current account surplus vis-à-vis the United States—a buildup of foreign claims on the United States). In Table 15.1, we see from the current account surplus for 1980 that U.S. foreign investment amounted to *$0.1 billion.*

You should also note in Table 15.1 that the balance on capital movements accounts is the same size, but of opposite sign, as the balance on current account. Indeed, given the nature of double-entry bookkeeping (discussed in Chapter 4), where each transaction involves both a debit and credit entry, thereby ensuring that the balance of payments balances in an accounting sense, *the balance on current account must be offset exactly by the balance on the capital movements account.* That is, a current account deficit implies a simultaneous capital account surplus of the same size. Accordingly, it is easy to see why economists refer to our balance on current account as a measure of our net foreign investment or disinvestment position with the rest of the world. A capital account deficit means we have built up more claims against foreign nations during this time period than they built up of claims against us, which is exactly what a *current account surplus* means.

The capital account and changes in official reserve assets. What is important is *not* the fact that the balance of payments balances, but *how* it balances. It is useful to make a distinction in the capital account between *private* capital flow transactions and *official* capital flow transactions. At the bottom of Table 15.1 we note separately the change in **official reserve assets** that took place in 1980. (Lines 12 and 13 are included in lines 9 and 10 respectively.) In general, official reserve assets consist of the foreign exchange holdings—the holdings of foreign currencies by a specifically designated "official" government agency—usually a central bank or an allied stabilization fund. When a country's official reserve assets *increase,* this frequently implies that the official agency undertook actions to *buy* foreign exchange through the sale of its domestic currency on the foreign exchange markets. Frequently these actions are undertaken for the purpose of changing the exchange rate from what it would otherwise have been. Such actions are termed **official foreign exchange market intervention.** The statistics reported at the bottom of Table 15.1 suggest that foreign official institutions ran up their holdings of dollar assets by more than $16 billion in 1980. This is a crude measure of the intervention operations conducted by foreign governments. U.S. holdings of foreign exchange increased by $8.2 million, a measure of U.S. foreign exchange intervention operations.

Official intervention is important for the following reason. Balance in the balance of payments was achieved in part by a sizable amount of intervention in foreign exchange markets. Had there been no official intervention, balance would have been achieved by a balancing of private capital flows and the current account balance. But

this would have meant a different exchange rate and therefore a different balance on current account and capital account. This will become clear once we come to an understanding of the forces that determine exchange rates. We turn to a discussion of exchange rate determination in the next section.

THE DETERMINATION OF FOREIGN EXCHANGE RATES

In order to buy goods and services from other countries or to purchase foreign financial assets, we need to acquire purchasing power that foreign residents will accept. In most circumstances, this means we have to acquire foreign currency. To do so, we (or our bank) must enter the **foreign exchange market,** purchasing foreign currency with American dollars. Residents of foreign countries who wish to purchase American goods and services or U.S. financial assets will likewise enter the foreign exchange market, selling their foreign currencies in exchange for dollars.

How much we must pay for foreign currency and, correspondingly, how much foreign residents must pay for U.S. dollars is reflected in the prevailing **exchange rate.** The exchange rate is simply a price—the value of one currency expressed in terms of another.

To develop a thorough understanding of the foreign exchange market, we will proceed in steps. For the moment, we will focus our attention on the financial transactions associated with our trade in goods and services; later we will introduce capital flows.

The U.S. demand for foreign goods and services and the demand for foreign exchange

The demand for any foreign-produced good or service is determined by the same factors that determine the demand for a domestically produced good or service—its price, the prices of other goods and services, people's incomes, people's tastes, and so on. However, what is different in the case of foreign-produced goods and services is that the price that is relevant to U.S. residents is the dollar price, *not* the foreign currency price. The exchange rate, the value of one currency expressed in terms of another, is the means whereby foreign currency prices can be translated into domestic prices. This can be illustrated simply as follows:

Suppose the yen price of a particular Japanese calculator is ¥2,000. What is its dollar price? It depends on the exchange rate. Suppose the exchange rate is $1 = ¥200. This means that, in exchange for $1, ¥200 can be obtained in return. A calculator having a yen price of ¥2,000 has a dollar price of $10.

The exchange rate between any two currencies can be expressed in either of two ways: (1) the number of units of domestic currency per unit of foreign currency (the domestic currency price of the foreign currency), or (2) the number of units of foreign currency per unit of domestic currency (the foreign currency price of the domestic currency). Obviously, either way of expressing the exchange rate is nothing other than the reciprocal of the other way of expressing it. To avoid confusion, it is best to define the exchange rate one way and stick with it throughout. For our purposes, the *exchange rate* will be defined as the domestic currency price of the foreign currency—i.e., the number of units of domestic currency per unit of foreign currency. The dollar-yen exchange rate used above ($1 = ¥200) will be expressed as $\frac{1}{200}$ or 0.005. In other words, each unit of Japan's currency costs ½ cent. Defined this way, the dollar price (P_{US}) of a Japanese good is equal to the Japanese currency price (P_J) times the exchange rate (e). That is:

$$P_{US} = P_J \times e.$$

From this expression the yen price of a U.S. product can be found by *dividing* the U.S. price by the exchange rate (i.e., $P_J = \frac{P_{US}}{e}$). Thus the yen price of a $25 item is ¥5,000 (i.e., 5,000 = $\frac{25.00}{0.005}$).

It is obvious from this relationship that the dollar price of foreign goods and services depends on two factors: (1) the price of such goods, expressed in their native currency, and (2) the dollar price of foreign currency. An increase in the foreign currency price of the goods we import, *given the exchange rate,* will increase their dollar price. Similarly, an increase in the exchange rate—an increase in the dollar price of foreign currency—will increase the dollar price of the goods we import, even if the foreign currency price remains unaltered. This last point is easily illustrated. Suppose the dollar-yen exchange rate is increased from ½ cent to 1 cent. The calculator with a price of ¥2,000 will now have a dollar price of $20 instead of the former $10.

The demand curve for foreign exchange

Because the dollar price of foreign-produced goods and services varies as the exchange rate varies, it is relatively easy to establish a relationship between the exchange rate and the quantity of foreign exchange demanded. The relationship is based on two propositions:

1. There is an inverse relationship between the quantity of foreign goods and services demanded and their *dollar* price; this is nothing more than the law of demand.
2. Payment for foreign goods and services must ultimately be made in the currencies of the relevant foreign countries; U.S. importers acquire foreign exchange through the sale of dollars on the foreign exchange market.[2]

An increase in the exchange rate will lead to a reduction in the quantity of foreign exchange demanded. Since an increase in the exchange rate raises the dollar price of foreign-produced goods and services, reducing the quantity demanded of those goods and services, there will be a corresponding reduction in the amount of foreign exchange demanded to finance the smaller volume purchased. This is illustrated in Figure 15.1; Figure 15.1 is based on the hypothetical data presented in Table 15.2.

---

[2] Even if payment is made in dollars, as frequently happens, these dollars will often be ultimately sold for foreign currencies. That is, exporters acquiring the dollars often turn around and sell them for their own domestic currencies.

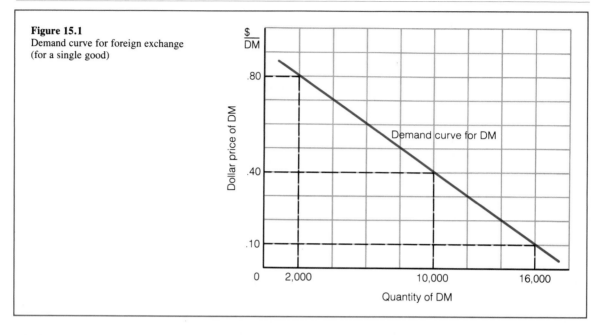

Figure 15.1
Demand curve for foreign exchange
(for a single good)

Examine first the data presented in Table 15.2. The hypothetical example is based on the assumption that the German camera in question has a fixed German currency price of 200 deutsche marks (DM200). However, as the dollar price of DMs rises from 10 cents to 80 cents (i.e., from $1 = DM10 to $1 = DM1.25), the dollar price of that camera rises from $20 to $160. Of course, as the dollar price of the German camera rises, the quantity demanded falls; the data in column (4) of Table 15.2 reflect this relationship. Once we know the quantity of cameras demanded, it is easy to figure out the quantity of DMs demanded: The quantity of cameras demanded times their DM price yields the quantity of DMs demanded.

From this discussion, it is clear why there is an inverse relationship between the exchange rate and the quantity of DMs demanded. This relationship yields the demand curve for foreign exchange illustrated in Figure 15.1.

Two final notes. First, in the hypothetical example just discussed, we were concerned with a single foreign-produced good only. By adding up the demand for DMs for all the German goods and services we import, we obtain the total de-

mand for DMs associated with our trade with Germany. Second, the demand for other foreign currencies associated with our trade with other countries can be derived in the same manner as the demand for DMs. Given the demand for each of the currencies of the countries with whom we trade, it is relatively easy to figure out the dollar value of our outpayments associated with our trade in goods and services with other countries at each exchange rate.

Shifts in the demand curve for foreign exchange. The demand curve for foreign exchange described above is a *ceteris paribus* relationship. *Ceteris paribus,* an increase in the exchange rate will cause a reduction in the quantity demanded of foreign exchange. This is reflected in a movement *along* the demand curve. But the demand for foreign exchange—the amount U.S. importers are willing to buy—is affected by more than just the exchange rate. Changes in those other factors will cause *shifts* in the demand for foreign exchange. Two of the more important other factors are discussed below.

First, increases in the foreign currency prices of the goods we import will increase or decrease the demand for foreign exchange, depending on how responsive U.S. buyers are to changes in

Table 15.2

The demand for foreign-produced goods and services and the demand for foreign exchange (the case of a single good)

(1) DM price of a German camera	(2) Exchange rate (dollar price of DM)	(3) Dollar price of a German camera (2) × (1)	(4) Quantity of German cameras demanded	(5) Quantity of DMs demanded (4) × (1)
DM200	0.10	$ 20	80	16,000
200	0.20	40	70	14,000
200	0.30	60	60	12,000
200	0.40	80	50	10,000
200	0.50	100	40	8,000
200	0.60	120	30	6,000
200	0.70	140	20	4,000
200	0.80	160	10	2,000

the prices of foreign goods. *Given the exchange rate,* we know that an increase in the foreign currency price of any good will raise its dollar price as well. We also know that an increase in the dollar price will result in a reduction in the quantity of foreign goods demanded. What will happen to total expenditures for the foreign-produced goods (measured in terms of the foreign currency)? We cannot tell at this point. The quantity of foreign goods demanded is less, which, by itself, would *reduce* total foreign currency outlays; but the foreign currency price for each unit sold is higher, which, by itself, would *increase* total foreign currency outlays. Which of these two opposing forces predominates is an empirical question. Virtually all of the empirical evidence to date suggests that the first factor predominates; that is, the negative effect of the reduction in the quantity demanded on total foreign currency outlays outweighs the positive effect of the increase in foreign currency prices. Accordingly, increases in the foreign currency prices of imported goods will cause a reduction in the demand for foreign exchange—i.e., the demand curve for foreign exchange will shift to the left.

In this context, although an increase in the foreign currency price of any single foreign-produced good will probably result in a decrease in demand for that particular currency, there may well be an increase in demand for some *other* foreign currency as U.S. consumers substitute in favor of a similar, relatively lower-priced product produced elsewhere. An increase in the foreign currency price of any single good may not result in an *overall* reduction in the demand for foreign currencies. However, *if foreign prices in general rise relative to U.S. prices, there is likely to be a general reduction in the U.S. demand for foreign currencies.*

Second, an increase in the level of income in the United States will generally result in an increase in the demand for foreign goods and services, as well as an increase in the demand for foreign exchange. Thus, an increase in the level of U.S. income will cause the demand curve for foreign exchange to shift up and to the right.

The foreign demand for U.S. goods and services and the supply of foreign exchange

Continuing our focus on a country's trade in goods and services, let us examine the factors that determine the supply of foreign exchange. As we shall see, the supply of foreign exchange derives from the foreign demand for U.S. goods and services—i.e., U.S. exports. When German importers purchase U.S. goods, they enter the foreign exchange market, selling their own domestic currency in exchange for dollars. In other words, the demand for dollars by German importers has as its counterpart the supply of DMs on the foreign exchange market. Therefore, what determines their demand for dollars in turn determines their supply of DMs to the foreign exchange market.

Consider the problem from the point of view of residents in Germany. What matters to them is the DM price of American goods, *not* the dollar price. The higher the DM price of American goods, the smaller will be the quantity of American goods demanded in Germany; again, this follows directly from the familiar law of demand.

The question we wish to consider is this: How will changes in the exchange rate affect the DM price of American goods and the supply of DMs on the foreign exchange market, *ceteris paribus?* The answer is given in two steps:

1. An increase in the exchange rate—i.e., an increase in the dollar price of DMs—lowers the DM price of American goods. This is easily illustrated. Suppose the dollar price of DMs rises from 10 cents (i.e., $1 = DM10) to 20 cents (i.e., $1 = DM5). Whereas at the lower exchange rate it took DM10 to acquire $1, it now requires only DM5. This means that an American good carrying a $10 price tag now costs DM50 in Germany instead of the former DM100. As a consequence, an increase in the exchange rate will lead to an increase in the quantity of U.S. goods and services demanded.

2. Although the quantity of U.S. goods demanded will rise in response to an increase in the exchange rate, it does not follow automatically that the value of expenditures in DMs will also rise. The increase in the *quantity* of U.S. goods demanded would serve to increase total DM expenditures on U.S. goods. But the *reduction in the DM price,* the consequence of the increase in the exchange rate, serves to lower total DM spending. Which effect predominates? Empirically, the evidence suggests that the percentage quantity change exceeds the percentage price change. What this means is that *an increase in the exchange rate will cause total DM expenditures on U.S. goods to rise. This, in turn, means that the quantity of DMs supplied will rise in response to an increase in the exchange rate.*

The supply curve of foreign exchange. These ideas are illustrated in Figure 15.2; Figure 15.2 is based on the hypothetical data presented in Table 15.3. We consider in this example the demand on the part of German residents for an American-produced electronic switch. The dollar price of the switch is assumed to remain fixed at $40. The DM price of the switch, on the other hand, varies as the exchange rate varies. This is seen in column (3) of Table 15.3. At an exchange rate of 10 cents (i.e., $1 = DM10) the $40 switch carries a DM price of DM400; at

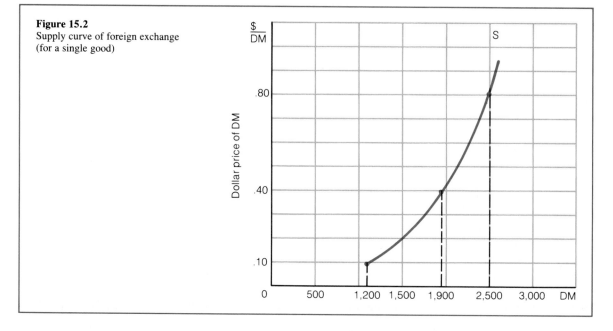

Figure 15.2
Supply curve of foreign exchange (for a single good)

Table 15.3

The foreign demand for domestically produced goods and services and the supply of foreign exchange (the case of a single good)

(1) Dollar price of an American- produced electronic switch	(2) Exchange rate (dollar price of DM)	(3) DM price of the electronic switch (1) ÷ (2)	(4) Quantity of American switches demanded	(5) Quantity of DMs supplied (3) × (4)
40	0.10	DM400	3	1,200
40	0.20	200	7	1,400
40	0.30	133.33	12	1,600
40	0.40	100	19	1,900
40	0.50	80	26	2,080
40	0.60	66.67	33	2,200
40	0.70	57.14	42	2,400
40	0.80	50	50	2,500

an exchange rate of 40 cents, that same switch carries a DM price of DM100; and so forth.

It is clear, then, that the DM price of the American-produced switch falls as the exchange rate rises, ceteris paribus. Correspondingly, as the DM price declines, the quantity demanded rises. This is shown in column (4). Finally, drawing on our earlier discussion of the effects of the price and quantity changes on total expenditures, it is clear in column (5) that the quantity of DMs supplied rises as the DM price of the switch falls.

From this, it follows that there is a direct relationship between the exchange rate and the quantity of DMs supplied. This relationship is illustrated graphically in Figure 15.2.

Two final notes. First, in the hypothetical example just discussed, we focused our attention on a single American good only. By adding up the supply of DMs for all of the American goods and services exported to Germany, we obtain the total supply of DMs associated with our trade with Germany. Second, the supply of other foreign currencies associated with our trade with other countries can be derived in the same manner as the supply of DMs.

Shifts in the supply curve of foreign exchange. Because the supply curve of foreign exchange described above is derived from the foreign demand for American goods and services, *shifts* in the supply curve will be determined by forces analogous to those that cause shifts in the

demand curve for foreign exchange. Our discussion can therefore be brief.

The supply curve of foreign exchange is a *ceteris paribus* relationship—i.e., *everything else unchanged,* an increase in the exchange rate will cause an increase in the quantity of foreign exchange supplied. This is reflected in a movement along the supply curve. In response to a change in those *other* factors (other than the exchange rate) that affect the amount of American goods and services foreign residents are willing to buy, the supply curve of foreign exchange shifts. An increase in the *dollar* price of American-produced goods and services will, assuming the empirical evidence discussed above is correct, cause the supply curve of foreign exchange to shift to the left—i.e., less foreign exchange will be supplied at each and every rate of exchange. Similarly, an increase in foreign income will generally result in an outward shift of the supply curve. The increase in demand for U.S. goods as a result of an increase in German income will raise the German demand for U.S. dollars and increase the supply of DMs.

The U.S. bilateral balance on goods and services: A graphic representation of the demand for and supply of foreign exchange

We are now in a position to show graphically our goods and services trade with one other foreign country. You will recall from our discussion earlier that the U.S. balance on goods and services was defined as the difference between the expenditures we make for foreign-produced goods and services, and the expenditures made by foreign residents on U.S.-produced goods and services. If inpayments (associated with the sale of our goods and services abroad) exceed outpayments (associated with our expenditures for foreign produced goods and services), we are said to be in surplus on goods and services account; if outpayments exceed inpayments, we are said to be in deficit on goods and services account.

The demand for foreign exchange measures the magnitude of our outpayments; the supply of foreign exchange measures the magnitude of our inpayments. Whether we are in deficit, in balance, or in surplus will depend on whether the demand for foreign exchange exceeds, equals, or is less than the supply. Moreover, since the demand for and supply of foreign exchange are both related to the exchange rate, the magnitude of the imbalance on goods and services account, or the absence of any imbalance, will depend on the exchange rate. This is illustrated clearly in Figure 15.3.

In Figure 15.3 we show the demand for and

supply of DMs associated with our trade in goods and services with Germany—our bilateral trade with Germany. If the exchange rate happens to be e_0, inpayments from Germany for our goods and services will equal the outpayments to Germany for German goods and services; our **bilateral balance** on goods and services account with Germany will therefore be zero. If the exchange rate happens to be higher than e_0—say, e_2—the United States will be in surplus on goods and services account with Germany. At an exchange rate below e_0, on the other hand—say, e_1—the United States will be in deficit with Germany on goods and services account.

Note the very important role the exchange rate plays in the determination of our balance on goods and services account. As is apparent from Figure 15.3, the goods and services deficit that exists when the exchange rate is e_1 would be eliminated entirely if the exchange rate were to rise to e_0. Similarly, the surplus that exists at the exchange rate e_2 would be eliminated if the exchange rate were to fall to e_0.

The reason the balance on goods and services varies as the exchange rate varies is straightforward. An *increase* in the exchange rate affects both the quantity demanded and the quantity

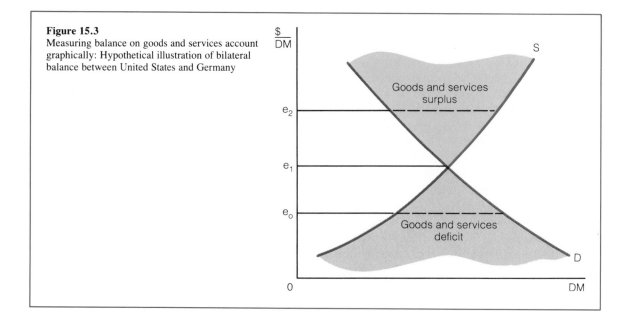

Figure 15.3
Measuring balance on goods and services account graphically: Hypothetical illustration of bilateral balance between United States and Germany

supplied of foreign exchange as follows: By *raising the dollar price of foreign produced goods and services,* a reduction in the quantity of foreign exchange demanded is induced; and by *lowering the foreign currency price of American goods,* an increase in the quantity of foreign exchange supplied is induced. If we define the balance on goods and services account (B) as the difference between our exports (E) and imports (M) of goods and services—i.e., $B = E - M$—it follows that B is positively related to the exchange rate: The higher the exchange rate, the larger positive or the smaller negative our balance on goods and services account will be.

A definitional aside. For our purposes we have defined the *exchange rate* as the dollar price of foreign exchange. An *increase* in the exchange rate, by raising the dollar price of foreign currency, is the same as the dollar *depreciating* in value on foreign exchange markets. This is because foreign currencies are worth more in terms of dollars and the dollar is worth less relative to those currencies. In the popular press, a depreciation of the dollar is referred to as a *decline* of the dollar. This decline is measured, using our definition, by an *increase* in the exchange rate. Dollar appreciation—or a rise in the dollar—is measured by a *decrease* in the exchange rate.

The overall balance on goods and services account

In the previous example, we discussed only our bilateral balance on goods and services account—i.e., the balance associated with our trade with one country, Germany. In order to obtain our overall balance, it is necessary to add together the bilateral balances of all the countries we trade with—Canada, Britain, France, Japan, Korea, etc. Moreover, just as our bilateral balance with Germany is affected by movements in the dollar–DM exchange rate, our bilateral balance with each of our trading partners will similarly be affected by changes in the bilateral exchange rates of those countries—by the American dollar–Canadian dollar exchange rate, the dollar–pound sterling exchange rate, and so on.

The overall balance on current account

As noted earlier, the balance on current account can be obtained by summing the balance on goods and services account and the balance on unilateral transfers account. In order to obtain the demand for foreign exchange associated with our *current account* transactions with Germany, we would add to the demand for DMs on goods and services account the demand arising out of "gifts" made by U.S. residents to German residents. Likewise, by adding to the supply of DMs on goods and services account the supply arising out of "gifts" made by German residents to U.S. residents, we obtain the supply associated with our current account transactions with Germany. The difference between the demand for and supply of DMs on current account yields our bilateral current account balance with Germany. The overall current account balance is obtained by summing up the bilateral current account balances of each of our trading partners.

Capital account transactions

Up to this point we have avoided any reference to an equilibrium exchange rate. Although this might surprise you, the equilibrium exchange rate *cannot* be found at the point of intersection of the demand and supply curves presented earlier. The reason for this is that the demand and supply curves illustrated before represent only *part* of the inpayments and outpayments associated with our financial transactions with the rest of the world. The intersection of these partial demand and supply curves does not provide us with the equilibrium exchange rate. Their intersection merely tells us what the exchange rate would have to be in order to have balance within one subaccount of our balance of payments. To determine the equilibrium exchange rate, we need to know the *total* demand for and supply of foreign exchange. We need, that is, to add the demand and supply arising out of capital account transactions.

In order to accomplish this, we need to settle one important question: Does the amount of foreign investment U.S. residents make, or the amount made by foreign residents in this country, depend on the exchange rate level? In general, the answer to this question is no. That is, the amount of foreign investment will not depend on whether the dollar–DM exchange rate is 40 cents or 80 cents. This can be seen easily on the basis of the following simple numerical example.

How much American residents are willing to invest in Germany (and, correspondingly, the amount German residents are willing to invest here) will depend on the difference in the relative yields of U.S. and German financial assets. Suppose the interest rate in the United States happens to be 5 percent, whereas in Germany it is 10 percent. Suppose further that the exchange rate is equal to 50 cents (i.e., $1 = DM2.0). Consider now an American resident who has $1,000 to invest. If the $1,000 is put into a U.S. security, it will yield at year's end $50 in interest (i.e., $1,000 × 0.05 = $50). If the $1,000 is put into a German security it will yield at year's end $100. This can be seen as follows: The $1,000 can be used to acquire DM2,000; at 10 percent interest, that DM2,000 will yield at year's end DM200; converting DM2,200 back into dollars at an exchange rate of 50 cents gives $1,100—$100 more than initially.

Suppose the exchange rate had been different. Would that have affected the yield to the American resident who invested in a German security? No. If the exchange rate had been 20 cents, the $1,000 would have bought DM5,000; at 10 percent interest, that DM5,000 will yield at year's end DM500; converting DM5,500 back into dollars at an exchange rate of 20 cents gives $1,100—$100 more than initially.

It is clear then that the actual value of the exchange rate does not affect in any way the relative yield on foreign and domestic financial assets. How much foreign investment will be undertaken by residents of the respective countries, therefore, will not depend on the exchange rate.

However, it is important to note that, whereas the actual value of the exchange rate does not matter, the relative yields on foreign and domestic assets *will change if the exchange rate changes* between the time when a foreign investment is undertaken and the time when the proceeds are converted back into domestic currency units. The following example illustrates this clearly.

Suppose at the time of the investment the exchange happens to be 0.50. The $1,000 will buy DM2,000, which, at 10 percent interest, will grow to DM2,200 in one year. Suppose, however, that in the interim the exchange rate fell from 0.50 to 0.40; suppose, that is, that the dollar appreciated in value (and the DM depreciated in value) in the interim. DM2,200 would now convert to only $880 (i.e., 2,200 × 0.40 = 880); the American resident would then realize a *loss* of $120. On the other hand, if the exchange rate had gone up from 0.50 to 0.60 (a dollar depreciation), DM2,200 would have converted to $1,320 (i.e., 2,200 × 0.60 = 1,320) yielding a net gain of $320.

In the examples just cited, we saw that when the dollar appreciated in value—when the exchange rate fell from 0.50 to 0.40—the American resident actually suffered a 12 percent loss on a foreign investment of $1,000; when the dollar depreciated, the American resident actually made a 32 percent return.[3] Thus, *changes* in the exchange rate do affect the relative yields on domestic and foreign financial investments. *Obviously, the yield on a foreign financial asset will*

---

[3] The following formula can be used to calculate the percentage return on a foreign investment: Percent return = $i_f + \left[\frac{\Delta e}{e} \times (1 + i_f) \right]$, where i_f is the foreign interest rate and e is domestic price of the foreign currency. Take the case where $i_f = 0.10$ and the dollar depreciates in value by 20 percent (i.e., the exchange rate rises from 0.50 to 0.60, a 20 percent increase). Using the formula, this implies a 32 percent return on a foreign investment abroad—$0.32 = 0.10 + [0.20 \times (1 + 0.10)] = 0.10 + 0.22$. If the dollar appreciates in value by 20 percent (i.e., the exchange rate *falls* from 0.50 to 0.40), there will be a 12 percent loss on a foreign investment abroad: $-0.12 = 0.10 - [0.20 \times (1 + 0.10)] = 0.10 - 0.22$.

Note also that if the exchange rate does not *change*—i.e., $\frac{\Delta e}{e} = 0$—the percent return is simply the foreign interest rate. This confirms the point made earlier that the return is independent of the exchange rate.

rise relative to the yield on a domestic financial asset if the domestic currency depreciates in value between the time the foreign investment is made and the time the proceeds are converted; the relative yield on a foreign financial asset will fall if the domestic currency appreciates in the interim.

Of course, at the time investors make their decisions, they cannot be absolutely sure how the exchange rate will change in the future. Nevertheless, their *expectations* of future exchange rate changes are an important consideration. If investors expect the domestic currency to depreciate in value in foreign exchange markets, this has the effect of raising the expected yield on foreign investments. If the dollar is expected to decline, this makes foreign financial assets more attractive to U.S. investors and U.S. assets less attractive to foreign investors. Such expectations can be an important source of capital flight from the United States. An expected appreciation of the domestic currency, on the other hand, can be an important force attracting capital from abroad.

Adding capital flows to the demand for and supply of foreign exchange

It is useful to divide capital flows into two distinct types—*private* and *foreign official.* Private capital flows are motivated by profit. Foreign official capital flows are made for the purpose of influencing the exchange rate. Let us focus our attention first on private capital flows. We will add foreign official capital flows later.

Private capital inflows and outflows. Large numbers of private U.S. residents, corporations, and banks hold in their portfolios all sorts of domestic and foreign financial assets. Continuously, they are confronted with the problem of determining how much of their portfolios they should hold in foreign as opposed to domestic assets. Presumably, their objective is to obtain a mix of foreign and domestic assets that yields as high an **expected return** as possible given risk and liquidity considerations. All sorts of complex factors influence these decisions.

Investors will be influenced by the interest rates prevailing in home markets compared with interest rates abroad. They will be influenced as well by the relative risks of holding domestic versus foreign securities. These risks include, among other things, unexpected changes in exchange rates (which will affect the returns investors will realize on foreign securities), unexpected changes in interest rates (which, given the inverse relationship between bond prices and interest rates, will influence the returns investors will realize if they sell bonds prior to maturity), and possible restrictions imposed by foreign governments on the repatriation of earnings.

The international flows of capital generated on the basis of these considerations can be captured easily graphically. This is illustrated in Figure 15.4. Since the amount of foreign investment undertaken by both domestic residents and foreign residents is independent of the exchange rate—i.e., the same whether the exchange rate is e_2 or e_1 or any other value—we can simply add to the amount of DM demanded for the purpose of purchasing German goods and services the amount of DM demanded by U.S. residents for the purpose of acquiring German securities. Likewise, we can add to the amount of DM supplied (to acquire U.S. dollars) to purchase U.S. goods and services the amount supplied by German residents for their purchases of U.S. securities.

In Figure 15.4, the curve labeled D represents the demand for DMs for the purchase of German goods and services; D_T represents the total private demand for DMs—the demand arising out of the demand for goods and services plus the demand for DMs for the purchase of German securities; the horizontal distance between D and D_T at each exchange rate gives the amount of DM demanded to purchase German securities. Similarly, the curve labeled S represents the supply of DMs for the purchase of U.S. goods and services by German residents; S_T represents the total private supply of DMs—the supply arising out of the German demand for U.S. goods and services plus the supply of DMs for the purchase of U.S. securities; the horizontal distance between S and S_T at each exchange rate gives the amount of DMs supplied to purchase U.S. securities.

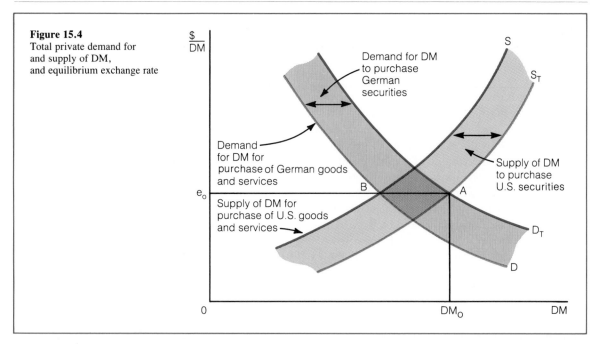

Figure 15.4
Total private demand for
and supply of DM,
and equilibrium exchange rate

The total demand for DMs, D_T, measures the total outpayments by U.S. private residents to German residents at each exchange rate. S_T, on the other hand, measures the total inpayments to U.S. residents by German private residents at each exchange rate.

At the point of intersection of D_T and S_T there exists balance-of-payments equilibrium with Germany—outpayments by U.S. residents (to German residents) equals inpayments to U.S. residents (by German residents). The exchange rate, e_o, therefore, is defined as the equilibrium exchange rate. For simplicity, we have assumed in Figure 15.4 that, at the exchange rate, e_o, there is equilibrium in the goods and services subaccount—outpayments for German goods and services equal inpayments from German residents for U.S. goods and services.

However, there is no necessary reason why an exchange rate that yields balance in our overall balance of payments should also yield balance in the goods and services subaccount. Indeed, one could have a surplus (or deficit) on the goods and services subaccount offset by a deficit (or surplus) of the same size on capital account.

These possibilities are illustrated in Figures 15.5A and 15.5B.

We see in Figure 15.5A that overall balance occurs at the exchange rate e_o. At that exchange rate, however, there is a surplus on the goods and services subaccount equal to EC—the difference between the inpayments (S) and outpayments (D) for goods and services. The deficit on the capital subaccount is also equal to EC: Outpayments on capital account equal EA (the horizontal difference between D and D_T), while inpayments on capital account amount to CA (the horizontal difference between S and S_T), the difference between inpayments and outpayments on the capital subaccount amounting to EC. In like manner, we see in Figure 15.5B that, at the equilibrium exchange rate e_o, the deficit on the goods and services subaccount of GF is equal to the surplus on the capital subaccount.

Foreign official capital inflows and outflows. We need to take into account now the capital flows generated by foreign official financial institutions. The distinction between private and foreign official capital flows is important because each is motivated by different consider-

Figure 15.5
Overall balance-of-payments equilibrium with offsetting imbalances in goods and services, and capital, subaccounts

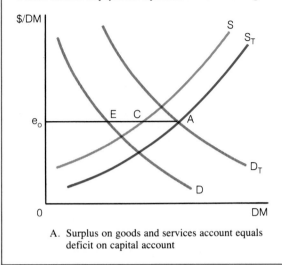

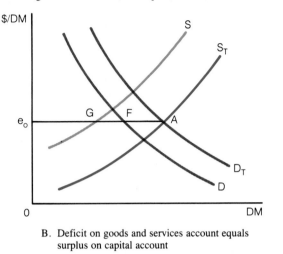

A. Surplus on goods and services account equals
   deficit on capital account

B. Deficit on goods and services account equals
   surplus on capital account

ations. Private capital flows are motivated by the returns investors expect to receive. Foreign official capital flows are motivated by a desire to influence the exchange rate itself.

To take an extreme example, let us suppose that governments here and abroad have agreed to buy or sell whatever amounts of foreign exchange are required to keep exchange rates fixed.

How this is accomplished is illustrated in Figure 15.6.

Assume to begin with that domestic and foreign governments have agreed to fix the exchange rate at e_0, the point of intersection of D_T and S_T. Under a regime of fixed exchange rates, the governmentally agreed upon rate of exchange is referred to as the **parity rate.** At the moment,

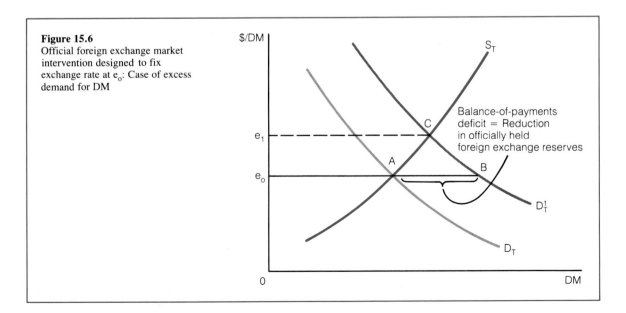

Figure 15.6
Official foreign exchange market
intervention designed to fix
exchange rate at e_o: Case of excess
demand for DM

Balance-of-payments
deficit = Reduction
in officially held
foreign exchange reserves

the fact that D_T equals S_T at the parity rate means the governments need do nothing to maintain the exchange rate at e_0.

Now suppose the demand for DMs increases, shifting the demand curve from D_T to D_T^1. Several factors could have been responsible for this increase in demand: a sharp increase in U.S. demand for German goods and services, the result, say, of an increase in U.S. incomes; an increase in the prices of U.S. goods relative to prices in Germany; tight money policies by German monetary authorities that raise German interest rates relative to U.S. rates of interest, making German financial assets relatively more attractive.

In the absence of any government commitment to fix the exchange rate at some level, the exchange rate would tend to rise to e_1—that is, the excess demand at e_0 (equal to the distance AB) would cause the dollar to depreciate in value relative to the DM. At e_1, the demand for and the supply of DMs are once again equal to one another implying balance-of-payments equilibrium. However, because of a government commitment to keep the exchange rate fixed at e_0, the German and U.S. governments are obligated to undertake actions designed to arrest the depreciation of the dollar.

At least two distinct kinds of actions may be undertaken by the U.S. and German governments. First, they could impose controls over the purchase and sale of foreign exchange. The United States, for example, could impose limits on the purchase of DMs by U.S. residents who wish to purchase German goods or German securities. This move would restrict the demand for DMs and forestall the depreciation of the dollar. Germany might loosen restrictions it has over its citizens' purchases of U.S. goods and securities. This would effectively expand the supply of DMs, thereby holding down the exchange rate.

Assuming there are no changes in restrictions governing the purchase and sale of foreign exchange, if any restrictions existed, there is a second avenue that can be used to hold the exchange rate at e_0—**foreign exchange market intervention.** Under this approach, either or both governments can step in to increase the supply of DMs to

wipe out the excess demand that exists at the exchange rate e_0. The U.S. authorities could sell some of the DMs they hold as part of their **foreign exchange reserves,** buying up dollars in return.[4] The German authorities, on the other hand, could add to their foreign exchange reserves by buying up dollars and selling DMs. In either case, the effect of the intervention is to cause the supply of DMs to increase; to keep the exchange rate fixed at e_0, official DM sales would have to equal the gap, AB, in Figure 15.6.

The effects of these intervention operations designed to hold the exchange at e_0 show up in our balance-of-payments accounts (and in those of Germany) as *changes in official reserve assets.* (The magnitude of such operations during 1980 for the United States and other countries is given at the bottom of Table 15.1. If the intervention takes the form of U.S. sales of DMs, this will show up as a *decrease* in U.S. official reserve assets (the reverse of a capital outflow); if the intervention takes the form of German purchases of U.S. dollars, it will show up as an increase in foreign official reserve assets (a capital inflow).

At the exchange rate e_0 in Figure 15.6, the United States will record a balance-of-payments deficit, the magnitude of which is given by the distance AB. In the technical jargon of economists, the deficit is *financed* by the reduction in U.S. reserve assets or the increase in foreign reserve assets.

In the event the dollar has a tendency to appreciate in value, foreign exchange intervention will be opposite to that described above. Consider Figure 15.7. The parity rate is assumed to be

---

[4] Because the United States does not own a great deal of foreign exchange, it acquires much of what it needs to conduct its intervention operations through **swap agreements.** A swap agreement is an arrangement between central banks where, for example, the Federal Reserve is given a line of credit with the German central bank (the Bundesbank), setting up a reciprocal line of credit in the United States. If the United States decides to intervene, it activates the swap (i.e., borrows DMs from the Bundesbank), using the loan proceeds to buy up dollars in the foreign exchange market.

Another popular method of acquiring foreign exchange is through the issuance of **foreign currency denominated bonds** for sale in, say, Germany; the DM receipts are then available to the U.S. authorities to support their intervention operations.

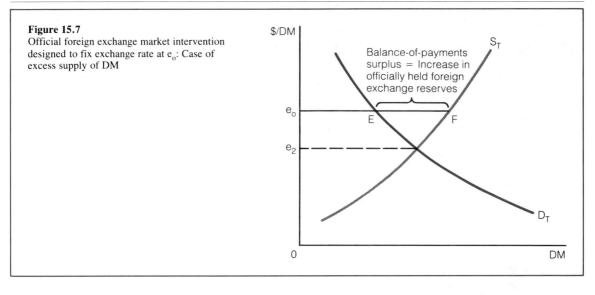

Figure 15.7
Official foreign exchange market intervention designed to fix exchange rate at e_o: Case of excess supply of DM

e_o. Given D_T and S_T, it is apparent that an excess supply of DMs exists at e_o. In the absence of any actions designed to arrest changes in the exchange rate, the exchange rate would fall to e_2—i.e., the dollar would appreciate in value relative to the DM.

Foreign exchange market intervention—the U.S. authorities adding to their holdings of DMs by selling dollars, or the German authorities selling off their holdings of dollars to buy DMs—could keep the exchange rate fixed at e_o. In this instance, the balance of payments will remain in surplus (equal to EF) at the exchange rate e_o.

FIXED VERSUS FLOATING EXCHANGE RATES: SOME OF THE ISSUES

We are now in a position to examine in detail some of the issues in the continuing debate over fixed versus floating exchange rates. The debate is important because the adoption of one or the other regime has significant implications for the conduct of macroeconomic policy and for the overall performance of the economy.

Defining fixed and floating exchange rates

Unfortunately, it is not easy to define the features of fixed and floating exchange rate systems

unambiguously. Under a **system of irrevocably fixed rates,** participating countries usually adopt rules to intervene—to buy or sell foreign currencies—whenever exchange rates have a tendency to depart from agreed-upon parity rates of exchange and to continue to buy or sell in amounts sufficient to ensure that such parity rates remain fixed. Under a **system of cleanly floating rates,** countries agree not to intervene—i.e., to let exchange rates be determined by the market forces of demand supply.

Using these two systems as polar extremes, it is possible to define various in-between exchange rate systems. Some systems permit exchange rates to float freely within a narrow band above and below agreed-upon parity rates; the foreign exchange intervention rules come into play once exchange rates reach those upper or lower limits. Under the **Bretton-Woods system**—the dominant exchange rate regime from the end of World War II to around 1971—exchange rates were allowed to fluctuate freely within a band 1 percent above or below parity rates; the **European Monetary System**—a regional payments system within the European Economic Community—has a permissible band of fluctuation of 2½ percent on either side of the parity rates for participating countries. Another kind of regime—variously described as **managed floating** or **dirty floating**—has no carefully defined intervention rules. Sometimes a group of countries reach a collective judgment that exchange rates have moved by "too much" or "too rapidly," sparking intervention to reverse the movement (partly or completely) or slow the movement down. Sometimes exchange rates will move a great deal with little or no intervention, whereas at other times even small movements will bring forth a sharp interventionist response. In short, a managed floating system can range the whole spectrum from near-clean to near-irrevocably fixed. Since the early 1970s the world economy has been on a managed floating system.

However, foreign exchange intervention is only one of the criteria that should be used to define an exchange rate system. Even if governments do *not* intervene in foreign exchange markets in order to influence exchange rates—a circumstance that would lead many to conclude that the system was cleanly floating—governments are still able to affect exchange rates by other policies.

To illustrate, if governments impose controls of one sort or another on the purchase or sale of foreign exchange by home residents, they can thereby influence the demand for and supply of foreign exchange and therewith exchange rates. Tariffs, quotas, and other nontariff barriers can influence exchange rates by affecting the demand for and supply of foreign exchange. **Capital controls**—for example, rules governing the foreign investments home residents can make and rules restricting the nature and magnitude of investments in the home country by foreigners—can also affect exchange rates by affecting the demand for and supply of foreign exchange. In other words, controls and trade barriers can accomplish, perhaps more effectively, what foreign exchange market intervention might be aimed to accomplish.

In addition, exchange rates can be influenced by monetary and fiscal policies. Expansionary monetary and fiscal policies pursued by country A that raise country A's real income relative to incomes abroad or that raise country A's prices relative to prices abroad will tend to raise country A's demand for foreign exchange and cause country A's currency to depreciate in value relative

to foreign currencies. In this manner, monetary and fiscal policy initiatives enable countries to exert some degree of control over the movement of exchange rates.

Maintaining fixed exchange rates: The need for coordinated macroeconomic policies

Foreign exchange market intervention is a tool of only limited usefulness in maintaining fixed rates of exchange. The reason? Countries are either unwilling or unable to intervene for an indefinite time period. Consider the case of a country that runs a persistent balance-of-payments deficit. What this means is that, at the parity rate of exchange, the demand for foreign exchange persistently exceeds the supply of foreign exchange. In order to keep the exchange rate at parity, the deficit country must continuously sell foreign exchange. It is impossible to do this indefinitely; the amount of foreign exchange at the disposal of the deficit country is limited, that amount depending on the amount of reserves the country holds plus whatever amounts can be borrowed. Alternatively, exchange rates could remain fixed indefinitely if *surplus* countries were willing to continuously build up their foreign exchange reserves. The surplus countries are likely to be reluctant to do this since it would require that they be willing to continuously finance other countries' balance-of-payments deficits.

There is also another reason the surplus countries would be willing to increase their reserves for a limited time only. Increasing their foreign exchange reserves results in an increase in the reserves of their depository institutions, a reserve increase that can be used to support an expansion of surplus country money supplies. This is easily explained. Suppose the German monetary authorities intervene in the foreign exchange market, puchasing dollars to arrest the tendency of the dollar to depreciate relative to the DM (or, alternatively, to arrest the appreciation of the DM). Suppose they purchase the dollars from German commercial banks. They pay for the dollars purchased by increasing the DM reserves of the German commercial banks. The expansion of bank reserves enables the German commercial banks to increase their loans and investments, resulting in an expansion of the German money supply, an outcome that could be inconsistent with the monetary policies the German monetary authorities want to pursue.

Given the limitations on the use of intervention as the means of maintaining fixed exchange rates, at some point either the deficit or the surplus countries, or both, will have to undertake other policy actions designed to shift the demand for or supply of foreign exchange. Put simply, other policy actions are required to shift the demand and supply curves so they intersect once again at the exchange rate corresponding to the agreed-upon parity rate. In short, other policies are needed to restore balance-of-payments equilibrium.

One possibility would be for the surplus or deficit countries, or both, to change their monetary and fiscal policies in ways that are consistent with balance-of-payments equilibrium. If the deficit countries pursue contractionary macroeconomic policies, the demand for foreign exchange will be reduced, which in turn reduces the balance-of-payments deficit at the parity rate. This is illustrated in Figure 15.8A; the reduction in aggregate demand occasioned by contractionary macroeconomic policies lowers the demand for foreign exchange, shifting the demand curve from D_T to D_T^1, restoring balance-of-payments equilibrium at e_0.

In Figure 15.8B we illustrate how the balance-of-payments deficit can be eliminated through the use of expansionary macroeconomic policies pursued by the surplus country. In this instance, the increase in aggregate demand in the surplus country raises the demand for dollars, which increases the supply of DMs (to pay for the dollars), restoring balance-of-payments equilibrium.

Although macroeconomic policies can be adjusted to bring about balance-of-payments equilibrium, it must be emphasized that countries are often very reluctant to change their monetary and fiscal policies for this purpose. Consider a country that is suffering both a balance-of-payments deficit and a less-than-full employment level of output. To achieve its domestic objective of full employment would require expansionary

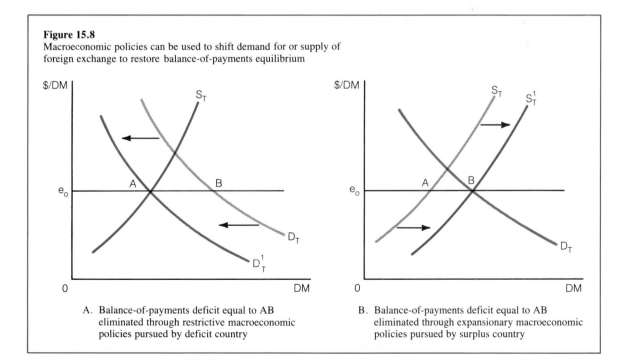

Figure 15.8
Macroeconomic policies can be used to shift demand for or supply of foreign exchange to restore balance-of-payments equilibrium

A. Balance-of-payments deficit equal to AB eliminated through restrictive macroeconomic policies pursued by deficit country

B. Balance-of-payments deficit equal to AB eliminated through expansionary macroeconomic policies pursued by surplus country

macroeconomic policies. But this is just the opposite of what would be required for balance-of-payments equilibrium at the agreed-upon parity rate. Or consider a surplus country that is suffering from inflation that is demand-pull induced. To slow inflation would require contractionary macroeconomic policies. But this is just the opposite of what would be required for balance-of-payments equilibrium.

In the face of such goal conflicts, countries are very reluctant to abandon domestic economic policy objectives in order to achieve the goal of balance-of-payments equilibrium. They often retain their domestic policy goals and the policies to support those goals, using, as long as is "reasonable," foreign exchange market intervention to arrest changes in the exchange rate. If the international payments imbalances persist, they will then frequently resort to controls as the means of restoring balance-of-payments equilibrium. The incentive to use controls is strong given the high priorities they each attach to the achievement of domestic goals.

The policy dilemma facing countries under fixed rates of exchange quickly becomes apparent. Intervention is of limited usefulness. It is satisfactory for the financing of temporary international payments deficits, but not indefinitely. Controls, while perhaps attractive, destroy the advantages that accrue to countries by having capital and goods move freely across international borders. And controls imposed by one country frequently invite the institution of controls by other countries in retaliation. That leaves us, then, with the question of how best to conduct macroeconomic policies under fixed rates of exchange.

We have seen before that the macroeconomic policies pursued by the various countries affect both the demand for and supply of foreign exchange. In order to maintain fixed exchange rates over the long run without resorting to the use of destructive controls or trade barriers, countries need to pursue macroeconomic policies that are *coordinated*—coordinated to ensure that the demand for foreign exchange equals the supply of foreign exchange at agreed-upon parity rates.

To accomplish the desired degree of coordination is easier said than done, however. Indeed, the failure of the Bretton-Woods system of *fixed-but-adjustable* par values in the early part of the 1970s was in large measure the result of the absence of effective international coordination. Under the Bretton-Woods system, which was started in 1944, the value of the U.S. dollar was fixed in terms of gold and the values of all other currencies were fixed in terms of the U.S. dollar. In order to keep exchange rates fixed, countries agreed to follow certain rules. The United States stood ready to convert gold for dollars at a fixed price; all other countries stood ready to buy or sell their own currencies at fixed dollar prices whenever market forces were pushing exchange rates up or down. This was the "fixed" part of the Bretton-Woods system.

Countries also agreed to change their exchange rates—i.e., to realign the foreign exchange value of their currencies—in case of "fundamental disequilibrium." This was the "adjustable" part of the Bretton-Woods system. The meaning of "fundamental disequilibrium" was never precisely defined, but was frequently interpreted to mean the existence of *persistent* international payments deficits or surpluses. However, as the Bretton-Woods system evolved, it became apparent that the world's nations frowned on frequent exchange rate adjustments. The emphasis was on the fixed, not the adjustable, part of the system. Exchange rate realignments were to be used only in response to a crisis, and only when all else failed.

During the first 20 years or so of Bretton-Woods there were remarkably few exchange rate alignments. In large part, this was caused by the fact that underlying world economic conditions over much of that period were stable enough that repeated exchange rate adjustments were not called for. In other words, macroeconomic policies and performances internationally were fairly effectively coordinated. However, they were not coordinated intentionally, in the sense of national governments reaching agreement on what constituted the best policies collectively. For the most part, effective coordination was accomplished quite by accident. That coordination was largely accidental is borne out by events in the late 1960s and early 1970s, when underlying world economic conditions became less stable. Most of the major industrialized countries responded to their growth-inflation-employment problems by pursuing policies they felt were in their own national interest. The effective macroeconomic coordination that had existed earlier began to come apart and significant exchange rate realignments took place with increasing frequency. Given the crisis atmosphere that surrounded each exchange rate parity change, the Bretton-Woods system became strained and finally gave way to a more flexible payments system.

Bretton-Woods collapsed sometime during the early 1970s. It is difficult to pin down the precise date of its collapse since between 1971 and 1973 the world economy vacillated between systems of floating rates and fixed rates of exchange. The suspension of gold convertibility by the United States on August 15, 1971, constituted the first official step toward abandoning Bretton-Woods. This was followed by a brief period of floating, which was followed in turn by the reinstitution of fixed rates in 1972. However, pressure to abandon support of fixed rates became overwhelming early in 1973 and the Bretton-Woods system died. Since that time, managed floating in one form or another has been a persistent characteristic of the international payments system.

It is not surprising that it was difficult to obtain the coordination necessary to ensure fixed exchange rates under Bretton-Woods. Nations have never shown enough enthusiasm for fixed rates of exchange to be willing to abandon domestic policy objectives to help to keep exchange rates fixed; domestic policy almost always received top billing, and understandably so. For the first 20 years or so under Bretton-Woods, the policy conflicts between domestic goals and fixed rates of exchange did not become evident. When they did, in the late 1960s and early 1970s, fixed rates were the first to go.

If all countries were identical, the prospects for the international coordination of economic policies would probably be quite good. But all countries are not alike. They differ not only in their growth, inflation, and employment outcomes, but in their policy goal priorities. Each country would willingly agree to coordinate policies if such policies served to better promote its own national interests. However, it is unlikely that coordinated policies to fix exchange rates would serve every country's best interests. Unless each country views policy coordination as a plus in terms of enhancing its own objectives, it is unlikely to go along. Under the circumstances, the destruction of a fixed exchange rate system is all but inevitable.

Incentives to adopt floating rates of exchange

In the absence of effective coordination and in the face of persistent international payments imbalances, it is not difficult to discover why countries have an incentive to adopt a system of floating exchange rates as the world did in the early 1970s. The single most important advantage of floating is that the exchange rate will adjust by whatever amount is necessary to equate the demand for and supply of foreign exchange. This ensures balance-of-payments equilibrium whatever the macroeconomic policies that the various countries pursue. However, though balance-of-payments equilibrium may be achieved with floating rates, this system is not without its costs. Consider the consequences for the U.S. and German economies of a depreciating dollar (an appreciating DM).

First, a decline in the value of the dollar relative to the DM will tend to make U.S. goods and services relatively less expensive and therefore relatively more attractive. This has the effect of expanding U.S. exports and reducing German exports. Germany is likely to view the reduction in its relative competitiveness as a decidedly negative outcome, whereas the United States is likely to view its increased relative competitiveness positively. What is important to realize here is that changing exchange rates bring about resource shifts within the U.S. and German economies, shifts that are costly.

Second, the decline in the foreign exchange value of the dollar, by raising the prices of imports in the United States, tends to raise the U.S. inflation rate. In line with our discussion in Chapter 14, the change in the exchange rate can be viewed as similar to a "shock" increase in the price level. To the extent that the shock increase in the level of prices raises inflationary expectations, and to the further extent that those expectations are accommodated by expansionary macroeconomic policies, a permanently higher rate of inflation in the United States will result. It is understandable, therefore, why the U.S. authorities view with some alarm declines in the value of the dollar on world currency markets.

The depreciation of the dollar—the appreciation of the DM—serves, on the other hand, to slow inflation in Germany. The reduced price of German imports reduces Germany's general level of prices in a manner opposite to the increases registered in the United States.

The need for macroeconomic policy coordination under floating rates

It is hardly surprising to find both the United States and Germany being alarmed by dollar depreciation. Declines in the value of the dollar hurt Germany's export industries and add to U.S. inflationary pressures. There is interest, therefore, in adopting policies aimed at achieving exchange rate stability. Again, in order to stabilize those rates, countries could adopt—as they were obligated to adopt under fixed rates—a policy of foreign exchange market intervention. Or they could take the controls and trade restrictions route. However, given the disadvantages of both approaches, over the long run at least, we come back again to the central weapon—**macroeconomic policy coordination.** In other words, if the world's economies are anxious to achieve long-run exchange rate stability, they must choose coordinated policies that are consistent with stable exchange rates. The real problem—and one that is far from solved—is how policy coordination ought to be achieved.

SUMMARY

1. The home country's *balance of payments* is a summary statement of the financial transactions between residents of the home country and residents of all other countries during some specified period of time. There are several balance-of-payments subaccounts: the *trade balance,* the *balance on goods and services,* the *balance on unilateral transfers,* the *current account,* and *the capital account.*

2. The current account balance is important because it measures, for the designated accounting period, the net *change* in financial claims between the United States and foreigners. A current account deficit means that we have increased our indebtedness to (or reduced our claim on) foreign countries; a current account surplus means that foreigners have increased their indebtedness to us (or reduced their claims on us). By the nature of double-entry bookkeeping, the balance on *capital movements account* will be the same size, but of opposite sign, as the balance on current account.

3. What is important is *how* the balance of payments balances. It is useful to view changes in *official reserve assets* as a measure of the magnitude of the intervention operations undertaken by our government for the purpose of affecting exchange rates and balances on current and capital account.

4. There is an inverse *(ceteris paribus)* relationship between the exchange rate (defined as the domestic price of the foreign currency) and the quantity of foreign exchange demanded. Since an increase in the exchange rate raises the dollar price of foreign-produced goods and services, reducing the quantity demanded of those goods and services, there will be a corresponding reduction in the amount of foreign exchange demanded. An increase in the foreign currency price of the goods we import, or a decrease in U.S. income, will lower the demand for foreign exchange. The demand curve for foreign exchange will shift down and to the left.

4. There is a direct *(ceteris paribus)* relationship between the exchange rate and the quantity

of foreign exchange supplied. An increase in the exchange rate, by lowering the non-U.S. price of American goods, induces an increase in the quantity demanded of U.S. goods and a corresponding increase in the supply of foreign exchange. An increase in the *dollar* price of American-produced goods and services, or a reduction in non-U.S. incomes, will cause a reduction in the supply of foreign exchange. The supply curve of foreign exchange will shift up and to the left.

5. The amount of foreign investment U.S. residents make, as well as the amount made by foreign residents in this country, does not depend on the exchange rate. However, *expectations* of future exchange rate changes are important to both foreign and domestic investors. If investors expect the domestic currency to depreciate in value, the expected yield on foreign investments will rise, making foreign financial assets relatively more attractive to both U.S. and non-U.S. investors.

6. *Balance-of-payments equilibrium* can be defined by the point of intersection of D_T and S_T, D_T being the demand for foreign exchange for U.S. current account transactions plus the *private* demand for foreign exchange for the purchase of foreign financial assets, and S_T being the supply of foreign exchange associated with U.S. current account transactions plus the *private* supply of foreign exchange for the purchase of U.S. securities. In equilibrium, the current account balance is equal to, but of opposite sign from, the capital account balance.

7. Foreign exchange market intervention takes the form of U.S. or foreign government purchases or sales of foreign exchange for the purpose of effecting exchange rate values different from those that would otherwise have prevailed.

8. It is difficult to define exchange rate systems unambiguously. Using foreign exchange market intervention as the distinguishing feature, one can define two polar extreme systems—*cleanly floating* and *irrevocably fixed*—and all kinds of systems in between—which, in general, one can describe as *managed*. However, because trade barriers, capital controls, and general macroeconomic policies can all affect exchange rates by affecting the demand for and supply of foreign exchange, defining exchange rate systems on the basis of whether or not, and to what extent, governments intervene is too narrow.

9. Foreign exchange market intervention is of only limited usefulness. It is satisfactory for the financing of temporary international payments deficits, but not indefinitely. Controls destroy the advantages of the free movement of goods and capital across international borders, and they invite retaliatory actions on the part of foreign governments. To achieve greater stability in exchange rates, it is necessary for the world's nations to pursue *coordinated* macroeconomic policies.

CONCEPTS FOR REVIEW

Balance of payments

Inpayments

Outpayments

Balance of trade

Balance on goods and services

Balance on current account

Invisibles

Unilateral transfers

Official reserve assets

Official foreign exchange market intervention

Foreign exchange market

Exchange rate

Parity rate

Foreign exchange reserves

Appreciation

Depreciation

Swap agreements

Foreign currency denominated bonds

System of irrevocably fixed exchange rates

System of cleanly floating exchange rates

Bretton-Woods system of fixed-but-adjustable par values

Managed (or dirty) floating

Fundamental disequilibrium

Macroeconomic policy coordination

QUESTIONS FOR DISCUSSION

(Those marked with an asterisk (*) are more difficult.)

*1.   Some economists prefer to define the exchange rate as the foreign price of the domestic currency, rather than as the domestic price of the foreign currency. Accordingly, on their demand and supply diagrams they would measure, for example, DM/$ on the vertical axis, $ on the horizontal axis.

   a.   Adopting that approach rather than the one used in this chapter, explain why there is an inverse relationship between dollars demanded and the exchange rate. Why is there a positive relationship between the quantity of dollars supplied and the exchange rate? (*Hint:* Remember who is buying dollars and selling DMs!)

   b.   Is it true that a decline in the foreign exchange value of the dollar will now be seen as a reduction in the exchange rate? Why?

   c.   Show, using either definition, that an increase in demand for U.S. goods on the part of German residents will cause the U.S. dollar to appreciate under a system of floating exchange rates.

2.   Assuming a system of cleanly floating exchange rates, illustrate the effect of each of the following on the dollar price of foreign currencies. Explain your reasoning carefully.

   a.   The growth of U.S. real GNP slows relative to the growth of real GNP abroad. (Assume in this question that the growth of imports in each country is directly related to the growth of real GNP.)

   b.   The U.S. inflation rate increases relative to inflation rates abroad.

What general conclusions can you draw from these two phenomena?

3.   Explain why a depreciation of the U.S. dollar adds to U.S. inflation.

*4.   Carefully evaluate the following statement: "If the U.S. balance-of-trade deficit increases, the dollar will decline and U.S. inflation will worsen." (*Hint:* Is this a *ceteris paribus* change?)

5.   It is sometimes argued that many foreign countries like to see the dollar fall because that helps their inflation rate, but they hate to see it fall because that harms their export industries. Explain the reasoning behind this view.

6.   Carefully evaluate: "If the countries of the world desire exchange rate stability, then it is essential that there be macroeconomic policy coordination internationally in order to ensure coordinated macroeconomic performances."

In awarding its fourth Nobel Prize in Economics (1972) to Sir John Hicks (a Briton) and Kenneth Arrow (an American), the Swedish Academy bestowed its highest honor on two economists who have played key roles in shaping the theoretical foundations of the science of economics. The highly abstract, mathematical, and esoteric works for which they were cited by the academy—specifically, "their contributions to general economic equilibrium theory"—are not well known outside the economics profession. Nevertheless, little is written by economists today that does not bear, if only indirectly, the imprint of the writings of these two men. Indeed, many of their ideals have become so much a part of the fabric of economic science that, to today's generation of graduating economists, they are conventional wisdom.

Sir John R. Hicks (1904–)

The method of partial equilibrium analysis dominated the study of the determination of market prices prior to the publication in 1939 of *Value and Capital*, a major work by John R. Hicks. In the partial equilibrium approach, each market is examined in isolation from all the rest; the links among markets are ignored. Hicks was the first to establish the general equilibrium properties of the economic market system, explicitly taking into account the interrelationships among markets. His findings were dramatic: Although the method of partial equilibrium permits definite conclusions about the impact of changes in demand and supply on market prices, those conclusions may prove faulty once the complex interrelationships among markets in an economic system are taken into account.

With hundreds and thousands of markets linked together interdependently, anything is possible—including the possibility of potato prices rising with the harvesting of a bumper crop. By showing what could and could not be predicted in a general equilibrium economic system, Hicks set the stage for revolution in economic research that continues to this day.

Sir John Hicks has also made important contributions to monetary theory, business-cycle theory, the theory of public finance, and development economics. Knighted in 1964, Hicks is a quiet, well-read man who is "not the easiest . . . to communicate with . . . a lone wolf in his thinking."

Kenneth J. Arrow (1921–)

Although cited by the Royal Swedish Academy for his work in general equilibrium theory and welfare theory, many regard Kenneth Arrow's Impossibility Theorem as his greatest achievement. Applying some "fairly elementary math" (which very few understand thoroughly) to a problem that even Aristotle and Hobbes grappled with—the discovery of the perfect voting system that would result in an ideal democracy—Arrow proved once and for all that such a perfect voting system is impossible to find. There can never be an "ideal form of democracy"; it is a self-contradiction in logic.

Less well known, but no less significant, was Arrow's path-breaking theory of risk that left its permanent mark on the economics of insurance, medical care, and the stock market. Although the work that the Swedish Academy cited is highly abstract and mathematical, Arrow's analyses and theorems were designed to be applied to such social problems as medical care, education, and racial and sex discrimination.

PART THREE

Microeconomics of consumer and business behavior: Price and output determination in product markets

Wide World Photos   *United Press International*

A Harvard professor since 1968, Arrow is noted for his rapid speech, his tendency to wear bright clothing, his general availability to students, and the pleasure he still derives from teaching even introductory economics.

Herbert A. Simon (1916–   )

The 1978 Nobel Prize in Economics was presented to a man whose work stands outside the mainstream of economic thought. Herbert Simon, a professor of psychology and computer science at Carnegie-Mellon University was cited by the Swedish Academy for "his pioneering research into the decision-making process within economic organizations."

Simon's study of business organizations led him to attack the classical economic assumption of profit maximization. According to Simon, this assumption is unrealistic, for people do not have the ability to obtain, let alone process, all the information required to make profit maximizing decisions. Rational decisionmaking is more "bounded"—i.e., people have only limited abilities to make comparisons, to see into the future, and to process data. Administrators are better described as "satisficers" rather than "maximizers" and, according to Simon, it makes sense in an uncertain world for the decisionmaking unit to set goals and to develop appropriate strategies for their realization.

Described by one colleague as "the one man in the world who has come closest to being a Renaissance man," and by another as "one of the few geniuses in the social sciences," Simon has taught courses in psychology, computer science, economics, and even an undergraduate course on the history of the French Revolution.

Simon has also been a pioneer in the development of "artificial intelligence" through computer technology—the development of soft-ware programs capable of solving problems in a "humanoid" fashion. His major current research interest is cognitive psychology.

A thorough familiarity with the concepts of demand and supply is a critical first step toward an understanding of how society allocates its scarce economic resources among alternative uses. A few of the basic ideas were developed at length in Chapter 3. It is the purpose of this chapter to extend our understanding of these concepts and to demonstrate how these analytical tools can provide us with insight into a number of highly significant economic problems.

In the first section of this chapter, the basic elements of demand and supply are reviewed. In the second section, the elasticity concept is introduced. The third section is devoted to a number of applications of these tools.

DEMAND, SUPPLY, AND THE MARKET PRICE

The laws of demand and supply are derived on the basis of a few reasonable assumptions about the behavior of consumers and producers. Consider first the basis for the **law of demand.** Consumers have limited incomes. Their incomes being limited means they cannot purchase everything they might want. They must, therefore, make decisions about how to allocate their incomes among the goods available for purchase. Presumably, they will allocate their incomes in ways that yield to them the greatest satisfaction. It is on the basis of such considerations that people make a determination of how much of each product they are willing and able to buy. How much of a product—any product—people are *willing and able to buy* we define as the **demand** for that product. The demand for a product, then, expresses more than a want or a desire for it; it expresses a willingness and ability to pay, a willingness to forego other things in order to acquire it.

The demand for any product—how much people are willing and able to buy—is determined by many factors: the price of the good itself, the prices of other goods and services, people's income and wealth, people's tastes, etc. On the assumption that all things other than the price of the product itself are unchanged, we are able

Chapter 16

Demand, supply, and the elasticity concept

to formulate the law of demand. It states: *Ceteris paribus*—holding everything else constant—*the price of a product and the quantity demanded are inversely related*. The downward-sloping hypothetical demand curve for steak portrayed in Figure 16.1 illustrates this law graphically. As steak prices rise, the quantity of steak demanded declines. What are the reasons for this inverse relationship? Basically, there are two. First, because the relative price of steak has gone up, many people will be induced to substitute other lower-priced goods for steak in their diets. Second, given the higher price for steak, people will not be able to buy as many goods and services with their fixed incomes as they could before. As a result of this reduction in their *real* incomes (their real purchasing power), people will normally cut back on their spending for most goods, *including steak*.

The basis for the **law of supply** is derived in an equally straightforward manner. The resources available for the production of goods and services are scarce. As a result, some mechanism must be developed for determining *what* shall be produced and *how much* of each. In market

economies, that mechanism is summarized in one word—*profits*. If the production of any one good is relatively more profitable than the production of others, more resources will be devoted to its production. It is on the basis of the relative profitability of the use of scarce resources that determines how much of each product producers are willing to produce and sell. How much of a product—any product—producers are *willing to produce and sell* we define as the **supply** of that product. Supply, therefore, expresses a willingness to use scarce resources for the production of one thing as opposed to the production of something else.

The supply of a product—how much producers are willing to produce and sell—depends on several factors: the price of the product itself, the price of other goods and services, resource prices, technology, etc. On the assumption that all things other than the price of the product itself are unchanged, we are able to formulate the law of supply. It states: *Ceteris paribus, the price of a product and the quantity supplied are positively related*. The upward-sloping hypothetical supply curve for steak in Figure 16.1 illus-

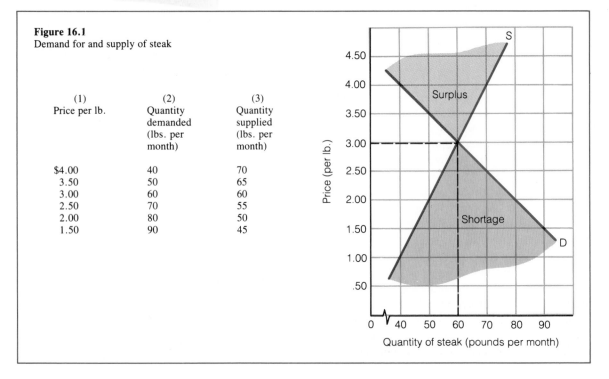

Figure 16.1
Demand for and supply of steak

(1) Price per lb.	(2) Quantity demanded (lbs. per month)	(3) Quantity supplied (lbs. per month)
$4.00	40	70
3.50	50	65
3.00	60	60
2.50	70	55
2.00	80	50
1.50	90	45

trates this law graphically. At higher steak prices, the quantity of steak supplied increases. What is the reason for this positive relationship? Faced with increasing costs, and to ensure at least as much profit as could be had with the employment of additional resources elsewhere, producers would generally have to receive higher prices to willingly increase steak production—i.e., to devote more resources to the production of steak.

It is important to remember that demand and supply must both be given an explicit time dimension. The amount of steak people are willing and able to buy in a week is undoubtedly different from the amount they are willing and able to buy in a month, year, or over their lifetimes. The same is true of the amount of steak producers are willing to produce and sell. Therefore, the quantities demanded and supplied must be expressed as *quantities per unit of time.* In our steak example, these quantities are expressed in terms of pounds of steak per month.

Market equilibrium—defined as a situation in which there is no further tendency for change—occurs at the point of intersection of the demand and supply curves. In Figure 16.1, the equilibrium price and quantity are, respectively, $3 per pound and 60 pounds per month. At a price of $3 per pound, the amount consumers are willing and able to buy matches precisely the amount producers are willing to produce and sell.

At any price other than $3, there will be **market disequilibrium**—i.e., there will be a tendency for further change. Above-equilibrium prices create surpluses (or excess supplies), prompting sellers to cut the price. The reduced price induces sellers to allocate fewer resources toward the production of steak (reducing the quantity supplied) and induces consumers to buy more (increasing the quantity demanded). Below-equilibrium prices, on the other hand, create shortages (or excess demands), prompting buyers to bid up the price. Higher prices induce sellers to allocate more resources toward the production of steak (increasing the quantity supplied) and induce consumers to buy less (reducing the quantity demanded). As a result of these price adjustments and the corresponding changes in the quantities

supplied and demanded, market equilibrium will ultimately be attained at a price of $3 per pound for steak. And note one very important, and frequently confused, characteristic of market equilibrium: In equilibrium, the market *clears;* neither shortages nor surpluses exist in equilibrium. Indeed, surpluses and shortages are features of market disequilibrium! *A surplus exists only because the price is too high to clear the market; a shortage exists only because the price is too low.* The price adjustments that take place in the face of surpluses and shortages illustrate the rationing function of prices.

Changes in demand and supply

By convention, economists draw a sharp distinction between *changes in the quantity demanded* and *changes in demand.* If the price of a good varies, the change in the amount of that good consumers are willing and able to buy will be reflected in a movement *along* the demand curve; this we call a **change in the quantity demanded. A change in demand,** by contrast, refers to a *shift* of the demand curve at each and every price; it reflects changes in the amount people are willing and able to buy as a result of changes in those factors—income, the prices of other goods and services, tastes, and so on—*other* than the price of the good in question. The distinction between a **change in the quantity supplied** and a **change in supply** is defined in a similar way.

Figures 16.2 and 16.3 illustrate the impacts on market equilibrium of changes in demand brought about by changes in income and changes in the prices of *other* goods and services. Let us consider each of these in turn.

Suppose consumers experience increases in their incomes. What impact will this have on market equilibrium? It all depends. If people are willing to buy *more* of the good, its price will increase; the demand curve will shift up and to the right, forcing up the market price. This outcome is illustrated in Figure 16.2A. If people express a willingness to buy *less* of the good, its price will fall; the demand curve will shift down and to the left, forcing down the market

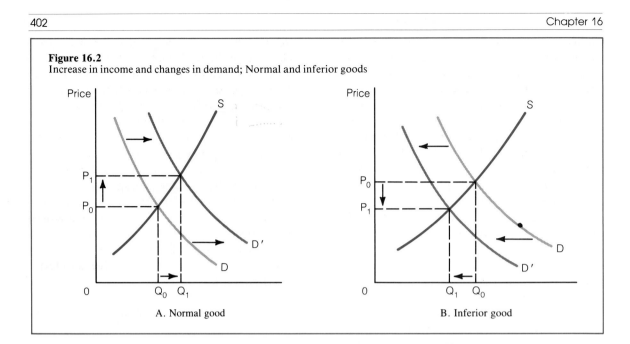

Figure 16.2
Increase in income and changes in demand; Normal and inferior goods

A. Normal good

B. Inferior good

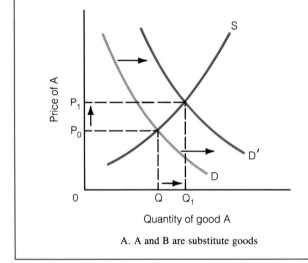

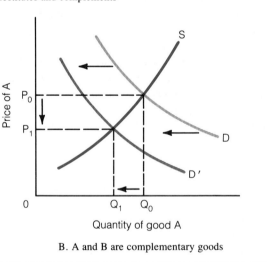

Figure 16.3
Increase in the price of a related good and changes in demand: Substitutes and complements

A. A and B are substitute goods

B. A and B are complementary goods

price. This outcome is illustrated in Figure 16.2B. *If income and the demand for some good are positively related,* we define such a good as a **normal good;** *if income and the demand for the good are inversely related,* such a good is defined as an **inferior good.** Figure 16.2A illustrates the impact of an increase in income in the case of a normal good; Figure 16.2B illustrates the mar-

ket impact of an increase in income in the case of an inferior good. Can you demonstrate the market impact of a *reduction* in income in the cases of both normal and inferior goods?

Figure 16.3 illustrates the market impact of a change in the price of some *other* good or service. Consider the market for good A represented in Figure 16.3. Suppose, for one reason or another, the price of some related good—good B—*increases.* What impact will this have on the market for A? It all depends. *If A and B are substitutes, the demand for A will increase.* People will be induced to cut back on their consumption of good B and substitute A in its place. The demand curve for A will shift up and to the right, forcing up the price of A. This shift in the demand for A is illustrated in Figure 16.3A. *If A and B are complementary goods,* meaning that an increase in the price of B raises the price of the complementary package—goods A and B together—*the demand for A will decline.* People will be induced to cut back on their consumption of *both* goods. The demand curve for A will shift down and to the left, forcing down the price of A. This shift in demand is depicted in Figure 16.3B. Can you demonstrate the impact on the market for good A of a *reduction* in the price of good B in the case where A and B are substitutes? Where they are complements?

In like manner, it is a relatively simple matter to illustrate the impact of a change in technology or a change in resource prices on market supply, and therefore on market equilibrium. Improved techniques of production that result in higher levels of output for given quantities of resource inputs, and reduced resource prices, will cause the supply curve to shift down and to the right. This will lower the equilibrium price and increase the equilibrium quantity. Be sure you can illustrate this change.

THE ELASTICITY CONCEPT

We know from the law of demand that changing steak prices will have an impact on the amount of steak people are willing and able to buy. We also know that the demand for steak will change as a result of a change in income, a change in the price of related goods, and changes in other things as well. In addition, on the basis of the law of supply, we know that producers will be willing to sell different amounts of steak at different prices and that the supply of steak will be affected by numerous other factors too. Frequently, we are interested in measur-

ing the responsiveness of buyers and sellers to changes in those factors that determine how much they are willing and able to buy and sell. How responsive are consumers to a change in the price of steak? To a change in income? To a change in the price of *other* goods? And how responsive are producers to a change in steak prices? The **elasticity** concept was developed explicitly for the purpose of enabling us to measure the magnitudes of these responses.

We develop below four frequently used elasticity measures. The first, called the **price elasticity of demand,** measures the responsiveness of the quantity demanded of some product to a change in its price. The second, called the **income elasticity of demand,** measures the responsiveness of demand to a change in income. The third, called the **cross-price elasticity of demand,** measures the responsiveness of demand for some good to a change in the price of some *other* good. The fourth, called the **price elasticity of supply,** measures the responsiveness of the quantity supplied of some product to a change in its price.

In principle, we could develop an elasticity measure for each of the many factors that affect the behavior of buyers and sellers. We choose not to develop any of these additional measures here for two reasons. In the first place, if the other determinants of demand and supply are easily quantifiable, the procedures one would use to construct the relevant elasticity measure would be precisely the same as those developed here. Second, many of the other determinants—such as tastes in the case of demand, or technology in the case of supply—are not easily quantifiable, making any elasticity measure of these factors difficult to quantify and interpret.

The price elasticity of demand

The **price elasticity of demand,** sympolically represented by E_d, is defined as the *percentage* change in the quantity demanded of a product divided by the *percentage* change in its price. That is,

$$E_d = \frac{\text{Percentage change in quantity demanded}}{\text{Percentage change in price}}.$$

Since the percentage change in any variable is defined as the change in that variable divided by its original value, the price elasticity of demand can be rewritten as

$$E_d = \frac{\Delta Q/Q}{\Delta P/P}.$$

(*Note:* Strictly speaking, the price elasticity of demand should be written with a negative sign preceding it. This is because the price and the quantity demanded are inversely related. By convention, however, the negative sign is ignored. Expressing the price elasticity of demand as a positive value makes it easier to speak of "larger" and "smaller" values. We follow that time-honored convention here.)

Why use percentages? The elasticity measure defined above is not, of course, the only possible measure of responsiveness. Alternatively, we could have defined some other measure of responsiveness, such as the *absolute* change in the quantity demanded divided by the *absolute* change in the price. The major difficulty with such a measure, however, is that it is not independent of the units in which the variables are measured. Consider the following simple example. Suppose the price of cashews fell from $4 per pound to $3, inducing an increase in the quantity demanded from 400 pounds to 600 pounds. Using our *alternative* measure of responsiveness, the change in quantity divided by the change in price, we would get a value of 200 (i.e., $\frac{\Delta Q}{\Delta P} = \frac{200}{1} = 200$); using our elasticity formula, on the other hand, $E_d = 2.0$ (i.e., $\frac{\Delta Q/Q}{\Delta P/P} = \frac{200/400}{1/4} = 2.0$). Now change the units in which the price variable is measured—from dollars to, say, cents. A 100-cent reduction in the price of cashews leads to a 200-pound increase in the quantity demanded. Using our alternative measure of responsiveness again, we would get a value of only 2.0 (i.e., $\frac{\Delta Q}{\Delta P} = \frac{200}{100} = 2.0$), not 200 as before. But are consumers less responsive? Not at all! The difference arises simply because we changed the unit of measurement from pounds per dollar to pounds per cent.

However, changing the unit of measurement does not change at all the measure of responsiveness defined by the price elasticity of demand. E_d equals 2.0, as before (i.e., $\frac{\Delta Q/Q}{\Delta P/P} = \frac{200/400}{100/400} = 2.0$). Because the price elasticity of demand is unaffected by the units of measurement, it has a distinct advantage over the alternative measure.

The arc-price elasticity of demand: The mid-points formula

Although E_d is not affected by the units of measurement of the price and quantity variables, the calculation of E_d *is* sensitive to the selected *original* or *base* values of P and Q. Consider once again our numerical cashew example. The price fell from $4 per pound to $3 and the quantity demanded rose from 400 to 600 pounds. The elasticity of demand was calculated, using the formula provided above, as follows:

$$\frac{\Delta Q}{Q} \div \frac{\Delta P}{P} = \frac{200}{400} \div \frac{1.00}{4.00} = \frac{1}{2} \div \frac{1}{4} = 2.0.$$

In this calculation, the *base* or original price was $4; the base quantity was 400. Suppose, on the other hand, that we calculated the elasticity of demand for a price *increase* from $3 to $4. Using the formula given above, E_d would be calculated as follows:

$$\frac{\Delta Q}{Q} \div \frac{\Delta P}{P} = \frac{200}{600} \div \frac{1.00}{3.00} = \frac{1}{3} \div \frac{1}{3} = 1.0.$$

Here, the elasticity of demand is 1.0 for a price *increase* from $3 to $4, whereas it was 2.0 for a price *reduction* over the same price range. The reason for the difference is obvious. In the case of the price *increase,* the *base* price used in the calculation was $3 and the base quantity was 600. Since the price range is the same in the two examples and since the change in the quantity demanded is also the same, it is annoying to be confronted with two different values for E_d. Consumers respond to a $1 change in price in the $3.00 to $4.00 range by changing the quantity demanded by 200 whether the price goes up or down. Yet, depending on whether the price increases or decreases, we get a different measure of responsiveness when in fact there is no difference. Clearly, the price elasticity cannot be 1.00 and 2.00 at the same time. Yet there is no obvious reason for choosing one over the other. That is, it is not at all obvious whether the base price selected should be $3 or $4, or whether the base quantity should be 400 or 600.

Because the calculated value of the elasticity is sensitive to the base selected, economists prefer to make the measurement using an *average* of the initial and final Ps and Qs as bases. The resultant calculation is often referred to as the **arc-price elasticity** since it is measured over a range of Ps and Qs—over an arc of the demand curve. The arc price elasticity can be calculated using the following **midpoints formula:**

> Arc price elasticity of demand
> $$= \frac{\text{Change in quantity demanded}}{(\text{Initial quantity} + \text{Final quantity})/2}$$
> $$\div \frac{\text{Change in the price}}{(\text{Initial price} + \text{Final price})/2}$$

On the basis of this midpoints formula, the elasticity of demand for cashews in the $3–$4 price range is 1.4 (i.e., $\frac{200}{(400+600)/2} \div \frac{1}{(3+4)/2}=$

$\frac{200}{500} \div \frac{1}{3.5} = 1.4$). While this method of calculation is more involved, it is a more accurate measure than if we had used the initial or final price and quantity bases. This is because, since we are dealing with a range over which the price varies, it is best to obtain a measure that reflects the *average* degree of consumer responsiveness.

Variations in the price elasticity of demand

Using the data on the demand for steak presented in Figure 16.1, we can readily calculate the arc-price elasticity of demand for each of five price ranges. These results are presented in column (1) of Table 16.1. Can you verify each of these calculations?

Note first how the calculated price elasticity of demand changes as we move from one price range to another. In particular, note how the price elasticity of demand declines as we move from the $4–$3.50 price range—the highest price range considered—to the $2–$1.50 price range—the lowest price range considered. It declines in value from 1.67 to 0.41.

At first glance, this result may appear to be somewhat peculiar. After all, each time the price

Table 16.1
The demand for steak: The arc-price elasticity of demand and total revenue

(1) The arc-price elasticity of demand	(2) Price per pound	(3) Quantity demanded (pounds per month)	(4) Total revenue
	$4.00	40	$160
$\frac{10}{90/2} \div \frac{0.50}{7.50/2} = 1.67$			
	3.50	50	175
$\frac{10}{110/2} \div \frac{0.50}{6.50/2} = 1.18$			
	3.00	60	180
$\frac{10}{130/2} \div \frac{0.50}{5.50/2} = 0.85$			
	2.50	70	175
$\frac{10}{150/2} \div \frac{0.50}{4.50/2} = 0.60$			
	2.00	80	160
$\frac{10}{170/2} \div \frac{0.50}{3.50/2} = 0.41$			
	1.50	90	135

$$\frac{\Delta Q}{Q} \div \frac{\Delta P}{P}$$

$$\frac{\Delta Q}{Q} \cdot \frac{P}{\Delta P}$$

changes by 50 cents, the quantity demanded changes by 10 pounds. Does this not mean that consumers are as responsive to a 50-cent price change when the price is $4 as they are to a 50-cent price change when the price is only $2? Absolutely not! A 50-cent price reduction in the $4.00 to $3.50 price range represents only a 13 percent price decline (i.e., $0.50/(7.50/2) = 0.13$); the quantity demanded, however, rises by 22 percent (i.e., $10/(90/2) = 0.22$). A 50-cent price reduction in the $2–$1.50 price range, on the other hand, represents a 29 percent price decline, yet the increase in the quantity demanded amounts to only 12 percent. The commonsense explanation for this result is that people's sensitivity to a price change depends on how much of the good they already have and how high its price is to begin with. A declining elasticity of demand as the price is reduced suggests that consumers become less and less responsive relatively.

9:00

The price elasticity of demand and total revenue

Knowledge of the price elasticity of demand is extremely useful because with it we are able to determine how *total revenue* or *total expenditures* change as the price of the product changes. Examine again the results presented in Table 16.1. Total revenue, the amount received by producers in the sale of their product—which is identical to the total expenditures of consumers—is obtained by multiplying the quantity demanded at each price times the relevant price. At a price of $4 per pound, total revenue amounts to $160 (i.e., $160 = 4×40); at a price of $2.50 per pound, total revenue equals $175. Note first that, as price declines from $4 to $3, total revenue *rises* from $160 to $180. Further price reductions, however, cause total revenue to decline. As the price is reduced from $3 to $1.50, total revenue declines from $180 to $135. Note further that the price elasticity of demand in the $4–$3 price range has a value in excess of unity; in the price range $3–$1.50, on the other hand, the price elasticity of demand is less than one. These results lead us to the following set of conclusions:

1. If the price elasticity of demand *exceeds one* ($E_d > 1.0$), a *price reduction* will cause total

revenue to *increase*. A reduction in the price of steak from $4 per pound to $3.50 causes total revenue to increase from $160 to $175; in this price range, $E_d = 1.67$.

2. If the price elasticity of demand is *less than one* ($E_d < 1.0$), a *price reduction* will cause total revenue to *fall*. A reduction in the price of steak from $3 per pound to $2.50 causes total revenue to fall from $180 to $175; in this price range, $E_d = 0.85$.

The explanation for these results is straightforward. Total revenue is a $P \times Q$ relationship. A price reduction means that sellers obtain less for each unit sold. On the other hand, they also sell more units. What happens to total revenue as a result of a price reduction depends on which of these two opposing forces dominates. If price falls by 5 percent and the quantity demanded rises by 10 percent—meaning that the price elasticity of demand exceeds one—the *loss* in revenue caused by the fact that sellers receive less for each unit sold is more than offset by the *gain* in revenue because they are selling so much more. The quantity demanded rises by a greater percentage than the price decline. Total revenue, therefore, rises. If, on the other hand, the price falls by 10 percent, causing an increase in the quantity demanded of only 5 percent—meaning that the price elasticity of demand is less than one—total revenue will fall because the quantity demanded rises less than in proportion to the price decline.

What would happen to total revenue if the price elasticity of demand equaled unity ($E_d = 1$)? Total revenue would not change as a result of a price decline. The price and the quantity demanded would change in proportion, leaving total revenue unaltered.

It becomes apparent, then, that values of E_d on either side of unity have significantly different implications for total revenue. If $E_d > 1$, a price reduction will cause total revenue to increase; if $E_d < 1$, total revenue will fall in the face of a price decline. Because of these differences, it has become conventional for economists to refer to demand as **price elastic** any time $E_d > 1$, and to refer to demand as **price inelastic** any time

$E_d < 1$. But note that the statement that demand is price inelastic does *not* mean that consumers are unresponsive to a change in price; it means only that the price elasticity of demand is less than one. If consumers were completely unresponsive to a change in price, the price elasticity of demand would be zero; demand would then be described as **perfectly price inelastic** and the demand curve would be vertical. It is possible that demand could be perfectly price inelastic over *some* range of prices, but it is unrealistic to assume it could be so over the range of all prices, especially very high prices. Indeed, it is always possible to find a price that is high enough to cause the quantity demanded to fall to zero. At the other extreme, it is possible for the demand curve to be **perfectly price elastic;** the demand curve would be horizontal, implying that a very small change in price would cause, in the limit, an infinite change in the quantity demanded. And finally, if $E_d = 1$, demand is said to be **unit price elastic.**

On the basis of these definitions, we can restate the relationships between the price elasticity of demand and total revenue as follows:

1. If demand is price elastic, a price *reduction* will cause total revenue to *rise.*
2. If demand is price inelastic, a price *reduction* will cause total revenue to *decline.*

What happens to total revenue if the price is *increased* instead? It should be apparent that *(a)* if demand is *price elastic,* an *increase* in price will cause total revenue to *fall;* and *(b)* if demand is *price inelastic,* an *increase in price* will cause total revenue to *rise.* Can you explain *why* these conclusions hold? Finally, can you explain why total revenue remains unchanged in the face of a change in price if demand is unit price elastic?

All of these relationships between the price elasticity of demand, the direction of price change, and the directional change of total revenue are summarized in Figure 16.4. These relationships are very important but frequently misunderstood. For example, in many of our major cities, mass transit authorities are continually appealing to the powers that be for a price hike for the purpose of raising revenue. Often these

Figure 16.4
Relationships between price elasticity of demand (E_d), direction of price change, and direction of total revenue (TR) change

E_d \ Direction of price change	Price increase	Price decrease
$E_d > 1$	TR↓	TR↑
$E_d = 1$	TR unchanged	TR unchanged
$E_d < 1$	TR↑	TR↓

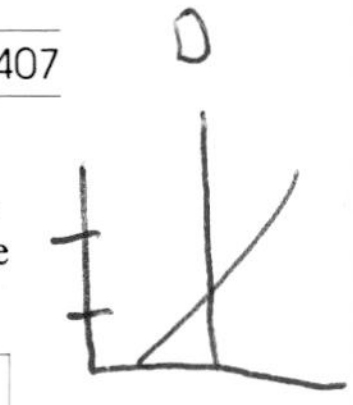

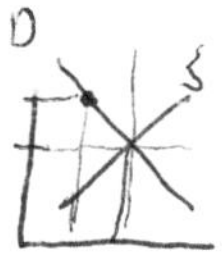

requests are made with little attention being paid to the responsiveness of consumers to the requested price increase. Will revenue actually rise as a result of the price hike? To hear the transit authorities, the answer would appear to be an unequivocal yes. But if the demand for mass transit is price elastic, total revenue will actually fall, not rise. If they want to increase total revenue, they should be calling for a price reduction!

Consider another example. A theater owner in your area has been complaining that her revenues are so small that she will be forced to close up unless revenues rise. She suggests a price increase from $2.25 a ticket to $2.75. You are asked to conduct a market survey to ascertain what will happen to the quantity of seats sold as a result of the price increase. You discover that, at a price of $2.25, the theater averaged 1,000 theatergoers per week; at a price of $2.75, you estimate that attendance will average only 800 people each week. How would you advise the theater owner? You should tell her not to raise her price to $2.75. The demand is price elastic in the $2.25–$2.75 price range (i.e., $E_d = 1.1$. Can you show why?); a price increase to $2.75 would reduce revenues.

Determinants of the price elasticity of demand

What forces determine how responsive consumers will be to a price change? That is, what are the factors that determine the price elasticity of demand? As you probably suspect, they are many and varied, and they vary in importance from product to product. We shall concentrate on only four: (1) the availability of close substitutes; (2) the importance of the item in the consumer's budget; (3) whether the good is viewed by the consumer as being a necessity or a luxury; and (4) time.

The availability of close substitutes. In general, the availability of close substitutes implies a high price elasticity of demand. If the price of the good in question rises by only a small percentage, the availability of many close substitutes suggests that consumers will cut back their consumption of that good by a sizable percentage as they switch to other goods. Charmin bathroom tissue and Gleem toothpaste probably each have a relatively high price elasticity of demand because of the availability of a large number of close substitutes.

These examples suggest a useful rule of thumb. The more narrowly defined the good is, the greater its price elasticity of demand will normally be. The price elasticity of demand for New York strip steaks is likely to be much higher than the price elasticity of demand for meat in general. There are close substitutes for New York strips—filet mignon, for example—but fewer close substitutes for meat. Similarly, the price elasticity of demand for Gleem and Charmin are each likely to be much higher than the price elasticity of demand for toothpaste and bathroom tissue in general. Can you explain why?

Importance in consumer's budgets. The more important the item is in consumers' budgets, the greater the price elasticity of demand for that good is likely to be. A relatively small increase in the price of a big budget item will force consumers to cut back their consumption of it by a relatively large percentage. A 10 percent increase in the price of a loaf of bread will lead to a small cutback in its consumption compared with a 10 percent increase in the price of housing. Moreover, it is also important to recognize here that the importance of any given item in the budget will depend in part on the size of the budget itself. For example, food has a tendency to assume a smaller and smaller proportion of people's income as their level of income rises. An increase in the price of food will cause people with relatively low incomes to cut back on their consumption of food products by more than those with relatively high levels of income. In other words, the price elasticity of demand for food is likely to be higher for people with low incomes than for people with high incomes.

Necessities versus luxuries. If a good is viewed as a necessity, its price elasticity is likely to be low compared with a luxury. Put simply, since a necessity is something we feel we cannot do without, a price hike is likely to elicit little responsiveness on the part of consumers. Luxuries, on the other hand, are items that, if pressed, we can do with less of. It must be pointed out, however, that the emphasis here is on how each consumer views his or her own situation. There are some goods we all agree are necessities: the basics of life like food, clothing, and shelter. Beyond that, however, we can say little. To pizza freaks, pizza may well be deemed a necessity; an increase in price will not lead to much of a reduction in the quantity demanded. To a commuter living in the suburbs, the auto may be viewed as a necessity; to city residents who feel that their transportation needs are served adequately by mass transit, the auto may be viewed as something of a luxury. In addition, the price elasticity of necessities will vary, depending on the importance of necessities in the entire budget.

Moreover, advertising may play an important part in shaping our views as to what goods should properly be viewed as necessities. Would any of us dare set foot outside without some kind of double deodorant protection? In addition, we may be convinced through advertising that truly substantive differences exist within a class of substitute goods when in fact the differences are miniscule. Witness the advertisements for Bayer aspirin or Charmin bathroom tissue. Such advertising, if successful, not only increases the demand for the product, it also reduces its price elasticity. Can you explain why? (*Hint:* What happens if people are led to believe that there are fewer close substitutes than there are?)

Time. In general, time is required for people to adjust their expenditures in response to a change in price. Thus, the price elasticity of demand could be decidedly smaller in the short run than in the long run. Consider the impact of rising gasoline prices on the demand for gas guzzlers. The immediate impact is likely to be negligible. People are unlikely to junk their large cars immediately in favor of economy models; nor will they necessarily trade them in for smaller cars immediately since the trade-in value for large models may also be reduced substantially. However, as time passes, as the gas guzzlers wear out, these cars will frequently be replaced with smaller, higher-mileage models. Can you think of reasons the price elasticity of demand for air travel, clothes, and pocket calculators should be higher in the long run than in the short run?

Table 16.2 presents some estimated values for the price elasticities of demand for a number of different goods purchased by consumers in the United States. Can you suggest some possible explanations for the results presented, especially for the differences among products, and for the short-run and long-run differences?

Table 16.2
Some empirical estimates of the price elasticity of demand for selected goods

Product	Estimated elasticity
Shoes	0.4
Stationery	0.5
Newspapers and magazines	0.1
Gasoline and oil	
Short run	0.2
Long run	0.5
Kitchen appliances	0.6
China and tableware	1.1
Jewelry and watches	0.4
Radio and television receivers	1.2
Sports equipment, boats, pleasure aircraft	
Short run	0.6
Long run	1.3
Physicians' services	0.6
Legal services	0.5
Taxis	0.4
Airline travel	
Short run	0.06
Long run	2.4

Source: H. S. Houthakker and L. D. Taylor, *Consumer Demand in the United States, 1929–1966* (Cambridge, Mass.: Harvard University Press, 1970).

The income elasticity of demand

Frequently, we are also interested in measuring the responsiveness of consumer demand to a change in income. Such a measurement is provided by the **income elasticity of demand.** It is defined as the percentage change in demand divided by the percentage change in income. Or,

Income elasticity of demand
$$= \frac{\text{Percentage change in demand}}{\text{Percentage change in income}}.$$

If income rises by 5 percent, inducing a 10 percent increase in the demand for steak, the income elasticity of demand for steak will equal 2.0 (i.e., $0.10 \div 0.05 = 2.0$).

Because the considerations underlying the income elasticity of demand are similar to those discussed in reference to the price elasticity of demand, our analysis here can be brief.

1. Why is it more appropriate to measure consumer responsiveness in terms of percentage changes than in terms of absolute changes? Because we want a measure of responsiveness that

is unaffected by differences in the units of measurement.

2. In actual practice, is it best to use a midpoints formula in making the calculations? Yes. Using the initial or final income and quantity bases would not give us a measure of the *average* degree of consumer responsiveness over an income range.

3. If the income elasticity of demand is positive, is this an indication that the good in question is a normal good or an inferior good? It tells us that the good is a normal good, because as income increases so does the demand. What if the income elasticity is negative? This tells us the good is inferior. An increase in income induces people to switch from "inferior" products to other, better-quality goods.

The cross-price elasticity of demand

Similarly, we can measure the responsiveness of the demand for some product to a change in the price of some *other* product. This measure we call the **cross-price elasticity of demand.** For two goods, A and B, the cross-price elasticity of demand for good A is defined as the percentage change in the demand for good A divided by the percentage change in the price of good B. Or,

Cross-price elasticity of demand for good A
$$= \frac{\text{Percent change in demand for A}}{\text{Percent change in price of B}}.$$

If the price of good B *falls* by 10 percent and the demand for good A *rises* by 15 percent, the cross-price elasticity of demand for good A will equal minus 1.5 (i.e., $0.15 \div (-0.10) = -1.5$). Since the cross-price elasticity is negative, goods A and B must be complements; the reduced price for B reduces the price of the package, AB, raising the demand for A. If the cross-price elasticity of demand for A were positive—a reduction in the price of B leading to a reduction in the demand for A—goods A and B would be substitutes; the reduced price for B induces consumers to substitute away from good A.

Changes in income and changes in the prices of *other* related products cause the demand curve for the product in question to shift. More or less of the product will be demanded *at each and every price*. The income elasticity and the cross-price elasticity enable us to calculate the

magnitude of the shift in demand attributable to these other forces. This is illustrated in Figure 16.5. Suppose income increases by 10 percent. An income elasticity of demand equal to 2.0 implies that the demand curve will shift outward by 20 percent at each and every price. Note that the change in demand is greater at lower prices than it is at higher prices. This result is easily explained. At a high price, the quantity demanded is relatively small; at a low price, the quantity demanded is much larger. A 20 percent increase when applied to a small base quantity (the quantity demanded at a high price) implies a smaller *absolute* change in demand than when it is applied to a large base quantity (the quantity demanded at a low price).

The price elasticity of supply

Analogous to the price elasticity of demand, the price elasticity of supply measures the responsiveness of sellers to a change in the product price. It is defined as:

Price elasticity of supply
$$= \frac{\text{Percent change in quantity supplied}}{\text{Percent change in the price}}.$$

Recalling our steak example in Figure 16.1, the price elasticity of supply can be readily calculated

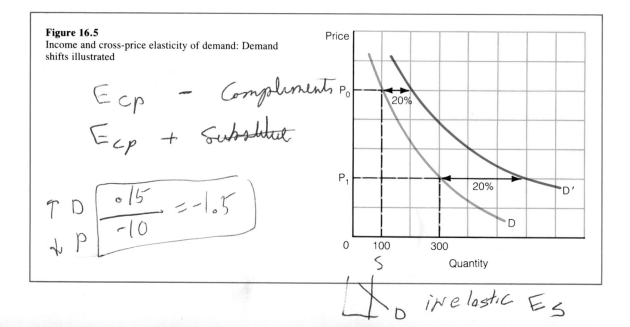

Figure 16.5
Income and cross-price elasticity of demand: Demand shifts illustrated

using the midpoints formula. In the \$3.50–\$4 price range for steak, the price elasticity of supply equals 0.56 (i.e., $\dfrac{5}{135/2} \div \dfrac{0.50}{7.50/2} = 0.56$). Because an *increase* in price induces an *increase* in the quantity supplied, the price elasticity of supply has a positive value.

As emphasized earlier, the amount of any product producers are willing to sell depends on its profitability vis-à-vis other goods and services. In general, the higher the relative price of the good in question is, the greater will be the incentive on the part of producers to devote more resources to its production. However, because time is required for these resource shifts to take place, time will be required for producers to adjust their rates of production in response to a given change in price. Very little if any adjustment may be possible in a very short time; much more adjustment will be possible over longer spans of time.

Conceptually, it is possible to divide the adjustment time into three distinct time periods: the *very* short run (sometimes called the market period), the short run, and the long run.

The very short run. The **very short run (or market period)** is so short that producers are unable to make any adjustment whatsoever in their rates of production in response to a change in price. The fact that a fixed quantity is available for sale, however, does not mean necessarily that producers will be willing to sell all of it *immediately* no matter what the price. That will depend in part on the nature of the product itself. If the good is perishable and cannot be stored, the fixed available supply will normally represent the amount producers are willing to sell, regardless of price. Under these circumstances, supply during the very short run will be perfectly price inelastic—i.e., the supply curve will be vertical. If the demand for the product increases, the price will rise. But this price rise will not—cannot!— elicit any change in the quantity supplied immediately. Moreover, the quantity supplied will not be reduced in the face of a price decline, even if that decline is substantial. It is better to sell the product at a low price, even if it means incurring a loss; if it spoils, the producer gets nothing.

Figure 16.6A illustrates these outcomes. Whether demand is D or D' or D'', the quantity producers are willing to supply, Q_0, remains unaltered.

In the case of a storable good, the very short-run supply response may be quite different. In Figure 16.6B, it is assumed that Q_0 represents the available fixed quantity of the good in question. If the price happens to be P_0, we assume that producers are willing to sell all of the available fixed supply. A higher price, however, will not elicit any change in the quantity supplied in the very short run. At prices above P_0, supply is perfectly price inelastic. However, if the price falls below P_0—let's say to P_2—producers may decide to cut back the amount they are willing to sell to Q_1. They will place the difference between Q_0 and Q_1 in storage in the hope that the future price will be higher. Under these circumstances—i.e., at prices below P_0—the very short-run price elasticity will not equal zero and, depending on the product, supply could be very price elastic.[1]

The very short run in the case of some products may be quite lengthy; in others it may be quite short. Not much can be done to change the rate of production of agricultural commodities during the current growing season; once the crops are harvested, nothing can be done to change the quantities produced until next season's crops are planted and harvested. For many other products, however, it is possible to alter the rate of production rather quickly; the very short run may be very short.

The short run. We define **the short run** as a period during which it is not possible for producers to alter their *productive capacity*. In the short run the "plant" capacity of producers is fixed. During that period, however, it is possible for sellers to change their rates of production through the more or less intensive use of their fixed plants. If producers deem it profitable to reduce their rates of production for a period, they can do so by laying off some workers. If

---

[1] Of course, if producers believe that prices will *not* improve in the future, they may not reduce the quantity supplied at all as the price goes from P_0 to P_2. The price elasticity of supply would then be zero—i.e., the supply curve would be vertical—even though the good is storable.

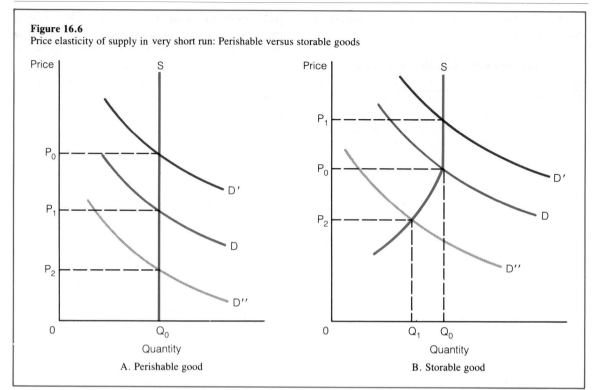

Figure 16.6
Price elasticity of supply in very short run: Perishable versus storable goods

A. Perishable good

B. Storable good

they find it profitable to step up production, frequently they are able to do so by going out and hiring more workers or by working at least some of their employees overtime. They could, if they wanted, shut down their operations completely. In the short run, these options are available to virtually all producers. Indeed, even farmers are able to change their production levels during any given growing season through the application of more or less fertilizer to their crops or through the use of more or less labor to cultivate and harvest crops already planted.

There is, of course, an upper limit beyond which production cannot expand in the short run. That limit is established by the productive capacity of existing plants. The lower limit is a zero rate of production (when firms shut down). Between a zero rate of production and the limit set by the existing productive capacity, there is in general a considerable range of variation of possible levels of production in the short run. The short-run supply curve, therefore, will in general be upward sloping. Producers are willing

to use their existing plants more intensively the higher product prices are; and they reduce plant use with lower product prices. This outcome is illustrated in Figure 16.7. Note there that, as the rate of production approaches the capacity rate (represented by the quantity Q_c), the supply curve gets steeper and steeper; at the capacity rate, it becomes vertical. (What does this imply about the short-run price elasticity of supply at capacity? Why?)

The short-run price elasticity of supply will, of course, vary from product to product. For most agricultural products, the short-run price elasticity of supply is probably fairly low, even at rates of production far below capacity. It is probably much higher for other goods such as automobiles or toothpaste. Can you think of reasons this would be so? The reasons for these differences will be explored in greater depth in Chapter 18.

The long run. In the long run, producers can vary not only the intensity with which they operate their plants, but their productive capacity as well. In the long run, the **scale of operation** can be changed. As a result of this fact, the supply curve in the long run is likely to exhibit a much higher price elasticity than that which characterizes the short-run supply curve. Two frequently discussed cases are presented in Figure 16.8. In Figure 16.8A, the long-run supply curve is depicted as a horizontal straight line; supply is *per-fectly price elastic* in the long run. This is often referred to as the "constant costs" case, meaning that producers can expand or contract their productive capacity without changing their costs per unit of output. If producers *double* their plant size, *double* their costs, and *double* their rate of production, costs per unit of output will remain unaltered; at the current price they are willing

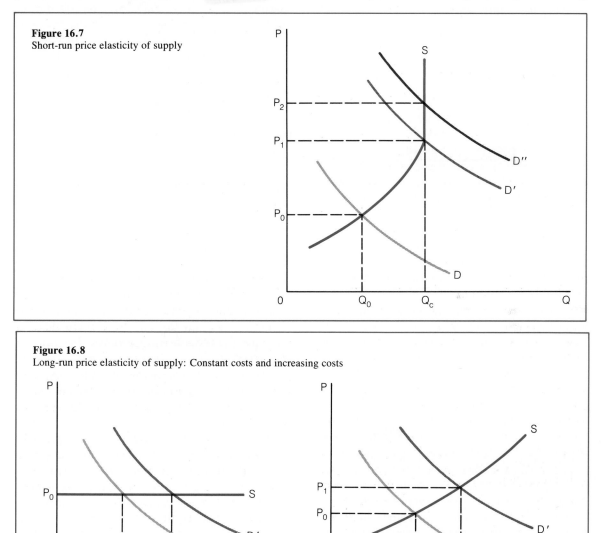

Figure 16.7
Short-run price elasticity of supply

Figure 16.8
Long-run price elasticity of supply: Constant costs and increasing costs

A. Constant cost

B. Increasing cost

to sell twice as much as before. Figure 16.8B depicts what many economists believe is the more realistic situation—namely, that of "increasing costs." As firms expand their productive capacity, they will frequently force up their resource costs, raising in turn their costs per unit of output. The long-run supply curve is not horizontal but upward sloping. These cases will be examined in detail in Chapter 18.

SOME APPLICATIONS OF THE ELASTICITY CONCEPT

The concepts of demand, supply, and elasticity are extremely powerful tools of analysis with many useful applications. We will discuss here only three: (1) price controls; (2) the U.S. farm problem, and (3) the incidence of an excise tax. First, a word of caution. In all of the applications discussed below, we concern ourselves with problems that are both highly complex and very emotional. We cannot possibly deal with all dimensions of these problems in the space of a few short pages, nor shall we attempt even to list all of the major questions raised by each issue. Our objectives are much more limited than that. We shall attempt, simply, to employ the tools developed in this chapter for the purpose of highlighting *some* of the economic dimensions of the problems discussed.

Price controls

Governments often interfere with the functioning of markets by establishing **price floors** (below which the price is not legally allowed to fall) and **price ceilings** (above which the price is not legally allowed to rise) on certain goods and services. The purpose behind these controls is to achieve a distribution of income and output *different* from the market-determined distribution. Prices are one means of rationing the supply of goods and services, but not the only means. Frequently, government officials are persuaded that *other* methods of rationing are fairer, more equitable, or more just. As a result, many governments impose price floors on such things as agri-

cultural products (in the form of **price supports**) and wages (in the form of **minimum wages**), and price ceilings on things such as apartment rents.

Rent controls. Figure 16.9 gives us insight into some of the economic implications of rent controls. Obviously, if rent control is to have any impact whatsoever, the authorities must establish a rent ceiling that is below the market-clearing rental price. At a rent-controlled price of $150 per month, an excess demand will exist for this type of rental housing. In other words, the existence of an effective rent control creates a shortage of housing.

Note some of the economic implications that arise from the imposition of such rent controls. In the first place, at a price of $150 per month, fewer rental housing units will be available for rent than at the market clearing price. Since the "production" of rental housing is less profitable at $150 than it is at $200, fewer resources will be devoted to the provision of this kind of housing. Of course, since the supply of rental housing units is relatively fixed over any given short period, such a reduction in the quantity supplied will take time. Some apartment owners may adjust in the short run by allowing their apartments to fall into disrepair; in the long run, some apartment buildings will be abandoned and fewer new units will be built. Put differently, although rent controls create short-run shortages, the fact that the elasticity of supply is so much smaller in the short run than in the longer run means that the long-run shortages will be much worse.

A second consequence is that, at the rent-controlled price, fewer rental units are available than people who are willing to rent. As a result, conditions are ripe for the formation of a **black market**—an illegal market in which unsatisfied buyers attempt to persuade landlords, usually with monetary compensation, to rent apartments to them as opposed to others.[2] To some extent, then,

---

[2] Some people in downtown Manhattan in New York City study the obituary columns religiously hoping to find a reported death of a tenant in a rent-controlled apartment. If they discover such a happy event, they will immediately rush to the landlord offering him or her as much as $2,000 to $3,000 or more in return for the right to rent the vacated apartment.

Figure 16.9
Some economic consequences of rent controls

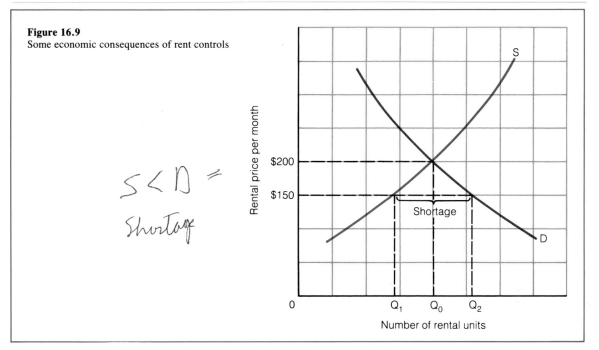

$S < D =$
Shortage

people who are willing to pay more can get what they want by circumventing the controls; the controls may not aid as many people as they were intended to assist.

Proponents of rent controls argue that a market-determined rental price would impose severe hardships on current tenants, many of whom can ill-afford to pay any more than the $150 rent-controlled price. Indeed it would. However, because rent controls have the undesirable effects of reducing the quantity of rental housing supplied and of creating an incentive for people to evade the controls illegally, many economists have suggested some alternative solutions. Let the price of rental housing be determined by the forces of demand and supply and *(a)* subsidize qualified tenants directly and/or *(b)* provide public housing directly to those people the government seeks to assist. Unfortunately, governments frequently balk at these suggestions, claiming they would "cost too much." What do you think of that response? Recalling the meaning of opportunity cost, do you think that, because rent controls do not appear on some line in the government's budget, there are no costs involved?

Absolutely not. The costs are reflected in the undesirable consequences that follow in the wake of rent controls. The problem is that, while the government may be able to control the price of housing, it cannot ensure that the desired quantity or quality of housing will be forthcoming.

Proponents of rent controls also make another pitch in their favor. By controlling rents, tenants are protected from having to move, which helps to keep neighborhoods stable. However, by regulating the price of apartments but not the costs of building and maintaining them, rent controls cause apartment building revenues to lag behind expenditures. Owners often respond by reducing maintenance and demanding a higher rent ceiling. Tenants deprived of service resist rent increases and threaten rent strikes. Owners speed up conversions to condominiums or abandon buildings. The result is that many neighborhoods are not stabilized, but destroyed.

A brief review of the U.S. farm problem

Throughout our history, American agriculture has been plagued by a number of long-run and short-run economic problems. Up until the 1970s, the long-run problem was essentially one of chronic excess capacity and low income returns to farmers. In the first 25 years following World War II, we observed declining *real* food prices—i.e., a declining ratio of food to nonfood prices—and a value for farm income per capita that was only about 60 to 65 percent of nonfarm income per capita. At the risk of oversimplifying, the root causes of that long-run problem are not difficult to discover: The growth in demand for food products fell far short of the growth of agriculture's productive capacity.

The long-run problem: A first approximation. Growth in demand can be broken into its two component parts: growth in domestic demand and growth in foreign demand (i.e., exports). Both advanced at about the same pace on average from World War II through the early 1970s; both advanced at a fairly sluggish pace. One reason for the sluggish growth can be found in the empirical fact that the demand for food products tends to be relatively income inelastic. Thus, although per capita income in the United States has increased substantially since the turn of the century, the per capita demand for agricultural products has gone up much less than in proportion.

By contrast, the growth in agriculture's productive capacity has been rapid. First, productivity advances in agriculture have been dramatic historically. As a result of *(a)* growth in the electrification and the mechanization of farms, *(b)* improved land management and soil conservation programs, *(c)* development of higher quality seeds, fertilizers, and pesticides, and *(d)* improvements in the breeding and care of livestock, the growth in agricultural productivity—growth in output per acre—has been brisk. Second, although the amount of labor resources devoted to farming has declined significantly since the turn of the century, the amount of land devoted to farming has not declined by anywhere near as much; *compared with farm labor,* we as a nation have not gobbled up much farm land for alternative uses. Combining these two elements— rapid productivity advance and only marginal reductions in farm land use—it is clear why agri-

cultural productive capacity has increased so much.

Figure 16.10 illustrates the net outcome of the influence of these various factors. The demand curve shifts outward over time as a result of increasing incomes. However, because of rapid increases in agriculture's productive capacity, the increase in supply is much larger than the increase in demand. As a result, farm prices fall (relative to the prices of other goods and services) and farm incomes improve little, if at all (relative to nonfarm incomes). This latter point requires a little explanation. There are two opposing forces operating on farm incomes. First, because the demand for agricultural products is price inelastic, the reduced price tends to *lower* farm incomes. Second, the increase in demand over time tends to partly offset this reduction.

Although Figure 16.10 captures in a sufficient way the long-run problem that plagued agriculture in the quarter century following World War II, the 1970s saw virtually all these circumstances change. Productivity growth remained high; a

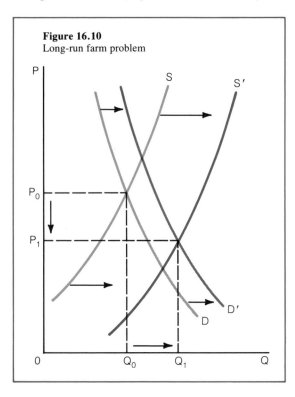

Figure 16.10
Long-run farm problem

factor that contributed to continued rapid increases in agriculture's productive capacity. But what was not foreseen was that growth in demand outstripped the growth in supply. As a result, *real* food prices increased and per capita incomes of farmers averaged nearly 90 percent of those earned by the nonfarm population, up sharply from the 60 to 65 percent average figure of the 25 years before. Moreover, the rapid exodus of labor from agriculture that had been going on earlier virtually stopped in the 1970s.

What accounted for the sharp increase in the growth of demand in the 1970s? An explosive growth in exports due to rising world population and the improved capability of some developing nations to purchase food and feed grains. U.S. grain exports tripled in volume and the dollar value of all our agricultural exports increased nearly 600 percent in the 1970s. Measured in terms of total farm sales, the numbers are even more impressive. Whereas agricultural exports represented about 10 to 14 percent of total farm cash receipts in the 40-year period from 1930 to 1970, they jumped sharply in the 1970s, reaching almost 30 percent in 1980. What this meant in terms of Figure 16.10 was that the demand

curve over the course of the 1970s increased by more than the supply curve, raising *real* food prices and farm incomes.

The short-run problem: A first approximation. Although the long-run problem is much less acute, at least for the time being, the short-run problem—income instability—remains. The reason farm incomes tend to be unstable, fluctuating markedly from one time period to another, is clear. Because the demand for and supply of agricultural products are so price inelastic in the short run, small changes in either demand or supply can lead to very large changes in prices and incomes. Many of these demand and supply changes are unpredictable. Therefore, unpredictable changes in weather conditions domestically often cause sharp variations in output; and unpredictable changes in weather conditions abroad often cause variations in demand on the part of foreign countries for our exports.

Figure 16.11 illustrates the influence of these factors on farm incomes. In Figure 16.11A we indicate the impact on farm incomes of short-run fluctuations in domestic supply in the face of a price-inelastic demand curve. A bumper crop, reflected in an increase in supply, forces

Figure 16.11
Effects of short-run fluctuations in demand and supply on farm prices and farm incomes

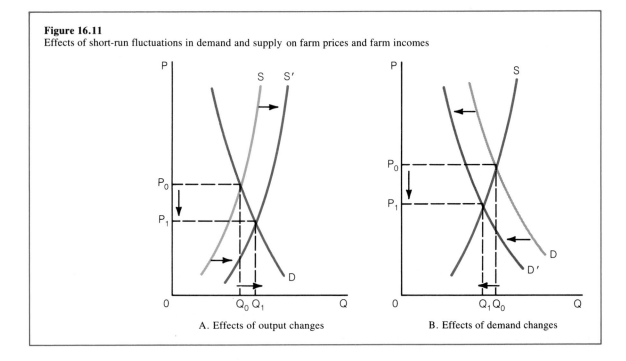

A. Effects of output changes

B. Effects of demand changes

down the price of farm goods; because demand is price inelastic, total farm income actually declines. The reason? Since $E_d < 1$, total revenue *falls* as a result of a price decline. What would be the impact on farm incomes of adverse weather conditions?

In Figure 16.11B we indicate the impact on farm incomes of short-run fluctuations in demand (largely due to variations in foreign demand) in the face of a price-inelastic supply curve. Any reduction in demand will be reflected in a sharp reduction in farm prices *and* farm incomes. Conversely, increases in demand will result in both increased farm prices and increased farm incomes.

The long-run farm problem is less acute today as a result of the growing importance of foreign markets for U.S. agricultural products. However, the short-run income instability problem has been aggravated because of that increased foreign dependence. This point has been emphasized repeatedly. The following quotation from the Council of Economic Advisers is illustrative:[3]

A clear demonstration that small variations in global food supply can lead to wide variations in producers' income and food prices was furnished by the events of 1972–74. World food production declined only about 2 percent globally in 1972. This modest decline led to an increase of 54 percent in U.S. crop prices in 1973 and to another 28 percent increase in 1974. Consumer food prices increased 31 percent over these 2 years. Net farm income was a record $33.3 billion in 1973, 78 percent higher than in 1972.

Government responses to the long-run and short-run farm problems. The above discussion provides only a thumbnail sketch of the economic problems that plague farmers. Nevertheless, it is clear why farmers have sought government assistance to improve their economic lot. The best goal and just how far government ought to go are matters of considerable debate. However, the most militant groups among farmers believe they have a simple answer, good for all times: Justice will be served only when farmers receive "100 percent parity."

[3] *Economic Report of the President,* 1980, p. 148.

Parity. The notion of **parity** has been more or less a part of our agricultural policy since 1933. The **parity ratio** is defined as the ratio of the prices farmers receive to the prices they pay in a given year compared to the value of that ratio in the period 1910–1914 (which, by the way, happened to be the heyday of agriculture). The statement that farmers are getting 75 percent parity in any given year means that prices received in that year, relative to costs paid, are 75 percent of what that ratio was in 1910–1914. It is clear, then, what 100 percent parity means: the ratio of prices received to costs are today the same as they were in the period 1910–1914. Loosely, the argument in favor of 100 percent parity can be put in the following way: If the income received from the sale of four bushels of wheat bought a pair of trousers in 1910–1914, the income received from the sale of four bushels today ought to buy a similar pair of trousers today.

Very few people, except perhaps farmers themselves, are persuaded that there ought to be a guarantee of 100 percent parity. In the first place, there is no good economic rationale for the selection of the base period—1910–1914—for which comparisons are made. That period was one of the most prosperous ever for American farmers. Why *they* might select such a period is obvious. But beyond that, it has no more claim to legitimacy than any other period. The second difficulty with 100 percent parity can easily be seen by recalling our earlier discussion of the long-run problem in the quarter century following World War II. Since the supply of agricultural commodities over time had a tendency to rise more rapidly than the demand, the free market would have dictated a decline in agricultural prices relative to the prices of other goods and services. In the eyes of most economists, this is precisely as it should have been. The decline in the relative price of agricultural products, by reducing the relative profitability of farming, acts as an inducement for resources to shift from agriculture toward the production of other goods and services for which a greater relative demand exists. A guarantee of 100 percent parity, on the other hand, would have forced the establishment of above-equilibrium prices for farm goods. The result would have been ever-increasing surpluses over time (since supply grew more rapidly than demand). You ought to be able to illustrate this outcome by showing that, over time, as the supply curve shifts further to the right than the demand curve, at the fixed price the agricultural surplus will grow. In order to maintain above-equilibrium prices, the government would have had to step in to buy up the surpluses created. Not only would it have been costly for government to purchase and store these surplus products. In addition, by ensuring that the relative price of farm goods did not fall, it would have forestalled the movement of resources out of agriculture into the production of other goods and services.

Although the concept of 100 percent parity has not been embraced by government for all goods, the milk lobby was able to get the federal government to agree to 100 percent parity in the case of milk products. At the time of this writing, the Reagan Administration was attempting to weaken that program by reducing its sup-port below 100 percent parity. Whether it will be successful remains to be seen. In other goods, the government has almost always stepped in to support agricultural prices whenever the parity ratio has fallen "too low," the definition of which has varied. In any event, the consequences of these government price supports are clear. Given the existence of a policy of government interference to ensure that the price does not fall below the established floor price, a surplus of agricultural products will emerge and the incentive for resources to shift out of agriculture will be diminished. Can you explain why?

Agricultural price supports. During the 1950s and 1960s, agricultural price support policies took one of two forms: government purchases of surpluses with and without crop restrictions. Under the program without restrictions, the government simply purchased the excess supply at the predetermined support price, placing the surplus in storage. The purpose was to support farm income by supporting price. This is illustrated in Figure 16.12A. What did the government do with these stored goods? The bulk of them were shipped abroad and given to foreign governments

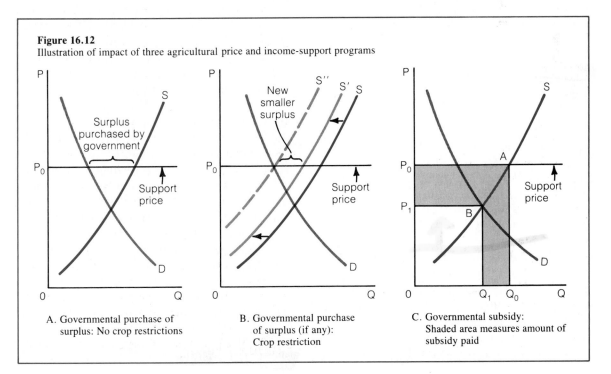

Figure 16.12
Illustration of impact of three agricultural price and income-support programs

A. Governmental purchase of
surplus: No crop restrictions

B. Governmental purchase
of surplus (if any):
Crop restriction

C. Governmental subsidy:
Shaded area measures amount of
subsidy paid

as part of our foreign aid program. Some were used to subsidize breakfast and lunch programs in public schools. The remainder was left to rot. Since there were no crop restrictions and since in the years following World War II supply grew faster than demand, this program meant growing surpluses over time at given fixed support prices. It is hardly surprising, therefore, that government decided to experiment at times with price supports combined with limits on production.

Under the program with crop restrictions, the government guarantees a support price only if farmers will cut back by some predetermined amount the number of acres they plant in any given growing season. By shifting the supply curve to the left, the government hopes to reduce the size of the surplus. This case is illustrated in Figure 16.12B. Often, crop restrictions were sufficient to eliminate entirely the surplus at the support price; the dashed supply curve in Figure 16.12B illustrates this outcome.

The philosophy underlying government support of farm incomes changed dramatically in 1973 with passage of the Agriculture and Consumer Protection Act. Before then, whenever market prices had a tendency to fall below the support prices, the government would step in and buy, maintaining prices at artificially high levels. The 1973 act changed all that. The government would now set a **"target price."** The market price could fall below this target price. When that happened, the government would provide farmers with a direct subsidy equal to the difference between the target price and the market price. This is illustrated in Figure 16.12C.

The market price is no longer limited by the support price. Rather, the market price is given by the intersection of the demand and supply curves (P_1 in Figure 16.12C). The government target price is given at P_0. In this instance, the government subsidy *per bushel* equals P_1P_0; the amount of the government subsidy equals the shaded area in Figure 16.12C.

The 1973 legislation limited the amount of the subsidy to $50,000 per farmer. Several attempts have been made since that time to cut the size of the subsidy to $20,000, but all such attempts have failed. The Reagan Administration

has taken a dim view of this subsidy program. At the time of this writing, it was a prime candidate to be slashed.

The farmer-owned national grain reserve program. The 1973 act changed the way farm incomes were protected. However, because market prices were permitted to fluctuate in accordance with changes in demand and supply, that act did not cushion farmers and consumers from the effects of instability resulting from increased reliance on market prices. In 1977, the government instituted a farmer-owned grain reserve program. The program was first applied to food grains (wheat and rice) and later extended to feed grains (corn, sorghum, barley, and oats).

The idea behind the farmer-owned grain reserve is straightforward. The government, in effect, directs farmers to add to their reserve stocks of food and feed grains when market prices fall "too low," thereby moderating the price decline; the farmers are directed to sell from reserve stocks when prices go "too high," the purpose being to moderate the price increase. Establishing what constitutes "too high" or "too low" a price is the difficult part. If the price at which farmers must begin adding to stocks to arrest price declines is consistently set above the market clearing price, farmers will, over the long run, always be adding to reserves; if the price at which farmers begin to sell from stocks to stop price increases is consistently set below the market clearing price, farmers will eventually run out of reserves. Neither outcome is desirable. Put differently, in order for the grain reserves program to operate as intended—to permit the smoothing out of price fluctuations—the longer-run target price must be set at a level corresponding to the long-run equilibrium price. Of course, since we cannot know beforehand what the long-run price will be, there will need be a lot of trial-and-error adjustments.

The incidence of an excise tax

It is frequently alleged that the imposition of an **excise tax**—a tax on each unit sold—on such items as automobile tires, cigarettes, and liquor is simply passed along to consumers in the form of higher prices so that they bear the full burden of the tax; it is the consumer who pays, not the producer. As Figure 16.13 makes clear, this view is generally incorrect. As a result of the imposition of the excise tax, the supply curve will shift upwards by the amount of the tax. If producers were willing to sell 100 units of the good at a price of $3 per unit, a $1 per unit excise tax means that they must now receive $4 per unit to sell the *same 100 units*. They are willing to sell 100 units at a price of $4 since the *net price*— the amount they receive per unit after paying the tax—is the same as before. However, as a result of the tax, producers will not be able to sell as much as they could before. At a price of $4.00, an excess supply of the good exists. Therefore, the price will be bid down from $4.00 until a new equilibrium is attained. In Figure 16.13, the new equilibrium is attained at a price of $3.40. Thus, consumers pay only 40 cents more for each unit consumed; producers receive 60 cents less for each unit sold. After paying the $1 tax, they receive only $2.40 for each unit they sell. The net price—defined as the gross price (the price paid by consumers) minus the tax— has fallen from $3 to $2.40. The burden of the

tax—or the **incidence** of the tax—is borne by both consumers and producers.

The excise tax has the obvious effect of reducing the quantity bought or sold. This result may have been one of the hoped-for results when the tax was levied. Excise taxes have often been levied on goods such as alcohol and cigarettes to discourage both their consumption and their profitable production.

The extent of the burden borne by consumers and by producers will depend on the price elasticities of demand and supply. Consider first the influence of the price elasticity of demand. In Figure 16.14, we draw two demand curves through point A; we assume point A represents the initial equilibrium price. The curve labeled D_1 is more elastic than the curve labeled D_0. As a result of the imposition of an excise tax that shifts the supply curve up from S to S^1, the price consumers will pay will be higher the *less* elastic their demand for the product is. This is seen by the fact that the new higher supply curve intersects D_1 at a price of P_1, but intersects D_0 at the higher price of P_2. Accordingly, the less elastic the demand for the product is, the greater the burden borne by consumers will be. There is an intuitive explanation for this result: the lower the price elasticity of demand, the less

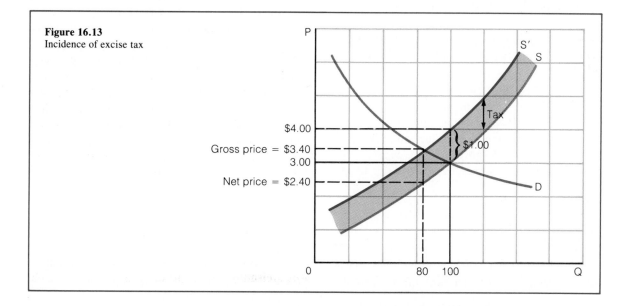

Figure 16.13
Incidence of excise tax

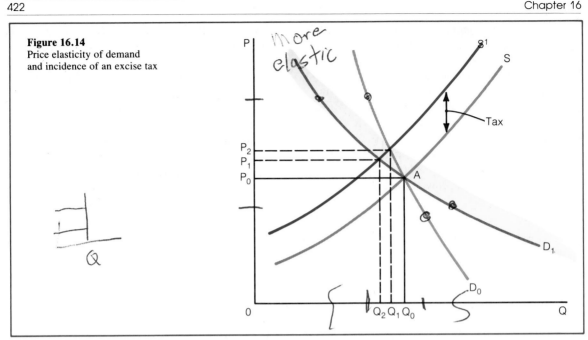

Figure 16.14
Price elasticity of demand
and incidence of an excise tax

responsive consumers are to a change in price; if they are less willing to cut the quantity they buy, it stands to reason that they will bear more of the burden of the tax.

Similarly, the less elastic the supply of the product is, the greater will be the burden borne by producers. This also can be understood intuitively: the less willing producers are to cut back production, the greater will be the adjustment thrust on them will be in the form of lower prices.

One final note is necessary. A careful examination of Figure 16.14 will reveal that the reduction in the equilibrium quantity as a result of the tax will be less the less elastic the demand for the product. If government imposed an excise tax primarily to raise revenue rather than to discourage consumption and production of the good in question, would government revenues rise more if demand were price elastic or price inelastic?

SUMMARY

1. The *demand* for a product—any product—is defined as the amount of the product

people are willing and able to buy. The *law of demand* is a *ceteris paribus* relationship; it hypothesizes that the price and quantity demanded are inversely related.

2. The *supply* of any product is defined as the amount producers are willing to produce and sell. The *law of supply* is a *ceteris paribus* relationship; it hypothesizes that the price and quantity supplied are positively related.

3. *Market equilibrium*—a situation in which there is no further tendency for change—occurs at the point of intersection of the demand and supply curves. At any price other than the equilibrium price—the *market-clearing price*—market disequilibrium will exist. Above-equilibrium prices create surpluses (or excess supplies); below-equilibrium prices create shortages.

4. Changes in demand or supply (as opposed to changes in the quantities demanded or supplied) change the market equilibrium.

5. A good is *normal* if income and the demand for the good are positively related; if the demand for the good and income are inversely related, the good is *inferior*. If the demand for one good and the price of another good are positively related, the two goods are *substitutes;* if

the demand for one good and the price of another good are inversely related, the two goods are *complements.*

6. The *elasticity* concept was developed to enable us to measure the responsiveness of buyers and sellers to changes in the factors that determine, on the one hand, how much people are able and willing to buy, and on the other, how much producers are willing to produce and sell.

7. The *price elasticity of demand* is defined as the percentage change in the quantity demanded of some product divided by the percentage change in its price. This elasticity measure, like all elasticity measures, uses percentages to ensure that the calculated value is unaffected by the units of measurements. The *midpoints formula* should be used to more accurately estimate the average degree of responsiveness over a range of prices and quantities.

8. If demand is *price elastic,* a reduction (increase) in price will cause total revenue to increase (decrease); if demand is *price inelastic,* a reduction (increase) in price will cause total revenue to fall (increase); if demand is *unit price elastic,* total revenue will remain unchanged in the face of a change in price.

9. In general, the price elasticity of demand for a product will be greater *(a)* the greater the availability of close substitutes, *(b)* the more important the item is in consumers' budgets, *(c)* if the good is viewed as a luxury, and *(d)* in the long run.

10. Other elasticity measures include the *income elasticity of demand,* the *cross-price elasticity of demand,* and the *price elasticity of supply.*

11. In *the very short run*—the *market period*—rates of production cannot be changed. Whether or not supply is perfectly price inelastic in the *very* short run, however, will depend on the nature of the good—specifically, whether the good in question is perishable or storable. *The short run* is defined as a time period for which the "plant" capacity of producers is fixed. The quantity produced need not be fixed, however, because producers can vary the intensity of operation of their fixed plants. In *the long run,* producers can vary both the intensity with which they operate their plants and their productive

capacity. In the long run, supply will be perfectly price elastic if expansion can take place under conditions of "constant costs"; under "increasing cost" conditions the price elasticity of supply will be less than infinite.

12. The elasticity concept has a great many applications. An understanding of the concept, for example, provides us with insight into rent controls, the U.S. farm problem, and the incidence of excise taxes.

CONCEPTS FOR REVIEW

Demand
Supply
Law of demand
Law of supply
Market equilibrium
Market disequilibrium
Surplus (excess supply)
Shortage (excess demand)
Change in demand versus change in quantity demanded
Change in supply versus change in quantity supplied
Price elasticity of demand
Arc-price elasticity of demand: the midpoints formula
Price-elastic demand
Price-inelastic demand
Perfectly price-inelastic demand
Unit price-elastic demand
Income elasticity of demand
Cross-price elasticity of demand
Price elasticity of supply
The very short run (the market period)
The short run
The long run
Price ceilings
Price floors
Rent controls
Black market
Parity ratio

Farmer-owned national grain reserve program

Excise tax

Incidence of an excise tax

QUESTIONS FOR DISCUSSION

(Those marked with an asterisk (*) are more difficult.)

1. Suppose the relationship between the price per pound of chocolate and the number of pounds of chocolate demanded is as follows:

Price per pound	Quantity (pounds)
$1	8
2	7
3	6
4	5
5	4

a. What is the arc-price elasticity of demand in the $1–$2 price range? In the $4–$5 price range? How would you explain the differences?

b. Convert the quantity column from pounds to ounces. Would this change affect your calculated arc-price elasticities of demand in (a)? If you had used some other measure of responsiveness, such as the change in the quantity demanded divided by the change in price, would your calculated measures of responsiveness have been different as a result of the conversion to ounces? Illustrate and explain.

*2. Assume for the moment that the price of gasoline is controlled and that, initially, the control price is equal to the market clearing price.

a. Suppose that foreign oil producers cut off their exports of petroleum products to the United States. Given the price ceiling, would the lines at the gasoline pumps be longer if the demand for motor gasoline were relatively elastic or relatively inelastic? (Hint: At the initial price, draw two demand curves, one more elastic than the other, as was done in Figure 16.14.)

b. Suppose price controls were lifted. Would the lines at the gasoline pumps be longer if the demand for motor gasoline were relatively elastic or relatively inelastic? What other effects would differences in the price elasticity of demand have?

3. The calculated cross-price elasticity of demand between good A and good B is zero. What conclusion can you draw about how goods A and B are related?

4. Many studies have found that the price elasticity of demand for automobiles lies in the 0.6–1.4 range. However, when you undertook a study of the demand for the Chevrolet Monte Carlo, you found that the price elasticity of demand was 4.2. In view of the results from other studies, should your findings be thrown out? (Hint: Is the elasticity of demand for a broadly defined good different from the elasticity of demand for a narrowly defined good?)

5. Carefully evaluate the following statement: "I will never understand farmers. They complain bitterly if weather conditions become adverse. However, if adverse weather conditions cause sharply reduced supplies, they are better off because their incomes will increase." (Hint: There are two issues raised here. One has to do with the effect of adverse weather conditions on farmers in the aggregate; the other has to do with the effects of bad weather on some individual farmers.)

6. In the city of Alpha the price elasticity of demand for mass transit has been estimated to be 1.6. The city manager asks you whether the price should be increased or decreased in order to increase mass transit revenues. What advice would you give?

7. Prior to the deregulation of the airline industry, many of the airline companies argued that the price reductions for air travel that would follow in the wake of deregulation would sharply reduce their revenues. In fact, the opposite happened. What does this tell you about what those airline companies thought the price elasticity of demand for air travel to be? What does this tell you about the actual price elasticity of demand?

Scarcity is the watchword of our economic system. And the forces of demand and supply are an embodiment of this principle. They reflect the choices made by buyers and sellers in the face of scarcity. If we are to understand how our economy functions, we must become thoroughly familiar with the forces that govern the choices people make. This is the task we set for ourselves in this chapter and in Chapter 18. In this chapter, the focal point of our attention will be on the **utility-maximizing principle** which underlies the concept of demand and provides the theoretical underpinning for the law of demand. In Chapter 18 we will examine in detail various **economic cost** concepts, which are critical to our understanding of supply.

THE THEORY OF CONSUMER CHOICE: THE INDIVIDUAL CONSUMER

Since the *market demand* for some good or service is nothing other than the sum of the individual demands on the part of all buyers in the market, it makes sense to begin our inquiry with a consideration of the factors that affect the individual consumer. Moreover, in view of how the demand for some good or service has been defined—i.e., as expressing a willingness and ability to buy, a willingness to forego other things in order to acquire it—it is important that we be able to illustrate this idea for the individual. We turn to an analysis of this issue now.

For the vast majority of us, it is inconceivable that we could have everything we could possibly want. The list of goods and services we would like to have is virtually endless. We would almost always like to have more, if not for ourselves personally, then for others. Realistically, however, we can't have everything we desire. Put bluntly, we simply can't afford it. Our limited incomes force us to settle for less, usually much less. It is necessary, therefore, for each of us to make choices—to choose, as best we can, how to dispose of our limited incomes. Of course, by choosing as we do from among the alternatives we face, we incur a cost—an *opportunity cost*—measured as the highest-valued alternative foregone.

Chapter 17

Utility theory and the theory of demand

In order to make deliberate choices, we must make comparisons among the alternatives available; that is, we must be able to compare the **want-satisfying qualities** of the goods and services available for consumption. The concept of **utility** was developed for precisely this purpose. *The utility of any good or service is a measure of its want satisfaction to the consumer; it is a measure of the amount of satisfaction the individual derives by consuming it.* Thus, the want-satisfying qualities of goods and services are reflected in their utilities.

All of this sounds simple enough. In fact, there is nothing simple about it. The problem is that no objective measure of utility exists; it is entirely a subjective construct. It measures for each consumer the amount of personal satisfaction he or she derives from the consumption of various goods and services. What could be more subjective than that! Moreover, it is highly unlikely that any of us could assign a *numerical* value to the utility we receive from each of the goods and services we consume. We could probably indicate whether driving a Rolls-Royce would give us more or less satisfaction than driving a Mack truck, or whether one bundle of goods would give us more or less satisfaction than some other. But we would be hard pressed to attach numerical values to each of these alternatives.

As we shall see later, the theory of consumer choice developed in this chapter does *not* assume that people are able to measure utility *numerically*. It does, however, assume that people do have the ability to rank the alternatives they face in terms of their preferences. They can state whether driving a Rolls-Royce will give them more or less satisfaction than driving a Mack truck, or whether one bundle of goods will give them more or less satisfaction than some other. As a result of this fact, the foundation of the theory of consumer choice is made more plausible than if numerical values had to be assigned. For the purpose of illustrating a number of important relationships, however, it is *convenient* to assume that people can and do measure numerically the utility they receive from the goods and services they consume. Because of its convenience (but

only because it is convenient, *not* because it is an essential part of the theory), we will retain this assumption until it ceases to be useful.

The law of diminishing marginal utility

The first fundamental proposition important to our understanding of the law of demand, is the **law of diminishing marginal utility. Marginal utility** is defined as the change in total utility brought about by the consumption of one additional unit of a good; it refers to the *extra* satisfaction, the *extra* utility received. The law of diminishing marginal utility tells us that *the extra utility diminishes with successive purchases.* As more and more is purchased (during some span of time), total utility will increase, but at a diminishing rate.

The law of diminishing marginal utility is illustrated in Figure 17.1. Column (2) of the table that accompanies Figure 17.1 shows how total utility changes as the consumption of the good in question changes. As is apparent, total utility increases, but at a diminishing rate, through the fifth unit consumed. The sixth unit adds nothing to total utility (the consumer is said to be *satiated* at that point). And note what happens to total utility as the seventh unit is consumed—it declines. Figure 17.1A depicts this relationship graphically.

A diminishing growth rate of total utility naturally implies a diminishing *marginal* utility. Since marginal utility is defined as the extra utility added by the last unit consumed, and since the extra utility diminishes as more and more units are consumed, marginal utility diminishes as consumption is increased. Column (3) of the table accompanying Figure 17.1 shows this relationship; its graphical counterpart is displayed in Figure 17.1B. As illustrated there, the MU curve has a negative slope throughout.

To help cement these ideas, consider the following analogy. Figure 17.1A looks like a hill that is less steep the higher one climbs. As you move up the hill, each step takes you to newer heights. But because the hill gets progressively less steep, each successive step raises your height somewhat less than the previous one. If you were to calculate the extra height added by each additional step—i.e., if you were to calculate the *marginal* height gain for each additional step—you would get a series of numbers, each one smaller than the previous one. Plotting those numbers, you would get a curve that looked like Figure 17.1B. As the number of steps taken increased, the marginal height gain would decline.

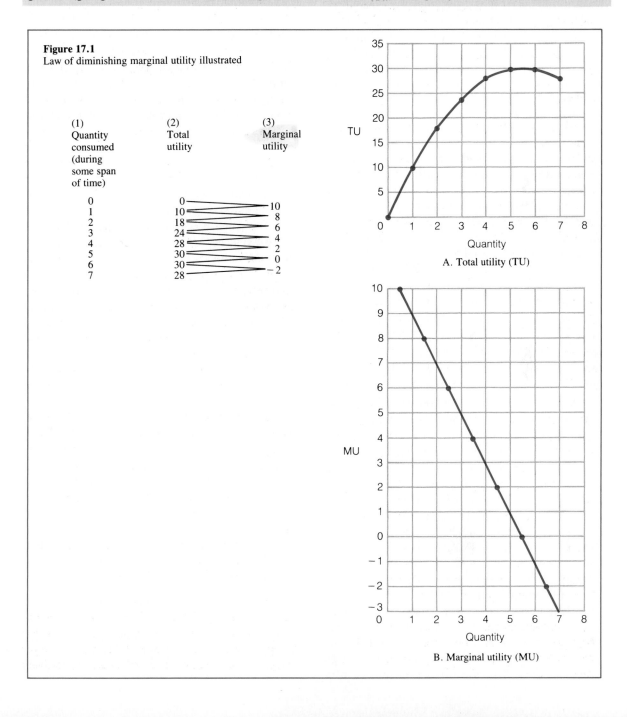

Figure 17.1
Law of diminishing marginal utility illustrated

(1) Quantity consumed (during some span of time)	(2) Total utility	(3) Marginal utility
0	0	
1	10	10
2	18	8
3	24	6
4	28	4
5	30	2
6	30	0
7	28	−2

A. Total utility (TU)

B. Marginal utility (MU)

Two final points are worth noting about Figure 17.1. First, if the consumption of an additional unit causes total utility to increase, it follows directly that marginal utility must be positive; the MU curve will lie above the quantity axis at that point. If an additional unit consumed causes total utility to decline, on the other hand, the MU curve will lie below the quantity axis at that point. The reason? If total utility declines, the extra utility added must have been negative. Second, it is equally important to recognize that a *reduction* in the amount consumed *raises* the good's marginal utility to the consumer. To see this, consider again the numbers presented in column (3) of the table accompanying Figure 17.1. At two units, the marginal utility—the extra utility added by consuming one more unit—is 6, whereas at four units, the marginal utility is 2. Put in terms of our hill analogy, if you slip and slide down the hill, the first step you take as you resume your climb will raise your height by more than the height *increase* you would have accomplished had you been higher up.

How reasonable is the law of diminishing marginal utility? Generally, you need look no farther than your own personal experiences to confirm its validity. The steak you eat on Monday night could well give you a great deal of utility. And probably, your total satisfaction for the week would rise if you had steak again on Tuesday, though probably the additional utility would be less than the initial portion of utility on Monday. And what would happen to your total utility for the week if you had yet another steak on Wednesday? And Thursday? Would you not eventually tire of steak if you had it night after night? Or consider the implications of your decision to tip a beer or two with friends after an evening of study. You studied hard all day and that first beer does wonders for your disposition. The second beer probably further increases your utility, but by the third or fourth beer, its marginal utility has fallen off considerably. (Perhaps at that point you give some consideration to the likely consequences for your head the morning after.) What is true of steak and beer is generally true of virtually everything else you consume.

Can you illustrate this point with yet other examples?

Utility maximization: The equimarginal principle

The second fundamental proposition in the theory of consumer choice is the **equimarginal principle.** This principle is a simple and intuitively plausible rule about how the consumer can obtain the "best" collection of goods possible given his or her budget limit. The principle is based on the assumption that *consumers desire to maximize their utility.* The principle seeks to answer the question, *Of all the possible combinations of goods and services that consumers could obtain with their limited incomes, which particular combination will maximize their utility?* The answer provided by the equimarginal principle is this: *Consumers should allocate their money incomes in such a way that the marginal utility per dollar spent is the same for all goods purchased.* Symbolically, this principle can be restated in terms of the marginal utilities and prices of the different goods and services (A, B, C, etc.) as follows:

$$\frac{MU_A}{P_A} = \frac{MU_B}{P_B} = \frac{MU_C}{P_C} = \cdots = \text{Common MU per \$ of income.}$$

Note that this rule does *not* state that consumers should allocate their money incomes in such a way that the marginal utility is the same for all goods purchased; what is important is the *marginal utility per dollar spent.* Nor does it state that consumers should allocate their incomes toward those goods that have the highest *total* utility or the highest total utility per dollar spent; to repeat, what matters is the marginal utility per dollar spent.

All of these points can be readily illustrated with the aid of a simple numerical example. You decide to join some friends on Saturday evening for some beer and pizza at Luigi's. The beer is priced at 80 cents a glass; each slice of pizza is priced at 60 cents. You have a budget limit of $5. The problem you confront is that of determining how to spend your $5 in a way that will maximize your utility—i.e., that will give you the greatest personal satisfaction. Using the equimarginal principle and given your subjective evaluation of the satisfaction to be obtained from consuming various quantities of beer and pizza as presented in Table 17-1, you will maximize your utility by consuming four beers and three slices of pizza. The fact that the marginal utility of the fourth beer is 20 and the marginal utility of the third slice of pizza is 15 means, given the respective prices of the two goods, that the marginal utility per dollar spent is the same for both goods (i.e., $\frac{15}{0.60} = \frac{20}{0.80} = 25 =$ Common MU per dollar of income). With this combination, your total utility for the evening comes to 280 (200 from beer and 80 from pizza). Can you do any better than that? No. There is no other combination that will yield you more utility and still be consistent with your budget limit of $5. Prove this to yourself by trying to choose some alternative combination.

A careful study of Table 17.1 will also reveal that the marginal utility per dollar spent will be the same for both beer and pizza if you select two slices of pizza and three beers (i.e., $\frac{30}{0.60} = \frac{40}{0.80} = 50 =$ Common MU per dollar

of income). Would not such a combination, therefore, represent a position of maximum utility? It would if your budget limit was $3.60 (three beers would cost you $2.40, and two slices of pizza, $1.20). However, given that you want to maximize your utility subject to a budget limit of $5, three beers and two slices of pizza will not satisfy the utility-maximizing rule; only four beers and three slices of pizza will accomplish that goal.

Of course, the utility-maximizing rule applies to more than just your decision of how best to spend $5 on beer and pizza during some given Saturday evening. It applies to *all* the goods and services you consume, including beer and pizza; the numerical example of Table 17.1 was designed for illustrative purposes only. It needs to be emphasized, moreover, that, as a description of consumer behavior, the equimarginal principle does *not* require that people be able to measure precisely—i.e., numerically—the utility they receive from each of the goods they consume. The principle is useful as long as people have the ability to make at least rough comparisons of the satisfaction they receive from the various goods and services they consume. Nor does the validity of the principle depend on people carrying their spending to the point where the mar-

Table 17.1
The equimarginal principle illustrated (budget limit = $5)

(1)	(2)	(3)	(4)	(5)	(1)	(2)	(3)	(4)	(5)
		Pizza					Beer		
Quantity	Price per slice	Total utility	Marginal utility	MU/P	Quantity	Price per glass	Total utility	Marginal utility	MU/P
0	.60	0			0	.80	0		
1	.60	35	35	58	1	.80	80	80	100
2	.60	65	30	50	2	.80	140	60	75
3	.60	80	15	25	3	.80	180	40	50
4	.60	85	5	8	4	.80	200	20	25
5	.60	80	−5	−8	5	.80	210	10	13
6	.60	65	−15	−25	6	.80	190	−20	−25
7	.60	40	−25	−42					
8	.60	5	−35	−58					

Note: In drawing up this table it has been assumed that the utility derived from beer is independent of the amount of pizza consumed, and vice versa. In other words, it has been assumed that whether you have one, two, or more slices of pizza, this in no way affects the amount of utility you obtain from beer. This is a bit unrealistic in view of the fact that your thirst, and therefore your utility from beer, will be affected by how much pizza you eat. Thus, there will be a different set of numbers for the utility derived from beer, depending on how many slices of pizza are consumed. We ignore such complications here.

ginal utility per dollar spent is *exactly* the same for all goods. Indeed, in the case of big-ticket items such as automobiles, refrigerators, clothes dryers, and the like—goods that are *not* divisible—the consumer could well decide to buy *one* unit (because the marginal utility of that first unit was sufficiently greater than the marginal utility of an equal number of dollars spent elsewhere), but not a second one (because its marginal utility per dollar spent was so much less).

The equimarginal principle: An intuitive restatement.   As a result of these important qualifications, it is possible to provide an intuitive restatement of the equimarginal principle: Because our incomes are limited, and because our wants are virtually insatiable, each of us is confronted with the task of having to make choices from among the alternatives we face. It is reasonable to assume that each of us makes choices in an effort to maximize our own utility. We can be assured of accomplishing this goal only if the additional satisfaction—*the marginal utility*—obtainable from any given purchase is at least as great as the additional satisfaction obtainable from *the same number of dollars spent elsewhere*. Notice the emphasis given to the marginal utility obtainable from the *same number* of dollars spent elsewhere. The marginal utility you derive from the purchase of a Mercedes Benz may be substantially greater than the marginal utility associated with the purchase of a Citation. But that difference alone is not sufficient to induce you to buy the Mercedes. The Mercedes is much more expensive than the Citation. If you buy the Citation instead, you will have much more income to spend on other things. You will buy the Mercedes only if the extra utility added by that purchase is at least as great as the extra utility you could obtain from all of the possible alternative uses of an equal number of dollars. This is the meaning of the equimarginal principle.

THE EQUIMARGINAL PRINCIPLE AND THE LAW OF DEMAND

With the aid of the equimarginal principle, the law of demand can be derived in a very straightforward manner. The law of demand, you will recall, states that, *ceteris paribus,* the price and the quantity demanded of any good are inversely related. This law, as we shall see, follows as a direct consequence of the utility-maximizing behavior implied by the equimarginal principle. To illustrate, suppose you have allocated your income in accordance with the utility-maximizing rule and that, initially (i.e., before any change in price), the marginal utility per dollar spent is the same for all goods purchased. Thus,

$$\frac{MU_A}{P_A} = \frac{MU_B}{P_B} = \frac{MU_C}{P_C} = \cdots.$$

Consider now the impact of a reduction in the price of good A, holding all else constant. The change in price means that the initial quantities purchased of A, B, and C, etc., are no longer optimal. Indeed, given the initial quantities, the reduced price for good A implies that the marginal utility per dollar spent on A now exceeds the marginal utility per dollar spent on other goods and services. You have an incentive, therefore, to buy a larger quantity of good A. As you buy more of good A, its marginal utility diminishes. Equilibrium is restored when the marginal utility per dollar spent is once again the same for all goods purchased. Utility maximization, then, combined with the law of diminishing marginal utility, provides us with one rationale for the law of demand.

The law of demand: Income and substitution effects

As the discussion above implies, the process whereby consumers adjust to a change in the price of any single good involves more than an adjustment in the quantity demanded of that good alone. It frequently involves an adjustment in the amount consumed of other goods and services as well. Given the budget constraint of consumers, then, it should be obvious that the price elasticity of demand for the good in question— i.e., the responsiveness of the quantity demanded of that good to a change in its price—depends on the nature and magnitude of the changes in the amounts consumed of *other* goods and services. This is easily illustrated. Suppose you have a budget limit of $100 a week. You maximize your utility by spending that $100 in such a way that the marginal utility per dollar spent is the same for all goods purchased. Suppose, given initial prices, that your utility is maximized by allocating $20 per week to good A, with the reminder, $80, allocated to all other goods and services. Suppose now that the price of good A falls. As a result of this price decline, a reallocation of your budget will be called for. According to the law of demand, the quantity demanded of good A will rise. But whether or not you spend more or less of your income on good A will depend on how price elastic your demand for this product is. But the price elasticity of your demand can only be determined on the basis of how you decide to reallocate your budget in response to a change in the price of good A. If in the process of readjusting your expenditures you decide to now spend $82 on "other" goods and services and only $18 on good A, this implies that your demand for good A is price inelastic. Why? Because a decline in the price of good A induced you to reduce your total expenditures for that good. If, on the other hand, you decide to now spend only $79 on "other" goods and services, this implies that your demand for good A is price elastic. Can you explain why? (If you are having difficulty understanding this discussion, you should go back and review the material in Chapter 16 on the relationship between the total expenditure for a good and its price elasticity of demand.)

We gain insight into the nature of these budgetary reallocations by recognizing that a change in the price of some good or service has associated with it both a **substitution effect** and an **income effect.** Let us consider each of these in turn.

Substitution effect. As a result of reduction in the price of good A, consumers have a tendency to buy more of it by substituting away from goods that are now relatively dearer. When the price of chicken falls while beef prices do not, people have a tendency to substitute some chicken for beef in their diets. Chicken is a better

buy in the sense that any given level of satisfaction can now be attained more cheaply with an increase in the consumption of chicken and a reduction in the consumption of beef. This is known as the substitution effect of a price change.

Income effect. In addition to the substitution effect, there is an income effect. That is, a reduction in the price of good A means that a given money income will enable people to buy more goods and services than before. A reduction in the price of chicken means that the budget stretches further; *real income* has increased. What will happen to the consumption of chicken as a result of this change in real income? It all depends. If chicken is a **normal good,** people will buy more of it. Here the income effect reinforces the substitution effect. If chicken is an **inferior good,** people will cut back on its consumption, offsetting in part the increased consumption of chicken attributable to the substitution effect.[1]

The price elasticity of demand for any given good will reflect the nature and strengths of these two effects. And, of course, the quantitative importance of these forces will vary from good to good and from consumer to consumer. The substitution effect in the case of some goods for which few close substitutes exist may be negligible (e.g., food), whereas for other goods, it could be sizable (e.g., individual food products, such as steak, for which there are several close substitutes). But the strength of this effect may not be the same for all people. Some people swear by steak, eating it to the exclusion of many other high-protein foods, whereas other people see it as "just like" so many other foods. Similarly,

---

[1] *If* chicken is an inferior good, and *if* the reduction in its consumption attributable to the income effect more than offsets the increased consumption attributable to the substitution effect, the law of demand will have been violated in the case of chicken. A reduction in the price of chicken will have induced a reduction in the quantity of chicken demanded. If people respond in this fashion to a change in the price of chicken, that good would be referred to as a **Giffen good,** named after Sir Robert Giffen, who observed that during the Irish famine of 1845, families increased their consumption of potatoes despite a sharp increase in their price. Other than this clear-cut historical example, economists have discovered few instances of Giffen goods. We shall, therefore, ignore such aberrations.

the income effect will vary from good to good and from consumer to consumer.

DEMAND: SOME CONCLUDING COMMENTS

It should by now be apparent why the demand for some good cannot be considered in isolation. The demand for any *single* good or service reflects the decisions people make regarding their purchases of *all* goods and services. Since our incomes are limited, we are forced to make choices from among the alternative goods available for purchase. Associated with each choice we make is a cost—an opportunity cost—measured by the highest-valued consumption alternatives foregone. We are assured of maximizing our utility only if the satisfaction we derive from each purchase is at least as great as the satisfaction to be obtained from a similar number of dollars spent elsewhere.

Changes in the prices of goods and services will generally call forth some readjustment in our spending patterns. The same is true of a change in income. How responsive we are to changes in these variables is measured by the price elasticity of demand, the cross-price elasticity of demand, and the income elasticity of demand.

We are each different from one another. In general, each of us responds in a quantitatively different way to a change in income and prices. The market demand obtained by summing up the individual demands of all buyers in the market reflects the relative preferences of all buyers in the aggregate. In a market context, the various elasticity concepts measure the average aggregate responses of all buyers.

For our purposes, it is extremely useful to examine the concept of demand in the following manner: The value of any commodity to a consumer is measured by the amount of the other commodities the consumer is willing to give up to obtain it. If the consumer is willing to give up four units of good A to obtain one unit of good B, good B is worth at least four of A to

that consumer. Since money is used to purchase most goods and services, the worth of any commodity can be expressed in terms of money. If the consumer is willing to pay $5 for one unit of some commodity, it means that the satisfaction obtained from its purchase is judged to be at least as great as that which could be obtained from spending that $5 elsewhere.

Consider the information displayed in Figure 17.2. At a price of $8 per pound, the consumer is willing and able to buy one pound of coffee per month. The consumer derives at least as much utility from this first pound of coffee as could be obtained by spending $8 on other goods and services. At a price of $6 per pound, the consumer is willing and able to buy two pounds per month. This means that the consumer derives at least as much utility from the *second* pound as could be obtained by spending $6 on other goods and services. What meaning can we attach to the fact that the consumer is willing and able to purchase three pounds of coffee at a price of $4 per pound? Each point on the consumer's demand curve, then, measures the *additional* satisfaction the consumer receives from the last unit purchased; the price of the good measures the *additional* cost the consumer must incur to obtain that last unit. Consumer satisfaction will be maximized, therefore, only if consumption is carried to the point where the additional satisfaction, the additional benefit, to be obtained from the last unit is equal to the additional cost that must be incurred to obtain it.

Suppose the *market price* for coffee is $4 per pound. You, as an individual consumer, are powerless to affect that price; whether you buy one pound of coffee or 10 pounds of coffee, its price will not change. How much coffee should you buy at this price in order to maximize your utility or satisfaction? Three pounds of coffee per month. The first pound of coffee is worth $8, but its cost to you is only $4. Since what you sacrifice (the $4 worth of other goods and services) is so much less than the benefits you receive, you should consume more than a single pound. Likewise, you should consume more than two pounds per month. Can you explain why?

Figure 17.2
Demand, price, and utility maximization

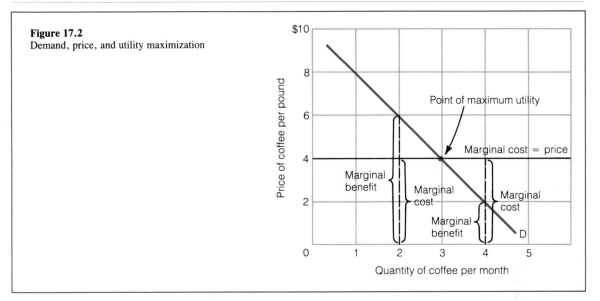

Only at three pounds is the *marginal utility, the marginal benefit* (the additional utility or benefit of the last unit), equal to the marginal cost (the additional cost incurred to obtain the last unit). Since the marginal benefit of the fourth pound is less than its marginal cost, you would be better off *not* purchasing it. Your utility is maximized at three pounds of coffee per month.

Consumer surplus

On the basis of the foregoing discussion, it should be clear that the total utility derived from the consumption of some good is generally larger than the total expenditure made to obtain it. This is easily demonstrated. Consider our previous coffee example. The price of coffee is $4 per pound. But the first pound is worth $8 to you. The first pound of coffee, therefore, yields a surplus value of $4. This $4 surplus value we refer to as the **consumer surplus** obtained from the first pound consumed. The second pound of coffee also yields a consumer surplus, this time of $2, because the marginal benefit of the second pound exceeds the marginal cost—the price—by that amount. Is there any consumer surplus associated with the purchase of the third pound? Why?

The total value you receive from the consump-

tion of three pounds of coffee, therefore, is $18 ($8 from the first pound, $6 from the second and $4 from the third). Your total expenditure, on the other hand, amounts to only $12 (3 × $4). You derive a consumer surplus of $6—the difference between its total value to you and its total cost. The reason a surplus exists is simple.

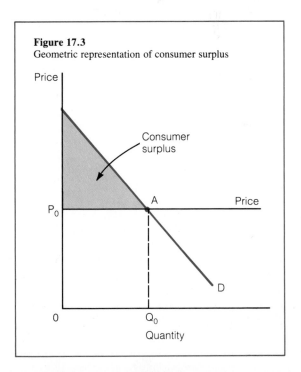

Figure 17.3
Geometric representation of consumer surplus

All units of the good sell for whatever the last unit brings on the market ($4). From the law of diminishing marginal utility, previous units are worth more than the last one; you earn a surplus on all previous units purchased. The shaded area under the demand curve in Figure 17.3 measures this consumer surplus geometrically. The area under the demand curve up to Q_0, the quantity purchased, measures the total utility or satisfaction obtained; the rectangle OP_0AQ_0, measures the total expenditure on the good; the difference between the two areas—i.e., the shaded area—is the consumer surplus.

The diamond-water paradox

With the aid of these concepts, economists years ago were able to resolve the following classic paradox. Water is clearly a much more useful commodity than diamonds; but diamonds command a very high price (upwards of $4,000 a carat today), whereas water is cheap. A number of classical economists, including Adam Smith, concluded from this that the utility of a good had nothing to do with its price; if it did, water would sell at a price substantially higher than the price of diamonds. They concluded, there-

fore, that each good had two different values— a use value and a value in exchange. Water has a very high use value, but a relatively low value in exchange; the opposite was true of diamonds.

Modern economists rejected this distinction, and rightly so. In the first place, the price of a good is not determined by its functional usefulness. Its price is determined by the demand for and supply of it. If the supply of some good is large *relative* to the demand for it, that good will command a low price; if the supply of it is small *relative* to the demand for it, it will command a high price. Water may be a much more useful product than diamonds, but that, per se, is irrelevant. Water is cheap and diamonds are expensive precisely because, compared with the demand for these goods, water is very abundant and diamonds are very scarce. This is illustrated in Figure 17.4.

There is a second problem with the thinking of the early classical economists with respect to this issue. It arises because they failed to recognize the crucial difference between the total utility received from each of the goods consumed and their marginal utilities. Because diamonds are scarce, their *marginal* utility is also high; as a result, they command a high price. Water,

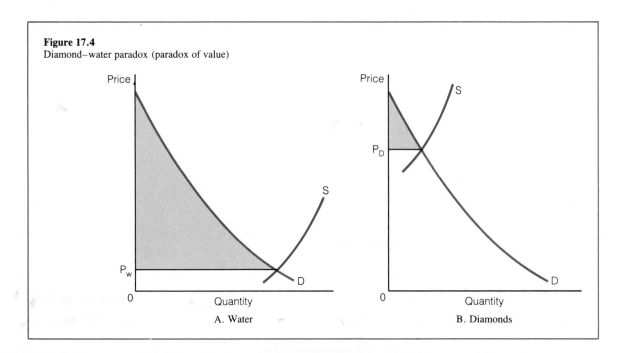

Figure 17.4
Diamond–water paradox (paradox of value)

A. Water

B. Diamonds

on the other hand, being relatively abundant, has a low *marginal* utility; it is, therefore, cheap. But the *total* utility derived from water is probably substantially larger than the *total* utility from diamonds. By this we mean that the consumer surplus earned in the consumption of water exceeds by a large margin the consumer surplus obtained from the purchase of diamonds. The shaded portions of the two diagrams in Figure 17.4 illustrate these differences dramatically.

The diamond-water paradox is thus easily resolved. Price is determined by the *relative* scarcity of a commodity. *And the relative scarcity of a good can only be determined by the demand for and supply of it.* It is the marginal utility of a good, not its total utility, that is important here. If a good is scarce, its marginal utility is high; therefore, so is its price. A good that is less scarce will command a lower price because its marginal utility is lower. On the basis of these considerations, can you now explain why a life-saving shot of penicillin might be cheap compared with mink coats for poodles?

SOME CONCLUDING OBSERVATIONS ON DEMAND THEORY AND THE THEORY OF CONSUMER CHOICE

In developing the theory of consumer choice, we did not address the question of what motivates consumers to choose as they do. This is not an easy question to answer, nor is it one that economists as economists are capable of answering. As far as the economist is concerned, this question is best left to be answered by psychologists, sociologists, anthropologists, and other students of human behavior. Economists merely take people's tastes as "given"; they do not inquire into all the factors that cause people to have the tastes they do. With that as a starting point, economists then proceed to make three reasonable assumptions:

1. Each of us has wants that far outstrip our means to satisfy those wants; we must, therefore, make choices.
2. The law of diminishing marginal utility is

a close approximation for each good consumed.
3. Consumers choose in ways designed to maximize their utility.

The theory of consumer choice developed in this chapter has followed directly from these three assumptions.

The utility the consumer derives from his or her choices is determined subjectively. There is no objective measurement of utility; the amount of satisfaction received is a subjective assessment. As a result of this fact, it is not possible for us to make comparisons among people in terms of the utility they receive from various goods and services. In the jargon of economists, we cannot make **interpersonal utility comparisons.** The failure to recognize this fact has led some people to draw wrong conclusions regarding the impact on consumer welfare of certain policy actions undertaken by the government. It is frequently argued, for example, that, because of the law of diminishing marginal utility, or more specifically, because of the law of diminishing marginal utility of income, total welfare for society as a whole can be increased by redistributing income from the rich to the poor. This conclusion will follow, of course, only if it can be shown that a dollar given to a poor person is worth more than the same dollar for the rich person. But how could that ever be proven? Just because the rich have more dollars than the poor does not mean that a dollar is therefore worth more to poor people. The worth of an additional dollar to people in each group is subjective; objective comparisons are impossible. This does not mean, of course, that it is impossible to make a case for redistributing income from the rich to the poor. It means only that the case cannot be made on the basis of interpersonal utility comparisons of income.

SUMMARY

1. The *utility* of any good or service is a measure of its want satisfaction to the consumer.
2. Utility underlies the theory of demand. Central to our understanding of the *law of de-*

mand is the *law of diminishing marginal utility,* which states that the extra utility added by any good or service diminishes as more and more is purchased (during some span of time).

3.   Another principle central to our understanding of the law of demand is the *equimarginal principle.* This principle provides a rule that indicates how consumers should allocate their limited budgets so as to maximize utility. The rule states that their budgets should be allocated so that the marginal utility per dollar spent is the same for all goods purchased. Thus, utility will be maximized when

$$\frac{MU_A}{P_A} = \frac{MU_B}{P_B} = \frac{MU_C}{P_C} = \cdots = \begin{array}{l}\text{Common } MU \\ \text{per \$ of} \\ \text{income}\,.\end{array}$$

4.   The equimarginal principle highlights fact that a change in the price of any single good or service involves more than an adjustment in the quantity demanded of that good or service alone; it frequently involves an adjustment in the amount consumed of other goods and services as well. The nature of the budgetary reallocations caused by a change in the price of any commodity is captured in the *income* and *substitution effects* of the price change.

5.   It is very useful to examine the concept of demand from the following perspective: The value of any commodity can be measured by the amount of the other goods and services that the consumer is willing to give up to obtain it. Put differently, each point on the consumer's demand curve measures the additional satisfaction, the marginal utility, or the marginal benefit, from the last unit purchased.

6.   In general, the total utility derived from the consumption of some good is larger than the total expenditure on that good. The difference between the two is referred to as the *consumer surplus.*

7.   Price is determined by the relative scarcity of a commodity. The relative scarcity can only be determined by the demand for and supply of a commodity. That being the case, it is clear that the total utility derived from some good does not determine price; the marginal utility represents the important determinant. Thus, we are able to resolve the *diamond-water paradox* and other similar paradoxes.

CONCEPTS FOR REVIEW

Utility

Marginal utility

Law of diminishing marginal utility

Equimarginal principle

Income effect

Substitution effect

Giffen good

Consumer surplus

Diamond-water paradox

QUESTIONS FOR DISCUSSION
(Those marked with an asterisk (*) are more difficult.)

1.   Carefully explain why the marginal utility of any commodity increases as less and less of it is consumed (over some span of time).

2.   Critically evaluate the following statement: "A Porsche, you tell me, would give you greater satisfaction than a Chrysler K-car. Yet you bought the K-car instead. Obviously you are not spending your income in ways to maximize your utility."

3.   If you have three wheels on your car when four are required to operate it, it is likely that the marginal utility of the fourth wheel will exceed the marginal utility of the third. Is this an instance where the law of diminishing marginal utility has been violated? Be explicit.

4.   Assume a world that has two goods only—X and Y. Construct a numerical example to show that, if $\frac{MU_X}{P_X}$ exceeds $\frac{MU_Y}{P_Y}$, total utility *must* increase, for any given level of total spending and given prices, by purchasing more of X and less of Y. (Your job will be made easier if you assume P_X is equal to P_Y.)

*5.   Assume a world of two goods only—X and Y. Assume initially that $\frac{MU_X}{P_X}$ equals $\frac{MU_Y}{P_Y}$. Now let P_X fall, holding constant P_Y. Show that, if the price elasticity of demand for X is less than one, the quantity of Y purchased will increase. What would happen to quantity of Y purchased if the price elasticity of demand for X was greater than one? Equal to one? (*Hint:* Hold constant the amount that is spent on both goods together.)

6. A local government wants to build a toll bridge. However, after estimating what the demand curve for the bridge would be, it was determined that the revenue the government would receive would be less than the cost of building the bridge. Therefore, the government decided not to build the bridge. Was this decision correct? (*Hint:* What if the revenue plus the consumer surplus exceeded the cost of building the bridge?)

TU

Total Utility — Total expenditure = Consumer Surplus

Appendix

Indifference curve analysis

The purpose of this appendix is to provide an alternative approach to the theory of utility developed in the main body of Chapter 17. The alternative approach is called **indifference curve analysis.** This alternative method has several distinct advantages, the chief one being that it does not depend on any precise measurement of utility, or even any knowledge of *how much* better off a consumer feels with one good (or a bundle of goods) versus another.

In the body of Chapter 17, the theory of utility was developed in terms of the amount—how many "utils"—of satisfaction consumers obtain from various goods and services. Unfortunately we have no idea how to measure "utils," and it is doubtful that consumers themselves think in terms of how many "utils" of satisfaction they get from the goods and services they purchase. The beauty of indifference curve analysis is that such precise calculations of satisfaction received are unnecessary. All that is required is that the consumer be able to say whether one bundle of goods yields more or less satisfaction than another, or whether they both produce the same level of satisfaction.

Indifference curves

What is an indifference curve? This question is best answered by means of a concrete example. Suppose we confront the consumer with a particular bundle of goods in order to get his or her reaction to it. Let the bundle consist of two goods highly desired by the consumer—tickets to Broadway plays and meals at fine restaurants. Assume to begin with that the original bundle consists of one ticket to a Broadway play and 50 meals at restaurants, to be used during some given month. We now ask the consumer the following question: "Are there other combinations of tickets and meals that would be equally satisfactory to you?" Because the consumer is assumed to be able to tell us which bundles yield equal satisfaction and which ones yield more or less satisfaction, we should be able to get our question answered.

Suppose the answers provided by the consumer are given in Table 17A.1. Bundle A is the original bundle consisting of one ticket and 50 meals. Combination B consists of two theater tickets and 25 meals. Thus, according to the answer provided, our hypothetical consumer is equally satisfied with either bundle A or bundle B. The consumer is *indifferent* between the two bundles. In effect, the consumer has declared that the reduction in total satisfaction resulting from 25 fewer meals (in that given month) is made up by the increased satisfaction resulting from an additional theater ticket.

Table 17A.1
Indifference schedule

	Theater tickets	Meals
A	1	50
B	2	25
C	3	15
D	4	10
E	5	8

The consumer has also indicated that bundle C provides the same level of satisfaction as A and B. In other words, the consumer is indifferent among bundles A, B, and C. Note carefully the differences among the bundles. The consumer, in moving from A to B, was equally well-off giving up 25 meals for one more theater ticket when the number of meals was initially equal to 50. In moving from B to C, the consumer is equally well-off by giving up only 10 meals to acquire an additional theater ticket. The reason? Because there are fewer meals and more theater tickets in bundle B than initially (bundle A), meals have become relatively more valuable and tickets relatively less valuable.

A similar pattern is evident in the movement from bundle C to bundle D. To obtain one more theater ticket the consumer is now equally well-off by giving up only five meals.

In the technical jargon of economists, the reduction in the number of meals the consumer is willing to give up to obtain an additional theater ticket reflects **the law of diminishing marginal rate of substitution;** the rate at which the consumer is willing to substitute meals for tickets diminishes as the number of tickets is increased.

The various combinations of the two goods in Table 17A.1 that leave the consumer equally well-off constitute the **indifference schedule.** The **indifference curve** is constructed from the indifference schedule. Specifically, plotting each combination of goods and connecting up the points yields the indifference curve presented in Figure 17A.1. What is important to note about the indifference curve is that the consumer is equally well-off at each and every point on the curve; the

consumer is indifferent among the various combinations of goods located on the curve.

Properties of indifference curves

Let us now examine carefully some of the properties of indifference curves. The first thing to note is that *the indifference curve slopes down and to the right.* This tells us that, in order to compensate for reductions in the quantity of one good consumed, the consumption of the other good must be increased in order for the consumer to be equally well-off. That is, the reduction in total utility occasioned by fewer meals must be compensated by an increase in the number of theater tickets.

Second, combinations of goods that lie *above* the indifference curve yield a higher level of satisfaction—a higher level of utility—than combinations that lie on the indifference curve. Consider point F in Figure 17A.1, which, we assume, lies directly above point A. At point F, the consumer has the same number of meals as point A but *more* theater tickets. Because the extra tickets raise total utility, the consumer is better off at point F than at point A; the consumer is *not* indifferent between points A and F. A similar line of reasoning would lead one to conclude that point G, a point below the indifference curve in Figure 17A.1 yields the consumer less satisfaction than any point along the indifference curve.

Third, the bowed shape of the indifference curve—the convex-to-the-origin shape—reflects the law of diminishing marginal rate of substitution. Indeed, the slope of the indifference curve measures the marginal rate of substitution—the increase in the quantity of one good required to compensate for reductions in the quantity of the other good. The fact that the slope of the indifference curve gets steeper as you move up towards the left, and flatter as you move down towards the right, implies diminishing marginal rate of substitution.

Fourth, there is not just a single indifference curve but a whole family of possible indifference curves. Thus, for example, one could construct another indifference curve through point F in Figure 17A.1. All points on that new indifference

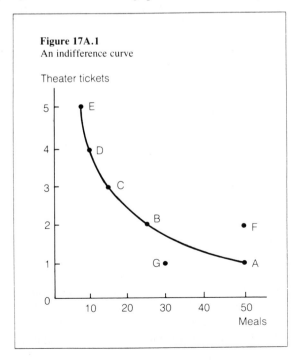

Figure 17A.1
An indifference curve

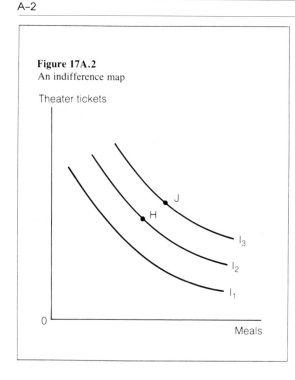

Figure 17A.2
An indifference map

Theater tickets

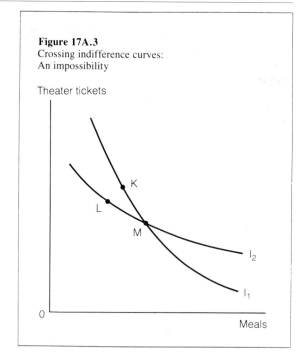

Figure 17A.3
Crossing indifference curves:
An impossibility

Theater tickets

curve would show combinations of meals and tickets that yield the same level of satisfaction or utility as point F. There are an infinite number of such indifference curves; every point representing a combination of the two goods has an indifference curve passing through it. The family of indifference curves is called an **indifference map.** The curves labeled I, I_2, and I_3 in Figure 17A.2 represent three different indifference curves in the indifference map for meals and theater tickets.

Fifth, indifference curves located farther from the origin are associated with higher levels of satisfaction. Thus, the level of satisfaction associated with I_3 in Figure 17A.2 is higher than the level of satisfaction associated with the indifference curves that are closer to the origin. This is easily demonstrated by comparing points H and J in Figure 17A.2. Point J is clearly preferred to point H because the consumer has more of *both* goods at J. And, since all points along I_3 yield the same level of satisfaction as point J, all points along I_3 must be preferred to all points along I_2.

Sixth, the fact that distinct indifference curves

represent different levels of total satisfaction means that indifference curves cannot intersect. To demonstrate why this must be, consider Figure 17A.3. There the indifference curves have been drawn so they do cross one another. That this is impossible can be seen by considering the meaning of points K, L, and M. Since points K and M are on the same indifference curve (I_1), the consumer is indifferent between K and M. Similarly, the consumer is indifferent between L and M since they both lie on the same indifference curve (I_2). However, if K is indifferent to M, and L is indifferent to M, that makes L indifferent to K. But point K represents a situation in which the consumer has more of both goods than at point L. Since more of both goods implies a higher level of satisfaction, the consumer cannot be indifferent between L and K; the indifference curves cannot intersect one another.

The budget line

An indifference curve reveals information—subjective information—about the consumer's preferences. In order to determine what bundle of goods the consumer will purchase, we need more information—specifically, objective information concerning the amount of money income the individual has available to spend—the **budget constraint**—and the prices of each of the goods. This objective information is summarized in the **budget line.**

The budget line tells us what the consumer's spending possibilities are. To illustrate, suppose the budget constraint amounts to $600. That is, the consumer in question has $600 per month to spend on theater tickets and restaurants. Suppose further that theater tickets cost $100 each (box seats, of course!) and meals at fine restaurants cost $20 per meal. Armed with this information, it is easy to construct the budget line displayed in Figure 17A.4.

The consumer has available several alternative choices. The entire $600 can be spent on theater tickets; at $100 each, that would permit the purchase of six tickets. This explains how the vertical axis intercept is found; in general, the vertical axis intercept is given by the value of money income (Y) divided by the price of theater tickets (P_T).

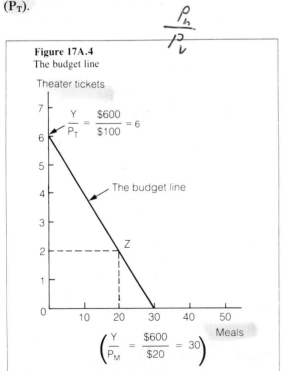

Figure 17A.4
The budget line

Theater tickets

$$\frac{Y}{P_T} = \frac{\$600}{\$100} = 6$$

The budget line

Z

$$\left(\frac{Y}{P_M} = \frac{\$600}{\$20} = 30\right)$$

Meals

Alternatively, the consumer could spend the entire $600 on restaurant meals. At $20 per meal, that would imply the purchase of 30 meals. This calculation gives us the horizontal axis intercept, which, in general, is determined by the ratio of money income (Y) to the price of restaurant meals (P_M).

The intercept points are not the only alternatives available. The $600 could be spent on various combinations of theater tickets and restaurant meals. Given the prices of the two goods, the market enables the consumer to trade five meals for each theater ticket (i.e., theater tickets command a price five times larger than restaurant meals). All of this information is summarized in the budget line in Figure 17A.4. Thus, if the consumer is initially spending the entire $600 on meals, by reducing the number of meals by 10, two theater tickets can be purchased (point Z in Figure 17A.4). All of the possible combinations of theater tickets and restaurant meals that exhaust the $600 are located on the budget line.

The slope of the budget line is given by the ratio of the price of meals to the price of theater tickets. That is, the slope of the budget line in Figure 17A.4 equals P_M/P_T.[1] And, *in general, the slope of the budget line will equal the ratio of the price of the good on the horizontal axis to the price of the good on the vertical axis.*

How can this be? The answer is fairly straightforward. The slope of the budget line in terms of the quantities of the two goods is given by the ratio 6 tickets to 30 meals; or alternatively, $\frac{1}{5}$.[2] But the vertical axis intercept point is given by Y/P_T, and the horizontal axis intercept point is given by Y/P_M. Thus, the slope can be calculated as:

$$\frac{6}{30} = \frac{(Y/P_T)}{(Y/P_M)} = \frac{P_M}{P_T} = \frac{1}{5}.$$

This result should occasion no surprise. The slope of one fifth corresponds precisely to the fact that the price of restaurant meals is one fifth the price of theater tickets. (This is what is meant by $P_M/P_T = \frac{1}{5}$.)

---

[1] This ratio should have a negative sign attached.

[2] Again, the negative sign is ignored.

Utility maximization: The indifference curve approach

We are now in a position to describe utility maximization using an indifference curve approach. What is needed is to bring together the indifference map (which summarizes the consumer's *subjective* valuations of the various bundles) and the budget line (which summarizes what the consumer is *able to do*). This will permit us to determine the quantities of the two goods the consumer will purchase. The results are shown in Figure 17A.5.

What we will now show is that the consumer will maximize utility by selecting the combination of theater tickets and meals given by point R—the point of tangency of the indifference curve I_2 with the budget line in Figure 17A.5. The reason? Given the budget constraint and the prices of the two goods, the consumer wants to allocate the money income in ways that will yield the highest level of satisfaction possible. Since the consumer cannot choose bundles of goods beyond the budget line, the highest level of satisfaction attainable is given by the highest indifference reached by the budget line; this is I_2.

It is true that the consumer could have purchased the combinations given by S or T (or any other combinations along the budget line). But the selection of those quantities would have put the consumer on a lower indifference curve; the consumer can do better than S or T.

Note that the slope of the indifference curve at the optimum point—point R—is the same as the slope of the budget line. This will always be true, since the highest attainable indifference curve must be tangent to the budget line. Given the meaning of the slopes of the budget line and the indifference curve, the following important conclusion is reached: *At the point where the consumer maximizes utility, the ratio of the prices of the two goods—P_M/P_T—is equal (in absolute value) to the marginal rate of substitution of theater tickets for meals.* In other words, in equilibrium, the rate at which the consumer is *willing* to substitute theater tickets for meals must equal the rate at which the market permits such substitution.

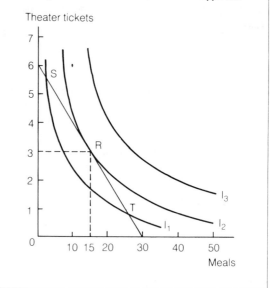

Figure 17A.5
Utility maximization: Indifference curve approach

This condition is analogous to the **equimarginal principle** developed in the main body of the chapter. The equimarginal principle applied to a world of two goods—theater tickets and meals—would give us:

$$\frac{MU_T}{P_T} = \frac{MU_M}{P_M}.$$

This condition can be rewritten as:

$$\frac{MU_M}{MU_T} = \frac{P_M}{P_T}.$$

The left-hand side of this expression can be interpreted as the rate at which the consumer is *willing* to exchange theater tickets for meals, the relative (subjective) valuation of the two goods being given by the ratio of the marginal utilities of the two goods. The right-hand side is, as before, the rate at which the market permits substitution between the two goods. The correspondence between utility maximization via the equimarginal principle and utility maximization via indifference curves is therefore clear.

Derivation of demand curve from an indifference curve

It is a relatively easy exercise to show how the demand curve for some product can be derived from an indifference curve. We show this result in Figure 17A.6 in the case of two commodities, X and W. The initial equilibrium is given at the point H_0, the point of tangency of the initial budget line with I_1. Now let the price of X fall, holding everything else fixed (specifically, money income, Y, and the price of W, P_W). Given the fixed money income, the reduction in price of X from P_X^0 to P_X^1 causes the horizontal axis intercept to shift from Y/P_X^0 to Y/P_X^1. The reason? If all the consumer's income were spent on X, the reduced price of X would permit a greater quantity of X to be purchased. Given the fixed price of W and the fixed money income, the vertical axis intercept remains unchanged. Thus, the effect of the reduction in the price of X is to rotate the budget line to a flatter position, yielding the new equilibrium position, H_1. Note that the reduction in the price of X increased the quantity of X demanded from X_0

to X_1, in accordance with the law of demand.

Suppose the price of X is reduced further to P_X^2, holding everything else constant. This will cause the budget line to rotate to an even flatter position. From the new equilibrium position, H_2, we see that the quantity demanded of X has increased from X_1 to X_2. The derivation of the demand curve from an indifference curve is therefore complete.

Two final notes. The discussion of the derivation of the demand curve highlights the fact that changes in the price of one good cause the consumer to reallocate the fixed budget among all goods, a point we emphasized in the body of the chapter. Thus, lowering the price of X causes the consumer to adjust his or her consumption of Y as well as X.

In Figure 17A.6, the reduction in the price of X results in an increase in the amount of Y consumed. This need not be the case; it depends on the price elasticity of demand for good X. Can you figure out whether the price elasticity of demand for good X implied in Figure 17A.6 is greater than or less than one? (*Hint:* Remember what is held fixed when the price of X is changed, and recall the relationship between the elasticity of demand and total expenditures.)

Income and substitution effects of a price change

Indifference curves can be used to highlight the income and substitution effects of a change in price. This is illustrated in Figure 17A.7. We show there, again, the two goods X and W. The initial equilibrium is given by point V, the tangency point between I, and the solid budget line. Now let the price of X fall; the budget line will rotate to a flatter position, giving us the new equilibrium position at point N.

Now the reduction in the price of X will cause the consumer to substitute in favor of more X, away from W. This is the **substitution effect** of the price change. In addition, because the reduction in the price of X raises the consumer's *real* income, the consumer will alter his or her consumption of X and W in response. This is the **income effect** of the price change.

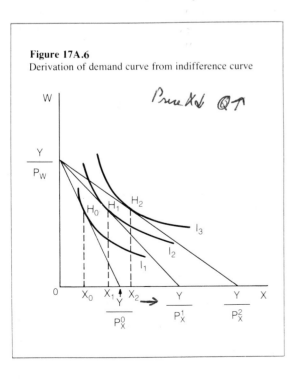

Figure 17A.6
Derivation of demand curve from indifference curve

Let us focus on the substitution effect first. Let us imagine that we reduce the consumer's real income to its former level. This means taking away income from the consumer in an amount that will put him or her back on the original indifference curve. Given the new relative price of X, this reduction in the consumer's real income means, in effect, confronting the consumer with the new "dashed" budget line. That new budget line, which is parallel to the new solid budget line (to reflect the fact that the new relative prices are in effect) gives us the "equilibrium" position, Q. The movement from V to Q reflects the substitution effect; the increase in the quantity of X consumed from X_1 to X_2 is the magnitude of the increased consumption of X due to the substitution effect.

Now return to the consumer the income that was taken away hypothetically. This will shift the budget line to the point of tangency—point N—with I_2. The movement from Q to N reflects the income effect; the increased consumption of X from X_2 to X_3 reflects the income effect on the changed price for X. In general, the shift from one indifference curve to another due to the change in price is a measure of the real income change occasioned by the price change.

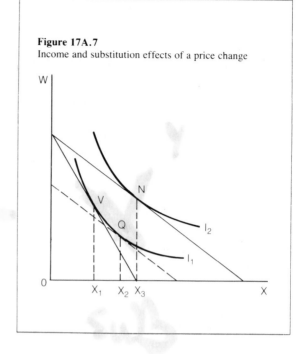

Figure 17A.7
Income and substitution effects of a price change

Chapter 18

Costs, profits, and product supply

In Chapter 17 we examined the theoretical underpinnings of demand. In this chapter we undertake an examination of the factors that determine supply. •

The market supply of some good or service, you will recall, refers to the amount that producers are willing to sell. Moreover, because the production and sale of any good or service requires the use of scarce resources, the supply of each good or service has associated with it a cost—an opportunity cost—calculated as the highest-valued alternative use of those scarce resources. Inevitably, therefore, we are forced to ask the following questions: What factors determine the uses toward which those scarce resources shall be put? That is, why are scarce resources used to produce soybeans, for instance, instead of something else? And why do we produce as many soybeans as we do? These are not easy questions to answer. In truth, the factors that determine supply are many and varied. However, one of the most important considerations is the profits producers expect to receive compared with the profits to be earned elsewhere. If the production of soybeans is viewed by some farmers as more profitable than the production of corn, more scarce land, labor, and capital resources will be devoted to soybean production and less to corn. Because of the importance of the profit motive, our efforts in this and the next chapter will be devoted to examining its implications for product supply. In this chapter, we will focus our attention on the factors that govern both the firm's costs and its revenues. In Chapter 19 we will examine product supply in the context of a perfectly or purely competitive market structure.

THE FIRM'S OBJECTIVE: PROFIT MAXIMIZATION

We begin our study of product supply with an important assumption. We assume that the decisions undertaken by sellers are motivated by one overriding consideration—**profit maximization.** If it is more profitable to produce product X than product Y, businesspeople will choose product X. If technique A is more profitable than some other technique, businesspeople will choose technique A. If more profits can be had through an expansion of production, businesspeople will choose to expand. If more profits can be had through production cutbacks, businesspeople will choose to cut back.

Profits are defined, simply, as the difference between the revenues received by the firm in the sale of its product and the costs it incurs in producing it. Letting TR represent the firm's total revenue, and TC the firm's total cost, profits can be defined symbolically as

$$\text{Profits} = \text{TR} - \text{TC}.$$

Obviously, if TC exceeds TR, the firm incurs a *loss*.

Given the definition of profits, it is easy to see what is meant by the notion that firms will undertake actions designed to maximize their profits. *Any decision that has the effect of raising revenues relative to costs will cause profits to rise; profits will be maximized when all actions designed to raise revenues relative to costs have been exhausted.*

In order to maximize profits, therefore, each firm must seek to determine, with some degree of precision, the impact of its actions on both its revenues and its costs. We turn to a consideration of these issues now.

COSTS

What does it cost to produce some good or service? To an economist, there is but one answer to this question—the foregone production of other goods and services. The cost of producing any good or service, therefore, is its **opportunity cost.** The cost incurred by the use of scarce resources to produce good X is the value of the other goods and services thereby foregone.

At this point you are probably asking yourself, But what does opportunity cost have to do with the production costs incurred by the individual firm? After all, do we not mean by the firm's production costs the payments made for land, labor, and capital resources? Precisely! However,

ask yourself the question, *How much must the firm pay in order to obtain the use of those scarce resources?* The answer is obvious: *Enough to attract those resources away from alternative uses.* If the firm is unwilling to pay resource suppliers at least as much as they can earn elsewhere, the firm will fail in its efforts to attract the resources that it needs.

Opportunity cost and production cost, therefore, are synonymous.[1]

The cost of production, defined as an opportunity cost, takes two forms. In the first place, the firm incurs certain **explicit**—or "out-of-pocket"—**costs** representing the payments it must make for outside labor services, fuel and electricity, material inputs, transportation, etc. The firm also incurs a second cost—an **implicit cost**—representing the payments it must make for the resources supplied by its owners. These include, for example, the payments that must be made for the buildings and equipment that are owned and used by the firm and for the labor services provided by the firm's owners.

At first glance, it may seem a bit strange to refer to these as "payments that must be made" since no out-of-pocket expenses are actually incurred by the firm in the use of its own resources. But if the firm's revenues are not sufficient to cover these costs—i.e., if these payments cannot be made—the firm's owners will shift their resources to alternative lines of production. The cost the firm incurs through the use of its own buildings is the rental income it foregoes by not renting those buildings to others; the costs that the firm's owners incur by using their own labor services are the wages and salaries they could obtain in some alternative line of production. Unless the resources supplied by the firm's owners can earn at least as much as those resources could earn elsewhere, they will be withdrawn from employment there. It is apparent, therefore, that *implicit costs* are every bit as much a cost of production as are *explicit costs. Production, or*

---

[1] This statement needs to be qualified. Opportunity cost and production cost are synonymous as long as there is no monopoly control of resources and as long as there are no externalities, subjects we will take up in Chapter 28.

opportunity, costs consist of the sum of the explicit and implicit costs.

Opportunity costs versus accounting costs

While the costs that are relevant to the individual firm are the opportunity costs of *all* the resources it uses, these are *not* the same as the firm's **accounting costs.** From an accounting point of view, the firm regards *all* explicit costs as costs of production, but *not all* implicit costs. Only a portion of the implicit costs are recorded as accounting costs (e.g., depreciation expenses that do not involve any out-of-pocket expenditures are included as an accounting cost of production). Other implicit costs are not (e.g., the costs of the labor services provided by the firm's owners). The exclusion of these implicit costs by accountants is justified on the grounds that they are difficult to measure objectively. But such a justification in no way implies that these costs do not exist.

The importance of this opportunity cost/accounting cost distinction is made apparent in Figure 18.1. The firm's production costs—its opportunity costs—consist of the sum of its explicit and implicit costs. If the firm earns revenues in excess of these costs, it is said to earn an **economic profit.** As should be apparent, the economic profit earned by the firm represents the payment received by the firm's owners over and above what their resources could fetch elsewhere. If firm revenues just covered the costs of production, no economic profit would exist. The firm's owners would earn an amount equal to what their resources could fetch in some other line of production.

Given that accounting costs are less inclusive than opportunity costs, **accounting profits**—the difference between the firm's revenues and its *accounting* costs—have a meaning to the firm that is different from the meaning of economic profits. In particular, unless the firm's owners cover *all* of their costs of production, they will

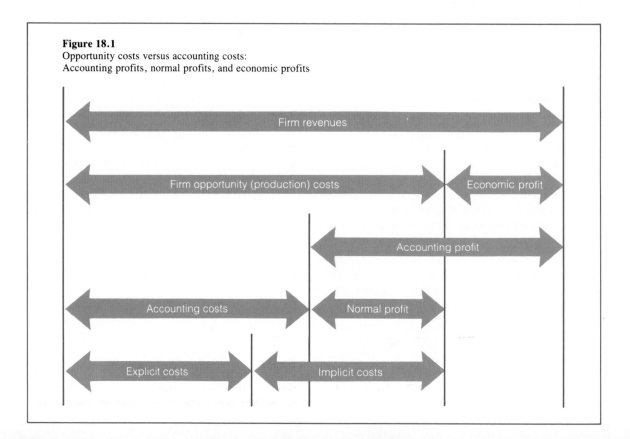

Figure 18.1
Opportunity costs versus accounting costs:
Accounting profits, normal profits, and economic profits

shift their resources elsewhere. *In an accounting sense,* then, the firm's owners must earn enough profit so that *all* of their costs are recovered. We call such profit a **"normal" profit**—a profit just sufficient to ensure that the firm's owners will retain their resources in that given line of production. *Accounting profits in excess of these "normal" profits are called economic profits.* Just because the firm makes accounting profits does *not* mean that the firm's owners will retain their resources in that line of production. If the resources owned by the firm can earn more elsewhere, those accounting profits are not large enough. Despite the presence of accounting profits, the firm actually incurs an economic loss; its revenues are less than its production costs. Can you explain why?

As a result of these considerations, whenever we talk of production costs we will be referring to opportunity costs. They include all implicit and explicit costs. *"Normal" profit, therefore, is treated as a cost of production.* When we talk of profit, we will mean economic profit, not accounting profit.

Short-run and long-run production costs

As the firm varies its rate of output, it will also normally experience a change in its costs of production. How much its production costs will vary, however, is highly dependent on the nature of the adjustments that the firm makes in the use of its scarce land, labor, and capital resources. These adjustments, of course, all take time. And the time required for the firm to make some kinds of changes will differ markedly from the time required to make others. Thus, the firm might be able to expand its production rate almost immediately by hiring additional workers and drawing down its inventories of material inputs. Much more time would be required for the firm to expand the size of its production facilities.

Because of these differing time requirements, economists find it useful to divide the adjustment process into two distinct time periods—the short run and the long run. In **the short run,** it is assumed that the firm is unable to alter the size of its productive facilities. In the short run, its productive capacity or plant size is fixed. Given that constraint, the firm in the short run can alter its rate of production only through more or less intensive use of its existing production facilities. The firm can change its production rate by hiring more or less labor and by operating its plant longer or shorter hours; it cannot, however, change its plant size. In the jargon of economists, the short run is characterized by the presence of both variable factors and fixed factors of production. In **the long run,** on the other hand, all factors of production are variable. Not only can the firm vary in intensity the use of its existing plant in the long run. It can also alter the size of its plant as well.

Corresponding to this distinction between the short-run and long-run adjustment periods is a distinction to be drawn between the firm's short-run and long-run costs of production. We will first study the factors that influence the firm's costs in the short run. Then we will examine the forces that determine its long-run costs.

Before turning to these issues, it is important to recognize that the short run and long run are analytical concepts. They do not refer to specific time periods. The long run, as mentioned earlier, refers to the time required for the firm to change the size of its operations; the short run is a time period so short that no change in plant size is possible. In the case of some productive activities, the long run is very long indeed; in the case of others, the long run is measured in terms of weeks or days. Expanding the productive capacity of a steel plant requires the addition of blast furnaces, which might take years to accomplish. Expanding the productive capacity of a taxicab company requires only the addition of another properly equipped automobile, which could be accomplished in a matter of days.

SHORT-RUN COSTS

The firm's short-run costs are of two sorts—its fixed costs and its variable costs. **Fixed costs** refer to those cost obligations that must be met no matter what the firm's rate of production.

These represent, for example, the interest costs associated with the firm's outstanding debt, the rental payments for buildings and machinery, and the contractual salaries of some administrative personnel. The important point to recognize about these fixed costs is that they do not vary with variations in the firm's rate of production. *Fixed costs are independent of the firm's level of output.* Whether the firm produces a small or large quantity of output or ceases production altogether, it incurs the *same* fixed costs of production. Moreover, although fixed costs do change as a result of changes in such things as the amount of debt outstanding or the expiration of leases, we will assume here that, over the short run at least, fixed costs remain fixed.

Variable costs, on the other hand, refer to *those production costs that do vary with the firm's rate of production.* These represent, for example, the firm's costs for fuel, power, lighting, material inputs, and most types of labor.

The firm's total costs (TC) in the short run consist of the sum of its fixed costs (FC) and its variable costs (VC). Symbolically,

$$TC = FC + VC.$$

Given the definitions of fixed and variable costs, it is apparent that any *change* in total costs is exclusively the result of changes in the firm's variable costs. As a firm expands its rate of production from, say, 1,000 units per month to 1,200, its variable costs per month will usually rise. To expand its rate of production, the firm will usually have to hire additional workers and/or step up its use of material inputs, causing its variable costs to increase. What is of interest to us here is the *rate* at which the firm's total costs rise as production is expanded through the application of additional variable factors of production to its fixed plant.

How much the firm's total costs will rise as a result of an expansion in its rate of production will depend, in general, on two things: (1) the number of additional factors of production required to produce a given increase in output, and (2) the prices that must be paid to obtain these additional factor inputs. In order to focus our attention on the first, we will assume for the moment that factor prices are fixed. This means, for example, that, if we are currently paying labor $6.00 an hour, it is possible for us to hire additional workers at that same wage rate. The magnitude of the increase in total costs will be determined solely by the number of additional variable factors of production that are hired or purchased at their given fixed prices.

The law of diminishing returns (or the law of diminishing marginal productivity)

The fact that the firm's plant size is fixed in the short run has important implications for its total costs as it varies its rate of output. In particular, as the firm expands its rate of production from relatively low levels of output to successively higher and higher levels of output, it becomes subject to **the law of diminishing returns.** That law—sometimes referred to as the **law of diminishing marginal productivity**—can be stated in two essentially equivalent forms:

1. As more and more of a variable input is applied to a fixed input, total output will rise, but at a diminishing rate.
2. Each successive increase in output of a given size will necessitate the use of successively larger amounts of some variable inputs.

The law of diminishing returns is illustrated in Figure 18.2. There we assume that labor is the only variable factor of production. Study first the table that accompanies the graphs. Notice that with a single worker the firm can produce 12 units of output per week. This 12 units of output represents the first worker's **marginal product;** it is the *change* in the firm's total output associated with the first worker put on the job.

With two workers the firm can produce 28 units per week; with the addition of the second worker, the firm's total output rises by 16. The second worker is therefore said to have a marginal product of 16. This represents the change in total output associated with the firm's second unit of labor. Does this mean that the second worker is inherently more productive than the first? Not necessarily. It simply means that two

Figure 18.2
Law of diminishing returns illustrated

(1) Labor input per week	(2) Output per week		(3) Labor's marginal product
0	0		
1	12	>	12
2	28	>	16
3	42	>	14
4	54	>	12
5	64	>	10
6	71	>	7
7	75	>	4
8	76	>	1
9	76	>	0

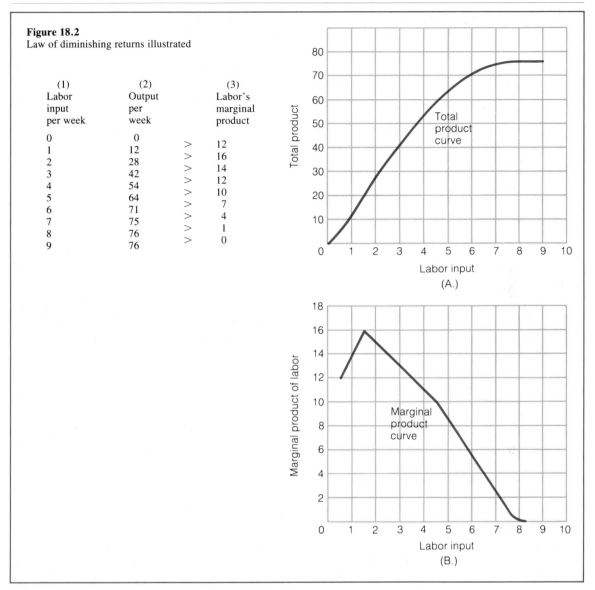

workers in the firm's employ are able to produce more than twice as much as one worker working alone. Given the firm's existing technology, two workers are able to divide the tasks to which they are assigned so as to produce 28 units per week—more than double the 12 units per week made possible by a single worker.

The fact that the marginal product of the second worker exceeds that of the first means the firm experiences, up to that point, *increasing re-*

turns. But note what happens to total output with the addition of the third worker. Total output rises, but only by 14 units. The marginal product of the third worker—14 units—is less than the marginal product of the second—16 units. Again, does this mean that the third worker is inherently less productive than the second? Not necessarily. It means only that three workers together are able to produce 42 units of output per week, and that the additional output associated with the third worker is smaller than the amount associated with the second. But since total output goes up by less with the addition of the third worker than it did with the second, should not the firm stop hiring at the second worker? Isn't the firm "less efficient" with three workers than it is with only two? Again, not necessarily. The firm is interested in maximizing its profits. Whether or not expansion is profitable will depend on, first, what it costs to obtain the extra output and, second, the additional revenues generated by the sale of that extra output. If the extra revenues obtained exceed the extra costs, it is profitable to proceed to hire the third worker; it is efficient to hire the third worker. Much more will be said on this later.

With the addition of the third worker, the firm enters the stage of diminishing returns. Each additional worker after the second adds successively less and less to the firm's total output. And note that the ninth worker adds absolutely nothing to the firm's output. Obviously, if it costs anything to hire the ninth worker, the firm will not do it. The firm could not otherwise maximize its profits. Can you explain why?

All of these relationships are portrayed graphically in Figure 18.2. The **total product curve** displayed in the upper diagram illustrates how the firm's total product changes as additional units of labor are hired. Note first how, through the second unit of labor, the total product curve rises at an increasing rate; this corresponds to the stage of increasing returns. Thereafter, the total product curve rises at a diminishing rate corresponding to the stage of diminishing returns. The total product curve also shows that production attains its highest value of 76 units with the hiring of the eighth worker; the ninth worker adds nothing.

The **marginal product curve** in the lower diagram of Figure 18.2 is derived from the total product curve. It shows the successive *additions* to total output brought about through successive additions of units of labor. Notice that the increasing portion of the marginal product curve implies that total output increases at an increas-

ing rate; the declining portion of the marginal product curve implies that total output increases at a diminishing rate. The declining portion of the marginal product curve corresponds to the stage of diminishing returns mentioned earlier. The law of diminishing returns and the law of diminishing marginal productivity are synonymous.

We can also see from our numerical example why the law of diminishing returns can be defined in two essentially equivalent ways. First, it is apparent that as additional workers are hired, total output rises, but, after the second worker, at a diminishing rate. Second, whereas the addition of the fourth worker causes total output to rise by only 12 units—from 42 to 54—three additional workers—the sixth, seventh, and eighth—are required to raise total output by 12 more units, from 64 to 76 units: *In order to generate an increase in output of a given size, successively larger amounts of labor are required.*

What is the basis for the law of diminishing returns? Why is it that total product rises at a diminishing rate? Put simply, *total output rises at a diminishing rate because, given the fixed size of the plant, each worker has less and less of the fixed input to work with as more and more labor is hired.* Therefore, the successive additions to total output will get smaller and smaller.

Total variable cost, average variable cost, and marginal cost

It is now a relatively simple matter to show the implications of the law of diminishing returns for the firm's total costs as it varies its rate of production. For simplicity we make the following two assumptions:

1. Labor is the only variable factor of production.
2. Each laborer hired is paid a fixed wage of $100 per week.

On the basis of these assumptions, it is easy to calculate the firm's **total variable costs (TVC).** It is nothing other than the quantity of labor hired per week times labor's weekly wage. TVC

Table 18.1

Total variable cost, average variable cost, and marginal cost

(1)	(2)	(3)	(4) Total variable cost	(5) Average variable cost	(6) Marginal cost
Output per week	Labor input per week	Labor's wage per week	(2) × (3)	(4) ÷ (1)	Δ(4) ÷ Δ(1)
—	—	$100	—	—	$ 8.33
12	1	100	$100	$ 8.33	6.25
28	2	100	200	7.14	7.14
42	3	100	300	7.14	8.33
54	4	100	400	7.41	10.00
64	5	100	500	7.81	14.29
71	6	100	600	8.45	25.00
75	7	100	700	9.33	100.00
76	8	100	800	10.53	∞
76	9	100	900	11.84	

for one unit of labor is $100; for four units of labor it is $400; and so on. The firm's TVC is shown in column (4) of Table 18.1.

Two other important concepts can be derived on the basis of the data presented in Table 18.1. They are **average variable costs (AVC)** and **marginal cost (MC)**. These concepts can be defined as follows:

$$AVC = \frac{TVC}{\text{Output}} = \frac{TVC}{Q},$$

$$MC = \frac{\text{Change in TVC}}{\text{Change in output}} = \frac{\Delta TVC}{\Delta Q}.$$

AVC measures the variable costs per unit of output; MC measures the *change* in variable costs per unit *change* in total output. These relationships are shown in Table 18.1, in columns (5) and (6), respectively. The output and labor input data in columns (1) and (2) of that table are the same as in Figure 18.2. Accordingly, the firm's AVC for a rate of production of 28 units is $7.14 (i.e., $200 ÷ 28 = $7.14). That is, in order to produce 28 units of output, the firm must hire two laborers at a cost of $200; the variable cost per unit of output is, therefore, $7.14. Marginal cost, on the other hand, is equal to the per unit *change* in total cost associated with a *change* in output. Hiring the second worker adds $100 to total costs and leads to a

16-unit increase in output. The per unit change in total cost associated with hiring the second worker is therefore $6.25 (i.e., $MC = \frac{\Delta TVC}{\Delta Q} = \frac{\$100}{\$16} = \$6.25$). Given these relationships, can you verify that the AVC for 64 units of output is $7.81, and that the MC associated with hiring the fifth worker is $10?

If we plot the numerical values presented in columns (5) and (6) on a graph, we obtain the results displayed in Figure 18.3. Study Figure 18.3 very carefully and note the following relationships.

1. The AVC curve declines as output is expanded from 12 units to 28. This is to be expected. *Since total output more than doubles with the hiring of the second worker, while total variable cost doubles exactly* (i.e., one laborer costs $100 whereas two cost $200), *variable costs per unit of output decline.*

2. The firm's AVC does not change as output is expanded from 28 units to 42 units. Since output per worker is 14 with three workers (i.e., 42 ÷ 3 = 14), the same as with two workers, variable costs per unit of output will not change with the hiring of the third worker. If total output had increased by *less* than 14 with the addition

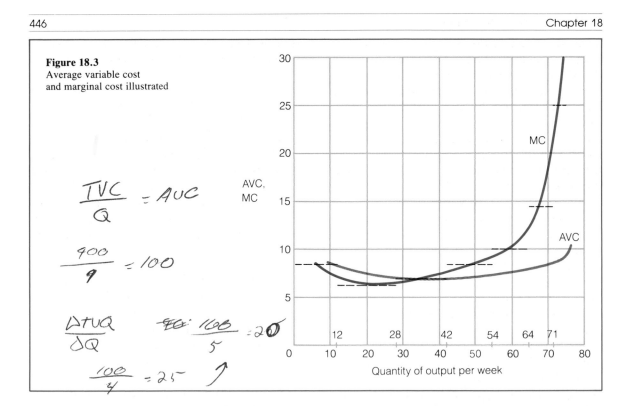

Figure 18.3
Average variable cost
and marginal cost illustrated

of the third worker, AVC would have increased. Can you explain why?

3. With the hiring of the fourth worker, and for additional workers thereafter, the firm's AVC rises. This is hardly surprising in view of the fact that each additional worker costs the firm $100, but output per worker diminishes as more workers are hired. As output climbs from 42 units to 75, AVC rises from $7.14 to $9.33. Suppose the additional output per worker did *not* decline as additional workers were hired. Suppose, that is, that each new worker added 14 units to the firm's total output. Can you explain why the firm's AVC would remain constant at $7.14 throughout?

4. As seen in Figure 18.3, the MC curve declines initially as output expands to 28 units; thereafter it rises, at first somewhat moderately, then more steeply. The shape of the MC curve is governed by the shape of the marginal product curve. Indeed, the rising portion of the marginal product curve corresponds to the declining portion of the MC curve; and the converse also holds

true. The reason for this correspondence is obvious. Each additional worker costs the firm $100. The second worker adds more to total output than the first. The *change* in total costs divided by the *change* in output, therefore, declines as output expands from 12 to 28 units. The third worker adds less to total output than the second, but costs the firm an additional $100. Therefore, marginal cost—the per unit *change* in the cost of output—rises with the third worker; as more workers are added, adding less and less to total output, MC rises more rapidly.

5. Note carefully the relationship between the MC curve and the AVC curve.

a. When the MC curve lies below the AVC curve the firm's AVC curve declines.

b. When the MC curve lies above the AVC curve, the firm's AVC curve rises.

c. The firm's AVC reaches a minimum at the point where MC is the same as AVC.

In other words, the MC curve intersects the AVC curve at the latter's minimum point. (*A note:*

Since MC refers to the per unit change in total costs over each of the respective *ranges* of output, the MC curve should be drawn as a "step function"; each of the "steps" are shown as dashed horizontal straight lines in Figure 18.3. The smooth MC curve was constructed by joining up the midpoints of these steps. Hereafter, we will ignore this complication and represent the MC curve as a smooth and continuous relationship unless otherwise noted.)

These relations between MC and AVC *must* hold; they are a matter of definition, not of economics. This is easily shown. Consider for a moment an analogy. Suppose you discover that the average height of the players on the basketball team is 6'8" and that "Shorty" Williams is about to be recruited. If Shorty is 7 feet tall, will the average height of the team rise or fall when he joins it? It will rise, of course. Since Shorty is above the average, the *average* height of the team will be pulled up by his presence. If, on the other hand, Shorty is less than 6'8" tall, the team's average height will fall. If he is precisely 6'8" tall, the average height will remain unchanged. In this example, Shorty is the marginal, or additional, player, whose height will raise or lower the average height of the team, depending on whether his height is higher or lower than the average. By the same reasoning, it should be clear that, if MC is less than or greater than AVC, AVC will decline or rise, respectively. Can you

now explain why the MC curve *must* therefore intersect the AVC at the latter's minimum point?

Other cost concepts: Average total cost (ATC) and average fixed cost (AFC)

Let us now complete our discussion of the firm's short-run costs with a brief analysis of the firm's **fixed costs.** As mentioned earlier, fixed costs do *not* vary as the firm varies its rate of output. What about the firm's **average fixed costs (AFC)**— that is, the fixed costs per unit of output? Obviously AFC declines continuously as output increases. This is shown in column (5) of Table 18.2, where it is assumed that the firm has $300 in fixed costs; its graphic counterpart is displayed in Figure 18.4. The reason for this relationship is clear: As output increases, the fixed costs are spread over increasing quantities of output. This is sometimes referred to as "spreading the overhead," where overhead refers to fixed costs. The data in columns (1), (2), (6), and (8) in Table 18.2 are taken directly from Table 18.1. The other data presented in Table 18.2 are easily explained. Since

$$TC = FC + VC,$$

the numbers presented in column (4) are obtained by summing across the numbers in columns (2) and (3). Moreover, since $ATC = TC/Q$ and $AFC = FC/Q$, it is apparent that

Table 18.2
Average fixed costs, average variable costs, average total costs, and MC

(1) Output per week	(2) Total variable cost	(3) Total fixed cost	(4) Total cost (2) + (3)	(5) AFC (3) ÷ (1)	(6) AVC (2) ÷ (1)	(7) ATC (5) + (6) or (4) ÷ (1)	(8) MC Δ(2) ÷ Δ(1) or Δ(4) ÷ Δ(1)
—	—	$300	$ 300	—	—	—	
							$ 8.33
12	$100	300	400	$25.00	$ 8.33	$33.33	
							6.25
28	200	300	500	10.71	7.14	17.85	
							7.14
42	300	300	600	7.14	7.14	14.28	
							8.33
54	400	300	700	5.56	7.41	12.97	
							10.00
64	500	300	800	4.69	7.81	12.50	
							14.29
71	600	300	900	4.23	8.45	12.68	
							25.00
75	700	300	1,000	4.00	9.33	13.33	
							100.00
76	800	300	1,100	3.95	10.53	14.48	
							∞
76	900	300	1,200	3.95	11.84	15.79	

$$\text{ATC} = \text{AFC} + \text{AVC}.$$

Thus, the data on ATC in column (7) are obtained by summing across the data in columns (5) and (6). Alternatively, ATC could have been found by dividing each number in column (4) by the corresponding number in column (1). All of these relationships are displayed graphically in Figure 18.4. You should note a number of other points from Table 18.2 and Figure 18.4.

1. Because the firm incurs certain fixed costs in the short run, any change in total cost is solely the result of changes in variable costs. Marginal cost can be calculated either as a change in total costs divided by the change in output, *or* as the change in variable costs divided by the change in output.

2. The AVC is somewhat U-shaped: As the level of output is increased, AVC declines and then rises. This is a consequence of our numerical example in which there was, first, increasing returns, then diminishing returns. If the firm experienced diminishing returns throughout, what would be the shape of its AVC? Why?

3. The ATC also has a U shape, but one more pronounced than that of the AVC. The reason? ATC is equal to the sum of AVC and AFC. Initially, ATC declines more sharply than the AVC since ATC consists of the sum of the declining portion of the AVC *plus* the decline in AFC. After a while, AVC rises, but, as shown before, AFC declines throughout. Therefore, the ATC will decline as long as the reduction in AFC more than offsets the increase in AVC; when the increase in AVC more than offsets the reduction in AFC, ATC will rise.

4. The vertical distance between ATC and AVC for any given level of output measures AFC. Since AFC declines throughout, becoming smaller and smaller as output expands, the gap between AVC and ATC will narrow. Given this relationship, it is no longer necessary to draw a separate curve for the firm's AFC.

5. Just as the MC curve must, *by definition,* intersect the minimum point of the AVC, it must also intersect the minimum point of the ATC—and for precisely the same reason. If the per unit change in total cost (i.e., the MC) exceeds average total cost, the average must rise; if MC is less than average total cost, the average must fall.

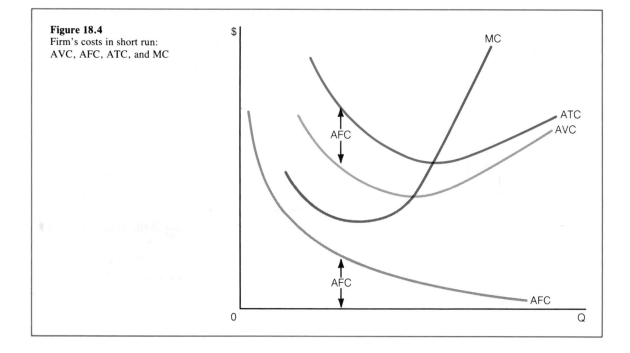

Figure 18.4
Firm's costs in short run:
AVC, AFC, ATC, and MC

Short-run production costs: A summary

The various shapes and positions of the firm's short-run cost curves are determined by four factors.

1. For given resource costs, the law of diminishing returns governs the shape and position of the firm's MC and AVC curves. The exact shape and position of these curves will vary from firm to firm, depending, of course, on *(a)* what it costs the firm to purchase additional variable resources, *(b)* the point at which the firm experiences diminishing returns, and *(c)* how rapidly the returns diminish. A firm that experiences sharply diminishing returns will have an MC curve that rises more steeply than one that has mildly diminishing returns. Can you explain why? A firm that has diminishing returns throughout will have an AVC and an MC that rise throughout. Why?

2. The height of the firm's AFC curve for any given level of output—and therefore the vertical distance between its AVC and ATC—will depend on the magnitude of the firm's fixed costs. A firm producing 50 units of output with a fixed cost of $300 will have an AFC that is less than the AFC of another firm producing 50 units of output with a fixed cost of $400 (i.e., $6 per unit as opposed to $8 per unit). Moreover, since, by definition, fixed costs do not vary as the firm varies its rate of output, *fixed costs have no impact whatsoever on the firm's variable costs or its marginal costs.*

3. The firm's ATC curve is affected by the presence of fixed costs, however. This is a result of the fact that ATC = AVC + AFC. Even in the case where the firm experiences diminishing returns throughout—implying an ever-increasing AVC curve—the ATC is likely to exhibit somewhat of a U shape. It will be U-shaped because, initially, the reduction in AFC more than offsets the increase in AVC, but eventually, the increase in AVC more than offsets the reduction in AFC.

4. If the firm must pay more to attract resources from alternative uses—if, for example, the firm must pay $105 per week to attract a second worker, $110 per week to attract a third, and so forth—its MC curve will rise more steeply,

as will its AVC curve. The reason? In addition to the increasing costs as a consequence of diminishing returns, there is the extra cost in the form of higher pay for each additional worker hired.

One final note. When the firm reaches the point of maximum output—the point beyond which a further expansion of production is not possible—its MC curve becomes vertical. Mathematically speaking, its marginal costs are infinite at this point. What this means is that the firm will simply experience an increase in its costs with no further increase in its output if additional variable factors of production are hired or purchased. At this point, the firm has reached its limit or capacity.

It should also be noted that MC can be interpreted in two ways. As we have emphasized before, MC represents the *additional* cost incurred by the firm *per unit increase* in its rate of production. It can also represent the additional "savings" to the firm per unit *reduction* in its rate of production. Recalling the information supplied in Tables 18.1 and 18.2, an MC of $8.33 shows the per unit increase in the firm's total costs associated with the hiring of the fourth worker; it is also a measure of the per unit "savings" in costs available to the firm if it reduces its work force from four to three workers.

LONG-RUN COSTS

In the short run, the size of the firm's production facility is fixed. Thus, the firm in the short run can alter its rate of production only through the more or less intensive use of its given production facility. The firm's short-run cost curves summarize the impact of changing rates of production on its costs under these circumstances. In the long run, however, the firm can alter the size of its plant by expanding or contracting the scale of its operations. All factors of production are variable in the long run. Since there are no fixed factors of production in the long run, there is no such thing as fixed costs in the long run. In the long run there are only variable costs of production. This may at first glance seem a bit strange. After all, doesn't the firm incur expenses in the long run that are similar to those incurred in the short run? Precisely. But, whereas some of these costs are fixed in the short run, they are variable in the long run. In the long run, the firm has the opportunity to reduce all of its costs to zero—it can close up its operations, settle all of its debts and dispose of its other contractual obligations as well. If it closes up its plant in the short run, it will still have to pay its fixed costs. Moreover, those costs that are fixed to the firm in the short run can be increased or decreased in the long run through changes in the scale of the firm's operations. It is not that the *nature* of these costs change, but only that the firm has the ability to vary them in the long run.

Economies and diseconomies of scale

As the firm alters its scale of operations, its per unit costs—average costs—will either rise, fall, or remain unchanged. These variations in the firm's long-run unit costs are summarized in its **long-run average cost curve (LRAC).** If the firm's long-run average costs decline as the firm expands its scale of operations, it is said to achieve **economies of scale;** if expansion is accompanied by rising long-run average costs, the firm is said to experience **diseconomies of scale.** It is frequently the case that, as the firm expands from a very small scale of operations to a larger plant size, it is possible to achieve certain economies of scale. But generally, there is some limit to the economies—the cost savings—that can be achieved. Further expansion beyond that limit will cause the firm to experience diseconomies.

Economies of scale refer to the cost savings made possible via expansion to larger-sized plants. Larger-sized plants often enable firms to achieve *greater specialization in the use of their labor.* Tasks can be divided more minutely and each worker can be assigned to fewer tasks. As a result, less time is lost in moving from one stage of the production process to the next. Also, each worker has the opportunity to become more proficient at the jobs to which he or she is as-

signed. *Larger plants also permit firms to make better use of management personnel.* Not only is it possible to specialize management functions—sales, finance, accounting, etc.—but larger-scale operations also ensure that management personnel will be more fully utilized. Finally, *a relatively large scale of operations may be required before it is profitable to employ the most efficient production techniques.*

Because many mass production techniques—e.g., assembly line techniques—are very expensive, they become viable alternatives only when the scale of operations becomes large enough. If the firm expects to sell only a few units per week, mass production techniques will probably not be justified.

As the firm continues to expand the scale of its operations, it is likely to encounter certain diseconomies of scale. Diseconomies of scale refer to the *higher* unit costs the firm incurs as a result of the shift to larger plants. As the plant size increases, decisionmaking becomes fragmented. The management problem becomes more difficult. Problems of communication and coordination arise. Sometimes, elaborate bureaucracies have to be constructed to deal with these communication and coordination problems. Frequently, the bureaucratic red tape becomes so onerous that the efficiency of the firm suffers. Management problems of these sorts are the most frequently cited examples of diseconomies of scale.

Economies and diseconomies illustrated. In Figure 18.5, four different plant sizes are represented. ATC_1 represents the short-run ATC curve for the smallest plant; ATC_2 represents the short-run ATC curve for the next larger plant; ATC_3 and ATC_4 represent the short-run ATC curves for two other larger plants. In the short run the firm can vary its rate of production only over the range of output given by its existing plant. In the long run, however, it can change its scale of operations by selecting some other plant size, some other scale of operations.

There are two questions for which we seek answers. First, over what range of plant sizes does the firm experience economies (diseconomies) of scale? Second, at what point—i.e., at

Figure 18.5
Long-run average cost curve (LRAC), or the envelope curve

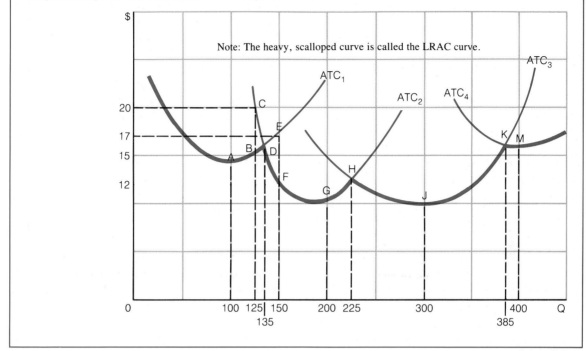

what rate of production—is it appropriate for the firm to alter its plant size?

Because the various short-run cost curves in Figure 18.5 are U-shaped and intersect one another, it is necessary for us to settle on some criteria for judging whether we achieve economies or diseconomies of scale as we move from one plant to another. The problem is that, at relatively low rates of production, lower unit costs are possible in the first plant than in the second; at higher rates of production, lower unit costs are possible in the larger plants. For example, to produce 125 units of output, unit costs are lower in the first plant than the second; at 150 units of output, the reverse is true. As a result of this fact, the following standard criterion is used: *If the minimum ATC declines as the scale of operations is increased, the firm is said to experience economies of scale; if the minimum ATC rises as the scale is increased, diseconomies of scale result.* As the plant size increases from the first through the third plants, the firm obtains economies of scale. This is evident from the fact that the minimum points—points A, G, and J—are successively lower as the scale is increased. Diseconomies of scale emerge as the largest plant is put into place. The reason? The minimum average cost point on ATC_4 lies above the minimum average cost point on ATC_3.

This brings us to the second question: At what rate of production is it appropriate for the firm to alter its plant size? Given that the firm has as its objective maximizing its profits, it should choose that plant size that yields the greatest profits. Suppose the firm is currently producing using the smallest plant and that the rate of output that maximizes its profits in the long run is 125 units. At that rate of production its ATC is $15 (point B). Should the firm expand its operations? No. If the firm did expand to the next largest plant, it would experience, *at a rate of production of 125 units,* higher costs per unit of output—$20 per unit (point C) instead of $15 (point B). It is better to stick with the original plant. Put simply, a rate of production of 125 units is too small to enable the firm to realize the cost savings associated with the larger plant—cost savings that are possible only at rates of production substantially in excess of 125 units.

If the profit-maximizing rate of production was 150 units, on the other hand, it would be profitable for the firm to expand its scale of operations to the next largest plant in the long run. *At that rate of production,* the second plant has an average cost of $12 (point F), whereas for the first plant it is $17 (point E). It is therefore profitable to expand. Indeed, at a rate of production in excess of 135 units—the point of intersection of ATC$_1$ and ATC$_2$ (point D)—it is profitable for the firm to undertake the investment necessary to expand its production facilities. Moreover, at a rate of production in excess of

225 units (point H), it is profitable for the firm to expand its scale to the third plant. At what point is it profitable to expand to the fourth plant? At rates of production in excess of 385 units (point K). And note that it is profitable to expand to the fourth plant *at such rates of production* even though diseconomies of scale set in. Why? Because it costs less to produce those quantities with that plant than with a smaller one; it costs less, for example, to produce 400 units per week with the fourth plant than the third.

Since it is profitable to operate the first plant up to point D, the second plant from point D to H, the third from H to K, and so on, the firm's LRAC can be represented by the heavy, scalloped curve depicted in Figure 18.5. This curve consists of various segments of the firm's short-run ATC curves. For obvious reasons, this scalloped curve is often called an **"envelope" curve.** In any event, the firm's LRAC constructed

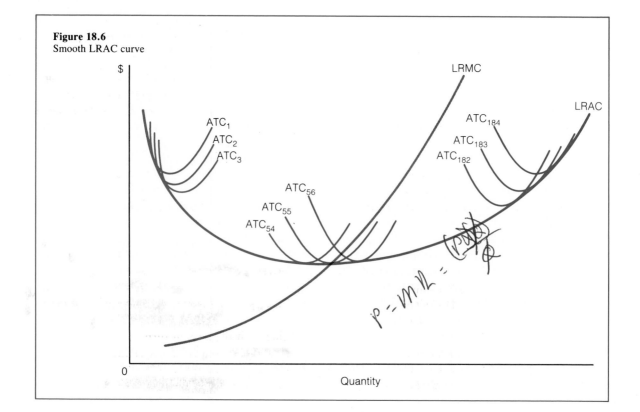

Figure 18.6
Smooth LRAC curve

in this way shows how the firm's unit costs vary as its output level varies under circumstances in which all factors of production are variable—i.e., in the long run, when it is able to choose the preferred plant size.

Often, the envelope curve—or LRAC curve—is drawn as a smooth curve that declines continuously over some range of output levels and rises continuously after attaining some minimum. If the number of plant sizes available to the firm is almost infinite and small changes in plant size are possible, the LRAC curve will appear as a rather smooth and continuous curve. This is illustrated in Figure 18.6. The numbers on each of the various short-run ATC curves represent the different plant sizes.

We also show in Figure 18.6 the firm's **long-run marginal cost curve (LRMC)**. For the usual reasons, the LRMC curve crosses the LRAC curve at the latter's minimum point. The LRMC curve consists of those segments of the short-run MC curves that correspond to those portions of each of the short-run ATC curves that make up the LRAC curve.

REVENUES

Not only is the firm concerned with the costs it incurs in producing any given level of output. It is also concerned with the revenues it will receive from the sale of its goods and services. We define the firm's **total revenue (TR)** for any good or service as the quantity sold times its price. Thus,

$$TR = P \times Q.$$

The firm's **average revenue (AR)** is nothing other than the price received for the particular good or service—i.e., the price represents the revenue received per unit sold:

$$AR = \frac{TR}{Q} = \frac{P \times Q}{Q} = P.$$

Finally, we define **marginal revenue (MR)** as the *change* in total revenue per unit *change* in the

quantity sold—i.e., the change in total revenue divided by the change in the quantity sold:

$$MC = \frac{\Delta TVC}{\Delta Q} \qquad MR = \frac{\Delta TR}{\Delta Q}.$$

$$AVC = \frac{TVC}{Q}$$

$$MP = \text{Marginal Product}$$

Individual firm demand and market demand

How much revenue the firm will receive from the sale of its output will depend on the demand conditions that it faces individually. If the firm happens to be the *sole producer* of some given product, the demand for its product will be the same as the market demand for that product. In other words, if people are willing to buy 100 units of good X at a price of $10 each, and if there is only one producer of good X, then the quantity demanded from that producer at a price of $10 will be 100 units. Since the firm is the only producer, it is said to have a **monopoly** over the production of good X. In the case of a monopoly firm, the demand for its product is identical to the market demand.

When the market is shared by more than one producer, the demand for the output of any single producer will not be identical to the market demand. The market demand refers to the amount that people are willing to buy from *all* of the producers of that product; the amount people are willing to buy from any single producer will generally be different. For the individual firm attempting to maximize its profits, what is important is the nature of the demand for its particular product, not the market demand (unless, of course, the firm is a monopolist, in which case they are one and the same).

Generally speaking, all firms can be divided on the basis of whether they are **price-takers** or **price-setters**. Price-takers are firms that, for various reasons, are powerless to influence the price of the good they produce. Price-setters, on the other hand, can influence product prices. Let us examine each of these in turn.

Price-takers. Consider first the classic case of a price-taker—that of a firm producing in a market that is **perfectly competitive.** In a perfectly competitive market structure, each firm

$$MC + MR$$

produces only a very small fraction of the industry's total output. If any given firm were to double its output or cease production altogether, it would have no perceptible effect on the total amount produced by the entire industry. In addition, each perfectly competitive firm produces a product that is indistinguishable from that of its competitors. Buyers, therefore, do not have any reason to prefer the output of any single firm over that of another.[2] Individual farmers selling tomatoes, lettuce, corn, cabbage, cotton, etc., are perhaps the best examples of perfectly competitive firms.

Consider the demand conditions confronting an individual firm under such circumstances. Suppose the firm produces corn. At any point in time a *market price for corn* will exist determined by the market demand for and supply of corn. Since the individual firm *acting on its own* cannot affect the market supply of corn (because its rate of production is but a minute fraction of total corn production), it cannot influence its market price either. Whether the firm sells a little of its output or a lot, the market price for corn will be unaffected. This means, then, that the individual firm can sell all it wants at the given market price. Moreover, since the firm's output is indistinguishable from that of its competitors, it will not be able to sell any output at a price exceeding the market price; if it did attempt to charge a higher price, buyers would purchase what they wanted from *other* producers. Also, the firm has no incentive whatsoever to lower its price below the market price since it can sell all it wants at the prevailing market price. From the point of view of the individual corn producer, therefore, the demand curve for its output is horizontal at the market-determined price; the individual corn producer is a price-taker.

The situation confronting our corn producer is illustrated in Figure 18.7. The market-deter-

mined price for corn is $3 per bushel. Since our firm can sell all it wants to at that price and can sell nothing at any higher price, it faces a demand curve that is perfectly horizontal—perfectly price elastic—at a price of $3. Whereas the market demand curve is downward sloping (in accordance with the law of demand), the demand curve faced by any individual firm in a perfectly competitive market is horizontal at the price determined by the intersection of the market supply and demand curves. Note in Figure 18.7 the difference in quantities between the individual firm and the market. In the market, the quantities are measured in terms of millions of bushels per month; for the firm the quantities are measured in terms of hundreds of bushels per month. If our firm were to double its output, its impact on the market would go unnoticed.

Note also that, for the perfectly competitive firm, the price of the product is the marginal revenue earned by the firm in the sale of its product. This is easily illustrated. If our producer sells one more bushel of corn, the firm's total revenue will rise by $3—the per bushel price of corn. Since each additional bushel sold fetches for the farmer three additional dollars in revenue, marginal revenue—the per unit change in total revenue—must equal $3. In the case of a perfectly competitive firm, then, it is true that:

$$AR = MR = P.$$

Price-setters. A price-setting firm faces a downward-sloping demand curve for its product. In general, the demand curve that each firm faces will be different from the market demand curve. However, for the moment, that distinction is unimportant. What is important is that, for such a firm, the price and the quantity sold are inversely related. A price-setting firm is *not* able to sell all it might want at any given price. On the contrary, the price-setting firm must cut its price in order to expand its sales volume. If it raises its price, its sales volume will decline—not necessarily to zero, as in the case of a price-taking firm, but to a lower level.

There are many reasons individual firms in some industries might face a downward-sloping

---

[2] If you prefer to buy brand X from Mr. Brown because he is friendlier, has a cleaner store, or because he is more conveniently located, then brand X purchased from Mr. Brown is a different product from brand X purchased from someone else. Under perfectly competitive market structures, such differences either do not exist or are immaterial to buyers. We shall discuss these issues at greater length in Chapter 21.

Perfectly Competitive
MR < P

Figure 18.7
Market demand and supply curves, market price, and price taker's demand curve

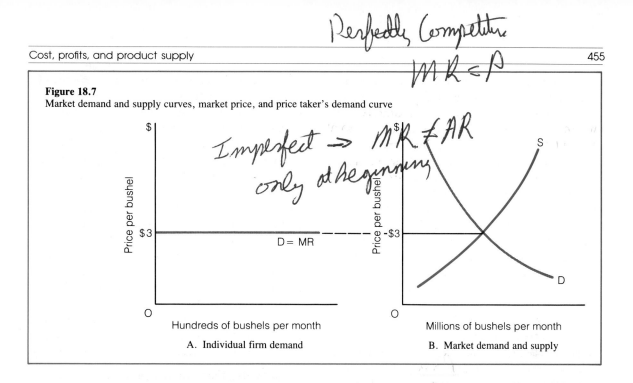

Imperfect ⇒ MR ≠ AR
only at beginning

A. Individual firm demand

B. Market demand and supply

demand curve. In the case of a monopolist, the reason is obvious: The market demand curve (whose shape is governed by the law of demand) *is* the firm's demand curve. In other industries, individual firms produce a substantial percentage of the total output (e.g., Ford or General Motors, in the case of autos). If any one of these firms changes its rate of production, the total supply of the product will be changed noticeably. Finally, in many industries, each of the firms produces a product that is at least somewhat differentiated from the products produced by others. In a sense, each firm has a monopoly in the production of its particular brand; Procter & Gamble has a monopoly in the production of Crest toothpaste, though obviously not in the production of toothpaste generally. Under any or all of these circumstances, the individual firm faces a downward-sloping demand curve for its product.

In the case of a price-setting firm, average revenue (i.e., the firm's demand curve) and marginal revenue are not the same. *With the exception of the first unit sold, average revenue (or price) will always exceed marginal revenue.* This is illustrated in Figure 18.8. At a price of $10 per unit, the firm sells nothing. At a price of $9, one unit is sold. Total revenue (TR) on the first unit is

$9. Marginal revenue (MR)—the change in TR brought about through the sale of the first unit—is $9 (i.e., $\frac{\Delta TR}{\Delta Q} = \frac{\$9}{1} = \$9$). For the first unit sold, MR = P.

To sell the second unit, price must be cut to $8. At a price of $8, the firm's TR is $16 ($8 × 2). MR, on the other hand, is only $7 (i.e., $MR = \frac{\Delta TR}{\Delta Q} = \frac{\$16 - \$9}{1} = \$7$). MR is less than price. How can MR be less than price? Simple. At a price of $9 per unit, the firm could sell one unit per month. In order to sell two units per month, the price had to be cut to $8. But the $8 price applies not only to the second unit sold per month; it applies to the first unit sold per month as well. *On a per unit basis,* the firm receives $1 less for the second unit sold *and* $1 less for the first unit sold, giving a total of $2 less as sales are expanded from one unit to two; MR falls, therefore, from $9 to $7. Can you explain why MR falls to $5 when the price is cut from $8 to $7? Why does MR fall to $3 when the price is cut further still to $6?

This relationship between MR and AR is shown graphically in Figure 18.8. (*A note:* Since MR refers to the *change* in total revenue *per*

Figure 18.8
Demand curve and marginal revenue curve of price-setting firm

Price per unit	Quantity sold per month	TR	MR
$10	0	0	
			> 9
9	1	9	
			> 7
8	2	16	
			> 5
7	3	21	
			> 3
6	4	24	
			> 1
5	5	25	
			> -1
4	6	24	

(handwritten: $\dfrac{P \times Q}{Q}$)

unit, the MR curve should be drawn as a "step function." The smooth MR curve was constructed by joining up the midpoints of these steps. Hereafter, we will ignore this complication and represent the MR curve as a smooth and continuous relationship.)

The firm's revenues: A summary

The shape and position of the firm's average revenue (AR) and marginal revenue (MR) curves will differ according to whether the firm is a price-taker or a price-setter. In the case of a price-taker, the firm's AR and MR curves are one and the same. AR and MR are each given by the product price. In the case of a price-setter, MR will be less than AR on all units sold except the first. In general, therefore, the MR associated with any given level of output will be less than the price at which that level of output can be sold.

(handwritten: Price Takers   D = MR = AR)

THE PROFIT-MAXIMIZING RULE

It is now a relatively simple matter to set forth the rule that must be followed if firms are to behave in ways that will maximize their profits. Profits, you will recall, are defined as the difference between the firm's total revenues and its total costs. That is,

$$\text{Profits} = \text{TR} - \text{TC}.$$

Obviously, a loss is incurred if TC exceeds TR.

Given the definition of profits, it is easy to state the **profit-maximizing rule.** Assume, for the moment, that the firm is actually earning profits (i.e., TR exceeds TC). In this situation:

1. The firm will undertake any and all actions that have the effect of raising its revenues relative to its costs.
2. Profits will be maximized when all actions designed to raise revenues relative to costs have been exhausted.

Consider a simple example. The XYZ Corporation is contemplating expanding its rate of production. An increase in output will cause its costs to rise. Since the firm also expects to expand its sales, its sales revenues are also expected to rise.

If the firm calculates that the expansion will add more to its revenues than it adds to its costs,

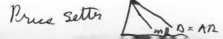

it should expand; if the expansion would add more to costs than to revenues, the firm should not expand. What is important to the firm, therefore, is the additional revenues it expects to receive compared with the additional costs it expects to incur. Recalling the meanings of marginal revenue (MR) and marginal cost (MC), the above discussion can be stated more succinctly as follows: If MR exceeds MC, the firm should expand its rate of production; if MR is less than MC, the firm should not expand.

The same considerations apply to a contemplated contraction in the firm's rate of production. In the case of a contraction, MC refers to the per unit "savings" in total cost; MR then refers to the per unit *reduction* in total revenue. *If MR exceeds MC, the firm should not contract its rate of production; if MR is less than MC, the firm should contract.* In other words, if MR exceeds MC, this implies that a reduction in output would cause total revenue to decline by more than the reduction in total costs. This, in turn, implies a reduced level of profits. The firm, therefore, should *not* cut back its rate of production.

The firm will have maximized its profits only if its rate of production is adjusted to the point where MC equals MR. Only at that point will it have exhausted all opportunities for raising its revenues relative to its costs by either expanding production (if MR exceeds MC) or contracting production (if MR is less than MC).

The same profit-maximizing rule applies to firms even if they are incurring losses. Losses are minimized by the firm undertaking actions in accordance with their MC and MR calculations. Sometimes losses are minimized by the firm staying open and continuing its production activities; sometimes losses are minimized by the firm shutting down.

The profit-maximizing rule applies to both price-setters and price-takers. In addition, the same rule applies whether we are dealing with short-run decisions or long-run decisions.

The next chapter will be devoted to the profit-maximizing behavior of the purely competitive firm. The profit-maximizing behavior of price-

setting firms will be studied in Chapters 20 and 21.

SUMMARY

1. Profits will be maximized when all actions designed to raise revenues relative to costs have been exhausted.

2. The cost of producing any good or service is its *opportunity cost.* This is reflected in the fact that the firm must pay at least as much for the resources it uses as they can command elsewhere.

3. If the firm earns revenues in excess of all *explicit* and *implicit costs,* it is said to earn an *economic profit.* Alternatively, economic profit can be expressed as the excess over and above what the owners' resources could earn elsewhere. *"Normal" profits* refer to the amount of accounting profits that yield to the firm's owners a return equal to what their resources could fetch elsewhere. "Normal" profit is viewed as a cost of production.

4. *The short run* is characterized by the presence of both variable and fixed factors of production; in *the long run,* all factors of production are variable. Corresponding to this distinction, it is useful to distinguish the firm's short-run costs from its long-run costs.

5. In the short run, there are both *fixed costs*—costs that do not change as the level of output is changed—and *variable costs*—costs that do change as the level of output is altered. In the long run, all costs are variable.

6. Assuming that the cost for each unit of the variable factor remains constant, the patterns of movement of *average variable cost* (AVC) and *marginal cost* (MC) will be governed by the nature of the relationship between output and the variable input. In the short run, the *law of diminishing returns* explains why AVC and MC both increase as output is increased.

7. The MC curve *must* cross the AVC curve at the latter's minimum point. The MC curve must also intersect the *average total cost* (ATC) curve at the latter's minimum point; this is a matter of definition, not of economics. Because

fixed costs do not vary as output varies, the *average fixed cost* (AFC) curve must decline throughout. Moreover, for the same reason, the vertical distance between the ATC curve and the AVC curve must get smaller and smaller as output is increased. Finally, the ATC curve will decline as long as the reduction in AFC more than offsets the increase in AVC; when the increase in AVC more than offsets the reduction in AFC, ATC will rise.

8.   If the firm's long-run average costs decline as the firm expands its scale of operations, it is said to achieve *economies of scale.* If expansion is accompanied by rising long-run average costs, the firm is said to experience *diseconomies of scale.*

9.   The amount of revenue any firm will receive from the sale of its product will depend on the demand conditions that it faces individually. Generally, all firms can be divided between *price-takers* and *price-setters.* Price-takers are powerless to influence the price of the good they produce. Generally, they can sell all they want at the *given* price; the demand curve the price-taker faces is horizontal (i.e., perfectly price elastic). Under the circumstances, average revenue (equal to price) is the same as marginal revenue. Price-setters can influence the market price. They each face downward-sloping demand curves for their product. Accordingly, the price-setting firm must cut price to expand sales volume. As a result, with the exception of the first unit sold, average revenue (or price) will always exceed marginal revenue.

10.   Whether firms are price-takers or price-setters, the profit-maximizing rule is the same: The firm will have maximized profits only if its rate of production is adjusted to the point where MC equals MR.

CONCEPTS FOR REVIEW

Profits

Profit maximization

Explicit costs

Implicit costs

Economic profit

"Normal" profit

Accounting profit

The short run

The long run

Fixed costs

Variable costs

Law of diminishing returns (law of diminishing marginal productivity)

Total product curve

Marginal product curve

Average variable costs (AVC)

Marginal cost (MC)

Average fixed cost (AFC)

Average total cost (ATC)

Economies of scale

Diseconomies of scale

Long-run average cost curve (LRAC) (the "envelope" curve)

Total revenue (TR)

Average revenue (AR)

Marginal revenue (MR)

Price-takers

Price-setters

Monopoly

Perfectly competitive

Profit-maximizing rule

QUESTIONS FOR DISCUSSION

(Those marked with an asterisk (*) are more difficult.)

1.   "Some firms report profits totaling $50,000–$60,000 a year, yet fold because they suffer 'losses.' I don't understand!" Explain the confusion.

2.   Suppose a firm encounters diminishing returns at the outset, the second worker adding less than the first, the third adding less than the second, and so forth. Show, using a numerical example, that the firm's average variable costs (AVC) will rise throughout, and that the firm's marginal costs (MC) will lie above AVC over all ranges of output (except for the first unit produced).

3. As a follow-up to question 2, although AVC rises throughout, is it likely that the ATC curve will have the conventional U-Shape? Explain your answer carefully. Explain also the circumstances under which the ATC curve will rise throughout.

*4. Suppose the ATC curve has a shape like a roller-coaster—it rises to a peak, then declines, reaches a trough and turns up, reaching yet another peak, and so on. Draw such an ATC curve. Now draw a possible MC curve to go along with this ATC curve. What does the MC curve look like? What relationship does it bear to the ATC curve? Be explicit.

*5. "If a firm experiences economies of scale (falling costs), it cannot also face diminishing returns (rising costs)." Do you agree or disagree? Explain your reasoning carefully. (Hint: Remember the short-run versus long-run distinction.)

*6. Evaluate the following statement. "I read in Atkinson's text that, for price-setters, marginal revenue (MR) will be less than price for all units sold except the first. This cannot be true. Why? Because if I sell one more unit for $10, my revenues must go up by $10. They can't go up by less since I have a $10 bill in my hand to prove it."

Chapter 19

Pure competition and competitive product supply

In this chapter we look at the consequences of the profit-maximizing behavior of firms operating in a market structure we call **purely competitive** or **perfectly competitive.** We open the chapter with a brief discussion of the characteristic features of a purely competitive market structure. This is followed by an analysis of the short-run and long-run behavior of purely competitive firms. On the basis of this study we are able to derive the short-run and long-run supply curves of both firms and industries in this type of market structure.

THE NATURE OF PURE COMPETITION

Of all the types of market structures we study in this text, our understanding of the purely competitive market structure is the most complete. In general, a purely competitive industry possesses the following four characteristics.

1. The industry is made up of a large number of relatively small firms. All firms need not be of uniform size. But one requirement that is essential is that each firm produce only a very small fraction of the total output of the industry. If any *single firm* were to double its rate of output or cease production altogether, the impact on the total output of the *industry* would not be noticed.

2. All firms in the industry produce a product that, for all intents and purposes, is homogeneous. We mean by this that the output of each of the firms is essentially indistinguishable from that of all the rest of the firms in the industry. A head of cabbage is a head of cabbage whether produced by farmer Brown or farmer Jones. In this context, what is important is that the product produced by each of the firms be indistinguishable *in the minds of the consumers.* If a number of consumers prefer to buy their cabbage from farmer Brown because he is friendlier or because his farm is closer, then it is fair to say that a head of cabbage purchased from farmer Brown is *not* the same product as a head of cabbage purchased from someone else. Here, the circumstances surrounding its sale differentiate farmer Brown's output from that of his competitors. In

a purely competitive market structure, such differences do not exist. As we shall see later, differences of this sort, and others as well, form part of the basis for another type of market structure—**monopolistic competition.**

3. A third feature of pure competition is that all market participants are fully informed. If two firms charge different prices for the same product, all consumers have knowledge of this fact; if firm A has profits of $500 per week and firm B has losses amounting to $300 per week, this is widely known. It may take time for such information to become known, but ultimately market participants will discover these kinds of information.

4. Finally, it is assumed that there are no significant **barriers to entry** to a purely competitive industry. That is, the capital costs required of would-be competitors are not so prohibitive that they are effectively barred from entering the industry. In addition, given that the product is homogeneous, it is not necessary for would-be competitors to break down consumers' attachments to certain products in order to be able to compete with existing firms. In short, it is not especially difficult to set up shop in a purely competitive industry.

At first sight, a number of these assumptions might appear to be overly unrealistic. Indeed they are. Pure competition is an extreme type of market structure. But that, in and of itself, is not a reason for excluding the purely competitive model from careful consideration. In the first place, a number of industries possess characteristics that approximate rather closely the features of a purely competitive industry. We can, therefore, obtain useful insights into the operation of these industries on the basis of our study of pure competition.

Second, a thorough understanding of pure competition is a necessary prerequisite to an understanding of more complex market structures. Although the purely competitive market structure is not applicable to a large number of U.S. industries, we do arrive at a number of conclusions that closely approximate the realities found in other market structures.

Finally, pure competition is frequently held up as having certain "ideal" properties, a standard by which to compare the actual performance of firms in our economic system. While a full evaluation of this proposition will have to wait until Chapters 27 and 28, it is important that we be clear on the principles underlying this particular market structure. This is our objective in the present chapter.

SHORT-RUN PROFIT MAXIMIZATION: THE PURELY COMPETITIVE FIRM

The ZZZ Corporation produces a single product only—programmable pocket-sized minicomputers. ZZZ is only one of a very large number of producers of minicomputers; and in the minds of consumers, all minicomputers are pretty much alike. Under these circumstances, the ZZZ Corporation, acting on its own, can have no discernable influence on the market price for minicomputers. The ZZZ Corporation is a price-taker; it faces a demand curve for its product that is perfectly elastic at the prevailing market-determined price for minicomputers. If ZZZ sets a price above the market clearing price, it will not sell any minicomputers; since it can sell all it wants at the market price, it has no incentive to sell for less.

In the short run, ZZZ incurs certain fixed costs—costs that are independent of the firm's rate of production. These costs include the rental payments made for plant and property, interest payments for outstanding debt, property taxes, and contractual obligations to some of the administrative personnel.

The production of minicomputers also imposes on ZZZ certain variable costs—costs that vary with the firm's rate of production. These costs include the material inputs utilized in the construction of pocket computers and the bulk of the labor employed by the firm. Table 19.1 summarizes these costs for the ZZZ Corporation. It is assumed there that ZZZ's fixed costs per week amount to $1,000. Whether ZZZ produces 120 units per week or shuts down completely, its *total* fixed costs remain unaltered. For obvious

$$TR = (P \times Q)$$

$$MR = \frac{TR}{p}$$

Table 19.1

ZZZ's short-run production costs and revenues: Profit maximization (market price of minicomputers = $54.00)

(1) Output per week	(2) Fixed costs per week	(3) AFC (2)÷(1)	(4) Variable costs per week	(5) AVC (4)÷(1)	(6) ATC (5)+(3) or (7)÷(1)	(7) Total costs (4)+(2)	(8) MC	(9) Total revenues	(10) MR (=P)	(11) Profits or losses (9)−(7)
0	$1,000	—	$ 0	$ 0	—	$1,000		$ 0		$−1,000
							8		$54	
10	1,000	$100.00	80	8	$108.00	1,080		540		− 540
							6		54	
20	1,000	50.00	140	7	57.00	1,140		1,080		− 60
							10		54	
30	1,000	33.33	240	8	41.33	1,240		1,620		380
							12		54	
40	1,000	25.00	360	9	34.00	1,360		2,160		800
							14		54	
50	1,000	20.00	500	10	30.00	1,500		2,700		1,200
							22		54	
60	1,000	16.67	720	12	28.67	1,720		3,240		1,520
							33		54	
70	1,000	14.29	1,050	15	29.29	2,050		3,780		1,730
							39		54	
80	1,000	12.50	1,440	18	30.50	2,440		4,320		1,880
							54		54	
90	1,000	11.11	1,980	22	33.11	2,980		4,860		1,880
							72		54	
100	1,000	10.00	2,700	27	37.00	3,700		5,400		1,700
							93		54	
110	1,000	9.09	3,630	33	42.09	4,630		5,940		1,310
							117		54	
120	1,000	8.33	4,800	40	48.33	5,800		6,480		680

reasons, average fixed cost (AFC) declines as ZZZ's rate of production is expanded. Can you explain why?

As ZZZ increases its rate of production, its variable costs rise. This is shown in column (4). Its variable costs per unit of output—its AVC—is shown in column (5). As is apparent from column (5), ZZZ's AVC at first declines, then rises, as output is expanded. The firm's average total cost (ATC), which consists of the sum of its AFC and its AVC, is shown in column (6). Like the AVC, the firm's ATC at first declines, then rises, as output is increased. As emphasized in Chapter 18, the ATC declines as long as the reduction in AFC more than offsets the increase in AVC; when the increase in AVC more than offsets the reduction in AFC, ATC rises.

ZZZ's total costs are shown in column (7). Total costs consist of the sum of the firm's fixed costs and its variable costs; it can also be obtained by multiplying the firm's ATC times its corresponding rate of output (i.e., TC = ATC × Q). Our firm's marginal cost (MC)—its per unit *change* in total costs—is shown is column (8). As is apparent from the data presented in Table 19.1, AVC declines or rises as MC is less than or greater than AVC; similarly, ATC declines or rises as MC is less than or greater than ATC. Can you explain why?

For purposes of illustration, we have assumed that the market-determined price for minicomputers is $54. Because of our earlier assumption that the ZZZ Corporation is a perfectly competitive firm, it can sell as few as 10 units or as many as 120 units, all at a price of $54 each. It should be obvious, therefore, that our firm's marginal revenue (MR)—its per unit *change* in total revenue—is also $54, the same as the price of the product itself. Can you explain why? This is shown in column (10).

Finally, in column (11), we show ZZZ's losses or profits at each rate of output. Profits or losses, you will remember, are calculated simply as the difference between the firm's total revenues and its total costs.

Profit maximization

It is obvious from the data in column (11) of Table 19.1 that the ZZZ Corporation will maximize its profits by producing either 80 or 90 units of output per week. At either of those rates of output, it earns a weekly profit of $1,880. At any other rate of output, its profits are lower. And note that *over that range of output,* MC equals MR. In other words, the ZZZ Corporation will maximize its profits by choosing that rate of production where MC equals MR. In order to see this clearly, examine the relationships that exist at other rates of production. Suppose the firm is currently producing at a rate of output of 70 units per week. Its weekly profits at that rate of output amount to only $1,730. It could obviously do better by expanding its output to 80 or 90 units per week. And the reason for this is apparent. As the ZZZ Corporation increases its production rate from 70 to 80 units, it incurs an *additional* cost for each additional unit of only $39, whereas it earns an additional $54 for each unit sold. In other words, since MR exceeds MC, it is profitable for ZZZ to expand.

Suppose, on the other hand, that our firm is producing at a rate of output of 100 per week. Its weekly profits at that rate of output amount to only $1,700. It could do better by *reducing* its rate of production to 90 or 80 units per week. Again, the reason for this is obvious. Since MC exceeds MR at rates of production in excess of 90 units, its cost "savings" exceed the reduced revenues associated with the production cutback. Profits are maximized only when MC equals MR. Moreover, since price is equal to MR for the perfectly competitive firm, the profit-maximizing rule can be restated as follows:

The perfectly competitive firm will maximize profits by producing at the point where MC = MR = P.

(*Note:* In our numerical example, profits are maximized by producing at either 80 units or 90 units of output. The reason we get two possible rates of output, not just one, is because MC refers to the per unit *change* in costs associated with the *change* in output over each of the respective ranges of output. As we go from 80 to 90 units of output, MC equals $54. Since MR is 54 at both 80 units and 90 units, the profits are the same at those two levels of output.)

Loss minimization

Suppose that the market-determined price for minicomputers happened to be $22 instead of $54. At that price, it is not possible for the ZZZ Corporation to make a profit. This is made apparent from the data presented in Table 19.2. The output and cost data in Table 19.2 are carried over from Table 19.1; the revenue data are different from Table 19.1 for the simple reason that the price of minicomputers is now different. At each rate of output, the ZZZ Corporation incurs a loss.

The question that now confronts the ZZZ Corporation is this: Should it continue to produce minicomputers or should it shut down operations completely? Isn't the answer to this question obvious? After all, since the ZZZ Corporation cannot earn any profit at a price of $22 per unit, would it not be better to simply cease production altogether? Not necessarily. Remember that, in the short run, the ZZZ Corporation incurs fixed costs totaling $1,000. These costs must be paid whether the firm stays open or shuts down completely. The question is: Can the firm do better than that? Granted, ZZZ cannot earn any profits at a price of $22. But is it possible to sustain a smaller loss than $1,000 by remaining open? Yes. ZZZ's losses will be less than $1,000 for all rates of output between 10 and 80 units per week. Therefore, ZZZ should remain open in the short run. By continuing to produce, the ZZZ Corporation is able to cover all of its variable costs *plus* make some contribution to its fixed costs. It cuts its losses by staying open; it would lose even more money—its $1,000 in fixed costs—by shutting down.

Obviously, the ZZZ Corporation will be interested in minimizing its losses. It will achieve that objective by producing a rate of output of either 50 or 60 units per week. At those rates of output it will sustain weekly losses of $400. It can do no better than that. But note that, at those rates of production, MC = MR = $22.00. In other words, the ZZZ Corporation will minimize its losses by following the same profit-maximizing rule as before—and for precisely the same reasons. At rates of production below 50 units, MR exceeds MC, implying that the firm can cut its losses by stepping up production; at rates of production in excess of 60 units, MC exceeds MR, implying that losses can be cut via production

Table 19.2
ZZZ's short-run production costs and revenues: Loss
minimization (market price of minicomputers = $22)

(1) Output	(2) Variable Costs	(3) Total Costs	(4) MC	(5) Total Revenues	(6) MR (=P)	(7) Profits or losses (5) − (3)
0........	$ 0	$1,000	$ 8	$ 0	$22	$−1,000
10........	80	1,080	6	220	22	− 860
20........	140	1,140	10	440	22	− 700
30........	240	1,240	12	660	22	− 580
40........	360	1,360	14	880	22	− 480
50........	500	1,500	22	1,100	22	− 400
60........	720	1,720	33	1,320	22	− 400
70........	1,050	2,050	39	1,540	22	− 510
80........	1,440	2,440	54	1,760	22	− 680
90........	1,980	2,980	72	1,980	22	−1,000
100........	2,700	3,700	93	2,200	22	−1,500
110........	3,630	4,630	117	2,420	22	−2,210
120........	4,800	5,800		2,640		−3,160

cutbacks. Only at the point where MC equals
MR will the firm's losses be minimized.

Loss minimization: The shutdown case

Will it ever pay to shut down completely in
the short run? Yes. Given the cost conditions
that prevail in the firm, it will pay to shut down
if the market price for minicomputers falls so
low that the firm loses more than $1,000 by re-

maining open. If the price falls below $7, it will
pay to shut down completely. This is illustrated
in Table 19.3. At a price of $7, the firm will
incur a loss of $1,000 by shutting down or by
producing a rate of output of 20 units. Any other
rate of output will leave the firm with losses in
excess of $1,000. At a rate of output of 20 units,
the firm is just covering its variable costs. At
any other rate of output, the ZZZ Corporation
cannot even cover all of its variable costs; at rates

Table 19.3
ZZZ's short-run production costs and revenues: Loss
minimization and the shutdown point (market price
of minicomputers = $7)

(1) Output	(2) Variable costs	(3) Total costs	(4) MC	(5) Total rev- enues	(6) MR (=P)	(7) Profits or losses (5) − (3)
$ 0	$ 0	$1,000	$ 8	$ 0	$7	$−1,000
10	80	1,080	6	70	7	−1,010
20	140	1,140	10	140	7	−1,000
30	240	1,240	12	210	7	−1,030
40	360	1,360	14	280	7	−1,080
50	500	1,500	22	350	7	−1,150
60	720	1,720	33	420	7	−1,300
70	1,050	2,050	39	490	7	−1,560
80	1,440	2,440	54	560	7	−1,880
90	1,980	2,980	72	630	7	−2,350
100	2,700	3,700	93	700	7	−3,000
110	3,630	4,630	117	770	7	−3,860
120	4,800	5,800		840		−4,960

of production other than 20 units (or zero), it incurs losses in excess of $1,000. At a price of $7 per unit, therefore, the ZZZ Corporation is indifferent between shutting down and staying open (and producing a rate of output of 20 units per week). If the price falls below $7, the ZZZ Corporation will close down in the short run. Can you explain why?

Some conclusions from the numerical examples

On the basis of the above numerical examples, the following conclusions can be stated.

1. If rates of production exist that enable the firm to cover at least *all* of its variable costs, the firm will maximize its profits or minimize its losses in the short run by producing at the "point" where MC = MR. Any other rate of production will cause the firm's profits to be lower or its losses larger.

2. For a perfectly competitive firm, the profit-maximizing or loss-minimizing rule can be stated as: MC = MR = P.

3. If the firm is unable to cover its variable costs with any positive rate of production, it will minimize its losses by shutting down.

If these conclusions are not understood thoroughly, you would be well-advised to study the examples once again before going on.

The profit-maximizing example illustrated graphically

The data for AVC, ATC, MC, and MR from Table 19.1 are plotted in Figure 19.1. The MC relationship is drawn as a step function. The profit-maximizing rate of production can be found at the point where MC equals MR. As is apparent from Figure 19.1, this equality can be found in the output range of 80–90 units. For simplicity, we will assume that the ZZZ Corporation will select a rate of output of 90 units. At that rate of output, its total cost can be found by multiplying its cost per unit (its ATC) times the number of units produced. Since ZZZ's ATC is $33.11 at the production rate of 90 units,

its total cost is $2,980 (i.e., $33.11 × 90 = $2,979.90). Its total revenue, on the other hand, can be found by multiplying the quantity sold times its price. In our numerical example, total revenue amounts to $4,860 (i.e., $54.00 × 90 = $4,860). Profits are calculated as the difference between total revenues and total costs. Profits here amount to $1,880 (i.e., Profits = $4,860 − $2,980 = $1,880). Graphically, profits can be found by calculating the difference between the price per unit ($54) and the cost per unit ($33.11), then multiplying that difference ($20.89) times the quantity (i.e., Profits = $20.89 × 90 = $1,880.10).

Profit maximization and loss minimization: A general graphic representation

The general graphic representation of profits or losses is given in Figure 19.2. Four alternative situations are presented there. In Figure 19.2A we illustrate the case of a perfectly competitive firm that is capable of earning positive short-run economic profits. Given the firm's cost conditions and the price of the product, P_1, profits will be maximized at the point—point D—where MC = MR = P_1. (In this, and all subsequent examples, MC is drawn as a smooth curve, not as a "step" function.) This implies a rate of production of A units. Since total revenue equals the price times the quantity sold, total revenue is given by the area of the rectangle OP_1DA. Price is given by the height OP_1; quantity is given by the distance OA; the product of price times quantity is given by the rectangle OP_1DA. Moreover, since total cost equals the ATC times the quantity produced, total cost is given by the area of the rectangle OCBA. ATC at the output level OA is given by the height AB (which equals OC); this times the quantity OA gives total cost, OCBA. Economic profits—the difference between total revenue and total cost—is given by the area of the rectangle CP_1DB.

Figure 19.2B illustrates the case of a firm earning zero economic profits in the short run. The firm "maximizes" its profits by producing at the point—point F—where MC = MR = P_2. This implies a rate of production of E units. At that

Figure 19.1

Profit maximization for ZZZ Corporation in the short run
(market price of minicomputers = $54)

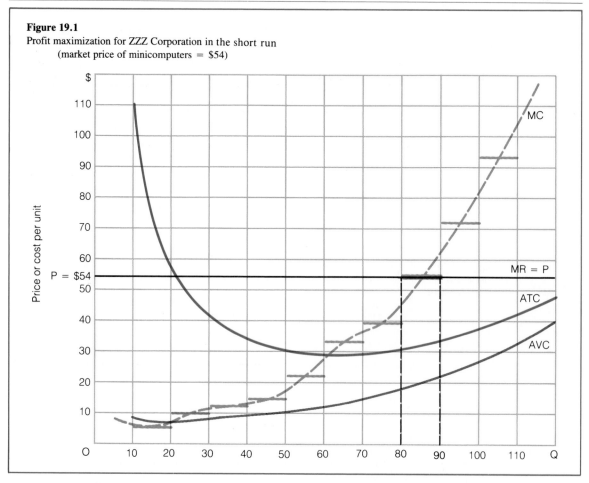

rate of production, the firm will be operating at the minimum point of its ATC curve. Can you explain why this must be so? (*Hint:* Remember the requirement that the MC curve crosses the ATC curve at the latter's minimum point.) Total revenue and total cost both are given by the area of the rectangle OP₂FE; economic profits are zero. In this case, the firm just breaks even. Economic profits are zero.

In Figure 19.2C we illustrate the case of a firm that incurs a loss. However, given the cost conditions confronting the firm and the price of the product, P₃, the firm minimizes its losses by producing at the point—point J—where MC = MR = P₃. This implies a rate of production of G units. Total revenue (given by the area of the rectangle OP₃JG) is less than total cost (given

by the area of the rectangle OLKG), leaving the firm with a loss (given by the area of the rectangle P₃LKJ). The firm will remain open because it is covering all of its variable costs and making some contribution to its fixed costs. The contribution that it makes to its fixed costs is given by the area of the rectangle MP₃JH. Total variable costs are given by the area OMHG; total costs are given by OLKG; the difference—total fixed costs—is given by MLKH; since total revenue exceeds total variable costs by the amount MP₃JH, that amount must represent the contribution made to fixed costs.

Figure 19.2D illustrates the case of a firm that is just covering its variable costs, but makes no contribution to its fixed costs. Given the cost conditions confronting the firm and the price of

Figure 19.2
Profit maximization and loss minimization: Four illustrative cases

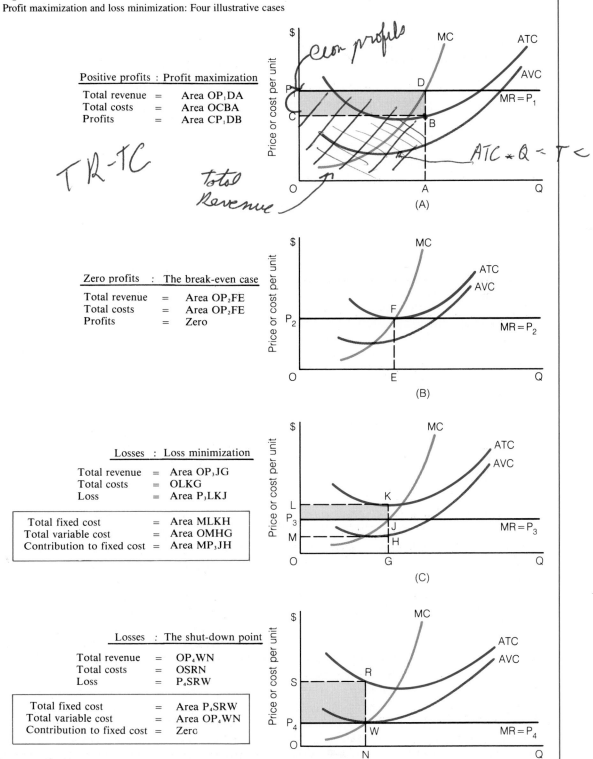

Positive profits : Profit maximization

Total revenue	=	Area OP_1DA
Total costs	=	Area $OCBA$
Profits	=	Area CP_1DB

(A)

Zero profits : The break-even case

Total revenue	=	Area OP_2FE
Total costs	=	Area OP_2FE
Profits	=	Zero

(B)

Losses : Loss minimization

Total revenue	=	Area OP_3JG
Total costs	=	$OLKG$
Loss	=	Area P_3LKJ

Total fixed cost	=	Area $MLKH$
Total variable cost	=	Area $OMHG$
Contribution to fixed cost	=	Area MP_3JH

(C)

Losses : The shut-down point

Total revenue	=	OP_4WN
Total costs	=	$OSRN$
Loss	=	P_4SRW

Total fixed cost	=	Area P_4SRW
Total variable cost	=	Area OP_4WN
Contribution to fixed cost	=	Zero

(D)

its product, P_4, the firm is at its shutdown point. At prices below P_4, the firm will minimize its losses by closing down its operations completely. Can you explain why?

The perfectly competitive firm's short-run supply curve

We are now in a position to describe the supply curve of the perfectly competitive firm in the short run. A firm's supply curve, you will recall, shows how much the firm is willing to produce and sell at various prices. In the case of a perfectly competitive firm, supply is derived from the profit-maximizing or loss-minimizing condition—MC = MR = P. The firm's supply curve can be described as follows: *It is that portion of the firm's MC curve that lies above the minimum point of its AVC curve.* This is illustrated in Figure 19.3. We have depicted there four alternative prices: P_1, P_2, P_3, and P_4. The question we wish to answer is this: How much is the firm willing to sell at each of the different prices?

At the price P_1, the firm is willing to sell Q_1 units of output, given by the intersection of its MC curve with the price. At the lower price, P_2, the firm will cut back its quantity supplied to Q_2. At P_3, the firm is willing to sell Q_3. At any price below P_4, the firm will shut down, causing its quantity supplied to fall to zero. It is apparent, then, that the firm's supply curve *is* that portion of the firm's MC curve lying above its AVC curve. Since the quantity of output that a profit maximizing (or loss minimizing) firm is willing to supply is determined by the intersection of MC and price, the MC curve depicts the supply response of the firm at different prices. The MC curve *is* the *firm's* supply curve.

The market supply curve

The total quantity supplied to the market will be the sum of the quantities supplied by each firm in the industry. Since, for each perfectly competitive firm, its MC curve is its supply curve, the market supply curve can be found by simply adding up horizontally the MC curves of all the firms in the industry. This is illustrated in Figure

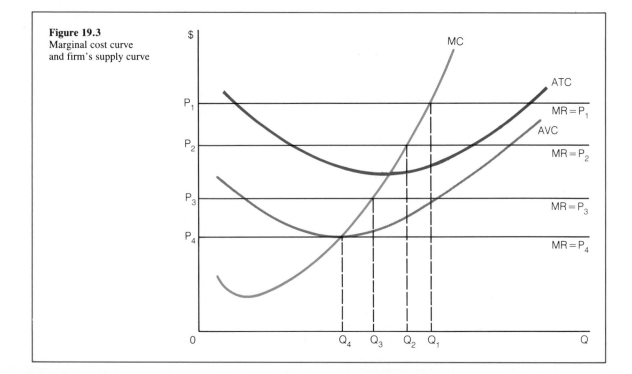

Figure 19.3
Marginal cost curve and firm's supply curve

Figure 19.4
Relationship between individual firm supply and market supply

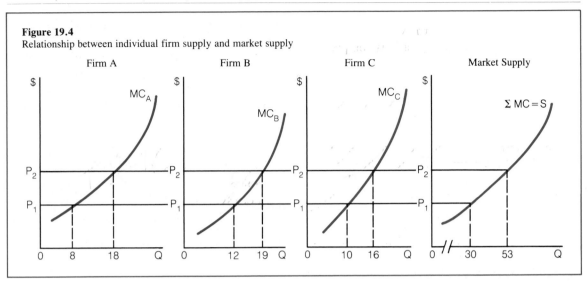

19.4. For simplicity, we will assume there are only three firms in the industry—firms A, B, and C. At the market price P_1, firm A will supply eight units; firms B and C will supply 12 and 10 units, respectively. The market supply at the price P_1—the sum of the individual firm supplies at the price P_1—will amount to 30 (i.e., 8 + 10 + 12 = 30). At the price P_2, firms A, B, and C will supply 18, 19, and 16 units, respectively, for a total market supply of 53 units. This is the meaning of "competitive market supply consists of the horizontal sum of all individual firm MC curves."

As we shall see in the next chapter, this relationship between the market supply curve and the individual firm MC curves is very important to our evaluation of the perfectly competitve market structure. Since each firm carries its production to the point where MC equals price, each point on the market supply curve corresponds to the aggregate marginal cost of the industry.

Producer's surplus

In Chapter 17 we developed the idea of *consumer's surplus.* **Producer's surplus** is an analogous concept. Consider Figure 19.5. A price of $4 per unit is required in order to have producers put the first unit of the good on the market for sale. At a price of $5 each, producers are willing

to expand supply from one unit to two units. But note that, although a price of $5 is required to coax the second unit out of producers, producers receive $5 for *both* the first and second units. Producers are therefore said to earn a "surplus" of $1 on the first unit since a $4 price was all that was required for that first unit.

At a price of $6.25, producers are willing to place three units on the market for sale. Produc-

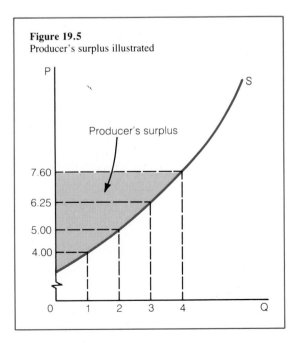

Figure 19.5
Producer's surplus illustrated

er's surplus now increases from $1 to $3.50 — $2.25 for the first unit (since $4 was all that was required to bring forth its supply) plus $1.25 for the second unit. Can you show that producer's surplus would amount to $7.55 at a per unit price of $7.60? If the market clearing price were $7.60, producer's surplus would be shown graphically in Figure 19.5 as the shaded area above the supply curve to the $7.60 price line.

LONG-RUN ADJUSTMENTS IN PURELY COMPETITIVE INDUSTRIES

In our earlier discussion of the characteristics of a purely competitive industry, two features were emphasized. First, the industry consists of a large number of small producers, each producing only a fraction of the total industry output. Second, each firm in the industry produces a product that is, in the minds of consumers at least, indistinguishable from that of its competitors. The purely competitive industry is also characterized by yet another feature—there are no effective **"barriers to entry"** to the industry. Put bluntly, it is relatively inexpensive and relatively easy for would-be competitors to set up shop and begin production.

It is not difficult to identify the reason new firms would consider entering a purely competitive industry. It is captured in one expression— **economic profits.** That is, as long as there are economic profits to be earned, the industry will experience the entry of new firms. In order to ensure that this is thoroughly understood, recall our previous discussion of economic profits. You will remember that "normal" profit was considered a cost of production, and that we meant by economic profit a return to the owners *in excess of what their resources would earn elsewhere.* In other words, the presence of positive economic profits in a purely competitive industry means that at least some firms are earning more than their resources could fetch in other production activities; the existence of such profits acts as a lure attracting resources to that industry. This simple fact has a number of highly signifi-

cant implications for purely competitive industries in the long run:

1. Only the most efficient firms will survive in the long run in a purely competitive industry.
2. In the long run, all firms in the industry will be earning zero economic profits.
3. In the long run, all firms in the industry will be operating at the minimum point on their long-run average cost curves. This means all firms will be using the best technology available and the most efficient plant possible, and each firm will operate its plant at its lowest cost point.
4. In the long run, the following relationship will prevail: $MC = P = $ Min. point on ATC.

To assist us in our understanding of these issues, two points require emphasis. First, the entry of firms into an industry will have the effect of increasing the market supply curve. That is, entry shifts the supply curve down and to the right. The exit of firms from an industry, on the other hand, causes the supply curve to shift upward and to the left. These supply curve shifts will affect the equilibrium price, lowering it in response to the entry of firms and raising it in response to the exit of firms. Second, the demand curve faced by each purely competitive firm is given by the horizontal straight line whose height is equal to the market price. Therefore, the market supply curve shifts resulting from firms entering or exiting from an industry will, because of their effects on the market price, cause corresponding shifts in the demand curves faced by each firm. These points are illustrated in Figure 19.6. At the initial price P_0, given by the intersection of the market demand and supply curves, the ZZZ Corporation faces a horizontal demand curve whose height is equal to P_0. If, as a result of the entry of firms into the minicomputer industry, the market supply curve shifts down and to the right from S to S_1, the demand curve facing ZZZ will be lowered by the amount that the market price is reduced.

With these points understood, let us now briefly demonstrate each of the four conclusions stated earlier.

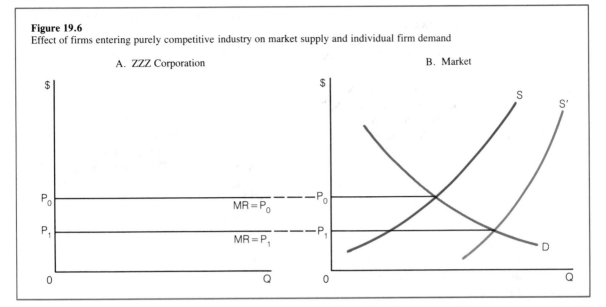

Figure 19.6
Effect of firms entering purely competitive industry on market supply and individual firm demand

A. ZZZ Corporation

B. Market

1. Only the most efficient firms will survive in the long run. At any point in time, each of the firms in the industry may be confronted with different costs as a result of differences in productive efficiency. On the other hand, each of the firms will face an *identical* market price for its output, that price having been determined by the forces of demand and supply in the *market.* As a result of cost differences, and because each firm faces an identical price, there will be differences in the levels of profits. This is illustrated in Figure 19.7.

In Figure 19.7 we represent the average total cost and marginal cost curves for three of the many firms that produce minicomputers. They are, respectively, the ZZZ Corporation, the AAA Corporation, and the BBB Corporation. In addition, we present the *market* demand and supply curves for minicomputers. (Note the different quantities represented on the market graph and the firm graphs.)

The market-determined price for minicomputers is $54. At that price, ZZZ and AAA make positive economic profits, but BBB just breaks even (i.e., earns zero economic profits). In the absence of barriers to entry, the presence of profits within the industry acts as a lure to potential

competitors. In the long run, as new firms enter the industry, the *market* supply curve will shift outward and to the right. The entrance of any single competitor will have an imperceptible impact on the market supply curve, but the cumulative impact of a number of entrants will cause the supply curve to shift noticeably. The increase in the supply of minicomputers will, of course, drive down their price. This, in turn, will lower the demand curves facing each of the individual firms.

Suppose that, after the initial burst of new entrants, the price falls to $39 as a result of a shift in the market supply curve from S to S_1. The new situation is depicted in Figure 19.7 by the use of dashed lines. As a consequence, the profits of each of the existing firms will be reduced. The BBB Corporation now incurs a loss; AAA just breaks even at $39; ZZZ continues to earn positive economic profits, though less than when the price was $54. The implications of these changes for the firms in the minicomputer industry are highly significant. Consider, for example, the implications for the BBB Corporation. Since all costs in the long run are variable, the BBB Corporation is not able to cover all of those costs at a price of $39. BBB has two choices

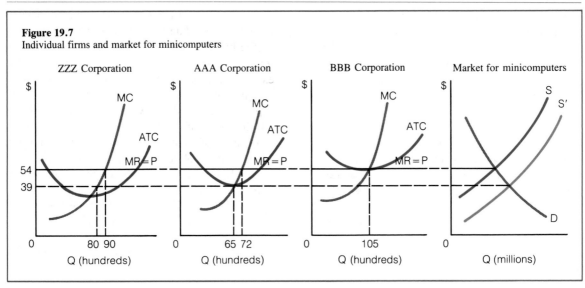

Figure 19.7
Individual firms and market for minicomputers

to make: It can either close down its operations and make its exit from the minicomputer industry; or it can undertake to change its operations so as to achieve a level of efficiency comparable to the most efficient firm in the industry. And why must BBB attain a level of efficiency comparable to the most efficient firm? Simple. As long as any firm in the industry makes positive economic profits, new entrants will be attracted into the production of minicomputers. This will cause supply to expand, forcing down the price. This process will continue until all profitable opportunities have been eliminated. The price will be forced down in the long run to the point where even the most efficient firm in the industry just breaks even. Therefore, if BBB is to just break even, it must achieve a level of efficiency like the best firm in the industry; it will incur a loss otherwise. And remember what is meant by the term *loss*. It means that the resources owned by the firm can earn more elsewhere.

The same conclusion applies to AAA. Although it breaks even at a price of $39, it must do something to cut its costs in the future or face the prospect of going out of business. That is, since ZZZ (and other firms as well) are still earning economic profits at a price of $39, the price in the future will fall below $39. Can you

explain why? Can you also explain why AAA must achieve a level of efficiency in the future comparable to the most efficient firm in the industry?

And what about the ZZZ Corporation? If it is as efficient as the best, it need not make any adjustments in order to survive. However, its long-run economic profits will eventually be whittled away to nothing. Ultimately, therefore, ZZZ will earn a return equal to what its resources could command elsewhere. If it is not as efficient as the best firms in the industry, it will inevitably be forced at some time in the future to attain a level of efficiency comparable to the best. Can you explain why?

2. In the long run, all firms in a purely competitive industry will earn zero profits. It should by now be apparent that, in the absence of any significant barriers to entry, new resources will enter the industry as long as there are firms earning positive economic profits. That is, resources will continue to enter as long as the potential returns in this perfectly competitive industry exceed those available elsewhere. Moreover, since the price will ultimately be bid down to the level necessary to eliminate the profits of the most efficient firms, and since all firms in the industry must ultimately attain a level of efficiency equal to that of the most efficient firms, it follows, therefore, that all firms in the long run will earn zero profits. Put differently, all firms in a perfectly competitive industry will earn a "normal" profit—a rate of return equal to what each firm's resources could command elsewhere—in the long run.

3. In the long run, each firm will operate at the minimum point of its long-run average cost curve. Not only will each firm earn zero profits in the long run, but competitive pressures are such that each firm will also put into place the most efficient plant size possible, and operate it at its lowest cost point. This is easily illustrated. Assume the ZZZ Corporation is at present producing minicomputers in a plant that is smaller than the most efficient plant size. This means, then, that it is operating at a point to the left of the minimum point of its long-run average cost curve—say, point B in Figure 19.8. If the price happens to be equal to P_1 initially, ZZZ will make some profits. But it can make even more profit by expanding the scale of its operations. Suppose that it adopts the most efficient plant size. If the price remains at P_1, it is apparent that its profits will rise. ZZZ has a strong incentive, therefore, to expand its scale from the plant

size associated with point B to the one associated with point A. The same is true for every other perfectly competitive producer of minicomputers. And, as long as positive economic profits exist, the supply of minicomputers will increase. Ultimately, therefore, the price must fall to P_0, a price equal to the lowest unit costs attainable on the most efficient plant size possible. In the long run, each firm will operate at the minimum point of its long-run average cost curve.

4. In the long run, each perfectly competitive firm will operate at the point where MC = P = min ATC. This fourth and final conclusion follows directly from the foregoing discussion. Can you explain why it must hold? (Remember again the relationship between MC and AC.) This conclusion is highly significant as it is frequently used by economists and others as a standard by which the performance of firms operating within the economy are compared. That is, when firms sell their goods at prices equal to their marginal cost—a phenomenon called **marginal cost pricing**—and when they produce their output at the point of least cost—the minimum point on their long-run average cost curve—society obtains the most that it can get from a given quantity of scarce resources. In short, the perfectly competi-

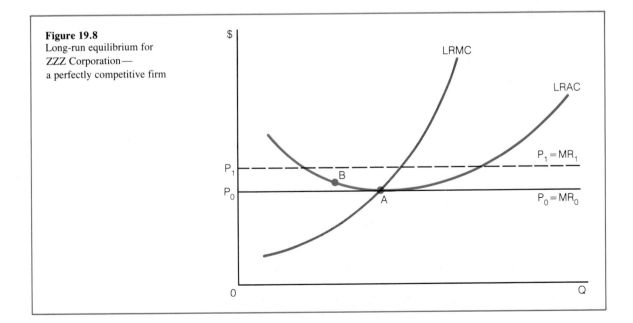

Figure 19.8
Long-run equilibrium for
ZZZ Corporation—
a perfectly competitive firm

tive market structure ensures the most efficient allocation of scarce resources possible. We shall examine this issue in greater detail in the chapters to follow.

The long-run supply curve in a perfectly competitive industry

In the short run, the supply curve of each perfectly competitive firm is that portion of its MC curve above the minimum point of its AVC curve. The short-run supply curve for the industry is obtained as the horizontal summation of the individual firm supply curves. The upward-sloping market supply curve obtained in this manner reflects the profit-maximizing behavior of firms that are subject to the law of diminishing returns.

The long-run supply relationships of the perfectly competitive industry are very different from the short-run supply relationships. As noted above, in long-run equilibrium, each firm operates at the minimum point of its long-run average cost curve, and each earns only a "normal" profit. The pressures of competition are such that the unit costs—the average costs—are, as noted earlier, the same for all firms. Moreover, since all firms in the long-run experience the same unit costs and all utilize the most efficient plant size, these circumstances would seem to imply that the long-run supply curve of the industry would be horizontal—perfectly price elastic—at a level corresponding to the common minimum point of all the firms' long-run average costs. That is, since entering firms will also ultimately be forced to adopt the most efficient plant size just as existing firms do, generating the same average costs of production, the implied long-run industry supply curve would be horizontal. This will be true as long as the expansion of industry supply does not raise the prices of resources for *all* firms in the industry. If, on the other hand, the expansion of industry supply raised the prices that *all* firms had to pay for their resources—for their land, labor, or capital—the LRAC curves of all firms would shift upwards. As a result, the long-run industry supply curve would slope upwards to the right. These different cases are illustrated in Figure 19.9.

Figure 19.9A depicts the case of a **constant cost industry.** The curve labeled S_{SR} shows the short-run quantity response to price changes; the curve labeled S_{LR} depicts the constant cost long-run supply curve. In this instance, the increase in industry supply resulting from the entry of new firms does not change the prices of the resources for the firms in the industry. Their costs, therefore, remain unaltered as production within the industry expands—hence the reason for the name *constant cost industry.* Assume initially that the industry is in long-run equilibrium, producing Q_0 units of output at a price of P_2. Now assume that the demand for the product increases from D to D^1. *In the short run,* the price will rise from P_2 to P_1, causing existing firms to earn positive economic profits. Can you explain why? Those profits will act as a lure, attracting new entrants into the industry. Since resource costs are not driven upward by these new entrants, and since new firms will enter as long as positive profits exist, the price will ultimately be forced back down to P_2, as represented by the shift of the short-run supply curve from S_{SR} to S^1_{SR}; the industry will now be producing an enlarged output equal to Q_2. The long-run supply curve of the constant cost industry, therefore, is perfectly horizontal—perfectly price elastic—at the price P_2.

Figure 19.9B illustrates the case of an **increasing cost industry.** Here, the expansion of industry supply in response to the increased level of profits forces up resource prices, raising in turn the costs for all firms—hence the reason for the name *increasing cost industry.* The new long-run equilibrium is obtained at a price of P_3 and a quantity of Q_3. The long-run supply curve of the industry is upward sloping.

Most economists believe that the increasing cost case constitutes the most common situation for most industries. The constant cost case would prevail only if the *total* demand for resources by the industry was but a small fraction of the aggregate of all demands by all firms—inside and outside this industry—for those resources. If that

Figure 19.9
Long-run industry supply:
Constant cost and increasing cost industries

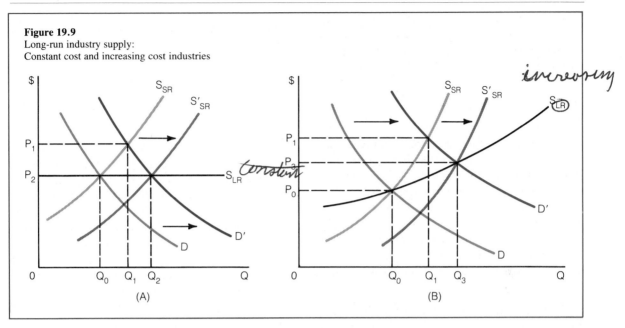

(A)

(B)

were not the case, resource prices would probably have to rise so that this industry could attract resources away from their alternative uses. This latter situation is probably the most realistic from the point of view of the bulk of American industries.[1]

A note on the perfectly competitive long-run equilibrium: Statics versus dynamics

It is doubtful that the long-run competitive equilibrium as we have described it can ever be attained. The reason for this is not difficult to discover. We live in an economic system that is ever changing, ever evolving. Population changes, as does its age distribution and its geographical location. People's incomes grow over time, not smoothly, but up and down in line with changes in the general level of economic activity. People's lifestyles change, as do their tastes. New products are continuously being introduced to the market, and a number of old ones are being phased out of existence. Techno-

logical advances frequently change production methods.

All of these forces, and others as well, cause many unpredictable changes in the forces of demand and supply, changing in turn the profit outlook from one year to the next. As a result of the operation of these forces, it is best to interpret our discussion of long-run equilibrium as reflecting the *tendencies* that exist in a purely competitive industry. That is, in a static, unchanging world, the long-run equilibrium would ultimately obtain as we have described it. In a dynamically evolving economic system, on the other hand, that ultimate equilibrium rarely occurs. The tendency toward one equilibrium position is interrupted by one change or another, setting in motion forces pushing us toward another equilibrium, which in turn is likely to be interrupted.

SUMMARY

1. Descriptively, a *purely competitive industry* possesses three characteristics: *(a)* the industry is made up of a large number of relatively small firms, each firm producing only a very

---

[1] Another theoretical possibility is that of a *decreasing cost industry*. We ignore this case here because it is not a common phenomenon.

small fraction of total industry output; *(b)* the product is homogeneous; and *(c)* there are no significant barriers to entry.

2. Because of the equivalence of MR and AR under pure competition, purely competitive firms maximize profits by carrying production to the point where MC equals P.

3. As long as the firm's revenues are sufficient to cover all of its variable costs *plus* make some contribution to its fixed costs, the firm should continue to produce in the short run even if it is suffering losses; loss minimization is accomplished by carrying production to the point where MC equals P.

4. If the firm's revenues are not sufficient to cover its variable costs, the firm will minimize losses by shutting down its operations.

5. The perfectly competitive firm's supply curve is that portion of its MC curve that lies above the minimum point of its AVC curve.

6. The market supply curve under conditions of pure competition is given by the horizontal sum of the MC curves of all the firms in the industry.

7. *Producer's surplus* is a concept analogous to *consumer's surplus.* It arises because the price at which *all* units are sold equals the price necessary to coax out the *last,* or the marginal, unit. All prior units that producers were willing to sell at lower prices now earn a surplus.

8. The presence or absence of economic profits governs the entrance and exit of firms in a purely competitive industry in the long run. This simple fact has a number of highly significant implications for purely competitive industries in the long run: *(a)* only the most efficient firms will survive; *(b)* all firms in the industry will earn zero economic profits; and *(c)* all firms will be operating at the minimum point on their LRAC.

9. The long-run supply relationships under pure competition are very different from the short-run supply relationships. If expansion of industry supply does not raise the prices of resources for the industry, the long-run industry supply curve will be horizontal; if expansion of industry supply raises resource prices for the in-

dustry, the long-run supply curve will slope upwards to the right.

CONCEPTS FOR REVIEW

Pure competition

Homogeneous product

Fully informed market participants

Barriers to entry

Profit maximization under pure competiton (MC = P)

Loss minimization

The "shutdown" case

The "break-even" case

Producer's surplus

Long-run equilibrium (P = MC = Min. LRAC)

Constant cost industry

Increasing cost industry

QUESTIONS FOR DISCUSSION

1. Explain why, under conditions of pure competition, the profit-maximizing rule, MC = MR, can be restated as MC = P.

2. The firm's MC curve is often drawn as sloping downward, then upward, as output is increased. Since the market supply curve is constructed on the basis of the individual firm MC curves, why is it that the market supply curve is never drawn as sloping downward, then upward, as the quantity is increased? (*Hint:* This is easy to answer if you know the definition of the firm's supply curve and if you understand the relationship between MC and AVC.)

3. Assume, to begin with, that a purely competitive long-run equilibrium has been established with all of the characteristics described in the body of this chapter. Then suppose that the ZZZ Corporation discovers a new technique of production that enables it to lower its unit costs (i.e. its average costs) by 10 percent at all levels of output.

a. Explain carefully the sequence of events that will occur as a consequence of ZZZ's discovery to change the long-run purely competitive equilibrium position of the industry. Will all firms ultimately adopt ZZZ's new technique? Under the circumstances, what incentive does ZZZ, or any other firm, have to use scarce resources to develop new cost-saving techniques of production?

b. Is it true that ZZZ's discovery will cause the equilibrium price to fall by 10 percent in the long run under conditions of constant costs? What about increasing costs?

4. Explain why any firm would continue to stay open in the short run if, month after month, it was in the red (i.e., incurring losses). When would it be appropriate for the firm to close up shop in the short run?

5. Explain in nontechnical language why any producer would remain in business if, year after year, its profits were zero. Doesn't the existence of zero profits mean that the firm's owners could do better elsewhere?

Chapter 20

Monopoly and pure competition: A study of contrasts

In Chapter 19 we studied in some detail the consequences of the profit-maximizing behavior of firms in a purely competitive environment. We direct our attention in this chapter to a market structure that is the extreme opposite of pure competition—that of **monopoly.** The characteristic feature of monopoly is that there is only one firm in the industry. It follows, therefore, that the demand curve facing the monopolist is the *market* demand curve.

The fact that the monopolist faces a downward-sloping demand curve means that the monopolist is a *price-setter,* not a *price-taker.* Its price-setting powers are limited, however (it cannot charge "any price it wants"), because lower prices are required if larger quantities are to be sold. As a consequence, the monopolist must determine simultaneously both its rate of output and its price. This is to be contrasted with the purely competitive firm, which must determine its rate of production only, subject to the market-determined price.

We will study first the short-run and long-run profit-maximizing behavior of the monopolist. The results emerging from this analysis will then be contrasted with the conclusions arrived at in our discussion of the purely competitive firm. Next, we will turn our attention to the case of a **"natural monopoly"** and the economics of price regulation. In the final section of this chapter we will examine the implications of the differences between the purely competitive and the monopolistic market structures.

PROFIT MAXIMIZATION UNDER MONOPOLY

We will assume that the monopolist has one primary objective—to maximize profits. As we will see, the monopolist attains this objective by following exactly the same rule as the purely competitive firm—that of equating marginal revenue and marginal cost. This is hardly surprising. If an action undertaken by a monopoly firm adds more to its revenues than it does to its costs, its profits will, of course, rise. The monopolist will have maximized profits when all actions designed to raise revenues relative to costs have been exhausted.

Unlike the purely competitive firm, however, the monopoly firm faces a downward-sloping demand curve for its product. That is, in order for the monopoly firm to expand its sales, it must cut its price. This is obviously different from the purely competitive firm, which can sell all it wants at the market-determined price. In the case of monopoly, it is the monopolist that determines the product's price. And associated with any given price is a *unique* quantity demanded. In addition, the price set by the monopolist and the quantity demanded of the product are inversely related, in accordance with the law of demand.

As a result of the fact that the monopolist faces a downward-sloping demand curve, the demand curve of the firm and its marginal revenue curve are no longer one and the same. Indeed, the marginal revenue generated through an additional unit of sales will generally be less than the price at which the unit sells. This difference was emphasized in Chapter 18, but bears repeating here in view of its importance to our study of monopoly.

Price, marginal revenue, and downward-sloping demand

Consider the hypothetical data presented in Table 20.1. At a price of $10 per unit, the quantity demanded equals one; total revenue at that price amounts to $10. Obviously, for the first unit sold, marginal revenue (MR) is the same as price. Marginal revenue—the change in total revenue per additional unit sold—is equal to $10 for the first unit. For the second unit sold, and for all subsequent units, marginal revenue is less than price. At a price of $9 per unit, the quantity demanded is two. Total revenue rises from $10 to $18, implying a marginal revenue of $8. That is, associated with a $9 price, the firm's MR amounts to only $8—$1 less than the price.

It is easy to explain why MR is less than price. The firm can sell one unit (per unit of time) at a price of $10. In order to sell two units (per unit of time) the price must be reduced to $9—for both the first and second unit. Thus, the firm earns one dollar less for *both* units sold. Its MR, therefore, falls from $10 to $8 when the quantity sold rises from one to two. Similarly, when the price is reduced to $8, three units (per unit of time) can be sold. But the MR—the additional revenue per additional unit sold—falls to $6. This is because in order to sell three units (per unit of time) the price must be cut to $8, not only for the third unit sold, but for the original two units, which previously had sold at $9.

At this point it is natural to ask, Why can't the firm sell the first unit at $10, the second at $9, the third at $8, and so on? Why must it sell all three units at $8 apiece? That is, why must there be a common price? The reason is this: The person buying the product at $8 could take advantage of the situation by reselling it at a price slightly higher than $8 to those who might otherwise buy at $9 or $10. Under these circumstances, the monopolist's market for the first two units would dry up. As long as the possibility of resale exists, this will force the establishment of a uniform price.

Of course, there are some markets where the possibility of resale does *not* exist. For example, psychiatric services cannot be resold to another person. Under these circumstances, it is possible for sellers to *discriminate* among buyers—selling the service, for example, to a wealthy person at a high price, but providing the same service to others at lower prices. Airline companies regularly practice such discrimination, as evidenced, for example, by their general practice of providing lower airfares for travel by night than for

Table 20.1
Downward-sloping demand: The divergence of price and marginal revenue

Quantity demanded	Price of product	TR	MR
0	—	0	
			$10
1	$10	$10	
			8
2	9	18	
			6
3	8	24	
			4
4	7	28	
			2
5	6	30	
			0
6	5	30	
			−2
7	4	28	
			−4
8	3	24	

travel by day. For the present, we will ignore these complications. We will concentrate our attention instead on markets in which the product can be, and will be, readily resold in the event of any attempted price discrimination.

An aside: Marginal revenue and the price elasticity of demand

Before turning to an explicit analysis of the behavior of a profit-maximizing monopolist, it is worth noting as an aside that a very simple relationship exists between MR and the price elasticity of demand. Recalling our discussion in Chapter 16 of the relationship between total revenue (or total expenditures) and the price elasticity of demand, we arrived at the following conclusions:

1. If the price elasticity of demand exceeds unity, a price reduction (rise) will cause total revenue to rise (fall).
2. If the price elasticity of demand is less than one, a price reduction (rise) will cause total revenue to fall (rise).
3. If the price elasticity of demand equals unity, a change in price—up or down—will leave total revenue unaltered.

Since MR is defined as the change in total revenue per unit change in the quantity sold— i.e., $MR = \dfrac{\Delta TR}{\Delta Q}$—it should be obvious that the following relationships must hold between MR and the price elasticity of demand:

1. If demand is price elastic, a price reduction will cause total revenue to rise, implying in turn that MR is positive.
2. If demand is price inelastic, a price reduction will cause total revenue to fall, implying that MR is negative.
3. If demand has a price elasticity equal to unity, a price reduction will leave total revenue unaltered, implying that MR is equal to zero.

Using the data presented in Table 20.1, can you tell, on the basis of the positive and negative

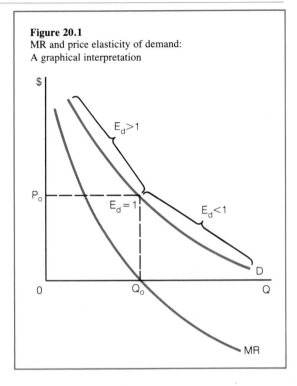

Figure 20.1
MR and price elasticity of demand:
A graphical interpretation

values of MR, the range of prices for which demand is elastic? Inelastic? Unit elastic? As should be apparent, demand is elastic in the $10–$6 price range, unit elastic in the $6–$5 price range, and price inelastic in the range of prices below $5.

The relationship between MR and the price elasticity of demand can be given a simple graphic interpretation. This is shown in Figure 20.1. It is apparent that the demand for the product has a price elasticity equal to unity at the price, P_0. The reason? At that price, MR equals zero. At prices higher than P_0, the price elasticity of demand exceeds unity; at prices below P_0, the demand curve is price inelastic. Can you explain why?

The relationship between MR and the price elasticity of demand can also be expressed by the following simple formula:

$$MR = P \times \left(1 - \frac{1}{E_d}\right).$$

Thus, if:

1. $E_d = 1$, $MR = 0$ [i.e., $MR = P \times (1 - 1) = 0$];

2. $E_d = \infty$, $MR = P$ [i.e., $MR = P \times \left(1 - \frac{1}{\infty}\right) = P \times (1 - 0) = P$].

This illustrates the case of a perfectly elastic demand curve, the kind faced by each firm in a perfectly competitive market;

3. $E_d > 1$, $MR > 0$;
4. $E_d < 1$, $MR < 0$.

The above formula will prove useful later in our discussions of markup pricing.

Short-run profit maximization: A numerical example

We are now in a position to study the implications of the assumption that the monopolist attempts to maximize profits. To start with, we will analyze the monopolist's behavior in a short-run context, leaving until later our discussion of the long run. In an effort to highlight the differences that exist between the purely competitive and the monopoly firm, we will assume for the moment that both kinds of firms face similar cost conditions.

Consider once again the market for minicomputers. In contrast to our discussion in the previous chapter, we will assume here that the ZZZ Corporation is the sole producer of that product; ZZZ is a monopolist, not a perfect competitor. As a monopolist, the ZZZ Corporation faces a downward-sloping demand curve for its product—the market demand curve. In Table 20.2, we have assumed that the demand curve facing the monopolist can be described as follows.

First, the consuming public will not buy any minicomputers at all at a price of $86.84 or above; the quantity demanded at that price (or at higher prices) is zero. Second, for each reduction in price of $4.14, the quantity demanded rises by 10 units. At a price of $82.70—$4.14 below the $86.84 price—the monopolist can sell 10 units; at a price of $78.56—$4.14 below the $82.70 price—the monopolist can sell 20 units; and so on. This information is given in columns (1) and (8) of Table 20.2.

The total revenue obtained by the ZZZ Corporation in the sale of its minicomputers is presented in column (9) of Table 20.2. It is obtained, simply, by multiplying each price times the corre-

Table 20.2
Short-run production costs and revenues: Profit maximization under monopoly

(1) Output (Q)	(2) Fixed costs	(3) Variable costs	(4) AVC (3)÷(1)	(5) ATC (6)÷(1)	(6) Total costs (2)+(3)	(7) MC	(8) Price (P)	(9) Total Revenue (8)×(1)	(10) MR	(11) Profits (+) or losses (−) (9)−(6)
0 ...	$1,000	$ 0	$ 0	—	$1,000		$86.84	$ 0.00		$−1,000.00
10 ...	1,000	80	8	$108.00	1,080	$ 8	82.70	827.00	$ 82.70	− 253.00
20 ...	1,000	140	7	57.00	1,140	6	78.56	1,571.20	74.42	+ 431.20
30 ...	1,000	240	8	41.33	1,240	10	74.42	2,232.60	66.14	+ 992.60
40 ...	1,000	360	9	34.00	1,360	12	70.28	2,811.20	57.86	+1,451.20
50 ...	1,000	500	10	30.00	1,500	14	66.14	3,307.00	49.58	+1,807.00
60 ...	1,000	720	12	28.67	1,720	22	62.00	3,720.00	41.30	+2,000.00
70 ...	1,000	1,050	15	29.29	2,050	33	57.86	4,050.00	33.00	+2,000.00
80 ...	1,000	1,440	18	30.50	2,440	39	53.72	4,297.60	24.76	+1,857.60
90 ...	1,000	1,980	22	33.11	2,980	54	49.58	4,462.20	16.46	+1,482.20
100 ...	1,000	2,700	27	37.00	3,700	72	45.44	4,544.00	8.18	+ 844.00
110 ...	1,000	3,630	33	42.09	4,630	93	41.30	4,543.00	− 0.10	− 87.00
120 ...	1,000	4,800	40	48.33	5,800	117	37.16	4,459.20	− 8.38	−1,340.80

sponding quantity demanded. At a price of $82.70 each, total revenue amounts to $827 (i.e., $82.70 × 10 = $827.00); at a price of $53.72 each, total revenue equals $4,297.60 (i.e., $53.72 × 80 = $4,297.60).

Given this information, it is a relatively simple task to calculate ZZZ's marginal revenue. For the first 10 units sold, ZZZ's total revenue rises from zero to $827; MR—the additional revenue per additional unit sold—amounts to $82.70 (i.e.,

$$MR = \frac{\Delta TR}{\Delta Q} = \frac{\$827}{10} = \$82.70).$$ On the other

hand, a price reduction from $62 to $57.86 raises the quantity demanded from 60 units to 70 units, raising, in turn, total revenue from $3,720 to $4,050; that $330 increases in total revenue implies an MR of $33 (i.e., $MR = \frac{\$330}{10} = \$33$).

For simplicity, we have assumed that the costs confronting ZZZ are exactly the same as those presented in Chapter 19. The cost data represented in columns (2) through (7) of Table 20.2 are nothing more than a reproduction of the data contained in Table 19.1 of the previous chapter.

We are finally in a position to answer the fundamental question posed earlier. What price and what rate of output will maximize ZZZ's profits? On the basis of the data presented in column (11) of Table 20.2, the answer is obvious. ZZZ will maximize its profits by producing either 60 minicomputers (per unit of time) and selling them all at a price of $62 each, or by producing 70 units and selling them at $57.86 each. Either choice will generate for ZZZ a profit of $2,000 (per unit of time). All other price/quantity combinations yield less profit.

Also note that, at the price/quantity combinations that yield the maximum profit, MC = MR = $33. This particular result should have been expected. Indeed, if MC differs from MR, it is possible for ZZZ to adjust its rate of output and its price in ways that will improve its profit picture. To illustrate, suppose ZZZ is currently producing 50 minicomputers (per unit of time) and selling them at a price of $66.14 each. Can ZZZ increase its profits by expanding its output and cutting its price? Yes. If it cuts its price to $62, it will sell 10 more units than before and its

MR—the additional revenue per additional unit sold—will amount to $41.30. Its MC, on the other hand, amounts to only $22. Since ZZZ adds more to its revenues than it does to its costs by expanding output by 10 units and cutting the price per unit by $4.14, its profits will rise with such a move.

Or consider the situation confronting ZZZ at a rate of production of 80 units and a price of $53.72. If ZZZ were to cut its production back to 70 units and raise its price to $57.86, its per unit "savings" in costs ($39)—its MC—would exceed its per unit reduction in revenues ($24.76)—its MR. The result would be that its profits would rise. Profits will be at their maximum only at the price/quantity combinations where MC equals MR.[1]

The numerical example: A more careful examination. There are a number of points worth noting about the results of our study thus far.

It is often alleged that monopolists will charge *the highest price possible* for their products. For a profit-maximizing monopolist, such a statement is sheer nonsense. ZZZ could have charged a price of $78.56, for example. But at that price its profits would have amounted to only $431.20, which is much less than its profits at a price of $57.86. Or, to be extreme, at a price of $86.84, ZZZ would not be able to sell any minicomputers at all; it would therefore not earn any revenues to offset its costs. ZZZ maximizes profits by choosing that rate of output and that price at which MC equals MR. To do otherwise would yield less profit.

Note also that at its profit-maximizing position, ZZZ's price of $57.86 exceeds its MC of

---

[1] In this numerical example, profits are maximized at two different prices and two different rates of production. Like our discussion in Chapter 19, this is easily explained. At a rate of production of 60 units and a price of $62, profits amount to $2,000. Since the per unit *change* in total cost (i.e., MC) is the same as the per unit *change* in total revenue (i.e., MR) as ZZZ expands its production by 10 units and cuts its price to $57.86, profits will, of course, be the same at 70 units as they were at a production rate of 60 units and a price of $62. ZZZ has no basis for choosing one of these price/quantity combinations over the other, but we will assume for simplicity that ZZZ will choose to produce at a rate of output of 70 units and a selling price of $57.86.

$33. This result is not surprising in view of the fact that *(a)* for a downward-sloping demand curve, MR will be less than price, and *(b)* maximum profits are attained at the point where MC equals MR. This result is, however, highly significant from the point of view of efficiency in the allocation of resources in a market economy. It means that the price that the consumer must pay for the last unit exceeds the additional cost that must be incurred to produce it. We shall have much more to say about this later.

In our numerical example, it was assumed that ZZZ could make positive economic profits. This need not always be the case. Indeed, given the cost conditions confronting the ZZZ Corporation, one could well imagine that ZZZ could face a demand curve for its product such that it incurred a loss at all price/quantity combinations. As was the case with a purely competitive firm, ZZZ would reduce its short-run losses by continuing to produce as long as there were price/quantity combinations that yielded revenues sufficient to cover its variable costs. Under these circumstances, it would minimize its losses by choosing that price/quantity combination at which MC equaled **MR**. If all price/quantity combinations generated revenues that were insufficient to cover its variable costs, ZZZ would, of course, minimize its short-run losses by shutting down completely. This will become clear in our subsequent graphic presentation of the monopoly firm.

The profit-maximizing monopolist: A graphic analysis

The entire preceding discussion can be summarized rather neatly in a single graph. This is done in Figure 20.2. The demand curve facing the monopolist is, of course, the market demand curve for the product. Its downward slope is dictated by the law of demand. The **MR** curve corresponding to this demand curve is labeled **MR**. In order to keep the graph as uncluttered as possible, we have included in Figure 20.2 only two of the firm's cost curves—its **ATC** curve and its **MC** curve.

The monopoly firm has to discover both the rate of output and the product price that will maximize its profits. Graphically, these decisions can be derived as follows.

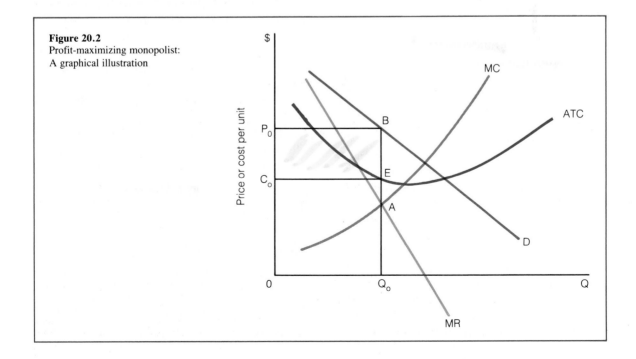

Figure 20.2
Profit-maximizing monopolist:
A graphical illustration

Figure 20.3
Profit-maximizing monopolist:
Graphical proof of profit-maximizing rule

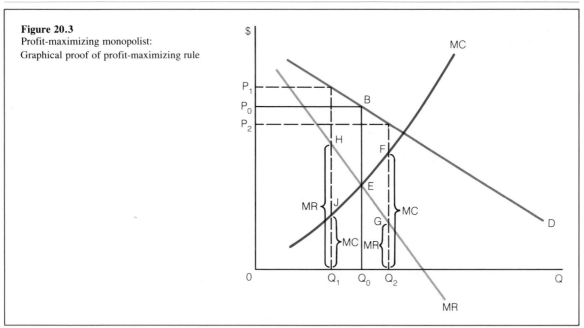

Identify the point where the MC curve and the MR curve intersect (point A). Directly below that intersection point, one can determine the profit-maximizing rate of production, Q_0. On the basis of the demand curve, it is clear that the quantity Q_0 can be sold at a price of P_0; P_0 is the profit-maximizing price.

How are profits determined graphically? Simple. Total revenue (TR) for the monopolist is given as the quantity sold times the price. Thus, TR is given by the area of the rectangle OP_0BQ_0. Total cost (TC), on the other hand, is arrived at by multiplying the cost per unit at Q_0—the ATC at Q_0—times the quantity produced. Thus, TC is given by the area of the rectangle OC_0EQ_0. Profits—the difference between TR and TC—are given by the area of the rectangle C_0P_0BE.

Given the firm's costs and the demand conditions for its product, can the monopolist improve its profits by selecting some price/quantity combination other than P_0 and Q_0? *No.* To see this, consider Figure 20.3, which is a reproduction of Figure 20.2 with the ATC curve eliminated. First, select some price/quantity combination other than P_0/Q_0—say, P_2 and Q_2. At the rate of production Q_2, the firm's MC is given by the height FQ_2, whereas its MR is given by the height

GQ_2. Since MC exceeds MR, the firm would "save" more costs than it would lose in revenues by cutting its production rate from Q_2 to Q_0. Or consider the price/quantity combination of P_1 and Q_1. Since at Q_1, MR equal to HQ_1 exceeds MC equal to JQ_1, the monopoly firm would add more to its revenues than it would to its costs by expanding its rate of output and lowering its price—to Q_0 and P_0, respectively. The monopolist can do no better than producing Q_0 units of output and selling that quantity at a price of P_0 for each unit.

Profit maximization and loss minimization illustrated

In Figure 20.4A we illustrate the case of a monopoly firm that earns positive economic profits by producing at the point where MC equals MR. The characteristic feature of such a firm is that, over some range of production, the demand curve lies above the ATC curve. The magnitude of the monopolist's profits is given by the shaded rectangle area of the graph, as explained earlier.

In Figure 20.4B we illustrate the case of a monopoly firm that incurs losses at all ranges

Figure 20.4
Short-run profit maximization and
loss minimization illustrated

A. Here the firm maximizes
profits by setting price
and quantity at levels consistent with equality
of MC and MR

B. Here the firm minimizes
losses by setting price
and quantity at levels con-
sistent with equality of
MR and MC
Loss: Area of rectangle P_1C_0AF
Fixed cost: Area of rectangle
EC_0AB
Contribution to fixed cost:
Area of rectangle EP_1FB

C. Here the firm minimizes
losses by shutting down
completely in short run

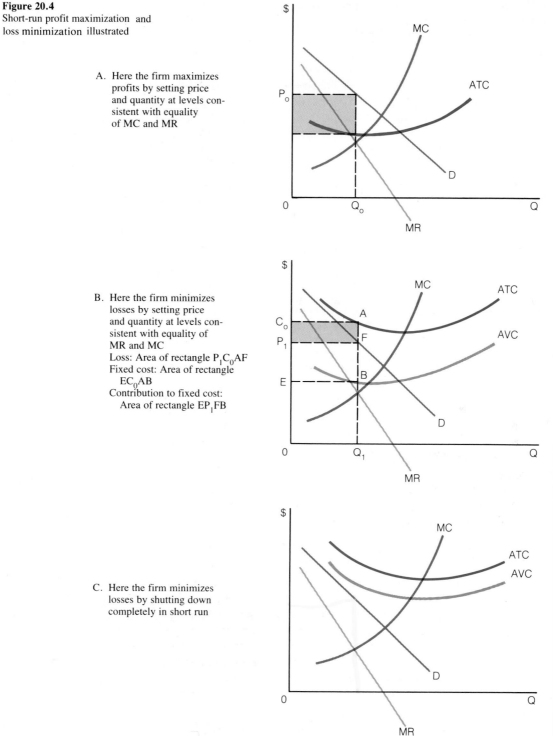

of production. Since the ATC curve lies everywhere above the demand curve, there is no possibility of economic profits here. However, since there are some rates of production for which revenues more than cover the variable costs of production, the monopoly firm will minimize its losses in the short run by producing at the point where MC equals MR—i.e. by producing the rate of output Q_1 and selling it at the price P_1. The magnitude of its losses is given by the shaded rectangle area of the graph—the area P_1C_0AF (i.e., total cost of OC_0AQ_1 exceeds total revenue of OP_1FQ_1 by this amount).

It is obvious that the losses incurred by the monopoly firm in Figure 20.4B are less than its fixed costs. The firm's AFC at the rate of output Q_1 is given by the vertical distance between AVC and ATC at the rate of output. Total fixed costs, therefore, amount to the area of the rectangle EC_0AB—i.e., AFC times the rate of output Q_1. The contribution that the monopoly firm makes to its fixed costs is given by the area of the rectangle EP_1FB.

Since the monopoly firm in Figure 20.4C is not able to cover all of its variable costs at *any* price/quantity combination, it will minimize its losses by shutting down in the short run. The loss it incurs by shutting down is smaller than the loss it would suffer by continuing to produce.

An aside: The profit-maximizing monopolist and the price elasticity of demand for the monopolist's product. It is a relatively easy matter to demonstrate that the only relevant portion of the demand curve facing a profit-maximizing monopolist is the price elastic portion—i.e., that portion of the demand curve for which the price elasticity exceeds one. This conclusion can be derived on the basis of two simple propositions.

1. The demand curve is price elastic over that range of sales for which MR is positive.
2. Since MC is generally positive over all ranges of output, profit maximization must occur at a point where MR is positive.

Can you demonstrate that the monopoly firm will maximize its profits by producing at the point where the price elasticity of demand equals unity if MC equals zero?

Monopoly and long-run equilibrium

Unlike the perfectly competitive firm, it is frequently the case that monopoly firms will earn positive economic profits, even in the long run. Perfectly competitive firms cannot earn profits in the long run for the simple reason that the existence of profits will act as a lure, attracting new firms into the industry and forcing down the price of the product until all such profitable opportunities have been eliminated. This result is inevitable since no significant **barriers to entry** exist in pure competition.

The barriers to entry in the case of monopoly, however, are generally very significant. This is not to argue that there can never be new entry into an industry that was previously monopolized. If the opportunities for profit are great enough, it still might be possible for one or more firms to enter the industry in an effort to obtain some of those profits. But in many instances, the barriers to entry are such that would-be competitors are effectively denied entrance.

And what are these barriers to entry? There are many. In industries where economies of scale can be exhausted only with very large production facilities, the huge capital costs required by would-be competitors to set up a plant that could compete effectively could be prohibitive. Moreover, there might not be "room" for competition in the sense that, if the market had to be shared by two or more firms, none could make a profit. Whether this is true, of course, will depend on both the cost conditions in the industry and the demand for the industry's output.

In some instances, firms are given exclusive franchises by the government. This effectively excludes all would-be competitors. Traditionally, public utilities are provided such exclusivity, though frequently they are subject to various types of government regulations.

In other cases, firms are granted exclusive rights over the control of a product by having it patented. Although patents are legally enforceable for only 17 years—eliminating all competition during the life of the patent—firms possessing such patent rights are frequently able to maintain their competitive edge for a much longer period. The experience that these firms acquire and the research and development (R&D) efforts they put into their product often keep them in the front of the pack long after the patent has expired.

An extremely effective barrier to entry arises whenever a firm acquires ownership or control over a raw material that is essential in production. For several years, the Aluminum Company of America (Alcoa) retained its monopoly position because of its control over all basic sources of bauxite. The International Nickel Company of Canada, by virtue of its control over approximately 90 percent of the world's proven nickel reserves, has enjoyed literal monopoly power.

There is one other important barrier to entry—the product produced by the industry itself. In order for new entrants to compete effectively, buyers must be enticed away from existing brands of the product. In some instances, buyer attachment to an existing brand may be so strong that would-be competitors stand little chance of earning a profit. In other cases, buyer attachment will be so weak that existing brands do not pose much of a barrier.

Barriers to entry are present, of course, in market structures other than just monopoly. They exist as well in market structures characterized by the presence of several firms. The point that needs to be made, however, is that the existence of significant barriers to entry means that profits may persist in the long run. The fact that would-be competitors are denied entry because of the presence of these barriers to entry means that no automatic mechanism exists that will ensure the elimination of profits in the long run.

THE EFFICIENCY LOSSES OF MONOPOLY

In the view of most economists, an industry that is monopolized will frequently produce less efficiently than one that is perfectly competitive. That is, a monopoly industry will often *produce less output at a greater cost per unit* and charge a *higher price* than firms in a perfectly competitive industry. Thus, fewer resources will be allocated to an industry that is monopolized than to one that is perfectly competitive. It is on the basis of these considerations that economists are led to the conclusion that there are efficiency losses associated with monopoly.

As long as the cost conditions facing the monopolist are the same as the cost conditions that would prevail if the industry were perfectly competitive, it is easy to demonstrate the efficiency losses of monopoly.

Consider the following hypothetical example. Suppose, initially, that minicomputers are produced by 1,000 small firms under conditions of perfect competition. Each individual firm is a price-taker; it faces a perfectly elastic demand for its product at the price determined by the intersection of the market demand and supply curves. The market supply curve, obtained by summing together the MC curves of all the firms in the industry, is nothing other than the MC curve of the *industry.* Each firm maximizes its profits by carrying its production to the point where $MC = MR = P$. In the long run, each firm will produce a rate of output that corresponds to the minimum point on its long-run cost curve; that is, each firm will select that plant size that will afford it the least cost per unit of output, and each will operate that plant at its least-cost point. The intersection of the market demand curve with the curve labeled $S = MC$—point E in Figure 20.5—represents the long-run competitive solution for this industry. In the long run, the competitive industry will produce a rate of output equal to Q_c at a price equal to P_c.

Now suppose that the ZZZ Corporation buys out all of the other firms in the industry so that ZZZ becomes the sole producer. Suppose further that ZZZ produces minicomputers, not with a single large plant, but with the aid of all the original 1,000 plants. Under these circumstances, the MC curve of the ZZZ corporation will be the same, we assume, as the industry MC curve

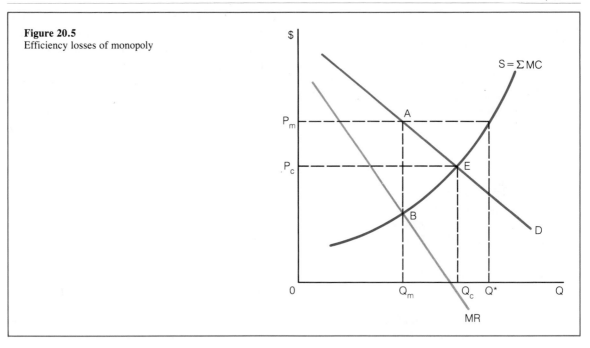

Figure 20.5
Efficiency losses of monopoly

that prevailed when the industry was perfectly competitive. ZZZ's MC curve is obtained by summing together the MC curves of its 1,000 plants. ZZZ's costs are thus assumed to be the same now as the industry's costs were when it was perfectly competitive.

What is different for ZZZ is that it now faces a downward-sloping demand curve for its product—the market demand. ZZZ cannot sell all it wants at any given price. ZZZ can sell more only if it cuts its price. Because ZZZ is the sole producer of minicomputers, it must determine both its rate of output and the market price for minicomputers. On the assumption that ZZZ desires to maximize its profits, it will produce at the point where MC equals MR. At that point, it will produce a rate of output equal to Q_m and sell minicomputers at a price equal to P_m. The fact that ZZZ's MR curve lies below its demand curve means that:

1. The rate of output that will maximize its profits—Q_m—is smaller than the purely competitive rate of output—Q_c.
2. The price that will maximize its profits—

P_m—is higher than the purely competitive price—P_c.

These points are emphasized graphically in Figure 20.5.

It should also be clear that, since ZZZ produces a smaller rate of output than the purely competitive industry, ZZZ will operate each of its 1,000 plants at a smaller rate of output than did each of the previously 1,000 competitive firms. This implies either that each of the plants will be reduced in size in the long run, leading to higher unit costs than those prevailing under pure competition, or that some of those plants will be closed down.

Note one other very important result in Figure 20.5. Whereas in the case of pure competition, the industry supply curve was the same as the industry MC curve, the amount that a profit-maximizing monopolist is willing to sell at different prices cannot be determined by reference to the monopolist's MC curve alone. The amount that the profit-maximizing monopolist is willing to sell at a price of P_m is Q_m, *not* Q^*, as would be implied by the MC curve. In other words, the monopolist's supply curve is *not* its MC curve. *The amount that the monopolist is willing to sell cannot be determined independent of demand.* In the case of monopoly, there is no independent supply curve.

The meaning of efficiency losses

It is true that a monopolist facing cost conditions identical to those of perfectly competitive firms will produce a smaller level of output and charge the buyer a higher price. But in what sense does the existence of monopoly power imply that there is an efficiency loss? That is, what do economists mean when they say that monopoly power results in a less efficient use of resources than pure competition? The answer: *It derives from the fact that, under conditions of monopoly, the price charged to buyers exceeds the monopolist's marginal cost of production.* In Figure 20.5 we observe that the monopoly price—given by the vertical distance AQ_m—exceeds marginal cost—given by the vertical distance BQ_m. Let us examine the implications of this difference closely.

First of all, recall the meaning of demand that was discussed at length in Chapter 16. The demand for minicomputers—or any other product—reflects people's preference for this product compared with other goods they could purchase. It expresses a willingness and an ability to buy, a willingness to give up other goods and services in order to obtain it. Moreover, in view of the equimarginal principle, consumer satisfaction will be maximized when the consumption of each good or service is carried to the point where the marginal utility per dollar spent is the same for all goods and services. Each point on the demand curve is a reflection of this principle. A willingness and an ability to buy the quantity Q_m at a price of P_m in Figure 20.5 tells us something about the value that people attach to this product in comparison with other goods and services. Specifically, their willingness to buy Q_m at a price of P_m means that, up to that point, consumers receive more satisfaction, more value, per dollar spent than they could receive from spending that amount on other goods and services, given their prices. The price of minicomputers, then, can be taken as a measure of the relative worth of minicomputers *at the margin.* The last unit purchased at the given price yields to the consumer more satisfaction than additional units of other goods and services given their prices. In this sense, *the price of any product can be viewed as a measure of its relative marginal value to consumers.*

The cost of producing any product, on the other hand, refers to its opportunity cost. The cost of producing minicomputers refers to the payments that must be made to attract and keep resources away from their alternative uses. And since additional resources are required to produce additional units of a product, it is easy to see what is meant by marginal cost. *Marginal cost is a measure of the relative marginal value of the other goods and services that must be sacrificed to produce additional units of the good in question.*

The significance of the difference between price and marginal cost characteristic of monopoly is now apparent. *If price exceeds marginal cost, people place a greater value on additional units of this product than they do on the alternative goods and services that could be produced with the same resources.* In view of this fact, society as a whole could be made better off if *more* resources were devoted to the production of this product. Whenever price exceeds marginal cost, an *underallocation* of resources to this product exists, from society's viewpoint.

If price is less than marginal cost, an *overallocation* of resources to this product exists. The reason for this is obvious. People place less value on additional units of this product than they do on the alternative goods and services that could be produced with the same resources. From the point of view of society, then, resources should be allocated to any product up to the point where price is equal to marginal cost. At this point—$P = MC$ for all goods and services—resources will be allocated efficiently.

Returning to Figure 20.5, it is clear that efficiency in the allocation of resources will take place only at the quantity Q_c and the price P_c. At that rate of production and price, P equals MC. But that result is obtained automatically under conditions of perfect competition. Each and every individual firm under conditions of pure competition maximizes profits by producing at the point where MC equals P. The price for the product is determined by the intersection of demand and supply. Since supply is nothing other than the sum of the individual firms' marginal costs, we are assured of the result that the price of the product will always equal the marginal cost of producing it. This is one reason economists view perfect competition as an ideal: Perfect competition ensures that resources are allocated efficiently.

In contrast, monopoly power results in a misallocation of resources. Specifically, when a product is produced under conditions of monopoly, fewer resources will be allocated to its production than society desires. In that sense, there is an efficiency loss associated with monopoly.

AN ADDITIONAL ADVANTAGE OF COMPETITION OVER MONOPOLY: PRICE EQUAL TO THE LOWEST COST PER UNIT

Recalling our discussion in Chapter 19, the forces of competition guarantee one additional result in the long run. Under perfect competition, we can be assured that P = min LRAC. This means that:

1. In order to survive, all firms must adopt the best technology available.
2. The cost per unit will be as low as possible.
3. The price charged to the consumer is as low as it can possibly be without firms suffering economic losses.

From the point of view of consumers, these results are highly desirable—a second reason economists frequently prefer the purely competitive market structure. Of course, as our earlier discus-

sion makes apparent, monopoly power will not, in general, yield such desirable results. On the contrary, the monopoly firm will generally not put into place plants comparable to those that would be put into place by perfectly competitive firms. The monopolist will not produce a quantity of output comparable to a perfectly competitive industry's output. And the monopolist will not charge a product price comparable to the price that would prevail under conditions of pure competition. The purely competitive solution would be inconsistent with the monopolist's maximization of profits.

AN OFFSET TO THE EFFICIENCY LOSSES: ECONOMIES OF SCALE

As long as the monopoly firm faces cost conditions similar to those confronting perfectly competitive firms, all of the above results will hold. The monopoly firm will produce a smaller level of output than the perfectly competitive industry and will charge the buyer a higher price than the perfectly competitive price. However, if the cost conditions confronting the monopoly firm are sufficiently dissimilar from those of the perfectly competitive firms, these results need not hold at all. In particular, if significant economies of scale exist in the production of a product, the profit-maximizing monopoly firm could well produce a greater output at a lower price to the consumer than would prevail under perfectly competitive market conditions. This possibility is illustrated in Figure 20.6.

Suppose the good in question is produced by 1,000 firms under conditions of perfect competition. Each firm produces only a fraction of the output of the industry—say, $\frac{1}{1,000}$ of the total. The plant size for each firm is assumed to be relatively small. The long-run competitive result for a single firm is shown in Figure 20.6A. There, P = MC = min AC = \$54; the quantity produced by the firm is 108 units per time period.

Suppose, by contrast, that the good in question is produced by a single firm—a monopolist—in

Figure 20.6
Pure competition and monopoly compared: The case of sizable economics of scale

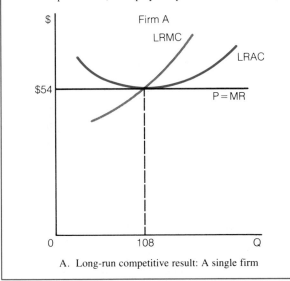

A. Long-run competitive result: A single firm   B. Long-run monopolistic result: A single-monopoly firm

a single large plant. If the single producer is able to obtain significant economies of scale—i.e., if unit costs on the large plant are significantly below those obtainable on a small plant—it is possible that the monopolist's profit-maximizing rate of production will be *larger,* and the product price *lower,* than would exist under conditions of pure competition. Thus, in Figure 20.6B, we illustrate a situation in which the monopoly firm will maximize its profits by producing 125,000 units at a price of $48 each—$6 less than the purely competitive price. And how do we know that the rate of output will be larger than in a purely competitive industry? Simple. The demand curve facing the monopolist is the *market* demand curve for the product. Because the demand curve is downward sloping in accordance with the law of demand, the quantity demanded at a price of $48 (the monopoly price) will be greater than the quantity demanded at a price of $54 (the purely competitive price).

The conclusion that follows from this discussion is rather obvious: *It is not necessarily true that pure competition will result in a lower price for the consumer and a larger rate of production. If significant economies of scale are present, con-* *sumers could obtain a larger output at a lower price under conditions of monopoly.*

It is also important to recognize what we have *not* demonstrated. Just because a monopoly exists does not mean that significant economies of scale are necessarily present, nor that the consumer is necessarily made better off in terms of a lower price for the product. If sizable economies of scale do not exist, the consumer could well be made worse off by the presence of monopoly power, as was suggested earlier. Moreover, even in the case where sizable economies do exist, it is not necessarily true that the product will be produced most efficiently in a single large plant. In some instances, that will be true. In other instances, greater efficiency is attained when the product is produced in a few large plants or several medium-sized plants. This will be discussed at greater length in the next chapter. The point that needs to be emphasized here is that, when economies of scale are present, perfect competition, characterized by the existence of a large number of small producers, may not result in the most efficient use of our scarce resources. Monopoly may be a more efficient kind of market structure, even if price exceeds MC, because it could bring about a lower average cost and price than pure competition.

NATURAL MONOPOLIES

If economies of scale are so pronounced that the total market can be served efficiently only with a single extremely large producer or a few very large producers, such an industry is called a **natural monopoly.** Many public utilities—electric, gas, water, rail, and communication—are often alleged to fall into this category. Frequently, these industries are given exclusive operating franchises by government, in return for which they are subjected to governmental regulation.

If a natural monopoly were allowed to set its price and rate of production at levels that would maximize its profits, the outcome might or might not be superior to that which would prevail under conditions of perfect competition. But even if the profit-maximizing price were lower and the rate of production higher than under competitive conditions, greater efficiency still could be achieved through an appropriate

regulatory policy. The reason? Since at the profit-maximizing point price exceeds marginal cost, an *underallocation* of resources will result if the monopoly firm is unregulated.

From the point of view of efficiency in the allocation of resources, it is appropriate for the regulatory authorities to establish a **marginal cost pricing policy**—that is, to set the price of the product in accordance with its marginal cost of production. In Figure 20.7A, such a policy would imply a regulatory price of P_r and a rate of production of Q_r. This price and quantity can be found at the point of intersection of the market demand curve with the monopolist's MC curve—point A. Unregulated, the profit-maximizing monopolist would choose the price/quantity combination at which MC equals MR—i.e., P_m and Q_m.

Although marginal cost pricing would bring about a more efficient allocation of resources, such a policy might prove to be impractical. In particular, marginal cost pricing might leave the firm with insufficient revenues to cover all of its costs. This situation is illustrated in Figure 20.7B. Given the cost and demand conditions facing the firm, a price of P_e and a rate of production

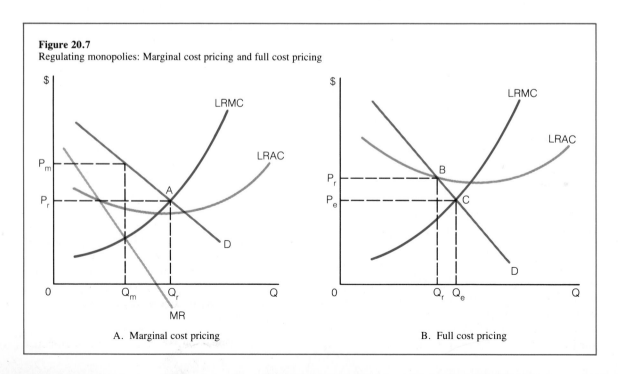

Figure 20.7
Regulating monopolies: Marginal cost pricing and full cost pricing

A. Marginal cost pricing

B. Full cost pricing

of Q_e would force the monopolist to absorb a loss. In the long run, the monopolist would be unwilling to continue to absorb losses. Can you explain why? Under these circumstances, an alternative regulatory policy would be one in which the monopolist charged a price and set a rate of production that enabled it to cover all of its costs. This is given by the point of intersection of the market demand curve and the monopolist's average cost curve—point B—yielding a regulated price of P_r and a corresponding quantity, Q_r. At this point, the monopolist just breaks even—hence the reason for the name **full cost pricing.**

At the break-even point, the firm makes zero economic profits. Its accounting profits are not zero, however. On the contrary, at that point, the firm's owners obtain a rate of return similar to what could be had elsewhere. Frequently, at regulatory hearings, one hears management insisting on a regulated price that will yield to the firm's owners a "fair" rate of return. Although no one knows what constitutes a "fair" return, management spokespeople usually mean a return comparable to the returns received elsewhere in the economy.

A CONCLUDING NOTE ON NATURAL MONOPOLIES

The point of the above exercise is simple. Pure competition does not necessarily result in the most efficient allocation of resources. Efficiency sometimes demands that the production of various goods and services be monopolized. This is especially so in those industries where economies of scale are very pronounced. However, in order to ensure optimum efficiency, it is necessary to regulate the monopoly. And optimum efficiency is attained at the point where MC equals P. In other words, regulators should be guided by the principle that monopolies be forced to operate *as if* they were perfect competitors. Therefore, *assuming that everything else remains unchanged,* a regulated monopoly can be an improvement over purely competitive results. We take up this subject in greater detail in Chapter 27.

SUMMARY

1. The monopolist maximizes profits by following exactly the same rule as the profit-maximizing purely competitive firm—that of equating marginal revenue and marginal cost. However, unlike the purely competitive producer, the monopolist must choose both the price and the quantity produced that will enable the profit maximum to be attained. This difference follows directly from the fact that the demand curve faced by the monopoly firm is not coincident with its marginal revenue curve. Indeed, because the demand curve faced by the monopolist is downward sloping in accordance with the *law of demand,* its MR curve will be below the demand curve for all units sold (except the very first unit).

2. Unlike the perfectly competitive firm, it is frequently the case that, due to significant barriers to entry, the monopoly firm will earn positive economic profits even in the long run.

3. A monopoly industry will often produce less output at a greater cost per unit and at higher prices than firms in a perfectly competitive industry. As a consequence, fewer resources will be devoted to an industry that is monopolized. This gives rise to possible *efficiency* losses associated with monopoly.

4. As long as the cost conditions facing the monopolist are the same as the cost conditions that would prevail if the industry were perfectly competitive, it is easy to demonstrate the efficiency losses of monopoly. The efficiency losses can be summarized as follows:

a. Since profit maximization involves the outcome that price exceeds marginal cost, people place greater value on additional units of this product than they do on the alternative goods and services that could be produced with the same resources; too few resources are being devoted to the production of this good.

b. The monopolist will not produce at the minimum point on its LRAC; the monopolist, therefore, will not produce at the lowest possible cost per unit.

5. If *economies of scale* are significant

enough, it is possible that the profit-maximizing monopoly firm will produce a greater output at a lower price than would prevail under perfectly competitive market conditions.

6. A strong case can be made for regulating a *natural monopoly*. From the point of view of efficiency in the allocation of resources, it is appropriate for the regulatory authorities to establish a *marginal cost pricing* policy or, if such a policy would leave the firm with less than "normal" profits, a *full cost pricing* policy.

CONCEPTS FOR REVIEW

Monopoly

Barriers to entry

Efficiency losses of monopoly

Marginal cost pricing

Natural monopoly

Marginal cost pricing policy

Full cost pricing policy

Absence of a supply curve in monopoly

Profit-maximizing monopolist produces in elastic portion of demand curve

QUESTIONS FOR DISCUSSION

(Those marked with an asterisk (*) are more difficult.)

1. State whether you agree or disagree with each of the following statements. Explain your answer carefully in each instance.

a. Monopoly firms set their prices as high as possible.

b. A profit-maximizing monopolist will always produce in the elastic portion of his/her demand curve.

c. The presence of significant barriers to entry guarantees that monopoly producers will earn economic profits in the long run. (*Hint:* Focus on the word *guarantees.*)

2. Assume that all firms in a perfectly competitive industry are merged into a single monopoly firm. Compare the long-run equilibrium of the perfectly competitive industry with that of the monopolist. Make explicit your assumptions about the cost differences, if any. What general conclusions can you draw?

3. Carefully evaluate. "Even if economies of scale are so large that a profit-maximizing monopoly firm produces a larger output at lower prices than would prevail under pure competition, the monopoly firm should be regulated because it is not producing efficiently."

*4. "Suppose that all firms in a perfectly competitive industry are merged into a single monopoly firm. Assume further that the price elasticity of demand for the output produced by the perfectly competitive industry prior to the merger was equal to 0.5. No matter how sizable the economies of scale, the merger will result in less output and higher prices as long as the monopolist maximizes profits." Do you agree or disagree. Explain carefully. (Hint: If MC is positive, in what portion of the demand curve does profit maximization require the monopolist to operate?)

Pure competition and pure monopoly are extreme forms of market structure. Some goods are produced under conditions that closely approximate our description of pure competition, the most notable example being agricultural commodities. And a few industries—particularly, public utilities—closely approximate our model of regulated monopoly. But the bulk of the products produced by U.S. business enterprises cannot be described accurately by either pure competition or monopoly alone. Rather, there are elements of both monopoly power and competition in the production of almost all goods and services. A number of industries in the United States are characterized by a little competition and a great deal of monopoly power; others are somewhat less monopolistic in character; and others still are characterized by only a modicum of monopoly power. Unfortunately, these different blendings of monopoly power and competition complicate considerably our study of market structures.

The focal points of our attention in this chapter will be on two kinds of loosely defined market structures—**monopolistic competition** and **oligopoly.** Neither of these market structures can be defined precisely; for our purposes, it would be inappropriate to draw very sharp distinctions between the two. The reason for this is simple. In our study of monopolistic competition and oligopoly we will attempt to gain insight into the behavior of a wide variety of firms and industries that are very different from one another. No single definition of either form of market structure can do justice to the manifold differences that exist. And the line dividing firms that are monopolistically competitive from those that are oligopolistic is somewhat arbitrary. But despite all of the problems we encounter in categorizing firms and industries, it is possible to define monopolistic competition and oligopoly in such a way that most firms and industries will fit into one or the other.

Chapter 21

Monopolistic competition and oligopoly

MONOPOLISTIC COMPETITION AND OLIGOPOLY DESCRIBED

Characteristics of monopolistic competition

Monopolistic competition and pure competition share much in common. Monopolistic competition is generally characterized by a sizable number of relatively small producers. The share of the total output accounted for by any single producer is generally fairly small. Moreover, although barriers to entry are present in monopolistic competition, for the most part they are not so effective as to preclude entry into the industry.

There are two essential differences between pure competition and monopolistic competition. First, each of the firms in a purely competitive industry produces a product that is indistinguishable from that of its competitors. In monopolistic competition, each firm generally produces a different product—a product that is in one way or another differentiated from that of its competitors. Second, whereas in pure competition it is assumed that buyers and sellers have complete information, it is assumed in monopolistic competition that people possess incomplete information.

Product differentiation and **incomplete information** are the main factors responsible for the monopoly power possessed by firms in monopolistically competitive markets. We mean by monopoly power, simply, that each producer faces a downward-sloping demand curve for his or her product. Consumers often form some degree of attachment to particular product brands. And frequently, they lack complete information with respect to other competitive brands. If the price of brand X is raised, the quantity demanded will decline. But, unless the price rise is very substantial, the quantity demanded will not fall to zero as would happen under perfectly competitive market conditions. Moreover, unlike perfectly competitive producers, monopolistically competitive firms cannot sell all they want to at any given price; in order to expand their sales, monopolistically competitive firms must cut their prices.

Because monopolistic competitors face down-ward-sloping demand curves for their products, the analysis of their profit-maximizing behavior will be similar to our study of monopoly behavior in Chapter 20, with one very important difference: Unlike the monopolist, the monopolistic competitor is not the sole producer of his or her product. The monopolistically competitive firm may be the sole producer of a particular brand, but that brand will generally be one of a large number of closely competing brands. The availability of close substitutes implies that the demand curve for any particular brand is likely to be highly price elastic, though, unlike pure competition, not perfectly price elastic.

Advertising plays a very important role in monopolistic competition. Not only does it inform the consumer about different product brands; producers also use it as a tool to maintain and extend the market for their individual brands.

Characteristics of oligopoly

Some of the features of monopolistic competition are also found in oligopoly. Product differentiation and the absence of complete information are frequently important sources of monopoly power in oligopoly. But the critical feature that distinguishes oligopoly from other forms of market structure is the fact that a very significant proportion of the industry's output is produced by a few large producers. Since producers are so few in number, a kind of interdependency exists in oligopolistic markets that is quite unlike that found in other forms of market structure.

Consider first the environment within which monopolistic competitors operate. The number of producers is relatively large and each producer accounts for only a small share of the total market. If any single producer captures a larger share of the total market, the impact of that increase on any other single producer will generally be quite small. The increase in the market share of one producer will be spread across such a large number of other producers that the reduction in the market share of each will be miniscule. Under these circumstances, each individual producer can safely assume that its actions will generally be ignored by the other producers. If firm A cuts its price, there is no reason to believe that this will elicit any change in behavior on the part of firm A's competitors. Likewise, firm A will generally ignore the individual actions undertaken by other firms.

The same is not true of firms in oligopolistic markets. The increase in the market share of any single large producer will have a noticeable impact on the market shares of the other firms in the industry. The individual oligopolist cannot legitimately assume that its actions will be ignored by its competitors. If firm A is contemplating a price change, it must give consideration to the impact of its decision on the behavior of its competitors. Will they maintain their prices in the face of a price cut by firm A? If so, then firm A will probably capture a somewhat larger share of the market. If the other producers react by cutting their prices, A's market share will probably not increase noticeably, if at all.

Recognized mutual interdependence is the key feature of oligopolistic markets. Two important consequences follow from its presence. In the first place, it complicates dramatically the analysis of oligopolistic markets. Since such a wide variety of reactions and counter reactions exists to any single decision, it is extremely difficult to draw conclusions that have general applicability. Second, because each firm can be adversely affected by the individual actions of other producers, they all have a strong incentive to collude in an effort to maximize their individual and collective welfare. **Collusion** may take many different forms, ranging all the way from tightly organized **cartels** to very loosely structured **gentleman's agreements**.

A word of caution

Although it is common to analyze monopolistic competition and oligopoly separately, it is not always appropriate to draw very sharp distinctions between the two types of market structures. From the point of view of the number of producers and the ease of entry, it might be appropriate

to classify some industries as monopolistically competitive. Gasoline stations and dry cleaners might be so classified. However, each gasoline station and each dry cleaning firm in a small geographical area is very much aware of the prices charged and the services performed by competitors; recognized mutual interdependence is very much in evidence. From that point of view, it would be reasonable to classify such industries as oligopolistic.

The point that requires emphasis is this. Although we will follow the time-honored tradition of analyzing each of these market structures separately, our focus will be on the behavioral effects of the *various characteristics* embodied in these market structures, rather than on the idea that most U.S. industries can be easily classified into one or the other type; they cannot be so easily classified.

PRICE AND OUTPUT DETERMINATION UNDER MONOPOLISTIC COMPETITION

Although it is difficult to identify industries that fit precisely our description of monopolistic competition, there are a number that do approximate this market structure rather closely. These include, for example, retail stores in metropolitan areas—grocery stores, department stores, gasoline stations, beauty shops, barber shops, dry cleaners, etc.; clothing manufacturers; book publishers; costume jewelry manufacturers; plywood producers; brick and concrete block producers; and wood and metal furniture producers. It is apparent from this list that monopolistic competition covers a wide variety of products.

In an effort to highlight the distinguishing features of monopolistic competition, we will carry forward our example of the minicomputer industry. It is assumed that a relatively large number of producers of minicomputers exists. Each producer manufactures a minicomputer that is differentiated from all the rest; ZZZ's model is known as "The Wizard."

The market demand for minicomputers is shown in Figure 21.1 by the curve labeled D; the demand for ZZZ's model is shown by the

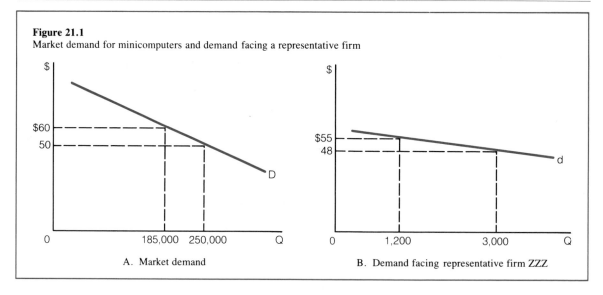

Figure 21.1
Market demand for minicomputers and demand facing a representative firm

A. Market demand

B. Demand facing representative firm ZZZ

curve labeled d. Note first the differences in the quantity scales between the market and the ZZZ Corporation. Whereas the market demand is calibrated in hundreds of thousands, the demand for ZZZ's "Wizard" is measured in thousands; ZZZ is assumed to be representative of the firms in the minicomputer business, and it produces a relatively small share of the industry's total output. The second feature worth noting is the fact that the demand for ZZZ's product is much more price elastic than the demand for minicomputers generally. The availability of many close substitutes for ZZZ's output and fewer close substitutes for minicomputers generally are the main factors responsible for this difference. What this means is that a slight change in price by ZZZ gives rise to a sizable change in the quantity demanded. If ZZZ lowers its price for "The Wizard" slightly, it will experience a sharp increase in its sales as large numbers of buyers switch away from other minicomputers in favor of "The Wizard." Symmetrically, a slight increase in the price of "The Wizard" will induce many of ZZZ's customers to switch to the competition.

Profit maximization in the short run

Technically, the analysis of profit maximization under conditions of monopolistic competition is exactly analogous to our analysis of profit

maximization under conditions of monopoly. Each firm faces a downward-sloping demand curve for its product. For the usual reasons, each firm's marginal revenue (MR) curve lies below its demand curve (except for the first unit sold). Profits are maximized, or losses minimized, at the point where MR equals MC. The firm will cease production altogether in the short run, thereby minimizing its losses, if it is unable to cover all of its variable costs of production with any positive rate of output. The three standard short-run cases are illustrated in Figure 21.2.

Long-run equilibrium under monopolistic competition

The equilibrium attained in the long run under monopolistic competition will correspond more closely to pure competition than it will to monopoly. The reason for this is obvious. Because of the absence of any significant barriers to entry, the presence of positive economic profits will act as a lure attracting resources into the industry. Remember that the existence of positive profits in this industry implies that resources here are earning more on average than comparable resources are earning elsewhere, which is the reason additional resources will enter.

As new resources enter a monopolistically competitive industry as a result of positive profits,

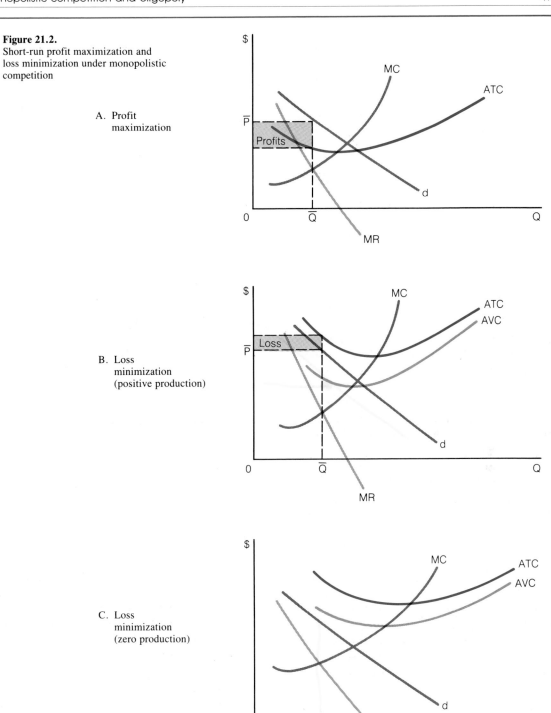

Figure 21.2.
Short-run profit maximization and
loss minimization under monopolistic
competition

A. Profit
    maximization

B. Loss
    minimization
    (positive production)

C. Loss
    minimization
    (zero production)

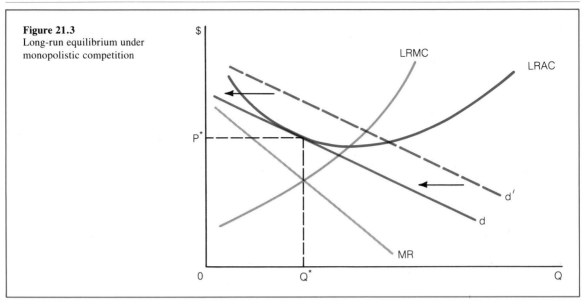

Figure 21.3
Long-run equilibrium under monopolistic competition

our representative firm will face a shrinking demand for its product—i.e., its demand curve will shift to the left. The reason? Each firm's share of the total market will be reduced somewhat with the entry of new firms. This is illustrated in Figure 21.3. The original demand curve facing our representative firm prior to the entry of new firms is drawn as a dashed curve, d′; the demand curve that prevails *after entry* is drawn as a solid line, d; at any given price, less will be sold after entry. Note the complete absence of any profits in the long-run equilibrium. It is important, of course, to add the appropriate qualifications to this discussion. It is not true that zero profits *must* obtain in the long run under monopolistic competition. The dynamics of any given industry may rule out such a result. The introduction of new products, as well as improvements of existing ones, continuously opens up new profitable opportunities. Nevertheless, the existence of positive profits means that there will always be the pressure from new entry to cause those profits to be reduced to negligible levels.

"The wastes of competition"

By comparison with pure competition, monopolistic competition is less efficient. Figure 21.4

illustrates the three respects in which monopolistic competition is less efficient.

1.   In long-run equilibrium, the profit-maximizing monopolistic competitor sets price in excess of marginal cost. This implies, of course, that fewer resources will be allocated to the production of this good than is optimal.
2.   Because the monopolistic competitor does not operate at the minimum point of its long-run average cost curve, the most efficient plant size will not be selected.
3.   For the plant size that is selected, the monopolistic competitor will not operate it at its minimum point.

For identical cost conditions, the purely competitive firm would set its rate of output at Q_c— the minimum point on its long-run average cost curve—and the product would sell at the market-determined price, P_c. The monopolistic competitor, on the other hand, will produce a rate of output equal to Q_0 and set a price of P_0 for its product. At that rate of output, price exceeds MC by the amount EB. *We refer to the difference between the competitive price and the price charged by the monopolistic competitor, and the difference between the competitive and the monopolistically competitive rates of production, as "the*

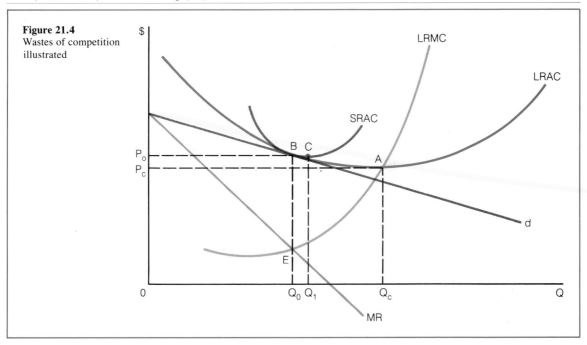

Figure 21.4
Wastes of competition
illustrated

wastes of competition," or, as this is sometimes called, the **wastes of monopolistic competition.**

In many monopolistically competitive industries, these wastes of competition are probably relatively small. This will be especially true in industries in which the product differences are small. Under those circumstances, the products produced will be very close substitutes for one another, implying that each firm will face a demand curve for its product that is very nearly horizontal; that demand curve will be tangent to the long-run average cost curve at a point very near the latter's minimum point. (Recalling our discussion in Chapter 20, this point can be put more formally. **MR**, price and the price elasticity of demand are related as follows: **MR** = P × (1 − 1/E_d). Since profit-maximization requires the equality of **MR** and **MC**, then the "markup" of price over marginal cost will depend on E_d, the price elasticity of demand. That is, with profit maximization, **MC** = P × (1 − 1/E_d). Thus, the greater the price elasticity of demand, the closer will be MC to P. Since all profits will be eliminated in the long run, the higher the price elasticity of demand, the closer

will be the tangency of the demand curve to the minimum point on the long-run average cost curve.)

From the point of view of the welfare of society, there is one important offset to these wastes of competition that is difficult to quantify. The offset is this: Under monopolistic competition, consumers are provided with greater product variety than they get under pure competition. People are not offered a single homogeneous product called "shirt." Rather they have the opportunity to purchase many different kinds of shirts that vary by fabric, style, color, and design. To the extent that people feel better off with these choices as opposed to having none, there will be an offset to the above-described wastes.

Product differentiation

Product differentiation is one key feature that distinguishes monopolistic competition from pure competition. Generally, it is this characteristic that provides each of the firms in the industry with some degree of monopoly power.

Products can be differentiated in several ways. The *location* of the retail or wholesale outlet for the product is one important source of product differentiation. If product X is available at a location one mile from your home, that alone is sufficient to differentiate it from the *same* product sold at some other more distant location. Indeed, since you have to spend more time and money (for motor gasoline and oil) to get to the more distant location, product X sold at these two different locations is not really the same product.

Moreover, the circumstances surrounding the sale of some product will frequently differentiate it from the sale of that *same* product under different circumstances. For example, the purchase of a beer at a sedate bar is certainly different from the purchase of the same brand of beer at a swinging singles bar; each bar can hardly be said to sell the same product.

Sometimes the differences between products are substantive; sometimes they are not. Multifunction pocket calculators are substantially different from simple-function brands; apparently, the many different brands of aspirin are not. However, what matters from the point of view of monopolistic competition is whether the various brands are differentiated from one another *in the minds of consumers.* To the extent that people are convinced that Bayer aspirin is superior to other marketed brands, the theory is useful only if it recognizes these differences. Indeed, the differences perceived by consumers are important to the explanation of why such wide discrepancies can exist in the prices of the various product brands.

Nonprice competition

Under monopolistic competition, firms compete not only on the basis of the prices they charge for their products, but also on the basis of the product differences themselves. *Given demand conditions,* each monopolistically competitive firm will attempt to maximize its profits by choosing a price and a rate of output for which marginal cost equals marginal revenue. However, each firm will usually attempt to change the demand conditions it faces in an effort to expand its market and its profits as well. The efforts that

the firm undertakes to change its demand conditions we call **nonprice competition.**

Nonprice competition can take several different forms. For example, many firms attempt to distinguish their brands by simply packaging them differently. They hope that attractive packaging will convince the consumer of the superiority of their particular product brand. To the extent that they are successful, such product brands will frequently command a somewhat higher price than other brands.

Sometimes firms will compete by producing a product that possesses one or more characteristic features not possessed by other brands. Again, this is a form of nonprice competition that, because it changes both cost and demand conditions, enables the producer to charge a different price. Of course, each producer hopes that these differences in cost and demand will yield larger profits. In any event, **product development** and **product betterment** are very important characteristics of monopolistic competition.

Advertising

Advertising is one of the most important, and most controversial, forms on nonprice competition. Through it, producers seek to obtain competitive advantages over their rivals, advantages they hope will be registered in the form of enlarged profits.

Most advertising campaigns are designed by firms with one or more of the following three purposes in mind:

1. To expand—i.e., to shift out—the demand for their products.
2. To maintain the demand for their products in the face of promotional efforts on the part of rival firms.
3. To reduce the price elasticity of the demand curve that they face.

The first two purposes require little explanation. To the extent that a firm is able, through advertising, to convince increasing numbers of people of the superiority of its products over those of its rivals, it will experience an increased demand for its products. Moreover, as a result of the advertising campaigns of its rivals, it is frequently necessary to undertake at least some amount of advertising in order to neutralize the impact of those campaigns on the demand for its product. If the firm did not advertise enough, its customers might be attracted away by the onslaught of ads from the competition.

The third purpose requires a bit more explanation. The high price elasticity of demand that each firm faces in monopolistic competition is largely because buyers view each of the products produced as very close substitutes; the greater the avialability of close substitutes, the higher the price elasticity of demand. If any single firm is able to convince buyers through its promotional efforts that its product is superior to all the rest and that competitive products are at best poor substitutes, it will have succeeded in reducing the price elasticity of the demand that it faces. As a consequence, it obtains a greater degree of monopoly power.

(This latter point can be illustrated formally. As shown earlier, in equilibrium,

$$MC = P \times \left(1 - \frac{1}{E_d}\right).$$

This formula tells us how much price is "marked up" over marginal cost as E_d varies. If E_d is infinite, as in pure competition, $P = MC$; there is no markup. The lower the price elasticity of demand, the greater the markup will be and the greater the degree of monopoly power will be.)

The advertising controversy

Advertising is extremely expensive. One minute on television during prime time viewing can cost $100,000 or more; a one-time full-page ad in *The New York Times* costs about $80,000. Moreover, from the point of view of the economy as a whole, it has been estimated that advertising and promotional expenditures totaled in the neighborhood of $40 billion in 1980. That amounts to $40 billion worth of other goods and services given up because those resources were used in advertising. The question is, Is it worth it?

There is no easy answer to this question, although there is no shortage of people who *think* they know the answer. To the ad people and most television producers, the answer is an unequivocal yes! To many social critics, the answer is an unqualified no!

The controversy over advertising is in large measure a *normative* issue—one that involves value judgments—for which there is no objective right answer. It is useful, nevertheless, to address some of the many pro and con arguments.

The case in favor of advertising is made on the basis of the following conditions.

1. Buyers do not have complete information about existing, let alone new and improved, goods and services available in the marketplace. In the absence of advertising, they would have to waste a very important scarce resource—time—in order to acquire the information they need to make rational choices. By comparison, advertising is a cheap way of providing consumers with the information they need. If this is true, society as a whole receives a net benefit from the promotional efforts of businesspeople.

2. Radio, television, magazines, and newspapers—in short, the media—are supported wholly or in large part by advertising. Whether or not, and to what extent, you view this as a positive attribute will depend on the benefits and costs you associate with the current media forms. In the absence of advertising, the full cost would be borne by the buyers of the product, which could well lead to more efficient use of our scarce resources insofar as media content would be more in accord with the preferences of consumers.

3. Advertising is alleged to play a very important role in determining our aggregate economic performance. By encouraging people to spend, spend, and spend some more, advertising promotes higher levels of production and employment than would otherwise prevail.

4. Advertising actually promotes greater competition, so it is argued, not less. Advertising provides people with greater information regarding available product substitutes and thereby

strips away much of the monopoly power each producer would possess in its absence.

5. Finally, one of the most important arguments that has been put forth in favor of advertising is that it frequently leads to *lower* production costs and hence *lower prices* for the consumer. An advertising program that expands the demand for some product often enables the producer to attain sizable economies of scale—sizable enough to generate lower average costs *inclusive* of advertising outlays. This is illustrated in Figure 21.5. In the absence of advertising, the profit-maximizing point for the monopolistic competitor would, we assume, be given by point A. As is apparent from the firm's LRAC cost curve (exclusive of advertising), the firm could, if the demand for its product were larger, achieve significant economies of scale. Suppose the firm undertakes an extensive advertising program. This will raise its average costs at the initial output level Q_0. However, if the firm succeeds in raising the demand for its product, it could ultimately end up with *lower* average costs, even including the advertising outlays. This is illustrated by the movement from A to B in Figure 21.5.

In the case against advertising, most of these points are disputed.

1. Consider first the economies of scale argument. *If* the advertising program did increase the producer's demand sharply, it is possible that the consumer would benefit through lower prices. However, a large proportion of the advertising outlays that are made by firms *do not* have the effect of raising the demands for their products. On the contrary, the effect of one firm's advertising program on the demand for its product is largely offset by the advertising campaigns of rival firms. Under those circumstances, demand does not increase and the potential economies of scale are not realized. On the other hand, both costs and prices rise. This is shown in Figure 21.5 as a shift from A to C, as opposed to the shift from A to B described earlier.

It is probably true that the failure on the part of any one firm to advertise would cause it to lose its share of the market—i.e., cause it to experience a reduction in the demand for its product. *From each firm's point of view,* advertising is a prerequisite for profits. But from the point of view of society as a whole, self-cancelling advertising is a social waste. Is variety in the consumption of toothpaste, beer, cigarettes, toilet tissue and countless other products worth such a huge expenditure of scarce resources? To many people, the answer is obvious.

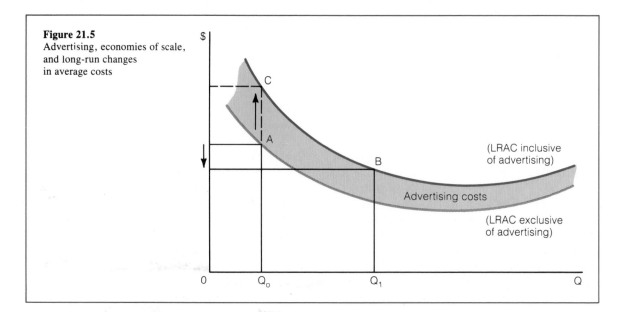

Figure 21.5
Advertising, economies of scale, and long-run changes in average costs

Additionally, if the advertising programs of a number of firms were extremely successful in the sense of sharply increasing the demands for their products, would the consumer benefit through lower prices even if sizable economies of scale were realized? Does not a huge expansion on the part of some existing firms imply at least a partial elimination of competing firms? And would not the increase in monopoly power accorded the successful advertisers lead to a smaller price decrease than otherwise, and perhaps even a price increase?

2. What about the argument that advertising is a cheap source of information about existing, new, and improved products? In the minds of a number of critics, the argument is not a persuasive one. In the first place, advertising is designed more to persuade the consumer than it is to simply provide him or her with information. The claims made about many products are highly exaggerated and frequently misleading. And the amount of information we obtain from the millions of dollars spent on toothpaste, shaving cream, and toilet tissue commercials is, by any standard of comparison, miniscule.

3. Advertising promotes the growth of monopoly power in two important respects. First, by creating brand loyalties, advertising reduces the price elasticity of demand and thereby makes consumers less responsive to price-cutting by rival firms. Second, the advertising outlays required to introduce a new product to the market are generally so large as to create for many would-be competitors a financial barrier to entry.

4. There is little evidence to suggest that advertising is an important determinant of the levels of output and employment in our economic system. Most economists believe that low levels of aggregate demand can be remedied through appropriate expansionary monetary and fiscal policies. Moreover, it is possible that advertising is itself a source of economic instability. During periods of prosperity, advertising outlays are increased, intensifying the demand pressures within the economy; during periods of recession, advertising expenditures are reduced, intensifying unemployment. Furthermore, to the extent that higher levels of consumer spending are created

in the wake of business promotional efforts, a smaller level of savings will result. This, during periods of prosperity, leaves fewer resources available for capital formation and growth.

5. It is true that advertising supports much of the media in this country. However, in the minds of a number of critics, a significant amount of control over the media is exerted by advertisers. Will a television station provide its viewers with an honest portrayal of a labor dispute if the corporation involved is one of its sponsors? Will reporters of a newspaper pursue leads with vigor that could embarrass a major advertising client?

In sum, it is extremely difficult to evaluate the pro and con cases of advertising. Nevertheless, an increasing number of economists are beginning to realize that the microeconomic effects of advertising are not as bad as originally believed. This is because the empirical evidence seems to support the view that advertising is an important and relatively cheap means of transmitting to the consumer information about products on the market. Time is a scarce resource. In the absence of advertising, huge chunks of time—i.e., huge costs—would have to be spent by consumers to acquire the information they need in order to make rational choices. This is not to imply that advertising necessarily generates marginal net benefits for society, nor that the adverse effects are inconsequential. It simply suggests that the negative effects are partially offset, at least, by the positive informational impacts.

Product innovation, technological advance, and monopolistic competition

Compared with firms under pure competition and monopoly, monopolistic competitors have a much stronger incentive to devote resources to the development of new and improved products. Unlike firms in pure competition, monopolistically competitive firms have the potential of earning, for at least some time, profits in excess of "normal" as a result of their innovative efforts. Unlike monopolists, they have a stronger incentive to undertake research and development activities because of the intense competitive pressures they face and because they desire to expand their market shares. However, by contrast with firms classified as oligopolists, monopolistically competitive firms are likely to undertake less research and development. Barriers to entry are weaker under monopolistic competition and overall profit margins are lower.

THE THEORY OF OLIGOPOLY

There is no single market structure that is more difficult to analyze than oligopoly. Put bluntly, it is very difficult to predict what will be the consequences of the profit-maximizing behavior of oligopolists. Indeed, the whole concept of profit maximization on the part of individual producers becomes ambiguous under oligopoly. This state of affairs is unfortunate since so many very important sectors of our economy are oligopolistic. Industries producing goods such as automobiles, steel, oil, natural gas, aluminum, synthetic fibers, communications equipment, metal cans, tires, electric bulbs, computers, photocopiers, telephone and telegraph equipment, soaps and detergents, sewing machines, and gypsum products are all produced under conditions of oligopoly. In each of these industries, 70 percent or more of the total output is produced by three or four firms. In short, each of these industries is highly *concentrated.*

Economies of scale as the cause of fewness

Frequently, the *fewness* of firms in these industries can be explained by the presence of sizable economies of scale. The existence of a large number of small firms in the industry would preclude these potential cost savings; efficient production is often possible only with a relatively small number of large producers. To the extent that this is true, the economic rationale for oligopoly is analogous to that for natural monopoly, which we studied in the previous chapter.

But while it is possible to explain the existence of some oligopolistic industries on the basis on economies of scale, it is not necessarily true that buyers will benefit simply because large-scale operations permit lower unit costs. The fewness of the firms implies the existence of a considerable degree of monopoly power—a power that can be used in ways that are undesirable from a societal point of view. Moreover, since would-be competitors are frequently unable to compete effectively unless they begin with large-scale operations involving investments of millions (and perhaps even billions) of dollars, economies of scale can act as a formidable barrier to entry. Under these circumstances, it is apparent that just as a case could be made for regulating a natural monopoly, so a case can be made for regulating an oligopoly. However, in view of the general distaste that exists throughout much of the United States to government control of private business activity, and of the widespread belief that government intervention is itself an important source of inefficiency, few oligopolistic industries are regulated as closely as are, say, public utilities. In any event, because each of the large producers in an oligopolistic industry possesses considerable monopoly power, it is very important from a welfare point of view that giant firm sizes can be justified on the basis of economies of scale. In other words, if an industry is dominated by a few large firms and if significant economies of scale are *not* present, those few firms could exercise their monopoly power in a way that would be clearly detrimental to public welfare. Under those circumstances, a rather strong case could be made for splitting up that industry into a much larger number of small firms. The increased competition that would ensue from a split-up would bring about lower product prices and a larger volume of output.

For this reason, in virtually every antitrust action involving a firm that the government feels is too large, the firm's owners invariably trot out the economies of scale argument as the justification for their huge size. Any one or all of the following sources of these economies are frequently cited:

1. Large-scale mass production techniques.

2. Efficiency in the use of existing management and sales personnel. ("Our people would be underemployed or underutilized in a smaller operation, with the result that our unit costs would be higher.")

3. Advertising efficiency. ("A small firm could never undertake the massive expenditures required for the national promotion of our product. And a national market is required in order to get our production level up high enough to justify the introduction of cost-saving mass-production techniques.")

(Arguments such as these are also used to justify **horizontal mergers** among firms—two or more previously rival firms merging or combining into one. And similar arguments are often cited as being of some importance in cases of **conglomerate mergers**—mergers involving firms in *different* industries. In Chapter 27 we will examine at length the difficulties encountered by antitrust officials as they attempt to dispute the claims made by business executives that their size is justified on the basis of their realized economies of scale.)

The point that needs to be made here is this. Each firm has an obvious interest in increasing its monopoly power. Monopoly power is frequently the source of greater profits. If sizable economies of scale are present, the monopoly power conferred on a few large producers may not be detrimental to public welfare and may even be beneficial. Of course, as with a natural monopoly, a theoretical case can be made for the proposition that welfare could be boosted further still through the enforcement of a policy of marginal cost pricing (or at least full cost pricing). Similarly, in the absence of economies of scale, the monopoly power conferred on large producers can be seriously detrimental to the public interest. Because monopoly power is profitable, firms go to great lengths to "prove" that their size is justified by the presence of economies. But the skepticism that is frequently expressed by public officials is similarly justified because of the incentives that exist for increasing each firm's monopoly power. Fewness may be justified on the basis of economies of scale. But fewness does not prove that those economies exist.

The consequences of fewness: Recognized mutual interdependence

If monopoly power were the only distinguishing characteristic of oligopoly, this type of market structure would be no more difficult to analyze than monopoly itself. However, monopoly power is *not* the critical distinguishing feature. What makes oligopoly unique is the existence of **recognized mutual interdependence.** This is best explained by means of an illustration.

Suppose minicomputers are produced by many small producers. Suppose further that ZZZ cuts slightly the price of its model—"The Wizard." Other producers will, as a consequence, lose some customers to ZZZ. In this sense, all firms are mutually interdependent. However, since ZZZ's gain in sales is spread across such a large number of other producers, the loss experienced by *any single producer* will probably be small. Under these circumstances, it would be reasonable for ZZZ to assume that competitors will ignore its price cut. Put differently, because ZZZ's influence on each of the rival firms is miniscule, ZZZ has no reason to believe that its behavior will elicit any sort of reaction on the part of the competition. Since the profits of each of the other firms is so weakly dependent on the actions taken by ZZZ, they are each likely to ignore ZZZ's price cut. *Each firm behaves as if its profits were independent of the actions of other firms; in this sense there is no recognized mutual interdependence.*

Consider now the production of minicomputers by an oligopolistic industry. Suppose there are only three firms in the industry—ZZZ, AAA, and BBB. Under these circumstances, would it be reasonable for ZZZ to assume that its behavior will be ignored by AAA and BBB? Probably not. If ZZZ cuts the price for its product, AAA and BBB *will notice* the loss of their customers to ZZZ. Therefore, in making its decision to lower price, ZZZ must take into account the reaction of AAA and BBB to its decision. Will the other two firms follow ZZZ's lead and cut their prices by a similar amount? If they do, people will have little incentive to switch to "The Wizard," with the result that the gain for ZZZ will not be as large as otherwise.

What if AAA and BBB react by cutting their prices by even more than ZZZ? As is obvious, ZZZ will probably lose customers to AAA and BBB, with a consequent reduction in its profits. Moreover, if ZZZ reacts by cutting its price further still, the stage is set for a **price war** that could prove costly to everyone.

Other reactions are also possible. AAA and BBB could step up their promotional efforts in reaction to ZZZ's price cut. The net result would be that ZZZ might gain little or nothing from its price-cutting initiative.

In any event, the point of this discussion is simply that, under oligopoly, there is a mutual interdependence that is explicitly recognized by all of the major firms in the industry. It would be folly for each firm to behave as if its actions would be ignored by the competition. *Each firm recognizes that its profits are heavily dependent on the actions of the other firms in the industry.* This state of affairs complicates considerably our study of the profit-maximizing behavior of the oligopolist. It is still true that profits will be maximized (or losses minimized) when producers equate marginal cost and marginal revenue. The difficulty is that the oligopolist really has no idea what its marginal revenue will be until it figures out what actions rival firms will take. This kind of uncertainty is nerve-wracking for the oligopolist. *Since the profits of each are so heavily dependent on the actions of a few other firms, they are all keenly interested in each other's behavior and are each hopeful that the actions of the other firms will be supportive of their quest for greater profits.*

The mood to collude

It is apparent from the foregoing that oligopolists have a strong incentive to **collude**. After all,

since each firm has the power to hurt the others, they all have a reason for getting together to establish workable "rules of conduct" that are beneficial to everyone.

Collusion can take many different forms. The oligopoly firms may band together to form a **cartel**—a highly formal arrangement that frequently involves written (or at least verbal) agreements among the participants respecting such things as the product's price, the size of the industry's output, and each member's share of the market. Frequently, cartel agreements contain provisions (or at least understandings) dealing with the punishments that will be meted out to those cartel members who would dare to violate cartel rules. The most famous and, in the minds of many, the most notorious cartel is the Organization of Petroleum Exporting Countries (OPEC), consisting of the vast majority of non-North American world oil producers. Within bounds, OPEC sets the prices for member country oil exports. Also, it sets production quotas for each member country, and therefore overall OPEC production levels. This we take up in greater detail in Chapter 25.

Gentlemen's agreements constitute a less formal means of collusion. Rarely are gentlemen's agreements put into writing; the terms are agreed upon verbally and sealed with a hand shake. Although such agreements are usually arrived at in secret, they are sometimes "negotiated" in the open. For example, at news conferences, in interviews, or in newsletters, corporate executives will frequently make known their views about what is "in the industry's interest." A careful reading of these statements by a number of these oligopolists over a period of time will often reveal an emerging consensus.

Price leadership is an even less formal means of collusion. In this case, a single firm emerges as a price leader. That firm pretty much determines the price of the product for the entire industry. Virtually all firms will price their product in line with the price leader. If the price leader raises the price by 10 percent, almost everyone else will follow suit. At a minimum, price leadership would appear to be present in such industries as copper, steel, cement, newsprint, farm machinery, automobiles, and gasoline.

Frequently, the price leadership form of collusion involves neither written nor verbal agreement. Indeed, this form of collusion may not involve any formal communication at all between the participants. Most firms simply know who the leader is and find it in their self-interest to follow that firm's lead. The leader may or may not be the largest firm in the industry, though that is the usual case. The leader may or may not be the firm that initiates a price change, although if the leader disagrees with the original price action, it can generally force the initiating firm, and the other firms as well, to adopt a price more in line with its own thinking by simply taking some alternative price action.

Collusion and monopoly

It is not difficult to discover why firms in an oligopolistic market structure desire to collude. Each firm's profits are visibly dependent not only on its own individual actions but on the actions of a *few others* as well. I might be able to do very well on my own, but that could change dramatically on the basis of actions undertaken by one or two other firms. And those other firms are in the same boat as I am. Its risky going it alone. Its almost impossible for me to predict how my profits will be affected by my own actions since I have no precise idea how my competitors will react. Therefore, wouldn't it be better if we could all get together to work out rules of behavior to ensure our individual and collective welfare?

If the firms do collude, the oligopolistic market structure gets converted to something more closely approximating monopoly. One could easily imagine a cartel-like arrangement that, in its effects, is indistinguishable from monopoly. All firms in the industry join together for the avowed purpose of maximizing *industry* profits. By acting in concert, they become like one firm. Given the cost conditions prevailing in the industry and the market demand for the product, industry profits are maximized at the point where the *industry's* marginal cost is equal to its marginal revenue. For obvious reasons, such collective action is referred to as **joint profit maximization.** To the extent that oligopoly firms do maximize their joint profits, the price and output decisions will be the same as those of the monopoly firm discussed in the previous chapter. Moreover, our discussion of the implications of monopoly power in Chapter 20 apply here as well.

The incentives to cheat

Although each oligopoly firm has an incentive to collude, they likewise all have an incentive to cheat on any collusive agreement if that would serve to enhance their individual profit prospects. This is one of the anomalies of oligopolistic firm behavior. However, it is not difficult to discover why the incentives to collude and cheat can exist simultaneously. At a minimum, by colluding, an oligopoly firm is able to reduce somewhat the risk and uncertainty that it faces in the marketplace. As long as everyone follows the rules of the game—be they rigid and detailed, as in some cartel arrangements, or loose, as in price leadership—they will probably all make out all right as far as their profits are concerned. It is possible that their individual profits will each be greater than if they had each tried to go it alone without any rules, without colluding. But if each firm is interested in maximizing its profits, it will always be on the lookout for ways to achieve even higher profits than is possible by colluding. Each firm knows that, by shaving its price a little, it will be able to attract customers away from its competitors. The trick, of course, is to achieve this without the others finding out; if they find out, they could react in ways that would cause the firm to earn smaller profits, perhaps substantially smaller profits. Firms that find it profitable to cheat by lowering their price will frequently do so by granting "secret" price concessions to some or all of their buyers; or they will attempt to accomplish the same thing by granting their buyers easier credit terms, more rapid delivery, and other services "free."

What determines the success or failure of collusion?

Many factors can affect the success or failure of any collusive arrangement. One of the most obvious is the *number of oligopolistic producers* in the market. In general, the larger the number of producers, the less the likelihood of success. It is more difficult to police an agreement when there are a large number of producers; it is even more difficult to reach agreement in the first place. Individual firm interests are less likely to be identified with those of the industry. Because the effects of any individual firm's actions will be spread across a relatively large number of producers, there is less likelihood of retaliatory action on the part of the others, either individually or collectively. In the presence of large numbers, the benefits of cheating and the likelihood of getting away with it are enhanced; the risks associated with acting on your own are reduced.

It is also easier to cheat when the market is characterized by significant *product differences*. When the various products are differentiated, it is frequently difficult to know whether or not the price differences that exist are a reflection of quality differences. Firms can, therefore, undertake to improve the quality of their product without altering its price. This form of cheating is difficult to police. Moreover, such nonprice competition cannot be quickly duplicated by rival firms. If the product is homogeneous, on the other hand, cheating must take the form of secret price concessions. Not only are these somewhat easier to discover, but once discovered, they can be quickly duplicated.

Collusive agreements are not likely to be very successful if the barriers to entry to new firms are low. For obvious reasons, the existence of abnormally high profits will attract new entrants. Not only does this wreck the market for existing producers, but because the numbers have increased, it is all the more difficult to establish and enforce any new collusive agreement. However, in instances where barriers to entry are not sizable, it is still possible for the existing few to effectively keep out the competition by practicing **limit pricing.** The idea here is straight forward. If prices were set at profit-maximizing levels, new firms would probably enter. To forestall such entry, less than profit-maximizing prices are agreed upon. This makes entry less attractive; it limits entry, hence the name **limit pricing.** Would-be entrants can also be kept out by the threat of limit pricing.

Recession is frequently the enemy of collusion. During periods when demand is low, all parties to a collusive agreement are likely to suffer profit losses *if* they stick to the agreement. But there will always be some producers who will feel that they can do better by striking out on their own. If the recession is prolonged enough and profits are severely depressed as a result, many firms may come to feel that they have little to lose by breaking with the others.

Finally, the stronger the antitrust laws and the more vigorously they are enforced, the greater will be the costs of colluding and the smaller will be the likelihood of firms undertaking such a costly venture.

The kinked demand curve

The *structure of prices* in most oligopolistic industries tends to be very inflexible. That is, even in the face of changing costs, the prices charged by oligopolists will often remain unchanged. If collusion among producers were widespread, such rigid price structures would be explained easily. But even if firms do not collude, rigid prices would tend to be observed as a natural consequence of recognized mutual interdependence. One hypothesis that has been set forth to explain these rigidities is the **kinked demand curve.** It is based on the notion that rival firms will respond differently to a price cut than they will to a price hike. Specifically, rival firms will match price cuts but not price increases.

The implications of the kinked demand curve hypothesis are illustrated in Table 21.1. There we consider the nature of the demand curve facing the ZZZ Corporation, depending on the assumed responses of ZZZ's rivals. If we assume

Table 21.1
The kinked demand schedule for ZZZ Corporation

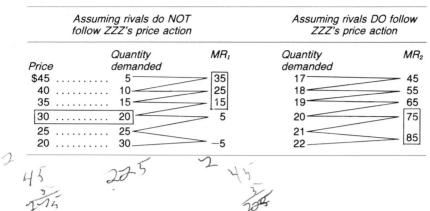

| | Assuming rivals do NOT follow ZZZ's price action | | Assuming rivals DO follow ZZZ's price action | |
Price	Quantity demanded	MR_1	Quantity demanded	MR_2
$45	5	35	17	45
40	10	25	18	55
35	15	15	19	65
30	20	5	20	75
25	25		21	
20	30	−5	22	85

that ZZZ's competitors will not change their prices in response to a price change by ZZZ, we obtain the demand response on the left-hand side of Table 21.1. Note there that a $5 price reduction will bring about a five-unit increase in the quantity demanded of ZZZ's product. The implied marginal revenue calculations are easily obtained.

If ZZZ's competitors match ZZZ's price change, the demand curve facing ZZZ will be much different. If ZZZ lowers price by $5, and its rivals follow suit, ZZZ will not attract customers away from its competitors. As a result, the increase in the quantity demanded will be much smaller. In Table 21.1 it has been assumed that the increase will be one unit for each $5 price reduction by ZZZ.

Suppose the initial price is $30. At that price, ZZZ sells 20 units. Suppose further that rival firms will match price reductions but will *not* match price increases by ZZZ. The demand curve facing ZZZ will differ, depending on whether ZZZ raises or lowers its price. For price increases, the more elastic schedule on the left-hand side of Table 21.1 applies; for price reductions, the less elastic demand schedule on the right-hand side applies. Graphically, these differences in the assumed responses of rival firms yield a demand curve that is "kinked," as shown in Figure 21.6; the kink in the demand curve occurs at the point representing the initial price.

Note first the sharp discontinuity—the gap—in the MR curve that occurs at the output level below the kink (point A) in the demand curve. This discontinuity occurs because the elasticity of the demand curve facing the oligopolist changes sharply at the kink. Elasticity is very high *above* the kink, as sales fall sharply when competitors refuse to match price increases; elasticity is much lower below the kink, as sales gains are small when competitors match price reductions. (This same point can be seen in Table 21.1. Recalling the relationship between MR and the price elasticity of demand, we see that for price increases, MR is positive; for price decreases, on the other hand, MR falls sharply taking on a large negative value in our numerical example.)

So where should the oligopolist produce and what price should be charged? The firm maximizes profits by producing at the point where MC equals MR. If the MC curve happens to intersect one of the two segments of the MR curve, the oligopolist will maximize profits by setting a price different from the initial price. If the oligopolist faces MC_3, a quantity Q_2 will be produced at a price of P_2—a price in excess of the initial price. On the other hand, if the MC curve passes anywhere through the gap in the MR curve, profits will be maximized by continuing to produce a quantity Q_1 at the initial price.

In general, the sharper the kink in the demand curve, the greater will be the gap of discontinuity in the MR curve. This implies that there may be a considerable range over which MC may vary

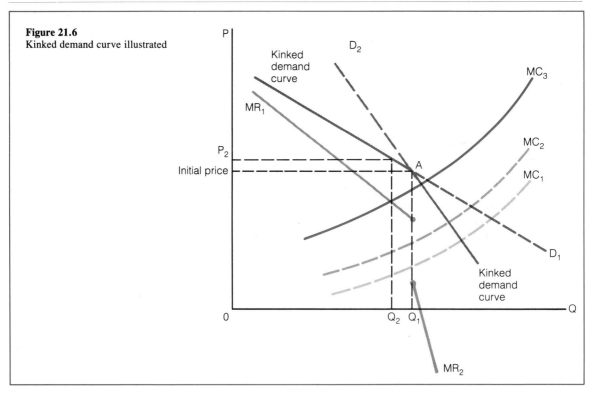

Figure 21.6
Kinked demand curve illustrated

without the firm varying either price or output—in sharp contrast to the perfect competitor or the monopolist. This is why a number of economists have argued that the kinked demand curve explains why prices in oligopolistic markets can remain sticky even in the face of sizable changes in marginal costs. The critical factor to remember here is that the existence and sharpness of the kink depends on how fellow oligopolists respond to each other's actions.

Price leadership and the kinked demand curve

One of the problems with the kinked demand curve theory is that it leaves unexplained how the *initial price* (where the kink occurs) is established. However, if we assume that the market is characterized by some form of price leadership, it is possible to identify the relevant initial price. In conjunction with price leadership, the theory behind the kinked demand curve has been found to be useful in the analysis of some oligopolistic markets. For example, it is alleged that the automobile industry is characterized by price leadership, with General Motors being the obvious price leader. GM may not be the first automaker to announce its new prices, but it is quite assuredly the price leader.

The price leader in the automobile industry is assumed to behave in the following manner. GM is assumed to look upon all automakers as if they were a single producer—a monopolist. Given the cost conditions confronting the "monopoly" and the demand conditions characterizing the market, GM is assumed to select price and output levels designed to maximize industry profits. Each of the automakers can accept the price or face the consequences of choosing some other price. That is, if Ford decides to establish a price in excess of GM's, GM will stick with its lower price and Ford will be confronted with a situation in which a large number of its customers will switch to GM cars. That is, the demand curve Ford faces for prices in excess of GM's is highly elastic. If Ford tries to price below GM,

GM will cut its price to ensure that Ford does not increase its market share. In other words, Ford faces a very inelastic demand curve for its autos for prices below GM's industry profit-maximizing price. Ford faces a kinked demand curve.

Does this imply that all automakers will price their automobiles at essentially the same price for similar models? Not necessarily. It all depends on the MR and MC conditions facing each firm. However, given the high degree of substitutability among the models produced by the automakers and given the relatively low price elasticity of demand for automobiles in general, there is considerable likelihood that the demand curve facing each of those who are not price leaders is very sharply kinked, implying that a large discontinuity in the MR curve exists. Even if large discrepancies exist in the MC conditions facing the firms, they are very apt to price their products similarly.

There is some evidence that such conditions prevail in the auto industry. Each year, one of the automakers announces price hikes for its new models; this is followed by other automakers who make similar announcements. But generally, the final price increase put into effect will be determined by GM. Suppose Chrysler announces first that its prices will rise by $180 on average. If GM follows with an announcement of a price hike in the neighborhood of $180, prices will probably rise throughout the industry by about $180. If, on the other hand, GM announces a price hike of only $100, it won't be long before Chrysler recognizes the implications of this difference and rolls back its announced price increase to around $100.

(Interestingly, this situation in the auto industry is changing due to ever increasing foreign competition. Thus, due to competition from Japan and Germany, in particular, the auto industry is becoming more competitive and less oligopolistic than was the case a few years back.)

SUMMARY

1. *Monopolistic competition* is generally characterized by a large number of relatively small producers; barriers to entry are weak; product differentiation is present; and people have incomplete information. Production differentiation and the absence of complete information are the important sources of the monopoly power firms possess in this market structure.

2. Product differentiation and the absence of complete information are also important sources of monopoly power in *oligopoly*. But the significant distinguishing feature of oligopoly is the *fewness of firms,* which gives rise to *recognized mutual interdependence,* a feature that complicates considerably the study of this particular market structure.

3. Firms producing under conditions of monopolistic competition face downward-sloping demand curves for their products. Each firm faces a demand curve that is much more elastic than the demand curve for the industry's output. The reason is the availability of many close substitute products within the industry. Ease of entry implies the absence of economic profits under monopolistic competition in the long run. However, because each firm faces a downward-sloping demand curve for its product, the long-run equilibrium will be characterized by *"wastes of competition."*

4. Product differentiation is the one key feature that distinguishes monopolistic competition from pure competition. Sometimes the differences are substantive, sometimes they are not. However, what matters is whether or not products are differentiated from one *another in the minds of buyers.*

5. *Advertising* is an important and controversial form of nonprice competition. Its purposes are threefold: *(a)* to expand the demand for the firm's product; *(b)* to maintain demand in the face of the promotional efforts of rival firms; and *(c)* to reduce the price elasticity of demand.

6. It is very difficult to predict what the consequences of the profit-maximizing behavior of oligopolists will be. As a result of *recognized mutual interdependence,* each firm recognizes that its profits are heavily dependent on the actions of the other firms in the industry; each firm cannot discover what its marginal revenue will be until it figures out what actions rival firms

will take. In view of the nerve-wracking uncertainty faced by oligopolists, it is clear why they are frequently in the *mood to collude.* However, just as oligopolists have an incentive to collude, they have an *incentive to cheat* on any collusive agreement.

7.   The *kinked demand curve* model provides us with some insight into why the structure of prices in oligopolistic industries tends to be very inflexible. When the kinked demand curve model is combined with the price leadership model, one obtains useful insights into the operation of some oligopolistic markets.

CONCEPTS FOR REVIEW

Monopolistic competition

Oligopoly

Product differentiation

Monopoly power

Recognized mutual interdependence

Price war

Collusion

Cartels

"Gentleman's agreement"

Wastes of competition

Nonprice competition

Advertising

Mood to collude

Incentive to cheat on collusive agreements

Limit pricing

Price leadership

Joint profit maximization

Kinked demand curve

QUESTIONS FOR DISCUSSION

(Those marked with an asterisk (*) are more difficult.)

1.   *a.*   The purely competitive firm faces a perfectly elastic demand curve for its output. The monopolistically competitive firm, by contrast, faces a downward-sloping (i.e., less than perfectly elastic) demand curve for its output. What accounts for this difference between the two kinds of firms? Explain your answer carefully.

b.   A monopoly firm faces a demand curve for its product that is the market demand curve. The monopolistically competitive firm, by contrast, faces a demand curve that is much more elastic than, and lies below and to the left of, the market demand curve. What accounts for these differences? Be explicit.

2.   The supply curve for the purely competitive firm consists of that portion of its MC curve lying above its AVC. Can the supply curve of a monopolistically competitive firm be defined similarly? What about the supply curve of an oligopolistic firm? (*Hint:* How is the supply curve of a monopoly firm defined?)

3.   Suppose, as a result of an extensive advertising campaign, ZZZ faces a much less elastic demand curve for its product than before. Suppose further that ZZZ makes zero profits in the long run. What effect will the reduction in the elasticity of demand have on the size of the "wastes of competition" in the case of ZZZ? Explain carefully.

4.   Explain why you agree or disagree with the following statement: "The greater the degree of product differentiation, the greater will be the price differences among producers, and conversely."

*5.   *a.*   Firm A, a monopolistic competitor, produces an unusual product—the Wojo. Not only are fixed costs zero, but the marginal cost of production is zero as well. Under the circumstances, firm A will maximize profits by setting price and output at levels corresponding to the point on the demand curve it faces that is unit price elastic. Do you agree or disagree?

b.   If firm A, described above, faces a demand curve for its product that is unit price elastic throughout, its profits will be the same for *any* positive level of output. Do you agree or disagree? (*Hint:* Ask yourself what the MR curve must look like if the demand curve is unit price elastic throughout. Then ask yourself what MC, AVC, and ATC must look like. What is you conclusion?)

6.   Carefully evaluate: "Because of recognized mutual interdependence, it is almost impossible to set forth a 'general' case illustrating profit-maximizing equilibrium under oligopoly."

*7.   *a.*   In the kinked demand curve model, certain assumptions were made regarding the responses of rival firms to price actions undertaken by any individual oligopolist. What were the assumed responses on the part of rival firms?

    b. Suppose rival firms matched any and *all* price changes. What would the demand curve facing our hypothetical oligopolist look like? How would it compare with the market demand curve?

    c. Suppose rival firms cut their prices in response to a price increase by our hypothetical oligopolist; and in response to price reductions, rival firms cut their prices even more. What would the demand curve facing our hypothetical oligopolist look like? How would it compare to the kinked demand curve?

*8   Although cartels and cartel-like arrangements have been declared illegal by the courts, producers in industries characterized by price leadership are immune from prosecution. Is it true that price leadership can lead to the same outcomes as joint profit maximization under a formal cartel? Why do you think it is difficult to prosecute producers in price leadership industries?

*9.   Carefully evaluate: "If each firm in an industry faces a demand curve for its product that has a price elasticity of demand greater than one, the market demand for the industry's output must have a price elasticity greater than one."

The Swedish Academy selected two economists who are political opposites for the sixth Nobel Prize in Economics (1974). Gunnar Myrdal (of Sweden) and Friedrich A. von Hayek (of Austria) were cited for "their pioneering work in the theory of money and economic fluctuations and for their pioneering analysis of the interdependence of economic, social, and institutional phenomena." Though their works have parallels in both timing and substance, their approaches, applications, and conclusions appear to be at direct opposites. Their influences have been on the extremes of economic thought. Myrdal's work argues for government intervention to smooth out the business cycle; Hayek's argues for the laissez-faire approach. The citation stressed their contributions to monetary analysis. But each man is better known for his work in other areas of social policy. The announcement of the award acknowledged the reactions their works have generated. Pointing out that each had found new and original ways of posing questions, the Swedish Academy stated that they had "put forward new ideas on causes and politics, a characteristic that often makes them somewhat controversial. This is only natural when the field of research is extended to include factors and linkages which economists usually take for granted or neglect."

Gunnar Myrdal (1898–   )

A proponent of government action to alter the distribution of wealth, Gunnar Myrdal has made waves in the fields of both economics and sociology. He is widely known for his work *An American Dilemma— the Negro Problem and Modern Democracy,* a study begun in 1938 and published in 1944, and for *Asian Drama,* an exhaustive work on the development of southeast Asia published in 1968.

Wide World Photos

Myrdal laid the foundation for his work in monetary analysis early in his career in his work *Monetary Equilibrium,* written in the early 1930s. In this he and others of the Stockholm School anticipated by nearly a decade the theories of John Maynard Keynes. An architect of the Swedish Labor Party's welfare state during the early 1930s, he began his career in the practice of law. His wife, Alva, a sociologist, persuaded him to study economics. Their joint works and activities helped to shape the post-World War II social democracy government of Sweden.

Myrdal saw the issues of equality and discrimination as two of the foremost economic problems. Described as an anatomist of nations, his work is frequently referred to as the study of the haves and have-nots. "Economists say that I'm a sociologist," he complains, "and they don't mean anything good by that." His methodology is multidisciplinary; he does not restrict himself to economics but combines studies from a variety of disciplines. Further, he argues that it is impossible for the social sciences to be neutral because they are based on the values by which people live.

His wife, a respected author, sociologist, former Swedish ambassador to India, United Nations director, and cabinet minister, has assisted him in many of his books. Together they are still writing about world political-social-economic relations.

PART FOUR

Microeconomics of consumer and business behavior: Price determination in resource markets and distribution of income

Friedrich A. von Hayek (1899–   )

A free market advocate who was one of the few economists to predict the economic crash of 1929, Friedrich von Hayek is recognized as an authority on monetary and economic policies and on constitutional rights.

Wide World Photos

In his early works on business cycles Hayek argued that a continued policy of deficit spending by government, financed by money creation, is the beginning of economic decline. Government action to cure our economic ills leads ultimately to only one result—economic collapse. According to Hayek, the best cure for a depression is a hands-off policy by government. He advises that it is best to sweat it out for a while—"a little suffering now is better than more suffering later."

His works fall into three main parts—pure economic theory, problems of economic policy, and social and political philosophy and legal theory. His main interest for the last several decades has not been economics but fundamental political and legal theory. *The Constitution of Liberty* (1960) is seen as the work of a political philosopher who is also an economist. In *The Road to Serfdom,* published in 1945, he argued that policies to intervene in the functioning of the private economy can lead to totalitarian societies. To Hayek's surprise, this book became a best seller.

In describing his works, Hayek said, "a strong interest in the history of ideas, which first had expressed itself in studies in the history of economics, combined with an acute awareness of the difference in character between the natural and the social sciences, led me more and more toward the general problems of the role of reason in the conduct of human affairs, which in a way had been my starting point."

Hayek spent several years in public service in his native Austria before taking a chair at the London School of Economics. In 1950 he moved to the University of Chicago as professor of social and moral science. Facing mandatory retirement age, he decided to return to his native Austria where he is a visiting professor at Salzburg University.

A reserved, courtly, Old-World scholar, he continues his writing and lecturing on social and political philosophy to this day.

For separate but broadly parallel "contributions to the theory of optimum allocation of resources," Leonid V. Kantorovich, a Russian, and Tjalling C. Koopmans, a Dutch-born American citizen, shared the seventh Nobel Prize in Economic Science (1975). In the citation, the Academy emphasized that their works "embrace whole national economies as well as individual corporations and even divisions, had led to improved economic planning. As they have formulated the problems and described the connection between production results and productive inputs in new ways, these two scholars have been able to achieve highly significant results." Their techniques of activity analysis are used in production planning—in economies organized along both capitalist or communist lines—and are applicable either at the individual business level, as in the United States, or at the national level, as in the planned communist economies of Eastern Europe. Both Kantorovich and Koopmans began their work by seeking answers to the questions fundamental to all economic activity: What goods should be produced? What methods of production should be used? How much of current production should be consumed and how much should be invested to create new resources for future production and consumption?

Leonid V. Kantorovich (1912–   )

In 1939 a young man of 27, Leonid Kantorovich, presented a paper on management and planning technique at a Leningrad seminar. The paper provided a formulation of an activity analysis model and outlined a computational technique for solving related linear programming problems. Kantorovich's work was in pure mathematics. But in his paper the problem of the allocation of resources was treated not only from a mathematician's point of view—it also dealt with the role prices played in reaching optimal decisions.

Although his innovations were considered "crackpot" by the party economists at the time, his standing as a mathematician was so secure he suffered

Wide World Photos

no direct harassment during the Stalin period. But his technique to improve central planning of the Soviet economy did not receive recognition until the 1950s. The Soviet political climate had to change for the work to be viewed in its best light.

Kantorovich has been an indirect critic of the Soviet economic system, although his criticism is couched in mathematical language. He has maintained that a deficient Soviet investment policy has caused less than optimal economic growth.

The Academy noted in its citation, "Early in his research, Professor Kantorovich applied the analytical technique of linear programming to demonstrate how economic planning in his country could be improved."

Described as very cautious politically and not given to gossip when with colleagues from outside the USSR, he often displays an ironic sense of humor when in familiar Soviet surroundings. Once, speaking before a conference of mathematical economists, he recalled the difficulties and delays in publishing some work, referring to the secrecy common during the Stalinist era. He related, "It was after all a highly sensitive study. For our calculations, for example, we had to establish such things as the rail distance between Moscow and Leningrad."

Since 1976 he has headed a mathematical-economics laboratory especially created for him at the Institute of Economic Management, the place where Soviet officials of ministerial rank receive training in uses of modern planning and in Western management science methods.

Tjalling C. Koopmans (1910–   )

Study of the efficient use of transportation facilities during World War II led Tjalling Koopmans to devise a formula—an activity analysis model—for routing empty ships to their next and most efficient destinations. After the war, as a member of the Cowles Commission, he extended his work about the relationship between prices and optimality.

Wide World Photos

The Academy noted that Koopmans had "shown, for instance, that on the basis of certain efficiency criteria it is possible directly to make important deductions concerning optimum price systems." His work defined the decentralization of economic activity, in response to considerations of profit, not only for a transportation problem but for the functioning of a whole economic system.

His work has been in the field of econometrics and mathematical programming—not in the more widely known areas of social and political economics. But his theories on resource allocation have wide application to business. The scheduling of oil refinery operations, the moving of wood pulp from the source to newspaper plants, the assigning of tasks to machines, and the cutting of metal and paper in the most economical ways are all examples of where activity analysis is used to select the best production technique.

Koopmans began his studies in the Netherlands in the fields of mathematics and physics but turned to economics for his doctorate. "I was halfway with math and halfway with physics when I found economics more challenging," he explained. At Yale, where he holds the Alfred Cowles Professor of Economics chair, he divides his time between research and teaching. He is described as "the father figure in our crop of mathematically sophisticated economists."

We now shift the focus of our study of microeconomics away from product markets toward resource markets. There are several questions of immediate concern to us here: What determines the demand for the resources that are used in the production of goods and services? What determines the supply of resources? What determines the income payments to the various factors of production—to labor, to the owners of capital goods, and to the owners of natural resources? What accounts for the marked differences in the incomes of various groups of individuals in our economic system—lawyers, doctors, economists, teachers, athletes, janitors? What accounts for the differences in the incomes of whites versus blacks and other minorities, and of males versus females? What role do unions play in determining wages? When monopoly power is present in product markets, does this affect the payments received by the various factors of production?

We begin our study of resource markets in this chapter by focusing our attention on the forces that determine the demand for a *single* factor of production. We will then look at the forces that determine the demand for *several factors* of production simultaneously. Finally, we will examine the supply side of resource markets and the interaction of the demand for and supply of resources.

In Chapter 23 we will examine in greater detail wage determination in perfect and imperfect market structures. Chapter 24 will be reserved for the study of other incomes—rent, interest, and profits. Finally, in Chapter 25, we will examine in detail the economics of reproducible versus exhaustible resources.

Resource demand and the concept of "derived" demand

Resources are not demanded for their own sake but for what they are capable of producing. Resources do not yield utility directly, but indirectly. Goods and services are the direct source of the want-satisfying characteristics people demand. The demand for resources is a reflection of the demand for the goods and services themselves. The demand for resources is a **"derived" demand.**

Chapter 22

Theory of production and resource use

The concept of derived demand is important for it highlights the nature of the interconnection between resource markets and product markets. It is essential to understand that the outcomes in resource markets reflect in very fundamental ways the outcomes in product markets.

At the same time, it is important not to be misled by the concept of derived demand. The nature of the relationship between resource and product markets is not one-way—from goods markets to resource markets. Indeed, the demand for goods and services does not come from out of the blue; it comes from the incomes earned by the resources as a result of their use in the production of goods and services. Recognizing economic activity as a *circular flow* will keep you out of the trap of thinking of the relationship between resource and product markets as one-way.

THE DEMAND FOR A SINGLE VARIABLE FACTOR OF PRODUCTION

Let us consider again the problem of factor demand from the point of view of our hypothetical firm—the ZZZ Corporation. In earlier chapters we were interested in ZZZ from its perspective as a *seller* in product markets. Now we want to focus on ZZZ from its perspective as a *buyer* of the resources that go into the production of minicomputers.

In our discussion of product markets we assumed that ZZZ wished to maximize its profits (or minimize its losses). That discussion led to the development of ZZZ's profit-maximizing rule: ZZZ will maximize profits (or minimize losses) by carrying its production of minicomputers to the point where marginal cost (MC) equals marginal revenue (MR). We want to extend that discussion here by focusing our attention on the amount of resources ZZZ will demand to produce that profit-maximizing rate of output.

A restatement of the profit-maximizing rule

Actually, the profit-maximizing rule that has guided much of our discussion up to this point can be restated in terms of the decisions firms make in resource markets. Marginal cost was defined before as the change in total cost that accompanied the production of an additional unit of output. However, since the additional unit of output produced requires additional resources, *MC must refer to the additional resource costs incurred to produce the additional output.* Also, marginal revenue was defined before as the change in total revenue that accompanied the sale of an additional unit of output. Additional sales ultimately being the result of additional production, *MR refers to the additional revenue generated by the additional output produced through the use of added resources.*

Our statement of the profit-maximizing rule earlier was put in the following terms: Whether a firm's profits will rise or fall as a result of an expansion of output will depend on whether the *additional* cost incurred in expanding production is less than or greater than the *additional* revenue generated by the increased level of production. Since more resources are required to expand production, the profit-maximizing rule can be restated in the following terms: *Whether a firm's profits will rise or fall as a result of hiring more resources will depend on whether the additional resource costs incurred are less than or greater than the additional revenue derived from the sale of the additional amounts produced by those added resources.*

We define **marginal factor cost** (MFC) as the change in total cost per unit change in the variable factor of production. Letting the variable factor input be represented by (V), MFC can be defined as:

$$\text{MFC of variable factor input} = \frac{\Delta \text{ total cost}}{\Delta \text{ variable factor input}} = \frac{\Delta \text{TC}}{\Delta \text{V}}.$$

We define **marginal revenue product** (MRP) as the change in total revenue per unit change in the variable factor of production:

$$\text{MRP of variable factor input} = \frac{\Delta \text{ total revenue}}{\Delta \text{ variable factor input}} = \frac{\Delta \text{TR}}{\Delta \text{V}}.$$

Whether it is profitable to hire an additional unit of the variable factor can only be determined by comparing the MFC of the variable factor input with that variable factor's MRP—i.e., by comparing the additional cost of hiring one more unit of the variable factor with the additional revenue that that added factor will fetch for the firm from the extra output produced.

In examining the profit-maximizing behavior of firms in resource markets, it is important—just as it was in our study of product markets—to separate the short run from the long run. In the short run, a fixed productive facility exists. Variations in output in the short run come about through the more or less intensive use of that fixed production facility. In other words, in the short run, production varies through the application of more or less variable factors of production given fixed factors. In the long run, all factors of production are variable.

In this section we will focus our attention on the short run, examining the case where we vary only one factor of production holding all others fixed. Later we will take up the more complicated case where all or several factors of production can be varied simultaneously.

The demand for a single factor of production: The short run

Let us assume for the moment that ZZZ can purchase a little or a lot of the variable factor of production at a fixed price per unit of the factor. This could arise, for example, because the market for that variable factor is perfectly competitive. Under those circumstances, ZZZ is only one of a great many buyers of the variable factor; because ZZZ's purchases are small relative to the market total, ZZZ pays a fixed price—the market price—for each extra unit it buys.

For ZZZ, therefore, marginal factor cost (MFC) is fixed at the per unit price of the variable factor. To illustrate, suppose the variable factor is labor and that the wage per hour is $5. Since the wage per hour is fixed whether ZZZ purchases the services of only a few hours of labor or a great many hours, the *change* in total cost

per *additional* labor hour purchased—the MFC of labor—is constant and fixed at $5.

The question that ZZZ then faces is this: Given the constant MFC of the variable factor, what quantity hired will maximize profits? That will depend on the variable factor's marginal revenue product (MRP)—the additional revenue ZZZ will receive from the extra units of output produced by the added units of the variable factor.

The MRP of the variable factor will depend on two things:

1. The additional output produced as a result of the purchase of one more unit of the variable factor.
2. The additional revenue received by ZZZ from the sale of the additional output.

On the basis of our analysis in Chapter 18, you should recognize the first item as the variable factor's marginal product, or, more accurately, its **marginal physical product**—the change in output divided by the change in the variable factor input. The second item is nothing other than ZZZ's marginal revenue—the change in total revenue divided by the change in output. Indeed, the MRP of the variable factor can be defined as the variable factor's marginal physical product (MPP) *times* marginal revenue (MR). That is,

$$\frac{\Delta TR}{\Delta \text{ variable factor}} = \frac{\Delta \text{ output}}{\Delta \text{ variable factor}} \times \frac{\Delta TR}{\Delta \text{output}}$$

or

$$MRP = MPP \times MR.$$

This makes sense, as the following example illustrates. If the additional unit of the variable factor raises ZZZ's output by five units, and if the additional revenue generated by the sale of *each* additional unit is $10, the extra revenue added by the extra variable factor—its MRP—must be $50—i.e., five additional units of output at $10 each yields $50 more in revenue.

The MRP schedule

The MRP of the variable factor depends on the factor's MPP *and* on the firm's MR. Therefore, to determine the MRP at various levels of employment of the variable factor, we must address two specific questions:

1. As ZZZ hires more and more of the variable factor, what happens to total output for each extra unit of the variable factor hired? In other words, what happens to the variable factor's MPP as more and more units are hired?
2. As ZZZ sells additional units of output, what happens to the additional revenue per additional unit sold? In other words, what happens to the firm's MR as more and more units of the product are sold?

On the basis of our discussion in earlier chapters, we already know the answers to both of these questions. As we saw in Chapter 18, when more and more units of a variable input are applied to a fixed input, total output will rise but at a diminishing rate. That is, the MPP of the variable factor diminishes as employment of the variable factor increases. This is the law of diminishing returns, or the law of diminishing marginal productivity.

What happens to MR will depend on the market structure for ZZZ's output. If ZZZ sells its product in a perfectly competitive market, its MR will be constant and equal in value to the market-determined price for minicomputers. Since ZZZ is only one of many sellers of minicomputers, the number of minicomputers sold by ZZZ will in no way influence their price; the

additional revenue per additional unit sold—MR—is simply equal to price.

If ZZZ faces a downward-sloping demand curve for its product—meaning that it must cut its price in order to expand its sales volume—then, with the exception of the very first unit sold, price will exceed marginal revenue. In addition, MR will decline with the sale of additional units.

Equipped with this knowledge about the behavior of MPP and MR, we are able to construct the MRP schedule of the variable factor of production for ZZZ. We will briefly examine two cases. In the first, we will assume that ZZZ is a perfect competitor in the sale of its output. In the second case we will assume that ZZZ faces a downward-sloping demand curve for its product, which covers instances where ZZZ sells its output in less than perfectly competitive market structures (e.g., monopoly, oligopoly, or monopolistic competition).

Case I: MRP schedule when firm sells its output in a perfectly competitive market.   Consider Table 22.1. On the basis of the data in columns (1) and (2), it is relatively easy to determine the marginal product of the variable factor; it is simply the change in output for each additional unit of the variable factor hired. The decline in the variable factor's marginal product after the second unit hired is a reflection of the law of diminishing returns.

ZZZ's MR is given in column (4). Because

Table 22.1

The MRP schedule of the ZZZ Corporation on the assumption that output is sold in a perfectly competitive market

(1) Variable factor input per week	(2) Output per week	(3) Variable factor's marginal product (MPP)	(4) ZZZ's marginal revenue (MR)	(5) Variable factor's marginal revenue product (MRP) (3) × (4)
0	0			
1	12	12	$10	$120
2	28	16	10	160
3	42	14	10	140
4	54	12	10	120
5	64	10	10	100
6	71	7	10	70
7	75	4	10	40
8	76	1	10	10
9	76	0	10	0

ZZZ sells its output in a perfectly competitive market, its MR does not vary with the number of units sold. Whether ZZZ sells 12 units or 76, its extra revenue per unit sold is $10.

The variable factor's MRP is given in column (5). It is obtained, simply, as the product of each pair of values in columns (3) and (4)—the MPP of the variable factor times MR.

To illustrate the concept of MRP more concretely, consider the following line of reasoning. Suppose ZZZ is currently using three units of the variable input per week. Output produced will then amount to 42 units. At a price of $10 per unit (the same as MR, since, given the assumption of pure competition in product markets, P = MR), total revenue comes to $420. Suppose now that ZZZ hires a fourth unit of the variable factor for a week. Total output rises to 54 units; given a price of $10 per unit, total revenue rises to $540. The additional revenue derived from the sale of the extra output produced with the aid of the fourth unit of the variable factor is $120—the difference between the total revenue received when three units of the variable input were hired ($420) and the total revenue received when four units were hired ($540). This difference is the MRP of the fourth unit of the variable factor input and is given by the fourth entry in column (5). Not surprisingly, the value $120 derived by the above reasoning is the same as the value derived by multiplying the appropriate entries in columns (3) and (4). All other entries in column (5) can be similarly derived.

The MRP curve: ZZZ's demand curve for the variable input. The MRP data in column (5) of Table 22.1 are plotted in Figure 22.1. The curve formed by connecting up the discrete points is referred to as the **MRP curve** of the variable factor input. Each point on the curve measures the additional revenue that will accrue to the firm for each unit of the variable input. At four units of the variable input, MRP amounts to $120; at five units, MRP comes to $100.

The MRP curve formed in Figure 22.1 looks almost exactly like the marginal product curve in Figure 18.2. This is as it should be. The MRP curve here was derived by multiplying MPP by MR. Since MR is constant throughout, by as-

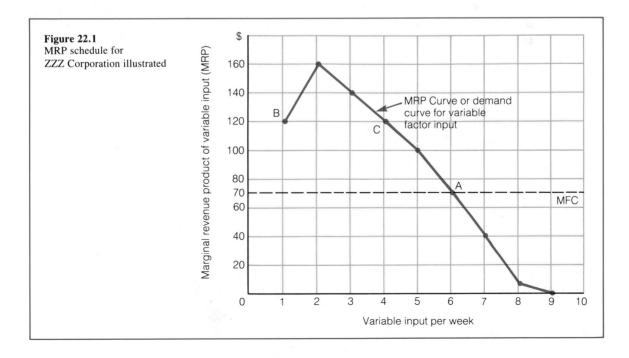

Figure 22.1
MRP schedule for
ZZZ Corporation illustrated

sumption, all changes in MRP are the result of changes in MPP. Since MPP at first rises, then falls, as the variable factor input is increased, MRP will at first rise then fall. Put differently, the rise and the fall of the MRP curve, and the steepness of its slope, are determined exclusively by the pattern of movement of the variable factor's MPP. As we shall see a little later, this is true only as long as the firm sells its output in a perfectly competitive market—i.e., as long as MR is invariant to the amount the firm sells.

The MRP curve also represents the firm's demand curve for the variable input. This can be shown quite easily. ZZZ's demand curve for the variable factor input shows the quantity of the variable input ZZZ is willing and able to purchase. But how much it is willing and able to purchase can only be determined by reference to the quantity of the input that is consistent with its goal of profit maximization.

Suppose ZZZ can purchase all of the variable factor input it wants at a cost of $70 per unit per week. Its MFC of the variable input, therefore, is $70. Suppose further that it is at the moment hiring three units of the variable factor input per week. Should it purchase more of the variable input or less? That's easy. It should purchase more.

As Figure 22.1 and Table 22.1 indicate, hiring one more unit of the variable input increases its total revenue by $120—the MRP of the fourth unit of the variable factor. Since a MRP of $120 exceeds a MFC of $70, the firm's revenues will rise by more than its costs—i.e., profits will rise—with the purchase of an additional unit of the variable factor.

What would happen to ZZZ's profits if it were to cut back its purchases from three to two? Its revenues would fall off by $140—the MRP of the third unit—but its cost savings would amount to only $70—its MFC. Its profits would be reduced if it were to cut back on its employment of the variable factor.

Therefore, it should increase its employment of the variable factor from three to four units per week. What about adding a fifth unit? Yes.

Since MRP of $100 exceeds MFC of $70, profits would increase.

Suppose, on the other hand, that ZZZ is currently hiring eight units of the variable factor per week. When MFC is $70, should it expand or curtail its employment of the variable factor? It should cut back. The reason? Since the MRP of the eighth unit is only $10, ZZZ would save more on its costs than it would reduce its revenues by cutting back on its employment of the variable factor.

The conclusion that follows from all of this is very straightforward. *If MRP exceeds MFC, it is profitable to expand employment of the variable factor input; if MRP is less than MFC, it is profitable to curtail employment of the variable factor.*

Equilibrium for the ZZZ Corporation is obtained at the point where MRP intersects with MFC. That is, it is profitable for ZZZ to carry its employment of the variable factor up to the point where MRP equals MFC. In Figure 22.1, equilibrium occurs at point A; the profit-maximizing level of employment of the variable factor of production is six units. The employment of more or less than six units when the MFC equals $70 would result in less profit for ZZZ.

If MFC equaled $100, it would be profitable for ZZZ to employ only five units per week of the variable factor of production; at a MFC of $40, it would be profitable to hire seven units. It is clear then why the MRP curve represents ZZZ's demand curve for the variable factor: It shows the amount of the variable factor that ZZZ is willing to purchase at the different prices of the variable factor.

A puzzle. Suppose MFC equals $120. It would appear, on the basis of Table 22.1 and Figure 22.1, that ZZZ could achieve its profit-maximizing optimum by hiring either one unit *or* four units of the variable factor. However, it is easy to show that point B, involving the employment of one unit, is "unstable," and that ZZZ would opt in favor of the employment of four units.

Point B is unstable in the following sense. It is true, at point B, that MFC equals MRP. However, if ZZZ were to increase its employment of the variable factor to two units, MRP would rise to $160—$40 more than the MFC associated with the employment of the second unit. Moreover, it would be profitable to hire the third unit, as well, since the MRP of the third unit exceeds MFC. By carrying employment of the variable factor to the fourth unit, ZZZ exhausts its opportunities for additional profit, assuming an MFC of $120. For this reason we ignore the rising portion of the MRP curve; any point along the rising portion is unstable, which means that more profit is obtainable by expanding employment beyond the intersection of MFC and the *rising* portion of the MRP curve. Hereafter we will represent as economically meaningful only the downward-sloping portion of the MRP curve. Interestingly, the rising portion of the MRP curve corresponds to the stage of increasing returns. What the discussion here tells us is that maximum profit is attainable *only* when the firm operates in the stage of decreasing returns.

Case II: MRP schedule when firm sells its output in an imperfectly competitive market. When the ZZZ Corporation sells its output in an imperfectly competitive market, its MRP schedule differs from the one described above in one very important respect. Because ZZZ faces a downward-sloping demand curve for its product, it must cut its product price in order to expand its sales volume. Its MR declines as output is increased.

In Case I, the shape of the MRP schedule was determined by only one thing—the pattern of movement of the variable factor's marginal physical product. This was because MR was constant (and equal to product price) at all levels of output. When ZZZ sells its output in an imperfectly competitive market, the shape of the MRP schedule is determined by *both* the pattern of movement of the variable factor's marginal physical product *and* the pattern of decline of ZZZ's marginal revenue. In this case, therefore, the downward slope in the MRP curve is the result of *both* diminishing marginal productivity *and*

the decline in marginal revenue as more and more units of output are produced and sold.

In all other respects, our discussion of the MRP curve in Case I applies here. The MRP curve represents the demand curve of the firm for the variable factor of production. Profit maximization involves the strategy of carrying the employment of the variable factor to the point where MRP equals MFC. And, on the assumption that the firm selling its output in an imperfectly competitive market can purchase all of the variable factor it wants at a constant price per unit, the MFC of the variable factor is the same as its price.

Marginal revenue product (MRP) *and* value marginal product (VMP)

Consider again the meaning of equilibrium described above in Cases I and II. The payment to each unit of the variable factor is given by MFC. The fact that, in equilibrium, MRP equals MFC means that the variable factor is paid an amount equal to the *marginal* contribution of the variable factor to the firm's revenues. However, the marginal contribution of the factor to the firm's revenues may not represent the worth of the factor to society at the margin.

The employment of an additional unit of the variable factor results in an increase in the firm's output measured by the factor's MPP. How much value does society attach to the additional output produced? It depends on how much people are willing and able to pay to obtain it. Since the product price measures the worth to society at the margin of an additional unit of output, the value to society of the additional output produced by the variable factor is the factor's MPP times the product's price. This value we define as the variable factor's **value marginal product (VMP)**. In other words,

Value marginal product
$$= \text{MPP} \times \text{Product price}$$

or

$$\text{VMP} = \text{MPP} \times \text{P}.$$

The variable factor's VMP differs from its MRP by the following magnitude:

$$VMP - MRP = (MPP \times P) - (MPP \times MR)$$

or, factoring out the common MPP

$$VMP - MRP = MPP \times (P - MR).$$

If the firm sells its output in a perfectly competitive market, VMP equals MRP. Why? Because, for a perfectly competitive firm, MR equals P.

If the firm sells its output in an imperfectly competitive market—meaning it faces a downward-sloping demand curve for its output—the factor's VMP will exceed its MRP. Why? Because P exceeds MR, which means that VMP exceeds MRP.

Figure 22.2 illustrates the distinction between the variable factor's MRP and its VMP for a firm selling its output in an imperfectly competitive market. Since for all units sold (except the first) MR is less than price, the MRP curve must lie below the VMP curve at the various levels of employment of the variable factor.

Some consequences for resource use of monopoly power in product markets

Less-than-optimum levels of resource use. In Chapter 20 we saw that the presence of

monopoly power resulted in a less than optimum level of output in the following sense. The profit-maximizing position of the firm yields an outcome where price exceeded MC. Since price is a measure of the marginal benefit buyers attach to additional purchases, the fact that price exceeds MC means that, from the point of view of society, "too little" of the product is being produced.

The less-than-optimum level of output in the face of monopoly power translates into a less-than-optimum level of resource use. This is seen clearly in Figure 22.2. The profit-maximizing level of use of the variable factor occurs at point A—where MFC = MRP. At that point, the firm hires V_1 units of the variable factor. However, the value that society attaches to the employment of an extra unit of the variable factor is given by VMP—the price of the product (which measures the marginal benefit society attaches to an extra unit of the good) times the additional output produced with the employment of an extra unit of the variable factor. Also, as is clear from Figure 22.2, the VMP of the variable factor at a level of employment of V_1 units is given by the vertical distance from V_1 to the VMP curve (point B); at that employment level, VMP exceeds MRP by the amount AB.

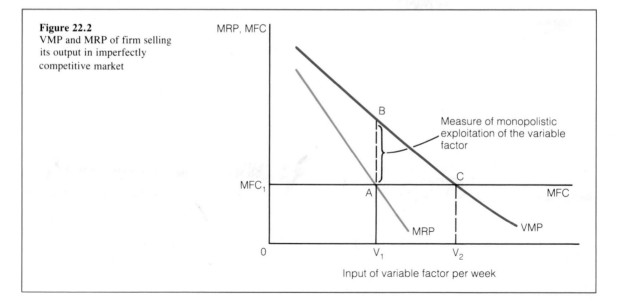

Figure 22.2
VMP and MRP of firm selling its output in imperfectly competitive market

Measure of monopolistic exploitation of the variable factor

Input of variable factor per week

Optimum resource use only occurs at the point where VMP equals MFC—point C in Figure 22.2. This optimum position is analogous to the MC = P optimum described in Chapter 20. The reason this is an optimum is clear. Employment of the variable factor should be carried to the point where the value to society of an additional unit of the variable factor—VMP—is equal to the extra cost to society—MFC.

If the firm sold its output in a perfectly competitive market, its MR would be the same as the market price and MRP would be the same as VMP. The profit-maximizing purely competitive firm, therefore, would carry its employment of the variable factor to the point where MFC equaled VMP. A firm selling its output in an imperfectly competitive market, on the other hand, will hire less than the optimum amount of the variable factor. The less-than-optimum level of employment of the variable factor, illustrated in Figure 22.2, is the counterpart of the less-than-optimum rate of production that emerges from the profit-maximizing strategy of a firm facing a downward-sloping demand curve for its product.

Monopolistic "exploitation" of the variable factor input. There is a sense in which the variable factor of production is "exploited" as a consequence of monopoly power in product markets. This can be illustrated with the aid of Figure 22.2.

At the point of profit maximization—point A—the variable factor is paid by the firm an amount equal to the firm's MRP. However, what the firm is willing to pay for the output of the extra unit of the variable factor is less than what the firm's customers are willing to pay for the extra output produced. To that extent, the variable factor is being exploited. The degree of exploitation is measured by the vertical distance between the MRP curve and the VMP curve—the distance AB in Figure 22.2.

It should be pointed out that the variable factor does not suffer any monopolistic exploitation when the firm sells its output in a perfectly com-

petitive market. The reason? Since MRP equals VMP, the variable factor is paid at the profit-maximizing equilibrium, an amount equal to the VMP.

Usually the term *monopolistic exploitation* is applied only to the variable factor labor. We talk about the monopolistic exploitation of labor in instances in which firms sell their products in imperfectly competitive markets, and about the absence of any monopolistic exploitation in instances where perfect competition prevails in product markets. However, there is no reason the concept cannot be applied to any and all variable factors of production; in these instances, it is the owners of the variable nonlabor resources that are *exploited*.

One final note. Although the term *exploitation* is almost always used in a pejorative sense, no such use of the word is implied here. The term as used here has only one meaning. The fact that VMP exceeds MFC means that "too little" of the variable factor is devoted to the production of the good in question.

RESOURCE MARKET EQUILIBRIUM: THE CASE OF PERFECT COMPETITION

Up to this point, we have dealt only with the profit-maximizing equilibrium position of a single firm. We now want to study the determinants of resource market equilibrium. We begin our study by focusing attention on perfectly competitive resource markets. In these markets, resource prices are determined by the now-familiar forces of demand and supply.

The peculiar feature of perfectly competitive resource markets is the fact that no single buyer or seller of resources has the power to influence resource prices. Such markets are characterized by the presence of large numbers of buyers and sellers. Each buyer and seller is such a small part of the total that their presence or absence in the market is immaterial as far as market prices are concerned.

The market demand curve for a factor of production

It is relatively easy to figure out the market demand curve for any given resource. It is nothing other than the aggregate of the resource demand curves of all producers using that resource. And since an individual producer's demand curve has been identified as its **MRP** curve, the market demand curve is simply the sum of all individual **MRP** curves. The market demand curve for the resource is illustrated in Figure 22.3 by the curve D_R.

The explanation for the downward slope of the market demand curve is straightforward. The first factor, a characteristic feature of all producers, is that of diminishing returns. The **MRP** curves of all firms are downward sloping because the marginal product of the variable factor diminishes with increases in its employment.

The second factor, a characteristic feature of those producers facing downward-sloping demand curves for their products, is declining marginal revenue. The **MRP** curves of those producers decline for the additional reason that, to sell more output, they must cut their product prices, causing their **MR** to decline.

The downward slope of the market demand curve is an outgrowth of both diminishing returns and declining **MR**. Of course, if all resource buyers are perfect competitors in their product markets, the downward slope of the **MRP** curve will be the result of diminishing returns alone.

One final point. In this section we are examining perfectly competitive resource markets. However, in the discussion above, some of the resource buyers were producers selling their products in imperfectly competitive markets. Is this consistent? That is, is it possible to talk about perfect competition in resource markets when some of the resource buyers are imperfect competitors in product markets? Yes. One can easily imagine monopolists or oligopolists, for example, who, in the purchase of their resources, are a small part of the total demand. It is this feature— a small portion of the total demand for the resource—that is of interest to us here. However, it is important to realize that, although the resource market may be perfectly competitive, the monopolistic exploitation of the variable resource can still exist. Can you explain why? This has important implications, as we shall see later.

The market supply curve of a factor of production

It is common practice to draw resource supply curves as upward sloping, meaning that larger quantities of resources will be forthcoming at higher resource prices. The rationale for the upward slope differs depending on the nature of the resource being studied.

Some resources—e.g., capital goods and raw materials—are "produced" by firms and sold as inputs to the productive activities of other firms. The study of resource supply in these instances is very straightforward and follows precisely our study of product supply in earlier chapters. Since the supply of these resource inputs represents the *output* of firms involved in their production, the supply curves of these resources are nothing more than the product supply curves of the firms producing them. In line with our earlier study

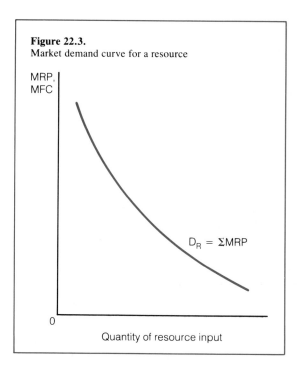

Figure 22.3.
Market demand curve for a resource

MRP, MFC

$D_R = \Sigma MRP$

0

Quantity of resource input

of pure competition and monopoly power, therefore, the following general conclusions apply:

1. The supply curve of a firm selling its (resource) output in a perfectly competitive market is simply that portion of its MC curve lying above its AVC curve; the market supply curve of the resource is the horizontal sum of all the individual firm supply curves.
2. The supply curve of a firm selling its (resource) output in an imperfectly competitive market is undefined; the market supply curve is undefined as well.

There is a second important difference between various kinds of resources. Some are **reproducible resources** (labor and capital), whereas others are not (extractive resources like oil, coal, etc.). In this chapter we will focus on reproducible resources, leaving until a later chapter the analysis of **exhaustible resources.**

There is a third difference between resources—that between labor, on the one hand, and other resource inputs, on the other. Let us examine the labor supply response to determine the unique considerations that apply there.

The market labor supply curve

The factors that determine how much people are willing to work and the occupations they choose are varied and complex. For the moment, we will address only one question: Given the occupational choices of people, how does the number of labor hours supplied to some given labor market vary as the wage is varied?

Figure 22.4 and the accompanying table depict the usual pattern of labor supply response for an individual according to the thinking of classical economists. At a low wage rate—say, $3 per hour—the hypothetical individual would be willing to offer only 15 hours of work per week. Increases in the wage rate would induce an increase in the number of labor hours supplied up to a wage of $10 per hour. An increase in the wage from $10 to $11 per hour would leave the number of hours offered unchanged. Increases beyond $11 per hour would result in an actual reduction in the number of hours offered. Beyond $11 per hour, the supply curve is said to be "backward bending."

The explanation for this kind of labor supply

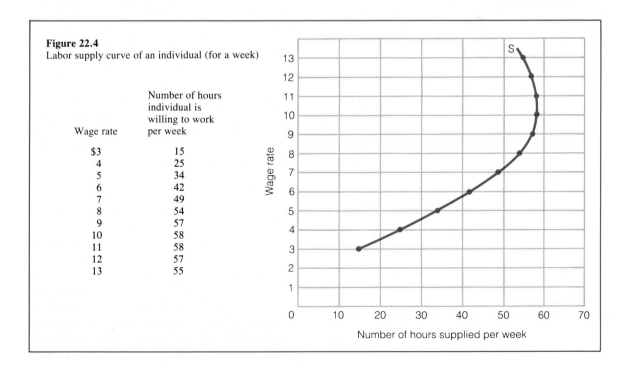

Figure 22.4
Labor supply curve of an individual (for a week)

Wage rate	Number of hours individual is willing to work per week
$3	15
4	25
5	34
6	42
7	49
8	54
9	57
10	58
11	58
12	57
13	55

response is based on the following considerations. People face a work-leisure choice. An hour of work is a foregone hour of leisure. The opportunity cost of working is leisure foregone. On the other hand, the cost of an hour of leisure is the foregone income an individual could have received from working. That foregone income represents a reduced command over other goods and services. The work-leisure choice, then, is fundamentally a choice between leisure and other goods and services, the acquisition of which requires expenditures out of income earned.

Labor supply as a reflection of income and substitution effects. The work-leisure choice involves both income and substitution effects analogous to the income and substitution effects discussed in reference to utility theory in Chapter 17.

The **substitution effect** works in the following way. An increase in the wage rate raises the cost of leisure relative to the goods and services that the additional income from work effort could purchase. Higher wages create for the individual an incentive to work more—to substitute away from leisure toward increased work effort.

The **income effect** operates differently. If our income rises, most of us desire to consume more goods and services, *including more leisure*. But more leisure implies less work. Thus, since a higher wage rate raises the level of income that can be received for a given level of work effort, the individual has an incentive to work less.

The income and substitution effects work in opposite directions. The labor supply response of the individual as a result of an increased wage reflects the net outcome of these opposite pulls. If the substitution effect exceeds the income effect, an increase in the wage rate will lead to an increase in the supply of labor; if the income effect dominates the substitution effect, an increase in the wage will call forth a smaller supply of labor effort.

The interpretation of the labor supply curve in Figure 22.4 is now clear. Up to a wage of $10 per hour, the substitution effect dominates the income effect; from $10 to $11 per hour, the income effect cancels out the substitution ef-

fect, leaving the number of labor hours supplied unchanged; beyond $11 per hour, the income effect dominates the substitution effect, causing the number of labor hours supplied to be reduced. The domination of the substitution effect by the income effect accounts for the backward bending of the supply curve.

Aggregating—adding horizontally—the labor supply curves of all individuals offering labor hours to this market yields the market supply curve. One such possible market labor supply curve is given in Figure 22.5.

You will note that we have ignored the backward-bending portion of the labor supply curve in Figure 22.5. There are two reasons for this. First, there is little empirical evidence to support the idea that the labor supply curves of *individuals* are backward bending. And second, there is virtually no evidence that the *market supply curve* is backward bending. It is possible that the reduced work effort of some people at higher wages is more than offset by the increased work effort of others.

Competitive labor market equilibrium

The point of intersection of the market demand and supply curves for labor yields the equilibrium competitive wage. This is shown in the left panel of Figure 22.5 as the wage W_0. A wage rate in excess of W_0 results in unemployed labor resources—i.e., an excess supply of labor—the existence of which will force the wage rate down to W_0. The excess demand for labor that exists at wage rates below W_0 will cause the wage rate to rise.

Each individual buyer of labor services in this perfectly competitive labor market is such a small part of the total that he/she is unable to influence the market wage. If a firm offers a wage less than W_0, it will not be able to attract any workers. Since they can get W_0 elsewhere, why would they offer their labor services for a wage less than W_0? On the other hand, the firm has no incentive to offer a wage in excess of W_0 since it can obtain all the labor it wants at the market determined wage. *From the point of view of a firm buying labor services in a perfectly competitive market,*

Figure 22.5
Labor market and firm equilibrium under conditions of perfect competition

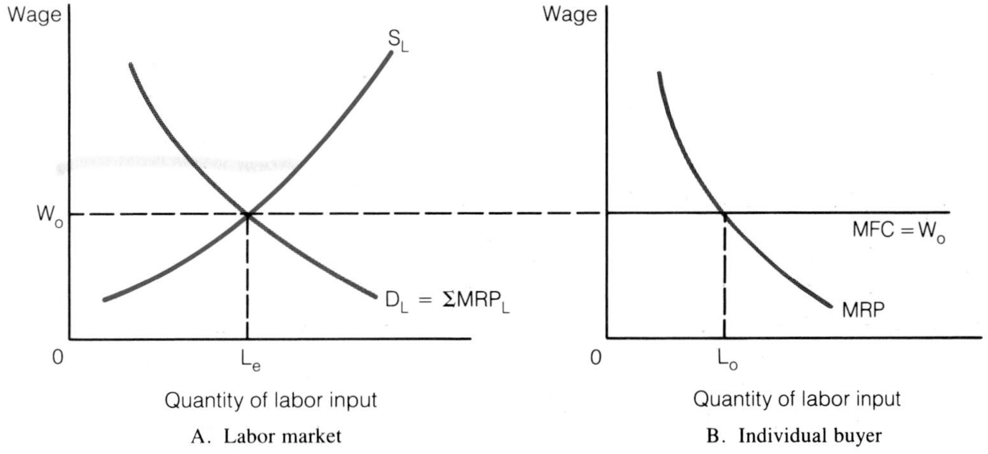

A. Labor market

B. Individual buyer

the supply curve of labor is perfectly elastic—i.e., horizontal—at the market-determined wage, W_0. The fact that additional workers can be added at the same constant wage means that the wage, W_0, represents each firm's MFC for labor—i.e., $MFC = \Delta TC/\Delta L = W_0$. Under the circumstances, equilibrium for the firm occurs at the point where MRP, the firm's demand for labor, equals the competitively determined wage. This is shown in the right-hand panel of Figure 22.5.

The competitive equilibrium position for labor illustrated in Figure 22.5 applies as well to other perfectly competitive resource markets. The demand for and supply of other resources yields the equilibrium resource price. Each resource buyer faces a perfectly elastic supply curve for the resource at its market determined price. And the resource price is the firm's MFC of that resource.

RESOURCE MARKET EQUILIBRIUM: THE CASE OF IMPERFECT COMPETITION

The existence of monopoly power in product markets has its counterpart in resource markets. It is known as **monopsony power,** and it refers to the *power of resource buyers* to influence resource prices.

Although, technically, *monopsony* means a single buyer, monopsony power is present any time a buyer faces an upward-sloping supply curve for a resource. Just as we have been using the term *monopoly power* to refer to instances in which product sellers face downward-sloping demand curves for their products—encompassing, thereby, more kinds of market structures than just monopoly—so *monopsony power* refers to more than simply the presence of a single buyer. Generally, monopsony power arises in those instances where individual buyers constitute a large enough share of the market that their presence or absence matters to the total.

As a consequence of the existence of monopsony power, the firm is no longer able to purchase all of the resource that it wants to at some market-determined price. On the contrary, the firm with monopsony power must raise its price offer to attract larger quantities of the resource. That firm, acting on its own, helps to determine the resource price, unlike the perfectly competitive buyer.

In the case of a firm facing an upward-sloping supply curve for a resource, the price it pays

Figure 22.6
Resource supply curve and marginal factor cost (MFC) curve of firm with monopsony power

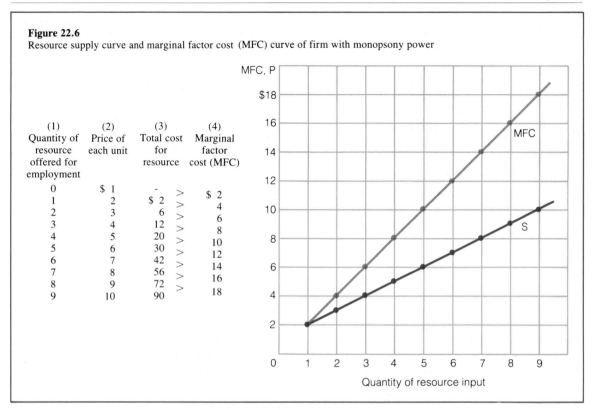

(1) Quantity of resource offered for employment	(2) Price of each unit	(3) Total cost for resource	(4) Marginal factor cost (MFC)
0	$ 1	-	
1	2	$ 2	$ 2
2	3	6	4
3	4	12	6
4	5	20	8
5	6	30	10
6	7	42	12
7	8	56	14
8	9	72	16
9	10	90	18

for the resource and its marginal factor cost (MFC) are not the same. With the exception of the first unit purchased, the price of the resource will always be less than MFC. This is illustrated in Figure 22.6.

Consider first the table that accompanies Figure 22.6. The first unit costs the firm $2, which yields a total cost for the resource of $2. Since the total cost for the resource was zero when none were purchased, the change in total cost with the purchase of the first unit—the MFC for the first unit—is $2, the same as the price. With the purchase of two units, the firm must pay $3 for *each* unit per time period for a total resource cost of $6. Since total cost with the addition of the second unit went from $2 to $6, the MFC for the second unit is $4 —$1 in excess of the price of the resource. The reason MFC exceeds price is straightforward. The $3 must be paid not only for the second unit, but for the first unit as well. Thus, the rise in the total cost of the resource from $2 to $6 can be decom-

posed into two parts: (1) the $3 cost that must be incurred to attract the second unit, and (2) the *additional* $1 that must be paid for the first unit. This is the meaning of an upward-sloping supply curve. One unit can be had for $2 when the firm is only buying one unit; for the firm purchasing two units, *each* unit will cost the firm $3.

With the addition of the third unit and the fact that $4 each much be paid for all three units, the total cost of the resource rises from $6 to $12; the MFC for the third unit is $6, $2 more than price.

All the rest of the numbers presented in the table accompanying Figure 22.6 are calculated in the same manner as described above. *The fact that the firm must pay a uniform price for all units purchased and that higher prices must be paid to attract additional resources means that, except for the first unit purchased, MFC exceeds the resource price.* This is shown graphically in Figure 22.6.

Monopsony equilibrium

Figure 22.7 shows the equilibrium of a firm that possesses monopsony power. As before, the firm adopting a profit-maximizing strategy will carry its employment of the resource to the point where MFC equals MRP. (Can you explain why some other level of resource use would be inconsistent with profit maximization?) This occurs, in Figure 22.7, at point A implying an equilibrium level of resource use of R_0 units. And how much must the firm pay to attract R_0 units? This is given by point B on the supply curve of the resource. The firm can attract R_0 units of the resource at a price of P_R^* for each unit.

Some consequences for resource use of monopsony power in resource markets

Less-than-optimum levels of resource use. You will have noticed from Figure 22.7 that the resource in question is paid less than its MRP— that is, less than the contribution of the last unit of the resource to the firm's total revenue. The reason for this is clear. MFC exceeds the price of the resource, and the profit-maximizing behavior of the firm would dictate a level of employment of the resource where MFC equals

MRP. That level of employment is forthcoming at a price of P_R^*—less than MRP.

Assume for now that the firm under consideration sells its product under conditions of perfect competition. The MRP curve in Figure 22.7 would then be the same as the resource's VMP. From the point of view of society, the (opportunity) cost of using one more unit of the resource is given by its price. However, the value to society of the additional output produced with the aid of the extra resource input is given by the VMP. It is clear from Figure 22.7 that, since VMP exceeds the resource price paid, society would benefit from the allocation of more units of the resource to the production of this firm's product. Indeed, if MRP equals VMP, the optimum allocation would not occur until the firm employed R_1 units—point C in Figure 22.7—an outcome that would also imply a higher payment to the resource.

Monopsonistic "exploitation" of the factor input. Earlier we discussed the monopolistic exploitation of a resource that arose because the firm had monopoly power—that is, it faced a downward-sloping demand curve for its product. There is also another sense in which the resource can be exploited. It is referred to as the **monopsonistic exploitation of the resource.** It

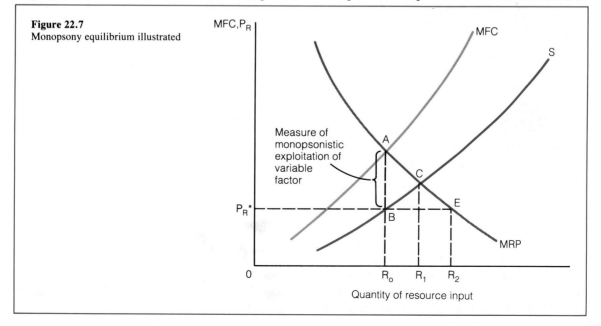

Figure 22.7
Monopsony equilibrium illustrated

arises when the firm faces an upward-sloping supply curve for the resource—that is, when the firm possesses monopsony power. The degree of resource exploitation is given by the difference between the price that is paid to the resource and the MRP of the resource. In Figure 22.7, it is given at the firm's profit-maximizing equilibrium position by the distance AB. When the price that is paid for the resource is less than the marginal contribution of the resource to the firm's revenue, the resource is said to be subject to monopsonistic exploitation.

As we noted in our discussion of monopolistic exploitation, we do not use the term *exploitation* in a pejorative sense. The term *monopsonistic exploitation* has only one meaning—the fact that MRP exceeds the price paid to the resource means that "too little" of the factor is devoted to the production of the good in question.

The presence of monopsony power results in an undefined demand curve for the resources. In our study of product markets, we were able to define rather clearly the supply curve of the product under conditions of perfect competition. For the individual, purely competitive firm, product supply was given as that portion of the MC curve lying above AVC; the market supply curve consisted of the horizontal sum of the individual firm supply curves. On the other hand, when monopoly power was present, we could no longer associate the firm's supply curve with its MC curve; the supply curve was undefined.

Analogously, it is quite simple to define the market demand curve for a resource under conditions of perfect competition in resource markets. The individual firm's demand curve for the resource is given by its MRP curve; the market demand curve is obtained by "adding up" the individual firm demand curves. But when monopsony power is present, it is no longer possible to associate the firm's demand curve for the resource with its MRP curve.

By definition, a demand curve shows how much the buyer is able and willing to purchase at given prices. However, if the monopsonist's MRP curve were its demand curve, it would try to purchase R_2 units at a price of P_R^* in Figure 22.7 rather than R_0 units—the quantity that maximizes its profits. The fact that it hires only R_0 at the price P_R^* means that the MRP curve is *not* the monopsonist's demand curve for the resource; the monopsonist's demand curve is undefined.

Monopolistic exploitation and monopsonistic exploitation combined

Figure 22.8 illustrates a situation in which both monopoly power and monopsony power are present. Monopoly power being present is reflected in the fact that the VMP curve lies above the MRP curve. Monopsony power being present is reflected in the fact that the MFC curve lies above the supply curve.

The profit-maximizing level of resource use, R_0, is given by point B—the point of intersection of MRP and MFC. Each unit of the resource is paid a price equal to P_R^*. The resource is being exploited as a result of the presence of both monopoly and monopsony power. The monopolistic exploitation of the resource is given by the distance AB; the monopsonistic exploitation of the resource is given by the distance BC. The exploitation of the resource alerts us to the fact that, from the point of view of society, "too little" of the resource is being employed by the firm. Optimum employment would occur only at point E—the point of intersection of VMP and S, implying a level of resource use equal to R^* and a resource price of P_R^1. Can you explain why?

THE FIRM'S DEMAND FOR SEVERAL VARIABLE FACTORS OF PRODUCTION: THE LONG RUN

In the long run all factors of production are variable. Under these circumstances, the firm must make a decision as to what constitutes the optimum combination of resources.

As we have emphasized repeatedly, the firm desires to maximize its profits. In order to accomplish this, the firm wants to obtain that mix of

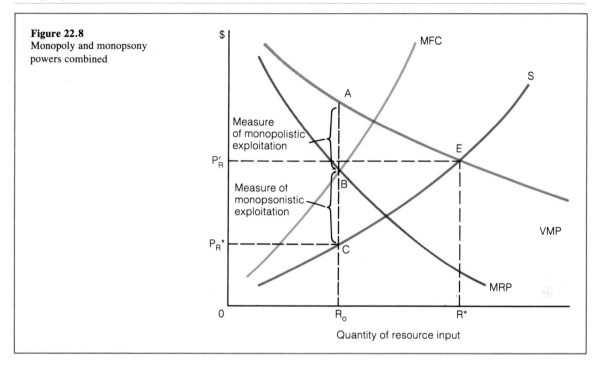

Figure 22.8
Monopoly and monopsony
powers combined

resources that will minimize its total costs for any given level of production. For this reason, *the optimum combination of resources is referred to as the least-cost combination.*

The least-cost rule

The problem confronting the firm is analogous to the problem confronting the individual consumer who wishes to maximize his/her utility. The consumer faces an income constraint. The consumer then must decide how to allocate that income across all possible combinations of purchases so as to yield the greatest utility possible. The utility-maximizing rule we developed earlier stated: Allocate a given income in such a way that the marginal utility per dollar spent is the same for all goods.

A very similar rule can be developed for a firm facing the choice of several factor input combinations. It is known as the **least-cost rule:** *To get the lowest total cost for any given level of production, the profit-maximizing firm will hire factors of production in amounts until the marginal physical product per dollar spent is equal for each factor of production.* In other words,

$$\frac{\text{MPP of factor A}}{P_A} = \frac{\text{MPP of factor B}}{P_B}$$

$$= \frac{\text{MPP of factor C}}{P_C}.$$

The least-cost rule can be illustrated quite simply. Most goods and services can be produced using factors of production in different proportions. We can produce automobiles using a lot of labor and relatively little capital—using, that is, labor-intensive methods. Or we could use much less labor and a relatively large quantity of sophisticated assembly-line pieces of capital— that is, capital-intensive methods. The question is, What techniques of production should the firm use? The least-cost rule provides us with the answer.

Suppose the **MPP** of labor and capital both are 100 units per week. That is, holding the quantity of capital fixed, adding one more employee will raise total product by 100 units. Or, holding the quantity of labor fixed, adding one more piece of capital equipment will raise total output by 100 units. Since 100 additional units of output will add the same to the firm's total revenue whether an additional employee is hired or an additional piece of equipment is purchased, the firm will make its decision on the basis of the prices of the factors of production. Obviously, if the price of labor services is less than the price of capital services, it will "pay" the firm to add an additional employee. Although its total revenue will rise by the same amount whether one more worker or one more piece of equipment is added, its total costs rise by less when one more worker is added.

Consider another example. The MPP of factor A is twice the MPP of factor B. If the price of factor A is more than twice the price of factor B, it will be profitable for the firm to add more of B in preference to A.

The long-run cost curve for a firm, discussed in Chapter 18, was derived, implicitly, using the above least-cost rule. Thus, in order for the firm to discover the least cost at each point on its ATC curve—that is, to discover the lowest total cost for each level of production—it should follow the above least-cost rule.

The substitution rule

An important corollary to the least-cost rule can now be stated. If the price of one factor—say, factor A—rises while other factor prices remain fixed, it will generally pay the profit-maximizing firm to substitute away from the now-dearer factor in favor of the relatively lower-priced factors of production. The reason for this is clear. The firm will be able to reduce its total costs for any given level of output by taking on additional factors of production (other than A) whose MPP per dollar spent is less than that of A and by reducing its employment of A. It should continue to substitute until the MPP of each factor per dollar spent is the same. This will ultimately occur because the increased employment of some other factor, for given amounts of A, will reduce its MPP, while the reduced employment of A, given the employment level of the other factor, raises A's MPP.

SUMMARY

1. The demand for any resource is a reflection of the demand for the goods and services whose production involves the use of that resource as an input; the demand for the resource is a *"derived"* demand.

2. The *marginal revenue product* (MRP) of a variable factor of production can be defined as the variable factor's *marginal physical product* (MPP) times marginal revenue (MR):

$$MRP = MPP \times MR.$$

The law of diminishing returns and the pattern of movement of MR govern the change in MRP as additional units of the variable factor are employed.

3. The MRP curve represents the firm's demand curve for the variable input. It shows how much the profit-maximizing firm is willing and able to purchase at each price for the variable factor. The horizontal sum of the individual firm MRP curves for each variable factor gives us the market demand curve for that variable factor.

4. The *value marginal product* (VMP) of a variable factor is defined as the variable factor's marginal physical product (MPP) times the product price (P):

$$VMP = MPP \times P.$$

5. VMP and MRP will be equal to each other only when the firm sells its output in a purely competitive market; there MR equals P. In imperfectly competitive markets, VMP will exceed MRP because P exceeds MR.

6. Monopoly power in product markets results in less-than-optimum levels of resource use; also, it causes the variable factor of production to be "exploited."

7. Although the market supply curve for any resource generally slopes upward to the right, firms buying resources under conditions of pure competition face a resource supply curve that is perfectly elastic—i.e., horizontal—at the market-determined price for the resource. When *monopsony power* is present, the firm faces an

upward-sloping supply curve for the resource in question.

8. When monopsony power is present, the MFC of a resource will, except for the first unit purchased, exceed the price of the resource.

9. Monopsony power results in less-than-optimum levels of resource use; it causes the variable factor of production to be "exploited." Also, it results in an undefined demand curve for the resource.

10. The *optimum* or *least-cost combination of resources* is obtained when factors of production are hired in amounts such that the marginal physical product per dollar spent is the same for each factor:

$$\frac{\text{MPP of factor A}}{P_A} = \frac{\text{MPP of factor B}}{P_B}$$
$$= \frac{\text{MPP of factor C}}{P_C}.$$

An important corollary of the least-cost rule is the *substitution rule*.

CONCEPTS FOR REVIEW

"Derived" demand

Marginal factor cost (MFC)

Marginal revenue product (MRP)

Value marginal product (VMP)

Monopoly power and less-than-optimal levels of resource use

"Produced" resources

Reproducible versus exhaustible resources

Work-leisure choice (income and substitution effects)

"Backward-bending" supply curve of labor

Monopsony power

Monopolistic exploitation

Monopsonistic exploitation

Least-cost (or optimum) combination of resources

Substitution rule

QUESTIONS FOR DISCUSSION

(Those marked with an asterisk (*) are more difficult.)

1. Explain, using words instead of graphs or equations, the difference between MRP and VMP. Why is the distinction important?

*2. "All firms in a purely competitive industry are merged into a single monopoly firm. Assuming that the monopoly firm keeps all the previously competitive plants open and uses the same techniques of production, and assuming that the demand for the industry's output has not changed, profits will be maximized by hiring the same number of variable factors of production as before." Do you agree or disagree? Explain carefully. (*Hint:* Is it true that the MRP curve of the monopolist can be found by adding up horizontally the MRP curves of the individual purely competitive producers?)

3. Explain why the profit-maximizing rule MC = MR can be restated as MFC = MRP? Is it true that the profit-maximizing rule for a firm selling its product under conditions of pure competition, MC = P, can be restated as MFC = VMP?

4. "The least-cost rule developed in this chapter is analogous to the equimarginal principle developed in Chapter 17." Do you agree or disagree? Explain, illustrating how they are or are not analogous.

5. How does a purely competitive resource market equilibrium differ from a monopsony market equilibrium? Be explicit. Which of the two market types is more efficient? Why?

6. Using nontechnical language, explain why the supply curve of labor could be backward bending.

Chapter 23

Labor income: Its determination and distribution

Traditionally, factors of production were classified under the headings of *land, labor,* and *capital.* Corresponding to these three categories, it was common to identify three "functional" categories of income—*wages* to labor, *rent* to land, and *interest* to capital. In feudal-based aristocratic societies, these distinctions were important politically and sociologically. Land was owned by the old aristocracy—the rentier class; capital (material assets other than land) was largely owned by the rising bourgeois class; and labor power was the only factor of production "owned" by the working class.

In today's modern industrial societies, at least, the political and sociological relevance of distinctions based on ownership of particular resources is questionable. Meaningful class lines are not easily drawn on the basis of such factor ownership. Is it meaningful to lump together as part of the working class below-the-poverty-line domestic workers and million-dollar-a-year corporate presidents? Is it meaningful to lump together as part of the aristocracy impoverished southern black landowners and wealthy western farmers? Is it meaningful to lump together as "owners of capital" the Rockefeller family trust and the Teamster's union pension fund?

Even the idea that factor incomes are "functionally" distinct does not stand up to careful analysis. Land, defined as the "natural productive powers of the soil," is different from capital and labor. *But the realization of the soil's actual powers is, in large measure, the result of human effort using capital goods.* The clearing of wasteland, the draining of marshes, and the reclamation of land (e.g., from the ocean) involve the use of capital resources, human power, and human ingenuity; the extraction of natural resources requires the use of both capital and labor; and even the maintenance of the fertility of land involves the use of human effort and capital. In other words, the production of output and income is the result of the cooperative efforts of land, labor, and capital. These factors are functionally distinct only in a very limited sense.

It is not possible to distinguish clearly between labor and capital either. Workers do not sell "raw labor power" alone; they sell their effort, their training, their education, their ingenuity, and their experience. Many of these attributes are part of their capital—"human capital"—just as the tools they work with are part of their capital. There is little functional difference between the act of sacrifice involved in workers adding to their human capital and the sacrifice of the current use of resources to equip workers with tools (capital).

To focus on the differences in the productive functions of land, labor, and capital, therefore, is not only difficult, it is unjustifiable, since production and income are the result of the cooperative efforts of resources working together. However, *it is useful to distinguish among land, labor, and capital as sources of productive services. And it is useful to look upon the incomes received by the various factors of production as the market-determined returns to the productive services provided by each source.*

In this chapter we will focus our attention on **labor income**—the return to labor for the productive services it provides. In Chapter 24 we will examine in detail the incomes earned by land and capital for the productive services they provide.

We open this chapter with a discussion of wage determination under perfect competition. In the first section we examine in detail the principles underlying competitive wage determination and the forces responsible for wage differences under pure competition. We address there the principles that govern the distribution of income between labor on the one hand, and the other sources of productive services—land and capital—on the other; those principles are known as the **marginal productivity theory of distribution.**

The second section of the chapter is devoted to an examination of wage determination in the face of monopoly power in product markets and monopsony power in labor markets. Most of our attention there is focused on labor unions and their role in the wage determination process.

WAGE DETERMINATION UNDER PERFECT COMPETITION

Throughout this chapter and elsewhere in the book we use the term *wage rate* to refer to the price people receive for the "sale" of their labor services for a given time period. We talk in terms of an hourly wage rate, or a weekly wage rate, or an annual wage rate—the latter two categories being commonly referred to as "salaries." Moreover, the "wage rate" designation means *gross pay* (i.e., employee compensation) for the relevant time period, including employee fringe benefits, payments for social security, and income taxes withheld.

It is important to note that the wage rate relevant to buyers and sellers is the *real* wage rate—the money wage rate corrected for changes in product prices. Workers are interested in what their money wages will buy. If the prices of the goods and services they buy double, a doubling of the money wage will leave them in the same *real* position as before. We will ignore the complications introduced by changes in the *general level of prices* by assuming an unchanged price level. But it is good practice to keep in mind that it is the real wage that counts. Somewhat differently, what interests employers is their real wage costs—the money wage they pay corrected for changes in the prices of *their* individual products.

We begin by focusing on wage determination under perfectly competitive labor market conditions. In this setting, no single buyer or seller has the power to influence the wage rate. There are a large number of individual buyers and sellers. Each worker "sells" his or her services for a given market-determined price. Workers who refuse to offer their services at the "going wage," hoping to receive more, will not be able to get work. They have no incentive to offer their services for less than the market-determined wage since they can get all the work they want at that wage.

Individual buyers must also pay the "going wage." If they offer less, they will not get any employees offering their services; the employees can do better elsewhere. They have no incentive

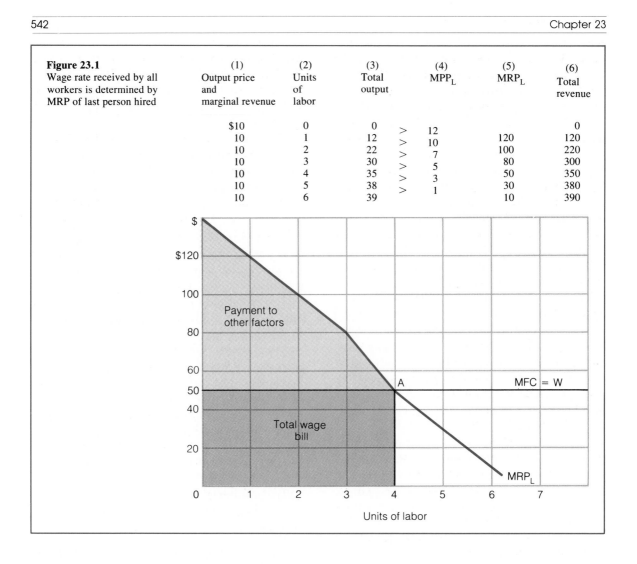

Figure 23.1
Wage rate received by all workers is determined by MRP of last person hired

(1) Output price and marginal revenue	(2) Units of labor	(3) Total output		(4) MPP_L	(5) MRP_L	(6) Total revenue
$10	0	0				0
			>	12		
10	1	12			120	120
			>	10		
10	2	22			100	220
			>	7		
10	3	30			80	300
			>	5		
10	4	35			50	350
			>	3		
10	5	38			30	380
			>	1		
10	6	39			10	390

to offer more since they can get all the workers they want at the market-determined wage.

Of course, not all labor markets are perfectly competitive. But the assumption of perfect competition is a useful starting point. Moreover, even if perfect competition were a realistic assumption, a uniform (real) wage rate would not exist for all workers. Not all workers are equally trained, equally experienced, etc. At a minimum, several perfectly competitive labor markets corresponding to the different "grades" of labor would exist. To keep things manageable, let us concentrate our attention first on the determination of the real wage for a single grade of worker.

The determination of the real wage rate for a single "grade" of labor

We will examine here the case of a labor market where all the people offering their services are *exactly alike* in all respects—in talent, skill, education, effort, etc. In this instance, competition will cause worker wage rates to be exactly equal. Employers would have no reason to pay more to one worker than to another; no single worker would have any basis for asking for more than the others receive.

To discover precisely what wage rate they *all* receive, consider Figure 23.1. There we show the demand curve for labor on the part of one of the firms that hires this "grade" of labor. The demand curve for labor, you will recall, is the firm's marginal revenue product (MRP) curve for labor. To keep things simple, let's assume that the firm represented in Figure 23.1 sells its output in a perfectly competitive market; in this instance, the MR it receives is the same as the price of the product.

How much would the firm be willing to pay for the first worker? Well, hiring the first worker raises output from zero to 12 units. Those 12 units can be sold for $10 a piece. Hiring the first worker raises the firm's total revenue by $120. The firm would be willing to pay *up to* $120 for the first worker. This is true as long as only one worker is hired.

What about two workers? Because of diminishing marginal productivity, the MRP of the second worker is only $100. The firm would never be willing to pay more than $100 to acquire the second worker. However, since the first and second workers are exactly alike in all respects, they must get exactly the same wage. But which wage will the firm be willing to pay? The MRP of the first person? The MRP of the second person? The answer should be clear. *The firm would never be willing to pay more for the services of the extra worker than the contribution of the extra worker to the firm's revenues.* The firm would, therefore, be willing to pay up to $100 for the second worker; and since both workers are exactly the same, the firm would be willing to pay up to $100 each for both workers.

Note. This may seem a bit strange. After all, isn't the first worker more productive than the second? *No.* They are both exactly the same. It is true that one person, working in cooperation with fixed amounts of the other factors of production, contributes $120 to the firm's revenues. But two workers combined produce a quantity of output sufficient to generate for the firm $220 in revenues. A second worker makes a marginal contribution of only $100, and that is all the firm is willing to pay to acquire the second. Since the first two workers are exactly the same, the firm is willing to pay for each only what it is willing to pay for the last worker hired.

The same is true for three workers. Since the MRP associated with the third worker is $80, the firm is willing to pay up to $80 to acquire the third. And it is willing to pay for all three workers only what it is willing to pay for the last worker hired.

We note from Figure 23.1 that the MFC of labor—the market-determined wage in this instance—is equal to $50. The firm adopting a profit-maximizing strategy would hire four units of labor, the quantity of labor that equates MRP and MFC. And note that all four workers receive $50 each, the MRP of the *last* worker hired.

Recalling our discussion in the previous chapter, we know how the wage rate was determined. It is the wage rate obtained at the point of intersection of the *market* demand curve for labor and the *market* supply curve of labor. Since the market demand curve for labor is nothing other than the sum of the MRP curves of all firms in the market, one very important conclusion becomes evident: *All workers in this market are paid the same wage rate; and since that wage rate is found at the point of intersection of the market supply and demand for labor (MRP_L), the wage rate paid is equal to the MRP of the last worker in this market.*

The marginal productivity theory of wages and distribution

We are now in a position to state two of the most celebrated theories in microeconomics—the **marginal productivity theory of wages** and the **marginal productivity theory of the distribution of income** among factors of production. First, the marginal productivity theory of wages.

To formalize the theory, we will assume that the labor market for any single "grade" of labor is perfectly competitive. We will also assume that all of the firms hiring the services of labor sell their products in perfectly competitive markets. This latter assumption means that P equals MR, implying, as you will recall from Chapter 22, that MRP equals VMP. Moreover, the fact that each firm can sell all it wants at the market-determined price for its output means that the downward slope of the MRP curve is the result of one fact alone—diminishing marginal productivity.

As demonstrated above, all workers in this market receive the same wage. That wage is equal to the MRP of the *last* worker hired. Since MR for each firm is constant (and equal to P), most economists express this equilibrium condition in a more simplified way: *All the people hired in this market receive a wage equal to the marginal product of the last person hired.* This is what is meant by the proposition that "labor is paid its marginal product under conditions of pure competition." The expression "paid its marginal product" means, more accurately, "paid the value of its marginal product," where it is understood that the marginal product that is important is the marginal product of the *last person hired.*

Now that we understand the marginal productivity theory of wage determination, it is fairly easy to explain the marginal productivity theory of income distribution. Study again the table that accompanies Figure 23.1. Given a wage rate of $50, the firm will hire four workers; the firm's **wage bill** (the number hired times the wage rate) comes to $200. But the output produced by four workers, cooperating with the other factors of production, yields the firm $350 of total revenue (35 units of output sell at a price of $10 each). The difference between the firm's total revenue and its total wage bill represents the income that is available to be distributed to the other factors of production. In this illustration, the excess amounts to $150.

Technically, this excess amount is nothing other than the excess of the MRP produced by the first person and all earlier persons up to the very last. To see this, look at column 5 of the table accompanying Figure 23.1. The MRP of the first person is $120; but the first person is paid only $50, meaning that the excess of $70 associated with the first person hired remains with the firm. In a similar way, the excess of $50 associated with the second person remains with the firm. Adding the excess associated with the first ($70) to that of the second ($50) to that of the third ($30) yields the total excess of $150. There is no excess associated with the fourth

worker. The MRP of the fourth worker equals the wage rate.

From this one can easily fashion the marginal productivity theory of distribution. The payment to labor is given by (the value of) the marginal product of the last unit of labor hired times the number of units hired. The excess of the value of the marginal product of the first person and all earlier persons up to the very last is available for distribution to the other factors.

The distribution of income between labor and the other factors can easily be shown diagrammatically. In Figure 23.1, the value of the product produced by this firm—$350—is given by the MRP of the first worker plus the MRP of the second plus the MRP of the third plus the MRP of the last worker. In other words, it is the total area under the MRP curve up to the fourth worker. The total wage bill is given by the heavily shaded rectangle—the wage rate times the number of units hired. The excess of the value of the product over the wage bill—the lightly shaded triangular area—represents the payment to the other factors of production.

Some generalizations. A number of important generalizations follow from the discussion above.

First, we saw in Figure 23.1 how, on the basis of the marginal productivity theory, it was possible to determine the distribution of income between this one grade of labor and the other factors of production for a single firm. Aggregating across firms yields the market demand curve for labor. The value of output produced by all the firms hiring this grade of labor is given by the area under the market demand curve up to the quantity hired. The total income paid to this grade of labor is given by the wage rate times the quantity hired. The excess of the value of output over the total wage bill—the remaining triangular area under the demand curve—represents the distribution to the other factors.

Just as we are able to calculate the wage for this grade of labor and the distribution of income between this grade and all other factors of production, we are able to do so for all grades of labor and all labor markets. In this fashion, the marginal productivity theory of distribution can be used to determine the division of our nation's income—national income—between labor and the other factors.

Second, the same principles operate in perfectly competitive markets to determine the payments to nonlabor factors of production. Up to this point, we have been holding all other factors constant and varying the quantity of labor hired. The law of diminishing marginal productivity holds, and from this one can show how wages are determined by the value of labor's marginal product. The same principles apply to the determination of the rewards to nonlabor factors of production.

Suppose there are only two factors of production—labor and land. Hold labor constant and vary the amount of land that is used in the production of some good. One could then easily construct a MRP curve for land; it would be downward sloping because the law of diminishing marginal productivity holds. The total rent payment to land would be determined by the "marginal product" of land. Diagrammatically, this payment would be represented, as in Figure 23.2, by the rectangular area FGHO; the remaining

triangular area, FGJ, represents the income payment to labor. Here land is paid (the value of) its marginal product. Its distributive share of output and that of labor are determined by their respective interdependent marginal products. (That is, the MP of any factor depends on the quantities of the other factors with which it works.) The marginal productivity theory is complete.

Third, we saw earlier that the excess of the MRP produced by the first worker and all earlier workers up to the last one was distributed to the other factors. Is this fair? Are the other factors—the owners of land and capital—"profiteering" at the expense of labor? No, at least not in the usual sense of the word.

The point that needs to be made is this: Output is produced with the aid of *all* the factors—land, labor, and capital. The MRP of labor is determined by varying the employment of labor holding the other factors constant. But the value of the output produced is not just the result of labor working alone; it is the result of the cooperative activities of land, labor, and capital.

The marginal productivity theory merely tells us that, under competitive conditions, labor is

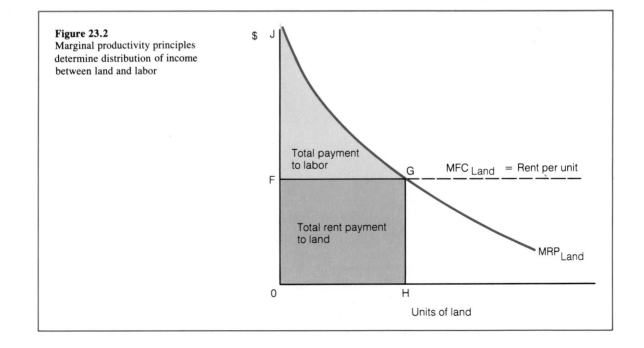

Figure 23.2
Marginal productivity principles determine distribution of income between land and labor

paid (the value of) its marginal product—by which is meant the value of the marginal product of the last worker hired. Labor is not in this instance "exploited" in some sense; there are no conspiracies here. To bring out the point more clearly, consider Figure 23.2 again. Would you argue that land was exploited because labor received the excess of the MRP of the first and all earlier units of land up to the last unit employed? If that were the case, we would be led to the strange conclusion that it is possible for all factors of production to simultaneously exploit one another.

Real wage differences in perfectly competitive labor markets

Imagine an economy in which *all* workers are identical in *all* respects, in which *all* jobs are identical in *all* respects, in which no single buyer or seller of labor services has the ability to influence the wages paid. Under those circumstances, each and every worker would be paid the *same* wage for their labor services. More explicitly, the point of intersection of the demand and sup-

ply curves of labor services would occur at the *same* wage rate in *all* the perfectly competitive labor markets.

To illustrate why this conclusion holds, consider Figure 23.3. There we show two different perfectly competitive markets for labor services. To keep matters simple we will assume that what makes them different is their geographical separation from one another. As a starting point, we will also assume a fixed supply of workers in each market; this is given by the vertical (perfectly inelastic) supply curves, S_A and S_B, in markets A and B, respectively.

We see from Figure 23.3 that the quantity of labor services available in *both* markets totals 260, *initially* distributed as follows: 100 in market A, 160 in market B. Given the demand for labor services in each market, this distribution gives rise to a *real* wage differential between the two markets. Equilibrium in market A yields an initial wage of W_1, which is higher than the initial equilibrium wage of W_2 in market B.

These real wage differences provide workers in market B with an incentive to shift their labor

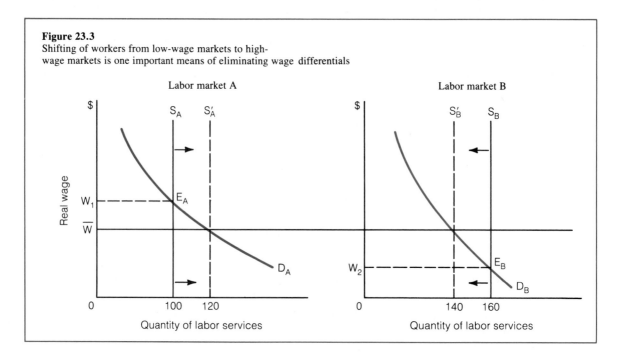

Figure 23.3
Shifting of workers from low-wage markets to high-wage markets is one important means of eliminating wage differentials

services from B to A. As workers shift from market B to market A, a narrowing of those wage differences will result. Specifically, the increased supply of labor services in market A will reduce real wages there; the reduced supply of labor services in market B will raise wages there. Assuming that these labor supply shifts occur *without cost*—an assumption that we will examine below—labor supply will continue to shift until real wages are completely equalized; the existence of the slightest real wage differential between the two markets will create incentives for workers to shift from markets where real wages are lower to those offering higher real wages.

Three points are worth emphasizing in this discussion. First, as noted before, the focus here is on *real* wages, not money wages. Huge discrepancies can exist in money wages with little or no discrepancies in real wages as long as money wage differences are compensated by corresponding cost-of-living differences. Much higher money wages prevail in labor markets in New York and Washington, D.C., than in small towns in the South and Midwest. But the cost of living is so much higher in New York and Washington that the real wage differences between these cities and many other parts of the country are much smaller. The labor supply shifts illustrated in Figure 23.3 resulted in the equalization of real wages, not necessarily money wages.

Second, in the discussion above, the real wage differences were eliminated because labor resources shifted from one market to the other. The same result could have been accomplished by the shift of firms—the buyers of labor services—from high real wage markets to markets with lower real wages. In terms of Figure 23.3, this could be illustrated by a leftward and downward shift of the demand for labor in market A and a corresponding rightward and upward shift of the demand for labor in market B as some firms shift out of market A to market B.

In the short run, labor is much more mobile than are most other factors of production. Therefore, it is reasonable to expect that the tendency toward real wage equality would be accomplished

by labor supply shifts. In the long run, it is not at all clear that capital is less mobile than labor. Firms can choose to relocate in the long run, though wage costs are only one consideration influencing their location decisions; proximity to the buyers for their products and proximity to suppliers of material inputs are also important, among other things. Nevertheless, there are some notable examples where wage costs have been important in determining the locational shift of industries. The shift of the textile industry from the Northeast to the Southeast after World War II illustrates the point well enough.

The shift of firms from high-wage markets to low-wage markets in those instances where wage costs are critically important might be explained as follows. The relevant real wage from the point of view of workers is their money wage divided by some *general* cost-of-living index. The real wage that is relevant from the point of view of employers is the money wage they pay divided by the prices of *their own individual products*. From the perspective of workers, there may be little difference in real wages between market A and B; nominal wages may differ substantially, but the cost-of-living differences just offset that difference. Workers would then have no incentive to move. However, from the perspective of employers, the lower nominal wages in one market could well imply much lower real wage costs if they shifted their location to that market; assuming that their other costs were not much different and given the prices they expect to receive for their output, lower money wages in one market could provide employers with a powerful incentive to relocate. Of course, if firms shift between markets where, from the point of view of workers, real wages were equal, this would change those real wages and induce labor supply shifts as well in the same direction. Can you illustrate this?

Finally, it is important, in terms of the illustration in Figure 23.3, to realize that all workers need not be mobile. A few movers are enough. As shown in Figure 23.3, the shift of 20 workers from market B to market A was sufficient to accomplish the equalization of the real wages.

Sources of wage differences under perfect competition

Now that it is clear what is required for a single uniform real wage to exist for all workers, it becomes equally clear how it is possible for wage differences among workers to exist—even in perfectly competitive labor markets. Workers are not alike in all respects; jobs are not alike in all respects; and the shift of labor resources from one market to another is not costless.

What we will do in this section is focus on these sources of wage differences, maintaining all the while the assumptions of perfect competition. In the next section, we will concentrate on yet other sources of differences in wages—i.e., those that arise because of labor market imperfections.

One source of real wage differences in perfectly competitive markets—all jobs are not alike

Even if workers were alike in all respects, the fact that all jobs are not alike is sufficient to explain *some* of the real wage differences we observe in everyday life. Jobs vary in terms of their attractiveness. Some are very unpleasant in the sense of being dirty, tiresome, strenuous, or of low social prestige; some involve a lot of training and education; some provide only irregular employment or seasonal layoff. It is frequently the case that higher wages have to be offered to coax more people to take these kinds of jobs.

The fact that all jobs are not all equally attractive is important to understanding the existence of wage differentials in our economy. Such differences are consistent with perfect competition. Indeed, many wage differentials can be explained simply in terms of the job choices people make—i.e., by the conditions of supply in the many and varied labor markets.

To illustrate the importance of labor supply conditions, consider Figure 23.4. We show there two perfectly competitive labor markets, one each for the two different occupations, A and B. It is generally agreed that occupation A is less attractive than B. Everything else the same, most workers would choose B. However, if 90 of the 100 available workers chose B and only 10 chose A, the wage differential would be huge. Given the demand for labor services in each market, the 10 workers choosing A would receive $12 per hour by comparison with the $1.20 per hour the other 90 workers would receive in B.

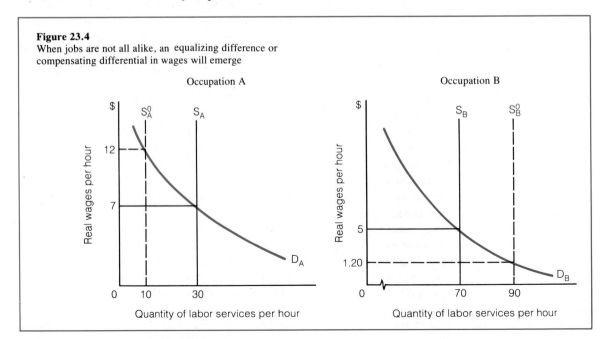

Figure 23.4
When jobs are not all alike, an equalizing difference or compensating differential in wages will emerge

Perhaps a wage differential of that magnitude would induce some workers out of occupation B into A. However, given that occupation B is more pleasant, it is doubtful that a sufficient number of people would shift to equalize real wages. Rather, *the shifting will cease at the point where the wage differential just compensates for the nonmoney differences between the jobs.* That wage differential is termed the **"equalizing difference"** or the **"compensating differential"**—a measure of the monetary value that people attach to the nonmoney differences between jobs. In Figure 23.4, we have assumed that the shifting will cease once the distribution of workers between A and B amounts to 30 and 70 workers, respectively. Although occupation A pays $7 per hour compared with $5 per hour in B, it constitutes an equilibrium position in the sense that a $2 per hour differential is insufficient to induce any further shifting from B to A. That $2 per hour differential represents the "equalizing difference."

The relative attractiveness of different jobs goes a long way toward explaining many of the wage differentials observed in our economy. Jobs that involve exposure to radioactive materials or other harsh chemicals frequently command very high wages compared with other jobs requiring comparable skills. Workers are generally paid more to work the "swing shift" from 4:00 P.M. to midnight, and even more to work the "graveyard shift" from midnight to 8:00 A.M. Jobs considered "dirty" or of low social prestige often pay relatively high wages, as do jobs that are mentally or physically strenuous. Indeed, conditions of supply go a long way toward explaining why many plumbers earn more than your college professors, and why nerve-wracked air controllers, who monitor and schedule traffic in and out of busy airports, are so highly paid. The fact that many white-collar clerical workers earn less than blue-collar workers is also partly a reflection of differences in conditions of supply. Even the extremely high earnings of doctors, lawyers, or chemists are partly a reflection of differences in supply—the pay difference being partly justified as a compensation for the educational costs incurred and the absence of pay during the years of training.

Of course, not all wage differences are explained by differences in these conditions of supply. That is, not all wage differentials are of the equalizing difference kind. But the conditions of supply are extremely important; as Figure 23.4 makes clear, such wage differentials are quite consistent with the assumption of perfect competition. The wage in each market is determined at the point of intersection of the demand for and supply of labor services; the absence of complete wage equality is the result of the refusal of enough people to shift out of the low-wage market to the higher-wage market.

Another source of real wage differences in perfectly competitive markets—all people are not alike

If all people were alike, all competitive wage differentials could be explained as an equalizing difference. But people are not all alike; the qualitative differences between real-world workers are substantial—differences that are important to understanding real wage differences in our economy.

The innate abilities of people are different. Some people are brighter than others; some are stronger; some people are more creative with their hands; some are more creative with their minds. People differ by training, experience, and levels and kinds of education. They also differ by color, sex, weight, age, and background. These quality differences give rise to what are called **nonequalizing differences** in wages.

The issue of quality differences among workers is highly controversial, and rightly so. Quality differences among workers enable employers to rank workers—from superior to inferior. In some instances, the criteria used to distinguish one worker from another can be justified by objective standards; in other instances, there is no legitimate basis for the criteria that are applied. Some jobs require that applicants hold advanced degrees—in engineering, in chemistry, in physics, in economics, etc. This is often legitimate since adequate job performance in some occupations is dependent on the job holder having advanced knowledge in these fields of inquiry. However, all too frequently (though much less so today than was true 20 years ago) preference is given to applicants who are white, males, young, and good looking—criteria that are unjustified in many instances, reflecting nothing more than the bigotry of those doing the hiring.

Whether legitimate to job performance or not, all criteria used in selecting employees serve to segregate workers into different categories of labor. It would be inaccurate to view each of these categories of labor as exclusive in the sense that workers within one group compete with each other for certain types of jobs, but do *not* compete for *other* kinds of jobs with *other* groups. It would be more accurate to view the groupings of labor in the following way: *Workers within any given group are closer substitutes for each other than they are with workers in other groups.*

In some instances groups will be *noncompeting.* Workers applying for janitorial positions are unlikely to compete with workers applying for college-level teaching positions. On the other hand, workers applying for jobs in mobile-home assembly plants are likely to be fairly close, though not necessarily perfect, substitutes for workers in auto assembly plants.

But even these distinctions are difficult to maintain under all circumstances. If wages for janitors became $150,000 a year, I might decide to quit teaching and direct my efforts toward fine-honing my floor-polishing skills. The point here is that the various groupings of workers are not frozen; the sizes of the groups can be, and often are, increased or decreased in response to the appropriate economic incentives. When the salaries paid to engineers rise relative to salaries in other occupations, this will frequently cause *some* college students to change their career choices in favor of engineering; some people who are now working may decide to quit to return to school to study engineering in an effort to acquire another job that holds out the promise of a higher income.

What is important to determining the numbers of people who will shift from one occupational grouping to another is people's responsiveness to changing wage differentials. This is measured by the *cross-price elasticity of supply*—the percent change in the quantity of labor services supplied in one occupation in response to a given percent change in the (relative) price of labor services in some other occupation.

Of course, in a society where some employers discriminate among workers on the basis of race,

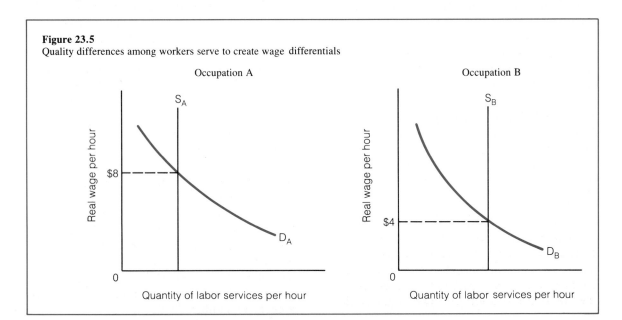

Figure 23.5
Quality differences among workers serve to create wage differentials

sex, age, etc., the mobility of some workers may be effectively blocked. The refusal of employers to consider certain "types" of workers keeps those who are discriminated against in lower-wage occupations.

The effects of quality differences among workers can be analyzed with the aid of Figure 23.5. As before, the conditions of supply become all important to determining real wage differentials among workers. To keep things simple, we will assume only two occupations. Occupation A has a requirement that only highly educated and highly trained people need apply; occupation B has only minimal educational and training requirements.

Given the demand and supply curves presented in Figure 23.5, it is clear that occupation A offers its workers a much higher wage than is offered to workers in occupation B. Whereas each worker in occupation A commands a wage of $8 per hour, workers in occupation B earn only $4 per hour.

Even if there were no restrictions on the movement of labor resources between occupations A and B, it is quite possible that little or no labor would shift from B to A, the result being that the $4 per hour wage differential would persist. Why? Because in order for workers in B to shift to A, they would have to acquire more training and education to qualify for jobs in the A category. The costs they would have to incur to make the shift could well be viewed as too high. If they retain their existing jobs, they would have to incur tuition or training costs as well as forego much of their leisure time; if they quit to return to school full-time, not only would they incur those educational expenses, they would also suffer another cost—foregone income. Of course, if the wage differential becomes high enough, the incentive to undertake those costs becomes stronger.

Figure 23.5 is useful for the analysis of other "quality" differences among workers—even those quality differences that are alleged to exist because of race, sex, weight, height, etc. Discrimination in labor markets based on these criteria often takes the form of occupational discrimina-

tion. One could think of occupation A as reserved for whites only, with blacks, whether highly educated or not, being forced to accept employment in category B. The large supply of workers in occupation B, relative to the demand for workers there, keeps black incomes depressed below those of whites. It is important to recognize here that white incomes are maintained at a higher level than otherwise because of this kind of racial discrimination. Were qualified blacks not blocked from moving to occupation A, the supply of labor services would increase in A, lowering the wage that would be paid to *all* workers in A. The counterpart of the movement of blacks from B to A would be higher wages paid to those remaining in B. Can you illustrate this?

With respect to the issue of quality differences among workers, a number of points need emphasis. Employers discriminate among workers on the basis of all sorts of worker characteristics. Some of the criteria that are applied are quite legitimate, some are questionable, and some are downright unjustifiable. But whether legitimate or not, all of the criteria used have the effect of establishing different supply curves of labor services across occupations.

The demand and supply curves of labor services in any given occupation establish its real wage. Combining all labor markets, it is reasonable to expect the emergence of real wage differentials even under conditions of perfect competition. An *equilibrium pattern* of real wage differentials will emerge when the incentive or opportunities for shifting from one market to another are eliminated.

The real wage effects of occupational discrimination based on race, sex, etc., can be studied relatively easily with the aid of diagrams like those presented in Figure 23.5. One can still retain the assumption of perfect competition in the analysis of discriminatory practices in the sense that no single buyer or seller has the power to influence wages. However, one important assumption characteristic of perfectly competitive labor markets is missing—the assumption that workers are free to move from one labor market category to another.

Of course, occupational discrimination constitutes only one dimension of discrimination in our economic system. Discrimination against blacks also often takes the form of segregated and inferior primary and secondary schools, which has the effect of limiting their future potential development. For women, discrimination in education often takes the form of pressures, both subtle and overt, to pursue different curricula from those of males and to limit their educational aspirations. As a result, the nature and extent of the human capital women acquire in our educational system is generally different from that of their male counterparts. As is true of blacks, this compounds the problems women face in the labor market. Not only must they overcome the prejudices that exist in the marketplace, but often the nature and extent of their education are not of the sorts that meet the requirements of existing high-paying job vacancies.

General equilibrium in perfectly competitive labor markets

As we saw earlier, a single uniform real wage will emerge under conditions of perfect competition only when all workers are all alike in all respects and when all jobs are identical. *Wage differentials will emerge under conditions of perfect competition as a result of both differences among jobs and differences among workers. In both of these instances, the conditions of supply become all-important to the determination of the overall equilibrium pattern of wage differentials.*

The equilibrium pattern of wage differentials that emerge under perfect competition will reflect both **equalizing differences**—wage differentials that compensate for nonmoney differences among jobs—and **nonequalizing differences**—wage differentials that reflect the qualitative differences among people.

IMPERFECTLY COMPETITIVE LABOR MARKETS

Although the perfectly competitive model discussed above does have relevance to the explana-

tion of the existence of a wide variety of wage differentials in the U.S. economy, it tells only part of the story. Indeed, in the minds of some observers, labor market imperfections play a more important role both in the determination of observed real wage differentials among workers and in the explanation of other labor market phenomena. It is one of the purposes of this section to explain how the real wages of workers are influenced by labor market imperfections—imperfections that can and do arise as a consequence of buyers or sellers, or both, exercising the market power they possess.

There is a second purpose to be served by our discussion here—namely, to explore some of the complex issues of unionism in the United States. The complex nature of the discussion is not difficult to discover. Unions are concerned with more than just the real wages of their members. They are concerned as well with how many of their members can get employment at the union wage scale; they are concerned with job security; they are concerned with job safety, job health, medical insurance programs, and pension plans.

We undertake our study of labor market imperfections in steps. We begin with a very brief history of unionism in the United States. This is followed by an equally brief discussion of union goals and the methods used to accomplish those goals. Finally, we will examine in a more formal way some of the economic consequences of both *monopsony power* and *monopoly power* in labor markets.

Brief history of unionism in the United States

Although it is difficult to date precisely the beginnings of the union movement in the United States, the factors that gave rise to the growth of unionism are clearer. Union activity was virtually nonexistent during the colonial and revolutionary periods. Most nonagricultural products were produced during those times in small retail establishments called **shops.** Products were largely custom-made to meet the specifications of individual customers; apprentices worked alongside journeymen (i.e., skilled craftsmen) and masters (i.e., the journeymen owners); and, most important, apprentices, journeymen, and masters alike all shared, to some extent, a common interest—that of maintaining the standards of the craft and product prices.

After the Revolutionary War, factories producing standardized products for the national market began to replace the small retail establishments. Put simply, the craft shops were unable to produce commodities as cheaply as the factories. As a consequence, increasing numbers of journeymen and their apprentices were forced to work in factories. However, as more and more factories were established and because of the limited sizes of the markets, competition among producers became very intense. Accordingly, producers focused on holding down their production costs as the means of staying competitive. Holding down production costs usually meant holding down wages, demanding longer hours for the same pay, and hiring cheaper labor. Many producers tried to increase the number of apprentices for each journeyman hired; eventually, they tried to abolish the apprenticeship system altogether, replacing apprentices with women and children who would work for less. Under the circumstances, conditions were ripe for the craftsmen to join together "to protect their rights."

The early unions: The Revolutionary War to the Great Depression

The earliest unions were not intended to be permanent organizations. They were formed as a consequence of specific disputes with employers over such things as reduced wages or the replacement of apprentices with women and children. Once the dispute was resolved, the "union" disappeared.

However, beginning around the 1790s, "permanent" unions began to make their appearance in the United States.[1] In 1792, some shoemakers in Philadelphia set up a union (the Federal Society of Journeymen Cordwainers) on a permanent

---

[1] The word *permanent* is put in quotes to emphasize the intentions of the union organizers rather than the realization of their intentions. Indeed, most early "permanent" unions disappeared soon after they were organized.

basis to counter what they saw as repeated employer attempts to reduce their wages and to reduce the status of their craft through the hiring of ever-greater numbers of low-paid, unskilled workers. Journeymen and their apprentices in other cities and other trades encountered many of the same threats to their status and wages. So they too pursued the union route. Accordingly, labor "societies" were established by printers, carpenters, cabinetmakers, and masons in several cities, such as New York, Baltimore, Pittsburgh, and Boston.

The objectives of most of these early unions were similar. Members would pledge not to work for employers who paid less than the union-determined wage or who hired a disproportionate number of unskilled workers. In addition, many of these unions tried to establish **closed shops**—work places where only union members were hired. If employers did not accede to the union's demands, what then? The union would threaten to **strike** or to **boycott** the firm's products.

Employers strongly resisted union demands. Wherever unions would grow up, an employers' organization would spring up whose primary objective was to smash the unions. To assist them, employers turned to the courts. In those early days at the turn of the 19th century, the employers generally got a very sympathetic hearing. What the courts did was strip the unions of their effective powers by declaring as illegal any of the actions unions might undertake in support of their cause—strikes, boycotts, closed shops—on the grounds that those actions injured others—namely, employers and nonunion members. In a few instances, the courts even ruled that labor unions were "illegal criminal conspiracies." Is it any wonder, then, that so many unions folded in this environment?

Despite these difficulties, the union movement did not come to a complete halt in America. It certainly suffered setbacks in the face of unfriendly court rulings. However, the economic factors that gave birth to the unions remained; and so, therefore, did the incentives to organize.

Gradually, in the early years of the 19th century, the courts shifted their opinions somewhat.

It would be incorrect to suggest that the courts turned prolabor. However, it is clear that they softened their strong antiunion rulings. But that changed legal environment merely caused employers and their associations to step up their union-breaking efforts. And the antiunion methods they employed were extensive.

One of the most frequent methods used to break unions was the employment of **strikebreakers** (called **scabs** by union people) to replace workers on strike. Often the strikebreakers were recent immigrants desperate for work. A second method used by employers was the **yellow-dog contract.** Before they were hired, workers would have to sign a contract agreeing not to join or support a union. If workers violated the contract, they could be both discharged and sued.

A third method used was the **blacklist.** Those thought to be connected with unions had their names put on a list. The lists were circulated among employers with the understanding that no one appearing on the list would be hired.

As a means of policing yellow-dog contracts and of updating their blacklists, many employers would use labor spies to infiltrate the unions. When deemed necessary, employers would return to the courts to try to obtain injunctions enjoining strikers from engaging in "illegal" and "dangerous" activities.

This hostile, antiunion climate persisted until the mid-1930s, which, understandably accounts for why unions up until then were so weak and why membership in unions was so small (accounting for less than 10 percent of the labor force, often substantially less than 10 percent). However, prior to the heyday of unionism in the United States—the mid-1930s until after World War II—there were two significant developments in the latter third of the 19th century. The first was the formation of the Knights of Labor in 1869, followed by the organization of the American Federation of Labor in 1886.

The Knights of Labor. The American labor movement took a giant step forward in 1869 with the formation of the **Noble and Holy Order of the Knights of Labor.** Under the visionary leadership of Terence Powderly, the Knights intended their organization to embrace *all* skilled and un-

skilled workers, to make labor a unified force for social reform. They aimed to end child labor, to replace the existing system of employers and wages with worker-owned cooperatives, and to nationalize the railway and telegraph industries.

The objectives of the Knights of Labor were radical. At first their social program had little appeal to workers whose immediate concerns were the bread-and-butter issues of higher wages and improved working conditions. However, as a consequence of the Knights' successes at striking the railroads at a time when other unions were failing miserably, workers flocked in droves to the Noble Order. In the single year from July 1, 1885, to June 30, 1886, the Knights' membership exploded from about 10,000 workers to over 700,000.

These successes of the Knights were short-lived. The worker-owned cooperatives set up with union funds were so poorly planned and so badly operated that they quickly collapsed. Because their social reform program was deemed so radical, the Knights met stronger employer resistance than ever. As soon as they became less effective in their use of the strike weapon, workers abandoned the Knights of Labor, their vague and idealistic goals being of little interest to them in the first place.

The American Federation of Labor. The second and more enduring development occurred at the peak of the Knights' power in 1886. Meeting in Columbus, Ohio, the representatives of several national labor union organizations established a national federation called the **American Federation of Labor** (AFL), under the leadership of the colorful, cigar-chomping Samuel Gompers.

Basically, there were two reasons the AFL survived where the Knights of Labor and other federations failed. First, the AFL was concerned with only one thing—improving wages and working conditions for its members. It did not have grand, utopian objectives or a program for social reform. Second, Gompers and his associates decided to stay out of politics. They would attempt to use their influence to gather votes to "reward their friends and punish their enemies." But they would not, unlike labor union organizations in Europe and elsewhere, form labor-oriented political parties. This characteristic persists to this day. True, the Democratic party has generally enjoyed more labor support than the Republican party. But that has not always been the case.

Although the AFL endured, it remained a weak federation until the mid-1930s. There were several reasons for this. First, employer resistance to unions persisted unabated over this entire period. Indeed, employers stepped up their resistance during the 1920s, successfully thwarting union growth. Second, the courts renewed their antiunion stance by prosecuting unions under recently enacted antitrust laws. The courts argued that workers joining together to raise wages served to restrain trade in the same way as collusive oligopolists seeking higher prices for their products. Finally, because the AFL represented *craft* union workers only, it failed to capitalize on the growth opportunities that would have been possible had it appealed to the rapidly increasing numbers of unskilled industrial workers.

The heyday of unionism: 1932–1947

Between 1932 and 1947, union membership exploded, rising from about 3 million to over 15 million. Two factors were largely responsible for this change: (1) the passage of new laws by the Congress that were decidedly prolabor, and (2) the rise of industrial unions. Let us look at each of these developments.

The prolabor laws of the 1930s. The first real legal break given to the unions occurred with passage of the **Norris-LaGuardia Act** in 1932 that outlawed yellow-dog contracts and that made it much more difficult for employers to obtain injunctions preventing union activities. However, the really dramatic change occurred in 1935. In that year the Congress passed the **National Labor Relations Act** (also known as **Wagner Act**)—the Magna Carta of American unionism. In that act, (1) workers were guaranteed the right to organize and to engage in collective bargaining without the "interference, restraint, or coercion of employers"; (2) employers were

forbidden to engage in "unfair labor practices" such as blacklisting of prounion workers and refusing to bargain with representatives of the employees; and (3) the **National Labor Relations Board** (NLRB) was established to police unfair labor practices and to resolve disputes among competing unions.

The growth of industrial unionism. The growth of the industrial unions was, perhaps, inevitable. As a consequence of technological advances and greater specialization in production, clear-cut distinctions between craft jurisdictions became increasingly difficult and, more important, new types of jobs grew up for which there were no craft unions. At first, the AFL steadfastly resisted attempts to organize workers along industrial lines, even if that meant leaving millions of workers without union representation. The craft organizations feared that their members would not be able to win sizable concessions from employers if *all* workers in the industry were organized, because wage increases for all workers would be more costly than for just craft workers. In addition, the craft unions were afraid of being swallowed up by the industrial workers, an outcome that would dilute their strength at the bargaining table and in union matters generally.

Because of these animosities, John L. Lewis, then president of the United Mine Workers, led the industrial unionists away from the AFL to form the **Congress of Industrial Organizations** (CIO) in 1936. The results were spectacular as millions of workers in previously unorganized mass-production industries such as autos, steel, and aerospace joined up.

It was not until 1955 that the AFL and CIO buried the hatchet and merged as a single federation, the AFL–CIO, which persists to this day.

Unionism since World War II

After World War II, and largely as a consequence of the willingness of the labor unions to flex their new-found muscles in the form of very damaging strikes, the tide of public opinion began to turn against organized labor. There was a growing sentiment that the unions were becoming too powerful, that there was a need for a Wagner-type of act to check unfair labor practices on the part of the unions.

The Taft-Hartley Act of 1947. The result was passage of the **Taft-Hartley Act** in 1947 (formally known as the **Labor Management Relations Act of 1947**) amending the Wagner Act. Among its provisions, the Taft-Hartley Act prohibited closed shops in industries engaged in interstate commerce. **Union shops**—work places where nonunion people can be employed as long as they join the union within 30 days—were permitted under the Taft-Hartley Act. However, one very controversial provision in the act gives states the right to deny contracts to firms whose union requires workers to join up, a provision that sometimes effectively outlawed union shops as well. This provision is still being hotly debated. (As of this writing, though, it appears that the Reagan Administration looks with disfavor on its repeal.) The Taft-Hartley Act further outlawed several "unfair" union labor practices, such as (1) coercing workers to join unions, (2) failing to bargain with employers in "good faith," (3) **jurisdictional strikes** (strikes aimed at settling disputes between competing unions over who has jurisdiction over what on the job), and (4) demanding that employers pay for "nonaccomplished" services. (The last provision was intended to combat the practice of **featherbedding,** wherein unions insisted that unnecessary workers be hired as a condition for obtaining necessary workers.)

The Taft-Hartley Act also included a number of provisions designed to stop misuses of union funds by union bosses. It required that unions give a 60-day notice before striking against the terms of a new contract. And in instances where the President determines that strikes "imperil the national health or safety," it gives the attorney general the right to seek a court injunction to order an 80-day "cooling off" period.

The Landrum-Griffin Act. The second significant piece of labor legislation was passed in 1959 despite the strong opposition of labor. Known as the **Landrum-Griffin Act** (formally the **Labor-Management Reporting and Disclosure Act**), this piece of legislation was intended to increase restraints on union officials, to strengthen the misuses-of-funds provisions of the Taft-Hartley Act, and to reduce corruption within certain unions. Toward these ends, this act limited the amount of money union officials could "borrow" from union treasuries. It made embezzlement of union funds a federal offense. And it required regularly scheduled elections of union officials by secret ballot. How successful the act has been in limiting corruption is hotly debated.

Slowdown in growth of union membership after World War II. After World War II, the growth of union membership slowed sharply. The absolute number of union members has increased, but as a percentage of nonagricultural employment, union membership has declined. Union members represented over 33 percent of nonagricultural employment in 1947; they represent only about 23 percent today.

Part of the reason for the slower growth of unions has to do with the change in public attitudes as reflected in such laws as the Taft-Hartley Act and the Landrum-Griffin Act. A more important factor probably has to do with the fact that employment in heavy industry (where union membership tends to be most heavily concentrated) has declined relative to employment elsewhere (especially the service sector and government).

Union goals and union methods

The essence of union-management relations is captured in the **collective bargaining process.** The outcome of the collective bargaining process is a contract that spells out the wages and working conditions agreed to by employers and union members. Most such contracts run for a time period of from one to three years. Once a contract negotiated by the union's leaders has been ratified by the union's members, it becomes a legally binding document.

Negotiations on each new contract generally begin several months in advance of the expiration date of an existing agreement. This is done to try to avert work stoppages that could result simply because there was no new contract to replace the one that expires.

At the beginning of the negotiating process, both sides frequently make contract demands that they each know are excessive. They do this partly to show that they are out to get all they can and partly to discover just how far the other side can be pushed. However, at some point, both sides have to get serious, because looming over the entire process is the threat of a work stoppage. Indeed, it is the threat of a work stoppage and the fact that work stoppages are costly to both sides that, except for conflict over very basic issues, force each side to be "reasonable."

The question is, What factors influence the negotiators and therefore the ultimate contract? In truth, the factors are many and complex. At the risk of oversimplifying, let us emphasize four: (I leave it to the reader to indicate how these various forces are likely to affect the outcome.)

1. *Financial status of employers and workers:* the past and expected future profits of the employer; the financial condition of the union (as a measure of its ability to withstand a protracted work stoppage); the financial resources (e.g., unemployment insurance and other government assistance) available to workers if they strike.
2. *Ease of passing on costs:* the ease with which increased wage costs can be passed on to buyers in the form of higher prices.
3. *Pattern bargaining:* the terms the union has been able to get from *other employers;* or the terms *other unions* have been able to get in other industries. (In many instances, a union contract with one firm in an industry establishes a pattern to be followed in negotiations with other firms in the same industry. Sometimes the package negotiated in one industry (e.g., steel) becomes the pattern to be followed by unions in other industries (e.g., autos). Pattern bargaining is the labor-market counterpart of price leadership).
4. *Government intervention:* Will the government intervene to ensure that any work stoppages are brief, and how will this affect the outcome?

Union goals and contract issues. Almost invariably unions try to incorporate in their contracts with employers rules and conditions that reflect their goals. Some idea of just how complex contract talks can get can be seen by consideration of the following issues.

Pay. There are a great many issues here. Should workers be paid by the hour or by the amount they produce? Unions generally prefer the former because it ensures that all workers are paid equally. Employers often prefer the latter—called **piece work**—because it provides workers with greater incentives to produce more. Sometimes unions will agree to some kind of modified piece work system in exchange for concessions elsewhere. However, unions try to ensure that workers continue to get paid some amount if machinery breaks down or if necessary materials are unavailable.

Employers sometimes like **profit sharing** because it gives workers more incentive to be productive. Unions are often skeptical because it makes workers incomes dependent on the decisions of owners and managers, whom union officials do not control.

There is also the issue of **wage differences** among union workers who perform different jobs and have different levels of experience.

Overtime pay involves more than just the overtime rate. There is also a question of how often workers will be called upon to work overtime. Unions frequently prefer that more workers be hired to work the extra hours as this increases their power and influence. Employers often prefer overtime to hiring more workers because, although the overtime rate is higher, they frequently do not have to pay more in the form of fringe benefits.

Fringe benefits—health plans and pension benefits—are desired by union members because of their insurance features. Moreover, unlike wages, most fringe benefits are not subject to taxes by government.

Finally there is the matter of **cost-of-living adjustment** (COLA) clauses.

Working conditions. Will there be a five-day workweek at 8 or 7½ hours per day? What about a four-day workweek? What about 10 days on and 6 days off? What about "flex time"—an arrangement whereby employees work out with employers more flexible hours, such as 6 A.M. to 2 P.M. instead of 9 A.M. to 5 P.M.? What about the health and safety of the work place? These are all questions that must be addressed.

Job security. Job security has always been a matter of considerable concern to labor. Often unions seem willing to grant concessions elsewhere in the contract for increases in security. The **seniority system** was established to grant the greatest job security to those employed the longest. The system can, of course, be abused by those with the most seniority. But it also prevents older workers from being arbitrarily replaced with younger, low-paid workers.

Work rules are also aimed at providing workers with greater job security. True, many work rules are designed to protect workers from such things as speeding up the assembly line. However, work rules are often used to ensure that the same production methods are used over the life of the contract—to ensure, that is, that workers are not replaced by machines, or that new labor-saving techniques are not introduced.

Settling disputes. Procedures must be worked out in advance for handling problems that inevitably arise. These procedures are often called **grievance procedures.** Most grievance procedures in most labor contracts follow the time-honored tradition of letting the shop steward try to first resolve problems that arise; if the shop steward is not successful, the problems are turned over to a grievance committee composed of union and company officials; and if that group is not successful, the problems are turned over to an arbitrator—a third (and hopefully impartial) party for settlement.

Economic effects of imperfect labor market conditions

We now turn to an examination of some of the economic consequences introduced by the presence of labor market imperfections. Specifically, we will study the effects caused by the presence of market power on the buyer's side—so-called **monopsony power**—and by the presence of monopoly power—labor union power—on the seller's side.

The exercise of monopsony power. Let us focus first on the consequences of market power in the hands of the *buyers* of labor services. To keep things simple, we will assume for now that the supply side of the market for labor services is competitive. There are a large number of indi-

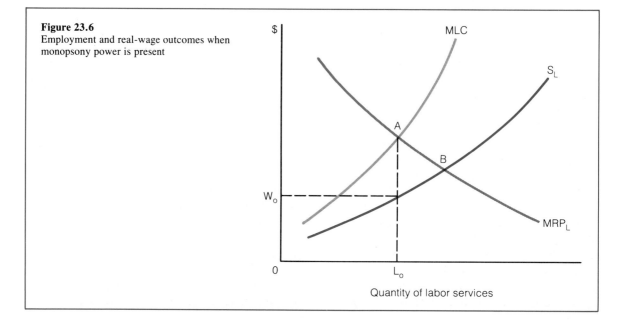

Figure 23.6
Employment and real-wage outcomes when monopsony power is present

vidual sellers of labor services. Each seller of labor services is so small relative to the market total that he/she is unable to influence the wage received for his/her labor services. Additionally, we will assume that workers have no choice but to sell their labor services to a single buyer—a monopsonist.

Figure 23.6 illustrates the employment and real wage outcomes under the circumstances just described. Because of our lengthy discussion of monopsony power in Chapter 22, we can be brief.

The monopsonist confronts an upward-sloping supply curve of labor services—the market supply curve. Because the monopsonist must pay higher and higher wages to attract additional labor resources, and because all workers are paid a uniform wage, the marginal cost of labor resources will generally exceed the wage that is paid. Thus, the marginal cost of labor services (MLC) curve lies above the supply curve.

The monopsonist adopting a profit-maximizing strategy will hire labor up to the point where MLC equals MRP_L. In Figure 23.6, this equilibrium position is attained at the employment level L_0.

The equilibrium wage paid to all L_0 units of labor can be read off from the supply curve. L_0 units of labor will be forthcoming at a wage equal to W_0 for each.

Had the market been perfectly competitive and characterized by the same demand curve for labor services (MRP_L) as in Figure 23.6, equilibrium would have occurred at point B—implying *both* a higher level of employment and higher real wages for workers.

By comparison with the outcomes that emerge in perfectly competitive labor markets, monopsony results in lower real wages and lower levels of employment, *ceteris paribus*.

Importance of monopsony power. One rarely confronts monopsony power in its pure form— only one buyer. True, there are single-company towns characterized, as their description implies, by a single employer. But such markets are few and far between. There have been instances in which several employers have banded together to bargain with labor, the "association" becoming, in effect, a pure monopsonist. Such associa-

tions, as noted before, were common during the early days of the labor union movement. They were formed both to crush the unions and to counter their bargaining power, a point we will examine formally below.

Much more important are labor markets characterized by the presence of a few "large" buyers—a labor market structure that is sometimes referred to as an **oligopsony.** How successful an oligopsony is in keeping wages depressed below their competitive levels is difficult to say. In markets where a few oligopsonists are present alongside a relatively large number of small employers, the competitive forces may be strong enough to force the oligopsonists to pay near-competitive wages. Of course, if a large enough group of employers collude—either overtly or covertly—the wage that would prevail might be much closer to its monopsony level.

In examining labor markets, it is important to realize that the exercise of monopsony power in any single market will be conditioned by forces in labor markets elsewhere. Indeed, if the single-company town employer pays wages dramatically below what workers elsewhere are receiving, that employer risks losing its labor services to those other markets.

Before passing on to the analysis of power on the sellers' side of the labor market, it is worth noting one extreme form of monopsony power— the "reserve clause" in baseball player contracts.

Prior to 1976, virtually all major league baseball club owners required their players to sign contracts containing a "reserve clause" that *(a)* gave owners exclusive rights over each player's labor services, and *(b)* denied players the right to sign contracts with anyone else until released (e.g., sold) by their existing owners. Even at the end of a contract, owners had exclusive negotiating rights with their players. That is, at the end of a contract, players were not free to negotiate with other club owners unless released.

In 1976, the "free agent" system began. Under certain circumstances, players were free to negotiate with other clubs. The effect on player salaries—particularly, the salaries of the superstars— was dramatic. A doubling, tripling, even quin-

tupling (or more) of many player's salaries occurred overnight, which served as testimony to
how severely depressed players' salaries had been
as a consequence of the monopsony power of
each owner.

The owners argued that the reserve clause was
essential to the preservation of competition *between teams*. Without the reserve clause, cities
with the largest gate receipts would be able to
"buy the World Series" by bidding away the best
talent from other teams; the game of baseball
would be ruined. Whether this argument is nothing more than a smoke screen designed to mask
the fact that it is in the owners' interests to pay
less for superior ballplayers than they are worth
is hotly debated. The players' argument in favor
of the free agent system should be apparent. As
many of you know well, controversy over the
free agent system was the source of the baseball
players strike during the 1981 season.

Consider another example of the possible exercise of monopsony power. It is sometimes alleged
that hospitals in a given geographical region band
together to keep down nurses' wages. Because
of attachments to their families, and because they
are often not the sole breadwinners in their fami-

lies, nurses have a hard time moving to alternative locations in search of higher wages.

**The exercise of monopoly power in labor
markets.** The counterpart of power on the buyers' side of the market is power on the sellers'
side. Generally, power on the sellers' side arises
because workers are organized into some sort
of union. It is the union acting on behalf of its
members that gives workers power in dealing
with employers.

Unions attempt to secure for their members
more than just high wages, narrowly defined.
They negotiate with employers over working conditions, fringe benefits, and employment security,
as well as over wages. For purposes of illustration, we will focus our attention here on the role
of unions in influencing the real wages of union
members. This focus need not be overly narrow,
however, since the other benefits unions secure
for their members can, to some extent, be translated into real wage equivalents. Real wages *per
hour worked* are somewhat less than they could
be because of paid sick leave, paid holidays, improved health insurance, etc. Workers are frequently willing to work for less per hour if they
are provided some guarantee that their jobs are

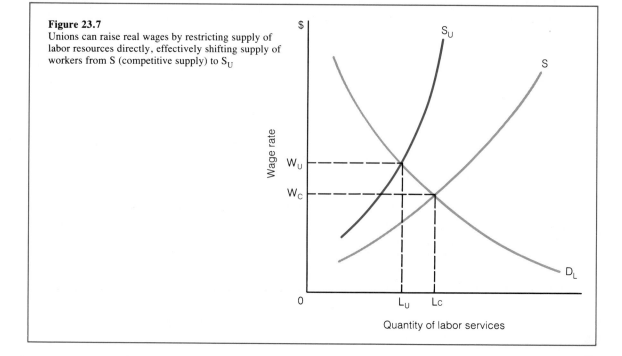

Figure 23.7
Unions can raise real wages by restricting supply of
labor resources directly, effectively shifting supply of
workers from S (competitive supply) to S_U

secure. They may soften their wage demands in return for safer and more pleasant working conditions. These other aspects of employment can be captured in our discussion here of how unions influence real wages.

> Basically, unions attempt to secure higher real wages for their workers either by restricting—directly or indirectly—the supply of workers to employers, or by raising—directly or indirectly—the employers' demand curves for workers, or both.

Restricting the supply of workers. Figure 23.7 illustrates the effects of labor supply restrictions on workers' real wages. In the absence of any restrictions, the competitive supply of labor to this market would be given by the curve labeled S; under competitive conditions, workers would be paid the real wage W_C. Enter the union, which, by one method or another, successfully restricts the supply of workers to S_U. The effects on the level of employment and the real wages of those who are union members is apparent. The level of employment falls to L_U and real wages rise to W_U.

There are many methods or tactics available to unions to restrict supply. Lobbying for the enactment and strict enforcement of immigration laws is one common tactic. Additionally, some unions levy high membership fees on new entrants, or they insist that new members serve inordinately long apprenticeships at low pay before being admitted as full members. Sometimes unions impose severe restrictions on union size and insist that employers hire only union members. (Many people have alleged that this tactic was used in the past by the American Medical Association (AMA). The AMA limited the number of schools it would license and the number of students each school could train.)

These methods serve to restrict the supply of labor resources directly. But unions can also restrict the supply of workers indirectly by forcing employers to pay a high standard wage to all those who are hired. The high standard wage must be in excess of the competitively determined wage. Otherwise there would be little advantage to workers in joining the union. This case of indirect supply restriction is illustrated in Figure 23.8.

The competitive wage in Figure 23.8 is given by W_C. Here we assume the absence of market power on either side of the market. Now suppose the sellers' side becomes organized into a union. The union insists upon the wage W_U for all members that are hired. The marginal labor cost to

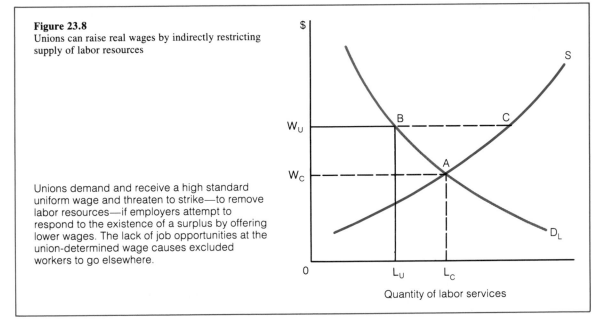

Figure 23.8
Unions can raise real wages by indirectly restricting supply of labor resources

Unions demand and receive a high standard uniform wage and threaten to strike—to remove labor resources—if employers attempt to respond to the existence of a surplus by offering lower wages. The lack of job opportunities at the union-determined wage causes excluded workers to go elsewhere.

Quantity of labor services

employers hiring in this market is W_U. They can hire all the workers they want at this uniform union-determined wage. Adopting a profit-maximizing strategy, employers would hire workers up to the point where MRP_L equals W_U. The level of employment under these conditions would equal L_U.

Isn't there a problem here? Given the competitive supply curve S, there is an excess supply of workers at the wage W_U. Wouldn't the existence of this labor surplus force down wages to the competitive level?

As a general proposition, the answer to this question is *no*. Normally, the excess supply of workers amounting the BC would force down the wage to W_C under competitive conditions. But these are not competitive conditions, and any attempt on the part of employers to lower wages below the union standard could lead to a strike—an outcome where the union withdraws all workers from the market until employers accede to union demands.

Of course, if the union wage standard is set too high, employers might risk a strike from the union and hire so-called scab (i.e., nonunion) workers as a means of smashing the union. How successful employers can be at this will depend heavily on how many workers are willing to offer their services at wages below the union standard (i.e., the excess of supply of labor at the union standard) and on how many are willing to cross strikers' picket lines. The higher the union standard, the greater the chance of employer success.

Presumably, the union will be sensitive enough to these pressures not to set its standard too high. Once that "correct" standard is discovered, what happens to those workers who, under competitive conditions, would be willing to work for less? They drift elsewhere. The lack of job opportunities at the union standard forces them out of this labor market. In this manner, the union successfully (and indirectly) restricts supply.

Let us examine a bit more closely the factors that enter into the union determination of the "correct" wage standard. The union might have considerable power in establishing the wage standard, but it is almost always the case that the number of persons hired at that standard will be determined by the producers. At a very high wage standard, relatively few workers will be hired. True, those who get the jobs at the very high wage rate will earn relatively high incomes, but not very many union people will be so fortunate. If that is what the union wants—i.e., if the union wants to reward "the few"—then the "correct" standard is a very high wage rate.

However, if the union wants to realize some other objective, such as achieving the greatest *total* income possible for its members, this would suggest quite a different wage standard. Recalling the relationship between the price elasticity of demand and total expenditures, the union should strive for the wage standard that corresponds to the point on the demand curve for labor that is unit price elastic. The reason for this is straightforward. If the price elasticity of demand—i.e., the wage elasticity—exceeds one, a reduced wage rate will induce producers to increase their *total* spending for labor; if the wage elasticity is less than one, a wage increase will cause total expenditures for labor to increase. Only at a wage elasticity equal to unity will total spending on labor (or total income earned by labor) be at its maximum.

Alternatively, if the union wants to achieve the highest level of employment for its members, it should seek a wage standard equal to the perfectly competitive wage rate. Only at the competitive wage rate will there be "full employment" in this labor market.

Expanding the demand for workers. Unions also frequently attempt to expand the demand for their members as a means of raising real wages. Sometimes unions will work with management to improve worker productivity. Given the definition of MRP, higher productivity levels cause an upward shift in the demand curve for labor, which enables the union to apply a somewhat higher wage standard. Or the union may help the industry to advertise its products—which, if successful, raises the demand curve for the industry's output and the demand curve for the labor resources used in its production. Alternatively, the union may attempt to lobby the administration and the Congress for tariffs or quotas against foreign produced goods; by diverting demand away from foreign toward domestic goods, tariffs and quotas have the effect of raising the demand for labor in affected industries.

These methods raise the demand curve for labor services indirectly. Sometimes unions use methods to increase the demand for labor directly. **Featherbedding** is, perhaps, the best known kind of tactic used. Generally, featherbedding is a practice whereby unions attempt to keep union-member employment at levels above what they would otherwise be. Sometimes unions specify the *number of workers* that must be hired on a particular project, even though employers would normally hire less. If the employers refuse to go along with the unions, they might not get any workers. Sometimes union rules specify that, in those instances when nonunion musicians are hired, employers must hire union musicians on a standby basis. Some printer union contracts specify that, where newspapers receive copy already completely set, union members must be hired to reset it.

Of course, many of these jobs are completely superfluous, and such featherbedding practices are frequently resented by employers and the public alike. Nevertheless, they persist. How successful such tactics are in raising real wages, however, is a debatable point. In the estimation of some observers, such practices contributed to the death of a number of newspapers and to the decline of railroads, outcomes that could hardly inure to the benefit of the unions involved.

Labor market imperfections and efficiency losses. When either monopoly *or* monopsony power is present in labor markets (or any other resource markets, for that matter), an efficiency loss results. To determine the efficiency loss we can proceed as we did in our study of product markets to show why perfectly competitive labor markets are efficient and why, in contrast, imperfectly competitive labor markets lead to an inefficient allocation of resources.

Consider a perfectly competitive labor market. The demand for labor is given by the MRP curve for labor. Since the marginal revenue that accrues

to the employers from the sale of their products enters into the determination of MRP, the demand for labor is a derived demand—derived, ultimately, from the demand for the products produced. Go one step further and assume that producers sell their products in perfectly competitive markets. Under those circumstances, P equals MR. Therefore, *just as the price of the product reflects the marginal benefit society attaches to extra units, so the MRP of labor measures the marginal benefit that society attaches to an extra unit of labor being employed in this market.*

Now consider the supply side of the labor market. The differences among jobs and people generally will establish a pattern of labor supplies across labor markets. *The labor supply curve in any individual labor market—the number of units of labor services willingly offered at various wage rates—measures the marginal cost to society of additional units of labor services in this market.*

Equilibrium that occurs at the point of intersection of the demand for and supply of labor services, is an efficient equilibrium. At that point, the marginal benefit to society of the use of the equilibrium quantity of labor services equals the marginal cost to society of employing that quantity.

This competitive equilibrium position, E_C, and its meaning are illustrated in Figure 23.9. Contrast this result with the ones that emerge when either monopoly power or monopsony power are present. The monopsonist will hire a smaller quantity of labor services and pay less per unit than under competitive conditions. Monopsony equilibrium is given by point E_M. (Although not shown here, imagine that the marginal labor cost curve *of the monopsonist* intersects the MRP curve directly above the point E_M, so that E_M is a profit-maximizing equilibrium position for the monopsonist.) There is an efficiency loss here. As is apparent, fewer workers are employed in this market than would be dictated by consideration of the marginal benefits and marginal costs to society; the undersupply here means an oversupply of workers elsewhere.

In the face of monopoly power, on the other

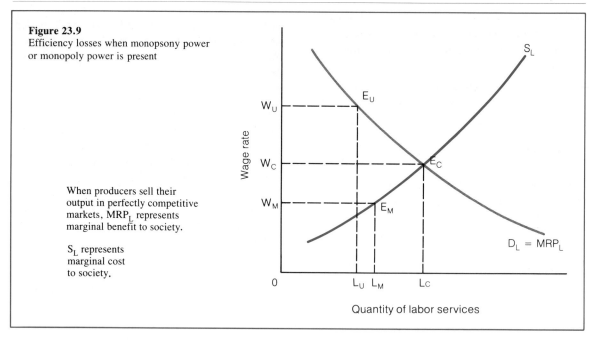

Figure 23.9
Efficiency losses when monopsony power
or monopoly power is present

When producers sell their
output in perfectly competitive
markets, MRP_L represents
marginal benefit to society.

S_L represents
marginal cost
to society.

hand, such as might be represented by a union of workers that insists upon a high wage standard, the union "equilibrium" might be represented at the position E_U. Here again, there is an efficiency loss. Too few workers in this market means too many elsewhere. (In Figure 23.9, L_U is less than L_M. This need not be the case. The quantity hired by the monopsonist will depend on where the marginal labor cost to the monopsonist equals MRP; L_U will depend on the magnitude of the union wage standard.)

While the presence of monopsony power *or* monopoly power will generate outcomes that are less efficient than under competition, when *both* monopsony power and monopoly power exist, the outcomes need not be less efficient. This remarkable conclusion is illustrated below.

Bilateral monopoly. When power exists on both sides of the market, we have a situation known as **bilateral monopoly.** One of the problems we encounter in the study of this kind of market is that the outcomes for wages and the level of employment are theoretically indeterminant. To see this, consider Figure 23.9 again. The union will be pushing for a wage equal to

W_U. If it gets it, that will result in an employment level of L_U. The monopsonist, on the other hand, will be pushing for a wage equal to W_M and a level of employment of L_M. There is no way to theoretically determine how these two extreme positions will be resolved. *The outcome will depend on the relative bargaining power of the two sides.* It cannot be determined by reference to the demand and supply curves (or the imaginary marginal cost of labor curve from the point of view of the monopsonist).

Many factors will influence the relative bargaining position of the two sides. If the union represents only a small minority of the workers in a geographical area, the outcome may be closer to that desired by the monopsonist since, at some point, the monopsonist may be able to go outside the union to satisfy its labor services needs. On the other hand, if the union represents the majority of workers and is in a financially strong position compared with the firm with which it is negotiating, the outcome is likely to be nearer the union standard. Of course, if the company is financially weak, too high a union wage standard could force it out of business. This could result in an outcome much closer to the monopsony solution. To insist on the union standard could destroy all the jobs for union members—hardly a constructive outcome.

One very interesting implication of bilateral monopoly is that we could observe an outcome that is much closer to the purely competitive result. That is, whereas the existence of *either* monopoly power or monopsony power alone will yield an outcome quite different from perfect competition, the presence of monopoly power on *both* sides of the market could result in an outcome much closer to the perfectly competitive solution.

This is one of the essential characteristics of what economists have come to call **countervailing power.** The idea is that, when those with monopsony power must sit across the negotiating table from those with monopoly power (e.g., a union), neither group is able to fully capitalize on its market power since each encounters countervailing power from the other side. The result is that the labor market outcome is closer to the perfectly competitive outcome than would otherwise be the case.

To illustrate, consider Figure 23.10, which depicts the classic bilateral monopoly problem. The union solution would imply a wage-employment outcome given by W_U and L_U. The monopsony solution would imply a wage-employment outcome given by W_M and L_M.

Generally, the union and the monopsonist will reach agreement on the wage rate somewhere between W_M and W_U. What wage will be agreed upon precisely cannot be determined theoretically since it depends on the relative bargaining strengths of the two parties.

Suppose they finally reach agreement on the wage rate W_0. Once the wage rate is determined, it is fairly easy to determine the level of employment. The union is willing to offer as much labor (up to the limit of its membership) as employers

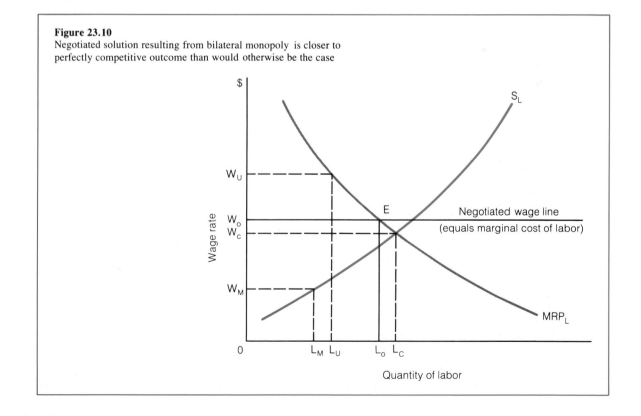

Figure 23.10
Negotiated solution resulting from bilateral monopoly is closer to perfectly competitive outcome than would otherwise be the case

want *at* the agreed-upon wage. The supply curve of labor facing the monopsony firm is no longer upward sloping. It is perfectly elastic (i.e., horizontal) at the negotiated wage. This means that the negotiated wage becomes the marginal cost of labor. The first, second, or last worker hired adds the same to the monopsonist's total costs. The profit-maximizing level of employment for the monopsonist facing a constant marginal cost of labor—the negotiated wage—occurs at the intersection of the negotiated wage line and the MRP_L curve.

We see from Figure 23.10 that the bilateral monopoly solution leads to a wage-employment combination given by W_0 and L_0, outcomes that are closer to the perfectly competitive outcomes, W_C and L_C. Indeed, had the negotiated wage been set at the point corresponding to the intersection of MRP_L and S_L, we would have seen wage and employment outcomes identical to the perfectly competitive solution. Of course, the negotiated wage could have been closer to either the monopoly or monopsony extremes. In such cases, we would have ended up with outcomes farther away from the perfectly competitive solution, but still closer to the competitive outcomes than otherwise.

The minimum wage

The federal government currently requires employers to pay workers a **minimum wage** of $3.35 per hour; many municipalities have established their own minimum wage standards, frequently at levels well in excess of the federal standard. The establishment of minimum wage standards is highly controversial. The reason such standards are enacted is clear. In the eyes of the government enacting such wage standards, workers *should* receive a wage that is sufficiently high to permit them to live decently.

We may all agree with this social objective (even if we do not know exactly what is meant by a decent standard of living). But most economists think the minimum wage is a rather poor tool for accomplishing that objective. Sure, the government can impose wage standards. But the government cannot compel employers to hire all the workers that might be forthcoming at that standard. Indeed, profit-maximizing producers will hire workers only up to the point where the MRP_L equals the minimum wage. It is frequently the case that the number hired will be less than the number of people who are willing to offer their services at the governmentally imposed standard.

Figure 23.11 illustrates this possibility. We show there a perfectly competitive market. In the absence of a minimum wage, perfect competition will yield an employment-wage combination of W_C and L_C that is found at the point of intersection of the demand for and supply of labor. If the minimum wage is set at $\overline{W}$, the results are clear. Employers will hire only L_1 workers; those workers who receive employment will experience an increase in their incomes but, at the minimum wage, unemployed labor resources remain—some workers cannot get jobs in this market even if they were willing to work for less.

What happens to those workers who are unable to find jobs at the mandated minimum wage? It depends. First, if there are other labor markets that do not have a wage minimum or a wage minimum as high as in this market, the effect will be to cause the unemployed workers here to spill over into those other markets, depressing wages there. The net outcome may be approximately the same level of overall employment as in the absence of a minimum wage, but there is an efficiency loss. Can you explain the nature of the efficiency loss?

On the other hand, if the market in question is the overall U.S. labor market and the minimum wage under consideration is the federal standard, those labor resources remain unemployed. There are no other markets into which these resources can "spill over." This leaves welfare, the underground economy, or street activities as the only viable alternatives for these unemployed resources.

SUMMARY

1. In a perfectly competitive market the equilibrium wage rate is obtained at the point

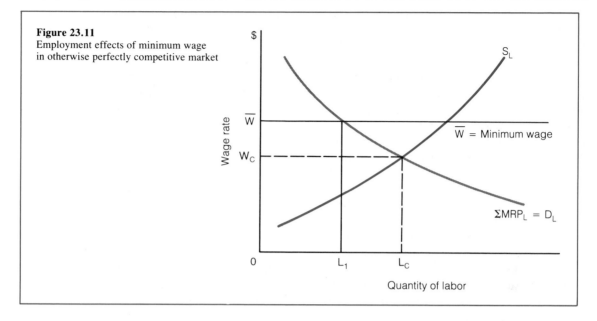

Figure 23.11
Employment effects of minimum wage
in otherwise perfectly competitive market

of intersection of the market demand curve for labor and the market supply curve for labor. Since the market demand curve for labor is nothing other than the sum of the *marginal revenue product* (**MRP**) curves of all firms in the market, the wage rate that is paid to each worker will equal the **MRP** of the *last* worker in this market. This is what is meant by the *marginal productivity theory of wage determination.*

2. The *marginal productivity theory of distribution* can be understood as follows. The payment to labor is given by the value of the marginal product of the last unit of labor hired times the number of units hired. The excess of the value of the marginal product of the first person and all earlier persons up to the very last is available for distribution to the other factors of production.

3. In an economy in which *all* workers are identical in *all* respects, in which *all* jobs are identical in *all* respects, in which no single buyer or seller of labor services has the ability to influence the wages paid, each and every worker would be paid the *same* wage for his or her labor services. Since it is clear what is required for a single uniform real wage to exist for all workers, it is also clear why wage differences exist among workers—even in perfectly competitive labor

markets. Workers are not alike in all respects; jobs are not alike in all respects; and the shift of labor resources from one market to another is not costless.

4. The earliest unions were not intended to be permanent organizations. They were formed as a consequence of specific disputes with employers over such matters as reduced wages or the replacement of apprentices with women and children; once the dispute was resolved, the "union" disappeared. However, beginning around the 1790s, "permanent" unions began to make their appearance in the United States. The objectives of most of these unions were similar: Members would pledge not to work for employers who paid less than the union-determined wage or who hired a disproportionate number of unskilled workers. In addition, many of these unions tried to establish *closed shops.* Employers strongly resisted the union's demands. Wherever unions would grow up, an employers' association would spring up whose primary objective was to smash the unions. To assist them, employers turned to the courts. At least through the early 1930s, court decisions were, for the most part, decisively antiunion. Moreover, employers associations employed a number of methods, ranging

from the employment of *strikebreakers* to use of the *yellow-dog contract* to *blacklisting* union personnel.

5. The American labor movement took a giant step in 1869 with the formation of the Knights of Labor. The objectives of the Knights were radical. At first, their social program had little appeal to workers whose immediate concerns were the bread-and-butter issues of higher wages and improved working conditions. The Knights membership rose sharply as a consequence of their success in the use of the strike weapon. But as soon as they became less effective in their use of this labor tool, workers abandoned the Knights, their vague and idealistic goals being of little interest to them in the first place.

The American Federation of Labor (AFL) succeeded where the Knights had failed. There were two reasons for this. First, the AFL was concerned with only one issue—improving wages and working conditions for its members. Second, the AFL decided at the outset to stay out of politics.

6. Between 1932 and 1947, union membership exploded, rising from about 3 million to over 15 million. Two factors were largely responsible for this change: *(a)* the passage of new laws by the Congress that were decidedly prolabor— the Norris-LaGuardia Act and the National Labor Relations Act, for example; and *(b)* the rise of industrial unions.

7. After World War II, and largely as the consequence of the willingness of labor unions to use their power effectively, the tide of public opinion began to turn against organized labor. This change in attitude was reflected in the Taft-Hartley Act and the Landrum-Griffin Act.

8. The essence of union-management relations is captured in the bargaining process. The outcome of the collective bargaining process is a contract that spells out the wages and working conditions agreed to by employers and union members. Whether the outcome will be more or less favorable to the union will depend on several factors: the financial status of employers and the union; the ease with which wage costs can be passed on in the form of higher prices; the nature of the agreements reached by the union with other employers; and the prospect of government intervention in the negotiations.

9. Union contracts cover a variety of issues of concern to both employers and employees— pay, profit sharing, overtime pay, fringe benefits, cost-of-living adjustments, working conditions, job security, work rules, and procedures for the settling of disputes.

10. Compared with the outcomes that emerge in perfectly competitive labor markets, monopsony results in lower real wages and lower levels of employment. The counterpart of power on the buyers' side of the market is power on the sellers' sid . Generally, power on the sellers' side arises because workers are organized into some sort of union. Basically, unions attempt to secure for their workers higher real wages either by restricting the supply of workers to employers, by raising the employer's demand curves for workers, or both. When either monopoly or monopsony power is present in labor markets, an efficiency loss results. The MRP of labor measures the marginal benefit that society attaches to an extra unit of labor being employed in any market; the labor supply curve, on the other hand, measures the marginal cost to society of additional units of labor services employed. Only at the intersection of the market MRP curve and the supply curve of labor will an efficient outcome result. By contrast, the monopsonist will hire a smaller quantity of labor services and pay less per unit than under competitive conditions. The union, on the other hand, will insist on higher wages than under competitive conditions.

11. When power exists on both sides of the labor market, we have a situation of *bilateral monopoly.* The outcomes will depend on the relative bargaining power of the two sides. Under bilateral monopoly we could observe an outcome that is much closer to the purely competitive result. This is partly because of the presence of *countervailing power.*

CONCEPTS FOR REVIEW

Marginal revenue product (MRP)
Marginal productivity theory of wages

Marginal productivity theory of the distribution of income

The "equalizing difference" or compensating differential

The notion of noncompeting groups

The "nonequalizing difference"

Closed shops

Union shops

Strike

Strikebreakers ("scabs")

Yellow-dog contract

Blacklist

Knights of Labor

American Federation of Labor (AFL)

Congress of Industrial Organizations (CIO)

Norris-LaGuardia Act

National Labor Relation Act (or Wagner Act)

Taft-Hartley Act

Landrum-Griffin Act

Pattern bargaining

Profit sharing

Overtime pay

Fringe benefits

Job security

Seniority system

Work rules

Monopsony power

Oligopsony

Featherbedding

Bilateral Monopoly

Countervailing power

Minimum wage

QUESTIONS FOR DISCUSSION

(Those marked with an asterisk (*) are more difficult.)

1. Explain carefully why the MRP curve for labor can be called the demand curve for labor.

2. Suppose the marginal product of the fourth worker to a perfectly competitive firm is five units per hour and the price of each worker is $10 per hour. Suppose further that the perfectly competitive firm attains its profit-maximizing equilibrium by hiring four workers. What is the market price of the product produced by the perfectly competitive firm?

3. Describe briefly why the Wagner Act is often called the Magna Carta of American unionism.

4. It is often argued that big unions, by pushing up the price of labor and reducing the level of employment, cause a misallocation of resources. Union supporters reply that this is not true; unions are needed to offset the monopsonistic power of producers, which, by itself, would push the price of labor too low and cause too-low levels of employment. Suppose monopsony power is present. Which of the two arguments is correct?

*5. "Assume initially a monopsony equilibrium—a large number of unorganized workers sell their labor services to a single producer. Now let government impose a minimum wage. The result will be an increase in the level of employment, not a reduction as would be the case under perfect competition." Evaluate carefully. (*Hint:* Take the initial equilibrium; set the minimum wage above the monopsonistic equilibrium wage; determine the new marginal cost of labor curve.)

Chapter 24

Rent, interest, and profits

According to statistics published by the U.S. Department of Commerce, approximately three quarters of U.S. national income goes to labor in the form of wages and salaries. The remaining quarter is distributed between the owners of the other two factors of production—land and capital—in the form of rent, interest, and profits.

Although the definitions used by the Department of Commerce to classify incomes are useful in some contexts, they are of only limited use when it comes to the study of the pricing of factors of production. As a means of better understanding factor prices, economists have developed very special definitions for wages, rent, interest, and profits that are not at all in conformity with most definitions used in official government publications.

Take wages and salaries. As defined in the national income accounts, wages and salaries include all take-home pay and fringe benefits plus income taxes withheld and social security taxes paid. However, as we shall see below, at least some portion of wages and salaries is more appropriately viewed as economic rent, and another portion really represents a return on capital—*human capital*.

We have already seen in Chapter 18 how the accountant's definition of profit, the one commonly used in published government statistics, differs from the economist's definition of profit. Again, as we shall see below, it is perhaps more appropriate from the point of view of understanding factor prices to consider some portion of the profits figures that are published as economic rent; some other portion is better viewed as a return to the labor services provided by the *owners* of land and capital.

And the concept of rent as used here will, at times, be seen to be at considerable variance with its more common usage as the payments made by tenants to landlords. We open this chapter with a discussion of the concept of economic rent. This will be followed by the study of interest and profits.

ECONOMIC RENT

Pure economic rent refers to the income that is earned by a factor of production—any factor—

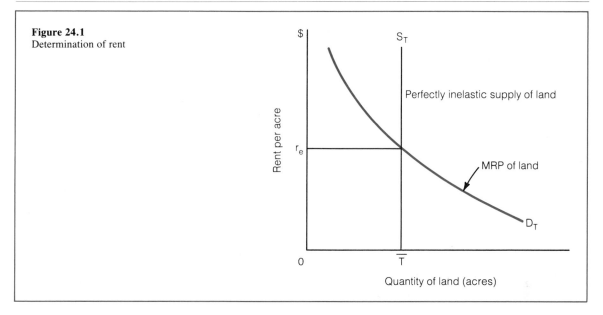

Figure 24.1
Determination of rent

Perfectly inelastic supply of land

MRP of land

that is completely price inelastic in supply. We mean by this that the quantity of the factor forthcoming will not change, no matter what price is offered for its services.

Classical economists of the last century used land—"the original and inexhaustible gift of nature"—to exemplify the concept. In Figure 24.1 we show a vertical supply curve for land over the point, $\bar{T}$, representing its fixed and unvarying quantity. Note that, whether the rent per acre is high or low, the quantity of land available for use to producers is unchanging.

The intersection of the demand curve for land, D_T —the marginal revenue product (MRP) of land—with the perfectly price inelastic supply curve yields the equilibrium rent per acre. The demand curve for land slopes downward for the usual reasons. As the amount of land used in production increases, holding other factors fixed, the marginal product of land declines, consistent with the law of diminishing returns. If the output produced is sold in imperfectly competitive markets, the **MRP** of land will decline for the additional reason that marginal revenue (**MR**) declines.

The rent per acre must tend toward r_e. Why? Because at a price above r_e, the amount of land demanded would be less than the available sup-

ply. Some landowners would not get anything at all for their land. Since receiving something is better than receiving nothing at all, these landowners would offer their land for less and thereby bid down its price. Likewise, a rental price below r_e could not long be sustained. Producers who did not get as much land as they want at a price less than r_e will offer more and thereby bid up its price. The only sustainable rental price is the one that equates the demand for land with its fixed supply.

Implications of perfectly inelastic supply

Two important implications of perfectly inelastic supply are deserving of note. First, in most resource markets, the supply curves are upward sloping. Given some equilibrium price and quantity combination, higher resource prices are necessary to coax additional resources into employment in any given market. That is, higher prices are necessary to attract those resources away from their next best alternative uses; the opportunity cost of resource employment in market A is the value of the next best alternative in some other market.

However, because the geographical location of land is fixed, landowners are denied the opportunity to shift that resource to other locations. From the point of view of its geographical location, then, the opportunity cost of land is zero. There are alternative uses of land *within any geographical location,* which means there is an opportunity cost associated with the use of land for farming—namely, the rent per acre that could be earned in its next best alternative use. But, locationally, its opportunity cost is zero.

An aside. Although the total supply of land is technically fixed, the total supply in the market is not. The fertility of land can be reduced by overcropping. Therefore, the supply of some grade of land could be reduced unless properly cared for. Moreover, additional land can be "created" through drainage of swamps or by the reclaiming of land from the ocean, as has been done on a grand scale in Holland. Nevertheless, it is not a serious violation of the truth to argue that the supply curve of land is vertical, or at least near vertical.

Second, the fixed supply of land means that the rent per acre is determined exclusively by the demand for it. If the demand for land in some geographical location is high, its rent per acre will also be high; if the demand for land is low, it will earn a small rent per acre. Since the demand for any resource is a derived demand, the rent per acre will largely be determined by the market value of the goods and services produced using land as an input.

Explaining rent differentials

It is not all that difficult to explain land rent differentials. Land rents differ because of differences in demand for different parcels of land. The question of interest, then, is this: What accounts for the observed differences in demand between different parcels of land? The short answer is: differences in the *quality* of different parcels of land.

Whether a given parcel of land is of high or low quality depends in large measure on how would-be purchasers of land intend to use it. Consider land that is used for farming wheat. The quality of different parcels of such land will be determined by the prospective yields per acre on each. Plots of land that have a high yield per acre will command a higher rental price than plots with a lower yield per acre. This is hardly surprising. Since the demand for land is given by the MRP_T, and since the productivity of land (in this instance, its yield per acre) enters into the computation of MRP_T, it is reasonable to expect the demand for high productivity land to be higher than the demand for low productivity land. That is, MRP_T for a given quantity of high productivity land will exceed the MRP_T on a similar quantity of low productivity land. The rent on the higher productivity land will be correspondingly higher.

Or consider land that is used for mining iron ore. The quality of different parcels of such land will be determined by how rich the veins of ore are and by the ease with which the ore can be extracted. It should be no surprise that parcels of land rich in easily accessible iron ore deposits command higher rents than do plots that are less rich in ore deposits or whose ore deposits are difficult to extract. Can you explain these rent differences in terms of the MRP of land for the different quality plots?

A third qualitative feature of land that is important in some instances is its location. We notice, for example, that land rents are much higher in the prime business districts of our cities than they are in the surrounding suburbs, and that suburban land rents are higher than those in more rural areas. For some businesses it is important that they be located in the prime business district; it may be important to be close to suppliers, close to competitors, and close to the population center from which it draws its labor resources and sells its products. The high land rents prevailing in prime business districts are the result of the very high demand for the given land area constituting the business district. In this regard, it is interesting to note that, partly as a result of the extremely high land rents in many business districts, there is a tendency to conserve on land acreage rented by constructing buildings up instead of building sideways. It is more costly to build up than it is to build sideways. But these construction cost differences are undoubtedly more than offset by what it would cost in some cities to rent additional land to take advantage of the lower sideways construction costs.

Land rents and land use

Many plots of land have several alternative uses. The question is, What determines the uses that will be made of the several different parcels of land? The short answer is land rents.

To illustrate, consider Figure 24.2. There we show a given fixed supply of land in a *given location*. All land in this market is uniform in quality. There are several possible alternative uses of the land in this location. It could be used for farming—for growing wheat, corn, lettuce, or oranges. It could be used for mining—of coal, iron ore, oil. Factories could be erected in this location, and so could single or multifamily residences, shopping centers, or office buildings. And the land may be put to one or more of these uses simultaneously; some portion of the available supply may be used for one alternative use and the remainder for other purposes.

We show in Figure 24.2 four possible alternative uses of the land in this location. It is not necessary, at this point, to specify what the alternative uses are. In fact, there is an advantage at this juncture in being vague about the alternatives; we will just call them alternatives A, B, C, and D.

The demand for land for each of the alternative uses is given by D_A, D_B, D_C, and D_D. The market demand curve for land in this location is obtained by adding up the quantity of land demanded for all of the alternative uses at each possible rental price. The intersection of the market demand curve with the perfectly inelastic market supply curve yields the equilibrium rent per acre in this market, r_e. This rental price per acre will determine how much of the fixed supply will be devoted to each of the alternative uses. As is apparent from Figure 24.2, none of the land will be devoted to alternative A; the amount of land demanded for alternative A at a rental price of r_e is zero. Only a very small portion of the available supply will be devoted to alternative C. Alternative B gets the bulk of the land. And alternative D gets somewhat less.

Actually, Figure 24.2 constitutes a fairly general representation of how the market determines land use in any particular location. The parcel of land in Figure 24.2 could represent the available supply of land in the downtown area of a major city. There are several possible alternative uses of that land. It could be used for farming,

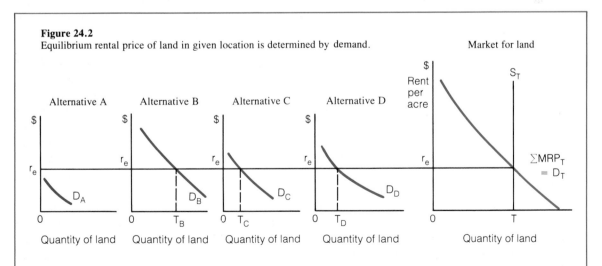

Figure 24.2
Equilibrium rental price of land in given location is determined by demand.   Market for land

Alternative A   Alternative B   Alternative C   Alternative D

The equilibrium rent represents for each of the alternative uses the marginal cost of land. Equating the rental price per acre with the MRP_T in each use determines how land will be distributed among the alternatives.

but such a use is unlikely. The demand for this parcel of land on the part of other users is likely to be such that the rent per acre would be too high to justify its use for farming. Even though this parcel of land might be the most productive for farming anywhere in the world, the rent per acre could be so high as to make its use for farming unprofitable. Alternative A could represent the farming use alternative of this land.

The important point to recognize here is the critical role played by the demand for land for each of the alternative uses. The demand for land, given by MRP_T, is a derived demand—derived from the demand for the products produced using land as an input. How much producers are willing to pay to use the land will ultimately be determined by how much people are willing to pay for the goods and services produced. With respect to alternative A, although the land in question may be extremely productive for farming, the rental cost per acre is so high relative to the value of the farm output that could be produced that it is unprofitable to use this land for farming. Put differently, the value of the output produced relative to the rental cost per acre is much higher for alternatives B, C, and D. This is why the available supply of land will be devoted to those uses.

Alternatively, one could imagine that the land supply represented in Figure 24.2 is a parcel of land located in the open plains of the western United States. In this instance, alternative B could well represent the wheat farming use of this land; alternative A could represent the office building use. Because of its location, the office building alternative would not be viable economically, even if the rent per acre in this location is a mere fraction of the rent per acre that land fetches in downtown Chicago, New York, or Los Angeles.

Land rents and land prices: Are they related?

Land rent refers to the cost of using some amount of land for a certain length of time. We speak of rent per acre per month, rent per square foot per year, etc. However, the rental value of land and the price of land are not the same. The price of land refers to the value at which each unit of land can be sold outright in the market.

However, there is a very close connection between the rental value of land and the price of land. Indeed, the price of land can be shown to be approximately equal to the **capitalized value** of its rent. To illustrate, suppose you own a piece of land. Whether you use it yourself or rent it to others, the land will yield rent in perpetuity. Suppose its current rental value is $1,000 per acre per year, and that you *expect* it to have a real rental value of $1,000 forever. The value of the land to you is easily determined. It is nothing more than the expected real rental value of the land divided by the expected real rate of interest. If the expected real rental value is $1,000 per year per acre and the expected real interest rate is 5 percent (0.05) per year, the value of an acre of land will be $20,000 ($1,000 ÷ 0.05); if the expected real interest rate is 4 percent (0.04), the value of an acre will be $25,000 ($1,000 ÷ 0.04). Note here the inverse relationship between the price of land and the interest rate. A lower real interest rate implies higher land prices; higher real interest rates imply lower land prices.

Note also that, for any given interest rate, the higher is the expected rental value of the land, the higher its price will be. If the expected real rental value were $2,000 instead of $1,000, the acre of land would be worth $40,000 at a 5 percent rate of interest ($2,000 ÷ 0.05) as opposed to $20,000.

This relationship between the rental value and price of land can be explained easily by recalling our discussion back in Chapter 11. We studied there a peculiar kind of bond known as a consol—a bond that paid a fixed amount to its owner in perpetuity. We also showed that the price of the bond was determined simply as the value of the coupon payment divided by the rate of interest. The problem we face here—that of determining the price of land on the basis of its rental value—is analogous to determining the price of the consol. That is, the land yields to its owner the rental value in perpetuity, like a consol; its price is determined like that of a consol.

There are some important respects in which land is not like a consol. First, unlike a consol, there is no guarantee of what the rental value of land will be in future years. It could rise, fall, or remain the same, depending on what happens in the future to the demand for land. In order to determine the price of land, it is necessary to make the calculation based on the rental value that is *expected* to prevail in future years. For illustrative purposes, we assumed that the real rental value would remain constant, but obviously there are other possibilities as well.

Moreover, what price the land will sell for need not correspond precisely—or even closely—to its value as calculated by its owner. As noted above, the calculated value is based on one's perception of the steam of rents the land will yield in future years. There is no reason to think that the seller's perception will be the same as the buyer's perception. Although in principle it is easy to see how land prices are intimately related to the rental values of land, in practice, the process of determining land prices is a complicated one.

Rent and other factors of production

Earlier we noted that rent refers to the income earned by a factor of production that is completely inelastic in supply. The perfectly inelastic supply feature is important because it suggests that the opportunity cost of the use of this factor of production is zero. Land is a good example; there are no alternative uses of land *outside* the place where it is located. *Land earns a return known as rent, where we mean by rent the return earned by a factor of production in excess of its opportunity cost.*

But other factors of production often earn an amount in excess of their opportunity costs. That excess we term the **rent portion** of their income. To illustrate, consider the extremely high incomes earned by many superstars—those individuals with very unique talents. We can find such individuals in acting, in singing, in sports, in management, etc. Now consider their next best employment opportunities. The next best alternatives provide us with a measure of the opportunity costs of their chosen lines of work. What is the next best employment alternative for Robert Redford? Maybe it is a job that would yield him an income of $40,000 a year. If that's the case, Robert Redford earns much more than his opportunity cost. That excess we refer to as the rent portion of Robert Redford's income.

There is one interesting sidelight to this discussion. Many people express outrage at the exceptionally high incomes earned by some individuals in our economic system. To many, such incomes are unjustified and unethical. After all, these people don't work any harder than many others. Why should they get more? Actually, these people are complaining largely about the rent portions of the incomes earned by the superstars—the excess income over and above the alternatives that most people find themselves in. Without getting into the question of ethics, those high incomes earned by certain unique individuals are determined by the same factors that determine high land rents for certain parcels of land—high levels of demand. Put differently, the high incomes received by certain people are a reflection of their high MRPs—the high revenues received by those to whom these individuals sell their labor services. According to some critics, having Robert Redford star in a movie virtually guarantees that it will be a blockbuster. And gate receipts for baseball games tend to be much higher when the roster includes one or two superstars.

There are many other illustrations of economic rent. Some cities restrict the number of taxicab licenses issued. These licenses, known as medallions, earn rents as long as their supply is less than the quantity demanded, the quantity demanded being determined by the MRP of operating a cab. The capitalized value of the rent earned by a cab determines the price of the medallion. In New York City, such medallions currently sell for about $75,000.

It is also quite appropriate to refer to profits in excess of normal profits as rental income. Above-normal profits arise when factors of production supplied by owners receive more than their employment would fetch elsewhere. If monopoly firms or oligopoly firms earn above-normal profits, we refer to those excesses as monopoly rent or oligopoly rent. Moreover, profits in excess of "normal" earned by perfectly competitive firms in the short run can also be termed rent; however, in the long run, those short-run rents will be competed away through the entry of new firms.

The taxation of rent

About a century ago, Henry George forged a powerful single-tax movement in the United States based on the proposition that only land rents should be taxed. His argument was largely based on equity considerations. Land is not produced; it is a gift of nature. Landowners do not work for their rental incomes; owners receive rents only because they own the land. Land rents represent a windfall. Henry George argued that land rents rightfully belong to the public and should accordingly be taxed away from the owners for public use.

One frequently hears similar arguments applied to OPEC. Oil is a gift of nature. Accordingly, it is unethical for the oil producers to amass the wealth that they do just because they happen to own it. No one has really solved the problem of how the rents earned by the oil producers should be taxed away.

Whatever the merits of the equity arguments, Henry George did fashion one valid efficiency principle regarding the taxation of rent. The efficiency principle is this: *Taxing economic rent does not distort production incentives or impair economic efficiency.*

The validity of this principle, in the case of land, is the consequence of the fact that the opportunity cost of land is zero. If the government taxes away 20 percent of the rent, or 80 percent— or indeed 100 percent—will there be any less of it used in production? *No.* What else can landowners do with it? The absence of an efficiency loss in this instance is in marked contrast to the efficiency losses that might result from the taxation of wage incomes. If taxes on wages cause less labor hours to be supplied, there would result an efficiency loss.

The same argument can be made with respect to the taxation of other rents. In this regard, it is interesting to consider once again the "reserve clause" that, prior to 1976, was a feature of most baseball contracts. In effect, the reserve clause was a means whereby club owners could tax away the rents earned by their ballplayers. Did the reserve clause impair efficiency? Apparently not. Ballplayers were still paid more than their next best alternative, so they remained in the game. However, many were paid less than they could have earned without the reserve clause "tax." The reserve clause "tax revenues" accrued to the club owners; the ballplayers demanded an end to this tax and, to date, have been largely successful in getting it reduced. Further progress was made as a result of the ballplayers strike during the 1981 season.

Consider the implications of taxing yet another kind of rent—economic profits. It is often argued that taxing producers' profits causes smaller rates of production and higher prices. In other words, taxing profits impairs efficiency and distorts production incentives. However, because profits are a form of economic rent, taxing those profits cannot distort production incentives or impair economic efficiency. If the owners are earning more than their resources can command elsewhere—more than is required to keep them where they are—how would efficiency be impaired by taxing those profits away? To see this more clearly, ask yourself how the firm's MC and MR curves would be affected by a profits tax. They aren't! Therefore, neither the rate of production nor the price of the product will be affected by a profits tax.

INTEREST, PROFIT, AND CAPITAL

The interest and profit shares of income are closely related to the process of capital accumulation. Indeed, some early economists used the two income concepts interchangeably as measures of the return to capital. Today, most economists distinguish between the two terms as follows.

1. *Interest* refers to the income return on **debt capital.** Many firms finance their purchases of capital goods by borrowing funds, paying interest to lenders on the debt they acquire. People can lend funds to business firms directly (by purchasing corporate bonds), or indirectly (by depositing funds in any of a number of financial intermediaries who in turn make loans).

2. *Profit* refers to the income return on **equity capital.** Equity capital represents the ownership claims on businesses. Profit income is earned by those who own their businesses outright or by those who own shares of stock in corporations.

We also need to recognize that, just as income is earned on physical capital (in the form of interest and profits), income is earned on **human capital.** Human capital is accumulated as a result of education, training, and experience. It is frequently the case that those in possession of greater amounts of human capital will be rewarded with higher wages—or if they own their own businesses, with higher profits—the extra wages representing, crudely, the return to human capital.

In this section we will focus first on interest income and follow up with a discussion of profits and the return on human capital. Before examining these income shares, however, it is important that we be clear on the nature and role of capital as a factor of production.

Capital as a factor of production

Land and labor are often referred to as the *primary* factors of production; capital is referred to as the *produced means* of production. Land and labor are primary in the sense that their supplies are largely determined outside the economic system—the supply of land being determined by nature and the supply of labor being largely determined by social and biological factors. Capital, on the other hand, is produced by the economic system itself.

Capital accumulation—whether in the form of physical capital goods or human capital—is

not an end in itself. It is a means to an end, a means to enlarge the production of *future* goods and services; the purpose of capital accumulation is to provide additional productive inputs to *further* increase the future production of the goods and services we want, over and above what would otherwise have been produced.

Capital accumulation requires that resources be diverted from other uses—specifically, from the production of goods and services for *current* use. There is a cost to accumulating capital—namely, foregone goods and services for current use. Moreover, to add to the stock of productive capital inputs, time is required. Capital accumulation requires a period of "waiting." What motivates the sacrifice of goods and services for current use—what makes the "waiting" worthwhile—is the prospect of a sufficient increase in future income and production. The payoff on capital accumulation is the *extra* goods and services over and above what would otherwise have been possible; that extra output is the return on "waiting."

The extra output produced as a consequence of capital accumulation is a measure of the **productivity of capital.** The value of that extra output represents the income return on capital accumulation. It can take the form of either interest income (the return to those who lend their resources to others for purposes of accumulating capital) or profit income (the return to those who used their own time, effort, and money.)

The **cost of capital** is measured as the value of current consumption sacrificed. The cost of the resources used to produce capital is measured as the value of those resources in their next best alternative use—consumer goods. Capital is productive only if the value of the future goods produced with it exceeds its cost. The return on capital is measured as the excess value. In order to compare quantitatively the return on diverse projects having different costs, we express the return on capital in *percentage* terms—the excess of the value of the output produced divided by the cost of capital for each project. Since the diverse projects yield benefits for time periods of different lengths, it is important to express the return on capital in terms of *percent per annum* (or percent per given time period). We will illustrate these ideas, first with respect to the accumulation of physical capital, then with respect to human capital.

Interest income: The return on debt capital

The interest rate—representing the cost of borrowing money—plays a very important role in determining the amount of investment that will be undertaken. To see this, consider the investment problem from the point of view of an individual producer.

Suppose the producer is considering the purchase of a new machine and is attempting to ascertain whether or not its purchase will be profitable. Let the cost of the machine be $1,000 and assume that it has a useful life of 10 years. Additionally, suppose that for each of the 10 years the machine is in use, the producer *expects* to receive $150 in additional revenues from the sale of the added output. Should the machine be purchased? Not necessarily. It is true that the machine costs only $1,000 and that, over its lifetime, it is expected to yield $1,500. However, whether these revenues will be enough to make this project profitable depends largely on the rate of interest.

The influence of the rate of interest can be looked at in several ways. First, if the funds to purchase the machines must be *borrowed,* repaying the loan in installments over the 10-year period, the $1,500 in revenues may not be sufficient to cover the principle of the loan (the $1,000) *plus* interest costs. As will become clear, if the interest rate happens to be 8 percent per annum, revenues will just be sufficient to cover costs; a higher rate of interest would make the purchase a distinctly unprofitable venture.

Second, if the firm uses its own internal funds (business income) instead of borrowing, interest costs are avoided but an opportunity cost is incurred. By using internal funds to purchase the machine, the producer foregoes the opportunity of using those funds in other ways that could yield an interest income return. If the interest rate at which the producer can lend funds exceeds 8 percent, it would be better off lending those funds to others rather than undertaking this investment project.

The third way of looking at this issue—the one commonly used by businesspeople and economists—is to calculate the present discounted value (PDV) of the stream of revenues associated with the use of the machine over its lifetime. The PDV concept was discussed at length in Chapter 11, so we can be brief here.

The basic notion behind the PDV concept is very straightforward. What is the value *today* of $150 that is expected some time in the future? It is worth less than $150. The reason? Money today is more valuable than the same amount of money earned in the future because money in hand today can earn interest in the interim. The question that needs to be asked is this: How much must I have in hand today so that, if it were invested at the rate of interest, it would yield $150 in some future time period? Your answer will tell us the worth today—the present value—of that future value.

To illustrate, if $142.86 were put into an interest-bearing asset offering a 5 percent rate of interest, at the end of one year the principal (the $142.86) *plus* interest would amount to $150. In other words, at a 5 percent rate of interest, the present value of $150 received a year from now is $142.86.

Now we know that: $142.86 \times (1 + 0.05) = $150. Rewriting this, we can see that $142.86 = \dfrac{\$150}{(1 + 0.05)}$. This tells us that the present value of $150 due one year from now is $142.86. This value is obtained by *discounting* the future value by 1 plus the rate of interest—hence the reason for the name *present discounted value.*

Going further, we can see that the $150 the machine will yield two years from now will be worth even less—that is, it will be more heavily discounted. If I place $136.05 in an asset for two years at the rate of 5 percent, it will be worth $150 at the end of two years—i.e., $136.05 \times 1.05^2 = $150. Or, reversing the procedure, the present value of $150 two years from now is $136.05—i.e., $150 ÷ 1.05² = $136.05.

But why go through all this? Because I will then be in a position to compare the present cost of the machine with the present value of the stream of revenues I can expect to earn on it. *As long as the PDV of the stream of revenues associated with an investment exceeds the present cost, it is profitable to invest.* One can show that, with a rate of interest of 5 percent, the PDV of the stream of revenues of $150 per year earned for 10 years will amount to $1,158.27—the PDV of $150 due one year from now *plus* the PDV of $150 due two years from now *plus* the PDV of $150 due three years from now, and so on. Therefore, at a 5 percent rate of interest, this investment project is profitable—the present discounted value of the revenues associated with its use ($1,158.27) exceeds its present cost ($1,000). However, at a rate of interest of 10 percent, the present discounted value of the stream of revenues on this project amounts to only $921.68—an amount that is less than its present cost. At a 10 percent rate of interest, this project is unprofitable. At an 8 percent rate of interest, the PDV of the stream of revenues

will just equal the cost of the project, which explains why so much importance was attached to the 8 percent figure earlier.

The investment demand for loanable funds. The rate interest is just as important whether an investment project is financed by borrowing or by using internal funds. To keep things simple, however, let us assume that firms finance their investment only by borrowing. Under these circumstances, the demand for capital as a factor of production has as its counterpart the demand for loanable funds.

Figure 24.3 shows an investment demand curve for loanable funds on the part of an individual producer. The curve is downward sloping; there is an inverse relationship between the interest rate and the quantity of loanable funds demanded by the firm for investment purposes.

As in the case for other factors of production, the downward-sloping demand curve here is fundamentally the result of the law of diminishing returns. Holding other factors of production fixed, the marginal productivity of capital diminishes as more and more capital is added. This can best be illustrated through consideration of the concept of the **rate of return on investment;**

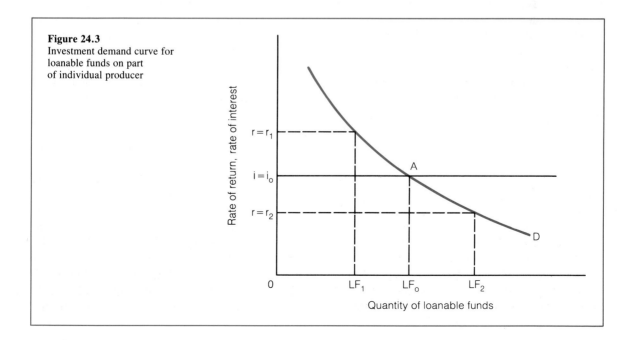

Figure 24.3
Investment demand curve for loanable funds on part of individual producer

in the macroeconomics portion of this text, we referred to the rate of return on investment as the **marginal efficiency of investment.**

The rate of return on investment has a very particular meaning that is different from the rate of interest. We saw earlier that, in order to determine whether it was profitable to undertake an investment project, it was necessary to compare the PDV of the stream of revenues with the cost of the investment. To calculate the PDV, we used the interest rate. We saw that, as long as the PDV of the stream of revenues exceeded the cost, it was profitable to proceed.

Now consider a somewhat different calculation. Take the stream of revenues associated with an investment project. Now find that rate of discount that, when applied to the stream of revenues, causes the value of that stream to just equal the cost of the project. That rate of discount we call the rate of return on investment. The following should therefore be clear. If the PDV of the stream of revenues exceeds the cost, it will take a rate of discount higher than the rate of interest to discount that stream by an amount to bring that value to the point of equality with the cost. The rate of return to investment exceeds the rate of interest. Since the rate of return exceeds the rate of interest—implying that the PDV of the stream of revenues exceeds the cost—it is profitable to undertake the project. Conversely, when the rate of return (r) is less than the rate of interest (i), it is unprofitable.

As the firm expands its investment programs, more and more loanable funds will be required for financing purposes. However, because of diminishing returns, the rate of return to investment will decline as more investment projects are undertaken. The stream of additional revenues associated with each additional project, other factors of production held constant, will diminish. This means that it takes a lower rate of discount to discount the stream of revenues for each added project to a point equal to cost—i.e., the rate of return declines.

The decline in the rate of return to investment—analogous to the now-familiar diminishing MRP—is what accounts for the downward

slope of the investment demand for loanable funds. The individual producer represented in Figure 24.3 will maximize profits by carrying investment to the point where the rate of return equals the rate of interest. This occurs at point A, implying a quantity of loanable funds demanded of LF_0.

To see why point A must be the equilibrium position, consider some quantity of loanable funds other than LF_0. If the firm borrowed only LF_1, the rate of return on the marginal investment project would amount to r_1, which exceeds the rate of interest i_0. Since additional projects are expected to yield a rate of return in excess of the rate of interest, the firm would add to its profits by expanding its investment—by borrowing more. It would not be profitable, however, to borrow more than LF_0. Borrowing a quantity equal to LF_2, for example, would be unprofitable since the rate of return on investment is less than the rate of interest; if LF_2 were borrowed, it would pay to cut back to LF_0.

The market for loanable funds.   Figure 24.3 illustrates well enough the situation confronting an individual producer. However, for any given individual producer, the interest rate is fixed. Whether the producer borrows a little or a lot, it will have no noticeable effect on the interest rate. Therefore, we need to examine how the market interest rate is determined.

In Chapter 11, we explained the determination of the interest rate in terms of the demand for and supply of money. A complementary, not competing, theory is presented here; it is known as the **loanable funds theory.**

The market demand for and market supply of loanable funds are given in Figure 24.4. The market demand curve represents the total, economywide demand for loanable funds. It consists of the investment demand for loanable funds on the part of all producers *plus* the demand for loanable funds on the part of consumers (representing those consumer purchases financed with the use of borrowed funds) *plus* the demand for loanable funds on the part of government (to finance government deficits—the excess of government expenditures over tax receipts). The investment demand curve for loanable funds is

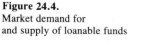

Figure 24.4.
Market demand for
and supply of loanable funds

given by D_I; the total demand curve for loanable funds is given by D_T. The horizontal distance between D_I and D_T measures the demand for loanable funds on the part of consumers and government.

The market supply curve represents the total, economywide supply of loanable funds—on the part of individuals, businesses, financial institutions, and governments in surplus. The supply curve is upward-sloping, indicating that, at higher interest rates, the supply of loanable funds will increase.

The response of the supply of loanable funds to changes in interest rates reflects in large measure the operation of income and substitution effects. Much of the supply of loanable funds represents personal and business saving. According to the **substitution effect,** the higher the rate of interest, the greater the incentive to save. A higher rate of interest implies that the price of future consumption has fallen relative to current consumption because a dollar saved today provides you with an even larger income in the future. Because of the change in relative prices, you have an incentive to substitute away from

current consumption toward future consumption—that is, you have an incentive to save more.

On the other hand, a higher interest rate implies that a given volume of savings will be larger in the future than at a lower rate of interest. Your total income (from work and savings) will be larger over time, providing you with an incentive to increase both your future consumption *and* your current consumption—to reduce your current savings. This is the **income effect** that operates to reduce your savings.

The supply curve of loanable funds reflects the pull of these two opposing forces. The fact that the supply curve in Figure 24.4 is upward sloping means that the substitution effect dominates the income effect. Of course, one could have a "backward-bending" supply curve of loanable funds, reflective of the notion that the income effect dominates the substitution effect after some point. We ignore this possibility here on the grounds that, empirically, the overwhelming preponderance of evidence suggests that the supply curve is upward sloping.

The intersection of D_T and S at point A yields the equilibrium rate of interest, i_e, and the equilibrium quantity of loanable funds, LF$_C$. At that interest rate, the quantity demanded for investment purposes equals LF$_1$; the difference between LF$_C$ and LF$_1$ represents the amount demanded by consumers and government.

One final note. Figure 24.4 is useful for examining the often repeated idea that government deficits are bad because the funds that must be borrowed to finance them "crowd out" at least some amount of private investment. There is no question but that the financing of larger deficits with borrowed funds leads to less investment than otherwise. If a government deficit raises the demand for loanable funds from D$_T$ to D$_T^1$, the interest rate will rise to i$_e^1$, reducing the quantity of loanable funds demanded for investment purposes from LF$_1$ to LF$_2$.

Does this mean that it is therefore inappropriate for the government ever to run deficits? Not necessarily. Indeed, as we saw in Chapter 8, the question of the appropriateness of government deficits can only be judged in the context of the multiple and often conflicting economic objectives of government policies. The reduced levels of investment spending that result from the financing of deficits with borrowed funds must be weighed against the positive benefits of the policies that caused the deficits in the first place.

Interest rates and risk. Up to this point we have been talking as though there were a single interest rate. In fact there are a whole variety of interest rates—different interest rates depending on the nature of the loans and the type of borrower. One of the central factors responsible for observed differences in interest rates is *risk.* We note, for example, that the large and financially sound corporations can frequently borrow funds at lower interest rates than firms that are smaller or less sound financially. The reasons? Loans granted to the former are relatively risk-free. A **risk premium** is generally added to the risk-free rate in the case of loans granted to the latter.

Differences in the riskiness of loans have become highly institutionalized in U.S. financial markets. We hear a great deal about the so-called **prime rate**—the interest rate charged by banks to their most creditworthy corporate customers. Less creditworthy customers must generally pay more than the prime rate for borrowed funds. In addition, a number of institutions exist that rate bonds according to riskiness. Aaa rated bonds—bonds issued by corporations perceived to be the most creditworthy—almost always offer lower interest yields than do, say, Baa rated bonds, the latter being adjudged more risky than the former.

Despite these differences in interest rates, however, it is still meaningful to talk in terms of *the* interest rate. Interest rates on bonds of a given maturity, at least, tend to move up and down over time in tandem, the result of changes in the *overall* demand for and supply of loanable funds.

Normal profit: The return to equity capital

Few words in the English language inspire as much emotional debate as does the word *profit.* To many people, profit represents an income share earned by exploiting others. Its existence is taken as evidence of the presence of economic injustice and corporate greed in our economic system. This hostile reaction is often disputed by others who view profits as essential to the growth prospects of our economy, an instrument critical to the improvement of living standards generally.

In order to understand profits and the role they play, we need to get away from these value judgments and address the issue squarely, in "positive economics" fashion. The matter of profits is complex. This is in large measure because it is not always perfectly clear what this income share represents a return to. As we shall see once again, the economist's usage of the term is often at variance with its everyday meaning.

We begin our discussion by recalling the notion of "normal" profit, which we studied at length in Chapter 18. As you will remember, at least part of the profit reported by producers is nothing other than the return to the owners for the factors that they supply themselves. Using the idea of opportunity cost, we know that some portion of what accountants and others refer to as profit really represents production costs—not explicit production costs, but implicit production costs. Part of what is referred to as profit represents a return on the labor effort supplied by the owners. Part may represent the equivalent of rent on the owners' natural resources. And part may represent the return on the owners' capital. *In other words, part of what is referred to as profit—what the economist calls "normal" profit—is really the (implicit) wages, rent, and interest costs associated with the factors of production supplied by owners themselves.* Because they are supplied by the owners, these costs are given a different name in everyday discussions, i.e., profits.

Once this point is understood, it is clear why economists refer to a firm that earns only a "normal" profit as earning zero *economic* profit; it is, after all, just covering its costs. Profits in excess of normal represent economic profits. As we noted earlier, because the owners earn a return in excess of what is required to keep their own resources where they are, economic profits are akin to pure economic rent.

Profit: Return on entrepreneurship and innovation. While the above distinctions are important to the study of profit, they are rather sterile. They do not capture the essence of the choices people make between selling the services of the resources they own to others and setting up their own business enterprises, or joining with others in a shared ownership of a business. This distinction is important to understanding why profit income is viewed as different from wages, rent, and interest.

From this perspective, profit is viewed as the return to entrepreneurship and innovation. Those who choose to "own" presumably feel that they can do better than to sell to others the services of the resources they own. No doubt the decision to become "boss" is, in some instances, motivated by psychological factors. Some people feel freer and more independent being their own boss. But one of the most important motivating factors is the lure of economic profits—the belief or dream that the financial rewards of ownership will be greater than those resulting from the sale to others of the services or the resources they own.

Many people go into business on their own because they feel they have more daring, greater vision, and better ideas; in short, they believe themselves to be more resourceful. Of course, not everyone succeeds. Only a few people are ever able to amass huge fortunes because of their daring and vision. Nevertheless, the lure of *economic* profit is a strong one, fully justifying the separation of profit income from other income shares.

Profit: Return on risk taking. Many economists carry these ideas one step further in an effort to better pinpoint what profit represents a return to. Yes, profit represents a return to entrepreneurship and innovation. But, since the future is *uncertain,* so too will be the prospective returns to ownership. Uncertainty means there are risks inherent in being your own boss or in buying shares of stock in corporations. From this point of view, profit can be seen as the return to risk taking.

Some economists think the risks inherent in ownership can help to explain why economic profits are positive in our economic system. To their way of thinking, people are generally *risk averse*. That is, the marginal disutility people attach to dollars they might lose exceeds the marginal utility they attach to dollars they might gain. Without special incentives, people would prefer steady *smaller* incomes to erratically changing incomes whose average value is higher. A profit risk premium is therefore necessary to compensate people for their aversion to risk and to coax out the supply of risk bearing. Those who assume such risk will, on average, earn positive economic profits.

Monopoly profits. **Monopoly profit** is often treated as distinct from the concept of profit as the return to risk taking or profit as the return to the labor, capital and natural resources supplied by the owners of the firms. Monopoly profit is different in that it represents the return to those who have, and who make use of, market power.

Of course, the mere presence of market power does not guarantee economic profits. As we saw in our study of monopolistic competition, although each individual firm possesses market power (the existence of which is given by the fact that they each face downward-sloping demand curves for their products), the ease of entry and exit serves to eliminate short-run profits in the long run. However, when significant barriers to entry exist—whether in the form of economies of scale (in the case of natural monopolies, for example), exclusive patent rights, or financial barriers—positive economic profits in the short run can persist into the long run.

The key to understanding monopoly profits lies in recognizing how those in possession of monopoly power are often able to earn higher returns than otherwise by creating artificial scarcities. An artificial scarcity is to be distinguished from what might be called a natural scarcity. Scarcity of resources is a fact of life and the problem we face in economics is that of achieving the optium allocation of scarce resources among their alternative uses. Pure competition ensures the optimum allocation of resources; the equality of marginal cost and price reflects this fact.

However, whenever sellers face downward-sloping demand curves for their goods and services, it is in their own individual interests to sell less than the societal optimum. Recognizing that larger quantities sold will command a lower price per unit, sellers will equate MR and MC. This profit-maximizing equilibrium generates an artificial shortage, evidenced by the fact that price exceeds MC. The exercise of such monopoly power may or may not result in monopoly profits, which may or may not persist into the long run; often it will.

There is some dispute among economists over whether monopoly profits should be treated categorically different from other income shares. Suppose, for example, that you hold an exclusive patent on some good that yields monopoly profits. You could, of course, lease your patent rights to others. Using our earlier definitions, you would earn a rent on the patent; the producer to whom you leased the patent would earn a normal profit.

The cost of leasing the patent would wipe out the income share defined as monopoly profit.

An aside. It is important to note that the mere presence of economic profit is not an indication of a contrived or artificial scarcity. Indeed, perfectly competitive firms, at least in the short run, can earn economic profits without violating the "marginal cost equals price" condition. The existence of such profits is important to efficiency in the allocation of resources. These profits act as signals, directing the flow of resources toward uses that are the most valuable from the point of view of private markets. Monopoly profit, on the other hand, is frequently the by-product of inefficiency in the allocation of resources.

Windfall profits. To add to the confusion, there is another category of profits, popularly called **windfall profits,** that has captured a lot of attention in recent years, especially in regard to oil company profits. The definition of windfall profits is not precise, although what most people mean by it is fairly straightforward.

A windfall is an *unexpected* gain or advantage. When the term is applied to profits, it means an unexpected increase in profits. Many people view windfall profits as unfair. When the OPEC producers raised their oil prices in 1973–74 and again in 1979–80, domestic oil producers were given a windfall. They were able to sell oil on the market at prices greatly exceeding what would otherwise have prevailed. Since, in the eyes of many observers, the price increases received by domestic oil producers could not be justified by increases in their production costs, the windfall gains were "unjustified." The windfall profits constituted an unfair transfer of wealth from those paying higher prices for petroleum products to domestic oil producers. The windfall profits tax signed into law by President Carter in 1980 was based on the idea that it was appropriate to tax away this unjustified advantage.

Economists generally feel uncomfortable with the windfall profits concept. They do not deny that, at times, some producers reap huge financial gains that were unexpected and not of their own doing. However, not every producer is necessarily in that position. Consider a producer who expected oil prices to rise to $30 a barrel. The producer, in anticipation of the price rise, undertakes investments that would have been unprofitable at a $20 per barrel price, but would just break even at $30. Let the per barrel price now go to $30. Can our hypothetical producer be said to reap a windfall? Hardly.

WAGES AND HUMAN CAPITAL

Many of the expenditures made on education, training, and health can be viewed as investments designed to increase human capital. Like investments in physical capital goods, investment in human capital is not an end in itself but a means to an end.[1] That end is higher future earnings than otherwise. Moreover, just as investment in physical capital requires the sacrifice of current consumption, so too does investment in human capital. Many resources are devoted to the provision of education and training that could be devoted to the production of other goods and services; and this is in addition to the lost production and earnings of those being trained and educated. Finally, it is possible to estimate the rate of return on investment in human capital in a manner similar to the estimation of the rate of return on physical capital. In principle, one compares the cost of the investment in human capital with the increased earnings made possible by the accumulation of human capital.

It is useful to view expenditures on education, training, and health as forms of investment. It gives us insight into the reasons some people are paid more than others, as noted in Chapter 23. Also, it indicates one way society can use its scarce resources to increase per capita income and growth.

However, in a number of respects, the analysis

[1] Of course, not all education is aimed specifically at increasing future earnings. Indeed, much education is aimed at acquainting you with dimensions of yourself and the world around you that have, at best, only an indirect bearing on your earning potential. Accordingly, economists often distinguish the investment aspects of education from the consumption aspects.

of human capital is a much more complex subject, in large measure because of the overwhelming importance of the human factor. Consider the problem of estimating the return on a college education. It is common practice to compare the average annual income of those who have a high school diploma with those who have a college degree; in 1979, the difference amounted to about $3,500. The question is, Can the higher incomes earned by college graduates be said to be the result of higher levels of education alone? Probably not. First, to the extent that college graduates are more talented and work harder, it is highly probable that they would have earned more than most other people who did not go on to college, even if they hadn't gone to college. Second, many employers hire college graduates and pay them more than those with high school diplomas, not because they are necessarily better suited or better able to perform the job, but because the college degree is viewed as evidence of perseverence, discipline, and an above-average ability to learn—attributes considered important by employers. In other words, the college degree gives the college graduate "credentials," the worth of which is reflected in higher wages.

The rent, interest, and profit components of wages

On the basis of the foregoing discussion, it should be clear that there is nothing simple about the forces that determine people's wages and salaries. On the contrary, the factors that determine wages and salaries are highly complex. For some purposes, however, it is useful to think of wage and salary differentials in terms of the following three items.

1. *The "labor time" component of wages.* This is perhaps best measured as the wages that unskilled workers—workers with little or no education or training—can command in the marketplace.

2. *The interest or profit component of wages.* This is the return people receive for their investments in their human capital.

3. *The rent component of wages.* This is the earnings some people receive because of their unique talents, talents that enable them to earn more than their next best alternative.

For some people, the "labor time" component explains all of their income. For others, the interest or profit component is much more important. And for still others, the rent component is the critical element. Most important, these three components of wages are not mutually exclusive. Indeed, for some individuals, the unique talents they have might not pay off unless they undertake a huge investment in human capital. And for some others, their talents are wasted because they chose to pursue one line of work as opposed to another.

SUMMARY

1. *Pure economic rent* refers to the income earned by any factor of production that is completely price inelastic in supply. Being completely price inelastic, the opportunity cost of the factor is zero. Given the fixed supply, the rent earned is determined exclusively by demand.

2. Land rent differentials are the result of differences in demand for different parcels of land. The differences in demand are the consequence of differences in the *quality* of the different parcels, the "quality" of land being determined by the contribution of each parcel to the MRP_T for each alternative use.

3. Land rent determines the uses that will be made of any given parcel of land.

4. The price of land can be shown to be approximately equal to the *capitalized value* of its rent.

5. *Rent* is the return earned in excess of opportunity cost. All of the income earned by a factor of production that is completely price inelastic in supply (e.g. land) is rent. For other factors of production, the rent portion of their incomes can be determined on the basis of the best alternative uses.

6. Taxing economic rent does not distort production incentives or economic efficiency.

7. The *interest* and *profit* shares of income are closely related to the processes of capital accumulation. For some purposes, it is useful to think of *interest* as the return on debt capital, and *profit* as the return on equity capital.

8. Capital accumulation is not an end in itself. It is a means to an end, a means to enlarge the production of *future* goods and services. There is an opportunity cost to capital accumulation—namely, foregone goods and services for current use. Whether the cost of capital accumulation is worthwhile can only be determined by identifying its *rate of return*—the value of the extra goods and services produced relative to the cost.

9. As long as the present discounted value (PDV) of the stream of revenues associated with an investment exceeds the present cost, it is profitable to invest. Alternatively, as long as the rate of return on investment exceeds the rate of interest, it is profitable to invest.

10. "Normal" profit is really nothing other than the (implicit) wages, rent, and interest costs associated with the factors of production supplied by the owners.

11. In order to understand why people choose to set up their own business enterprises or join with others in a shared ownership of a business, it is important to view profit as a return on entrepreneurship and innovation or as a return on risk taking.

12. It is useful to view many of the expenditures made for education, training, and health as forms of investment—investment in *human capital.*

13. For many purposes it is useful to examine wage and salary differentials in terms of the following three components: (*a*) the "labor time" component of wages; (*b*) the interest or profit component of wages; and (*c*) the rent component of wages.

CONCEPTS FOR REVIEW

Pure economic rent
Capitalized value

Capital

Debt capital

Equity capital

Human capital

Productivity of capital

Cost of capital

Rate of return

"Normal" profit

Profit: Return on entrepreneurship and innovation

Profit: Return on risk taking

Monopoly profit

Windfall profit

QUESTIONS FOR DISCUSSION

(Those marked with an asterisk (*) are more difficult.)

1. Using the general definition of *rent*—the return to any factor of production in excess of its opportunity cost—explain *(a)* why economic profits are rent; *(b)* why the return to land is rent; *(c)* why much of the return to superstars is rent; and *(d)* why the "rent" you pay your landlord for your apartment is not all rent.

2. How does the economist's definition of *rent* differ from the everyday use of that term? Give an example where the use of the term by an economist differs from its everyday use; give an example where they are the same.

3. State whether you agree or disagree with each of the following statements. Explain your reasoning carefully in each instance.

  a. "If all land in the state of Iowa is equally fertile, then every acre of land in that state should command the same rent."

  b. "An increase in the world price of wheat will increase agricultural land rents."

  c. "The difference in income between an unskilled construction worker and a Ph.D. physicist is rent."

*4. *a.* According to Henry George's single-tax proposition, taxing land rent would not result in any efficiency losses. Explain this proposition.

  b. Suppose other forms of rent were taxed. Would it be fair to say that such taxes would not result in any efficiency losses? (*Hint:* Suppose government taxes the rent portion of the incomes of very talented people. Given the work-leisure discussion in Chapter 23, what result would you expect? What conclusion then?)

  c. Would your answer to *(b)* have been different if the individuals in question were workaholics? (*Hint:* What does the supply curve of a workaholic look like?)

  d. What general conclusions can you draw from your answers to *(a), (b),* and *(c)*? (*Hint:* What importance should one attach to the price elasticity of supply?)

5. Are the notions of *(a)* profit as a return on entrepreneurship and innovation, *(b)* profit as a return on risk taking, and *(c)* monopoly profit inconsistent with the notion of profit as rent? Explain.

Chapter 25

The economics of depletable resources

The last few chapters have been concerned with what might be called the **economics of reproducible resources.** Capital and labor are reproducible. Even land that is employed in the production of goods and services is not "used up"; the amount of land available tomorrow will be the same as today. (Of course, its quality may be lower unless we take care to protect the soil and replace the nutrients extracted through use.) However, for many natural resources, it would be inappropriate to classify them as reproducible. They are better classified as **depletable resources** in the sense that the quantity available tomorrow depends very much on the quantity we use today. Timber, fish, iron ore, coal, natural gas, and oil are all examples of depletable resources.

It is important to note that not all our depletable resources are alike. Some, such as oil, coal, natural gas, and iron ore, are essentially **nonrenewable.** Such long periods of time are required for new supplies of these resources to be created that it is meaningful to think of their quantities as fixed in supply. Every barrel of oil we extract from the ground today means one less barrel available for tomorrow.

Other depletable resources are **renewable.** Fish can reproduce themselves and forests can be replanted. However, just because they are renewable does not mean that their supplies cannot be exhausted. On the contrary, fishing too heavily or harvesting too many trees could ultimately exhaust the supplies of both fish and trees.

The purpose of this chapter is to explore in detail the economics of depletable resources, focusing our attention on the difference between renewable and nonrenewable resources. We begin with a discussion of the economics of renewable resources, then turn our attention to the economics of nonrenewable resources. In regard to the latter discussion, we will undertake a brief analysis of the role played by the OPEC cartel in the pricing of energy products. We end the chapter with a very brief review of the findings of a 1980 presidential study entitled *Global 2000 Report to the President.* It points to a world in the year 2000 that will be more precarious than it is now unless, among other things, we better manage the use of our depletable resources.

THE ECONOMICS OF RENEWABLE RESOURCES

Although renewable resources can be reproduced, they also can be exhausted. To illustrate, consider a body of water that currently has a fish population of 4 million. Assume further that, for every 1 million fish, the natural rate of increase is ½ million per unit of time; with a parent population of 4 million the natural rate of increase is 2 million. Thus it would be possible to harvest 2 million fish per unit of time indefinitely. The parent population would remain at 4 million; the amount fished in each time period would just equal the natural rate of increase of the fish population. But suppose the body of water were more heavily fished and the rate of extraction amounted to 3 million instead of 2 million. The result? The parent population would decline. The initial 4 million plus the 2 million increase minus the 3 million harvested would, after the first round, reduce the parent population to 3 million. That 3 million plus the 1½ million added naturally, minus the 3 million harvested would, after the second round, reduce the parent population to 1½ million. At this rate of extraction—3 million per time period—it would not take long before the supply of fish was exhausted.

Of course, if the rate of extraction amounted to less than the 2 million natural rate of increase, the parent population and the supply of fish would rise. If only 1 million were extracted per time period, the initial 4 million plus the 2 million increase minus the 1 million harvested would, after the first round, increase the parent population to 5 million. That 5 million plus the 2½ million natural increase minus the 1 million harvested would, after the second round, raise the parent population further, to 6½ million. Certainly, the parent population cannot increase without limit; any given body of water can support only so many fish. Once that point is reached—once the body of water becomes that loaded, that saturated—there can be no further increase in the supply of fish. For each new fish added, one must die.

The concept of sustainable yield

These ideas lead directly to one of the most important concepts in natural resource economics—the concept of **sustainable yield**. The ideas underlying this concept are fairly straightforward and can be illustrated with the aid of Figure 25.1. Two points are important to remember.

1. The *rate of increase* of the natural resource (e.g., fish) depends first on the *size of the population*, and second on the *carrying capacity of the environment*. If a given body of water can support

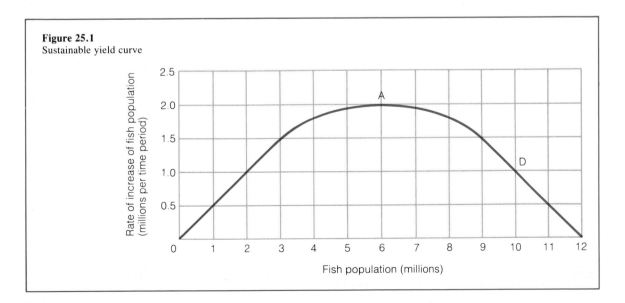

Figure 25.1
Sustainable yield curve

Rate of increase of fish population (millions per time period) — vertical axis: 0.5, 1.0, 1.5, 2.0, 2.5
Fish population (millions) — horizontal axis: 0 1 2 3 4 5 6 7 8 9 10 11 12

only 12 million fish, that 12 million represents the carrying capacity of that pond; the population cannot increase beyond 12 million. Generally the rate of increase of the fish population will be greater the larger the size of the population. A parent population of 4 million will result in a larger population increase per time period than will a parent population of only 2 million. But this need not always be true, which brings us to the second point.

2. The rate of population increase will be subject to diminishing returns. When the food supply in the pond is abundant and the pond is uncrowded, it is possible for there to be a large increase in the fish population relative to the initial parent population. However, as the pond becomes more crowded and as food to support fish life becomes more difficult to find, the rate of population increase will diminish.

These two points are illustrated in Figure 25.1 by what is known as the **sustainable yield curve.** We plot on the vertical axis the rate of increase of the fish population per time period. The horizontal axis measures the size of the fish population. The curve rises at first, reaches a maximum, and slopes downward thereafter, touching the horizontal axis at 12 million fish. The 12 million point represents the carrying capacity of the pond.

Each point on the sustainable yield curve tells us the number of fish that can be extracted per time period *indefinitely*—hence the reason for the name, *sustainable yield.* If the fish population happens to be 2 million, it is possible to harvest 1 million fish per time period indefinitely. The parent population will remain constant at 2 million since the natural rate of increase just equals the rate of extraction. Of course, since the natural rate of increase is larger when the population is 3 million, it is possible to harvest more fish per time period on a sustained basis—1½ million per time period according to Figure 25.1.

Because of diminishing returns, the natural rate of increase diminishes with the size of the population. Whereas the natural rate of increase was 1½ million per time period at a population of 3 million, it rises to only 2 million when the

population is 6 million—point A in Figure 25.1. At even higher populations, the natural rate of increase *falls* below 2 million per time period. For example, at point D, the sustainable rate of extraction consistent with maintenance of a population of 10 million is only 1 million. By extracting *more* than 1 million per time period when the population is 10 million, it is possible to *increase* the sustainable yield above 1 million. The reason? Although the parent population falls below 10 million, the smaller population is better able to regenerate itself, increasing the sustainable yield per time period.

Conservation and sustainable yield

If the pond is not fished, the population will tend naturally toward 12 million and remain there indefinitely. This point, however, is hardly interesting from an economic point of view, since the "no-fishing" outcome means denying us fish resources. The most relevant point, from an economic perspective, is point A—the point representing the **maximum sustainable yield.** At point A, we are able to harvest 2 million fish per time period forever. That is the most we can extract from the pond period after period after period. If more than 2 million are extracted per period, the fish supply will soon become exhausted, which is hardly a desirable outcome.

Using Figure 25.1 we can give real meaning to the idea of **conservation** as that term is used by economists. *It means, in this fish example, preventing the fish population from falling below 6 million; at population levels above 6 million, there is no conservation problem.*

This definition of *conservation* is at variance with its common usage—namely, using as little as possible. This usage of the term may be relevant under some circumstances, but certainly not all.

Taken to its logical conclusion, using as little as possible would mean using none. Ultimately, we would end up with a fully stocked pond of 12 million fish where each new fish reproduced would displace one other. We can surely do better than this. Indeed, it is possible to extract fish from the pond time and time again without endangering future supplies. The only question is, How much can we extract? The answer to this question revolves around the considerations that are relevant to determining the point of maximum sustainable yield—the rate at which the population can reproduce itself and the rapidity with which diminishing returns sets in.

Consider the following. Suppose 1½ million fish are extracted each year. Is there a conservation problem? We don't have enough information yet to answer this question. If the parent population is below 3 million, we have a real problem; the rate of extraction exceeds the rate of natural increase. Soon the supply of fish will be depleted. However, if the parent population is above 3 million, the extraction of 1½ million per time period will be less than the natural rate of increase. The fish population will grow. And it will continue to grow past 6 million. According to Figure 25.1, the population will settle down somewhere between 8 and 9 million, where the natural rate of increase of 1½ million per time period equals the rate of extraction.

As long as the fish population is 6 million or more, and as long as 2 million fish or less per time period are extracted, we do not encounter a conservation problem. Of course, if we extract more than 2 million fish per time period, we will fail to conserve our fish resources *no* matter how large the fish population initially was. Can you explain why? Moreover, only by maintaining the fish population at 6 million can we ensure the maximum sustainable yield of 2 million per time period. These considerations lead economists to conclude that conservation involves preventing the fish population from falling below 6 million.

Conservation and property rights

The fish example represents only one application of the concept of sustainable yield. The concept has relevance as well to the harvesting of timber and animal resources. Once again, from a conservation perspective, it is important to ensure that the populations of these resources do not fall below those levels associated with their maximum sustainable yields.

In order to bring about the conservation outcome—preventing the population from falling below its maximum sustainable yield level—it is often necessary to restrict harvesting in some manner. We have ample evidence to demonstrate that unrestricted harvesting can lead to the exhaustion or near-exhaustion of many of our resources. Buffalo that were once in abundance in the United States were almost made extinct by the unrestricted slaughter that took place years ago. The absence of careful restrictions on fishing almost wiped out the herring population in 1969. And several other species of fish are likewise threatened today because fish catches exceed maximum sustainable yields. Moreover, the failure to carefully restrict the harvesting of timber is resulting in sharp reductions in the world's tree population. Most experts estimate that the current rate of deforestation is well in excess of maximum sustainable yields. If continued, it could ultimately exhaust the world's timber supply.

In general, our failure to conserve these resources—our failure to ensure maintenance of the appropriate sizes of populations and appropriate rates of extraction—is a by-product of our failure to resolve the question of who has property rights over these resources.

Conservation and common property resources

Many of these resources are **common property resources.** Their uses are available to anyone and everyone.

The problem that can arise with a common property resource is this: No single individual has any incentive to restrict his or her current use of the resource to ensure its availability in the future. Since this is true of all individuals, there is nothing to guarantee that the resource will not be used excessively. One should not jump to the conclusion that the resource will necessarily be used excessively. It may or may not. The point is nothing guarantees that it will not be used excessively.

The now-familiar demand and supply apparatus illustrates well enough the issues under consideration here. We will assume, as we have always assumed whenever we have used demand and supply curves, that the resource in question—in this example, fish—is harvested and sold under conditions of perfect competition. Thus the supply curve in Figure 25.2 represents the horizontal sum of the marginal cost curves of all the fish producers. The intersection of the supply and demand curves gives us the competitive equilibrium position.

To keep matters simple, let us assume initially that the fish population equals or exceeds the size necessary to generate the maximum sustainable yield (i.e., at or to the right of point A in Figure 25.1). The maximum sustainable yield is given by Q* in Figure 25.2.

In Figure 25.2A, no conservation problem presents itself. The equilibrium quantity har-

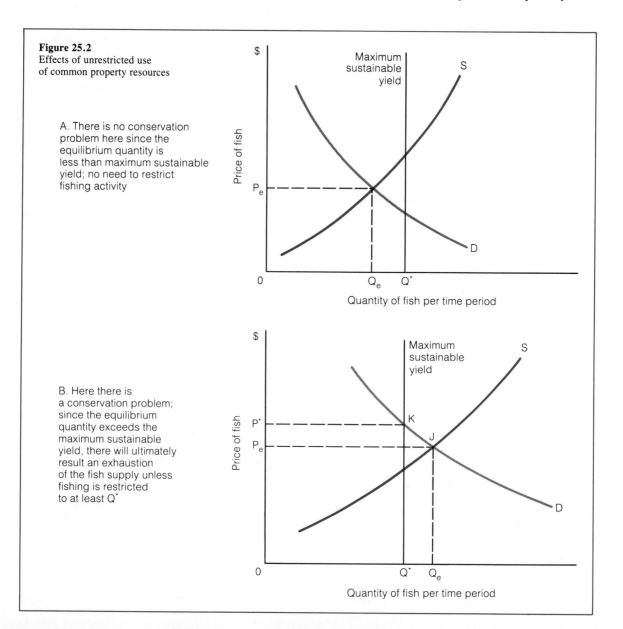

Figure 25.2
Effects of unrestricted use
of common property resources

A. There is no conservation
problem here since the
equilibrium quantity is
less than maximum sustainable
yield; no need to restrict
fishing activity

B. Here there is
a conservation problem;
since the equilibrium
quantity exceeds the
maximum sustainable
yield, there will ultimately
result an exhaustion
of the fish supply unless
fishing is restricted
to at least Q*

vested is less than the maximum sustainable yield. This means that, at current rates of consumption, there is no prospect of resource exhaustion. There is no need for anyone to intervene to restrict fishing activity. The perfectly competitive solution will yield the optimum amount of harvesting. There is no need to worry about the future; the future will take care of itself.

The result presented in Figure 25.2B is quite different. There, unrestricted fishing will cause an ultimate depletion of the fish supply. This is because the equilibrium quantity exceeds the maximum sustainable yield. In order to conserve future supplies, it is necessary to restrict fishing to *at least* Q*. We say "at least" because, if the amount harvested has for some time exceeded the maximum sustainable yield, the population could well be below that necessary to produce Q* on a sustained basis. It may be necessary to harvest below the sustained yield for a time to permit the fish population to build to its optimum level.

One way of achieving a quantity harvested equal to the maximum sustainable yield is to impose a tax on fish producers to drive up the price to P*; the quantity demanded at P* is just equal to Q*. If a further reduction is deemed necessary, an even higher tax would be called for. Of course, nonprice solutions are possible. Restrictions could be placed on both the number of people permitted to fish and the number of fish extracted.

The question that naturally arises in Figure 25.2B is, Why don't those harvesting the fish, acting on their own, restrict their harvests? Don't they realize that unrestricted fishing will ultimately deplete the supply of fish? They might know it, but each individually has no incentive to restrict supply. Even if I cease my fishing activity altogether, this will not affect the outcome since the amount I harvest is such a small part of the total market. Moreover, since I do not "own" the resource and cannot therefore restrict other people's use of it, the only cost that is relevant to me is the cost of harvesting the fish, *not* the cost in the form of damage to the future supply of fish. For these reasons, there is a need for government intervention to restrict free market activity.

When the common property resource is within national borders, it is often fairly easy for governments to impose the necessary use restrictions. This does not mean that all governments do so; many do not. Nor does it mean that they will meet no resistance; they often meet much resistance from those private producers whose profits would be adversely affected by restrictions. However, the most difficult problems of all occur when the common property resources reside outside national borders. Not only would unrestricted fishing rights in international waters to all comers destroy an individual nation's conservation attempts. It would, if the total catch exceeded the maximum sustainable yield, damage future catches, perhaps severely and irreversibly. It is understandable, therefore, why many nations have attempted to expand their territorial limits. The United States in 1977, for example, extended its territorial water limits from 12 to 200 miles. However, not everyone is comfortable with the expansion of territorial limits. Indeed, such extensions are hotly disputed by those whose access is denied.

Conservation and private property rights

The problems that can and do arise with common property resources often do *not* arise when the resource in question is owned privately. The owners have an interest in ensuring continued future supplies—at least this is usually the case.

In earlier sections of this book, when we were dealing with reproducible resources (where the quantity available tomorrow was *not* dependent on the quantity used today), we were able to define efficiency in terms of marginal cost pricing. The marginal cost that was relevant was the marginal cost of producing the goods and services in question. Determining the efficient price in the case of depletable resources is much more difficult. In general, marginal cost pricing, as we have defined it, will *not* be an efficient solution.

To illustrate, let us assume that the market for fish in some regions consists of a very large number of buyers on one side, and a very large number of sellers on the other side, each of whom owns a small pond from which the fish are harvested. In this perfectly competitive setting, each producer is a price-taker, the price being set by the market. However, *unlike other markets, the supply curve that is relevant to determining the market price is not, in general, the curve formed by summing up the MC curves of the individual sellers. Rather, the relevant supply curve will generally lie above and to the left of our usual supply curve, reflecting the extra cost—the loss in future harvests—caused by today's harvest.*

Figure 25.3 depicts this outcome. In the left panel we show an individual producer; in the right panel we show the market. Focus first on the individual producer. Assume the market-determined price equals P_e. (How this price is arrived at will become clear in a moment.) How much will the producer be willing to fish and sell at this price? If the only relevant consideration were production cost, our hypothetical producer would be guided by marginal cost and would, in accordance with the profit-maximizing rule, produce at the point where MC equaled P_e—i.e., the quantity Q_e. However, if the fish

harvested today meant that there would be fewer fish available for harvest tomorrow, the producer would look at more than just production cost in determining the optimum harvest. The reduction in future harvests represents a cost to the producer that must be added to production cost. The curve labeled MC* incorporates this added cost. MC* includes both the marginal cost of harvesting the fish plus the added cost attributable to the fact that fish harvested today are unavailable for harvesting tomorrow. Therefore MC* lies above and to the left of MC. From the point of view of the individual producer, the profit-maximizing rate of production occurs at Q*—the level corresponding to the point of intersection of MC* and P_e.

The relevant supply curve for the market is formed by adding up horizontally the individual MC* curves—*not* the MC curves. That supply curve—S^1 in Figure 25.3—intersects the market demand curve, yielding the equilibrium price, P_e. How the market price for fish was determined is now clear.

One final technical note. Economists refer to the *vertical* difference between MC and MC*—and correspondingly, the vertical distance be-

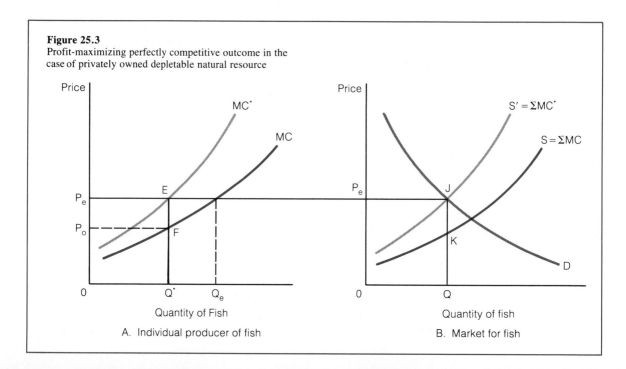

Figure 25.3
Profit-maximizing perfectly competitive outcome in the case of privately owned depletable natural resource

A. Individual producer of fish

B. Market for fish

tween S and S^1—as the **reservation price** for the resource in question. In the left panel of Figure 25.3, the reservation price for the individual producer is given by the distance EF at the output level Q*; in the right panel, the market reservation price is given by the distance JK at the output level Q. *It is called a reservation price because it represents the price differential that is necessary to compensate for the reduced future output.* Put differently, if marginal production costs were all that mattered, only a price of P_0 would have been necessary to induce the individual producer to harvest Q*. The difference between P_0 and P_e represents the individual producer's reservation price—the amount necessary to compensate this producer for reduced future harvests.

What influences an individual producer's reservation price?

Up to this point we have been discussing the idea of reservation price as though it were some easily calculable amount and as though it was relevant to depletable resources under all circumstances. In fact, it is not easily calculable and not always relevant.

To see why this is so, consider some of the factors that will influence an individual producer's reservation price.

1. The *interest rate* is important. If I leave fish in the pond for future harvests, I forego the interest income on the revenue I could have earned by the sale of those fish today. If the interest rate is low, the income I forego is smaller than when the interest rate is high. *Ceteris paribus,* the higher the interest rate, the lower the reservation price since I have less incentive to withhold fish from the market.

2. The *expected future price of the resource* is important. If the future price is expected to rise substantially, the individual producer has an incentive to curtail harvesting in order to sell at the higher future price. Under these circumstances, the reservation price could be sizable. Moreover, note how the expected future price and the interest rate interact. Suppose fish prices are expected to rise by 10 percent per year over the next several years. Should I sharply curtail

harvesting? Maybe and maybe not. Suppose the interest rate is currently 12 percent and is expected to remain there indefinitely. Couldn't I do better by harvesting now, collecting the revenue, and banking it at 12 percent? I would earn 12 percent more per year in contrast to the 10 percent additional I would earn by leaving the fish unharvested.

3. The *expected future cost of harvesting* is important. *Ceteris paribus,* the higher the expected future cost of harvesting, the less incentive I have to withhold fish from the market; the smaller, therefore, my reservation price will be.

4. The *carrying capacity of the pond,* the *current fish population,* and the *maximum sustainable yield* are important, too. If the fish population is equal to the carrying capacity of the pond, I have no incentive to withhold *all* my fish from the market, even if the future price I expect is dramatically higher than today's prices. I can harvest some fish with no loss in ultimate yield. The reservation price would thus be zero. (MC would coincide with MC* in Figure 25.3.) Of course, the reservation price would not be zero for *all* rates of production. For low rates of production it might be zero; for higher rates of production—rates of production that cut significantly into future growth—the reservation price could be positive and sizable.

5. Finally, since ponds can be restocked and harvested trees replanted, the reservation price—the excess over marginal harvesting cost—will be affected by such activities. Whether such activities are profitable will depend on the four items just listed. Because the future is at best uncertain, there is no simple mechanical procedure for calculating the reservation prices for our depletable resources. The concept of reservation price is nonetheless important. Its inclusion in the market prices of those resources is critical as far as efficiency in the allocation of our resources is concerned.

Monopoly power and depletable resources

The perfectly competitive outcome discussed above resulted in a price for fish in excess of its marginal production or harvesting cost. Yet

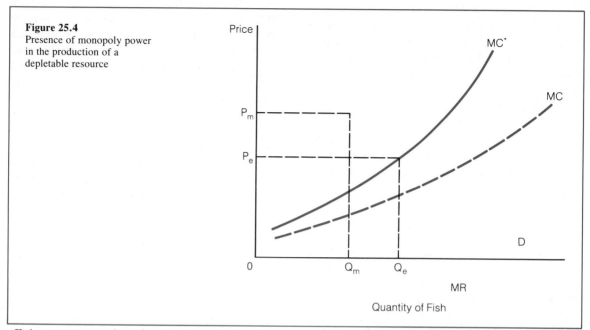

Figure 25.4
Presence of monopoly power
in the production of a
depletable resource

efficiency was not impaired. Indeed, in the face of positive reservation prices, efficiency obtains only when price equals MC*. However, if monopoly power were present—if, for example, all ponds were owned by a single individual or corporation—efficiency would be impaired. Figure 25.4 illustrates this possibility.

The market demand curve for fish is the demand curve faced by the individual producer. Rather than charge the price that equates MC*—marginal production cost plus the reservation price—and demand, the monopolist would maximize profits by selecting that output that equates MR and MC*, charging a price of P_M, a price well in excess of P_e. In this instance, efficiency is impaired in the same manner as it was impaired in our prior discussion of monopoly power.

THE ECONOMICS OF NONRENEWABLE RESOURCES

The above ideas are all highly relevant to the pricing of **nonrenewable resources**—such resources as coal, oil, and iron ore, which, unlike fish and trees, cannot be reproduced. Of course, in these instances, the notion of maximum sus-

tainable yield makes no sense. Since these resources are nonrenewable, it is not possible to extract given fixed amounts on a sustained basis *indefinitely*. Depending on the amounts available and the rate of extraction, it may be possible to stretch out the supply for a long period. But, because the extraction of any amount today means that much less available for use tomorrow, this cannot go on indefinitely.

Although the notion of sustainable yield is not relevant, the idea of reservation price is relevant to the study of nonrenewable resources. Because a barrel of oil extracted today means lost future production, the "cost" of each barrel of oil extracted today exceeds the cost of extraction itself.

Although nonrenewable resources are finite, we must be careful not to draw conclusions that are unwarranted. Take oil as an example. We are often told that, at current rates of extraction, we will run out of oil at some point in the not-too-distant future; as a consequence, our economic system will grind to a halt. This is reckless thinking.

First, from the point of view of the physical quantity of oil available from the earth's crust, we are a long way from exhausting the supply of oil. There are huge untapped quantities of oil available from tar sands and oil shale; and it is widely believed that a great deal of oil exists under the floors of our oceans. The reason these sources of oil have not been exploited to a greater extent than they are now is straightforward. The price of oil, although very high by the price standards of the 1960s and earlier, is not yet high enough to make these alternative sources of oil commercially viable (i.e., sufficiently profitable) options.

Second, oil is not our only energy source. As is well known, we have huge supplies of coal and natural gas. True, the quantities of coal and natural gas are finite and cannot last forever. But besides these energy sources, there are uranium, wind, oceanic, and solar sources of energy that are nearly infinite in their capacity to supply energy. However, as is the case with the alternative sources of oil identified earlier, many of these alternate energy sources are not now viable commercially. Today, the costs of most of these alternatives are so high that they are unprofitable even at current energy prices.

What is important to note about these two ideas is this: *The various energy sources are substitutes for one another. As conventional sources of energy become scarcer, their prices will rise, making it profitable to tap unconventional energy sources.* The conclusions that follow from these observations can be stated directly.

First, even if oil production is stopped altogether, that will not mean that we will have "run out of oil" in the sense that we will have completely exhausted our oil supplies. On the contrary, oil production is likely to cease long before we have reduced the supply of oil to zero. To extract the last few barrels of oil from most existing wells is frequently very costly. At some point, alternate sources of oil and nonconventional sources of energy will prove to be more profitable options. Once that point is reached, existing wells will be shut down and resources will shift from well production to the alternatives, even though some oil remains in the wells. Moreover, it is conceivable that very little oil will ultimately be

extracted from oil shale and tar sands, despite the vast quantities that are known to exist in these forms. This is because the prices at which these sources of supply become profitable could well be in excess of the prices at which nonconventional energy sources such as solar and nuclear become profitable.

Second, it is not true that the economic system will inevitably grind to a halt if oil production were to cease. On the contrary, the economy would probably continue to *grow,* the principal reason being that ever-increasing amounts of energy can be had from nonconventional sources of supply.

The conservation of nonrenewable resources

In our study of the economics of renewable resources we defined *conservation* as preventing the parent population of the resource from falling below the level associated with the maximum sustainable yield. Since the idea of sustainable yield has no significance in the case of nonrenewable resources, the definition of *conservation* needs to be altered accordingly. *In the case of nonrenewable resources, conservation means achieving the optimum—the best—allocation over time.*

Discovering the optimum allocation over time for nonrenewable resources is not simple. To see why this is so, consider a highly simplified example.

The optimum allocation over time under perfect competition. Assume that (*a*) the market for oil is perfectly competitive, (*b*) the amount of oil available is known with certainty, (*c*) all oil is privately owned, and (*d*) the costs of extracting oil are zero. Under these circumstances it is easy to show that the price of oil will rise over time at a rate equal to the rate of interest. If the rate of interest happens to be 10 per cent per annum, the price of oil will advance at a rate of 10 percent per year, *ceteris paribus.*

To see why this is so, consider the situation from the point of view of individual producers. They all know they face only one choice—to remove their oil and sell it *today* or to leave part or all of it in the ground for *future extraction.* For each barrel they remove and sell today they receive a price equal to, say, P_0. That amount of money can be used to purchase an interest-bearing asset offering a yield of i percent. A barrel of oil sold today could yield the owner an amount equal to $P_0 \times (1 + i)$ one year from now. Two years from now that amount would grow to $P_0 \times (1 + i)^2$. In three years, the amount would grow to $P_0 \times (1 + i)^3$. And so on.

Now the question each owner must ask is, Can I do better financially by leaving part or all of the oil in the ground for future extraction? That will depend on the expected future price of oil. If oil prices are expected to rise by less than the rate of interest, I have an incentive to remove the oil now, sell it, and invest the proceeds in interest-bearing assets. Suppose the price of oil is expected to rise by 5 percent per year and the interest rate is equal to 10 percent. If I leave the oil in the ground for future extraction, my wealth will rise over time at an annual rate of 5 percent. If I were to sell all of my oil now and invest the proceeds in assets paying 10 percent interest, my wealth would grow at 10 percent per annum. The incentive to extract the oil and sell it now is apparent. On the other hand, if the future price of oil is expected to rise at a rate in excess of the rate of interest, owners have an incentive to withhold oil from the market.

It is important to see that decisions made by producers to sell or not to sell today cause changes in the conditions initially presumed to prevail. If several producers decide to step up production to sell *now* (because the prevailing rate of interest exceeds the expected future price of oil), this will reduce today's oil prices and raise future oil prices (because increased sales today reduce future supplies, causing increased future prices). The reduction in current oil prices and the increase in future oil prices serve to eliminate the incentives producers have to sell now. Ultimately, rates of extraction will be adjusted until the expected rate of price increase equals the rate of interest.

Now consider the problem from the other end. Suppose, at first, that the expected rate of increase in oil prices exceeds the rate of interest. Producers have an incentive to withhold oil from the market. This raises current prices and, because future supplies will be larger than otherwise, lowers future prices. Ultimately, the rate of the price increase expected will equal the rate of interest.

Some qualifications. Although the tendency for the rate of oil price increase to match the rate of interest is clear enough, there are many reasons the patterns of oil price changes may be quite different. Consider for a moment the assumptions that were used in establishing the relationship between the rate of price increase and the interest rate.

The known fixed quantity. We assumed that the amount of oil available was known with certainty. This is far from the truth; the quantity of oil available is highly uncertain.

We can divide the quantity of oil into three types of deposits—**proven reserves** (*known* quantities of oil reserves), **potentially recoverable reserves** (estimated quantities of oil that are believed to exist), and **other reserves** (unknown and unsuspected quantities of oil). The only amounts of oil known for sure are proven reserves. But proven reserves constitute the absolute minimum of our oil resources. As new discoveries are made—i.e., as potentially recoverable reserves and other reserves are converted to proven reserves—the known quantities of oil will increase.

The point is, we have only a rough idea of how much oil is locked away in the earth's crust. We know that oil supplies are dwindling—indeed, we started running out of oil the day we removed the very first barrel—but how much is left is very much an open question.

How much oil people *believe* is available is important to the determination of oil prices under perfect competition. If only a small quantity of oil is believed to be available, the reservation price for each barrel of oil extracted is likely to be very high, a reflection of its perceived high degree of scarcity. If large quantities of oil are believed to be available, on the other hand, the reservation price will be correspondingly lower.

It is important to note that the amount of oil people believe to be available changes over time for reasons other than just the fact that oil extracted yesterday leaves that much less oil available today. Thus, as new discoveries are made—particularly large discoveries that cause people to revise upward their estimates of the amount of oil available—there will be downward revisions in the reservation prices of the oil producers, an outcome that will serve to lower future prices more than would otherwise have occurred. Under the circumstances, oil prices will rise for a while at a rate less rapid than the rate of interest. Future oil prices could actually fall for a while. On the other hand, if exploration and development programs fail to discover oil in quantities that people believed existed, the consequence will be downward revisions in their estimates of the amount of oil available, and upward revisions in the reservation prices of the oil producers. This will cause even higher future oil prices than those implied by the rate of interest.

In the face of revised expectations about th quantities of oil available, prices will change over time at rates different from the rate of interest. And, if those expectations change frequently enough, the pattern of oil price change over time may be dramatically different from the pattern described earlier.

Alternative energy sources. Of course, the quantity of oil available is not the only important consideration. The quantities of substitute energy sources are also important. These substitute energy sources include not only conventional sources, such as natural gas and coal, but less conventional sources, such as solar, oceanic, and nuclear. It should be clear that major new natural gas discoveries will cause the future price of oil to be lower than it would otherwise have been. And if a scientific breakthrough permits nonconventional sources of energy supply to come on stream earlier than expected, this too will moderate future oil prices.

Extraction costs. We assumed earlier that extraction costs were zero. Admittedly, this assumption is unrealistic, though it is worth emphasizing that, for a great many oil wells both here and in other countries, the costs of extraction are negligible relative to the price of oil.

According to many studies, the costs of extraction in the Middle East averaged less than $1 per barrel in 1981 compared with a per barrel price of around $35.

The assumption of zero extraction costs was convenient because it enabled us to focus attention better on the nature of the trade-off between the present and the future inherent in each producer's decision to extract oil now or to wait. It also enabled us to talk in terms of a given *fixed quantity* of oil, because as long as costs are zero (or negligible), they will not play an important part in the determination of how much is available for use by buyers; the total amount "available" to be extracted does not depend on price. However, when costs are not negligible, and particularly when the costs of extraction for the *marginal* barrel of oil are not negligible, the quantity "available" to be extracted is very much dependent on price. We find, for example, that it is often only profitable to employ **secondary** and **tertiary recovery methods**—increasingly expensive techniques for extracting oil that are often needed after wells have been partially depleted in order to recover more of what remains—when oil prices rise sufficiently to cover the extra costs of these methods. Under these circumstances, the quantity available, far from being fixed, depends on current and prospective oil prices; the amount of oil "available" rises with the price of oil. Moreover, increasing oil prices provide producers with incentives to step up expenditures for exploration and development of both conventional and nonconventional sources of oil, further changing the amount "available." In addition to the extra spending to produce more oil, higher oil prices stimulate the production of oil substitutes. All of these developments influence the pattern of movement of the price of oil over time.

Private ownership. We assumed earlier that all oil was owned privately. When that is the case, profit-maximizing producers will be motivated to accomplish the "correct," optimum allocation of oil over time. The reason? The optimum allocation is the one that provides producers with the greatest wealth possible. On the other hand, if oil is a common property resource whose production is uncontrolled by government, the result will be an inefficient use of oil over time. Why? First, everyone has an obvious incentive to extract as much oil as possible (subject to cost constraints) *immediately*. There is a danger that if you don't get yours now you won't get any since others, whom you do not control, have free access as well. Second, although those who are fortunate enough to get the oil because they got to it first could store it up and spread its allocation over time in accordance with the thinking enunciated above, storage costs will frequently *not* be negligible. To avoid large storage costs you have an incentive to sell off more now than would be deemed desirable. Thus, to ensure the optimum allocation of a common property nonrenewable resource over time, it is necessary for government to intervene to control its extraction and use.

Perfect competition. Finally, we earlier assumed a world of perfect competition. This too is an unrealistic assumption. Given the existence of the OPEC cartel, the world oil market is probably more accurately described as monopolistic than competitive. The contrast between the monopoly outcome and the perfectly competitive outcome is captured in Figure 25.5.

The curve labeled MC* is *not* the usual mar-

ginal cost curve; it is the reservation price curve discussed in the first section of this chapter. The perfectly competitive outcome would be given by the point E_C, implying the competitive quantity, Q_C, and the competitive price, P_C. The monopoly (or cartel) outcome, by contrast, is given by the point E_M, implying the monopoly quantity, Q_M, and the monopoly price, P_M. As is apparent, the cartel serves to both raise price and reduce quantity relative to the result that would emerge under pure competition. And, importantly, the allocation over time by the cartel will, in general, be different from that under pure competition.

As is made clear from Figure 25.5, a profit-maximizing cartel is more conservational than a perfectly competitive market. That is, the profit-maximizing cartel will put fewer barrels on the market for sale today, with the result that more will be left for future years. In a time when a great many people tout the advantages of greater conservation, this point has not been lost on OPEC leaders. OPEC often declares that its cartel pricing and production policies are actually doing the world a favor. By ensuring that less will be consumed today, it guarantees that more will be available tomorrow.

This argument is frequently trotted out by

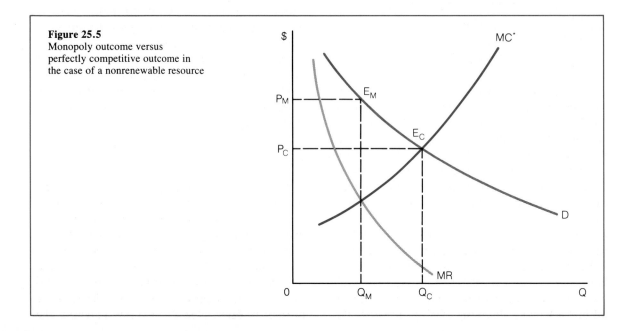

Figure 25.5
Monopoly outcome versus
perfectly competitive outcome in
the case of a nonrenewable resource

OPEC leaders to "demonstrate" that whereas other monopolies might cause undesirable outcomes, the OPEC cartel is "needed" to ensure that the available oil will last longer. This line has not been warmly received by the oil importing nations, and for good reason. First, if the objective is to conserve as much as possible, the logical conclusion would be to set a price so high that none is consumed! This is not even an interesting outcome from the point of view of what constitutes the best use of our nonrenewable resources. Also, it doubtless holds little appeal for the OPEC producers because such an outcome would imply zero revenue. However, addressing the issue in this way makes clear that *the objective is not to conserve as much as possible, but to achieve the optimum allocation over time.*

In this regard, there is good reason to think that the OPEC cartel would produce a less optimum distribution over time than would be the case under perfect competition. The reason?

By setting a price in each time period that is higher than the competitive price, the OPEC cartel hastens the day when oil will be replaced by nonconventional sources of energy; oil shale, tar sands, solar, oceanic, and other energy sources become commercially viable options that much sooner. At the time when the switchover to nonconventional energy sources is complete, more oil will be remaining in the ground than would have been the case under perfect competition.

This discussion brings us to another widely misunderstood issue—namely, the objectives of Saudi Arabia in pursuing the policies it does within OPEC. Saudi Arabia is frequently held in high esteem in the West because of its "restrained" pricing policies and its refusal to go along with some of the more radical OPEC producers who seek ever higher prices and production cutbacks. Is Saudi Arabia behaving as a friend of the West for its actions? Perhaps. But there is an alternative view of Saudi actions. First, if Saudi Arabia desired to be so "good" to us, how does one explain Saudi support of a policy that caused a fourfold increase in the price of oil in 1974 and a doubling of oil prices in 1979,

actions that caused massive disruptions throughout the world economy? Our skepticism of Saudi Arabia's motives is further bolstered by the fact that increases in oil prices by magnitudes desired by some OPEC nations may be entirely inconsistent with the maximization of wealth by OPEC. That is, insofar as higher oil prices spur the exploration and development of alternative energy sources, hastening the day when OPEC oil will be replaced by other kinds of energy, the run-up of oil prices at too rapid a rate could mean less wealth overall. In other words, the actions of Saudi Arabia to curb oil price hikes and to maintain high levels of production may have nothing to do with "friendly feelings" toward the West. It may be that such actions are justified simply on the grounds of profit maximization.

THE THEORY OF DEPLETABLE RESOURCES AND ECONOMIC GROWTH

The theory of depletable resources developed in this chapter is very relevant to the debate over whether the world economy has the capacity to grow continuously well into the forseeable future. Some doomsday predictions imply that production must ultimately come to a grinding halt because the supply of nonrenewable resources is fixed and because production activity gobbles up those resources. This was the conclusion reached by a group of MIT scientists writing in the late 1960s and early 1970s in a series of widely publicized studies that caused alarmed reactions throughout the world.

Limits to growth

One of these studies, by Prof. Jay W. Forrester, entitled *World Dynamics* (published in 1971), came to the following conclusion: *The material standard of living for the world will peak in 1990 and decline thereafter.* Forrester argued that (*a*) industrialization "may be a more fundamental disturbing force in world ecology than is population," (*b*) "there may be no realistic hope of the present underdeveloped countries reaching the standard of living demonstrated by the present industrialized nations," (c) "a society with a high level of industrialization may be unsustainable," and (d) "the present efforts of underdeveloped countries to industrialize may be unwise."

Is there any way to avert the decline in living standards after 1990? Yes, Forrester tells us, but only under very stringent conditions. The natural-resource-usage rate must be reduced by 75 percent; gross investment must be reduced by 40 percent; pollution generation must be reduced by 50 percent; food production must be reduced by 20 percent; and the birthrate must be reduced by 30 percent.

This is strong stuff. Without the adoption of some incredibly dramatic policies, our quality of life will deteriorate. The hopes and aspirations of the teeming millions of people who live in underdeveloped countries cannot possibly be satisfied. Even if stringent policies are enacted, the best we can hope for is approximately today's average world standard of living.

The main reason Forrester came to these conclusions stemmed from (a) his explicit assumption that the stock of exhaustible, nonreproducible resources was fixed in supply at a level equal to 400 times the quantity consumed in a single year, and (b) his implicit assumption that no possibilities exist of substituting plentiful for scarce resources and that there will be no new discoveries of nonreproducible resources or the development of synthetic substitutes.

With these assumptions it is obvious that the economic system will eventually grind to a halt. As long as production goes on, nonrenewable resources will continue to be gobbled up until there are no more. After that point is reached, production will stop.

How reasonable are Forrester's assumptions? According to most studies by economists, his assumptions are not reasonable at all. First, there is no evidence whatsoever to suggest that the stock of exhaustible, nonreproducible resources is fixed in supply at 400 times current consumption for a year, or at any other amount times current consumption. Actually, the degree of scarcity among resources varies dramatically. Whereas the known reserves of gold, mercury,

and silver are only about 10 times current annual consumption, the known reserves of oxygen, nitrogen, chlorine, and uranium are tens of millions times larger than current annual consumption.

Second, the implicit assumption that plentiful resources cannot be substituted for scarce resources enjoys no empirical support. Iron and aluminum can be used to replace copper in communication satellites. Chlorine can be used to replace iodine. The xerography process can be used to replace tin and lead in printing. Uranium used in the generation of nuclear power can replace oil and natural gas as sources of energy. And solar power, which is essentially infinite in its capacity to supply energy, can be used to replace other energy sources.

Finally, no allowance has been made by Forrester for the development of synthetic and nonsynthetic substitutes, an outcome that is certainly possible but at considerable variance with our history.

The point of this whole discussion can be put simply: There is no necessary reason economic growth must inevitably come to a halt just because nonrenewable resources are fixed in supply with no possibility of further increase. The reason? If the economy functions as it has in the past, adaptive adjustments will be wrought in the face of the relative price changes that will occur as existing nonrenewable resources become increasingly scarce. Forrester's conclusions would ring truer if all production required the use of these nonrenewable resources, if new discoveries were ruled out, and if there were no prospects of developing substitutes, synthetic or otherwise. However, such an economic system would be very different from the one we live in now and not at all descriptive of how our economic system has evolved over time. Indeed, the price mechanism operates in our economic system to induce the substitution of plentiful resources for scarce resources. This is accomplished directly through the substitution of renewable and reproducible resources for nonrenewables, and indirectly through the substitution of goods that are less intensive in nonrenewable resources for those that are more nonrenewable-intensive. Moreover, as the prices of scarce non-renewable resources rise relative to the prices of other resources, investment tends to be spurred to search out and discover new sources of supply and to develop synthetic and nonsynthetic substitutes.

The fact that we will eventually "run out" of nonrenewable resources does not mean that economic growth must necessarily come to a grinding halt once that point is reached. True, growth may be less robust than when nonrenewable resources were more abundant, and the mix of goods will undoubtedly change over time. But the idea that growth must cease altogether cannot be supported.

Global 2000

Although most public attention has been focused on the need to conserve nonrenewable resources, which must eventually run out, a 1980 report issued by the U.S. government entitled *Global 2000 Report to the President* points to serious stresses currently operating to threaten our renewable resources.

The major findings and conclusions of *Global 2000* are summarized in the following two paragraphs.

If present trends continue, the world in 2000 will be more crowded, more polluted, less stable ecologically and more vulnerable to disruption than the world we live in now. Serious stresses involving population, resources, and environment are clearly visible ahead. Despite greater material output, the world's people will be poorer in many ways than they are today.

For hundreds of millions of the desperately poor, the outlook for food and other necessities of life will be no better. For many it will be worse. Barring revolutionary advances in technology, life for most people on earth will be more precarious in 2000 than it is now—unless the nations of the world act decisively to alter current trends.

In greater detail, *Global 2000* suggested that, *in the absence of changes in current policies and practices,* the world in the year 2000 could be characterized as follows:

6.4 billion people will populate the Earth, an increase of 55 percent since 1975. Fully 77 percent of that population—5 billion people—will live in the Less Developed Countries (LDCs). Already crowded LDC cities will become more crowded: Mexico City will have more than 30 million people; Calcutta will have nearly 20 million; and Greater Bombay, Jakarta, and Seoul will all be in the 15–20 million range. And what will life be like for those teeming millions? Miserable. Most of the people in those LDC cities will live in "uncontrolled settlements"—slums and shanty towns where sanitation, water supplies, and health care will be minimal at best. And difficult as urban conditions are likely to become, conditions in the rural areas of many LDCs will be worse.

Will food production grow by an amount sufficient to sustain 6.4 billion people in the year 2000? The U.S. Government's globalists tell us yes, but then add that most of the increase will go to countries that are already well fed. For the LDCs, rising food output will barely keep pace with population growth; and for the poorest LDCs—in parts of the Mideast, Asia and Africa—a "calamitous drop" in food per capita will occur: More than one billion people—about 20 percent of the world's population—will not have enough to eat; and "the quantity of food available to the poorest groups of people will simply be insufficient to permit children to reach normal body weight and intelligence."

Rapid population growth and the increased incidence of poverty pose a serious threat to the globe's renewable resource base: Half the world's forests will be gone by the year 2000; arable land per person will decline, on the average, by more than one-third; the resources essential for agriculture will deteriorate further in many parts of the world, the result of enlarged desert areas (estimated to grow by 20 percent by the year 2000), increased soil erosion, further loss of nutrients, increased air and water pollution, increased salination of both irrigated land and water used for irrigation, and more frequent and more severe regional water shortages; and, between 500,000 and two million plant and animal species—15 to 20 percent of all species on earth—will face extinction, a rate of extinction unprecedented in human history.

From 1975 to 2000, petroleum reserves per capita will decline by at least 50 percent, and energy supplies generally will tighten further, an outcome that is all the more troubling in view of the Report's conclusion that virtually all of the increase in food production will be the consequence of a marked increase in energy-intensive inputs and technologies such as fertilizers, pesticides, herbicides and irrigation.

In the period from 1975 to 2000 the world's water supply will decline by 35 percent and its quality will deteriorate.

As grim as this picture is, it could be overly optimistic. For example, the energy projections made in *Global 2000* were prepared in late 1977 using price assumptions that implied lower energy prices through the year 2000 than many people now believe will be the case. If the higher energy prices prove to be correct, this will raise the costs of energy-intensive production processes, an outcome that may slow food production more than the report suggests.

Additionally, the higher real price of energy could raise the rate of deforestation (as more wood is consumed for cooking and heating); and hasten the loss of soil nutrients (as growing amounts of dung and crop residues are shifted to cooking fires).

It was also assumed in the report that the world fish catch would increase at about the same rate as population, a projection that could prove optimistic as well. The world catch of naturally produced fish actually leveled off in the 1970s. Most estimates now suggest that the world fish harvest will rise little, if any at all, by 2000.

Of course, it is also possible to argue that the report paints too pessimistic a picture. The report claims, for example, that land under cultivation will increase by only 4 percent by 2000 "because most good land is already being cultivated." However, some studies suggest that cropland could be 50 percent greater than today. In addition, many farm specialists believe that much food production is now so inefficient that improved management techniques alone could produce sizable yield gains. Technological advance could further greatly expand agricultural output per acre.

Moreover, the transition of the world away from petroleum dependence may occur more rapidly than was anticipated at the time the energy projections were made. This is in part because

the real price of energy has increased so much more than was then anticipated. The change would provide incentives to speed up the timetable of transition. According to many experts, *aquaculture* could, given adequate financial and technical support, raise sharply the production of freshwater and marine species—a fivefold to tenfold increase by 2000, according to the 1976 FAO World Conference on Aquaculture. Moreover, although the base of many natural resources will undoubtedly be further eroded, other resources will remain abundant. And many more mineral resources in our oceans, such as manganese and copper, have yet to be tapped.

> The point is that we have no clear fix on what is in store for planet Earth in the year 2000. However, it was not the purpose of the *Global 2000* report to predict what will occur, but to project what could occur if today's policies and practices continue unaltered for the next two decades. The message that comes through loud and clear is this: If today's global policies and practices continue into the future, we will see an increasingly crowded world, a world in which growing numbers of people are suffering hunger and privation, a world that will, as a consequence, be more vulnerable to violence and upheaval than the world we live in now.

In any event, one of the most important findings of *Global 2000* is the apparent threat to the earth's renewable resource base. In the view of the report's authors, the earth's carrying capacity—the ability of biological systems to meet human needs—is being eroded. By the year 2000, matters could be considerably worse.

It was this alarming projection, perhaps more than any other, that led the U.S. government to issue an urgent plea for "prompt changes in public policy" all around the world. Unfortunately, the report failed to indicate just how dramatic the policy changes would have to be in order to avert the catastrophe that might otherwise occur. As the analysis in the first section of this chapter makes clear, there is a need to aim for that optimum-sized renewable resource base that is capable of generating maximum sustainable yields. Whether the optimum-sized resource bases for many resources are larger or smaller than at present is an open question—and a question that the report failed to address specifically.

It is important to address this question in order to determine more precisely the magnitude of the global efforts that must be undertaken to avoid the disaster that *Global 2000* envisions. If the globe's renewable resource base has been pushed below its optimum size, the pace of development that can be sustained will be less than its maximum. In order to achieve the optimum-sized resource base and the maximum pace of development, it may be necessary to cut consumption of renewable resources below current sustainable yields in order to build up the resource base itself. Of course, if the renewable resource base has not yet been reduced to its optimum size, it is possible to continue to step up resource consumption at a rate equal to the maximum sustainable yield; such a rate of consumption could be sustained indefinitely.

The problem is that we do not know with any precision what the optimum resource base is. Many suspect, however, given the progressive impoverishment of our renewable resource base, that we have passed the optimum point for a great many resources. If this is true, the problems we face are truly formidable, because it implies that without massive income and wealth transfers from the developed to the less developed nations, that we could witness ever-growing numbers of desperate, poverty-stricken people throughout the world. Of course, because so many of the pressures on renewable resources are, as the *Global 2000* report put it, "the result of the desperate struggle of poverty-stricken peoples to stay alive," it will be all the more difficult to accomplish the goals of sound resource management and environmental protection. But implementing the resource management and environmental protection that will ultimately improve conditions for the poor means also to restrict their use of resources now, reducing their current below-subsistence level of existence even further.

SUMMARY

1.   Although renewable resources can be reproduced, they can also be exhausted. Resources exhaustion will occur, for example, if the rate of extraction of the resources exceeds the natural rate of increase. The *sustainable yield* of a resource refers to the amount of the resource that can be extracted, period after period, indefinitely. The *maximum sustainable yield* refers to the maximum amount of the resource that can be extracted, period after period, indefinitely.

2.   From the point of view of renewable resources, *conservation* means preventing the parent population of the resource from falling below that level associated with the maximum sustainable yield.

3.   In order to bring about the conservation outcome for renewable resources, it is often necessary to restrict harvesting in some manner. In the case of *common property resources,* it is necessary to intervene if the unrestricted depletion rate exceeds the maximum sustainable yield. The problems that can and do arise with common property resources often do *not* arise when the resource in question is owned privately. Unlike common property resources, the owners of renewable resources have an interest in ensuring continued future supplies.

4.   In the case of renewable resources, the supply curve that is relevant to determining the market price is not, in general, the curve formed by summing up the MC curves of the individual sellers. Rather, the relevant supply curve will generally lie above and to the left of our usual supply curve, reflecting the extra cost—the loss in future harvests—caused by today's harvest. The extra cost is referred to as the *reservation price* for the resource in question. It is called a reservation price because it represents the price differential that is necessary to compensate for the reduced future output.

5.   The reservation price is influenced by several factors: the interest rate, the expected future price of the resource, the expected future cost of harvesting, the maximum sustainable yield,

the current parent population of the resource, and the carrying capacity of the environment.

6. In the case of *nonrenewable resources,* the notion of maximum sustainable yield makes no sense; it is not possible to extract given fixed amounts on a sustained basis *indefinitely.* However, the idea of reservation price is relevant to the study of nonrenewable resources. Because the amount extracted today means lost future production, the "cost" of the amount extracted today exceeds the cost of extraction itself.

7. In discussions of nonrenewable resources, it is important not to draw conclusions that are unwarranted. Take oil as an example. It is important to recognize that the various energy sources are substitutes for one another. As conventional sources of energy become scarcer, their prices will rise, making it profitable to tap nonconventional energy sources.

8. In the case of nonrenewable resources, conservation means achieving the optimum—the best—allocation over time.

9. Under a number of restrictive assumptions—(*a*) the market for oil is perfectly competitive, (*b*) the amount of oil available is known with certainty, (*c*) all oil is privately owned, and (*d*) the costs of extraction are zero—the price of oil will rise over time at a rate equal to the rate of interest. Violate those assumptions and the pattern of price change will be different from the rate of interest.

10. A profit-maximizing cartel is more conservational than a perfectly competitive market; that is, the profit-maximizing cartel will put fewer barrels on the market for sale today, with the result that more will be left for future years. However, to be more conservational does not necessarily better serve the public interest. The objective is not to necessarily conserve more, but to achieve the optimum allocation of the nonrenewable resource over time. There is good reason to think that the OPEC cartel would produce a less optimum distribution over time than would be the case under perfect competition.

CONCEPTS FOR REVIEW

Reproducible resources

Depletable resources

Renewable resources

Nonrenewable resources

Sustainable yield

Maximum sustainable yield

Conservation and property rights

Common property resources

Reservation price

Proven reserves

Potentially recoverable reserves

Other reserves

Secondary and tertiary recovery methods

QUESTIONS FOR DISCUSSION

(Those marked with an asterisk (*) are more difficult.)

1. We have all seen numerous television commercials requesting that we conserve our oil and natural gas resources. One very popular ad depicts a young boy who pleads with us to save energy for his generation; the background is a barren, wind-swept desert. What message is the ad attempting to convey? How truthful is the ad? Carefully evaluate.

*2. Price controls on oil and natural gas were in effect during most of the 1970s. It was felt by a majority in Congress that, among other things, controls were necessary to prevent the oil companies from reaping huge windfall profits as a consequence of the very sharp increase in world oil prices engineered by OPEC late in 1973 and early 1974. "Why," many in Congress asked, "should the oil companies get a huge increase in profits on oil that has already been discovered and in the ground? It isn't fair."

Without attempting to address the question of what is fair or not fair, many critics of controls argued that the controls themselves encouraged "wasteful consumption" of energy; controls actually discouraged exploration and development of not only alternative sources of oil and natural gas, but alternative energy sources generally. Evaluate this case against controls. (*Hint:* Use your knowledge of demand and supply to illustrate your answer.)

3. "The reservation price for a renewable resource will be zero as long as the parent population is in excess of the rate associated with the maximum sustainable yield." Carefully evaluate.

4. Explain why models used to forecast the future may be unrealistic if they assume that production requires the input of nonrenewable resources that are fixed in supply.

*5. The *Global 2000 Report* suggests that the renewable resource base will erode sharply by the year 2000 unless policy actions are taken to reverse present trends. If, in fact, the renewable resource base has eroded so much that renewable resources are below the levels associated with their maximum sustainable yields, how will market forces operate to slow the erosion of the base? Are "policy changes" absolutely essential to slow the erosion of the natural resource base?

6. The man on the street argues that we will soon run out of oil; the economist says, "Nonsense. We will never run out of oil." Who is probably right, and does it matter?

Chapter 26

Income inequality

The previous four chapters examined in detail the forces that determine the income returns to the various factors of production—land, labor, and capital. The income returns to these factors of production were divided into four types—wages, rent, interest, and profits. The proportion of our total national income accruing to each of the factors of production yields what is known as the **functional distribution of income.** In this chapter we turn our attention from the functional to the **personal distribution of income.**

The functional and personal distributions of income are related to one another in a fairly straightforward manner—on the basis of **factor ownership.** As a result of our earlier study of resource markets, we have a fairly good understanding of what determines the income flows to land, labor, and capital; to whom these income flows accrue is determined by who owns these resources.

The income inequality that we observe in the United States is largely the consequence of inequality in the distribution of ownership of our factors of production. By most reports, capital ownership is very unequally distributed—40 percent or more of the stock of physical capital in the private sector is owned by 1 percent of the population. Ownership of land, including natural resources, is also apparently very unequally distributed. Ownership of labor is more equally distributed when defined in terms of the number of hours supplied. But it is much less equal when defined in terms of the *quality* of labor services provided, this being extremely important to the explanation of observed differences in the distribution of labor-source income, as we saw in Chapter 23.

Taking all sources of income into account and distributing them according to who owns the resources, one comes up with the personal income distribution statistics widely reported in the press. For example, the poorest 20 percent of our population gets only 0.6 percent of our nation's total personal income (before taxes and government transfers); the richest 20 percent, on the other hand, receives almost 50 percent.

It is the purpose of this chapter to examine the magnitude of income inequality in the United

States and to assess the effects of government policies aimed at narowing income differentials among individuals, particularly government policies aimed at eliminating poverty. We will also attempt to tackle the thorny question, What degree of income equality should we strive for? Complete equality? Less inequality than now exists? More equality? As we shall see, consideration of this issue will place us squarely in the murky area known as normative economics.

MEASURING INCOME INEQUALITY

Figure 26.1 and the accompanying table represent two alternative ways of highlighting the magnitude of the income differences observed in the United States. The table tells us, for example, that the lowest-income 20 percent of the population receives only 0.6 percent of total income (before taxes and government transfers); the next

higher-income 20 percent receives 8.0 percent of total income; the next fifth of the population gets 16.5 percent; and so on. It is clear that the distribution of income is far from equal.

Just how unequal income is distributed in the United States is portrayed vividly in the graph in Figure 26.1. The curve shown in the graph is known as a **Lorenz curve.** In order to translate the data in the table onto the graph, we need to explain how to convert the income distribution data into a *cumulative* distribution.

The meaning of cumulative distribution is most easily explained by example. We see that the first 20 percent of the population receives 0.6 percent of total income. The first 40 percent receives 8.6 percent of total income—the 0.6 percent received by the lowest-income 20 percent *plus* the 8.0 percent received by the next 20 percent. And what about the first 60 percent? It is 25.0 percent of total income—the first 40 percent (8.6) *plus* the next 20 percent (16.4). In the same way it is easy to see that the first 80 percent

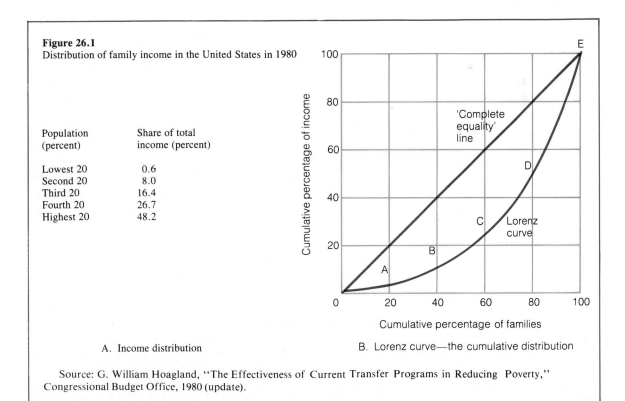

Figure 26.1
Distribution of family income in the United States in 1980

Population (percent)	Share of total income (percent)
Lowest 20	0.6
Second 20	8.0
Third 20	16.4
Fourth 20	26.7
Highest 20	48.2

A. Income distribution

B. Lorenz curve—the cumulative distribution

Source: G. William Hoagland, "The Effectiveness of Current Transfer Programs in Reducing Poverty," Congressional Budget Office, 1980 (update).

receives 51.7 percent of total income. And, obviously, the total population receives 100 percent.

The cumulative distribution is formed by adding—accumulating—the percentages of total income received as we add successive percentages of the population. The Lorenz curve represents this cumulative distribution. Thus we see from point A in the graph that 20 percent of the population receives 0.6 percent of total income; 40 percent of the population receives 8.0 percent of total income; and so on.

We also show in the graph a line labeled the *complete equality line*. This is what the Lorenz curve would look like if family income were distributed equally—i.e., if all families received exactly the same income. Under an equal distribution of income, 20 percent of the population would receive 20 percent of total income; 40 percent of the population would receive 40 percent of total income; and so on.

A useful summary measure of the degree of income inequality is given by what is called the **Gini ratio.** This ratio expresses the area of the bow-shaped portion of the graph—the area between the Lorenz curve and the complete equality line—as a percent of the total area of the triangle. The closer the Lorenz curve lies to the diagonal, the lower the Gini ratio will be; conversely, the farther away the Lorenz curve is from the complete equality line, the larger the Gini ratio will be. Inspection of the graph implies a Gini ratio of around 0.56. What would the value of the Gini ratio be if income were distributed equally?

Some international income distribution comparisons

It is clear from our discussion that incomes are far from equally distributed in the United States. Yet, compared with other countries in the world, there is generally less income inequality here than elsewhere. In fact, the greatest income inequalities are found in the less developed nations of the world, where one generally finds a very few, extremely rich people in contrast to the impoverished masses. In Thailand, for example, it has been estimated that the poorest 60

percent of the population receives only about 12 percent of total income (before taxes and government transfers), while the top 2 percent receives over one third. Compared with a Gini ratio of 0.56 in the United States, the Gini ratio in Thailand is about 0.81, nearly one and one-half the U.S. ratio. Sweden, on the other hand, has less income equality than does the United States; the Gini ratio for Sweden is only about 0.34.

A brief look at the figures behind the U.S. Lorenz curve

In one important respect, the Lorenz curve and the Gini ratio exaggerate the extent of income inequality in the United States. The reason? The data on family income for *any one year* will contain a source of inequality that would not be present if incomes were measured *over the entire lifetimes of all families*. Generally speaking, families in the earliest and latest stages of their life cycles earn *less* than those in their middle years.

Let us look at the "typical" life cycle income of a family. Because of lack of skill and experience, the typical young worker has a relatively low earning power. The earning power of young families is further held down because of children and the withdrawal of one spouse from paid employment.

As the family matures, family earnings typically rise. Workers become more skilled and experienced; the spouse who in earlier years did not work—or worked only part time—is increasingly likely to work more after the children begin school. However, family earnings usually peak in the 50–55 age bracket, then begin to decline somewhat. This is partly the result of the loss of young income earners as they begin their own family units, of early retirement and increasing illness and disability.

The point of this discussion can be put as follows.

There is less inequality of income among families when measured over their lifetimes; the inequalities observed at any single point in time in part reflect differences in stages of life cycles of different families. Even if lifetime family incomes were the same, the Lorenz curve would not coincide with the complete equality line because not all families would be in the same stage of their life cycle. Young and elderly family units would be earning less than those in their middle years, causing the Lorenz curve to "bow."

However, even when these differences are taken into account, a substantial amount of income inequality still exists in the United States. According to many economists, the bulk of the remaining income inequality can be attributed to differences in human capital—to differences in education, skill, and experience—which translate into substantial income discrepancies among U.S. families.

Income differences also result because *wealth* is very unequally distributed. Indeed, if one were to construct a Lorenz curve for the *income earned on property alone,* it would be very severely "bowed." About 65 percent of all families earn little or no income in the form of rent, interest, dividends, or royalties. By contrast, about 10 percent of all families receive approximately 70 percent of all property income. The Gini ratio for personal income from property exceeds 0.75!

There are other important sources of income inequality—the exercise of *monopoly power, discrimination* (racial, sexual, age, national origin), and pure *luck.*

In assessing the various factors responsible for the income differences we observe it is important to recognize that many are dynamically interrelated. The tremendous concentration of property and property income is partly due to the amassing of wealth by those families whose earning power is high due to education, for example. As those families mature, their growing wealth adds further to their incomes, which permits even faster accumulation.

The dynamics of wealth accumulation do not terminate with the life of the family. Wealth is passed on to the children, from one generation to the next, perpetuating both future wealth and income inequalities. Moreover, the higher earning power of many families is passed on to children in the form of better health and larger in-

vestments in education than is generally true of a lot of low-income families. While far from being the complete truth, there is much that is accurate in the notion that *high income begets high income.*

Government programs and the distribution of income

The data in Figure 26.1 and the accompanying Lorenz curve describe the distribution of income in the United States *before taxes and government transfers.* The question that now arises is, What does the distribution of income look like *after taxes and government transfers?* Figure 26.2 illustrates the difference government makes.

The outer curve is a reproduction of the Lorenz curve in Figure 26.1. It shows the cumulative distribution of income *before* taxes and government transfers. The inner curve is the Lorenz curve calculated *after* taxes and transfers. The fact that the inner Lorenz curve lies closer to the complete equality line than does the outer curve means that government tax and transfer programs, on balance, reduce inequality in the distribution of income. How much? Before taxes and transfers, the Gini ratio had a value of 0.56; after taxes and transfers, the ratio fell to 0.44, a reduction of approximately 21 percent of the before-tax-and-transfer-income inequality.

It is clear, then, that government produces a fairly substantial reduction in income inequality in the United States. Put differently, government policies have had the effect of redistributing a substantial amount of income from those higher up on the income scale to those lower down. You will note that I avoided saying that income was redistributed from the rich to the poor. To some extent, income is so redistributed. However, the greatest proportionate amount of the redistribution is from those in the middle and upper-middle income classes to those lower down. Basically, there are two reasons for this. First, most of the reduction in income inequality is accomplished by government transfer programs, not our tax system. And second, taxes are much less progressive than is commonly believed. Even federal income taxes (which are generally much

Figure 26.2
Distribution of family income in the United States in 1980, after taxes and governmental transfers

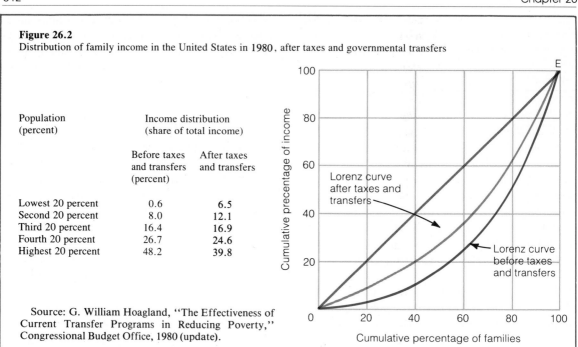

Population (percent)	Income distribution (share of total income)	
	Before taxes and transfers (percent)	After taxes and transfers
Lowest 20 percent	0.6	6.5
Second 20 percent	8.0	12.1
Third 20 percent	16.4	16.9
Fourth 20 percent	26.7	24.6
Highest 20 percent	48.2	39.8

Source: G. William Hoagland, "The Effectiveness of Current Transfer Programs in Reducing Poverty," Congressional Budget Office, 1980 (update).

more progressive than state and local income taxes) are not as progressive as the rate schedules would imply since, as their incomes rise, people increasingly are able to avail themselves of tax loopholes that keep their effective tax rates from rising as rapidly as otherwise. Property taxes are not very progressive, if at all. And most other taxes—e.g., sales and excise taxes—are regressive.

If taxes were proportional to income, the before-tax and aftertax distribution of incomes would be the same. If everyone paid 20 percent of their income to government, everyone's after-tax income would be 20 percent lower than their before-tax income and the percentage differences in incomes that existed before taxes would be preserved after taxes. To illustrate, consider two individuals, A and B, whose before-tax incomes are $10,000 and $100,000, respectively. They each pay 20 percent of their income to government, leaving them with aftertax incomes of $8,000 and $80,000, respectively; both before tax and after tax there is a tenfold spread—a 1,000

percent difference—between the incomes of A and B.

If, on the other hand, taxes are progressive, aftertax incomes would be more equal than before-tax incomes. If individual A paid 20 percent in taxes and B 40 percent, after taxes their incomes would be $8,000 and $60,000, respectively; this is a difference of only 750 percent after taxes in contrast to a before-tax difference of 1,000 percent. Finally, to the extent that taxes are regressive, incomes would be less equal after taxes than before.

Because taxes overall (federal, state, and local) are not especially progressive, we should not expect a dramatic reduction in the aftertax distribution relative to the before-tax distribution of income. And we don't. According to the careful research of some economists, of the 21 percent reduction in income inequality due to all government programs—taxes *and* transfers—only about a 5 to 6 percent reduction can be attributed to taxes. The remaining 15 to 16 percent reduction is the result of government transfers.

Government transfers are categorized into three types—social insurance, cash transfers, and in-kind transfers. The largest and by far the most important from the point of view of the overall distribution of income is **social insurance,** comprising such programs as social security (old age and survivors benefits, medicare, and disability benefits), federal employee retirement, and unemployment compensation. Of the reduction in income inequality due to taxes and transfers, almost half is the result of our social insurance programs. **Cash transfers** are second in importance, responsible for about 4 percent of the 21 percent decrease in inequality. The largest single cash transfer program consists of aid to families with dependent children (AFDC). Finally, **in-kind transfers**—the government provision of goods and services such as food, housing and medicaid—are responsible for a little more than one tenth of the reduction in income inequality.

The reduction in income inequality over time

Although incomes are far from equally distributed, even after taxes and transfers, incomes today are much more equally distributed than they were 50 years ago. Whereas the Gini ratio after taxes and transfers stands at about 0.44 today, in 1929 it stood at 0.65. A number of factors are responsible for this shift. Of considerable importance has been the widening of educational opportunity, which provided increased access to higher-paying occupations. Another important factor has been the slow but perceptible widening of occupational opportunities to blacks, other nonwhite minorities, and women. Yet another factor has been the increased mobility of the American people, migrating from lower- to higher-opportunity areas.

To a considerable extent, moreover, the reduction in income inequality has been the result of extensive changes in the system of governmental tax and transfers. Although an income tax was levied for a brief period during the Civil War, it was not until 1913 that the income tax became a permanent feature of our system of government. And tax rates in the early days were much lower than those in effect today. Whereas the highest marginal tax rate on *personal income* was only 24 percent in 1929, it is 50 percent today; and whereas the *corporate income* tax rate was only 11 percent in 1929, it varies today from 16 percent (on corporate incomes below $25,000) to a maximum of 46 percent (on corporate incomes above $100,000).

The existence of loopholes in both the income tax and inheritance tax make our tax system less progressive than is commonly believed. Nevertheless, it is much more progressive today than it was 50 years ago. This difference has had a substantial impact on the concentration of income:

1. Rising tax rates on corporate income leave smaller earnings after taxes and correspondingly smaller dividends. Since stock ownership tends to be concentrated among those families having the highest incomes, the effect of rising corporate rates has been to reduce income inequality.
2. Higher tax rates on personal income also make it more difficult today to amass a sizable estate.
3. Higher inheritance and estate taxes have reduced the transmisssion of wealth from one generation to the next.

Of even greater importance, perhaps, has been the change in the system of government transfers. Fifty years ago, unemployment insurance did not exist; nor did social insurance. Today, eligible workers who are laid off are paid nearly 66 percent of average weekly earnings; and frequently this amount is supplemented by special collective bargaining arrangements with employers—so-called supplemental unemployment benefits (SUBs). Likewise, old-age social security pensions and disability insurance contribute to the support of nearly 20 percent of the population; increasingly, retirement incomes are being supplemented by private pension plans. Finally, the transers to low-income people in the form of aid to the disabled, aid to families with dependent children, food stamps, public housing, and general assistance were virtually nonexistent 50 years ago. Although these programs have been cut sharply by the Reagan Administration, they still remain quite substantial.

THE PROBLEM OF POVERTY

Not all government transfer programs are designed specifically to aid the poor. Many very wealthy families receive old-age social security benefits. And a great many workers in high-wage cyclical industries who are temporarily laid off are eligible to receive unemployment compensation. Nonetheless, the great bulk of the monies transferred by government are concentrated at the low end of the income scale. Social security payments represent, for the majority of elderly recipients, the only significant source of retirement income. A lot of unemployment compensation goes to those at the low end of the income scale. (The less-skilled and less-well-educated workers whose earnings are near the bottom are most likely to be the first laid off.) And the monies distributed from most other transfer programs are specifically directed at those with low in-

"How could the government possibly *afford* a guaranteed annual income? As I see it, the average family needs at *least* $65,000 per year."

Reprinted by permission The Wall Street Journal.

comes and little wealth. That is, recipients must satisfy a **"means test"**, somewhat arbitrary low-income and low-wealth dividing lines that separate the eligible from the ineligible.

Defining the nation's poor

The question that naturally arises is this: How successful have governmental transfer programs been in reducing poverty in the United States? To answer this question we need to identify who the poor are. And to do that, we need to establish criteria by which we can divide the population into those that are poor and non-poor.

Establishing the appropriate criteria is not as easy as you might think. It part, it depends on whether you subscribe to a *relative poverty standard* or an *absolute poverty standard*.

The relative poverty standard. Some believe that poverty is best defined in *relative* terms. Whether or not you are poor can only be determined by comparing your income with the incomes of others. For example, it has been suggested that a family is poor if it is in the lowest 10 or 15 percent of the income distribution. The 10 percent or 15 percent figures are, of course, arbitrary: Why not 5 percent, or 25 percent? How should one decide? But there is a more fundamental problem with this particular relative definition: It is impossible to eliminate poverty as there will always be a lowest 10 percent or lowest 15 percent. Even if every family had annual earnings in excess of $1 million per year (and the prices of goods and services were the same as today), the lowest 10 or 15 percent would be defined as poor even though everyone lived luxuriously; the point of this definition is that some live more luxuriously than others. On the other hand, if earnings on average were abysmally low, a 10 or 15 percent figure could well fail to reflect the extent of the poverty prevalent generally.

Given these problems, it is apparent why this particular relative definition of poverty has not found widespread acceptance. But consider an alternative definition of poverty in relative terms: A family is poor if it earns less than, say, one half of the *average* family income or one half of the *median* family income.[1] According to this definition, it would be possible to eliminate poverty. If the income distribution were compressed so that no family earned less than 50 percent of the median or average, poverty would cease to exist. However, this definition has two problems. First, if the average or median income happens to be very high—so high that those families earning the average or median live in luxury—families earning 50 percent less than these amounts could still be very well-off by conventional standards. Or suppose the average or median happens to be very low—so low that those families earning the average or median live miserably. Would we just consider those families earning somewhat less than 50 percent of the median or average nonpoor?

The second problem with this standard is that it implies acceptance of a normative judgment about the "correct" distribution of income. We as a society are anxious to eliminate poverty, and to accomplish this no family should receive less than 50 percent of the median or average family income. Is this reasonable? Who can say?

The absolute poverty standard. It is understandable why people desire a relative poverty standard. After all, most of us judge our own well-being by comparing our position relative to others. However, as suggested above, a relative poverty standard fails to address the central question most often asked—namely, what level of income is necessary to provide a decent standard of living? What this question seeks is *not* a *relative* poverty standard but an *absolute* poverty standard.

---

[1] The average and the median family incomes are *not*, in general, the same. To get the average family income, one takes the total income of all families and divides that figure by the number of families. The median family income is that family income level that divides the family population into halves; half of the families earn more and half earn less. To illustrate the difference, consider five families in a block that earn the following amounts, respectively: $5,000, $10,000, $15,000, $20,000, and $150,000 per year. The average is $40,000; the median is only $15,000. The average is much higher than the median because one family earns so much more than the others; the $40,000 average gives a distorted picture because four out of the five families earn much less than $40,000. The median is a more accurate portrayal; it is less affected by extreme values.

It is one thing to suggest that we need some objectively determined minimum decent standard. It is quite another thing to define that standard. Ideally, we would like to be able to spell out in detail the quantities of goods and services that we consider essential to the survival or welfare of the family unit in order to arrive at our standard. But is it possible for all of us to reach agreement on what this bundle of goods and services should consist of? Some will argue that it should consist of only the minimum caloric intake essential to human existence plus the minimum required amount of shelter and clothing. A continuous diet of powdered skim milk, soy meal, and a vitamin and iron supplement would probably come close to satisfying the minimum food standard and cost very little. Flour sacks and rubber boots might even satisfy the minimum clothing requirement. And a heated room 10 feet by 12 feet in size with a toilet and wash basin is probably sufficient shelter to assure the survival of a family of four. Should we define poverty as anything less than these minimums? Or should we be more generous to make allowance for items like:

A two- or three-bedroom housing unit with a refrigerator and stove in a separate kitchen.

Hot and cold running water.

Two or three changes of clothing for each member of the family.

Cotton underwear, leather shoes, sweaters, overcoats, shirts, ties, dresses, suits, scarves, caps, and gloves.

A radio and a television (black-and-white and used, of course).

A used car (or an allowance for public transportation).

Meat, bread, potatoes, fruits, and vegetables in the diet.

A six-pack of beer now and then.

Comprehensive medical health-care coverage.

Savings (to help finance the children's education).

Obviously, the list could be extended to include yet other amenities. The point is, however, that there is no universally acceptable definition of what it means to be poor in an absolute sense. Any definition we concoct is bound to be influenced by what we feel is fair. Normative judgments will enter into any standard we devise.

It is important to recognize, moreover, that the acceptability of any absolute standard is bound to be influenced by the distribution of incomes generally. To illustrate, suppose we were to attempt to discover that level of income below which family members experience **privation**—the sense of being deprived of the usual necessities or comforts. Obviously, the higher the standard of living generally—i.e., the greater the "usual" comforts and necessities—the higher that minimum income standard will be. And can you imagine people agreeing on a minimum income defined that way? In any event, any absolute standard is likely to be influenced by prevalent relative income standards.

The official definition of poverty

Although there is no completely satisfactory way of defining *poverty,* there is an official definition used by the U.S. federal government that is best described as an absolute poverty standard. In first arriving at this standard, however, government officials did *not* attempt to set forth in detail all the goods and services deemed essential to the survival or welfare of the family unit. The U.S. standard was based on a minimum nutritionally sound food plan designed by the Department of Agriculture. The plan estimated the food requirements for each member of the family on the basis of age and sex. These requirements were combined to yield a family total. The cost of this minimum family food plan was then multiplied by 3, the resultant total being defined as the *poverty line.* The number 3 reflected the judgment of federal government officials that an amount equal to twice the food plan would be sufficient to provide people with the other bare necessities of life.

Table 26.1 shows the poverty-line income levels for farm and nonfarm families of various sizes

Table 26.1

Official poverty-line income levels for farm and nonfarm families, 1981

Number of family members	Nonfarm poverty-line income	Farm poverty-line income
2	$ 5,690	$4,850
3	7,070	6,020
4	8,450	7,190
5	9,830	8,360
6*	11,210	9,530
Unrelated individuals ("one-person families")	4,310	3,680

*For family units with more than 6 members, add $1,380 for each additional member in a nonfarm family, and $1,170 for each additional member in a farm family.

Source: U.S. Deaprtment of Commerce, Bureau of the Census.

in 1981. Since somewhat lower costs are prevalent in rural areas and many rural families grow for themselves at least some of the food they consume, the poverty-line income level for farm families is set at 85 percent of the level for nonfarm families.

As a consequence of increasing prices—in particular, increasing consumer good prices—the poverty-line level of income has increased overtime. Whereas the poverty line level for a family of four was $4,369 in 1973, it was $8,450 in 1980.

How many Americans are poor?

Many of you will no doubt be surprised at how low the official poverty-line income levels are in the United States. Indeed, many families having income levels two, three, or four times the poverty-line levels complain that they hardly have enough to make ends meet. They do not feel well off; they feel poor. Of course, many subjective considerations enter into one's assessment of one's own well-being. Nevertheless, for the vast majority of people, a family income of $8,450 per year to support four people would constitute for them a state of abject poverty.

To illustrate, suppose our hypothetical family of four spent one third of its poverty-line income on food. That would imply an expenditure of around $8 per day for a family of four, or an expenditure of less than 70 cents per person per meal. A single meal at McDonald's would blow the whole food budget for a day! Is it any wonder why people who earn well in excess of the poverty line complain.

Yet, as low as the poverty-line levels are, many families in the United States have incomes below these levels. According to U.S. government statistics, around 12 percent of families—one out of every eight—have incomes below the poverty-line levels. And as large as this number is, it is well below the 20 percent or more families measured as poor in the 1950s.

These statistics have been the subject of much heated debate. Many argue, with some justification, that poverty is much more widespread than implied here. The poverty line levels are too low. If, instead of measuring poverty as it does now, the federal government were to measure poverty in terms of income levels below which people suffer privation, perhaps 50 percent or more of the American population would be classified as poor. On the other hand, even if we accept the official poverty-line levels as constituting "acceptable" minimal levels—or at least as appropriate benchmarks—there is evidence that the official count of poverty is too high. The official poverty count is based on cash income alone (including earned income and cash transfer income

such as payments for social security, unemployment compensation and aid to families with dependent children) and excludes such in-kind transfers as public housing, food stamps, medicare, and medicaid. Translating these benefits into income equivalents and using the official poverty-line benchmarks, the poverty population falls to 3 to 6 percent of all families in 1980, according to some estimates. Whatever you think of the reasonableness of the now-official poverty-line income levels, it is certainly appropriate to adjust for in-kind transfers. Indeed, because in-kind transfers have become increasingly important over the course of the past decade, many believe that the official poverty count—based as it is on cash income alone—has become increasingly inaccurate. Although official poverty statistics show a near halving of the percent of families defined as poor between 1959 and 1969—from 22.1 percent to 12.1 percent—they show little improvement since then. However, as noted above, once account is taken of the income value of in-kind transfers and the fact that such programs have grown in importance, it is clear that steady progress has been made in reducing the incidence of poverty.

The uneven incidence of poverty

Tables 26.2 and 26.3 provide us with greater detail about the characteristics of our nation's

Table 26.2
Persons below poverty level, by age, race, and Hispanic origin: 1978

Age	Number below poverty level (000)				Percent below poverty level			
	All races	White	Black	Hispanic origin	All races	White	Black	Hispanic origin
All ages	24,497	16,259	7,625	2,607	11.4	8.7	30.6	21.6
Under 14 years	7,583	4,468	2,898	1,115	16.5	11.7	42.0	27.7
14 to 21 years	4,384	2,710	1,563	480	13.4	9.8	35.4	23.9
22 to 44 years	5,794	4,004	1,596	674	8.2	6.6	20.9	17.0
45 to 64 years	3,502	2,547	905	213	8.1	6.6	22.3	13.9
65 years and over	3,233	2,530	662	125	13.9	12.1	33.9	23.1

Source: U.S. Bureau of the Census.

Table 26.3
Mothers with children under 18 years old, by work experience, poverty status, and race: 1978.

Work experience	All races		White		Black	
	Total number (000)	Percent below poverty level	Total number (000)	Percent below poverty level	Total number (000)	Percent below poverty level
All women with own children	30,493	12.6	26,112	9.2	3,740	35.0
Worked in 1978	18,964	8.4	16,135	6.3	2,431	22.1
50–52 weeks	9,459	3.7	7,850	2.6	1,386	9.9
27–49 weeks	4,341	7.8	3,784	5.7	489	25.2
1–26 weeks	5,163	17.4	4,501	13.2	556	49.8
Did not work in 1978	11,529	19.4	9,976	14.0	1,309	58.8
Families and subfamilies headed by women with own children	5,719	41.5	3,792	32.9	1,822	59.2
Worked in 1978	3,924	26.1	2,769	20.1	1,085	41.3
50–52 weeks	2,254	9.3	1,617	5.4	597	19.6
27–49 weeks	808	29.6	581	22.4	216	50.0
1–26 weeks	863	66.7	571	59.2	273	81.7
Did not work in 1978	1,795	75.1	1,023	67.8	737	85.5

Source: U.S. Bureau of the Census.

poor. As is apparent from the tables, poverty afflicts people of all races, at all ages, and in different family situations. However, a careful reading of those tables reveals that the incidence of poverty is far from uniform. Consider some of the highlights:

In Table 26.2: Although the absolute number of white people experiencing poverty exceeds the number of blacks, only 8.7 percent of all white people are poor in contrast to 30.6 percent of blacks.

In Table 26.2: Note the tremendous disparity among age groups and across races. Poverty tends primarily to afflict the young and the elderly. Also, whereas 11.7 percent of white youth under the age of 14 are poor, 42.0 percent of all black youth in that age category are poor. Moreover, in contrast to the

12.1 percent of whites aged 65 years and over that are poor, more than one third of all elderly blacks are poor.

In Table 26.3: In the upper portion of the table we see that the incidence of poverty among women with children was less among whites than among blacks. Not surprisingly, the incidence of poverty was less the greater the number of weeks women worked. Of the 9.5 million women with children who worked 50–52 weeks, only 3.7 percent were below the poverty level, in contrast to 12.6 percent overall. Among black women with children who worked 50–52 weeks, only 9.9 percent were below the poverty level, in contrast to 35 percent overall.

In Table 26.3: In contrast with the upper portion of the table, the lower portion indicates the extremely high incidence of poverty among families and subfamilies headed by women with children, the heaviest incidence occurring among black female-headed families and subfamilies. Nearly one third of white female-headed families and subfamilies were below the poverty level, in contrast to nearly 60 percent for black female heads.

Government policies to assist the poor

There is no question but that government plays a major role in helping the poor. Just how big a role it plays, however, is difficult to nail down precisely. The reason for this is that no unambiguous overall measure of government assistance exists in this area. The most commonly used measure of assistance to the poor is given by a statistic known as **social welfare expenditures.** In fiscal year 1979 (October 1, 1978, to September 30, 1979) social welfare expenditures reached $480 billion for all levels of government (federal, state, and local)—nearly 20 percent of the gross national product.

However, this measure of government assistance to the poor is deficient in one very important respect. Some portion of the monies categorized as social welfare expenditures is distributed to people other than those defined as poor. The $480 billion referred to above includes all federal, state, and local social insurance expenditures. It includes all public assistance, health, and medical program expenditures. And it includes expenditures for veterans' programs, education, housing, and a whole host of social services programs. As should be apparent from this list, many nonpoor people are on the receiving end of these government transfers. Nevertheless, the bulk of the monies go to those who officially are categorized as poor.

There are important differences among the several forms of social welfare expenditures. Some programs are designed to attack the root *causes of poverty;* others are designed to remove the *symptoms of poverty*—to provide poor people with cash or in-kind goods and services to better enable them to live more decently. Moreover, while some social welfare programs, such

as aid to families with dependent children (AFDC), are specifically aimed at the poor, other programs, such as social security payments to the aged, are not since both poor and nonpoor retired participants receive benefits. Let us examine some of these different programs and program objectives in greater detail.

Removing the causes of poverty

There is a popular saying in Washington, D.C., that "You can't solve a problem by throwing money at it." When used in the context of government antipoverty programs, there is one sense in which this flip saying is wrong. If you define poverty as a lack of adequate income, then you can eliminate poverty by making sure, through transfers, that everyone has an adequate income. However, this approach by itself only eliminates the *symptoms of poverty;* it does not solve the poverty problem. In a fundamental sense, the poverty problem will be solved only when people's earnings are high enough that supplementary assistance from government is not required to keep people at or above the poverty line. For government antipoverty programs to be truly successful, therefore, it is necessary to attack the root *causes* of poverty.

The causes of poverty are many and varied. Inadequate skills, training, and education are among the most commonly cited causes. Discrimination against blacks, other minorities, and women is another widely recognized cause. Physical and mental disabilities constitute yet other sources of poverty.

It is also clear that these many causes of poverty are not necessarily independent of one another. Discrimination in education or in on-the-job training programs could be partly responsible for the inadequate skills, training, and education of many poor people. Job discrimination could prevent many blacks, other minorities, and women from earning enough to provide the required educational training for their children, perpetuating the cycle of poverty. And improper prenatal care, which occurs all too frequently among women who are poor, can result in offspring who grow up with physical or mental handicaps or a diminished capacity to learn.

A whole host of government policies exist designed to attack the many causes of poverty. Among the most important are those aimed at improving the education, skills, and training of the poor. The provision of free elementary and secondary education—which, of course, benefits both the poor and nonpoor—are extremely important. But in the minds of our legislators, free education is not enough; more must be done to deal specifically with the problems of the poor. This kind of thinking led to the development of a variety of other programs—for example, the Comprehensive Employment and Training (CETA) program (which, at this writing, the Reagan Administration intends to scuttle), under which the federal government provides subsidies for the training of hard-core unemployed workers, and the Work Incentive Program (WIN), which subsidizes the training and employment of people on welfare and provides day-care facilities for their children. In addition, the government has passed legislation that outlaws discriminatory hiring, firing, and employment practices (e.g., the Civil Rights Act of 1964 and the Equal Pay Act of 1963).

Government policies aimed at eliminating the causes of poverty have not been an unqualified successs. In the minds of some, they have been conspicuously unsuccessful. However, it is extremely difficult to judge the extent of our successes or failures. Clearly, poverty has not been eliminated despite the expenditure of billions of dollars. It is true that the overall incidence of poverty is much lower today than it was 20 or 50 years ago. But it is not obvious how much of that reduced incidence can be attributed to government policies. To discover the answer would necessitate that we be able to answer a prior hypothetical question: How much worse would the problem of poverty have been in the absence of these programs? It is impossible to answer such "What if" questions definitively. And it is not entirely clear what meaning we would attach to the answer even if the definitive response was possible. The full effects of these government programs may not become evident until years after their introduction. Judging their success or failure before the appropriate amount of time has elapsed would be illegitimate.

It is not the purpose here to debate at length the several controversial issues surrounding our educational, training, and antidiscrimination statutes and programs, nor their effects on the incidence of poverty. We do know that it is important to come to grips with the root causes of poverty. Perhaps the programs now in effect will ultimately prove to be very successful; perhaps they will not, in which case it is probably reasonable to expect yet other approaches in the future.

Income maintenance programs for the poor

The fact that government efforts to eliminate the causes of much of the poverty we see may ultimately prove successful is small consolation to those who are now living in poverty. There is a need for programs to boost the incomes of the poor. It is hoped that many such income maintenance programs can be phased out in the future as we make headway in the fight against the causes of poverty. However, it is unlikely that all such programs will be phased out of existence entirely. Many people, because of their physical or mental disabilities or because of their age, will stand in need of government assistance even if we discover successful solutions in eliminating poverty for everyone else.

Social security. The largest of the income maintenance programs is **social security.** Many object to calling this an antipoverty program although the bulk of the recipients depend on this transfer program for their livelihood. They would prefer that it be referred to as an insurance program—a program into which they and their employers contributed (through the payroll tax) during their working years and from which they withdraw retirement income, disability benefits, and assistance in payment of their medical bills.

To a certain extent it is appropriate to refer to social security as the equivalent of an insurance program. However, many social security recipients are today receiving in benefits much more than they would have received had benefits been calculated on the basis of their original contributions. Moreover, social security checks account for more than half of the total income of 56 percent of the elderly couples and 73 percent of the single people who are receiving benefits. Finally, the formulas used by the government to calculate benefits are heavily tilted toward those who during their working years were low wage earners. Although there are insurance aspects to the social security system, the benefit formulas have been deliberately designed to ensure at least a minimum subsistence income for the elderly; the antipoverty features of social security are quite prominent. (For a more detailed discussion of social security, see Chapter 4.)

One important difference between social security and other specific anti-poverty programs is that social security benefits are received as a **matter of right;** the program recipient is not required to demonstrate a need for the cash benefits. This feature of the social security system is deemed by many as desirable, especially by those who believe that a "means test" (where the recipient would have to demonstrate the need for government assistance) is a demeaning experience.

The matter-of-right concept is based on the principle that, since beneficiaries paid for their benefits in the form of payroll taxes deducted from earnings, they are rightfully entitled to receive benefits. But do beneficiaries really pay for their benefits? There is no simple answer to this question. We know that low-paid workers receive in benefits much more for their tax dollars than high-paid workers. And many low-paid workers, while they are working, receive a tax break in the form of the *earned income credit* that offsets in whole or in part their payroll taxes. Thus, many beneficiaries are really paying for only a small part of their benefits, whereas others are paying more than their share. All of this means that the principle on which the matter-of-right concept is based is much weaker than proponents would have us believe. This does not mean that a means test should be applied to the benefits received by at least some classes of beneficiaries. But it does mean that the sharp distinction often drawn between social security and other forms of welfare is not entirely justifiable. For those beneficiaries whose earnings were low during their working years and whose benefits are now large compared with the tax dollars they paid to the system, social security is as much a welfare program as is AFDC. In the latter program, however, beneficiaries are subjected to a means test.

Other matter-of-right income maintenance programs. Besides social security, there are a whole host of other matter-of-right income maintenance programs. They include, for example, government employee pensions, unemployment compensation, workers' compensation, and veterans' compensation. As is true of social security, people covered by these programs receive benefits not because they need them necessarily but because events take place that legitimize their receiving benefits. They retire, become unemployed, or become disabled.

Means-tested income maintenance programs. The above-described matter-of-right programs constitute fully two thirds of all government expenditures on income maintenance programs. The remaining one third consists of programs, the beneficiaries of which are subject to a means test.

Aid to families with dependent children (AFDC). This is the best known of the means-tested income maintenance programs. In fiscal year 1979, total government expenditures for AFDC amounted to $11.1 billion. The bulk of these monies were used to provide assistance to cover the costs of food, shelter, and clothing for needy dependent children in single-parent households.

The AFDC program is extremely controversial. Many allege that it provides incentives for men to desert their families and for women to bear additional children. Whether the latter is true is difficult to discover. But it does appear that the program does encourage fathers—especially those whose incomes are low or who have difficulty finding and holding jobs—to abandon their families. The reason? Benefits are frequently smaller, or denied altogether, if there is an able-bodied man in the house. While this feature was designed to encourage able-bodied fathers to go to work to support their families, it sometimes drives them out of the home instead. Those fathers who do not earn enough to support their families or who cannot get steady work may feel they can do more to support their dependents by leaving home, thereby allowing their families to qualify for AFDC. In order to counter these kinds of perverse incentives, many states have reformed their eligibility rules; at the federal level, an AFDC–unemployed father program was added in 1968. However, these reforms have not gone far enough. The perverse incentives have been far from eliminated.

Means-tested in-kind transfers. The bulk of government means-tested assistance to the poor takes the form not of *cash* benefits as under the AFDC program but of in-kind transfers—transfers in the form of goods and services. **Medicaid, food stamps,** and **housing assistance** are examples of such in-kind transfers.

Medicaid is the largest of the means-tested in-kind transfer programs to the poor. Fiscal 1979 expenditures under this program amounted to about $20 billion; over 25 million people a year receive medical care benefits from medicaid. Unlike many other welfare programs, whose benefit formulas call for gradually reduced benefits at higher levels of income, the medicaid program uses an all-or-nothing formula. Low-income families either qualify for full medical benefits or they get no assistance at all. Families that qualify for AFDC benefits automatically qualify for medicaid; a modest number of somewhat higher income families also qualify.

Food stamps, the second largest means-tested in-kind transfer program, provide benefits to about 18 million people. The fiscal 1979 cost of this program amounted to $6.5 billion. Under this program, qualifying poor families receive vouchers from the federal government. The vouchers can be used to buy food only (with some restrictions on the nature of food products that qualify). The magnitude of the government subsidy declines as income increases. As family income increases, the dollar value of the voucher is reduced. This is intended to ensure that the poorest of the poor families get the greatest assis-

tance. As of this writing, the food stamp program is being slashed sharply by the Reagan Administration.

Although food stamps can be spent only on food, this program provides indirect assistance for other budget items. The food stamp subsidy frees money for other items that would otherwise have been spent on groceries.

Housing assistance represents the third major in-kind transfer program. Under this program, the federal government subsidizes the purchase of low-income housing by local governments. Qualifying poor families rent these subsidized housing units at a cost equal to 25 percent of their income. The benefit they receive falls as their income increases.

Income maintenance programs and the incentive to work. One of the most troubling aspects of our income maintenance programs is that they provide very strong incentives for people *not* to work. The reason is simple. Because benefits are gradually reduced or eliminated altogether as income increases, many people would not be made much better off—in fact, might be made worse off—as a consequence of their working. Goods and services that were formerly provided or heavily subsidized by the government must now be paid for out of the money they earn at work.

The reduction in benefits that comes about as earned income increases is the equivalent of the government levying a tax on those earned income increases. And the magnitude of the "tax" that is levied is extremely hefty. For example, for each $1 of income that a family earns in excess of $30 per month, AFDC benefits are reduced by 67 cents; food stamp benefits are reduced by 11 cents; and social security taxes, which are levied on each $1 of earned income, take away an additional 7 cents. Adding up these three items alone, we see that the poor family loses 85 cents for each $1 of earned income in excess of $30 per month. That amount is the equivalent of a 85 percent *effective marginal tax rate*—an effective marginal rate that is 35 percentage points higher than the statutory maximum marginal tax rate that applies to the incomes of only the wealthiest people in the country.

But the 85 percent effective marginal tax rate is really only a lower-bound estimate for many poor families. Suppose the family in question was receiving housing assistance. Then, for each $1 of increased earned income, the family would have to pay more in rent for the same apartment. The effective marginal tax rate is raised further still. And that's not all. If earned income rises enough, the family may no longer qualify for medicaid benefits. It is difficult to tell how much medicaid benefits are worth since the benefits the family receives depend on the use that the family must make of medical services. In the family whose members are often sick, medicaid benefits could be sizable.

In any event, it is clear that poor people who choose to work are subjected to extremely high effective marginal tax rates. In many instances, the effective marginal tax rates approach 100 percent. If they reach 100 percent, they are not better off; effectively, government has taxed away all of their extra earned income in the form of reduced benefits (which they must now pay for themselves). In some instances, the effective marginal tax rate exceeds 100 percent. Under these circumstances they are made worse off. Who would work under such conditions?

All of this must be put in perspective. Why, you might ask, would *anyone* work given the benefits that are available from the government? This is not difficult to answer. The government provides benefits in amounts that barely enable recipients to eke out a subsistence standard of living. Most people would elect to work because the incomes they can earn enable them to attain a living standard much in excess of the governmentally defined minimum—even after taxes.

The point that needs emphasis is this: The vast majority of poor people lack the education, skills, or other attributes that would permit them to obtain jobs that would offer them an income sufficient to attain a substantial above-subsistence standard of living. The best many could do would be to take jobs, if available, at the minimum wage. During 1981 the minimum wage standard set by the federal government was $3.35 per hour. At 40 hours a week and 52 weeks a year, this minimum wage standard implies an annual income of $6,968.

Consider now a single parent with three children. If the parent does not work, the family might receive $4,500 in AFDC benefits and $2,000 in food stamps—a total of $6,500. In addition, the family is eligible for medicaid assistance, which, for purposes of illustration, we will assume amounts to $2,500 per year—a figure that is close to the actual national average. The total of all benefits received to this point amount to $9,000—without any work whatsoever. If housing assistance is also given, the total is even higher.

Now consider the alternative—working. The single parent earns the minimum wage for a total income of $6,968 per year. However, because the family has earned income, its benefits under AFDC and the food stamp program are reduced and it must now pay social security taxes; it might still, however, qualify for medicaid. Taking account of all of these effects, the family is only about $2,400 richer than when earned income was zero. If the single parent had to pay $46 per week for child care—a figure that is not outrageous for *three* children—the family would be no better off.

Pressing the point further, suppose the single parent, because of training, education, or the removal of discriminatory employment practices, was able to earn on the job about twice the minimum wage? The family would lose its remaining AFDC benefits and would no longer qualify for food stamps; it would now be ineligible for medicaid assistance; and its social security taxes and income taxes would be higher. After adjusting for all of these changes, the family might be only about $2,000 richer than when it had no earned income—an amount that is even smaller than when the minimum wage was earned. And that is before child care (after the child care tax credit) or other work-related expenses are taken into consideration. Not much incentive to work, is there?

The implications of all this are serious. We know that, in the absence of any welfare programs, many of the poor who are not now working would be forced to work. They would not have any other choice. Some might do fairly well—well enough to support themselves and their families at a subsistence standard of living, at least. Others—especially many of the physically and mentally handicapped—would not be able to support themselves. Without any government assistance, and with inadequate private charity, it does not require much imagination to figure out what would happen to the latter group of poor people.

Through our elected representatives, we as a society have rendered a judgment that calls for some minimal amount of assistance for those who would otherwise not be able to make it on their own. We have decided as well that such assistance should be reduced in accordance with increases in the earning power of beneficiaries. We hope that those receiving assistance will get off the welfare rolls by going to work. However, the reduction in benefits as earned income increases discourages work effort, all the more so the steeper the reduction in benefits per additional dollars of earned income (i.e., the higher the effective marginal tax rate).

The welfare system that now exists does more than just encourage people to stay on welfare. It encourages some low-wage earners to join the system. Some people might figure they could do *almost* as well by not working. Take a breadwinner who earns on the job just a bit more than the basic benefits available through welfare. Why work?

One way around this work disincentive problem is to reduce the effective marginal tax rate on earned income—i.e., cut benefits less severely as income increases. But this solution creates another problem: The cost of welfare would rise dramatically. Also, many people who are not poor (as defined officially) would begin receiving benefits, and those who are poor now would continue to receive benefits long after their earned incomes had moved them above the poverty line.

To illustrate, suppose government agreed to give to the family that earned no income $5,000 in basic benefits; for each $1 increase in earned income, basic benefits would be reduced by 25 cents—implying an effective marginal tax rate of 25 percent. If the family's earned income rose to $5,000, the family would continue to receive $3,750 in welfare benefits. (The original $5,000 in basic benefits *minus* $0.25 \times \$5,000$). If family earned income rose to $10,000, it would still receive $2,500 in welfare benefits. Indeed, it would continue to receive welfare benefits until its earned income reached $20,000. And any and all families whose earned incomes were less than $20,000 per year—even those who were not then on the welfare roles—would be eligible for welfare benefits if such a scheme were adopted. The cost of such a plan could be prohibitive.

One way around this dilemma would be to reduce the level of basic benefits below $5,000— say to $2,500. Under these circumstances, and assuming an effective marginal tax rate of 0.25, benefits would cease once family earned income reached $10,000. However, if family members are unable to work for one reason or another, the level of basic benefits would be inadequate to provide anything close to a minimum decent standard of living.

In short, the problems with our welfare system are the result of a conflict of objectives. We desire *(a)* to provide people with an adequate income to ensure a minimum decent standard of living, *(b)* to provide incentives for welfare recipients to seek gainful employment, *(c)* to help only those in need, and *(d)* to hold down the costs of welfare. Unfortunately, these four goals are not easily reconcilable, as the above discussion makes clear.

The negative income tax

The basic problem of welfare policy is to fashion acceptable compromises among these apparently irreconcilable objectives. One possible solution—and the one proposed by a number of economists—is to replace most existing welfare programs (including AFDC and most in-kind transfers) with a **negative income tax.** The basic idea behind this proposal is straightforward.

1. *Establish a guaranteed minimum level of income for all families (the guaranteed minimum amount varying in size, depending on the size of the family)*. For purposes of illustration, assume the guaranteed minimum for a "typical" family of four amounts to $6,000 per year. If this family earns no income whatever, it will receive $6,000 in cash from the government.

2. *Establish the effective marginal tax rate on earned income*. Again, for purposes of illustration, assume an effective marginal tax rate of 40 percent.

3. With the establishment of the first two items, it is possible to discover the *crossover level of income*. Families earning incomes below the crossover level receive cash from the government—hence the name *negative income tax*. Families with earned incomes above the crossover level pay a portion of their incomes to the government in the form of taxes.

The crossover level of income is given by the formula:

Cross over level of income

$$= \frac{\text{Guaranteed minimum family income}}{\text{Effective marginal tax rate}}.$$

Using the numbers chosen for purposes of illustration, the crossover level of income occurs at $15,000 (i.e., $6,000 ÷ 0.40). This means that all families with earned incomes below $15,000 will receive cash from the government. The amount they receive depends on their earned incomes. Families with earned incomes above $15,000 pay taxes to the government.

These ideas are captured succinctly in Figure 26.3. On the horizontal axis we measure family earned income; on the vertical axis is measured family disposable income. The 45° line is a reference line showing the relationship between earned income and disposable income in the absence of any government taxes—positive or negative. The reference line tells us, for example, that if earned income equaled $8,000, disposable income would equal $8,000 in the absence of positive or negative taxes.

The second line in Figure 26.3 shows the relationship between earned income and disposable

income in the face of government negative and positive income taxes. That line is less steep than the 45° line and intersects the vertical axis at $6,000. That point of intersection with the vertical axis represents the guaranteed minimum family income. Families with no earned income will have $6,000 of disposable income.

With an assumed marginal tax rate equal to 0.40, each $1 of earned income will increase disposable income by 60 cents. A family with an earned income of $1,000 will have a disposable income of $6,600. (Because of its $1,000 in earned income, the family gets $400 less from the government than the family with zero income; $1,000 in earned income plus $5,600 in cash from the government results in $6,600 of disposable family income.) A family with an earned income of $10,000 will have a disposable income of $12,000. (Because of $10,000 in earned income, the family gets $4,000 less in cash from the government than the family with zero income; it therefore gets to keep the $10,000 of earned income and receives $2,000 in cash from the government.) And a family with $20,000 in earned income will have a disposable income of $18,000. Once the crossover level of earned income is reached, cash benefits from the government cease; for each dollar of earned income above that level (here, $15,000), 40 percent goes to the government in the form of taxes.

Under this scheme, it is easy to figure out the level of disposable income for any given level of earned income:

Disposable income
= Minimum guaranteed income
+ Earned income
× (1 − effective marginal tax rate).

In Figure 26.3, the slope of the disposable income line is equal to 1 minus the marginal tax rate—the change in disposable income per dollar change in earned income.

Several important conclusions follow from the analysis presented in Figure 26.3.

1. Suppose, for the moment, that the poverty-line level of income is defined as $6,000 per year. As is apparent from Figure 26.3, many peo-

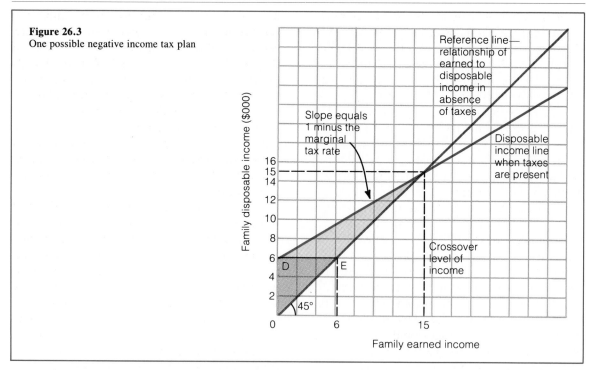

Figure 26.3
One possible negative income tax plan

This cost can be cut in either of two ways, or both. First, the government could cut the minimum income guarantee from $6,000 to, say, $2,400, maintaining all the while the same 40 percent effective marginal tax rate. Under this scheme, the crossover level of income would oc-

ple will be receiving a check from the government who, by definition, are nonpoor; and many of those whose *earned* incomes are below the poverty-line will be receiving cash from the government that enables them to enjoy disposable incomes in excess of poverty-line levels. Indeed, every family with any earned income whatsoever will have a level of disposable income that is above the official poverty line. Because of the government transfers of cash, the symptoms of poverty will be eliminated under such a program.

2.   However, it should also be clear that a program like this will be very expensive. Every family with an earned income of less than $15,000 will receive cash from the government. A great many (officially defined) nonpoor will be receiving assistance.

cur at $6,000 instead of at $15,000. Given a poverty-line level of income of $6,000, this plan would guarantee that only the poor would get assistance. (Those families above $6,000 would pay taxes.) There is one problem with this "solution." Because the effective marginal tax rate is the same under this program as under the original one discussed above, people have the same incentive to work as before. But what about those families who, because of, say, physical or mental disabilities, can't earn $6,000? This scheme would guarantee that they would have an income to dispose of that was less than the poverty line—a value that government has already determined to be necessary for a bare subsistence standard of living. These poor families would be forced to live at less than subsistence standards.

Second, the government could reduce cost by *raising* the effective marginal tax rate (i.e., the disposable income line would be rotated downward to a flatter position). This would reduce the crossover level of income and thereby reduce the number of nonpoor families receiving assistance. It would also cause the disposable income of poor people to rise by less than before for increases in earned income. However, while this change would *appear* to reduce the total welfare cost, it might in fact raise the cost. The reason? By raising the effective marginal tax rate, this scheme would reduce people's incentives to work. Thus, it is possible that many of those who would otherwise work might stop altogether. Before, under a scheme that had a lower effective marginal tax rate, the government was subsidizing families by an amount equal to the difference between the 45° reference line and the disposable income line in Figure 26.3 for each level of earned income (an amount that would be less than $6,000 for each family with positive earned income up to $15,000); now the government might be forced to give many of those families full support. True, fewer nonpoor would be receiving assistance and less earned income would be retained by the poor because of more sharply reduced benefits—factors that would serve to lower cost. But more poor people would be receiving *larger amounts* because of the disincentives to work. To illustrate this latter point, take an extreme example. Suppose government provided poor people (those earning less than the poverty-line amount) with a subsidy equal to the difference between the poverty-line level and their level of earned income. If their earned income were $4,000, they would receive a subsidy equal to $2,000; if their earned income were $6,000, they would receive no subsidy. Here, the effective marginal tax rate would equal 100 percent; for each dollar increase in earned income, the subsidy would decline by one dollar. The line DE in Figure 26.3 illustrates just such a situation. For people earning $6,000 or less, their disposable income will just equal $6,000; for people earning more than $6,000, the relationship between their earned income and disposable income will be determined by the tax laws. (What that relationship is, or might be, is not shown to avoid cluttering the diagram.) Now, the question that needs to be asked is, Why would anyone earning $6,000 or less ever work? They get $6,000 without working and $6,000 if they work. Some, those who do not like being on welfare, will choose to work; but from a purely economic point of view, they certainly have no incentive to work. Under this scheme, people who formerly were working, receiving a subsidy from the government of less than $6,000, will now receive the full $6,000 without any work whatsoever. But the situation may be worse than that. What about people who earn only $7,000 or $8,000 a year? They have to pay social security taxes, child care, and other work-related expenses. Might not many of them choose not to work and receive $6,000 instead from the government? As you can see, the cost could become sizable.

Will a negative income tax work? We could go on and on talking about various alternative negative income tax schemes, but such an exercise hardly seems worth the effort. The ideas behind each of the possible alternatives are straightforward, but don't answer the fundamental question, Will the negative income tax work? The results from some experimental *temporary* negative income tax programs do not provide us with clear answers to this question. Overall, the results are not strong enough to demonstrate the superiority of the negative income tax over the hodgepodge of existing welfare programs.

And what were the various negative income tax experiments? From about 1967 through 1978, the Department of Health, Education, and Welfare (HEW) experimented with a number of negative income tax programs to ascertain their effects on work incentives. For the most part, the experiments were conducted in two cities—Seattle and Denver. About 5,000 families participated in the experiments.

HEW used six different negative income tax formulas. The formulas were differentiated from one another in two respects. Either the "basic benefit" (the amount of assistance paid to a family that had no earned income) differed from plan to plan, or the "effective marginal tax rate" (the rate at which family assistance is reduced as earned family income rises) differed. They selected three different basic benefit amounts—50 percent of the poverty line, 75 percent of the poverty line, and 100 percent of the poverty line. For each of these three, they experimented with two effective marginal tax rates—50 percent and 70 percent.

Several important results emerged from these experiments.

1. Compared with the number of hours worked before the experimental programs were introduced, people, on the average, reduced their work effort. But the reduction in work effort was not uniform. In general, the reduction in work effort among female heads of families was much less than the reductions by husbands and wives in husband-wife families. In husband-wife families, the greatest percentage reduction in number of hours worked was among the wives.

2. As expected, the three plans with the higher effective marginal tax rate (70 percent) resulted in a greater reduction in work effort than the lower (50 percent) effective marginal tax rate plans. The higher the effective marginal tax rate, the smaller the incentive is to work.

3. For a given effective marginal tax rate, some reduction occurred in work effort among female heads of families as the basic benefit amounts were increased. Among husband-wife families, there was no real change in work effort. However, there were different responses on the part of husbands and wives. Wives reduced their work effort, and husbands increased theirs, as basic benefits increased.

The reduction in work effort suggests that replacing current welfare programs with a negative income tax might not be as desirable as many proponents believed. However, one needs to interpret these experiments with caution. The programs were designed to be temporary only, and this was well understood. Whether this result would hold under a permanent program is not known. Of course, one cannot rule out the possibility that the reduction in work effort might be more sizable under a permanent program. Families who knew the program to be temporary may have tried to maintain their attachment to the labor force, which they might not do under a permanent scheme.

HOW UNEQUAL SHOULD THE DISTRIBUTION OF INCOME BE?

After this lengthy discussion on income distribution and the problems of poverty in the United States, we come now to the question that is, on the one hand, the most difficult to answer, yet, on the other hand, the easiest to answer. How unequal should the distribution of income be? We do not know.

The question of the optimum degree of inequality is a matter of normative economics. It depends on people's value judgments. And there is no reason why the value judgments of economists should be deemed superior to (or inferior to) those of others.

What is of interest is that there needs to be justification for the absence of equality. We tend to believe that an equal division is fair or equitable. If a birthday cake is divided equally among party guests, that is considered fair; unequal pieces must somehow be justified. No justification is apparently required for equal-sized slices.

It is, of course, possible to *explain* many of the observed differences in people's incomes; this is not a justification for those differences, only an explanation. People differ from one another in their skills, levels of education, work effort, skin color, family background, luck, etc. Given these differences, is there some justification for redistributing incomes among people?

We, as a society, have consciously deemed it appropriate to redistribute income in favor of the least advantaged in our society—to the poor, the sick, and the disabled. Beyond that, we have not faced squarely the issue of how income ought to be otherwise distributed. True, we have passed many laws that have had the effect of redistributing income—for example, tax laws that have provided loopholes for those in the highest income brackets, and oil and gas price controls that have had the effect of distributing income from oil and gas producers to consumers. But the full effects of these many laws on the distribution of income are not well understood. Nor is it clear exactly how income is redistributed as a consequence of these many laws.

What economists would argue is this: Any time you deal with matters affecting the distribution of income you are likely to have some effect on economic efficiency. The higher the level of economic efficiency, the greater will be the size of the pie to be divided. Competitive markets are the most efficient; they result in the largest pie possible. But it is in the nature of competitive markets that the pie gets distributed in accordance with dollar votes. Those dollar votes are distributed in accordance with the incomes made possible by peoples' earning power. The unequal distribution of earning power will result in an unequal division of the national pie.

If we as a society select some distribution of income other than that characterizing competitive markets, we have to ask whether the redistribution we call for will cause the size of the pie itself to shrink by impairing efficiency—by impairing incentives to work or invest, for example. It is alleged by some that many redistribution schemes could so shrink the size of the pie that the absolute amounts going to those to whom income is distributed will not rise much, if at all; the fact that they get a larger *share* does *not* make them better off. Unfortunately, we have no good answers to these difficult questions.

SUMMARY

1. The degree of income inequality in the United States can be measured using a *Lorenz curve*. The Lorenz curve measures the cumulative distribution of income. A useful summary measure of the degree of income inequality is given by what is called the *Gini ratio*.

2. In one important respect, the Lorenz curve and the Gini ratio exaggerate the extent of income inequality in the United States. This is because these measures attempt to gauge the extent of inequality at a single point in time. There is less inequality of income among families when measured over their lifetimes.

3. Government policies have produced a fairly substantial reduction in the degree of income inequality in the United States. Most of the reduction in income inequality is accomplished by government transfer programs, not our tax system; taxes are much less progressive than is commonly believed.

4. Not all government transfer programs are

designed specifically to aid the poor. Many wealthy families receive old-age social security benefits; and a great many workers in high-wage cyclical industries who are temporarily laid off are eligible to receive unemployment compensation. Nonetheless, the great bulk of the monies transferred by government are concentrated at the low end of the income scale.

5. There is no universally accepted poverty standard. In practice, most poverty standards are a blending of a relative poverty standard and an absolute poverty standard. Neither of these standards are easy to define unambiguously.

6. According to U.S. government statistics, around 12 percent of all families—one out of every eight—have incomes below the poverty-line level. These statistics, however, are the subject of much heated debate. Many argue, with some justification, that poverty is more widespread than implied here. The poverty-line levels are too low to be meaningful. On the other hand, if we accept the official poverty-line level as constituting an "acceptable" minimum, there is evidence that the official count of poverty is too high. The official poverty count is based on cash income alone and excludes such in-kind transfers as public housing, food stamps, medicare, and medicaid. Translating these benefits into income equivalents and using the official poverty-line benchmark, the poverty population falls to 3 to 6 percent of all families in 1980.

7. The incidence of poverty is far from uniform. Although the absolute number of white people experiencing poverty exceeds the number of blacks, only 8.7 percent of all whites are poor in contrast to 30.6 percent of blacks. Poverty tends to afflict primarily the young and the elderly. The incidence of poverty among women with children is less among whites than among blacks. Not surprisingly, the incidence of poverty is less the greater the number of weeks women work. And the incidence of poverty among the families and subfamilies headed by women is exceptionally high, the heaviest incidence occurring among black female-headed families and subfamilies.

8. One needs to distinguish between policies aimed at eliminating the *symptoms of poverty* and

programs aimed at attacking the root *causes of poverty.*

9.   One of the most troubling aspects of our income maintenance programs is that they provide very strong incentives for people *not* to work. The reason is simple. Because benefits are gradually reduced or eliminated all together as income increases, many people would not be made much better off, and might in fact be made worse off, as a consequence of their working. The reduction of benefits that comes about as earned income increases is the equivalent of the government levying a tax on those earned income increases. And the magnitude of the "tax" that is levied is extremely hefty, in many instances exceeding the statutory maximum marginal tax rate that applies to the incomes of only the wealthiest people in the country.

10.   The problems with our welfare system are the result of a conflict of objectives. We desire *(a)* to provide people with an adequate income to ensure a minimum decent standard of living, *(b)* to provide incentives for welfare recipients to seek gainful employment, *(c)* to help only those in need, and *(d)* to hold down the costs of welfare. Unfortunately, these four goals are not easily reconcilable.

11.   The basic problem of welfare policy is to fashion an acceptable compromise among these apparent irreconcilable objectives. One possible solution—and the one proposed by a number of economists—is to replace most existing welfare programs with a *negative income tax.* The basic idea behind this proposal is straightforward: *(a)* establish a guaranteed minimum level of income for all families; and *(b)* establish the effective marginal tax rate on earned income. However, there are several problems with the negative income tax. If government establishes a guaranteed minimum that is "too low," many who, because of, say, physical or mental disabilities, can't earn up to the poverty-line level would be forced to live at less than subsistence standards. If government were to *raise* the effective marginal tax rate, people's incentives to work would be reduced.

12.   There is no unambiguous way to answer the question, How unequal should the distribution of income be? This question is a matter of normative economics; it depends on people's value judgments.

CONCEPTS FOR REVIEW

Functional distribution of income

Personal distribution of income

Lorenz curve

Gini ratio

Social insurance

Cash transfers

In-kind transfers

Supplemental unemployment benefits (SUB)

Notion of "means test"

Relative poverty standard

Absolute poverty standard

Social welfare expenditures

Aid to families with dependent children (AFDC)

Comprehensive employment and training act (CETA)

Work incentive program (WIN)

Medicaid

Food stamps

Housing assistance

Negative income tax

Crossover level of income

QUESTIONS FOR DISCUSSION

(Those marked with an asterisk (*) are more difficult.)

1.   "If all taxes were proportional to income, the tax system would not matter at all as far as the distribution of income is concerned." Carefully evaluate.

2.   Explain carefully the problems with establishing both a relative poverty standard and an absolute poverty standard.

3.   Explain carefully why the problems with our welfare system are the result of a conflict of objectives—a conflict between *(a)* providing people with an income adequate to ensure a minimum decent standard of living, *(b)* providing people on welfare with

incentives to work, and *(c)* holding down the costs of welfare. Does the negative income tax "solve" these conflicts? Explain why or why not.

4. "The poverty problem is truly exaggerated in this country. The welfare system is a mess precisely because many people can do almost as good as working, and sometimes better, by being on welfare. If you eliminated welfare, the poverty problem would be much reduced because those not working now would not have any choice." Carefully evaluate.

*5. You have been asked to develop a negative income tax proposal to "solve" the poverty problem. The total outlay the government is willing to spend is $30 billion each year. At present, 10 million families are in need of some welfare assistance. It is "generally agreed" that a family can barely eke out a subsistence standard of living at $8,000 per year. Carefully analyze the problems you are likely to encounter in setting up the negative income tax. Be specific.

Chapter 27

Government and the private sector: Antitrust policies and other government regulations

In this chapter and the one to follow we will examine a whole range of controversial issues dealing with the role of government in our economic system. For the most part we will avoid attempting to answer the question of whether we have too little or too much government. There is no way to answer this question in a completely objective manner. The question itself is a matter for normative economics, and any answers we might give would be heavily laden with value judgments. Our purposes are more limited. What we want to do is examine the nature of, and rationale for, some of government's activities in our economic system.

We have dealt at length elsewhere in this book on many aspects of government's role in our economy. Much of our attention in the first half of this book was focused on government's **stabilization function**—government's use of monetary, fiscal, and other policies aimed at effecting changes in our macroeconomic performance. We have also examined such matters as government agricultural price supports, energy programs, antipoverty initiatives, and minimum wage and rent controls. Specific considerations of these issues will not be repeated here.

The specific focus of these two chapters will be on the role of government in *improving* economic efficiency. The idea that government can contribute to efficiency may surprise you, especially in view of the common complaint that government is the root cause of many (most?) of our economic ills. However, care must be exercised in the evaluation of this complaint. As we shall see, the rationale for much of government activity derives from the fact that the allocation of resources that would best serve the welfare of society as a whole will be different, and perhaps substantially different, from the allocation that would result from the actions of people promoting their own individual welfare. In the absence of government, too few resources would be devoted to the provision of some goods and services; too many would be devoted to others. When government enters the picture to "rectify" the allocation of resources, its actions will often come in conflict with some private interests; those private interests adversely affected by government policies will often complain.

You will notice that the word *rectify* was put in quotes. There is a good reason for this. The fact that government does have an important role to play does not mean necessarily that it will do a good job. There is no guarantee that government will accomplish the "correct" reallocation of resources, the one that best serves the public interest. There is no guarantee that the functions of government will be carried out efficiently. Indeed, as will become clear in the discussion that follows, it is exceptionally difficult, if not impossible, to develop objective standards by which to determine how large government should be, the nature and extent of its activities, and the quality of its performance.

We open this chapter with a very brief review of how a purely competitive economic system would allocate resources among alternative uses. In this system, prices are all-important. There is no government to guide the economy; resources are allocated by an invisible hand.

We then ask, What can go wrong? Our answer: Many things. First, monopoly or monopsony power can distort the allocation of resources. Government intervention to encourage more competition seems justified. Second, some goods that are produced may not be safe, and there may be health and safety hazards on the job in many occupations. Again, government intervention to ensure safer products and a safer and more healthy work environment seem justified. Third, even if competition prevails, and even if health and safety are not issues of concern, the allocation of resources may be distorted as a consequence of the presence of **externalities.** *Externalities arise when the voluntary actions of economic agents—in the production or consumption of goods and services—result in adverse or beneficial side effects for which no compensation is made.*

It is the purpose of this chapter to examine in detail the issues of federal government antitrust policies and occupational and product health and safety regulations. We leave to Chapter 28 a detailed examination of the important subject of externalities.

THE THEORY OF THE INVISIBLE HAND

The **theory of the invisible hand**—first enunciated by Adam Smith over 200 years ago and refined by modern economists—is an extremely powerful and influential idea and the source of considerable controversy. This theory lies at the heart of the laissez-faire philosophy that countenances the nonintervention of government in markets. At the same time, it is this theory—or rather its alleged failure—that lies at the heart of non-laissez-faire philosophies that countenance the active intervention of government in markets.

The theory of the invisible hand concerns itself with only one thing—economic efficiency. What the theory states is this: *Given certain ideal conditions, the utility-maximizing behavior of individuals and the profit-maximizing behavior of producers will lead to the most efficient social outcome. Each individual acting in his or her own self-interest promotes the interests of society at large.*

According to the theory of the invisible hand, there would appear to be no justification for government intervention in markets. However, before one can accept this conclusion it is necessary to inquire into the "ideal conditions" that must be met in order for the theory to hold. There are three important ideal conditions: (1) perfect competition, (2) absence of externalities, and (3) a fair distribution of income (and wealth). The first we will examine in detail in this chapter; the second will be taken up at length in Chapter 28; and the third we dealt with at the end of the last chapter.

Ideal condition number one: Perfect competition

We have already examined in depth the meaning and implications of perfect competition—in both product and resource markets. We can, therefore, be brief.

Under perfect competition, no single buyer or seller possesses any market power; each economic agent is a price-taker. Put differently, there is no monopoly or monopsony power here.

Equilibrium in each market is given by the intersection of that market's demand and supply curves. Moreover, the activities in each market depend on the activities in others. Indeed, all the demand and supply curves form one huge *interdependent* process that economists refer to as **general equilibrium.** We know, for example, that we cannot speak of some person's demand for product X as though it were independent of his/her demand for products Y, Z, and all other goods. The individual consumer maximizes utility by allocating his/her income in such a way that the marginal utility per dollar spent is the same for all goods purchased.

Similarly, one cannot speak of a firm's demand for some resource as though it were independent of its demand for other resources. Pure competition forces producers to operate at minimum average cost, which in turn means using the least costly combination of resources.

The supply curves—in product markets and resource markets—are also linked interdependently. Profits guide the decisions of producers in terms of both *what* to produce and *how much.* If it is more profitable to expand the production of good X than Y, more resources will be devoted to X. Under pure competition, there are no barriers to entry or exit; firms are free to enter or leave industries. In long-run equilibrium, all firms will earn zero *economic* profits; this is not zero accounting profits, but zero economic profits—a level of accounting profits just sufficient to maintain resources where they are. Let positive economic profits appear anywhere and resources will shift in that direction until all further profitable opportunities are exhausted. The profit-maximizing behavior of producers ensures that the supply of any one good or service is interdependent with the supplies of other goods and services.

Likewise, the supply curves in resource markets are interdependent. Resource owners will sell their resources, or the services of their resources, in those markets offering the highest returns.

Recognizing these interdependencies, it is easy to see how all of the decisions people make are synchronized and coordinated. And, importantly, such coordination and synchronization is accomplished without the "hand" of government; they are accomplished by an invisible hand—by people acting in their own self-interest. Moreover, the outcomes that emerge result in the production of that collection of goods and services that is efficient.

That the perfectly competitive system is efficient is seen in the intersection of each market's demand and supply curves. Consider product markets. The demand curve in each market reflects the choices people make to maximize utility. Any point on the demand curve tells us that, because people are willing to purchase the particular quantity indicated at the given price, they value that quantity at least as highly as the other goods and services they might purchase given their prices. The purchase of either more or less than the indicated quantity would make people worse off; that quantity, and only that quantity, will maximize utility. The last unit of good X purchased by each individual in the market is the one that brings the marginal utility (MU) per dollar spent on X into line with the MU per dollar spent on all other goods and services.

For the individual consumer, price is fixed. Price represents to the individual the product's marginal cost—the cost of acquiring the last unit. Demand measures the marginal benefit to the consumer. Utility is maximized when the individual purchases the product in an amount up to the point where the marginal benefit equals marginal cost—i.e., where marginal benefit equals price. For this reason, the price of each good or service is a measure of its relative worth at the margin; price measures the *marginal benefit* people attach to the product.

The supply curve, on the other hand, reflects the choices producers make to maximize profits. Each perfectly competitive producer maximizes profits by carrying production to the point where marginal cost (MC) equals price. The competitive supply curve consists of the horizontal sum of each producer's MC curve. Any point on the competitive supply curve tells us that, because producers are willing to produce and sell the particular quantity indicated at the given price, it is at least as profitable to use the resources required to produce the indicated quantity of that good as to use those same resources in the production of other things. The production and sale of either more or less than that quantity would mean less profit; that quantity, and only that quantity, will maximize profits.

For the individual producer, price is fixed. Price represents to the producer the product's marginal benefit—the revenue received by selling one more unit. Supply measures the marginal cost of producing one more unit; profits are maximized when production is carried to the point where marginal benefit is equal to marginal cost—i.e., where marginal cost is equal to price. Recalling the notion of opportunity costs, we know that the marginal cost of good X represents the value—the sacrifice—of the other goods and services that the resources used in the production of an extra unit of X could otherwise have produced. As long as MC is less than price, society values additional resources devoted to the production of X more than it does additional resources devoted to other goods and services.

Competition ensures that the equilibrium price will be the one that equates demand and supply. Thus, competition ensures that the value of each product to society (measured by its price) will be brought into equality with the marginal cost of the resources used in its production; that is, marginal benefit will equal marginal cost. Put differently, competition ensures that additional units of any product will be produced as long as they are valued more highly than the alternative products that the required resources could otherwise produce. This means that the "right" quantity of each good and service will be produced—"right" in the sense of maximizing consumer satisfactions. Competitive prices ensure that scarce resources are used with maximum efficiency.

If, for any reason, production of any good is carried to a point different from MC = P, social welfare is reduced in the sense that scarce resources will be used with less than maximum efficiency. If price exceeds MC, this signals that "too few" resources are being devoted to this good. The added benefits of more resources being devoted to the production of this good will exceed the value of the extra resources needed. Similarly, if MC exceeds price, this signals that "too many" resources are being used in the production of this good.

Imperfect competition and the competitive ideal

In the real world, most markets are not competitive. Indeed, it is more accurate to describe most resource and product markets as imperfectly competitive. At first blush, this would seem to indicate that our resources are not being efficiently allocated. It would also seem to establish a case for government intervention in markets to attempt to accomplish more competition among buyers and sellers. However, one needs to evaluate this case carefully.

Welfare benefits under imperfect competition

In some instances, it might be argued, society's interests are promoted by the presence of imperfect competition.

Product variety. If all markets were perfectly competitive, each producer would produce a product that was indistinguishable from the products of rival firms. There would be no product variety. Product differentiation introduces some monopolistic elements, but the departure from marginal cost pricing these elements cause may be justified because of the welfare benefits that result from variety. Unfortunately, we have no way of knowing how much product variety is optimal, or whether markets, left alone, produce the right amount of variety. Whether product advertising is, on balance, a net plus or minus in this regard is an open question.

Rapid technological advance. It is also argued by some that purely competitive markets are not conducive to rapid technological advance. It is true that each competitive producer, in order to survive, has a strong incentive to *adopt,* and to adopt quickly, the best available (least-cost) techniques of production. However, does it have an equally strong incentive to undertake the costs necessary to develop on its own better techniques of production? Some researchers think not. If a new and better technique is developed by one firm, it will earn economic profits that will be quickly whittled away as rival firms adopt the better technology. The incentive to develop new techniques may therefore be weak. Moreover, to the extent that rapid technological advance is the by-product of large research programs involving huge sums of money, it is doubtful whether such programs could be financed by the typical small perfectly competitive producer; large, imperfectly competitive firms may be a necessary accompaniment of rapid technological progress.

Needless to say, this line of reasoning is controversial. Those firms being attacked because of their bigness will frequently trot out this technological advancement argument. But in many instances the evidence is less than convincing. Unfortunately, the degree of market power in the hands of producers that is appropriate to promote rapid technological progress, and the degree of the departure from marginal cost pricing therefore justified, is an open question. The answer to the question also probably varies from industry to industry. Nevertheless, many researchers have concluded that, in at least most industries where market power is highly concentrated, the biggest of the big firms cannot be justified on these grounds.

Economies of scale.   There is a third possible justification for departing from the competitive ideal—economies of scale. As we saw in Chapter 19, when economies of scale are substantial, it may be in the interests of society to permit the concentration of production within one or a few large firms. In the cases of such "natural monopolies," however, there is also some justification for government regulation to bring about an outcome more in line with the efficiency conditions dictated by pure competition—i.e., price regulation to bring about the condition where MC equals P, or at least P equals AC.

The question that naturally arises is this: How far should government go in regulating the prices of so-called natural monopolies? In the case of some public utilities—e.g., gas and electric companies—it is common for government to regulate price in return for the granting of an exclusive

franchise to particular producers. This could be efficient if those firms that are regulated also produced at minimum cost. However, because competition has been eliminated, they do not have the same incentives to keep costs as low as perfectly competitive producers do. It is often alleged that the "costs" of regulated activities are higher, perhaps much higher, than they would otherwise be. (This is evidenced by plush executive offices, inordinately high executive and worker salaries, excessively large staffs, and unnecessary or little-used expensive office equipment.) Whether the "costs" are high or low makes little difference to many of the firm's owners, so it is alleged, because either way the regulatory authorities will set a price that gives only a "normal" return. Policing costs is a major problem confronting regulatory commissions.

There are, however, many industries where the high degree of concentration can be partly explained by the presence of economies of scale—e.g., autos. Should government intervene in these industries to regulate their prices as well? This is a much more difficult question to answer. It is also a question that has never been answered completely satisfactorily. Many people feel uncomfortable with the idea of government extending its arm to regulate these industries in the way it does the public utilities. Such regulation smacks of socialism; it is inconsistent with the spirit of capitalism. The government did not give these producers an exclusive franchise. Entry to such an industry has not been limited by government. Therefore how can price regulation be justified? What this argument ignores is that the presence of sizable economies of scale may be as effective a barrier to entry as the granting of an exclusive franchise.

On the other hand, would regulation introduce inefficiencies of the sort that are alleged to exist in the public utilities? Would costs swell once incentives to keep costs at a minimum are eliminated? Or would those firms who are subject to government price regulation cut their research and development expenditures, thereby slowing the pace of technological advance? After all, if the regulatory commissions were to set producer prices at levels that provided them with a "normal" rate of return only, what incentive would these producers have to engage in research and development to improve their products or to cut their costs? Moreover, in many instances, the degree of concentration among *domestic* producers misrepresents the extent of competition that actually prevails. Stiff competition from *foreign* producers is often pointed to as an important force in bringing about outcomes closer to the competitive ideal than might otherwise prevail.

THE NEED FOR ANTITRUST POLICY

From our earlier discussion it is clear that the economy benefits materially when competitive rivalry exists among firms. It is also clear that it is in our own interests to attempt to prohibit business practices that stifle competition. However, this does not mean that we desire an economic system structured along exclusively purely competitive lines. Sometimes society is better off with large firms (e.g., in those instances where economies of scale are sizable or where rapid technological advance requires resources in quantities that only large firms can provide). And presumably we are better off having some product variety rather than none, an outcome that allows some departure from the purely competitive solution.

Once monopoly power is permitted to exist, however, we immediately encounter a problem. In the interests of increasing their profits, firms have a very strong incentive to acquire as much monopoly power as possible. They have a strong incentive, that is, to avoid the discipline of competition—to eliminate, if possible, competitive rivalry and to stifle competition.

This means that, left to their own devices, producers will try all kinds of techniques to eliminate competition. To counter these tendencies, there needs to be some societal forces to ensure the continuation of competitive rivalry. However, if we reject the socialist route, involving as it would the detailed regulation of virtually all aspects of private sector activity, we are left with only one alternative—the development of an antitrust policy and other forms of government regulation.

Objectives of antitrust policy

In order to promote the efficient use of our scarce resources, antitrust policy must be designed in ways to negate those actions of producers that result in the stifling of competition.

Eliminate unfair competition. One objective of antitrust policy is the elimination of **unfair competition.** Unfortunately, there is no generally accepted definition of what constitutes "unfair competition." Indeed, when a firm is forced out of business, its owners will frequently point to their demise as having been the consequence of unfair practices engaged in by rival producers. This is all the more likely if the rival producers happen to be foreign producers. However, we must be careful to distinguish between healthy competition, which forces out of existence inefficient producers, and trade practices designed to stifle competition. One such unfair trade practice is known as *cutthroat* or *predatory competition.* What happens here is that one producer (or a group) slashes prices in order to drive rival firms into bankruptcy. Once the competition is eliminated, the predator raises prices to levels consistent with his/her newfound monopoly power. Would-be entrants are kept out by the predator's threat to cut prices to levels so low that entry becomes unprofitable.

In order to stop such ruinous competition, the government has occasionally stepped in to regulate those industries where cutthroat pricing practices, among other things, were found to exist. The Civil Aeronautics Board (CAB) was set up to eliminate unfair competition among the airlines. And the Interstate Commerce Commission (ICC), originally established to regulate various aspects of railroad transportation across states because of alleged unfair trade practices by the railroads, became involved later in the interstate regulation of the trucking industry as well. Although the reasons for regulating these industries were motivated by good intentions—the public welfare—research by economists over the course of the past 20 years made clear that the regulatory commissions had gone much too far. They had reached the point where they were downright detrimental to the goal of economic efficiency. Indeed, in the minds of many researchers, the regulations actually stifled competition. Regulations seemed directed more at protecting producers than consumers; and the regulations had the effect of protecting established industry interests at the expense of would-be entrants. In the end, it was also discovered that the regulations were actually detrimental to industry interests, too. This was partly evidenced by the near bankruptcy of many of our railroads in the early 1970s, due in large measure to regulations. It was also seen in the sharp increase in airline profits in the late 1970s, when many of the CAB price regulations were lifted. The removal of those price regulations, by lowering air travel prices generally, benefited the traveling public as well. Similar kinds of improvements are expected to follow in the wake of price deregulation actions undertaken by the Congress in 1980 for the railroad and trucking industries.

One important lesson seems to have been learned from our history of government regulations designed to negate the effects of unfair competition among producers. The regulations themselves often result in more harm than benefit as far as efficiency is concerned. There are other ways of dealing with "unfair" practices and with the consequences of the exercise of monopoly power that are probably more effective than government regulation of the industries themselves. We will examine these alternative methods below.

Eliminate collusive actions among producers. Why producers have an incentive to collude is clear. Each producer entering into a **collusive agreement** is able to share in the monopoly profits afforded by group action. The group acts as though it were a single producer, and the resultant "monopoly" generates aggregate profits larger than the aggregate profits that would have existed under more competitive conditions. Obviously, the larger pie can be shared in ways that make *all* producers better off.

In view of the stiff penalties, including jail sentences, that are imposed on those producers found to participate in collusive agreements, it is not surprising that we do not witness much overt collusive activity in this day and age. But this does not mean that collusion does not exist. Since the incentives to collude are strong, much collusive behavior may have been pushed underground.

However, some economists have alleged that open, overt collusive behavior on the part of producers still exists, only today it takes on forms that are much more subtle than signed agreements. Indeed, the producers need not ever get together to accomplish what signed agreements accomplish. Price leadership has been identified as one such form of subtle collusive behavior. The argument goes as follows: Producers have a common interest; the leader sets the price as if the industry were monopolized; the followers accept the leaders' decision and set their prices at the same level; all producers thereby share in the monopoly profits of the industry.

Why isn't price leadership outlawed? The answer: What is there to outlaw? The fact that producers announce their prices? This can hardly be used as a justification. Indeed, the courts have ruled that it is illegal for bar and medical associations to deny their members the right to advertise prices of the grounds that such practices actually stifle competition. If this line won't work, what about the fact that producers charge similar prices? This also has problems. Indeed, how can this be used as a justification when, under perfect competition, every producer sells at the same price? Moreover, how do you counter the argument that all the firm is doing is meeting the competition?

In short, it is extremely difficult to build a case against an industry where, at least on the surface, it appears that price leadership is being practiced to suppress competitive rivalry among firms. In the absence of an explicit agreement among producers, it is often too difficult to discover whether firms have acted to stifle competition; the fact that prices are quoted and similar to each other hardly constitutes the proof one needs.

Prevent mergers that tend to lessen competition. When firms are taken over by other firms, the possibility arises that competition will be reduced. However, as will become clear, not all takeovers necessarily reduce competition; it depends in part on the nature of the takeover.

The takeover of a firm by a competitor *in the same market*—a **horizontal merger**—is often alleged to reduce competition. Yes, horizontal mergers do cause a reduction in the number of firms competing with one another. But whether they serve to reduce economic efficiency is an open question. If economies of scale are realized, or if the environment is made more conducive to rapid technological advance as a consequence of such takeovers, economic efficiency need not suffer.

Vertical mergers—takeovers involving a supplier firm and its customer—are also widely viewed to be detrimental to competition. Once again we need to acknowledge that such takeovers need not adversely affect the public interest if, for example, economies of scale are realized in the process. Moreover the fact that vertical takeovers do not necessarily reduce the number of competitors within the affected industries—the number of supplier firms and the number of customer firms in each industry remaining the same—complicates the argument considerably. However, if one or a group of customer firms are able, through merger, to gain effective control over essential supplies, economic efficiency could suffer considerably. The merged firms would then have erected a very effective barrier to entry that could stifle competition sharply.

The issue is complicated still further in cases of **conglomerate mergers**—diverse enterprises from several industries being combined under a single management. Perhaps the best known conglomerate is International Telephone and Telegraph (ITT). Its management controls, among others: the Sheraton Corporation, the largest hotel chain; Continental Baking, the largest manufacturer of bakery products; and Hartford Fire Insurance, one of the largest insurance companies. Other well-known conglomerates include Litton Industries, Gulf & Western, and Textron.

The conglomerates constitute an important part of the American economy. Since World War II a sharp increase has occurred in the size of the largest firms relative to the total economy. Whereas the value added of the 200 largest industrial corporations accounted for about 14 percent of GNP in 1950, it accounts for about 19 percent today; the value added of the largest 200 as a percent of total *manufacturing* value added has increased by even more—from about 48 percent in 1950 to around 61 percent today. Most of this increase in the relative size of the top 200 firms occurred during the 1960s, when the merger fever, particularly the conglomerate merger fever, was at its height.

The fact that a great deal of the increase in relative size of our industrial giants is accounted for by the growth of conglomerate mergers raises doubts about the extent of the reduction in competition that may have occurred as a result. Yes, conglomerate mergers have increased the relative size of the largest corporations. However, because conglomerates combine diverse enterprises from several industries, such mergers do not bring about a corresponding increase in concentration *within* industries. Once again, it is important to acknowledge that conglomerates may provide economies of scale in management and marketing, at least. By the same token, the huge concentrations of economic power within conglomerates can, and often do, lead to an increase in their political influence, both at home and abroad. Conglomerates constitute an important lobbying force in Washington and other capital cities of the world. Not only do they seek to influence elections. They frequently have an important voice in the design of legislation as well.

Antitrust policy in the United States

As the foregoing discussion makes clear, the question of how government ought to deal with concentrations of economic power is not cut-and-dried. On the one hand, when economic power becomes more concentrated, competition is often reduced and economic efficiency suffers. On the other hand, increased concentration may offer substantial benefits in the form of enlarged economies of scale and an increase in the pace of technological advance. Balancing these diverse outcomes is not easy.

It is important to recognize, however, that the balancing of these economic considerations constitutes only one aspect, and not necessarily the most important aspect, of antitrust policy in the United States. At times, such considerations seem to play little or no part at all. Indeed, during the earliest days of antitrust policy—the 1890s—Congress and the courts seemed intent on going after the big businesses, not to make the economy more efficient necessarily but to cut the rich and powerful down to size (including labor unions). This attitude is perhaps best illustrated in one of the most famous early Supreme Court decisions—*United States* v. *Trans-Missouri Freight Association,* in 1897. In that case, the Court ruled that, although large businesses may "permanently" reduce the prices of the goods traded, trade may "nevertheless be badly restrained by driving out of business the small dealers and worthy men whose lives have been spent therein and who might be unable to readjust themselves to their altered surrounding."

Interestingly, such concern for "small dealers and worthy men" continues to play a decisive role to this day in some Supreme Court decisions. One of the most celebrated cases occurred in 1966. The case involved the merger of two grocery firms in Los Angeles—Von's Grocery Company, the third largest food chain in the area, and a direct competitor, Shopping Bag. The court ruled against the merger. The grounds were not that the two merged firms caused a dramatic increase in economic concentration. In fact, after the merger the two firms accounted for only 7.5 percent of sales—smaller than the leader, Safeway. The grounds were that the number of single-store operators in the retail grocery market had been on the decline. Yes, the number of operators had declined—from over 5,300 in 1950 to around 3,800 in 1960, the date Von's merged with Shop-

ping Bag. But rather than ask whether 3,800 firms was sufficient to ensure competition, the Court in 1966 cited the 1897 Supreme Court decision, based as it was on concern for the fate of "small dealers and worthy men." The Court argued, "Where concentration is gaining momentum in a market we must be alert to carry out Congress' intent," which was "to prevent economic concentration in the American economy by keeping a large number of small competitors in business."

But the courts have not always been consistent on such matters. Many mergers have been allowed when the facts would have indicated a sharp increase in economic concentration. Moreover, although the intent of Congress has generally been to encourage competition and to oppose monopoly, some decisions, especially those rendered under the Robinson-Patman Act, as we shall see below, have had the opposite effect—that of supporting monopoly power.

Major antitrust legislation

Antitrust policy is much too complicated a subject to deal with in a few pages. We will therefore deal here with just the highlights. The foundation of U.S. antitrust policy is formed by six major legislative acts—the Sherman Act, the Clayton Act, the Federal Trade Commission Act, the Robinson-Patman Act, the Miller-Tydings Act, and the Celler-Kefauver Act.

The Sherman Act (1890). This law, which constitutes the cornerstone of U.S. antitrust policy, was passed largely in response to the wave of mergers that occurred in the latter half of the 19th century. The two most important provisions of the act state:

1. "Every contract, combination in the form of trust or otherwise, or conspiracy, in restraint of trade or commerce among the several states or with foreign nations, is hereby declared illegal."

2. "Every person who shall monopolize, or attempt to monopolize, or conspire with any other person or persons, to monopolize any part of the trade or commerce among the

several states, or with foreign nations, shall be guilty of a misdemeanor."

The language of the Sherman Act is vague. No clear understanding was provided for such phrases as "to attempt to monopolize" or "conspire with another person." About the only practice the Court has consistently outlawed under this act is price fixing. Competing firms must set their prices independently of one another; the establishment of prices cooperatively is illegal. However, as noted earlier, the courts have not, as a rule, seen fit to apply the Sherman Act to instances of price leadership. If price fixing is overt and open it is illegal; if it is tacit, the court has been hesitant to rule it illegal.

Initially, the courts used the act not to go after individual firms who controlled substantial shares of their individual markets but to go after the formation of **trusts.** The establishment of a trust constituted one important way whereby producers could collude to limit competition. The common stock of different firms would be placed in a trust, with an agreement that they would all work together and share profits collectively. It was not until 1911 that the courts, as a consequence of Teddy Roosevelt's trust-busting platform, began to apply the act to the tactics employed by individual firms to restrain trade. In 1911, the Court ruled that Standard Oil, which then controlled 90 percent of the country's refinery capacity, and American Tobacco, which then controlled 75 percent of the tobacco manufacturing market, had to be broken up into several smaller rival firms.

These actions did not constitute a prohibition against monopoly per se. Standard Oil and American Tobacco were broken up because each had used "unreasonable" tactics to restrain trade. In later cases, the Court refused to break up U.S. Steel and American Can, even though they each controlled substantial shares of their market. The cases were thrown out because the government had failed to show that these companies had followed "unfair or unethical" business practices. The ineffectiveness of the Sherman Act led the Congress to pass two other antitrust laws in 1914.

The Clayton Act (1914). This act attempted to spell out in detail the specific "unfair and unethical" business practices Congress sought to prohibit. Five such practices were prohibited if they "substantially lessened competition or tend to create a monopoly."

1. *Price discrimination*—charging purchasers different prices that are unrelated to transportation costs. This section was not actively enforced until the Robinson-Patman Act of 1936.
2. *Interlocking directorates*—the practice whereby the director of one firm sits on the boards of directors of competing firms. The opportunities for collusion are obvious when interlocking directorates are present.
3. *Interlocking stockholding*—the practice of taking over another firm by the purchase of its common stock. Interestingly, this provision was evaded easily. All the firm had to do was purchase the *physical assets* of the other firm, instead of its common stock. This loophole was finally closed in 1950 with passage of the Celler-Kefauver Anti-Merger Act.
4. *Tying contracts*—the practice whereby the sale of one item is conditional upon the buyers purchasing another item. One celebrated tying agreement declared illegal by the court was one in which IBM made the sale of its business machines conditional on the purchase of IBM-brand punchcards. The Court ruled that this tying contract gave IBM a virtual monopoly over the punchcards.
5. *Exclusive dealings*—the practice whereby company X makes the sale of its product to retailer Y conditional on Y *not* selling products produced by X's competitors.

The Federal Trade Commission Act (1914). This act is very direct and to the point. It declares that "unfair methods of competition in Commerce are illegal." What constitutes unfair was to be determined by an independent board of five members—the Federal Trade Commission (FTC). Shortly after coming into existence, however, the commission ran into trouble with the courts. The courts, so the justices argued, not the commission, would determine whether practices were unfair. The commission, of course, may bring suits against companies for engaging in what it believes are unfair practices, as it has against the Exxon Corporation and IBM, but the final determination will be made by the courts. (The primary function of the FTC today is to control misleading advertising and the misrepresentation of products.)

The Robinson-Patman Act (1936). Since 1914 there have been three major amendments to the Clayton Act. They are the Robinson-Patman Act (1936), the Miller-Tydings Act (1937), and the Celler-Kefauver Act (1950).

The Robinson-Patman Act was designed to strengthen the law against price discrimination. However, there is considerable evidence that this act has actually served to impede rather than promote competition. Indeed, the Department of Justice in 1976 issued a report calling for the repeal of this act on grounds that it decreased competition.

The act itself was aimed at protecting not the consumer but small business from larger competitors. In line with the "small dealers and worthy men" arguments used in the 1897 Supreme Court case, the Robinson-Patman Act sought to curb, among other things, price cutting by large discount and chain stores. It also prohibited selling to the public at "unreasonably low prices."

According to some economists, the perverse effects of this act are amply illustrated in the 1967 *Utah Pie* v. *Continental Baking Co.* court decision. Utah Pie was a local bakery with a near monopoly in the production of frozen pies in Salt Lake City. To gain a large share of the Salt Lake City frozen pie market, Continental Baking Co. and two other national bakery firms engaged in intense price competition with Utah Pie. These national firms sold their frozen pies in Salt Lake City at prices lower than elsewhere in the country. Utah Pie's share of the market fell to below 50 percent and that firm brought suit against Continental and the others. The Court ruled in favor of Utah Pie; the national firms had engaged in "predatory" price cutting to harm Utah Pie. Their tactics had injured a local firm, an outcome that the Robinson-Patman Act was designed to prohibit. Was the effect of

this decision perverse? It is difficult to say. The fact is that, despite the court action, Utah Pie went out of business two years later.

The Miller-Tydings Act (1937). Like the Robinson-Patman Act, the Miller-Tydings Act seeks to put the interests of small business above the interest of consumers. This act exempted "fair trade" agreements from prosecution under antitrust laws. A fair trade agreement permits manufacturers to prohibit retailers from selling their products below a "fair trade" price.

It's hard to imagine a law more at odds with economic theory than this one. It was finally repealed by the Congress in 1977.

The Celler-Kefauver Act (1950). This act prohibited a firm from acquiring the physical assets of a competitor when the effect of the transaction was to lessen competition. This closed the loophole in the Clayton Act, which, as noted before, prohibited mergers through stock acquisition, but which did not prohibit mergers formed as a result of asset sales.

Antitrust policy: A few closing notes

While there is fairly broad agreement among economists regarding the need for an antitrust policy with teeth, there is much less agreement as to where we ought to go from here. The Sherman and Clayton acts are widely perceived as having exerted a positive influence in favor of more competitive markets. They raised dramatically the costs of overt collusion. And the specific anticompetitive practices they prohibited have probably served to reduce barriers to entry below what they would otherwise have been.

However, many problems remain. First, what, if anything, should be done about oligopolistic industries that act as if they were monopolies? There is a term that describes such industries— **shared monopoly.** In these industries, collusion is not overt. The suspicion is strong, however, that the oligopolists do collude, only they do it tacitly. Price leadership is one frequently identified form of shared monopoly.

What should be done about shared monopolies? No one knows. Some think they should be attacked vigorously; any firm holding a market share of 15 to 20 percent or more should be broken up into smaller independent units unless the larger size can be justified on efficiency grounds.

A second problem area concerns conglomerate mergers. To date, antitrust law has not been effective in preventing such mergers. This is primarily because it is difficult, if not impossible, to identify clearly what kinds of adverse economic effects they create. Nevertheless, many legislators feel that something ought to be done to limit the size of conglomerate mergers on grounds that the "dispersion of power" is good in and of itself. Senator Edward Kennedy proposed just such a bill in the 96th Congress. But it died as a consequence of the change in administration and the Republican takeover of the Senate in the 1980 election. Whether it will be revived again in the near future is doubtful in view of President Reagan's policy position that such mergers ought not to be discouraged.

A third problem area deals with the question of whether antitrust laws should be used to protect small businesses from competition from larger enterprises. We saw earlier how the Robinson-Patman Act has been used as a tool to protect small business to the detriment of consumer welfare. Some think protection of small business is an inappropriate goal, but the lobbying efforts on behalf of small business are so intense that efforts to repeal Robinson-Patman will have a tough time.

A great many economists feel we should use the theory of the invisible hand as our guide to antitrust policy. According to that theory, competitive markets allocate resources in line with consumer wants. Consumer welfare is thereby maximized. The overriding concern of antitrust policy should be consumer welfare. We should not be concerned with protecting small business per se. If larger enterprises force small firms out of business and if consumer welfare is promoted as a consequence, so be it.

Bigness per se is not inconsistent with the theory of the invisible hand. The question again is one of whether or not big firms, on balance, promote economic efficiency. The anticompetitive effects of monopoly power must be weighed against the advantages resulting from, say, realized economies of scale.

Of course, because predatory actions designed to harm competitors for the purpose of acquiring monopoly power are inconsistent with the goal of maximizing consumer welfare, the invisible hand guide would outlaw such practices. It would also outlaw horizontal mergers unless such mergers promote consumer welfare (e.g., if such mergers resulted in beneficial economies of scale effects). It would also outlaw price-fixing arrangements among producers. However, unless shown to be contrary to consumer welfare, the guide would not necessarily outlaw vertical mergers, conglomerate mergers, or price discrimination.

GOVERNMENT REGULATORY ACTIVITY

Much of this book has already dealt with the subject of government regulation. The monetary and fiscal policies that occupied much of our attention in the first half of this book are forms of government regulation. We dealt at length in Chapter 9 with the issues surrounding the regulation and deregulation of financial institutions. The regulation of natural monopolies was a subject of intense study in Chapter 21. In the second section of this chapter we examined a variety of issues relating to U.S. antitrust policy.

It is the purpose of this section to expand our discussion of government regulation to deal with a number of controversial issues that have been the subject of intense debate in recent years. Specifically, we will examine the dramatic shift of direction toward deregulation of what might be called, for want of a better name, **traditional regulatory activities**—government regulations designed to control prices and the entry of firms in such diverse industries as communications (telephones and broadcasting), interstate transportation (railroads, airlines, and trucking companies), and pipeline transportation (natural gas pipeline companies). We will also examine the factors responsible for the rapid surge of health and safety regulations during the 1970s, and, ironically, the equally rapid surge of second thoughts about the desirability of undertaking these regulatory initiatives in the late 1970s and early 1980s.

Justifications for government regulation

Traditional regulatory activities were justified on grounds that the monopoly power possessed by companies in certain industries would result in inordinately high prices for the goods produced, as well as the absence of "adequate" service both to people located in outlying regions and to infrequent users. The trick for the regulatory agencies was to discover a price for each of the services as close to the competitive price as possible, but far enough above it to permit the subsidization of services to people and places that would otherwise not have it.

Over time, these arguments began to lose force as a consequence of increasing numbers of competitors and inefficiences in the regulatory processes themselves. Correspondingly, the voices clamoring for the deregulation of these traditional sectors held sway. Since passage of the Airline Deregulation Act of 1978, Congress has also substantially deregulated common carrier trucking, interstate movers of household goods, and railroads.

Health and safety regulations were justified on quite different grounds. Producers who strive to maximize profits will fail to take into account the harm to workers caused by unhealthy and unsafe work places. They will fail to take into account the damage to the environment caused by the dumping of waste products. And they will fail to undertake the expenditures necessary to ensure safe and healthy products. Since the harm caused by these nonactions of producers are properly treated as costs—costs imposed on others but not absorbed (or internalized) by producers—it is appropriate for government to intervene to control those costs.

Where's the problem?

In the minds of many economists, it is difficult to fault the *justifications* for both traditional regulatory activities and social regulation. So, what is all the debate about? Why did the Reagan Administration set as one of its major objectives a sharp reduction in federal government regulatory initiatives? And why did the Carter and Ford Administrations before that put regulatory reform high on the agenda of issues to be dealt with? Oversimplifying somewhat, it probably is fair to say that most of the furor over government regulations has little to do with the goals of government regulations per se; most people in government think the goals are worthwhile (or at least they pay lip service to them). If the problems do not lie with the objectives, what then? Most critics contend that the problems are a consequence of the failure of government regulations to produce desirable outcomes. This criticism comes in several guises:

"Health and safety regulations have not produced marked improvements in working conditions or in the environment. The methods or processes we use to regulate are wrong and need to be reformed."

"Government regulations have gone too far. We simply cannot afford the cleanest air and water and the safest workplaces. In short, the costs of government regulation exceed the benefits."

"A great many regulations are unnecessary, and a great many others require those being regulated to use methods of compliance that are much more costly than alternatives that would 'get the job done' just as well. Either these regulations only raise the cost side of the benefit-cost equation, or they add to the cost side unnecessarily. Moreover, many regulations are in conflict. At a minimum the conflicts ought to be eliminated."

Regulatory reform

It is difficult to evaluate the claims made by the critics of government regulation. There is no question but that many government regulations are unnecessary. The *Code of Federal Regulations*—the manual containing the bulk of all federal government regulations—is loaded with *nit-picking rules* that are costly but of dubious social value. (One of the more humorous nit-picking rules of the Occupational Health and Safety Administration (OSHA) concerned the detailed specifications that had to be met in the design of toilet seats! In fairness, however, OSHA claimed that it had merely used existing industry standards.) It is also true that a great many government regulations go beyond the mere specification of standards that must be met. They also set forth in detail *the means* that must be used to comply with the standards without regard to the costs of compliance. In many instances, other less costly techniques are available that would meet the standards of performance. And even if less costly techniques were not *then* available, the mandating of the standard of performance itself would cause the affected businesses to seek the least costly means of complying. Moreover, there is no question but that many *conflicting regulations* exist on the books. (For example, as Raymond Hasty, president of Park Sausage Company pointed out in testimony before the Joint Economic Committee in 1978, "USDA requires that our sausage kitchen floor be washed repeatedly for sanitary reasons. Yet OSHA rules floors must be dry. What's a man to do?")

The need to accomplish reforms in these three areas is widely shared. The nit-picking rules that cannot withstand the usual cost-benefit test should be discarded. Rather than detail the *means* that must be used to comply with government imposed standards, it is probably almost always preferable to leave the means of compliance up to those being regulated. And where regulation conflicts are present, they need to be resolved.

The notion that we have gone too far, that the costs of regulation exceed the benefits is much more difficult, if not impossible, to evaluate. Let us examine this criticism in parts.

First, a great many statistics are brought to bear to "prove" that government regulations have grown too rapidly and too costly. Congressman Clarence Brown, for example, stated, "Currently, the *Code of Federal Regulations* totals 800,000 pages and occupies 52 large bookshelves. Twenty years ago the whole thing was about ankle-high on me, but now I cannot reach to the

top of that shelf of books stacked end-to-end, and I am six foot four."[1]

Moreover, much has been made of a study done for the Joint Economic Committee by Murray Weidenbaum, chairman of President Reagan's Council of Economic Advisers, that stated that the costs of regulation exceeded $100 billion in 1979. In addition, according to a U.S. Department of Commerce study, the percentage of GNP under regulation rose from a total of 8.2 percent in 1965 to 23.7 percent by 1975, with fully 77 percent of that increase accounted for by the growth of health and safety regulations.[2]

Finally, many critics point to the existence of a whole host of regulatory agencies—the most notable being the Environmental Protection Agency (EPA), the Consumer Product Safety Commission, and the Occupational Safety and Health Administration (OSHA)—all of which did not exist until the 1970s, as evidence of government regulation out of control.

What should one make of all this evidence? Actually, very little. None of these statistics really answers the question, What did we get for our money? Nevertheless, the costs of regulation have swelled so much and government regulation has become so pervasive that it has caused many critics to propose the adoption of a **regulatory budget** as a solution.

The regulatory budget

The idea behind the regulatory budget is straightforward. It would establish a ceiling on the amount of costs that government could impose on individuals, private firms, and other institutions in order to meet government regulations. In principle, it is analogous to the familiar fiscal budget, and its role in the analysis and weighing of alternatives would be similar. There is an opportunity cost to using scarce resources to ac-

---

[1] Clarence J. Brown, "Legislating a Regulatory Budget Limit," in *Reforming Regulation,* eds. T. B. Clark, M. H. Kosters, and J. C. Miller III (Washington, D.C.: American Enterprise Institute, 1980).

[2] Reported in Paul W. MacAvoy, "Overview of Regulatory Effects and Reform Prospects," in ibid.

complish regulatory objectives just as there are opportunity costs to using scarce federal dollars for national defense or education. Choices have to be made.

Cost-benefit analysis

Unfortunately, the regulatory budget only addresses one side of the issue—the cost side. What about the benefits of regulation? How is it possible to determine the optimum size of the regulatory budget without knowing what that budget will "buy"? This suggests, of course, that there is need for a cost-benefit analysis, not only for individual regulatory activities but overall.

Requiring that all regulatory agency decisions meet the cost-benefit test is really nothing more than a requirement that those decisions pass the test of common sense. After all, what sensible person would propose a regulation where the costs decisively exceeded the benefits?

Unfortunately, it's not all that simple. In a great many cases, the costs of regulatory proposals are extremely difficult to measure. Generally speaking, measuring benefits is even more difficult, especially in cases where the result of the proposal is a reduction in the risk of accidental injury or death. Nevertheless, despite its shortcomings as a tool, and certainly as a *precise* tool of analysis, many economists would argue for its continued use—indeed, its extended use. The discipline it brings to bear on the regulatory processes could force into the open many facts that regulators might be prone to overlook.

The need to reform the methods of regulation

All of this discussion leads us back to the critics' first complaint—namely, that the social regulations have not worked as well as they might have because the methods or processes used by the regulators have been wrong. In order to assess this view, it is necessary to inquire into the issue of externalities. That subject is reserved for the next chapter.

SUMMARY

1. The theory of the invisible hand is a very powerful and influential idea and the source of considerable controversy. This theory lies at the heart of the laissez-faire philosophy that countenances the nonintervention of government in markets. At the same time, it is this theory—or rather its alleged failure—that lies at the heart of non-laissez-faire philosophies that countenance the active intervention of government in markets.

2. The theory of the invisible hand concerns itself with only one thing—economic efficiency. What the theory states is this: Given certain ideal conditions, the utility-maximizing behavior of individuals and the profit-maximizing behavior of producers will lead to the most efficient social outcome; each individual acting in self-interest promotes the interests of society at large. However, before one can accept the conclusion of this theory, it is necessary to inquire into the "ideal conditions" that must be met in order for the theory to hold. There are three important ideal conditions: perfect competition, absence of externalities, and a fair distribution of income and wealth.

3. In some instances, it might be argued, society's interests are promoted by the presence of imperfect competition. Imperfect competition may result in greater product variety that more than offsets the monopolistic elements introduced thereby. It may result in more rapid technological advance. And it may permit the realization of greater economies of scale.

4. In order to promote the efficient use of our scarce resources, antitrust policy must be designed in ways to negate those actions of producers that result in the stifling of competition. Antitrust policy should have as its objectives (1) the elimination of unfair competition, (2) the elimination of collusive actions among producers, and (3) the prevention of mergers that tend to lessen competition.

5. The question of how government ought to deal with concentrations of economic power is not cut-and-dried. On the one hand, when economic power becomes concentrated, competition

is often reduced and economic efficiency suffers. On the other hand, increased concentration may offer substantial benefits in the form of enlarged economies of scale and an increase in the pace of technological advance. Balancing these diverse outcomes is not easy. However, the balancing of these economic considerations constitutes only one aspect, and not necessarily the most important aspect, of antitrust policy in the United States. At times, such considerations seem to play little or no part at all.

6.   Traditional regulatory activities were justified on grounds that the monopoly power possessed by companies in certain industries would result in inordinately high prices for the goods produced, as well as the absence of "adequate" service both to people located in outlying regions and to infrequent users. Health and safety regulations were justified on quite different grounds. Producers who strive to maximize profits will fail to take into account the harm to workers caused by unhealthy and unsafe workplaces. They will fail to take into account the damage to the environment caused by the dumping of waste products. And they will fail to undertake the expenditures necessary to ensure safe and healthy products.

7.   Most of the furor over government regulations has little to do with the goals of government regulations per se. The problems are a consequence of the failure of government regulations to produce desirable outcomes.

8.   The nit-picking rules that can not withstand the usual cost-benefit tests should be discarded. Rather than detail the *means* that must be used to comply with government-imposed standards, it is probably almost always preferable to leave the means of compliance up to those being regulated. And where regulation conflicts are present, they need to be resolved.

9.   The idea behind a *regulatory budget* is straightforward. It would establish a ceiling on the amount of costs that government could impose on individuals, private firms, and other institutions in order to meet government regulations. In principal, it is analogous to the familiar fiscal budget.

10.   Unfortunately, the regulatory budget only addresses the cost side of the issue. What is needed is a thoroughgoing cost-benefit analysis of all agency decisions. Unfortunately, it is not all that simple. In a great many cases, the costs of regulatory proposals are extremely difficult to measure. Generally speaking, measuring benefits is even more difficult, especially in cases where the result of the proposal is a reduction in the risk of accidental injury or death. Nevertheless, despite its shortcomings as a tool, and certainly as a precise tool of analysis, many economists would argue for its continued use or the discipline it brings to bear on the regulatory process.

CONCEPTS FOR REVIEW

Theory of the invisible hand

Economic efficiency

Externalities

General equilibrium

Antitrust policy

"Unfair competition"

Collusive agreement

Horizontal merger

Vertical merger

Conglomerate merger

The Sherman Act (1890)

The Clayton Act (1914)

The Federal Trade Commission Act (1914)

The Robinson–Patman Act (1936)

The Miller–Tydings Act (1937)

The Celler–Kefauver Act (1950)

Shared monopoly

Traditional regulatory activities

Social regulation

Regulatory budget

Cost-benefit analysis

QUESTIONS FOR DISCUSSION

1.   What accounts for government encouragement of some monopolies and the outlawing of others?

2. "Despite the lofty ideals of antitrust policy, from an economist's perspective, the actual conduct of antitrust policy does not fit those ideals well." Discuss.

3. "The elimination of all barriers to international trade would prove to be one of the most effective antitrust policies of all." Do you agree or disagree? Explain.

4. "Government social regulations have grown too rapidly. The need to slow their growth is therefore apparent. After all, if they continued to grow at the same pace they have since 1965, 100 percent of our GNP would be under regulation by the year 2000." Carefully evaluate.

*It is now time to turn our attention to the prob-
lem of **externalities**. Externalities occur when the
voluntary actions of producers, consumers, or
both, cause adverse or beneficial side effects for
which no compensation is made.*

Examples of externalities abound. Consider
briefly an adverse externality, the problem of *pollution.* A firm is permitted to discharge its effluent
back to the river, degrading its quality and adversely affecting the operations of water users
downstream. The cost to the users downstream
is imposed on them by the firm upstream. That
cost is not considered a cost of production to
the upstream firm. Therefore, it will not be reflected in that firm's product price. Under these
circumstances, as we will see, market prices will
give the wrong signals and cause a misallocation
of resources. Accordingly, government intervention would seem to be justified.

Or consider an example of a beneficial externality, the construction of a dam by a group of
farmers to control flooding. Those other farmers
in the valley who do not pay for any of the cost
of the dam will still benefit from the presense
of the dam. Once again, market prices will give
the wrong signals and cause a misallocation of
resources. Government intervention would seem
to be justified in this instance as well.

In this chapter, we will study first the issue
of beneficial externalities. This will be followed
by a discussion of adverse externalities.

Chapter 28

Government and the private sector: The general problem of externalities

BENEFICIAL EXTERNALITIES, RESOURCE MISALLOCATION, AND THE "FREE RIDER" PROBLEM

The theory of the invisible hand presumes that
social welfare is promoted when each individual
pursues his or her own self-interest. However,
the validity of this proposition depends heavily
on the absence of externalities in production and
consumption. When externalities are present,
perfectly competitive markets can cause a misallocation of resources.

To see this, let us delve a bit more deeply
into the assumptions that underlie the theory of
the invisible hand. This theory implicitly assumes

that all the benefits of the products produced are *private benefits.* Only those who purchase the products receive the benefits they provide; non-buyers receive no benefits. This assumption is important. If true, it means that the market demand curve for each product, obtained by adding up the demand curves of individuals, accurately represents the relative benefit of this good to society as a whole. The social benefit is indistinguishable from the sum of the private benefits; social welfare is promoted when people promote their own individual welfare.

If beneficial externalities are present, on the other hand—i.e., if people receive benefits without paying for them—the market demand curve, obtained in the usual way, will *not* accurately represent the relative benefit of this good to society as a whole. It will understate the relative benefit of the good. What matters from the point of view of social welfare is not the private benefits alone—which is what the demand curve measures—but the social benefits—the private benefits *plus* the beneficial externalities.

Let us examine this important issue in greater depth. Some goods are private in the sense of providing benefits only to those who buy them. People who buy apples get the enjoyment and nourishment apples provide; people who do not buy apples are excluded from these benefits. However, there are many goods that provide benefits to people other than those who buy them; there are spillover benefits—beneficial externalities.

To illustrate, examine the benefits that result when some people pay for vaccinations to protect themselves against contagious diseases. Those who are vaccinated certainly receive protective benefits. However, there are spillover benefits as well. Those not vaccinated receive some protective benefits since the likelihood of the disease spreading is reduced. In this instance, the social benefits of vaccination exceed the private benefits, the private benefits being those that are received by the people who pay for the vaccinations.

Consider another example. Mr. Jones farms a piece of land located in a valley that is subject to repeated flooding. If a dam were erected, flood control would be possible. Suppose Jones builds such a dam at his own expense. Jones benefits from the dam, but so do all of the other farmers in the valley even though they paid none of the cost. Here again, social benefits exceed private benefits. The benefits received by *all* the farmers in the valley exceed the benefits received by Jones alone.

Some might argue that it's unfair for people to receive benefits when they did not pay for them. However, it is not our purpose here to discuss whether the outcomes are fair or not fair; that is a side issue. What is important, though, is that, in the face of beneficial externalities, the outcomes may be inefficient. More pointedly, *perfectly competitive markets will not allocate resources efficiently when beneficial externalities of the kind described above are present.* The reason is clear. The spillover or external benefits are *not* reflected in the demand curve for the product. The market demand curve consists of the horizontal sum of the individual demand curves. Each individual demand curve tells us how much each person is willing to pay to obtain various quantities of the product. How much each individual is willing to pay is a measure of how much he or she expects to benefit personally from buying it; any benefit others might receive is irrelevant. The market demand curve reflects only the benefits received by those who buy the product; it reflects only the private benefits.

In a private goods market (where the benefits accrue only to those who buy the good), the market demand curve will yield not only total private benefits at the margin but social marginal benefits as well. The reason is clear. Since the only benefits received are those that people are willing and able to pay for, total private benefits—obtained by the horizontal addition of the individual demand curves—must equal the total of all benefits received by society as a whole—total social benefits. However, in markets where beneficial externalities are present, social marginal benefits cannot be found by adding the individual demand curves horizontally. As we will see below, it is possible, in principle, to construct a curve that reflects marginal social benefits. That curve will lie above and to the right of the demand curve. However, that marginal social benefit curve is *not* a demand curve. And since perfectly competitive markets allocate resources on the basis of market demands (and supplies) only, resources will be misallocated to the extent that they fail to accurately reflect social benefits.

These ideas can be illustrated with a simple numerical example. Consider a product—such as vaccinations—that has beneficial spillover effects. I am willing to pay $10 for a unit of the product. The $10 I am willing to pay reflects the marginal benefit I expect to receive from the product. My friend Oscar, on the other hand, is willing to pay only $6 for a unit, reflecting the marginal benefit he attaches to the product. If the price is $10, I will buy one unit and Oscar will not buy any. However, because of the spillover effects, Oscar receives some benefits even though he didn't buy any. Oscar gets a *free ride;* he gets something for nothing. Let's assume, for the sake of argument, that Oscar gets 50 cents worth of benefits because of my purchase. The marginal social benefit consists of my marginal private benefit ($10) plus Oscar's "free ride" (worth 50 cents), plus whatever other benefits spill over onto others. Now, although the mar-

ginal social benefit exceeds $10, this will not influence the market-determined result. Indeed, if the price exceeds $10, I will not purchase the product and the benefit I would have received plus the spillover benefits resulting from my purchase will not be realized. The market-determined result depends only on demand (and supply). The signal that marginal social benefit provides does not get transmitted to the marketplace; only marginal private benefits are transmitted. The reason? Since Oscar was unwilling or unable to pay anything when the price was $10, the market receives no signal from Oscar that he received any benefits because he didn't spend any funds to acquire those benefits.

These ideas are portrayed graphically in Figure 28.1. The demand curve D, which shows how much people are willing to pay for the good, measures the relative value of the good at the margin *to those who buy it.* If this good were sold in a perfectly competitive market, equilibrium would occur at point A. At that equilibrium position, marginal private benefit is equal to marginal cost.

This looks like an efficient outcome, but it is not. At point A, marginal cost equals marginal *private* benefit; not marginal *social* benefit. The

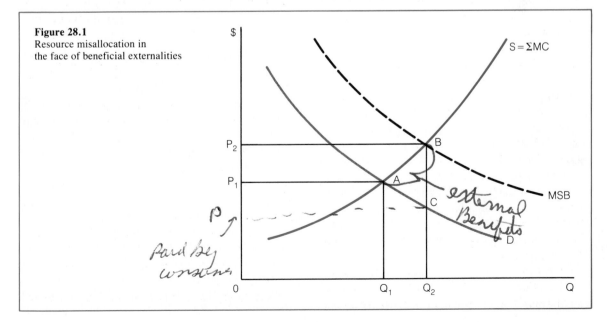

Figure 28.1
Resource misallocation in
the face of beneficial externalities

demand curve reflects only the additional benefits that accrue to those who buy it; it does not reflect the additional benefits to all members of society of an additional unit purchased.

The dashed line labeled MSB measures the marginal social benefits associated with different quantities of the good in question. The MSB line lies above and to the right of D. The vertical distance between the D curve and the MSB curve at any point measures the marginal spillover or external benefits.

In order to achieve an efficient outcome, it is necessary to equate MSB with MC. Using Figure 28.1, this is accomplished only when the quantity Q_2 is produced. Perfect competition will not bring about this outcome, however. The MSB curve is *not* a demand curve; the demand curve is labeled D. The perfectly competitive market will cause only Q_1 to be produced. Perfect competition allocates resources in accordance with marginal *private* benefits and marginal costs. Marginal social benefits over and above those that accrue to people who buy it are irrelevant. The result? *Perfect competition will cause too few resources to be allocated to the production of goods having beneficial externalities. These goods will be undersupplied by private markets.*

Solving the "free rider" problem that results from beneficial externalities

There are a great many ways this "free rider" problem can be solved. Basically, however, all "solutions" are based on one or the other of two principles. Devise some mechanism to (a) exclude those who do not pay from receiving benefits, or (b) make sure that everyone who receives benefits pays.

Consider the second alternative. When there are beneficial externalities, as is true of vaccinations, a case can be made for collective action. Specifically, government could use some portion of its tax revenues to *subsidize* the consumption or production of this product. Using Figure 28.1 to illustrate this solution, the government would subsidize each unit purchased by an amount equal to BC. Those who are vaccinated pay a

price equal to the height of the demand curve at point C. Producers would receive a price equal to the height of the supply curve at point B. Q_2 would be produced, the quantity that equates MSB and MC.

A variant of the second alternative is to have the government itself provide the good. This might be most appropriate in the example cited earlier—that of providing a flood control dam for the farmers in the valley. The reason? Each farmer might be willing to pay $10,000 to have the dam. However, in the absence of collective action, the dam might not be built because its cost—say, $1 million—exceeds by a considerable margin the amount that any individual farmer is willing to pay. In other words, the private market would not cause any resources to be committed to the construction of the dam even though the marginal social benefit was greater than the marginal cost.

Government provision need not be inevitable, however, even in this instance. Imagine that farmer Jones bought up all the farms in the valley. The benefits of the dam would then accrue to Jones. The dam might then be built privately. As long as marginal private benefits exceeded marginal cost, the dam would be constructed. Why did Mr. Jones not build the dam on his own when he was but one of many farmers in the valley? Because the benefit he would receive personally was less than the cost of the dam. Even if Jones could afford it, he has no incentive to give the others a free ride. However, when Jones buys up all the farms, he *internalizes* all the benefits that previously would have gone to others. Previously external benefits now become Jones' private benefits. Accordingly, as long as the marginal private benefits to Jones exceed the marginal cost, the dam will be built.

The idea that a single farmer might buy up all the land in a valley might be extreme. But there are many other examples of private market participants acting to internalize the externalities that might otherwise accrue to others. Suppose a developer decides to set up a large marina on a water inlet. If the marina is built, the restaurant located next door is likely to profit immensely.

It would hardly be surprising if the developer bought the restaurant first (probably even before revealing his intentions) in an effort to internalize the external benefits that would otherwise have gone to the existing owner.

Consider another example. Rather than just buy one house at a time for purposes of renovation, real estate developers will often purchase whole city blocks of houses and renovate them all. The reason? If the developer renovates one house at a time, it not only raises the value of that house, but the value of neighboring houses as well. There is much greater profit to be had by internalizing those external benefits through the purchase of other houses in the neighborhood.

Public goods

In contrast to the situations given above, there are many instances in which private markets will fail to solve the externalities problem systematically. It is unlikely, for example, that the flood control dam will be built. The marginal benefit that accrues to any individual farmer will probably be less than the cost of the dam. And in private markets, no one will be willing to pay more than the marginal private benefit he or she expects to receive. Without a sufficient increase in the marginal private benefit (such as might occur if Jones were to purchase other farms in the valley, thereby internalizing the externalities), private markets will fail to allocate resources toward its construction. Yet, from a social point of view, the dam should be built; the added benefits to the farmers (and perhaps others) exceed the cost. One solution would be for at least some of the farmers to pool their funds, to join together collectively, in order to have the dam built. For reasons to be explained below, this might not be a viable solution. An alternative solution would be for the government itself to provide the dam, paying for it out of tax revenues. In any event, either method promotes social welfare; either leads to a more efficient allocation of scarce resources.

In the jargon of economists, the dam is a **public good.** *What makes a good "public" as opposed to "private" is the presence of beneficial externalities that are nonexclusive.* People cannot be excluded from the benefits no matter who pays for the goods. Once built, none of the farmers in the valley can be excluded from the dam's benefits. National defense is another example of a public good. Because national defense is available to everyone no matter who pays for it, no one can be excluded from the benefits it provides. Police and fire protection are yet other examples of public goods.

Interestingly, many different goods are to varying degrees public goods. We saw earlier that vaccinations provide benefits to those who are vaccinated (a private benefit). However, nonexclusive external benefits are provided to those not vaccinated because the likelihood of the disease spreading is reduced; to that extent, vaccinations are a public good. There are both private good and public good aspects to education. The individual receiving the education surely benefits; but, insofar as we are all better off when the general level of education is higher, there are nonexclusive external benefits as well.

A "pure" public good defined

On the basis of these considerations, it is possible to set forth a definition of a *pure* **public good.** One aspect of the definition is clear: Benefits must be nonexclusive. However, some goods whose benefits are nonexclusive are not properly *pure* public goods. Consider again vaccinations. The benefits are nonexclusive. But, unlike national defense, which provides the *same* protection to everyone no matter who pays for it, those paying to be vaccinated receive more benefits than those who do not pay. *In order to qualify as a pure public good, the benefits must not only be nonexclusive; its consumption by one person or one economic agent must not reduce the amount available for others. Its availability for anyone makes it available to everyone without additional cost.* Each person receives benefits equal to what they would have received had they paid for the quantity of the public good they consume. The mere fact that the pure public good is available to everyone

Table 28.1

Pure private good and pure public good distinguished:
Hypothetical demand schedules for product X

Quantity demanded by	Price				
	P_1 ($100)	P_2 ($80)	P_3 ($60)	P_4 ($40)	P_5 ($20)
Person A	—	1	2	3	4
Person B...........................	1	2	3	4	5
Person C	—	—	1	2	3
The market demand (quantity)	1	3	6	9	12
MSB (pure private good)	P_1 ($100)	P_2 ($80)	P_3 ($60)	P_4 ($40)	P_5 ($20)
MSB (pure public good)	$(P_1 + P_2 + P_3)$ ($240)	$(P_2 + P_3 + P_4)$ ($180)	$(P_3 + P_4 + P_5)$ ($120)		

means they each receive those benefits no matter who pays for it.

The distinction between a pure private good and a pure public good can be highlighted in another way. In the case of pure private goods, the marginal social benefit is indistinguishable from the marginal private benefit. The marginal social benefit (MSB) for any given quantity of a pure private good can be read directly off of the market demand curve, the MSB being given by the price of the last unit sold. In the case of a pure public good, on the other hand, the marginal social benefit is *not* equal to the price of the last unit sold; it is generally much greater. This distinction is shown in Table 28.1.

We assume, for simplicity, that there are only three buyers—individuals A, B, and C. First examine the pure private good case. At a price equal to P_1 ($100), only individual B would buy any of the good. The marginal private benefit— equal to P_1—is the *same* as the marginal social benefit because there are no external benefits. At a price equal to P_2 ($80), B will buy two units and A will buy one. Again, the marginal private benefit for A and B—equal to P_2—is the same as the marginal social benefit because external benefits are absent.

Now look at the pure public good case. For simplicity, assume that Table 28.1 accurately represents the quantities of the good that persons A, B, and C would be willing and able to pur-

chase at the various prices. If the price were P_1, B would buy one unit; the marginal private benefit to B of the first unit is P_1. However, the marginal social benefit is much greater than P_1. Why? Because the good is a pure public good, the purchase of one unit by B yields to A and C a unit's worth of benefits even though they did not pay anything. The quantity of the good available to everyone is the same regardless of who pays. Accordingly, since the first unit has a marginal private benefit to B equal to P_1, a marginal private benefit to A equal to P_2, and a marginal private benefit to C equal to P_3, the MSB of the first unit consists of the *sum* $P_1 + P_2 + P_3$. (Or, using the numerical values, at a price of $100, the MSB is $240.)

What is the MSB of the second unit? It is the marginal private benefit of the *second* unit for B (equal to P_2) plus the marginal private benefit of the *second* unit for A (equal to P_3) plus the marginal private benefit of the *second* unit for C (equal to P_4). In short, the MSB of the second unit is equal to the *sum* $P_2 + P_3 + P_4$. (Or, using the numerical values, at a price of $80, the MSB is $180.)

At first, this outcome might seem a little puzzling. We see that, if the price of the public good equaled P_1, B would buy one unit; A and C would buy none. Now, if price falls to P_2, it appears that B would buy two and A would buy one. Isn't that right? No. When B bought the first unit, both A and C received benefits equal in value to the price they each would have been willing to pay for the first unit. They get the benefits of the first unit without paying anything; they get a "free ride." Since A and C are already getting benefits equal to what they were each willing to pay for the first unit (even though B purchased it), what they will be willing to pay now will be determined by the marginal private benefit of the *second* unit. For person A this is P_3, and for C, it is P_4. If the price happens to fall to P_2, B will buy a second unit (since P_2 represents the marginal private benefit to B of a second unit). And because the good is a pure public good, A and C are given yet another "free ride," the value of which is given by the prices that they each would be willing to pay for the *second* unit. The MSB of the second unit, therefore, is equal to $P_2 + P_3 + P_4$. The MSB of the third unit is figured similarly—as the *sum* $P_3 + P_4 + P_5$. The MSB of the fourth, fifth, and all other additional units (not shown in Table 28.1) are figured similarly.

On the basis of the foregoing example, it is clear why the MSB curve in Figure 28.1 was positioned above and to the right of the demand curve. The MSBs for any given quantity exceed the marginal private benefits by the magnitude of the external benefits. And, importantly, if the cost of the pure public good exceeds the maximum price that anyone is willing to pay to obtain the first unit, the private market will fail to allocate resources toward its production. The fact that MSB may exceed cost is immaterial as far as private markets are concerned.

The problem of determining the what, how, and for whom of public goods

In the face of beneficial externalities, a case can be made for government involvement to ensure that resources are allocated efficiently. However, this does not mean that government should intervene in all instances where positive externalities might exist. There are times when the private market will do the job adequately—e.g., the real estate developer who purchases all the housing

units in a block or the marina developer who purchases the restaurant adjoining the proposed marina. In these instances, the externalities that would otherwise exist are internalized via the actions of private market participants. There is no need for government here.

Strictly speaking, government involvement is appropriate in instances where excluding people from the external benefits is unfeasible. It is agreed, for example, that government should provide national defense, flood control dams, and police and fire protection. Each of these goods comes about as close to satisfying the definition of a pure public good as is possible. Moreover, it is also agreed that government should subsidize education and vaccinations at least to the extent of the difference between the social and private benefits provided by those goods.

Beyond these generalities, very little can be said concerning the goods and services government should provide to promote efficiency in the allocation of resources. Moreover, it is clear that, in terms of the goods and services it provides or subsidizes, government does not follow a strict rule of limiting its involvement to instances where excluding people from the external benefits is unfeasible. Government often provides goods such as parks and swimming pools—goods from whose benefits nonpayers could be excluded. Government is also involved in the insurance business (social security) when, from a strictly economic point of view, such involvement is questionable. How should one evaluate government involvement in these cases? This is not an easy question to answer. If efficiency were the *sole* consideration, government would provide or subsidize goods only in instances where excluding people from the external benefits was unfeasible. But efficiency in the allocation of resources is only one of many goals of government. Sometimes the nature and scale of government involvement will be governed by other considerations such as justice and equity—concepts that are difficult to evaluate in economic terms.

Let us ignore for now these other considerations and focus our attention on the efficiency argument. From an efficiency point of view we know, *in principle,* what should determine whether a good or service should be provided by government. The question is, can we translate that principle into practice to determine what goods and services, and in what quantities, the government should actually provide? Unfortunately, the answer to this question is no.

The central problem: Determining benefits for public goods. One of the major reasons it is difficult to apply the principle in practice is that there is no easy way of measuring the benefits provided by public goods. In the case of private goods, it is easy to measure benefits. The benefits provided by private goods are measured in terms of how much people are willing to pay to obtain these goods. Would it not be possible to measure the benefits provided by public goods by determining how much people would be willing to pay to obtain those goods? Possibly, but probably not. Let's see why.

One could imagine that everyone had a demand schedule for, say, national defense. *In principle,* one could calculate the MSBs associated with various levels of national defense by adding up the marginal private benefits of everyone for those levels of national defense. The marginal private benefits would be determined by how much each person was able and willing to pay. But how do we go about determining how much people are willing to pay? The private market will not allocate resources for national defense purposes because the cost of any minimal level of national defense will probably exceed by a considerable margin the amount that any individual would be able and willing to pay. Thus we will not observe any market transactions that would enable us to calculate the benefits people attach to national defense.

Suppose the government were to ask each individual how much he or she would be willing to pay for various levels of national defense. The government might then levy a charge on each person for any level of defense equal to the marginal private benefit they attach to national defense. Would this approach work? Probably not. You would have an incentive to tell the government that you would benefit little from national defense even if the opposite were true. If you value national defense highly and tell the govern-

ment that, it will have virtually no effect on the level of national defense the government will provide. You are but one of millions of people being interviewed by the government, and it will be the collective assessment of those others, not your own assessment, that will determine the outcome. All you will get by telling the government you value national defense highly is a big tax bill. You could understate the value you attach to national defense and thereby minimize your tax bill without in any way affecting the level of national defense that will be provided. So why not lie a little?

Everyone else has the same incentive to understate the benefits of national defense. The benefits overall will therefore be understated. The government, if it acts on the basis of the interview results, will end up allocating too few resources for national defense purposes.

Suppose you are given assurance that your tax burden will not be influenced by your valuation of national defense. Will government then be able to get a better reading of the benefits of national defense? Not likely. If you are the kind of person who views a strong national defense as essential to deter nuclear attack and to preserve freedom in the world, you have an incentive to overstate the benefits to you personally. You hope that the appropriate level of resources will be devoted to national defense, knowing full well that your stated evaluation will not enlarge your tax bill. What do you have to lose by overstating the benefits? On the other hand, if you feel that increased expenditures for national defense will intensify the arms race and thereby heighten world tensions, you are likely to understate the benefits. Under the circumstances, people's estimations of the benefits will prove wholly unreliable.

We began with a proposition that private markets will fail to allocate sufficient resources toward the production of goods for which *exclusion* of nonpayers is unfeasible. This justified government provision or subsidization in the interests of efficiency in the allocation of resources. We end up with a conclusion that is somewhat disturbing. Because we have no way of determining with any degree of accuracy the benefits people receive from the goods provided or subsidized by government, we have no way of answering some of the most vexing questions of our time. Should more or less of our resources be devoted to public expenditures? (In order to answer this we would need to know the relative marginal social benefits and costs of private versus public expenditures. Since we cannot determine the benefits from public expenditures accurately, there is no way to answer the question objectively.) Should more or less resources be devoted to national defense, health, education, bridges, dams, and roads? (Once again, we would need to examine the relative marginal social benefits and costs of these different kinds of public expenditures, an exercise that is difficult to perform given the problems inherent in measuring benefits.)

Of course, we do get these questions answered. They are answered by elected officials at the federal, state, and local levels of government. However, there is no reason to think that the decisions made by these officials are the "correct" ones from the point of view of efficiency in the allocation of resources. In the first place, even if all our elected representatives were well-intentioned, there is no reason to think they would thereby have the ability to correctly assess the benefits and costs of public expenditures. They may try hard to do their job well, but they can't read minds. Second, it is in the nature of elected officials not to admit to mistakes—at least not if they want to get reelected. For this reason, some public expenditure programs continue in existence even when it is clear that, *from an economic point of view,* they have failed or have outlived their usefulness. In an effort to offset this natural tendency, many governments have adopted a procedure known as **zero-base budgeting.** This procedure requires that all public expenditure programs, even those that have been in existence for a long time, be justified anew from time to time (by going back to a "zero base", hence the name, zero-base budgeting). The success of zero-base budgeting is very much an open question. You still have the problem of evaluating benefits

and costs, and you must remember that most such programs have strong vested interests who can be expected to lobby intensely against expenditure cuts. Those vested interests have a strong incentive to play down the costs and to blow out of proportion the benefits to keep the program alive.

Finally, even if we could measure costs and benefits more accurately, there is no guarantee that the political process would allocate resources correctly. For example, given the same costs, project A might yield many more benefits than project B, but the majority of the people might favor B over A; although the benefits from A are sizable, they accrue largely to only a few.

EXTERNAL COSTS AND RESOURCE MISALLOCATION

We have already seen how private markets will cause too few resources to be devoted to the production of goods that provide beneficial externalities. Conversely, *private markets will cause too many resources to be devoted to the production of goods that yield harmful externalities.* The reason is clear. The spillover or external costs are *not* reflected in the supply curves of products in private markets. The market supply curve under pure competition consists of the horizontal sum of the individual firm marginal cost curves. Each MC curve tells us by how much the *individual producer's costs* rise as output is expanded. Any costs that might be imposed on others as a consequence of the production or consumption of the commodity will not be reflected in the producers' MC curves. These external costs, therefore, will *not* be reflected in the market supply curve. The market supply curve measures only marginal private costs; marginal private costs will be the same as marginal social costs only when harmful externalities are absent.

When external costs are present, marginal social costs cannot be found by adding the individual MC curves horizontally. In principal, it is possible to construct a curve that reflects marginal social costs; that curve will be above and to the left of the supply curve. However, that marginal social cost (MSC) curve is not a supply curve. And since perfectly competitive markets allocate resources on the basis of market supplies (and demands) only, resources will be misallocated to the extent that they fail to accurately reflect social costs.

Figure 28.2 illustrates clearly the distinction between marginal private costs and marginal social costs when harmful externalities are present. We consider in Figure 28.2 a commodity whose production involves the discharge of waste materials into a river; the discharged waste adversely affects water users downstream. The curve labeled S is the market supply curve. It consists of the sum of the individual MC curves of all producers. It shows the added costs incurred by the producers at different levels of output. The fact that producers are able to dump waste materials into the water without charge means that the cost of fouling the water is imposed on others. Adding this external cost to the cost borne by the producers yields the **marginal social cost** of this commodity; the vertical distance between the supply curve (representing marginal private costs) and the MSC curve measures the external costs at the margin for each level of output.

Efficiency will be promoted when production of this commodity is carried to the point where MSC = MSB. For simplicity, we will assume in Figure 28.2 that the demand curve for the commodity measures the marginal social benefit of the product. The efficient solution would be given by point E, implying a rate of production of Q* and a price of P*. However, the private market would lead to the price-output combination given by point A. The problem? Too many resources are being devoted to the production of this good. At the competitively determined level of output, Q_c, MSC exceeds MSB. This implies the need to cut back production to the level Q*. However, there is no mechanism in private markets to bring about the optimum social solution, P* and Q*. MSC is *not* a supply curve; the presence of external costs will not affect the market outcome.

One possible solution would be for the government to impose a per unit tax equal to the vertical distance between the supply curve and the MSC curve. In effect, the MSC curve would become the supply curve. Accordingly, equilibrium would occur at point E. Producers would get

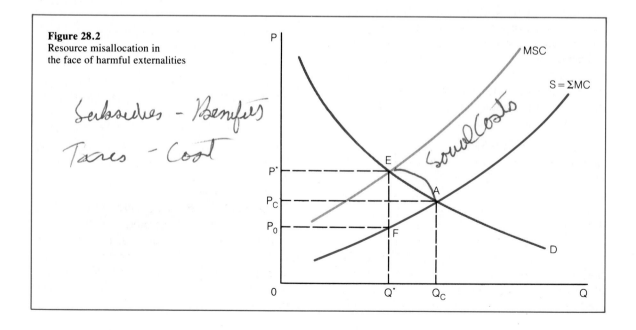

Figure 28.2
Resource misallocation in
the face of harmful externalities

only P_0 for each unit produced; as a result, they would be willing to produce only Q^*. Government would collect a per unit tax equal to EF. The price to buyers would be P^*; at that price they would be willing to purchase Q^*.

The revenue collected by the government might be used either to compensate those whose interests are adversely affected by the dumping of waste materials into the river, or the funds might be used to "clean up" the river proper.

An alternative solution? Government intervention to limit the output level to Q^*. By limiting supply in this manner, a market clearing price of P^* would emerge ultimately, resulting in an optimum social outcome. However, as we will show later, this "solution" is defective.

External costs and the problem of pollution

In the above example, government intervention caused at least part of the external cost to be "internalized" by those producing the product. This is most obvious in the case where government imposes a per unit tax equal to the marginal external cost. In addition to the marginal private cost (given by the height of the supply curve at any given level of output), producers had to shoulder the external cost burden themselves through payment of the per unit tax. Producers also had to bear a cost when government restricted the output level of Q^*. The profit-maximizing level of production is Q_c, not Q^*. True, profits are larger at Q^* without the tax than with it; but profits are not as large as they could otherwise have been.

However, the problem of pollution and how to deal with it are much more complex than this example suggests. First, although for purposes of illustration we have assumed that external costs are easily measured, in reality they are very difficult to measure. For example, what value should be attached to the recreational uses of the river adversely affected by the pollution? The highly subjective nature of people's valuations of water for recreational uses should be obvious. And as was the case with public goods, people

may have an incentive to misrepresent their valuations. Or suppose the pollution has adverse effects on some people's health. How should one value these consequences? How should one value the days lost from work due to increased sickness? By the wage per day times the number of days lost? How about the pain and suffering or the shortened life span? How should these be valued? Is good health really priceless? Or suppose the pollution harms the fishing industry or other water-using industries downstream. How should one value the damage done here? Downstream producers have an obvious incentive to overstate the damage done by those upstream. So is there any prospect of getting an accurate measurement?

Our inability to measure the external costs accurately has obvious implications for the solutions proposed above. If the difference between marginal private cost and marginal social cost is not known with precision, it is not possible to determine the precise size of the per unit tax that should be imposed. Likewise, it is not possible to determine by precisely how much output should be restricted.

A second complication arises because not all producers using the river contribute equally to its pollution. The nature and magnitude of the waste materials deposited into the river will vary from producer to producer because of differences in size of productive facilities, techniques of production, and the kinds of goods and services produced. These differences would suggest the need for a differential treatment of producers based on the contributions they each make to the external costs that arise because the river is used as a receptacle for the deposit of wastes.

A third and very important complication is that no simple fixed relationship exists between the amount of waste generated and the amount of pollution. Indeed, a great deal of waste material may be deposited in the environment without creating any pollution whatever. At first this might seem contradictory. After all, isn't pollution caused by the generation of waste materials?

Yes. But as long as the environment is able to assimilate the waste materials generated, there is no pollution problem. If the capacity of the environment to absorb waste products were infinite, there could never be a pollution problem.

Pollution defined

Unfortunately, the absorptive capacity of the environment is not infinite; it is limited. And when the absorptive capacity is overused, a pollution problem emerges. Put another way, *if the rate at which waste products are being generated exceeds the rate at which the environment can absorb or assimilate those wastes, the result is pollution.* It is not just a question of the production of wastes per se. It is a question of the rate at which they are produced and the types of waste produced in comparison with the capacity of the environment to absorb these wastes.

The materials balance approach to pollution

We need to go one step further and recognize that the environment both provides the raw materials used in the production of goods and services and serves as the receptacle for the unwanted by-products of consumption and production—the wastes, or residuals. What needs emphasis, however, is that *the mass of wastes ultimately returned to the environment will be approximately equal to the mass of the materials withdrawn from the environment and used in the production and consumption of goods and services.* That is, the fuels, foods, minerals, and other raw materials that we "consume" are in reality only processed into useful forms. After we have consumed the *services* of those products, we deposit them as waste in the environment. Since it is not possible to consume these products in a physical manner—our consumption and production merely transforming these products by mechanical, chemical, or biological processes—the mass of what entered into their production and consumption must ultimately be deposited as waste. In sum, the environment provides us with materials in one form, and we transform, process, and ulti-

mately redeposit them in another form. The masses of the two forms must be more or less equal—hence the term **materials balance.**

The nature of our pollution problem

Once the concept of materials balance and the definition of pollution are understood, the nature of our pollution problem and policy alternatives become clearer. Two implications of the materials balance problem are worth noting?

First, it is not possible to eliminate waste if we mean by that the disappearance of material. We might be able to transform the waste generated and reuse it (e.g., recycling). But we cannot get rid of the material itself. Second, a reduction of one type of waste must be accompanied by an increase in another type of waste or greater use of attendant by-products.

These ideas are easily illustrated. It is often suggested, for example, that the amount of air pollution could be reduced by installing scrubbing devices in smokestacks to remove the sulfur dioxide from the exhaust gases of coal-burning plants. But what does one do with the sulfur-laden waste water from the scrubbers? Dump it in the river? If so, increased water polution naturally accompanies reduced air pollution. Or again, what about regulations designed to reduce the amount of particulate matter emitted into the air from trash-burning incinerators? Is it not true that we merely change the form of the waste? The problem of air pollution is lessened; the problem of solid-waste disposal is made worse.

What about recycling? Would this not solve our pollution problem? It might help, but it is unlikely to solve the problem. First, unless 100 percent of our waste is recycled indefinitely, some waste products will ultimately emerge. Moreover, in order to convert waste materials into a reusable form, it is often necessary to make use of additional material inputs from the environment. This implies a larger flow of wastes subsequently. In general, recycling enables us to obtain larger quantities of goods and services with a smaller flow of wastes (because of a smaller flow of environmental inputs) than would have been possible had we not recycled. But it is important to determine whether the waste materials generated in reprocessing waste materials cause more damage to the environment than if we had not recycled. That is, can the environment better assimilate the original waste material than it can the waste material generated in reprocessing? Or can that additional waste material itself be transformed into an alternative form of waste for which the assimilative capacities of the environment are greater?

Consider the case of paper. If we do not recycle it, waste paper products will be disposed of in a solid-waste form. What about recycling? Only about 60 to 70 percent of the paper is reusable pulp. The rest is filler, ink, and coating. In order to recycle paper, it is necessary to separate the reusable pulp from the other waste material. And what do we do with the other waste material? Release it into our waterways? Here, recycling had two effects. First, the flow of waste to produce a given volume of paper was reduced by making use of the pulp component of the waste paper to make yet more paper. Second, the unusable solid waste portion of the paper changed form. Are we really better off? Is the damage to the environment smaller when a smaller quantity of waste material takes the form of suspended solid waste material in our waterways? The answer is not at all obvious until we know something about the assimilative capacity of our waterways as compared with land for the disposal of waste paper products.

Given that the amount of waste is determined by our use of materials from the environment, the materials balance approach forces us to think in terms of how we must change biologically, chemically, and/or mechanically—the form of the waste so as to reduce or eliminate the damage to the environment.

The materials-balance approach also points the way the economy must go if it is to reduce the flow of waste materials. We can *use our material inputs more efficiently*—i.e., devising means whereby we can *obtain a larger quantity of output per unit of material input*. A second alternative is *recycling*. A third possibility lies in *altering the composition of our output* in favor of goods and services that require less material input. And finally, we could take the rather drastic step of *reducing production and consumption* within the economy.

Consider this last alternative for a moment. It has long been popular with some environmental groups. However, it has not enjoyed widespread support. The reasons are simple. Unemployment would rise as a consequence of reduced production, and in the face of a growing labor force, unemployment could become an ever-larger problem. Improvements in living standards overall would be impossible unless population were reduced by more than production. Not only would it be more difficult to solve the poverty problem (since the improved living standards resulting from transfers to the poor would, by definition, mean reduced living standards for the nonpoor as well); it would mean no improvement in the living standards of our children. And note that the amount of pollution is not reduced by simply bringing growth to a halt. Zero growth simply means no *growth* in waste materials. *More bluntly, zero growth means generating the same amount of waste as before.*

Many people believe that we can deal with the pollution problem in a better way. Ending economic growth is simply too drastic. We must, therefore, search out ways to reduce pollution directly.

The optimum level of pollution

It is certainly possible to imagine a situation in which the American economy would have no pollution problem. But our material standard of living and the composition of our output would be dramatically different from what they are at present. To most people, the opportunity cost of a pollution-free environment is so high that they would not opt for such a drastic change in their lifestyles. Nevertheless, most of these same people are concerned about the environment and would probably prefer less pollution than what exists currently.

Even if we suppose the government is willing

to take whatever action is necessary to bring about a level of pollution that society considers tolerable, what criteria should be employed to determine what is tolerable? A partial answer to this question can be obtained by adopting an approach similar to the benefit-cost approach discussed earlier.

Let us imagine for the moment that only one type of pollution exists—water pollution—and that we are interested in finding out the optimum level of water pollution for a river that runs through one of our major cities.

There are two considerations of utmost importance in determining the optimum amount of pollution. The first is the **marginal social cost of pollution.** This represents the added cost to members of society of an additional unit of pollution. Presumably, as the quantity of pollution increases, the marginal social cost of pollution increases as well.

The relationship between the marginal social cost of pollution and the quantity of pollution is given in Figure 28.3. The curve labeled the marginal social cost of pollution begins at the origin. The reason? There is no pollution, and thus no external cost problem, until the rate of generation of wastes exceeds the rate at which the environment can absorb those wastes. Once that point is reached, a pollution problem arises. And as pollution concentrations increase, so does the marginal social cost of pollution—hence the reason for the upward slope.

The second important consideration is the **marginal cost of pollution elimination.**[1] This represents the added cost of eliminating an additional unit of pollution. In Figure 28.3, the curve labeled "marginal cost of pollution elimination" is downward sloping, which tells us that the marginal cost of eliminating *a unit* of pollution when the level of pollution is low is higher than the marginal cost of eliminating *a unit* of pollution when pollution concentrations are high. This makes sense. When pollution concentrations are high, a lot of water pollution might possibly be eliminated with the use of a relatively simple and cheap filter system. To reduce pollution concentrations even further would require more sophisticated and costly techniques. And to eliminate the last little bit of pollution might be very costly indeed.

The intersection of the two curves—the marginal social cost of pollution curve and the marginal cost of pollution elimination curve—yields the optimum amount of pollution, Q*. At that point, the added cost of an additional unit of pollution just equals the additional cost of reducing pollution by one more unit.

Why not eliminate pollution entirely? The answer is clear from Figure 28.3. The marginal cost of eliminating the last little bit of pollution would exceed by a considerable margin the marginal social cost of that little amount.

The optimum pollution tax

There is a need for government intervention to bring about the optimum pollution outcome discussed here. The external costs imposed on others as a consequence of the dumping of waste products in the river are not reflected in the costs of those doing the polluting. They, therefore, have no incentive to reduce pollution; the river, as a consequence, would in time become an open sewer were there no government intervention.

One solution would be for government to impose a pollution tax—a **residual charge**—on those who dump waste products into the river. Each type of waste product from all sources would be charged a fixed amount per unit of waste. In terms of Figure 28.3, the optimum tax would be T*—a rate of tax set by the height of the intersection of the marginal cost of pollution eleimination curve and the marginal social cost of pollution curve.

How can we be sure that a tax equal to T* would cause the optimum amount of pollution, Q*, to occur? This is not difficult to discover. Those doing the polluting will make sure that no more than Q* is generated.

In order to see why those who dump waste will bring about the optimum result, consider

---

[1] This could be called the *marginal benefit of pollution* on grounds that it measures the "free ride" polluters obtain; it measures what they don't have to pay!

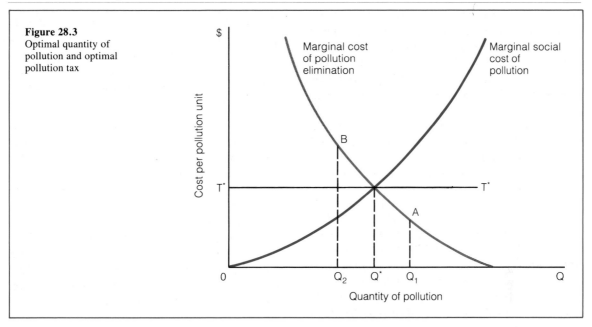

Figure 28.3
Optimal quantity of pollution and optimal pollution tax

again the meaning of the marginal cost of pollution elimination curve. The height of the curve at each point tells us the marginal cost of reducing pollution by one more unit. Suppose the quantity of pollution equals Q_1 in Figure 28.3. Will those who dump waste reduce their pollution levels to Q^* once a tax equal to T^* is imposed, or will they continue to produce Q_1 or more of pollution? If they are profit maximizers, they will cut back their pollution to Q^*. For each unit of pollution they dump, they pay T^*. Since the cost they incur by cutting pollution back by one unit at Q_1 is less than T^*, it is less costly to eliminate this unit of pollution than to pay the tax. It is not, however, less costly to cut back pollution at Q_2. Indeed, since the marginal cost of pollution elimination at Q_2 exceeds the tax, profit maximization would dictate dumping the waste materials; producers would continue to do so until pollution concentrations reach Q^*. In this manner, a tax of T^* will accomplish the desired objective.

We have, of course, assumed that it is easy to measure the two curves in Figure 28.3. In fact, it is extremely difficult to measure both the marginal social cost of pollution and the marginal cost of eliminating various amounts. It is proba-

bly most difficult to measure the marginal social cost of pollution since so many subjective considerations lie behind people's evaluations of the damages done. In any event, the measurement problems mean that it is difficult to discover either the optimum amount of pollution or the optimum pollution tax.

Objections to a pollution tax

Measurement problems aside, many groups in our society object *in principle* to the argument that residual charges—pollution taxes—are the best means of controlling pollution. Instead, they prefer the **legal-control approach.** Government establishes an agency with the authority to control particular types of pollution in certain areas.

In principle, the legal-control approach can be effective. But is it really better than the residual-charges approach? Economists are skeptical. The main advantage of the residual-charges approach is that it lets market participants discover the least costly ways of reducing pollution. Polluters react to the tax signal. If some device can be installed to cut pollution by X amount, and if this method is less costly than payment of a tax, polluters will adopt it; they will search out and install those devices that are the least costly. In this way, we are assured that a given reduction in pollution will be accomplished with the fewest real resources.

Can the same be said of the legal-control approach? Possibly. In some instances, regulators merely specify the maximum amount of waste permitted from each source and leave the choice of abatement up to each individual polluter. In other instances, regulators specify the kinds of abatement procedures that must be followed without regard to cost or differences among firms. As you might imagine, such an approach could well result in more resources than are necessary to accomplish a given reduction in pollution, and it could misallocate resources as well. The regulators could specify procedures that are much more expensive than need be; this is inefficient. Moreover, regulators could insist that all producers adopt the *same* devices, whether they generate a little or a lot of a particular chemical waste that government seeks to control. The costs per unit of pollution are disproportionately large for those producers generating very little pollution, which contributes to resource misallocation. Under a pollution tax scheme, those generating only small amounts might not limit their pollution at all, choosing instead to pay the tax.

If the residual-charges approach is superior to the legal-control approach from an economic perspective, why do so many people oppose the former in favor of the latter?

Many consumer groups oppose residual charges on the grounds that such charges are passed along in the form of higher prices. True enough. But is this really a legitimate objection? The legal-control approach that forces businesses to install pollution control devices also results in higher business costs and therewith higher prices as well. Insofar as regulators insist on devices that are more costly than the least-cost methods, prices could be even higher under a legal-control approach. In addition, it is wrong to conclude that prices in general will rise by the same amount as the tax. A pollution tax is like an excise tax; as we saw in Chapter 16, part of the burden will be borne by consumers and part by producers, the relative burden being de-

termined by the relative supply and demand elasticities. Finally, since a pollution tax will cause the prices of pollution-intensive commodities to rise relative to those that are less pollution-intensive, consumers will be given an incentive to change their spending patterns in ways that promote welfare.

Many environmentalist groups oppose residual charges on grounds that such an approach gives people a license to pollute: Pay the tax, then pollute all you like. In a sense, this is true. But it is besides the point. If the tax is set optimally, an optimum amount of pollution will occur—the amount that equates the marginal social cost of pollution and the marginal cost of pollution elimination. The tax will cause polluters, acting in their own self-interest, to curtail pollution to that level; they are free—have a license—to pollute up to that point. Perhaps this is what some environmentalists find objectionable—that any positive level of pollution can be optimal. However, unless evidence is forthcoming that raises the marginal social cost of even small positive amounts of pollution above the marginal cost of eliminating those small amounts, a policy that called for zero pollution would be nonoptimal.

Many industrialists—especially those who generate large amounts of harmful wastes—oppose residual charges on grounds that such charges discriminate against them unfairly. It raises the prices of their products relative to those that are relatively cleaner to produce and consume. However, isn't this outcome required from an efficiency point of view? That is, isn't such an outcome in accord with the efficiency requirement that relative product prices should reflect underlying relative costs—including both private and external costs?

On the other hand, it is easy to see why it is in those industrialists' own interests to oppose such charges—or, indeed, to oppose any and all restrictions on polluting. However, if some controls are to be imposed, would it not be better for them to argue in favor of a policy that requires everyone to cut their pollution? In that way, everyone's costs rise and the relative price differential that would emerge would be smaller than under a residual-charges scheme. It sounds fair to have everybody shoulder the burden. But is it really? You will have to answer that for yourself.

SUMMARY

1. *Externalities* arise when the voluntary actions of economic agents—in the production or consumption of goods and services—result in adverse or beneficial side effects for which no compensation is made. When externalities are present, perfectly competitive markets will cause a misallocation of resources. Specifically, in the face of *beneficial externalities,* perfectly competitive markets will cause too few resources to be allocated towards those goods. In the presence of *adverse externalities* (external costs), perfectly competitive markets will cause too many resources to be devoted to their production.

2. For goods that generate beneficial externalities, those benefits will *not* be reflected in the demand curves. Market demand curves reflect only the benefits received by those who purchase the products; they reflect only private benefits. Since perfectly competitive markets allocate resources on the basis of *market* demands and supplies only, resources will be misallocated to the extent that they fail to accurately reflect all the benefits received, private plus external.

3. Government provision of goods yielding beneficial externalities is not inevitable. To the extent that private market participants act to internalize the externalities that might otherwise accrue to others, private markets will successfully solve the externalities problem. However, there are many instances in which this outcome is unlikely. In many instances, the wherewithal required to provide even a minimum quantity of the goods in question may exceed by a considerable margin the resources at the disposal of any individual or small group of individuals (for example, national defense).

4. In the case of *public goods,* people cannot be excluded from the benefits these goods offer, no matter who pays for them. In order to qualify as a *pure public good,* not only must the benefits be nonexclusive, but benefits will be the same

as if each individual had paid for the good on his/her own. For example, if the price of a public good were equal to P_1, causing individual A to purchase one unit, the marginal social benefit would be much larger than the marginal private benefit to A. The marginal private benefit to A of the first unit is equal to P_1. The marginal social benefit is higher because the purchase of one unit by A yields to B and C the *same* benefits as if they had purchased one unit themselves.

5. If the cost of the pure public good exceeds the maximum price that any individual is willing to pay to obtain it, private markets will fail to allocate any resources towards its production. The fact that the marginal social benefit may exceed cost is immaterial as far as private markets are concerned. Strictly speaking, government involvement is appropriate in instances where excluding people from the external benefits is unfeasible.

6. Is it possible to determine what goods and services, and in what quantities, the government should actually provide? Unfortunately, the answer to this question is no. One of the major reasons has to do with there being no easy way of measuring the benefits provided by public goods. If government were to ask each individual how much he or she would be willing to pay for various levels of public goods, and if a charge were levied on each person equal to the marginal private benefits they attach to those goods, everyone would have an incentive to understate the values they attach in order to minimize their tax liabilities. On the other hand, if government gave assurance that one's tax burden would not be influenced by one's evaluation of the public goods, people's responses would prove to be unreliable. Some would tend to overstate the benefits, while others would tend to understate them.

7. The reason private markets will cause too many resources to be devoted to the production of goods that yield harmful externalities is that the external costs are *not* reflected in the supply curves of products in private markets. Since perfectly competitive markets allocate resources on the basis of market supplies and demands only, resources will be misallocated to the extent that they fail to accurately reflect social costs.

8. If the rate at which waste products are being generated exceeds the rate at which the environment can absorb or assimilate those wastes, the result is *pollution.* According to the *materials-balance approach,* the mass of wastes ultimately returned to the environment will be approximately equal to the mass of materials withdrawn from the environment and used in the production and consumption of goods and services. The materials-balance approach points the way the economy must go if it is to reduce the flow of waste materials. We can use our material inputs more efficiently; we can recycle; we can alter the composition of our output; and finally, we could reduce production and consumption.

9. When the *marginal social cost of pollution* is equal to the *marginal cost of pollution elimination,* we will have discovered the *optimum amount of pollution.* In other words, at that point, the added cost of an additional unit of pollution just equals the added cost of reducing pollution by one more unit. One way to achieve the optimum amount of pollution is for government to impose a pollution tax—a *residual charge*—on those who pollute. Alternatively, one could use the *legal-control approach.* From the point of view of efficiency in the allocation of resources, the residual charges approach is deemed superior to the legal-control approach.

CONCEPTS FOR REVIEW

Externalities

Beneficial externalities

Adverse (or harmful) externalities

Private benefits versus social benefits

The "free rider" problem

Internalizing the externality

Public goods

"Pure" public goods

Private goods

Zero-base budgeting

Pollution

Materials-balance approach to pollution

Optimum amount of pollution

Marginal social cost of pollution

Marginal cost of pollution elimination

Residual-charges approach

Legal-control approach

QUESTIONS FOR DISCUSSION

(Those marked with an asterisk (*) are more difficult.)

1. In nontechnical language explain why perfectly competitive markets will tend to allocate too few resources to goods that have beneficial externalities and too many resources to goods that have harmful externalities.

*2. In Figure 28.1 we examined the case of resource misallocation in the face of beneficial externalities. One way to solve the problem would be a government subsidy, the magnitude of the subsidy being equal to the vertical distance between the D curve and the MSB curve at each level of output. Would this solve the problem, parallel to the way a tax can be used to solve the external cost problem? Explain carefully.

3. It is widely agreed that government should subsidize education because of its public-good features. Discuss the problems with estimating how much of the educational burden should be borne by government and how much by the individual. Would your answer be different for students in business administration versus students in schools of social work?

4. Carefully evaluate each of the following statements:
   a. "Governments govern best that govern least."
   b. "Because government regulations force firms to use scarce resources that would otherwise be used for expansion to reduce pollution, those regulations must reduce economic efficiency."
   c. "Firms that pollute are socially irresponsible."
   d. "If economic growth were reduced to zero, pollution would cease."

*5. "I just don't understand you economists. You agree that pollution is bad, but rather than stop those activities that cause pollution, either through an extremely high tax or closing their operations down, you propose a tax to give the "optimum" amount of pollution—an amount of pollution that is nonzero!" Carefully evaluate.

Two pioneers in international trade theory were awarded the ninth Nobel Prize in Economics (1977). The late Bertil Ohlin (a former professor of economics at the University of Copenhagen and former minister of trade in Sweden) and James Meade (a former professor at Cambridge University) were cited for "their path-breaking contributions to the theory of international trade and international capital movements." The Academy noted that although the works for which they were cited appeared much earlier (Ohlin's in 1933 and Meade's in 1950–55) "the breadth and importance of [their] contributions have not become obvious until the 1960s and 1970s in conjunction with the growing internationalization of the economic system."

Bertil Ohlin (1889–1979)

Ohlin passed his university matriculation exams at the age of 15 and earned the equivalent of a master's degree at 18. At the age of 25 he was appointed a full professor at the University of Copenhagen.

Wide World Photos

His doctoral dissertation formed the basis of one of the most celebrated theories of international trade—the so-called Heckscher-Ohlin theory—that explains the international trade patterns on the basis of relative resource endowments in different countries. Capital-abundant countries export capital-intensive goods, labor-abundant countries export labor-intensive goods, and so on. That theory also explained why trade tended to equalize the prices of factors of production in different countries.

Ohlin turned his midlife energies to politics. He was minister of trade in Sweden's 1944–45 coalition government and a leader of the Swedish Liberal Party for 23 years, from 1944 to 1967. He considered himself a "social liberal." Social welfare programs and government interventions for social purposes were as much a part of his philosophy as his belief in the need for decentralized decision making through a system of markets and prices for most aspects of economic life. Ohlin had hopes of becoming prime minister of Sweden. Although he was disappointed at not achieving this political goal, he said that receiving the Nobel Prize "means that the other half of one's life was not altogether without reward."

Asked if he would prefer to be remembered for his work as an economist or for his political leadership, Ohlin stated, "I'd rather be remembered in some measure for both, but if I have to choose, I would say that I have long worked to bring about a favorable economic development in Sweden and to check the growth of socialization . . . I think it's probably this I'd like to be remembered for, because it's most important."

PART FIVE

The United States and the world economy

James E. Meade (1907–   )

Meade's principal contribution is his path-breaking two-volume study, *The Theory of International Economic Policy,* which examines the conduct of economic policies in an "open" economy context. In this work, Meade established himself as the preeminent authority on the problems and prospects of stabilization policies in a world of restrictive trade practices under both fixed and floating exchange rates.

Meade is recognized internationally as a leading pioneer in the field of macrotheory in economics—the behavior of large groups such as whole economies. He first acquired international fame as a result of his brilliant editing of the *League of Nations World Economic Surveys* in the late 1930s. In 1940, Meade joined the economic section of the Cabinet and he was its director—the Labour Party's chief economist—in 1946–47. After that he played an important part in the establishment of the General Agreement on Tariffs and Trade (GATT).

Meade is described as a quiet man who rarely travels or accepts invitations to speak at or attend seminars. He is an abstract thinker of whom it is said, "His heart is to the left—but his thinking is above. . . . He takes a blank sheet of paper and a certain amount of algebra and just thinks in terms of pure theory."

Meade retired as a professor at Cambridge some years before mandatory retirement age and is now a senior research fellow at Christ's College, Cambridge.

United Press International

Sir Arthur Lewis of Princeton University and Theodore W. Schultz of the University of Chicago—both with lifelong interests in the economics of developing nations—were named for the 11th Nobel Prize in Economics (1979). The citation said that both men "are deeply concerned about the poverty in the world, and both are engaged in finding ways out of underdevelopment." Lewis and Schultz made significant contributions to practical policy questions. Both emphasized the need for investment in "human capital" as critical in dealing with the problems of poverty that still plague most of the human race.

Arthur Lewis (1915–   )

A native of the island of St. Lucia in the British West Indies, Lewis was knighted for his services as vice chancellor of the University of West Indies, and was a professor of political economy affairs at Princeton University. Sir Arthur Lewis has had a lifelong concern for the poor and underdeveloped countries of the world.

Wide World Photos

Lewis was specifically cited by the Academy for his theoretical models of Third World development. He emphasized the role of agrarian reform as a prelude to industrialization and as the means for improving the terms of trade between the "North" and the "South."

Lewis sees progress for the poor countries as dependent on rapid growth of the rich countries. He considered the instability of the rich countries—which ruined the markets and earnings of the poor countries—the real menace to the stability and economic well-being of the poor countries. In the long run, he said, "our salvation lies in recognizing that what is good for the developing countries is also good for the developed."

Lewis teaches economics through ideas, not numbers—a nonmathematical approach that endears him to students. His fourth-floor office has no name on the door.

He is considered somewhat cynical, not expecting to "see much happen." He insists on emphasizing the realism of the political or institutional pitfalls along the road of beautiful models and perfect policies.

Theodore W. Schultz (1902–   )

Schultz, recognized as the dean of agricultural economists, is best known for his work on the importance of human resources for economic and social development. The Swedish Academy stated, "Schultz and his students have shown that for a long time there has been a considerably higher yield on 'human capital' than on physical capital in the American economy."

Wide World Photos

Schultz was honored for developing a detailed critique of industrialization policies of developing countries. According to the citation, he was the first to systematize "how investments in education can affect productivity in agriculture as well as the economy as a whole."

Schultz stressed the importance of agriculture to development, but his greatest contribution, perhaps, lay in his emphasis on the importance of investment in human beings as the major factor responsible for technology improvements and rapid growth. By comparing rates of return on investment in humans with more conventional types of investment, Schultz attempted to show the extent of underinvestment in education and training. His work has been oriented toward classical market analysis, stressing the factors that inhibit agricultural production in developing nations. He is particularly critical of massive shipments of U.S. grain to poor nations, contending that the American largess destroys the incentives for farmers in developing countries to increase their output.

Schultz never tires of teaching. By his own admission he is "always trying to provide a small room for poverty in the house economists have built."

Few areas are subjected to as much intense debate as those involving our trading relationships with foreign countries. Hardly a day goes by that we do not hear someone somewhere complaining about the undesirable consequences of imports, and applauding the efforts of those firms that export.

> "Foreign steel producers do not trade 'fairly.' Not only do they 'dump' their excess production on world markets to the detriment of U.S. steel producers, but their governments actually subsidize steel production in ways that the U.S. government does not."

> "U.S. firms, workers, and industries are injured by imports. Imports provide employment to foreign workers and steal employment from the United States. Imports are a cause of idle productive capacity in a number of industries, including steel, textiles, and automobiles."

> "Imports of things like oil pose a threat to our national security."

> "Imports are the cause of our balance of payments deficit and of the weakness of the dollar in foreign exchange markets."

> "Exports, by contrast, provide additional employment opportunities for U.S. residents. They help to keep our plants busy and they help to keep the dollar strong."

It is the purpose of this and the next chapter to provide a framework with which to evaluate our trading relationships with the rest of the world. As we shall see, there is a kernel of truth in each of the passages above. However, they do not provide us with a complete picture. In this chapter we shall attempt to construct part of the required larger picture.

In the first section of the chapter we will examine briefly the nature of the patterns of U.S. trade with the rest of the world. In the second section we will study the theory of comparative advantage, which provides the essential basis and rationale for international trade. The third section will examine the implications and consequences of restrictive trade practices through the use of tariffs, quotas, and other measures.

Chapter 29

Trade and trade restrictions

673

PATTERNS OF U.S. TRADE

The United States is the world's largest trading nation. In 1980, we exported $341 billion worth of goods and services and imported $314 billion. U.S. exports and U.S. imports each make up about 12 percent of the world's total of exports and imports. However, because of the relatively huge size of the U.S. economy, foreign trade makes up a smaller fraction of total production and consumption in the United States than it does for any other noncommunist country. Whereas imports and exports each are about 13 percent of U.S. GNP, they are each 15 percent of GNP in Japan, 25 percent of GNP in Canada, 28 percent of GNP in West Germany, 30 percent of GNP in the United Kingdom, and over 50 percent of GNP in the Netherlands.

Interestingly, the relative importance of international trade to the United States has been increasing. This is the result of several factors:

1. A sharp increase has taken place in U.S. dependence on foreign sources of supply for petroleum products. Whereas U.S. petroleum imports amounted to only $4.6 billion in 1972, they came to about $80 billion in 1980.
2. U.S. agriculture has become an increasingly important source of production for the world economy. Whereas U.S. agricultural exports amounted to $9.5 billion in 1972, they came to $42 billion in 1980.
3. The rapid growth of Western Europe and Japan has created competition for many U.S. products. However, this growth has also created expanding markets for many U.S. goods, particularly high-technology items such as computers and sophisticated machinery. U.S. exports of capital goods increased from $17 billion in 1972 to $64 billion in 1980.

U.S. exports

U.S. exports have increased from around 6 percent of GNP in 1969 to over 13 percent in 1980. In some sectors of our economy, however, exports make up a considerably larger percentage of total production. In manufacturing, exports account for 71 percent of the production of medicinals and botanicals, 55 percent of the production of rice milling equipment, 47 percent of pulp milling equipment, 27 percent of fertilizers, 26 percent of aircraft equipment, 26 percent of sewing machinery, and 26 percent of construction machinery. In agriculture, exports account for 55 percent of our production of wheat, 55 percent of our production of hides, 51 percent of soybeans, 40 percent of cotton, 30 percent of tobacco, 27 percent of rice, and 27 percent of corn.

In terms of employment, about 5 percent—or one out of 20 people employed in the private sector—is directly export-related. The figures are estimated to be about 13 percent for agriculture and 9 percent for manufacturing. Can there be any doubt, therefore, as to the importance of exports to the U.S. economy?

U.S. imports

Imports are important to the United States for several reasons. In the first place, although the United States has only 6 percent of the world's population, it produces 26 percent of the world's production of goods and services. Our factories use over 3 billion tons of raw materials each year. Some of these materials either are not found at all in the United States or they are in short supply. As a consequence, we import about one fifth of the raw materials we consume. Indeed, of our total imports, over two thirds are for raw materials that we do not or cannot readily produce—either at all or in sufficient quantities to satisfy domestic demands. Automobiles, telephones, newspapers, missiles, jet aircraft, household appliances, tools, and machinery are just a few of our manufacturers that depend heavily on imported raw materials.

The 1973 oil embargo impressed on all Americans the importance of imports to the American economy. But this dependence extends far beyond petroleum to many other important industrial raw materials. The natural rubber used by American industry is 100 percent imported; 99 percent of our bauxite (essential to the production of aluminum) is imported; 98 percent of manganese ore, 97 percent of cobalt, 86 percent of tin, 83 percent of asbestos, 70 percent of nickel, 57 percent of mercury, 42 percent of petroleum, and 33 percent of iron are likewise imported. If imports of these basic raw materials were cut off, several factories would be either slowed down or idled completely.

Imports are important to the United States for a second reason. How much we are able to export abroad is heavily dependent on how much we buy from foreign countries. If the rest of the world could not sell their goods and services to the United States, many of those countries would be hard pressed to find alternative markets for their goods. With their earnings reduced, their ability to import from the United States would fall and our export industries would suffer.

U.S. relations with industrial countries

The industrial economies of the United States, Western Europe, Japan, and Canada are closely linked by trade. Well over half of our foreign trade is with these countries.

About one fifth of our foreign trade is with Canada—our largest single trading partner. The United States takes more than two thirds of Canada's exports and more than two thirds of all Canadian imports come from the United States. Canada is a source of raw materials for U.S. industry, especially newsprint, wood pulp, crude petroleum, lumber, iron ore, nickel, and aluminum. A highly active two-way trade takes place in industrial products (automotive products in particular) and agricultural goods.

Japan is today our third largest market, accounting for nearly one tenth ($21 billion) of total U.S. exports of goods in 1980. Japan imports many types of sophisticated machinery from the United States and substantial amounts of raw materials as well. Outside of the 10 nations of the European Economic Community (EEC), Japan is the largest single buyer of U.S. farm products. On the other hand, the United States is a major importer of Japanese goods, ranging all the way from automobiles and sophisticated electronic consumer durables to steel.

The EEC figures prominently in U.S. trade. In 1980, U.S. exports of goods to the EEC of $50 billion represented about 22 percent of our foreign sales; U.S. imports of goods from the EEC amounted to more than $45 billion. The nine-nation EEC has been the largest market for our farm products, accounting for almost one third of our agricultural exports.

U.S. relations with developing countries

Trade between the United States and the less developed countries (LDCs) has been undergoing significant change. Just 10 years ago, U.S. imports from those countries were heavily concentrated in raw materials and agricultural products. Today, we import sizable quantities of manufactured goods. In 1980, 27 percent of our imports from the LDCs consisted of manufactures.

As a group, the developing countries are much more important to our trade than is often realized. Of the $224 billion worth of goods we exported in 1980, more than $82 billion—about 37 percent—went to the LDCs, which was more than we sold to the EEC and Japan combined. We imported about $120 billion worth of goods from these countries, representing about 48 percent of our total imports of goods.

The nature of our trade with the LDCs is extremely diverse. We import oil from the OPEC nations, oil and agricultural products from Mexico, coffee from Brazil, textile and leather goods from India, textiles, footwear, steel, and petrochemicals from Korea, and textiles and electrical and electronics equipment from Taiwan. Our main exports to these countries are feed grains, cereal, industrial raw materials, machinery, and transport equipment.

East-West trade

Trade between the industrialized West and the communist countries exceeded $100 billion in 1980, more than triple the volume of trade in 1970. Among Western nations, Germany and Japan are the largest traders with communist countries. Machinery and equipment are the most important Western exports; raw materials constitute the major imports.

U.S. trade with communist countries is relatively small. In 1980, U.S. exports to the communist world amounted to only $3.5 billion; imports came to only $1.4 billion. U.S. agricultural products constitute the bulk of our exports to the communist countries; raw materials and light manufactures are the main imported items. The U.S. maintains controls on the export of strategic goods to the communist world.

THE THEORY OF COMPARATIVE ADVANTAGE

It is not difficult to discover why the world's economies engage in international trade: *It is to their advantage to trade.* Trade permits people to become more productive through specialization, thereby enabling them to buy a wider variety of goods at lower prices. Nations that try to become self-sufficient will frequently have to settle for lower standards of living for their citizens. Different nations are differently endowed with various kinds of economic resources. Some countries are rich in capital resources; others are rich in labor resources; and still others are rich in natural resources. *Trade enables countries to specialize in and export those goods that use intensively those resources that are for them most abundant and most cheap. Trade also enables them to import at lower prices goods that use intensively those resources that are for them most scarce and therefore most expensive.* Put differently, trade enables each country to export on favorable terms those goods for which it has a *comparative advantage* and to import on favorable terms those goods for which it has a comparative disadvantage.

Through trade, the world's resources are used more efficiently. Greater efficiency in turn means a greater quantity of goods and services for any given volume of world resources. Potentially, all countries can gain from this greater abundance of goods and services. These gains would be de-

nied to countries who attempted to be completely self-sufficient.

Absolute advantage versus comparative advantage

We can illustrate the gains from trade with a series of simple numerical examples. Let us imagine a world economy consisting of two countries only—Japan and the United States. Assume further that each country produces only two goods—wheat and 10-speed bicycles. Each economy is a *barter* economy; that is, goods are exchanged directly for goods and not through the intermediary of money.

From Table 29.1, we see that a single worker in the United States can produce two bushels of wheat *or* 10 bicycles in a normal day. In Japan, on the other hand, one worker can produce one bushel of wheat *or* eight bicycles in a day. The reason for these differences in labor productivity need not concern us for the moment. According to this example, the United States is *absolutely* more efficient in the production of both goods. That is, it takes fewer resources in the United States to produce a unit of either good than it does in Japan. Thus, the U.S. can be said to have an **absolute advantage** over Japan in both commodities.

Table 29.1
Output per person per day in the United States and Japan: Wheat and 10-speed bicycles

	Wheat (output per person per day)	10-speed bicycles (output per person per day)
United States	2	10
Japan	1	8

Since the United States can produce both commodities with fewer resources than Japan, it would appear that the United States has nothing to gain from trading with Japan and that Japan has everything to gain from trading with the United States. But is this so? Let us study Table 29.1 more carefully to see if this is correct.

The first point we need to determine is how much it costs to produce wheat and bicycles in Japan and the United States. In this context, the only relevant concept is *opportunity cost.* The cost of producing two bushels of wheat in the United States is 10 bicycles; the use of scarce labor resources to produce two bushels of wheat means the United States foregoes the opportunity of producing 10 bicycles. Put differently, the cost to the United States of producing one bushel of wheat is five bicycles. But the cost to Japan of producing one bushel of wheat is eight bicycles. Thus, it costs *relatively* less to produce wheat in the United States than it does in Japan. Japan must give up more bicycles to produce a bushel of wheat than does the United States.

With the same reasoning, it is easy to see that the cost of producing bicycles is relatively lower in Japan. The cost of producing eight bicycles in Japan is one bushel of wheat; the cost of producing five bicycles in the United States is one bushel of wheat. Since more bicycles can be had for each bushel of wheat given up in Japan, bicycles must cost relatively less in Japan.

In sum, although the United States is absolutely more efficient than Japan in the production of both goods, it is *not* relatively more efficient in both. Whereas the United States is *relatively* more efficient in the production of wheat, Japan is *relatively* more efficient in the production of bicycles. Because of these differing degrees of relative efficiency, it follows that the United States has a **comparative advantage** in the production of wheat; Japan, on the other hand, has a comparative advantage in the production of bicycles.

The gains from trade: A first approximation

According to the theory of international trade, each country will have a tendency to specialize in and to export those goods for which it has a comparative advantage. Obviously, each country will tend to undertake the required shift of resources only if there are clearly demonstrable gains to be had from trading. Thus, Japan will be willing to shift some of its resources to bicycle production *if* for each group of eight bicycles it sends to the United States it gets in return *more* than one bushel of wheat (or, to state it differently, if fewer than eight bicycles are required in order to get in return a bushel of wheat from the United States). Similarly, the United States will be willing to shift some of its resources to wheat production *if* for each bushel of wheat it sends to Japan it gets in return more than five bicycles.

Are such gains possible? Yes. *As long as one bushel of wheat exchanges for more than five but less than eight bicycles, each country gains from international trade.* This is easily illustrated. Suppose one bushel of wheat exchanges for six bicycles:

1. The United States gains from trade. For each bushel of wheat the United States sends to Japan, it receives six bicycles in return. Shifting labor resources out of bicycles into wheat and trading the excess makes sense. Only five bicycles can be had per bushel of wheat given up through the shifting of resources from wheat to bicycles in the United States; through international trade, the United States can get six bicycles per bushel of wheat given up.

2. Japan gains from trade. Japan need only give up six bicycles to get a bushel of wheat from the United States; to get a bushel of wheat via the shift of domestic resources into wheat production, it would have to give up eight bicycles. Shifting labor resources out of wheat into bicycle production and trading the excess makes sense for Japan.

There are two other simple propositions that are left to the reader to demonstrate:

1. If one bushel of wheat exchanged for five bicycles in international trade, Japan would gain but the United States would not; the United States would have no incentive to trade.

2. If one bushel of wheat exchanged for eight bicycles, the United States would gain, but Japan would not; Japan would have no incentive to trade.

Note: What determines the ratio of exchange of bicycles for wheat internationally will be discussed later.

The gains from trade further illustrated

In order to illustrate the magnitude of the gains to be had from trading, let us expand our earlier numerical example somewhat. Assume for the moment that the United States has 20 laborers in total, whereas Japan has 40. They are divided *before trade* as follows. In the United States 8 laborers work on wheat and 12 on bicycles; in Japan 20 on wheat and 20 on bicycles. This division is dictated by the relative preferences of U.S. and Japanese residents for bicycles and wheat. The total production and consumption of bicycles and wheat *before trade* are given respectively as follows. For Japan, 160 bicycles and 20 bushels of wheat are produced and consumed; for the United States, 120 bicycles and 16 bushels of wheat. These are shown in the upper half of Table 29.2. Note that prior to trade—i.e., the state of **autarky**—the world production and consumption of bicycles and wheat amount to 280 and 36 respectively.

Suppose the United States and Japan decide to engage in trade with each other. Suppose further that the international ratio of exchange of bicycles for wheat happens to be 6:1. (Why this ratio is possible will become clear later.) The United States will specialize in wheat by devoting all of its labor resources to wheat production;

Japan will specialize in the production of bicycles. Note at this point that, compared with the former levels of production, such specialization results in an increase in the world production totals of *both* wheat and bicycles. This is shown in the lower half of Table 29.2. There is no mystery here. When each country specializes in the production of the good for which it has a relative or comparative cost advantage, more can be produced of both goods. The fact that there is more is the reason both countries can, via trade, expand their consumption of both goods beyond that which is possible in a state of autarky. This is easily illustrated.

At an international exchange ratio of six bicycles for each bushel of wheat, the following outcomes are possible. If the United States is willing to sell 22 bushels of wheat to Japan in exchange for 132 bicycles (i.e., $6 \times 22 = 132$), and if Japan is willing to sell 132 bicycles in exchange for 22 bushels of wheat, a bargain can be struck that enables both Japan and the United States to consume more wheat *and* bicycles than was possible in the absence of trade. This is made clear in the lower half of Table 29.2. The advantages to be had from specializing and trading are obvious.

One final note: In the simple kind of example presented here, the only conceivable after-trade consumption points in Japan and the United States are those for which world imports equal world exports. The export of 22 bushels of wheat from the United States must correspond to the

Table 29.2

Comparison of before-trade and after-trade production and consumption possibilities

	Production before trade			Consumption before trade		
	United States	Japan	World total	United States	Japan	World total
Bicycles	120	160	280	120	160	280
Wheat	16	20	36	16	20	36
	Production after trade			Consumption after trade		
	United States	Japan	World total	United States	Japan	World total
Bicycles	0	320	320	132	188	320
Wheat	40	0	40	18	22	40

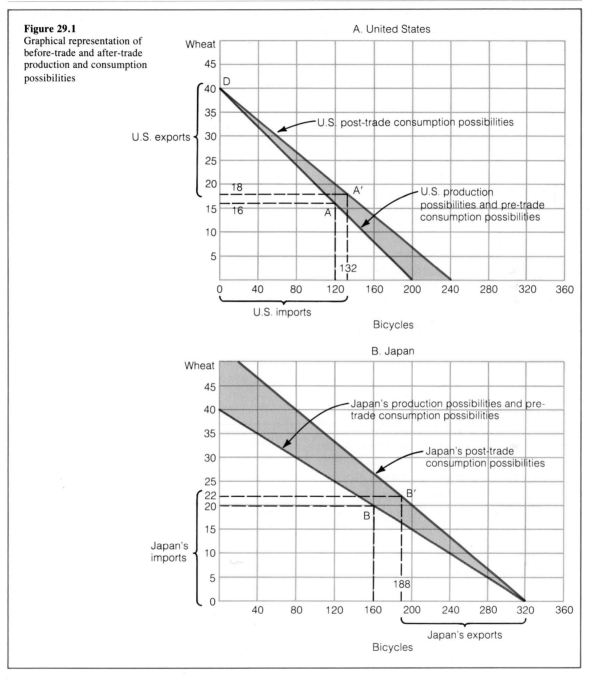

Figure 29.1
Graphical representation of before-trade and after-trade production and consumption possibilities

A. United States

B. Japan

22 bushels of wheat imports for Japan; and the 132 bicycles exported from Japan must be equal to the 132 bicycles imported into the United States.

The graphic representation of the gains from trade.[1] It is easy to show the gains from trade graphically. Given the volume of each country's labor resources, and assuming constant opportu-

---
[1] This section can be ignored without loss of continuity.

nity costs (i.e., for each additional bushel of wheat produced, the United States must give up the production of five bicycles and Japan the production of eight bicycles), each country's production possibilities curve can be represented as a straight line, as shown in Figure 29.1. This also represents each country's *pretrade* consumption possibilities line. If there is no trade, each country can consume only what each produces separately. Prior to trade, the United States selects the wheat-bicycle combination given by point A. The corresponding pretrade position for Japan is given by point B. Before trade, bicycles exchange for wheat in the United States at the ratio 5:1; in Japan, the corresponding pretrade exchange ratio is 8:1.

Let trade begin. Japan specializes in bicycles and shifts all of its resources to point C; the United States specializes in wheat by shifting all of its resources to point D. Since in the world market bicycles exchange for wheat at the ratio of 6:1, each country has the opportunity to trade along a line that lies above its production possibilities. This new line represents for each country its *post-trade* consumption possibilities. *With trade each country's consumption possibilities exceeds its production possibilities*. With trade, each country can obtain consumption points A′ and B′ as opposed to points A and B obtainable before trade. The magnitude of each country's exports and imports as given in Table 29.2 is shown graphically in Figure 29.1.

Comparative advantage: A restatement

It will prove very useful to our later discussion to restate the theory of comparative advantage somewhat differently. Consider first the pretrade circumstances confronting the United States and Japan. Before trade, five bicycles in the United States exchange for one bushel of wheat. This implies that a bushel of wheat in the United States before trade commands a price that is five times as much as a bicycle. Since one laborer can be used interchangably to produce either one bushel of wheat or five bicycles in half a day, a bushel of wheat is worth five times as much as one bicycle. Thus, before trade, the relative price

of wheat—the price of wheat (P_w) relative to the price of a bicycle (P_b)—equals 5 in the United States. Symbolically,

Pretrade relative price of wheat in the U.S.
$$= \frac{P_w}{P_b} = 5.$$

Similarly, since the pretrade exchange ratio of bicycles for wheat is 8 in Japan, this implies, that the pretrade relative price of wheat must be 8. Thus,

Pretrade relative price of wheat in Japan
$$= \frac{P_w}{P_b} = 8.$$

The relatively greater efficiency of the United States in the production of wheat translates directly into a lower *relative* pretrade price for wheat in the United States. *The lower relative price for wheat in the United States prior to trade is evidence of the United States' comparative advantage in wheat.*

A lower relative price for wheat in the United States before trade implies *simultaneously* a lower relative price for bicycles in Japan. Since the relative price of bicycles is nothing more than the reciprocal of the relative price of wheat, this is easily demonstrated.

Pretrade relative price of bicycles in Japan
$$= \frac{P_b}{P_w} = \frac{1}{P_w/P_b} = \frac{1}{8} = 0.125.$$

And,

Pretrade relative price of bicycles in the U.S.
$$= \frac{P_b}{P_w} = \frac{1}{P_w/P_b} = \frac{1}{5} = 0.20.$$

The lower relative price for bicycles in Japan before trade is evidence of Japan's comparative advantage in bicycles. Once trade is opened up between the United States and Japan, a *common* international price ratio will be established; *relative price differences are eliminated* (or at least reduced) after trade. The international price ratio is referred to as the international **terms of trade.**

One important conclusion follows from this discussion. Although our numerical example implied that the United States had an *absolute advantage* in the production of both goods, it has a *comparative advantage* in the production of wheat alone. The United States does *not* have a comparative advantage in *both goods*. Indeed, that is impossible. *The fact that the relative price for wheat is lower in the United States prior to trade is itself evidence that the relative price of bicycles is higher; the United States is comparatively disadvantaged in the production of bicycles.* It is not possible for one of the world's economies to have a comparative advantage in all goods—an absolute advantage, perhaps, but not a comparative advantage. And as long as relative prices differ between countries before trade, these countries can gain from trade.

There is a second important conclusion that needs to be emphasized. Both Japan and the United States will gain from trading with each other as long as the common international terms of trade lies between the pretrade price ratios. Be sure that you can explain why this must be so.

Relative prices, absolute prices, and the exchange rate

Up to this point we have assumed that the United States and Japan were both barter economies. Goods were exchanged directly for goods without the use of money as an intermediary. Additionally, we have been assuming that production was carried on in both countries under conditions of constant opportunity costs; no matter what the levels of production of wheat and bicycles, every bushel of wheat exchanges in production for five bicycles in the United States and eight bicycles in Japan. In this section we drop both assumptions in the interest of greater realism.

In the United States, the monetary unit is known as the dollar ($); in Japan, it is known as the yen (¥). The **exchange rate** is simply the price of one currency in terms of another. It tells us, for example, the number of yen that exchange for each dollar. For our purposes, we will assume a fixed exchange rate of 200 yen for each dollar—i.e., ¥200 = $1. This means, for example, that

a good selling for ¥1,000 in Japan is worth $5 in the United States. (In Chapter 15 we studied the factors responsible for the movements of exchange rates.)

Throughout we will assume that the costs of transporting goods between Japan and the United States are zero. This is done in the interests of simplifying the problem. As we shall see, if Japan and the United States trade freely with each other, all traded goods will command the *same* price in each country. When transport costs are present, *free trade* will bring about a situation in which the price differences between the traded goods in the two countries will equal the per unit differences in transport costs.

Assume to begin with that the pretrade relative prices for Japan and the United States are as follows. The relative price of wheat in the United States is 5—i.e., $\left(\frac{P_w}{P_b}\right)_{U.S.} = 5.0$; the relative price of wheat in Japan is 8—i.e., $\left(\frac{P_w}{P_b}\right)_J = 8.0$. The United States has a comparative advantage in wheat; Japan has a comparative advantage in bicycles. Assume further that bicycles sell for ¥300 in Japan; wheat therefore sells for ¥2,400 per bushel. This is a result of the fact that P_w in Japan is, before trade, 8 times P_b. For the United States, assume that bicycles sell for $2; wheat therefore sells for $10 per bushel (i.e., $P_w = 5 \times P_b$).

Given the exchange rate (¥200 = $1), it is easy to see that at the pretrade prices, it would be cheaper for U.S. residents to buy their bicycles in Japan and for Japanese residents to buy wheat in the United States. Whereas a bushel of wheat costs $10 in the United States, it costs the equivalent of $12 in Japan (i.e. ¥2,400 ÷ the exchange rate = $12.00). Similarly, whereas a bicycle costs ¥300 in Japan before trade, it costs the equivalent of ¥400 in the United States (i.e., $2 × exchange rate = ¥400).

Because of these price differences, each country has an interest in trading with the other. When trade is opened up, U.S. residents will try to buy bicycles from Japan; Japanese residents, wheat from the United States. The increased demand for bicycles in Japan will cause bicycle prices to rise in Japan, creating incentives for Japan's wheat producers to shift resources out of wheat into the production of bicycles. The increased demand for wheat in the United States will cause U.S. wheat prices to rise, creating in-

centives for U.S. bicycle producers to shift resources out of bicycles into wheat production. These resource shifts will continue until, given the exchange rate, Japanese and U.S. prices for wheat and bicycles are equalized. This is illustrated in Figures 29.2 and 29.3.

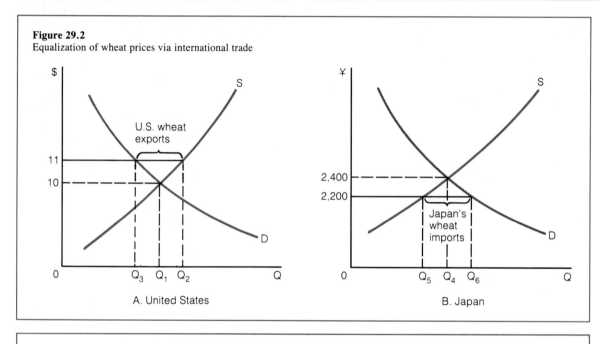

Figure 29.2
Equalization of wheat prices via international trade

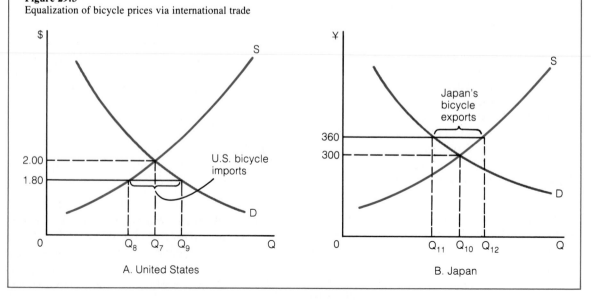

Figure 29.3
Equalization of bicycle prices via international trade

Consider first Figure 29.2. Before trade, wheat in Japan is priced at ¥2,400, at the point of intersection of the Japanese domestic demand for and supply of wheat; the pretrade price for wheat in the United States is $10. At the exchange rate of ¥200 = $1, wheat is much more expensive in Japan. The purchase of wheat from the United States by Japan raises the demand for wheat in the United States and lowers it in Japan. The U.S. price for wheat will rise; the price for wheat falls in Japan. Wheat production in the United States rises to Q_2; in Japan wheat production falls to Q_5. Because of the higher price for wheat in the United States, U.S. consumption of wheat falls to Q_3; the lower price for wheat in Japan induces an increase in Japanese consumption to Q_6. The U.S. exports the difference between its domestic production and consumption (Q_2Q_3); Japan imports the amount Q_5Q_6. In equilibrium, U.S. wheat exports equal Japan's wheat imports. Otherwise, there would be further price adjustments in both Japan and the United States until they did equal one another. Moreover, in equilibrium, wheat sells for the same price in Japan and the United States. Given the exchange rate (¥200 = $1), $11 per bushel is equivalent to ¥2,200. If prices were not equal, there would be a further incentive to expand or contract the volume of trade.

Similar conclusions are arrived at in Figure 29.3 with respect to bicycles. As is apparent from the pretrade prices for bicycles in the United States and Japan, bicycles are much cheaper in Japan. The increased demand for Japanese bicycles raises Japan's prices and lowers U.S. prices. The consumption of bicycles falls in Japan and rises in the United States; the production of bicycles rises in Japan and falls in the United States. In equilibrium, U.S. bicycle imports equal Japanese bicycle exports. Additionally, given the exchange rate, U.S. and Japanese bicycle prices are equalized after trade.

The above demand and supply analysis is very useful in highlighting a number of outcomes caused by international trade. These can be summarized as follows.

1. Since the supply curves for each of the goods in both countries are upward sloping, this indicates that production is subject to increasing costs. As a consequence, there will *in general* not be complete specialization with free international trade. There will be a reallocation of resources in each country away from the production of those goods for which each has a comparative disadvantage and toward those for which each has a comparative advantage. But as long as both goods were produced prior to trade in each country, it is likely that both goods will be produced by each after trade. Japan continues *after trade* to produce both wheat and bicycles, though less wheat and more bicycles than *before trade*. Similar considerations apply to the United States. It is not surprising, therefore, to find countries importing goods from abroad that are produced at home. The domestic production of a good that is imported will be cut back to the point where the price differences between foreign and domestic markets are eliminated.

2. It should also be noted that the higher price received by producers for the export good and the lower price received by producers for the *import-competing* good are the mechanisms that cause the shift of resources toward the export good. The higher relative price received for the export good raises its relative profitability, thereby inducing the shift of resources.

3. The higher price for the export good and the lower price for the import-competing good induce domestic consumers to shift their consumption away from the export good toward the good that is imported. In other words, domestic consumers have to pay more for the good that is exported than they did prior to trade. Offsetting this, of course, is the lower price they pay for the good they now import.

4. One could easily take account of the existence of transport costs. Because of transportation charges, the tendency toward the equality of prices between countries will be incomplete. There will be a tendency toward the equality of **landed prices** only. That is, under free trade, and given the exchange rate, there will be a tendency toward the equality of (*a*) the price in the exporting country *plus* transport costs and

(*b*) the price in the importing country. In some instances, transport costs are of negligible importance; in others, they are prohibitive. Where transport costs are small relative to the value of the product shipped—as in the case of diamonds—we can safely ignore their influence. Where transport costs are high relative to the value of the product—as in the case of coal—such transport costs could prove prohibitive to the movement of such goods to distant countries. Of course, in some instances high transport costs may be an important source of trade between some countries. For example, it may be cheaper for the northern states to import some goods from Canada than to buy those same goods domestically because of the greater distances that must be traveled within the United States.

Sources of comparative advantage

Although the demand and supply apparatus presented earlier allows us to identify some of the likely consequences of international trade, it does not help us to understand *why* the various demand and supply curves intersect where they do prior to trade. That is, it does not help to explain *why* each country has a comparative advantage in one good as opposed to another. It is the purpose of this section to discuss briefly some of the factors responsible for each country's comparative advantage. *Since pretrade relative prices tell us in which goods a country has a comparative advantage, and in which goods it does not, the sources of comparative advantage can be found in those factors that determine the relative demands for and the relative supplies of each of the goods produced.*

Technology. If a country possesses a production process that is technologically superior to the processes used abroad, this could be a source of that country's comparative advantage in that product. Technological supriority here means more output per unit of input. Technological differences between countries are often important sources of cost differences.

In some discussions, the technology differences between countries are frequently ignored.

Many people argue that U.S. industry is not able to compete with foreign producers because wage costs are so much lower in foreign countries. But wage costs alone do not tell us what we need to know to determine *unit costs*—the costs for each unit of output. If wage costs are low and each worker produces a very small output, unit costs could be very high compared with a country whose wage costs are high but whose technique of production brings about a high level of output per worker. In other words, the technological superiority of some production processes may overcome the wage cost differences between countries.

It needs to be recognized, however, that the existence of a superior production process in one country does not mean that those technological differences will persist over time. Indeed, the **transmission of technology** from one country to another is an important factor responsible for changing the comparative advantage position of countries in various goods and services. Initially, country A may have a comparative advantage in the production of good X because of its superior technology—a technological superiority that overcomes its wage cost disadvantage. Country A, therefore, exports product X. In time producers in country B imitate the technology used in country A. If wage and other input costs are lower in country B, country A may lose its comparative advantage in X. In time it may begin to import X from B. Moreover, B may eventually lose its newly acquired comparative advantage in X as the technology is transferred to yet other countries whose wage and other input costs are lower still. Countries A and B may both ultimately end up importing X from, say, country C.

These ideas form the basis of what is known as the **product cycle theory of international trade.** A new product is discovered in country A, produced and marketed there, and subsequently exported. During the introductory stages of a product, the methods and techniques of production are often very crude and the scale of production is fairly small. As the new good matures and becomes more standardized, the introduction of cost saving mass-production techniques become feasible. For a while, then, country A can maintain and perhaps enlarge its comparative advantage in this product, even when confronted with higher wage and other input costs. However, the standardization of the product and the processes used to produce it facilitate the transmission of these technologies abroad.

Once a promising market exists abroad, foreign producers have an incentive to imitate the good, as well as the technology used to produce it. If wage and other input costs are low enough, this process of imitation may well cause country A to lose its technical lead. Eventually country A may lose its export market in the good in question. The "cycle" is complete once country A begins importing that good. Of course, the technical lead that is lost in the production of any single good may well be offset by product innovations in other goods. In a *dynamic* world economy, any single country's comparative advantage could well be changing continuously.

The international transmission of technology explains, in large measure, why the United States has been losing out to foreigners in the production of such traditional goods as steel and textiles. Technological advance has not been rapid in these industries, and U.S. producers have been subjected to ever-increasing import competition—first from other major industrialized countries, such as Canada, Germany, and Japan, and now from a number of the less developed countries, such as Korea. Increasingly, the LDCs will acquire advantage in the production of these goods, displacing production from even Japan and Germany.

Resource endowments. One of the most important explanations of each country's comparative advantage lies in the fact that different countries are endowed with different quantities scarce resources. Given the further fact that the production of different goods requires the use of scarce resources in different proportions, differences will emerge in production costs for similar goods between countries. Eli Heckscher and Bertil Ohlin are the two economists most responsible for the development of the theory of comparative advan-

tage based on differences in resource endowments among countries.

*The **Heckscher-Ohlin theory** can be stated as follows: Each country will tend to export those goods that use most intensively the country's relatively abundant resources.* The essentials of the theory can be explained in the following way. Assume a world of only two resources—capital and labor. Assume country A has a *relatively* larger amount of capital than country B. This means, of course, that country B has a *relatively* larger amount of labor. As a consequence of these differences in relative resource endowments, capital will be *relatively* cheaper in A and labor will be *relatively* cheaper in B. Now, the various goods produced in A and B employ capital and labor in different proportions. Some use capital *relatively* intensively; others use labor *relatively* intensively. *Because capital is relatively cheaper in country A, it should cost relatively less for A to produce capital-intensive products. By the same reasoning, it should cost B relatively less to produce labor-intensive products.* These relative cost differences were presumed by Heckscher and Ohlin to form the basis for each country's comparative advantage. Capital-rich country A will have a comparative advantage in goods that use capital relatively intensively. Labor-rich country B will have a comparative advantage in goods that use labor relatively intensively.

Of course, in the real world there are more than just two kinds of resources. Indeed, there are a large variety of resources. Not only are there natural resource differences between countries. There are also differences internationally in the qualities of labor and capital. Nevertheless, despite these differences, there is considerable empirical support for the notion that differences in resource endowments and differences in the intensity of use of those resources in the production of various goods explain a great deal of the trade that takes place between nations. The fact that high-technology products require highly skilled technical personnel—both in their development and during the initial stages of their production—and that the United States is abundantly endowed with such workers, goes a long way toward explaining why the United States enjoys a comparative advantage in the production of a number of newly developed high-technology products. Relatively lower wages abroad are explained in part by the relative greater abundance of labor, which explains in large part why we import so many labor-intensive products and why, given the similarities of technologies in some fields caused by the transmission of those technologies abroad, we import goods that are relatively capital-intensive. Relative resource endowments explain why they OPEC nations export oil and why countries like Colombia and Brazil export coffee. The United States could produce much more oil than it now does—through coal liquefaction and the use of advanced techniques to extract oil from shale and from tar sands. It could also produce its own coffee—in greenhouses, for example. Under current technology, however, it is much cheaper to import these items from abroad.

Of course, trade between nations is more complicated than can be captured by any simple theory. In some fields the United States has a comparative advantage in newly developed products; in others that lead is held by other industrial countries such as Japan and Germany.

Differences in tastes or demand. The technology and resource endowments explanations of comparative advantage emphasize the conditions of *supply* in the various countries. The forces of *demand* are also important in the determination of a country's comparative advantage. We saw earlier that we could discover which goods a country had a comparative advantage in from knowledge of the pretrade relative prices. And since relative prices are determined by both demand *and* supply, it is easy to see why differences in demand between countries are important. Consider, for example, the following circumstances. Suppose countries A and B produce goods X and Y using the same techniques of production; assume further that resource endowments are identical in A and B. On the basis of the technology and resource endowments explanations of comparative advantage, it would appear that A and B would have little to gain from trading with each other. In the absence

of technology and resource endowments differences, there would appear to be no differences in comparative costs and hence no differences in relative prices. Neither country has a comparative advantage in goods X or Y.

However, relative prices cannot be determined on the basis of supply considerations alone. For example, if consumers in A have a relative preference for good X, whereas consumers in B have a relative preference for good Y, pretrade relative prices will differ between A and B. Specifically, the relative price of X—i.e., $\frac{P_x}{P_y}$—will be lower in B prior to trade (implying, of course, that the relative price of Y is lower in A). These relative price differences imply that A has a comparative advantage in Y, and B has a comparative advantage in X. Both countries can gain from trading with each other.

Tastes or demand differences are obviously important in international trade. Religious, cultural, sociological, and climatic differences between countries are some of the more critical factors shaping the consumption decisions of the nations of the world. Additionally, differences in the levels of economic development help to explain differences in the consumption patterns of different countries. In poor countries characterized by low per capita incomes a sizable market exists for necessities, but only a small market for luxury goods. The market for luxury goods is much more extensive within developed countries. This partly explains why the major trading partners of the developed countries tend to be other developed countries. At least this is true in the case of trade in consumer goods.

RESTRICTIVE TRADE PRACTICES

In this section of the chapter we will examine in detail some of the consequences of restrictive trade practices. We have already emphasized the advantages that accrue to countries as a result of trade. But, despite these advantages, most countries adopt measures designed to restrict trade. These restrictive trade practices take several different forms. They include **tariffs, quotas, orderly marketing agreements, multiple ex-**

change rates, and some kinds of **anti-dumping statutes.** These measures are all designed to restrict imports. **Export subsidies** constitute a different kind of restrictive trade practice designed to promote a country's exports.

Restrictive import practices

The effects of a **tariff** can be analyzed usefully with the aid of Figure 29.4 . The upward-sloping supply curve measures the different levels of *domestic* production; the downward-sloping demand curve measures different levels *domestic* consumption. In the absence of trade, equilibrium would take place at the price P_0 and the quantity Q_0.

Assume for simplicity that we can import all the goods that we want at the prevailing international price for the good—P_2. (This, in other words, means that the international supply curve for the product is perfectly elastic at the price P_2.) Under free trade, then, the price will fall from the pretrade price of P_0 to P_2. Domestic production will be cut back from Q_0 to Q_2, and domestic consumption will increase to Q_4. Imports will amount to Q_2Q_4.

The reduction in the production of the good caused by free trade is frequently viewed as a

negative factor as far as the producers of this good are concerned. The reduced price for the product causes a reduction in producer profits. The least efficient producers will be forced to either shut down completely or cut back their output levels severely. Some workers will be laid off. And the communities in which these plants are located will suffer the consequences of these reduced levels of income and spending. In a well-functioning economy, these displaced resources will ultimately find employment in more efficient industries elsewhere in the economy. However, these adjustments take time—frequently, a great deal of time—to take effect. Moreover, to those who are displaced, there is considerable uncertainty as to their future prospects. Often they have no idea where they can obtain employment in the future. Adjusting to changed economic circumstances is almost always difficult, and it is almost always strongly resisted. Is it any wonder, then, that producers and workers in industries facing stiff import competition exert a great deal of pressure on Congress to pass legislation restricting the importation of such goods?

Offsetting these negative effects, of course, is the fact that the consumer benefits through lower prices. However, consumers are not in general well organized for the purpose of lobbying Con-

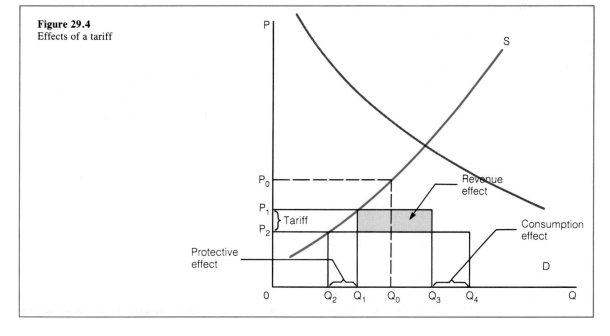

Figure 29.4
Effects of a tariff

gress. Moreover, while the benefits in the *aggregate* are often large, for each individual consumer they are likely to be small *for any particular good.* By contrast, workers and producers tend to be better organized, and the negative effects tend to be substantial in those regions of the country where the good is produced. As a consequence, it is not difficult to discover why Congress frequently gives in to those seeking import relief.

Tariff relief

In any event, suppose Congress does grant import relief by imposing a tariff on the good in question. For simplicity, let us assume that the government imposes a *specific tariff* on the imported item. A specific tariff is nothing other than a tax of a certain fixed amount for each unit of the good that is imported. For purposes of illustration, we will assume that government imposes a tariff equal to the distance P_1P_2.

The tariff raises the price of the domestic good from P_2 to P_1. Because of the higher price, it now becomes profitable to expand domestic production from Q_2 to Q_1. On the other hand, domestic consumption falls from Q_4 to Q_3. Likewise imports are reduced from Q_2Q_4 to Q_1Q_3.

There are three readily identifiable effects of a tariff. The first, called the **protective effect,** refers to the increase in (less efficient) domestic production made possible by the presence of the tariff. In Figure 29.4, this is measured as the distance Q_2Q_1. The **consumption effect** refers to the reduction in domestic consumption caused by the tariff; this is measured as the distance Q_3Q_4. The third effect is called the **revenue effect.** It refers to the revenue collected by the government as a result of the imposition of the tariff; it is equal in value to the quantity imported times the size of the tariff and is given by the area of the shaded rectangle in Figure 29.4. Note further that the tariff represented in Figure 29.4 is not prohibitive. A **prohibitive tariff** would eliminate imports altogether. A tariff equal to P_0P_2 would be prohibitive. Such a prohibitive tariff would yield the maximum protection to domestic producers and no revenue for the government.

A single demand and supply diagram cannot capture all of the complexities associated with the imposition of a tariff. The diagram does make clear that a tariff will cause more of the product to be produced domestically than under free trade. This would appear to be a decided benefit. However, the production of more domestically means using resources that could potentially be better used elsewhere. This is the key lesson to be learned from the theory of comparative advantage. If tariffs are required in order to maintain resources in the production of some good, resources will not be allocated in the most efficient manner possible. Indeed, tariff protection maintains the employment of resources in industries that are the least efficient. This is reflected in the fact that, in industries receiving tariff protection, buyers must pay higher prices than otherwise.

Quotas

When restrictions are placed on the *quantity* that may be imported, this is referred to as a *quota.* In a limited sense, quotas have effects similar to tariffs. This is easily explained. When a tariff is imposed, it has the effect of reducing the quantity imported. Suppose that, instead of a tariff, Congress passed legislation limiting imports by a quota to the amount Q_1Q_3 in Figure 29.4. Under these circumstances, the price in the domestic economy will rise to P_1. This is exactly the same price that prevailed after the tariff was levied. At that price, domestic demand equals total supply (domestic supply of Q_1 and foreign supply of Q_1Q_3). The protective and consumption effects of the quota are the same as those for the tariff. However, unlike the tariff, there is no automatic revenue effect. The government could obtain the revenue by issuing "quota tickets" for sale to importers carrying a price equal to P_1P_2 for each unit imported. In that case, the revenue effect for the quota would be the same as for the tariff. In the absence of "quota tickets" the revenue that would otherwise be obtained by the government will be divided in some indeterminate way between importers and exporters. If exporters charged P_1 instead of P_2, they would gain the additional revenue. If exporters continued to charge P_2, importers would charge P_1, thereby gaining the additional revenue. A third possible outcome will arise if exporters charge more than P_2 but less than P_1, in which case the additional revenue will be split in some fashion between exporters and importers.

In other senses, quotas are quite unlike tariffs. Quotas are frequently more restrictive (and therefore more protective) in their effects. For example, suppose the domestic demand for the product rises as a result of, say, an increase in income. For any given tariff, the larger quantity demanded will be satisfied at least in part through an increase in imports. The increase in imports in this instance serves to limit somewhat the magnitude of the price increase in the domestic market. A rigid quota, on the other hand, will not permit any increase in imports. The increased domestic demand will have to be met by domestic producers. And since higher levels of domestic production are more costly than additional imports, the price in the domestic market will rise by more than under the tariff. As a result, domestic producers are accorded more protection.

The situation gets more complicated still with the introduction of **variable import quotas.** Instead of establishing a quota that fixes for all time the quantity that may be imported, some countries will impose quotas on some goods specified as a percentage of domestic consumption; for example, a quota that allows no more than 10 percent of the amount consumed domestically to be imported. Here, increases in demand will in all likelihood be met with some increase in imports. Whether such a variable import quota is more or less restrictive than a tariff will depend on the differences in the amounts imported under the different schemes. Generally, quotas are viewed as much more restrictive.

Orderly marketing agreements

On the surface, **orderly market agreements** do not appear to fall under the heading of restrictive trade practices. Representatives from the countries involved get together for the purpose of reaching agreement on a "fair" division of the market between foreign and domestic producers. Everyone agrees that trade ought to be "fair" and "orderly." However, these terms have little meaning to an economist. Generally, the importing country initiates these agreements with the exporting countries because its domestic industry is being threatened. Rather than impose tariffs or quotas outright, the importing country will try to reach an agreement with the exporting countries on the amounts that will be admitted. The exporting countries agree to participate, hoping to get a better deal than they would be dealt if the importing country imposed tariffs or quotas. The effects of the orderly marketing agreement, however, are nonetheless the same as those for tariffs and quotas. The exact formula agreed upon may be complex. But the net result is the limitation of imports for which there are both consumption and protective effects.

Multiple exchange rates

In some countries, it is illegal for residents to own foreign currencies except by permission of the government. All foreign exchange earned by exporters must be turned over to the government in exchange for local currency. And all importers must buy the foreign exchange they need from the government. Since the government controls all foreign exchange dealings, it can charge, or pay, in local currency different prices depending on its objectives. If the government wants to limit imports, it can charge importers a very high price in terms of local currency to acquire foreign exchange, thereby making imports very expensive. And different prices can be charged for different categories of imports. Luxury goods are frequently discouraged by insisting upon a very large payment of domestic currency for each unit of foreign currency purchased. Similarly, if the government wishes to encourage exports, it will frequently pay large amounts of domestic currency in exchange for foreign currencies. In effect, the government subsidizes the production of exports. And different prices can be paid for different categories of exports, depending on which goods the government wishes to subsidize the most. The government chooses, therefore, to use **multiple exchange rates**—different prices for foreign currencies, depending on their purposes—to achieve the allocation of resources it deems most desirable. Obviously, however, the effects on trade are similar to a system of tariffs and export subsidies.

Some antidumping statutes

According to U.S. law, any country that sells its goods in the U.S. market at prices less than its own domestic market is said to be guilty of **dumping.** If dumping is present, the United States has the authority to levy tariffs and/or to otherwise restrict the imports of such goods until such violations cease.

Antidumping statutes were written into law for the express purpose of stopping two kinds of disadvantageous trade practices. The first, called **distress-goods dumping,** occurs when producers find themselves overloaded with inventories. If they unloaded those inventories on domestic markets, the price received for *all* they sold would fall, and their profits would suffer as a result. Given the option, they would prefer to dump their distress goods at low prices on foreign markets. This disrupts foreign markets, harms foreign producers, and disrupts normal production patterns there. In order to stop this practice, antidumping statutes were enacted.

The second kind of dumping is called **predatory dumping.** Foreign producers charge inordinately low prices in the domestic market to drive out domestic producers. Once the domestic competition is eliminated, they raise their prices to high levels, threatening all the while to lower them again if domestic producers try to reenter the market in competition. Obviously, such a practice does not serve the interests of domestic consumers.

There is, however, no reason to think that just because foreign producers charge less in our market than they do in their home market that there is either distress-goods or predatory dumping. If foreign producers have a near-monopoly position in their own market but are confronted

with a great deal of competition in world markets, it would be quite consistent with a profit-maximizing strategy to charge a higher price in their home market and a lower price in foreign markets. For the United States to impose a tariff under such circumstances would be detrimental. The problem, however, is that there is no clear-cut way of determining whether or not this is the source of the price disparity.

Export subsidies

In an effort to enhance the competitveness of their export goods, a number of governments subsidize their production. This lowers production costs, which in turn lowers prices in world markets. This is a restrictive trade practice because it distorts the allocation of resources. Resources are allocated in a less efficient manner than otherwise. For countries using subsidies, more resources are devoted to export goods than would be dictated by efficiency considerations. Their trading partners suffer because fewer resources will be devoted to the production of the affected import-competing industries than would be appropriate from an efficiency point of view. Of course, subsidies provided to import-competing industries would have similar distortive effects.

SUMMARY

1. The United States is the world's largest trading nation. U.S. exports and imports each make up about 12 percent of total world trade. However, because of the relatively huge size of the U.S. economy, foreign trade makes up a smaller fraction of total production and consumption in the United States than it does for any other noncommunist country. Interestingly, the relative importance of international trade to the United States has been increasing. This is the result of (*a*) the sharp increase in U.S. dependence on foreign sources of supply for petroleum products, (*b*) the increased importance of U.S. agriculture in world markets, and (*c*) rapid economic growth abroad. The United States main-

tains important trading relationships with both the developed and the less developed countries of the world.

2. Countries trade because it is to their advantage to trade. Trade enables countries to specialize in and export those goods that use intensively those resources that are for them most abundant and most cheap. Trade also enables countries to import at lower prices the goods that use intensively those resources that are for them most scarce and therefore most expensive. What is important is *not* the *absolute advantage* that any one country or group of countries holds over others, but their *comparative advantage.*

3. Are gains from trade possible? As long as the exchange ratios that exist before trade differ between countries, then gains from trade are possible. With trade, each country's consumption possibilities exceeds its production possibilities.

4. The theory of comparative advantage can be restated in terms of pretrade relative product prices. When one takes account of the exchange rate, pretrade relative price differences can be translated into pretrade absolute price differences. Under free trade, and in the absence of transportation costs, both relative and absolute price differences that existed pretrade will be eliminated.

5. In the face of increasing costs, specialization and production will in general be incomplete.

6. Since pretrade relative prices tell us in which goods a country has a comparative advantage and in which goods it does not, the sources of comparative advantage can be found in those factors that determine the relative demands for and the relative supplies of each of the goods produced. The most important sources of comparative advantage include differences in technology, differences in relative resource endowments, and differences in tastes or demand.

7. Despite the advantages that occur to countries as a result of international trade, most countries adopt measures to restrict trade. These restrictive trade practices take several forms. They include *tariffs, quotas, orderly marketing agreements, multiple exchange rates,* some kinds of *antidumping statutes,* and *export subsidies.*

CONCEPTS FOR REVIEW

Absolute advantage

Comparative advantage

Autarky

Consumption possibilities can exceed production possibilities with international trade

Exchange rate

Commodity price equalization as a consequence of free trade

International transmission of technology

Product cycle theory of international trade

Heckscher–Ohlin theory of international trade

Tariffs

Quotas

Orderly marketing agreements

Antidumping statutes

Export subsidies

Protective effect of a restrictive trade practice

Consumption effect of a restrictive trade practice

Revenue effect of a restrictive trade practice

Prohibitive tariff

Variable import quotas

Dumping

Distress-goods dumping

Predatory dumping

QUESTIONS FOR DISCUSSION

1. *a.* Consider the following table, which reports output per person per week in the United States and Germany for motorcycles and cameras. Assume constant costs of production.

	Motorcycles (output per person per week)	Cameras (output per person per week)
U.S.	20	40
Germany	16	20

Does either country have an absolute advantage in the production of both goods? Which country has a comparative advantage in motorcycles? Explain in terms of (1) opportunity costs and (2) pretrade exchange ratios.

b. State the pretrade relative price ratios in Germany and the United States. Explain.

c. Assuming that Germany has 10 workers and the United States has 20, show the gains from international trade. Be explicit.

d. Assume an exchange rate of $1 = DM3 and pretrade prices as follows: $50 for cameras in U.S. and DM200 for cameras in Germany. Identify the dollar and DM prices for motorcycles in the United States and Germany respectively; show that the absolute prices differ in accord with the relevant comparative advantages.

e. Show how trade will cause an equalization of prices for motorcycles and cameras.

2. Consider the following table, which reports output per person per year in the United States and France for wine and cheese. Assume constant costs of production.

	Wine (output per person per year)	Cheese (output per person per year)
U.S.	20	6
France	8	8

Does either country have an absolute advantage in the production of both goods? Which country has a comparative advantage in wine?

3. Explain why it is possible for a country to have an absolute advantage but not a comparative advantage in the production of all goods.

4. Does the product cycle theory shed any light on the question of why U.S. auto companies have experienced a reduced share of the U.S. auto market? What hypothesis might you advance?

5. Although Japan is one of the world's major producers of steel, the government there is cutting back on steel production. They argue, "Our future is not in steel. In time we will not be able to compete effectively with Korea and Brazil." How might this be explained by the product cycle theory?

6. Explain in words the rationale for the Heckscher-Ohlin theory of international trade.

7. Explain the circumstances under which a tariff and a quota will yield the *same* outcomes.

The call for free trade is a strong one. With trade, the world's resources are used more efficiently. This means, of course, that a greater volume of goods and services can be produced from a given quantity of resources. Why, then, would countries elect to impose restrictions on the movement of goods internationally? Why, that is, would countries choose freely to reduce the real incomes of their citizens by imposing tariffs or quotas on goods they import and by subsidizing the production of their exports? If the interests of the United States are best served by policies designed to raise the growth of its output and income, why would we favor trade restrictions that are inconsistent with that goal? If the United States seeks to achieve better relations with other nations, why would we favor policies to close off foreign access to our markets? And why would other nations that have goals similar to those of the United States similarly restrict their trade?

In an effort to assess the reasons trade restrictions are applied, it is important to recognize that there are both gains and losses associated with restrictive trade practices. *The losses take the form of reduced levels of real income.* This is evidenced by the fact that we have to pay more domestically to obtain goods that are cheaper on world markets. However, the losses generally are spread rather thinly. Even though the magnitude of the losses in the aggregate may be sizable, it is frequently the case that the cost to any single individual or group is not particularly burdensome. We pay perhaps a few extra dollars for each ton of steel, and therefore a few extra dollars for our cars and home appliances. We pay a dollar or so extra for each pair of shoes. And we pay 10 to 20 cents extra for a T-shirt or towel.

Not only do restrictive trade practices reduce a nation's real income, they also cause a redistribution of income in favor of workers and producers in those industries receiving import protection. Restrictions on imports of cotton textiles, meat, and steel *raise* the incomes of workers and firms in those industries producing them. Irving B. Kravis, an economist from the University of Pennsylvania, put the issue as follows:

Chapter 30

Trade liberalization and U.S. commercial policies

Every one of these restrictions benefits the individuals concerned at the expense of the rest of the people. *Each involves a reduction of production and of the national income and a redistribution of the smaller amount of income in favor of the beneficiaries of the restriction.*

Every current claim for protection, no matter what its guise, is a claim for special preference at the general expense.

Whatever the desired objective that is described, there is no getting around the fact that every successful claim for protection makes a select few better off at the cost of making everybody else worse off.[1]

It is true that those groups adversely affected by import competition are highly visible. Often they possess sufficient political clout to persuade Congress to pass legislation restricting imports of the goods they produce. These groups do not, however, argue that it is appropriate national policy to provide them with protection at the expense of the rest of the nation. On the contrary, they argue that it is *in the nation's interest* to restrict imports.

It is the purpose of this chapter to assess many of the arguments that are brought to the fore favoring import limitations. This will be followed by a brief analysis of U.S. commercial policies, past and present.

SOME ARGUMENTS FOR IMPORT RESTRICTIONS

1. Increased imports cause a reduction in our trade surplus. Since a trade surplus is a desirable national objective, a general case can be made for import limitations.

This argument is highly controversial. Its validity depends on three propositions: (a) a trade surplus is a desirable national objective; (b) import restrictions will increase the trade surplus; and (c) import restrictions are the best way of increasing the trade surplus.

[1] Irving B. Kravis, "The Current Case for Import Limitations," in *Commission on International Trade and Investment Policy,* Albert L. Williams, chairman, United States International Economic Policy in an Interdependent World (Washington: U.S. Government Printing Office, 1971), vol. 1, pp. 141–42; emphasis added.

A trade surplus is a desirable goal

It is difficult to provide an objective assessment of this goal since it is a matter of *normative* rather than *positive* economics. We can, however, ask ourselves whether the reasons put forth in support of this objective are sound. In the first place, it needs to be recognized at the outset that it is impossible for *all* countries to achieve a trade surplus. If country A achieves a trade surplus with its trading partners, those countries together must have a trade deficit with country A. A trade surplus for one country must be offset by a trade deficit elsewhere. If we export more than we import from others, their trade with us must involve an excess of imports over exports. If all countries tried to achieve a trade surplus, some will inevitably be frustrated.

Nevertheless, many people feel that the realization of the goal of an export surplus is desirable because of what it implies about the strength of our economy in comparison with the rest of the world. To these people, an export surplus is evidence of economic strength; a deficit is a sign of weakness.

In order to evaluate this argument, it must first be recognized that the trade balance refers to the difference between our exports and imports of *goods* alone. It does not include our exports and imports of *services* (sometimes referred to as our trade in *invisibles*). The question that needs to be answered is this: Should our objective be to achieve a surplus for goods *and* services, or for goods alone? If the former, a *trade* deficit could be more than offset by a surplus on services account, yielding an overall surplus for goods *and* services. From the point of view of the "strength" of our economy, why the emphasis should be put on goods alone and not on goods and services is not at all obvious. Why would an export surplus of goods imply economic strength whereas an export surplus of services would not?

Unfortunately, the view that a trade deficit is *invariably* a sign of economic weakness is a prevasive and harmful fallacy. The volume of goods that we export and import is determined by many complex factors. In the first place, how much we are willing to buy from foreign countries and how much they are willing to buy from us will be determined by *relative prices*. This will be affected not only by differences in productivity between nations but also by the exchange rate, *ceteris paribus*. It is true that low levels of productivity in the United States could be a source of the lack of competitiveness of our export goods abroad. And this could be a sign of weakness in the U.S. economy. In addition, a high value for the dollar on foreign exchange markets could make U.S. goods more expensive in foreign markets and foreign goods less expensive in U.S. markets. A low value for the dollar on foreign exchange markets would have the opposite effects. (In Chapter 15 we examined in detail the host of factors that determine exchange rates.)

Moreover, a high rate of inflation in the United States relative to foreign inflation rates would, *ceteris paribus,* cause the prices of U.S. goods to rise continuously relative to the prices of foreign goods. The rise in imports (and the reduction in exports) caused by the more rapid inflation in the United States could reflect a weakness in the U.S. economy, namely the inability to curb inflation.

There is a second very important influence on our exports and imports—relative growth of *real incomes*. As real income increases, part of the induced increase in spending will take the form of increased imports. If real income grows more rapidly in the United States than abroad, there is a natural tendency for imports to rise relative to exports. Indeed, sluggish growth abroad implies a corresponding sluggish growth for our goods in foreign markets. In this case, the growth of imports relative to exports is a sign of the economic strength of our economy relative to foreign nations; it is not a sign of economic weakness! The point must be made that the presence of a trade deficit cannot invariably be considered a sign of weakness of an economy.

Can import restrictions increase the trade surplus?

Although controversial, let us accept for the moment the proposition that a trade surplus is a desirable goal. The question that then needs to be addressed is whether trade restrictions will in fact cause an increase in the trade surplus. The evidence on this issue is far from clear. However, it is generally believed that trade restrictions will not do the trick. This is the result of the fact that restrictive actions taken by the United States will almost always call forth retaliatory restrictive actions on the part of other nations. Any diminution of imports into the United States as a result of trade restrictions is likely to be matched by a corresponding diminution of U.S. exports. Under these circumstances, the trade balance will not improve.

It needs to be emphasized that retaliation against a country imposing trade restrictions is a widely accepted principle among the nations of the world. The **General Agreement on Tariffs and Trade** (GATT), the international agency responsible for overseeing the implementation of a code of commercial conduct agreed to by most of the world's economies, has as one of its basic principles the preservation of the "balance of benefits" that each country derives from trade restrictions. According to this principle, any country that finds its interests adversely affected by the trade practices of some other nation is entitled to restore its "balance of benefits" through restrictions of its own. Thus, efforts by the United States to limit its imports through restrictive devices is almost certain to set off a chain of self-defeating restrictions by others.

Are import restrictions the best way to increase the trade surplus?

Even if other countries allow the United States to improve its trade position through restrictive trade devices, are trade restrictions the best way of bringing about that objective? Since the trade balance is defined as the difference between exports and imports, consideration should at least be given to schemes designed to promote exports. Moreover, if more rapid inflation in the United States is the cause of its deteriorating trade position, is it better to restrict imports or to pursue proper monetary and fiscal policies designed to slow its inflation rate? If sluggish productivity growth is the source of the problem, would it not be better to pursue policies aimed at increasing productivity? And what about the policy alternative of allowing the value of its currency to fall in foreign exchange markets—a policy that would make imports more expensive, and exports more competitive in world markets? The point is, there are a number of alternatives available that could well be better than import restrictions. Additionally, since trade restrictions almost invariably invite retaliation, these policy alternatives could be more effective.

2.   Imports reduce employment opportunities for U.S. citizens; a trade deficit raises the U.S. unemployment rate.

Few arguments favoring import restrictions carry as much force as this one. On the face of it, there would appear to be no effective way of disputing this argument. After all, if U.S. residents buy goods from foreign producers instead of domestic firms, workers in those U.S. firms will have to be laid off, boosting the unemployment rate. Actually, the argument is very weak, if not completely fallacious.

Those who advance this argument implicitly assume that employment opportunities are frozen. If workers are laid off as a result of, say, import competition, they will not be able to find employment elsewhere. This belief violates the basic tenet of economics. Resources are scarce and they have alternative uses. The opportunity cost of using scarce resources to produce one thing is the other things we must forego. To argue that there are no alternative uses for the resources displaced by import competition is tantamount to arguing that there is no longer any economic problem. That would mean, therefore, that all wants were satisfied. Moreover, according to the theory of comparative advantage, imports displace resources from their least efficient uses. In other words, if the displaced resources were shifted to the production of other goods, they would be put to more efficient uses. This means the resources so relocated can now command higher incomes than in their previous employment. Labor can receive a higher income, and

the return on capital can be greater. This does not mean, for example, that every worker will be better off; but, on average, workers can be made better off.

These gains, however, came about only in the long run, only after the resources have found new employment in areas offering higher wages and greater profit. In the short run—a period of time that could last for months or even years—the people affected are forced to bear the huge costs of adjusting to changed circumstances. In some instances, entire communities will suffer. Workers are thrown into the ranks of the unemployed; firm profits are depressed; spending by community residents declines, which causes additional layoffs elsewhere, further reducing spending within the community. People are forced to look for new jobs, often far away from their current homes. Many will be forced to acquire additional training and/or education. There will be moving expenses and other costs associated with the sale of their existing homes and the purchase of new ones. There are other costs as well, which, though difficult to quantify, are nonetheless important—moving away from friends, familiar surroundings, and breaking community ties.

The people affected would find these **adjustment costs** less burdensome if they could be assured that they would ultimately be better off economically. There are, of course, no such assurances; no one can be guaranteed a better job or greater profit. This kind of uncertainty makes people very resistant to change. It is understandable, therefore, why they would seek protection from import competition.

In a fundamental sense, the dislocations caused by import competition are really no different from the adjustments necessitated by dynamic change *within* our economy. One of the fundamental factors responsible for the improvement of living standards in the United States (and elsewhere) has been the mobility of capital and labor. The goods and services that we produce and consume today are markedly different from those produced and consumed 25 and even 10 years ago. New products and new product varieties are being developed continuously. Some product lines produced in an earlier day are no longer produced. Some old industries have folded completely. Many new industries have come into being. And there is no reason to believe that future changes in production and consumption will be any less dramatic than they have been in the past.

All of these changes have brought about significant reallocations of resources. Labor and the owners of capital have had to bear sizable adjustment costs similar to those described earlier. However, for the most part, the labor and capital resources dislocated by these dynamic adjustments within the economy were absorbed either within the same industries or within other industries. And most important, the relocations were almost always to employment offering higher wages and greater profit. This was true, for example, when the textile industry moved out of Pennsylvania and other northern states into North Carolina and other southern states. In this instance, thousands of workers suffered tremendous economc and social injury through no fault of their own. They were victims of changes in the marketplace.

The question we must ask is, Should government have intervened in order to prevent the shifting of those resources from the Northeast to the South, in order to prevent a great many lives from being disrupted? It is not possible to answer this question in a completely satisfactory way. However, to have denied the shift would have been to deny producers the freedom to choose the location that permitted lower production costs and therefore lower product prices. The protection of those adversely affected by the shift would have been achieved, as we noted earlier, at the expense of everyone else. Moreover, as Irving Kravis has emphasized,

> Such protection tends to freeze patterns of employment that are not in the long-run interests of workers or of the U.S. at large. The jobs that are protected tend to be low-wage jobs relative to those that would be available without protective policies. The Pennsylvania textile workers of yesterday were injured by the shift to the South. Today, their successors are better off than they would be if the government had intervened to keep the textile in-

dustry in that stage; they are working in industries that pay higher wages than the textile industry.[2]

The situation is really no different when the source of dislocation comes from foreign countries. If the government intervenes to restrict imports, workers and employers in those affected industries will be better off. But the cost of such restrictions is shouldered by the rest of the economy, which is denied the opportunity of obtaining those goods at lower prices from abroad. However, the gains to workers and employers are short-run gains only. In the long run, even the workers and employers in protected industries will be worse off than otherwise. For the most part, the industries requiring protection are low-wage industries, and restrictions also prevent the expansion of our export industries, which generally pay high wages. There are two reasons this is so. First, restrictions on our purchases from abroad give foreigners fewer dollars with which to buy American goods. Second, because import restrictions invite retaliation, we are able to sell fewer goods abroad.

To those workers and employers dislocated by imports, vague assurances of higher standards of living in the future seem all too inadequate. They will surely want to know where they can move to in order to improve their economic lot. However, since this kind of exact information can almost never be provided, that in no way justifies a policy favoring restrictions. In this respect, there are essentially three policy actions the government can undertake to facilitate the relocation of displaced capital and labor resources.

1. *Improve the flow of information about the availability of employment opportunities elsewhere.* Better information about possible job prospects would provide people with greater hope and make them somewhat less resistant to change. Of course, the availability of such information would be beneficial not only to workers and employers displaced by imports, but to others displaced by internal dynamic economic readjustments.

---

[2] Ibid.

2. *Give adjustment assistance.* To ease the burden of adjustment, the government could provide financial assistance to those displaced by imports. This could take the form of loans, grants, and/or tax credits to help defray educational, retraining, and moving expenses incurred by affected workers and employers. This assistance could be extended as well to aid the communities adversely affected by the readjustments.

3. *Conduct macroeconomic policies to ensure a buoyant economy.* Whether or not the adjustments occasioned by rising imports will take place readily will be heavily dependent on the state of the economy generally. If growth is rapid and the unemployment rate low, it will be relatively easy to absorb the displaced resources. If the economy is in a recession, on the other hand, the required readjustments will take considerable time and the losses to adversely affected individuals will be greater. It is easy to adjust when domestic demand is rising and the economy is healthy. Even where imports enter in large volume, it is frequently easy for workers and employers to find other lines which they can pursue with higher wages and greater profit as long as the economy is buoyant. Import restrictions are not the proper means of achieving the objective of high employment. Rather, it is more appropriate to use monetary and fiscal policy to achieve this objective.

When the economy is buoyant and other employment opportunities abound, the voices favoring import restrictions are stilled. During recessionary periods, those individuals adversely affected by imports clamor for protection. It's not difficult to figure out why. Policies designed to liberalize international trade almost never receive a sympathetic hearing when growth is sluggish and unemployment is high.

Net exports and the unemployment rate

Finally, it is important that we examine the evidence on the relationship between net exports and unemployment. Proponents of import restrictions frequently argue that a decline in net exports is an important factor responsible for raising unemployment. However, there is virtually no evidence to support this proposition. More often than not, declining net exports are associated with a *falling* unemployment rate; the converse is also true. From 1960 to 1961, a rise occurred in U.S. net exports from $4.4 billion to $5.8 billion, accompanied by a simultaneous rise in the unemployment rate from 5.5 percent to 6.7 percent. From 1962 to 1969, there was a fairly steady decline in the unemployment rate from 6.7 to 3.5 percent. Over that same period net exports both rose and fell. The rise in net exports from 1962 to 1965 is consistent with the view that rising net exports should cause unemployment to fall; the decline in net exports from 1965 to 1969 is inconsistent with that view.

A look at the years since 1969 reveals the same varying pattern. From 1969 to 1971, the unemployment rate rose; net exports rose from 1969 to 1970 and fell from 1970 to 1971. The unemployment rate fell from 1971 to 1973; net exports continued to fall in 1972, followed by a very sharp rise in 1973. The unemployment rate rose from 1973 to 1975; net exports fell in 1974 and rose in 1975. The unemployment rate fell during the period 1976 to 1978; net exports rose during 1976 and fell sharply in 1977, followed in 1978 by a moderate rise. Finally, corresponding to the increase in the unemployment rate from 1979 to 1980, net exports rose sharply.

The point of this exercise is simple. There is virtually no merit to the argument that a decline in net exports will cause the unemployment rate to rise. There are at least two reasons this is so. First of all, the level of employment is determined by the level of economic activity overall. Net exports is but one component of aggregate demand. It is true that a decline in net exports, *ceteris paribus,* will reduce aggregate demand and therewith employment. This reduction could be offset by an increase in aggregate demand emanating from the public or private sector; such an offset could have been brought about by expansionary monetary and fiscal policies.

There is a second and equally important criticism of this simple view. Net exports are defined as the difference between our exports and our imports. The volume of goods we export is dependent on the foreign demand for our goods; the volume of goods we import depends on domestic demand for foreign goods. If aggregate demand grows more rapidly in the United States than abroad, our net exports will decline—and so will our unemployment rate. It is true that our unemployment rate would have been lower still had all of the increase in aggregate demand taken the form of expenditures on domestically produced goods and services. But that would necessitate interfering with the people's choices in the marketplace. In addition, it would mean forcing people to pay higher prices for goods that were cheaper abroad. Proponents of freer trade would argue that it would be more appropriate to pursue somewhat more expansionary monetary and fiscal policies to offset the "leakage" caused by rising imports.

Jobs lost by imports and jobs gained by exports

All too often it is argued that a given dollar volume of imports displaces more workers from our import-competing industries than the number of jobs created by an equivalent dollar volume of exports. This fact is then presented as evidence of the employment benefits our country would obtain if imports were restricted. In fact, this is one of the most powerful arguments one can present in *favor* of freer trade. As we emphasized in Chapter 29, a country gains from freer trade because, *given its resources,* trade enables it to obtain a larger volume of goods and services than would be possible in a state of autarky. This point was emphasized by Irving Kravis:

> In a statement before the Joint Economic Committee . . ., a representative of the Trade Relations Council reported upon an analysis of the trade position of 313 . . . manufacturing industries of the United States. In 1967, 128 of these industries had a foreign trade deficit aggregating $9 billion. The excess of imports over exports in these industries was calculated to involve a net loss of 367,552 jobs. The other group, consisting of 185 industries, had trade surpluses which amounted to $10.4 billion. The job-equivalent of this trade surplus was estimated at 201,532 jobs. Although apparently cited

as an argument for protection, these data constitute a powerful argument for freer trade. For the labor of a little more than 200,000 men, we received $10.4 billion. This was enough to obtain goods from abroad that it would have taken (almost) 400,000 men—twice as many—to produce. To advance these figures as an argument for protection is to embrace a make-work philosophy. It is to argue that we should devise policies that will lead to more, rather than fewer, hours of work to produce a dollar's worth of real income. If this is what we want, protection is a good way to get it. If we want to find ways to increase man hours per dollar of output, international trade is not for us. International trade increases real product per hour of work rather than raising the hours required to produce a dollar's worth of product.[3]

3. International trade is unfair because foreign wages are so low.

There are several things wrong with this argument. In the first place, what matters is not wages alone, but *unit labor costs*—i.e., labor costs per unit of output. In some industries, our workers are so much more efficient than foreign workers that our unit labor costs are in fact lower here than abroad. This is the characteristic feature of many of our export industries. Indeed, wages in our export industries are generally higher than in our import-competing sectors. The argument can hardly be said to hold universally. It is interesting to note, moreover, that many foreign producers facing competition from U.S. firms argue that trade with the United States is unfair because American workers are so much more efficient, so much more productive!

Second, those who argue that trade with foreign countries is unfair because of low foreign wages are frequently connected with our import-competing industries. But it is precisely in those industries that we would expect a comparative cost disadvantage. The point is that not only are wage costs lower abroad but the productivity differential between foreign and some U.S. import-competing industries is not sufficient to offset those wage differences. In short, in those instances, unit labor costs are lower abroad.

---

[3] Ibid.

Beggar-thy-neighbor policies

All of the arguments favoring import restrictions discussed up to this point have as their basis the protection of certain special interests. What is frequently ignored in these arguments is that the protection of special interests comes at the general expense. Some are made better off, at least temporarily, but at the cost of making everyone else worse off.

There is another aspect to import restrictions that also needs emphasis. Policies to limit imports are frequently advocated for the purpose of solving, or helping to solve, one or another domestic ill. When unemployment is high and/or rising, import protection is often sought in order to help alleviate the domestic employment problem. However, if we are successful in protecting some domestic jobs, we do so at the expense of employment in other countries. In other words, the alleviation of some of our domestic employment problems serve to aggravate the employment problems in foreign countries. Such policies designed to promote domestic goals at foreign expense have been aptly described as **beggar-thy-neighbor policies.** Is it any wonder that these kinds of policy initiatives invite foreign retaliation?

4. Some industries need to be protected in the interest of national security.

The national security argument is a complicated one. The difficulty is that it is almost never clear how the national security is to be protected by import limitations. Apparently, to advocates of this view, the fact of a national security issue is sufficient proof of the need for protection. On careful examination, however, the national security argument does not fare well.

For years import quotas were imposed on foreign oil, the object being to protect the domestic petroleum industry to ensure adequate domestic supplies in the event of an emergency. How a more rapid rate of depletion of our own petroleum resources is supposed to guarantee us adequate domestic supplies has never been satisfactorily explained, however. In reply, the petroleum industry advanced the argument that high domestic prices (attributable to quotas) were necessary to ensure a viable domestic industry. High prices encourage domestic exploration and development. This response raises the inevitable question: Are import restrictions the best way of ensuring adequate supplies? Many economists would argue no. If national security is the issue, why not purchase foreign oil at cheaper prices and stockpile it? Or why not subsidize the exploration of petroleum *reserves* and restrict domestic production to levels to keep the domestic industry operational and capable of rapid expansion in the event of an emergency?

This was the situation prior to the actions taken by the Organization of Petroleum Exporting Countries (OPEC) to raise the world price of oil fourfold in 1974. Immediately after the OPEC oil embargo and the oil price increases, the United States embarked on a plan called *Project Independence*—a policy goal aimed at reducing significantly our dependence on foreign oil. That policy goal is all but dead now. The U.S. policy objective today is much more modest: to raise the domestic price of oil to world levels in order to both curtail domestic consumption and stimulate domestic production; to adopt new efficiency standards in the interests of conservation; and to stockpile limited quantities of oil (called **strategic reserves**) to be used in the event of an emergency.

In any event, given that about 50 percent of the oil consumed in the United States is imported, our national security would be under even greater threat if we attempted to become completely or almost completely self-sufficient in energy. The costs would be monstrous. The rate of discovery of new oil sources in the United States has slowed considerably in the past several years, thereby severely limiting our oil production potential. Restrictions designed to severely curtail imports in the face of a limited production potential would cause a rapid escalation of energy prices—a consequence that would be very detrimental to our growth prospects generally. A weak economy would probably pose a greater threat to our national security than would continued high levels of oil imports.

In the case of oil, the national security argument depends for its validity on the proposition that, in the event of an emergency, we could be cut off from existing sources of oil supply. This would strangle production and make us very vulnerable to attack. Alternatively, the threat of a cutoff could force a change in our foreign policy. Given the diverse sources of supply and the fact that the United States is on friendly terms with a number of the major oil-producing countries of the world, many people feel that it would be inappropriate to restrict foreign supplies severely or to engage in anything but a modest stockpiling program.

A quite different national security argument has been used to justify the protection of the steel industry. In this case, it is argued that protection is necessary in order to maintain skills and to ensure that the full range of steel products is produced. Actually, this is a weak argument. As was amply demonstrated during World War II, human skills and ingenuity managed very quickly to produce what was needed. This was true not only of the United States, but of England, Japan, and Germany as well. Indeed, during World War II, the United States quickly produced large quantities of airplanes, the designs of many of which had never been produced before.

It must also be emphasized that the national security argument has applicability only to a large-scale conventional war of long duration. If the next war were nuclear, the extent of our steel- and oil-producing capacity would not matter much.

Finally, protection for national security reasons could well prove to be inconsistent with the goal of improving our political and diplomatic relations with foreign countries.

5. Protection is necessary in order to allow an "infant industry" the opportunity to attain the size and experience required to enable it to compete with foreign firms.

The "infant industry" argument is used most frequently to justify the protection of new industries in LDCs. However, such protection is legitimately justified only under very particular circumstances. If the industry is able to demonstrate that it will be able to compete in world markets once it matures, a policy that provides *temporary* protection until maturity is attained can be justified. In its early stages of development, industry size is frequently small. In later stages, as the industry expands, it may be possible to achieve sizable economies of scale. Only at maturity will the industry be able to compete in world markets with well-established foreign producers.

The legitimacy of this argument hinges on the fact that the industry will ultimately be able to survive on its own without protection once it matures. If sizable economies of scale are not potentially available, the case for protection becomes suspect. Moreover, it is important to recognize that only *temporary, not permanent,* protection is justified by this argument. Import restrictions should not be maintained to protect the inefficient use of resources. Unfortunately, such temporary measures all too easily become permanent fixtures.

U.S. COMMERCIAL POLICY: PAST AND PRESENT

International trade was of critical importance to the United States in the early years of its development. As a young "have not" nation, the United States in colonial days followed the classic pattern now being repeated in many of the developing nations. Manufactured goods were imported from Europe and paid for by exports of farm products and raw materials. During that time, a very modest tariff equal to about 5 percent of the value of import goods was imposed on most imported items. Its purpose was not to protect domestic producers but to provide revenue for the colonial governments.

During the 1800s, U.S. tariff policies changed dramatically. At the beginning of that century the infant industry argument was invoked to justify increasing tariff rates to encourage the development of a number of new industries. By the time of the War of 1812, import duties reached a level of about 12½ percent.

The War of 1812 was so costly, however, that

import duties were doubled. These high rates provided U.S. firms with a taste of protectionism, causing many producers to press for higher rates still. This led in 1828 to the establishment of near-prohibitive rates on imported woolen and cotton products. The New England textile manufacturers were delighted. As a result, the textile industry flourished.

The delight of the textile manufacturers was not shared, however, by growers of cotton, tobacco, and rice. They feared that high import duties would kill their profitable sales to England. Understandably, they pressed for lower duties.

During the next half century, import duties seesawed as one group or the other gained influence in Congress. The overriding consideration that determined which group would win, however, was the state of federal revenues.[4] Tariffs provided the bulk of the revenues for government. When times were good and the government ran surpluses, those favoring lower tariff rates generally prevailed. In hard times when customs collections declined, the protectionists often prevailed.

1890–1920: The era of rapid industrialization

America's industrial development was explosive from 1890 onward. This was attributed by protectionists to the benefits wrought by high tariffs. Proponents of lower tariffs attributed the growth to the abundance of natural resources. Initially, the protectionists held sway in Congress. They succeeded in obtaining passage of the **Tariff Act of 1897,** which established very high tariff walls against imported products. Import duties under that act averaged 57 percent of the landed prices of imported goods.

As the United States prospered and federal budget surpluses grew, a sentiment developed favoring lower tariffs. At the beginning of the century, both parties declared themselves in favor of reduced import duties. Some tariffs were re-

duced along the way, but it was not until 1913, when then President Woodrow Wilson called a special session of Congress for the purpose of enacting legislation to reduce tariffs to a point consistent with the revenue needs of the government alone, that significant cuts were made. That special session passed a bill establishing tariff rates averaging about 29 percent.

The Hawley-Smoot Tariff Act of 1930

Immediately after World War I, U.S. tariff policy shifted direction again toward increased protectionism. At first, public sentiment favored limiting tariff increases to agricultural products. World farm prices had dropped dramatically after World War I and increased tariffs were viewed as necessary to protect farmers. Once the tariff question was reopened, however, Congress received a flood of petitions from manufacturers demanding higher tariffs for their products as well. Congress responded in 1930 with the passage of legislation erecting the highest tariff walls in U.S. history. The act, called the **Hawley-Smoot Tariff Act of 1930**, established tariff rates averaging almost 60 percent! This piece of legislation brought forth retaliatory tariff legislation from almost every country around the world. As a result, world trade plummeted.

The Reciprocal Trade Agreements Act of 1934

The Hawley-Smoot Tariff Act of 1930 is generally viewed as one of the most destructive pieces of legislation ever passed by the U.S. government. That act, and the retaliatory measures adopted by other countries, contributed significantly to the depth and length of the worldwide Great Depression of the 1930s.

The world economy stagnated during the Great Depression. In an effort to maintain their levels of economic activity, country after country erected higher and higher trade barriers. Beggar-thy-neighbor policies became the order of the day. The tariff warfare fed on itself until, by 1934, world trade all but vanished.

The disastrous reductions in world trade gave dramatic evidence to the self-defeating nature of

---

[4] Until the end of the 19th century, customs receipts accounted for about half of all U.S. government revenues. By the outbreak of World War II, the share had fallen to less than 6 percent of all federal receipts. Today they represent less than 1 percent.

beggar-thy-neighbor policies and unilateral tariff restrictions. Recognizing this, President Franklin D. Roosevelt introduced, and Congress passed, one of the most important bills in U.S. history—the **Reciprocal Trade Agreements Act of 1934.** That piece of legislation initiated a movement worldwide reducing trade barriers.

The unique feature of the Reciprocal Trade Agreements Act of 1934 was the authority given to the President to negotiate reciprocal trade agreements with individual countries. *Reductions in trade barriers were to be granted to countries only if corresponding concessions were granted to the United States.* The provisions of the act empowered the President to negotiate reductions of duties by as much as 50 percent.

The effect was both immediate and dramatic. As a result of the agreements arrived at between the United States and other countries, U.S. and world trade expanded sharply. Between 1934 and 1939, U.S. foreign trade expanded 39 percent. The gain with countries that signed the agreements was nearly 60 percent.

The Reciprocal Trade Agreements Act was renewed 11 times. In the process the President was granted authority to negotiate further tariff reductions beyond the original 50 percent limitation. From 1934 to 1961, the value of U.S. trade increased 15-fold as the average tariff on dutiable goods dropped to 12 percent.

General Agreement on Tariffs and Trade (GATT)

In an effort to avoid a repetition of the disastrous spiral of trade restrictions that characterized the world economy in the early days of the Great Depression, the United States invited 22 other trading nations to Geneva in 1947 to create the General Agreement on Tariffs and Trade (GATT). The approach of GATT was fundamentally different from that of the Reciprocal Trade Agreements Act. Under the latter, all trade negotiations involved one country at a time. Such **bilateral negotiations** were very time consuming. Under GATT, trade negotiations became **multilateral.** GATT enabled the United States to bargain simultaneously with all other participating countries. *Concessions agreed upon by individual*

negotiating teams were then extended to all other members of the agreement. This arrangement, which continues to this day, is known as **most favored nation (MFN)** treatment. During the first round of GATT talks in 1947, the United States successfully completed exchanges of tariffs with all 22 countries in less than seven months. Seven rounds of intergovernmental tariff talks have been held under the auspices of GATT since 1947. The seventh round—known as the **Tokyo round**—was recently completed in 1979.

In order to protect tariff concessions from being nullified by other trade barriers, GATT members have developed a code of conduct governing their international trade relations. Additionally, GATT has been an important forum for removing trade restrictions, resolving trade disputes, and promoting trade liberalization generally. Since 1947, the membership in GATT has grown from 23 to 94 nations, with 21 others associated with it.

The Kennedy round

With the growing complexity of the world economy, the rapid expansion of trade, and the growth of regional trading blocks—most notably the European Economic Community (EEC), and to a lesser extent the European Free Trade Association (EFTA)—new approaches to trade negotiations were required. The **Trade Expansion Act of 1962** was designed to meet those needs. Previously, all negotiations were done on a commodity-by-commodity basis. The Trade Expansion Act of 1962 changed all of that. It authorized the negotiation of tariff cuts by all participants on *all* products, except those specifically excluded. Across-the-board tariff cuts of up to 50 percent were authorized. In some cases, reductions of up to 100 percent were allowed.

The negotiations under this act—known formally as the **Kennedy round**—were started in Geneva, Switzerland, in May 1964. Fifty-three nations accounting for over 80 percent of world trade participated. After three years of difficult negotiations, the talks were completed in June 1967. The results were quite impressive. Tariff concessions on about $40 billion worth of goods were agreed to. On a broad range of industrial goods, tariff cuts averaging 35 percent were successfully negotiated. Some tariff concessions were achieved on agricultural products, though less than the United States desired. The participants also agreed to adopt a set of procedures to prevent "dumping." And finally, an agreement was reached whereby the industrialized countries would grant tariff concessions to LDC exports without requiring *full* reciprocity.

The Trade Act of 1974

Following the Kennedy round, a continuing effort was made by GATT to identify persistent trade and tariff problems. It was quickly discovered that, although tariff barriers were being reduced, **nontariff barriers** were becoming more prevalent. By the early part of 1972 it was clear that a new round of multilateral negotiations was needed that would focus attention not only on tariff barriers but on nontariff barriers and other trade distortions as well.

The negotiating basis for the United States was provided for in the **Trade Act of 1974.** That bill authorized the President to:

1. Negotiate a maximum 60 percent reduction on duties above 5 percent, and the complete elimination of duties of 5 percent or less (e.g., a 20 percent tariff could be reduced to 8 percent; a 3 percent tariff could be reduced to zero).
2. Enter into agreements for the reduction, elimination, or harmonization of nontariff barriers (NTBs), provided approval is obtained from both Houses of Congress.
3. Negotiate improvements in the rules of conduct of GATT members and associates. For example, the Trade Act of 1974 authorized the President to seek revisions in the rules to permit *temporary* trade restrictions to ease the adjustment to new imports on the domestic market. In the same vein, the President was authorized to seek a new code of conduct governing *export subsidies* and *countervailing duties* (a charge placed on imports to counteract the subsidies granted to exporters in foreign countries).

4. Take measures to relieve injury to domestic producers caused by imports. If the U.S. International Trade Commission finds that serious injury has been sustained by domestic producers, the President must act to restrain imports and/or provide *adjustment assistance, unless he or she determines that such actions are contrary to the interests of the United States.*
5. Implement a system of generalized tariff preferences for the benefit of the LDCs.

The Tokyo round

The mulitlateral trade negotiations (MTN) began formally in February 1975, in Geneva. Known popularly as the Tokyo round (because they were the outcome of the 1973 meeting of the world's economic ministers in Tokyo), these negotiations involved the participation of over 100 countries. The MTN agreement was completed in 1979.

Although it has been billed by many of its signatories as one of the most successful rounds of negotiations under GATT, it was not as successful as many proponents of the "free trade" persuasion would have liked. True, the participants successfully accomplished sharp reductions in many existing tariff barriers. However, by the time of the negotiations, tariffs had become much less important than nontariff barriers (NTBs) as trade restriction devices. The best the participants could work out for NTBs was an agreement that spelled out certain codes of conduct. Unfortunately, many of the codes are worded to permit more than one legitimate interpretation (meaning that country A could interpret those codes in one way, while country B could interpret them differently). And many kinds of NTBs were not covered by the agreement at all. For example, while most types of *direct* subsidies for export goods were made illegal, many types of *indirect* subsidies were left out of the agreement. Apparently, it is illegal to make a government subsidy outright to firms producing export goods, but it is not necessarily illegal if the government subsidy takes the form of government loans at below-market (i.e., subsidized) rates of interest.

This state of affairs has led many critics to contend that we still have a long way to go to realize the ultimate goal of free trade. If the participants were all very serious about eliminating NTBs, why not negotiate to eliminate them outright rather than to write up codes of conduct that can be interpreted differently?

There are other issues that were not handled within the MTN framework. Many products that were already covered by other agreements—such products as coffee, textiles, footwear, and steel—were specifically exempted from the MTN discussions. Given the growing importance of orderly marketing agreements (OMAs), these are major exemptions. Finally, the participants could not reach agreement on a system of generalized tariff preferences aimed at assisting the LDCs. This led many countries in the latter group to contend that the MTN was an agreement between and among the developed nations that had little in it of interest to the LDCs.

In sum, the MTN agreement took the world economy one step closer toward the goal of free trade. Just how big a step this agreement represents is a matter of considerable dispute. Nevertheless, much more progress is required before the nations of the world can declare, 'We are finally there."

SUMMARY

1. Not only do restrictive trade practices reduce a nation's real income. They also cause a redistribution of the smaller amount of income in favor of workers and producers in those industries receiving import protection. Why would countries choose freely to impose trade restrictions if these are the outcomes? Several "objective" reasons are frequently advanced, but most arguments for protection cannot withstand critical review.

2. Frequently the case for import limitations is made on the grounds that reduced imports will better enable us to achieve the desirable national objective of a trade surplus. There are several problems with this case. First, it is mathematically impossible for all countries together

to achieve a trade surplus. If country A achieves a trade surplus, A's trading partners together must have a trade deficit with country A. Second, although many view an export surplus as evidence of economic strength, in fact a trade surplus can arise as a consequence of either economic strength or economic weakness. Third, why the emphasis should be put on goods alone and not on goods and services is not at all obvious. Fourth, it is not at all obvious that trade restrictions will in fact cause an increase in the trade surplus. This is because almost any restrictive action taken by the United States will almost always call forth retaliatory restrictive actions on the parts of other nations.

3. A second argument advanced in favor of import restrictions emphasizes the role of trade deficits in increasing the unemployment rate. This argument is very weak, if not completely fallacious. Those who advance this argument implicitly assume that employment opportunities are frozen. This belief violates a basic tenet of economics—that resources are scarce and have alternative uses. Empirically, there is no evidence to suggest that a decline in net exports is an important factor responsible for raising unemployment. More often than not, declining net exports are associated with a *falling* unemployment rate. Finally, it is often argued that a given dollar volume of imports displaces more workers than the number of jobs created by an equivalent dollar volume of exports. This is apparently presented as evidence of the employment benefits our country would obtain if imports were restricted. In fact, this is one of the most powerful arguments one can present in *favor* of freer trade. A country gains from a free trade because, *given its resources,* trade enables it to obtain a larger volume of goods and services than would be possible in a state of autarky.

4. A third argument in favor of import restrictions is that international trade is unfair because foreign wages are so much lower than the United States. However, what matters is not wages per se, but unit labor costs. Moreover, the theory of comparative advantage tells us that there will be some goods in which we have a relative cost disadvantage precisely because there are other

goods for which we have a relative cost advantage.

5. A fourth argument in favor of import restrictions is that some industries need to be protected in the interest of national security. Unfortunately, it is frequently not clear how the national security is protected by import limitations. For example, a number of years ago import quotas were imposed on foreign oil. The object was to protect the domestic petroleum industry to ensure adequate domestic supplies in the event of an emergency. How a more rapid rate of depletion of our own petroleum resources was supposed to guarantee adequate domestic supplies was not explained satisfactorily.

6. A fifth argument is that protection is necessary in order to permit an *infant industry* the opportunity to attain the size and experience required to enable it to compete with foreign firms. It is important to recognize that only temporary, not permanent, protection is justified by this argument.

7. During the colonial era, import duties were designed not so much to protect domestic producers as to provide revenue for the colonial governments. During the 1800s, however, U.S. tariff policies changed dramatically. At the beginning of that century, the infant industry argument was invoked to justify increasing tariff rates to encourage the development of new industries. The delight of those manufacturers who received protection from imports was not shared by export interests who feared that high import duties would be met in kind by import restrictions imposed by the governments in Europe.

8. In the period from 1890 through World War I, import duties seesawed from very high to very low rates. The *Tariff Act of 1897* established very high tariff rates on the order of 57 percent. In 1913, President Woodrow Wilson was successful in accomplishing tariff cuts to about 29 percent. After World War I, on the other hand, U.S. tariff policy shifted direction again toward increased protectionism. This led in 1930 to the passage of legislation establishing the highest tariff walls in U.S. history—the *Hawley–Smoot Tariff Act of 1930.* This piece of legislation brought forth retaliatory tariff legislation from almost every country around the world. As a result, world trade plummeted.

The Hawley–Smoot Tariff Act of 1930 was followed in 1934 by an equally sharp departure in the opposite direction. Congress passed the *Reciprocal Trade Agreements Act,* which gave the President the authority to negotiate reciprocal trade agreements with individual countries. The provisions of the act empowered the President to negotiate reductions of duties by as much as 50 percent.

9. The bilateral negotiations under the Reciprocal Trade Agreements Act was time-consuming. Under the *General Agreement on Tariffs and Trade* (GATT), trade negotiations became multilateral. Seven rounds of intergovernmental tariff talks have been held under the auspices of GATT since 1947. The sixth round—the *Kennedy round*—was completed in 1967; the seventh round—known as the *Tokyo round*—was completed in 1979.

CONCEPTS FOR REVIEW

Notion of import restrictions as facilitating a trade surplus

General agreement on Tariffs and Trade (GATT)

Import restrictions help reduce U.S. unemployment rate

Beggar-thy-neighbor policies

"Infant industry"

Tariff Act of 1897

Hawley–Smoot Tariff Act of 1930

Reciprocal Trade Agreements Act of 1934

Bilateral negotiations versus multilateral negotiations

Most favored nation (MFN)

Kennedy round

Trade Expansion Act of 1962

Trade Act of 1974

Tokyo round

Nontariff barriers

QUESTIONS FOR DISCUSSION

(Those marked with an asterisk (*) are more difficult.)

1. "If the trade balance is defined as the difference between exports and imports, and if trade restrictions reduce imports, then restrictive trade practices must result in an improved trade balance." Carefully evaluate.

*2. "The notion that tariffs and quotas raise prices is crazy. The rates of increase in prices of a great many imported goods that are subject to tariffs are less than the rate of inflation generally." Critically evaluate. (*Hint:* Even assuming that the *rates* of increase are higher than inflation generally, what does this have to do with the statement in the first sentence? And regarding the statement in the first sentence, if prices were not increased, why have tariffs or quotas?)

3. Explain why restrictive trade practices are more likely to be imposed during periods of recession than during periods of prosperity.

4. If a trade surplus is a desirable goal for all countries, what is to stop every country from having a trade surplus?

5. A modified form of the infant industry argument is often advanced to justify temporary protection for the U.S. auto industry, beleaguered as it has been by small foreign imports. The argument goes as follows: "We were caught off guard by the fourfold increase in oil prices in 1974 and the sharp oil price increases again in 1979, which made large U.S. cars unprofitable. Time is required to enable us to retool to meet the onslaught of auto imports from Japan in particular."

Evaluate this argument. Speculate, using the product cycle theory developed in Chapter 29, whether the U.S. industry will ever again be able to acquire a 90 percent or more share of the U.S. auto market without protection from imports.

James Tobin (1918–)

The 13th Nobel Prize in Economic Science (1981) was awarded to James Tobin for his work on portfolio selection theory, which examined how people "actually behave when they acquire different assets and incur debts." The Yale University professor explained that his theory "sets forth the principle of not putting all your eggs in one basket because then, if something goes wrong, you lose them all at once."

United Press International

In singling out his portfolio selection theory, the Academy acknowledged that it was only part of Tobin's distinguished works "which cover a broad spectrum of economic research. . . . Few economic researchers of today could be said to have gained so many followers or exerted such influence on contemporary research."

The selection committee added that Tobin had "unquestionably inspired substantial research during the 1970s on the effects of monetary policy, the implications of budget deficits, and stabilization policy in general."

The public's willingness to diversify financial holdings, and the awareness that "money" can be held in different forms—certificates of deposit or money market funds—are the practical things that have come out of Tobin's work. He showed that every time control of one kind of "money" is attempted, ingenious markets devise different forms of it.

Tobin is also noted for the development of the Q-ratio, a measure of the market value of physical assets relative to their replacement costs. When the Q-ratio is low, many business firms expand by acquiring the assets of existing companies rather than by building new plants or new equipment; when the Q-ratio is high, expansion takes the form of additions to plant and equipment.

Among the economics fraternity Tobin is considered one of the nation's most creative economic thinkers and one who cares deeply about public policy, his students, and his work. On campus he has a reputation as being "enormously rigorous and highly demanding," and his colleagues call him "brilliant" and "shy." He is well known for his sense of humor. Each year, when he lectures about the Q-ratio, he wears a T-shirt given him by former graduate students. On the front it says, "Q is all that matters."

Index